D1731559

Leipziger Altorientalistische Studien

Herausgegeben von
Michael P. Streck

Band 8

2018
Harrassowitz Verlag · Wiesbaden

Jacob Jan de Ridder

Descriptive Grammar of Middle Assyrian

2018
Harrassowitz Verlag · Wiesbaden

Publication of this volume has been made possible by the generous funding of the Deutsche Forschungsgemeinschaft (German Research Council).

Bibliografische Information der Deutschen Nationalbibliothek
Die Deutsche Nationalbibliothek verzeichnet diese Publikation in der Deutschen Nationalbibliografie; detaillierte bibliografische Daten sind im Internet über http://dnb.dnb.de abrufbar.

Bibliographic information published by the Deutsche Nationalbibliothek
The Deutsche Nationalbibliothek lists this publication in the Deutsche Nationalbibliografie; detailed bibliographic data are available in the Internet at http://dnb.dnb.de.

For further information about our publishing program consult our website http://www.harrassowitz-verlag.de

© Otto Harrassowitz GmbH & Co. KG, Wiesbaden 2018
This work, including all of its parts, is protected by copyright. Any use beyond the limits of copyright law without the permission of the publisher is forbidden and subject to penalty. This applies particularly to reproductions, translations, microfilms and storage and processing in electronic systems.
Printed on permanent/durable paper.
Printing and binding: Hubert & Co., Göttingen
Printed in Germany

ISSN 2193-4436
ISBN 978-3-447-10979-6

ܚܙܝ ܠܟܘ ܓܝܪ ܠܡܫܟܚܐ ܠܚܝܐ ܕܡܢ ܕܘܟܬܗ ܡܫܬܢܐ. ܟܕܡܐ ܓܝܪ ܕܪܓܫ
ܠܘܩܕܡ: ܠܐ ܫܒܩ ܠܚܝܐ ܕܢܣܬܟܠ܀
ܡ̈ܠܐ ܕܢܚܡܬܐ ܕܡܪܝ ܐܝܣܚܩ ܕܢܝܢܘܐ

voor Leo de Ridder

Table of contents

List of figures

Preface and Acknowledgements

This study is the result of my PhD research, which I started after my graduation in 2011. The following year, the project received three years' funding from the Deutsche Forschungsgemeinschaft, enabling me to fully concentrate on my research. I was introduced to Middle Assyrian studies by J. G. Dercksen in the form of two seminars at Leiden University, although the theme of my dissertation was suggested to me by Prof. M. P. Streck. He continued to support me as my first supervisor and, without his valuable comments and ideas, this dissertation could not have been finished.

Prof. Wiggermann allowed me to use many of his unpublished Tell Ṣabī Abyaḍ texts, which represent a significant contribution to our knowledge of Middle Assyrian grammar. Meanwhile, N. J. C. Kouwenberg sent me some early drafts of his Old Assyrian grammar. His ideas, expressed in his manuscript and in personal correspondence, helped shape this study in many respects. J. C. Johnson kindly provided me with an early version from his edition of the M 6 archive. This study uses his numbering of the tablets in the Istanbul Museum. P. Gauthier sent me his dissertation on the large M 4 archive, F. Schmidt her master's thesis on the M 14 archive and O. Vinnichenko her dissertation on Neo Assyrian syntax. I consulted these unpublished manuscripts.

I furthermore want to thank various scholars who helped me in several ways by providing comments or suggestions: G. Barjamovic, Y. Bloch, Prof. E. Cancik-Kirschbaum, Prof. J. Hazenbos, S. Jakob, Prof. M. Krebernik, J. Llop, D. Shibata, Prof. M. Stol and M. Worthington. I would also like to thank M. Hilgert, J. Marzahn of the Vorderasiatisches Museum in Berlin and A. Lassen of the Yale Babylonian Collection for allowing me to collate some Middle Assyrian tablets. Various people read parts of my dissertation and helped me to improve my English and other aspects: R. Essam, B. McGrath, B. Kemperman, A. Kungl and M. Greiner-Siebert. Most notable is B. McGrath, who was kind enough to read the manuscript on multiple occasions. I would like to particularly express my gratitude to M. Luukko who gave me many constructive and insightful comments during the revision process. Thanks are also extended to the students who attended my classes on Middle Assyrian at the Leipzig university for their input and various suggestions on interpreting the documents.

During the writing of my dissertation, my loving wife, Elyze Zomer, was my biggest support. Moreover, her comments and remarks on Middle Assyrian incantations and Middle Babylonian palaeography also proved to be invaluable.

Leipzig, February 2018 — Jacob Jan de Ridder

Bibliographical abbreviations

1 Bibliographical abbreviations[1]

AbB	Altbabylonische Briefe in Umschrift und Übersetzung.
Adad Ritual	KAR 154, as edited in Menzel 1981, T 2–T 4 no. 2; translation in Pongratz-Leisten 2015, 382–85.
ADD	C. H. W. Johns, *Assyrian Deeds and Documents: Recording the transfer of property, including the so-called private contracts, legal decisions and proclamations preserved in the Kouyunjik collections of the British Museum, chiefly of the 7th century B.C.* Cambridge: Deighton Bell and co., 1898–1923.
AfO	Archiv für Orientforschung.
AfO Beih.	Archiv für Orientforschung, Beiheft.
AHw	B. Meissner/W. von Soden, *Akkadisches Handwörterbuch*, Volume I-III. Wiesbaden: Harrassowitz Verlag, 1959–1981.
AJA	American Journal of Archaeology.
AKT	Ankara Kültepe Tabletleri.
ALCA	O. Pedersén, *Archives and Libraries in the City of Assur*. Acta Universitatis Upsaliensis 6-7. Uppsala: Almqvist & Wiksell, Volume 1=1985; Volume 2=1986.
AnOr	Analecta Orientalia.
AO	Museum siglum of the Louvre museum, Paris (Antiquités orientales).
AOAT	Alter Orient und Altes Testament.
AoF	Altorientalische Forschungen (Schriften zur Geschichte und Kultur des Alten Orients).
AOS	American Oriental Series.
ArOr	Archiv Orientální.
ARu	M. David/E. Ebeling, *Assyrische Rechtsurkunden*. Stuttgard: Verlag von Ferdinand Enke, 1929.
AS	Assyriological Studies (Oriental Institute, Univ. of Chicago).
ASJS	Acta Sumerologica (Japan) Supplementary (Series).
Assur	Assur. Monographic Journals of the Near East.
Aššur Ritual	VAT 10598+KAV 144, as edited in Menzel 1981, T 5–T 7 no. 3.
AT	Ancient Textiles Series.
AuOr	Aula Orientalis.
AuOrS	Aula Orientalis Supplementa.
AuOrS 1	D. Arnaud, *Textes syriens de l'age du bronce recent*. Barcelona: Editorial AUSA, 1991.
BAI	H. Freydank/C. Saporetti, *Bābu-aḫa-iddina, die Texte*. Corpus Medio-Assiro Roma: Denicola, 1989.
BATSH	H. Kühne (ed.), Berichte der Ausgrabung Tall Šēḫ Ḥamad/Dūr-Katlimmu (Berlin 1991ff)
BE	Babylonian Expedition of the University of Pennsylvania, Series A: Cuneiform Texts.
Billa	Finkelstein, J. J.: Texts from Tell Billa, *JCS* 7 (1953) 111–76.

1 Abbreviations for text references outside the MA corpus are in principle not covered in this list, except for some major series such as AbB and SAA. For OA see the OA bibliography in Michel 2003 with additions in AfO 51 and 52. For the other corpora, see Streck (2014/16), RlA 14, III–LIX.

BiOr Bibliotheca Orientalis.
BM Museum siglum of the British Museum, London.
BMCG H. Freydank, *Beiträge zur Mittelassyrischen Chronologie und Geschichte*. Schriften zur Geschichte und Kultur des Alten Orients 21. Berlin: Akademie-Verlag, 1991.
BSOAS Bulletin of the School of Oriental and African Studies.
BVW E. Ebeling, *Bruchstücke einer mittelassyrischen Vorschriftensammlung für die Akklimatisierung und Trainierung von Wagenpferden*. Deutsche Akademie der Wissenschaften zu Berlin Institut für Orientforschung: Veröffentlichung 7. Berlin: Akademie-Verlag, 1951.
BWL W. G: Lambert, *Babylonian Wisdom Literature*. Oxford: Clarendon Press, 1960 .
CAD A. L. Oppenheim et al. (eds.), *The Assyrian Dictionary of the University of Chicago*. Chicago: Oriental Institute, 1956–2010.
CDA J. Black/A. George/N. Postgate, *A Concise Dictionary of Akkadian, 2nd edition*. SANTAG 5. Wiesbaden: Harrassowitz Verlag, 2000.
CGSL S. Moscati/A. Spitaler/E. Ullendorff /W. von Soden, *An Introduction to the Comparative Grammar of the Semitic Languages*, 3rd Printing. Porta NS 6. Wiesbaden: Harrassowitz Verlag, 1980.
CM Cuneiform Monographs.
Coronation Ritual Edited as Krönungsritual aus der Zeit der Nachfolger des Tukulti-Ninurta I, in Müller (1937) 4–58. See also Parpola 2017, SAA 20 7. For colum iv (KAR 217), see Panayotov 2015.
CTMMA Cuneiform Texts in the Metropolitan Museum of Arts.
CTMMA 1 E. Spar (ed.), *Tablets Cones and Bricks of the Third and Second Millennium B.C.*. CTMMA 1. New York: Metropolitan Museum of Art, 1988.
CTN Cuneiform texts from Nimrud.
CUSAS Cornell University Studies in Assyriology and Sumerology.
CUSAS 34 J. Llop-Raduà, Middle Assyrian, in: *Assyrian Archival Texts in the Schøyen Collection and Other Documents from North Mesopotamia and Syria*, ed. A. R. George, 61–76. Bethesda: CDL Press, 2017.
DeZ Siglum Deir Ez-Zawr Museum, see Chapter 25.6.
DSC Cybernetica Mesopotamica Data Sets: Cuneiform Texts.
DSC 1 C. Saporetti, *Assur 14446: La Famiglia A*. DSC 1. Malibu: Undena Publications, 1979.
DSC 2 C. Saporetti, *Le Leggi Medioassire*. DSC 2. Malibu: Undena Publications, 1979.
DSC 3 C. Saporetti, *Assur 14446: Le altre Famiglie*. DSC 1. Malibu: Undena Publications, 1982.
EA J. A. Knudtzon (ed.), *Die El-Amarna-Tafeln*. VAB 2/1-2. Leipzig: Hinrichs, 1907–1915.
EMA C. Saporetti, *Gli Eponimi Medio-Assir*. Bibliotheca Mesopotamica 9. Malibu: Undena Publications, 1979.
Giricano K. Radner, *Das mittelassyrische Tontafelarchiv von Giricano/Dunnu-ša-Uzibi*. Excavations at Giricano 1. Subartu 14. Turnhout: Brepols, 2004.
GAG W. von Soden, *Grundriss der Akkadischen Grammatik*, 3., ergänzte Auflage. AnOr 33. Roma: Pontificio Istituto Biblico, 1995.
GAV N. J. C, Kouwenberg, *Gemination in the Akkadian Verb*. Studia Semitica Neerlandica 32. Assen: Van Gorcum, 1997.
GKT K. Hecker, *Grammatik der Kültepe Texte*. AnOr 44. Roma: Pontificio Istituto Biblico, 1968.
GOA N. J. C. Kouwenberg, *A Grammar of Old Assyrian*. Handbook of Oriental Studies: Section 1 the Near and Middle East. Brill: Leiden/Boston 2016.

HALOT	L. Koehler/W. Baumgartner, *The Hebrew and Aramaic Lexicon of the Old Testament*. Brill: Leiden/Boston/Köln 2001,
HdO	Handbuch der Orientalistik.
HANE M	History of The Ancient Near East, Monographs.
HSAO	Heidelberger Studien zum Alten Orient.
HSK	Handbücher zur Sprach- und Kommunikationswissenschaft.
HSS	Harvard Semitic Studies.
IAMY	Istanbul Arkeoloji Müzeleri Yilliği.
IM	Museum siglum of the Iraq Museum, Baghdad.
Iraq	Iraq (British School of Archaeology in Iraq).
Ištar Ritual	KAR 139, edited in Menzel 1981, T 1–2 no. 1; as 'Ritual im ^{é}ēqi in Kār-Tukultī-Ninurta' in Meinhold 2009, 349–54 no. 9; a translation in Pongratz-Leisten 2015, 386–90. See also Parpola 2017, SAA 20 29.
JAOS	Journal of the American Oriental Society.
JBVO	Jenaer Beiträge zum Vorderen Orient.
JCS	Journal of Cuneiform Studies.
JEOL	Jaarbericht Er Oriente Lux.
JNES	Journal of Near Eastern Studies.
K	Museum signatur of Kuyunjik (British Museum).
KAI	H. Donner/W. Röllig, *Kanaanäische und aramäische Inschriften*, 3 volumes. Wiesbaden: Harrassowitz Verlag, 1962/64.
KAJ	E. Ebeling, *Keilschrifttexte aus Assur juristischen Inhalts*. WVDOG 50. Leipzig: J. C. Hinrich'sche Buchhandlung, 1927.
KAM	Keilschrifttexte aus mittelassyrischer Zeit. nos. 1−6 as MARV 1−8, no. 8−9 as MARV 9−10.
KAM 7	J. Llop(-Raduà), *Mittelassyrische Verwaltungsurkunden aus Assur: Texte aus den "großen Speichern" und dem Ubru-Archiv*. WVDOG 124, Wiesbaden: Harrassowitz, 2009.
KAM 10	H. Reculeau/B. Feller, *Mittelassyrische Urkunden aus dem Archiv Assur 14446*, WVDOG 130, Wiesbaden: Harrassowitz Verlag, 2012.
KAM 11	V. Donbaz, *Middle Assyrian Texts from Assur at the Eski Şark Eserleri Müzesi in Istanbul*, WVDOG 146, Wiesbaden: Harrassowitz Verlag, 2016.
KAR	E. Ebeling, *Keilschrifttexte aus Assur Religiösen Inhalts*. WVDOG 28, 34. Leipzig: J. C. Hinrich'sche Buchhandlung, 1919ff.
KAV	O. Schroeder, *Keilschrifttexte aus Assur verschiedenen Inhalts*. WVDOG 35. Leipzig: J. C. Hinrich'sche Buchhandlung, 1920.
KBo	Keilschrifttexte aus Boghazköi.
KTN inventory	VAT 16462, as edited in Köcher 1947/58. Collations, Freydank 1971, OLZ 66/11–12, 534.
KUB	Keilschrifturkunden aus Boghazköi.
LANE	Languages of the Ancient Near East.
LAS 2	S. Parpola, *Letters from Assyrian Scholars to the Kings Esarhaddon and Assurbanipal II: Commentary and Appendices*. AOAT 5/2. Neukirchen-Vluyn: Neukirchener Verlag, 1983.
LB	Siglum Liagre Bohl Collection, Leiden.
LKA	E. Ebeling, *Literarische Keilschrifttexte aus Assur*. Berlin. Akademie-Verlag, 1953.
LVUH	W. Röllig, *Land- und Viehwirtschaft am unteren Ḫābūr in mittelassyrischer Zeit*. BATSH 9 Texte 3. Wiesbaden: Harrassowitz Verlag, 2008.
MAH	Museum signatur of the Musee d'Art et d'Histoire, Geneva.
MAL	Middle Assyrian Laws, as edited in Driver/Miles 1935; Roth 1997.

MAOG	Mitteilungen der Altorientalischen Gesellschaft.
MAOG 3/3	B. Meissner, *Studien zur assyrischen Lexikographie*. MAOG 3/3, Leipzig: Verlag von Otto Harrassowitz, 1929.
MAOG 7/1–2	E. Ebeling, *Urkunden des Archives von Assur aus mittelassyrischer Zeit*. MAOG 7/1–2, Leipzig: Verlag von Otto Harrassowitz, 1933.
MAPD	Middle Assyrian Palace Decrees, as edited in Roth 1997; cf. Weidner 1954/56b.
New Year Ritual	VAT 16435, as edited in F. Köcher 1952; translation in Pongratz-Leisten 2015, 384–86.
MARV	Mittelassyrischen Rechtsurkunden und Verwaltungstexte. no. 1 by H. Freydank as VS 19, Berlin: Akademie Verlag, 1976; no. 2 ibid. as VS 21 (1982); no. 3 ibid. as WVDOG 92 (1994); no. 4 ibid. as WVDOG 99, Saarbrücken: Saarbrücker Druckerei und Verlag, 2001; no. 5 ibid. by H.Freydank/B. Feller as WVDOG 106 (2004); no. 6 ibid. as WVDOG 109 (2005); no. 7 ibid. by H. Freydank as WVDOG 111 (2006); no. 8 ibid. by H. Freydank/B. Feller as WVDOG 119, Wiesbaden: Harrassowitz Verlag, 2007; no. 9 ibid. as WVDOG 125 (2010); no. 10 ibid. by D. Prechel/H. Freydank as WVDOG 134 (2011).
MATC	S. Jakob, *Die Mittelassyrischen Texte aus Tell Chuēra in Nordost-Syrien*. VFMOS 2, III. Wiesbaden: Harrassowitz Verlag, 2009.
MATSH	E. C. Cancik-Kirschbaum, *Die Mittelassyrischen Briefe aus Tall Šēḫ Ḥamad*. BATSH 4 Texte 1. Berlin: Dietrich Reimer Verlag, 1996.
MCS	Manchester Cuneiform Studies.
MDOG	Mitteilungen der Deutschen Orientgesellschaft zu Berlin.
MKA	B. Kh. Ismail-Sabir, *Mittelassyrische Keilschrifttexte aus Assur*, Diss. Berlin, 1967.
MPR	S. Saleh, *Die mittelassyrischen Personen- und Rationenlisten aus Tall Šēḫ Ḥamad/Dūr-Katlimmu*. BATSH 18 Texte 6. Wiesbaden: Harrassowitz Verlag, 2014.
MVAeG	Mitteilungen der Vorderasiatisch-Agyptischen Gesellschaft.
MZL	R. Borger, *Mesopotamisches Zeichenlexikon, Zweite, Revidierte und aktualisierte Auflage*. AOAT 305. Münster: Ugarit-Verlag, 2010.
N.A.B.U.	Nouvelles Assyriologiques Bréves et Utilitaires.
Ni	Tablets excavated at Nippur, in the collections of the Archaeological Museum of Istanbul
NKRA	P. Koschaker, *Neue Keilschriftliche Rechtsurkunden aus der El-Amarna Zeit*. Abhandlungen der philologisch-historischen Klasse der Sächsischen Akademie der Wissenschaften 39/5. Leipzig: Hirzel Verlag, 1928.
NTA	V. Donbaz, *Ninurta-Tukulti-Aššur: zamanina ait orta Asur idarî belgeleri*. Ankara: Türk Tarih Kurumu, 1976.
OAAS	Old Assyrian Archive Studies.
OBO	Orbis Biblicus et Orientalis.
OIP	Oriental Institute Publications.
OLA	Orientalia Lovaniensia Analecta.
OLZ	Orientalistische Literaturzeitung.
OMA 1	C. Saporetti, *Onomastica Medio-Assira, Volume I: I Nomi di Persona*. StP 6. Roma: Pontificio Istituto Biblico, 1970.
OMA 1	C. Saporetti, *Onomastica Medio-Assira, Volume II: Studi, Vocabolari ed Elenchi*. StP 6. Roma: Pontificio Istituto Biblico, 1970.
Or	Orientalia.
OrAnt	Oriens Antiquus.
Phoenix	Phoenix. Bulletin uitgegeven door het Vooraziatisch-Egyptisch Genootschap Ex Oriente Lux.

Porta	Porta linguarum Orientalium, AS: Alte Serie, NS: Neue Serie.
PIHANS	Publications de l'Institut historique-archéologique néerlandais de Stamboul.
PKT	E. Ebeling, Parfümrezepte und kultische Texte aus Assur, *Or* 17/2 (1948) 129–45, *Or* 17/3 (1948) 299–313, *Or* 18/4 (1949) 404–18, *Or* 19/3 (1950) 265–78.
PNAE	The Prosopography of the Neo-Assyrian Empire.
PRU 4	J. Nougayrol, *Le Palais Royal d'Ugarit IV: Textes accadiens des Archives Sud.* Mission de Ras Shamra 9. Paris: Imprimerie Nationale, 1956.
RA	Revue d'Assyriologie et d'Archéologie Orientale.
RGTC	Répertoire géographique des textes cunéiformes.
RGTC 4	K. Nashef, *Die Orts- und Gewässernamen der altassyrischen Zeit.* Wiesbaden: Dr. Ludwich Reichert Verlag, 1991.
RGTC 5	K. Nashef, *Die Orts- und Gewässernamen der Mittelbabylonischen und Mittelassyrischen Zeit.* Wiesbaden: Dr. Ludwich Reichert Verlag, 1982.
RIMA	The Royal Inscriptions of Mesopotamia, Assyrian periods.
RIMA 1	A. K. Grayson, *Assyrian Rulers of the Third and Second Millennia BC (to 1115 BC).* RIMA 1. Toronto: University of Toronto Press, 1987.
RIMA 2	A. K. Grayson, *Assyrian Rulers of the Early First Millennium BC I (1114-859).* RIMA 2. Toronto: University of Toronto Press, 1991.
RlA	Reallexikon der Assyriologie (und Vorderasiatischen Archäologie).
RIAA	L. Speleers, *Recueil des inscriptions de l'Asie antérieure des Musées royaux du Cinquantenaire à Bruxelles.* Bruxelles: Vanderpoorten, 1925.
Rm.	Tablets in the collections of the British Museum.
RS	Siglum of Raˀs Šamra (Ugarit).
SAA	State Archives of Assyria.
SAAB	State Archives of Assyria Bulletin.
SAAS	State Archives of Assyria Studies.
SANER	Studies in Ancient Near Eatern Records.
SCCNH	Studies on the Civilization and Culture of Nuzi and the Hurrians.
SNAG	J. Hämeen-Anttila, *A Sketch of Neo-Assyrian Grammar.* SAAS 13. Helsinki: The Neo-Assyrian Text Corpus Project, 2000.
StAT	Studien zu den Assur-Texten.
StCh	Studia Chaburensia.
Stelen	W. Andrae, *Die Stelenreihen in Assur.* WVDOG 24. Leipzig: J. C. Hinrich'sche Buchhandlung, 1913.
StMes	Studia Mesopotamica.
StOr	Studia Orientalia.
StP	Studia Pohl.
Subartu	Subartu. European Centre for Upper Mesopotamien Studies.
Sumer	Sumer. Journal of Archaeology and History in Iraq (سومر).
Syllab	W. von Soden/W. Röllig, *Das Akkadische Syllabar, 4. Auflage.* AnOr 42. Roma: Pontificio Istituto Biblico, 1991.
Syria	Syria. Revue d'art oriental et d'archéologie.
T	Siglum Tell Ṣabī Abyaḍ tablets, see Chapter 25.4.
TabT	Siglum of the Tell Ṭābān tablets, see Chaper 25.5.
TCS	Texts from Cuneiform Sources.
TCS 5	A. K. Grayson, *Assyrian and Babylonian Chronicles.* New York: J. J. Augustin Publisher, 1975.
THet	Texte der Hethiter.
TIM	Texts in the Iraq Museum.
TR	Siglum Tell El-Rimāḥ texts, see Chapter 25.3.

TUAT NF	Texte aus der Umwelt des Alten Testaments, Neue Folge.
UF	Ugarit-Forschungen.
Ugaritica	Ugaritica. Mission de Ras Shamra.
UGM	W. Mayer, *Untersuchungen zur Grammatik des Mittelassyrischen.* AOATS 2. Neukirchen-Vluyn: Neukirchener Verlag, 1971.
UŠA	J. N. Postgate, *The Archive of Urad-Šerūa and his family, a Middle Assyrian Household in Government Service.* Corpus Medio-Assiro. Roma: Denicola, 1988.
VAB	Vorderasiatische Bibliothek.
VAT	Siglum of the Staatliche Museen, Berlin.
VDI	Vestnik Drevnej Istorii.
VS	Vorderasiatische Schriftdenkmäler der (Königlichen) Museen zu Berlin.
WAW	Writings of the Ancient World.
WO	Die Welt des Orients. Wissenschaftliche Beiträge zur Kunde des Morgenlandes.
WVDOG	Wissenschaftlichen Veröffentlichungen der Deutschen Orient-Gesellschaf.
WZKM	Wiener Zeitschrift für die Kunde des Morgenlandes.
VFMOS	Vorderasiatische Forschungen der Max Freiherr von Oppenheim-Stiftung.
YBC	Tablet siglum, Yale Babylonian Collection (New Haven).
ZA	Zeitschrift für Assyriologie und vorderasiatische Archäologie.
ZDMG	Zeitschrift der Deutschen Morgenländischen Gesellschaft.

2 Languages

Akk	Old Akkadian
AlAkk	Alalaḫ Akkadian
AmAkk	Amurru Akkadian
BH	Biblical Hebrew
HattAkk	Ḫattuša Akkadian
EgAkk	Egyptian Akkadian
EmAkk	Emar Akkadian
MA	Middle Assyrian
MitAkk	Mittani Akkadian (Tušratta)
MB	Middle Babylonian
NA	Neo-Assyrian
NB	Neo-Babylonian
OA	Old Assyrian
OB	Old Babylonian
SuAkk	Susa Akkadian
Sum.	Sumerian
UgAkk	Ugarit Akkadian

3 Sites and archaeological context

KTN	Kār-Tukultī-Ninurta
M 1ff	MA archives following ALCA
N 1ff	NA archives following ALCA

TaR	Tell Ar-Rimāḫ
TṢA	Tell Ṣabī Abyaḍ
TŠḪ	Tell Aš-Šēḫ Ḥamad

4 Middle Assyrian kings

Aššur-nērārī II	1424–1418/1414–1408	Aššnīr II
Aššur-bēl-nišēšu	1417–1409/1407–1399	Abn
Aššur-rîm-nišēšu	1408–1401/1398–1391	Arn
Aššur-nādin-aḫḫē	1400–1391/1390–1381	A.n.aḫḫē
Erība-Adad I	1390–1364/1380–1354	EAd
Aššur-uballiṭ I	1363–1328/1353–1318	Aub
Enlil-nērārī	1327–1318/1317–1308	En
Ārik-dēn-ili	1317–1306/1307–1296	Adi
Adad-nērārī I	1305–1274/1295–1264	Adn
Shalmaneser I	1273–1244/1263–1234	Sa
Tukultī-Ninurta I	1243–1207/1233–1197	TN
Aššur-nādin-apli	1206–1203/1196–1193	A.n.apli
Aššur-nērārī III	1202–1197/1192–1187	Aššnīr III
Enlil-kudurri-uṣur	1196–1192/1186–1182	Eku
Ninurta-apil-ekur	1191–1179/1181–1169	Nae
Aššur-dān I	1178–1134/1168–1134	Ad
Ninurta-Tukultī-Aššur	1133	NtA
Mutakkil-Aššur	1132	MtA
Aššur-rēša-iši I	1131–1115	Ari
Tiglath-pileser I	1114–1076	Tp
Ašāred-apil-ekur	1075–1074	Aae
Aššur-bēl-kala	1073–1056	Abk

Figure 1: Overview of Middle Assyrian kings.[2]

2 This table is a slightly edited version from BMCG, 188–89; cf. Freydank 2016, 198.

Chapter 1: Introduction

1.1 Terminology

§ 1 Akkadian is the oldest attested Semitic language and the first to split from the Semitic family tree; together with Eblaite, it formed the Eastern Semitic (ES) branch. As ES split from the other Semitic languages, Akkadian contains a number of innovations and archaisms unknown in the other Semitic languages. Akkadian itself is attested from 2600 BCE until the first century CE, a long period, which, in terms of length, is third only after the other Middle Eastern languages, Egyptian/Coptic (about 3000 BCE and from about 1700 CE onwards as a literary language) and Aramaic (about 1000 BCE to the present time). Like Aramaic, the large geographical area in which Akkadian was spoken or written caused the development of a number of vernaculars that may be called independent languages, instead of dialects. The contrast between North and South Akkadian is well known in the Assyrian and Babylonian languages. Moreover, different vernaculars of Akkadian existed in peripheral cities, written by scribes with a different linguistic background. Despite these linguistic differences, official languages were developed in Standard Babylonian (SB) and the hymnic-epic dialect to be used for official and monumental inscriptions, and religious and literary texts. The situation resembles the Arabic world, where the written language is dominated by the official Modern Standard Arabic, but where dialectal forms often appear. This is the situation in the Late Bronze Age (1550–1200 BCE), where Akkadian reached its highest geographical extent, and Akkadian cuneiform was written from Kabnak (Elam) in the east to Amarna (Egypt) and Ḫattuša (ancient Anatolia, modern Turkey) in the west. The situation of North-West Mesopotamia is of particular interest, where Akkadian was the main scribal language in the kingdoms of the Hittites, Mittani and Aššur. Akkadian archives were mainly found in the cities of Emar, Nuzi, Alalaḫ, Ugarit, Ḫattuša, Amarna and Aššur.[1] In this study, we will refer to this group as "Western Peripheral Akkadian" (WPA), as the different vernaculars that can be found in each city have a lot in common in terms of scribal traditions (see § 61).[2] The Akkadian of Aššur differs in one important respect from the rest of WPA, that is, it was written by scribes with an Akkadian linguistic background, as opposed to other WPA dialects where the native language was Hurrian, Hittite or a variant of North-West Semitic (NWS). In this

1 For smaller find spots, see the overview in Pedersén (1998). Note that our main sources for the cuneiform of Mittani are the diplomatic letters were found in Amarna (Egypt).

2 Some confusion seems to exist about the exact extent of the term WPA (Izre'el 1992, 172). For this reason, it is best to give our own definition of the term here, which will be retained during the rest of the study. WPA includes all non-Babylonian native dialects written west of Babylonia. This excludes the Canaanite-Amarna dialects found, for instance, in the Byblos correspondence. This is due to the large extent of local North-West Semitic influences in these letters, as opposed to AmAkk and UgAkk, which makes these letters less suitable for comparison. MA is sometimes included here, since it has a scribal tradition borrowed from Babylonia, in common with all other WPA dialects.

situation, we find the Middle Assyrian (MA) corpus. While the royal inscriptions and literary compositions, such as the Tukultī-Ninurta epic, were written in SB, while texts with a more practical use, such as laws, letters and contracts, were written in the language of the people, albeit often with a number of Babylonianisms. Nowadays, there is some dissension as to when the Old Assyrian (OA) period ended and when the MA period started (cf. Veenhof/Eidem 2008, 23–24 § 1.2; Miglus 2011, 221). In our study, there can be no misconception: the MA period started, as determined by the oldest dated tablet (KAJ 177), with the reign of Aššur-nērārī II.[3] Disregarding royal inscriptions, MA texts are attested from the reign of Aššur-nērārī II (1424–1418/1414–1408) until the reign of Aššur-bēl-kala (1073–1056).[4] The obscure period between the end of level 1b archives in Kültepe and this first MA legal text has to be regarded as an intermediate period. Anything else belongs to the field of social and political historical studies, and is of little interest to our grammatical research.

§ 2 The map presented below attempts to approach the linguistic landscape in the late second millennium prior to the Assyrian conquest in a very global fashion. It should not be taken as gospel, especially as it does not take the overlap of different languages into account and omits the possibility of bilingual communities. Even nowadays, language distribution is very erratic, especially in the more elevated areas that contain small pockets of linguistic enclaves, which continue to thrive due to their remoteness. As for the late second millennium period, we can state that we know relatively little about the ethnic and linguistic composition of Northern Mesopotamia in this period. Most of our material comes from the aforementioned cities, such as Alalaḫ, Emar and Nuzi, where scribes did not write in their native languages. As such, we must mostly rely on PNs to approach the distribution of different ethnic groups. It seems that Hurrian and related groups were mostly centred around the northern part of the Tigris River and the Ḫabur Triangle, where the main cities of the Mittani Empire were centred. NWS groups, such as the Suteans, were found along the Mediterranean coast and the Euphrates River (cf. Kärger/Minx 2012, 367). As a nomadic

3 It appears that the marriage contract TIM 4 45 is actually the oldest MA text, but its eponym Urad-Šerūʾa cannot be dated, while the origin of the text itself is of unknown origin. It has some features not known from later MA, such as the values <áb> used in OA and <lib> (LUL). The particle *-mi* (§ 418ff) is also atypical for MA. Note also the absence of VA in l. 10 *aš-*[*š*]*a-ti-mi*. Another indication of an early date of the texts is the use of ZU and ZA for assimilated pronominal suffixes (§ 225) in l. 5 *mu-sà* and l. 6 *aš-ša-sú*. In terms of palaeography, Saporetti (1968) notes the uncommon PNs, with the palaeography being closer to Nuzi than MA. Again, in EMA (108f), Saporetti suggests an early dating to before EAd–Aub. Freydank gives a broader estimate and dates the eponym Urad-Šerūʾa to the reign of Aššrnīr II–Aub (BMCG, 177), based on its occurrence in KAM 10 20. However, there is no reason to assume that there could only be one eponym of the name Urad-Šerūʾa in Assyrian history, for instance, there were two eponyms during the reign of TN by the name Abattu. It seems, therefore, quite possible to date the said text to the period before Aššrnīr II, based on the Nuzi-like palaeography, unknown PNs and the odd sign values. Donbaz (2001) attempted to connect this Urad-Šerūʾa to two post OA tablets with the said eponym; however, these texts are clearly very close to the OA period, and therefore Donbaz' claim cannot be accepted. See also Veenhof (1982, 363 n4). KAM 10 25 is another possible early Middle Assyrian tablet.

4 Aššur-nērārī is mentioned in KAJ 177:10. The Giricano texts have been dated to the reign of Aššur-bēl-kala; see Giricano, 52 § III.2. At least three texts from the M 7 archive date to the reign of the king; see ALCA 1, 70–71; MARV 10, 1.

group, their geographical distribution overlapped to a great extent with Hurrians. Akkadian distribution continued from the south up until Aššur, but probably not north of it. The population of such places as Tell Ar-Rimāḫ (cf. Sasson 1979) and Nineveh (cf. Veenhof 1999) was most probably ethnic Hurrian. If there was a dialect continuum with Babylonian, direct contact was only possible through the area of the Euphrates River as the Zab area was home to the Hurrian kingdom of Arrapḫa.[5] We cannot be certain to what extent the Assyrian destruction of Ḫanigalbat changed the linguistic landscape. It is probably safe to say that Assyrian spread to cities such as Nineveh and Arbail. But, despite the colonization of Ḫanigalbat, the presence of Assyrian in Ḫanigalbat was less permanent and, if anything, seems to have opened up the possibility of the rise of Aramaean tribes. The settlement of these nomadic people probably ended the linguistic expansion of Assyrian over this area.

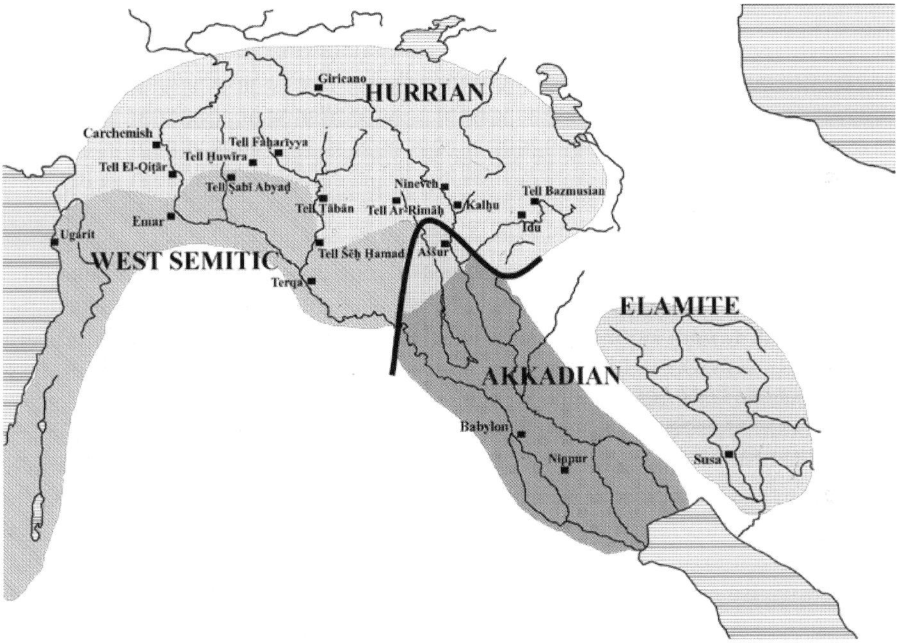

Figure 2: Map of the linguistic landscape.[6]

§ 3 The Assyrian language is usually regarded as a dialectal form of Akkadian.[7] The terminology of dialect has, until the present day, has been viewed negatively. It is usually seen as a corrupted form of the standard language, while many unjustly claim that their own

5 This does not mean that Akkadian-speaking communities were not present in this area. In fact, the influence of Assyrian Akkadian in the Nuzi corpus is well known (e.g., Wilhelm 1970, 35–38) and Assyrian people are certainly attested in Nuzi as having participated in Nuzi society (e.g., Maidman 2010, 15).

6 This map is a view of the linguistic landscape surrounding the Assyrian enclave, prior to the fall of Mittani. A possible Akkadian dialect continuum boundary is indicated by the black line. The map does not account for language overlapping.

7 For a discussion of the terminology of 'dialect', see Finegan (2008, 14–18).

speech is free of dialect (see Finegan 2008, 15). Such claims are unjustified, as dialects usually develop independently from the standard language, although they do share a common origin. Moreover, to a degree, every person speaks in dialect, which is regionally motivated; differences between social classes exist as well. One well-known example is the difference between Jewish and Christian Aramaic (NENA), spoken in the same region (Khan 2011, 709). At the same time, mutual intelligibility is known to have existed between different languages or is absent within one language because people do not want to communicate with people of another group (cf. Chamber/Trudgill 2004, 3–4). For Akkadian, the latter situation remains difficult to detect, but regional differences are quite apparent. Certainly, we will see that the Assyrian dialect of this study is sometimes more archaic than Standard Akkadian. This does not mean that there cannot be a corrupted form of a language. A famous example is the Canaanite-Akkadian language in some of the Amarna letters (Rainey 1996), but this did not reflect a spoken language, meaning that the terminology of "dialect" can be somewhat misleading. It should also be noted that there are no firm rules to establish the difference between a language and a dialect. This is mostly political or even religiously dictated, e.g., one can hardly claim that vernacular Moroccan and Egyptian are dialects of the same language (Arabic), as they are certainly not intelligible to each other. Moroccan Arabic is especially distant from Modern Standard Arabic and, in its daily use, is full of code-switching between Moroccan Arabic and non-Semitic languages, such as French, Berber and even Spanish in some areas.[8] Based on political and religious motives, the different Arabic dialects are usually not officially recognized or only partly. This brings us to another possible criterion of dialect: it is usually not written. If we applied this definition, Assyrian would not be regarded as dialect because it is often written. Moreover, the Assyrian texts are rather uniform and hardly betray any variety between speakers, be it regionally or socially motivated. This is actually a problem in most Akkadian dialects. An attempt by Goetze (1945) to prove different regional dialects based on sign values was accepted by some (e.g., Oppenheim 1964, 55), while Kraus (1973a, 32–34) rightfully pointed out that these dialectal differences are no more than orthographic variation. In addition, despite the structural differences between Assyrian and Babylonian it has been pointed out that both dialects had a remarkably parallel development, e.g., in MA/Middle Babylonian (MB), we have the loss of mimation, sound change /št/ > /lt/, the increased use of the perfectum over the preterite, and the loss of the t-stems. It could be argued that these changes were caused by the mutual intelligibility between the two dialects, where grammatical changes could easily spread over the different vernaculars (Parpola 1988c, 294). Moreover, the lexicon between the vernaculars did not show remarkably large differences (Kogan 2006; Streck 2007, 67ff). This has led to the conclusion that both dialects were mutually intelligible by some (Kouwenberg 2010, 12). Although Geller (2002, 563) compared the difference with Dutch and German, when referring to Neo-Assyrian (NA), he pointed out that both languages are only mutually intelligible when written. As a Dutch native, I must confess that I (and most other Dutch people) had to learn German in order to understand it. I therefore doubt whether this comparison is valid for Akkadian and question the extent of mutual intelligibility between Dutch and German. Blau

8 Code-switching is not an alien phenomenon to Akkadian. The royal archive of Qatna contains a number of instances where an Akkadian sentence is suddenly followed by a Hurrian verb; see Richter/Lange (2012).

(2012, 19ff) applied the wave model (Wellentheorie) to the Canaanite languages. According to this model, different languages, which separated at different moments in time from a proto-language, could later become more similar to each other because of long periods of intensive contact and geographic proximity. Thus, applying this model to Akkadian languages, Assyrian and Babylonian may originally have been quite different, but grew much closer to each other in the course of the second millennium BCE because of the intensive cultural contact. This has some merit when we compare OA and Old Babylonian (OB) with the smaller differences in MB and MA.

1.2 Historical setting

§ 4 After the OA period had come to a political climax with the reign of Šamšī-Adad I, the city of Aššur lost its political importance and fell into obscurity for centuries, together with most of Mesopotamia. The end of the OA period could have been formally marked with the deposition of Šamšī-Adad's dynasty, as well as the short intercession of usurper Puzur-Suen, a king who was erased from the Assyrian King List.[9] Around this period, the last OA texts were found.[10] During the following "Dark Age" (1759–1350) (see Cifola 1995, 17ff; Yamada 2017), the Hurrian people rose to prominence and several Hurrian states, such as Arrapḫa (modern Kirkuk) appeared, which were dependent on the Mittani Empire. A historical reference in the treaty, between the Mittani king Šattiwaza and Suppiluliuma of the Hittites, mentions that Šauštatar, one of Šattiwaza's predecessors, had carried away the two doors from Aššur to his own palace in Waššukanni.[11] This essentially meant the end of the political independence of Aššur, but the continuity of the Assyrian King List suggests that the royal dynasty continued as vassals of their Mittani overlords. A short interim period lacking any Assyrian royal inscription is believed by some to be related to the Hurrian dominion.[12] However, during the reign of Šuttarna II, the doors were returned, which signalled the renewed independence of Aššur and possibly even supremacy over Mittani.

§ 5 The details of Assyria's independence are unclear, but, under Aššur-nērārī II, the oldest known MA text (KAJ 177) was written. Less than a century later, Aššur-uballiṭ I wrote to the Egyptian court (letter EA 15 and EA 16) referring to himself as great king (LUGAL GAL in EA 16:1). The early MA texts from Aššur refer to the monarch as king for the first time (e.g., KAJ 162:10) since Šamšī-Adad I, instead of the traditional ÉNSI (*iššiʾakku*) "steward". However, the title "great king" equalled that of the contemporary kings of Hatti, Babylonia and Egypt. This caused the Babylonian king, Burnaburiaš II, to complain to the pharaoh as he regarded the Assyrians to be his vassals (EA 9). Nonetheless, Aššur-uballiṭ was also militarily successful as he boasts in his inscriptions to have conquered Muṣru and other Hurrian territory (RIMA 1 A.0.76.1). The city of Tell Ar-Rimāḥ is believed to have

9 See Grayson (1985); RIMA 1 A.0.40; Reade (2001, 5–8). The Puzur-Suen inscription featured a typical OA palaeography, orthography and language, which were used before the time of Šamšī-Adad I.

10 See Gelb/Sollberger (1957); Donbaz (2001). Many of the OA tablets from Aššur appear to be slightly younger than the material of Kültepe; for a more complete list, see Michel (2003, 121ff § 2.1).

11 See Weidner (1923, 38–57 no. 2); Beckman (1999, 42–54 no. 6A–B).

12 See Yamada (1994, 30f); Lion (2011, 155).

fallen at this time and was shortly thereafter reoccupied by the Assyrians.[13] In the south, another Mittani vassal, Arrapḫa (modern Kirkuk), was destroyed, supposedly by the armies of Aššur-uballiṭ I; with its destruction, the archives of Nuzi ended.[14] However, no evidence of an imposed Assyrian administration exists in the area, while the Babylonians ultimately annexed the country.[15] The sudden military supremacy of Assyria was due to Hittite military activities to the east of the Euphrates, when King Suppiluliuma had driven Tušratta of Mittani out of his capital of Wašukanni in the Ḫabur region and conquered his territories to the west of the Euphrates. Eventually, Mittani authority was restored by the Hittites in the Ḫabur region, involving treaties between the two countries drawn. Furthermore, the Mittani Empire lost its territory west of the Euphrates to the Hittites, while its eastern borders were threatened by the Assyrians (Bryce 2005, 161–63, 185–87). Relations with Babylonia were intensive, but uneasy according to the Assyrian chronicles. One of them tells us that Aššur-uballiṭ married his daughter into the Kassite royal household, whose son inherited the throne. The new monarch was deposed in a rebellion and, in response, Aššur-uballiṭ marched south and placed a son of the enthroned king, Burnaburiaš, on the throne (TCS 5 21:8'–17'). Little is known of Aššur-uballiṭ's direct successors, but Assyrian power seems to have waned again. Enlil-nīrārī is known for a battle with Babylonians at Sugāgu, close to Aššur (TCS 5 21:18'–23').

§ 6 Under Adad-nērārī I, the tables were turned and new skirmishes along the borders resulted in a Babylonian defeat (TCS 5 21:24''–31'). Such skirmishes continued until the end of the MA period without much effect. Adad-nīrāri I wrote in one of his inscriptions how he first turned Ḫanigalbat (former Mittani) into a vassal, while later totally incorporating it into his own kingdom after a campaign, which ended in the defeat of the Hurrians (RIMA 1 A.0.76.3). The king is likely to have destroyed the kingdom as inscriptions were prepared for a new palace in the former Hurrian capital of Taidu; however, these never left Aššur, as Hanigalbat recovered temporarily and regained independence (RIMA 1 A.0.76.4, 128).[16] Although the king's activities are not reflected in Assyrian archives from former Ḫanigalbat territory, the projects signalled the start of Assyrian colonial expansion in the west. International correspondence shows that this also frustrated diplomatic relations with the Hittites, who rejected a formal alliance (KUB 23 102). However, the Hittites ultimately opted for better relations, as they needed the Assyrians to bring stability and security to the Hurrian territory, which they had ravished (KBo 1 14). During the reign of Shalmaneser I, Hanigalbat was defeated once more and new Assyrian colonies were founded at former Hurrian settlements. Assyrian archives were established at the sites of Tell ʿĀmūdā, Tell Billā, Tell Faḫariyya, Tell Ar-Rimāḥ and Tell Aš-Šēḫ Ḥamad. Assyrian expansion reached the Euphrates and military expeditions took place in the mountain regions north of the empire. This caused even more tension with the Hittites, with whom they now shared borders, while

13 For further literature, see Llop (2011a, 600 n80).

14 See Harrak (1987, 52ff); Wilhelm (1989, 35); Maidman (2010, 16ff).

15 See Brinkman (1972, 275). Under Sa/TN, the region fell at last into Assyrian hands, as is shown by the reference to Arrapḫean works in KTN, as well as the Tell ʿAlī archive from the region, which dates back to the two kings (Llop 2011b, 211–12).

16 The total loss of Ḫanigalbat is disputed by Bloch (2012, 105 n34), who suggested that at least Tell Aš-Šēḫ Ḥamad and Tell Faḫariyya remained in Assyrian hands.

the conflict came to a head in the battle of Niḫriya, which brought about the defeat of the Hittites at the hands of the Assyrian king, Tukultī-Ninurta.[17] After this event Tukultī-Ninurta waged war with Babylonia and conquered the country, bringing the size of the MA Empire to its apex. This victory was celebrated in the Tukultī-Ninurta epic describing the wars between the two countries. The king installed a governor in Babylonia and carried off slaves and booty to Assyria. Together with Hurrian slaves from Hanigalbat, these spoils of war were used to build a new capital 3 km north of Aššur, which the king named after himself, namely, Kār-Tukultī-Ninurta. The king's reign ended violently when he was murdered by his son, Aššur-nādin-apli, who managed to succeed his father for a few years (Yamada 1998; Jakob 2017, 132).

§ **7** With the death of Tukultī-Ninurta, the capital shifted back to Aššur. Coincidently, many archives in the periphery did not continue (Tell ʿAlī, Tell ʿĀmūdā, Tell Billa, Tell Faḫariyya, Tell Ḫuwīra, Tell Ar-Rimāḥ, Tell Aš-Šēḫ Ḥamad), with only the archives of Tell Ṣabī Abyaḍ and Tell Ṭābān continuing and informing us of the developments in Ḫanigalbat. During this crisis, the governors of conquered territory gained more independence, which eventually resulted in the foundation of vassal (or independent) kingdoms at the end of the MA period, as attested in the land of Māri (Maul 1992, 47), and the land of Ḫana (cf. Podany 2002, 73–74). With the installation of Tiglath-pileser I as king in Aššur, a short period of (at least military) revival took place. The monarch writes in his inscriptions how his empire was threatened by Aramean tribes, which he ultimately defeated. The campaigns of the king brought his armies as far as Lebanon in the south and Lake Van in Turkey in the north. At least this last claim can be confirmed by a rock relief and inscription of the king in this area (RIMA 2 A.0.87.15; Schrader 1885, 1*). After securing the western and northern borders, the king marched to Babylon and conquered the city once more (RIMA 2 A.0.87.4). Despite these military achievements, texts from Aššur show a decline in the number of provinces since the reign of Tukultī-Ninurta. This testifies to the fact that the Assyrians were unable, for unknown reasons, to stabilize their conquered territories for a long period. After the reign of Aššur-bēl-kāla, the empire seems to have collapsed, except for the core area, while Assyria fell into obscurity again until the early first millennium BCE (Jakob 2017, 132–40).

1.3 Previous scholarship

§ **8** Given the lack of studies that concentrate on MA grammar, it is necessary to consider studies of the other Assyrian dialects which often make reference to MA material and have therefore shaped our current knowledge. In general, the first studies on the Assyrian dialect concentrated on NA material, which especially in the early history of Assyriology was better known. The first substantial study of NA was carried out by Ylvisaker (1911), who published a grammar based on the Sargon II correspondence. Around this time, the MA laws (MAL) attracted some interest from scholars, particularly in terms of the unique verbal system, resulting in a monograph by Lewy (1921) and one review by Landsberger (1924). The

17 See Harrak (1987, 257–61); Bryce (2005, 313–19).

handwritten text of Lewy's study made his results difficult to access. Driver and Miles (1935, 7–12) listed a number of examples highlighting the development and differences in orthography in the law text. For letters and administrative documents, Finkelstein (1953, 115a) was the first to discuss the MA grammar of letters and other administrative documents by listing the few peculiarities of the Tell Billā texts. Von Soden (1957/58) made a number of short remarks on NA phonology and morphology. Unfortunately, Deller's dissertation on NA phonology (1959), which contained a number of references to MA, has remained unpublished, but several articles were published with relevance to Assyrian grammar (see bibliography).

§ 9 An important contribution to our knowledge of Assyrian grammar was made by von Soden. In his grammar on Akkadian, he consistently refers to the situation in the Assyrian dialects, while listing some of the main features of MA in the appendix of his grammar (GAG, 301 § 195). Two dissertations on the Assyrian dialects were published by his former students: Hecker on OA (GKT 1968) and W. Mayer on MA (UGM 1971). Mayer's grammar was initially well received by reviewers (Aro 1972; Fohrer 1972; Roberts 1972; Hecker 1972–73; Lambert 1973). However, some criticism of the hasty conclusions reached by the author was made by Postgate (1974) and a number of mistakes had to be corrected (Freydank 1975), while more recently his results have been regarded more critically (e.g., Cochavi-Rainey 2011, 8). The grammar was modelled after the example of von Soden's GAG, but was brief in the actual description of the grammar. Mayer based his work on a considerably smaller number of texts than is nowadays available; an estimation of about 750 texts could be too high as (following the indices) less than 200 texts were used. Like many older grammatical treatments of Akkadian dialects, no attention was given to the chronological and geographical distribution of the different genres.[18] During his study, few texts from the later periods and colonies were known; however, with our current knowledge of Assyrian, better results are possible.

§ 10 Since W. Mayer's study, little has been done with regard to Assyrian grammar. The main contribution was made by Parpola (1974), who discussed the Assyrian verb *naša'u* for both MA and NA. A short discussion on moods and tempus in the Tell Aš-Šēḫ Ḥamad letters was carried out by Cancik-Kirschbaum (MATSH, 62–65), with the discussion continued in Streck's (1997) review of her study. Farber (1990) briefly discussed the possibility of the *i-modus* in MA, although the relevant forms occur in no more than a handful of texts. Our knowledge about the transition of MA to NA has increased, due to texts from the late MA and short discussions on their grammar; see Maul (1992, 18–19) and Radner (Giricano, 53–54). Parpola continued to publish on NA, often with references to grammar relevant to MA as well (e.g., Parpola 1972; various notes in LAS 2 etc.). A grammar (SNAG) and a study on orthography (Luukko 2004) were published in the context of the "The Neo-Assyrian Text Corpus Project". Furthermore, four short overviews on Assyrian or MA appeared (Huehnergard 2005, 599–603; Kouwenberg 2010, 18; Streck 2011, 371–73; Luukko/Van Buylaere 2017). Studies on the grammar of the MA onomasticon must be mentioned as well. Most important is OMA 2 (90ff) and a short study

18 Cf. Hasselbach (2005, 19–20) on Gelb's (1961) grammar of OAkk.

by Streck (2002b, 116). A short discussion by Salah (MPR, 63–65) on the grammatical peculiarities of the lists from TŠḪ mostly revolves around the onomasticon.

1.4 Geographical setting

1.4.1 Aššur

§ 11 The name of the land of Assyria and of the Assyrian language derived etymologically from the city of Aššur, which is the place of origin of the Assyrian people. It was not until the NA period that natives from cities such as Nineveh, Erbil and Nimrud (ancient Kalḫu) could be regarded as essential parts of the Assyrian heartland. This process only started during the MA period when these cities were incorporated into the kingdom of Aššur for the first time. Unfortunately, no archives from the MA period were found in archaeological excavations, besides a few royal inscriptions.[19] This makes Aššur and Kār-Tukultī-Ninurta the only two sites in the Assyrian heartland that have provided us with significant philological material from the MA period. It should therefore not come as a surprise that about 60% of MA texts come from Aššur, although this percentage has steadily decreased over recent decades with the excavations of new MA sites in Syria. All the different MA archives were described together by Pedersén in ALCA 1, then again by Pedersén (1998), and by Postgate (1986) and in selected archives in more detail also by Postgate (2013), while a few texts have turned up in NA archives (ALCA 2). Pedersén numbered the archives M 1–M 14, a classification that is still commonly used and will be applied in this study as well.

§ 12 The table below shows the number of texts per archive, resulting in about 2,000, as counted by Pedersén in his two studies.[20] However, as the tablet collection from Aššur and Kār-Tukultī-Ninurta is shared by the museums of Berlin and Istanbul, a proper inventory of all tablets has yet to be made. As such, Pedersén (1998, 88f) could only account for a maximum of 56 tablets from Kār-Tukultī-Ninurta, but this number was soon outdated following the publication of 173 tablets in MARV 4 (2001) and a number of additional texts in the other MARV volumes. The table comprises all the main genres of literary and religious texts, edicts, letters, contracts and notes. As many of the literary and religious texts are in SB, the actual amount of truly MA texts is slightly smaller. Most archives are centred around the reigns of Adad-nērārī I and Tukultī-Ninurta. Only M 6 has no texts dating back to this period. Two archives start before it, with M 9 centring around the reigns of Erība-Adad I/Aššur-uballiṭ I, but with the first texts dating back to the reign of Aššur-nērārī II. Still, this archive attests a few land sales from the post-Kültepe OA period (e.g., de Ridder 2013a). The biggest archive, M 4, centres around the latter MA kings. The chronological spread of the Aššur archives is rather similar to the periphery.

19 Our lack of knowledge is, to some extent, caused by the excavations in Nineveh having been concentrated on the two citadels of Kuyunjik and Nebi Yunus; see Pedersén (1998, 158ff).

20 The actual number of tablets often proved to be higher, partly due to the lack of excavation numbers for a large amount of tablets. This has become obvious with the more recent publications of M 4 and M 7 in the MARV series.

	Texts:	Period:	Main persons/type:	Primary publication:
M 1	6		Library	–
M 2	About 160		Library	–
M 3	4		School tablets	–
M 4	About 650	Ad–Tp (?)	*ša muḫḫi/rab ginā'e*	MARV 1–3; 5–9; Gauthier forthcoming
M 5	65+	Adn–TN, Abk?		Unpublished
M 6	115	Ad		NTA, Johnson forthcoming
M 7	420+	Sa–Abk		MARV 10; KAM 11; StAT 5
M 8	140+	Sa–TN	Ubru	KAM 7
M 9	140	Aššnīr II–And	Kidin-Adad, Iddin-Kube and others	KAJ; DSC 1; DSC 3; KAM 10
M 10	83	Adn–TN	Urad-Šerū'a family	UŠA
M 11	60+	Adn–TN	Bābu-aḫa-iddina	BAI; Donbaz 1997
M 12	About 60	Adn–Tn	Uṣur-bēl-šarra and others	KAJ; KAV; MARV 1; MARV 2
M 13	56	Sa–TN	Ṣillī-Aššur and others	KAM 11
M 14	35	EAd–TN	Adad-zēra-iqīša and others	KAJ; Schmidt forthcoming
	1,994+			

Figure 3: Archives from Aššur.

1.4.2 Peripheral territory

§ 13 With the annexation of new territories, archives were started in their administrative centres. The first example was Tell Ar-Rimāḥ, possibly during the reign of Aššur-uballiṭ I (Llop 2011a, 600). Soon thereafter, the archives of Tell Alli and Tell Billa were started during the reign of Adad-nērārī I. With the conquest and pacification of Ḫanigalbat by Adad-nērārī, the archive of Tell Faḫariyya was started in the Ḫabur region, which was presumably the former Mittani capital of Wašukanni. Under Shalmaneser I, the Assyrians built a large number of new local administrative centres and outposts. Most archives from this period are dated from the reigns of the said king and Tukultī-Ninurta I. From all available find spots, at least a few examples are available. As the map in Figure 6 shows, a few smaller archives have been found in the areas east and south of Aššur. Some diplomatic letters written by Assyrians or in Assyrian dialect were found outside Assyria in Nippur, Ḫattuša and Amarna. The few letters from Amarna and Nippur are from the reigns of Aššur-uballiṭ I and Enlil-nērārī, while those from Ḫattuša date from between the reign of Adad-nērārī I and that of Tukultī-Ninurta I.

§ 14 The statistics for the available data on archives show that as much as 58% of the corpus originates from Aššur and Kār-Tukultī-Ninurta. This number used to be well over 75% in the period before the excavation of the three main sites in former Ḫanigalbat. Both Tell Aš-Šēḫ Ḥamad and Tell Ṣābī Abyaḍ comprise over one quarter of the corpus, while exact numbers are still unknown. The letter forms of correspondence were published first (MATSH), while administrative texts have more recently been published (LVUH; MPR); a considerable amount awaits publication (Cancik-Kirschbaum forthcoming). Likewise, the (semi-)published Tell Ṣābī Abyaḍ texts total no more than 28, with the vast majority of the texts still awaiting publication (Wiggermann forthcoming). Most of the Tell Ṭābān and Tell

Faḫariyya texts that were excavated during recent decades remain unpublished and could not be consulted. The only large peripheral site, which has been completely published, is Tell Ḫuwīra (MATC).

Find spot	Period	Published texts	Total	Primary publication
Aššur	Aššnīr II–Abk	1,000+	1,994+	See above
KTN	TN	173 in MARV 4	173+(?)	MARV 4
Amarna	Aub	2	2	EA 15–16
Ḫattuša	About Ad–TN	12	12	KBo/KUB series
Giricano	Abk	15	15	Giricano
Nimrud	–	1	1	Lambert 1969
Nippur	En	3	3	Chapter 25.7
Nineveh	–	3	3	Chapter 25.7
Ugarit	About TN	4	4	Chapter 25.7
Kulišḫinaš	Adn–TN, Ari[21]	About 14	About 14	Chapter 25.7
Šuri	Sa	1	1	Chapter 25.7
Tell ˁAlī (Ali)	Adn–TN	25	25	Ismail/Postgate 2008
Tell Barri	?	?	4	Chapter 25.7
Tell Bdēri	Tp	Only royal	–	Maul 1992
T. Bazmusian	-	7	7	Chapter 25.7
Tell Billa	Adn–TN	67	67	Billa
Tell Faḫariyya	Adn–TN[22]	12	62	Chapter 25.7
Tell Fray	<Unknown>	–	11	–
Tell Ḫuwīra	TN	101[23]	101	MATC
Tell Ar-Rimāḥ	Aub, Adn–TN	132	216	Chapter 25.3
T. Šēḫ Ḥamad	Sa–TN	About 242	570[24]	MATSH; LVUH; MPR
T. Ṣabī Abyaḍ	TN–Ari	18	315	Chapter 25.4
Tell Ṭābān	Sa–Nae, Tp?	6	141[25]	Chapter 25.5
<Ḫana>	TN, Ad–Tp	2	2	Chapter 25.7
			About 3,743	

Figure 4: List of the MA find spots.

21 One text published in Maul (2004, 2–5 no. 1) is linked to the eponym Mušēzib-Aššur. This is an eponym that belongs to the reign of Tiglath-pileser I following the studies of Bloch (2012, 290 n34); Freydank (2016a, 90). Additionally, there may have been an eponym of the same name around 1150 BCE, which would be the reign of Aššur-dān I. See BGMC (154); Maul (2004, 3). In any case, following the date formula of this text, scribal activity in Tell ˁĀmūdā continued for a significant period following the reign of Tukultī-Ninurta.

22 Following the study of Bloch (2012), the eponym Mudammeq-Nusku (OIP 79 5–6) belongs to the end of the reign of Adad-nērārī I, which indicates that the Ḫabur region and Tell Faḫariyya continuously stayed under Assyrian control following the conquest of the said king.

23 Ninety-seven numbered texts plus four envelopes.

24 See Llop (2012b, 218).

25 According to Shibata (2016, 101), there are 64 complete tablets, 77 tablet fragments and 307 small tablet fragments. Only the first two categories are included in this inventory.

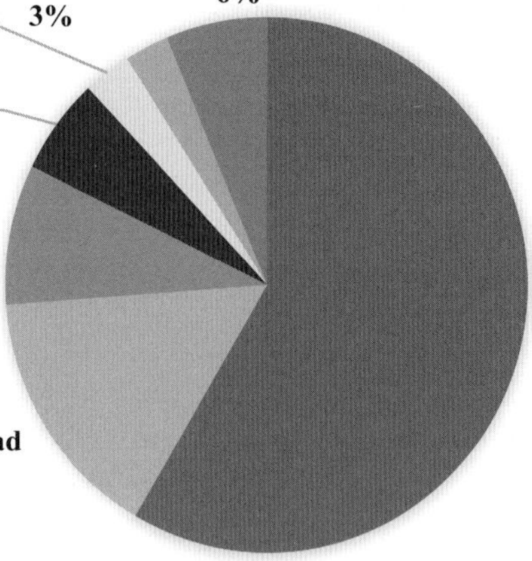

Figure 5: Circle diagram of find spots.

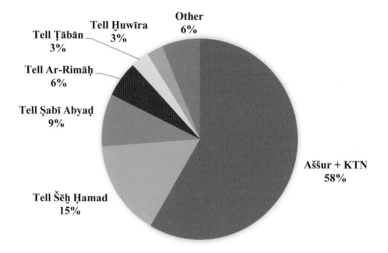

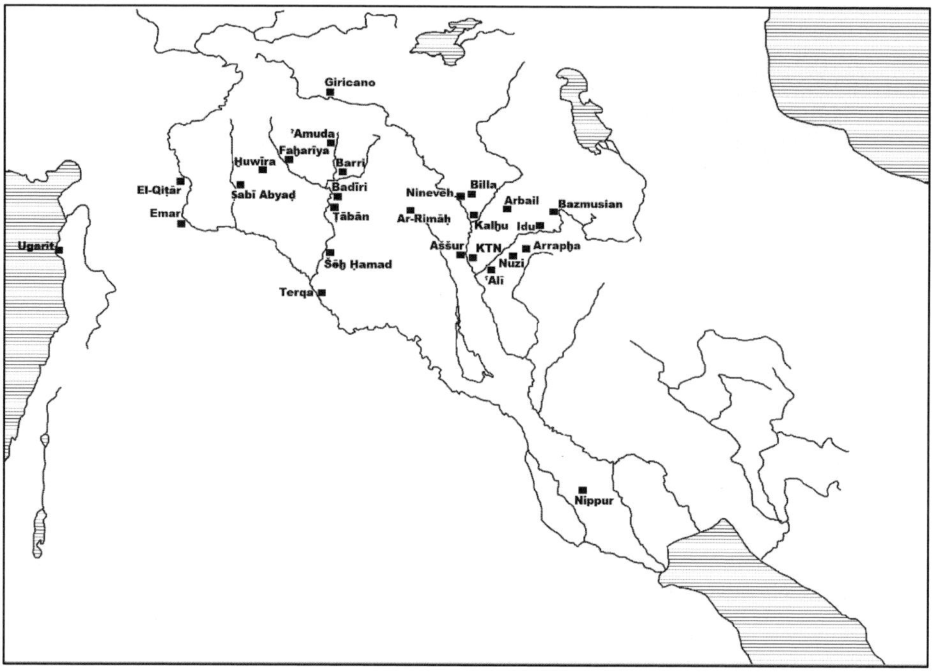

Figure 6: Geographical spread of sites with MA texts.[26]

26 Amarna and Boğäzkale are not included. For modern GNs, the noun 'tell' is omitted.

1.4.2.1 Chronology of peripheral texts

§ 15 Before discussing evidence from these sites, we should first look at the chronology of the expansion of the Assyrian Empire. Unlike some studies, we will limit ourselves to what can be deduced from the date formula of archives. What royal inscriptions and archives from Aššur tell us is of less relevance. Leaving aside the discussion of the reliability of these texts, this study does not concentrate on the moment when a hostile city was pacified, but on the moment when scribal traditions in the conquered city continued. The site of Tell Ar-Rimāḥ is the first site where archives continued outside of Assyria and Aššur-uballiṭ I, which is somewhat expected as it lies relatively close to the Assyrian heartland.

§ 16 Most archives flourish under Sa/TN and do not continue after the murder of the latter king (cf. Llop 2012b, 214–15), with the exception of the Tell Ṣābī Abyad archive, which continued even until the reign of Enlil-kudurri-uṣur (Wiggermann 2010, 19, 59). Tell Ṭābān seems to have continued as well, following the eponym Saggiu (Nae) in TabT 05-11:13 (Shibata 2007, 65–66). However, only about 10 out of the over 100 tablets have been published (cf. Shibata 2012, 490–91), so there is little information on the actual chronological orientation of said archive. A fragment of a seal from Aššur-dān I was found in Tell Ḥamidīya in the Ḫabur Triangle, which suggests the building of a palace during this period (ḤT 6 in Deller 1990, 330). However, it may be noted that most of the peripheral text concentrations earlier than 1400 deal with royal inscriptions: Tell Badīri, Satu Qala, Tell Ṭābān and Ḫana (see below). All except for Satu Qala consist of royal inscriptions and administrative documents/letters, although there is only one damaged tablet from Tell Badīri, while there are only two Ḫana texts. When we put the numbers of tablets in this chart, we find that over 65% of the texts date to no earlier than the reign of Tukultī-Ninurta. Only 1% are exclusively later (Giricano), while the rest are mainly the unpublished texts of Tell Ṭābān and Ṣabī Abyaḍ dating to both periods (Shalmaneser I and later), meaning that no definitive statistics can be provided here. However, it is safe to say that at least 75% of the texts date to the very short period of And–TN, a period of no more than 70 years. This picture is confirmed in Figure 7, with most of them dating back to this short period.[27]

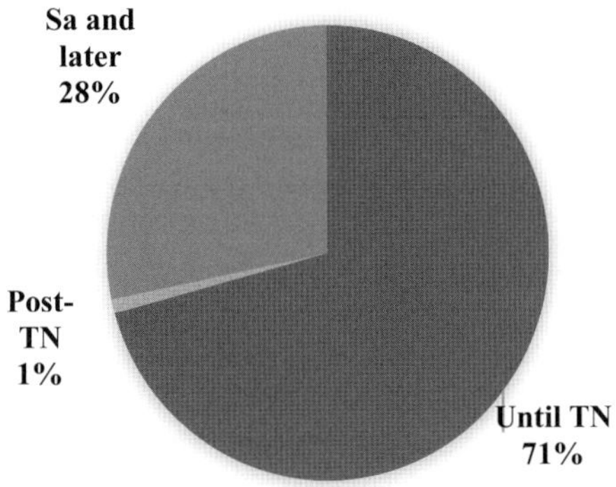

Figure 7: Chronology of texts according to the archives.

§ 17 The extent to which regional differences in Assyrian dialect could develop in such a short period is questionable, especially given that the authors of the letters from this period

27 This is difficult to say, as there are no preliminary proposals for a sequence of the eponyms of Adn as there are for Sa and TN.

(at least) appear almost exclusively to be of Assyrian descent. Even in the slightly more ethnically diverse area of contact, however, Machinist pointed out that Assyrian personal names (PNs) are overrepresented and explained this as being in part due to the filling of a void left by the deportation of the natives (Machinist 1982, 18–19). This is reasserted by the publication of lists of persons from TŠḪ in MPR, showing that this town, in former Ḫanigalbat territory, was inhabited by people with a largely Akkadian onomasticon. Hurrian and other ethnic groups are well attested in texts from the Assyrian heartland, especially KTN, where there is a number of lists dealing with entire families living and working there.[28] In the other direction, we find a small number of Elamite families in Tell Ḫuwīra (MATC, 14). These people show a degree of integration and assimilation in Assyrian society, as some of them adopted partly or fully Assyrian names, including the theophoric element of Aššur (Jakob 2005, 184–85). Yet, it would be unreasonable to assume that people from former Mittani territory could not ascend the social pyramid. Natives from Ḫanigalbat could also obtain high positions. There was a Sutean governor in Ḫarbe (Tell Ḫuwīra; see MATC, 11b); similarly, we have a Katmuḫean governor of the province of Dūr-Katlimmu (Tell Aš-Šēḫ Ḥamad) according to DeZ 2211 (Jakob 2003, 370; cf. LVUH, 70), a Hurrian mayor of Aššur (KAJ 106:6–9), and a scribe named Kidin-Sîn, who was the son of a Sutean (Jakob 2003, 243 no. 64), among other examples (cf. Jakob 2005, 181). One may even argue that Adad-nīrārī I initially tried to govern Ḫanigalbat through a native vassal king, Šattuara I (RIMA 1 A.0.76.3.), before the local royal house was replaced by the family of Aššur-iddin, which was related to the Assyrian dynasty. Rather than assuming a large distance between the native population of Ḫanigalbat and the Assyrian occupiers, Szuchman (2007, 96–97) pointed out that the archaeological evidence shows coexistence and cultural continuity in at least some settlements. However, the governing of local provinces ultimately led to the semi-independence of a number of vassal kingdoms. So far, we know of the kingdoms of Ḫana, Māri and Idu, each of which ruled was by its own royal house during the reign of Tiglath-pileser I. But at least for Māri and Ḫana, the royal house has traces going back to the reigns of Shalmaneser I and Tukultī-Ninurta I, with the first mention of a local king occurring at the end of the reign of Aššur-dān I and the start of the reign of Ninurtī-Tukultī-Aššur.[29] We could explain this by the inability of the capital to effectively govern its new territories. We already noted that, during the reign of Tukultī-Ninurta I, the archives ended because the site was abandoned (Tell Ḫuwīra) or even destroyed (Tell Aš-Šēḫ Ḥamad) (cf. Llop 2012b, 214–15), while the king had to campaign in the region against insurgencies and remnants of Ḫanigalbat. It is therefore not inconceivable that some provinces started to take the defence of their territory into their own hands and thus gradually became independent.[30] This tradition of semi-

28 For example, MARV 2 6; cf. Freydank (1980).

29 Evidence of early references to the royal house of Māri has been gathered on multiple occasions, most notably by Maul (1992, 47–54) and Shibata (2012). For an early reference to a Ḫana dynasty, see RIMA 2 A.0.89.2001. A reference to a king of Ṭābētu is found in a note from the M 6 archive, dating to the end of the reign of Aššur-dān I; A 1736 (NTA, 18):2. Ṭābētu, modern Tell Tābān, is the site from where most textual evidence for this kingdom was found; see Maul (1992, 48).

30 The situation resembles the early Abbassid caliphate, which is traditionally regarded as having reached its apex during the Hārūn Ar-Rašīd period (786–809 CE), a mere 30 years after it started; but, even during this rather short reign, parts of the empire began to segregate from the centre. Morocco was

autonomous vassal kingdoms, officially being loyal to the central authority, is reflected by the MA royal inscriptions of Māri, still paying homage to Tiglath-pileser I.

1.5 Selection of texts

1.5.1 Criteria

§ 18 At this point, it may be worthwhile to look at the different points of view from other Akkadian grammarians on different dialects. Huehnergard (1989), in his grammar on the Akkadian of Ugarit, made a strong distinction between texts that originate from elsewhere and those that were of genuinely Ugaritic composition.[31] This is certainly of relevance in the case of literary texts, which were no more than copies from Babylonian examples. A failure to make any division in the material of any kind would only render an imprecise grammar and reduce its value (see Flemming 1999, 701–2). However, a "minimalistic" approach to the letters meant that every letter for which an Ugaritic origin could not be proven was excluded from the corpus as well. Even texts from Ugarit's port, modern Raˀs Ibn Hānī, were excluded despite the fact that they were so similar to Ugaritic tablets, they could have been written by the same scribes. Akkadian literary and lexical texts were regarded as being of little relevance because of their lack of WPA features; however, they were nonetheless still considered because some of them showed WPA peculiarities in the orthography. However, Huehnergard chose to always mention them as a distinct group, as they were still very different from the other texts. Ultimately, this brought the corpus of 960 cuneiform tablets down to 577 used for the research. Huehnergard's goals are certainly different from ours; rather than researching the actual grammar of UgAkk, his goal was to describe the scribal tradition as Akkadian (Akkadian was never a spoken language in the city). A different approach to the same corpus was taken by van Soldt (1991), who included the most material, but ordered the data by genre and date of the texts. Like Huehnergard, this approach is suitable for describing scribal traditions with the advantage that the differences between genres are clearer.

§ 19 For NA, Hämeen-Anttila (SNAG) and Luukko (2004) based their grammatical research for a large portion on the letters from the correspondence of Sargon II and the Assyrian scholarly letters from the reigns of Esarhaddon and Assurbanipal. This approach is somewhat understandable, considering the relatively large size of the NA letter corpus and the rich language that the letters contain.[32] For example, we have royal letters by

permanently lost by the caliphate to the local Zayid Shīˀa dynasty of the Idrissids, while a governor, who was sent to quell a rebellion in the province of Ifriqīya, seized the opportunity to found the dynasty of the Aghlabids, but remained a formal vassal and paid tribute as such. During the reign of Harun's son, al-Ma'mun, Persia acquired a similar position as a semi-independent vassal under the Tahirid dynasty.

31 Similar criteria to Huehnergard's were used by Izre'el (1991a–b) in his grammar on Amurru. However, as all Amurru texts have been found either in Amarna or in Ḫattuša, his selection was more straightforward.

32 The Sargon II correspondence alone already consists of 1,300 letters. See Luukko (2004, 18 n70); cf. this amount with the 600 texts used in W. Mayer's UGM and the 599 texts in Huehnergard (1989).

Sargon (SAA 1, nos. 1–27) and letters from his governors from various places of the empire (SAA 1, 5, 15, 19). Furthermore, we also have a lot of seventh century letters from scholars (SAA 10), priests (SAA 13), Esarhaddon's royal letters and letters by various officials (SAA 16). This is a luxury that we do not have in MA, where most letters come from high officials born in Aššur, while the few letters from Assyrian kings are rather heterogeneous in language and in orthography. Only letters of the Ḫanigalbat kings and the Sutean governor of Tell Ḫuwīra were likely written by people of a different linguistic background. However, just as most MA letters come from the reign of Tukultī-Ninurta I, the vast majority of the NA letters are from the reigns of Sargon II, Esarhaddon and Assurbanipal. In theory, the restricted corpus of Hämeen-Anttila and Luukko helped focus their research. They mostly disregarded the majority of literary texts and the Babylonized language of royal inscriptions. Additionally, the authors argued that the language of administrative and economic texts was more linguistically conservative than the letters. This restricted group of selected texts is, however, a luxury that cannot be afforded for grammatical research of MA, given how limited our corpus is.

1.5.2 Definition of Middle Assyrian grammar

§ 20 In order to analyse irregularities in texts within the MA context, we will first need to define the MA language and when a text can be called MA. A preliminary diagnostic sign may be the orthography. MA developed perhaps the most accurate orthographic system compared to other systems of cuneiform. It could indicate vowel length and the gemination of consonants together, unlike OA. Moreover, it was in the process of developing a system to indicate all emphatic consonants with an independent sign: <ṭí/é> (TÍ); <ṭu> (GÍN); <qa> (QA); <qi/e> (KIN); <qu> (KUM); <ṣu> (ZUM); <ṣi/e> (ZÍ); the exceptions to this rule are <d/ṭa> (DA) and <ṣ/za> (ZA). Of course, contemporary and later dialects incorporated some of these values as well; however, in NA, the value /ṭi/, for instance, is shared by DI and TÍ (cf. Luukko 2004, 45), whereas, in MA, only TÍ was used regularly. Additionally, there was the tendency to use some signs for special combinations: <šá> (NÍG) for the relative pronoun *ša*, ŠÚ for pronominal suffixes *-šu* and *-šunu*, and Ù for the conjunction *u*. Additionally, unlike OB/OA, the labials /b/ and /p/ are usually distinguished by using PI for <pi/e>. For /b/pu/, there is still no difference. Although /w/ ceased to be indicated by PI, /ʔ/ and /y/ received their own signs with ʔA and IA. However, MA orthography is certainly not limited to texts written in the Assyrian dialect of Akkadian. In addition, texts are not grammatically explicit. There is a number of additional characteristics, which can be used to more pragmatically identify a text as being MA.

§ 21 *Main criteria: a text needs to derive from an MA archaeological context.* While these criteria seem natural, it is inapplicable when archaeological context is unknown because the text was obtained from the antiquities market. Still, regardless of these problems, even texts from Aššur can present issues. The population of Aššur was never homogeneous and, during the MA period, a Hurrian segment with relatively high social status can be expected, given the occurrence of a mayor of the city with a Hurrian name, that is, Eḫlipi, son of Alguza (KAJ 103:7–10 TN). Secondly, a Babylonian element was present in the city, at least since the meddling of Aššur-uballiṭ I in Kassite affairs (Wiggermann 2008b). Scribes with Babylonian names, including theophoric elements, such as Marduk and Nabû, occur throughout MA history (cf. Jakob 2003, 243–44). A Babylonian background could result in some misunderstanding when writing legal formulae in MA dialect. A good example is the tablet KAJ 6, written by Nasḫira-Marduk, son of Yāku-limmer[33]: *a-na pa-i* (=*a-na pi-i*) KAJ 6:4; *mi-i-mu-ú-šu ga-BI-e* (=*mi-(im)-mu-šu gab-be*) l. 9; *li-ba-a-la* (normally *lìb-bi-*URU) l. 11; *i-BA-la-aḫ-šu* l. 12; *ú-BA-sú* l. 20; *TE-e-ni* (*dēni*) l. 20; *ka-ús-pí* (=*ṣarpu*? 'silver?') l. 23. A text like this has previously convinced some Assyriologists that the difference between /b/ and /p/ had been lost in MA (Dahood/Deller/Köbert 1965, 37 § 8.9); but, in this case, it is more likely due to a foreign misunderstanding than anything else. The issue with archaeological context goes two ways: letters by Assyrians to outlying regions were found in places such as Ugarit (e.g., RS 06.198). Some Assyriologists dealing with the same issue in other areas often take the minimalist approach and refrain from analysing these works in their studies, such as Huehnergard (1989, 8), who omitted the Raʾs ibn Hāni texts from his study of Ugaritic Akkadian, even though he deemed it likely that they were written by the same scribes. While there are valid arguments to be made for restricting one's field of research, at the same time, it creates the need to separately analyse such otherwise forgotten texts.

§ **22** *Second criteria: A text has to have an Assyrian date formula, with* a limmum *eponym; or, in absence of a preserved eponym, it must contain Assyrian month names.* This is an important point, since only texts from the Assyrian Empire are dated by a *limmum* eponym. There are some (albeit a few) exceptions to this rule; for instance, the OB text Ḫarādum 2 29, with an eponym date formula, derives from an OB site, but otherwise has no Assyrian features.[34] These criteria identify texts as MA, which otherwise are atypical. Most notable are the Ḫana-style texts, which we will discuss in more detail below. Unfortunately, many texts do not have a date preserved, or never had one to begin with, such as the Tell El-Qiṭār text (Snell 1983/84) and most (but not all) letters. Additionally, a date according to the Assyrian calendar is helpful, but its absence is not decisive. First of all, from the reign of Tp onwards, double date formulas with both Babylonian and Assyrian calendars can be found, as well as documents with only a Babylonian month. In the Giricano archive (Abk), only Babylonian months are attested, while, in the NA period, the calendar had been abolished. Moreover, we will see that local calendars could also be used.

§ **23** *Third criteria: A text must be written by an Assyrian scribe.* These criteria can be applied when no date is present, for instance, in letters. The main problem is how to establish whether a scribe is Assyrian, as their name is often not attested or not unambiguously Assyrian. HoweverHowever, in the case of the Tell El-Qiṭār text, the scribe Anumae, son of Talmae, appears to be of Hurrian descent (Snell 1983/84, 166), thus precluding the classification of the text as MA. We already discussed some of the errors that could arise in relation to texts written by non-native Assyrians. Moreover, these criteria

33 Cf. the remarks of Saporetti, who concluded that the scribe was from a different non-Assyrian school (DSC 3, 11).

34 This text features the eponym Abī-Suen (l. 30) unknown from the OA eponym list (cf. Ups and downs). Nor do we find any other typical OA features in this text; on the contrary, gemination is attested (*an-ni-im* l. 7), while Amorite people, such as Yasmaʿ-Addu (l. 17), are featured.

are not flawless, since Assyrian monarchs especially had the tendency not to use the Assyrian dialect when writing to outlying areas, most clearly in EA 16 (Mittani-Akkadian, according to von Soden 1952a, 434), RS 34.165 8 (Babylonian) and possibly Ni 669 (Babylonian$^{?}$). The language of the king is Assyrian in the letters MATSH 9 and MARV 4 8, which, in the very least, show that the choice of language was intentional. For this reason, we have to be careful with letters such as the Ugarit RS 06.198 (AO 18.889), even though it was written by an Assyrian and appears to have some characteristics of Assyrian grammar.

§ **24** *Fourth criteria: MA palaeography.* This criterion deserves a dedicated study and will not be applied here. Studies of palaeography are somewhat hampered by the lack of proper copies of the texts from KAJ, which contain the most important and oldest MA documents up until the Sa/TN period. The publication of the M 4 and M 6 archives in the MARV series and NTA are good resources for the later period.

§ **25** Nonetheless, for some controversial texts, the situation is not clear because, for instance, the identity of the scribe may not be known, or the date of the tablet may be omitted or not preserved. These texts could be quoted, but only when essential to a discussion of the grammar. They may provide valuable information on MA grammar, but this information cannot in itself be trusted to represent the Assyrian dialect, rather than other (unknown) vernacular Akkadian dialects. Some examples will be discussed below.

§ **26** The tablets Rm 376 and Lambert 1969 are two large tablets containing a number of incantations. There is a number of other known MA incantations, but their language is clearly not Assyrian (Zomer 2018). However, these two tablets feature a number of typical Assyrianisms (Lambert 1965, 285; Lambert 1969, 35; Veldhuis 1991, 63f). However, Babylonian influence on this genre of texts has led to a rather inconsistent use of the language, e.g.:

- *ul pa-ṣu-na-at* 'she is not veiled' Lambert 1969:45=Babylonian *ūl pussumat* ~ Assyrian *lā paṣṣunat*
- *ul ta-pa-te* 'she cannot open it' Lambert 1969:42=Babylonian *ūl ipette* ~ Assyrian *lā tapatte*
- *an-nu-ú te-šu-ú* 'this is chaos' Lambert 1969:47=Assyrian *anniu tašēˀu*$^{?}$
- *ú-ter-šu-nu* Rm 376 r. 17, 18 (SB *utēršunūti*; MA *uta*$^{??}$*eršunu*)

Other MA incantations usually show no sign of the MA dialect at all (e.g., KAL 2 22, 47). Nevertheless, the two texts treated by Lambert feature a few interesting Assyrian forms and phonological features relevant to our discussion on phonology, e.g., /k/ > /ḫ/ spirantization (§ 207); /w/ > /m/ (§ 181); *i-modus* (§ 510f). Not all of these features are necessarily a reflection of Assyrian, rather than Babylonian; but, because of their difficulty, they need to be discussed. For this reason, many forms of these two tablets are quoted in this study, although typical Babylonian forms are left out of the discussion, along with logograms in the sign list.

§ **27** From the El-Qitār excavation in Syria, one Late Bronze Age contract was uncovered, dealing with inheritance, as published by Snell (1983/84). The original editor pointed out that the text was written in the Assyrian dialect (159, 166f; cf. Llop 2012b, 213). While this opinion may be accepted, it does not mean that the scribe of the text was actually a native speaker of Akkadian. This immediately becomes apparent from the fact that the people involved bear Hurrian, rather than Akkadian, names. The lack of an Assyrian date formulas shows that the text was certainly not written in Assyria proper. In terms of grammar, the pronominal suffix is used erroneously (Snell 1983/84, 167), showing that the scribe was not well educated in the language. In terms of orthography, we find a strange use of signs, e.g., *a-ḫa-MÈŠ* 'together' l. 11; *al-ta-KÀ-a-an* 'I placed' l. 24; *lu-ú-ŠÌB* 'he may dwell' l. 36. On the other hand, we find a typical Assyrian case of the metathesis of quantity (*lu-ú-la-a-mi-id* l. 34). The formulation of the legal stipulations is odd at best, e.g., l. 5 *riksa irku*s 'he issued a decree'. I am not aware of this clause being used in private administrative documents, as issuing a decree seems limited to the king (MAPD passim), although a reference to the private sphere can be found in MAL A § 34. Secondly, take l. 9–10: *aššat* PN *ša ana mārruttēšu epušūni* 'the wife of PN, which he took as his daughter'. MA adoption documents generally use the construction *ana mārutte laqā'u* 'to take into adoption' (e.g., KAJ 3:4). I am therefore less certain than Kouwenberg (2010, 365) who quotes this text as the sole example of a Gt-stem other than *alāku* in MA. In our opinion, this text is highly unreliable for a discussion on MA grammar and thus only the Gt-attestations and plene spellings of /a/ are quoted in this study.

1.5.3 Genres

§ 28 We have already discussed the archaeological context and distribution of the MA corpus, counting a corpus of between 3,000 and 4,000 texts. With these data, we can make some rough estimations of the percentage of different genres in this corpus. Royal inscriptions are not included, as they are usually not written on clay tablets; besides, their language is literary Babylonian (see below). Pedersén counted about 160 literary texts and school exercises in the M 1–3 archives, most of which are Babylonian compositions and therefore not used in our study. Nonetheless, many of these literary texts demonstrate a certain degree of Assyrianisms, which may (to a certain degree) have been added unintentionally by scribes when copying a Babylonian original. On the other hand, the absence of Assyrianisms in certain compositions suggests that scribes often corrected Babylonian forms and brought them in line with how they experienced the Akkadian language (Worthington 2012, 160–62 § 3.7). Among the 160 literary tablets are 59 fragments of genuine Assyrian "literary" compositions. These two numbers have to remain as rough indications, as an unknown number of MA literary texts come from NA archives, which have not been indexed by Pedersén, or are found in smaller collections without any archaeological background. The MA literary fragments, combined with the letters, constitute about 10% of the total corpus in the MA dialect.[35] That said, these numbers may fluctuate with the publication of archives as the statistics are not always clear. In this study, we sometimes include this corpus of texts, along with letters, which are sometimes referred to as private. This is only partly true, as some of the largest archives (e.g., M 4) are of an official character. As they still deal with individual people, however, unlike "literary" texts,

35 Llop (2012a, 297) counted 238 letters in a corpus of 1,924 texts, not including any literary compositions, from the libraries in Aššur, which explains how the 12% figure for letters was arrived at.

the term private is used as a common term. The distribution and statistics of the different genres in MA will be discussed below.

	Find spots	Tablets	Period
Babylonian	Aššur	About 100	Nae–Tp[36]
Literary texts	Aššur, Nineveh, Nimrud, (TSA)	60 counted	(TN)–Nae–Tp
Letters	Not in Tell ʿĀlī/Kulišḫinaš	245 counted[37]	Adn–Aššnīr III[38]
Administrative texts	Not in Amarna/ Ḫattuša/Nippur	± 3,300	Complete period

Figure 8: Statistics of MA main genres.

§ 29 The above table gives an overview of the chronological and geographical spread of MA texts according to genre. As a side note, most MA literary compositions are older than the period ascribed to them. This is especially true for the palace edicts, going back as far as the reign of Aššur-uballiṭ I. The copies of these texts are earlier and date from the period shown in the table. As for letters, all of them essentially centre around the period of Adn–TN, with only letters from Tell Ṣābī Abyaḍ (and possibly Tell Ṭābān) being dated with certainty after this period. Older letters, going back to the era of Aub, are without exception diplomatic. Diplomatic letters are often not written in Assyrian dialect, as we will see below. In general, only administrative documents, such as loans and notes, cover the entire MA chronological period. However, there are more criteria to concern ourselves with than chronology. For our grammatical research, it is necessary to narrow down the definition in order to define the research more exactly and to keep the work sustainable. Some considerations need to be made, primarily the linguistic features of the texts; however, orthography and even palaeography can also be used as criteria. It is obvious that Sumerian material or copies of Babylonian texts, such as the Codex Hammurapi from MA Aššur, are of little relevance to our research into MA language; but, even these texts could give possible information on the orthography or palaeography. Even if these appeared to be orthographically Babylonian, palaeography could show a native hand, while some orthographic features of Assyrian could be present as well. In order to keep the research feasible, the field of research has to remain limited. Essentially, it comes down to strictly defining our corpus by separating texts that are relevant or essential to our research and those that are irrelevant. The Babylonian compositions can be attributed to the latter group, but even some of the administrative documents can be considered as they are very formulaic. Therefore, it is unavoidable to review each individual text and include or exclude them in this study, based on their content. This task becomes easier when an edition of the texts is available, but often there are only copies available. In this case, it is sometimes necessary to make a decision on some of the specimens. The task of reviewing the corpus appears to be easier than in the case of OA in OB corpuses, as there should be no more than 3,000 published MA texts, as opposed to 20,000-plus for OA or OB. The difficulty remains for the many different genres that MA possesses: literary religious

36 See Pedersén (1998, 83–84); Weeden (2012, 235–36 n46–47).

37 A total of 238 letters is found in Llop (2012a). Add to this four (fragmentary) letters from Aššur: KAM 11 65, 106, 114, 121, and three more from an uncertain origin: BM 103203; Llop/Cohen (2017); NP 46.

38 Letters from Tell Ṣabī Abyaḍ may continue up until the reign of Ninurta-apil-ekur, but at least seem to continue until Aššur-nīrarī III.

compositions from the "libraries", monumental inscriptions from the temples, letters and different types of administrative texts. In some of these genres, there is a thin line between documents in Assyrian dialect and those in the literary SB, whereas orthographic features of north and south are not equally distributed according to the linguistic features. This is different from OA texts, where most texts were letters, with even other administrative types of documents being in a minority. It is therefore necessary to divide documents between those in literary Babylonian and those that in more typically Assyrian; the difficulty comes with the question as to where to draw the dividing line. The increasing influence of Babylonia on Assyrian culture and language is a problem that will be discussed in more detail below.

1.5.3.1 Literary texts

§ 30 For the most part, defining the MA corpus is straightforward. Every Assyrian archive from the Late Bronze Age outside of Aššur consists of letters and legal and administrative texts. All these archives consist of texts written, at least partly, in MA dialect, although most administrative texts are very formulaic in terms of language and make extensive use of logograms. For archives from the city of Aššur, the situation becomes more complicated, since some archives mainly feature "literary" texts.[39] However, even here, only the M 1–3 archives were designated as libraries, with M 4–14 containing official or private administration.[40] Judging from the content of the only significant "library", that is, M 2, the texts can be divided into three basic groups: royal inscriptions, Assyrian literary texts and Babylonian copies of literary texts.[41] The royal inscriptions are a problematic group (see below), but are certainty not limited to this archive. The Babylonian compositions are, for obvious reasons, not included; examples are a copy of the Codex Hammurapi (KAV 190–192) and the hymn to the sun god (KAR 19), which was also found in Ḫattuša (KBo 1 12). There is even a small amount of Sumerian literature, e.g., KAR 13; KAR 9 358. To this group of Babylonian compositions, we can attribute the MA texts published in KAL 1–4; these divinations and incantations are mostly in literary Babylonian dialect. When looking at the actual Assyrian compositions, most of them feature sufficient grammatical characteristics to label them Assyrian; those that are Assyrian are MAL, MAPD, BVW and PKT. Why these texts were written in Assyrian dialect is not entirely clear. It has been suggested that such compositions simply could not have had a Babylonian equivalent (cf. Aro 1955b, 132); however, this is only partly true for the law texts. Moreover, all these texts feature considerable Babylonian influences (see below). It is perhaps more likely that the answer lies in the function and the target group of these texts. Assyrian literary

39 The term "literary" is used in its broadest context, encompassing not only mythological texts, hymns and epics, but also rituals, divination texts, incantations and even laws. Royal inscriptions are a problem on their own and will be discussed below.

40 This study uses the same archival classification as Pedersén in ALCA 1-2. MA archives are numbered with M, and NA archives with N. For other studies on MA archives, see Pedersén (1998) and Postgate (1986b, 2013).

41 Weidner (1952/53) has suggested that this library was actually founded by Tiglath-pileser I. Most of the MA literary texts indeed seem to belong to the reign of this king. This idea has largely been rejected in recent years as many literary texts from M 2 were written during the period prior to the reign of Tiglath-pileser (e.g., Pedersén 1998, 83-84).

compositions that are written in literary Babylonian are mostly limited to the epics (see below). The individual fragments of those literary texts in genuine Assyrian amount to almost 50% of the M 2 texts, while accounting for more than 50% of the total literary texts that are written in the MA dialect.[42] A considerable part of the literary texts are of unknown provenance, so that their share in the M 2 archive could be even larger. Fewer than 25% of texts are classified in NA archives. Most of these texts are from the N 1 archive, which is a "library", of which M 2 is believed to have originally been a part. [43] This leaves only the Ištar Ritual, which derives from a purely NA context, but this is not surprising as some texts from earlier areas tend to turn up in later archives.[44] In conclusion, the texts in Assyrian dialect in the MA library archives in fact constitute a considerable part of the corpus, rather than a small minority. Only a few literary texts remained undiscovered in Aššur. The New Year Ritual could originate from KTN (Köcher 1952, 192 n2). Note also that the occasionally quoted MA incantation Rm 376 (§ 26) possibly derives from Nimrud, and an NA fragment (K 10135) of MAL A from Nineveh (Postgate 1973, 19–20 no. 4; cf. Roth 1997, 154). Outside Central Assyria, a few literary texts have been found in Tell Ṣabī Abyaḍ. As these are not written in the Assyrian dialect, it is better to refrain from commenting on them here.

MAL[45]									
A	M 2 17	B	M 2 35	G	N 1 47	D	–	E	–
F	M 2 11	G	N 1 47	H	–	J	–	K	M 14: 36
L	M 14 31	M	–	N	–	O	M 2 15	x	Nineveh
MAPD									
A	N 1 37	B	N 1 123	C	M 2 20	D	M 2 20	E	N 1: 37
F	M 2 20	G	M 2 20	H	M 2 20	x	N 1 134		
BVW									
A	M 2 3	Ab	M 2 39	Ac	M 2 46	B	M 2 34	C	M 2 6
D	M 2 1	E	M 2 24	F	M 2 56	G	M 2 5	H	M 2 42
I	N 1?	K	M 2 37	L	M 2 44	M	M 2 53	N	M 2 53
O	M 2 55	P	M 2 54	Q	M 2 52	R	M 2 48	S	M 2 45
T	M 2 43	U	M 2 26	Ko	–				
PKT									
1:Stambul I–II	–	2:VAT 8711	M 2 33	3:KAR 220	N 1 34				
4:KAR 222	M 2 65	5:VAT 9659	N 1 56	6:VAT 9493	M 2 21				
7:VAT 9493	M 2 30								
Other texts									
Ištar Ritual	N 4 472	Adad Ritual	–	Coronation Ritual	N 1 70				
Aššur Ritual	?	New Year Ritual	KTN?	(KAR 217)	N 1 100				

Figure 9: Overview of literary fragments.

42 These literary compositions are numbered according to fragments, mainly because they are included in the same way as in ALCA. Letters and administrative texts are numbered according to composition.

43 The M 2 and N 1 archives supposedly belong together, although it should be pointed out that M 2 is situated at the Anu-Adad Temple, while N 1 was found at the Aššur Temple; see ALCA 1, 31ff.

44 Notice, for example, that OA tablets were found in MA archives; see ALCA 1, 27.

45 It should be noted that the different fragments of MAL are not small pieces of the same tablet; nor were they all written at the same time (Weeden 2012, 235–37). Fragment x is even an NA copy from Nineveh of MAL A (see Postgate 1973, 19–20 no. 4). Concerning the other fragments, it is disputed that they are actual law texts. Especially in the case of MAL H (KAV 144), it is clear that the damaged text was part of a ritual. It can probably be linked to the larger Aššur Ritual (VAT 10598); see Menzel 1981, T 6–7.

§ 31 In the previous discussion, it was claimed that some of the "literary" texts feature characteristics of the Assyrian dialects. This conclusion derives from a few main points that are known from MA grammar, which do not occur in literary Babylonian or contemporary MB. These features can be summarized as follows, with the paragraph reference to their discussion in this grammar: VA (vowel assimilation) (§ 143ff); w/o Babylonian VA (§ 165); genitive *-i(m)* > *-e* (§ 240); uncontracted aleph (§ 188ff); I/a > *e-* (§ 553ff); subj *-ūni* (§ 659ff); D-stem base *PaRRuS* (§ 521); *(u)wa-* > *u-* (§ 176); pronominal suffixes (§ 370ff); /qt/ > /qṭ/ (§ 211); /šb/ > /sb/ (§ 222); *-m/n-* > *-ʾ-* (§ 233); 3fs verbal prefix *ta-* (§ 504); independent personal pronouns (e.g., *šūt*) (§ 348ff); irregular verb *naṣṣ-* (§ 602ff); /w/ > /b/ (§ 178). Inevitably, not all texts are long enough to have each characteristic attested, with the exception of MAL archives. As can be seen in the list below, most of the longer texts are fairly complete in the number of attested Assyrianisms. These features are only based on phonology and morphology, as orthography is a different discussion (see below).

	MAPD	Coronation Ritual	PKT	Ištar Ritual	Adad Ritual	BVW	New Year Ritual
VA	x	x	x	x	x	x	x
w/o Bab. VA	x	x	x	x	x	x	x
-i > *-e*	x	x	x	x	x	x	x
Uncont. aleph	x	x	x	x	x	x	x
I/a > *e-*	x	x	x	x	x	x	x
Subj. *-ūni*	x	x	x	x	x		
D *PaRRuS*	x	x	x				
(u)wa- > *u*	x	x			x		
Pron. suff.	x	x				x	
/qt/ > */qṭ/*	x	x					
/šb/ > */sb/*	x	x					
-m/n- > *-ʾ-*	x		x				
3fs *ta-*	x			x			
Indep. pr.	x						
naṣṣ-		x					
/w/ > /b/		?					

Figure 10: Grammatical features in literary texts.

§ 32 It can be observed that most texts are relatively limited in their range of Assyrian features. This is mainly due to the damaged state of the fragment and the formulaic repetition of many lines in such compositions as BVW and PKT. Other texts, such as the Adad Ritual, Ištar Ritual and the New Year Ritual, are fairly short. Still, these texts and the smaller compositions are of some interest to our research as they are significantly different in content from the main MA letter corpus and administrative texts. It should also be pointed out that, syntactically, the texts may differ significantly from the rest of the MA corpus. This is especially apparent in MAL A–B, with the preterite still commonly used in main clauses, whereas it had virtually disappeared from main clauses in the rest of the MA corpus. As the situation was similar in MB, the texts are likely to represent an older phase of the Assyrian dialect, despite the fact that their known copies date from the middle of the MA period (MAL A dates to Nae, see BCMG, 97).

§ 33 Aside from statistics and linguistic features, the orthography is a point of interest. Some texts feature characteristics that are difficult to explain, such as the archaic syllabic values in BVW and possible plene spelling of stressed vowels in MAL A–B (see § 107ff). More significant are those features that are known from OB and MB, but that are mostly limited to MAL A–B in MA:

- Initial plene spelling of I/weak verbs in the present of the G or preterite/present of the D-stem (see § 101ff)
- The spelling ˀA+V of the intervocalic aleph (see § 182)
- Nasalization, also in PKT (see § 231)
- Occurrences of Babylonian *nadānu* (see § 606)

Despite these characteristics, the literary texts feature typical Assyrian forms that are rare in the administrative texts and letters. The origin of MA scribal traditions remains problematic and will be discussed in Chapter 2. It can be expected that those literary texts shed light on this issue, although the orthography of MAL A–B is typical Babylonian. Weeden (2012) has already highlighted the relation in palaeography with Mittani cuneiform. It has been suggested that some features of the laws were archaic and thus a composition date before 1250 BCE was favoured; however, later collations revealed an eponymic date formula of the later MA period.[46] In any case, the literary texts are indispensable for a discussion of MA grammar, if only because they cover completely different topics than the texts from private archives. However, as shown above, their distinctive orthography cautions us to treat them carefully and, if necessary, discuss them separately from the other genres.

1.5.3.2 Royal inscriptions and epics

§ 34 The Assyrian royal inscriptions of the early second millennium represent a difficult genre to categorize linguistically. The oldest examples date from the OA period to the stewards Šalim-aḫum, Ilu-šumma and Erišum I. Orthography and grammar show typical OA features, e.g., the values <kà>; <ší>; <ṭí>; <tù>. The sound change /ay/ > /ē/ is attested in *e-né-en* 'two wells' RIMA 1 A 0.32.2:35. On the other hand, some orthographic and phonological forms appear, which t are less typical for OA, e.g., the values <la>; <ti>; <tì>. Some morphologic forms are Babylonian as well, as can be seen in *i-pu-uš* RIMA 1 A.033.6:16 (Ass. *epuš*), but *e-pu-uš* RIMA 1 A.0.33.3:16. With the exception of the reign of Šamšī-Adad, the royal inscriptions remained mixed with typical Assyrian characteristics and Babylonian forms. Some new values can be detected in the inscriptions of Puzur-Aššur III, e.g., <la> i/o <lá> (LAL); <ṭi> (DI) i/o <ṭí> (TÍ): *ba-la-ṭi-⸢šu⸣* RIMA 1 A.0.61:5. At the same time, the old and new values were used, side by side, as late as the reign of Aššur-rêm-nišēšu, e.g., *ba-lá-ṭí-ia ù ša-lá-am* RIMA 1 A.0.70.1:9. Typical Assyrian grammatical forms can still be found, e.g., uncontracted *ru-ba-ú* RIMA 1 A.0.61:11, I/e preterite *e-pu-šu* RIMA 1 A.0.61.1:10. However, mixed forms appear, such as the contracted *lu-ti-ir* (Ass. *lutaʾʾer*; Bab. *litīr*) RIMA 1 A.0.69.1:15. During the early MA period, Assyrian forms steadily disappeared from the inscriptions until they were virtually gone by the reign of Adad-nērārī I and the succeeding monarchs (Reiner 1962, 159). Given the standardized character of the inscriptions, which is especially true for the earliest examples, they are of limited use to our research. Difficult and unique morphological forms that occur cannot

46 See Driver/Miles (1937, 12); revised date formula in Weidner (1937/39, 38); BCMG, 97.

usually be labelled with certainty as Assyrianisms. For this reason, caution is required in using this genre in our research, such that the genre will be avoided when possible. The royal inscriptions of the Māri kingdom do feature more Assyrianisms and show some features closer to NA than MA (see Maul 1992, 18f).

§ 35 A similar genre is that of the royal epics, attested for the first time in Assyria's history for the contemporary kings.[47] The first is the epic of Adad-nērārī's wars against Babylonia, which is too fragmentary to be considered here.[48] Better preserved is the large Tukultī-Ninurta epic consisting of multiple tablets and fragments, most recently edited by Machinist (1978) and Chang (1981). The epic consists of many fragments, while new pieces still surface, most recently, a part of a copy from the Ugarit library (Arnaud 2007 no. 37). The new material could eventually help us with a better reconstruction of the order of the different columns, which is still problematic (e.g., see the discussion in Chang 1981, 78ff). Another smaller text deals with the battles of Tiglath-pileser I (LKA 63).[49] Although all of these texts were written in literary Babylonian, it has been pointed out that Assyrianisms do occur.[50] Most significant is the sound change /i/ > /e/ in the prefix conjugation of I/weak verbs, which is also common in the royal inscriptions and seems to outweigh the Babylonian variant (Machinist 1978, 477ff). However, it has been demonstrated that this change is common in all peripheral Akkadian (Jucquois 1966, 102–5 § 2 c). We can therefore hardly regard this as a strong indication of an Assyrian substrate.

§ 36 The scarceness of true Assyrianisms in the royal inscriptions and epics limits their relevance to our study. We already mentioned that some characteristics of MA also occur in contemporary MB and literary Babylonian, such as the sound change of /a/ > /e/ in the prefix conjugation of I/weak verbs. To this example, we can add the sound change /št/ > /lt/ (Aro 1955a, 37f). In general, some genuine Assyrian features, which are already attested in OA, also occur in southern vernaculars, e.g., the 3fs prefix *ta-* in the prefix conjugation is an archaic feature, which can also be found in literary Babylonian (GAG, 123 § 75h). Similarities in the different vernaculars of Akkadian make it potentially difficult to analyse texts where different traditions come together. This danger is at its highest in royal inscriptions and the epics; for this reason, they are mostly excluded from our research.

1.5.3.3 Letters

§ 37 The letter corpus is relatively small, compared to OA and NA, where the total numbers run into the thousands. Inventories of the letters were made on three occasions: Saporetti (1970) counted 65 letters, Cancik-Kirschbaum (MATSH, 232–45) included 132 texts in her catalogue and, most recently, Llop (2012) listed as many as 238 published and unpublished letters.[51] As both Cancik-Kirschbaum and Llop discussed the characteristics of MA letters

47 From the OA period, there is one epic text describing the deeds of the OAkk king Sargon; see Günbattı (1997, copy); Dercksen (2005).

48 See Weidner (1963a); Wilcke (1977, 187–91); Machinist (1978, 141–42; 401).

49 LKA 62 does seem to belong to the NA period. See Edzard 2004.

50 See Machinist (1978, 431ff); Chang (1981, 21ff).

51 While Llop's number is used in this study, not all his counted letters are really in MA. Llop included the pre-MA letters from Tell Ar-Rimāḥ, as well as letters with Assyrian characteristics that did not originate

in more detail, we will try to limit the repetition of their studies to the most basic points. The number of letters is likely to rise, as not all archives from Aššur have been published and the samples of the tablets from Tell Ṣabī Abyaḍ suggest a large share of letters. A selection of letters from the Aššur archives has been published by Llop (2012), while a further overview of the tablets from different find spots can be found in Figure 11 and the circle diagram in Figure 12.

§ 38 The majority of the letter corpus can be divided into two subcategories: letter orders and letter reports (MATSH, 50). The group of letter orders is the most common and consists of officials writing instructions to their subordinates. As an example, all letters from the BAI archive (M 11) belong to this category. The introduction is of the following type: *ana* PN_1 *qibīma umma* PN_2, 'speak to PN_1 thus PN_2. The second group of letter reports consists of subordinates reporting to their superiors. Only a few examples are known from Aššur, but they are more common in the TŠḪ and Tell Ḫuwīra letters. The introduction is different: *ana* PN_1 *bēlīya tuppi* PN_2 *urdika* 'to PN_1 a tablet of PN_2 your servant'. Letters always start with the addressee, followed by the author. On envelopes, the order is the other way around. Only one Hittite letter from Tudḫaliya IV to Tukultī-Ninurta I is known to have changed this arrangement (KUB 3 74). However, this has little to do with Assyrian scribal habits.

§ 39 The two most important archives from Aššur, which contain a good number of letters, are the Bābu-āḫa-iddina (M 11/ Assur 14440/5) and the Ubru (M 8/ Assur 11018) archives. These two are rather formulaic in character, especially the Ubru letters, which are mostly standardized summons to gather legal evidence for the court. Letters from Tell Ḫuwīra are equally formulaic in the majority of cases, while more variated content can be found in the Tell Ṣabī Abyaḍ and Tell Aš-Šēḫ Ḥamad letters. In general, we should expect more grammatical irregularities and features closer to daily speech in the letters that were dictated to a scribe. This was unlikely to be the case in formulaic letters, such as the summons from the Ubru archive, which makes these irregularities rare. However, we do have a valid passage available in the diplomatic letter RS 06.198:[52]

> *kīma PN marā šipre [an]a muḫḫīya illaka u anā⌜ku mī⌝ nummê aḫūya [i]ṣabbutū[ni an]āk[u a]na muḫḫi [aḫ]īya ušebbala [arḫi]š* 'when PN, the messenger, will come to me then I shall send to my brother quickly whatever my brother wants to take' RS 06.198:21–27

The construction of main and dependent clauses in this passage is corrupt.[53] At the same time, one may argue that, despite irregularities, these dictated letters are the closest that one

from Assyria, such as the Cypriote letter found in Ugarit (RS 20.18); see also the discussion below.

52 This letter, found in Ugarit, was possibly written by a person from the Bābu-aḫa-iddina archive, meaning that and therefore the it letter can be regarded as in core MA (cf. Jakob 2003, 301).

53 The scribe introduces a temporal adverbial clause by introducing *kīma* 'when', but changes it again to a main clause by omitting the subjunctive *-ni* on the verbal predicate *illaka*. He follows the finite verb with the conjunction *u*, rather than a governing main clause. This is followed by the subject *anāku* 'I', then continuing with an asyndetic relative clause without *ša*. The dependent clause is followed by an unnecessary repetition of the subject *anāku* 'I', while adding the adverb *arḫiš* 'quickly' behind the verbal predicate as an afterthought.

may get to the spoken language. Unfortunately, scribes of letters remain anonymous and the formulaic character of many makes it unlikely that they were dictated.

§ 40 A difficult group is that comprising royal letters and letters from peripheral or foreign areas. The latter, almost without exception, consists of royal letters. Royal letters found in Assyria proper are rare; to date, one letter by Tukultī-Ninurta I from TŠḪ (MATSH 9) and two from KTN (MARV 4 8 and 10) have been identified. The two oldest royal letters are the two Amarna tablets EA 15–16 from Aššur-uballiṭ I to the Egyptian court, from which no. 15 is claimed to be in the Assyrian dialect (Moran 1992, xix), as opposed to the Hurro-Akkadian character of no. 16.[54] Indeed, EA 16 features a number of forms that do not belong in the MA dialect, e.g., ⸢*qí-NE-ma*⸣ (MA *qí-BI-ma*) l. 2; *aš-*⸢*bu*⸣ (MA *usbū*) 8; *i-ip-pu-uš* (MA *ēpuš*) 16. Even EA 15 is not completely MA in character, e.g., *ka-ša* l. 4 (MA *ku*^{w}*āša*) no subjunctive *-ūni* in *išpurū* l. 10. Aside from a few (possible) forms (*a-di an-ni-ša ab-ba-ú-a* l. 9; [*ú*]*-še-bi-la-ku* Bab. *ušābilakku* l. 15), it is hard to distinguish this text from Babylonian. From the period of Aššur-uballiṭ's successor Enlil-nīrārī, there are three letters written to Enlil-Kidinni in Nippur (BE 17 77; BE 17 91; Ni. 669). While these are very fragmentary, most features seem to support the identification of the Assyrian dialect. Other letters were found in Ḫattuša and Ugarit. Some of these were already identified as Assyrian by W. Mayer (UGM, 3 § 1f) and a different list was found in the two more recent inventories of MATSH (232ff), while a maximalist approach was adopted by Llop (2012a). Without trying to pass judgement on their actual content, some letters from these two cities are not Assyrian in language at all. One of these is RS 20.18, written by the king of Cyprus(!) and henceforth included in Cochavi-Rainey's (2003) short grammar on Cypriot Akkadian. I am in the dark as to why Mayer and Llop regarded this letter as Assyrian. It was certainly not due to palaeography. The occurrence of the Assyrian form *a-ba-te*^{meš} 'words' l. 7 may have been a reason.[55] In general, the orthography and language are certainly very different in this letter from the core of Assyria. Note the following examples of unusual sign usage: <ka$_4$> (QA) in KUR-*ti-ka*$_4$ 'your country' l. 13 (passim); <dú> (TU) in *it-ta-dú*$^{!}$*-ú* l. 23; <de$_4$> (TE) in *ni-i-de*$_4$*-me* 'we know' l. 24. In terms of grammar, we find: the otherwise unattested preposition *itti* in *it-ti-*[*i*]*a-ma* 'with me' l. 14; 3ms of I/*ā-ē* verbs is *i-* instead of *e-*, e.g., *i-te-ep-šu-ni* l. 11; atypical use of the particle *-me* and the lack of VA in *it-ta-mu-uš-me* l. 22. Another example is the letter KBo 28 82, of unknown authorship. Some features are common in Assyrian, with most of them being Babylonian, while the use of the Hurro-Akkadian verbal form *ultuḫeḫin* 'I prostrate myself' convincingly shows that the text is not Assyrian at all (cf. § 547). More problematic is the text RS 34.165, which was probably written by Tukultī-Ninurta (Schwemer 2006). The letter is most certainly not written in MA dialect. Unusual values are relatively few compared to the letter's length: <qè> (GI) in *ta-al-qè* l. 14; <kà> (GA) in *a-al-kà* l.15 and r. 32. Grammatically, we find a contracted *ana mīnim* 'why?' in *ammīne* passim, e.g., *am-mi-ni-e* r. 8, rather than normal MA *ana*^{ʔ}*īne*. It must be added that we also find *ammīne* in OA (see § 407). Interestingly, the only other MA letter with this form is EA 16 (l. 50). Again,

54 See von Soden (1952a, 434); Moran (1992, xix n35); Artzi (1997, 324).

55 The reading *a-ba-te*^{meš} (also l. 10) is far from secured as the copy allows us to read the sign MA instead of BA.

we find *itti* (e.g., l. 32), Babylonian conjugated forms of *ušābu* (e.g., *aš-bu* l. 9 vs. *usbū*), Babylonian /w/ > /m/ (e.g., *a-ma-te* r. 1) and the preposition *ultu* (e.g., l. 43 and passim; see Aro 1957, 41). It is another question as to why this letter was not written in Assyrian dialect, but it is unusable for a study on the MA language. The situation for texts from Ḫattuša is somewhat better; however, even some "Assyrian" letters also fail to follow the Assyrian grammar with complete accuracy. For instance, the letter KBo 1 14 seems to be written by a Hittite king(!) (Wilhelm 2006). It is therefore unsurprising that the language is not Assyrian, as discussed by Mora/Giorgieri (2004, 67–69); in terms of sign values, consider <tù> (DU), as in *ul-tù* l. 7'; *tù-ud-da* l. 12'; <pá> (BA) *e-pá-ši* l. 26', to name just a few examples. The grammar is not much better. Again, we find *ultu*, e.g., *ul-tù* l. 7', as well as the absence of the subjunctive *-ūni*, e.g., *ša áš-pu-ra* l. 28' or Babylonian *adīni* i/o *udīni*, e.g., *a-di-ni* l. 22'. As this letter features some typical morphological forms, it will be quoted in the chapter on pronouns, given that, here, extant attestations are too meagre to justify disregarding this letter. The two texts discussed earlier will be mostly omitted from this study. Other texts are mostly damaged, but seem to be written in the Assyrian dialect. KBo 1 20 was probably written by a Hurrian king (Harrak 1987, 80); however, the preserved part seems to be mostly following MA grammar and palaeography (Mora/Giorgieri 2004, 82). The other damaged letters are usually not quoted because of the uncertainty of their language. Foreign letters were also found in Assyria proper. Sometimes, they seem to mimic the Assyrian style, such as the letter T 93-8a from Carchemish. The texts feature some confusion in the gender of pronominal suffixes, betraying the hand of a non-native Assyrian scribe.

Find spot	Letters
Aššur	86
Kār-Tukultī-Ninurta	10
Amarna	2
Ḫattuša	12
Nippur	3
Ugarit	6
Tell Bazmunian	7
Tell Billa	9
Tell Faḫariyya	5
Tell Ḫuwīra	25
Tell Ar-Rimāḥ	7
Tell Ṣabi Abyaḍ	20+[56]
Tell Aš-Šēḫ Ḥamad	32
Tell Ṭābān	14
<Other/uncertain>	6
	244

Figure 11: Number of letters found at different archaeological sites.

56 According to the counting in MATSH (50), at least 12 letters were found during the excavations of the 1990s. As this publication was finished in 1995, we can safely count the letters discussed by Wiggermann in papers and lectures with excavation numbers dating to 1996 onwards. This brings us to at least eight more letters, resulting in a total of 19 known instances.

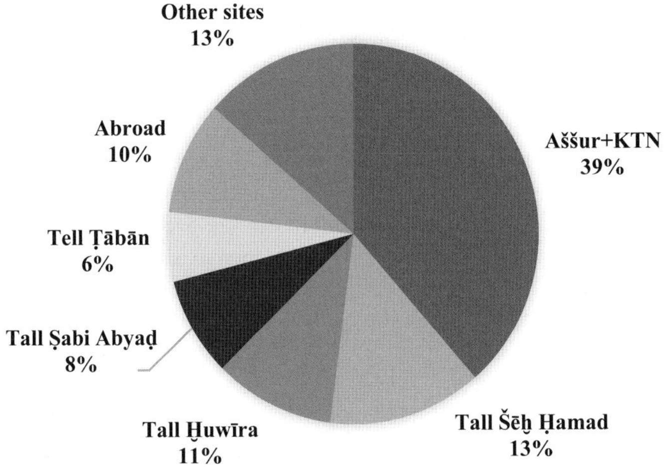

Figure 12: Share of the different find spots of letters.

1.5.3.4 Administrative and legal documents

§ **41** Having discussed the literary texts and letters, we are left with a large group of over 3,000 tablets.[57] This figure has to remain a rough estimation until all archives have been published and a thorough inventory of all museum collections is made. Every MA site that has yielded tablets includes administrative texts. As the archives outside Aššur belonged to the local administration, this comes as no surprise. The corpus can be divided into two groups, as the terminology already suggests.

§ **42** The group of legal documents deals with all kinds of transactions and has judicial value, as it features a list of witnesses and seals. The texts usually feature land grants and, on some occasions, other subjects, such as adoption agreements. The details of the different types of transactions are varied, although they are sometimes formulaic and therefore of interest to our studies. Most examples of this corpus have been published in KAJ, which was dedicated to this type of text. Koschaker studied a number of the KAJ texts, together with contemporary examples in NKRA. Other classical text editions of these legal documents can be found in ARu and MAOG 7/1–2. The dissertation of Ismail-Sabir (MKA) on this subject has remained unpublished. In recent decades, more examples have been published, mainly in the MARV series, although the majority of the MARV texts belong to the second category.

§ **43** The second group of texts is much larger and contains all kinds of transactions and lists, which only have an administrative function. Despite the vast number of texts, this

57 This numbering is by default; it is arrived at by deducting the literary texts and letters from a rough estimation of about 3,000 MA texts. Theoretically, the number could be reduced somewhat if, among the unpublished texts, a large number of letters is found. However, this is highly unlikely as many Assyriologists have tended to find letters more interesting and, as a result, published them more often.

genre is of limited use for our understanding of MA grammar. The texts make use of a standard formulae that does not make for a good representation of Assyrian syntax. Many texts deal with transactions of goods, which were recorded for administrative reasons. The common clause, *ana la mašāʾe šaṭir* 'it was written down in order not to forget', is revealing in this respect. Larger multiple deliveries have been recorded in the case of the M 4 *ginā'u* archive on large tablets (see Freydank 1997a). This type of text does not provide us with a great deal of grammatical detail about the Assyrian language. In particular, the *ginā'u* tables (e.g., MARV 7 5) can hardly be regarded as actual texts, as any syntactical sequence is often absent. These texts are generally limited in the use of syllabic script, as they rely, for a large part, on logograms. On the plus side, many technical terms are only attested in this corpus, while being a welcome addition to our knowledge of the Assyrian lexicon. Lists of PNs without any other designation occur as well (e.g., Jas 1990).

1.5.4 Regional variation

§ 44 Regional variation in MA can be divided twice into two groups. The first main division is grammatical variation, based on foreign influence on one side in the form of non-Akkadian-speaking people who were in contact with the Assyrians. On the other side, there is the possibility of regional differences within the Assyrian dialect. We can also make a second division, which is based on orthography. The Assyrian kings conquered large new areas, in which Akkadian cuneiform was already known. Here, too, we can distinguish between the variation among Assyrian natives and the variation because of underlying foreign influences.

§ 45 The expansion of the MA Empire in the 14th and 13th centuries introduced a large number of new ethnic groups into Assyria, of which the Hurrians can especially be found in the MA onomasticon. Aramaic and other NWS groups also existed in the empire, but remained mostly invisible in the onomastic record, with the notable exception of the Sutean governor of Tell Ḫuwīra.[58] Campaigns into Babylonia brought a large number of Southerners to the empire, namely, Kassites. Most of them could have been captives, although a large number of people moved voluntarily and could have secured high positions in the social pyramid. Babylonians are found as early as the reign of Aššur-uballiṭ I in Aššur (Wiggermann 2008). An Elamite workforce has been attested in the Tell Ḫuwīra archive, but they are otherwise not attested as a significant ethnic group. Royal inscriptions mention Hittite and Luwian captives, but they are not referred to in the administrative documents. Linguistic background aside, the empire contained many cities and realms where Akkadian cuneiform was practised before the conquest and continued to be practised afterwards. Most of these scribal centres may not be very well known to us, but some traditions could have continued to a certain extent. Nonetheless, regional variation in general remained minor. This can largely be explained by the government of the Assyrian Empire. First of all, it was not until Shalmaneser I that a structural government of former

58 Most of our onomastic evidence about Suteans derives from the few examples known from Tell Ṣabi Abyaḍ; cf. Minx (2005, 8–12). As these people often occur as Nomads, one may question whether a clear North-West Semitic influence would be visible in the TSA archive when published, but it is possible.

Ḫanigalbat can be observed by the appearance of the first large archives in peripheral sites. Therefore, we can safely assume that most scribes were recent immigrants from Aššur and its direct vicinity, with little dialectal difference to be expected. Salah claimed that the script of the TŠḪ lists displayed the standard cuneiform from Aššur, leading to the conclusion that the scribes received their education in this city (MPR, 63a). Moreover, as Machinist (1982, 19) highlighted, with respect to the nature of the government, the peripheral archives only sporadically record native non-Assyrian names. In Machinist's opinion, this points to enclaves of Assyrians in their newly conquered territories and cities, with limited direct contact with native people. If the Assyrian dialect was widespread outside Aššur before the expansion, we would not be able to notice it as a result of these politics.

§ 46 As we will discuss below, the MA cuneiform model seems to be partly transmitted through Mittani scribal traditions. A mixture of Assyrian and Nuzi (Arrapḫa) scribal traditions is found in the letter BM 103203 (Fincke 2014, 23–28). This text is thought to have been written shortly after the incorporation of former Arrapḫa territory following the conquest by Aššur-uballiṭ I. However, it remains the only example of this blending of traditions. The use of the Hurrian adverb *entu* in Tell Billa texts is noteworthy. In the case of the NA features in the Giricano texts (Giricano, 53–54), it is probably better to speak of chronological variation due to the late date formula of these texts. With the publishing of new material from Syria, the evidence of a mixture of different cuneiform traditions becomes more evident. One major aspect is the unique calendar used in Tell Ṭabān in combination with the Assyrian eponyms (Shibata 2007, 67–69). From the borderland between Assyria and the kingdom of the Hittites, we find unusual texts such as RE 19 (Assyrian date formula) and Snell (1983/84; no date formula). The unpublished material of Tell Ṣabī Abyaḍ, in particular, is very interesting. There are some Assyrian style letters written from abroad. For instance, the letter T 93-8a from Carchemish does not properly distinguish between the grammatical genders, which is a strong indication that the native language of the scribe did not feature any grammatical gender (probably either Hittite or Hurrian). Otherwise noticeable is the *-āni* morpheme in T 02-3 (see § 642) and the Canaanite(?) text T 97-37. These texts await closer examination, particularly in combination with its palaeography, until more accurate conclusions can be drawn. The West Semitic influence in MA is non-existent, except for some attested PNs, mostly from Tell Ṣabī Abyaḍ. It has been suggested that Chaldean caused the sound change /št/ > /lt/ (Keetman 2006), which is absurd as contact between Assyrians and Chaldeans in the second millennium is not attested (for other objections, see Streck 2008, 251 n8).

§ 47 One of the few cases of grammatical and orthographic local variation can possibly be found in Ḫana. We cannot be certain as there are only two texts published (Kümmel 1989; HSM 1036688), which are mostly identical in formula. They formally belong to our corpus since both are dated with eponyms, yet the formulae are atypical for MA, along with some orthographic and grammatical features that do not fit with our grammar as they do not occur elsewhere. Most relevant for us are the following features:

- *a-na* É.GAL-*lum* HSM 1036688:17 (usually MA uses LIM under all circumstances)
- ^{m}*Ṣil-li-*^{d}*Me-er* Kümmel 1989:9 ≠ /w/ > <B> (see § 178)

- KI-*i* Kümmel 1989:13; HSM 1036688:7=*itti?* (or *iltu?*) (see Kümmel, 196; Tsukimoto, 88)
- *te-di-nu* Kümmel 1989:21 ≠ *iddinū/tadnū* 'they gave/it is given'
- ^{id}*a-tap-pa maš-qi-ti* 'ditch of the irrigation outlet(?)' Kümmel 1989:5[59]

In some of these, the use of LUM, for example, could be purely orthographic. The occurrence of ^{d}Mēr, rather than Bēr, could indicate a phonetic difference. Of particular interest here is the verbal form *teddinū*, since it could refer to the 3mp prefix *ta-*, known from OAkk Mari and Eblaite.[60] Podany (1997, 424) noted differences in the Kümmel (1989) texts from earlier Ḫana texts. However, these features show that some regional variation surfaced in the Assyrian-style Ḫana texts.

1.6 Methodology

§ 48 This study features an analysis of the MA dialect on two levels: synchronic and diachronic. On the one hand, the linguistic features of the language are described and the differences with other relevant dialects are noted, particularly the other two stages of the languages OA and NA, but also contemporary MB, the standard language SB and the WPA dialects to which MA is related. On the other hand, an attempt was made to describe and explain the linguistic developments of MA and how this relates to OA and NA. This is done in order to provide the reader with a broader understanding of the language and the mechanics behind it, but also to place this study in a broader context of linguistic studies to the Akkadian language itself, and to Semitic in general. In order to reach this goal, the study is divided into three parts: orthography/phonology, morphology and syntax. However, we will mostly focus in this study on the first two parts. Orthography and phonology are discussed together because our knowledge of phonology follows on from orthography.

§ 49 An important part of the MA corpus concerns the PNs, especially given that a large number of texts comprises lists. Some caution is justified when studying MA PNs as they often contain archaic and foreign elements, which have little to do with MA grammar.[61] For this reason, W. Mayer mostly avoided discussing the onomasticon (UGM, 4f), while others referred to Babylonian examples.[62] In his short study, Streck (2002b, 116) highlighted several Assyrian phonologic features in the MA onomasticon that separated it from Babylonian. Babylonian influences can still be seen in the large number of PNs with the theophoric element Marduk (OMA 1, 311ff), resulting in some clearly Babylonian names, e.g., ^{m}*Šu-zu-ub*-^{d}AMAR.⸢UTU⸣ KAJ 13:35; *Mu-tir-gi-*⸢*mil*⸣*-li* (*Mutīr-gimilli*) KAM 10 10:5. Typical archaic features are the occurrence of Gt-stems and the lack of the sound

59 This must be a status construct, with the irregular construct form *atappa* instead of *atap*. Otherwise, the two forms have the wrong case ending, as a nominative is required.

60 Cf. Edzard (1985); Catagnoti (2012, 126–27 § 4.5.2).

61 Cf., for OAkk, Hasselbach (2007, 23–24 n8).

62 Hecker (1973/74, 168); Jas (1990, 35 n10); Kouwenberg (2010, 404 n166; 466 n74). On some occasions, Kouwenberg still based his conclusions concerning MA grammar on PNs (e.g., Kouwenberg 2010, 64–65 n71).

change /št/ > /lt/: ᵐ*Muš-te-piš*-DINGIR KAJ 173:3; however, this is rare. Typical Assyrian characters (as found in Streck 2002b, 116) are as follows:

- In I/a verbs *i-* > *e-*: ᵐ*E-šar-de-en*-ᵈNUSKA (*Ešar-dēn-Nusku*) KAV 99:7
- *w-* > *u-* over *w-* > *a-*: ᵐᶠ*A-ḫa-at-uq-ra-at* (*Aḫāt-uqrat*) KAJ 3:3
- Lack of Babylonian VA: [ᵈA]MAR.UTU-*ki-na-i-šam-me* (*Marduk-kēna-išamme*) OIP 79 5:23
- D-imperative *PaRRiS* over *PuRRiS*: ᵐᵈ*A-šur-šal-lim-a-ni* (*Aššur-šallimanni*) KAV 99:5
- Š-imperative *šaPRiS* over *šuPRiS*: ᵐᵈUTU-*še-zi-ib* (*Šamaš-šēzib*) KAJ 154:9

Notice also that Babylonian and Assyrian forms can appear next to each other: ᵐ*Šu-zu-ub*-ᵈAMAR. ⸢UTU⸣ KAJ 13:35 ~ ᵐᵈUTU-*še-zi-ib* KAJ 154:9; [ᵐ*M*]*u-ši-ib-ši*-ᵈ7-*ta* Billa 3:27 ~ ᵐ*Mu-šab-ši*-ᵈIŠKUR-*ma* KAV 168:3. There seems to be sufficient reason to regard most of the onomasticon as Assyrian; thus, names are often quoted in this study. As for the issue of metathesis (§ 226), a feature typical for MA, the evidence from PNs is indispensable as most forms occur here. For Hurrian PNs in MA, see Freydank/Salvini (1984); and, for North-West Semitic, see Minx (2005, 8–12).

1.6.1 Method of citation

§ 50 As a grammatical study, examples are provided for the different grammatical aspects. Since MA is a dead language, the corpus can only be extended by the excavation and publishing of new texts. Therefore, an attempt is made to be thorough when providing attestations where reasonable standards are possibly involved. Attestations of single morphological forms are, by default, not transcribed, but given in transliteration. When longer phrases are cited, they are transcribed (except for the main point of discussion) in a style similar to the CAD. For instance, in the discussion on using the pronouns, all of the cited passages, save for the relevant pronoun, will be transcribed. Reconstructed words are put between brackets in transliterations and transcriptions. These brackets are not repeated in the translations for the convenience of keeping them readable.

§ 51 Quoted normalized forms are given in their Assyrian variant, rather than following the OB/SB forms quoted in most dictionaries. This is done in order to represent the Assyrian language in its own right, although, when the normal Babylonian form is ambiguous, it is usually given to avoid confusion. As a result, an infinitive such as *epāšu* is found in the CAD/AHw under *epēšu(m)*.

§ 52 Texts are cited according to their numbering in the most recent text publication, while citation by museum number is avoided. However, unpublished letters and legal documents only known by their museum number are listed in the concordances at the end of this study. Texts from old publications, such as KAJ and KAV, are sometimes included in MARV and KAM 7, e.g., KAJ 316=MARV 1 22=KAM 7 140; in this case, the text is cited according to its initial publication in copy form. Texts published in articles are cited according to their museum number, with a bibliographical index found in the concordances. In two cases, texts from a large find spot are listed by museum number: as the Tell Ar-Rimāḫ texts are ordered after their museum numbering in their primary publication (Iraq 30) as TR, this numbering is repeated here. Secondly, as the Tell Ṣabī Abyaḍ texts remain unpublished (with a few exceptions), they are listed according to their museum number as well (T).

When there is no museum number available, we refer to the author of the initial publication, e.g., Kümmel (1989). If texts are not numbered, they are cited with a page number, e.g., PKT 1 I right:19. Recent text publications have been allocated an abbreviation in order to make quoting more practical, e.g., LVUH; MATSH; MATC etc. Abbreviations of the classic text publications are relatively widespread, e.g., KAV and KAJ. Inevitably, an explanatory list of all abbreviations can be found in the bibliography. When relevant, dated texts from Aššur are quoted with an abbreviation of the monarch (Figure 1) to which the eponym is ascribed. For this purpose, I used the indices and abbreviations of BMCG and, to a lesser degree, EMA, supplemented by the new studies of the chronological order of eponyms in the period Shalmaneser I–Tukultī-Ninurta I and Aššur-rēša-iši–Tiglath-pileser I.[63] In the case of the undated letters from the Bābu-aḫa-iddina and Urad-Šerūa archives, the abbreviations BAI and UŠA are used. The dating of the other texts from the archive suggests that most texts in this case date from the reign of Shalmaneser I, or shortly before and after. For texts from the periphery, no dating is provided. As a general rule, all colonial texts are from the reigns of Shalmaneser I and Tukultī-Ninurta, while the Giricano texts date from Aššur-bēl-kāla. There are very few exceptions to this, although at least some of the Tell Ṣabī Abyad and Tell Ṭābān texts seem to date from the period after the reign of Tukultī-Ninurta I.

1.6.2 Transliteration

§ 53 The character of the cuneiform script makes it impossible to ensure that transcriptions are factual. A clear example is the lack of consistent distinction of the vowels /i/ and /e/, so that one cannot be certain with a sign such as RI whether to read <ri> or <re>. The only solution we have is to set a number of rules, based on orthography and phonology, which are provided to us by MA and Akkadian in general. The basic rules of transcriptions used in this study are:

- Each Cv syllabic sign has one basic value, with vC signs used for consonants of similar places of articulation, e.g., velars <ug/k/q> (UG). Sign values normally have only one possible vowel; however, /e/ is regarded as allophonic and can therefore double with /i/.
- If the phoneme /e/ is not distinguishable in the orthography, /i/ is transliterated. This rule is also valid in basic instances where it can be assumed on phonologic grounds, such as the genitive (see § 240). The vowel /e/ is an allophone and does not usually differentiate the meaning of a form with /i/. An exception to this methodology involves the cases where /e/ results from e-colouring through an etymologic guttural (see § 182f, 186). If the orthography allows us, we can read /e/ in these instances as this sound change is a key feature of the Assyrian dialect.
- In the cases where orthography is conflicting, italic capital letters are used to transliterate the signs. If the reading of a sign remains uncertain on other grounds, capital letters are used as well.
- Capital letters are also used for the logograms, which are usually Sumerian in origin. The more common logograms are repeated in the sign list (Chapter 24), where the transcribed Assyrian form is given when possible.

---

63 Most notably, Bloch (2012); Freydank (2016a).

– Some common abbreviations are used for proper names to simplify the transliterations: DN=divine name; GN=geographical name; ^(m/f)^PN=personal name (male/female); RN=royal name. These abbreviations are written with cursive capital letters. The original form will be used only when proper names are very common and simple (e.g., Adad, Aššur etc.).

Features of MA and Akkadian orthography and phonology in general are discussed in their respective chapters, where choices in transcription are further explained.

1.6.3 Transcription

§ 54 This study makes use of transcriptions when the orthography is not under discussion. This is done in order to make this study more accessible for readers who are not familiar with the cuneiform script, but who are interested in Assyrian grammar. Reading MA phrases in transliteration is made especially difficult by the many logograms and determinatives involved, which sometimes obscure the genuine Akkadian forms. At the same time, transcribing a text is deceptive because there is no consensus on how to transcribe Akkadian, let alone the MA dialect, with its own features. In addition, as MA uses logograms extensively, the underlying Akkadian form is often not clear and must be left alone. Transcribing a text is also interpreting; in many cases, spelling allows for multiple interpretations and transcriptions. For instance, what should one transcribe when reading the logogram UD^{meš} 'days', as the plural form of the Akkadian underlying *ūmu* can be morphologically both masculine or feminine (see § 271). It is therefore necessary to choose the most fitting interpretation, as different people can have different opinions. For this reason, it is necessary to lay out a few conventions to be used for the transcriptions presented throughout this study:

– In the case of vocalic sequences, generally the first vowel is lengthened when it is /i/ or /u/, e.g., *idūak* 'he will kill'; *išīam* 'he will buy'. In cases where the first vowel is /a/ and followed by a nisbe type ending (§ 254ff), the /a/ is lengthened and an intervocalic /y/ is transcribed, e.g., *šanāyīu* 'second rate'. If alternative spellings have a /y/ written by the sign IA (or PI), the consonant is transcribed in other forms as well, e.g., *šanāyīu* 'second rate'; *Sūtīu* 'Sutean'.
– Frequently, exceptions or mistakes occur in the cuneiform texts, for instance, a wrong case ending, an unexpected sound change or abnormal syllabification. These "mistakes" are not corrected; instead, when forms are unusual, they are transcribed following their spelling, but with the addition of the postscript …^{sic}. to make the reader aware that the irregularities in the form are already present in the cuneiform text.
– When a vowel /e/ can be reconstructed on the basis of Assyrian phonology, it is represented in the transcription, unless the orthography goes against this interpretation. This stands in contrast to the transliteration, when /I/ is taken as the basic value.
– An attempt is made to transcribe the logograms, although, in the case of plurals, this is difficult because the plural forms are often unclear. For this reason, the singular form is usually quoted, together with determinatives; usually, the plural marker …^{meš} is used, except when the abbreviation …$^{pl.}$ is written.
– In some cases, the Assyrian form underlying a logogram is too uncertain to attempt transcription. In these cases, they are left alone. The most common example is the logogram ŠE(*-um*) for 'barley', supplemented by some technical terms.

Chapter 2: Orthography

2.1 General features of Akkadian cuneiform

§ 55 Before discussing the peculiarities of MA scribal traditions, a brief discussion of Akkadian cuneiform in general needs to take place. The following section is therefore aimed at the reader with an interest in Semitic languages or linguistics, but who is not familiar with syllabic cuneiform. This study uses the names and numberings of cuneiform signs as they can be found in the final version of Borger's sign list MZL. Another important sign list is that of Labat, which is especially useful for the palaeographic development of the signs. A list arranged according to MZL can be found at the end of this study.

§ 56 Akkadian cuneiform, in general, can be regarded as syllabic writing where each sign ideally represents a syllable. We can best compare the system to the Geʿez script still used in living Ethiopian languages, such as Amharic, which has, in its most recent form, well over 400 characters. These characters represent Cv or simply C to indicate the absence of a following vowel, effectively making the script semisyllabic. Unlike the Ge'ez script, Akkadian uses true CvC and vC syllabic values, which Ge'ez lacks, e.g., *ul-te-bi-lak-ku-nu* 'I sent to you' KAV 99:40=*/(ˀ)ul/tē/bi/lak/ku/nu*. As can be seen, there are three types of syllabic readings that can be connected by a hyphen (-): Cv, vC and CvC. In addition, Akkadian has one or more signs for each of its vowel colours: A; I; E; U; Ú; Ù. The reader may note the use of an acute and a grave accent, respectively, Ú and Ù. These occur in order to distinguish the different signs for the vowel /u/. Alternatively, it is also possible to number different values U; Ú; Ù > U$_1$; U$_2$; U$_3$. The use of numbering becomes obligatory when there are more than three values for the same sign. Normally, the numbering for the primary value is omitted. However, it should be emphasized that not all primary values are common in MA. For instance, we predominantly find <ṭí> (ṭi$_2$), rather than the value <ṭi>. The cause of this deviation lies in both the changing cuneiform tradition and the system that Assyriologists have applied to number values. However, the essential difference in values is caused by different possible readings of cuneiform signs. For closed syllables, MA does not exclusively resort to CvC signs, as we will see below (§ 82ff). Instead, we often find the two sign construction Cv+vC and rarely a Cv+v+vC construction. The reader may also observe that, in the final construction, an optional vowel sign is used, which can indicate vowel length or stress. However, these types of plene spellings are mostly limited to open syllables. Similarly, gemination can optionally be indicated with plene spellings (§ 88ff), but such instances are often, in fact, erroneous (§ 120f). MA cuneiform generally respects word borders and the ends of lines. Only rarely does a word continue on the next line or do we find sandhis (see § 122ff for these peculiarities). It should furthermore be noted that there are no word dividers in MA, a feature that was present to a certain extent in OA. Likewise, there is no kind of interpunction, with the exception of lines drawn on tablets to divide different sections of a text.

§ 57 A second point of importance is the polyvalence of cuneiform signs, which means that each sign can have multiple readings. In general, it can be stated that a syllabic sign usually has multiple related readings, with a variation in vowels, often between /i/ and /e/ (see § 132ff) and/or homorganic consonants, e.g., the sign Á can be read <id/t/ṭ> or <ed/t/ṭ/>. The values vC use significantly more related syllabic values, while, for Cv values, a clear attempt is made to distinguish between different phonemes. For all positions, the sign use is discussed in the chapter on phonology. We do not always find related values; often, they are unpredictable, e.g., the sign RI (MZL no. 142) can be read <ri/e> or <d/tal>. Thirdly, a sign can also have a logographic or determinative reading, which we indicate in our transcriptions with capital letters and separate by periods or, in the case of determinatives, in superscript. Logograms usually derive from Sumerian and are themselves not in congruence with case or gender, unless they include a phonetic complement (see § 66). Special attention may be given to plural markers (mostly the attached .MEŠ; see § 74ff) and determinatives, both of which are also attested in syllabically written nouns and indicated here in upper case letters, e.g., ^{na4}KIŠIB^{meš} 'seals' KAV 99:35=determinative NA$_4$ for 'stones'+logogram KIŠIB 'seal'+the plural marker MEŠ.

2.2 Historical development

§ 58 The use of the cuneiform script in MA times has never been properly researched. A differentiation must be made between palaeography and orthography, which are both of interest to our grammatical research. Palaeographic knowledge could be used for dating the cuneiform tablets. Freydank pointed out the possibilities and difficulties of studying MA palaeography; in particular, the close connection with NA is discussed.[1] Following his article, four sign lists for limited corpora have been published.[2] A sign list based on a limited number of texts from Aššur was published by Schwemer in his comparison between different WPA ductus in Ḫattuša.[3] Weeden's (2012) study followed on from Schwemer's, but both studies focus on the cuneiform of Ḫattuša rather than MA scribal traditions (see below). Therefore, a full study on the palaeography of letters and administrative texts in Aššur and Kār-Tukultī-Ninurta is still a necessity. The available lists also give us much information on the orthographic reading of the signs, forming the basis of any further research. Given the close connection between MA and NA palaeography and orthography, the study of Luukko (2004) is a useful addition. One of the main problems with MA cuneiform script is the origin of the model. It is immediately apparent that in both palaeography and orthography, it bears very little resemblance with the OA model. Kouwenberg (2004, 99) noted: "*No doubt the similarity between MB and MA is caused by the fact that MA orthography, which is completely different from that of OA, is derived from an OB or MB model.*" Below, we will discuss the validity of this statement and nuance

1 See Freydank (1988; 2010b).

2 See MATSH, 69–87; Giricano, 54–61; MATC, 26-40; MPR, 387-402. Additionally, for the royal inscriptions of Māri, we now have Maul (1992, 55–62; Maul 2005, 83–91. Tell Ṭābān paleography is discussed in Shibata (2016, 105ff).

3 See Schwemer (1998, 17ff). The selection of texts is listed on page 15 n47.

it where necessary. We will do so by comparing the MA model with the situation elsewhere in contemporary Mesopotamia.

§ 59 As we have already noted, MA cuneiform bears little resemblance to OA in terms of orthography and palaeography.[4] One of the few characteristics of MA, which can be traced back directly to OA, is the use of the sign TÍ for <ṭí/é>, which was originally used for all dentals (<dí/é>, <tí/é>, <ṭí/é>). The Babylonian equivalent DI is only used in MA for <di/e> and in OA only rarely for the value <sá>. This exceptional preservation of a traditional sign value is to be explained by the MA–NA tendency to use separate signs for emphatic consonants. Rarely, we find the OA value <ší/é> (SI) i/o <ši> (IGI) in MA texts, e.g., *a-na ší-im a-na ši-im ga-me-er* (…) *i-din* 'he sold it for the full price' KAJ 146:7–11 (Aub). The same value may occur in contemporary Akkadian.[5] It should be noted that, in the OA period, the script developed continuously; however, the script seems to have initially developed away from the contemporary OB, rather than approached it. Kryszat (2008) pointed out that OA uses a number of shorter signs (e.g., <lá>), uncommon in OB, but more convenient for scribes to write, which explains their popularity. On the other hand, signs such as <la$_1$> and even <bí> (NE) in letter introductions were used among the better-educated scribes. That said, the active use of these signs died out during the history of level II texts, with their occurrence eventually limited to copies of older compositions.[6] In the few post-OA texts from Aššur, more features familiar to the Babylonian model were introduced. This is well documented in the three texts found in the MA archive M 9 or Assur 14446: MAH 15962+env. (Gelb/Sollberg 1957); Izmir 1439 (Donbaz 2001); KAM 10 1 (de Ridder 2013a). These three texts feature a number of changes, which are still relevant in MA. The palaeographic development of these texts, and late OA in general, was commented on by Veenhof (1982, 366–67). In terms of orthography, the following new features are most notable: we find a few examples of gemination in orthography (*da-an-na-at* MAH 15962:37, see GKT, 14 § 7a);[7] once in the case of the value <ši> i/o <ší> (PN: *Ri-ši-a* MAH 15962:39); for the first time, the use of *Personenkeile* before an introduced PN, but not after the logogram DUMU (^{m}*Šu-mu-li-ib-ší* DUMU *Da-da* MAH 15962:8); and, instead of the exclusively OA plural marker ḪI.A, we find MEŠ in these texts (e.g., DUMU^{meš} KAM 10 1:16). Due to the scarcity of textual material following the end of the OA period, we cannot be certain of the extent to which scribal traditions developed into the MA model, or whether it was replaced without a transition period. For instance, two of the three Assur 14446 texts (MAH 15962; Izmir 1439) seem to have been written by a scribe with a suspiciously Babylonian sounding name, that is, Nabû-qarrād. One may suspect that the dynasty of Šamši-Adad stimulated southern influences in the scribal tradition. This is especially true for his royal inscriptions, but no change can be observed in the Ib-level Kültepe texts following Šamšī-Adad's accession in Aššur. Initially, Veenhof (1982) believed that an Assyrian manumission from an unknown archaeological context (APM

4 For OA scribal practice, see the sign list in TC 2, (4ff) and the grammatical treatment in GKT.

5 For UgAkk, cf. Huehnergard (1989, 37); for AmAkk, cf. Izre'el (1991b, 116). Both instances are very uncertain. It does not seem to occur in HattAkk; see Durham (1976, 104).

6 For <bí> (NE), see *qí-bí-ma* BIN 4 22:3; pace MATSH (55 n32).

7 According to Lambert, the relative scarceness of gemination in MA is still a remnant of OA; see Lambert (1965, 285).

9220) had to be dated to Šamšī-Adad I, due to its many Babylonian influences and the mention of a king, namely, Šamšī-Adad. Nowadays, it seems more likely that this text should be dated to either Šamšī-Adad II or Šamšī-Adad III (cf. Barjamovic/Hertel/Larsen 2012, 22–23 n63). As the text is neither truly OA nor MA in style, it seems that there very much must have been a formative period in which OA was gradually replaced. This was probably due to economic decline; since OA scribal traditions stood alone in a cuneiform world dominated by OB scribal traditions, it is quite likely that it was not profitable for the Assyrians to retain their own scribal traditions. Another text from this period is TIM 4 45, resembling APM 9220 and containing some MA and OA and Babylonian features, which had disappeared in later MA, e.g., the absence of VA in some forms (*in-na-ma-ru* APM 9220:21; *aš-*[*š*]*a-ti-mi* TIM 4 45:10) and the use of a Sumerian verbal logogram (Ì.LÁ.E APM 9220:16; TIM 4 45:12) still found in MA texts (§ 70). Veenhof (1982, 366ff) extensively discussed the palaeography and syllabary of these late texts.[8] The few texts that we have from the post-OA period seem to confirm a more fluid transaction period, but we will now look at the evidence from contemporary Mesopotamia.[9]

§ 60 OB scribal traditions not only influenced MA, but also reached more distant areas. It is assumed that the Hittite scribal traditions were copied from the OB model used in level-VII Alalaḫ. Before this period, the OA model was used in Anatolia, but that would have ended during the campaign of Ḫattušili I to Alalaḫ around 1550 BCE (Rüster/Neu 1989, 15; van den Hout 2012), although Syrian scribal traditions were already present in OA Anatolia (Hecker 1996; Michel 2010). Moreover, plene spellings of I/weak verbs in MAL A–B is a feature known from OB, but mostly absent in MB (see Kouwenberg 2003/4). This can only be explained in terms of being passed down through an OB cuneiform model, especially given that plene spelling was erroneously used with I/n verbs (see § 102).[10] This suggests that the scribal tradition in question was in the process of being forgotten and certainly not freshly introduced; indeed, we hardly find these plene spellings outside MAL A–B. Texts similar in formula to the loans from the reign of Aššur-uballiṭ I and earlier from the M 9 archive have been found in Dūr-abī-ešuḫ (CUSAS 8) and especially in the Tell Muḥammad texts dating from around the fall of the first dynasty of Babylon (Al-Ubaid 1983, cf. Sassmannshausen 2004, 69); see below § 71. Podany (2002, 185) points out that the palaeography of the Terqa texts from the Middle Ḫana period (about 1600–1400) is comparable to MA.[11]

---

8 This does not mean that the text in question is younger than Gelb/Sollberger 1957. The related text KAM 10 1 dates to Aššur-bani, son of Išme-Dagan I, which would date the text to be from later in the reign of Išme-Dagan.

9 It has been suggested that OA influenced the orthography of level-IV Alalaḫ, and the statue of Idrimi in particular; see Greenstein/Marcus (1976, 60). However, our current state of knowledge of West Syrian cuneiform traditions in the early second millennium BCE does not allow us to reach such preliminary conclusions.

10 The plene spelling of I/weak is not a feature known in OA. See also the discussion on plene spelling in verbs and nouns in AKT 6, 30ff § 6.a.3.

11 On the other hand, she also pointed to differences in terminology between the MA Ḫana text (Kümmel 1989) and earlier Ḫana texts (see Podany 1997).

§ 61 MA cuneiform has a remarkable amount in common with contemporary WPA, as opposed to OA. Fortunately, for most vernaculars, a grammatical treatment exists: Tušratta correspondence (Adler 1976); Nuzi (Wilhelm 1970); Alalaḫ (Giacumakis 1970); Alašia Akkadian (Cochavi-Rainey 2003); Canaanite Akkadian (Rainey 1996a–d); Egyptian Akkadian (Müller 2010; Cochavi-Rainey 2011); Ugarit (Huehnergard 1989); Amurru (Izre'el 1991); Emar (Seminara 1997). However, the dialect of Nuzi and Alalaḫ are particularly in need of an updated study. I am aware of only one comparative study (Jucquois 1966), which included early second millennium material as that from Mari, while unfortunately excluding Assyrian. The reason for the similarities in WPA cuneiform has to be sought partly in the ever-changing political situation of Northern Mesopotamia. In the late second millennium, the area was initially dominated by the Hurrian state of Mittani/Ḫanigalbat. Although an actual cuneiform archive from Mittani remains undiscovered, a number of diplomatic letters from the Mittani king, Tušratta of Amarna, have surfaced (EA 17–29).[12] As the Assyrian mainland was situated along the borders of Mittani, and in fact part of the empire at some point, one would expect a considerable influence on the Assyrian scribal traditions. The first MA texts probably date from the period in which Assyria was a vassal of Mittani (Lion 2011, 158). They already demonstrate most characteristics of the MA script that were typical of the entire period up until the reign of Aššur-bēl-kāla, leaving a gap of about 250 years between the few post-OA tablets and the first MA texts.[13] Similarities between the palaeography of Mittani texts and early MA documents raise the question as to whether this new model was ultimately derived from the Mittani.[14] In this regard, van Dijk claims in the preface of TIM 4 that the early MA text, TIM 4 45, was, in fact, closer to Nuzi palaeography than to MA, whereas Nuzi palaeography is not derived from Mittani cuneiform (Weeden 2016, 163). It is, of course, possible that multiple traditions existed in Aššur before the late 15th century, during which Mittani cuneiform became dominant. Despite the possibility that MA cuneiform could have derived from Mittani, it does not suffer from a lack of distinction between voiced, voiceless and emphatic consonants, which is typical of the Hurro-Akkadian texts (cf. Weeden 2012, 242–43). It is to be expected that the lack of proper distinction between sounds in Mittani cuneiform would negatively influence MA (cf. Adler 1976, 1). However, the absence of these phonemes in Mittani orthography could have prompted Assyrian scribes to introduce old and new innovations to write these values.

§ 62 Unlike the unclear origins of MA cuneiform traditions, we can still be certain that the scribal schools of different realms and cities in Mesopotamia continued to influence each other during the Late Bronze Age. According to Izre'el, such an influence from Assyrian

12 Mittani script is found in a number of other texts from Northern Mesopotamian (origin). For lists, see Schwemer (1998, 15); Weeden (2012, 231–32).

13 This number is roughly estimated by dating the last OA texts to 1700 (after Šamšī-Adad I) and the first MA texts after 1450 (before Aššur-uballiṭ I).

14 See Schwemer (1998, 15); Weeden (2012, 245; 2016, 163). Note that the Assyrian Amarna letter EA 16 was also written in Nuzi-Akkadian, which ultimately belonged to the Mittani tradition as well. See von Soden (1952a, 434); Artzi (1997, 327). Schwemer claimed that the earliest Ugaritic-Akkadian texts were also in a Mittani ductus, but no actual study on UgAkk palaeography exists to date. See Schwemer (1998, 16 n52); van Soldt (1991, 375ff § 8).

scribes was caused by the changing political landscape (Izre'el 1991a, 357ff, 385f). EmAkk mostly seems to follow MA in terms of sign values, although the chronological development is difficult to verify using current studies.[15] In general, MA has the tendency to introduce new sign values for emphatic consonants, a trait it shares, to some degree, with other WPA dialects, such as UgAkk and EmAkk. We have already seen that <ṭí> (TÍ) was retained from OA to distinguish <ṭi> from <di> (DI) and <ti>. Typical for MA is <ṭu> (GÍN), which replaced <ṭú> (TU) in MA from 1325 onwards and first occurred in MB in 1250 (Syllab, 63 no. 322); however, <ṭú> is relatively common in older texts. For /q/, we find <qa> (QA), which is one of the emphatic distinctions it shares with contemporary Akkadian, possibly derived from OB.[16] Likewise, <qu> (KUM) is widespread in Late Bronze Age Akkadian and could have been introduced from Elam (Syllab, 23 no. 129). On the other hand, <qi> (KIN) remains more limited to WPA, being rare in MB (Syllab, 58 no. 294). It seems to have been introduced relatively late in MA, while, in earlier texts, <qí> (KI) is still common. In the MAL A, it only occurs in two instances: *ta-al-ti-qe-ú-ši-ni* MAL A § 23:29; *qi-ra* MAL A § 40:76. In MAL B, the sign KIN is more frequent, while, in the Coronation Ritual, MAPD and most other literary compositions, KIN is used almost exclusively. Likewise, in the earlier text, we find KI preferred over KIN. In Ugarit, the values <qi> (KIN) could have been introduced as late as the reign of Niqmaddu III (see Huehnergard 1989, 35). For /ṣ/, the common value <ṣi> ZÍ was used, which can occasionally be found in OA (Syllab, 20 no. 109). In older texts, <ṣí> (ZI) is still found. It is possible that, in MB, <ṣu> (ZUM) is present (cf. Aro 1955a, 20); however, this value seems to have been more or less simultaneously introduced around 1400 in most of Late Bronze Age Akkadian (Syllab, 59 no. 299; Durham 1976, 116; Huehnergard 1989, 37). Here, too, in older texts, <ṣú> (ZU) is common. The process for emphatics was never completed, as the values <ṣa> (ZA) and <ṭa> (DA) share signs with <za> and <da>. The development of special signs for emphatics is a new development in Late Bronze Age Akkadian, as it was mostly absent in OAkk and OA and rather limited in OB (GAG, 32 § 26b). We also find <šú>, which first occurs in the royal inscriptions of Shalmaneser and frequently in MB from the reign of Nebuchadnezzar I onwards (Aro 1955a, 25; Syllab, 58 no. 296). However, unlike the southern dialect, MA mostly seems to prefer its use in pronominal suffixes, a feature it shares with Ḫattuša (Durham 1976, 202ff), e.g., *pa-ni-šú-n[u]* Coronation Ritual i 28; *ma-za-al-te-šú-nu* Coronation Ritual iii 11; GÙB-*šú* Ištar Ritual:4; ŠEŠ^{meš}-*šú* Giricano 4:25 (exceptions are: *ú-na-šú-qu* Coronation Ritual iii 3; *tu-be-šú-ni-ma* PKT 4 r. left; see also de Ridder 2016c, 299–300 § 1.2). Similar is the use of <šá> (NÍG), which was first introduced for the particle *ša*, e.g., ^{iti}*šá sa-ra-a-te* MAL A § 59:64; *šá* SAG MAN(^{meš}) MAPD § 3:26; § 21:103; šá SAG LUGAL § 22:121; ^{lú}*šá*-SAG-MAN^{meš} Coronation Ritual ii 37; 2 BÁN *šá qa-ni-šu* PKT 3 i 1; *šá* UGU LUGAL PKT 3 iv 8. It must be admitted that <šá> is also frequently used syllabically. In terms of vowels, MA breaks from OA by at least attempting to distinguish /i/ and /e/. The system for doing so was far from complete, but signs were used to differentiate the Cv position as well as that of vC. This aspect is discussed in more detail in § 132.

15 See Seminara (1998, 171ff). Typically, MA values are present, such as: <ṭu> (GÍN); <ṣu> (ZUM); <pi>; <ṭi>.

16 See Syllab, 7 no. 36; cf. Finet (1956, 19).

	Ca	Ci	Ce	Cu	aC	iC	eC	uC
b	BA	BI	BAD	BU	AB	IB		UB
p	PA	PI		BU	AB	IB		UB
m	MA	MI	ME	MU	AM	IM		UM
d	DA	DI		DU	AD	Á		UD
ṭ	DA	TÍ		GÍN	AD	Á		UD
t	TA	TI	TE	TU	AD	Á		UD
n	NA	NI		NU	AN	IN	EN	UN
š	NÍG/ŠA	IGI	ŠE	ŠU (ŠÚ)	AŠ/ÁŠ	IŠ		UŠ
s	SA (ZA)	SI		SU (ZU)	AZ/ÁŠ	EŠ		UZ (UŠ)
z	ZA	ZI		ZU	AZ	GIŠ		UZ
ṣ	ZA	ZÍ (ZI)		ZUM	AZ	GIŠ		UZ
l	LA	LI		LU	AL	IL	EL	UL
r	RA	RI		RU	AR	IR		UR
y	IA	IA		IA	(IA)	(IA)		(IA)
g	GA	GI		GU	AG	IG		UG
k	KA	KI		KU	AG	IG		UG
q	SÌLA	KIN; KIN		KUM	AG	IG		UG
ḫ	ḪA	ḪI		ḪU	AḪ	AḪ		AḪ
ˀ	ˀA	ˀA		ˀA	ˀA	ˀA		ˀA

Figure 13: MA syllabic values.

§ 63 In conclusion, MA cuneiform seems to be based on three pillars: a Babylonian, an OA and a Mittani. All of them influenced MA to different extents. It appears that the core of the MA cuneiform model was borrowed from an unknown OB scribal tradition, which was in use in Northern Mesopotamia in order to replace the OA model. However, a few features of OA can still be found in MA. The developments in later OA suggest that the transition could have been a fluid process, instead of an abrupt change. The Babylonian model could have been transmitted through the Mittani overlords; however, the myriad of different scribal traditions in every Northern Mesopotamian city does not suggest an especially uniform Mittani school. Rather, it seems that Mittani merely had some amount of influence on the Assyrian scribes, visible in the palaeography. Mittani cuneiform was also ultimately based on a number of OB scribal traditions, which were in use in the region and continued to be used, even after the ultimate demise of Mittani. This explains why remnants of the scribal tradition known from OAkk and OA were still in use in MA and other WPA forms. If we regard MA as part of a family of cuneiform traditions, with a common origin, which kept influencing each other, then we can explain the common innovations, e.g., emphatic signs and the distinction between /i/ and /e/. The introduction of these innovations did not happen all at once, while the texts preceding Shalmaneser I demonstrate some older traits disappearing from the language. However, around the period of this king's reign, the orthographic system had become stable, albeit rigid, leaving room for very little variation or exceptions. Some degree of innovation continued, as the development of scribal traditions never halted. However, the orthographic model developed for MA was unprecedented in terms of the accuracy with which it enabled scribes to write.

2.3 Cuneiform signs

2.3.1 Logograms

§ 64 The number of logograms or logographic combinations used in MA has increased significantly compared to OA, both quantitatively as well as qualitatively (for a representative list of combinations, see the sign list at the end of this study). Cancik-Kirschbaum estimated the number to be as much as 20% of the words in her Tell Aš-Šēẖ Ḫamad letter corpus (MATSH, 71). In some administrative texts, the number of logograms may even breach the 50% mark, although admittedly this remains uncommon.[17] Logograms are most common in notes and, with decreasing frequency, in legal documents, letters and literary texts. They are also frequently used in PNs, resulting in some difficulties when analysing the Akkadian forms behind them. For instance, it is not entirely clear whether to read names of the type DN-KAR as DN-*šēzib* or DN-*ēṭir*.[18] At the same time, difficulties arise as to whether to reconstruct a Babylonian or Assyrian form, as can be observed in the case of Assyrian ^{md}*A-šur-mu-še-zi-ib* KAJ 14:27 vs. Babylonian *Šu-zu-ub*-^{d}AMAR.⌜UTU⌝ KAJ 13:35. Another problematic PN is the type *Mannum-balu*-DN (see *balu* § 447). Although the term suggests otherwise, logograms do not have to be singular, as often multiple signs are necessary to express one word, e.g., ŠE.Ì.GIŠ 'sesame' T 93-7:6. Additionally, sometimes multiple signs are read as one: UD.KA.BAR > ZABAR. Logograms are usually of Sumerian origin, although some Akkadian forms exist as well, such as the preposition *iš-tu*, the measurement MA.NA and the semi-Sumerian É.GAL-*lim*, but these are well known in Akkadian. Other Akkadograms outside the sphere of numbers and measurements are rare. Hurrian logograms are uncommon, but probably attested in TUR.DAN (< *turtānu*) 'deputy' LB 2532:4 (Richter 2012, 448), which is otherwise written syllabically. Many Sumerian loans can still be found in vernacular MA, as will be demonstrated in § 265.

§ 65 We can arrange logograms according to a number of different categories, some of which we will discuss in more detail below. The main category comprises substantives, which form the vast majority of logograms in terms of application, as well in the number of different words. Somewhat related is a small group of adjectives, e.g., DÙG.GA (*ṭābu*); GAL (*rabīu*); GIBIL (*eššu*); SIG_5 (*damqu*); SUMUN (*labēru*); TUR (*ṣeḫru*). While the number is small, they are frequently used. Another expanding group comprises prepositions. *iš-tu* (*iltu*) can be regarded as an Akkadogram, but KI is also used. For *ina*, we find the first instances expressed by the sign DIL, although one may argue that the grapheme *i+na* could be regarded as an Akkadogram as well. A very small group comprises the verbal forms expressed in Sumerian; while these are not applied very often, they are one of the most obvious instances of southern influences on orthography, as they are much more common in OB and MB. These forms are discussed below.

§ 66 In order to ease the reading of a logogram, a phonetic complement is often added to the logogram. This is usually limited to the final syllable of the base of a word. Attached

17 For instance, the text T 98-44 has the relative pronoun *ša* only once and only consists of logograms (Sumerian and Akkadian).

18 See OMA I/II and, in particular, the indexes of the MARV/KAM volumes.

pronominal suffixes and other morphemes are not considered to be phonetic complements. For some logograms, phonetic complements are so common that most studies tend to read them syllabically, e.g., ŠÀ-*bi* > *lìb-bi*. A list of the most common examples is given below. Other logograms are less common and their phonetic complements are optional:

annuku	AN.NA-*ku* 'tin' KAJ 18:2 (Ead/Aub)
	AN.NA-*ki* KAJ 159 r. 11 (Sa)
bētu	É-*ti-ka* 'your house' VAT 8851:5 (Sa)
emūqu	^{md}NIN-[URTA]-Á-*qa-i*[*a*] (Ninurta-emūqāya) KAJ 76:28
emāru	ANŠE-*ra* 'donkey' VAT 8851:27 (Sa)
kunukku	KIŠIB-*ku* 'seal' KAJ 101:1 (Aššnīr III)
paṣīu	BABBAR-*ú* 'white' KAJ 273:4
rabīu	GAL-*ú* 'big' MARV 10 82:8
sūtu	^{giš}BÁN-*ti* 'seah' Billa 35:6 (Adn/Sa)
šarrutu[19]	MUNUS.LUGAL-*ti* 'queen' RS 06.198:15
tupšarru	DUB.SAR-*ri* 'scribe' KAJ 74:9 (Ead/Aub)
urḫu	ITI-*ḫi* 'month' KAJ 29:6 (Aub)
zittu	HA.LA-*ti-šu* 'his share' KAM 10 14:5 (Aub)

§ 67 Although phonetic complements usually comprise the final syllable of a noun, sometimes the phonetic complements do not agree with syllabic rules. For these exceptions, different explanations can be given. In the case of ⌜EN-*ī*⌝-*ni* (*bē/lī/ni*) 'our lord' KAV 217:16', the sign I is used to indicate a long, binding vowel. In another text, we find the PN ^{m}*Aš-šur*-⌜SIG$_5$⌝-*iq* 'Aššur-dameq' MARV 2 1 vii 5, which could in fact be in accordance with syllabic rules, provided we reconstruct the sound change /m/ > /ʔ/ (see § 233). In this case, the value <iq> (IG) indicates a closed syllable: *Aš/šur/da/ʔiq*. It is also possible for a phonetic complement to indicate a morpheme, rather than the final syllable, as in the case involving the plural (adjective) morpheme *-ūt/-utt* in LÚ-*ut-ta* MATC 4:15. That said, it should be pointed out that the morpheme *-utt* can also be indicated by a single sign of the TA series, e.g., NINDA^{meš} GAL-*tu* (< *rabīuttu*) 'big breads' MARV 1 7:9 (cf. NINDA^{meš} *arrukuttu* 'long breads' l. 6). This may cause some confusion with forms that can take a feminine ending *-(a)t* or feminine plural. Another case of a phonetic complement indicating a morpheme, rather than a syllable, is found in the pronominal suffix *-anni* in PNs, such as ^{md}*Še*-KAR-*a-ni* 'Šēzibanni' KAJ 226:5. Another related, albeit limited, group comprises logographic spellings with mimation; here, ITI-*im* and ŠE-*um* are attested (see § 86f). Prefixed phonetic complements also occur on a number of forms:

balāṭu D	^{md}IŠKUR-*ú*-TI.LA 'Adad-uballiṭ' KAJ 221:3
damāqu D	^{m}*Mu*-SIG$_5$-^{d}EN 'Mudammeq-Bēl' MARV 5 20:18
ezabu Š	^{md}*Še*-KAR-*a-ni* 'Šēzibanni' KAJ 226:5
	^{d}UTU-*mu*-KAR 'Šamaš-mušēzib' MARV 5 8:55
nukarippu	*nu*-^{giš}KIRI$_6$ MARV 4 1:25
šalāmu D	^{md}30-*mu*-SILIM 'Sîn-mušallim' MARV 9 96:3

19 The word *šarrutum* 'queen' was probably not common in MA, as the NA logogram MUNUS-É.GAL for this noun should probably be understood as *issi ēkalle*; see Parpola (1988a); Postgate (2001). Some MA attestations (*iltu ēkalle*?) are found in MUNUS-É.GAL-*lim* (Franke/Wilhelm 1985:2; MUNUS.É.GAL.LIM-*lu* T 04-2:17). The presence of *šarrutu* in this Ugarit letter could be explained by the fact that the Assyrian scribe was writing from Aššur to a foreign queen (of Ugarit), thus using different terminology.

It may be observed that most of these examples are limited to PNs. Moreover, there is a clear tendency to use them with the prefix of the participle of derived stems, where the logogram is used for the base of the verbal form.

§ 68 A small group of nouns involves bases, which are indicated with one individual (C)vC sign or sometimes two different signs. There is some inconsistency in the preference of scholars when it comes to transcribing these words as logograms or as syllabic spellings, e.g., DUB (*tuppu*) 'tablet': DUB-*pu*; DUB^{pu}; *tup-pu*. Most of these are often used without phonetic complements, so that we are obliged to transcribe them as logographic, at least in some cases. Examples such as DUB and ŠÀ also occur in OA with similar phonetic complements and have to be read in these instances as logograms because of the absence of geminated spelling in the said orthography. Nonetheless, for the convenience of the reader, this study chooses to use the syllabic reading, where possible. The most important of this group of nouns are:

<tup> DUB in *tuppu* 'tablet': *tup-pu/tup-pi/tup-pí/tup-pa* etc.[20] DUB can also be used logographically, but never occurs outside the context of the word *tuppu*. The unusual phonetic complement <pí> (BI) can be explained as a scribal tradition, as it appears in both OA (e.g., CCT 4 40b:11) and OB (e.g., TCL 17, 12:22). However, the OA complement <pì> (BAT) is not used here (e.g., BIN 6 188:5).

<lìb> ŠÁ in *libbu* 'heart': This semi-logogram is usually written with the phonetic complement BI for the genitive or status constructus. The use of BI, instead of the preferred BAD, makes it possible to regard this form as an Akkadogram. We also find LUGAL [*ki*]-*i li-ib-bi-i-šu* MAL B § 3:23. Other phonetic complements are rare: *lìb-bu-šu-ma* (VA) MAL A § 37:16. Rarely, we find irregular spellings: *li-ba a-li* KAJ 6:11; *li-be* T 93-11:34; ⸢*li-be*⸣ T 96-36:22. BAD is also rarely found: *lìb-be-ši-na* KAJ 277:6.

<u$_4$> UD in *ūmu* 'day': *u*$_4$*-m*v. This sign must be regarded as logographic, rather than syllabic, as UD is never used in variations of *ūmu*, such as *ūmmakkal* 'for one day'. The sign is used syllabically to express the series <ud/t/ṭ>. The semi-logographic use is most notable in the plural: UD^{meš}-*ú* T 96-1:4. Forms without UD should also be noted: *ú-mu*^{meš} MATC 3:7; *ú-me* KAJ 127:15; as should *u*$_4$*-um* KAJ 182:7; KAJ 184:5.

<muḫ> UGU in *muḫḫu* 'top': *muḫ-ḫe* passim. This noun occurs in prepositional phrases, always in the genitive. Other spellings are occasionally found, e.g., *i+na mu-ḫi* KAJ 23:5.

§ 69 A special group of semi-logographic spellings comprises numbers and measures. We will discuss the numbers in Chapter 9, but list the measures below. They appear to be abbreviations or static forms of their counterparts in spoken language. As such, they are never inflected, except for ŠE-*um*:

MA.NA (Akk. *manû*): Despite being an Akkadian word, *manû* is never inflected, but used as an Akkadogram. Different spellings are not known to me.

QA (*qaʾu*): As MA-NA; this Akkadogram is, for convenience, transcribed as SÌLA in this study.

20 The transcription <tup>, rather than <ṭup>, is intentional as the presence of /ṭ/ in this Sumerian loan is based on a misconception; see Streck (2009, 136–139). There is a possibility that Sumerian DUB became *tuppu(m)* in Babylonian, yet was realized with /ṭ/ as *ṭuppu(m)* in Assyrian; see Streck (2009, 139).

ŠE-*um/im/am*: It has been shown that ŠE should be read as *eyyû(m)* in Akkadian.[21] The phonetic complement is equally difficult because of the lack of mimation in MA, while it only occurs with ŠE. If we read it syllabically, a reading such as ei_x-u_{16}/e_x/a_{16} would make little sense. It appears that ŠE was originally used as a determinative; otherwise, we cannot explain the Akkadian entry in the lexical list BVW Ko:12 ŠE: ŠE-*um*. ŠE can also occur independently, e.g., MATSH 1:12. For the incorrect use of case endings, see § 275.

2.3.1.1 Sumerian verbal forms

§ 70 Verbal forms could be expressed with Sumerograms, usually (but not necessarily) accompanied by a phonetic complement (cf. Postgate 1997, 159 n2). Most attestations derive from loans from the early MA archive M 9; however, attestations from the literary corpus are also known. Sumerian verbs in letters are highly unusual, but one is attested in GAR-*nu* BE 17 91:5. While some verbs behave in the same way as normal logograms (e.g., DU), others are actually conjugated according to Sumerian grammar (e.g., Ì.LÁ.E). The latter are limited to loans and other administrative documents.

Logographic, with conjugation through optional phonetic complements:

alāku	DU (*illak*) in passim *a-na* MÁŠ DU 'it goes for interest', e.g., KAJ 83:22 (Sa); KAJ 87:7 (EAd/Aub); DU-*ak* KAJ 85:21 (Arm)
danānu	KALAG-*at* (*dannat*) 'it is valid' BM 108924:22 (Adn$^?$)
epāšu	DÙ-*aš* (*eppaš*) Coronation Ritual ii 16; iv 23 ~ ⸢DÙ⸣ Adad Ritual:2
šakānu	GAR-*nu* (*šaknū*) 'they are placed' BE 17 91:5
tadānu	SUM-*na* (*iddina*) 'he gave' Giricano 4:30 (Abk)
ṭiābu	*lu* DÙG.GA (Akk. *lū ṭāb*) Coronation Ritual ii 32

Sumerian conjugated verbal forms:

lā dagālu	LÚ^{meš} IGI NU DU[Ḫ]^{meš} 'blind People' KAJ 180:2 (Sa)
laqā'u	ŠU.BA.AN.TI (*ilqe*) 'he took' passim, e.g., KAJ 11:7 (Aub); 22:7 (Abn); 50:5 (Abn); TR 2903:7; 3007:8; Kümmel 1989:20 (TN); HSM 1036688:10 (Ari)
madādu N	Ì.ÁG.E (*imaddad*) 'he will measure out' passim, e.g., KAJ 60:9 (Aub); KAJ 70:8
šaqālu	Ì.LÁ.E (*išaqqal*) 'he will pay' passim, e.g., KAJ 11:8; 22:8; 50:6; TR 3021:7; TIM 4 45:12; Kümmel 1989:28; HSM 1036688:18
šiāmu	IN.ŠI.ŠÀM (*išīm*) 'he bought' Kümmel 1989:18 (TN)[22]
tadānu	IN.NA.AN.SUM (*iddin*) 'he gave' HSM 1036688:12 (Ari)
lā zuāzu	NU *zu-zu-tum* 'who have not divided' Kümmel 1989:17 (TN)

In the case of ŠU.BA.AN.TI we sometimes find a different phonetic complement (see CAD L, 131), e.g., ŠU.BA.AN.TI-*ú* KAJ 32:7; SU.BA.AN.TI-*e* KAJ 37:6. Even a plural marker is used in ŠU.BA.AN.TI^{meš} KAJ 12:7 for the plurality of the agents of this verb. On one occasion, we find a mixture: ^{ŠU}*il-qe* MARV 3 32:13-14. Admittedly, these variations on the Sumerian verbs are relatively rare; however, Ì.LÁ.E; ŠU.BA.AN.TI and DU are used passim in loans from the EAd/Aub period. Only rarely do we find their syllabic equivalent in the strict formula of these texts, e.g., *il-qé* MARV 1 19:8. In PNs, we often find the element Ì.GÁL (*ibašši*), e.g., Ì.GAL-DINGIR MARV 1 19:16, and the element *ú*-TI.LA (*uballiṭ*), e.g., ^{d}UTU-*ú*-TI.LA KAJ 262:14=Šamaš-uballiṭ.

21 See Weeden (2009); Dercksen (2011).

22 Note that the sign ŠÀM is an apparent mistake for the correct ŠÁM, possible signalling a decay in scribal traditions.

§ 71 The phenomenon of logographic/Sumerian verbs is totally absent from OA, but can be found in OB, e.g., ŠU.BA.AN.TI Ḫarādum 2 99:8; Ì.ÁG.E Ḫarādum 2 100:7; IN.ŠI.IN.ŠÁM Ḫarādum 2 113:10. We find them for the first time in Assyrian in the two Babylonian-influenced texts Veenhof 1982:16 and TIM 4 45:12, both times as Ì.LÁ.E. It seems that, when Assyrian scribes replaced their OA scribal system, they introduced not only orthographic and palaeographic changes, but also legal formulae from a Babylonian curriculum. As such, we find these logograms in legal formulae, known from Babylonian equivalents as far away as Elam. The most direct link with Babylonian can be found in the Tell Muḫammad texts (cf. Alubaid 1983), where loans are similarly formulated to their MA counterparts. It should furthermore be noted that, in the kingdom of Ḫana, texts continued to attest these legal formulae after the Assyrian occupation.

n šeqel kaspim ištu PN_1 PN_2 *ilqi ana warḫim n*-KAM *kaspim u ṣibtašu išaqqal*
'PN_2 took *n* shekel of silver from PN_1 after n month he will pay the silver and its interest'

Babylonian:

[*n*] GÍN KÙ.BABBAR [...] KI PN_1 PN_2 ŠU.BA.AN.TI *a-na* ITI 1-KAM (...) KÙ.BABBAR *ù* MÁŠ.BI-*šu* Ì.LÁ.E '*n* shekel PN_2 took from PN_1, after one month he will pay the silver and its interest' IM 92139:1–10 (Tell Muḫammad)

5 GÍN KÙ.BABBAR MÁŠ ^{d}[UT]U *ú-ṣa-ab* PN_1 *ù* PN_2 ŠU.BA.AN.TI^{meš} *a-na maškānim* KÙ.BABBAR *ù* MÁŠ-*bi* Ì.LÁ^{meš} 'five shekels of silver, he (no PN) will add the interest of Šamaš, PN_1 and PN_2 will take it and pay the silver and interest at the harvest period' IM 43599:1–11 (Reschid 1965 no. 7).

Middle Assyrian:

9 MA.NA AN.NA KI PN_1 PN_2 ŠU.BA.AN.TI *a-na* 3 ITI-*ḫi* SAG.DU AN.NA Ì.LÁ.E 'nine minas of lead PN_2 took from PN_1, withing three months, he will pay the capital of the lead' KAJ 45:2–7

ana n warḫī qaqqad ŠE *inaddin/imaddad*
'within *n* months, he will give/measure out the capital of barley'

Babylonian:

ŠE-*am* (...) Ì.ÁG.E^{meš} 'he will measure out the barley' IM 92721:11-13 (Tell Muḫammad); cf. CUSAS 8 53:11 et passim

a-na ^{iti}*ša-ad-du-ut-tim* ŠE-*a-am* ù MÁŠ.BI Ì.ÁG.E 'in the month of *Šadduttum*, he will measure the barley and its interest out' IM 10688:8–9 (Reschid 1965 no. 128)

i-na ^{iti}*ab-è* KÙ.BABBAR Ì.LÁ.E 'in the month of *Abu*, he will measure the silver out' IM 43487:8–9 (Reschid 1965 no. 135)

Assyrian:

a-na 6 ITI-*ḫi* SAG.DU AN.NA Ì.LÁ.E 'within six months, he will pay the capital of lead' KAJ 11:7–8 *a-na* 7 ITI-*ḫi* SAG.DU ŠE-*im* Ì.ÁG.E 'within seven months, he will measure the amount the capital of the barley out' KAJ 60:7–9

ina ūmi irrišušu inaddin/imaddad
'on the day that he requests it from him, he shall give it/measure it out'

Babylonian:

u₄[!]*-um é-kál-lum i-te-er-šu-šu* (…) Ì.ÁG.E 'the day the palace requests it from him, he will measure it out' IM 43904:7–12 (Reschid 1965 no. 75)

Middle Assyrian:

i+na u₄-me e-ri-šu-šu-ni id-da-an 'on the day that he requests it from him, he shall give it' KAJ 82:6–8

tuppašu ana ḫepê nadât
'his tablet is liable to break'

Babylonian:

iš-tu tup-pa-šu (...) *a-na ḫe-pi na-du-ma* 'when this tablet is liable to break' MPD 23 275:11–12 (Susa)

Middle Assyrian:

[*tu*]*p-pu ši-it* (…) *a-na ḫe-pé na-ṭa-at* 'this tablet is liable to break' KAJ 142:12–15[23]

ezub tuppīšu
'aside from the wording of the tablet'

Babylonian:

e-zu-ub KA *tup-pí* 'aside from the wording of the tablet' IM 43892:10 (Reschid 1965 no. 109)

Assyrian:

e-zi-ib KA-*i tup-pí-šu pa-*[*n*]*i-ti* 'aside from the wording of the (earlier) tablet' KAJ 31:1

SUBJECT OBJECT *išīm* (Ḫana)
'Subject bought object'

Ḫana (Babylonian):

PN É IN.ŠI.ŠÁM 'PN bought the house' Podany 2002 3:14–15

Ḫana (Assyrian):

ŠEŠ[meš] NU *ze-zu-tum* ⸢A⸣.ŠÀ IN.ŠI.ŠÀM 'the brothers, who have not (yet) divided (the estate), bought the field' Kümmel 1989:17–18

n šeqlam kaspam iddin (Ḫana)
'he paid *n* shekel of silver'

Ḫana (Babylonian):

26 GÍN KÙ.BABBAR *ṣar-pa* IN.NA.AN.SUM 'he paid 26 shekels of (refined[?]) silver' Podany 2002 15:14–15

Ḫana (Assyrian):

5/6 GÍN KÙ.BABBAR *za-ku-a* IN.NA.AN.SUM 'five sixths of a shekel of pure silver he paid' HSM 1036688:11–12

23 Not only is the formula a loan from Babylonian, but we may even regard the infinitive *ḫepê* as Babylonian. For the transcription *naṭṭat* from *nadāʾu,* see Kouwenberg (2003, 85).

The use of Sumerian verbs continued into the MB period, where we still find these Sumerian verbs frequently in contracts, e.g., IN.ŠI.SA$_{10}$ ŠÁM.TIL.LA.BI.ŠÈ Gurney 1983 22:7'; 27:7'; NU.TUK^{meš} Gurney 1983 22:15'; IN.ŠE.ŠÁM HS 161:7 (~ *i-ša-am* HS 144:9). This type of verb is familiar to contemporary Nuzi, but it is not used frequently, e.g., DU-*ku*^{meš}-*ni* HSS 15 14+:60; DU-*ku-ni* HSS 15 99:19; ⸢ì⸣.LÁ.E JNES 6 613:18. Sumerograms used as verbs also occur in religious/literary texts in OB: ZU-*da* CUSAS 10 12:36, 37; they are found in literary MB too: KAR-*ib* AOAT 251, 178: 9; DU-*ak* 16. In MA, both types are used, but they remain limited to a few formulae in contracts, mostly in KAJ and Tell ar-Rimāḥ texts, along with some additional forms in the Coronation Ritual.

2.3.1.2 Determinatives

§ 72 Determinatives are frequently found in their normal function in MA. They can be placed either before or after a noun; however, the latter category is limited to the plural markers (see below). Most determinatives are placed before logograms, but they can also come with syllabic words, as is amply attested with nouns, e.g., ^{giš}*pa-ás-ru* 'pole' MARV 3 36 iii 8; ^{túg}*ḫu-la-na-t*[*e*] 'wraps' MARV 10 54:1. It is often difficult to determine whether a Sumerogram has to be read logographically or as a determinative. This feature for Sumerogram É 'house' has been discussed in Faist/Llop (2012, 24–25) (cf. É in NA, Parpola 2008, 70–71). Likewise, it is often difficult to establish whether to read KUR or URU for geographical names or LÚ before nisbes, as nisbes can be used as adjectives. Logographic, as well as determinative, readings are probably open to interpretation, even among contemporary scribes.

With a plural marker:

ummiānu	$^{\text{lú.meš}}$*um-mi-a-na-a-tu* 'creditors' MARV 4 151:62
urdu	$^{\text{érin.meš}}$ÌR^{meš}-*ni* 'slaves' T 97-2:11
zammāru	$^{\text{munus.meš}}$*za-ma-ra-te* '(female) singers' MARV 4 59:15

In administrative texts, determinatives are often omitted before nouns where they are otherwise expected. This is most apparent for the determinative LÚ, which is used for professions and other kinds of human designations. For instance, from among the 75 or so attestations of the *malāḫu* 'shipper' in the MARV series, spellings are roughly divided between ^{lú}MÁ.LAḪ$_5$ and MÁ.LAḪ$_5$ without the determinative. Other professions are stricter with their application of the determinative, although exceptions are frequent, e.g., LUNGA 'brewer' MARV 3 61:2 or *a-láḫ-ḫi-nu*^{meš} 'bakers' MARV 9 96:10. The frequency of omitting a determinative seems to be directly related to the frequency of the use of the noun that it comes with. For instance, KUR and URU, for geographical names, are only rarely omitted, whereas the measurement ^{giš}BÁN 'seah measurement' omits its determinative in the majority of attestations.

§ 73 On the subject of determinatives, the use of *Personenkeile* for masculine and feminine names may be noted: ^{m}(DIŠ) and ^{f}(MUNUS). They appear in OB (cf. MZL no. 748), but are found for the first time in Assyrian in the late OA texts from Aššur, e.g., APM 9220; KAM 10 1; MAH 15962+. In MA, they are obligatory before PNs, but not in genealogical statements, e.g., IGI ^{d}UTU-*na-da* DUMU *Uz-za-ia* 'Aššur-nāda son of Uzzāya' KAJ 3:16. That said, exceptions are relatively rare; given the frequency of the construction, a large number can still be found. Examples from Aššur:

ina bēt ^{md}MAR.TU-PAP DUMU ^{md}*A-šur-i-qí-ša* MARV 1 37:4–5
ina qāt ^{m}DUMU-*ṣíl-lí-ia* DUMU ^{m}*Aš-šur*-KAR MARV 5 39:9
^{m}*Ṣíl-lí-ḫúb-bu-ši-ša* DUMU ^{m}*A-bi*-DINGIR-*li* AO 20.154:4–5
^{m}⸢*Ki*⸣*-ti-de* ⸢DUMU⸣ ^{m}*Ki-din-Taš-me-te* LB 1848:3–4
^{md}*A-šur*-A-PAP DUMU ^{md}UTU-*ú-ma-i* VS 1 102:3–4

Some peripheral attestations from Tell Ṣābī Abyaḍ and Tell Aš-Šēḫ Ḥamad:

IGI ^{m}*Ge-el-zu* [D]UMU ^{m}*A-la-ie-e* T 97-05:13–14
[PN DUMU] ^{m}*Tam-ši-i-lu* T 98-40b+ ii 104
^{md}UTU-⸢*i-din*⸣ DUMU ^{md}UTU-*ši-me-ik-r*[*i-bi*] T 98-125:5–6
[*P*]*N* DUMU ^{m}*qa-ab-ba*-[(x)] T 04-31:2'
^{md}*Iš₈-tár-ki-i-a-bi-ia* DUMU ^{m}*Ia-a-tal-li* MPR 28:33

Both MA Ḫana texts feature *Personenkeile*, following the logogram DUMU:

^{md}30-MU-SUM-*na* DUMU ^{md}IŠKUR-*ú-ma-i* Kümmel 1989:15–16
IGI ^{m}*A-ḫi-li-ka* DUMU ^{md}AMAR.UTU-PAP HSM 1036688:19 (Ḫana)

With the plural marker MEŠ, both are possible:

DUMU^{meš} ^{md}MAR.TU-PAP KAJ 8:8
DUMU^{meš} ^{d}IŠKUR-*mu*-KAR KAJ 54:7
DUMU^{meš} *Ad-ma-ti*-DINGIR KAJ 57:23
ša DUMU^{meš} ^{md}*Be-er*-SUM-MU^{meš} KAJ 122:6
DUMU^{meš} KI-DINGIR-TI.LA KAJ 175:29
DUMU^{meš} ^{m}DINGIR-KAM KAV 26 r. 17

In lists of witnesses, the use of a *Personenkeil* is optional following IGI, occurring in some texts while absent in others throughout MA history. I am uncertain how this distribution of *Personenkeile* developed. Their use following DUMU^{meš} and IGI are atypical for Nuzi or late OB; on the other hand, this use is common in MB. Very rarely, a feminine marker precedes a logogram to indicate that the form is feminine:

tuppa ^{f}KALAG.GA (*dannata*) 'strong tablet' KAJ 14:17 cf. *tup-pa* KALAG.GA KAJ 149:22

2.3.1.3 Markers

§ 74 A special type of determinatives is attached behind a word instead of in front of it. Quite unlike normal determinatives, they are less strictly bound to logograms and can be attached just as well to syllabic spellings. There are only two kinds of markers in MA: plural markers and distributive TA.ÀM. Some exceptions are found, e.g., 4 *su-ku-ni-*[*n*]*u*$^{mušen.meš}$ 'four doves' T 98-7:3; 1 *me-su-ku*^{mušen} 'one falcon' T 98-77:3. Determinatives can sometimes involve a plural marker. It is perhaps better to interpret them as nouns in some cases.

šēbu	$^{lú.meš}$*še-bu-te* 'witnesses' MAL A § 40:70
tappāu	$^{lú.meš}$*tap-pa-ú-šu* KAJ 32:5
sukanninu	4 *su-ku-ni-*[*n*]*u*$^{mušen.meš}$ 'four doves' T 98-7:3

§ 75 Plural markers represent a special type of determinatives, since they can basically be attached to any noun. In MA, we find three different pluralizing determinatives: MEŠ, ḪI.A and DIDLI. Of these three, only MEŠ occurs with a large variety of animate and inanimate logograms. The minor variant ME.EŠ can be found in the late OA texts from the M 9 archive (e.g., KAM 10 1), but is otherwise unusual in MA, and perhaps in 7 UD$^{me.eš}$ KAM

10 40:1 and DUMU$^{me.eš}$ MARV 8 47:25. As we may see below, MEŠ has an overlap with the other plural markers, creating variations and sometimes words with two plural markers. The variant ME only occurs on very rare occasions: UDU.U$_8$^{me} 'ewes' Ali 2:11 TÚG$^{ḫi.a-me}$ Whiting 1988:6; ÉRIN$^{meš.me}$ Billa 48:9; ^{iti}*a-ab*-LUGAL^{me} KAJ 127:19; LAL^{me} MARV 2 20:28. In general, MEŠ can be used with any logogram.

aḫu	ŠEŠ^{meš} 'brothers' MAL A § 25:84
dayyānu	DI.KU$_5$^{meš} 'judges' MAL A § 15:48
emmeru	UDU^{meš} 'sheep' A 113 (NTA, 15):1
eṣu	GIŠ^{meš} 'wood' KAJ 108:2
ḫaṭṭu	^{giš}GIDRU^{meš} 'sticks' MAL A § 7:77
kitāʾu	GADA^{meš} 'flax' KAV 200 r. 2
kunukku	^{na4}KIŠIB^{meš} 'seals' KAV 109:23
marāʾu	DUMU^{meš} 'sons' KAJ 6:15
nikkassu	NÍG.KA$_9$^{meš}-*šu* 'his account' KAJ 80:1
šamnu	Ì^{meš} 'oil' KAJ 306a:10
ŠE	ŠE-*um*^{meš} 'barley' KAJ 101:2
šīpātu	SÍG^{meš} 'wool' KAV 106:9

§ 76 Often, the logogram takes a phonetic complement, indicating the case ending. Basically, this suffix always involves one syllable and follows the plural marker. Pronominal suffixes are also added directly to the plural marker.

emmeru	UDU.NÍTA^{meš}-*tu* 'sheep' A 1740 (NTA, 20):8
ilu	DINGIR^{meš}-*ni* 'gods' MAL A § 25:90; KAJ 232:3
nāqidu	NA.GADA^{meš}-*te* 'herdsmen' A 297 (NTA, 16):3
urdu	$^{érin.meš}$ÌR^{meš}-*ni* 'slaves' T 97-2:11
šarru	LUGAL^{meš}-*nu* 'kings' T 02-32:10
urḫu/ūmu	ITI.UD^{meš}-*te* MAL A § 19:91

The attached (pronominal) suffixes, of which we will present only a very small selection, are similar:

kunukku	^{na4}KIŠIB^{meš}-*ia* 'my seal' KAV 98:15
ṣābu	ÉRIN^{meš}-*šu* 'his troops' MARV 7 48:13

Combinations of the previous two categories are noticeably rare. Two cases from the Tell Ḫuwīra archive can be presented:

ešartu	10^{meš}-*tu-ma* 'group of 10' MATC 80:5
ūmu	UD^{meš}-*te-šu-nu* 'their days' MATC 40:13

§ 77 The sign MEŠ is the only marker of plurality that comes with syllabically written nouns. In this case, it follows the plural ending and additional suffixes. It is not used often, unlike in certain WPA dialects, where it more commonly occurs as an additional aid for the scribes whose native language was not Akkadian (e.g., UgAkk: Huehnergard 1989, 86ff). In addition, Adler (1976, 34 § 22) points to a preference for the use of an extra plural marker in the cases in which a substantive is orthographically identical in both the singular and plural form. For MA, it may be partly caused by the shortening of final vowels, which is a feature known from NA (SNAG, 78). This would cause confusion with the masculine plural forms, thus resulting in the need for a logographic plural marker. However, it is also found with the feminine plural ending *-āt*, which, when written defectively, is identical to the singular ending *-at*. It must be stated that, in absolute numbers, the use of plural markers on syllabic spellings is not preferred.

alaḫḫinu	*a-láḫ-ḫi-ni*^{meš} ‘bakers’ A 1750 (NTA, 24):10
Aššurāyu	*Aš-šu-ra-ie-e*^{meš} ‘Assyrians’ KAJ 310:22
azamru	*a-za-am-ru*^{meš} ‘fruit’ MARV 5 42:4
gu(r)rutu	^{udu}*gu-ra-tum*^{meš} ‘ewe’ KAJ 9:6
ḫamsu	*ḫa-am-sa-te*^{meš} ‘maltreatments’ PRU 4, 289:5
ḫīṭu	*ḫi-ṭa-a-ni*^{meš} ‘sins’ MAPD § 21:110
ḫuṣābu	*ḫu-ṣa-a-be* ^{meš} ‘twigs’ PKT 1 II left:14
maʾišu	2 ^{udu}*ma-i-šu*^{meš} ‘(a type of sheep)’ KAJ 120:10
pāḫutu	*pa-ḫa-te*^{meš} ‘provinces’ A 113 (NTA, 15):4
panu	*pa-ni* ^{meš} MAPD § 8:50
qarrātu	^{iti}*qar-ra-tu*^{meš} KAJ 118:24
qēpu	*qe-pu-tu* ^{meš} ‘representatives’ MAPD § 8:51
	qe-pu-tu-šu^{meš} ‘his representatives’ MAPD § 21:109
qermu	*qé-er-mu*^{meš} ‘(a garment)’ MARV 10 18:3
ṣāmidu	*sa-mi-di-šu*^{meš} ‘his grinders’ MARV 1 49:10
ṣēnu	*ṣe-na*^{meš} ‘flock’ Ali 3:6
šēḫtu	*še-ḫa-a-te*^{meš} ‘incense burners’ Coronation Ritual i 39
šerku	*šer-ku*^{meš} ‘palace functionary’ MAPD § 20:97
tuttubu	^{túg}*tu-ut-tu-bu*^{meš} ‘(a woollen fabric)’ MARV 10 14:1
tuppu	*tup-pa-te*^{meš} ‘tablets’ KAJ 310:38
zāriqu	*za-ri-q*[*i*]^{meš} (a palace employee) MAPD § 8:49

In this light, we may also note its use on adjectives: ^{kuš}*gu-sa-na-te* BABBAR^{meš} KAV 104:7. We may assume the use of MEŠ with determinatives as well (cf. Huehnergeard 1989, 88), but it is more likely that most of them were actually logograms, e.g., ÉRIN^{meš} *Kaš-ši-e* ‘Kassite troops/Kassites’ MARV 1 1 i 21’–22’.

§ 78 The use of the plural marker ḪI.A (or ḪÁ) is limited to three logograms: A.ŠÀ (*eqlu*) ‘field’, É (*bētu*) ‘house’ and TÚG (*ṣubātu*) ‘textile’.

A.ŠÀ	A.ŠÀ$^{\text{ḫi.a}}$ MAL B § 17:6; MARV 1 3:3’; A.ŠÀ$^{\text{ḫi.a}}$-*šu* KAJ 61:19 but A.ŠÀ^{meš}-*š*[*u-nu*] KAJ 39:13
É	É$^{\text{ḫi.a}}$ Coronation Ritual iii 39; É$^{\text{ḫi.a}}$-*šu* KAJ 61:20
TÚG	TÚG$^{\text{ḫi.a}}$ MAL A § 40:48; KAJ 123:2; TabT05-85:1; VAT 8237 passim; MARV 3 5:1

Exceptionally:

ālu	URU$^{\text{?.ḫi.a}}$ ‘cities’ MARV 4 151:12
karānu	GEŠTIN $^{\text{ḫi.a}}$ ‘wine’ MARV 10 84:3

However, for these logograms, MEŠ is attested as well. It seems that TÚG forms an exception here and cannot occur without ḪI.A as a plural logogram.

A.ŠÀ	A.ŠÀ^{meš} ‘fields’ KAJ 32:17; KAJ 310:12; A.ŠÀ^{meš}-*šu-nu* KAJ 47:26; MATSH 8:29’; VAT 8873:13
É	É^{meš}-*šu* ‘his houses’ TR 3001:5 (Adn); TR 3002:5 (Adn); É^{meš}-*šu-nu* ‘their houses’ KAJ 47:26; VAT 8236 r. 17

Although the plural TÚG cannot occur without ḪI.A, it is attested with É, together with a double plural marker:

É	É$^{\text{ḫi.a-meš}}$-*šu-nu* ‘their houses’ MATSH 12:34
TÚG	TÚG$^{\text{ḫi.a-me}}$ ‘textiles’ Whiting 1988:6
	TÚG$^{\text{ḫi.a-meš}}$ TabT05a-623:6; KAV 103:10; KAV 108:4; MARV 10 82:1

Note also the discrepancy between noun and adjective pluralizers in É$^{\text{ḫi.a}}$ GIBIL^{meš} 'new houses' A 3061 (NTA, 33):4.

§ 79 The plural marker DIDLI is the most limited of the three. It can only be found with URU, e.g., URU^{didli} MAL A § 24:44; KAJ 159 r. 9; George 1988 2 r. 11'. On one occasion, we even find a double use of DIDLI with MEŠ, as it also occurs with ḪI.A and MEŠ: URU$^{\text{didli.meš}}$-⸢*ni*?⸣ KAJ 193:5. In ^{uru}KA-KUR^{didli} (Billa 48:6), the plural marker is based on URU and not KUR.

§ 80 Relatively often, we find plural markers attached to a singular nomen. Sometimes, the singularity can be deduced from the syntax; in other cases, the number 1 occurs before the noun. At the same time, we also find syllabically spelled nouns in the singular, while the preceding number and plural marker indicate that a plural form is meant.

ālu	URU^{didli} *šu-a-tu* 'that city' KAJ 159 r. 9
ebirtu	7 *e-bir-ta*^{meš} 'seven steps' MAPD § 21:108
epinnu	1 ^{giš}APIN^{meš} 'one plough' LVUH 77:10
marʾu	*ina bēt* DUMU^{meš}-*ša ašar panūšani tuššab* 'she shall reside in the house of (one of) her own sons, wherever she chooses' MAL A § 46:93–94
pursītu	1 ^{dug}*pur-si-te*^{meš} 'one (offering) bowl' MARV 9 70:3
ṣubātu	1 TÚG$^{\text{ḫi.a}}$ 'one textile' KAJ 231 passim; KAV 99:16; VAT 8236 passim
	1 TÚG$^{\text{ḫi.a}}$ MARV 1 24:4 (but otherwise correct in this text!)
ūmu	*a-di* 1 ITI UD^{meš} *i-dan* 'within a month he will give it' KAJ 128:14

Attestations of TÚG$^{\text{ḫi.a}}$ are so abundant that one may wonder whether the scribes actually realized that ḪI.A was a plural marker. This may explain the double spelling, such as in the case of TÚG$^{\text{ḫi.a-meš}}$TabT05a-623:6. Some nouns that are plural in meaning, but not morphologically plural, can receive a plural marker:

immeru	80 UDU '80 sheep' MARV 1 47:2
	70 UDU '70 sheep' LVUH 51:16
ṣēnu	5 *me* 29 *ṣe-na*^{meš} 'a flock of 529' Ali 3:6
	3 *me* 76 *ṣe-na* Ali 5:6
šīru	[n+]20 UZU *ša-ša-lu* '20 pieces of meat tendon(?)' KAJ 130:7

Sometimes, a plural marker is not written; for instance, it is not found with measurements, such as *10 ANŠE^{meš} '10 homers'. Nonetheless, there are some exceptions, e.g., 100 ANŠE^{meš} KAJ 47:2; 20 ^{giš}BAN^{meš} MARV 1 20:2. With normal logographic nouns, it is often omitted from administrative documents. A case can be made that the presence of a plural number preceding the noun was sufficient to indicate plurality. The few examples here are therefore to be regarded as a small sampling:

alpu	2 GU_4 *ša-ku-lu-ú-tu* 'two fed oxen' A 3190 (NTA, 37):1
enzu	30 ÙZ MU 4$^{!}$ '30 goats aged four years old' Ali 6:12
immeru	3 UDU 'three sheep' A 1740 (NTA, 20):4
	2 UDU.NÍTA 'two sheep' KAJ 280:1
	PAP 3 UDU 'total of three sheep' A 2602 (NTA, 26):4
šēpu	*ina* GÌR DINGIR 'at the feet of the god' Coronation Ritual i 37

§ 81 Another marker is TA.ÀM, having a distributive that means 'each'. It is often used with measurements or even attached to numbers themselves. According to Kouwenberg (GOA § 2.7.3), there may not be a phonetic realization of the marker in the actual language;

this is supported by its use over different categories of words in our corpus. A few attestations:

3$^{\text{ta.àm}}$-*a-te iddan* 'he will pay back three times' MAL B § 8:16

šumma umāti lā eppaš 12 GÍN$^{\text{!ta.àm}}$ *annaka iḫīaṭ* 'if he does not work (the agreed) days, he will weigh out 12 shekels of lead (for each day)' KAJ 99:19–21

2 *šabartu ša erīe* 45 MA.NA$^{\text{ta.àm}}$ *ana šuqulte* 'two blocks of copper, its weight is 45 minas each' KAJ 178:1–2

40$^{\text{ta.àm}}$ *libnāte* (…) *taddana* 'you will give 40 bricks each' MATC 4:25–27

2 SÌLA$^{\text{ta.àm}}$ ŠE-*am ekkulūni* 'they will eat two litres each' MATC 22A:9–10

1 *biltu šīpātu ana lubulte ša* x x *sinnišāte* 16 MA.NA$^{\text{ta.àm}}$ *tadnā* 'one talent of wool for clothing is given to x woman for 16 minas each' Ali 23:9–11

2.3.2 CvC signs

§ 82 As opposed to their scarce use in early second millennium OA, MA intensively makes use of CvC signs. As a common rule, all closed syllables, which are preceded or succeeded by a different phoneme, use a CvC sign, e.g., *a-píl* KAJ 169:13; *tar-ba-ṣ*[*i*] KAV 96:14. If a syllable is part of a geminated consonant, it is still preferable to use a CvC sign, despite being less common, e.g., *ú-bi-il* MAL A § 42:17; *a-laq-qe-a* MATC 9:25. Alternation between spellings with CVC and Cv-vC signs was normal, as Akkadian does not recognize standardized spellings (see Sommerfeld 2006). Consider the following two lists, which compare alternate spellings:

Nouns:

šul-ma-nu KAJ 75:10	*šu-ul-ma-nu* KAJ 76:11
ar-ḫiš MATC 1:5	*ar-ḫi-iš* MATSH 15:18
tam-le-e LVUH 91:5	*ta-am-le* LVUH 87:10
pár-ru-tu LVUH 16:19	*pa-ru-tu* LVUH 14:24
pi-šèr-ti LVUH 70:18	*pi-še-er-ti* LVUH 93:3
pi-qit-te MATC 54:17	*pi-qi-te* MATC 54:2
⸢*ur*⸣-*kiš* Giricano 7:13	*ur-ki-iš* MAPD § 21:110
ḫi-bur-ni KAJ 53:3	⸢*ḫi-bu-ur-ni*⸣ KAM 10 11:2
na-mur-tu KAJ 186:2	*na-mu-ur-tu* A 2615 (NTA, 31):2
mul-la-e MATSH 2:59	*mu-ul-la-e* MATSH 2:54
pi-šèr-ti LVUH 60:7	*pi-še-er-ti* LVUH 93:3

Verbs:

ú-bíl MAL A § 43:20	*ú-bi-il* MAL A § 42:17
i-laq-qé MAL A § 10:104	*i-la-qe* Coronation Ritual ii 41
i-qab-b[*i-ú*] PKT 5 r. 8	*i-qa-bi-ú* MAPD § 8:50
liq-bi Ištar Ritual:11	*li-iq-bi* MARV 1, 22:18
i-laq-qé-ú MAL A § 41:13	*i-la-aq-qé-ú* MARV 1 41:7
ta-šap-pa-ka-šu-nu BVW F:10	*ta-ša-pa-ka-šu-nu* BVW A:4
taḫ-te-pe MAL A § 8:86	*ta-aḫ-te-e-pe* MAL A § 8:79
la-áš-pur MATSH 7:19'	[*l*]*a-áš-pu-ur* MATSH 36:6
ú-kal-lu-ni Coronation Ritual iii 11	*ú-ka-lu-ni* KAV 128:6
šaṭ-ra-at KAJ 122:14	*šaṭ-rat* MAL A § 28:5
a-pi-il KAJ 171:23	*a-píl* KAJ 169:13

pa-qíd KAJ 178:21	*pa-qi-id* KAJ 210:10
im-taḫ-r[*u*] MARV 1 48A r. 5'	*im-ta-aḫ-ru* MAL A § 4:48
ma-ḫír Giricano 15:4	*ma-ḫi-ir* MARV 8 55:12'
maḫ-ru KAJ 66:29	*ma-aḫ-ru* KAJ 163:27
i-ḫap-pi KAJ 101:18	*i-ḫa-pí* KAJ 74:10
iš-kun MARV 5 80 r. 9'†	*iš-ku-un* MARV 5 80:4†

§ 83 A group of exceptions are formed by syllables of the type C_1vC_1, probably because of the lack of suitable sign values, e.g., [*l*]*i-id-bu-ub* MATC 11:31; [*l*]*i-il-li-ku-ni* MATC 7:17 (but *te-lil-te* Adad Ritual:8); *ka-ak-ke* MATC 1:7. However, there are some exceptions, e.g., *ú-lal* Adad Ritual:4. Ultimately, there remains a considerable group of examples that simply do not use CvC signs despite expectations: *e-ta-az-ba* MATC 4:30; *im-ta-aḫ-ru* MATC 40:15; *ma-ḫi-ir* MATC 38:4; ⸢*ta*⸣*-di-in* MARV 10 53:16; *ša-ki-in* PKT 5:24. Variation in the frequency of CvC use is visible in different texts, with MAL A seeming to use CvC less frequently. In conclusion, the use of CvC remains largely unpredictable. The main problem with this type of sign is that it is more difficult to distinguish closely related consonantal and vocalic values from each other, e.g., BAL being used for /*bal-pal*/ and ḪAR for /*ḫar-ḫír-ḫer*/. Even scribes of Akkadian may sometimes have been confused by this issue (e.g., Huehnergard 1989, 31). Variation between different CvC signs for the same value is less common in MA, but is attested a few times.

Some cases of CvC variation:

^{d}*A-šur*$^{!}$*-BI-laḫ* KAJ 57:24	^{d}*A-šur-BI-láḫ* KAJ 145:12
^{túg}*lu-bùl-ta* Coronation Ritual i 35	*lu-búl-ta-ša* MAPD § 6:45
ša-kín MARV 2 17a+:36 et passim.	*šá-kin* A 3196 (NTA, 39):28
ú-kar-ru-ú KAJ 159 r. 13	*ú-kar*$_5$*-ru-ú* TR 2057B:4'

§ 84 Most likely because of the common fluctuation of the vowel in CvC signs, some scribes seem to have had problems applying the right sign in the right place in the few cases where the vowel in the CvC sign is fixed. This is attested a number of times for the present and preterite of the verb *tadānu*, for which the correct use is <dan> (KAL) in the present *i-dan* 'he gives' (*iddan*) (e.g., KAJ 71:16) against the preterite DIN in *i-din* 'he gave' (*iddin*), e.g., KAJ 149:12. The problem arose when the preterite *iddin* disappeared from main clauses and was limited to the expression *iddin-ma ušappi* 'he gave and caused to acquire'. I have already discussed elsewhere how preterites were more often preserved in formulaic legal documents and notes than letters, where they almost completely disappeared (de Ridder 2016b, 231). The confused spellings of *iddin* and *iddan* are ultimately due to the coexistence of two past tenses in the administrative documents. For an Assyrian scribe, there was thus no question that *i-DIN* with the value <dan$_5$> could be used in the present tense, even though <dan> (KAL) was more precise. This leaves us with the following verbs, which are written as if in the preterite tense, while functioning in the present (cf. UGM, 11):

tadānu	*i-DIN-šu* 'he will give him' KAJ 6:23
	i-DIN KAJ 53:7; KAJ 88:14; TR 2913:9
	i-DIN-ma TR 3036 r. 3'

On one occasion, with the graphemic gemination of R_3:

tadānu	*i-DIN-na* KAJ 114:17

We may possibly add a case where MUR is used instead of MAR in the present *emmar* 'he sees': *e-MUR* KAJ 98:9 and *ik-ta*$^{?}$*-ṣúr/ṣir* (=*iktaṣar*) KAJ 300:9. A phonologic change seems unlikely for both *i-DIN* and *i-MUR*, since this would presume that present and preterite had (nearly) become indistinguishable.

§ 85 As discussed above, MA uses phonetic complements on logograms. There are a few examples where these phonetic complements occur following or preceding a CvC sign. Examples remain relatively rare:

batāqu	*ib-ta-*^{ta}*táq* 'he made accusations' MARV 1 13:8
Erībīu	*E-rib*^{bi}*-iyu* (PN) KAM 10 10:20
ḫapāʾu	*i-*^{ḫa}*ḫap-pi* 'he will break' KAJ 95:12
nakkamtu	^{é}*na-kám*^{ma}*-te* 'treasure' KAV 100:10, 31 (pl.); cf. ^{é}*na-kám-a-te* 109:23
našlamtu	*na-aš-*^{la}*lam-ti* 'final instalment' KAJ 28:12
šalāmu	*i-*^{ša}*šal-lim-ma* 'he will redeem' KAJ 152:4 (Aub)

An additional form of phonetic complement is found in the preposition *ṭí-*^{ḫi}*ḫi* (SUḪUR). As we will discuss in § 476, this complement is more palaeographic than phonetic.

2.3.3 Signs used to indicate mimation

§ 86 A special group of vC and CvC signs was originally used for mimation. When mimation was lost in MA, the signs were still used in the final position. As we will see, this group of (C)vM signs started to be used in word forms that never required /m/ (e.g., *ša-aṭ-ru-TUM-ni* KAJ 79:8). It is therefore sometimes difficult to retain the original reading (Reiner 1973, 27). Gelb (1970, 535) decided against correcting these signs, mainly because the decay in case endings in later periods would have necessitated the use of these signs to amend the case endings as well. In later MA, this group of signs became very restricted and was only found in the fixed spellings É.GAL-*lim*, UGULA-*lim* and ŠE-*um*. By the Sa/TN period, the commonly occurring TUM had become very rare. In general, most of the signs are used as semi-logograms, as discussed above. Orthographic remnants of mimation are much more frequent in MB, where they are very common, e.g., *maḫ-RUM* (DIL) Gurney 1983 no. 22:14'; *i-ta-nap-pa-LUM* no. 25:18; *kab-TUM* no. 28:9'. In MA, similar spellings are very rare: *it-ta-na-bu-KUM* PKT 4 r. left 7, 11.

§ 87 The main syllabic values are as follows:

<lum> (LUM); <lim> (IGI); <lam> (LAM): Of these three values, we mostly find <lim> IGI in the logographic spellings of É.GAL-*lim* (*ēkallum*) 'palace' and UGULA-*lim* (*uklum*) 'steward'. In MA, we may read the sign as <lì/è>; however, É.GAL is usually not inflected with other case endings, e.g., É.GAL-*lim* GAL-*tu* 'big palace' MATSH 10:8. Some exceptions to this statement exist, e.g., É.GAL-*la* MARV 4 27:26; 30:24. We may also note some spellings from a TSA letter, where the phonetic complement *-lu* and *-li* was added to *-LIM*, confirming that the latter sign is no more than graphic: É.GAL.LIM-*lu* T 04-2:15; É.GAL.LIM-*li* T 04-2:10. According to Cancik-Kirschbaum (2012, 28 n30), the fixed use of LIM for all three case endings was a Babylonian influence, which took place in the post-OA period. However, É.GAL-*lim* is used passim in OA, even when the case ending is not correct, e.g., Pa. 17 (L 59-572):6. In OA, *ālum* is used as a synonym for the

city, which, to a certain extent, was still the case in the early MA texts. For various spellings in OA, see RGTC 4, 14–30. Different case endings are more frequently found for UGULA, especially in palace edicts and early EAd/Aub documents, e.g., UGULA-*lum* KAJ 160:8 (EAd); KAV 212:6 (Aub); MAPD § 33:22; UGULA-*lim* KAJ 162:8 (Abn); MAPD § 7:46; UGULA-*la*[*m*] MARV 4 151:69. The value <lim> is also used in other contexts: ^{m}*A-šur-mu-šal-lim-šu-nu* MARV 6, 86:4. There are a few attestations of LIM before a pronominal suffix: *Ap-LIM-ia* (PN) KAJ 17:25 (Aub); *a-LIM-šu* 'his city' KAJ 53:15 (Aub). It is probably better to interpret this form as an Akkadogram (UGM, 10 § 6) or an erroneous spelling. We also find *ṣa-lam* 'stele' in Stelen passim.

<rum> (DIL) passim in DUB.SAR-*RUM* KAJ 33:13; KAJ 164:25; Jankowska 1962 r. 10; cf. DUB.SAR-*ru* T 97-15:23 (TN); PN *Uš-šu-rum* TIM 4 45:25; KAM 10 25:27; *Za-du-rum* KAM 10 25:21. All attestations seem to date from the EAd/Aub period or earlier.

<tam> (UD) perhaps *da-al-t*[*am*$^{?}$] 'door' KAJ 8:17.

<tum> (TUM), as <tu$_4$> in most text editions. This group of signs is not restricted to one word, e.g., *a-bu-ZA-tum* 'stables' VAT 8923:6; *maš-ka-tum* 'depot' MAL C+ § 9:12; 5 UDU *gu-ra-TUM Aš-šu-ra-a-TUM* 'five Assyrian *g*.-sheep' Billa 36:2; *la sa-aḫ-pa-tum* MARV 1, 20:3. This sign is also inaccurately used in other positions: *ša-aṭ-ru-TUM-ni* KAJ 79:8; KAJ 142:6, *ka-tum* KAJ 32:16; Billa 19:17; *lā TUM-ka-*⸢*as*⸣*-sú* (< *ka*$^{??}$*usu* D) 'do not delay him' EA 15:18; *ta-kúl-tum* '(cultic) meal' TabT105A-151:13. Notice also its use in the plural: ^{udu}*gu-ra-TUM*^{meš} 'ewe' KAJ 9:6. Some lists frequently feature <tum> for female nouns, e.g., *nàr-ma-ak-tum* 'washbasin' KAJ 303:1; *ša-na-i-tum* 'second rate' KAJ 303:4; *an-nu-tum* 'these' KAJ 303:12; *an-ni-tum-ma* 'this' BM 108924:22. The same is true for many attestations in Billa 36: ^{udu}*gu-ra-tum* 'ewes' Billa 36:1; *aš-šu-ra-tum* 'Assyrian' Billa 36:2; ^{udu}*gu-ra-tum* Billa 36:3; *ḫa-ab-ḫa-a-tum* '(meaning uncertain)' Billa 36:4; ^{udu}*zi-pu-tum* 'fat-tailed sheep' Billa 36:5; ^{udu}*pár-ra-tum* 'she lamb' Billa 36:6. Saporetti (1981, 21) reconstructs an uncertain *TUM-*[*re-zi*] in Billa 1:14. As for the distribution across the corpus, we find no attestations of texts from after the reign of TN; moreover, <tum> is not used in letters, with the exception of peripheral letters found outside Assyria proper, such as EA 15. It is furthermore notable that, while <tum> is rarer in peripheral settlements, we find a large number of attestations in Tell Billa and Tell Ar-Rimāḥ texts, which are consequently the two oldest peripheral archives. Otherwise, <tum> does not occur outside the centre. The sign TUM seems to always be used with correct nominative nouns.

<um>; <im>; <am> (UM; IM; AM): These are mostly limited in use as semi-phonetic complements to ŠE. Otherwise, IM can also be found in ŠÀM-*im* KAJ 153:8, unexpectedly in *a-na* 1 ITI-*im* A 320:7 (Aub) i/o *a-na n* ITI-*ḫi* passim, e.g., KAJ 11:7, and in DN *Nabīum*, e.g., ^{md}*Na-bi-um*-EN-PAP LVUH 39:24, cf. § 236ff.

2.4 Spelling

2.4.1 Plene spelling of gemination

§ 88 Gemination or the doubling of consonants happens frequently in MA in a number of different environments. At the same time, orthographic representation is considerably less frequent and inconsistent. The most important reason for gemination is the doubling of the second radical in the present tense or D-stem. A consonant can also be doubled because the same phoneme is added to it, which is most common with suffixes, e.g., *šanīe(m)+ma* (e.g., *ša-ni-em-ma* MAL A § 3:28). Additionally, contact with different phonemes can result in the assimilation of a consonant into the following consonant, which happens most frequently with /n/ e.g., I/n verbs *insuḫ* > *issuḫ*. It is also possible that the two phonemes merge into a different doubled consonant, as with the suffixes, e.g., *bēt+šu* > *bēssu*. Gemination of ʾ$_{1-7}$ is not visible in the orthography, but did exist, based on the absence from VA in syllables closed by a geminated aleph.

§ 89 Gemination can either be written plene or remain defective. Plene and defective geminated forms can approximately be divided equally. This is the common situation in WPA, which seems to be an inheritance from Mittani scribal traditions.[24] However, the equal estimation is partly reinforced by a number of common words, which are always geminated (see below); otherwise, the number would be considerably lower. Gemination appears to be less common than in contemporary MB, although it differs in both dialects between genders and dialect. In general, literary texts have the most gemination, with some exceptions, such as the Coronation Ritual, while the least gemination occurs in the administrative genre. In OA, gemination was usually not expressed (GKT, 14–15 § 3; GOA § 2.4), but the few known post-OA texts already feature gemination to some degree (Gelb/Sollberger 1957, 174). Lambert (1965, 285) believed that the scarcity of gemination was in fact caused by an OA substratum in the MA scribal traditions, which is even reflected in some SB compositions. As gemination remains relatively rare, some confusion may occur, e.g., *ú-ta-er-šu-nu* MATSH 7:7'' (perfect) ~ *ú-ta-e-ra-ni* KAV 98:17 (preterite). A list of selected verbs without gemination of the second radical, or the third radical (in the case of II/weak verbs), follows below:

bakāʾu	*i-ba-ki-a* 'they will cry' MAPD § 2:19
epāšu	*lā te-pu-šu-ni* 'you do not do' T 93-3:6
ezābu	*lā te-zi-ba* 'do not leave' T 93-2:11
ḫabālu D	*lā ḫa-bu-la-ku* 'I am not indebted' A 748:6
ḫapāʾu	*i-ḫa-pí-ú* 'they will break' KAJ 134:17
labānu	*i-la-bi-in*$^{!}$ 'he will make bricks' KAJ 111:12
lapātu	*i-la-pa-at* 'he will touch' Coronation Ritual i 25
malāʾu D	*la-a ú-ma-lu-ú* 'they will not restore' MAL A § 4:56
nakāsu D	*la-a ú-na-ku-su-ma* 'they will not cut off' MAL A § 4:55
pasālu	*i-pa-si-lu-ni* 'he will distort' KAJ 1:25
rakāsu	*i-ra-ka-su-ni* 'he will set up' Coronation Ritual i 40
ṣabātu D	*ú-ṣa-bi-tu-šu-ni* 'he seized him' A 3196 (NTA, 39):11
šakānu	*i-ša-kan* 'he will place' Coronation Ritual i 36
tabāku	*i-ta-ba-ak* 'he will pour' KAJ 119:16
ušābu	*la-a ú-šab* 'he will not reside' MAPD § 1:2

§ 90 In attestations where gemination is attested, we can observe the tendency to use CvC signs. As we will see, the use of CvC seems to be learned, meaning that CvC signs occur more frequently in some forms than in others. A definite pattern is not apparent.

---

24 Adler (1976, 16 § 6) seems to think that consonant doubling could have been expressed by a plene-written vowel, but limits his evidence solely to the suffix *-utt* (see § 113). In UgAkk, the situation was 50/50, according to Huehnergard (1989, 47ff). However, in AmAkk, doubling was the rule, rather than the exception (see Izre'el 1991, 61ff).

CvC signs:
i-qar-ri-i-bu MAL A § 2:22
ḫab-bu-ul MAL A § 39:28
i-šap-pa-ar MAPD § 9:53
i-qar-rib Coronation Ritual i 39
ú-kal-lal-šu Coronation Ritual i 26
lid-di-na-ku Coronation Ritual i 36
ú-kal-lu-ni MARV 10 5:6
^{dug}*kal-la-a-te* New Year Ritual:16'
i-rad-de George 1988 1 r. 6'
i-ḫap-pe KAJ 73:16
tu-qa[*r*]*-ri-ba-ni* MATSH 5:13'
ú-ḫal-li-qu-ú-ni KAJ 128:13
uz-zak-ki-ši KAJ 7:8
i-laq-qé KAJ 169:23

vC+Cv signs:
i-ma-ag-gu-ur MAL A § 30:32
ta-at-ta-la-ad MAL A § 36:10
i-na-áš-ši-ú MAPD § 8:51
la-a ta-ap-pa-al MAPD § 10:59
ga-am-mu-ri Coronation Ritual i 37
ta-ṣa-al-li MATSH 9:39
i-la-aq-qe KAJ 306:a9
na-ap-pí-ša KAV 99:22
ul-te-bi-la-ak-ki A 845:13
ma-ad-du MARV 3 60:4
i-ša-ak-ku-nu MARV 4 13:5'
tu-ud-da T 97-10:14
ša ša-at-ti-šu T 97-34:8

§ 91 As gemination is optionally represented in orthography, we can compare spellings with and without gemination.

Verbal:

it-tal-ka LVUH 60:9	*i-tal-ka* LVUH 68:6
in-ni-ṣi-id LVUH 70:16	*i-ni-ṣi-id* LVUH 74:22
il-li-ka-ni MATC 43:12	*i-li-ka-ni* MATC 56:4
i-ba-aš-ši T 96-1:7	*i-ba-ši* MATSH 7:26'
la i-ma-ad-da-ad Jankowska 1962:17	*i-ma-da-ad* Jankowska 1962:6
i-pa-⸢*al-làḫ-ši*?⸣ Tsukimoto 1992 D r. 5'	*i-pa-láḫ-šu* Giricano 4:23
i-na-ak-ki-su MAPD § 2:21	*i-na-ki-su* MAPD § 5:46
i-qa-ab-bi MAPD § 2:17	*i-qa-bi* MAPD § 2:13

Nominal:

pi-it-ti MATSH 9:22	*pi-ti* MATC 3:11
qa-as-su MATSH 8:49'	*qa-sú* MAL B § 6:45
ši-id-di MATSH 2:7	*ši-di* MATSH 3:14
ši-il-la-ta MAL A § 2:16	*ši-la-ta* MAL B § 3:23
qu-up-pa KAV 99:25	*qu-pi* KAJ 310:4
mu-ul-la-e MATSH 2:54;	*mu-la-ú* Billa 30:1

§ 92 Gemination occurs with some of the assimilated pronominal suffixes, but usually these are written defectively. This subject will be discussed in more depth in § 224f.

aḫāzu	*eḫ-ḫa-a-si* 'he will seize her' MAL A § 55:36
epāšu	*e-pa-a-*[*s*]*u* 'he will do to him' MAL A § 14:40
kallutu	*kal-la-a-su* 'his daughter-in-law' MAL A § 30:34
maḫāṣu	*ta-ma-ḫa-si* 'she will hit her' MAPD § 18:85
qātu	*qa-sú* 'his hand' MAL B § 6:45
ṣabātu Š	*ul-ta-aṣ-bi-si* 'he has arranged for her' MAL A § 22:108
tarqītu	*tar-qi-su* 'its perfume taking' PKT 6 ii 27

Sometimes, however, geminated forms are found. This feature remains very rare in MA and is mostly confined to MAL A.

epāšu	*e-pu-us-si* 'he will do to her' MAL A § 9:89
mutu	*mu-us-sa/sà* 'her husband' MAL A (27x)
rēšu	*re-es-su* 'his head' T 02-3:22

ṣabātu	*iṣ-ṣa-ba-as-si* 'he has seized her' MAL A § 12:18
	i-<ṣa>-ba-as-si MAL A § 40:69
šaptu	[*ša*]-*pa-as-su* 'his lip' MAL A § 9:94

§ 93 Some words are always geminated in orthography; this is especially true for pronouns (personal, relative and determinative). They can be regarded as 'learned' forms, as little variation occurs within them, e.g., *at-ta; gab-bV; am-mar; ma-am-ma; mìm-ma; muḫ-ḫu* etc; the exceptions are few: *ga-BI-e* KAJ 6:9 (Aub); *mu-ḫi* KAJ 37:10; KAJ 66:4; TR 3007:6'; and the tentative *a-na-te-ka* MATSH 29:10'†. Likewise, some participles are always geminated: *aš-šum/šúm*; *šum/šúm-ma*; *um-ma*; the exceptions are: *a-šúm-ka* A 877:6; *šu-ma* KAJ 6:17; KAJ 62:14; T 93-07:8; *šú*$^{!}$*-ú-ma* KAJ 58:19. The evidence demonstrates that mostly learned forms were geminated. This is also confirmed by the evidence from proper names, where some parts are always geminated: *Kaš-šV* 'the Kassite'; *Aš-šurāyV* 'the Assyrian'; ^{iti}*Al-la-na-tV*; ^{iti}*Qar-ra-(a)-tV*; ^{m}*Aš-šur-dan-ni-ni* MARV 9 23:6'; ^{Id}*A-šur-dam-me-eq* KAJ 123:14; ^{Id}*Be-er-tap-pu-ti* KAJ 158:23 etc. Semi-logographic nouns with phonetic complements are geminated by default, e.g., *lìb-bi*; *lìb-be*, but **lìb-i*; *li-bi* KAJ 175:9; *tup-pu; tup-pì*, but **tup-ú* (see § 68). However, as these spellings also occur in OA, where gemination does not occur, one may wonder if these are really to be read syllabically, instead of logographically.

2.4.2 Plene spelling of long vowels

§ 94 MA uses plenty of plene spellings of the type Cv_1-v_1 and v_1-v_1C for vowels. Traditionally, it is assumed that this is an indicator of vowel length; indeed, this seems to be the case in MA as well. The lengthening of vowels can be based on either morphologic or etymologic grounds. The latter occurs due to the contraction of vowels, which is something that is considerably rarer in OA and MA than in the other dialects of Akkadian. Numerous plene spellings implicate specific reasons, which will be discussed elsewhere. We often find the sign IA followed by a vowel sign in order to indicate the vowel quality of the sign (§ 172), whereas prefixes of the prefix conjugation of verbs use plene spelling for historical reasons (§ 101ff). Lastly, some unexplained plene spellings could be related to stress, rather than length. We will concentrate on plene spellings for vowel length below. Plene spellings of long vowels mostly focus on penultimate syllables and are more limited for ultimate syllables. Despite a word being able to contain more than one long syllable, it is rare to find plene spellings of more than one vowel in MA/NA (see Worthington 2010, 186). Plene or defective spellings of long vowels are rarely fixed, with the exception of a few particles (see below) and the subjunctive. The variation of the different spellings can be summarized in the table below, which provides a good overview of the different positions of plene spellings.

Verbs:

ú-qar-ri-bu-ú-ni A 297 (NTA, 16):5	*ú-qar-ri-bu-ni* Coronation Ritual iii 8
it-tu-ú-ra MAL A § 24:70	*it-tu-ra* MAL A § 22:10
pa-al-ḫa-a-ku Billa 63:21	*pal-ḫa-ku* MATSH 16:20
li-qa-a-al MATSH 12:31	*li-qa-al* MATSH 6:10'
iz-zu-ú-zu LVUH 22:36	*iz-zu-zu* KAV 168:10

Nouns:

de-e-na Franke/Wilhelm 1985:5	*de-na* KAJ 8:11
ad-ra-a-te Giricano 9:6	*ad-ra-te* MARV 1 8:16
ták-ba-a-ru A 2606 (NTA, 28):10	*ták-ba-ri* A 2606 (NTA, 28):1
na-mu-ra-a-tu A 3186 (NTA, 35):10	*na-mu-ra-tu* A 113 (NTA,):6
nap-ša-a-te MAL B § 2:16	*nap-ša-te* MARV 7 14:8
ša-ku-lu-ú-tu A 3190 (NTA, 37):1	*ša-ku-lu-tu* MARV 4 65 iv 1
a[r]-sa-a-n[u] KAJ 277:13	*ar-sa-nu* KAJ 226:10
pi-i KAJ 113:32	*pi* KAJ 199:4
gi-na-a-e MARV 3 22:3	*gi-na-e* MARV 10 90:13
ṭé-e-ma MARV 2 22:12	*ṭé-ma* MATSH 2:22
tup-pa-a-te MAL B § 6:48	*tup-pa-te* KAV 102:11

§ 95 Particles specifically need to be mentioned. In MA/NA, there is an unequal distribution of plene spellings. The table in SNAG (29 § 2.4.3) is mostly valid for the MA period as well, with *ša* almost never written plene, *kī* almost always and *lā* usually, while *lū* uses both spellings. Plene spellings for the particle *ša* do occur in the law texts, but they are a minority in such cases: *ša-a* MAL A § 3:43; § 9:95; 21:91; B § 3:33; § 8:12; see also KAJ 6:5. Similar to the I/weak verbs, this spelling was probably adopted by analogy with the other particles, whereas *ša* has a short vowel. Defective spelling for *kī* can also be found in the formula *ki ša-pár-ti* 'as pledge', e.g., KAJ 11:16; KAJ 13:10 passim. Here, too, plene spelling can be found, e.g., KAJ 14:8; KAJ 163:6. In other texts, we find defective *kī* as well, e.g., KAJ 60:12; Billa 3:14; Gircano 14:14; T 3001:6. Still, *ki-i* outnumbers defective *ki* by about 10 to 1.

§ 96 Plene spellings of final long vowels, such as the 3mp ending *-ū* on finite verbs (cf. § 506) or the plural ending *-ū*/*ī* for masculine nouns, are not frequent. Verbs in questions are an exception (§ 682). On the other hand, plene spellings of final vowels are better attested in OA.[25] The decrease in frequency could be due to the shortening of final vowels. Hämeen-Anttila claimed that all final vowels had shortened in NA because they were post-tonic (SNAG, 29 § 2.4.3, 32 § 2.4.7). The actual number of arguments given for this claim is small at best. As the defective spellings are orthographically identical to singular forms, MA often attaches the plural marker MEŠ to the base (see § 77). Examples of plene spellings are as follows:

Nouns:

bitqu	*bi-it-qé-e* (=*bitqē*?) 'losses/levy(?)' KAJ 294:2
ēṣidu	5 *e-ṣi-du-ú* 'five reapers' Giricano 9:8

Verbs:

tadānu	*i-ta-nu-ú* 'they have given' AO 20.154:13
ubālu	*it-ta-ab-lu-ú* 'they have brought' KAJ 212:9

Cf.:

bakāʾu	*ib-ti-ki-i-ú* 'they have cried' T 02-32:13

25 See Veenhof (2010, 30–31); GOA § 2.3.1.

In comparison with the plural endings *-ū/ī*, it may be noted that plene spellings for III/ē verbs are just as rare.

laqāʾu	*i-la-qé-e* 'he will take' AO 19.228:20

Perhaps because of the shortening of long final vowels, we find a limited number of plene final vowels where no lengthening is expected. These attestations should not be confused with the lengthening of the final vowel in question.

apil zaku	*a-píl za-ku-ú* 'it is paid and cleared' KAJ 12:16
ŠE.ÀRA-*šu*	ŠE.[À]RA-*šu-ú* Giricano 2:10; Giricano 3:8
tuppu	*tup-pí-e* 'tablet' KAJ 6:4

§ 97 The vowel /ū/ of plural verbs is usually spelled plene when followed by the subjunctive *-ni*. This somewhat supports Hämeen-Anttila's claim about the shortening of final vowels, if we assume that /ū/ in *-ūni* is both lengthened and stressed. The same plene spelling is also attested with the subjunctive *-ni* following a pronominal suffix ending in /u/ (e.g., *-šu*, *-kunu* etc.).

etāqu	*e-ti-qu-ú-ni* 'they passed' MARV 1 6:3
ḫamāṣu	*iḫ-mi-ṣú-ku-nu-ú-ni* (*iḫmiṣūkununi*) 'they robbed you' T 04-37:12
ḫiāru	*i-ḫi-ru-ú-ni* 'they checked' MAPD § 8:50
laqāʾu	*li-il-qe-ú-ni* 'they must take' MATC 9:11
muātu	*me-tu-ú-ni* 'he is dead' MAL A § 46:89
pašāru	*ip-šu-ru-ú-ni* 'he withdrew' KAJ 113:9
qarābu D	*ú-qar-ri-bu-ú-ni* 'he presented' A 297 (NTA, 16):5
tadānu	*it-ta-nu-ni-šu-ú-ni* 'he has given to him' A 1746 (NTA, 22):8

Plene spelling is not obligatory, nor is it influenced by the grammatical number of the subject, unlike NA (cf. Fabritius 1995).

akāku	*e-ku-lu-ni* 'they eat' T 93-3:19
laššu	*la-áš-šu-ni* 'is not available' MATSH 6:9'
šakānu	*ša-ak-nu-ni* 'it is placed' KAV 103:12
urādu	*ú-ru-du-ni* 'they will descent' MATC 4:24
ušābu	*us-bu-tu-ni* 'she is settled' MAL A § 24:57

Similar to the subjunctive *-ūni*, plene spellings are attached before pronominal suffixes.

buāru D	*ú-ub-ta-e-ru-ú-uš* 'they will prove him' MAL A § 15:49
kuānu D	*ú-uk-ta-i-nu-ú-uš* 'they will convict him' MAL A § 15:40

§ 98 For feminine plural nouns, plene spellings are relatively common in the plural morpheme *-āt*. Sometimes, the plural marker MEŠ is added to the base, although the word does not need to distinguish itself from the singular.

adru	*ad-ra-a-te* 'threshing floors' Giricano 9:6
gišḫurru	*giš-ḫu-ra-a-te* 'building plans' MAPD § 1:10
kablu	*ka-ab-la-a-te*^{meš} 'legs(?)' KAJ 121a:3
mākaltu	*ma-ka-la-a-te* 'wooden dishes' Adad Ritual r. 15'
nāmurtu	*na-mu-ra-a-tu* 'audience gifts' A 1751 (NTA, 24):10
napšātu	*nap-ša-a-te* 'life' MAPD § 10:58
pahutu	*pa-ḫa-a-te*^{meš} 'provinces' MARV 7 22:4
tuppu	[*tu*]*p-pa-a-te* 'tablets' MAPD § 2:18

Defective spellings are just as frequent as plene spellings. Unlike masculine plural nouns, MA rarely attaches the plural marker MEŠ in order to distinguish between singular and plural. In fact, MEŠ is found more frequently with plene spellings.

adru	*ad-ra-te* 'threshing floors' Billa 4:6
abātu	*a-ba-ta* 'words' MAL A § 19:83
namšartu	^{giš}*nam-ša-ra-te* 'threshing sledges' Billa 25:5
šuršurrātu	*šur-šu-ra-tu* 'chains' MARV 1 4:2
tupninnu	^{giš}*tup-ni-na-te* 'chests' KAV 98:36
tuppu	*tup-pa-te-šu-nu* 'their tablets' MAL B § 6:37

It should be emphasized that the frequency of plene spellings is influenced by position. As we have seen, ultimate plene spellings are rare, while penultimate plene spellings are optional. As plural feminine nouns with pronominal suffixes demonstrate, plene spellings in antepenultimate syllables are non-existent. Thus, we find *tup-pa-a-te* 'tablets', but never **tup-pa-a-te-šu* or **tup-pa-a-te-šu-nu*.

§ 99 The lengthening of long vowels in *PāS* and similar two-consonantal nominal constructions is related to the question of whether the long vowel is retained when the syllable is closed. There is a famous quote from Edzard (1986, 361) addressing this matter: "*Wir wissen es nicht!*" Nonetheless, Worthington (2010) recently concluded, based on quantitative evidence from NA, that, in this particular dialect of Akkadian, the long vowel seems to have been retained in the singular status rectus and construct. Some examples are found in MA: *ma-a-te* KAJ 268:6; *de-e-na* Franke/Wilhelm 1985;5; *qe-e-pu* MARV 4 18:1; *pu-ú-ḫi* MARV 6 88:27; *si-i-ra* MATC 12:17; *ṭé-e-ma* MATC 15:22. Despite there being many defective spellings present in NA, Worthington (2010, 184) alludes to the scarcity (in NA) of the lengthening of long vowels. The same can be said for MA, but cf. *pu-ḫi* KAJ 91:1; *qe-pu* MARV 4 31:24; *mu-še* MATSH 22:6; *ṭé-ma* MARV 1 15A:8. On the other hand, in bound constructions where the syllable was closed, plene spellings of vowels are almost totally absent, thus making the shortening of the long vowel likely, e.g., [*qe*]*-ep-šu* MARV 3 14:19; *ṭé-em-ša* A 845:20; *mu-us-sa* MAL A § 3:33. Long spellings in these cases are rare but signal a case of the metathesis of quantity, e.g., *qa-a-sú* MAL B § 10:32. Double spellings, such as **qa-a-as-su*, are not known to me. The same is also true when the CvC syllable of the base is opened by a suffix or morpheme starting with a vowel; this includes plural endings, e.g., *be-lí-šu* 'his lord' KAM 10 25:4; *qe-pu-tu* 'representatives' MARV 4 12:6'; *mu-ši-šu* 'its night' MATC 12:14. At the same time, the relatively few forms in genitive construction do not indicate vowel length either, e.g., *ri-iš* 'head' KAJ 148:8; *ra-aṭ* 'pipe' KAV 205:28; *ṭé-em* 'message' T 93-2:3; MARV 8 23:4; *de-en* 'lawsuit' KAV 159:7.

§ 100 Plene spellings involving word-final closed syllables are rare, although a few attestations can be found, especially in the literary corpus. Most of the given attestations do not have an expected long vowel in the position of the plene spelling cf. § 107ff.

epāšu	*e-pa-á-aš* 'he will do' MAL B § 14:33
šagarruru	*tu-uš-ga-ra-a-ar* 'you will let them go free(?)' BVW F:4
laqā'u	*la-qé-a-at* 'she is taken' MAL A § 32:52, 53
muātu	*mi-ta-a-at* 'she died' MAL A § 53:99
	me-e-et 'he died' MAPD § 2:14

nakāru	*it-ti-ke-e-er* 'he has denied' MAL A § 24:65
našāʾu	*na-ṣa-a-at* 'she carried' MAL A § 28:3
qaʾālu	*li-qa-a-al* 'may he take care of it' MATSH 12:31
zuāzu	*zu-ú-uz* 'divide!' PKT 3 i 6

Usually, bound vowels of construct forms with pronominal suffixes are written defectively. There are a few exceptions, mostly found in MAL A–B.

abu	*a-bi-i-ša* 'her father' MAL A § 55:13
	a-bi-i-šu-ma KAJ 6:5
akālu	*a-na ša-ku-li-i-ša* 'to provide for her' MAL A § 46:104
emu	*e-mu-ú-ša* 'her father-in-law' MAL A § 29:14
ḫimsātu	*ḫi-im-sa-te-e-ni* 'our wrongful possessions' KAV 217:13'
ilku	*il-ki-i-šu* 'his *ilku*' Giricano 4:26
libbu	*li-ib-bi-i-šu* 'his heart' MAL B § 3:26
narkubu	^{na4}*nár-ka-bi-i-šu*^{meš} 'his grindstones' MARV 1 30:16
našāru	*na-ša-a-ri-i-ka* 'your deducting' MATC 4:20
qaqquru	*qa-qí-ri-i-šu* 'his territory' MAL B § 13:19

2.4.2.1 Initial plene spellings

§ 101 The present *iparras* or D-stem present/preterite of verbal roots from the type I/weak is sometimes spelled with an extra vowel, as if the initial sound was long (e.g., *i-id-da-an* MAL A § 3:42). This characteristic, which is certainly not unique, was studied at length by Kouwenberg (2003/4), who later revised his findings (2010, 542–46).[26] He concluded that, in OB, regarding the present and the preterite/present of the D-stem the initial aleph was replaced by a long vowel by analogy with the preterite. This is also confirmed by the lack of 'plene spelling' for the perfect of the D-stem: that is, all forms where the initial weak radical comes into contact with a succeeding consonant and, in some cases, merges with it. Already in OB, the I/w verbs were added to this group, either by analogy or because present forms alternated between having lengthened or short first syllables (Kouwenberg 2003/4, 100–1). In late second millennium Akkadian, the tradition of plene spelling mostly disappeared, except in some vernaculars of WPA, where it still occurs. Kouwenberg, therefore, suggested that plene spelling had become a learned form, while it did not reflect the actual lengthening of the first syllable. For this reason, it could continue in WPA, where Babylonian was not the native language. In this context, we also find it in MA, albeit mostly confined to MAL A. Consider the following list (all attestations are from MAL A, unless indicated otherwise):

akālu	*e-ek-ku-lu* 'they will eat' MAL A § 36:94
alāku	*i-it-tal-ka-an-ni* 'he has come' MAL B § 19:9
emādu	*e-em-me-ed* 'he will impose' MAL A § 3:39

26 Streck (1997, 310–11 § 23d; 2011, 12 § 21c) presented a different solution and claimed that the plene spelling of I/weak verbs was in fact used for syllables that begin with a stop. This convention would, thus, be merely orthographic and explained by the original use of the vowel sign to indicate /ʾ/ or /y/. Kouwenberg (2006, 156–159) argued that word-initial forms could theoretically have an aleph, but there is no reason to assume they do. The only dialect containing evidence of a word-initial aleph would be OA, where the prepositions *ana/ina* could assimilate into an aleph in forms such as *a-am-tí-šu* (*ana* +*amtīšu*) 'for his slave' AKT 3 32:3. In MA, a spelling such as *ḫi-ri-ṣa-*⸢*ḫi*⸣ (< *ḫirīṣu* +*aḫu*) could point to the loss of an aleph because the spelling indicates a syllabic structure *ḫi/rī/ṣa/ḫi* i/o *ḫi/rīṣ/ʾa/ḫi*. See MATC 3:6 (commentary).

	e-em-mi-id 'he will impose' MAL A § 16:62; § 23:39
idāʾu	*ú-ud-di-ú-ni-šu-ni* 'he assigned him' MAL A § 43:28
epāšu	⸢*e*⸣*-ep-pu-šu-ú-ši* 'he will do to her' MAL A § 1:13
	e-ep-pu-ú-šu-uš 'he will do to him' MAL A § 22:13
	e-ep-pa-áš MAL B § 7:10; § 15:38; § 18:27
uṣāʾu	*tu-ú-uṣ-ṣa* 'she will go out' MAL A § 37:19; § 46:91
ušābu	*tu-ú-uš-ša-ab* 'she will dwell' MAL A § 45:70; § 46:94
	tu-ú-uš-šab 'she will dwell' MAL A § 46:101
ušāru	*ú-uš-šu-ru-šu-nu* 'they will release them' MAL A § 23:26

§ 102 In OB texts, plene spellings (*e-ep-pa-áš*) and defective spellings (*e-pa-áš*) are more common than "normal" spellings of the type *ep-pa-áš*. In MAL A–B, plene spellings are most frequent, but otherwise no such restriction seems to apply in these two texts or in MA in general, e.g., *ep-pu-šu-ú-ni* MAL A § 23:20; *eḫ-ḫa-az-ma* MAL A § 43:30. It seems, therefore, that the OB orthographic influence of I/weak verbs was limited to plene spellings. As a result of these forms being learned, plene spellings also penetrated the paradigm of other weak or irregular verbs. The most frequent is the irregular verb *tadānu* "to give" (Bab. *nadānu*), which never had a lengthened vowel in the first place, but was apparently regarded by the scribe as I/weak because the first radical is not visible.

tadānu	*i-id-da-an* 'he will give' MAL A § 3:42; § 24:71; MAL B § 14:30
	i-id-dan 'he will give' MAL A § 22:111; § 24:59; § 29:19; § 43:26; 45:88; § 51:86; § 55:41; 47
	i-id-du-nu-né-eš-še 'he will give to her' MAL A § 45:67
	i-id-dan-ši 'he will give her' MAL A § 33:66; § 55:32
	i-id-du-nu MAL B § 6:37

Similar plene spellings can be found in a number of other weak verbs, which correspond to each other in terms of having a weak second radical. To this group, three perfects can be added, which is unusual because this type of plene spelling is usually limited to present verbs. Similar to *tadānu*, the scribe did not recognize the second radical and therefore wrote the prefix plene by analogy with the I/weak verbs:

bāuru D	*ú-ub-ta-e-ru-ú-uš* 'they will prove him' MAL A § 15:49
kiānu D	*ú-uk-ta-i-nu-ú-uš* 'they will convict him' MAL A § 15:50
Niāku	*i-it-ti-a-ak-ši* 'he had intercourse with her' MAL A § 14:37
qaʾʾuʾu D	*tu-ú-qa-a* 'she will wait' MAL A § 36:95

On one occasion, we find a stative, which is probably spelled that way by analogy with present I/weak verbs.

ušābu	*ú-us-bat* 'she dwells' MAL A § 24:47

§ 103 Outside MAL A–B, this kind of plene spelling is significantly rarer. Only a few examples can be given, none of them from after than the reign of TN.

agāru D	*ú-ug-ga-ra* 'I will hire' MATC 4:11
alāku	*i-il-la-ak* 'it will go' T 97-15:15
amāru	*e-em-mu-ru* 'they will examine' MARV 2 20:20 (TN)
apālu	*e-ep-*⸢*pal*⸣ 'he will pay' MARV 4 151:61 (TN)
erāšu	*e-er-ru-*⸢*šu*⸣ 'they will cultivate' KAJ 52:18 (EAd/Aub)
epāšu	*e-ep-pu-šu-ni* 'they will make' MARV 4 34:20' (TN)
	e-⸢*ep*⸣*-pa-ša-na-ši-in-ni* MATSH 11:17
epāšu D	*ú-up-pi-šu-ni* 'he performed' MATSH 9:20
	ú-up-pi-šu-ú-ni DeZ 2521:19

idā'u	*ú-ud-du-ni* 'they know' MATSH 6:5'
ubālu	*ú-ub-bu-lu-né-eš-šu* ''they will bring to him' MATSH 9:46

Some cases of plene spelling in the preterite and imperative can be found.

akālu	*le-e-kúl* 'may he eat' MATC 5:24
alāku	*a-al-ka* 'come!' T 93-7:13
tadānu	*i-id-di-nu-ma* 'they gave it' KAJ 152:13 (Aub)

For strong verbs, plene spellings are very rare. However, some examples are found in OA as well, e.g., *a-aṣ-ba-ṣú-ma* CCT 4 3b:6; *e-ep-šu-ma* TC 3 249:10 (GKT, 43–44 § 27c).

makāsu	⌜*i*⌝-*im-ti-ki-is* 'he has collected' KAJ 301:9 (BAI)

2.4.3 Stress

§ 104 Given that stress influences phonology, it will be worthwhile briefly summarizing this aspect. Beforehand, it must be noted that, as the classic Semitic languages have a number of exceptions to the basic stress rules, it may not be possible to explain all examples in Akkadian.[27] In general, Assyriologists seem to agree that stress is non-phonemic, meaning that there are no minimal pairs that differ in stress from each other.[28] However, opinions vary on where the stress is placed, simply because it is not clearly indicated in writing, while a living Akkadian tradition does not exist to help us. The evidence for stress is thus limited to three aspects: plene writing, where it is not expected (which makes the assumption that plene spelling can be used for this purpose);[29] word building, when concentrating on the elision of vowels and the variation in syllables;[30] and the evidence that other living Semitic languages give us. Nonetheless, a dedicated study of Akkadian stress is necessary for us to at least get an idea of the basics for Akkadian (Kogan 2004, 379). As this is perhaps too ambitious for the current study, we will try to limit ourselves to a few remarks.

§ 105 The traditional view assumes that stress is penultimate (e.g., *nad'ānu; 'uznu; š'umu* etc.).[31] In words with more than two syllables, the antepenultimate syllable is stressed if the antepenultimate is open (e.g., *z'ikaru;* verbal form *'iškunū*). The ultimate syllable is stressed if the word has more than one syllable from which the ultimate is closed, has a long vowel or is open, and has a contracted vowel (e.g., *id'ûk*; *ibn'û*). These rules are based on the situation in classical Arabic. One may assume that stress in Akkadian and Arabic are similar to each other, as it is clear that the loss of case endings strongly influenced the placement of stress.[32] Unfortunately, the theory is hardly founded on Akkadian evidence, while the evidence for the situation in classical Arabic itself is disputed (Knudsen 1980). According to Reiner, stress falls on the first syllable of a word. A few arguments for this

27 See Dillmann (1907, 110–12 § 59) (Ge'ez); Joüon/Muraoka (2006, 94–95 § 31) (Hebrew); Fischer (2006, 19–20 § 32) (Arabic).

28 The possibility of such minimal pairs was briefly considered by Buccellati (1996, 21–23 § 1.5).

29 See Aro (1953; 1971, 250); Knudsen (1980). Plene-written /e/ in Hittite is also a sign of stress see Kloekhorst (2012).

30 See Reiner (1996, 38–39 § 3.2).

31 See Meissner (1907, 12–14 § 9a); Ungnad (1992, 28–29 § 24); CGSL, 66–67 § 10.5–10.6, GKT, 68–70 § 44; Knudsen (1980, 3–7); GAG, 46–48 § 38.

32 Cf. the situation in Hebrew: Blau (1993, 30–37 § 9).

case are mentioned: languages that stress another syllable tend to elide the vowel in the first syllable (e.g., numerous instances in Syriac[33]: *qəṭ'al* (ܩܛܠ) < **qaṭ'alū* 'they killed'). Moreover, with this assumption, variations in word constructions of the type *damiqtum/damqatum* can be explained, but remain unexplained if the stress is penultimate. Reiner adds that this type of stress can certainly be proven in the case of the Assyrian dialect, making it an interesting case for us to consider.[34] Hämeen-Anttila (SNAG, 27f § 2.4.2) offered a number of convincing counterarguments to Reiner's ideas. The occurrence of a *Murmelvokal* (SNAG: dissimilation of vowels) in NA seems only to be possible before a stress, rather than following a stressed first syllable, e.g., *iš/pu/r'ū/ni* i/o *išpurūni* (cf. § 151). He continued to claim that the stress falls on the first long syllable in NA (Cv:/CvC), counting backward from the penultimate, or on the first, if no long syllable is present (e.g., *id'ûk*; *'iškanu*; *'imḫaṣ*). Ultimate stress can occur, but is limited. The syllable before an enclitic particle (e.g., *-ni/-ma* etc.) is stressed. Stress involving open short syllables lengthens the vowel, thus explaining plene writings where it is not expected. Unexpected plene spellings show that stressed vowels are lengthened.[35]

§ 106 Establishing the rules of stress for MA is not an easy task (if it is indeed possible at all). The Akkadian language gives us only a few hints about stress. For instance, simple nominal constructions, such as *PaRiS* > *PaRSu*, are examples of where the stress is clearly on the first syllable *P'aRSu* (unless one assumes stressed case endings). Continuing in this vein is the feminine construction *PaRiSat* > *PaRSatu/PaRiStu*. The occurrence of both constructions makes it unlikely that, in both cases, the penultimate syllable is stressed, based on the assumption that a stressed vowel is less likely to elide. However, we cannot be certain in what way stress developed over the course of Assyrian history, meaning that it is hard to argue against the possibility that stress became penultimate in *PaRS'atu/PaR'iStu*. In MA, some evidence for a shift in stress is visible in the prefix conjugation with the subjunctive *-ūni*. In some forms, VA is absent for the theme vowel, while a secondary /a/ appears, which is never written plene, suggesting that its realization was not strong. Thus, we find *iprasūni* instead of *iprusūni*. As we will discuss below (§ 151), this secondary /a/ is likely to be a *Murmelvokal*, which occurs because of a change in stress involving the subjunctive marker. What also follows is that stress must fall on the theme vowel in forms without the subjunctive. NA provides further examples of substantives wherein the first syllable /u/ > /a/. This has led to the assumption that this secondary /a/ appeared before a stressed syllable (Postgate 1974, 274; Kouwenberg 2010, 269 n4). For MA, we can thus assume that the subjunctive was stressed, which is further supported by the frequent plene spellings of /ū/ in the subjunctive. However, similar examples are absent in OA, meaning that we cannot be completely certain about the situation in Assyrian. Considering these arguments, this study assumes that, in general, the penultimate syllable (not including pronominal suffixes) is stressed.

---

33 For the complex rules regarding accents in Syriac, see Brockelmann (1960b, 43–47 § 71–78).

34 Reiner (1996, 38–39 § 3.2); Buccellati (1996, 21–23 § 1.5).

35 See SNAG, 27–28 § 2.4.2; Hämeen-Antilla's ideas are largely based on what was first proposed by Deller (1959, 182 § 38u).

2.4.3.1 Unexpected plene spellings in MAL A–B

§ 107 We are left with a large number of unexpected plene spellings in MAL A–B. It was first suggested by Aro (1971, 250), following earlier research (1953), that such spellings in Akkadian could indicate stress, although he himself admitted that this would present us with a number of new problems. Hecker (1973/74, 169; cf. SNAG, 28) also suggested that open syllables were stressed in MA in his review of UGM. That plene spellings of short vowels may be a sign of stress can also be expected in respect of plene spellings in the final vowel of the verbal predicate in polar questions. This is attested in all three dialects of Assyrian.[36] Assuming Aro's claim is at least partially correct, there are at least five possibilities that could render plene spellings:

1. Vowel length
2. Reflex of an etymologic long vowel in I/weak verbs
3. Metathesis of quantity (see § 111ff)
4. Stress
5. Random/no function or unknown function

Of these options, the first is logical to assume, as we have discussed above how MA often spells long vowels plene. On the other hand, options 1 and 4 can overlap in the cases where we expect the stressed syllable to include a long vowel, such as the subjunctive. All cases of plene spelling in MAL A–B deal with the ultimate or penultimate syllable, except for option 2. In other words, if Aro's assumption is correct, stress would be either ultimate or penultimate, meaning that we can reject plene spelling of long vowels in these texts. On the other hand, plene spellings in short form, such as *kī* and *lā*, are clearly motivated by length, even though they could be learned spellings. Option 3 overlaps with option 4 in a similar way to option 1. We will list a number of attestations that are candidates for option 4, with the exception of cases where we expect a long vowel, such as feminine plurals.

Open penultimate syllable:

alāku	*il-lu-ú-ku* 'they will go' MAL A § 17:71; 24:67
epāšu	*e-ep-pu-ú-šu-uš* 'they will do to him' MAL A § 22:13
ḫadāʾu	*ḫa-di-i-ma* 'he wishes' MAL A § 43:34
	ḫa-a-di MAL A § 55:38
ḫapāʾu	*ta-aḫ-te-e-pi* 'she has crushed' MAL A § 8:79
laʾāʾu	*i-la-a-ʾe-e* 'he is able' MAL A § 19:88
laqāʾu	*tal-te-e-qé* 'she has taken' MAL A § 23:15
nakāsu D	*ú-na-ku-ú-su* 'they will cut' MAL A § 40:92
palāšu D	*ú-pal-lu-ú-šu* 'they will pierce' MAL A § 40:84
qarābu	*i-qar-ri-i-bu* 'they will become close' MAL A § 2:22; MAL A § 56:45
rašāʾu	*tar-ti-i-ši* 'it has gotten' MAL A § 8:84
ṣabātu	*iṣ-ṣa-ab-bu-ú-tu* 'they will be seized' MAL A § 25:94
šakānu	*i-ša-ak-ku-ú-nu-uš* 'they will assess him' MAL A § 52:90
tuāru	*it-tu-ú-ra* 'he has refused' MAL A § 24:70; cf. § 45:73, 85
zakkāʾu	*ú-zak-ka-a-ši* 'he will clear her' MAL A § 48:44

Nouns:

panu	*pa-nu-ša-a-ni* 'of her choice' MAL A § 46:106

36 OA in GOA § 23.2.2; NA in SNAG, 35 § 2.4.10 cf. GAG, 255 § 153d.

Regressive metathesis of quantity:

Verbs:

aḫāzu	*eḫ-ḫa-a-si* 'he will marry her' MAL A § 55:36
alāku	*il-la-ka-a-ni* 'they will go' MAL A § 40:57
epāšu	*e-pa-a-*⌜*si*⌝ 'he will do to her' MAL A § 14:40
izuzzu	*iz-za-a-zu* 'they will stand' MAL B § 18:25
ṣabātu	⌜*iṣ*⌝*-ṣa-ba-a-sú* 'he has seized him (=her)' MAL A § 12:15
ubālu	*ub-ba-la-a-ši* 'he will bring her' MAL A § 40:71
zuāku	*za-a-ku* 'he is clear' MAL A § 14:38; § 24:74; § 29:60; § 38:25; § 47:17

Nouns:

emūqu	*e-mu-qa-a-ma* 'with force' MAL A § 16:63
esertu	*e-se-er-tu-ú-ma* 'concubine' MAL A § 41:10
kallutu	*kal-la-a-su* 'his daughter-in-law' MAL A § 30:34

Progressive metathesis of quantity:

Verbs:

agāru N	*in-na-gu-ú-ru* 'they will be hired' MAL A § 36:94
našāʾu	*na-ṣa-a-at* 'she is carrying' MAL A § 28:3
šaṭāru	*i-ša-ṭu-ú-ru* 'they will write' MAL B § 6:49

Ultimate closed syllable:

epāšu	*e-pa-á-aš* 'he will do' MAL B § 14:33
laqāʾu	*la-qé-a-at* 'she is given' MAL A § 32:52, 53
muātu	*mi-ta-a-at* 'she died' MAL A § 53:99
nakāru	*it-ti-ke-e-er* 'he has denied it' MAL A § 24:65
paṣānu	*pa-aṣ-ṣu-ú-na-at* 'she is veiled' MAL A § 40:60
rakāšu	*ra-ki-i-EŠ* 'it is bound' MAL A 34:72

Penultimate preceding subjunctive:

aḫāzu	*aḫ-zu-ši-i-ni* 'he has not married her' MAL A § 40:63
idāʾu	*ud-du-ši-i-ni* 'he assigns to her' MAL A § 24:45
šakānu	*iš-ku-nu-ši-i-ni* 'he bestowed upon her' MAL A § 26:98
tamāʾu	*ta-am-ʾa-ta-a-ni* 'you swore' MAL A § 47:30

§ 108 An analysis of the preceding examples is difficult to carry out, as it is impossible to prove on the basis of the stress of two MA texts. On the other hand, length is in most of these examples unlikely, while patterns can be recognized. This strongly suggests that we are not dealing with option 5: random plene spellings or without function. The following observations on possible stress must therefore be regarded as purely theoretical, in the hope that they will eventually help an all-encompassing study on stress in Akkadian. If we leave the case of potential metathesis as undecided, then we may note that all cases are penultimate open syllables or ultimate closed syllables. Another important point is the frequent occurrence of these plene spellings for syllables, which are affected by Assyrian VA. On the basis of these plene spellings, we cannot prove that all syllables affected by VA are stressed, but it certainly seems to indicate that VA is not a sign of weakening. The vowel preceding the subjunctive *-ni* results in stress: *ez-bi-lu-ú-ni* MAL A § 30:36; *aḫ-zu-*

ši-i-ni MAL A § 40:63. Pronominal suffixes do not result in stress, as has been observed by others.[37] In our corpus, this is shown in ⸢*da-ba*⸣*-a-ab-šu-nu* MAL B § 6:14. Notice a possible change of stress if suffixes are added: *ḫa-a-di* MAL A § 55:38 ~ *ḫa-di-i-ma* MAL A § 43:34. In the case of *ta-am-ˀa-a-ta-ni* MAL A § 47:27, ˀA+A is not a true plene spelling (see § 182); that said, a similar form with the subjunctive should be noted: *ta-am-ˀa-ta-a-ni* MAL A § 47:30. On the other hand, it must be recognized that the examples often do not agree with the rules, as stated in Deller (1959) and SNAG: *ta-aḫ-te-e-pi* MAL A § 8:79 would be *t'aḫ/te/pi*; *mi-ta-a-at* MAL A § 53:99 would be *m'î/tat* etc.

§ 109 As Hecker (1973/74, 169) pointed out, more examples can be found in the private archives, although they remain rare.

Verbs:

alāku	*a-al-ka* 'come!' T 93-7:13
barāˀu	*ba-a-re* 'it starves' T 97-10:18
emādu	*e-mi-i-id* 'impose' T 97-10:25
erābu	*e-er-ra-ba* 'I enter' MATSH 12:30
ḫadāˀu	*ḫa-di-a-ta-a-ni* 'as you wish' MATC 15:9
ḫabāqu	*ḫa-bi-i-qa* (meaning uncertain) MATSH 3:23
laqāˀu	*la-a-qe-ú-ni* 'it is taken' MARV 3 24:8
	la-qé-a-at 'it is taken' Jankowska 1962 r. 2 cf. *la-qé-a-at* MAL A § 35:52, 53
malāˀu	*ma-a-al-li* 'fill up!'MATC 11:19
našāru	*na-ša-a-ri-i-ka* '(lit.) your deducting' MATC 4:20
našāˀu	[*na*$^{?}$]*-a-ši* 'it is brought' MARV 10 69:11
	na-ṣa-ku-ú-ni MATC 10:18
qabāˀu	*aq-ti-bi-a-áš-šu* 'I have said to him' MATC 15:16
radāˀu	*ra-a-di* 'it is followed' Billa 63:14
sasāˀu	*si-i-si* 'read!' RS 06.198:16
šakānu	*al-ta-kà-a-an* 'I have put' Snell 1983/84:24
tadānu	*i-da-a-an* 'he will give' CUSAS 34 40:11
	ta-a-din A 842:3, 6, 8, 11, 16, 19
	ta-a-din$^{?}$ AuOrS 1 105:5
	di-na-a 'give' (ms) A 1476 r. 8'
	id-da-a-an MARV 3 52:10
upāˀu	*up-pu-a-*[*a*]*t* 'it is acquired' Jankowska 1962 r.1
zakāˀu	*za-a-k*[*u*] 'he is clear' MARV 4 115:6

Nouns:

Ab-šarrāni	^{iti}*a-ab*-LUGAL^{me} (name of a month) KAJ 127:19
atta	*at-ta-a-ma* 'you' T 97-10:13
attune	*at-tu-*[*n*]*u-ú-ma* 'you' MATSH 7:6'
balu	*ba-a-lu* 'without' KAJ 6:20
ildu	*i-il-du* 'foundation' CUSAS 34:6
mīnu	*mi-nu-*⸢*ú-ma*⸣ 'what' T 93-3:4
mutu	*mu-ú-te* 'husband' KAJ 2:13
šumma	*šú-ú-ma* 'if' KAJ 58:19
tuppu	*tup-pí-e* (sg.) 'tablet' KAJ 6:4

37 See Peust (2009, 228–29); Luukko (2004, 96–97), which has a list involving murmel-a in NA pronominal suffixes.

Regarding these examples, one may review the cases involving the metathesis of quantity, especially the case of progressive metathesis, which does not occur in NA.

§ 110 It is necessary to trace the MA tendency in relation to the opening of closed syllables (§ 157) and shortening long vowels (§ 158), as these developments resulted in, or were the result of, changed stress. For instance, the shortening of *ramānu* > *ramanu*, when applying the rules of Hämeen-Anttila, shifted the stress *ram'ānu* > *r'amanu*. In the case of the change *-ūt* > *-utt* (see § 113f), it should be noted that the syllabic structure remains intact > *šar/rū/tu* (CvC/Cv:/Cv)=*šar/rut/tu* (CvC/CvC/Cv), such that a change is not necessary here. In the case of the opening of closed syllables, the evidence is meagre; indeed, it is not clear how this would affect stress, e.g., *re-ḫi-ti* TR 2049:6'=*rē'ḫ/tu* > *rē'/ḫi/tu* or *rē/hi'/tu*. It must be noted that, in Biblical Hebrew, stress does not change in similar environments: *m'alku* > *m'e/lek̲* (מֶ֫לֶךְ) 'king' (Blau 1993, 34 § 9.1.5.). It appears that there were no set rules for stress in this period, yet the opening of several closed syllables may point to a gradual development of stress occurring at the end of a word.

2.4.4 Metathesis of quantity 1: vC: > v:C

§ 111 The metathesis of quantity concerns the variation between the alternation of the etymologically lengthened consonants and vowels with its environment. We frequently find plene spellings of a vowel instead of a geminated consonant. This type of alternation is especially common in NA.[38] Reiner (1966, 45–46 § 4.1.2.5) concluded that the phenomenon represented syllabic lengthening, which could vary between vocalic length or gemination of the succeeding consonant as a free phonetic variation: v:C ~ vC:. The alternation between these spellings in Assyrian may not, in that case, represent dialectal variation between Assyrian and Babylonian, but variation within the Assyrian dialect itself. While this assumption does seem to work well for NA, judging from the extensive evidence gathered by Luukko and Deller, it cannot be accepted beyond doubt for MA.[39] As we will see, the metathesis of quantity not only occurs before a geminated consonant, as in NA (e.g., MA *al-tap-ra-a-ku* MATSH 1:4 < *altaprakku*), but also occurs following a geminated consonant (e.g., *lu-pa-ši-i-šu* MATSH 3:37 < *lūpaššišu*). In this case, we would have to accept an additional form of free variation: C:v ~ Cv:. For this variation, three forms of lengthening would be possible: v:C ~ vC: ~ Cv:. Based on the Assyrian reluctance to geminate consonants in orthography, it seems more likely that they would alternate with plene-written vowels, rather than seek a phonetic explanation. It should be noted that the metathesis of gemination especially occurs in a number of environments: before pronominal suffixes *-anni* and a geminated second radical. We will list a number of attestations below, while trying to distinguish between different corpora of texts. The

38 For NA, see Deller (1959, 164–187 § 48); Deller/Köbert/Dahood (1966, 38 § 10.4); GAG, 24 § 20d–e; Parpola (1988b, 79); SNAG, 30 2.4.4; Luukko (2004, 123–28 § 4.14). The phenomenon remained unnoticed for MA in UGM, except for pronominal suffixes (see UGM, 25 § 22).

39 Notice a parallel development in the South and Central Semitic of quantitative metathesis in relation to geminated (Arabic II: فعّل *faˁˁala*) and lengthened stems (Arabic III: فاعل *fāˁala*). It has been argued that both stems derived from one single stem, which would explain the overlap in semantic functions (Lipiński 2001, 393ff).

examples of MAL are discussed in § 107f.[40] The following examples are normal cases of the metathesis of quantity, where lengthening moves backwards (regressive): vC: > v:C:

billu	[*b*]*i-i-*⸢*la*⸣ 'mixture' MATSH 16:18
erāšu	⸢*e*⸣*-ri-ša-a-ni* 'he requests me' MATSH 16:17
ḫaṭṭu	*ḫa-a-ṭé* 'sceptre' MATSH 16:13; *ḫa-aṭ-ṭu* BVW Ko r. 9
maḫāru	*im-taḫ-ra-a-ni* 'he has confronted me' KAV 169:5; MARV 1 13:5
maṭā'u	*i-ma-a-ṭí* 'it will become less' T 96-8:17
mazziz(z)ū	^{lú}*ma-zi-i-zu* 'witness(?)' MARV 1 41:8
našā'u	*ša* (…) *na-ṣa-a-ni* (*naṣṣanni*) 'who brings here' MATC 3:14
ša'alu	*il-ta-a*$^{?}$*-la-a-ni* 'he questioned me' T 02-32:8
šapāru	*al-tap-ra-a-ku* 'I have sent to you' MATSH 1:4
	iš-pu-ra-a-ni MATSH 10:6, 18, 37, 41
	iš-pu-ra-⸢*a-ni*$^{?}$⸣ MARV 10 3:1
tadānu	*id-du-ú-nu* 'they will give' KAM 11 79:29
	la-a-din 'I shall give' Faist 2001, 252:22;
	la-a-d[*i-i*]*n* T 96-15:13

§ 112 Cases of the progressive metathesis of quantity are rare (*C:v* > *Cv:*). In the cases where the subjunctive *-ni* or other suffixes are added, we can expect that the preceding vowel indicates stress or is lengthened.

alāku	*a-la-a-ka* 'I will come' MATC 2:18
	i-la-a-ka MATC 12:4
šagarārru	*tu-uš-ga-ra-a-ar* 'you will let them go free(?)' BVW F:4
ḫābāqu D	*ḫa-bi-i-qa* (meaning uncertain) MATSH 3:23 (imperative)
maṭā'u D	*la-a tu-ma-ṭa-a* 'do not deduce' A 877:10
našā'u	*na-ṣa-ku-ú-ni* (*naṣṣakkunni*) 'it is brought to you' MATC 10:18
pašāšu	*lu-pa-ši-i-šu* (meaning uncertain) MATSH 3:37
tadānu	*it-ta-nu-ni-šu-ú-ni* 'he has given to him' A 1746 (NTA, 22):8
	⸢*i*⸣*-di-na-šu-ú-ma* 'MATSH 7:3''
tadānu Š	[*a-na š*]*a-du-ú-ni* 'for distribution' KAJ 113:31

Note also the following examples in the peripheral Assyrian text published by Snell (1983/84):

alāku	*li-it-ta-a-lak* 'let him go away' Snell 1983/84:18
lamādu D	*lu-ú-la-a-mi-id* 'let him teach' Snell 1983/84:34

Attestations with a mixture of the metathesis of quantity and the expected geminated consonant are also found in MA. These are especially more frequent in the Tell Ḫūwira texts and seem to show that the quantity of metathesis was indeed merely orthographic. Note that Llop and Luukko regarded *ma-a-al-li* as a scribal mistake.[41]

laššu	[*l*]*a-a-áš-šu* 'not available' Billa 62:10
malā'u D	*ma-a-al-li* 'fill!' MATC 11:19
qabā'u	*aq-ti-bi-a-áš-šu* 'I said to him' MATC 15:16
šalāmu D	*a-na šal-lu-ú-me* 'to carry out' MARV 8 7:10
tadānu	*la-a-ad-di-na-ak-ku* 'I shall give you' NP 46:17
	la-a-ad-di-na-ku NP 46:20

---

40 For some attestations in PNs, see MPR, 64b n530.

41 Following an unpublished paper. The Llop and Luukko interpretation of *ma-a-al-li* as a 'bed' (*mayyālu*) is of course possible, but this complicates the interpretation. Moreover, a geminated /l/ is more difficult to explain than an extra /a/.

2.4.5 Metathesis of quantity 2: v:C > vC:

§ 113 The progressive metathesis of quality of the type v:C > vC: is mostly limited in MA to the abstractum/plurality morpheme *-ūt*, which is the standard form in Akkadian, compared with the Assyrian variation *-utt*.[42] This form is used for abstracta (see § 252) and plural iterations of normal nouns (see § 281), but is not attested for normal masculine plural adjectives, which remain defective in writing (see § 310). A related form is the feminine nisbe *-īt* > *-itt*, but only a few examples have been observed to date. The feminine plural marker *-āt* > *-att* would be expected, but is not attested. On the other hand, this feature is attested for singular feminine forms ending in *-āt*: the feminine adjective *le-a-at-ta* 'usable' (< *lēʾatu*) MATC 3:10 and the possessive pronoun *ni-a-at-tu* (< *niātu*) 'our' MATC 80:7. The function of the metathesis of quantity seems to be to indicate the length of a syllable, rather than an actual switch in length from a long vowel to the following consonant. Chronologically, we may trace this phenomenon back to OA, where it occurs once in geminated spelling, such as *an-ni-ut-tù-um* 'this' ATHE 24A:43 (GKT, 93 § 59f; GOA § 9.8.1 n25). Admittedly, this pronoun has no geminated spellings in MA (see § 373f). Geographically, the suffix *-utt* is not limited in MA; in fact, it can be found in most of the WPA dialects (Nuzi: Wilhelm 1970, 39; HattAkk and WPA: Durham 1976, 473ff; MittA: Adler 1976, 16f). In this light, Adler (1976, 17) suggested that it is likely that the use of the metathesis of quantity goes back to a Hurro-Akkadian influence on MA, rather than sole examples from the OA corpus. However, Kouwenberg (GOA § 4.3.2) points out that the status constructus examples of some OA forms prove the phonetic reality of the metathesis of quantity, e.g., *šé-bu-ta-áš-nu* (*šēbuttašnu* ≠ *šēbussunu*) 'their testimony' ICK 1 185 r. 5. We should, however, highlight the following attestation in a TSA prayer: MAN-*ut-ka* (*šarrūt-ka*) 'your kingship' T 96-31c:2''†. Nonetheless, the said literary text is mostly written in a literary dialect. It is notable that Luukko (2004, 126–27; cf. Deller 1959, 166) only presented a few examples of *-utt* for NA, while it is not mentioned in SNAG (78f). It therefore seems that a decrease in the use of the metathesis of quantity for the suffix *-ūt/utt* took place in this period.

§ 114 Attestations for the morpheme *-ūt* > *-utt* are common in our corpus; however, spelling varies significantly. As we will see, the spelling with the geminated consonant *-utt* is not the most common spelling, yet attestations are still frequent. There is a total absence of the metathesis in the demonstrative pronouns (e.g., *annūtu* 'these').

aʾīluttu	*ri-it-ti a-i-lu-ut-te* 'the hand of humanity(?)' KTN inventory iv 23'
	a-i-lu-ut-te 'people' T 93-2:9
aššuttu	*aš-šu-ut-ti-šu* 'his wifebeing' KAJ 7:9
ayyāruttu	*ayya-a-ru-ut-te* 'flowers' PKT 6 ii 24
ḫaziānuttu	*ana ḫa-zi-a-nu-ut-te* 'for governing' KAV 217:4'
marʾuttu	*mar₅-ut-ti-šu* 'his adoption' MAL A § 28:5
namuttu	*na-mu-ut-ta* 'mockery' MAPD § 19:92
panuttu	*mazziz pa-nu-ut-te* 'court attendants' MAPD § 8:51
rīmuttu	*ri-mu-ut-te* 'gift' MATSH 1:13
šanuttu	*ša-nu-ut-te-ka* 'a second time' PKT 5 r. 9
	ša-nu-ut-te-šu MAPD § 20:98
šarruttu	MAN-*ut-te* 'kingship' Coronation Ritual ii 47

42 See GAG, 24 § 20d; UGM, 25 § 22.1; MATSH, 94.

	LUGAL-*ut-ta* 'kingship' KBo 1 14 r. 5'
šēbuttu	*še-bu-ut-te* 'witnesses' T 04-37:21

Unfortunately, the evidence is not entirely unambiguous, with a long vowel often written instead. Examples where Ú follows a weak radical are perhaps better analysed as defective spellings, since Ú represents an open syllable rather than a long vowel.

labbukuttu	ŠIM^{meš} *la-bu-ku-ú-te* 'steeped aromatics' PKT 1 I right:10, 29
panīuttu	*pa-ni-ú-te* 'former' MATC 29:7
qēputtu	*qé-pu-ú-te* 'representatives' MAL B § 6:43; MARV 4 18:3; *qe-pu-ú-*[*tu*] MARV 1 72:10
qurbuttu	*qur-bu-ú-te* 'nearby' MAL A § 24:44
šākuluttu	[*š*]*a-ku-lu-ú-tu* 'fattened' MARV 4 65 r. iv 11'†
šalmuttu	*šal-mu-ú-*⸢*te*⸣ MARV 7 1:25†
šēbuttu	*še-bu-ú-tu* 'witnesses' MAL A § 17:69
urkīuttu	⸢*ur*⸣*-ki-ú-tu* 'the latter' MATSH 10:33
zēzuttu	*la-a ze-zu-ú-tu* 'who did not divide' MAL A § 25:89

Very rarely do we find double spellings. These seem to be based on two premises: the scribe added Ú following a weak radical in line with spellings, such as *pa-ni-ú-te*, and thereafter added the geminated Assyrian suffix *-utt*.

bāriyuttu	[*ba*]*-ri-ú-ut-te* 'divination' MATSH 9:19
*mar*ʾ*uttu*	*mar-ú-ut-ti* 'adoption' KAJ 1:6

Both the spellings with geminated consonants and a long vowel (*-utt* ~ *-ūt*) most frequently occur in literary texs. In fact, MA mostly resorts to defective spellings in all three main corpora: literary, letters and administrative documents. A few examples suffice.

*ba*ʾʾ*eruttu*	*ba-e-ru-te* 'extispicy' Ali 7:9
dannuttu	*dan-nu-te* 'strength' MATC 11:26
maḫīranuttu	*ma-ḫi-ra-nu-te-ma* 'recipients' MAL A § 3:30
*mar*ʾ*uttu*	*ma-ru-ti-ša* 'her adoption' KAJ 3:4
qēputtu	*qe-pu-tum* 'representatives' KAJ 247:8
sabsuttu	^{f}*sa-ab-su-tu* 'midwife' MAPD § 1:11
šangûttu	*ša-an-gu-ta* 'priesthood' Coronation Ritual ii 33
šanuttu	*ša-nu-te-šu* A 1828 (NTA, 25):10
*ṭe*ʾ*īnuttu*	*ana ṭé-i-nu-te* 'for grinding-corvée' KAV 107:12
urduttu	*ur-du-ti* 'slavery' KAJ 7:29

As we argued above, it is likely that, in all instances, /t/ was geminated. This can be observed in the status constructus attested in the genitive construction. Already in OA, we find the construct *-utti*, rather than *-ūt* (GOA § 4.3.2). For MA, the evidence is limited:

*ba*ʾʾ*eruttu*	1 UDU.NÍTA *a-na ba-e-ru-te* UD.8.KÁM 'one sheep for the extispicy of the eighth day' MARV 2 29:15
qēputtu	*ša qāt qe-pu-te* LUGAL 'in the charge of the representatives of the king' MARV 4 51:20

§ 115 Analogous to the change *-ūt* > *-utt*, we find a similar change in the feminine nisbe ending *-īt* > *-itt*. As we already pointed out, the same change never took place in the plural morpheme *-āt* (> **-att*). However, even for the feminine nisbe ending, the evidence is rather limited. It is attested twice in the adverbial *urkittu* (see § 495) and a few gentilic adjectives.

Aššurittu	*Aš-šu-ri-it-tu* KAJ 167:3

šanāyittu	*ša-na-it-*[*te*] 'second quality(?)' MARV 10 63:3'
Šubrittu	[f]*Šu-ub-ri-it-tum* KAV 211:3
urkittu	⌜*ina ur-ki*⌝*-it-te* 'afterwards' MAL A § 24:51
	ina ur-ki-it-ti KAJ 9:25

We can observe the metathesis of quantity in a number of feminine nouns with a root of the type III/ī. This indicates that this feature is not motivated by the nisbe morpheme, but can occur in all types of word construction. It also indicates that we should transcribe /i/ as being lengthened in the masculine counterparts (e.g., *šaniu* > *šanīu* 'second').

berittu	1[et] *be-ri-it-te* 'one clasp' KAJ 123a:3; 12 (√*barû*)
littu	[Id]*Be-er*-EN-*li-it-te* KAJ 217:12=with (*lītum* > *littu*)
šanittu	*ša-ni-it-te* T 02-32:11

2.4.6 Metathesis of syllables/inverted spellings

§ 116 The inverted readings are an NA feature proposed by Deller (1962, 188–93) for Cv and vC signs, where the vowel and consonant switch places, e.g., *i+na tar-IṢ* i/o *i+na tar-ṣi*. Many of Deller's examples can be explained phonologically by metathesis caused by a change in stress (cf. NA Luukko 2004, 128–31 § 4.15). Luukko therefore calls the phenomenon the "metathesis of syllables", rather than the pure orthographic "inverted readings." Nonetheless, a rare case of actual inverted spellings may be found in MA, e.g., UM-ŠE KAJ 85:6 i/o ŠE-*um* 'barley' passim. The metathesis of syllables is attested for the stative *tabik* > *tabki*.

rēḫtu ina 2 *karmāni tab-ki*[!] 'the remainder is poured out into two granaries' LVUH 75:22

1 *me* 90 *emāru* ŠE *ina* (…) *karme* (…) *tab-ki* '190 homers of barley are poured out in the granary' LVUH 75:30–31

ŠE-*am utru* (…) *ina karme tab-ki* 'the extra barley is poured out in the granary' LVUH 75:35–36

Otherwise, inverted spellings are rare and difficult to distinguish from epenthetic vowels; one example could be *ip-tu-a-KA*=(*iptuag*[?]) T 02-32:29. Another possible example can be found in [*ba*]*-ri-ú-ut-ta* 'divination' MATSH 9:19. This depends on the etymology of the noun, as it is often taken to be from III/weak *barāʾu* 'to see' (AHw, 110; CAD B, 131–32). At the same time, there is the well-attested variant *ba*[??]*eruttu* in MA, also previously translated as 'divination' (CAD B, 28a; Roth 1995, 155), which could derive from the D-stem *ba*[??]*uru*. It was first attested in *ba-e-ru-ta* MAL A § 1:9 and, more recently, in texts such as *ba-e-ru-te* MARV 3 75:4; *ba-e-ru-ti* Ali 7:5. These latter texts deal with a flock for the *ba*[??]*eruttu*, which points to divination. Deller (1987, 65 no. 29) suggested that *ba*[??]*eruttu* replaced the Akkadian noun *bīru*. Despite some similarities between the two nouns, *bārûtu* is the normal noun for divination in Akkadian, which would make MA a strange exception. It has been suggested that *ba*[??]*eruttu* should be taken as a form of oath-taking, which was accompanied by an offering of animals (Ismael/Postgate 2008, 161; see also Driver/Miles 1935, 518; AHw, 96). This has been disproven by Shibata (2015b, 148–50), with the clear application of *ba*[??]*eruttu* for divination in the letter, TabT05a-134:22. However, this would leave us with two similar terms (*ba*[??]*eruttu* and *bārīuttu*) for apparently the same phenomenon. I am uncertain about Shibata's attempt to solve the matter phonologically and would assume (if the reading in MATSH 9 is correct) that it is an inverted spelling of a syllabic sign: RI instead of IR. Alternatively, we simply have to accept that there are two similar nouns with an entirely different etymology, which refer to the same ritual practice of divination or, at least, to very phenomena.

§ 117 A true example of inverted reading can be found in spellings of the noun *šiltāḫu* 'arrow', which shows a kind of metathesis in MA, e.g., *LIŠ-ta-ḫu*^{meš} MARV 10 3:11; *LIŠ-ta-ḫi* MARV 1 63:1.[43] Note that spellings without metathesis can be found, e.g., *ši-il-ta-ḫu* Billa 46:1. This has led to the assumption that the metathesis of arrows is an orthographic metathesis of the value <liš>, which would have to be read <šil$_4$> (Reiner 1982). Indeed, the forms without metathesis use a combination of Cv+vC signs to indicate the word-initial syllable. Note that spellings such *liš-ta-ḫu* may feature an unusual contact of /š/ and /t/, which always becomes /lt/ in MA (see § 220ff). Another example of <šil$_4$> can be found in *mi-LIŠ* UDU 'half a sheep' MARV 3 16 ii 24' (cf. Llop 2009/10, 27). This kind of inverted reading has been suggested for NA with Cv and vC signs by Deller (1962, 188–93), but, to date, remains limited for MA with LIŠ. Other examples of signs with inverted syllabic readings are rare. We should note <šat> (KUR) with the inverted reading <taš$_x$> in the PN ^{f}*Taš$_x$-me-*^{d}IDIGNA MPR 48:3 (see MPR, 209).

2.4.7 Abnormal syllabification

§ 118 A number of spellings has been unable to confirm syllabic rules, e.g., *i-maḫ-aṣ* (=*i/maḫ/ḫaṣ*) Coronation Ritual i 28. Previous studies have sometimes tried to solve these spellings by suggesting (C)vCv readings of some signs, e.g., *mu-šal-lima-a-nu* KAJ 92:10.[44] Some of these CvCv values are basically logograms with CvC stems, which are read with a theme vowel. In short, this means that, for example, in UgAkk, we find that *qí*-É (Ug. 6 394ff. iii 24') is read as *qí-biti* because the word has nothing to do with a house *bītu* (É). There are two main arguments against this type of reading. First of all, this goes against the principle of a syllabic script (there being no such thing as a CvCv syllable), which only strengthened with the increased use of CvC signs in the late second millennium. Secondly, the quoted example is in the genitive; if it were in the nominative, we would have to read *qí-bitu* (e.g., *ša-ilu* Ug. 5 162:6'). This would mean that any CvCv sign would have to have three different values according to a triptotic case system. This demands a logographic reading according to a true rebus principle. In NA, this type of sign became more widespread, being used before a case ending and verbs (Deller 1962; Deller 1965, 473). However, according to Luukko's orthographic study, even these examples are "distorting the reality by forcing the orthography to conform to morphologically desired forms and thus to the more 'correct' grammatical interpretations" (Luukko 2004, 69 n187). For this reason, we accept Luukko's (2004, 27–29 § 3.5) terminology of 'abnormal syllabification' and make no attempt to the restore these forms. The attestations feature a vowel sign or vC sign following a (C)vC sign: *i/maḫ/ḫaṣ* ≠ *i-maḫ-aṣ* Coronation Ritual i 28. For this reason, abnormal syllabification can be regarded as purely orthographic.

---

43 See MARV 1, 14 (Commentary no. 63); Hecker (1980, 275).

44 For MA, see UGM, 8ff; for NA, see Deller (1962; 1965, 473). Note that this section does not contain a discussion of the bisyllabic readings of IA and A+A, as these are both composite signs to begin with. For a discussion of their bisyllabic readings, see the section on /y/ in § 170.

§ 119 In NA, considerably more attestations can be observed (Luukko 2004, 27ff § 3.5). In MA, the feature is rarer, but spread across the entire corpus and found in literary texts, letters and other types of administrative documents.

Nouns:

Ab-šarrānu	^{iti}*Ab-Šar-a-nu* (name of the month) KAV 212:12 (Aub)
	^{iti}*a-bu*-LUGAL-*a-nu* RE 92:17; ^{iti}*a-bu*-MAN-*a-ni* MARV 7 70:1
Admat-ilī	*Ad-mat*-DINGIR (*Admat-ilī*) VAT 8722:10
adru	*ad-ar-šu* 'his threshing floor' MARV 1 36:7'
aššum	*áš-šúm-i-ka* 'concerning you' T 02-32:7
danniš	*dan-iš*$^{!}$ 'very' PKT 1 I right:3; cf. *dan-níš* KBo 28 59:4, 6
mušallimānu	*mu-šal-lim-a-nu* 'delivery man' KAJ 92:10
muttaḫṣu	*mu-ut-taḫ-iṣ* < *mumtaḫṣum* 'warrior' Lambert 1969:40
nakkamtu	^{é}*na-kám-a-te* 'treasury' KAV 109:23
namāšu	[*i*]*m*$^{?}$*-mu-uš-ú-ni* 'they departed' MARV 3 9:31
našpertu	[*n*]*a-áš-pár-a-te* 'messages' MARV 2 17a+:98
qiāšu	^{d}UTU-*i-qiš-a* (*Šamaš-iqīša*) TR 2012+:8
šallimanni	DN-*šallimanni* 'o DN, make me whole' passim, e.g., ^{Id}30-*šal-lim-a-ni* KAJ 223:8; also in similar imperative forms with 1cp-suffix e.g., ^{md}30-*še-zib-a-ni* MARV 2 27 v$^{?}$ 13'; ^{md}*A-šur*-KAR-*an-ni-ma* (*Aššur-šē/zi/ban/ni*) A 2615 (NTA, 31):8

Verbs:

akālu N	⸢*i*⸣*-na-*⸢*kíl*⸣*-ú-ni* 'it is consumed' MARV 5 70:18
alāku	*i-lik-a-ni* 'he came' CTMMA 1 101:4
anāḫu	*At-na-ḫi*-DINGIR (*Atannaḫ-ilī*) Jankowska 1962:3 cf. ^{m}*A-ta-na-aḫ* KAM 10 34:20'
karāru D	*ú-kar-ú* 'he will deduce' TR 102:11
laššu	*la-áš-ú* 'there is none' Cohen/Llop 2017:5
maḫāru	*im-ḫur-ú-ni* 'he received' KAJ 129:13
	im-ta-ḫur-ú-ni$^{!}$ KAM 11 23:10
maḫāṣu	*i-maḫ-aṣ* 'he will hit' Coronation Ritual i 28
tadānu N	*in-na-din-ú-*[*ni*] 'it was given' MARV 7 1:8

As for the CvCv sign values, it can be seen that one or two examples for each form do not make a strong case for a new type of sign value. Rather, this confirms that these examples should be examined according to our own understanding of Akkadian and cuneiform, as opposed to representing a study in their own right.[45] In general, it may be observed that certain scribes had some peculiar writing habits, but their irregular spellings were not frequent enough to justify them being systemized, as W. Mayer did (UGM, 8–11 § 6). It could be argued that spellings such as ^{Id}30-*šal-lim-a-ni* KAJ 223:8 show that the accusative pronominal suffix *-anni* was added directly to the base: = *šallim'anni*.

2.4.8 Graphemic gemination

§ 120 In general, it can be stated that gemination in orthography is more frequent in literary texts than in letters and administrative texts. Especially in the last corpus, gemination is rare and limited to a few standard forms. One can easily conclude that the gemination of consonants was a learned feature, which was not easy to distinguish by the scribes of administrative documents and letters. Perhaps they had difficulties with it because gemination was historically not a feature of Assyrian scribal traditions. That said, it is

45 See also Postgate (1974, 273); Luukko (2004, 69 n187).

possible that gemination did not take place in the spoken language either. In any case, the scribes tended not to use it, such that we do not find many mistakes. For the following examples, I cannot provide a satisfactory explanation.

Verbs:

amāru	*et-ta-mar* (< *ētamar*) 'he has seen' TabT05a-134:10
	e-ta-⸢*a*⸣[*m*]*-mar* MARV 4 32:13 (sign AM uncertain)
batiqtu	*bat-ti-iq-tu* 'loss' Maul 2004 1:4 (cf. Freydank 2012b, 211)
emādu	*le-me-du-un-ni* (*lēmedūni*) 'may they impose' AO 19.227:23
maḫāru	*im-taḫ-ḫar* 'he has received' KAJ 242 r. 4
ušābu	*us-ba-ak-*[*k*]*u* 'I dwell' T 96-6:10

Nouns:

Allānātu	^{iti}*A-la-an-na-tú* (name of the month) TR 3003:13
ḫaziānu	^{lú}*ḫa-zi-an-ni* 'mayor' A 1736 (NTA, 18):13; ^{lú}*ḫa-zi-an-ni* Giricano 4:19 cf. ^{lú}*ḫa-zi-a-ni* KAJ 133:11

§ 121 One of the more common types of "erroneous" gemination is the so-called morphographemic spellings. In the forms, the base of a noun or verb was written as a separate unit with a phonetic complement (cf. AmAkk: Izre'el 1991a, 62). "Graphemic consonantal gemination" occurs frequently in NA, but it is rarer in MA, probably because gemination is still limited.[46] Only a few examples can be given:

Morphographemic verbs:

baqānu N	*i-ba-qa-an-na* 'they are plucked' LVUH 48:26
tadānu	*i-DIN-na (iddana*) 'he will give' KAJ 114:17
	it-ta-an-⸢*nu*⸣ 'they gave to each other' MATSH 13:16
	i-din-nu 'they gave' KAJ 163:25
	id-din-nu-ni 'they gave' KAJ 157:6

Morphographemic nouns:

edānu	*e-da-an-nu* 'period' KAJ 25:8; KAJ 58:11
šalāmu D	*lu-šal-lim-mu* 'may they keep whole' MARV 7 14:10
šapārtu	*ša-pár-r*[*a*]*-te* (pl.) 'pledges' T 97-37:16
taklīmu	*ták-lim-mu* (type of offering) A 602:8 cf. *ták-li-mu* l. 7
ṭēmu	*ṭé-em-ma* 'instruction' T 96-14:18

2.4.9 Defective writings, aphesis and breaking of words

§ 122 MA is not free from scribal mistakes. This is clear from instances where the order of signs is confused, e.g., *UM*-ŠE KAJ 85:6 instead of the normal ŠE-*um* 'barley'. Other mistakes have less obvious reasons, e.g., *i-al-qé-ú-ni* A 333:11 and probably for *ilqeūni* 'they took'. More frequently, a sign is omitted, in which case it is not always totally clear whether this was an actual scribal mistake or vowel syncope had taken place (cf. defective spellings in Luukko 2004, 36–37 § 3.8).[47]

ḫadā'u	*ḫa-di-*<*a*>*-*⸢*tu*⸣*-ú-ni* 'she wishes' MAL A § 33:70
maḫāṣu	*i-maḫ-Ø-ṣu-ú-ši* 'they will hit her' MAL A § 40:75 ~ *i-maḫ-ḫu-ṣu* MAL A § 40:81

46 For NA, see Deller (1959, 188–192 § 39a–d); Luukko (2004, 31–35 § 3.7).

47 Defective writings of the subjunctive *-ūni* are a different category, as discussed in § 662.

The distinction is especially unclear in the following two verbal forms of the same stem, from the same archive (BAI) and probably the same scribe:

tadānu *a-ta-na-ad-nu-*[*ni*] 'I keep giving' KAV 96:12 (Adn)
ta-ta-na-ad-nu-[*ni*$^{?}$] 'you keep giving' KAV 194:16 (Adn)

Both forms are presents in the Gtn-stem, which would have the expected forms with Assyrian vowel assimilation *attanaddunūni* and *tattanaddunūni*. If we assume a secondary *Murmelvokal* [ə], syncope of this weak sound is expected to take place. If these are not scribal mistakes, this could point to a gradual loss of /a/ > /ə/ > zero in this position.

§ 123 Aphesis may be attested in the following forms (cf. NA: Luukko 2004, 121–122 § 4.12). Given the scarcity of attestations, these could be scribal mistakes.

Arrapḫa ^{kur}*Rap-ḫa-ie-e* KAJ 212:3 (NtA)
Aḫu-maššil ^{m}*Ḫu-maš-ši-il* Giricano 10:26 (Abk)
ēṣidu ^{lú}*ṣi-du* 'reapers' MARV 1 47:37, 42 (TN)
Waššukannu *Šu-ka-nu* MARV 5 1:16 (Nae$^{?}$); MARV 5 64:9 (Nae$^{?}$)

§ 124 Examples of words continued on the next line are rare. Similarly, Luukko (2004, 26 § 3.3) found only seven examples in NA. However, this is unexpected, as OA has a long tradition of breaking words and writing them directly below, resulting in a subline (GOA § 2.1.2). In MA, we find a limited number of attestations, all of which are in the dating of the tablet (usually the name of the eponym). The only attestation not occurring in the date formula is found in TR 3003.

līmu *li-/mu* 'eponym' AO 20.153:19–20
PN ^{md}EN.LÍL-SUM-/IBILA KAJ 319 15–16
^{m}*Ṣíl-lí-/*^{d}É$^{!}$.ŠAR.RA TR 3003:5–6
^{md}*Iš*$_{8}$*-tár-/tu-bal-l*[*i-su*] T 98-15:6–7
^{md}*Iš*$_{8}$*-tár-tu-bal-/l*[*i*]*-su* T 98-106:7–8
^{md}*Sál-ma-nu-/*A-PAP T 96-1:22–23

An unusual case of breaking a word can be found in MARV 1 30. In this text, the first two lines specify the two columns containing the content of the tablet. The two words that specify the columns are both broken in two lines so as to fit on the small horizontal space available:

$^{\text{na4}}$/UR$_{5}$ | $^{\text{na4}}$*nàr-/ku-bu* 'grind-stone | upper grind-stone' MARV 1 30:1–2

The separation of a small section of a tablet into two columns is attested in a few other texts. For instance, in the testament MARV 8 47, there are two columns for the group of witnesses (ll. 42–45).

2.4.10 Sandhis

§ 125 While the issue of the existence or absence of a word-initial aleph is not entirely clear, it seems that this aleph was, at least, omitted in some instances in the Assyrian dialect.[48] In effect, this often resulted in a merger of a word-final vowel with the succeeding word-initial vowel. This can be especially observed on several occasions in OA, with

48 Cf. Kouwenberg (2006, 156–59), especially his summary of previous literature in n21. Cf. also the present discussion of the weak consonants in § 164ff

sandhi writings of the prepositions *ana/ina*, where /a/ in the second unstressed short syllable is elided and /n/ is assimilated (GKT, 177f § 103b; GOA § 3.2.4.1). Different types of sandhis are also found in NA.[49] Sandhis can be regarded as a natural feature of Akkadian. By default, the *anlaut* vowel seems to win over the *auslaut* vowel, e.g., Libbi-ālim: *Lib/bi/-ā/le* > *lib/bā/le/* (Worthington 2012, 175). As can be seen in this example, the syllabic structure of the word changes through the loss of one vowel. This feature of two resyllabificated nouns is called sandhi. The loss of one vowel can also be called crasis (Worthington 2012, 174–75). Judging from the examples below, crasis takes place through the elision of the *auslaut*, rather than contraction, as we never see lengthening or a change in vowel colour of the *anlaut*. For MA, note the following examples (cf. UGM, 26 § 23):

Admati-ilī	*Ad-mat*-DINGIR VAT 8722:10
emittu	*a-na e-mi-it-ta-a-na paššure* (< *ana emitte ana*) 'to the right side, to the table' Ištar Ritual:2
ḫiriṣ aḫe (?)	*ḫi-ri-ṣa-*⌜*ḫi*⌝ (*ḫi/riṣ/+a/ḫi* > *ḫi/ri/ṣa/ḫi*) 'ditch of the shore' MATC 3:6 see commentary
izuzzu	*la-za-az* 'I will not stand' (*lā azzaz*) MCS 2 1:23
kāl ūme	*ka*$^{!}$-⌜*lu*⌝-*mi* 'the whole day' MATSH 22:6
kamāṣu	*ik-ta-mi-ṣi i-ḫa-al* 'she crouched down, went into labour' Rm 376:26 (probably sandhi; see Röllig 1985, 266)
laʾû	*la-la-ʾe* (< *lā alaʾʾe*) 'I am unable' MATSH 12:28
Libbi-āle	*li-ba-a-la* 'the inner city (Aššur)' KAJ 6:11
nuggāt ippê	*nu-ga-ti-pi* 'rage of the 19th day' A 3187 (NTA, 36):5 (see W. Mayer 2016, 118); cf. *i-pi* A 1724 (NTA, 17):4.
šiknāte utturat	*ši-ik-na-te-mu-tu-rat* 'exalting of shape' Rm 376:20 (see Röllig 1985, 264)
šīt tattaṣbat	*ši-i-*⌜*ta-at*⌝*-ta-aṣ-bat* 'she has been seized' MAL A § 24:51–52[50]
ina tēbe ṣē	*i+na ti-be-ṣe-e* 'at the departure' MATC 40:14 see commentary

Sandhis that derive from prepositions will be discussed in § 423ff. A few select examples are given below:

mīnu	*a-na-i-ni* 'why?' passim (*ana+mīnu*, see § 406f)
panīu	*a-pa*-LUGAL (*appāššare* < *ana pan šarre*) 'in the presence of the king' KAJ 151:22
qātu	*aq-qa-at* (< *ana qāt*) 'at a distance' MAPD § 2:18
qību	*i-qí-bi* DINGIR^{meš} 'by the command of the gods' Franke/Wilhelm 1985:8
šērtu	*iš-še-er-te* (*ina+šērtu*) 'tomorrow' MATC 2:16

Some notes about the examples above now follow. In the case of the Ištar Ritual, progressive vowel assimilation could be at work (cf. NA Luukko 2004, 90–93 § 4.5). The PN in KAV 217 may contain a short Assyrian stative of the form *parsāk*, which has been attested in the other Assyrian dialects (see § 516).

§ 126 External sandhis occur frequently with elements of PNs:

^{md}[*A*]-*šur-ki-ti-di* LVUH 4:12; ^{d}*e-kur-ki-ti-di* KAJ 94:17 cf. ^{md}*A-šur-ki-ti-i-di* AO 21.380:25

A-be-⌜*li*⌝ (< *abī-ilī*) TR 2903:3

^{m}*Mil-*⌜*ka*⌝*-a-bi* (Milki-abi) MARV 2 ii 28 cf. ^{m}DÙG.GA-*mil-ki-a-bi* KAJ 224:14

^{d}*A-šur-ke*$^{!}$*-nu-ú-ṣur* (Adad-kēna-uṣur) KAJ 37:17 cf. ^{md}IŠKUR-*ke-na-ú-ṣur* MARV 3 80:6'

49 Cf. SNAG 37f; Luukko (2004, 188ff § 4.11).

50 This example is more difficult because the verb continues on another line. The pronominal *šī* would not be the first example of a Babylonianism in MAL A.

^{md}IŠKUR-SAG-*ši-i-ši* (*Adad-rēša-iši*) Franke/Wilhelm 1985:11
^{m}*Ták-lak-a-na-*^{d}⸢*A-šur*⸣ (< *Taklāku-ana-Aššur*) KAV 217:21'
^{m}*I-gar-še-mi-id* 'Igāršu-emid' MARV 1 41:4

The particle *mā* forms a special category. It is always spelled *ma-a*, unless it is followed by *anlaut a-*. Usually, this is the preposition *ana*. In this case, we should find a double sequence of the sign A, which is omitted, creating a sandhi spelling: **ma-a a-na* > *ma-a-na*. However, spellings with some pronouns, such as *attunu*, are also found; in this case, <A> is omitted altogether: *ma-at-tu-nu*.

ana	*ma-a-na* (*mā ana*) MATSH 3:14, 4:10'; T 04-13:12 (et passim)
anaʾīne	*ma*$^{!}$*-a-na-i-ni* (< *mā+ana+mīnu*) 'thus, why …?' MATSH 2:54; 12:41 cf. *ma-a-a-na-i-ni* VAT 8851:7
	ma-a-na-i-ni (< *mā ana mīnim*) MATSH 12:41
	ma-a-na-i-ni T 02-32:9
attune	*ma-at-tu-nu* 'thus, 'you'' (< *mā attune*) MATSH 7:12'
ayyēša	*ma-a-ie-e-ša-mi* (*mā ayyēša-mi*) MATSH 3:12

Chapter 3: Phonology Part 1: Vowels

§ 127 MA uses the set of PS vowels /a/, /i/, /u/ and lengthened /ā/, /ī/, /ū/. In early Akkadian, /e/ and /ē/ were added; the possibility of /o/ and /ō/ will be discussed below. The set of vowels comprises opposition short and lengthened forms: with and without a macron. It is common in Assyriological studies to use another set of vowels with a circumflex: /â/, /î/, /û/, /ê/. In contrast to the opposition short and long vowels, the circumflex simply denotes contraction, in which a guttural is elided. The pronunciation of these vowels seems to be no different than the lengthened ones.

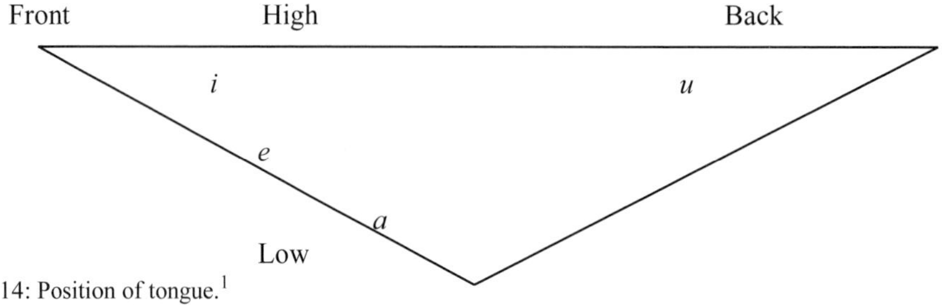

Figure 14: Position of tongue.[1]

§ 128 The opposition between long and short vowels and consonants is phonemic in Babylonian, as there are numerous minimal pairs in Akkadian that show the difference, e.g., *šarratum* 'queen' ~ *šarrātum* 'queens'; *idin* 'give' ~ *iddin* 'he gave' (cf. Buccellati 1996 § 1.4). For MA, this difference is less clear, as Assyrian vowel assimilation changes the colour of short vowels, so that there are more differences than only length. A phonemic difference in masculine plural forms (e.g., *ēṣidu* ~ *ēṣidū* 'reaper(s)') cannot be confirmed because the shortening of long final vowels is suspected (cf. § 97). Likewise, an imperative such as *idin* does not exist in MA. As for consonant length, we may expect that the D-stem of I/t-verbs in the perfect and preterite are differentiated by the doubling of /t/ e.g., *utta*$^{??}$*er* ~ *uta*$^{??}$*er*. In general, we may state that, in MA, the lengthening of vowels and consonants is probably phonemic, similar to Babylonian, although it is difficult to find clear examples.

3.1 Vowel /a/

§ 129 The vowel /a/ is a primary vowel in MA and only rarely (if ever) is it derived from another vowel. Orthographically, it has only one vowel sign (A), without variation. For the sequence A+A, see § 169.

§ 130 There is also a small number of nouns that always have /a/ in the first syllable, whereas Babylonian has /i/. It is not clear to me which vowel was original. The most frequent example is *pāḫutu* (Bab. *pīḫātu*) 'province'. To this common noun, we can add

1 Based on Izre'el/Cohen (2004, 10); Lipiński (2001, 106ff).

two less frequent substantives: *sāpīu* 'felt worker' (cf. Jakob 2003, 431), which is only once attested as *sepû*, similar to Babylonian spellings (cf. CAD S, 227; AHw, 1037). The other substantive is *kanūnu* 'kiln', where Babylonian has *kinūnu* (CAD K, 393-5; AHw, 481–82).

kanūnu	[1] *ka-nu-nu ša libnāte* (Bab. *kinūnu*) 'one brazier of bricks' New Year Ritual:13' also 18'
sāpīu	^{lú}*sa-pi-u* (Bab. *sepû*) 'felt worker' MARV 3 53:11; cf. *se-pi-*[*e*] MARV 2 15 r. 4'
pahutu	*pa-ḫa-te-ia* (Bab. *pīḫātu*) 'my provinces' MATSH 26:12'
šumālu	*šu-ma-la* 'the left' LVUH 69:30 (< *šu-mi-la* LVUH 86:4)

§ 131 In NA, /u/ often becomes /a/ in the first syllable of a noun. It is possible to regard this /a/ as a *Murmelvokal* [ə].[2] On the possibility of this *Murmelvokal* in verbal forms, when Assyrian vowel assimilation is expected, see § 151. One NA example is the adjective *šaklulu* 'perfect', which sometimes becomes *šaklalūtu* in the plural (CAD Š$_{3}$, 220f), e.g., SAA 10 353:23); MA *urutḫu* 'a pair of implements' (*ú-ru-ut-ḫu* KAJ 303:8; MAH 16130:7') becomes *arutḫu* in NA (e.g., *a-ru-ut-ḫe* CTN 2 155 iv:17); MA *šu-ku-ut-ta-ša* 'jewellery' MAL A § 40:72 is found in NA as *ša-kut-tum* SAA 13, 134 r. 3. For MA, there are only two examples so far (for *apparā* see Bloch 2012, 228 n92):

apāru D	*ap-pa-*⸢*ra*⸣ (< *appurā*) 'covered' MARV 4 34:17'
gušūru	^{giš}*ga-šu-ri* 'beams' T 97-17:18; cf. ^{giš}*g*[*u-š*]*u-ru*^{meš} T 96-9:5

3.2 Vowels /i/ and /e/

§ 132 The vowel /e/ is not part of the stock of Proto-Semitic phonemes, but an innovation in Akkadian and most other Semitic languages, such as Hebrew and Ge'ez. Arabic does not accept /e/ as a phoneme, while it is regularly found as an allophone for short /a/ (Lipiński 2001, 113 § 10.11). Assyrian regards /e/ as a phoneme according to the cuneiform script, but it is difficult to see the difference between /e/ and /i/. A phonemic differentiation can be derived from only a few different minimal pairs. We do find *de-en* 'case' (KAV 159:7 and PNs) always spelled with <en>, rather than the imperative *di-in* 'give!' with <in> (e.g., KAJ 316:14). However, it is likely that *dēnu* 'case' has a long vowel. Another minimal pair is found in the pronominal suffixes: *-še* (dative 3fs) vs. *-ši* (accusative 3fs). Admittedly, the evidence is thin and the difference could merely be allophonic (cf. NA in Luukko 2004, 40 § 3.10). Note also spellings such as ^{md}*A-šur-ki-te-i-di* (*Aššur-kitte-idē*) KAJ 113:28, where the sequence /e+i/ is maintained. In Akkadian, there are two phonetic oppositions, /a-e/ ~ /i-e/, where /e/ is etymologically derived from /a/ and /i/, respectively (Edzard 1959, 305). Unlike Arabic or Hebrew and, in particular, Babylonian, the vowel /e/ in Assyrian only derives from /a/ on rare occasions, but does so under the influence of e-colouring through ʾ$_{3}$ and ʾ$_{4}$ (see § 165). In fact, in most instances, /e/ developed out of the original /i/, often making it impossible to distinguish between the two phonemes. The spread of the vowels /e/ and /i/ is a problem in the Assyrian dialect, particularly due to the weak differentiation in the cuneiform script. This differentiation in script was almost completely absent during the OA period (cf. GKT, 24 § 14a). However, a better system for differentiation between the two vowels developed for some signs from the MA period onwards (cf. HattAkk in Durham

2 See Postgate (1974, 274); Postgate (1995, 7); Deller/Finkel (1984, 82.1); Luukko (2004, 93f); Kouwenberg (2010, 49). Hämeen-Anttila referred to this feature as the dissimilation of vowels (SNAG, 31–32 § 2.4.6).

1976, 352; NA Luukko 2004, 40–42 § 3.10). An overview of the distribution between the signs now follows.[3]

bi ≠ *bé*	*il* ≠ *él*	*ki* ~ *ke*	*ši* ≠ *še*$_{20}$
be ≠ *bi*	*el* ≠ *il*$_{5}$	*li* ~ *le*	*še* ≠ *ši*$_{x}$
di ~ *de*	*im* ~ *em*	*mi* ≠ *mé*	*te* ≠ *ti*$_{7}$
ḫi ~ *ḫe*	*in* ≠ *en*$_{6}$	*me* ≠ *mì*	*ti* ≠ *te*$_{9}$
gi ~ *ge*	*en* ≠ *in*$_{4}$	*pi* ~ *pe*	*ṭi* ~ *ṭe*
ib/p ~ *eb/p*	*ir* ~ *er*	*qi* ~ *qe*	*ṭí* ~ *ṭé*
id/t/ṭ ~ *ed/t/ṭ*	*iš* ≠ *eš*$_{15}$	*ri* ~ *re*	*ze* ~ *zi*
ig/k/q ~ *eg/k/q*	*eš* ≠ *ìš*	*si* ~ *se*	
iḫ ~ *eḫ*	*is/ṣ/z* ~ *es/ṣ/z*	*ṣi* ~ *ṣe*	

§ 133 Variation between /i/ and /e/ is common, with the vowel signs E and I even appearing when they are not expected. These unexpected spellings mostly occur in the word-medial and word-final positions, but not in the word-initial position; for the few verbal exceptions, see § 507 and § 555. It has been assumed that these spellings suggest actual pronunciation (LAS 2, 48 r5; Luukko 2004, 87 § 4.3.3). It is more probable to assume that the difference between the two vowels was so thin that scribes often confused them. This explanation is more straightforward than to assume unmotivated /e/ > /i/ and /i/ > /e/ changes based on exceptional spellings. Below is a list of forms with the alternating spelling of /i/ and /e/ in (almost) identical forms.

I ~ E:

PI-i KAV 100:8	*PI-e* MAL A § 2:17
ki-i MATSH 7:15''	*KI-e* MATSH 7:12''
^{lú}*i-ṣi-du* MARV 1 47:1	^{lú}*e-ṣi-du* KAJ 11:3 passim.

BI ~ BE (BAD):

ta-bi-ik MATC 80:3	*ta-be-IK* Coronation Ritual i 33
bi-IR BVW Ab:12:8	*be-IR* BVW D:2; G r. 9; MAPD § 2:17
lìb-bi MATSH 1:6	*lìb-be-ku-nu* MATSH 9:31
e-ra-bi LVUH 69:3	*e-ra-be* LVUH 83:4
tu-bi-áš PKT 1 II right:4	[*t*]*u-be-a-áš* PKT 1 I right:17
gab-bi MAPD § 21:111	*gab-b*[*e*] MATSH 30:2'
il-bi MAL B § 20:20	*il-be-ú-ni* KAV 119:11
bi-ri-šu-nu KAJ 39:15	*be-ri-šu-nu* KAJ 1:25
na-aṣ-bi-[*t*]*e* KAJ 130:17	*na-aṣ-be-te* KAJ 226:4

IL ~ EL:

il-mi-il-t[*a*] MATSH 4:34	*el-me-el-te* MATSH 2:17

MI ~ ME:

ga-mi-IR KAJ 160:14	*ga-me-IR* KAJ 174:10
mi-tu LVUH 43:4'	*me-tu* LVUH 37:20
e-em-mi-id MAL A § 16:62	*e-em-me-ed* MAL A § 3:39
am-MI-ša MATC 2:17; 4:21	*am-me-e-ša-ma* MATC 9:24
e-mi-ta LVUH 83:4	*e-me-ta* LVUH 93:10
[*u*]*t-ta-mi-iš* MATSH 14:18	*ú-ta-me-ša-ma* MATSH 3:39

3 The symbol ≠ is used to indicate differentiation between two signs for /i/ and /e/, while ~ is used to indicate the lack thereof.

kar-mi LVUH 81:19	*kar-me* LVUH 60:24
mi-il-te LVUH 37:19	*ME-il-te* LVUH 43:3'; 48:10, 23
šu-mi-la LVUH 78:21	*šu-me-la-ni* LVUH 91:7
mi-it-ḫar-šu MAL K § 3:9	*me-et-ḫar-šu* KAJ 101:15
li-mi KAM 10 30:2; KAM 11 25:14; MARV 1 49:1	*li-me* KAJ 80:4 et passim
mi-it-ḫar-šu MAL K § 3:9	*me-et-ḫar-šu* KAJ 91:22
mi$^{!}$*-iš-la* KAJ 67:8	*ME-iš-lu* KAJ 310:28
tal-mi-du MPR 2:19	*tal-me-du* MPR 60:15
tal-mi-tu MARV 1 57 iv 17' et passim	*tal-me-tu* MARV 1 57 iv 26'

IN ~ EN:
No variation is attested.

ŠI (IGI) ~ ŠE:

mu-ši-šu MATC 12:14	*mu-še* MATSH 22:6

IŠ ~ EŠ:
Here, the difference is based on the sibilant, rather than the vowel (see § 221).

TI ~ TE:

bir-ti MATSH 12:29	^{uru}*bi-ir-te* (GN) MATSH 14:6
pi-ti MATSH 8:58'; MATC 3:11	*pi-te-[ka]* MATSH 16:27
a-sa-i-ti LVUH 86 vs. 12	*a-sa-i-te* LVUH 83:13; 86 vs. 10
pa-ḫi-ti 'province' A 3185 (NTA, 35):2	*pa-ḫe-te* MARV 1 39:1
nap-ti-ni A 3198 (NTA, 40):8 (rare)	*nap-te-ni* A 1742 (NTA, 21):3
it-ti-ši KAJ 293a:5	*it*$^{!}$*-te-ši* KAJ 293a:8
i-ti-din KAJ 172:12 (passim)	*i-te-⸢din⸣* YBC 12860:12
ti-ru-ub-ti (*tērubtu*) KAJ 79:16	*te-ru-bat* MATC 80:1
ša-pár-ti KAJ 60:12	*ša-pár-te* KAJ 30:12
ba-e-ru-ti Ali 7:5	*ba-e-ru-te* Ali 7:9

Sometimes, broken spellings occur where both phonemes are expressed in the orthography:

emu	*e-MI-e-ša* 'her father-in-law' MAL A § 29:17
Mennazu	^{f}*MI-EN-na-za* MARV 1 40:2
šamāʾu	*ši-me* (*šeme*) 'hear!' A 850:18
zabālu	*iz-zi-BI-EL* 'he has delivered' MAL A § 30:21

However, one way of writing prevailed, such that the number of exceptions remains rather small (see Luukko 2004, 41 § 3.10.). Based on the frequent interchangeability of /e/ and /i/, Hecker and W. Mayer (GKT, 24 § 14a; UGM, 15 § 9) argued for a closed pronunciation. Hecker suggested Anatolian influence because of a similar situation in Hittite (cf. Friedrich 1960, 25 § 10), where the orthography was also confusing and suggested an Anatolian influence on the Assyrian language, with /e/ pronounced closed and similar to /i/. One should not overestimate the influence of the Anatolians on Assyrian during the OA period; despite the absence of statistics, it is not likely that a major portion of the population lived (at least temporarily) in Anatolia. Even if they did, a large number stayed abroad and never returned, meaning that they could hardly have influenced the language at home. In any case, it is unlikely that this limited linguistic contact between both populations was able to change something as fundamental as phonology; indeed, this change would certainly not survive long enough to be visible in MA.

§ 134 Given the demonstrated scribal variation, it is often difficult to establish when /e/ or /i/ should be read. The instances where we can be certain of either vowel are quite limited, e.g., the prefix conjugation of verbs /e/ for I/a and I/e verbs (§ 555) and /i/ for all other (regular) verbs (§ 507). Again, exceptions are found: *i-ta-mar* KAJ 89:15; *i-pu-šu* TIM 4, 45:15; *i-ri-šu-šu-ni* KAJ 48:11; *i-te-te-eq-šu-ma* KAJ 101:19. A regular exception is the verb *alāku*, which always takes /i/ signs. This can be explained by the doubling of /l/, which compensates for the loss of the original guttural /h/. In this light, we should explain why the N-stem of I/weak verbs takes /i/ signs: *IN-NI-pa-áš* MATSH 8:44. We also often find /e/ in stative 3ms, so that a change in this position should be expected: *ga-me-IR* (KAJ 174:10) ~ *ga-mi-IR* (KAJ 160:14); *ta-be-IK* Coronation Ritual i 33 ~ *ta-bi-IK* MARV 6 14:10 (see § 516). In verbal forms of the type I/w in the Š-stem a strong distinction is made between /e/ and /i/ by always using the sign ŠE for */šē/*: *ú-še-ši-ib-ši* (*ušēšib+ši*) § 36:84; *ú-še-bi-il-áš-še* (*ušēbil+am+šī*) MAL A § 36:90. Type II/weak Assyrian verbs have, in the stative, a long vowel /ē/, independent of their original consonant: *me-tu* LVUH 37:20. In the case of lost mimation, the preceding /i/ changes to /e/ (see § 240). In line with many I/weak roots, we find nominal forms where R_1 is written as /e/, rather than /i/, as in Babylonian, e.g., *e-šar-te* (Bab. *išartu*) 'justice' Coronation Ritual ii 34; *e-mi-it-ta* (Bab. *imittu*) 'right side' Ištar Ritual:2.

§ 135 Rather than the aforementioned instances, where /i/ becomes /e/ on (partly) morphological grounds, there are also a few instances where this sound change is directly caused by a succeeding consonant. The vowel /i/ before /r/ seems more susceptible to a change to /e/, which is a feature that MA shares with other dialects of Akkadian (cf. GAG, 44 § 35b). An exception to this rule is *si-i-ra* 'plaster' MATC 12:17. Attestations come from all different genres:

āmirānu	*a-me-ra-a-ni* 'eyewitness' MAL A § 47:9
buāru D	*ú-ba-e-er* 'he proved it' MAL A § 18:77
ešāru Š	*lu-še-še-ru* 'they must put it in order' MATC 12:16
labēru	*la-be-ru-tu* 'old' LVUH 83:2
magāru	*im-me-ge-er-ma* 'she(!) agreed' KAJ 3:2
pišertu	*pi-še-er-ti* 'clearance' LVUH 93:3
mišertu	*mi-še-er-t[a]* 'a net(?)' MATSH 2:11
mummirtu	*mu-um-me-er-ta* 'procuress' MAL A § 23:35
šabiru	*ša-be-ru* (Bab. *šawiru*) 'ring' MATC 63:5
ušāru	*la-a tu-še-er* 'you did not give up' KAV 201:18
uššir	*uš-še-er* 'excluding' KAJ 120:1

This preference can also be observed with /i/ > /e/ before /ḫ/ (GAG, 31 § 25b), e.g., *me-ḫi-ir-ti-ša* MAPD § 21:104. It is also known that /a/ becomes /e/ in this environment, although von Soden labels this sound change as Babylonian (GAG, 13–14 § 9b). Before /ḫ/, this is attested in *ma-ni-ḫa-te* MAL B § 13:24; MAL M § 1:4, 12 cf. *ma-na-ḫa-te* MAL B § 1:9; *ma-na-ḫa-ti* KAM 10 25:12 (√*anāḫu*, see AHw, 601). Before /r/, this is attested in *na-áš-per-ta* 'message' MATC 11:19; ^{túg}*lu-be-ru* (OB *lubārum*) Postgate 1973 no. 1:22; KAJ 256:1. The noun *lubēru* is notable because it derives from long /ā/. Most attestations are found in the status absolutus of *gamru* in the expression *ana šīm ga-me-er* 'the full price' MAL A § 44:43; KAJ 147:10; KAJ 149:7 (et passim); there is one instance of [*ana šīm*] *ga-*

mi-ir KAJ 160:14. As this expression and spelling (*ga-me-er*) are attested in OB and OA, it may possibly be a direct loan (CAD G, 37a). In addition to the environment of /ḫ/ and /r/, there are a few other forms where /e/ derives from /a/, but it is not entirely clear why:

etû	GAL *e-te* 'the chief gatekeeper' (Bab. *atû*) KAJ 102:7; *e-te-e* MARV 2 17a+:7
edānu	*e-da-nu* 'fixed date' (Bab. *adānu*) MAL B § 6:21
šelippāyu	^{lú}*še-lip-pa-iu-ú* 'engineer' KAJ 188:22; ^{lu}*ši-*⸢*lip*⸣*-pa-ie* KAJ 300:6 (< *Šalim-pî-Ea*) (see § 259)

The sole example of /u/ changing into /i/ is obscure: *si-ma-ti* (< *summatu*) 'dove' KAJ 177:4; it also occurs (but not exclusively MA) in *ku-ri-le* 'for the harvest' (< *kurullu*) KAV 99:39; MARV 1 58:9; MARV 10 50:5 (cf. CAD K, 572–73).

3.3 Vowels /u/ and */o/

§ 136 MA uses four distinct signs to express /u/: U; Ú; Ù and UD for <u$_4$>. The sign Ú is most commonly used to express the vocalic value of /u/. For the conjunction '*u*' (see § 689ff), Ù is used, but U$_1$ also occurs in some texts, including the Coronation Ritual, which does not use Ù, e.g., *Aš-šur u* ^{giš}TUKUL^{meš} Coronation Ritual ii 15. We also find it in some M 9 texts, again as a conjunction: KAM 10 9;16, 17; KAM 10 18:16 (Both EA/Aub); KAJ 169:13. The sign UD is only used for *ūmu* 'day' and can therefore be regarded as semi-logographic (see § 68). Interchangeability between /a/ and /u/ is attested, but on a much lower scale than for /i/ and /e/.

§ 137 There are a few attestations of the sound change /a/ > /u/. These were already gathered by W. Mayer (UGM, 13, 16 § 8.1, § 10.1).[4]

arāru	*ta-ta-ru-ur*/*ra-ar* 'she has cursed' MAPD § 17:79 vs. *ta-ta-ra-ar* MAPD § 17:81
napāšu D	*nu-pu-ša* 'airing' KAV 99:14; KAV 109:12
pāḫutu	*pu-ḫa-at* 'responsibility' KAJ 100:20
ša kenāte	^{iti}*šá ke-nu-te* (*ša kenāte*) (name of the month) TR 2910:21
šaṭāru	*šu-ṭar* (*šaṭar*) 'write!' KAV 104:16, 22

Mayer (UGM, 13) connects the change /a/ > /u/ with the Arabic *tafḫīm* (تفخيم), but this makes little sense since *tafḫīm* concerns a velarized pronunciation of consonants (cf. Fischer 2006, 18 § 29.2). The exact causes of these changes are therefore not entirely clear. A few suggestions can be made. In the case of *nuppuša*, one could reasonably assume a Babylonian D-stem infinitive. Three examples (*puḫat, tattarur, šuṭar*) have the affected vowel preceding /r/ or /ḫ/, which also causes changes with /i/ and /a/ changing into /e/ (see § 135). One may also note that *tattarur* only occurs in one version of MAPD, while another version has *tattarar* attested twice; here, one may suspect a confusion with the preterite, which involves /u/. Moreover, Mayer adds that the emphatic consonant /ṭ/ in *šuṭar* may also have influenced the change (UGM, 16). This leaves us with *ša kēnūte*, for which I cannot think of a solution. In any case, the above discussion does not attempt to reject the interchangeability of /a/ <> /u/, but merely attempts to point out that, for most forms, an

---

4 Some of Mayer's findings are not correct (and thus are not included here), see Freydank 1975, 143. Note also the change of /a/ > /u/ in the GN *Katmuḫi* > *Kutmuḫi* (see RGTC 5, 165).

alternative explanation is possible. A related phenomenon is possibly the change /i/ > /u/ (see below).

§ 138 Attestations of /i/ > /u/ are somewhat more common than vice versa: [iti]*Ḫu-bur* (*Ḫubur*) KAM 10 15:39 (common variant); [é]*Ḫu-bur-ni* (*Hiburnu*) KAJ 65:3; *ku-ri-il-ti-e* 'fodder' KAJ 255:6 (usually as *ku-ru-ul-te-e* KAJ 127:11); see also MA royal inscriptions from Māri: *muq-ta* 'collapse' (*miqtu*) Maul 1992, 38:9 and perhaps *m*[*uq-ta*] Maul 1992, 25:12B, but *mi-iq-ta* Maul 1992, 25:12A/M. W. Mayer's suggestion (UGM, 16), that we are dealing with a *Murmelvokal*, is probably not correct. Attestations for interchangeability are few and far between; thus, such a conclusion is not warranted. Moreover, we argue that <A> is more likely to be used as an orthographic representation of *Murmelvokale* (§ 131). Maul (1992, 33) pointed to the variation of /u/ in final vowels as discussed by Deller (1959, 113–15 § 24). It is doubtful that these are comparable phenomena, as variation in the final vowel is also attested for MA in the paradigms of independent personal pronouns. Note that /i/ and /u/ are, to a certain extent, interchangeable in Akkadian (CGSL, 47f § 8.71).

§ 139 The existence of /o/ in Akkadian has been suggested by a number of scholars.[5] Aside from the aforementioned *a/u* variation, there are two other arguments used to make the claim for the existence of /o/ in the Assyrian dialect:

- Between a labial/emphatic sound and /r/, e.g., *qurbu* (*qorbu* < **qerbu*), e.g., *qur-bu* A 983:10
- The perfect of the D-stem I/weak, e.g., *ūtuḫḫir* (*ūtoḫḫir* < **ūtaḫḫir*) ~ NA

Additionally, it has been suggested that the /a/ ~ /u/ alternation in the syllable preceding the subjunctive *-ūni* may have been pronounced [o] (von Soden 1948; GAG, 19 § 15d). However, as we will discuss below, a *Murmelvokal* in this position is more likely. The theory of [o] has been criticized on a number of occasions.[6] Most recently by Kouwenberg (2005/6) argued that *qurbu* comes from the true Assyrian adjectival pattern *purus*, while the perfect I/weak may be analogous to the D-stem stative, which has become *uḫḫuz* (instead of the earlier *aḫḫuz*), thus an extension of /u/ from one class to another. In the case of the I/n D-stem infinitive *nuppušu* i/o *nappušu,* von Soden suggested /o/ under the influence of the labial (GAG, 143 § 88b). We may point out that *nuppušu* is essentially a Babylonian D-stem infinitive, of which more attestations are known in MA (see § 521). With respect to the variation, Reiner's comment is still relevant: "*In this sense, the letter o is a notation for a diaphoneme (comparable to the notation used by some linguists for the pronunciation of English, as in sɔrij [for the word spelled sorry]), which means that some speakers pronounce sorij and others sarij*" [Reiner 1973, 48]. Thus, the alternation /a/ ~ /u/ could be a sign of variant speech in Assyrian between /a/ ~ /u/, but an independent phoneme /o/ is, thus far, not visible.

5 See Deller (1959, 54–78 § 19–21); GKT, 18–20 § 9; UGM, 12–13, 16; GAG, 14 § 9e; SNAG, 26 § 2.4.1; Luukko (2004, 84–85 § 4.3.1). See also Westenholz (1991) on the situation in Babylonian.

6 See Gelb (1955, 97–98); Reiner (1973, 47–48); Kouwenberg (2005/6, 322).

3.4 Diphthongs

§ 140 Akkadian originally recognized two common diphthongs: /au/ and /ai/. The first changed into /ū/ in Assyrian, which can be observed in common words, such as *u_4-mu* 'day' (*(y)awm* > *ūm*) and *mūtu* 'dead' (*maut* > *mūt*). The diphthong /ai/ changes to /ē/ in Assyrian as opposed to Babylonian /ī/.; cf. *ēnum* (eye/spring) in *e-nu-ma* 'well' MATSH 3:30 as opposed to *i-ni-ka* 'your eyes' TCL 17 68:10 (OB). Other diphthongs, such as /uw/iw/uy/, have changed to /u/, as can be seen, for instance, in *uwbil* > *ubil* 'he carried' (Lipiński 2001, 176 § 22.13). For MA, it can simply be stated that all diphthongs disappeared due to this sound change. In the cases in which the semivowel /w/ or /y/ remains, it is not necessary to assume a diphthonic pronunciation, cf. English 'awful' and 'raw' (but the Dutch diphthonic cognate 'rauw', pronounced *rau*). As such, we presumably find /ay/ not realized as a diphthong when /y/ is doubled or followed by a vowel (see Gelb 1955, 99 § 8f). Likewise, /aw/ forms do occur in MA, where /w/ is represented in the orthography with <B>, e.g., *a-bat* 'word' (OB *awātum*), but never **ú-bat*. As has been pointed out by Gelb (1955, 99 § 8f), the diphthong /au/ is not found in Akkadian, leading to the conclusion that the sound change /au/ > /ū/ was no longer functional in historic Akkadian.

§ 141 In this study, it is assumed that verbal roots of the type II/ū-ī (e.g., *tuāru; ḫiāru*) are, in fact, two-radical roots with a long vowel (e.g., GAG, 179 § 104a). However, in Semitic languages, this long vowel can turn into the semivowel /w-y/ in certain conjugated forms (Lipiński 2001, 447f § 44.5), which can also be observed in some OA spellings of II/ū verbs in the G-stem. In the D-stem forms such as *ú-ta-e-ra-ni* KAV 98:17 occur, which show no sign of a semivowel or make use of the sign IA. This prompts the question about which consonant takes the place of the long vowel (Kouwenberg 2010, 482f). According to Lipiński, a third long vowel root existed in CāC, which produced an aleph in some conjugated forms, e.g., *šaʾālu* 'to ask' (Lipiński 2001, 447 § 44.5). We do not need to concern ourselves with the question about whether this etymology of two-radical roots is correct. What is important here is the knowledge that this type of root is able to render a non-etymologic aleph in some conjugations; hence, it should be constructed in the D-stems: *uba*^{ʾʾ}*eranni* KAV 98:17.

§ 142 In line with the above, we analyse verbal forms such as *i-mu-at* (√*mūt*) with the glide > *imū*^{w}*at*. The same is true for II/ī roots, such as *i-ṭé-an=iṭē*^{y}*an*. This assumption becomes more difficult to assert when variation occurs and we find forms with and without a vocalic sequence. This is well attested in the GN *Šadikannu*; it is not unthinkable that foreign names contain sounds that were difficult to express in MA cuneiform.

Šadikannu ^{uru}*Šu-a-di-ka-nu* T 97-2:7 (TN); T 97-5:6 (TN); T 97-6 (TN); MARV 5 1:15 (Nae); 2:15 (Nae)
^{uru}*Šu-di-ka-nu* MARV 5 10:5 (Nae); cf. T 02-2:3
^{uru}*Ša-di-ka-an-*[*ni*] MARV 5 27:7 (Tp)
^{uru}⸢*Ša*⸣*-di-ka-ni* MARV 5 10:16 (Nae)
⸢*Ša*⸣*-a-di-*⸢*ka*⸣*-nu* MARV 5 64:8 (Nae); cf. T 96-23:3

In normal Akkadian nouns and verbs, these presumed diphthongs are very rare as discussed above. The two attestations provided below are probably scribal mistakes. In the case of *i-*

ma-du-ad$^{!}$, we may assume a mixed form, where the scribe began writing a plural form (*imaddudū*), but realized he needed the singular (*imaddad*).

epāšu D   *ù-pa-UZ-sí* (< *uppaš-ši*) 'he will treat her' KAJ 2:12 cf. *ú-pá-su* KAJ 6:16 (Aub)
madādu   *i-ma-du-ad*$^{!}$ (< *imaddad*) 'he will measure out' KAJ 27:21 (Aub)

3.5 Assyrian vowel assimilation

§ 143 Assyrian vowel assimilation (henceforth abbreviated as VA) or vowel harmony is an important characteristic of Assyrian. It is not to be confused with Babylonian VA, where /a/ assimilates into /e/.[7] VA has been attested in OA, MA and NA, with only minimal changes in the conditions.[8] The sound change can be briefly summarized thus: short /a/ in an open syllable assimilates into the vowel of the succeeding syllable. This mostly occurs in the penultimate position, excluding most suffixes. Some slight differences have been reported in previous studies: Hecker, Buccellati and Hämeen-Anttila claimed that the open syllable Ca was post-tonic (GKT, 19ff § 10a; Buccellati 1997, 25), while the latter also assumed that only /a/ assimilates into a short following vowel (SNAG, 30f § 2.4.5). Peust (2009), on the other hand, assumed a stressed realization of the affected syllable. Under the assumption that the subjunctive *-ūni* is stressed, the opposite can be stated: VA can be pre-tonic (but not necessarily) and is not stressed. The long vowel /ā/ is generally not affected, e.g., *pa-ṭa-ri-ša* (*paṭār+īša*) MAL A § 5:66; *ma-ḫi-ra-a-nu (maḫir+ānu)* § 6:72. A possible attestation is the feminine plural *qu-BE-te* (sg. *quppu*) 'boxes' MARV 3 4:10 (see the commentary on p. 21 n24). For specific nouns, it may be reasonably assumed that the long /ā/ was shortened, although this can rarely be proven.

§ 144 Pronunciation of the affected vowel is strong and often (but not always) stressed, as most examples are penultimate. Buccellati (1997, 25) suggested that VA could be graphic for [ə], whereas Babylonian used /a/ to write this allophone. One needs to assume that the VA concerns *Murmelvokale*. We have already seen that VA often occurs in stressed syllables. Moreover, Buccellati's claim suggests a greater degree of similarity in phonology between Assyrian and Babylonian, but a large dissimilarity in orthography. Concerning the extensive geographical spread of the two languages, as well as the considerable influence of southern culture on writing, the opposite is more likely. Moreover, VA is visible in all stages of Assyrian, despite replacing its entire scribal system in favour of an updated southern variant in the transition period from OA to MA/NA.

3.5.1 Assyrian vowel assimilation in nominal forms

§ 145 In MA, VA remains an active sound change and can be found in a large number of different environments. Below, we will discuss the most common environments and provide a selection of attestations. The most neutral environment of VA is in nouns and

7 See GAG,14ff § 10a–b, e.g., *ilaqqe* > *ileqqe* 'he will take'.

8 OA: Bar-am 1935, 10ff; GKT, 19ff § 10; GOA 3.81–5; MA: UGM, 11ff § 7; NA: Deller (1959, 145ff); SNAG, 30f § 2.4.5. In general: Landsberger (1924, 723); Goetze (1947, 240); Ungnad (1992, 15 § 5b); GAG, 15f § 10.5 e–g; Buccellati (1997, 25); Huehnergard (2005, 599); Peust (2009); Luukko/Van Buylaere (2017, 323). However, VA is absent from the dialectal variations of Old Akkadian. See Hasselbach 2005, 121f § 3.2.4.2.

adjectives in the penultimate syllable, caused by the case ending. In effect, we can find three different variations of the same noun according to case ending, e.g., nominative: *qaqquru*; genitive: *qaqqere*; accusative: *qaqqara*.

maškunu	*maš-ki-ni* 'pledge' TR 04-37:23
naglubu	*na-ag-li-b*[*e*] 'nail clipper' KAV 205:18
naptunu	*na-ap-te-né* 'meal' TR 2037:37
qaqquru	*qa-qi-ri* 'earth' New Year Ritual 194:19'; *qa-qu-ru* T 97-10:18
simunu	*si-mu-nu* 'time' Ištar Ritual:1 ~ *si-mi-ni* r. 9'

Similar to the masculine nouns, substantives with the feminine ending *-at* are affected. Thus, we find three possible forms, i.e., nominative: *pāḫutu*; genitive: *pāḫete*; accusative: *pāḫata*.

aḫḫuzutu	*a-ḫu-ze-te* 'marriage gift' MAL A § 30:28
ēṭirutu	[f]*E-ṭí-ru-tum (*PN) KAJ 2:7
pāḫutu	*pa-ḫu-tu* 'province' MARV 4 127:33
terḫutu	*te-er-ḫe-te* 'bride payment' MAL A § 38:23

This type of VA basically affects the ultimate syllable of the stem of a noun. It remains unaffected by additional suffixes, such as a pronominal or *-ma*, regardless of whether it concerns a noun or verb.

qaqquru	*qa-qí-ri-i-šu* 'his territory MAL B § 13:19; 14:26 (cf. *qa-qa-ra* B § 14:30)
šaṭāru	*i-ša-aṭ-ṭú-ru-ni-iš-šu* 'they will write for him' KAJ 177:17
šamāʾu	[*a*]*l-te-me-ma* 'I have heard' MATSH 4:4'
šillutu	*ši-il-le-te-ša* (< *šillate*+*ša*) 'her impudence' MAPD § 18:89
taḫāḫu D	*ú-ta-ḫu-ḫu-šu* 'they will douse him' MAPD § 5:37
uṣāʾu	*ta-at-ti-ṣi-ma* 'she went out' MAL A § 13:26

Rarely do we find the first syllable affected by VA:

ḫarīṣu	*ḫi-ri-ṣi* (< Bab. *ḫarīṣu*) 'channel' MATSH 8:33'

§ 146 We find VA frequently applied to the infixed construct vowel /a/ before the pronominal suffixes. Initially, this change was purely penultimate in OA: *tup-pá-šu-nu* 'their tablet' (no VA) CCT 2 42:5. However, from the MA period onwards, the syllable in front of longer pronominal suffixes was affected as well: *tup-pu-ku-nu* 'your tablet' KAV 98:40 (Deller 1959, 145ff). In light of OA pronominal suffixes beginning with a consonant cluster (*-knu; -šnu; -šna*, see GKT, 76 § 49a; GOA § 9.5.3), this change becomes understandable. This type of pronominal suffix would close the preceding syllable (e.g., *naš/par/tak/nu* 'your writing') and thus make them unsuitable for VA. When this type of suffix disappeared from MA, VA penetrated in order to construct /a/ before the bisyllabic pronominal suffixes by analogy with the one-syllable pronominal suffixes. However, in NA, VA before bisyllabic pronominal suffixes had again become the exception rather than the rule, perhaps due to change of stress (Deller 1959, 149). In MA, the absence of VA before pronominal suffixes on substantives is still rare:

ḫīṭu	*ḫi-ṭa-šu* 'his punishment' MAL A § 16:66 (perhaps *ḫiṭaʾšu*, see § 168)
idu	*i-da-šu* 'his arm' MATSH 8:36'
immēru	ANŠE-*ra-šu* 'his donkey' VAT 8851:26 (cf. ANŠE-*ra* l. 27)
mazzaltu	*ma-za-al-ta-šú-nu* 'their post' Coronation Ritual iii 11
ṣupru	*ṣu-up-ra-šu-nu* 'their hoof' KTN inventory iv 9'

In the attestation ANŠE-*ra-šu*, the sign RA could be semi-logographic, instead of syllabic, in which case we would have to transcribe ANŠE.RA-*šu*. In any case, VA would have taken place in this form in all three stages of Assyrian, since the pronominal suffix is short. Otherwise, we commonly find the construct vowel /a/ affected by VA. A selected list of examples is given below:

appu	*ap-pu-šu* (…) *i-na-ki-su* 'they will cut off his nose' MAPD § 5:36
esertu	*e-se-er-tu-šu ú-*⌜*pa*⌝*-ṣa-an* 'he will veil his concubine' MAL A § 41:1
kutallu	*ku-tal-lu-šu e-em-mar* 'he will investigate his case' MAL A § 47:22
lubultu	*lu-bu-ul-tu-šu i-laq-qé-ú* 'they will take his clothing' MAL A § 40:82-83
nubattu	*nu-bat-tu-šu* 'in the evening' PKT 1 I right:26 (adverbial use, see GAG § 146)
rēḫtu	*re-eḫ-tu-šu* 'its remainder' MARV 3 10:12'
šapārtu	*ša-pár-tu-šu* 'his pledge' KAJ 22:15
tuppu	*tup-pu-ku-nu* 'your tablet' KAV 98:40
	tup-pu-šu-nu 'their tablet' MARV 1 47:28
zittu	*zi-te-ki-na* (< *zittakina*) 'your (2fp) share' KAV 194:21

§ 147 Other exceptions of VA into nouns are rare.[9] However, attestations are relatively numerous in OA (cf. GOA § 3.4.9.5). We can therefore suggest that VA was better standardized in MA scribal traditions.[10] Only a few exceptions can be presented, of which most are of uncertain reading.

aššutu	*a-ša-tu* 'woman' T 93-54:17†
šiguru	*ši-ga-ri* 'lock' Aššur Ritual ii 2', 4'
ikkuru	^{lú}*i-ka-ru* 'ploughmen (pl.)' T 98-58:7
qaqquru	*qa-qa-ri* 'terrain' KAJ 175:20 ~ *qa-qí-ri* l. 2

There is not a lot to say about these examples, other than that they are exceptions. As there are so few attestations, it is difficult to categorize them. Sound changes can take centuries to fully cover all words and forms in a language, and even individual speakers may vary on some occasions (cf. Aitchison 2001 84ff). The substantive *qaqqar-* 'terrain' is particularly known to have been subjected to VA in other cases: *qa-qú-ru* KAJ 174:3; *qa-qí-ri* KAJ 175:2, 8. In general, it must be stated that these types of exceptions are to be expected, while plenty of possible reasons can be given. For example, a scribe writing a substantive could easily have lost his perspective on the syntax, causing the lexical base and, at the last moment, the case ending to be written. It could even be possible that an ethnic Babylonian scribe or Babylonian educated scribe would have sometimes allowed a southern form to prevail, cf. the situation in OA: *za-kà-ri* (Bab. *zikaru*) OIP 27 55:53; *dan-na-té* JNES 16, 164:35; *ú-tá-tum* BIN 4 90:5 (see GKT, 20 § 10a; GOA § 3.4.9.4–5).

3.5.2 Assyrian vowel assimilation in finite verbs

§ 148 In verbal forms, VA usually occurs under a few conditions. In conjugated verbs, we find VA often caused by an attached vowel /u/, which can either be the masculine plural morpheme *-ū* or part of the subjunctive *-ūni*. There is no difference in the effect of both morphemes on VA. A selected list of examples is given below:

---

9 Attestations are gathered by W. Mayer in UGM, 14. However, some of the given examples are not valid; see the comments of Postgate (1974) and Freydank (1975, 173).

10 For exceptions in NA, see Deller (1959, 151–52 § 35e). Deller suggested that they are probably Babylonianisms, while emphasizing that the exceptions are most frequent found in literary texts, such as rituals.

alāku — *i-lu-ku-ni* 'it goes' KAJ 53:10
amāru — *im-mu-ru-šu-nu* 'they will see them' MAPD § 1:5
batāqu — *ta-ab-tu-qu-ú-ni* 'you accused' KAV 201:13
epāšu — ⸢*e*⸣-*ep-pu-šu-ú-ši* 'they will do to her' MAL A § 1:13
erābu — *er-ru-bu* 'they will enter' TR 04-37:5
našāqu — *ú-na-šú-qu* 'they will kiss' Coronation Ritual iii 3
ṣabātu N — *iṣ-ṣa-ab-bu-ú-tu* 'they will be seized' MAL A § 25:94
ṣarāḫu N — *iṣ-ṣa-ru-ḫu* 'they will become hot' PKT 1 I right:12
šakānu — *i-ša-ku-nu* 'they will place' Coronation Ritual i 24
šalāmu D — *ú-*⸢*šal*⸣-*lu-mu* 'they will pay in full' MAL J § 3:7
tadānu — *i-id-du-nu* 'they will give' MAL B § 6:38
i-du-nu-ú-ni KAJ 88:20

§ 149 In the perfect, the infixed morpheme *-ta-* creates a new open syllable, which is affected by VA. When the theme vowel is either /i/ or /u/, we find the patterns *iPtiRiS* and *iPtuRuS*.

bakāʾu — *ib-ti-ki-i-ú* 'they have cried' T 02-32:13
erāšu — *e-te-ri-iš* 'he has requested' KAV 106:6
laqāʾu — *al-te-qe-ma* 'I have taken' KAV 217:7'
il-te-qe 'he has taken' A 1765 (NTA, 25):15
maqātu — *im-tu-qu-ut* 'he has fallen' MATSH 4:7
maṭāʾu — *ta-am-ti-ṭí* 'it has been defective' MARV 3 38:10
našāqu — *it-ti-ši-iq-ši* 'he kissed her' MAL A § 9:93
qabāʾu — *táq-ti-bi* 'she spoke' MAL A § 2:16
ragāmu — *tar-tu-gu-um* 'she has called' MAPD § 21:105
šarāqu — *tal-ti-ri-iq* 'she stole' MAL A § 3:25

Some exceptions are found; in the following verbal form with an epenthetic vowel, VA does not penetrate the antepenultimate syllable, whereas the penultimate suffix is affected:

madādu — *im-ta-du-du* 'they have measured out' MARV 7 7:8

§ 150 Exceptions without VA are very rare; nonetheless, a few attestations can be found. Most notable are the three attestations in the Giricano archive, all of which occur in the same text. In this text, we find another exception of VA (*a-ie-e-ša-mi-ni* Giricano 12:18').[11] It is, of course, possible that these forms are actually Gtn preterites; however, given the position of the preterite in MA, this seems highly unlikely.[12] For some reason, VA is often applied inconsistently or erroneously to the word *parrutu* 'a youg female lamb' (see LVUH, 12).

balāṭu D — *ú-ba-la-ṭu* 'they will maintain' KAJ 168:13 (TN)
ḫalāqu — *iḫ-ta-li-iq* 'he has lost' Giricano 12:19'; T 98-94:18[13]
kallumu — *ú-kal-la-mu* 'they will show' Ni. 669:7 (En)
maḫāru — *im-ta-ḫur-ú-ni*$^{!}$ 'they have received' KAM 11 23:10

11 According to Radner (Giricano, 62), only two texts from this anonymous scribe are known. The other text does not feature any exceptions of VA, but is still notable for the occurrence of NA *ussērib* (< MA *ultērib*), as discussed in § 220.

12 Kouwenberg suggested that some OA verbal forms without VA can be read as Gtn-stems; see GOA § 3.4.9.4. Of course, the absence of orthographic gemination in OA makes such a reinterpretation more viable.

13 The fact that this verb is attested on two occasions suggests that this is a Gt-stem present form (*iḫtalliq*). However, this Gt-stem is not attested in other dialects of Akkadian, nor is it clear what it could mean.

namāšu	*it-ta-mu-uš-me* 'he has departed' RS 20.18:22 (Cypriote letter)
parrutu	*pa-ra-tu* 'young lamb' LVUH 4:28; *pa-ru-te* LVUH 23:25; cf. *pár-re-te* LVUH 51:7
qabā$^{?}$*u*	*aq-ta-bi* RS 18.54a (possibly not Assyrian)
ṣabātu	*la i-ṣa-ba-tu* 'they will not seize' TR 2020:6'
tadānu	*it-ta-din* 'he has given' Giricano 12:9', 11' (cf. OA *i-ta-dí-in* AKT 6 110:34)
	it-⌜*ta-din*⌝ 'he has given' MARV 10 16:6 (signs hardly visible)
	it$^{?}$*-t*[*a-din*] 'he has given' KAJ 275:3
ušābu	⌜*uš-šá-bu*⌝ 'they will sit' T 04-37:21 (signs hardly visible)

The situation becomes more complicated in the cases where suffixes are added, with the syllable of the *-ta-* infix closed and the succeeding vowel eliding: *imtuqut* > *imtuqtū*. According to Kouwenberg (2010, 140), the *-ta-* infix remains affected by VA if the elided vowel is /u/; however, in the case of /i/, the original /a/ remains.[14] We will call this type of VA, when the causing vowel has disappeared, virtual VA. For the perfect of (*u/u*) verbs, only three attestations are known to me:

namāšu	*it-tu-um-šu-ni* 'they have departed' MATSH 6:25'
	it-⌜*tu*⌝*-um-šu* TabT05a-623:1
zakā$^{?}$*u*	*i-zu-ku* (*izzuk*^{w}*ū* < *iztuku*^{w}*ū*) 'they have cleared' KAJ 162:19

Kouwenberg's claim is not unproblematic, since he only presented one attestation and I can only find one more involving the same verb. Nonetheless, it seems to hold in combination with his presented NA evidence where verbs with *i* theme vowel were also affected. In NA, this feature extended to some verbs while, in others, the original vowel pattern *iptaqdū* was preserved. Therefore, with the present evidence, it cannot be confirmed how far this feature was extended across the MA verbal paradigm, other than in terms fo the verb *namāšu*. In the semi-Assyrian text, the Alašia letter, we find *it-ta-mu-uš-me* RS 20.18:22, instead of the expected *ittumuš-me*, possibly due to the addition of *-me*.

For the (*i/i*) class:

ḫalāqu	*iḫ-ta-al-qu* 'they are lost' RS 18.54a:2' (peripheral Assyrian)
qarābu	*iq-ṭar-bu* 'they approached' KAV 159:4 cf. *aq-ti-ri-ib* MATSH 2:29

For the (*i/a*) class:

tadānu	*i-ta-nu* (< *itadnū*) 'they gave' MATSH 6:21' ~ *ta-ti-din* KAJ 100:19

However, there are very few attestations where this change can be observed; moreover, in OA, /a/ remains in all instances. It therefore seems that VA had started to become lexicalized for perfect verbs and extended to the paradigm, but had not yet covered all forms. Nonetheless, in general, VA is retained in forms, even when the original vowel is apocopated. For instance, in the edicts published by George, we find an apocopated pronominal suffix, with the virtual VA of the preceding vowel /a/: *ikalla+šu* > *ikallušu* > *ikalluš*.

kalā$^{?}$*u*	*i-kal-lu-uš* (*ikalluš*) 'he will hold it' George 1988 1 r. 7'

Interestingly, virtual VA does not take place in the preterite of the N-stem, even though this was still the case in OA, cf. *it-ti-bi-ik* KAJ 306a:4 vs. *iš-ša-ak-nu-ú-ni* MARV 7 3:7.

---

14 This type of VA is only rarely attested in OA; see GOA § 3.4.9.

§ 151 Sometimes, verbal forms with the subjunctive *-ūni* are not affected by VA (See UGM, 12 § 8.1.a; Postgate 1974, 274). This seems to have been a recent innovation, rather than an archaism (cf. OA *ṭa-aṣ-bu-tù-ni-ma* ATHE 59:13). The absence of VA is attested in this type of verbal form with *-ūni* and the plural ventive *-(ū)ne* in NA (Deller 1959 71f). This is an NA feature referred to as regressive vowel dissimilation by Luukko (2004, 93–97 § 4.6.). For this reason, we find most attestations in MAPD, a text redacted in the period of Tp, which never features VA in subjunctive verbs.[15] However, attestations in other texts are also known. Still, all attestations are found in the literary corpus, which are generally late MA copies or compositions that confirm the late date of this development; cf. *im-⸢ma⸣-gur-ú-ni* Giricano 4:17 (Abk). The only exceptions to this are two Gtn-stem preterites from the same TSA letter, which does not contain an eponym but dates back to the reign of TN.

alāku	*il-la-ku-ú-ni* 'who go' MAPD § 6:39
erābu	*er-ra-bu-ú-ni* 'he enters' MAPD § 8:49
	er-ra-b[u]-ni 'they will enter' MAPD § 20:97
	er-ra-bu-ni 'that he enters' MAPD § 9:54
maḫāṣu Gtn	*i-ta-ḫa-ṣu-ni* 'they beat' T 96-15:12
pašāḫu	*i-pa-ša-ḫu-ni* 'as it cools down' PKT 5 r. 9
rakāsu	*i-ra-ka-su-ni* 'that he sets up' Coronation Ritual i 40
šakānu Gtn	*il-ta-ka-nu-ni* 'they placed' T 96-15:13
urādu Gtn	*it-ta-na-ra-du-ni* 'he goes down repeatedly' A 1748 (NTA, 23):12
	it-ta-na-ra-du-ú-ni KAJ 204:11

On the basis of the NA evidence, it has been suggested that this change of /u/ > /a/ was caused by the doubling of the final radical, resulting in the closing of the syllable (von Soden 1948, 301; GAG, 19 § 15d). Evidence for this claim is rather abundant in NA (e.g., *pa-qid-du-u-ni* < *paqdūni* SAA 13, 161:19'; *im-ra-aṣ-ṣu-ni* SAA 10, 316:10, Deller 1959, 190; Luukko 2004, 31ff § 3.7). Von Soden suggested that the alternation of /u/ and /a/ in this position indicated a pronunciation of /o/ (von Soden 1948, 301; see § 139). However, no geminated spellings in MA are known. This is possibly due to the awareness among scribes that gemination of the third radical is not desirable in Akkadian. It is, therefore, more likely that the geminated verbal forms in NA are morphographemic spellings, where the base of the verb is written with the endings added as phonetic complements. If this is correct, we must discount the possibility that the change of /u/ > /a/ was caused by the closure of the syllable. It is perhaps more likely that the spelling with <A> represented a *Murmelvokal* [ə].[16] The addition of the subjunctive resulted in a change of stress, which probably shifted to the /ū/ of the subjunctive *-ūni*. This would result in a *Murmelvokal* in the closed syllable preceding the subjunctive, as represented in the orthography with <A> (Postgate 1974, 274; see also Kouwenberg 2010, 49). According to Fabritius (1995), NA uses the original *iṣbutūni* and the secondary *iṣbatūni* to distinguish between singular and plural, respectively.[17] There is no evidence for a similar differentiation in function in MA;

15 A possible exception is caused by the reading of the aleph sign Aˀ as either <ˀa> or <ˀu> in *la-a iš-ˀA-lu-n[i]* 'he did not ask' MAPD § 3:25.

16 Cf. the similar use of <A> in Cv-signs within Hittite texts in order to write consonant clusters that are otherwise not possible with the Cv/vC/CvC syllabic values. See Hoffner/Melchert (2008, 12–13 § 1.11).

17 Notice also a comparable dissimilarity in the stative with the subjunctive: *paqidūni* (3ms) ~ *paqdūni* (3mp); see SNAG, 91. Fabritius' claims were discussed and, to a large extent, rejected by Luukko

however, the occurrence of both variations could have been representative of the spoken language, which would allow for such a development over time. Moreover, the *Murmelvokale* can also be found in NA substantive; see also § 131. Most examples without VA are probably explained this way: an unstressed *Murmelvokal* indicated by the scribes with /a/.[18]

§ 152 Of interest is the 3fs stative *PaRSat*, which features VA when the subjunctive *-ūni* is added. Attestations are frequent in MAL A, but are also found in administrative and legal documents:

aḫāzu	*aḫ-zu-tu-ú-ni* 'who was married' MAL A § 45:75 ~ ⸢*la-a aḫ*⸣*-za-tu-ú-ni* MAL A § 55:11
laqā'u	*la-qé-ú-tu-ni* 'who is taken' KAJ 167:6
marāṣu	*mar-ṣu-tu-ú-ni* 'she is sick' A 1765 (NTA, 25):5
našā'u	*na-ṣu-tu-ú-ni* 'what she carried' MAL A § 29:13 ~ *na-ṣa-tu-ú-ni* MAL A § 35:77
niāku	*ni-ku-tu-ú-ni* 'that she was raped' MAL A § 23:33
paṣānu D	*pa-ṣu-nu-tu-ú-ni* 'who is veiled' MAL A § 41:7
šakānu	*ša-ak-nu-tu-ú-*[*ni*] KAJ 310:66
šaṭāru	*šaṭ-ru-tú-ni* 'which is written' TR 3012:7 ~ *šaṭ-ru-t*[*u-ni*] KAJ 122:9
	ša-aṭ-ru-tu-ni KAJ 114:10
ulādu	*ul-du-tu-ú-ni* 'who bore' MAL A § 45:77
ušābu	*us-bu-tu-ú-ni* 'who dwelled' MAL A § 24:69
	us-bu-tu-ni 'who dwelled' MAL A § 24:57

There is a considerable number of attestations without VA, which seem centred around MAL A, with one further attestation in the Ištar Ritual.

aḫāzu	⸢*la-a aḫ*⸣*-za-tu-ú-ni* 'who is not married' MAL A § 55:11
namāru	*nam-ra-tu-ni* 'which is bright' Ištar Ritual:12
našā'u	*na-ṣa-tu-ú-ni* 'what she carried' MAL A § 35:77
patā'u	*pa-te-a-tu-ú-ni* 'who is opened' MAL A § 55:10

The following is uncertain:

ḫadā'u	*ḫa-di-*<*a*>*-*⸢*tu*⸣*-ú-ni* (perhaps *ḫadêtūni*) 'she wishes' MAL A § 33:70

It should be noted that the examples where /a/ remains are fairly numerous, but mostly limited to MAL A and other literary texts. It is possible to assume mixed Babylonian/Assyrian forms; however, it is more likely that they are late Assyrian forms and represent another form of the regressive VA of /u/ > /a/, even though Luukko does not list the feminine singular stative in his categories with attestations.

3.5.3 Sound changes related to vowel assimilation

§ 153 There are a few nouns known in Akkadian where a (long) /a/ in word-initial syllables becomes /i/ or /e/. The examples are mostly limited to a small number of specific nouns, meaning that it is difficult to accept them as an additional case of VA. The most common noun is the Assyrian *pā'u* 'mouth' > *pi-i/pe-e*, which occurs passim in the genitive (cf. GAG, 15 § 10e). In this short word, /ā/ usually takes the colour of the case ending, e.g., *pi-i* KAV 100:8/KA-*i* TR 2037:13, and with pronominal suffixes: *pi-i-k*[*a*] T 02-32:31. As the

(2004, 95–96 n304).

18 See Postgate (1974, 274); cf. Deller/Finkel (1984, 82.1).

genitive has become *-e* in MA, we also find this reality reflected once in *PI-e* MAL A § 2:17. However, one example shows the original form, i.e., *pa-i* KAJ 6:4 (Aub). Given the Babylonian background of this scribe and other peculiar forms in this text (cf. § 21), we may assume that *pa-i* reflects how the scribe understood Assyrian, as well as the spoken language, as opposed to the orthographic *pi-i*.[19] In OA, *pû* is attested in all three case endings, indicating variation between forms with and without VA. The length of the vowel is therefore uncertain (GOA § 5.5.1.8.2).

§ 154 Another common noun is *adru* 'threshing floor', which is often attested as *edre* in the genitive, although certainly not in all cases, e.g., *ad-ri* KAJ 52:13; 81:15; MARV 3 4:9. The CAD A_1 (130) connects the form with Aramaic *iddar* (cf. Syriac *ˀeddrā* ܐܶܕܪܳܐ Payne Smith 1903, 4). But this is improbable because, even if there was Aramaic influence on MA, we should expect it in peripheral cities from the period of Sa/TN or later. Instead, *edre* is found most frequently in the Ead/Aub-centred archive M 9. The second option offered by W. Mayer (UGM, 14) is a case of sound change, known in Arabic as *ˀimāla* (إمالة), who uses it to explain different cases of /a/ > /e/.[20] The fact that *edre* is solely found as a genitive makes this claim unlikely. It is, therefore, better to acknowledge that a sound change similar to VA, caused by the genitive endings, would appear to be the more likely. This is also attested in OA for genitive forms of *ašrum* 'place' > *ešrem*, e.g., *iš-ri-šu* KTH 6:13.[21] At the same time, *edru* is only found in this variant in the phrase *ana idre gire u zaruqqe lā iqarrrib* 'he may not encroach on the threshing floor, road and well', whereas *adru* is found in more varied contexts. This raises some doubt as to whether *idr-* is actually identical to *adru* or if another technical term is meant.

edru *ed-re* or *id-re* (normal *adru*) 'threshing floor' KAJ 151:1; 152:3; 153:3; 154:3; 155:3
cf. *ad-re* KAJ 147:15; 149:14; 160:3; 162:6; KAM 10 14:3

There is one possible attestation of the VA of /i/ in PN ^{m}*Be-lu-bu-ur* RS 06.198:1 ~ ^{m}EN-*li-bur* KAV 96:2 (UGM, 16). According to Saporetti (OMA 1, 174), the interpretation Bēlu-būr is more favourable. However, this person is likely to be identified with Bēl-libur, a *qēpu* of Bābu-aḫa-iddina (Jakob 2003, 301). Another isolated form is the change of /a/ > /e/ in a closed syllable of a Gtn participle: *mu-te-li-ú* (< *mumtalliˀu*) MPR 69:27.

19 The morphology of *pāˀum/pīˀum* is complicated in OA as the status constructus in inflected triptotically, as in the case of family members, such as *abu* (see § 292). Moreover, both basic forms seem to have existed next to each other (cf. GKT, 102 § 62c). In the status constructus, *pāˀi* is not attested in OA, but it is in the status rectus (GOA § 5.5.1.8.2). The pronunciation of *pi-i* as *pāˀi* is furthermore supported by the similar spelling of the name Šalim-pî-Ea (§ 259).

20 The *ˀimāla* (إمالة) concerns the palatalized pronunciation of the etymologic /a/; see Fischer (2006, 18 § 29.2).

21 See GKT, 20 § 10c; GOA § 3.4.9.1. cf. GAG, 15–16 § 10f.

3.6 Other vocalic changes

3.6.1 Syncope/elision

§ 155 In Akkadian there is a tendency against two successive open syllables with a third (or more) added. Usually the second vowel elides, effectively making the first syllable closed: $C_1v/C_2/C_3$, e.g., we find *kalb-um* 'dog' for the pattern $C_1aC_2vC_3$. This process took place in the early development stage of the language because, as we will see, in MA, the stress is likely to have been partly penultimate, such that *kal'ab-um* is unlikely to have the second vowel elided.

§ 156 In Akkadian, we find this rule applied in all nominal cases with a short vowel. Long vowels are usually retained. The situation regarding loan words is not entirely clear; it has been suggested that long vowels in loan words should be retained (Greenstein 1984, 31–32 § 5.2.2.), but, because we often know little about the vowel length or gemination in loan words, it is difficult to draw conclusions (cf. OA in GOA § 3.4.8).

Nouns:
- Feminine nominal constructions, e.g., *PaRvSat* > *PaRSat/PaRvSt*
- Feminine plural forms, e.g., sg. *bitiqtu* > *bitqātu* 'losses'
- Adjectives of the G-stem, e.g., *baliṭum* > *balṭu* 'alive'

Verbal forms:
- Perfect with an added morpheme, e.g., *imtaḫurū* > *imtaḫrū* 'they received'
- Imperatives with added morphemes, e.g., mp *muḫurā* > *muḫrā* 'receive!'
- Statives with a suffix, e.g., 1cs *paliḫ+āku* 1cs > *palḫāku* 'I am afraid'
- I/w preterite with an added morpheme, e.g., *ubil-ūni* > *ublūni* 'that they brought'
- Various forms of the Gt-stem (e.g., *imtagur-ū* > *imtagr-ū*), this is hardly attested

A more complete list of common examples of this sound change can be found in Streck (2014a, 19 § 39). In NA, some $C_1vC_2vC_3$ forms have even changed to $C_1vC_2C_3v$, which Hämeen-Anttila labelled as the metathesis of syllables (SNAG, 38 § 2.4.13.). So far, this is only known within MA for the imperatives of II/gem verbs: *dubub* > *dubbu*.

3.6.2 Epenthetic vowels

§ 157 In MA, the original rule to elide the second open syllable is no longer actively applied. There are a few reasons to justify this assumption. In Akkadian, the I/voc can be understood to have had an initial long vowel in the prefix conjugation. This becomes apparent when we posit a preterite 3mp with the subjunctive *ē/pi/š'ū/ni*, where the vowel in the second syllable does not elide (as opposed to I/w verbs: *ub/l'ū/ni* < *u/bi/l'ū/ni)*. In the non-prefixed forms, this vowel is certainly not long and thus we find an imperative mp *epšā* or stative 1cs *epšāku*. Kouwenberg (2003/4) argued that this initial long vowel can be found in plene spellings in OB, but that they are only orthographic in MA and not found in NA (99–100). Still, we find forms where the vowel in the second syllable is not elided, e.g., *e-šu-ru-ú-ni* (*e/šu/rū/ni*) 'which he inspected' MARV 1 6:30. In its turn, this makes it unclear whether the initial vowel is shortened only in the present tense, or in the perfect and preterite as well. We may point to I/u spelling, such as *it-tab-la* (*ittabla*) 'he has brought here' MAL A § 15:48 and *ub-lu-ú-ni* (*ub/lū/ni*) 'what he brought' MAL A § 38:24. The I/u verbs following these examples have R_1 assimilated into the *ta-* infix of the perfect, but, according to the vowel syncope, they have no long vowel in the preterite. For I/voc verbs, such spellings are not normal; thus, we maintain their lengthening in the perfect and preterite. In NA, it appears that the I/u developed analogously to the I/voc verbs, while the vowel in the second syllable no longer elided (SNAG, 96 § 3.13.2). Secondly, closed unstressed syllables in NA tend to be opened by an epenthetic or anaptyctic vowel, creating the sequence of two open unstressed syllables.[22] Sometimes, the final closed syllable is opened *a-ri-ši* (< *ariš* stative) LVUH 80:17.[23] In MA, the examples are rarer, but do occur for the second category.[24] Nonetheless, many of them do not meet the condition set by Hämeen-Anttila and Luukko: an epenthetic vowel has to have the same colour as the vowel in the preceding syllable.[25] It should be pointed out that many of the following examples could be instances of inverted spellings, as discussed in § 116f.

Nouns:

erbiyu	*e-re-bi-ú* 'locust' MATSH 2:7 (TN)
ḫulqu	6 KUŠ [*ḫu*]-*lu-qú* 'six lost hides' LVUH 43:10' (TN)
	2 ANŠE.NÍTA *ḫu-lu-q*[*u*!] 'two lost donkeys' LVUH 6:14 (Sa)
	1 ANŠE.N[ÍTA *ḫ*]*u-lu-*<*qu*> LVUH 2:15 (Sa)
mētu	1 *li-im* 2 *me-ti libnātu* '1200 bricks' KAJ 87:1 (EAd/Aub)
miṭru	*mi-ṭí-ru* '*m.*-bread' MARV 8 92:6; *me-ṭí-ru* YBC 12864:4, 5, 6, 10
nakru	*n*[*a-k*]*i-ri-ka* 'your enemies' T 02-3:19
rēḫtu	*re-ḫi-ti* 'remainder' TR 2049:6'
šēbu	*še-bi* 'old (one)' Giricano 10:17 (Abk); MPR 43:65[26]

Most examples occur in finite verbs; however, no attestations of opened syllables in I/w verbs are known. NA features an innovation of opening the second syllable of a 3ms stative *parsūni* > *parisūni* in order to distinguish it from the 3mp *parsūni* (Fabritius 1995; SNAG, 91); but this is not attested for MA.[27]

apālu	*ap-la-ta* 'she is paid for' Tab T05A-43:15
arāšu	*la a-ri-ši* 'not cultivated' LVUH 80:17 (TN)
epāšu	*e-pa-ša-ni* 'they worked' Tsukimoto 1992 B:10, r. 9' (Sa)
ḫalāqu	*me-et ḫa-la-qa* 'he dies or he flees' RE 19:16 (Nae)
	tu-ḫu-ta-li-qa T 93-11:28†
ḫalāṣu	*li-ḪI-lu-ṣu* (*liḫluṣū*) 'may they filter' T 93-7:7, 17, 23
ḫarāṣu Št	*tu-ša-ḫa-ru-ṣu-ni* (*tušaḫaruṣūni*) 'it has been deduced' KAJ 120:7 (Sa)
madādu	*im-ta-du-du* (*imtaddū*) 'they have measured out' MARV 7 7:8 (TN)
maḫāru	*la ma-ḫa-rat* (*lā maḫrat*) 'it is not received' LVUH 105:8 (TN)
	ma-ḫa-ru T 97-38:22 (A.n.apli−Eku)
naḫāru	*na-ḫa-rat* 'it is invalid' TR 2061:11
paqādu	*pa-qi-du* (*paqdū*) 'they entrusted' A 3196 (NTA, 39):4 (NtA)

22 Cf. Deller (1959, 20–53 § 8-17); SNAG, 34f § 2.4.9; Luukko (2004, 102–9 § 4.8); cf. OA GKT, 51 § 32b; also Emar in (Seminar 1998, 153–54).

23 For NA, cf. Luukko (2004, 105–6). For this specific attestation, see Freydank (2010a, 98).

24 Cf. Deller/Saporetti (1970a, 45); cf. Postgate (1986a, 37 n53).

25 See SNAG, 35; Luukko (2004, 102).

26 Both cases are probably nominal statives, as is attested passim in MPR, e.g., *še-eb* MPR 18:1.

27 Some attested preterites of I/weak verbs could be contested as statives. For instance, *e-ti-qu-ni* MAPD § 21:108 could be analysed as a stative having an epenthetic vowel.

puāgu	*ip-tu-a-KA*=(*iptuag*?) 'he has taken away' T 02-32:29
saḫāru	*la-sa-ḫur (lāsḫur)* 'I will find' KAJ 316:15[28] (TN)
šakānu	*iš-ku-nu-ši* 'he placed her' KAJ 7:19†[29] (EAd/Aub)
	šu-ku-nu 'place!' T 93-11:13
šaqāʾu Š	*ú-ša-šá-qa* 'he will give to drink' T 98-17:16 (TN)

Of these examples, a very rough 50% derives from texts in the peripheral archives. It is not clear whether these epenthetic vowels are an early adaptation of NA phonology or a sign of bad scribal scholarship. We can even increase this number if we include a few attestations from the Māri royal inscriptions (Maul 1992, 18–19): *áš-ku-nu* Maul 1992, 24:8; IGI-*ru-ma* (< *lēmur-ma*) Maul 1992, 26:13. We may add the following attestation: *ma-ḫe-ru-te* (< *maḫruttu*) Maul 1992, 22:3, although the inserted vowel /e/ has a different colour than the vowel preceding it. Maul (1992, 32) rightfully points out that /a/ has a tendency to become /e/ before /r/, which is the best explanation for the unexpected colour of this epenthetic vowel.

3.6.3 Shortening of long vowels

§ 158 In light of the epenthetic vowels, we may also point out some instances of Assyrian VA on a vowel expected to be long. It appears that /ā/ shortened in a number of substantives, but did not elide. Most relevant material on these words was gathered by Goetze (1947), who concluded that these substantives have short vowels, something that was accepted in their entries in the CAD; however, AHw maintains that their vowels are only short in Assyrian. We will list the examples relevant for MA below. The possibility cannot be excluded that some of these nouns did not shorten /ā/, but were affected by VA nonetheless. This explanation seems plausible on the basis of the orthography, except for the cases of (*ramānu*), where /a/ is known to have elided.

abātu 'word(s)': So far not attested with VA in MA (only potential cases in *a-ba-tu-šu* MATSH 8:41'; *a-ba-a-te* 'words' Tsukimoto 1992 D:7; the Alašia letter *a-ba-te*^meš RS 20.18:7 and the unusual *a-ma-te*^meš*-ia* RS 06.198:18, see § 181 for this attestation), but usually only found in the construct *a-bat* passim and *a-ba-su* in *šulmānu* texts passim). That said, examples in NA are more numerous.[30] It therefore seems that the long vowel was retained in MA, just as it was in OA (cf. Kouwenberg 2008, 169). Despite originally being a plural form, we can already observe that Assyrians regarded it as singular: *a-ba-te an-ni-te* 'this message' KBo 28 61/62:19'; singular accusative *a-ba-te* MAL A § 19:83. There is a possible case of VA in a fragment from the same letter, yet this is uncertain: *a-be*?*-te* KBo 28 64:6.

simānu 'time', in *si-mu-nu* Ištar Ritual:1; *si-mi-ni* Ištar Ritual r. 9'

usātu 'help', in *a-na ú-si-ti-šu* KAJ 46:5 (Kouwenberg 2008, 170 n23).

kallātu 'daughter-in-law', in *kal-le-te* (*kallātu*) MAL A § 46:97.

This noun is realized with a short /a/ in CAD (CAD K, 82ff), but a long /ā/ by von Soden (AHw, 426). In Assyrian, there always seems to have been a short /a/, as confirmed by VA

28 An alternative explanation, that this form is an N-stem, seems unlikely since *saḫāru* does not show the theme vowel /u/ in this stem. See CAD S, 52–54.

29 The passage is partly damaged; however, context makes a 3mp subject unexpected and a relative clause without an Assyrian subjunctive unlikely.

30 See Deller (1959, 145); Greenstein (1984, 37).

in OA (e.g., *kà-li-tí-ni* TCL 21 202:16). We do find a single plene spelling: *kal-la-a-su* MAL A § 30:34. However, this example is typical of penultimate plene spellings.

pāḫatu (Bab. *pīḫātu*), in *pa-ḫe-te* 'province' MAPD § 1:7; *pa-ḫu-tu* MARV 1 56:47. Babylonian *pīḫatu* (< *puḫḫu*) is once attested, probably as a loan: EN *pi-ḫa-te* 'district governor' MPR 67:43. The attestations of VA in MA leave no doubt that the penultimate /a/ in this substantive is short (cf. Edzard 1982, 84–85). The morpheme *-at* is in fact the singular feminine gender marker, which is confirmed by the plural form without VA, *pa-ḫa-te*^{meš} A 113 (NTA, 15):4; *pa-ḫa-a-tu* MARV 5 20:1. Of some interest are Radner's (Giricano, 89) claims of the existence of an alternative form for *pāhātu* (sg. *pāḫutu*) 'provinces/
responsibility', that is, *pa-ḫa-nu* Giricano 9:9. Radner connects this plural form to the singular *paḫnu* and claims that this is the same noun as *pāḫutu* (Giricano, 89). This noun is attested three times in MA: *pa-ah-nu* KAJ 307:5; *a-na pa-aḫ-ni-šu-nu* KAJ 307:11; ^{lú}*pa*$^{!}$*-ah-nu* TR 3006:10.[31] As these studies point out, it is more likely that *paḫnu* refers to a person. While this meaning does not seem to fit directly into the passage of Giricano 9, we are reluctant to accept Radner's claim based on only one attestation.

31 See AHw, 811; CAD P, 33; Postgate (1982, 305–6); Jakob (2003, 194 n9).

Chapter 4: Consonants

§ 159 The following chapter discusses the phoneme inventory of MA and the changes it undergoes in this phase of the language. Although the number of consonants seems unchanged from OA and OB, their realization did change. This is mostly notable in the deaffrication process regarding the sibilants. Sometimes, the changes are not easy to analyse, especially the fate of the semivowel /w/ and the realization of /š/.

		Bilabial	Dental	Alveolar	Velar	Lateral	Palatal	Laryngeal
Stops	Voiceless	p	t		k			ʔ
	Voiced	b	d		g			
	Glottalic		ṭ (/t'/)		q (/k'/)			
Sibilant	Voiceless			s		š (/ɬ/)		
	Voiced			z				
	Glottalic			ṣ (/s'/)				
Fricatives		v$^{?}$			ḫ			
Nasal		m	n					
Approx.		w$^{?}$	r			l	y	

Figure 15: Consonants in MA.[1]

4.1 Emphatic consonants

§ 160 The realization of the three emphatic consonants in MA is part of the greater debate in the context of Proto-Semitic. Opinions vary between pharyngealized realization, such as in Arabic, and glottalized realization in South Semitic such as Amharic. It was originally suggested that the glottalized realization in the South Semitic languages of Ethiopia was influenced by neighbouring Cushitic; however the discovery of similar sounds in Modern South Arabic has made this view unsustainable.[2] As stated by Kouwenberg (2003, 84 n56; cf. Luukko/Van Buylaere 2017, 323), it is likely that, if one emphatic consonant was glottalized, all were glottalized, making it necessary to discuss them as a whole.

§ 161 The most common evidence for the existence of glottalized emphatics in Akkadian is perhaps "Geers' law", which stipulates that no two emphatic consonants can be part of a root (Geers 1945; GAG, 65 § 51e); likewise, NA dissimilation of two successive emphatics, e.g., *qaqqadu* > *kaqqadu* (Knudsen 1961). Dissimilation is more likely if the emphatics were glottalized.[3] As Streck pointed out to me, Geers' law may be applied actively in MA in the GN *Qatāra*, e.g., ^{uru}*Qa-TA-ra* TR 2031:6. OB evidence indicates that, originally, there was a /*ṭ*/ in the proper name, e.g., *Qa-ṭà-ra-a*^{ki} Dalley/Walker/Hawkins no. 79:4, but rarely TA in *Qa*$^{!}$*-TA-ra*^{ki} no. 155:20. The use of TA in this latter OB spelling and MA

1 Based on Kouwenberg (GOA Table 3.1).

2 A small selection of the discussion: Ullendorff (1955, 151–57); Lipiński (2001, 111–12 § 10.9–10.10); Kogan (2011, 59-69).

3 See GAG, 32 § 26b; Edzard (1983, 134–35); Huehnergard (1997a, 438); Kogan (2011, 60 § 1.3.1.2).

points to the weakening of /ṭ/ > /t/, caused by the preceding emphatic /q/. A notable development against Geers' law is the appearance of /ṭ/ (< /t/), following /q/ in perfect forms of *qabāˀu* and *qarābu*, e.g., *iqtibi* > *iqṭibi* (see below).

§ 162 For MA, the most important evidence derives from the verbal base *naṣṣ*-, an irregular construction of *našāˀu*, as proven by Parpola (1974). However, the progressive assimilation of an aleph to double /s/ (*našˀ*- > **nass*-), as suggested by Parpola, does not follow from the orthography, which clearly suggests double /ṣ/. Suggestions to limit these changes to those instances that involve contact with the vowels /a/ and /u/ (excluding /i/) cannot be sustained, as forms with /i/ directly following /š+ˀ/ are not attested (Voigt 1986, 57 n28). Moreover, it appears that forms with <Š> and <Ṣ> could alternate as well.[4] Aro suggested that /ṣ/ had a glottal pronunciation [s'], such as in the Ethiopian languages (Aro 1977, 8). This idea was initially not well received, mainly because similar examples in other roots are difficult to find (e.g., *šaˀālu* > *išˀal* never **iṣṣal*, SNAG, 15 § 2.1.5.). Kouwenberg (2003) did discover similar forms in OA, where they had remained unnoticed because of the lack of gemination in the orthography. However, given the peculiar spelling of the aleph or, better still, the absence of the aleph, he concluded that the guttural had assimilated into preceding /ṣ/. Examples were found in the roots *waṣāˀum*; *maṣāˀum*, and *kaṣāˀu*. Unlike *našāˀu*, we do not find /š/ as an affected radical in these verbs because that would be a sign of the weakening of /š/ to /s/, which did not take place in OA. However, the roots do show signs that indicate gemination when /ṣ/ is followed by an aleph. In other words, /ṣ/ has assimilated into the following aleph. Likewise, sequences of /d+ˀ/ in OA *nadāˀu* are written with TA, which are best read as <ṭá>. Examples without this sequence use the expected DA. Evidence of similarly geminated forms occur in NA, e.g., *ma-aṣ-ṣa-ku-ni* SAA 10 294:28; *lu-uṣ-ṣu-u-ni* SAA 10 259:12. Once, in MA, we find *ku-uṣ-ṣu* 'winter' BVW Ko r. 17 for *kuṣˀu* (Bab. *kūṣu*). In MA, the following verbs are known to have this type of regressive aleph assimilation: *maṣāˀu; nadāˀu*; *našāˀu*; *uṣāˀu*.

§ 163 Two other verbs that suggest a glottalized realization are *qabāˀu* and *qarābu*, where the infixed *-t-* is partially assimilated with *-t-* > *-ṭ-*: *iqtibi* > *iqṭibi* (see § 211).[5] Hämeen-

4 Parpola himself noted the variation in orthography: *na-ša-at* Lambert (1969:59); cf. *na-ṣa-at* KAJ 100:23. See also Parpola (1974, 5 n17). It is questionable how far we can hold the orthography from the incantation treated by Lambert as being representative of MA as a whole.

5 It is perhaps useful to consider whether consonants (partially) assimilate into neighbouring emphatics and how this is distributed between languages with glottalized or pharyngealized emphatics. In general, when partial assimilation concerns emphatics it is also used for voiced and voiceless consonants. The closest parallel with MA could be Ṭuroyo, where /t/ > /ṭ/ on following the emphatics /ḍ-ṣ-ṭ/ (but not /q/), e.g., *rahátṭo* < *rahátto* 'running (f.)'; see Jastrow (1993, 18 § 17). Already this type of assimilation occurs in Egyptian Aramaic, but is limited to one substantive: *עתיק > עטיק 'old'; see Muraoka/Porten (2003, 17). Perhaps the best-known example is the VIII stem with the infixed *-t-* in Arabic, where partial (and sometimes complete) assimilation of the infixed consonant occurs, when preceded by an interdental or dental fricative, e.g., **iztihār* > *izdihār* (ازدهار) 'to flourish'; **iḍtirāb* > *iḍṭirāb* (اضطراب) 'to confuse'; **iṣtibār* > *iṣṭibār* (اصطبار) 'to endure'; see Brockelmann (1960a, 39 § 29); Fischer (2006, 25–26 § 46); Badawi/Carter/Gully (2004, 61). On the subject of the glottalized languages, full assimilation is attested in Ge'ez, where it must be remarked that this language has no infixed *-t-* verbal stem. For this reason, assimilation is found in nouns, yet it is not restricted to interdentals; it also covers

Anttila adds, on the bases of *iqṭibi*, that the pronunciation of the emphatic consonants was velarized, rather than glottalized (SNAG, 15 § 2.1.5). However, this is circular reasoning since it assumes that the velarized /ṭ/ can only assimilate into /q/ if this phoneme is velarized as well; it would be just as true if we replaced velarized with glottalized. Huehnergard (1997a, 438) suggested a shift towards pharyngealized pronunciation of /qt/ > /qṭ/ under the influence of Central Semitic. It is unlikely that Assyrian and Central Semitic experienced intensive contact during this period, which could have influenced such fundamental parts of the language, such as pronunciation; therefore, the suggestion has to be rejected. The assumption that the emphatics had a glottal pronunciation seems to be the only solution in explaining the progressive assimilation of an aleph in a large number of nouns and verbs.

4.2 Weak consonants

§ 164 Proto-Semitic contained a set of 29 consonantal phonemes. During the earlier periods, Akkadian was in the process of losing a number of them, mostly in the area of the gutturals; thus, by the second millennium, only 21 consonants were left. Only the PS guttural /ḫ/ was retained in all instances. Moreover, Assyrian reduced /w/ to an allophone of /b/, or to a glide, lowering the number to 20 in MA. The development of the gutturals is a difficult subject in Assyriology. The traditional view, that the gutturals had developed in a weak sound, numbered aleph$_{1-7}$, is imprecise and needs to be altered. As such, the table below shows the traditional vs. a revised model of the different aleph types, based on the table in Kouwenberg (2006, 150).

Traditional				Modern view based on Assyrian			
PS		Akkadian	E-colouring	PS		MA	E-colouring
ʔ	>	$ʔ_1$	-	ʔ	>	ʔ	-
h	>	$ʔ_2$	-	*h*	>	Ø	-
ḥ	>	$ʔ_3$	+	*ḥ*	>	*Ø/ḫ*	+
ʕ	>	$ʔ_4$	+	ʕ	>	ʔ	+
ġ	>	$ʔ_5$	+	*ġ*	>	*ḫ*	-
w	>	$ʔ_6$	-	*w*	>	*Ø/w/u*	-
y	>	$ʔ_7$	+	*y*	>	*Ø/y*	+

Figure 16: Types of aleph.

velars, e.g., **wadaqkəmu* > *wadaqqəmu* (**ወደቅሙ**) 'you have fallen'; **ḫadagku* > *ḫadaggu* (**ኀደጉ**) 'I have abandoned'; *śəṭəṭt* > *śəṭəṭṭ* (**ሥጥጥ**) 'ripped (f.)'. See Tropper (2002, 35 § 36.6–36.7). We could even look at a modern Ethiopic language with glottalized emphatics, such as Zway, where the same (both partial and full assimilation) occurs, even though Zway belongs to the Southern Ethiopian languages, as opposed to the Northern group of Ge'ez, e.g., *yätgōba* > *yäggōba* 'let him down'; *atgūbi* > *adgūbi* 'deposit'; see Leslau (1999, 4–5 § 9.1–3). For Argobba, Leslau considers the verbal prefix conjugation *šeqqe* 'you sold it' to have been derived from **šeṭke*. He further suggested an intermediate stage, where /k/ is partially assimilated into emphatic /q/, which resembles the development *iqṭibi*: **šeṭke* > **šətqe* > *šeqqe*. For similar examples, see Leslau (1997, 5 § 7.3). Considering this sampling of a few Semitic languages, it seems that partial assimilation into emphatics is not confined to either group of emphatic realizations.

§ 165 In MA, ʔ$_{1-4}$ are still distinguishable in the orthography, even though their original value was lost. For this reason, we will refer to their etymologic value rather than a numbered aleph value. Both etymologic /ʔ/ and /ʕ/ are still represented as a strong stop in the orthography, while /h/ and /ḥ/ have disappeared. On the other hand, /ʔ/ and /h/ form an opposite pair to /ʕ/ and /ḥ/, which changed the colour of short /a/ > /e/, commonly known as e-colouring. This sound change took place when following a vowel (e.g., *ilaqqaḥ* > *ilaqqe*), as well as when preceding the vowel (e.g., *ʕabārum* > *ebāru*). Long vowels are not affected (e.g., *laqāḥum* > *laqāʔu*).[6] The original view assumes a strengthening of the gutturals /ʕ-ḥ-ġ/ to an aleph, where they cause the e-colouring before reducing to zero. Such behaviour involving these phonemes would be very unusual. Kouwenberg argued that this was caused by a glide, in which the PS sounds changed as they disappeared. In light of the diphthong /ay/ > /e/, it is most likely that this glide was /y/: *iptē*^{y}*ū* < *yiptaḥū* (Kouwenberg 2006, 150–151). This explanation cannot be applied to ayin in II/ʕ and III/ʕ verbs since it remains a stop and does not change to a glide, while ayin does come with e-colouring. Perhaps we need to consider Dolgopolsky's (1991, 334–37) hypothesis that e-colouring was caused by the pharyngalization of /ʕa/ (and /ḥ/), which brought upon the palatalization of the surrounding /a/. The main difference between e-colouring in Assyrian and Babylonian is that it spreads in the latter to all /a/ vowels in a word, e.g., the Babylonian VA: *alaqqaḥ* 'I will take' > Babylonian *eleqqe*/Assyrian *alaqqe*. In the case of Assyrian VA, /e/ can spread to a preceding syllable: *iltaqe* 'he took' > *ilteqe*. Another difference is that, in Assyrian, e-colouring also occurs on /i/ in the prefix conjugations: *iḫpuš* 'he did' > MB *ipuš*/MA *epuš*.[7] E-colouring of the long vowel /ā/ is unusual, but occurs passim in the participle *ṭé-i-nu* 'miller' (√*ṭḥn*). Nonetheless, there are a few isolated instances where *ṭāʔinu* is found, e.g., *ṭa-i-nu*^{meš} MARV 6 90:14.[8] It may be that, in some infinitives of III/y-ʕ-ḥ, the same type of e-colouring of the long /ā/ took place, but, as the *LaQāʔu* pattern prevails here, it is not clear if this is the same sound change.

§ 166 In numerous instances, /ḥ/ changed to /ḫ/ instead of ʔ$_{3}$.[9] In MA, an example can be found in *pa-la-ḫi-šu-nu* 'their serving' KAJ 1:11, which derives from the root √*plḥ*. A form such as *i-pa-láḫ-šu* 'he will serve him' (Giricano 4:23) confirms the lack of e-colouring. Other examples include: *tu-pa-ša-aḫ-šu* 'you will cool it' (√*pšḥ*) PKT 5 r. 7; *ú-sa-aḫ-ḫi-ru-ni* 'he restored' (√*sḥr*) KAJ 177:9. According to the traditional view, PS /ġ/ changed to ʔ$_{5}$ and inflected the e-colouring (GAG § 23b, 24e). Both aspects have since been disproven as /ġ/ changed equally to /ḫ/ and /ʔ/ in the Akkadian roots, while unconditional e-colouring was "*extremely rare*" (Kogan 2001, 292). Only a few roots with /ġ/, which can be found in

---

6 See GAG, 13 § 9a. I am not entirely convinced by Kouwenberg's (2006, 151) chronological sequence of *iptaḥ* > *iptä*^{y} > *iptē*. A similar kind of e-colouring takes place in Ge'ez, when the gutturals are still present (see Tropper 2002, 36–37). Moreover, as we will discuss below, the change in the genitive *-i(m)* > *-e* took place before the loss of mimation, rather than *-im* > *-e*, indicating that, in Assyrian, vowel changes also took place prior to the loss of consonants.

7 See Kouwenberg (2010, 543); cf. GKT, 26 § 15c; GOA § 18.1.

8 See MPR, 63a n502. Note that CAD Ṭ (83) makes no mention of *ṭāʔinu*.

9 A list of examples was presented by Tropper (1995), while Huehnergard (2003) suggested the use of another PS laryngeal to explain the differentiation in Akkadian.

Akkadian, occur in Assyrian, with *ṣeḫēru* being one of the few.[10] In most instances, /ġ/ appears graphically as <Ḫ>.The presumed e-colouring in the root *ṣeḫēru* (< √*ṣġr*) is more likely to be caused by the radicals /ṣ/ and /r/[11], e.g., *ṣe-eḫ-ru* MAL B § 1:10; *ṣe-ḫe-ra-tu* KTN inventory ii 15; note also without e-colouring *ṣa-ḫa-ra-te* 'the small ones' VAT 9410:32. However, in MA, we also find some examples of /ġ/ > /ʔ/: one reconstructed form of *apāru* (Kogan 2001, 279); *li-t*[*ep-p*]*u-ru-ka* 'they may keep crowning you' Coronation Ritual ii 31.[12] More frequent are forms of the verb *ba*^{ʔʔ}*û* 'to search' (AHw, 145; Kogan 2001, 275). In general, the number of words in MA with the etymologic ġayin is even smaller than in OA, while no direct influence on the surrounding vowels is demonstrable.[13]

§ 167 The position of the word-initial aleph is not entirely clear. However, Kouwenberg (2006, 158) noted that, aside from possible e-colouring, all different etymologic alephs behave the same in OA. We already mentioned that the R_1 aleph had disappeared in the prefix conjugation of I/weak verbs (see § 101). We can also see this loss in the N-stem, where /n/ is visible, rather than assimilated into an aleph, e.g., *li-na-me-ru*$^{!}$ (≠ **li*^{ʔʔ}*amerū*) MATC 11:29. The loss of an aleph continued in substantives of these I/$^{ʔ-ʕ}$ roots, which show no signs of gutturals: ^{f}*mu-um-me-er-ta* (√^{ʔ}*mr*) MAL A § 23:21; *mu-si-pi* (√^{ʔ}*sp*) PKT 1 II left:21. A possible example of a word-initial aleph may be found in *a-na-i-ni* (< *ana mīni*) 'why?'. In this secondary form, /m/ changed to /ʔ/, yet the syllabic boundaries remained. At the same time, some sandhi spellings of PNs show vowel contraction between their succeeding components: ^{m}*Mil-*⸢*ka*⸣*-a-bi* (< Milki-abi) MARV 2 ii 28; ^{d}*A-šur-ke*$^{!}$*-nu-ú-ṣur (*Aššur-kēna-uṣur) KAJ 37:17; ^{Id}UTU-*ki-ti-d*[*i*] (Šamaš-kitti-ide) MARV 4 130:10'; cf. also the following literary passage: *a-na e-mi-it-ta-a-na* ^{giš}BANŠUR (< *ana emitte ana*) Ištar Ritual:2.

§ 168 The nominal constructions of III/weak roots tend to lose their third radical and lengthen the vowel between R_1 and R_2 as compensation for the loss of R_3 (GAG, 19 § 15b; cf. Worthington 2010). This process resembles the behaviour of original bi-radical or II/vowel roots. In MA, we can find this change in the construction *ḫi-i-ṭa* 'punishment' (*ḫīṭu* < *ḫaṭāʔu*) MAL A § 3:39 (and passim MAL A); MARV 4 153:9; *ḫi-pi* 'break' (< *ḫapāʔu*) KTN inventory ii 24; *mu-še* 'night' MATSH 22:6; *ni-še-šu-ma* 'his installation' KAJ 179:20; *ši-i-qí* 'irrigation' MAL B § 17:3; and perhaps *zi-be* 'food offering' (unclear context) MARV 6 75:14'–15'.[14] In the case of *būšu* 'property' (as per AHw, 144; CAD B, 353ff), the situation in MA is not unambiguous. The realization *būšu* 'property' (< **bašāʔu* from *ibašši*)

10 The root *ḫamāṣu* 'to plunder' should be mentioned here. In Arabic, the root is √*ġmṣ* (غمص); however, this is likely a secondary development, as R_1 behaves rather unpredictably in the different Semitic cognate roots. The root is further discussed in n79.

11 See GAG, 13 § 9a; Kouwenberg (2006, 152 § 2).

12 AHw, 57; CAD A_2, 167; UGM, 32. However, Müller reads *li-i*[*p-p*]*i-ru-ka,* while Menzel (1981, T 7) reads *li-t*[*e-pi*]*-ru-ka*.

13 For OA, see Kouwenberg (2006, 151–53 § 2). Notice also *ebāru*, which has been connected to Arabic √*ġrb* (غرب); on the other hand, it is √*ʕrb* in Ugaritic (see AHw, 234). However, it has also been suggested that √*ʕrb* changed to √*ġrb* due to the presence of /r/ close to /ʕ/ (see Nöldeke 1900, 154; Leslau 1987, 69; Kogan 2001, 267–68).

14 Cf. Worthington (2010, 189–90) for a short list of relevant nouns.

is supported in spellings as *bu*$^{!}$*-ši* KAM 10 25:1; *bu-ši-šu* Jankowska 1962 r.4. However, this is made unlikely by the spelling *bu-ši-ú* KAJ 174:5. Other exceptions can be found in ^{giš}*ri-qi-ú* 'aromatic' (*rīqu/riqqu*) T 98-63:5; *ni-qi-a-te* 'offerings (pl.)' KAJ 256:1 (Bab. sg. *nīqu*). In other nouns (e.g., *kūṣu* 'winter'), an original stop causes progressive assimilation (> *kuṣṣu*). The situation of the common noun *marʾu* 'son' (Bab. *māru*) remains unclear for MA. While the noun is exclusively written with the logogram DUMU, the addition of a vocalic sign (e.g., DUMU-*ú* MAL B § 1:10) points to the preservation of the original III/ʾ. For this reason, this study presumes that MA retains the original form *marʾu* (construct *marā*).[15] Meanwhile, in other cases, the aleph may have been lost, such as in the derived form *ma-ru-ti-ša* (*maruttīša*) 'her adoption' KAJ 3:3. As for the feminine form, the direct object DUMU.MUNUS-⸢*šu*$^{!}$⸣-*ma* 'his daughter' can only be read as *mārtušuma*, without the stop retained. Unlike Worthington (2010) for NA, I have found too few examples from MA of such *PāS* nouns in order to make any observations based on quantity. Kouwenberg claims that this type of lengthening does not take place at all in Assyrian.[16] In this case, we would have to explain our few instances differently, perhaps as an example of orthographic vocal metathesis, e.g., *ḫi-i-ṭa=ḫiṭṭa* 'crime'. Moreover, we also find a curious spelling without VA *ḫi-ṭa-šu* (≠ *ḫīṭušu*) 'his punishment' MAL A § 16:66. It is possible that we can interpret the unexpected /a/ as an indication of R_3; *ḫiṭaʾšu*). Nonetheless, Worthington (2010, 183–84) points to the sparseness of Assyrian plene spellings for long vowels and suggests that their absence may actually indicate a shortening of these vowels in later Assyrian, or even to different degrees of vowel length. In any case, Worthington's suggestions here remain just that. The occurrence of such evidence as *bušīu* 'property' and the feature of progressive assimilation of stops, as discussed below, make Kouwenberg's claim more likely.

4.2.1 Semivowel /y/

§ 169 The original PS semivowel /y/ is retained in only a few instances in MA. In some Akkadian grammars, /y/ is also referred to as $ʾ_7$, although it is never realized as a stop. We mostly find the phoneme as a secondary development, while the etymologic /y/ has become rare in MA. In MA cuneiform, there is one basic sign (IA) for all vocalic combinations with /y/, which seems to be a Babylonian influence occurring for the first time in Assyrian in TIM 4 45 *Ap-pa-ie-e* l. 17 and ÌR-^{d}*Še-ru-ia* l. 27. The sign occurs passim in the texts from the Ead/Aub period and earlier documents and is used with all vocalic combinations. In a limited number of instances, we seem to find the value <ya/i/e/u> PI, which is also attested in OB. Note that some sign lists transcribe the value <ia$_8$>.[17] All attestations are in the word-final position, although it is not clear, based on the few attestations available, whether this position is obligatory.

baʾʾuʾu	*ú-ba-ʾa-PI* 'to search for' KAJ 175:38 (EAd/Aub)
rabāyīu	*ra-ba-i-PI* 'fourth rate' KAJ 139:16 (Arn)
šanāyīu	*ša-na-i-PI* 'second rate' KAJ 139:2 (Arn)

15 For OA, Kouwenberg referred to the alternating basis of *merʾ-* and *mār-*, varying between the retained III/ʾ and the original vowel /a/ (GOA § 5.6.3).

16 See Kouwenberg (2006, 164 n40; cf. 2003, 85 n59); (Gelb 1955, 100).

17 Cf. Syllab, no. 223: MZL, no. 598.

Spellings with the combination A+A are rare (cf. W. R. Mayer 2003). They may be regarded as the bisyllabic <aya>, since it consists of two signs similar to IA. This type of spelling has become common in NA (e.g., *a-a-ši* SAA 1, 181:9 ~ *ia-a-ši* SAA 16, 99 r. 5). Perhaps this signals the sound change /iy/ > /ay/.

dayyānu	^{m}*da-a-an-*^{d}x x MARV 1 57 i 31
	da-a-an 'judge' KAV 159:7
	^{d}*A-šur-da-a-an*$^{!}$ AO 20.153:19
yāši	*ana A-A-ši* 'to me' K9-T1:4
nayyālu	^{lú}*na-a-a-lim* 'defaulter' KAV 212:5 (Aub)
Nisbe	EN-*a-a* '*Bēlāya*' (PN) A 1476 r. 6'

§ 170 In the word-initial position of the sign, IA is only found in a limited number of words, most noticeably personal pronouns (e.g., *yāši* 'for me'). As Gelb (1970, 537) points out, the word-initial /y-/ usually disappears in Akkadian, such as in the verbal prefixes (*yiprus* > *iprus*) or nominal forms (*yašarum* > *išarum* 'straight'). The word-initial /y-/ should, therefore, be rejected for all other forms in Akkadian.[18] In Gelb's opinion, the word-initial IA should be read either as <ai> with a variable vowel or even the bisyllabic <ay(y)a>. This bisyllabic reading is possible because the cuneiform sign IA is a composite of I+A, which suggests two successive syllables. At the same time, the presence of the composite I in the composite sign favours tge reading <iy(y)a>, which is in fact supported by MB evidence (Gelb 1970, 538).[19] The suggested sound change /yV/ > /iyV/ is also attested once in the 1cs genitive pronoun *i-iya-ú* MATSH 29:7' (NA *iyû* < *yāʾum*). Similar spellings with an extra initial I sign are also found in Egyptian Akkadian, e.g., *i-ia-nu-um-ma* EA 162:52 (Cochavi-Rainey 2011, 35 § 1.9.1.). In MA, there is one spelling with an additional vocalic suggesting the reading <aya>, rather than <iya>, in the pronoun *a-ia-ši* T 93-17:3 (*yāši* > *ayāši*). It is possible that such spellings result from the assimilated and fossilized preposition *ana*, thus *ana yāši* > *ayyāši*. A monosyllabic reading <ii> or <ai> may be preferred when followed by a vowel (e.g., *IA-a-ši*); however, the syllabic character of Akkadian cuneiform makes a bisyllabic reading more correct (*IA-a-ši=iy/ya/ši*). Some MA pronominal forms started with IA:

yāmattu	*iya-a-ma-at-tu* 'each' KAV 205:29
yāši	*ana iya-a-ši* 'to me' AO 19.227:22
yāʾûm	*iya*$^{!}$*-i*$^{!}$*-e* 'mine' MATSH 17:11'

It is rather unclear how far this change spread across the entire MA lexicon, but it cannot be assumed for all forms without orthographic evidence pointing in that direction. If correct, we may exclude foreign PNs, where this sound change is unlikely to have taken place, e.g., ^{m}*Ia-ap-ša-aḫ* KAJ 171:7; ^{m}*Ia-ab-na-an* MATC 23:9. Note also the plene spelling of the nisbe *I-iu-ú-ra-ie* AO 21.382:4 vs. the normal spelling *Iyi-ú-ri* (see RGTC 5, 145). As type I/i do hardly occur in MA (though note the irregular verb *idāʾu* 'to know'), we cannot determine how /y/ is represented in the stative of the infinitive. A few nouns occurring in

18 Seemingly, the only exceptions in OA are the independent personal pronouns of the first person, i.e., *yāši*, *yaʾum* etc, which should perhaps be interpreted as *iāti*, *iāʾum* instead (see GOA § 3.3.3.2 n58). These exceptions probably ceased in MA; see below.

19 Gelb's claims have been accepted by a number of scholars of NA, most notably Parpola in LAS 2, 139; Hämeen-Anttila in SNAG, 11 § 2.1.3; Luukko (2004, 37ff § 3.9). Cf. UGM, 8f § 5; Reiner (1964); W. R. Mayer (2003, 305f).

MA start with IA, but are traditionally regarded as examples of the reading <ai> instead of <ia>.

Nouns:

ayyakku	'sanctuary' in PN ^{m}*Ayya-a-ku-*⸢ZALÁG⸣*-er* KAJ 17:11
ayyulu	*ayyu-ú-lu* 'deer' KTN inventory i 31; *ayye-e-le*^{meš} RIMA 2 A.0.89.7 iv:20
ayyuru	*ayyu-ú-ru* 'rose' KTN inventory i 14; *ayye-e-re* RIMA 1 A.0.86.1:21; *ayu-ru-ur-t*[*u*$^{?}$] MARV 2, 28:11 (uncertain!); Ì *ayyu-ru-te* MARV 4 146:22'
Ayyaru	^{iti}*Ayye-e-ru* Giricano 2:14; 3:11

In the case of *ayyulu*, this noun is included in CAD A_1 (225–226) as *ayalu*, which is confirmed by a large number of spellings with A+A, rather than IA. The same can be said for *ayyuru* (*ayaru* CAD A_1, 229–230) and *ayyakku* (*ayaku*, CAD A_1, 224–225). The month of *Ayyuru* is mostly spelled as A+IA (*ayaru* CAD A_1, 230). In all examples presented above, we have reconstructed a double /y/, as the sign IA is used word-initially in all instances. If we accept the reading <ai>, representing the initial syllable /ay/, we can only reconstruct another /y/ in the following syllable.

§ 171 In the medial position, the occurrence of the sign IA to indicate /y/ is equally rare. Its use is limited to a few selected nouns and pronouns. In order to indicate the vowel following /y/ in IA, MA often attaches a vowel sign.

asayutu	*a-sa-ia-a-te* 'towers' MATC 4:18[20]
ayyēša	[*a*]*-ie-e-ša* 'whither' KAV 104:11 (< *ayyu+ša*)
	a-ie-e-ša-mi-ni (*ayyēša(m)-mi-ni*) Giricano 12:18'
nayyālu	^{lú}*na-ia-a-li* 'defaulter' KAJ 160:7, 162:4[21] cf. ^{lú}*na-a-a-lim* KAV 212:5
^{m}*Siyutu*	^{m}*Si-ie-e-te* MARV 8 60:1; ^{m}*Si-iu-ú-tu* l. 70 (PN)

Sometimes, no such vowel sign is added and we thus find defective spellings:

mayyālu	*ma-ia-*[*le*] 'bed' MAPD § 17:80; É *ma-ia-li-ia* KAV 102: 7, 14
qa$^{??}$*u*$^{?}$*u* D	*qa-iyi-ni* (*qayyīni*) 'wait for me' Billa 63:20
qayyāpu	*qa-iyi-pa-nu* 'creditors' MAL K § 3:7

As the use of IA remains scarcely attested in MA, in relative terms, such use in these substantives could be strong, as opposed to its representation as a glide in II/ī and III/ī verbs. W. Mayer claimed the opposite, suggesting that IA could also be used for an inlaut aleph (UGM, 20 § 15; cf. W. R. Mayer 2003, 303–305). However, in the examples shown above, IA is used where an etymologic /ī/ can be assumed, making a glide natural. Moreover, no instance is known where IA occurs for etymologic aleph$_{1-5}$. The only example usually written with A-A in Akkadian is *mayyālu* (CAD M_1, 120f); however, even this combination can be used to represent /y/ in other forms of Akkadian (see Mayer 2003).

§ 172 In word endings, /y/ is mostly limited to nisbe endings and the pronominal suffix *-ya* 'mine'. Sometimes, the sign IA directly follows the base of the GN, while, on other

20 Notice its cognates in other Semitic languages: BH *ˀošyā* (אָשְׁיָה); Aramaic *ˀāšīṯā* (אָשִׁיתָא); Arabic *ˀāsiya(tun)* (آسية).

21 The noun is probably connected with the verb *nâlu* 'to lay down', which was originally a II/i verb (Streck 2014a, 112 § 257, e.g., *tá-ni-al* OSP 1 7 i 2 OAkk). For its meaning, see Jakob (2003, 35 n230).

occasions, it is separated by the vowel sign A. These are examples of morphographemic spellings.

Aššurāyu	$^{\text{uru.d}}$*A-šur-a-ia*^{meš} KAV 217:10'; $^{\text{uru.d}}$*A-šur-a-iu* l. 13'; $^{\text{uru.d}}$*A-šur-a-ie*^{meš} l. 16'
Kargamisāyu	^{uru}*Kar-ga-mis-ayu*(IA)-*ú* MATSH 6:2'
Napširāyu	DUMU *Nap-šir-aya* MARV 1 73:10

Spellings with IA in feminine singular nisbe forms do not use the IA signs:

Assurāyittu	^{f}*Aš-šur-*˹*ra*˺*-i-tum* MAL C § 3:20

In attestations of nisbe endings the sign IA does not indicate its vowel quality; hence an extra vowel sign is usually added (Gelb 1970, 542-43), although never to the pronominal suffix *-ya* 'mine'.

Nisbe:

Kilizāyu	^{uru}*Ki-li-za-ie-e* 'the Kilizean' KAJ 158:7
Ninūʾāyu	^{m}*Ni-nu-a-iu-ú* KAJ 92:9 rather than ^{m}*Ni-nu-a-ia-ú*
Suḫāyu	*Su-ḫa-iu-ú* TabT105a-085:1

However, MA sometimes omits this vowel sign. In these instances, we often have to reconstruct case endings by context.

Aššurāyu	*Áš-šu-ra-iu* 'Assyrian' MATC 9:6
Ḫattāyu	*ub-ru Ḫa-ta-iu* 'Hittite envoy' MATC 56:2
Kargamesāyu	LUGAL ^{uru}*Kar-ga-mis-a-ia* 'the Carchemishean king' T 96-1:14-15
Kilizāyātu	*Ki-li-za-i*[*a*]*-tu* (pl. *Kilizāyātu*) T 93-54:21
Ninūʾāyu	^{m}*Ni-nu-a-ie* 'man from Nineveh' KAJ 101:10 cf. ^{m}*Ni-nu-a-iu-ú* MATC 22B:29

As we already stated, the pronominal suffix *-ya* 'mine' is usually written with IA, but does not take an extra vowel sign.

abu	*ab-ba-ú-ia* 'my forefathers' EA 15:9
bētu	É-*ia* 'my house' MAL A § 5:62

§ 173 In word patterns where IA is never used, we could expect the occurrence of /y/ as an allophonic glide. The basic rule for recognizing these is the vocalic sequence /i-e/, plus another vowel, when no etymologic /ʿ–ʾ/ is to be expected. These can be found in various forms of II/ī verbs with either an etymologic /ī/ or a guttural /ḫ–ʿ/ changed into /y/ as a second radical. The occurrence of /ē/ following the first radical appears to have been created out of a diphthong resulting from the second radical (see § 165), e.g., *mu-be-i-še* (*mube*^{yy}*iše* < **mubaḫḫišum*) PKT 4 r. left 4. However, a glide also occurs in some non-verbal or derived forms of type II/ī, e.g., *qe-pu* (< *qiāpu*) MARV 4 31:24). Most are from the demonstrative *anniu* 'this', or III/ī-ē verbs with a vocalic suffix attached, such as:

anniu	*an-ni-ú* 'this' KAJ 48:7
	an-ni-e A 320:20
	an-ni-a MAPD § 21:108
bētu	É : *bi-e-tu* (*biyetu*?) 'house' BVW Ko: 7
ḫapāʾu	*i-ḫa-pí-*[*ú*] 'they will break' KAJ 134:17
ibašši	*i-ba-ši-ú-ni* 'is available' MARV 1 13:12
qabāʾu	*a-qa-bi-a-ku-ni* 'I say to you' T 93-3:5
rabāʾu	*ra-bi-ú* (√*rby*) 'commander(?)' MAL M § 1:4

For a supposed glide between two identical vowels, evidence is more uncertain, e.g., ^{dúg}*ḫar-RI-e* (< *ḫarie* or *ḫarê*) PKT 1 II right:9; *an-NI-e* passim. The NA evidence seems to suggest that intervocalic vowels between /i-e/ need not contract: *an-ni-i-e* (*annie*) SAA 10 39:16.

§ 174 Only rarely do we find the elision of /y/, i.e., when in contact with a preceding consonant. Attestations do occur passim in plural forms of the demonstrative pronoun *anniu*: *annūtu* (< *anniūtu*) and *annātu* (< *anniātu*). Similarly, we always find the quantifying adverb of the number 2 spelled with elision, e.g., *ša-nu-te-šu* (< *šanīuttu*) MAL B § 4:33. Only once do we find the original form in *ša-ni-ú-tu*$^{!}$ T 96-1:6. In verbal forms elision is in fact very rare (e.g., *iq-ti-bi-ú* MATSH 2:58), yet an instance of elision is found in *la-qú-ú-ni* (< *laqyūni*) MAL C+ § 3:21, and possibly in the N-stem preterite: [*ša i*]*b-ba-šu-ni* (< *ibbašyūni*) 'whoever is available' MAPD § 2:16. Examples in nouns are mixed:

bušīu	*bu*$^{!}$*-ši* 'property' KAM 10 25:11
	bu-ši-ú KAJ 174:5
gabīu	$^{\text{na4}}$*ga-bi-ú* 'alum' KAJ 223:1
labiānu	*la-ba-ni* 'neck' Coronation Ritual ii 48
	la-ba-n[*a-t*]*i-ki-na* 'your necks' MARV 3 64:42
masīu	*ma-si-ú-tu* 'washed' KAV 103:23 (Bab. *mesû*)
paṣīu	BABBAR-*e* (*paṣīe*) 'white' MARV 10 3:1
rabīu	GAL-*ú* 'great' MARV 10 82:8

4.2.2 Semivowel /w/

§ 175 Due to the lack of the phoneme /w/ in Sumerian, Akkadian is limited in its means to express this semivowel (GAG, 25 § 21b). For this reason, in some grammars, it is referred to as $^{?}{}_{6}$ (e.g., GAG, 28 § 23b); however, representation as a stop is limited to a few instances. The OA corpus shows that /w/ was still retained as a strong phoneme in the early Assyrian dialect, as we find it frequently expressed with the sign PI in inlaut as well as intervocalic words (GKT, 38f § 25a; GOA § 3.3.2.4). This use of the sign PI for /w/ continued in some WPA dialects, where it was only rarely used for the actual labial /p/ (e.g., UgAkk: Huehnergard 1989, 35). However, in core Akkadian, we find /w/ expressed with <M> in MB and <B> in MA; additionally, spellings occur where /b/ is omitted or changed into /u/. It is questionable as to what extent these spellings were merely orthographic or if they represented a phonetic change. In spellings of adjectival numbers (such as *ša-na-i-PI* KAJ 139:2; *ra-ba-i-PI* KAJ 139:16; *ú-ba-*$^{?}$*a-PI* KAJ 175:38), it is probably better to assume the reading <yV>. True examples of <wV> (PI) could be found in two PNs. The first is *I-din-*^{d}*We-e*[*r*] LVUH 45:25, which is usually represented as Bēr in the MA onomasticon.[22] Saporetti also suggested the foreign PN ^{m}*E-šu-WA-ra*, the king of Cyprus, in RS 20.18:1 (OMA 1, 214–15). However, as discussed above (§ 40), this letter is not Assyrian.

§ 176 In the initial position, /w/ is usually reduced to a vowel: *(u)wa-* > *u-* (e.g., *wabālu* > *ubālu*) and /iw/ > /u/ (*iwbil* > *ubil*). Given this sound change, verbal roots of the type I/w

22 This reading by Röllig may be incorrect as, following the sign DIN, the copy of the text reads PA rather than DINGIR. The reading is based on the patrimony of the eponym Aššur-mušabši (l. 24), which is attested as having been Iddin-Wēr (e.g., KAJ 116 r. 6, collated by Postgate in UŠA no. 74). As such, I offer no better reading.

are written with *u*-, e.g., *ušābu* < *wašābu(m)*. These verbal forms are discussed in § 609. In nominal forms, this sound change is found in a number of *PaRS* pattern words.

ubru	^{lú}*ub-ri* 'foreigner' MAL L § 2:5 (< *wabru*, cf. OA *ub-ri* KUG 24:10)
	ub-ru MATC 23b:8
urdu	^{m}*Ur-di* 'slave' MARV 4 5:1 (< *wardu*)
	ur-di T 02-32:31
urḫu	*ur-ḫi* 'month' TabT05a-134:19
urku	*ur-ki* 'after' MAL B § 1:7; MATSH 2:3
urqu	*ur-qí* 'vegetables' MAL B § 13:21 cf. *ur-qi* MARV 3 16 i 18', but notice also *er-qa* 'green' KAV 98:19

Note that the sound change *wa-* > *u-* already started in OA, judging by some alternating spellings, such as *wardum* for 'slave': *wa-ar-di* BIN 4 200:5; *ur-dim* CCT 3 12a:13, but *bar-dí-šu* CCT 4 6b 14 (GKT, 41 § 26e; cf. GOA § 3.3.2.3).[23] From Hurrian(?) we find the following loans: É *ut-na-na-[te]* KAJ 306:2; ^{giš}*ut-na-na-a-tu* MATSH 10:14 < Hurr. *u̯atnann-* (cf. Deller 1987, 61–62; von Soden 1988; MATSH, 152f; Richter 2012, 307–8). When word-initial /w/ is followed by a long vowel, it simply drops off; thus, we find a number of instances of *wā-* > *ā-*.

ālidānu	*a-li-da-ni-šu* 'his begetter' MAL A § 28:9
(w)āṣû	*a-ṣi-e* 'departure' Billa 62:5
āšīpu	*a-ši-pi* 'exorcist' (√*wašāpu*) MARV 1 5:2

In this light, we can also present the various adjectival forms of the verb *wiāṣum* 'to be little/small', which probably had either /ḥ/ or /ˁ/ as R_2 because we find e-colouring in all attested forms. It seems that the adjective underwent the following changes: *waˁṣum* > *weˀṣum* > *ēṣu*. The reconstructed *ēṣu* is supported by the obscure plene spelling: *i*$^{!}$*-e-eṣ*$^{!}$AO 19.228:8'. This reconstruction would also explain the attestation *e-a-ṣi* (MAL C § 8:8), which von Soden analysed as an infinitive (AHw, 1496). Under this assumption, the second syllable remained lengthened and unaffected by e-colouring: *waˁāṣum* > *eˀāṣu*. Other examples are more uniform:

eˀāṣu	*e-a-ṣi* MAL C § 8:8
ēṣu	*e-ṣú* KAJ 149:3; KAJ 174:7
	i$^{!}$*-e-eṣ*$^{!}$AO 19.228:8'
ēṣuttu	*e-ṣu-tum* KAJ 8:9; TR 105:9
	e-ṣú-tum KAJ 32:5
	e-ṣu-tu TR 3025:16

Sometimes, variation took place, which is attested in a few instances of the GN Waššukannu, usually written with an *a-* prefix; however, on two occasions, we find the expected Assyrian sound change *wa-* > *u-*.

Waššukannu	^{uru}*Áš-šu-ka-ni* MARV 5 10:16 (Ad$^{?}$); MATSH 2:58; MATC 55:6
	^{uru}*Áš-šu-ka-an-ni* MATC 57:11
	⌜*Uš*⌝*-šu-ka-nu* MARV 5 2:17 (Nae$^{?}$); ⌜^{uru}*Uš-šu*⌝*-ka-nu* MARV 7 93:6 (Tp)

Although the two attestations spelling *Uššukannu* are from the ltter period, they are too few in number to 'date' a possible sound change in this GN. The city is already spelled with a *u-* in an Adad-nērārī I royal inscription:

---

23 For the so-called *birdum* (sic = *pirdum*) instead of *wardum* 'slave', readings of Hecker, see for instance Farber 2001, 142.

Waššukannu ^{uru}*Uš-ša-ka-na* RIMA 1 A.0.76.3:30

Twice, we find this GN with aphesis. If the syllable had dropped off in MA vernacular, both variations would have been artificial. In any case, the city was known in NA by the simplified spelling Sikan.

Waššukannu *Šu-ka-nu* MARV 5 1:16 (Nae$^{?}$); MARV 5 64:9 (Nae$^{?}$)

Some substantives of I/w roots appear to be bi-radical; these forms never had the initial *w*- (see Kouwenberg 2010, 460), e.g., *li-da-ni-ša* 'her children' KAV 211:4; [*b*]*i-la-at* A.ŠÀ 'yield of the field' KAJ 81:20; *ṣi-it* 'offspring' Hall 1983:7. There is one example of the word-initial *wa*- > *mu*-, which is possibly an erroneous spelling: *mus-ba-a-ku* (< *wašbāku*) TR 2083a+:9.[24] No similar spellings for I/w statives exist. However, the following fragment from an incantation should be noted: *ši-ik-na-te-mu-tu-rat* (*šiknāte utturat*) Rm 376:20. According to Veldhuis (1991, 63), the unexpected appearance of /m/, representing /w/, could only be explained as occurring in sandhi spelling with the previous word. If these examples are correct, we may assume that MA did indeed retain the word-initial /w/, but omitted it from the orthography.

§ 177 A number of uncontracted vowels shows a sequence of /u/+/a/, where /w/ is retained as a glide (Reiner 1966, 36; GAG, 26 § 21h). The semivowel /w/ in these instances is not etymologic but is used to ease the pronunciation of a sequence of two different vowels. This is visible in the G-stem of the weak verbs II/w: *duāku*; *kuānu*; *kuāšu; muātu; puāgu; quālu*; *suāku; tuāru; zuāzu*. In general, the glide /w/ manifests itself in the present and infinitive of the G-stem in a typical /u/ following the first radical. An interpretation of a glide over an aleph is furthermore strengthened by the OA evidence, where II/w is sometimes spelled with the sign PI, e.g., *i-tù-wa-ar* EL 105:9; *i-du-wa-ak* TCL 21 253:16. No glide is found in derived stems, such as D and Š, where the etymologic R_2 has become indifferent. This class of verbs will be discussed in detail in § 561ff. Reconstructed /w/ glides in oblique/dative personal pronouns (e.g., *šu(*^{w}*)ātu*) are equally not etymologic, but a secondary development (see § 354). We may also note the GN Nineveh (*Ninuwā*), with spellings such as ^{uru}*Ni-nu-a* MARV 8 47:41 (et passim) vs. OA *Ni-nu-wa-a*^{ki} RIMA 1 A.039.2 ii 11 (Šamšī-Adad I royal inscription) (see Lipiński 2001, 121 § 11.12); however, note the contraction in PN ⌜^{m}⌝*I*-⌜*sa*$^{!}$⌝-*na-at-ša*-^{uru}*Ni-na-a* MPR 40:6.

§ 178 Often, we find the etymologic /w/ represented as <B> in the orthography (e.g., UGM, 19f; GAG § 21d; Kouwenberg 2008, 169f). As both /b/ and /w/ are labials, one could argue for the sound change /w/ > /b/ being the cause of this new graphic representation. On the other hand, such a phonemic shift is rare in the classical Semitic languages; therefore, the change is probably graphic (see Lipiński 2001, 121 § 11.12).[25] The representation of <B>

24 The reading is as suggested by Postgate (1979b, 92). The change /w/ > /m/ in I/w verbs may very well be a Mittani/Hurrian influence. Cf. the following Mittani attestations: *um-te-eš-šìr-šu-nu* (Cooper/Schwartz/Westbrook 2005:6); ⌜*ú-ma-ʾa-ar*⌝ l. 15. See also the royal correspondence of Tušratta (Adler 1976, 44-45). This is analogous to MB (Adler 1955, 32).

25 The only case of the shift /w/ > /b/ known to me occurs in Samaritan Hebrew, e.g., *bayle* (ויילה) 'woe to him' (see Tal 2013, 26–27 § 2.2.2).

may have derived from spirantization, which is a common feature in Semitic languages. According to traditional grammar, Akkadian was perhaps be the only Semitic language where no spirantization/lenition took place.[26] However, a degree of spirantization involving /k/ and /m/ can reasonably be assumed (see § 207 and § 233). The spelling of /w/ through <B> led von Soden (1968, 216) to the conclusion that the etymologic /b/ was spirantized to /ḇ/ or /v/ on a regular basis in MA.[27] The fricative labial /v/ is close to /w/, while it is not unthinkable that /v/ developed further into /w/. Note Ṭuroyo, where the spirantized /b/ > /v/ > /w/, when preceded by a vowel, developed into /u/ (e.g., ptc. *kōteḇ* > *kōtew* > *kōtu*, Jastrow 1992, 16, 40). 28 As the written <B> does not seem to colour preceding /a/ into /u/, it seems likely that the sound change /aw/ > /u/ was no longer productive in MA. Evidence of the orthographic <B> used for the etymologic /w/ is already attested during the OA period,[29] and it seems that MA uses *-be* (BAD) in order to express the genitive Hurrian suffix *-ve* in proper names.[30] It is unfortunate that there is no evidence for the etymologic /b/ being spirantized; however, the orthographic representation of the etymologic [w] shows that this must have happened fairly frequently. Examples of /w/ > /b/ are given below:

abātu	*a-bat* 'case' passim.
	a-ba-a-te 'words' Tsukimoto 1992 D:7
bābu[31]	md*Ba-bu*-ŠEŠ-SUM-*na-ma* (Bābu-aḫa-iddina) KAV 105:4
	mKÁ-A-PAP (Bābu-aḫa-iddina) KAV 104:5
šabiru	*ša-be-ru* 'ring' MATC 63:5
šubāʾu	*šu-ba-e* 'roasting pan' KAJ 303:7
ṭibittu	*ṭí-be-ta* 'yarn, twine' (Bab. *ṭimītu* < *ṭawû*) MATSH 7:17'

Instances of the orthographic <B> for the word-initial /w/ are rather limited. They are largely limited to the DN Wēr. The noun *biblu* (√*wbl*) 'dowry' could be a Babylonian loan and, if so, would not be representative for MA.

biblu (√*wbl*)	*bi-ib-la* 'marriage gift' MAL A § 30:21
Bēr[32]	d*Be-er* (DN *Wēr*), e.g., md*Be-er*-PAP MARV 6, 29:16 cf. Ḫana text m*Ṣíl-lí*-d*Me-er* Kümmel 1989:9 and *I-din*-d*Me-er* KAJ 116:17'; m.gišTUKUL-*ti*-d*Me-er* DeZ 3281:14.

26 See von Soden (1968, 214). Central and South Semitic languages, such as Arabic and Ge'ez, feature the standardized change /p/ > /f/. Northwest Semitic Canaanite and Aramaic feature a complex system of spirantization of BGDKPT letters. For this phenomenon, see Muraoka (2006, 76f § 19). Spirantization in Ugaritic is not certain, but the phonology of Ugaritic is a problem in itself.

27 In OA, there are some spellings where the intervocalic /b/ is written as <W>, including with broken spellings (see GOA § 3.2.5.3). The spirantization of /b/ is also expected to occur in NB, where the etymologic /b/ sometimes disappears in broken spellings, which seems to suggest a glide (see W. R Mayer 1992, 51).

28 Ṭuroyo is notable because of the merging of both the etymologic /w/ and /v/ from the spirantized B into one phoneme, /w/. Similarly, Mlaḥsô retains the differentiation (see Jastrow 1994, 19).

29 See GKT, 41 § 26e. Note that *berdum* has since been proven to be a type of horse. See CAD P, 394f: Farber 2001, 142.

30 See UGM, 20 § 14.2. The same phenomenon was also noted in Nuzi-Akkadian, see Chiera/Speiser 1924/25, 77. For the Hurrian genitive suffix *-ve*, see Hazenbos 2007, 144–46 § 2.2.3; Wegner 2007, 65 § 2.2.4; Wilhelm 2008, 93-94 § 4.4.9. In Hurrian, the genitive is usually spelled with PI, e.g., *ni-ḫa-a-ri-i-we* (*niḫar=i=ve*) EA 24 iii 36 (see Wegner 2007, 160, 162). Some examples in MA: uru*Ḫar-be* MATC 4:4; uru*Pa-an-di-be* MATC 81:6; uru*qu-a-be* KAJ 158:11; uru*Ši-ba-ni-be* Billa 2:8.

31 For a discussion of the DN Bābu < *Ba(w)u*, see von Soden (1968, 216).

32 The original form Wēr is based on OA spellings of the theophoric element in PNs (see UGM, 20 no. 2; cf. Hirsch 1972, 34b).

cf. also *I-din-*^{d}*We-e*[*r*] LVUH 45:25

In etymologic II/w verbs, /w/ remained strong, but changed into /b/, caused by a weak third and/or first radical. Admittedly, the examples are numerous, but mostly limited to instances of one verb with the substantives *lawāʾu* > *labāʾu* (Kouwenberg 2010, 474 n98):[33]

labāʾu	*ta-la-bi* 'you will surround' BVW F:7, H:9; T:1
	il-bi 'he surrounded' MAL B § 20:19
	lā il-bi 'he did not surround' Maul 1992, 23:5, *al-be* p. 24:8, *lu al-bi* p. 38:6 (Māri)
libītu	*li-be-et* IGI^{meš}-*šu-nu* 'the rim of their eyes' KTN inventory i 19
	li-be-t[*e*] 'area' MATSH 13:21
nalbētu	*na-al-be-ta* 'wrap' KAV 99:17

§ 179 Bloch (2017, 121) has suggested that the verbal forms of the, otherwise unknown, verb *ḫabāqu* have to be represented in terms of another example of a strong II/w verb. A problem with his argument is the connection made between this verb and the lexically attested NB *ḫuāqu/ḫâqu*, which is a weak II/ū, rather than a strong II/w verb (cf. AHw, 322b; CAH Ḫ, 87a). Moreover, other grammarians have clearly demonstrated that II/w can only have a strong R_2, where either or both R_1 is /n/, or R_3 is weak (GAG, 179 § 104b; Kouwenberg 2010, 474 n98). I do not wish to reject Bloch's claim outright, especially given the lack of a better solution for this verb. It should, however, be stated emphatically that the proposed etymology and behaviour of this verb go against the grammatical rules of both MA and Akkadian in general. Moreover, as the foundations of Bloch's claim lay in two lexical NB texts, the connection is anything but necessary. Basically, the representation of /b/ seems little more than a scribal convenience where the limited sign PI was replaced with the more flexible BA series. It also shows that /b/ became close in pronunciation to /w/, so that /b/ was probably spirantized on a regular basis.

§ 180 We have seen how the intervocalic /w/ is represented as <B> in MA cuneiform; however, there is one notable exception. The noun and derivations from *awīlu* 'man' are represented by broken spellings where no consonant is indicated. Attestations are few, but occur in different text genres:

aʾīlu	*a-i-la* 'man' MAL A § 15:52
	a-i-lu-šu-⸢*nu*⸣ 'their man' MATSH 19:1'†
aʾīluttu	*a-i-lu-ut-te* 'men' T 93-2:9
	a-i-lu-ut-t[*e*] MARV 4 151:18

It is clear that there is a direct relation between similar spellings for nouns where the intervocalic /m/ disappears (see § 233). According to Reiner (1966, 113f n1), this MA form derives from an MB loan (*amīlu*) 'man', where the intervocalic /m/ had elided.[34] This is not very likely since the representation of /w/ as <M> is just as orthographic as MA <B> (W. R. Mayer 1992, 48–54). The broken spellings are caused by the vocalic sequence /a+i/,

33 The only possible exception is the verb *ṭaʾāʾu* 'to spin, braid' (√*ṭwī*, AHw, 1382b), which may be attested twice in the unpublished VAT 19544 as an infinitive [*a-n*]*a ṭa-ʾa-e* l. 15, and as a present 3ms *i-ṭa-ʾe* l. 16. A full publication of the said text is necessary to be certain. Admittedly, even if correct, one may argue that R_2/w is still strong, but realized as an aleph.

34 Cf. OA *a-mì-lá-ni* 'we are lord' BIN 4 33:51 (GKT, 41 § 26e). The use of MI could be a misreading or a scribal mistake for similar iterations of PI. None of the other studies of the text refers to this form, but do read as PI (e.g., Ichisar 1981, 398ff).

where /w/ was probably realized as a glide. This explains the difference with spellings such as *abātu* 'word', although notice the exception *ša-be-ru* 'ring' (Bab. *šawiru*) MATC 63:5. However, this exception also shows that there was a (phonetic) difference between the reflexes of etymologic /w/ in *šabiru* and *a*$^{?}$*īlu*, at least according to the interpretation of the scribes.

§ 181 While have listed attestations for the verb *lawā*$^{?}$*u* > *labā*$^{?}$*u*, another II/w verbal root shows the Babylonian sound change /w/ > /m/; *nawāru* > *namāru*.[35] We find one instance in the stative with additional substantives. It is not unthinkable that the verb is a Babylonian loan similar to *biblu* 'dowry'. In OA, the root had already become *namāru*, e.g., (*i-na-me-er* TCL 19 13:17), so the change was not recent. In fact, Edzard (1994) argued that √*nmr*, as a secondary root, gradually replaced √*nwr*.

namāru	*nam-ra-tu-ni* 'it is bright' Ištar Ritual:12
	i+na na-ma-re 'at dawn' MATSH 2:23; PKT 3 i 8
nāmurātu	*na-mu-ra-a-tu* 'audience gifts' (sg. *nāmurtu*) Coronation Ritual iii 7
kannamāri	*ka-na-ma-ri* 'early morning' (< *kal+namāre*) MATC 1:5

The occurrence of sandhis, such as *ka-na-ma-ri* (< *kal-namāri* 'in the early morning' § 491) MATC 1:5 suggests once more that the /m/ in *namāru* was part of the spoken language. It should be noted that the NB evidence suggests that /w/ written <M> was still pronounced as /w/, while at the same time, intervocalic /m/ appears to be pronounced /w/ as well.[36] Another example of /w/ > /m/ is found in the Hurrian loan *re-eš ḫa-me-lu-ḫi* 'head of the *ḫawalḫu*' Coronation Ritual ii 42, where this noun derives from *ḫalw+uḫli* (cf. Richter 2012, 123). Quite exceptional is *a-ma-te*^{meš}*-ia* SIG$_5$^{meš}*-te* 'good words' RS 06.198:18. Perhaps, here, we should read <ba!> instead of <ma>; the same applies to *a-*[*ma*]*s-su-ú-na* (< *abāt-šunu*) 'their words' T 04-35:12 (see Minx 2005, 95 no. 84). One other instance of the II/w > II/m substantive can be found, but its context remains unclear: *na-mu-ut-ta* MAPD § 19:92 (< *nawātu*, CAD N$_1$, 255–56). It is not unlikely that both roots occurred in MA as Babylonian loans, where the intervocalic /*w*/ is usually represented by <M> (Aro 1955a, 32f; GAG, 26 § 21d). The difference between <B> (< /w/) and <M> (< /w/) may not have only been logographic, as indicated by the orthographic variation of the DN Wēr in PNs. Texts consequently use Mēr for people from Ḫana and Māri (e.g., $^{m.giš}$TUKUL-*ti*-^{d}*Me-er* DeZ 3281:14), rather than the expected Bēr (e.g., ^{md}*Be-er-iš-ma-ni* MARV 1 47:55).

4.2.3 Etymologic aleph and ayin

§ 182 As mentioned above, aleph and ayin are both represented as strong stops in MA. The only difference between the two is the e-colouring of the preceding short /a/ before ayin. In order to express both gutturals, the sign $^{?}$A is introduced in MA and can be used for any vC or Cv combination. Early attestations of the value are already found in TIM 4 45, with one example from the Ead/Aub period: *ú-ba-*$^{?}$*a-PI* KAJ 175:38. It was most often used in roots with etymologic $^{?}{}_{1}$, e.g., *i-ša-*$^{?}$*a-al* MAL O § 5:8; *ša-a*$^{?}$*-la* KAV 107:19; *ṣa-al-*$^{?}$*a-at* Coronation Ritual ii 46, as well as roots with ayin, e.g., *ra-*$^{?}$*e-e* (√*r*^{ʕ}*i*) KAJ 127:12.

35 It must be admitted that the etymologies presented by von Soden (AHw, 768) are not unambiguous, although it seems unlikely that /m/ was the original R$_2$. Note that forms with <B> are actually attested in some PNs from OB texts (see Edzard 1994, 7 n11, 11–14).

36 See W. R. Mayer 1992, 48–54; Blasberg 1997, 126–31.

Surprisingly, the aleph sign is also used for elided /m/ and /n/ (see § 233). In verbal forms, ˀA is mostly limited to II/ˤ–ˀ forms; they are sometimes found in III/ˤ–ˀ statives, but rarely in prefix conjugations (both only literary) and never for I/ˤ–ˀ verbs. When the aleph is intervocalic, sometimes an extra vowel sign is added after the aleph sign ˀA. This does not necessarily indicate a long vowel, but is an extra designation of the vowel colour. This characteristic is typical for MB.[37] In a few cases, an extra vowel sign precedes ˀA.

laˀāˀu	*i-la-ˀe-e* 'he is able' MAL A § 18:76; MAL N § 2:8; cf. *i-la-a-ˀe-e* § 19:88
	i-la-ˀu-ú-ni MAL A § 47:20
mazāˀu D	*ú-ma-an-ze-e-eˀ-ši* 'he intends to rape her' MAL A § 55:22
	ana ma-an-zu-ú-ˀe 'for raping' MAL A § 55:26
qaˀˀuˀu D	*tu-qa-ˀa-a* 'she will wait' MAL A § 36:98
šaˀālu	*i-ša-ˀa-a-al* 'he will ask' MAL A § 48:35; 39; B § 17:13 cf. *i-ša-ˀa-al* MAL O § 5:8
	i-ša-ˀu-ú-lu MAL A § 45:63
šaˀāˀu	[*ni*]-*il-ta-ˀe-e-ma* 'we have sought' MATSH 18:34[38]

As can be observed, most of these attestations come from MAL texts. In other texts, extra vowel signs are often omitted.

ṣaˀālu	*la-a i-ṣe-ˀa-la* 'he will not quarrel(?)' MARV 8 62:6
šāˀālu	*la-a iš-ˀu-lu-n*[*i*] (*lā išˀulūni*) 'he asked' MAPD § 3:25
	al-ta-ˀa-al Billa 62:8
šaˀmu	10$^{?!}$ *li-tu* (…) [*š*]*a-aˀ-ma-tu* 'ten bought cows' AO 21.157:1-2

We frequently find a vowel sign instead of ˀA in order to express an etymologic aleph and ayin, a scribal practice already in use in OA.

maˀādu	*ma-a-ad-ma* 'much' MAL C+ § 8:8
	ma-a-di (*maˀdu*) MARV 4 151:22
šaˀālu	*ni-ša-a-al* 'we will ask' MATSH 2:60
	ša-a-li MAL F § 2:10 cf. *ša-ˀa-a-li* MAPD § 6:44

It will come as no surprise that the spellings with Aˀ(+V) are mostly limited to the literary texts, and MAL A–B specifically. Even the sign ˀA is relatively rare in private archives where an extra vowel sign seems to be the preferred way to spell aleph. Aside from writing ˀA and/or a vowel sign for stops, it is also possible to simply use a vC /V sign if it follows another consonant or vowel.

kalāˀu	*ik-kal-ú-ni* 'he was held' MAL A § 36:105
marˀuttu	*mar-ú-ut-ti* 'adoption' KAJ 1:6
nadāˀu	*na-ad-at* 'it is laid down' KAM 10 31:11
pirˀu	*pír-e* 'shoot' KTN inventory i 3 cf. *pi-ir-ˀi* l. 9
ṣabˀu	*ṣab-e* 'troops' MATC 11:28
ṣalāˀu	*ṣi-il-a* (*ṣilˀā*) 'lay down' KAV 98:25
	ṣi-il-a-šu-nu (*ṣilˀaššunu*) MATC 3:5

The cuneiform syllabary does not allow for the gemination of the aleph. However, there is no reason to assume that the aleph does not geminate in II/ˤ–ˀ verbs. Hämeen-Anttila claimed that, in NA, the sign ˀA was mostly used for a geminated aleph (SNAG, 13–4 §

37 See Aro 1955a, 21; Stein 2000, 18.

38 Streck (1997, 275) claims that this form derives from *labāˀu*. This cannot be accepted for two reasons. Firstly, etymologic /b/ is always written <B> for this root (cf. § 178). Secondly, etymologic /w/ is never written <ˀ> in MA.

2.1.4). This does not follow on from MA (e.g., the infinitive *ša-ʾa-a-li* MAPD § 6:44; the perfect *al-ta-ʾa-al* Billa 62:8); even Hämeen-Anttila has to cite a number of exceptions in NA. The aleph sign is never used in any form of the demonstrative *anniu*, with a glide /y/ probably expected here.

§ 183 As we discussed above, e-colouring took place when /a/ precedes or follows an etymologic ayin. As such, it is attested in the limited group of I/ˁ verbs, e.g., *la-a er-ru-bu* T 04-35:5; *e-zi-ba-ni* 'I left' MATC 3:23. There are no II/ˁ known in MA, but, for III/ˁ, the verbs *šamāʾu* 'to hear' and *raʾāʾu* 'to pasture' show e-colouring.

raʾāʾu	*i-re-a* 'they will pasture' KAJ 88:17
šamāʾu	*ta-áš-me-ú-ni* 'she heard' MAPD § 14:72
	[*a*]*l-te-me-ma* 'I have heard' MATSH 4:4'
	a-šam-me 'I will hear' KAV 96:16

However, exceptions exist as well; as for *raʾāʾu*, there are also attestations without e-colouring. For a discussion of this verb, see § 587.

raʾāʾu	*RA-ʾa-e* 'pasturing' KAJ 127:12
	i-ra-ʾu-ši 'he pastured her' Rm 376:23 (incantation)

§ 184 We already mentioned that aleph and ayin are represented as a stop, usually written with an aleph or an extra vowel sign. However, there is a number of instances where this stop is lost, some of which are predictable, and some not. Verbs with an etymologic I/ˀ–ˁ root lost their guttural, which initially caused the lengthening of the vowel preceding the second radical before being shortened again (cf. § 101). This loss continued in the substantives of these I/ˀ–ˁ roots, which show no sign of gutturals: ^{f}*mu-um-me-er-ta* MAL A § 23:21; *mu-si-pi* PKT 1 II left:21 (√*ˀsp*). In general, it can be stated that a post-consonantal aleph is usually retained.

garāʾu	*ga-ar-ʾa-at* 'she quarrelled' MAPD § 21:104
malʾutu	*ma-al-ʾu-tu* 'full' MARV 7 5 r. 3'†
marʾu	*mar*$_5$*-e* 'son' MAL A § 43:32
marʾuttu	*mar-ú-ut-ti* 'adoption' KAJ 1:6
nadāʾu	*na-ad-at* 'it is put down' KAM 10 31:11
pirʾu	*pír-ʾa* 'student' MATC 1:4
ṣalāʾu	*ṣa-al-ʾa-at* 'it is set up' Coronation Ritual ii 46
šaʾālu	*lā iš-ʾu-lu-n*[*i*] *išʾulūni*) 'he did not ask' MAPD § 3:25
tamāʾu	*ta-am-ʾa-a-ta-*(*a-ni*) 'you swore' MAL A § 47:27, 30, 31

However, MA demonstrates a number of exceptions where the aleph assimilates into the preceding consonant. Most notable is the common stative *na-aṣ-ṣu* 'they brought' (inf. *našāʾu*), which developed as a result of /s/ (< /š/)+/ˀ/ becoming indistinguishable from the geminated /ṣ/ [s']. It seems likely that progressive assimilation also occurred with other non-emphatic consonants and in nouns. Kouwenberg pointed to one of the earliest occurrences of the month name *ṣippu* (< *ṣip'u*), already present in OA (e.g., MA ^{iti}*Ṣi-ip-pu* MARV 8 84:11). However, a rare attestation with the aleph retained can be found in MA: ^{iti}*Ṣi-ip-ú* KAJ 4:32 (EAd/Aub). Another example is the noun *ku-uṣ-ṣu* (< *kūṣʾu*) 'winter' BVW Ko r. 17; *na-ma-te* (< **namʾadtu* from *maʾādu*) KAJ 146:6. The gemination of the preceding consonant keeps the syllabic structure of these forms intact. A selected list of examples of verbs with progressive assimilation can be given:

marˀuttu	[*m*]*a-ru-ut-ti-šu* 'adoption' KAJ 4:7, but *mar-ú-ut-ti* KAJ 1:6
maṣāˀu	*ma-ṣa-ta* (< *maṣˀāta*) 'you are able' MARV 1 15:13
nadāˀu	*na-ṭa-a*[*t*] (*naṭṭat* < *nadˀat*) 'it is laid down' Billa 19:24
našāˀu	*na-ṣa* 'it is brought' MARV 7 5:8
	na-aṣ-ṣú-ni TabT105A-151:12
	it-ta-ṣu KAV 98:45
	i-ta-ṣu MARV 7 7:3
salāˀu	*la sa-la-ku* 'I am no slanderer' KAV 169:7
šaˀāmu	*i-ša-mu-ú-ni* (*iššamūni*) 'he bought' KAJ 175:25 (EAd/Aub)
uṣāˀu	*ú-ṣa-an-ni* A 3196 (NTA, 39):22
	uṣ-ṣa-ni Giricano 4:21
uṣāˀu Š	*ú-še-ṣu-ni* 'they let go out' Adad Ritual:1

In NA, the progressive assimilation of the aleph has become common, although variation can be found in the attested nouns.[39]

§ 185 In many spellings, it is not clear from the orthography whether the aleph was retained or not. This confusion can occur when the aleph appears in the syllable-final position, e.g., *ma-di-iš=mādiš/maˀdiš* < *maˀdiš* A 845:9. Kouwenberg (2006, 159–61) argued that stops in the syllable-final position would naturally be weak and were therefore bound to have dropped off. This is, of course, attested in the prefix conjugation of all I/ˁ-ˀ verbs, where R_1 had disappeared completely. Otherwise, it is difficult to confirm, since gutturals in the final position are most often not indicated in orthography. We may assume that the aleph is retained in *ik-la-šu* (*iklaˀšu*) MAL B § 19:6† from the verb *kalāˀu*, since this form does not feature VA. There are a few cases of II/ˀ verbs where the MA orthography suggests the preservation of the aleph where it disappeared from OA: the imperative *ša-aˀ-la* (< OA *šālā*) KAV 107:99 and ⸢*il-ta*⸣*-aˀ-la-ni* (< OA *ištālanni*) MATC 15:12 are rare examples that indicate the aleph was retained in the syllable-final position. At the same time, the aleph is weakened in forms of the verb *šaˀāmu* 'to buy' in *i-ša-mu-ú-ni* (*išāmūni*) KAJ 175:25, and similarly in *i-ša-mu-ši* KAV 195+:18 vs. the adjective [*š*]*a-aˀ-ma-tu* (*šaˀmātu*) '(10) bought (cows)' AO 21.157:2. It is easier to believe that the reintroduction of the aleph in the verb *šaˀālu* is a scribal analogy for the forms without a suffix than believing that MA had strengthened the aleph, which was lost in OA. It may be noted that all attestations of *šāˀālu* in MA demonstrate aleph spellings, even where the *šaˀāmu* spellings do not (see Kouwenberg 2006, 160; 2010, 561–62). However, the contradictory evidence continued into the NA period, e.g., *i-sa-aˀ-lu-šú* for OA *ištāl-šu* (SNAG, 13 § 2.1.4); also note the III/ˀ verb *našāˀu*: *i-ši-iš-šu* (*iššiššu* < *inšiˀ-šu*†) KAJ 179:4.

4.2.4 Laryngeals /h/ and /ḥ/

§ 186 As we have already discussed above, both /ḥ/ and /h/ disappeared from Assyrian; however, the etymologic /ḥ/ is still visible through e-colouring, even in the secondary

39 For NA, see: Parpola (1974, 3 n10) (cf. Deller 1967); Parpola (1984, 206f n39); SNAG, 13 § 2.1.4. Cf. also Kouwenberg (2010, 580), but note that the MA text quoted by him is actually a NA ritual: [*i*]*t-tab-bu* < *ittabˀū* PKT 15a:13'.

stems.[40] This sound change is significant in the roots of etymologic II/ḥ and III/ḥ verbs, where e-colouring differentiates them from II/ī and III/ī verbs (see § 561ff and § 573ff).

baʾāšu D	*tu-be-áš* 'you will stir' PKT 1 II right:17 (cf. Syriac √*bḥš* ܒܚܫ)
laqāʾu	*i-laq-qé-e-ši* (√*lqḥ*) 'he will take her' MAL A § 5:68
patāʾu	*ip-TI-ú-ni* (√*ptḥ*) 'he opened' MARV 3, 23 r. 7
ṭeʾānu	*ṭé-a-ni* (√*ṭḥn*) 'grinding' KAJ 318:7

Of these attestations, the D-stem *tubeʾʾaš* 'you will stir' is significant, as it is the only case in MA where R_2/ḥ is visible in the D-stem by e-colouring. This is attested in more forms of the same text: *tu-be-šú-ni-ma* PKT 4 r. left 5; [*t*]*u-be-a-áš* PKT 1 I right:17; *mu-be-i-še* (*mube*^{yy}*iše* < *mubaḥḥišum**) PKT 4 r. left 4 (cf. OA in GOA § 18.8). In the case of /h/, e-colouring is absent, e.g., *na-ar-te* 'river' KAJ 129:12; *i-lak* MATSH 16:15. What is unusual is the occurrence of an aleph for the etymologic /ḥ/ in *peʾettu* 'charcoal:' *pe-ʾe-et-ta* 'charcoal' PKT 1 II right:1; *pe-ʾe-et-ta* New Year Ritual:15', related to the Arabic *faḥm* (فحم) (see AHw, 854), with the variations *pemtu* and *pentu* in Akkadian. According to Kouwenberg (2010, 518), the spellings in MA and NA with an aleph indicate a rare appearance of /ḥ/ > /ʾ/, which is possibly a secondary development. This opinion is confirmed by the geminated /t/, which resulted from an assimilated /m/ or /n/. In NA, we also find /n/ reappearing in the plural *pe-ʾe-na-a-te* SAA 2 6:533. Notice also *pe-eʾ-ta* PKT 4 r. left 8; *pe-ʾe-te* A 1748 (NTA, 23):9.

§ 187 The case becomes more complicated in III/e-i verbs. In a number of forms, R_3 follows R_2 directly, e.g., *il-te-qi-ú* 'they took' KAV 217:11', 12; *qí-bi-a* 'speak' MARV 3 64:6; *ḫa-di-a-ku* 'I rejoice' MATSH 9:43 etc. In these examples, the glide and the diphthong, which resulted from it, are cancelled. Instead, R_3 is treated as a strong consonant /y/. This can be observed from the following imperative: *pe-TI-a* 'open!' KAV 98:12. One would expect this imperative, derived from etymologic root √*ptḥ*, to use an <E> sign rather than an <I> sign, i.e., **pe-TE-a*. The use of the sign TI can only be interpreted as a reflection of /y/ directly following /t/; thus, we can transcribe *petyā* 'open!'. Strictly speaking, this is a broken spelling, since it does not follow the syllabic structure (*pet/yā*); but, as we have already seen, the orthographic representation of /y/ in MA was underdeveloped.[41] Unfortunately, similar spellings with a clear <I> sign, where <E> would be expected, are not known. However, unlike III/ʿ-ʾ verbs, R_3 is always retained in some form, with only a few known cases of vowel contraction: *la-qú-ú-ni* MAL C+ § 3:21; *i-la-qu-ú!-ni* MARV 1 71:19. These forms are, however, different from OA, where defective spellings could be used to indicate the original guttural (cf. Kouwenberg 2010, 580). This is not possible in the provided attestations because the spellings are broken, rather than defective.

40 There is a number of exceptions where the original /ḥ/ is represented with <Ḫ>; these are discussed in § 199.

41 Admittedly, this does not explain the TI sign in *ip-ti-ú-ni* MARV 3 23 r. 7. In OA, broken and glide spellings occur next to each other, e.g., broken *pì-it-a(-ma)* TCL 14 31:4 ~ glide *pí-tí-a* AKT 1 11:37 (see Kouwenberg 2010, 577).

4.2.5 Vowel contraction

§ 188 One of the characteristics of the Assyrian dialect is the preservation of syllabic boundaries in the case of a weak consonant. In effect, this means that two successive vowels can be separated by a glide or stop without vowel contraction, e.g., Assyrian *rabīum* 'big' vs. Babylonian *rabûm*. In the case of two successive vowels separated by a weak consonant, the preservation of this consonant is difficult to prove, except when a sign such as IA or ˀA or an extra vowel sign is used. Despite the better preservation of weak radicals in Assyrian, many cases of contraction are known in MA.[42] We have already mentioned the weak state of the aleph and semivowels in the word-initial position, observing a number of crasis spellings of two succeeding words where vowel contraction took place. We concluded that, in a succession of two different vowel colours, the second vowel replaced the colour of the preceding vowel. This is also true for vowel contraction inside morphological units. In general, it seems that semivowels are less vulnerable to vowel contraction than the aleph and ayin; indeed, we presented a few exceptions above. Semivowels can be found (sometimes as glides) in many morphologic categories, such as II/ī-ḫ and II/ū verbs, a number of pronouns (e.g., *šu(ʷ)ātu*) and the nisbe endings *-īy* and *-āy*, which never contract with succeeding case endings. It may be noted that, in the case of a geminated aleph (*i-ra-ˀu-mu-ši-ni* MAL A § 46:97), contraction is unlikely to take place. Contracting alephs may partly be caused by the addition of suffixes to a verb or substantive, which causes the stress to shift. It can therefore be observed that contraction is especially frequent with the R_3 of III/weak verbs. All possible vowel combinations will be discussed below, regardless of their vowel quantity.

4.2.5.1 Contraction of a+a

§ 189 The first vocalic sequence of /a+a/ does not seem to allow for contraction in the case of II/ˀ verbs. However, we have no reliable information on III/ˀ roots, which theoretically allow for contraction.

maˀādu	*ma-a-ad* 'more' BVW F r. 1
šaˀālu	*ša-a-li* 'asking' MAL F § 2:10
	ša-ˀa-a-li MAPD § 6:44

Cases of clear contraction are rare. We do find a case with a present III/ˀ verb followed by the dative suffix *-a(m)*. The following exception of the verb *šaˀālu* in the D-stem is uncertain, but could be the only case with contraction.

malāˀu	*ú-ma-al-la-ku-nu* (< *umallaˀakkunu*) 'I will compensate you' T 04-37:13
šalāˀu? D	*la-a ú-ša-la* (*ušâla* < *ušaˀˀalam*) (meaning uncertain) MATSH 6:7'

4.2.5.2 Contraction of a+i

§ 190 Cases of /a+i mostly maintain syllabic boundaries. The change of /a+i/ > /ê/ is typical Babylonian and not something to be expected in MA. On the other hand, unless /a/ is lengthened, we would expect cases of VA. Strangely enough, there are no attestations for this phenomenon; instead, /a/ seems to be lengthened for the most part. There are a few cases of etymologic /m/ > /ˀ/, which are expected to be preceded by a short /a/. However, as we discussed above, even these examples are not affected by VA, for reasons unclear.

aḫāˀiš	*a-ḫa-iš* 'together' OIP 79 6:13

42 A first attempt to make some observations on contraction in MA can be found in UGM, 18.

aˀīlu	*a-i-la* 'man' MAL A § 15:52
ālāyittu$^{?}$	[^{f}]⸢*a*⸣*-la-i-tu* 'villager (fem.)' MAL A § 45:52
anaˀīne	*a-na-i-ni* 'why' T 93-3:7
Arbāˀil	^{uru}*Ar-ba-il* 'the city of Erbil' TabT05-182:5
damāqu	in ^{d}IŠKUR-*da-iq* KAM 10 16 r. 4'
šakayyunu Š	*ul-ta-ka-in* 'I will have prostrated myself' A 1476:4
raˀāmu	*i-ra-ˀu-mu-ši-ni* 'they love her' MAL A § 46:97
šāˀiltu	*ša-il-te* 'demand$^{?}$' MATSH 6:22'
šaˀāmu	*ša-im* 'bought' LVUH 74:24
šamāˀu	*ša-ma-e* 'heavens' MARV 1 2:6
tappāˀu	*tap-pa-i-šu* 'his comrade' MAL A § 18:72
ukullāˀu	*ú-ku-la-i-ša* 'her ration' MAL A § 45:65
uṣāˀu	*ú-ṣa-i-ša* 'when she leaves' MAL A § 23:32

The exceptions where we do find contraction seem to be limited to III/weak roots. We may expect some Babylonian influences here; this is especially true for the infinitive *ḫapāˀu* 'to break', as we will argue in the discussion on the said verb (§ 570). Rather than an assimilation of the initial vowel to the second vowel, these instances show a merge with /ê/.

ḫapāˀu	*a-na ḫa-BI* (< *ḫapāˀu*) 'for breaking' MARV 1 38:10
laqāˀu	*le-qe* 'taking' KAJ 167:4
rubāˀu	*ru-bi-e-šu* (*rubêšu*$^{?}$ < *rubāˀīšu*) 'increase' MARV 3 29:8 (cf. *ru-ub-ba-ú* MARV 9 95:27)
ṣalāˀu	*i+na ṣa-le-e* 'during the abortion' MAL A § 53:99

4.2.5.3 Contraction of a+u

§ 191 As a short /a/ is affected by VA, we should expect it to be more vulnerable to vowel contraction (UGM, 18). In general, many spellings leave room for interpretation because contraction would lead to lengthening. This could be indicated by an extra vowel sign, e.g., *ú-ma-lu-ú* (*umalluˀū/umallûni*) MAL A § 4:56. There is no reason to assume that this sound change was complete in MA; thus, both forms should be expected.

No clear contraction:

kalāˀu D	*lā i-kal-lu-ú-*[*ši*] 'he will not detain her' MAPD § 6:45
karāˀu D	*ú-kar-ru-ú* 'they will deduct' KAJ 159 r. 13'
malāˀu D	*lā ú-ma-lu-ú* 'they will not compensate' MAL A § 4:56
	ú-ma-al-lu-ú MAL M § 1:6
sasāˀu D	*ú-sa-su-ú* 'they will make proclaim' MAL B § 6:36
uṣāˀu Š	*ú-še-ṣu-ú* 'they let go out' MAPD § 6:44

Contraction:

idāˀu	*ú-ud-du-ni* (< *udduˀūni*) 'they know' MATSH 6:5'
kalāˀu D	*ú-kal-lu-ni* (< *ukalluˀūni)* 'they withhold' KAJ 159 r. 13'
uṣāˀu	*ú-ṣu-ni* (< *uṣṣāˀūni*) 'they go out' Adad Ritual:6
uṣāˀu Š	*ú-še-ṣu-ni* (< *ušēṣuˀūni*) 'they let go out' Adad Ritual:1
zakāˀu D	*ú-zak-ku* (< *uzakkuˀū*) 'they will clear' KAJ 12:17 cf. *ú-za-ku-ú* KAJ 66:30

We also find one attestation in a verbal form in an MA Māri royal inscription. The verb is an Assyrian form (cf. Babylonian variant [*i-š*]*em-mu-ú* Maul 2005, ASJS 2 4:14).

šamāˀu	*i-šam-mu-šu* (*išammûšu* < *išammuˀūšu*) 'they will hear' Maul 1992, 26:15M

When the vowel /a/ is lengthened, no Assyrian VA can take place. As such, vowel contraction does not seem to take place in these instances either. This is especially true with the many instances of the nisba ending *-āy*; see § 254ff.

buāru D	*ba-ú-ra* 'to prove' MAL A § 18:7
*ginā*ʾ*u*	*gi-na-ú* 'regular offerings' MARV 5 39:5
*ku*ʾ*ā*ʾ*u*	*ku-a-ú* 'your' MATSH 29:8'
*muṭṭā*ʾ*u*	*mu-ṭa-ú* 'loss' LVUH 48:30
*rubbā*ʾ*u*	*ru-ub-ba-ú* 'increase' MARV 9 95:27 (cf. *ru-bi-e-šu* MARV 3 29:8)
*tappā*ʾ*u*	*tap-pa-ú-šu* 'his comrade' KAJ 32:5
tuāru D	*ta-ú-re* 'returning' KAV 98:30

4.2.5.4 Contraction of i+a

§ 192 In general, the sequence i+a is not susceptible to VA, which is true for Akkadian as a whole. We may point to the geographically near dialect of OB Mari, which is rather typical of this change and where the contraction to /ê/ is one of the few peculiarities of the said dialect (Finet 1956, 8–9 § 6). This is, however, not reflected in MA i+a; cf. II/ī and II/ḥ verbs; also the pronominal suffix *-ya* and independent personal pronouns of the type *šiāti*.

anniu	*an-ni-a* 'this' passim
*elā*ʾ*u*	*ti-li-a-ni* 'it comes up' KAJ 142:13
ḫaziānu	*ḫa-zi-a-ni* 'mayor' KAJ 106:8
niqīu	*ni-qi-a-te* 'offerings' KAJ 256:1
panīu	*pa-ni-a-ti* 'previous' KAJ 26:2
*radā*ʾ*u*	*ir-de-a-ni* 'he brought' Ali 11:11
šiāmātu	*ši-a-ma-at* 'purchased goods' KAJ 149:6
ummiānu	⸢*um*!⸣*-mi-an-šu-nu* 'their creditors' KAJ 32:9
*uṣā*ʾ*u*	*ṣi-a* 'come out' A 877:6

If contraction does take place, it seems that /i/ loses it to /a/. Note, furthermore, that none of the examples has a stop. In the case of a noun such as *abu* 'father' in the PN Milki-abi, a stop may originally have been present, regardless of the etymologic background of the weak consonant (< ʾ*abum*). While such a stop could still have been present in OA, there is no evidence for it in MA; in fact, this sandhi spelling pleads against it (cf. Kouwenberg 2006, 156–59).

asītu	*a-sa-te* (< *asīātu*) 'towers' KAJ 254:5
*elā*ʾ*u*	[f]*E-la-at-*[d]*Taš-me-tu* MARV 1 57 iv 8' cf. [f]*E-li-at*-DN MARV 1 57 ii 4'
labiānu	*la-ba-ni* 'neck' Coronation Ritual ii 48
	la-ba-n[a-t]i-ki-na 'your necks' MARV 3 64:42

There is only one possible indication of the contraction /i/+/a/ > /ê/; however, this is uncertain and probably a faulty spelling:

*ḫadā*ʾ*u*	*ḫa-di-<a>-*⸢*tu*⸣*-ú-ni* (perhaps *ḫadêtūni*) 'she wishes' MAL A § 33:70

4.2.5.5 Contraction of i+i

§ 193 Contraction in this sequence is not well attested. We may note that spellings allow for the preservation of the aleph by having an I sign followed by an E sign.

ammiu	*am-mi-e-em-ma* 'that' MAL A § 23:43
anniu	*an-ni-e* 'this' passim
šanīu	*ša-ni-e-ma* 'second' MAL A § 5:58
šanāyīu	*ša-na-i-e* 'second' MAL A § 30:26

If e-colouring causes two similar succeeding vowels, the glide may elide: *mu-be-i-še* (*muPaRRiSu*) PKT 4 r. left 4 ~ *mu-be-še* PKT 2 i 15.

mušaqqīu	*mu-ša-qí* 'giver of water (to cattle)' MARV 3 25:6
tamlīu	*ta-am-le* 'terrace' LVUH 87:10; cf. *ta-am-le-e* l. 8

4.2.5.6 Contraction of i+u

§ 194 Contraction of the vocalic sequence /i+u/ is relatively common. This mostly concerns the verbal forms of III/ī and III/ḫ verbs. Double-weak verbs, such as *baʾʾuʾu* and *elāʾu*, seem to be the most vulnerable to contraction, whereas, in verbs with two strong radicals, such as *laqāʾu* and *qabāʾu*, contraction is rare or uncertain.

baʾʾuʾu D	*ub-ta-ʾu-ni* (< *ubtaʾʾeūni*) Giricano 4:27
elāʾu	*i-lu-ú-ni* (< *eliūni*) MARV 8 7:11
elāʾu Š	*ú-še-lu-ni* (< *ušēliūni*) 'they brought up' KAV 98:22; cf. *ú-še-⸢li⸣-ú-ni* Billa 49:13
(*laqāʾu*)[43]	(*la-qú-ú-ni* 'he is taken' MAL C+ § 3:21)
	(*i-la-qu-ú*$^{!}$*-ni* 'they will take' MARV 1 71:19)
mudiʾu	*mu-du* (< *mudiʾu*) 'experience' Giricano 10:2
udāʾu D	*ud-du-ši-i-ni* 'he assigned to her' MAL A § 24:45
uṣāʾu Š	*ú-še-ṣu-ú-ni* 'they leased(?)' MAL J § 5:1†

Similar to the sequence /a+u/, there are some instances where the contraction is uncertain. This can be caused by the unambiguous orthography.

baʾʾuʾu	*ub-ta-ʾA-ú-ni* (*ubtaʾʾiʾūni/ubtaʾʾûni*) Franke/Wilhelm 1985:6

In addition, we find a number of cases without contraction. Many of these examples concern roots with etymologic ayin or aleph.

elāʾu	*e-te-li-ú* 'they have gone up' MATSH 14:13
laqāʾu	*lā il-qe-ú* 'they did not take' MATC 9:19
maṭāʾu D	*ú-ma-ṭí-ú-ni* 'he has deducted' KAJ 129:14
panīu	*pa-ni-ú-tu* 'previous' A 1735 (NTA, 18):19
qabāʾu	*iq-ti-bi-ú* 'they have said' MATSH 2:58
raqāʾu D	*lu-ra-qi-ú* 'they must make perfume' KAV 194:24
radāʾu	*ir-de-ú-ni* 'they led' KAJ 134:15
ṣalāʾu D	*lā ú-ṣa-li-ú* 'they may not have been idle' T 93-7:16
šamāʾu	*iš-mi-ú-ni* 'he heard' MAPD § 21:109
tāriū	*ta-ri-ú* 'children' KAJ 180:4

4.2.5.7 Contraction of u+a

§ 195 Basically, all sequences, shown below, are considered in the context of this study to involve the glide /w/. As such, they are discussed in § 177. For the sake of completeness, a few attestations are included below.

duāku	*du-a-ki* 'to kill' OIP 79 3:19
kuāša	*a-na ku-a-ša* 'to you' T 97-10:4
Ninuʾāyu	^{m}*Ni-nu-a-iu-ú* 'man from Nineveh' MARV 4 119:34
Šerūʾa	DN Šeruʾa, e.g., ŠU-^{d}*Še-ru-a* MARV 4 16:2; ^{m}ÌR-^{m}*Še-ru-ia* MARV 10 31:3

---

43 Contraction in the verb *laqāʾu* may be palaeographic, rather than phonologic, as the signs <qú> KU and <qé> KI are very similar. This uncertainty would not be present if <qu> (KUM) was used instead.

Contraction is attested for the dative pronoun *kuāša*, but this could be a Babylonianism.

kuāša	*ka-a-ša* 'to you' MARV 10 90:4

4.2.5.8 Contraction of u+i

§ 196 There are no reliable attestations in MA. However, we may note the DN Sîn, which was spelled *Sú-en* in OA, e.g., *Šu-Sú-in* (Šu-Suen) AKT 4 19:34. The MA spellings of ^{d}30 are generally transliterated as Sîn. Although I have been unable to find a syllabic spelling to confirm contraction in this DN, there is some evidence from the OA onomasticon, e.g., PN *Sí-in-iš-me-a-ni* (Sîn-išmeʾanni) ICK 1 79:16+ (see GOA § 3.4.11.4).

4.2.5.9 Contraction of u+u

§ 197 The attestations mostly concern the 3mp statives of D-stem III/weak verbs and the plural form of III/ū verbs. In some forms, the possibility of contraction remains open due to the plene spelling of the final vowel.

karāʾu D	*kar-ru-ú* 'they are deducted' LVUH 34:32'
zakāʾu D	*zak-ku-ú* 'they are cleared' KAJ 175:341
	perhaps *za-ku-*[*ú*] KAJ 66:29; KAJ 152:16
zarāʾu	*e-za-ru-ú* (*izarruʾū/izarrû*) 'they will sow' LVUH 103:16

A slight majority of the forms does point to contraction:

karāʾu D	*ka-ar-ru* 'they are deducted' MARV 1 10:14; *kar-ru* MARV 1 10:18
patāʾu D	*lu-ú pa-tu* MATSH 12:38†
zarāʾu	*i-za-ar-ru* 'they will sow' MARV 3 10:18'
	[*i-z*]*a-ar-ru* MATC 61:4
	i-za-ru LVUH 73:26; 77:8

4.3 Guttural /ḫ/

§ 198 The phoneme /ḫ/ is the only retained guttural. It was realized as a velar fricative (GAG, 31 § 25*), which explains why it behaved differently from most other gutturals and seldom used aleph spellings.[44] As /ḫ/ was realized as a velar, we find spellings where it was used as the spirantized version of the velar plosives [k] > [k̲], and perhaps even spirantized /q/ (see § 208). On the other hand, its fricative value explains how it could be used for the other gutturals /ġ-ḥ-h-ˁ/ (e.g., Mari in Finet 1956, 17 § 10). This also explains why <Ḫ> is not used for ʾ$_1$, which is a plosive laryngeal. The sign ḪI, used for <ḫi>, has become identical to TÍ, which is used mainly for <ṭí>. On the use of these signs, the following observations can be made.

/ḫa/	The sign ḪA is always used.
/ḫi/	The sign ḪI is almost always used. No distinction is made between /e/ and /i/. The value <ḫí> (GAN) is very rare: ^{lú}*al-ḫí-nu* 'the baker' Billa 7:7 cf. Billa 8:5†.
/ḫu/	The sigh ḪU is always used.
/aḫ/	Normally AḪ is used. No distinction is made between /a/, /i/ and /e/. There are two examples where ʾA is used, perhaps because of palaeographic similarity (see below).
/uḫ/	Normally UḪ is used.

44 This explains why the phoneme /k/ is sometimes represented by <Ḫ> in the script (see below) as both are velars. See GAG, 31 § 25d; Kouwenberg (2006, 152 n2).

§ 199 In Akkadian, the ḪA series is sometimes used for the etymologic /ḥ/ (ˀ$_3$) (Tropper 1995), but rarely for other gutturals, e.g., *i-pa-ša-ḫu-ni* 'it will cool down' PKT 5 r. 9 (√*pšḥ*); *pal-ḫa-ku* 'I am afraid' MATSH 22:20 (√*plḥ*); *i-sa-ḫa-ra-áš* 'he will turn' MATSH 27:7' (√*sḥr*). Notice the lack of e-colouring in these forms. Perhaps we should also add the noun *lēˀu* 'wooden tablet' to this group, if we accept that it derives from the root √*lwḥ*, cf. the Arabic *lawḥ* (لوح) (AHw, 547b). Some spellings of this noun seem to use the sign ḪI, which we would otherwise have to read <i_{11}> e.g., *ša pi-i le-*i_{11} *ša* É.GAL-*lim* 'according to the wording of the wooden tablet of the palace' MARV 3 5:36; *ša ki le-*i_{11} *ša* PN 'according to the wording of the wooden tablet of PN' MAH 1608 ii 5'.[45] An original /ḥ/ can be found in the Sutean name *al-qa-ḫa-ú-ni* T 04-37 r. 3, with a verbal form of the root √*lqḥ* (MA *laqāˀu*) (cf. Minx 2005, 8). Alternations between <ˀ> and <Ḫ> are rare, but much more frequent in OA and rarely in NA.[46] For MA, we only have two examples: *re-ˀA-ti* Adad Ritual:12' (< *reḫtu*) and, in a SB text, *i-na-as-sà-Aˀ-ma* < *inassaḫ-ma* KAR 19 r. 9 (see CAD N_2, 4c). These two examples may have occurred because of the palaeographic similarity between AḪ and ˀA. Notice also the variation in *perˀu* 'descendant' and *pír-e* KTN inventory i 3 ~ *pír-ḫi* AO 21.382:1. It is also attested in the verbal form *ul-tum-ḫe-ḫi-in* (*ultuḵeˀˀin*) KBo 28 82:3, which is a non-Assyrian verbal form from *šakayyunu* (see § 547) in a letter of questionable Assyrian character (§ 40). If we accept ^{kur}*ki-na-ḫi* Faist 2001, 252:5 and T97-37:5 as early attestations of Canaan (Hebrew *knāˁan* כְּנַעַן), it is another example of a guttural (ayin) represented in script as <Ḫ> (GAG, 31 § 25a).

§ 200 Consonant clusters starting with /ḫ/ sometimes receive an epenthetic vowel (cf. § 157). This may be compared with the situation in OA, where such syllables sometimes received an epenthetic /i/ or /e/, but rarely a /u/ (GOA § 3.2.2.3). In MA, this vowel is usually /a/, which could be a *Murmelvokal* [ə].

ḫalāṣu	*li-ḪI-lu-ṣu* (*liḫluṣū*) 'may they filter' T 93-7:7, 17, 23
ḫarāṣu Št	*tu-ša-ḫa-ru-ṣu-ni* (*tušaḫaruṣūni*) 'it has been deduced' KAJ 120:7
maḫāru	*la ma-ḫa-rat* (*lā maḫrat*) 'it is not received' LVUH 105:8
naḫāru	⌜*na*⌝-*ḫa*-⌜*rat*⌝ 'it is invalid' TR 2061:11 cf. *na-aḫ-ra-at* TR 3001:9
rēḫtu	*re-ḫe-ti* (< *rīḫtu*) 'remainder' TR 2049:6'

4.4 Labial plosives b/p

§ 201 MA has two labial plosives: voiced /b/ with allophone [ḇ], [w] or even [v], and voiceless /p/, possibly with allophone [f].

/ba/	Normally, BA is used. There are a few examples where PA is used (see below).
/pa/	Normally, PA is used. There are a few examples where BA is used (see below).
/bi/	A strong distinction between /i/ and /e/ is made by the use of <bi> (BI) and <be> (BAD).
/pi/	Normally, PI is used. No distinction is made between /i/ and /e/. In other WPA and OA dialects, PI is used almost exclusively for <wa/i/e/u>; but, in MA and MB, this value is not attested. We find BI used for <pí>, but this is mostly limited to combinations with DUB (see below).
/bu/	The sign BU is always used. No distinction is made between /b/ and /p/, which is uncommon for Cv signs.

45 Cf. Freydank in MARV 3, 9 no. 5. However, this sign value would seem to be very rare, making a reflection of /ḥ/ preferable.

46 See OA in GKT, 48f § 30; GOA § 3.2.5.3; NA in SNAG, 15 § 2.1.4.

/ab/ The sign AB is mostly used. No distinction is made between /b/ and /p/. We find ÁB once: *i-qa-áb-bi* TIM 4 45:11; and in some PNs, e.g., ^{m}*Na-áp-še-ru* KAJ 33:4; ^{I}*Ṭà-áb-*^{d}*A-šur* KAJ 132:28. Note also the unusual value <àb> (AD) found only in ^{na4}*àb-na ga-bi-a* KAV 109:20; *àb-na ga-bi-ú* T 93-28:2. For <áb(a)>, see also Syllab, 19 no. 108; MZL no. 258.

/ib/ The sign IB is always used. No distinction is made between /i/ and /e/, nor between /b/ and /p/.

/ub/ The sign UB is always used. No distinction is made between /b/ and /p/.

§ 202 It is not unlikely that, in every Semitic language, some kind of spirantization took place. That said, in most languages, this phenomenon was mostly limited to /p/ > /f/ (e.g., Arabic; Old South Arabic; Ge'ez), while, in Hebrew and Aramaic, it was more extensive and affected all so-called "*BGDKPT letters*" (e.g., Joüon/Muraoka 2006, 76f § 19). In light of this, von Soden argued for spirantization in Akkadian on the basis that the sign PI was used for values of the type <wV>.[47] In MA, our evidence is limited because etymologic /w/ was no longer written with PI. We do find the writing of <B> for etymologic /w/, which could be reflection /ḇ/ or [v] (see above § 178). Based on the evidence discussed there, it seems that, at least for /b/, a spirantized allophone existed, which was possibly strongest in intervocalic environments (as in Hebrew). Outside the orthography of etymologic /w/, evidence for a spirantized /b/ is difficult to find. It is possible that /b/ spirantized and elided, as it did in MA *aʾīlu* 'man' or, alternatively, that we are dealing with a spirantized /m/ (see § 180). Another attestation may be found in a version of the Cow of Sîn, where we find *mi-nu-ta* Rm 376:20, instead of the expected *binûtu* 'form' found in the NA versions (see Röllig 1985). A rather difficult example is *te-ze-em-me* (> *ezābu*) RS 20.18:15. As we will discuss below, /m/ is likely to have spirantized as well; thus, it seems that we have to analyse the form as follows: *tezzeb-me* > *tezzewwe*. On the other hand, the Assyrian character of RS 20.18 remains open to discussion (§ 40), the more so because the Assyrian present of *ezābu* is *ezzab*.

§ 203 The distinction between /b/ and /p/ is relatively strong in MA in signs of the type Cv. In vC, no such distinction is made. Exceptions exist, with instances known where BI is used for <pí>. This usage is largely limited to the phonetic complement for DUB, forming the word *tup-pí* 'tablet', e.g., *tup-pí-šu* KAJ 43:13 EAd/Aub, but *tup-pi-šu* KAJ 147:23. We find attestations of this spelling prior to the end of the MA period, e.g., *tup-pí* MARV 6 1:29 (Tp). This could be a leftover of archaic scribal traditions, when this spelling was common and no distinction between the labials took place. The orthography *tup-pí* is frequent in OA, but the equally common *tup-pì* is not attested in MA. For this reason, this orthography probably derives from Babylonian traditions, as we find OB dialects that use BI (e.g., *tup-pí-a* AbB 14 73:7). However, especially in NA, /p/ and /b/ are often confused, which led von Soden and Deller to believe that, in NA, /b/ and /p/ had become interchangeable, a process that had already started in MA.[48] Note the following examples:

<B> stands for /p/:

aškāpu	AŠGAB-*BE* 'leatherworker' MARV 10 5:18
nupāru	^{é}*nu-BA-ri* 'prison' AO 19.227:12 (TN) ~ ^{é}*nu-pa-ri* KAJ 254:9 (NtA)

47 See von Soden (1968); GAG, 33 § 27a*.

48 See von Soden (1957/58a, 122); Deller (1959, 234ff, specifically 242); Dahood/Deller/Köbert (1965, 37 § 8.9). Deller's (1959) example of *ṣu-pa-a-t*⸢*e*⸣ for *ṣubātu* has since been rejected as a form of *ṣuppu* 'pressed'. See BAI, 27 and CAD Ṣ, 249. Cf. also Maul (1992, 32 n107).

epāšu D	*ú-BA-su* 'he will treat him' KAJ 6:16 (Aub)
ḫasāpu D	*ḫa-su-BE* 'tweezers' KAV 205:20 (Sa) ~ *ḫa-su-pi* KAV 205:27 (Sa)
Izquppīya	^{m}*Iz-qup-BI-*⸢*ia*⸣ KAM 10 11:1 (Aub); ^{m}*Iz-qup-BI* KAM 10 11:8 (Aub)
kaspu	*ka-ús-BI* 'silver' KAJ 6:23 (Aub) i/o MA *ṣarpu* 'silver'
Mannu-iqip	^{m}*Ma-nu-qip-BI* Giricano 10:24 (Abk)
napāšu	*na-BI-ša* 'air!' KAV 99:14 (Sa); *na-ap-BI-ša* KAV 109:12 (TN)[49]
naqalpā'u	*us-qa-al-BI-ú-*⸢*ni*⸣ 'they came upstream' MARV 4 35:7 (TN)
^{m}*Piqabāyašea*	*BI-qa-ba-[ia-ši-e-a]* KAM 10 5:2' (Ead/Aub) cf. ^{m}*Pi-qa-ba-ia-ši-e-a* KAJ 66:28 (Ad)
pittu	É-*ti* 'responsibility' Coronation Ritual i 41
pû	*BI-i* 'message' KAJ 165:5, 11, 21, 23 (Aub); KAJ 172:12 (Ead/Aub); MCS 2 1:17 (TN)
	BI-ši-na KAJ 164:14 (Aub)
	BI-i t[up-pí-šu] 'message of his tablet' KAM 10 2:2 (EAd)
qalāpu	*a-*⸢*na*⸣ *qa-la-a-*⸢*BE*$^{?}$⸣ 'to strip off' MARV 10 74:12 (Tp)
quppu	*qu-BI=quppu*$^{?}$ 'box' LB 1848b r. 3' (Sa)
ṣarāpu	*a-na ṣa-ra-BE* 'to burn' A 305:14 (TN)
ṣippu	^{iti}*ṣi-ip-BI* KAJ 11:24 (EAd/Aub)

The verb *ḫapā'u* 'to break':

ḫapā'u	*a-na ḫa-BI* (< *ḫapā'u*) 'for breaking' MARV 1 38:10 (EAd/Aub); KAM 10 31:11
	a-na ḫe-BI KAJ 142:15 (Aub) cf. *a-na ḫe-pe* MARV 3 11:22 (UŠA)
	i-ḫa-BI 'he will break' KAJ 74:10 (EAd/Aub) cf. *i-ḫap-pi* passim, e.g., KAJ 51:13 (Sa)

The verb *upā'u* Š 'to acquire':

upā'u Š	*ú-šap-BI* 'he acquired' passim, e.g., KAJ 153:11 (Aub); KAJ 154:12 (Aub)[50]
	ú-šap-BI-ú KAJ 170:12 (M 9)

The verb *palāḫu* 'to fear':

palāḫu	^{md}*Iš*$_{8}$*-tár-BI-láḫ* KAJ 48:4 (Sa)
	^{d}*A-šur*$^{!}$*-BI-laḫ* KAJ 57:24 (Adn$^{?}$); ^{d}*A-šur-BI-láḫ* KAJ 145:12 (Adn); cf. *Pa-láḫ-Ku-be* KAJ 314:3
	i-BA-la-aḫ-šu KAJ 6:12 (Aub)

<P> stands for /b/:

abu	*a-PI=abī* 'father' KAR 9 r. 6
banā'u	in ^{md}IŠKUR-*PA-ni* (Adad-bani) TR 3012:5 (Sa)
bappiru	*pa-pi-[ri]* (*bappiru* < Sum. BAPPIR) 'beer-bread' MARV 2 23:12' (Sa)
be'ālu	*a-PI-el* 'I ruled over' RIMA 1 A.76.3:43 (Adn)
gabbu	*gáb-PI* 'everything' A 1020:13' (?)
ibašši	*i-PA-ši* 'there is' Cohen/Llop 2017:4
^{m}*Ipittu*	^{m}*I-BI-it-te* MARV 10 21:7 (Tp)[51]
qabā'u	*Qí-PI*-DINGIR (Qibi-ilī) A 845:1
ṣabātu	*tup-pu ṣa-*⸢*BI*⸣*-te* 'executed tablet' TR 2058:13 (Sa) cf. *tup-pi-šu ṣa-bi-it-te* MARV 1 1 i 8'
zību	*zi-PI* 'black cumin' KAJ 123:3 (Sa) vs. *zi-bi* RIAA 311:2 (Sa/TN)

49 Both examples for the root √*npš* are from the Bābu-aḫa-iddina archive. A change of root may be suggested as √*npš*, which becomes √*nbš* in Old Aramaic as well, e.g., KAI 218:7.

50 The Š of the verb *wapā'u* may, as an exception, be comparable to the BA series' use with DUB (*tuppum*). The normal variant with PI occurs as well: *ú-šá-pi-ú* KAJ 169:13.

51 This PN is attested with both BI and PI (see de Ridder 2013b, 143–144).

§ 204 The issue of the *bēt ḫašime* 'granary' must be addressed separately. We find a number of unexpected spellings. These readings have led some authors to read all occurrences of É *ḫašimi* as *pitti ḫašime* (e.g., Postgate 1986a, 27–28). Harrak (1989) pointed out that, up until recent times, Northern Iraqi Arabic and Syriac dialects still maintained the term *bēt lḫšim/lšḫim* (Arabic) and *bēt ḥšīmā* (Syriac), which he claimed were direct descendants of an Assyrian loan in Syriac and Arabic, which supported the claim for *bētu* over *pittu*. We would therefore have to read the rare <bì> or, better still, <be$_6$> (PI; see UGM, 10) in these examples. On the other hand, this does not explain the construct form *bēti*, instead of the normal *bēt*, in MARV 1 47. As both texts derive from the UŠ archive and possibly the same scribe (Farber 1990, 93), we may wonder whether these were erroneous spellings.

bēt ḫašimi	*ša PI-et* ḫa-[*š*]*i-me* 'granary' KAJ 101:5 (Aššnīr III)
	ša PI-te ḫa-še-me MARV 1 47:7, 11, 13-14 (TN)[52]
	i+na P[*I-t*]*e* [*ḫa-še-me*] MARV 1 47:22
	ša É*-ti ḫa-še-me* MARV 1 47:38
Cf.:	
bētu	*a-na* É*-te* PN MARV 6 27:18 (Tp)

§ 205 In general, von Soden and Deller's ideas on the weakening of the differentiation between the labials were not universally accepted.[53] If the two phonemes had truly merged, we could expect a much larger list of examples. Compared to other WPA dialects, the instances of labial confusion are remarkable small.[54] It certainly does not account for foreign scribes with a native language, such as Hurrian, which does not distinguish between the two labials. Perhaps a (similar) substratum explains the following alternation of a GN in the same text: ^{uru}*Ša-da-ba-iu-ú* A 3198 (NTA, 40):7 ~ *Ša-da-pa-a-iu-ú* l. 13. Likewise, in KAJ 6, we find as many as three instances of labial confusion, which could certainly be caused by the linguistic background of the scribe. Moreover, some confusion between the two phonemes is not unheard of in other Semitic languages and should therefore not surprise us much.[55] There are two further arguments against the interchangeability of /b/ and /p/. Etymologic [w] is never written with <P> signs in our corpus. This is probably because of the possible spirantization of /b/ > /ḇ/, whereas there are no changes in the spirantization of /p/ > /f/. Moreover, the sound change /šb/ > /sb/, amply attested in *ušābu* (§ 222 and § 609), is not once found with /p/.[56] There are very few minimal pairs to help us differentiate between the two phonemes:

---

52 Note that Harrak's (1989, 65) reading of É*-pi* MARV 1 47:38 must be incorrect, as this text consequently spells PI*-te*, making the reading É*-te* preferable. Cf. UŠA, 138 no. 56.

53 Accepted in CGSL, 26 § 8.9; GAG, 33 § 27; Lipiński (2001, 110 § 10.8); but criticized in SNAG § 2.1.6.1; Luukko (2004, 72ff § 4.1.1).

54 See, for example, the situation in UgAkk where PA is regularly used for <bá>, while BI is normal for <pí/é>. See Huehnergard (1989, 35). For MitAkk, see Adler (1976, 4). Cf. also Mandaic, which indicates frequent alternation between the two labials and where a regular switch in roots has taken place; see Nöldeke (1875, 47ff § 51), e.g., *auṭpuiẖ* ࡀࡅࡈࡐࡅࡉࡄ 'do him good' (√*yṭp* < √*yṭb*). We do not find such structural interchangeability in MA.

55 See Lipiński (2001, 116 § 11.4).

56 Surprisingly, there is very little evidence to actually support this claim. Consider the following: in the case of ÁŠ, this is not possible to distinguish because of the two equal readings <ás> and <aš> (§ 221),

battu 'side'	*ba-at-te* MAL A § 36:83	*pattu* 'canal'	–
būru 'bull'	*bu-ru* Lambert 1969:55	*pūru* 'lot'	*pu-ru* KAV 125:2
šabārtu 'bar'	*ša-bar-tu* KAJ 178:1	*šapārtu* 'pledge'	*ša-pár-te* MAL A § 39:28
usbu 'they sit'[57]	*us-bu* MATSH 2:20	*ušpu* 'slinger'	*uš-pu* MATC 71:10(?)[58]

The occurrence or absence of such minimal pairs does not completely resolve the issue, since we must assume the possibility of homonyms and even heterographs. Ultimately, we only have the spellings of the scribes to rely on, which show that the two phonemes are usually differentiated, for what it is worth.

4.5 Plosive velars /g-k-q/

§ 206 MA has the typical Semitic stock of three velars /g/, /k/ and /q/. As opposed to OA, all velars are strongly distinguished from each other in the signs of the type Cv, making it clear that they were still independently realized in speech. MA could have had another (fricative) velar /ḫ/ (see above).

/ga/ The sign GA is always used. We probably should not accept <ga$_{14}$> (KA) based on the erroneous spelling *ip-tu-a-KA* (*iptuag*?) T 02-32:29.

/ka/ The sign KA is always used.

/qa/ Normally, QA is used. Once we find <qá> (GA) in *GA-qí-ri* MARV 1 4:9' (Aub), which could refer back to the OA use of the sign GA. <qá> (GA) can also be found in SIG$_5$-*qá* KAJ 151:2; KAM 10 14:2. Cf. below SIG$_5$-*qú*. Perhaps it is better to read SIG$_5$.GA based on the following spelling: SIG$_5$.GA-*qú* KAJ 35:10. The value <qà> (KA) may be attested once: *qà-ni* 'border' KAJ 232:8 (Adn) and in PNs with the element *batqa* (OMA 2, 206), e.g., DUMU.MUNUS-*bat-qà* KAJ 51:2.[59]

/gi/ Normally, GI is used. No distinction is made between /i/ and /e/.

/ki/ Normally, KI is used. No distinction is made between /i/ and /e/.

/qi/ The representation of <qi/e> is equally divided between <qí/é> (KI) and <qi/e> KIN. The use of KIN for <qi> and <qe> is an Assyrian innovation, which is rare in MB, but frequently occurs in later UgAkk.[60] Other WPA dialects tend to use <qì> (GI), especially for the verb *leqû*. This is

e.g., *na-áš-pér-ti* MATC 11:21. CvC signs rarely involve an unambiguous reading, e.g., *liš/lis-pu-uk* KAV 205:29. However, in forms such as *iš-pu-ra-ni* MATSH 2:15 and *li-iš-pu-ra* MARV 1 71:30, the value of IŠ is at least clear, even when we take into account the differentiation between /š/ and /s/ through the signs IŠ and EŠ (§ 221). It is possible to read <bu> (BU) instead of <pu>, but this would refute the sound change /šb/ > /sb/, making such a reading undesirable. Other instances with a clear /p/ reading are *na-áš-pi-i*[*r-te*] Billa 13:11; *iš-pu-tu* 'quiver' BM 108960:1. Overall, the evidence against a change /šp/ > /sb/ is meagre at best; on the other hand, evidence in favour is totally absent.

57 The stative *usbū* derives from *ušābu*. An adjective (*usbu* 'seated') and participle (*ūsbu* 'seating') are to be expected in MA

58 This noun is always written with UŠ, even though Postgate (2008, 87 n12) suggested the etymologic root √*wsp*. This is further confirmed by OB evidence for the cognate *(w)aspu* (CAD A$_2$, 339; cf. AHw, 1475b). It is probably better to assume the value <ús> instead of assuming a phonologic change, in line with the many similar attestations of <ús> provided in § 221.

59 The attestation *kà-ni* is problematic given its palaeographic similarities to the logogram EZEN, found in a similar context, e.g., KAV 111:5.

60 See Aro (1955a, 19); Knudsen (1961, 60); MZL, 429 no. 815 "*qi/e (ass.-n., selten bab.-n.)*". However, in late UgAkk texts from the reign of Niqmaddu III, the use of KIN becomes more common. See Huehnergard (1989, 34–35). KIN is also used in Amarna and Boğazköy; see von Soden/Röllig (1991, 58 no. 294).

perhaps attested in *za-ru-qì* (Bab. *zuruqqu*) ‘shaduf’ KAJ 154:3. The use of <qí> (KI) is the traditional value in OB and OA, as both /k/ and /q/ are voiceless, as opposed to the voiced /g/ (Aro 1955a, 19). In earlier texts, KI is more common, whereas, in texts from around the reign of Tukultī-Ninurta, the sign KIN became more common. This can be seen in the table below, where the most conservative orthography is found in the M 9 and the Tell Ar-Rimāḫ archives. The distribution of the two signs is partly semantic; *qabāʾu* always uses <qí>, whereas, for *laqāʾu*, both are attested.[61] In the late MA Giricano archive, <qí> is not attested.

/gu/ Normally, GU is used. Syllabic use of GÚ is obscure and may occur in ^{túg}*pi-GÚ-ra-a-t*[*u*^{meš}] MARV 10 27:9, 11.

/ku/ Normally, KU is used. The value <ku$_{13}$> (KUM) occurs once in the verb *tabāku* in *it-ta-na-bu-KUM* PKT 4 r. left 7, 11. This is clearly a mistake; either the scribe had the value <qu> (KUM) in mind or was confused by the old value <kum>, used for the dative 2ms because mimation had disappeared in MA.

/qu/ The sign KUM was used for qu, but was already known in Babylonian and previously used in OA for the dative ending *-kum*. Spellings with <qú> KU have become rare and are archaic, usually occurring in early texts. With regards to the private archives, there are no certain examples after the reign of Sa, except for Dūr-Katlimmu. The attestations are: *la-qú-ú-ni* MAL C+:21; SIG$_5$-*qú* KAJ 14:9 (Adn/Sa); KAJ 63:3 (Aub); KAJ 146:2 (Ead/Aub); SIG$_5$.GA-*qú* KAJ 35:10 (Ead); *qa-qú-ru* KAJ 174:3 (Arn); ^{d}*A-šur-ni-me-qú* KAJ 37:16 (Arn); *e-ti-qú-ni* KAJ 142:8 (Aub); *ḫu-ul-qú* LVUH 7:16 (Sa); LVUH 13:13 (Sa); [*ḫu*]-*lu-qú*$^!$ LVUH 43:10’ (TN); *i-na-su-qú-ni* BM 108924:7.

/ag/ The sign AG is always used.

/ig/ The sign IG is always used for /g-k-q/. No distinction is made between /i/ and /e/.

/ug/ The sign UG is always used for /g-k-q/.

	<qí>	<qi>
MAL A	+++	+
MAPD	–	+
Coronation Ritual	–	+
PKT	(?)	+
M 4	*qabāʾu*/+	++
M 6	–	+
M 7	*qabāʾu*/+	+
M 9	++	+
M 10	*qabāʾu*/+	++
M 11	*qabāʾu*	+++
MATSH	*qabāʾu*/(+)	++
MATC	*qabāʾu*	++
LVUH	*qabāʾu*/(+)	+
TaR	*qabāʾu*/++	+
TṢA	*qabāʾu*	++
Giricano	–	+

Figure 17: Distribution of <qí> and <qi>.[62]

The distribution of <qí> and <qi> over the chronology of the MA and different genres can be summarized in the following table. As the verb *qabāʾu* never uses <qi> in its conjugated forms, it is indicated separately. This confirms that <qí> is more common in the older and archaic texts.

61 Spellings such as *qa-bi-ú-ni* (KAJ 142:9) of the verb *qabāʾu* show that R$_1$ remains /q/ in MA, despite its subsequent spellings with the sign KI.

62 Distribution of <qí> and <qi> over the main archive from absent (–) to common (+++).

§ 207 Spirantization of the velars is a possibility in Akkadian, with many examples of variations in these velars written as <Ḫ> (see von Soden 1968, 217f; Knudsen 1969; GAG, 31 § 25d*). Instances of /ḫ/ being written <G> or <K> would suggest that the spirantized value of the velars made them suitable for use in etymologic /ḫ/ as well. Some of these attestations seem allophonic, while, in other cases, they are phonemic, with the meaning changed by spirantization. In Assyrian, the evidence is scarcer, but does occur.[63] For MA, only two possible examples are apparent, both in the same incantation text.

kamās/šu	*ta-aḫ-ti-me-iš* 'she kneeled' Lambert 1969:57 Being derived from *ḫamāšu* is unlikely, pace Röllig 1985, 266.
šaḫāṭu	*il-ti-ki-iṭ* 'he leaped' Lambert 1969:55 (also CAD Š₁, 88, 89)

Despite the SB features of this text, the occurrence of VA shows that these forms are Assyrian. Spirantization is also attested in the verbal form *ul-tum-ḫe-ḫi-in* (*ultuḵeˀˀin*) KBo 28 82:3, which is a non-Assyrian verbal form from *šakayyunu* (see § 547) in a letter of questionable Assyrian character (§ 40).

§ 208 The sound change /ḫ/ > /q/ was proposed by Köcher (1957/58, 311) on the basis of MA *šu-⸢UG⸣-ri* KTN inventory i 36 and *šu-UG-ri* ii 7, instead of the normal *šuḫru/šūru*, which Köcher read as *šu-⸢uq⸣-ri*. He claimed a similar change in the verb *abātu* 'to destroy', which is common in the royal inscriptions. In the perfect tempus variations, /ḫ/ occurs as the first radical (*uḫ-DA-bi-it* RIMA 1 A.0.76.10:39; 13:39; *iḫ-DA-bit* RIMA 1 A.0.78:16) and /q/ (*ú-qa-ba-tu-ma* RIMA A.0.78.1. v:23.).[64] This is a problematic verb, as it is one of the few roots that displays a retained stop with ˀA (e.g., *iˀ-ab-ta* RIMA 2 A.0.87.1 vi 99 Tp). Sommerfeld assumed an emphatic constant of the series /ḫ-ġ-ẖ/ (in GAG, 31 § 25*), while Luukko (2004, 71) alternatively suggested the value /ṣ́/ based on similar variations between <Q>, <ˀ> and <Ḫ> in NA. Perhaps we should reconstruct the spirantized /q/, represented in the orthography as <Ḫ>, which could be a possibility. Another possibility is the change /q/ > /ˀ/, written with <Ḫ>, as found in vernacular Egyptian Arabic and other vernacular Arabic (cf. Woidich 2006, 12). The alternation between <Ḫ>, <Q> and <ˀ> show that Köcher and Sommerfeld are probably right in assuming that the first radical was an unusual phoneme; however, strictly speaking, all examples are in royal inscriptions that do not belong to this study. Moreover, the assumption of a unique phoneme, preserved in one verb of a dialect, was criticized as unlikely by Huehnergard (1997a, 438). In NA, spellings with <NN> occur in the position of the first radical. According to CAD (A₁, 44), these forms derive from the confusion among scribes with regard to the verb *nābudu* 'to flee', making the situation even more complicated. Recently, a new verb, *ḫ/qabbudu*, was found in the Tell Aš-Šēḫ Ḥamad texts (in MPR), presumably referring to a kind of sickness that made people unable to work. Salah suggested that the verb derives from *kabādu* 'to be heavy', attributing to it a new D-stem intensive meaning of G-stem 'to aggravate' (MPR, 76 Z. 4), e.g., *ḫab-bu-da-at* MPR 3:4; *qa-bu-da-at* MPR 12:56. I object to this interpretation, for two reasons: the alternation

63 For OA, see GKT, 50 § 31; GOA § 3.2.4.9. For NA, see SNAG, 17 § 2.1.6.2.

64 Supposedly a second example (*iq-ta-bit* RIMA A.0.78.14:16) would be a variation of a Tukultī-Ninurta inscription. I was unable to locate this variation in the copy or the RIMA edition (see Köcher 1957/58, 311; von Soden 1968, 214).

between <Q> and <Ḫ> for etymologic /k/ is something that cannot be logically explained. In fact, Salah probably hit the mark with his suggestion *ḫuppudu* 'to cause an eye-injury/blindness'. His objection that we would expect *lā dāgilu* (IGI NU.TUKU) 'blind' in this case is not very strong, because this is a participle used as an attributive for persons, while *ḫ/qabbutu* is used as a predicative. Secondly, it seems to me that there could be more conditions of the eyes, other than blindness. If we accept a verb *ḫappudu* it would fit well with our attestations of *šuḫ/qru* and *(ḫ/q)abātu*. The interchangeability of ḫ/q is also attested in PN *ḫ/qabbūtu*: ^{f}*ḫab-bu-tu* MPR 6:8; ^{f}*qa-bu-tu* MPR 8:5'; ^{f}*qa-bu-ú-tu* MPR 40:44 (also de Ridder 2016a, 124).

§ 209 Variation between the velars is very rare in MA. Judging by the few examples presented by Luukko (2004, 70-71), distinction between the phonemes remained strong. In the case of *ip-tu-a-KA* (T 02-32:29), we may be dealing with an inverted spelling for *iptuag*$^{?}$ (see § 116). Another example is /q/ > /g/: *za-ru-gi* KAJ 152:3 (< *zarāqu*, Bab. *zuruqqu*). Also note /g/ > /d/: *ni-id-na-ki* Ištar ritual:8 (< *nignakku*).

4.6 Dental plosives /d-t-ṭ/ and interdentals

§ 210 MA retained three dental plosives /d/, /t/, /ṭ/. The interdentals /ṯ/, /ḏ/ and /ẓ/, since OAkk, at least merged with the interdental fricatives (/š/ < /ṯ/; /z/ < /ḏ/; /ṣ/ < /ẓ/). Likewise, the lateral dental /ṣ́/ merged with /ṣ/. On the orthography, the following remarks can be made.

/da/ Normally, DA is used. A few times, we find the value <dá> (TA) in *ú-ša-TA-na* KAJ 114:15 (Sa); *tup*$^{!}$*-pa d*[*á*]*-na-ta* 'a strong tablet' KAJ 155:19 (Aub); [*tup-pa T*]*A-na-ta* 'a strong tablet' KAJ 146:16–17 (Aub). Perhaps also *la i-na-*⌜*TA*⌝*-a-an* KAJ 146:6, although we may restore <da> here (cf. Weeden 2012, 306; see also § 606). Notice also the PN ^{f}KUR-*TA-i-tu* (*Šaddaytu*) A 3184 (NTA, 34):1 cf. ^{f}KUR-*da-it-*⌜*te*⌝ A 3188 (NTA, 36):2. These could be scribal mistakes or a reflection of the OA use of TA for values <ta/ṭá/dá>; however, it is also present in peripheral Akkadian (Syllab, no. 102; cf. Nuzi in Wilhelm 1970, 87).

/ta/ Normally, TA is used.[65]

/ṭa/ There is no common special writing for emphatic /ṭa/, as, for instance, for <qa> (QA); instead, the sign DA is used. Once, we find the value <ṭá> (TA) in *na-TA-at* TR 3012:12 (Sa). According to Kouwenberg (2003, 85), this is a remnant of OA orthography; however, the value is also present in WPA (Syllab, no. 102). Given the fact that the text derives from Tell Ar-Rimāḥ, rather than Aššur, a remnant of local traditions is just as likely. The value <ṭà> (ḪI) was never common in Assyrian and only appeared in PNs, e.g., ^{I}*Ṭà-áb-*^{d}*A-šur* KAJ 132:28 Arn; ^{m}*A-ḫu-ṭà-bi* KAJ 172:10, 13 (or DÙG.GA$^{!}$); ^{m}*Ṭà-áb-ṣíl-lí-*^{d}*A-*⌜*šur*⌝ KAM 10 20:14; see also, in a broken context, *ṭà-ab* OIP 79 4:21. The sign value is rare in Akkadian, but does not appear to be a direct Mittani or MB influence.[66]

/di/ Normally, DI is used. No distinction is made between /di/ and /de/. Once, we find <de_4> (TE) in the usual text KAJ 6:20 de_4*-e-ni* 'case'. Unlike MB, DI is not used to express emphatic <ṭi> (see below).

---

65 Note the value <tá> in *im-tá-ši* 'he has forgotten' BM 103203:12 (Nuzi/Ass.). This reading should probably be changed to *em-da-ši* 'impose on her!', following Freydank (2016b, 97).

66 Cf. Adler (1976, 4); Syllab, no. 229.

/ti/ A strong distinction between /i/ and /e/ is made by the use of <ti> (TI) and <te> (TE). We also find <ti$_4$> (DI) on one occasion in *i-ti$_4$-iq-ma* KAM 10 20:8 and in the PN *Si-kil-ti$_4$-^{d}Be-er* MARV 1 10:17. For the use of TE with value <ṭe$_4$> and TI with <ṭì>, see below.

/ṭi/ Unlike in Babylonian, the sign DI is not used for emphatic <ṭi>. MA uses the value <ṭí> TÍ, probably as a remnant of OA, where it was used for all three dentals. Note that we also find this sign as the default in Ugaritic-Akkadian (Huehnergard 1989, 33). The legal document Jankowska 1962 features TI for <ṭe$_6$>, or perhaps <ṭì> in *TI-ḫi* (*ṭiḫi*) Jankowska 1962:9; see also *ne-re-ṭì* 'fear?' (< *narāṭu*$^{?}$) MARV 1 71: In some PNs, TE is used with the value <ṭe$_4$> or <ṭi$_4$>: ^{m}EN-[*l*]*e-ṭe$_4$-e*[*r*] KAV 98:5 (OMA 1, 166); *E-ṭe$_4$-er* KAM 10, 18:17; *mi-ṭi$_4$-ti* KAJ 151:7.

/du/ Normally, DU is used.

/tu/ Normally, TU is used. The sign UD is rarely used with the value <tú>, which is so far limited to a few attestations. In the final position, the reading <tú> may be preferable to the faulty accusative ending <tam> (cf. § 87): ^{iti}*a-la-*⸢*an*⸣*-na-tú* TR 3003:13 (see § 87; UGM, 10); perhaps *an-na-*⸢*tú*$^{?}$⸣ (nom.) KAJ 94:6 or, better still (?), *an-na-*⸢*TE*⸣ KAJ 94:6; *nap-*⸢*ša*⸣*-a-tú* A 2994:24. However, the two forms from Tell Ar-Rimāḥ (*šaṭ-ru-UD-ni* TR 2018:4; 3012:7) need to be read as *ut* with the archaic subjunctive *-Øni* (see § 661; pace UGM, 10). The writing *ši-iḫ-tú* (Giricano 8:4) is problematic, since it requires an emphatic /ṭ/. We find the sign TUM, which was also used in older dialects for the final closed syllable *-tum* in the intervocalic position with values <tu$_4$>, e.g., *ša-aṭ-ru-TUM-n*i KAJ 142:6, Billa 19:17; *ma-gír ḫi ib-ku-TUM-ni* Billa 19:5; *TUM-ka-*⸢*as*⸣*-sú* EA 15:18. The OA value <tù> (DU) is attested in *ma-du-DU* TR 3025:16.

/ṭu/ An innovation of WPA (UA: Huehnergard 1989, 34), Assyrian uses GÍN for this emphatic value in order to better distinguish it from <du>. In private archives, <ṭú> (TU) also occurs, most frequently in the root *balāṭu*, e.g., *bal-ṭú-šu-nu* KAJ 1:8; *i-ša-aṭ-ṭú-ru-ni-iš-šu* KAJ 177:17; *i-bal-laṭ-ṭú-ni* Giricano 8:20; ^{f}*Ú-ba-li-ṭú* MPR 20:4''. In OA, the value <ṭù> is found once in *i-ḫi-ṭù* 'they will weigh out' KAJ 85:21 (Arn).

/ad/ Normally, AD is used.

/id/ Normally, <id/t/ṭ> (Á) is used.

/ud/ Normally, UD is used. This sign is also used in limited contexts as <u$_4$> in *ūmu* 'day' (see § 68) and sometimes as <tú> (see above).

§ 211 We already mentioned that, in verbal forms of the type I/q, partial assimilation takes place with the emphatic velar /q/ resulting in /qt/ > /qṭ/ (see § 161). This phenomenon presumably occurred to make pronunciation of the emphatic value of /q/ easier. While this sound change is regularly featured in the NA corpus, in MA, it is still absent in many texts, including MAL.[67] This led Lewy (1921, 16) to state that the change was not fully adapted during this period. The list of examples in MA is fairly limited; we find <ṭí> (TÍ) for the VA-affected perfect of *qabāʾu* and <ṭa> (DA) in *qarābu*. A complete list of attestations is given below:

qabāʾu	*iq-ḪI-bi* 'he said' MAPD § 2:29; § 8:51; KAV 217:2', 10, 13, 21; KAJ 209:12 (NtA); A 1765 (NTA, 25):13 (NtA)
	iq-ḪI-bi-a-šu 'he said to him' TabT05a-134:14 (TN)
	táq-ḪI-bi 'she said' MAPD § 14:71
	aq-ḪI-bi 'I said' MARV 10 3:17 (Abk$^{?}$)
qarābu D	*uq-DA-na-ru-bu* 'they will offer' Coronation Ritual iii 5
	uq-DA-ri-bu-ni-šu 'they offered to him' KAJ 205:11 (Ad)

Looking at the datings of the texts, we may very carefully propose that the change in orthography only took place in the late MA period. The earliest attestation is no doubt from the Tell Ṭābān text TabT05a-134, which, according to Shibata, dates to the end of the reign of TN. However, some innovations may be found earlier in the peripheral texts than in

67 For NA, see Deller (1959, 221–24 § 42); SNAG, 21 § 2.2.3.1.

Aššur, of which Giricano is a good example (see de Ridder 2017a). Another early attestation could be the Coronation Ritual, which refers to Kār-Tukultī-Ninurta. However, Hecker (2008, 96) suggests that at least the copy of the text may date from the reign of Tiglath-pileser I. For MAPD; A 1765 (NTA, 25); KAJ 205; KAJ 209, a date back to the reign of Ad–Tp is certain, while MARV 10 3 could date from the period of Abk (de Ridder 2013b, 142). This leaves only KAV 217 as a possible earlier attestation (see Freydank 1992, 222–23). As such, we find many attestations of these two verbs without the sound change:

qabāʾu	*iq-ti-bi* 'he said' MAL A § 17:67; T 04-37:11
	iq-ti-bi-a 'he said (to me)' KAV 104:14; Billa 63:18; T 93-2:4; MARV 4 8:13
	iq-ti-bi-ú-ni 'they said to me' MATSH 6:6'; T 93-54:6
	aq-ti-bi 'I said' MATC 15:24
qarābu	*aq-ti-ri-ib* 'I approached' MATSH 2:29

Outside of the two verbs *qabāʾu* and *qarābu*, the sound change is not attested. Admittedly, the actual number of attestations, where /q/ and /t/ are in context, is limited:

damiqtu	^{f}*Da-a-*⌜*am*⌝*-mi-iq-tu* MATC 65:3
ḫaliqtu	*ḫa-li-iq-ta* 'lost' KAV 168:8; [*ḫ*]*a-liq-ta* MAPD § 15:73
^{m}*Nasiqtu*	^{m}*Na-si-iq-ti* KAJ 9:21
quālu	*iq-tu-a-al* 'he looked after' MATC 15:29
rāqtu	*ra-aq-ta-*(…) 'empty' KAV 103:28; KAV 205:13

The examples of *qabāʾu* without the sound change must be regarded as the result of hypercorrection by Assyrian scribes, as they must have been well aware that a perfect comes with a *-ta-* infix, rather than *-ṭa-*. This probably has little to do with any Babylonian influence, as both /t/ and /ṭ/ are in free variation here: there is no difference in meaning between *iqtibi* and *iqṭibi*. For this reason, we can expect the more traditional spellings with /t/, rather than suspecting a Babylonian influence.[68] Unfortunately, there are no examples of this sound change in nouns, but the relatively rare sequence of /q/+/t/ does not exclude the possibility that it happened. On this point, I disagree with Saporetti (1966, 277), who argued that <ṭì> (TI) is a normal value for MA and has to be read in the perfect forms of *qabāʾu*. It is true that the value can be found more often in literary texts, but only rarely in letters and administrative documents. This included the onomasticon (cf. OMA 2, 207). This brings us to two main problems. First of all, we would have to introduce this value in many archives solely for the verb *qabāʾu*. Secondly, it suggests that we know MA better than did the Assyrians themselves. If they intended to express /ṭ/, nothing was stopping them from writing the widely used TÍ. What is problematic is the attestation of the change /d/ < /t/ and the appearance of the initial /ḫ/ in the verb *abātu* (e.g., *uḫ-DA-bi-it* RIMA 1 A.0.76.10:39; 13:39; *iḫ-DA-bit* RIMA 1 A.0.78:16; see Köcher 1957/58, 311). However, this must be related to the literary Babylonian sound change /mt/ > /md/.[69] Attestations of this sound change in *qabāʾu* are widely attested in NA.[70]

68 Unlike SNAG, 21. § 2.2.3.1. As can be observed, the sound change was still valid in NA, but cannot be found in OA because the orthography does not distinguish between the dentals.

69 See Machinist (1978, 441–442); cf. GAG, 40 § 31f.

70 See Deller (1959, 221ff); SNAG, 21 § 2.2.3.1.

§ 212 The dental /t/ assimilates into the preceding /ṣ-z/ in finite verbs with the t-infix of the perfect (UGM, 25 § 21.7). This type of assimilation of the t-infix is common in Akkadian.[71]

samāḫu D	*ús-sa-am-me-eḫ* 'he has selected' MAL B § 8:12
sasā'u	*is-si-si* 'he has proclaimed' MAL B § 6:40
ṣabātu	*iṣ-ṣa-bat* 'he has seized' MAL A § 15:41; KAJ 307:7; Giricano 7:11
	iṣ-ṣa-ab-ta 'he has seized' MAL A § 15:47
	iṣ-ṣa-ba-as-si 'he has seized her' MAL A § 12:18
	iṣ-ṣa-ab-tu 'they have seized' MARV 6 22:8'
	ta-ṣa-ba-ta-ni 'you have seized' KAV 102:18
	aṣ-ṣa-bat 'I have seized' Hall 1983:19
ṣabātu D	*uṣ-ṣa-bi-it* 'I have taken' KAV 217:6; Halle 1983:8
	ú-ṣa-bi-it 'I have taken' AO 19.227:11
ṣabbu'u D	*ú-ṣ[a-b]i-šu-n[u]* 'he has inspected them' T 04-35:16
ṣalā'u	*ta-aṣ-ṣi-li* 'she has aborted' MAL A § 53:93
	a-ṣi-li 'I have cast' AO 19.227:13
zabālu	*iz-zi-bi-il*$_5$ 'he has brought' MAL A § 30:21
zakā'u	*i-zu-ku* 'they have cleared' KAJ 162:19
zakā'u D	*uz-zak-ki-ši* 'he has freed her' KAJ 7:8

A similar type of progressive assimilation takes place in the perfect of the I/d verbs.

dabābu	*ad-du-bu-ub* 'I spoke' Tsukimoto 1992 D:8
	ni-id-du-bu-ub 'we spoke' NP 46:7
dabābu Gtn	*[ta-ad]-da-na-⸢ab⸣-bu-ub* 'you will keep speaking' MATSH 9:37
duāku	*id-du-ku* 'they killed' MATSH 2:49

It also takes place in an SB literary text of the period: *e-za-qa-ap* 'he planted' BWL, 162:12 (cf. p. 152). This may not be so much an actual sound change as an orthographic convention. Traditionally, this type of assimilation has been used to argue for a spirantized pronunciation of /z/ and /ṣ/ in early second millennium Akkadian.[72] If we assume an affricative realization of /ṣ/ and /z/, then we can conclude that the scribes interpreted the consonant cluster /ṣ+t/ and /z+t/ as a double affricate and thus wrote it that way. In the case of MA, the affricative realization may have been something of the past, but nonetheless its previous realization may still be reflected in the orthography, as it continues to observed in the use of <Z> for regressive assimilated pronominal suffixes (see § 225). Alternatively, and possibly more plausible for MA, is Kogan's (2011a, 66–67) suggestion that these spellings represent metathesis, e.g., *izzibil* ≠ *i-*^{d}*z-t-ibil*, but *i-t-z-ibil*. This type of metathesis is attested in MA with infinitives of *ta(n)*-stems involving R_1/s–š (§ 226), although it is also known to occur in Akkadian with R_1/ṣ-z-d (GAG, 44 § 36a). While this assumption still requires <Z> to be read with an affricate value, at the same time, it does not require an affricate realization of /z/ as a phoneme. The same cannot be said for spellings such as *ta-aṣ-ṣi-li* MAL A § 53:93, given that <ṣi> (ZÍ) cannot be read as <zí> (an affricate) in MA. We would thus need to assume that it was also possible to read <Ṣ> as an affricate, even though the phoneme /ṣ/ itself was probably deaffricated in MA. The examples of /st/ > /ss/ are even more difficult to explain in a deaffricated context. Therefore, a comprehensive explanation of this type of assimilation in MA has still to be found.

71 See GAG, 35 § 29e; cf. OA in GOA § 3.2.4.8.
72 See Tropper (1996, 648); Streck (2006, 218).

§ 213 When in contact, /d/ assimilates into a following /t/, usually in the case of a feminine ending *-tV*, e.g., *ki-ši-it-ti* (< *kišidtu*) 'spoil' MARV 1 14:24; *pi-qi-te* (*piqittu* < *paqādu*) MATC 54:2; *ṣi-mi-te* 'yoke team' (*ṣimittu* < *ṣamādu*) MATC 22A:8; *e-mi-it-tu* 'punishment' (*emittu* < *emēdu*) MAL A § 24:81; *e-mi-it-ta* 'right side' Ištar Ritual:2; *ni-mat-te* (*emēdu*) KTN inventory ii 9; *ta-li-ta* (< **tawlidtu*) KAJ 96:16. Two verbal roots feature a shift of /t/ > /d/, one of which is *biātum* > *biādum*. In Babylonian, no such sound change takes place and we have *bâtu* (CAD B, 169ff), cf. *bētu* 'house' and the Arabic √*bīt* (بات) 'spend the night', e.g., *be-du-ú-ni* PKT 1 I right:30. The other root is *nābutu* > *nābudu* 'to flee' (N-stem): *i-na-bi-da-an-ni* MATSH 12:8; *in-na-bi-du-ni* MATSH 2:4, 22. This was interpreted by Cancik-Kirschbaum as evidence of the declining differentiation between the two dental plosives (MATSH, 99); however, the fact that this change is limited to two verbal roots makes such a far-reaching conclusion unnecessary.[73] Free variation between the two phonemes is more common and varied in NA; but, even here, Luukko (2004, 70) presents relatively few attestations. Perhaps we should add *tu-uḫ-ni* 'millet' MATSH 3:14' (Bab. *duḫnu*). The occurrence of the PN *Munnābittu* 'fugitive' (e.g., ^{m}*Mu-na-bi-it-te* KAV 168:1; also, OMA 1, 330) vs. PN *Nabudu* (e.g., *Na-bu-di* Tr 100:17; OMA 1, 341; see Kouwenberg 2004, 338) is not a very good example because of the unexpected doubling of the dental in the first PN; cf. *mu-nab-di* 'refugee' MARV 4 30:17' (cf. Kouwenberg 2004, 339). In fact, the Babylonian sound change /t/ > /d/ in Assyrian for R_3 seems to have worked in both directions. The verb *kabātu* is realized as *kabādu* in Assyrian, which conforms to its Semitic root √*kbd* (AHw, 416b; cf. Kouwenberg 2010, 43 n37). For some possibly unusual cases of *kabādu* in MA, see § 208. Before /š/, the dental plosives seem to assimilate: *qa-aš-ša* (< *qadšu*) KAM 10 25:3; ŠE *eš-šu* 'new barley' TR 3005:1 (GAG, 35 § 39d).

§ 214 There are a few examples from MA where /t/ > /š/ or /š/ > /t/ (UGM, 21f § 17). If these examples are correct, they could reflect the spirantization of /t/ > /ṯ/. Consider the following change of /š/ > /t/: *ut-ra-a-aq* (< *ušrâq*) 'he will empty' MAL B § 19:12; *kī ti-ru* (< *šīru*) (…) *lā ṭābūni* 'because the flesh (of the sheep) was not good' KAJ 209:5–7.[74] Evidence for the reverse /t/ > /š/ is more problematic:

i+na UDU *šu-a-šu* (…) 'from that sheep; (pieces of meat)' Adad Ritual r. 8'

tup-pu KALAG.GA A.ŠÀ *šu-a-šu* (…) *a-na* PN *za-ku-at* 'the strong tablet of that field is cleared for PN' KAJ 149:22 (Aub)

[*ša/i+na*] ⌜*pi*⌝ DUB$^{?}$ *šu-a-ša* 'according to the wording of that tablet' Billa 19:6

[*ša/i+na p*]*i tup-*⌜*pi šu'*⌝*-a-ša* 'according to the wording of that tablet' Billa 19:18

These are three masculine singular oblique pronouns derived from *šuātV*. It will be argued in § 353ff that these data are likely an indication of a merger of the oblique and dative

73 Some evidence for the decline of differentiation may be found in an NA syllabic Sumerian transcription where Sumerian /d/ > /t/. See Maul (2010).

74 See CAD Š$_3$, 113b; cf. CAD T, 430b. It is possible that the spelling resulted from confusion because of the graphic similarity between <ši> and <ti>. Judging by the CDLI photo, Ebeling's original copy is correct in his reading of <ti>, with a clearly visible extra wedge that excludes the possibility of <ši>.

paradigm of the independent personal pronominal. This is confirmed by the situation in NA.

4.7 Sibilants

4.7.1 Sibilants /s-ṣ-z/

§ 215 MA uses three basic sibilants as phonemes, which belong to the Common Semitic stock of fricative dentals: /s-ṣ-z/. Of these, /s/ is voiceless, /ṣ/ is a voiceless emphatic and /z/ is voiced. In earlier Akkadian, these three sibilants were realized as the affricates /^{t}s-^{t}ṣ-^{d}z/; however, in this study, we will assume that all had become deaffricated in this period.[75] Most scholars accept that /s/ and /š/ changed positions in MA and NA phonology; this will be discussed in § 219. In the orthography, /ṣ/ and /z/ are grouped together under the ZA series, with /sa/ being grouped under SA. For details, see below:

/sa/ Normally, SA is used. We find <sà> (ZA) in the pronominal suffix *-ša* (3fs) assimilated into a dental (see below). Other attestations are more obscure and mostly occur in BVW, e.g., *ZA-am-mu-tu* 'fragrance(?)' BVW S r. 4; *ta-ZA-làḫ* 'you will sprinkle' BVW A:5; G:12; H :4; I:9, r. 2; S:7, r. 5; KÁ *ZA-mu-uḫ* Adad Ritual:9; *a-bu-ZA-tum* 'stables' VAT 8923:6. In a SB text, we find *i-na-as-ZA-a*$^{?}$*-ma* < *inassaḫ-ma* KAR r. 9 (see CAD N_2, 4c).

/ṣa/ The sign ZA is always used.

/za/ The sign ZA is always used.

/si/ Normally, SI is used. No distinction is made between /i/ and /e/. In one PN, we find <sè> (ZÍ): [^{m}]^{d}*Sè-e*-KAR Giricano 7:29. Perhaps we also have a case of <sí> (ZI) in ^{d}*li-sí-ku-ti* (uncertain meaning) VAT 8923:2, 8, cf. ⌜^{d}⌝*li-si-ku-ti* SAA 13 46:12' (see Weidner 1963b, 122).

/ṣi/ Normally, <ṣi> (ZÍ) is used. No distinction is made between /i/ and /e/. In early texts, we sometimes find <ṣí> (ZI), e.g., *e-ṣí-de* KAJ 50:6 (Abn); KAM 10 2:12 (Ead); *Ma-ṣí*-DINGIR KAJ 87:12, 21; perhaps also *ḫal-ZI* 'district' Billa 6:8.

/zi/ Normally, <zi> is used. No distinction is made between /i/ and /e/. Sometimes, we find <zí>, e.g., *e-zí-ib* KAM 10 2:2.

/su/ Normally, SU is used. We find ZU for the pronominal suffix *-šu* assimilated into a preceding dental (see below). The attestation *i-na-ak-ki-ZU* MAL B § 8:17 (cf. *i-na-ki-su* MAL A § 8:80) is probably best explained as a spelling analogue, along with the assimilated pronominal suffixes, which both express the final *-su*.

/ṣu/ Normally, <ṣu >(ZUM) is used. This sign is probably a symptom of recent southern influence, where it had become common (Aro 1955a, 20). Eventually, ZUM replaced <ṣú> (ZU) completely; however, especially in the earlier texts, we still find the older value: *e-ṣú-tum* KAJ 32:6 (Adn/TN); *e-ZU* 'little' KAJ 174:7 (Aššnīr II/Abn); ^{m}*Tar-ZU-ša-lim* KAJ 160 9 (EAd), but also *iḫ-mi-ZU-ku-nu-ú-ni* T 04-37:12; *na-aṣ-ZU-ni* TabT05a-151:12; for <ṣu$_{x}$> (SU) only: *li-SU-ru-ka* RS 06.198:7.

/zu/ Normally, ZU is used. As SU and ZU highly resemble each other, it is not unlikely that there was some confusion among the scribes; hence, we have to introduce zu$_{x}$ (SU): *ta-na-ḫi-SU-ú-ni* MAL A § 36:13. We also find <zu$_{x}$> (SU) in all attestations of the PN Aššur-zuqupanni, who is a regular feature in the Bābu-āha-iddina archive, e.g., (^{m})^{d}*A-šur-SU-qup-pa-ni* KAJ 203:2; KAJ 293:20; KAV 99:2; KAV 108:1 but ^{md}*A-šur-zu-qup-pa-ni* KAV 102:2 (see OMA 1, 148f). Cf. *i-za-qu-pu-ú-ši* MAL A § 53:96. In an MA incantation, we find: *SU-um-ri-ia* 'my body' Rm 376:10. Borger did not number the reading <zu$_{x}$> for the sign, despite there being some other evidence (MZL, 252 no. 16).

/az/ Normally, AZ is used for aṣ/z. For the difference between <ás> (ÁŠ) and <as> (AZ), see § 221. On one occasion, <áṣ> (ÁŠ) is found in ^{zi}*ma-áṣ-ḫe-te* New Year Ritual:17'. The spellings in *na-áṣ-be-te* (TabT105a-085:2; TabT05a-623:7) for *naṣbutu*$^{sic.}$ can be removed, as we should read

75 Cf. Streck (2006); Kogan (2011, 66–67).

this noun as *nasbītu*.[76] Spellings with <áṣ> are still common in Nuzi (cf. HSS 14 140:23; 15 267:13; 16 87:11 etc.).

/iz/ Normally, (GIŠ) is used for <iṣ/z>. For the difference between <is> (GIŠ), <ís> (IŠ) and <és> (EŠ), see § 221. Of these values, <ís> (IŠ) is unusual.

/uz/ Normally, UZ is used for <uṣ/z>. For the difference between <us> (UŠ) and <ús> (UZ), see § 221.

§ 216 As can be seen above, the ZA series of signs is sometimes used for /s/. Although these values were the standard in OA, the fact that they are limited to pronominal suffixes shows a strong southern influence on orthography; see also § 225. We have already mentioned that, historically, all three sibilants were affricates; thus, they were realized as [ᵗs] (S), [ᵗs'] (Ṣ) and [ᵈz] (Z).[77] While originally all three affricates were already being expressed with the ZA series around the OAkk period deaffricatization of /s/ ([ᵗs]), which resulted in /s/ being written with SA.[78] In OB, the ZA series was still used for affricates, leading to the conclusion that /z/ and /ṣ/ remained, at least partially, affricated (cf. Streck 2006). The sibilant /s/ seems to have been separated in an affricated and deaffricated allophoneme judging by the distribution of SA and ZA signs to express the etymologic phoneme. As the orthography of OA does not give us much information about the process of 'deaffricatization', we know little about the situation in MA. However, the preferred use of <S> for dentals assimilated into pronominal -š suggests that the sibilants became deaffricated (for a more extensive discussion on assimilated pronominal suffixes, see § 224f).

§ 217 There is a number of small sound changes concerning the three sibilants. We find /s/ > /ṣ/ in *pa-aṣ-ṣu-ú-na-at* MAL A § 40:60 (Bab. *pasāmu*); /z/ > /s/ in *si-bi-bi-a-ni* 'black cumin' (< *zibibiānum*) KAJ 277:10; *ar-sa-nu* 'barley goats' (< *arzānum* > Sum. AR.ZA.NA) KAJ 226:10; *a*[*r*]-*sa-a-n*[*u*] KAJ 277:13; interchangeability of /s/ and /z/ in the PN Paʾus/zu, e.g., [ᵐ]*Pa-u-si* MARV 7 39:5'; ᵐ*Pa-u-zi* MARV 6 25:7. The progressive assimilation of /t/ into the preceding sibilant in verbal forms is discussed above in § 212. Note that /z/ assimilates into /t/ in *zīttu* 'share' (GAG, 38 § 30g), e.g., *zi-ti* KAJ 148:4; *zi-tu-šu* KAJ 179:9; *zi-it-tu* OIP 79 6:7. There remains the possibility of the change /ṣ/ > /s/ in the root *ḫamāṣu*, although the evidence and the Semitic etymologies are not unambiguous.[79]

---

76 According to Deller, the noun *nasbītu* refers to a festival (see UŠA, 47). This idea is confirmed by the OA evidence (Dercksen 2015, 52–53). Spellings from Aššur use <as> (AZ), rather than <ás> (ÁŠ), in the Tell Ṭābān material, e.g., *na-aṣ-bi-*[*t*]*e* KAJ 130:17; *na-aṣ-be-te* KAJ 226:4; MARV 2 19 4. r. 19'; MARV 10 5:23. Earlier publications read *naṣbutu*, rather than *nasbītu*. Given the presence of the OA plural *nasbiātu* (Dercksen 2015, 52), we can exclude the reading *naṣbutu*. In addition, the use of the signs AZ and ÁŠ only allow for one common value <as> ~ <áṣ>, which leads to the abandonment of /ṣ/ for /s/. This is permissible as there is still no convincing etymology available for this noun (see also de Ridder 2015d).

77 See Farber (1985); GAG, 35 § 30a.

78 See GAG, 36 § 30a: Hasselbach (2005, 97–97 § 2.7).

79 The problem is created by the root *ḫamāṣu* 'to plunder' and the MA plurale tantum *ḫamsātu* 'stolen goods', e.g., *ḫi-im-SA-a*-te 'stolen property' T 04-37:14; also, on one occasion, as *ḫamsu* in *ḫa-am-su* George 1988 1 r. 12'. In terms of the verbal root, von Soden (AHw, 315b) suggests a connection with Ge'ez √ʿ*mḍ* (ዐመፀ) 'to do wrong/act unjustly etc'. However, more possible cognates, such as the Arabic √*ġmṣ* (غمص), are available (see Leslau 1987, 63a). At the same time, von Soden connected *ḫamāṣu* to

4.7.2 Sibilant /š/

§ 218 The sibilant /š/ is the result of multiple phonemes (/š/, /ś/, /ṯ/) merging together. It was probably pronounced as a voiceless alveolar lateral fricative [ɬ] (see below); however, it has often been assumed that <Š> and <S> also swapped positions in MA and NA. A remarkable feature of the orthography is that there are no less than five new signs for /š/ introduced in MA; remarks on them are given in the following:

/ša/ Normally, ŠA is used. The syllabic value <šá> (NÍG) was first introduced in MA and contemporary MB, where the development is visible, as the sign is used more often in later texts.[80] In the prescriptive texts, the sign is mostly limited to the relative pronoun ša; however, even in the few texts where the sign is used (e.g., MAPD; Coronation Ritual), <ša$_1$> is still preferred. In other literary texts, such as MAL A, the value <šá> is mostly absent, occurring only once in the text *nap-šá-a-te* § 52:91 and in the date formula ^{iti}*šá sa-ra-a-te* MAL A viii 64. Its occurrence in the month name is a clear indication that the text is a literal copy of an earlier composition, whereas <šá> slipped by error into *napšāte*. In the case of MAL A, the absence of <šá> is certainly due to its archaic Babylonian orthography, where the value is rare (MZL no. 859). BVW is a literary text that uses <šá> in the most diverse situations, in alternation with the more frequent <ša> (ŠA), e.g., *ta-šá-qi* BVW Ac:5; *tu-šá-áš-ku* BVW I r. 8. It may be noted that, in the M 6 archive (Ad period), <šá> becomes frequent, although still not dominant over <ša$_1$>, e.g., URU *šá sa-ma-ia-a* A 1749 (NTA, 23):5; *ú-šá-kal* A 113 (NTA, 15):29; ^{lú}*mu-šá-ki-lu* A 1735 (NTA, 18):16; *a-na la ma-šá-e* A 3182 (NTA, 33):10. On the other hand, <šá> is not used in the Giricano archive (Abk period). The use of <šá> is most common in the relative pronoun *ša*, e.g., KAJ 110:11; KAJ 191:2; MARV 7 19:9; MARV 10 8:1; LVUH 8:9. Using a pronominal suffix is uncommon, except in *šul-ma-šá* T 97-5:11. The value <šá> seems to have been avoided in letters and does not occur in the letters of Tell Aš-Šēḫ Ḥamad and Tell Ḫuwīra, but does occur in the administrative documents from these sites. In the Bābu-aḫa-iddina/Ubru letters, it is only found in some fixed spellings, such as the month names in the date formula at the end of letters, e.g., ^{iti}*šá sa-ra-t*[*e*] KAV 98:49.

/ši/ A strong distinction between /i/ and /e/ is made by the use of <ši> (IGI) and <še> (ŠE). Some confusion in the use of both values can be found. In this grammar, these spellings will be regarded as erroneous. Rarely, we find the OA value <ší> SI in early M 9 texts: *ší-im* A.ŠÀ-*šu* 'price of his field' KAJ 153:14; *a-na ší-im ga-me-er* 'for the complete price' VAT 9034:5. Perhaps *ší-im-ta* MARV 4 151:56 (TN).

/šu/ Normally, ŠU is used. The sign ŠÚ was first used in MA, usually for pronominal suffixes, except in one instance: *ú-na-šú-qu* Coronation Ritual iii 3. Nowhere is the sign ŠÚ a frequent value in MA, although its application seems to have increased over time. According to Syllab no. 296, the value first appears in a royal inscription from Shalmaneser I; however, we already find the sign a number of times in KAJ 7 (e.g., DUMU^{meš}-*šú*), which is an early MA marriage document (EAd/Aub). This text is an exception and no other uncontested attestation dates back this far. During the Adn–TN period, the sign occurs occasionally, e.g., DUMU-*šú* MARV 5 53+:11 et passim (Sa); however, it does not occur at all in the Tell Aš-Šēḫ Ḥamad and Tell Ḫuwīra corpora, but is attested in Tell Rimāḥ: *a-bu-šú* 'his father' TR 3029:4. There are also a few attestations in TSA material, e.g., ŠEŠ-*šú* T 98-45+ vi 23''; T 04-7:12'. Attestations do seem to increase in late MA: *bi-ḫir-šú* KAJ 306a:9 (Nae); ^{ú}*áp-ru-šú* MARV 2 28:5 (Abk). In this light, we find the sign also used in the Giricano archive: *tup-pu-šú* Giricano 1:15; $^{\text{na4}}$KIŠIB-*šú* Giricano 4:1, 14:1;

ḫamsu and the derived pattern *ḫamsātu*, which he connected to Hebrew √*ḥms* (חמס) 'to treat violently'. While seemingly close in meaning, the Hebrew root seems incompatible with the Ge'ez/Arabic roots. Note also the Hebrew √*ḥmṣ* (חמץ) 'to be ruthless', probably connected to Ge'ez/Arabic roots. What this means for the Assyrian attestations of the verbal root *ḫamāṣu* and the nominal form *ḫamsātu* is not clear, but the total absence of signs of the AŠ series (also used for /s/; see § 221) to indicate R$_3$ suggests that it was /ṣ/, e.g., *tu-uḫ-tam-mi-iṣ* MAL N § 1:3. However, the use of the sign SU in *iḫ-mi-SU-ku-nu-ú-ni* T 04-37:12 should also be noted.

80 See Aro (1955a, 25).

ŠEŠ^{meš}-*šú* Giricano 4:25. The idea that the use of the sign was due to the preference of the scribe can be confirmed by the fact that all these attestations are from texts written by the same scribe (Aḫu-teribīya; see Giricano, 62). In literary texts, it is absent from the laws and palace edicts, but does occur in the Coronation Ritual, which is believed to be a late copy (Hecker (2008, 96): *ma-za-al-te-šú* Coronation Ritual iii 14. It also occurs once in another ritual from KTN: GÙB-*šú* Ištar Ritual:4. This could be a southern influence as the syllabic value was first used in MB texts in a broader context than later MA. The value became frequent during the reign of Nebuchadnezzar I (contemporary with Aššur-rēša-išī I), but occurred before this king. This suggests that the sign was an MB invention, intended as an easier alternative for ŠU (Aro 1955a, 25).

/aš/ There is an almost equal division between <aš> (DIL) and <áš> (ÁŠ). When checking the signs AŠ/ÁŠ, it can be observed that the older texts from before the period of EAd/Aub use DIL, instead of the ÁŠ, e.g., *ta-ad-na-aš-šu* KAJ 177:15 (Aššnīr II); *it-ta-na-aš-ši* KAJ 132:18 (Arn); KAJ 139:19' (Arn/Abn). This is probably a matter of chance, but is not unexpected. Since we stated that MA cuneiform is based on an OB model, we should expect to find OB *aš* (DIL, cf. Syllab, 1 no. 1) next to OA/OB *áš* (ÁŠ). While, in OB, there may have been a difference in function between the two signs (cf. Streck 2006, 217), this is not visible in MA. In MAL, both are used, while MAPD uses only ÁŠ. Texts from Tell Aš-Šēḫ Ḥamad and Tall Ḫuwīra use ÁŠ. The earliest MA texts from Giricano do not present any evidence outside of the DN *Aš-šur*. To date, no conclusion can be drawn concerning the variation in the usage of these two signs, other than that it was caused by the scribe's preference or education.[81]

/iš/ Normally, IŠ i/o EŠ is used, as will be discussed in § 221. In the DN Ištar, we find the spelling U-DAR for *Iš*$_8$*-tár*.

/uš/ The sign UŠ is always used.

	<šá> (rel.)	<šá> (free)	<-šú> (pron.)	<šú> (free)	<aš>	<áš>
MAL A	(+)	(+)	-	-	+	++
MAPD	+	-	-	-	-	++
Coronation	+	-	+	(+)	+	-
PKT	+	+	+	-	-	+++
M 4	+	+	(+)	-	-	++
M 6	++	++	-	-	-	(+)
M 7	+	(-)	-	-	-	++
M 9	-	(+)	+	-	+++	+
M 10	+	+	-	-	(+)	++
M 11	+	-	-	-	-	++
MATSH	-	-	-	-	-	+++
MATC	++	++	-	-	-	+++
LVUH	+	-	-	-	-	+
TaR	+	+	+	-	+	+
TṢA	+	+	(+)	-	+	++
Giricano	-	-	+	-	-	-

Figure 18: Distribution of the syllabic values for /š/.

As we discussed above, the orthographic sign uses for /š/ display some variation. This is best summarized in the following table, which distinguishes between free use (i.e., any syllabic construction) and fixed writings. In the case of <šá>, this includes the relative pronoun (rel.) and, for <šú>, the pronominal suffixes (pron.).

§ 219 The phonetic realization of /š/ in NA, and to a lesser extent in MA, has been the subject of extensive debate with the most prominent opinion being that /š/ and /s/ changed

81 Driver and Miles wrongfully assumed that ÁŠ was more frequent in older MA texts and could be used to date texts (see Driver/Miles 1935, 8).

position.[82] The evidence for this assumption is mainly based on NA, while it appears that the process was not yet complete in MA. The suggestion that /š/ was to be pronounced [s] was made by Parpola, in his article on the verb *naṣṣ-*, in which he showed that it was a by-form of *našā'u* with /'/ assimilated into <Š>. This suggests that /š/ changed into [s] in Assyrian, a change that is commonly accepted for NA.[83] However, as we will see below, in order to account for the sound change /št/ > /lt/, a realization as [ɬ] is assumed. Sound changes of /š/ are regular and mostly confined to one systematic, but common, condition.[84]

4.7.3 Sibilants before dentals

§ 220 A shared MB/MA sound change occurs when a /š/ or /s/ comes in direct contact with a dental (/d-t-ṭ/) the sibilant transforms into /l/.[85] There are very few and isolated exceptions to this sound change, which are already attested in the earliest texts. In the majority of attestations, the exceptions involve the sibilant /š/ and dental /t/, most notably in the perfect of Š-stems and G or D-stem of I/š verbs.

ebāru Š	*ul-te-be-ru* 'they made enter' MARV 1 14:36
ṣabātu D	*ul-ta-aṣ-bi-it* 'I posted' MATSH 2: 7, 10
šamā'u	*al-te-ma* 'I have heard' T 96-1:11
šapāru	*al-tap-ra-ma* 'I sent' TR 2031:8
šakayyunu Š	*ul-ta-ka-in* 'I prostrate myself' T 96-15:3

This is also attested in substantives:

altammu	^{é}*al-tam-me* 'tavern' MAL A § 14:31
lubaltu	^{túg}*lu-bal-ta* 'clothing' Coronation Ritual i 35
maltu	*ma-al-ti-ša* 'drink' MAL A § 45:96
mereltu	*mé-re-él-te* 'wish' T 96-6:7
piriltu	*pi-ri-il-ta* 'secret' Ištar Ritual:14
qēltu	*qe-el-tu* 'gift' New Year Ritual:7'

Examples with /d/ are rarer, but do occur as well:

ildu	*il-du* 'base' PKT 3 iv 7
	il-da KAJ 310:6
kašādu	*ik-tal-dam-ma* 'he has reached' MAL C § 8:7
	ik-tal-da! MATSH 14:5
	kíl-du 'acquisition' KAM 11 34:10
šadādu	*tal-du-du-ú-ni* 'she has drawn away' MAL A § 24:73 (cf. *tal-ta-da-ad* l. 42)

A few examples with /ṭ/ are known:

multu	*mul-ṭ[u]* 'comb' BVW Ko r. 21.
	mul-ṭu KAJ 310:6
šaṭāru	*il-ṭu-ra-áš-še* 'he wrote to her' MAL A § 46:92

---

82 The realization /š/ is an issue in all Akkadian dialects. For OAkk: Hasselbach (2005, 135–37 § 3.3.3); for OB: Streck (2006, 241–50 § 2.9).

83 Notice also the situation in contemporary Hittite where the value of /š/ is also unclear, but was probably closer to [s] (see Hoffner/Melchert 2008, 38 § 1.92–1.93).

84 There are few exceptions: note the assimilation of /š/ into /ḫ/ in ^{uru}*Ku-liḫ-ḫi-na-áš* MARV 5 64:5 (Nae); cf. ^{uru}*Ku-liš-ḫi-na-áš* MARV 9 12:12. See Freydank in MARV 5, 13b. The similarities between the signs for <liš> and <liḫ> suggest a scribal mistake.

85 See UGM, 24–25 § 21; Streck (2011, 371 § 4.2). For MB, see (Aro 1955a, 37f).

The sound change applies to /s/ as well. However, in most cases, when the sibilant /s-ṣ-z/ comes in contact with a dental, progressive assimilation takes place (see § 212):

masduru	*ma-al-de-re* 'duration' Billa 23:8
mazzaltu	*ma-za-al-ta-šú-nu* (<**manzastu*) 'their position' Coronation Ritual iii 14
saḫāru	*il-tu-ḫu-ur* 'he has tarried' MAPD § 21:106

Hecker (1973/74, 167) has attempted to date this sound change to the reign of Aub, based on the expected spelling from the PN *Aššur-multēpiš* in a Sa era text vs. two archaic spellings from an eponym of the Aub period. ^{d}*A-šur-mul-te-piš* KAJ 54:20 (Sa) ~ ^{d}*A-šur*$^{!}$*-muš-ti-piš* KAJ 41:24; ^{md}*A-šur*$^{!}$*-muš*$^{!}$*-ti-<piš>* KAJ 69:22. The older forms are atypical, even as archaic forms, and therefore not suitable on their own in order to date this sound change.[86] Other instances of the retained /št/ sequence are extremely rare and not confined to the period of Aub or before, usually appearing in (foreign) PNs: *ṭí-iš-ṭí-ša* 'residue' PKT 3 iv 6 (hapax); ^{uru}*Ḫi-iš-ta-ri-ba* KAJ 91:7 (Adn$^{?}$); *šu-ri-is-ta* '(meaning uncertain, see CAD Š$_{3}$, 349a)' KAV 99:26 (Sa); ^{m}*Iš-ta-ie-e* MPR 7:4; ^{m}*Iš-ta-re-e-ni* MPR 2:34; 12:38; 18:32 (de Ridder 2016a, 123). There is an odd exception to the sound change in the verbal form *uš-ta-ab-ši-lu* A 1748 (NTA, 23):10.[87] Fixed spellings of the preposition *ištu* (*iš-tu*) or DN Ištar (*Iš*$_{8}$*-tár*) cannot be considered as evidence for dating such a sound change.[88] However, *ištu* becomes *iltu* with pronominal suffixes and, on one occasion, is written as *ul-tu* KAJ 209:13 (Ad). Moreover, examples of /št/ > /lt/ are known from the reign of Aub and before: *il-ta-kan* KAJ 7:9 (EAd/Aub). Admittedly, the evidence is scarcer than one might expect. It has been suggested that the spellings are little more than orthographic influences from a real sound change in Babylonian (Aro 1972, 275). However, the complete adaptation in MA makes it unlikely that we are merely dealing with an orthographic tradition from the south. The sound change /št/ > /lt/ proves that /š/ could not have been pronounced [s], since this fails to explain how it would acquire lateral pronunciation.[89] Therefore, the only valid explanation for the sound change is a lateral /š/ value, presumably [ɬ], as has been suggested by a number of scholars.[90] Streck suggested a variation in the lateral with the voiceless lateral affricate value [ᵗɬ], which would become a deaffricated [ɬ] before the dental plosives.[91] This has the advantage that <L> needs to be nothing more than a scribal convenience for [ɬ], which is otherwise not present in MA. Although the exact realization of /š/ will probably be debated for a long time, it seems likely that /š/ was deaffricated in the MA. There are two related reasons for assuming this. First of all, we mentioned above that it is likely that the three sibilants /s-ṣ-z/ were deaffricated in this period, and that /š/ should be an unexpected exception. Secondly, the swapping of /s/ and /š/ (see below) strongly

86 A Št-participle is very rare in MA. Moreover, we should expect *multēpiš* in all Akkadian dialects, yet TI is written twice.

87 The verbal form *uštabšilū* 'they roasted' A 1748 (NTA, 23):10 is the only MA attestation included in the CAD B (137a) of the Š-stem of *bašālu* in this meaning.

88 Although it must be admitted that there seems to have been some exceptions to the rule /št/ > /lt/ in later Akkadian. Streck (1995, 9 § 12) points out that the numeral *išten* and derivations were never written with /lt/ in NB.

89 See Streck (2006, 241 § 2.9.1).

90 For example, Steiner (1977, 144–48); Diakonoff (1991/92, 52–53); Streck (2006, 244); Westenholz (2006, 257); Kogan (2011, 76–77 § 1.3.3.14).

91 See Streck (2006, 245; 2007, 48 § 2.1.2.; 2011 § 25); for MA: Streck (2011a, 371). This suggestion has met with some criticism (see Yakubovich 2007, 153; Kogan 2011, 71).

suggests that both phonemes were rather similar in this period. Indeed, as we will see, they use the same set of syllabic signs to a certain extent. For this similarity, it seems necessary to assume that /š/ was deaffricated and that the similarity was caused by both phonemes being a voiceless alveolar fricative. We therefore have to regard the sound change of /št/ > /lt/ as dissimilation (see Streck 2006, 244). Difficulties remain with the sound change of MA /lt/ to NA /ss/. Moreover, etymologic /lt/ and derived /lt/ (< št) could not have sounded different in MA, as they both changed into /ss/ in NA, e.g., *is-se-eq-qé* (< *ilteqe*) SAA 12 94:10.[92] NA examples of this shift (/št/ > /lt/ > /ss/) are rare in MA:

erābu Š	*ú-se-rib* (< *ulterib*) 'he has brought in' Giricano 15:11 (Abk$^{?}$)
kurultu	LÚ *ša ku-ru-se-e* (< Sum.) 'animal fattener' A 3186 (NTA, 35):12; A 3192 (NTA, 38):13, but *ku-ri-il-ti-e* 'fodder' KAJ 255:6 (TN) *ku-⸢ri⸣-il-*[*te*]-⸢*e*⸣ MARV 10 32:14 (Ari/Tp)

Nonetheless, as far as a phonetic explanation for /št/ > /lt/ > /ss/ goes, we should perhaps compare this assimilation with the other sibilants /s-ṣ-z/. We have already seen that, in verbal forms with a t-infix, progressive assimilation into the preceding sibilant took place, e.g., **iztibil* > *izzibil* (see § 212). The lack of difference between etymologic /lt/ and derived /lt/ should be indicated in some construct forms where the two consonants were separated. However, as far as we can see, derived /l/ did not always return to its original sibilant value: *ma-za-la-at* TN.-Epic ii 23 (cf. *ma-za-al-ta-šú-nu* (< **manzastu*) Coronation Ritual iii 14).[93]

4.7.4 Interchangeability between /s/ and /š/

§ 221 In the above, we discussed the phonetic developments of the phonemes /s/ and /š/ in MA. As a result of the developments in their realization and the change in Assyrian scribal traditions, some confusion arose, which we will discuss below. An unexpected feature of MA orthography is the representation of vS with the AŠ series, rather than the expected AZ series. This use is rather unique, even in the Assyrian dialect, since NA generally seems to use the AZ series (see Luukko 2004, 44ff § 3.13).[94] We will provide a selected list of attestations:

<ís> IŠ:

saḫāru	*IŠ-ḫu-ur* 'he turned back' New Year Ritual:25'

<és> or <is$_5$> EŠ:

esāpu	*te-EŠ$^{!}$-si-ip* 'you will gather' PKT 4 obv. left 3, 24
esertu	*EŠ-ra-a-te* 'concubines' MAL A § 41:12
ḫamāsu	^{m}*Ḫa-mi-EŠ-*^{d}*Da-gal* Faist 2001, 251:2
makāsu	*im-ti-ki-EŠ* 'he has levied customs' AO 20.157:14; ⸢*im-ti*⸣*-ki-EŠ* MARV 4 32:14;

92 See GAG, 44 § 33d; Deller (1959, 225ff); SNAG, 21–22 § 2.2.3.2.; § 2.2.3.3. Some cases remain, most notably before /d/; however, some expect a Babylonian or even an MA influence on these spellings, rather than a realization. See LAS 2, 243; SNAG, 22 § 2.2.4.

93 However, cf. the singular and plural forms *na-pal-tu* 'life' KAJ 316:15 and *nap-ša-a-te* 'life' MAL B § 2:16.

94 Note that Syllab is incorrect in assigning the AŠ series in brackets for the values <a/i/us> in no. 192 (ÁŠ) and no. 275 (EŠ); however, it can be accepted for no. 138 (UŠ) and no. 139 (IŠ). This misunderstanding of von Soden/Röllig is likely to have been caused by the exceptions introduced below.

	TR 2059:11
nakāsu	*i-na-ke-EŠ* 'he will cut' MAL A § 15:53
nasāhu	*EŠ-su-ḫu-*[…] 'he/they uprooted' MARV 4 97 r. 4'
	EŠ-su-ḫa-šu-nu-ni MARV 4 123 r. 6'
nisqu	*ni-EŠ-qu* 'first rate' KAJ 231:8
	A.ŠÀ *ni-EŠ-qi* MARV 4 127:62
palāsu N	*nap-le-EŠ* 'look!' KAJ 316:8
rakāsu	*ra-ke-EŠ* 'it is bound' KAJ 182:12; *ra-ki-i-EŠ* MAL A § 34:72
rakāsu D	*ur-ták-ke-*[?]*-EŠ* 'he bound up' MARV 8 76:5'[95]
saḫātu	*le-EŠ-ḫu-ut* 'may he wash off' MAL K § 3:8
sasāʾu	*li-EŠ-si-ú* 'they must read' MATSH 9:11'

<ús> UŠ:

esāqu D	*UŠ-sa-aq* 'he will apportion' MAL B § 1:10
kamāsu D	*ka-mu-UŠ* 'he squats' Coronation Ritual iii 4
kaspu	*ka-UŠ-pí* 'silver' KAJ 6:2; 3
rakāsu	*ir-ku-UŠ* 'he decreed' MAPD § 7:46; MARV 1 17:6; MARV 4 151:6
	[*r*]*u-ku-UŠ* 'bind!' T 93-4:13
samāḫu D	*UŠ-sa-am-me-eḫ* 'he incorporated' MAL B § 8:12
uspu	*UŠ-pu* 'slinger' MPR 74:37'; UŠ-*pi* MARV 4 89 i 9'[96]

<ás> ÁŠ:

ḫašlu	*ḫa-áš-la-a-te* 'bruised grain' MARV 4 151:16
kasāmu	*ka-ÁŠ-ma* 'chopped' New Year Ritual:16'
masīu	[*m*]*a-ÁŠ-su-ú-tu* 'washing' PKT 2 ii 9
nakāsu	*ú-na-ak-ka-ÁŠ* 'he will cut off' MAL A § 5:65
nasāḫu	ÉRIN^{meš} *na-ás-ḫu-te* 'deported people' KAJ 121:6
	it-ta-ás-ḫa-x-x-[*ni*] MARV 8 76 r. 8'†
sasāʾu	*la-a ás-si-šu-nu* 'I did not call them' A 2994:10
sasāʾu D	*ú-sa-ÁŠ-sa* 'he will proclaim' MAL B § 6:6, 8

On the other hand, we do find the AZ series commonly used for assimilated pronominal suffixes, e.g., *iṣ-ṣa-ba-as-si* 'he has seized her' MAL A § 12:18 (see § 224). This use was fixed and based on OB scribal traditions; as such, we never find the AŠ series used in such instances. Similar sign use also occurs in WPA, e.g., we find MA *ir-ku-UŠ*, also found in UgAkk, perhaps as a learned form (Huehnergard, 1989, 38).[97] It is important to note that the new use of the sign DIL for <aš> is never used for <às>. It is not inconceivable that <aš> (DIL) was introduced partly to better distinguish between /s/ and /š/. The value <ís> (IŠ) is rarely used; instead, we mostly find <és> (EŠ). It is likely that no distinction was made between /is/ and /es/ in the orthography. This brings us to another point: that is, the statistical evidence suggests that MA makes a distinction between /i-es/ and /i-eš/ by means

95 Reading follows the copy and photo of the (very damaged) tablet. Cf. Freydank (2017, 182).

96 As discussed in n58, this noun is best transcribed as *uspu*, rather than *ušpu*.

97 A more systematic analysis of the MA application of the AZ/AŠ series in contemporary Akkadian needs to be made, although the grammars do not seem to be in favour of a more widespread use of the MA system, e.g., HattAkk: Durham (1976, 217ff); AmAkk: Izre'el (1991, 55); UgAkk: Huehnergard (1989, 38 cf. 111–14); UgAkk: Cochavi-Rainey (2011, 41) (for a different kind of interchangeability). Confusion may have been caused by conflicting OAkk and OB scribal practices (see also § 58ff; Huehnergard 1989, 113). Confusion between sibilants continued well into the first millennium, partly caused by the swapping of the phonetic values /š/ and /s/ (Luukko 2004, 74–76 § 4.1.3.).

of the signs IŠ (values <iš/eš$_{15}$>) and EŠ (values <és/is$_{5}$>).[98] This would explain otherwise unexpected spellings, such as *ú-še-IŠ-šu-b*[*u*] New Year Ritual:12’, where we would normally expect EŠ. There are some exceptions, where EŠ is clearly used to express /š/:[99]

*aḫā*ʾ*iš*	*a-ḫa-eš* ‘each other’ PKT 4 obv. left 20
rakāsu	*i-ra-ak-ku-su-ni-eš-še* ‘they will decree for her’ MAL A § 46:98
rēšu	*re-eš* ‘head’ Coronation Ritual ii 42
*ṣalā*ʾ*u* Š	*ul-ta-aṣ-le-eš* (< *ultaṣle*$^{?}$+*še*) ‘he caused her an abortion’ MAL A § 21:99
šadaqdiš	*ša-da-aq-de-eš* ‘last year’ MARV 7 14:14†
ubālu	*ú-ub-bu-lu-ni-eš-šu* ‘they will bring to him’ MATSH 9:46

Three of the attestations deal with assimilated pronominal suffixes. Although spellings of the type *-eš-šV* for pronominal suffixes are atypical for OB, they could still be a fixed spelling for MA: in all three cases, we expected an /e/ vowel, either from the ventive *-nim* > *-ne* or the dative suffix *-še* (*ultaṣleš* < *ultaṣle*$^{?}$+*še*). Moreover, all but the two final attestations occur in literary texts, which could explain the difference. This also explains the spelling *a-ḫa-eš*, which is atypical and usually occurs as *a-ḫa-iš* in other texts (see § 383ff); meanwhile, for *rēšu* ‘head’, e.g., *ri-iš* TabT05a-134:19; PN *Ri-iš-*^{d}AG KAJ 11:4 (cf. OMA 1, 381–85). We already mentioned that there is only one case of <eš$_{15}$> (IŠ): *ú-še-IŠ-šu-bu* New Year Ritual:11’, 12’. Cases with CvC signs are rare; only one occurrence was found, i.e., *ma-sik/šik-te* MAPD § 10:57 (*masiktu/mašiktu*). The use of the signs ÁŠ/EŠ/UŠ for /s/ seems to have been caused by the deaffricated character of the sibilant as opposed to /ṣ/ and /z/. It is possible that this was the phonetic reality in the MA era, but this is not strictly necessary as we have claimed that the scribal system was adapted from an unspecified OB scribal system.

§ 222 The opposite use can also be observed: the AZ series used /š/. This phenomenon is limited to verbal forms where /š/ and /b/ are in direct contact, most noticeably in the roots *ušābu* and *šubalkutu*.[100]

nabalkutu Š	*us-bal-ki-it* ‘he transferred’ MAL B § 9:21
ušābu	*us-bu-ni* ‘they dwell’ MARV 1 71:9
	lu-us-bu ‘they must stay’ MATC 4:5
	ú-us-bat ‘she dwells’ MAL A § 24:47
	⸢*us*⸣*-ba-a-ku* ‘I dwell’ MATSH 12:29

Notice also, in some SB texts from Aššur, the following:

ušābu	*us-*⸢*ba*⸣*-at* ‘she is seated’ BWL, 162:6 (cf. p. 152)

According to J. and H. Lewy, this sound change was regular and also occurred when /š/ and /b/ were not separated by a long stressed vowel. Thus, the OA collective *subr'ûm* ‘slaves’ derived from *Šubarûm* ‘Subartu’ (Lewy/Lewy 1967, 14f). There may be some truth in J. and H. Lewy’s claim, but it is difficult to test as √*šb-* roots, such as *šabā*ʾ*u* and *šabāru*, which are rare in MA. On the other hand, *šabā*ʾ*u* is common in OA and most finite forms

98 Again, this is unexpected following NA studies (e.g., Luukko 2004, 44ff § 3.13).

99 This list of attestations excluded some (foreign) PNs and nouns without unambiguous roots.

100 See Lewy/Lewy (1967, 14–15); UGM, 24 § 21.4; Streck (2011, 371). Girbal claims that /š/ > /z/ and reaches conclusions on that assumption. There is no evidence in MA to support his claim. We would have to explain how /z/ became /š/ (=[s]) again in NA in forms of *ušābu* (see Girbal 1997, 174–175). A response to Girbal’s article can be found in Tropper (1996; published in 1997).

have the syllable binding /š/ and /b/ unstressed (e.g., *ú-ša-be-e-ma* KTS 1 16:9). Notice also PN *Šubrûm: Šu-ub-ri-im* AKT 6a 151:32. Even in MA, a few exceptions can be found:

nabalkutu Š	*tu-uš-ba-la-kat* 'you will move' PKT 3 i 4
Šubrīu	*Šu-ub-ri-e* 'Hurrian' MATC 15:31
	ᶠ*Šu-ub-ri-tu* MPR 58:40
ušābu	*aš-bu* 'they dwell' KBo 1 14:15', 17' (peripheral letter)
uš?!-*bu*	*uš*?!-*bu* MARV 10 6:25'–26'†

Nonetheless, as orthography is not always representative of spoken language and sound changes gradually spread throughout a language (Aitchison 2001, 84ff), we should not totally disregard J. and H. Lewy's claims. The sound change /š/ > /s/ does not appear to be limited to the position before the labials. One possible example is *tu-UZ-ga*[*-ra-a*]*r* BVW A:12 (but *tu-uš-ga-ra-(a)-ar* BVW F:4, 9.).[101] More obvious is the following verbal form of a Š-stem:

šaqalpuʾu Š	*us-qa-al-pí-ú-*⸢*ni*⸣ 'they came upstream' MARV 4 35:7

In relation to our claim that the use of ÁŠ/EŠ/UŠ was used because of the deaffricated character of /s/ (and of course /š/), at least originally, we may ask ourselves what the use of the AZ series in these few selected verbs might indicate. It seems most likely that the swapping of position between /s/ and /š/ is first visible in these selected verbs (SNAG, 10).

§ 223 The sibilant /š/ also becomes /s/ in the verb *sasāʾu* 'to call' (Bab. *šasû*) (§ 603); see also GAG, 37 § 30d, e.g., *ú-sa-ás-sa* MAL B § 6:8; *sa-su* KAJ 310:20; ⸢*si-si*⸣*-a* MARV 3 64:10. Related to the interchangeability of /s/ <> /š/ is the irregular verb *našāʾu*. When R_2/š and R_3/ʾ are in direct contact, geminated <ṢṢ> is written instead. The merger between [ɬ] and /ʾ/ would then result in an alveolar lateral ejective affricative [ɬ'], written as <ṢṢ>. Therefore, unlike earlier suggestions, the irregular forms of the *našāʾu* are no evidence for the alternation between /š/ and /s/ (pace Parpola 1974, 2). Nonetheless, this alternation does exist in a few nouns: *ma-as-qi-e* 'watering place' (< √*šaqāʾu* 'to give to drink') MATSH 4:18''; *si-ip-sa-te* BVW Ac:2, B:11, D:7, E r. 3, F:7, r. 13, T r. 3 (cf. NA *šipšate* CAD $Š_3$ 85 a), but notice the lexical entry: *ši-ip-sa-tu* BVW Ko r. 7. Confusion between Š and S is most common in Sumerian loan words. For instance, we find [ᵏᵘ]ˢ*šu-ḫu-pa-a-te*/ᵏᵘˢSUḪUBᵐᵉš MAPD § 6:43, which in SB is the singular *suḫuppu*; note also, ᶠ*sa-ab-su-tu* 'midwife' MAPD § 1:11 (CAD *šabsūtu* or *tabsūtu*, *šabšūtu* etc.), a loan from Sumerian ᶠŠÀ.ZU; possibly *sa-su-ur-tu* Ištar Ritual:8 (derived from *šassuru?*), which originates from ᶠZÀ.SUR₅, but this is not certain (see CAD S, 196); and the Indo-European loan *šušānu* 'horse trainer' occurs as *susānu* in MA, e.g., ˡᵘ́*su-sa-a-ni* KAJ 310:27.[102] It should be pointed out that the alternation of the two sibilants is already attested in the OA period and not unexpected in Akkadian (cf. OA in GOA § 3.2.5.1).

101 This reading was proposed by Girbal (1997, 3). However, according to the copy, there is no place for a sign as big as AR in the gap.

102 See CAD $Š_3$, 378–380; AHw, 1288; CDA, 389.

4.7.5 Assimilation of pronominal suffix -š

§ 224 Some orthographic variations occur with the pronominal suffixes. If a verb or substantive ends in a dental plosive or a sibilant, and a pronominal suffix *-š* is directly attached, both merge into /ss/. Gemination of /s/ is not always written. For instance, MAL A usually indicates the assimilation with plene writing, while the few examples in other literary texts, such as MAPD and PKT, have defective spellings.

abātu	*a-ba-su* 'his case' KAJ 48:8
aḫātu	⸢*a-ḫa-su*⸣ 'his sister' MARV 4 28:13'
	a-ḫa-su 'his sister' MPR 2:22 et passim MPR
aḫāzu	*eḫ-ḫa-a-si* 'he will marry her' MAL A § 55:36
amtu	GEME-*sa* 'her slave girl' MAPD § 18:89
balāṭu D	*la-a ú-bal-la-*⸢*su*⸣ 'I will not let him live' MARV 4 24:13'
ḫubtu	*ḫu-ba-su-nu* 'their plunder' MATSH 7:18''
idu	*i-sa* 'her hand' TR 2083a+:19
išātu	IZI-*su* 'its fire' PKT 1 I right:14
maḫāṣu	*ta-ma-ḫa-si* 'she will beat her' MAPD § 18:85
martu	DUMU.MUNUS-*su* 'his daughter' MAL A § 39:26
mutu	*mu-us-sa* 'her husband' MAL A § 3:33
pāḫutu	[*pa-ḫ*]*a-su* 'his office' Coronation Ritual iii 13
	pa-⸢*ḫa*⸣*-as-su-nu* 'their province' KAJ 47:18
qaqqadu	*qa-qa-sa* 'her head' TR 2083a+:2
qātu	*qa-su-nu* 'their hand' MATSH 8:63'
ṣabātu	*iṣ-ṣa-ba-as-si* 'he has seized her' MAL A § 12:18
ṣabātu Š	*ul-ta-aṣ-bi-si* 'he has directed her' MAL A § 22:108
šaptu	[*ša*]*-pa-as-su* 'his lip' MAL A § 9:94
tarqītu	*tar-qi-su* 'its perfume-making' PKT 1 I right:14
unūtu	⸢*ú*⸣*-nu-us-su* 'his equipment' T 96-8:14

Note also nasals:

ezābu	*e-ta-az-bu-ni-su* (< *ētazbū-nem-šu*) 'they have left him' MATSH 2:63

We may also note the following rare double form, where, despite the assimilated pronominal suffix, the preceding dental is still expressed in the orthography. This example should be regarded as a morphographemic spelling.

kašādu D	⸢*ú*⸣-[*k*]*a-šad-*⸢*su*⸣ 'he will chase him away' Giricano 10:15

When the final radical of the substantive or verb is *-s* or *-š*, the merger with pronominal suffixes still results in double <SS>, such as:

epāšu	*e-pu-us-si* 'he did to her' MAL A § 9:89
	e-pa-a-[*s*]*u* 'he will do to him' MAL A § 14:40
epāšu D	*ù-pa-UZ-sí* 'he will treat her' KAJ 2:12
	ú-pá-su 'he will treat him' KAJ 6:16
erāšu	*le-ri-su* 'may he request him' K9-T1:14
rēšu	*re-es-su* 'his head' T 02-3:22
riksu	*ri-ka-sa* 'her contract' MAL A § 34:72

§ 225 More archaic are the spellings with Z instead of S. We find both ZU and ZA; however, no examples with ZI are known, although this may well be arbitrary. As is to be expected, Z spellings are most prominent in MAL A (we have already discussed how this text leans on OB orthography). It appears that gemination plene spellings are another mixed remnant of OB scribal traditions, where spellings of the type AZ-ZA were common.[103]

aḫāzu Š *ú-ša-aḫ-ḫa-ZU* 'he will make him marry' MARV 1 37:6 (Aub)
amtu GÉME$^{!}$-*sà-ma* 'her maid' T 93-17:2[104]
aššutu *aš-ša-ZU* 'his wife' TIM 4, 45:6
bētu É-*ZU* 'his house' KAJ 50:19 (Abn)
erāšu *e-ta-na-ri-sú* 'they will keep requesting him/it' KUB 3 77:16'†
kibtu *ki-ba-ZU-nu* 'their wheat' T 93-54:19
kuāšu *lā TUM-ka-*⌜*as*⌝*-ZU* 'do not delay him' EA 15:18
martu *ma-ra-as-ZA* 'her daughter' KAJ 3:7 (EAd/Aub)
DUMU.MUNUS-*ZA* 'her daughter' TR 2037:7
mutu *mu-UZ-ZA* 'her husband' MAL A § 27:105 § 36:85, 101
mu-ZA 'her husband' TIM 4, 45:5
mu-ut-ZA 'her husband' KAJ 7:10 (Ead/Aub)
qātu *qa-(a)-ZU* 'his hand' MAL B § 6:45; § 10:32; KAM 11 2:5'
ṣabātu *iṣ-ṣa-ba-a-ZU* 'he has seized him (=her)' MAL A § 12:15
iṣ-ba-at-ZU-ma 'he seized him' MAL A § 36:106

Meanwhile, in PN:

dannuttu in *A-mur-da-nu-ZA* 'Amurru is her strength (PN)' KAJ 151:31; KAM 10 14:26; BM 108924:27

The use of <Z> is limited to substantives and verbs ending in a dental. The spellings date from the OB period, where <Z> was still the affricate [^{t}z]. Streck (2006, 245) explained that this makes sense if Š was pronounced [^{t}ɬ]. If the lateral articulation was lost, the affricate realization of [^{t}ɬ] would justify a spelling with <Z>, especially when /š/ followed /t/: [t^{t}l] > [t^{t}s] > [^{tt}s]. Unlike OB, only one spelling in MA is known with double <ZZ>: *mu-UZ-ZA* MAL A passim occurs next to *mu-us-sa* MAL A passim. On the other hand, MA is known to resist gemination at the end of a word. In this light, we can also explain spellings such as *iṣ-ba-at-ZU-ma* MAL A § 36:106, which maintain the dental that could also be heard in the pronunciation (also in OB; see Streck 2006, 231). More likely, these were simple scribal mistakes or morphographemic spellings, as confusion with pronominal suffixes is not unknown in WPA.[105] All these spellings lean on OB scribal traditions and are therefore unlikely to contain any information about the actual pronunciation of <Z>, which is likely to have become deaffricated. It can be noted that most examples with <Z> occur in Babylonian-influenced MAL A, with only a few occurrences in early KAJ texts and one in Tell Ar-Rimāḥ. Furthermore, the erroneous spelling *i-na-ak-ki-ZU* MAL B § 8:17 (cf. *i-na-ki-su* MAL A § 8:80) indicates that pronominal spellings with <Z> are erudite and thus could have spread erroneously to all word-final Sv syllables. Moreover, the preference to write <S> or double <SS> points to the fact that /z/ had deaffricated. This not only affected etymologic /z/ but also the secondary affricates that occurred when pronominal *-š* geminated with the proceeding dental plosive.

103 Streck (2006, 228–30) collated a large number of OB attestations of spellings of the type AZ-ZA for assimilated pronominal suffixes. The spellings AZ-SA occur but are rare (cf. Finet 1956, 35).

104 In this particular instance, we would actually expect the pronominal suffix *-ki*, since the noun is part of a letter introduction: ana ^{f}PN$_1$ *qibīma umma* ^{f}PN$_2$ *amatki* (not *amassa*) 'to ^{f}PN$_1$ speak, thus ^{f}PN$_2$ your maid'; cf. MATSH 4:1–2.

105 Notice UgAkk where spellings such as *i-ḫu-uz-ši* also occur next to *mu-da-at-šu*. See Huehnergard (1989, 102f).

4.7.6 Metathesis of sibilants and interdentals

§ 226 Metathesis is a phenomenon in linguistics where two different sounds are swapped. In MA, this is limited to the sibilants and the *-ta-* infix of the t-stems. This is not unexpected, as we find a similar form of metathesis in Biblical Hebrew and Ugaritic (CGSL, 63). Note also the general tendency to make prefixed *ta-* stems from infixed *-ta-* stems (cf. Lipiński 2001, 404ff). In the verbal forms of all attested *-ta-* stems with a sibilant as first radical, and in which the /t/ and sibilant swap positions, metathesis with other interdentals can be expected; but this is not attested in MA. Metathesis can only occur in verbal forms without prefixes (GAG, 155 § 96e). Metathesis in these forms is common in Akkadian, with the exception of metathesis with /š/.[106] However, in MA, it is found with /š/ in a few attested *ta(n)*-stems, e.g., Gtn-stem *tišappuru*. In fact, this type of metathesis with /š/ can be used as evidence that this phoneme had a (lateral) affricative realization in MA ([ᵗɬ]), since the metathesis of /s-ṣ-z/ and /d-ṭ/ with the t-infix may have been shared because of the affricative character of these three sibilants in early Akkadian (cf. Kogan 2011, 66–67). At the same time, the MA evidence of metathesis of deaffricated /s/ (Dtn *tusaḫḫuru*) indicates that the metathesis was irreversible. It is therefore neither strictly necessary that /š/ was still affricative in MA, as forms with metathesis were already found in the OA period.[107] In OA, we still find forms with and without metathesis next to each other; however, in MA, the material is rather ambiguous (cf. GKT, 66 § 41e also p. 145f § 87; Kouwenberg 2010, 580). Note also the additional /a/ in the Štn-stem stative with the subjunctive *tušaḫaruṣūni* (< *šutaḫruṣūni*). This vowel is not found in the morphologically similar Štn-stem infinitive *ina tušaḫruremma* MATSH 9:37. A complete list of attestations of metathesis can be found below.[108]

Gt:

šamāru	ᵈIŠKUR-*tiš-mar* KAJ 75:17; KAM 10 13:28

Gtn:

šamāʾu	ᵈ*A-šur-ti-šam-me* MARV 4, 151:59 (MARV 4 passim.)
	ᵈU-*ti-šam-me* CTMMA 1 99:9
šapāru	*a-na ti-šap-pu-r*[*e*] 'for repeatedly sending' MARV 2 17b+:97

Dtn:

saḫāru	ᵗᵘ́ᵍ*ša tu-sa-ḫu-ri* 'wrapping(?)' MAH 16086 A ii 10; B ii 11' (cf. Postgate 2014, 424)

Št$_2$:

ḫarāṣu	*tu-ša-ḫa-ru-ṣu-ni* 'it has been deduced' KAJ 120:7

---

106 See von Soden (1983, 289); Postgate (1986a, 37 n53); GAG, 44f § 36a; Reiner (2001, 393).

107 Metathesis with /š/ is already attested in OA; see GAG, 44 § 36a; GOA § 3.2.7.2. Von Soden's (1968, 219) initial explanation of spirantization (*tišmar* = *ṯiṯmar*) cannot be accepted. In addition, metathesis is rarely attested in PNs in MB (Hölscher 1996, 10). Perhaps the PN in question is of Assyrian origin.

108 Von Soden lists as an exception to the metathesis of /ṭ/ with /t/ in MA and gives the following example from a diri lexical text: *ṭi-ta-bu-ú* MAOG 3/3, 6 i 40 (GAG, 155 § 96e). However, the occurrence of the value <ṭi> (DI) is atypical for MA and this text is not regarded as part of our corpus.

Štn:

šaḫruru *i+na tu-ša-aḫ-ru-ri-ma* 'while keep being silent' MATSH 9:37

Štn:

ubālu ⸢*a*⸣*-na tu-še-bu-li* 'for repeatedly sending' MARV 2 17a+:99

4.8 Nasals /m-n/

§ 227 MA has two nasal sounds: /m/ and /n/. Originally, both were used for the mimation and nunation of nominal forms, with /m/ being used for the singular and /n/ for the dual. In MA and all contemporary Akkadian forms, these final nasal sounds had dropped off in all instances.[109] The use of old final signs, such as <lim> and <tum>, were originally used for mimation and are discussed in 86f.

/ma/ The sign MA is always used.

/mi/ A strong distinction between /i/ and /e/ is made with the use of <mi> (MI) and <me> (ME). 'Confusion' in the use of both values can be found, e.g., *e-MI-e-ša* MAL A § 29:17 *am-MI-ša* MATC 2:17; 4:21 (~ *am-me-e-ša-ma* 9:24). It is therefore difficult to assess to what extent the distinction was active or only based on some fixed spellings.

/mu/ The sign MU is always used.

/am/ The sign AM is always used. For its use as a phonetic complement with ŠE, see § 69 and § 87. Perhaps we find <àm> (A.AN) in *e-be*$^{!}$*-er-ta*$^{!}$*-A-AN* MAL M § 2:9 (see DSC 2, 179), although in this case a non-congruent dual remnant is more likely (see § 6.2.1; § 457).

/im/ The sign IM is always used. No distinction is made between /i/ and /e/. For its use as a phonetic complement with ŠE, see § 69 and § 87.

/um/ The sign UM is always used. For its use as a phonetic complement with ŠE, see § 69 and § 87.

/na/ The sign NA is always used.

/ni/ Normally, NI is used. No distinction is made between /i/ <ni> and /e/ <né>. For convenience, in this grammar, the reading né is avoided unless necessary. The sign NI has a limited use of the value <lí> (see § 241).

/nu/ The sign NU is always used.

/an/ The sign AN is always used.

/in/ A strong distinction between /i/ and /e/ is made by the use of in (IN) and en (EN). Both signs are, together with IL and EL, the only cases in MA where /i/ and /e/ are distinguished in the vC value, e.g., *ri-še-en* MAL A 15:54.

/un/ The sign UN is always used.

§ 228 As is common in Akkadian and East/North-Semitic in general, /n/ often assimilates into the following consonant. This occurs most prominently in the I/n verbs. As for the other way around, assimilation of R_2 to R_3/n is attested in the perfect of the verb *tadānu* 'to give', e.g., *it-ta-nu* (*ittannū* < **intadnū*) MARV 10 3:3; and perhaps also in the stative of *tadānu* > *ta-*<*ad*>*-na-at* (MARV 10 73:7), but this could just as well be a scribal mistake. Assimilation also occurs in nouns as shown in this list of /n/ when assimilated into the short feminine ending *-t*:

**almantu* > ^{f}*al-ma-at-tu* 'a widow' MAL A § 35:75

**kisintu* > *ki-si-it-te* 'trunk' KTN inventory i 6

**kēntu* > *ke-et-ta* 'truth' Coronation Ritual ii 36

**mandantu* > *ma-da-te* 'tribute' KAJ 106:13

109 See GKT, 54f § 35c; Gelb/Sollberger (1957, 171).

**marsantu* >	1 ^{dug}*mar-sa-tu* 'one soaking-vessel' KAJ 182:7
**maškantu* >	*ma-áš-ka-at-ta* 'a deposit' MAL A § 6:70
**šantu* >	*ša-at-te* 'year' MATSH 6:8'
**šukuntu* >	*šu-ku-ut-ta-ša* 'her jewellery' MAL A § 40:72

Substantives ending in *-n* with the feminine suffix *-tV* do not always assimilate into the dental. But this is rare and, so far, seems limited to a D-stem adjective of the verb *paṣānu*:

paṣṣuntu	*pa-aṣ-ṣu-un-⸢ta⸣* 'veiled' MAL A § 40:68
	pa-ṣu-un-ta MAL A § 40:77, 89, 94
	pa-ṣu-un-te MAL A § 41:12

If /n/ is the final consonant of a root, it is less likely to assimilate into suffixes in Babylonian, but this rule does not apply to OA, e.g., *i-da-ší* (*iddan+ši*) TCL 21 252:28.[110] Forms of assimilation continue to a certain degree into the NA period and are even attested in royal inscriptions (cf. Worthington 2012, 161). In general, though, assimilation is often not represented in the NA letter corpus (SNAG, 19–20 § 2.2.2). Similarly, the evidence of MA in MAL A–B suggests the preservation of /n/ before pronominal suffixes. While this also suggests the dissimilation of /n/ in comparison with OA, the difference is probably only orthographic.

arnu	*a-ra-an-ša* 'her offense' MAL A § 2:20
batiqānu	*ba-ti-qa-an-šu* 'his informer' MAL A § 40:82
nāikānu	*na-i-ka-an-ša* 'her rapist' MAL A § 55:36
paṣānu D	*ú-pa-ṣa-an-ši* 'he will veil her' MAL A § 41:3
ramānu	*ra-ma-an-ša* 'herself' MAL A § 24:42
ṣābitānu	*ṣa-bi-ta-an-ša* 'her arrester' MAL A § 40:93 cf. *ṣa-bi-ta-áš-ša* MAL A § 40:73
tadānu	*ta-ti-din-ši* 'he has given her' MAL A § 23:16
	i-id-dan-ši 'he will give her' MAL A § 30:28
ubānu	*ú-ba-an-ša/šu* 'her/his finger' MAL A § 8:80; B § 8:17

In other texts, substantives ending in *-n* before another consonant are rare; therefore, it is not clear whether this was only a scribal convenience, which did not affect the actual pronunciation. Some examples in other texts where it does occur are:

āmirānu	*a-me-ra-an-šu* 'his witness' MAPD § 21:106
bātiqānu	*ba-ti-qa-an-šu* 'their informer' MARV 1 41:12 Arn
napunu	*nap-ta-an-šu* 'his meal' T 04-2:28
ummiānu	*um-mi-a-an-šu-nu* 'their creditors' KAJ 32:9
šakānu	*i-ša-ka-an-šu* 'he will place it' MATSH 21:7'
šulmānu	*šul-ma-an-ša* 'her *šulmānu*-gift' A 845:21
tadānu	*i-din-šu* 'he gave him' TR 2082:18
	i-din-ma 'he gave' TR 3004:7'

On the other hand, many letters and administrative texts do show assimilation similar to the OA praxis (UGM, 23 § 19.2):

bātiqānu	*ba-ti-qa-šu-nu* 'their informer' RE 92:12 cf. *ba-ti-qa-an-šu* MARV 1 41:12
dēnu	*de-šu* 'his case' Billa 66:11
kanāku	*ku-uk-ka* 'seal!' KAV 103:18 ~ *kak-ka* 'seal' Lambert 1969:48 (cf. GAG, 42 § 33g)
ṣābitānu	*ṣa-bi-ta-áš-ša* 'her arrester' MAL A § 40:73
šakānu	*šu-ku-uš-šu* 'instruct him' MATC 11:31

110 See GKT, 55 § 36a; GOA § 3.2.4.1; cf. GAG, 42f § 33h.

šakānu N	*na-áš-ku-ša-ni* 'which is deposited' KAV 99:38
šulmānu	*šul-ma-šu* 'his *šulmānu*-gift' KAJ 54:13; 56:13; 72:13; 76:15
	šul-ma-šá 'her *šulmānu*-gift' T 97-5:11 ~ *šul-ma-an-ša* A 845:21
	šu[*l*]-*ma-k*[*a*] T 04-2:6
tadānu	*i-da-ši* 'he will give her' KAJ 2:13
	it-ti-di-ši 'he has sold her' TR 2083+:16
	i-di-ma 'he gave' KAJ 169:12
	i-di[!]-*im-ma* KAM 10 7:11'

PNs:

banā'u	[m]10-*ba-*⸢*ka*⸣-*la* (Adad-bān-kāla) MARV 3 41:14

Progressive assimilation is attested in the (irregular) infinitive of the irregular verb *tadānu* 'to give' in *ta-da-šu-nu-ni* (< *tad(i)n-aššunu-ni*) MARV 3 35:6 (see § 606); cf. normal *ta-da-a-ni* T 97-2:14. Perhaps we also find the NA form of *rāmunu* > *ramnu* with regressive dissimilation: *ra-mi-šu* 'his self' MATSH 9:42 (cf. SNAG, 51 § 3.1.4.2.). The dissimilation of /n/ in plural forms is shown below:

šattu	*ša 7 panī ša-na-te* 'of seven springs' MARV 2 9:6'
šikittu	*ši-ik-na-te-mu-tu-rat* (*šiknāte utturat*) 'great of stature' Rm 376:20

The example of *šanātu* may be a plural form of *šattu* 'year', conforming to the reading by Freydank (MARV 2, 9 Commentary no. 9) and von Soden (1983, 289). It is perhaps more logical to read 7 QA Ì *ša-na-te*, whereas the final noun stands for the aromatic plant *šanâtu* (CAD $Š_1$, 371; AHw, 1162), which is otherwise attested in PKT, e.g., Ì *ša ša-na-*[*a-te*] PKT 6 i 42.

§ 229 In NA, the assimilation of /n/ became a relatively rare phenomenon, mostly limited to I/n verbs and N-stems, but not occurring before pronominal suffixes (SNAG, 19 § 2.2.2). It is therefore difficult to understand what triggered the preservation of /n/ in MA in this position. We could consider the possibility of lene vs. allegro spellings. Here, allegro spellings are closer to the actual spoken language, where /n/ would assimilate in an ongoing sentence in order to ease pronunciation. The lene spellings would then refer to an absolutive or vocative version of a word, where sound changes, such as assimilation, would not take place due to a clear and emphasized pronunciation (see Sommerfeld 2006, 364ff). The problem with applying this theory to this MA phenomenon is the ongoing process from OA to NA; or, more specifically, what caused the switch from allegro to lene spellings. Considering that many allegro forms occur in the NA letter corpus, it is difficult to label the preservation of /n/ as merely lene spelling, as it rather appears to be a phonologic development. On the other hand, the process is not unambiguous and the frequency of forms with /n/ in literary MAL A–B also demonstrate some hypercorrect forms influenced by Babylonian. This picture is somewhat balanced by the assimilated forms in the letters and administrative documents.

§ 230 The nasal /m/ is less likely to assimilate; however, with the dative pronominal suffix and the ventive /m/ functions as a ghost phoneme assimilating to additional suffixes, e.g., *iq-bi-áš-šu-un-ni* 'he said to him' MAL A § 47:11; *ta-ta-na-áš-šu* 'you have given him' OIP 79 3:18; *ḫa-*⸢*ab*⸣-*bu-*⸢*la*⸣-*šu-un-ni* 'he is indebted to him' MARV 4 151:37. Although this is usually not visible in the orthography, one may wonder to what extent this is a scribal tradition instead of a phonetic reality. In the Kassite PN *Melim-Saḫ*, the nasal /m/ is mostly assimilated into /s/ > *Melissaḫ* (see OMA I, 323f). Notice also some peculiar spellings of a profession derived from the PN Šalim-pî-Ea (Jakob 2003, 461ff): *ša-li-pa-ie-e* MARV 4 34:15'; [lú]*še-lip-pa-iu-ú* KAJ 188:22; [lu]*ši-⌜lip⌝-pa-ie* KAJ 300:6.

§ 231 A curious feature of MA is nasalization, where an /n/ appears before a consonant, instead of the expected gemination, which is a phenomenon limited to the voiced phonemes /d-g-z/.[111] The number of attestations is small, such that a complete list can be presented:

madādu	*i-ma-an-da!-ad* 'he will measure out' KAJ 63:9 (Aub) ~ MB: [*i*]*-ma-an-da-ad* Peiser 95, 13
magāru	*im-ma-an-ga-ar* 'he will be in consent' MAL B § 2:20 ~ MB: *i-man-gu-ru* UM 61, 13
mazāʾu D	*ú-ma-an-ze-e-eʾ-ši* 'he intends to rape her' MAL A § 55:22 *ma-an-zu-ú-ʾe* 'raping' MAL A § 55:26

Perhaps we can add the following rare Akkadian word of foreign origin, where /n/ may also be original, but attestations without /n/ are also known:

minduḫru	*mi-in-du-uḫ-ra* 'residue' PKT 3 i 11, ii 10 but *mi-du-uḫ-ra* PKT 3iv 6 (CAD and AHw give *minduḫru*)

One case of nasalization with /m/ is known: *i-NAM-di* PKT 1 I right:15; II right:2; II right:20; 5:15 (MB: *i-NAM-du* Hinke iii 21). Although more likely, this spelling is probably related to the loss of mimation. Nasalization is more frequently observed in Babylonian, with no trace of it in OA and NA.[112] The phenomenon is also productive in later Imperial Aramaic and Mandaean, bringing about remnants of Imperial Aramaic nasalization in other dialects, such as Syriac. It has therefore been argued that the feature was caused by an Akkadian (i.e., Babylonian) substratum (Kaufman 1974, 121f). For this reason, it seems unlikely that nasalization was ever productive in Assyrian and instead was a Babylonian influence (Landsberger 1924, 723).[113] It occurs already in OB (Streck 2014a, 30 § 83) and its concentration in MAL A–B could therefore be connected to the OB influence of the initial plene spellings (cf. § 101ff). Note that only one example occurs outside the literary genre. Moreover, as indicated in the given examples, Babylonian cognates of most of the attested forms are easy to find.[114] Some of the examples may have been lexicalized (e.g., *mazāʾu* > *manzāʾu*). According to von Soden, the /n/ of nasalization was probably a different phoneme [ṅ], which sounded like the French "*nasalen n*" or "*dem ng-Laut in Deutsch 'Engel'*" (GAG. 41 § 32).

111 See UGM, 23–24 § 20; GAG § 32b; Kouwenberg (2010, 469).

112 For Babylonian, see Aro (1955a, 35ff); GAG, 41 § 32. Note that nasalization is widespread in other WPA dialects, where it is relatively common. HattAkk: Durham (1976, 440ff); MitAkk: Adler (1976, 19); AlAkk: Giacumakis (1970, 29); Nuzi: Wilhelm (1970, 17f); UgAkk: Huehnergard (1989, 114f).

113 Nasalization is an atypical feature for Semitic languages; outside Aramaic and Babylonian, it is most common in the Gurage languages (Southern Ethiopic). In these languages, it functions quite differently from our MA examples by being triggered most commonly by non-geminated /m-m^w-w-b-f-n/, e.g., *ãf^w* 'mouth' and *ãfuna* 'nose' (see Leslau 1992, 8–12 § 1.3). Considering the Babylonian origin of nasalization in Aramaic, its presence in Assyrian is anything but self-evident.

114 Note also a case of nasalization in the diplomatic Tukultī-Ninurta letter KBo 34.165: *la-a i-ma-an-gur* l. 13. This is clearly no reflection of Assyrian, as the text is written in Babylonian.

§ 232 In both MA and NA, /m/ often drops off or assimilates into the perfect infix /t/ in a limited number of verbs (SNAG, 19). Although it has been claimed otherwise, this type of assimilation is attested in texts as early as those from the reign of TN and is not limited to the later dialect (pace George 1988, 30).

maḫāru	*i-ta-ḫar* 'he has received' George 1988 1 r. 12'
	i-taḫ-ru 'they received' MARV 7 57:6 (Tp)
	ni-ta-ḫa-ar 'we have received' MARV 1 71:13
maḫāṣu	*i-ta-ḫa-ṣu-ni* 'they beat' T 96-15:12
	ni-ta-ḫa-aṣ 'we have stamped' MARV 1 71:15

However, notice *im-ta-aḫ-ru* MAL A § 4:48; [*i*]*m-taḫ-ra-an-*[*n*]*i* T 93-54:5. On one occasion, this sound change is attested in the substantivized Gt-participle: *mu-ut-taḫ-iṣ* 'warrior' Lambert 1969:40. The assimilation is also attested in a Gtn-participle: *mu-te-li-ú* (< *mumtalliʾu*) MPR 69:27; and a noun: ^{lú}*ta-ka-ru* (< *tamkāru*) 'merchant' T 97-18:16. Here, it needs to be noted that a sound change first occurs in the most frequent forms to which it can be applied, before slowly spreading to less frequent forms, hence explaining the limited group of verbs that this applies to in NA. The few examples in MA demonstrate the first phase. In the context of the slow spreading of a sound change, it is not unexpected to find forms with and without the change applied, with even an individual being able to alternate randomly (cf. Aitchison 2001, 84ff). Alternatively, /m/ > /n/ before /t/ in a perfect (GAG, 40 § 31g). This is only found in *ta-an-ti-ši-an-ni-i* 'did you forget me?' T 93-12:4. It is possible that this is the intermediate stage of the sound change described above, as we know that /n/ is more vulnerable to assimilation. Thus, /mt/ > /nt/ > /tt/.

§ 233 In the specific case of the root *danānu*, we find a number of attestations where II/n elides. Unlike the elided /m/ (see below), the aleph sign is always used in the instances where /n/ elides. This suggests a realization as a strong aleph.

danānu	*kī da-ʾa-ni* 'with force' MAL A § 55:20
danānu D	*lā tu-da-ʾa-an* 'you will not make it strong' PTK, 304:209

So far, this sound change is only attested in the root √*dnn* and may therefore be lexically motivated, instead of phonologically. According to Hämeen-Anttila, the change in verbal root derives from the stative *dān* > *daʾan* (SNAG, 100 § 3.14.3). The two-radical statives were thus conjugated in the prefix conjugations as II/ʾ verb, with non-etymologic /ʾ/. A similar phenomenon can be observed with intervocalic /m/:

aḫāʾiš	*a-ḫa-eš* 'together' MATSH 10:22 et passim.
	a-ḫa-iš (Bab. *aḫāmiš*) MAL B § 1:7
anaʾīnu	*a-na-i-ni* 'why?' passim (see § 406f)
aššum	*áš-šúm-i-ka* (*aššuʾīka*) 'concerning you' T 02-32:7[115]
azaʾillu	*a-za-i-la* (Bab. *azamil(l)um*) 'sack' MATC 6:5
gammuru	*kī ga-ú-ru-*⌜*te*⌝ T 96-36:26
peʾettu	*pe-ʾe-et-ta* 'charcoal' PKT 1 II right:1 (see § 186)
šamiʾu	*ūmū lā ša-iʾ-ú* 'days not propitious' TabT05A-134:16 (TN)[116]

115 The value <šúm> does represent mimation; pronunciation of the final /m/ is not obligatory and may be only scribal (§ 86f). Therefore, we should read *áš-šu*$_x$*-i-ka*, which solves the abnormal syllabification.

116 This follows the etymology of these forms, according to Shibata (2015b, 148), who connected it to

ūmū ša-ˀi-⸢*ú-tu*⸣ 'days propitious' TabT05A-134:18

Different cases of *damāqu* in PNs:

damāqu(?) — ^{m}*Da-*⸢*a*⸣*-qu* MPR 76:43.
DN-*damiq* — ^{d}IŠKUR-*da-iq* KAJ 162:31 (Abn); KAM 10 16 r. 4'; cf. ^{Id}*A-šur-dam-me-eq* KAJ 123:14 (*dammiq* is a D-stem imperative).
Ša-DN-*damqā/at* — in *Ša-Iš*$_8$*-tár-da-qa* MPR 51:31; ^{f}*Ša-Iš*$_8$*-tár-da-a-qa* MPR 56:7, cf. ^{f}*Ša-Iš*$_8$*-tár-dam-qa-at* MPR 60:3.

To this list, we could add *aˀīlu* 'man' as discussed above (see § 180). This sound change is well known from NA. It has been suggested that /m/ spirantized to > [ɱ] and ultimately > /w/.[117] The change of /m/ > /w/ is in fact confirmed by the NB evidence, where similar broken spellings are also found (W. R. Mayer 1992, 48–54). It seems that /m/ was reduced to a fast intervocalic glide in these examples. The sound change was also applied to geminated /m/ as can be seen in the PN variations DN-*dammeq* and DN-*daˀiq*. It further seems that, between a sequence of the vowels /a+i/, spirantization of /m/ is most common. However, Bloch (RAI 2012) also suggested a similar attestation in *ga-ú-ru-*⸢*te*⸣ T 93-36:26, which should be a nominalized form of the D-stem *gammuru*, probably *gammurtu* (CAD G, 133b). The original *aḫāmiš* can also be found in NA next to *aḫāˀiš* (Luukko 2004, § 4.1.2). We may also refer to *i-ra-aˀ-ši* Lambert 1969:54, which, according to Lambert (38), was derived from *irāmši* > *irāšši* > *irāˀši*. However, we cannot exclude the possibility that this aleph also derived from a spirantized /m/ when the verb was followed by a vowel, which then spread across the entire paradigm. It should be pointed out that, in the majority of cases, intervocalic /m/ is retained as can easily be observed with the enclitic particle *-ma*. Further selected examples include:

amāru — *e-ta-mar-ma* 'he has seen' MAL A § 40:78
māmītu — *ma-mi-te* 'oath' KAV 217:10'
namāšu — *a-na na-ma-še* 'for departure' Billa 63:20
rāmunu — *ra-mi-ni-ia* 'myself' MATSH 14:40
ṣimittu — *ṣi-me-te* 'cross-beam' MARV 8 52:4
taḫūmu — *ta-ḫu-mi* 'border' KAV 126:3

§ 234 There are a few rare instances where the value of both nasal sounds swapped. In the case of /m/ > /n/, this is caused by the labial in the root (GAG, 39 § 31b-c): *pa-aṣ-ṣu-ú-na-at* 'she is covered' MAL A § 40:60 (< *paṣāmum*); *pa-ṣu-na-at* Lambert 1969:45; *i-ba-aq-qa-an* MAL A § 44:44; *i-ba-qa-an* KAJ 188:18; *bu-qu-ni-ša* KAJ 97:2; *i-ba-qa-an-na* LVUH 48:26; *ba*$^{!}$*-aq-na* LVUH 21:19.[118] The change /m/ > /n/ also occurs in the prefix *ma-* of nominals, e.g., *na*[*r*]*-kab-tu* 'chariot' BVW Ko:20; *nap-se-me* 'nose bag' BVW Ko:17; *na-ag-li-b*[*e*] 'razors' KAV 205:18; *na-áš-pér-tu* 'message' MATSH 12:42. As for *mu-*, this phenomenon is limited to the noun *nubattum* 'night', e.g., *nu-bat-tu-šu-nu* MATC 41:7'. Partial assimilation of /m/ before a dental is attested (cf. NA in SNAG, 18): *emdu* > *en-*

Babylonian equivalent *šemû*. I assume the adjective *šaˀiˀu*, rather than *šaˀû*, in analogy with the ordinal *šanīu* 'second'. The orthography allows for this.

117 See Reiner (1966, 36–37, 113–14 n1); SNAG, 24 § 2.3.; Lipiński (2001, 118f § 11.8). Spirantization of /m/ is not unknown in Semitic languages; for instance, it is common in Gurage, e.g., *aɱära* 'bird of prey'; *äɱər* 'why?', even further /m/ > /w/, e.g., *ˀəwān* 'louse', *gʷäwaňä* 'hippopotamus' (see Leslau 1992, 26 § 4.13).

118 The verb seems to have been *baqānu* in OA as well, although the evidence is flimsy (see CAD B, 97).

du^{meš} 'cypress' MARV 10 30:2; *en-da-a-tu* 'impositions' MARV 8 59:7 (< sg. *emittu*?, see Freydank 2011, 359). On the other hand, /n/ > /m/ occurs as well, e.g., *im-ḫa* Adad Ritual:4 cf. *in-ḫa* Adad Ritual:4, 8, 9, 10, 14; *ka-am-ku-ú-ni* 'they are sealed' MARV 5 19:6'†; *ku-um-ka* 'seal!' KAV 195+:30 (Sa), cf. *ku-uk-ka* KAV 103:18 (Sa).[119]

§ 235 Rather unusual is the possible m/b alternation found in the PN ^{md}*Iš*$_{8}$*-tár-re-bat* (< DN-*rēmat*) MPR 58:46 (see MPR, 63b), and the PN ^{f}*Ra-mat-*^{d}*Še-ru-a* (< *Rabʔat*-DN) MPR 58:41. For similar alternation in the GN Šimanibe/Šibanibe, see de Ridder (2015c; 2016a, 123–124).

4.8.1 Loss of mimation

§ 236 While mimation in Akkadian was a common feature in the early second millennium, signs of decay became visible towards the end of the OB and OA archives. In the Late Bronze Age, mimation had fully dropped off as can be observed in Amurru (Izre'el 1991a, 43fff § 1.7); Ugarit (Huehnergard 1989, 99f); Nuzi (Wilhelm 1970, 16f); MitAkk (Adler 1976, 18 § 7); SB (Stein 2000, 22ff); limited in HattAkk (Durham 1976, 483ff); and most radically disposed of in MB (Aro 1955a, 32), where even the conjunction *aššum* > *aššu* was affected. A gradual loss of mimation can already be observed in OA. The increased frequency of mimationless forms in the Ib archives shows a steady development (GKT, 54f § 35c). The loss of mimation only affects the final /m/, which does not belong to a root, as can be seen in the following verbal forms: *i-šal-lim* MAL A § 39:31; *tar-tu-gu-um* MAPD § 21:105; *tu-kal-lam* BVW B:7; *tu-ka-tam* PKT 1 I right:17; *ša-im* LVUH 74:24. Nunation is always retained in the dual, but the evidence is flimsy.

§ 237 The loss of mimation most notably affected the case endings of the singular substantives of both genders, e.g., *šurqa* (< acc. *šurqam*) MAL A § 5: 64; ^{f}*qa-di-il-tu* (< nom. *qadištum*) MAPD § 1:11. The declined demonstrative pronouns belong to this group: *an-ni-ú* passim (< *annium*). The use of syllabic values (e.g., <lim>) with a maintained /m/ when used in other positions was discussed above (§ 86f), with the conclusion that they reflect a scribal tradition, rather than a phonetic reality. Most of them are CvC signs and were used as phonetic complements, e.g., *a-lim*; É.GAL-*lim*, UGULA-*lim*. The signs UM/IM/AM only occur in this position with the logogram ŠE.

§ 238 In verbal forms, the mimation had dropped off in the ventives *-a(m)* and *-ni(m)*. With another suffix added, the original /*m*/ assimilated into the following consonant, resulting in gemination.

aḫāru D	*ú-ḫi-ra-an-ni* 'he was delayed' MAL A § 36:104
rakāsu	*i-ra-ak-ku-su-né-eš-še* 'they will decree for her' MAL A § 46:98
ṣabātu	*i-ṣa-ba-ta-aš-ši* 'he will seize her' MAL A § 40:90
šapāru	*ta-šap-pa-ra-am-ma* 'she will send' MAPD § 6:44
ubālu	*it-ta-ab-lu-né-en-ni* 'they have brought' MAL B § 6:23

119 We may also note the m/n alternation in *šim/ngu*, e.g., *ši-im-gi* Ali 17:1; Ali 18:1; *ši-in-g*[*i*] MARV 1 54:2; *ši-in-ga* TabT05-11:5. This noun, however, remains obscure (see Postgate 2014, 405).

The loss of mimation eliminated the short ventive *-m* used for the prefix conjugation 2fs *taprusī*. Since there are no 2fs forms known in MA, it is not known how the language solved this problem, but it most likely left the feminine unmarked. It is possible that the ending /ī/ changed to /ē/ before mimation dropped off (see below). A similar problem was created in the pronominal suffixes, where the singular dative traditionally ended in -(*m*), but had now become indistinguishable from the accusative aside from the second-person masculine *-ku* vs. *-ka*. Similar to the ventive, /m/ was reflected in the gemination of a following consonant, usually the subjunctive. The known examples also attest a geminated /m/ of the ventive.

qabāʾu	*iq-bi-áš-šu-un-ni* 'he said to him' MAL A § 47:11
tadānu	*id-di-na-áš-še-en-ni* 'he gave to her' MAL A § 29:15

§ 239 The drop of mimation is also visible in the other morphological categories. In the possessive pronouns, mimation dropped off as expected, e.g., 2ms *ku-a-ú* KBo 1 14:10, 15, 16 (< *ku^{w}āʾum*). Again, this /m/ resurfaces in some examples with enclitic *-ma*: *šu-a-am-ma* MAL A § 27:106; *ku$^{!}$-a-ú-um-*[*ma*] MATSH 29:8'. Most adverbs of spatial deixis used to involve mimation as can be seen in the spellings where it resurfaces: *an-na-ka-am-ma* MATC 15:7 (cf. *a-na-kám* KAV 106:6 Sa); however, note *am-ma-ka-ma* MATSH 22:27–28. In the conjunction *aššum*, mimation is retained: *áš/aš-šum* passim. However, the construction *ana kīam* merged with the preposition *ana* into *akīa* without mimation: *a-ki-a* Coronation Ritual i 28, ii 29. In the DN name *Nabīum* (*Nabû*), mimation is retained.

Nabīum	^{d}*Na-bi-um*-EN-PAP KAJ 93:7; KAJ 97:12
	^{md}*Na-bi-um-ke-te* KAJ 158:5
	^{md}*Na-bi-um*-LUGAL-DINGIR^{m}[^{eš}] TR 96-15:5
	^{md}*Na-bi-um*-EN-SIG$_{5}$ KAV 105:2
	^{md}*Na-bi-um*-EN-PAP LVUH 39:24

§ 240 The loss of mimation could have set another sound change in motion, where /m/ coloured the preceding /i/ > /e/, before dropping off.[120] There are two grounds on which to assume that the final /i/ changed to /e/, but only where there used to be /m/. Hecker pointed to the probability that the genitive in OA was pronounced *-em*, instead of *-im*.[121] Singular substantives in the genitive in MA texts predominantly show Ce signs; but, unfortunately, we have little material for the plural. Secondly, the dative suffix 3fs *-šim* changed into *-še* in MA, without exceptions. This distinguished it from the accusative *-ši*, forming the only minimal pair in MA: /i/ vs. /e/. For the ventive *-nim* > *-ne*, W. Mayer pointed to a few spellings where NI is followed by EŠ for a pronominal suffix in *ir-ti-*⸢*ši*⸣*-ú-n*⸢*é-e*⸣*š-šu* MAL A § 39:39; *i-id-du-nu-né-eš-še* MAL A § 45:67 (UGM, 15 n2). However, as discussed above (§ 221), MA does not distinguish /i/ and /e/ in the syllables EŠ and IŠ. The two attestations given here are rather exceptional and literary in character. Nonetheless, in line with the above, we should still construct the ventive as *-nim* > *-ne*.

120 Cf. GAG, 14 § 9h; Gelb (1995, 100).
121 See GKT, 94f § 60b; GOA § 3.4.5.3.

4.9 Liquids /l/ and /r/

§ 241 Both /l/ and /r/ are part of the Common Semitic stock of phonemes. Although they belong to the same phonemic group of dental liquids, they are never confused in the orthography.

/la/ Normally, LA is used. In OA, the common sign is <lá> (LAL); however, in MA, we find it mostly as a phonetic complement of IDIGNA, e.g., DUMU-^{d}IDIGNA-*lá* KAJ 22:21 (Abn) and more rarely in other PNs: [*t*]*ák*$^{!}$-*lá-ku-a-na*-^{d}AMAR.UTU KAJ 47:6 (EAd/Aub). Obscure: *ta-ḫa-LÁ-LÁ* BVW A:12.

/li/ Normally, LI is used. No distinction is made between /i/ and /e/. We find <lí> (NI) in PNs of the type Ṣilli-DN (e.g., ^{m}*Ṣíl-lí-Ku-be* MARV 4, 139:8) and in ^{m}DINGIR-*be-lí-iš-ma-ni* HSM 1036688:22; DUMU.MUNUS-*ì-lí* A 2704:1. The last example may be a direct leftover from OA, where <lí> (NI) was especially common in the spellings *be-lí* 'my lord' and *ì-lí* 'my god'. See also the variant <lé> in *pa-par*$_5$*-da-lé-e* BE 17 91:5. In the final position, LIM is sometimes used for >lè>; however, its use remains mostly limited to a phonetic complement of É.GAL and UGULA (see § 87). Notice also ^{m}*A-ḫu-ṣil-LIM* HSM 1036688:24, where <lí> (NI) is expected for *ṣillī* 'my protection'. Quite exceptionally, we once find <lí> in a noun: *be-lí-šu* 'his lord' KAM 10 25:4 This spelling has become standard in NA, see Luukko (2004, 142).

/lu/ The sign LU is always used.

/al/ The sign AL is always used.

/il/ A distinction between /i/ and /e/ is made with the use of <il> (IL) and <el> (EL). Both signs are (together with <in> (IN) and <en> (EN)) the only cases in MA where /i/ and /e/ are distinct in a vC value. However, unlike the other opposite pair, attestations where the two values are used incorrectly are relatively frequent with <il$_5$> (EL) and <él> (IL), e.g., *iz-zi-BI-EL* MAL A § 30:21; *IL-MI-IL-t*[*a*] MATSH 4:34 ~ *EL-ME-EL-ta* MATSH 2:17); *ni-EL-lu*$^{!}$*-ku-ú-ni* T 97-10:1; *me-IL-te* LVUH 43:3'; 48:10, 12 (cf. *mi-il-te* LVUH 37:19). It should be pointed out that the value <il$_5$> is very common in OA, as the sign IL was rare in this period. At the same time, in the Hurrian areas, the differentiation between <il> and <el> was strong with very few deviations. This can be observed in the corpora of Nuzi and the Tušratta correspondence. In general, the use of <il$_5$> occurs in Late Bronze Age Akkadian, but is rare.[122] If we accept the presence of <il$_5$> in MA, it may be regarded as a remnant of OA traditions, similar to the use of <ṭí> (TÍ). At the same time, in absolute numbers, the sign IL is used significantly more often than EL. Therefore, we may not exclude the possibility that scribes had a tendency to use IL over EL, even in cases where it did not belong. In the NA period, there seem to be no cases were <il$_5$> was used, although <él> (IL) was still known (Luukko 2004, 46–47). Perhaps this indicates that IL was the preferred sign. On most occasions in MA, the signs are used as expected, e.g., (EL) usually in the paradigm of *elāʾu* (see § 580) and IL in the paradigm of *alāku* (see § 598f one exception above), as well as precative R$_1$/l verbs.

/ul/ The sign UL is always used.

/ra/ The sign RA is always used.

/ri/ Normally, RI is used. No distinction is made between /i/ and /e/.

/ru/ The sign RU is normally used. The MB <rù> (DIL), which derived from <rum>, is normally not used in MA, but can still be found in exceptional cases, e.g., DUB.SAR-*rù* Jankowska 1962 r. 10 (see § 87).

/ar/ The sign AR is mostly used. On one occasion, we could have <ár> (UB): [*a-m*]*a-ár* MARV 4 119:32 (Freydank 2012a, 233).

/ir/ Normally, IR is used. No distinction is made between /i/ and /e/.

/ur/ The sign UR is normally used. The value <úr> is unusual, but is found once in a letter from Ḫattuša with Assyrian influences in a Hittite name: ^{m}*Úr-ḫi*-^{d}IŠ[KUR] KBo 1 14:15'. The use of the value <úr> in this Hurrian PN Urḫi-Teššub is actually common in the Hittite 'Apology of Ḫattušili III' (CTH 81).

---

122 See Durham (1976, 232); Syllab, 60 no. 306.

§ 242 An odd sound change occurs in the Hurrian loan *ḫalzuḫlu* 'commander of a *ḫalṣu*'.[123] Two broken spellings of the old Hurrian form can be found in the Tell Billa texts: [^{lú}*ḫa*]*l-zu*$^{?}$*-uḫ-li*$^{?}$ Billa 21:5; ^{lú}*ḫa*$^{??}$*-al-zu-uḫ*$^{??}$*-li*$^{??}$ Billa 37:4. In the other attestations, /l/ and /z/ have merged into /*ss*/: ^{lú}*ḫa-síḫ-lu* KAJ 224 (=296):15; ^{lú}*ḫa-síḫ-li* Billa 25:3 etc. The liquid /l/, assimilating into the following sibilant, is common in Late Bronze Age and first millennium Akkadian.[124] Similar in this regard is *šalšu* 'third', written as *ša-áš-šu* MAPD § 19:92 (CAD Š$_1$, 264), and *ša-áš-šu-te-šu* 'the third time' PKT 4 obv. left 5.[125] This assimilation of /l/ has to be explained by the lateral realization of /š/, which could not sufficiently be distinguished from /l/ in consonant clusters. The change could therefore have been purely orthographic.

§ 243 Unusual is the form where /r/ > /š/, which is found in *ta-áš-qí-su* (< *tarqīt+šu*) 'perfume-making' PKT 6 i 37. The original form is also attested in *tar-qi-tu* PKT 3 iv 8. This could be an early example of the sound change /r/ > /š/ before /t/ and /k/, which occurs in NB and LB, e.g., *pirku* > *pišku*; *šipirtu* > *šipištu*.[126] Considering that the provided attestation comes from a 'literary' text, it may not be a feature of MA, as it could just as well be a Babylonian influence. We possibly find the sound change /l/ > /r/ in *ammar*, if we assume that it derives from *ana mala* (AHw, 43b).[127]

123 This may not be a direct loan as *ḫalṣu* was already known in OB Mari texts (see Streck 1997, 271).

124 See GAG, 43–44 § 34c. For MB, see Balkan (1954, 131–32, 199 n64).

125 Note also a similar loss of /l/ in the root √*ṯlṯ* in the Amharic equivalent *sost* (written *śost* ሦስት) 'three' (see Leslau 2000, 50 § 45.1).

126 See CAD P, 403ff; CAD Š$_3$, 65ff; cf. GAG, 44 § 35c; Woodington (1983, 24 § 12).

127 Note that we also find the change /l/ > /r/ in the MA incantation ritual VAT 10034+. Here, we unexpectedly read *ip-pa-ra-saḫ-ma* l. 58; *ap-pa-ra-si-iḫ* l. 59. Both derive from the verb *napalsuḫu* 'to fall to the ground' (see Farber 1977, 186, 204).

Chapter 5: Structure of Nouns

§ 244 The following chapters deal with nominal forms in Akkadian. These are word classes inflected according to case ending, which set them apart from the verbs and most pronouns. In this category, the normal nouns belong together with adjectives and numbers. These forms are also inflected according to gender. Nominal forms can occur in three states. Most important is the status rectus, which is the normal state with full declination. The status constructus occurs in the genitive construction and with pronominal suffixes. Rarely do we find status absolutus forms without endings. Note that the inflection of numbers and adjectives is slightly different.

§ 245 Concerning the structure of the noun, there are a few basic points to make. These are also true for Semitic languages in general. First of all, most nouns seem to use a tripartite root consisting of three radicals. As is traditional in Akkadian, we use the radicals P-R-S from the verb *parāsu* to create theoretical forms, similarly to the use of the roots F-ˁ-L in Arabic and P-ˁ-L/Q-Ṭ-L in Hebrew. The radicals are supplemented by vowels and prefixes, infixes or suffixes, creating basic noun patterns, such as *PaRS* or *maPRaS*. We can furthermore make a distinction between verbal noun and non-verbal nouns. The first category consists of verbal adjectives, participles and infinitives. They can also be inflected to the verbal stem and, in the case of the participle and infinitive, were used originally as the verbal predicate. They can also be used as lexicalized nouns and therefore belong in this discussion. Non-verbal nouns consist of nouns that do not belong in these verbal categories, but do contain a normal root, such as the patterns *PiRS, PaRRāS* and *maPRaS*. It must be admitted that we do find some word patterns for non-verbal nouns, which are connected to verbal stems, such as *PitRāS to* the Gt-stem. Words that do not fall into either category are naturally foreign loan words, as well as primary (or isolated) nouns, which do not contain a clear tripartite root, but are nonetheless good Semitic or Akkadian words. The most common examples are *abu* 'father'; *ummu* 'mother'; *libbu* 'heart'; *pû* 'mouth'; *appu* 'nose'. Primary nouns can take the feminine marker *-t*, e.g., *šattu* 'year'; *šaptu* 'lip'. Nouns with a seemingly tripartite root, but one that is not shared by any other nominal form or verbal root, are also regarded as primary nouns (Fox 2003, 61), e.g., *batultu* 'girl' and *uznu* 'ear'. As can be observed from these examples, primary nouns generally seem to refer to core family members or body parts and other basic concepts.

5.1 Noun patterns and roots

§ 246 This chapter will provide an overview of the different nominal patterns in MA and discuss foreign loan words. We will try not to delve into the etymology of individual nouns, no matter how interesting this may be, nor try to categorize all of them. The aim of this chapter is merely to provide an overview of the character of MA nominal patterns. The lexical inventory of the Assyrian dialect, in general, deserves a study on its own, but it is hoped that the Jena/Moscow/Leipzig 'Etymological Dictionary of Akkadian' project will do most of the work that remains to be done. In the meantime, we should mention the article of Kogan (2006), which compares the OA lexical inventory with Babylonian. For an overview of nominal patterns in MA, the scheme used in GAG, 66–90 § 53–59, and subsequently by Hecker in GKT, 82–89 § 53–57, is put into practice here.[1] The best general source on simple Semitic noun patterns is probably Fox (2003).

§ 247 When using this scheme, the reader should be aware of a few choices made. II/weak roots are usually ordered as two consonantal forms in the simple paradigm, while expanded patterns are treated as strong roots. On the other hand, I/weak and III/weak are ordered, together with strong roots, in order to account for them starting or ending in a vowel, rather than a consonant. In the same vein, III/weak roots with expanded patterns are ordered with strong verbs, since most of these are verbal nouns, built after the tripartite root system. Discussion on the function of the patterns is limited, if there is one, since this is a study of grammar, rather than semantics. It would require the assembling of a large lexical list to make such a discussion possible. For the same reason, attestations are not complete, including for the loans. In the framework of grammatical research, it is not deemed feasible to gather all technical terms, which are often Hurrian, but more often have an unclear etymology and meaning. These attestations, then, are simply meant to be representative of the corpus, but not the complete corpus.

§ 248 Compound words are rare in MA. This is not unexpected as word compounds are an unnatural feature in Semitic languages (GAG, 90 § 59a). Nonetheless, a few forms can be found in MA, which are mostly adverbs (cf. OA in GOA § 4.5). In relation to this, we should also mention the lexicalized *ša* construction (e.g., *ša-rēšēn* 'eunuch') mentioned in § 302.

ayyarzibne	*ayya-ar-zi-ib-ni* (an aromatic plant) < *ayyuru+zibnu* (?) KAV 98:3
kannamāre	*ka-na-ma-ri* 'in the early morning' MATC 1:5 (see § 491)
mār šipre	DUMU KIN 'messenger' RS 06.198:8; DUMU *ši-ip-ri-ia* T 05-1:8. pl. DUMU *ši-ip-r⸢u-ut-te⸣* 'messengers' MATSH 9:25
mazziz pane	*ma-zi-iz pa-ni* 'court attendant' MAPD § 8:50 (while the governing noun remains in the genitive, in the plural it refers the plural morpheme: *ma-zi-iz pa-nu-ut-te* MAPD § 8:51)
paddugānu[2]	*pa-du-ga-ni* (festival or banquet) KAJ 190:21; ⸢*ša*⸣ *pa-du-ga-na-a-*[*te*] MARV 3 77:8
pētḫalle[3]	*pe-et-ḫal-li* 'horse rider' CTMMA 1 99:5 ⸢*pet*⸣*-ḫal-li* T 93-2:11
šaddaqde	*ša-da-aq-di* 'last year' KAV 107:9 (< perhaps *šattu+√qdm*)
šalšene[4]	*šal*[!]*-še-ni* 'the year before last' MATSH 26:6'
ūmakkal	*ú-ma-kal* 'for the length of one day' MATSH 2:13 (< *ūmam-kala*)

These compounds are built from genitive constructions, where, at least originally, the governed noun occurred in the genitive. Moreover, as these compounds were

1 Cf. Ungnad (1992, 39–44 § 36); Streck (2014a, 40–47 § 110–38); GOA § 4.2.

2 This form is derived from *(ša) pan Dagan*, following Parpola (1979, 29).

3 This is derived from *pētû+ḫallu*, literally 'the opener of thighs' (AHw, 858a). Note the Babylonian VA in the participle of *patāʾu* 'to open'. This indicates that *pētḫallu* itself is a loan from Babylonian.

4 This is found s.v. *šaluššani* in the dictionaries. It is probably a compound of *šalšu* 'three' and *šattu* 'year' (see AHw, 1153a; CAD Š$_1$, 285b).

grammaticalized, the plural suffix was placed on the governed, rather than the governing, noun, e.g., [DUM]U *ši-ip-ru-ut-te* MATSH 9:8 (Streck 2014a, 47 § 138c). Etymologically, this appears to be odd, as the governed noun functions as a specification of the governed noun. For this reason, we also find an additional plural marker in the following attestation: DUMU^{meš} *ši-ip-ru-ut-te* MATSH 9:8. Note that some designations of professions of the type *rab X* 'chief of x' have the governing noun occurring in the nominative, as if a compound: GAL *mu-ra-qi-a-tu* 'chief of the perfume makers' MARV 3 i vi 13'; GAL *pi-ir-ḫu* 'chief of the apprentices(?)' CUSAS 34 45:22' (see CUSAS 34, 73–74).

5.1.1 Two-radical roots

§ 249 Many of the nouns in this category are primary nouns. However, some words have no Semitic cognates and could be Akkadian primary nouns or loans, e.g., *mātu* 'country' and *ḫaṭṭu* 'sceptre'. There is a strong distinction between patterns of short and long vowels. The latter group mostly consists of non-verbal nouns, such as *kīttu* (< *kīntu*) 'truth', *rēḫtu* 'remainder' and *ḫīṭu* 'punishment'. Nouns with a geminated final radical often seem to have an unknown origin.

a) With a short vowel:

PaS — Primary nouns, usually referring to family members: *a-bu* 'father' MAL A § 30:20; *a-ḫu-(...)* 'brother' MAL A § 22:106; *a-si* 'myrtle' MARV 2 22:1; *e-mu-ú-(...)* 'father-in-law' MAL A § 29:14; *pa-an* 'face' MARV 1 10:9.

PaSt — Primary nouns: *da-al-t*[*am*$^{?}$] 'door' KAJ 8:17; *ša-at-te* 'year' MATSH 6:8'. Deverbal nouns: *sa*-[*a*]*r-ta* 'crime' MAPD § 18:83.

PaSāt — Primary noun: *a-ḫa-su* 'his sister' (*aḫātu*) MPR 2:22. Deverbal noun: *a-bat* 'command' MATSH 1 :4.

PiS — Primary nouns: *i-da-(...)* 'hand' MATSH 8:36'; *il* 'god' MAPD § 8:48.

PiSt — Primary nouns: ^{kuš}*ḫi-im-t*[*u*] 'a leather skin' KAJ 250:1; *kim-tu* 'family' KAJ 179:21; see also *(Pi)RiSt*.

PuS — Primary nouns: *mu-tu* 'husband' MAL A § 40:61; *šúm-šu* 'his name' MARV 4 151:19.

PuSt — Primary noun *zu*$^{?}$*-ta* 'sweat' BVW M:7; *zu-ú-tu* BVW Ko r. 7. See also *(Pu)RuSt*.

b) With a long vowel:

PāS — Primary nouns: *ba-a-be* 'door' MATSH 8:51'; *e-na-(...)* 'eye, source' MATSH 3:30; *le-ú* 'wooden tablet' LVUH 92:3; *ka-ri* 'quay' KAJ 169:17; *ma-a-te* 'country' MAL A § 36:4; MATSH 2:14; *re-ša* 'head' KAJ 223:11; *ṣe-ni*^{meš} 'flock' MARV 3 73:3; *ša-ri-(...)* 'wind' MATC 2:15; *ša-ḫu* 'basis' KAJ 303:11; *ṭé-ma* (√*tḫm*) 'instruction' MATC 4:19. Deverbal nouns: *qe-el-t*[*u*] 'gift' (*qēltu*) New Year Ritual:7'.

PāSt — Primary noun: *na-ar-te* 'river' KAJ 128:12. Deverbal nouns: *ṣa-al-te* 'quarrel' MAL A § 8:78;

PāSat — Deverbal(?) noun *pa-ḫe-te* (*pāḫutu*) 'province' MATC 23A:1.

PīS — This group mostly concerns II/ū and II/ī roots. Primary nouns: *be-er* 'double hour' MATSH 6:28'; *ki-i-di* 'outside' MAL A § 6:71; *ki-si-(...)* 'bag' Coronation Ritual iii 10; *li-ṭu* 'hostage' MATSH 2:20; *še-pi-(...)* 'foot' MATC 56:4; UDU *zi-pu-te* 'a type of sheep' KAJ 230:8; *zi-qu* 'torch' Ištar Ritual:12. Deverbal nouns: *de*$_4$*-e-ni* KAJ 6:20; *li-tu* 'cow' AO 21.157:1; *re-eḫ-tu-(...)* 'remainder' A 1747 (NTA, 23):12; *ši-im* 'price' KAJ 147:10; *ši-qu* 'irrigation' Kümmel 1989:2. Note also the III/weak roots: *ḫi-pi* 'break' (< *ḫapāʾu*) KTN inventory ii 24; *ḫi-i-ṭa* 'punishment' (< *ḫaṭāʾu*) MAL A § 3:39; MARV 4 153:9; *(...)-qi-bi* 'command' Franke/Wilhelm 1985:8; *si-i-ra* 'plaster' MATC 12:17.

PīSt — Primary noun: *še-er-te* 'morning' MATC 5:11; Deverbal nouns: *ki-it-ta* 'truth'

Coronation Ritual ii 36; *ši-im-ti* 'testament' TR 105:5.

PūS Primary nouns: *ḫu-li* 'road' MARV 3 58:3'; *mu-še* 'night' MATSH 2:22; *pu-ru* 'lot' KAV 125:2; *u_4-me* 'day' MAPD § 9:52. Deverbal nouns : *mu-tu* 'dead' KAJ 316:14.

PūSt Primary noun : *um-te* 'day' T 93-3:17. Deverbal noun *tu-ur-ta* 'requital' MAL A § 42:18.

c) With geminated R_2:

PaSS Primary nouns: *ga-ap-pu-(...)* 'wing' KTN inventory i 22; *ḫa-aṭ-ṭu* 'stick' BVW Ko r. 9; *šam-ma* 'medicine' KAJ 221:4. Note also the primary nouns of the type *CaCC* with identical radicals: *ka-ak-ka* 'weapon' MATC 1:7; *sa-su* 'floor' (*sassu*) KAJ 310:3. Deverbal nouns and adjectives of the type *PvRS*, but with R_2=R_3. Deverbal noun: *sa-ar-[ri]* 'crime' MAL A § 36:107. Adjective: *da-an-ni* 'my valid declaration' KAV 159:4; *e-mi-(…)*'hot' PKT 1 I right:18; *ma-gu-tu* 'tight' BVW Ac r. 1.

PaSSat Primary nouns: *am-me-te* 'cubit' (*ammutu*) KAJ 128:4; *kal-le-te* 'daughter-in-law' (*kallutu*) MAL A § 46:97; *pár-ru-tu* 'young lamb' LVUH 19:25; ^{dug}*šap-pat-tu* 'a vessel' KAJ 277:1.

PiSS Primary nouns: *ge-ri* 'road' KAJ 152:3; ^{túg}*li-pu* 'wrap' MARV 1 24:55; ^{giš}*li-it-te* 'stool' (pl. *littātu*) MAPD § 17:80; EN^{meš} *pír-ri* 'enrolment officers' MARV 2 17a+:59; *pi-it-ti* 'responsibility' MATSH 9:22; *ri-te* 'hand' BVW F:5; *ši-in-ni* 'ivory' KAV 99:27. Deverbal nouns of II/gem roots: *[b]i-i-⸢la⸣* 'alloy' MATSH 1:18.

PiSSat Primary nouns: *si-ma-ti* (< *summatu*) 'dove' KAJ 177:4. Deverbal nouns of II/gem roots: *bi-la-te* 'alloy' KAV 205:25; *miḫ-ḫa-tu-(...)* '*m.*-beer' (pl.) MATC 12:5; *qi-im-ma-te* 'crown of trees' KTN inventory i 11; *ši-il-la-ta* 'blasphemy' MAL A § 2:16

PuSS Primary nouns: *um-me* 'trunk' KTN inventory ii 7; *qu-up-pa* 'box' KAV 99:25. Deverbal nouns of II/gem roots: ^{uru}*du-un-ni* 'fortified settlement' T 96-20:88; ^{giš}*mur-ru* 'myrrh' MARV 10 41:6.

PuSSat Primary nouns: ^{udu}*gu-ra-tum* 'ewes' Billa 36:1; ^{zì}*qu-pa-tu* (a type of flour) MARV 3 16 :9. Deverbal noun of II/gem roots: *nuggatu* 'rage' in *nu-ga-ti-pi* A 3187 (NTA, 36):5 (see W. Mayer 2016, 118).

5.1.2 Three-radical roots

§ 250 Various patterns occur.

a) Simple patterns:

PaRS Primary nouns: *a-ra-an-*(…) 'offense' MAL A § 2:20; *ḫar-šu* '(crumbled$^{?}$) bread' MARV 5 32:1; *kal-zi* 'precinct' MAPD § 1:4; *qar-ni-(...)* 'horn' KTN inventory i 20; *ub-ru* 'foreigner' MATC 56:2. Nouns derived from verbal roots or the other way around: *na-ak-ru* 'enemy' MATSH 3:10; *qa-bal* 'middle' MATC 81:5; *tar-⸢ṣi⸣* 'proper' MAL C+ § 5:29. Adjectives (§ 308ff): *ṣe-eḫ-ru* 'young' MAL B § 1:10; *sa-al-qi* 'boiled (meat)' Aynard/Durand 1980 12:12.

PaRaSt Primary noun: *ta-ḫa-al-te* 'a foodstuff' KAM 11 30:11. Deverbal noun: *ra-pal-te* 'loins' Rm 376:7. See also see *PaRaSSat*.

PaRiSt This group deals with substantivized adjectives (cf. OA in GOA § 4.2.2.4): *a-ri-ik-ta* 'length' Adad Ritual r. 4'; *e-mi-it-tu* 'punishment' MAL A 24:81 (Bab *imittu*); *e-ri-il-ti* 'desire' T 93-11:34; *ma-sik-te* 'blasphemy' MAPD § 10 :57 ; ^{f}*qa-di-il-tu* 'priestess' MAPD § 1:11; *ša-píl-ti-(...)* 'remainder' MATC 71:53. Many nouns refer to feminine entities: ^{f}*e-si-ir-tu* 'concubine' MAL A § 41:6; *qa-di-il-tu* 'a priestess' MAL A § 40:61.

PaRuSt Primary noun ^{f}*ba-tu-ul-te* 'young girl' MAL A § 55:23. Deverbal nouns: *za-ku-tu* 'cleansing' KAM 10 7:14'†; *ša-qúl-te* 'weight' (Bab. *šuqultu*) KAJ 178:18. Both examples are uncertain.

PiRS — Primary nouns: ^{túg}*bir-še* 'a textile' Coronation Ritual ii 17; *in-be* 'fruit' KTN inventory i 9; *in-ḫa* 'a song' Adad Ritual:8; *iš-ka* 'testicle' MAL A § 8:78; *kiš-pi* 'sorcery' MAL A § 47:2; ^{níg}*mi-iṭ-ru* '*m.*-bread' KAJ 306a:7; *pi-it-nu* 'chest' KTN inventory iii 11'; *ši-in-g*[*u*] 'a type of wool' MARV 1 54:2. Deverbal nouns: *ig-ri-(...)* 'wages' MAL E § 3:8'; *ki-iṣ-ri* 'rib' Adad Ritual r. 10'; MATSH 17:9; *pír-si* 'weaned (child)' MATC 64:26; *ri-ik-sa* 'decree' MAPD § 2:19; *ši-pár-(...)* 'instruction' MATC 4:17; *ši-ir-ki-(...)* 'gift' MAL A § 29:12; *zi-im-ri-(...)* 'song' Adad Ritual r. 14'.

PiRaS — Primary noun *si-mu-nu* 'occasion' Ištar Ritual:1.

PiRSat — Primary nouns *te-er-ḫe-te* 'bridal gift' MAL A § 38:23; UDU *zi-bu-tu*^{meš} (< **zinb*) 'fat-tailed sheep(?)' Ali 9:5.

(Pi)RiS — Nouns that have a I/w root do not have its first radical in nominal patterns; as such, they appear as *PiS* and *PiSt* forms; cf. *(Pu)RuSt*): *li-da-ni-(...)* '(her) children' KAV 211:4; cf. *(Pu)RuS*.[5]

PiRiSt — Deverbal nouns: *ki-ṣir-tu* MARV 5 42:14; *pi-qít-ta* 'allocation' MATSH 10:19; *pi-šèr-ti* MARV 3 10:20'; *qi-bi-te* 'command' MATSH 8:64'; *ri-qi-ta* 'perfume' MARV 4 146:4' *ṣi-mi-te* 'team' MATC 24B:6; *ši-pi-ir-te* 'instruction' KAJ 118:5

(Pi)RiSt — Deverbal nouns *bi-la-at* 'yield' KAJ 81:20; *ṣi-ib-ta* 'interest' T 04-37:26; *ṣi-it* 'offspring' Hall 1983:7; cf. *(Pi)RiS*.

PuRS — Primary nouns: *ḫur-di* 'posthumous son' Faist 2001, 251:9; *ṣu-up-ra-(...)* 'fingernail' KTN inventory i 26; *uz-ni-(...)* 'ear' MAL A § 40:84. Pattern with the same function as *PiRS*. The difference in theme vowel may have been caused by labials in the roots that occur in the majority of attestations (Krebernik 2006, 93–95). Most examples are deverbal nouns: *ḫu-ub-te* 'plunder' KAJ 103:14; *lum-ni* 'cruelty' MAL B § 39:34; *mu-ḫur* 'appeal' MATC 17:7; *mur-ṣi* 'illness' T 04-2:9; ⌜*p*⌝*u-uḫ-ri* 'assembly' MATSH 17:5; *pu-uz-ri* 'secret' MAL A § 18:73; *ṣu-u*[*ḫ*]*-ri* 'children' T 97-34:17; *up-ru* 'head cover' A 893:8.

PuRSat — Exceptionally, we once find the deverbal *pu-uq-du-tu* 'spike' KAJ 310:61. This is a variant of *puquttu* (see Edzard 1982, 81 § 4.2; UŠA, 115).

PuRuSt — Deverbal nouns: *šu-ku-ut-ta-(...)* 'jewellery' MAL A § 40:72; ^{túg}*lu-bùl-ta* Coronation Ritual i 35; *ú-gu-ra-t*[*e*] 'documents' KAJ 310:37.

(Pu)RuSt — Deverbal noun *šub-ta* 'dwelling' Faist 2001, 252:24; see also *(Pi)RiSt*.

b) With long vowels:

PaRāS — Primary noun: *te-še-ni* (wild animals) VAT 8236:3. Deverbal nouns, with infinitive pattern *PaRāS*: *da-ˀa-ni* MAL A § 55:20; *ša-la-ma* 'well-being' Ištar Ritual:13; *e-ṣa-da* 'harvest' MATSH 2:26.

PaRāSt — Deverbal nouns, consisting of an infinitive pattern *PaRāS*+feminine ending *-t*: *a-lak-ta* 'road' MATC 18:8; *na-pal-tu* 'life' KAJ 316:15; *ša-bar-tu* 'bar' KAJ 178:1; *ša-pár-te* 'pledge' MAL A § 39:28.

PaRīS — Primary nouns: *a-i-la* 'human' MAL A § 15:52; É *ḫa-ši-me* MATC 49:16; *sa-me-di* 'seed of s.' KAJ 277:8. Deverbal noun ⌜*ka*⌝*-ni-ka* 'sealed document' TabT05a-134:23; *na-ḫi-ri-*(…) 'nostrils' KTN inventory i 21. Also in the adjective *la-be-ru* 'old' KAJ 256:2

PaRīSat — Deverbal noun *ḫa-ri-be-ti* 'waste land' KAJ 164:3.

PaRūS — Primary nouns: *a-bu-sà-tum* 'stables (pl.)' VAT 8923:6; *e-bu-ri* 'harvest' KAJ 262:3; *ka-lu-mi-(...)* 'lamb' MATSH 12:28; *ka-mu-n*[*u*$^{?}$] 'cumin' NBC 4599:4; ^{sa}*pa-gu-me* 'a harness strap' BVW A:10; *ta-ḫu-ú-ma* 'boundary' MAL B § 9:20.

---

5 Note that, based on plene spelling, von Soden lengthens the vowel of *lidu* 'child' > *līdu* (AHw, 552a; GAG, 69 § 54k). If this is the case, we should, by analogy, lengthen the vowel of all *(Pv)RvS(t)* patterns of I/w roots. Analogous to other Semitic languages, it seems likely that the medial vowel was short, e.g., the Arabic *maṣdar* (infinitive) of two I stem (G) verbs: *ṣila* 'link' (صلة); *ṯiqa* 'trust' (ثقة).

PaRūSt	Deverbal noun *ba-tu-ul-ta* 'girl' MATSH 17:7. We should construct a long vowel in this noun by analogy with the masculine cognate *batūlu*.
PāRiS	The normal pattern for participles of the G-stem. See § 321ff.
PāRiSt	Feminine participles. Note also the plural *da-ri-a-te* 'eternity' Coronation Ritual i 41.
PiRāS	Primary nouns: *i-ga-ri* 'wall' VAT 8923:1; *li-ša-na* 'tongue' MATSH 16:9.
PuRāS	Primary nouns: *[b]u-ra-šu* 'juniper' MARV 10 41:10; *ḫu-ṭa-ri* 'staff' AO 19.227:9; *ku-na-šu* 'emmer' Billa 29:2; ^{túg}*lu-be-ru* 'ceremonial garment' KAJ 256:1; *nu-pa-ri* 'workhouse' Giricano 4:21; *qu-ma-ša-a-tu* 'capitals (of columns)' MARV 1 14:12; *ú-ba-an-(...)* 'finger' MAL A § 8:80; *u-ra-e* 'stable' T 98-43:1. Deverbal nouns: *du-ma-qi* 'jewels' (pl. tant.) Adad Ritual:6'; *mu-ṭa-ú* 'missing' MARV 6 86:7; *šu-ba-e* 'roasting pan' KAJ 303:7.
PuRāSt	Deverbal noun *qu-la-ap-te* (Bab. *qulīptu*) 'skinned' KAV 104:9.
PuRīS	Primary nouns, usually animal names in MA: *ḫu*$^{!}$*-zi-ri* 'pigs' T 98-123:4'; *su-ḫi-*⸢*ri*⸣ 'foal' MATC 11:23. The pattern is used in Semitic *PuRīS* for diminutive nouns, e.g., Arabic *quṣayr* 'small palace' (قصير). See von Soden (1991); Testen (2006). Cf. deverbal *uzību* 'foundling' in GN ^{uru}*<Du>-un-ni-/ša-*$^{\text{uru!}}$*Ú-zi-bi* Giricano 1:5–6.
PuRīSt	Primary nouns ^{f}*ḫu-zi-ir-te* 'sow' KAJ 80:12; *su-ḫi-ir-ta* 'foal' MATC 3:9.Deverbal noun: *ḫu-rib-te* 'desert' MATSH 13:21.
PuRūS	Deverbal noun: *bu-qu-ni-(...)* 'shearing' KAJ 97 :2.
PuRūSī	In the numeral *šu-nu-i*$^{!}$*-tum* 'two-year-old' KAJ 96:2. See § 347.

c) With gemination:

PaRRaS	Primary noun: *an-nu-ku* 'tin' KAJ 37:1; This pattern is used for adjectives as a type of infixed plural (Reiner 1966, 64; GAV, 52–55; cf. OA in GOA § 7.4.4). Most attestations are found under the feminine pattern *PaRRaSt* (below). The following nominal stative *ṣe-eḫ-ḫe-ru* 'they are (very) young' MAL A § 43:32, which is also related, is a Babylonian form for the Assyrian *ṣaḫḫurū* (cf. *ṣaḫḫarātu* below).
PaRRaSt	Feminine variant of *PaRRaS*: *ṣa-ḫa-ra-te* 'small ones' VAT 9410:32; *šap-pa-la-te* 'low one' Ali 23:13. See also the Babylonian form *ṣe-ḫe-ra-tu* 'small' (non-verbal adjective) KTN inventory i 15.
PaRRiS	Primary nouns: *kal-li-e* '(post) station'; ^{lú}*ka-li-*⸢*ú*⸣ 'messenger' MATC 58:4 (cf. § 490).
PaRRuS	Pattern of the verbal adjective of D-stem, occurs instead of Babylonian *PuRRuS*: ^{lú}*ḫab-bu-li-(...)* 'debtor' MAL A 48:32; *ṣa-am-mu-da* 'equipped(?)' KTN inventory i 12.
PaRRuSt	As above, feminine forms. All deverbal nouns: *pa-ṣu-un-te* 'veiled' MAL A § 41:12: *ta-mu-a-ti* 'oath' pl. tnt. Giricano 14:7.
PiRRiS	In deverbal *ṣe-eḫ-ḫe-ru* 'they are (very) young' MAL A § 43:32. See *PaRRaS*.
PiRRiSt	Primary nouns: *si-mil-ti* 'staircase' VAT 8923:3; *si-ni-il-te* 'woman' KAJ 311:9.
PaRRāS	The pattern is used for professions or other activities that a person might commit, much like the participle (GAG, 76 § 55o). Notice also the identical Arabic nominal pattern *ḫabbāz* (خبّاز) 'baker' (cf. GAV, 61–64 § 3.3): *pa-ḫa-ru* 'potter' MARV 3 80:11', 24; MATC 60:5; *gal-la-be* 'barber' A 3184 (NTA, 34):7; ⸢^{lú}⸣*na-ia-a-le* KAJ 160:7; *pár-ra-ṣa-ie-e* (?) 'liar' MATC 2:13; ^{lú}*za-ma-ru* 'singer' KAJ 221:3.
PuRRāS	Deverbal nouns, mostly III/weak roots as variant of *PuRāS*: *mu-ul-la-e* 'compensation' MATSH 2:54; *mu-ut-ta-qe* 'sweet cake' MARV 4 13:4'; *ru-ub-ba-ú* MARV 9 95:27 (but *ru-bi-e-šu* MARV 3 29:8).
PuRRiS	Primary nouns: *ku-ud-di-li* 'a type of textile' KAV 103:9; *pu-ni-gu* 'a type of bread' (Bab. *pannigu*) MARV 1 7:4, also *pan-gu* l. 18. See CAD P, 83b.
PuRRuS	Primary noun: *ku-ku-ba-tu* (sg. *kukkubu*) 'vessels' KAJ 292:6. Deverbal noun *uk-ku-lu* 'very dark' A 602:4. Probably a Babylonian form of the D-stem adjectival pattern *PaRRuS*.

d) R_3 geminated:

PaRaSS	Primary nouns: [dug]*a-ga-nu* 'a cauldrons' T 98-131:5; *a-sa-lu* 'a copper vessel' KAJ 303:3; *ka-lam-me* 'part of a chariot' KAJ 310:8.
PaRRaSS	Primary noun [*š*]*a ab-ba-áš-še* (a textile worker) YBC 6954:8; ⌜lú?!⌝ *ša ab-ba-še* KAM 11 96:6 (see Postgate 2014, 414).
PaRaSSat	Occurs as a plural pattern for singular *PaRaSt* in *ša-ḫar-ra-tu*? 'cloaks (pl.)' MARV 10 64:3'; [túg]*ša-ḫar-ra-*[*te*[meš]] MAPD § 6:43. See CAD Š₁, 81b.
PaRuSS	Primary noun: [kuš]*na-ru-qu* 'leather bag' KAJ 136:7'; [kuš]*na-ru-qu* DeZ 3441:18. Deverbal noun: *za-ru-qì* (Bab. *zuruqqu*) 'shaduf' KAJ 152:3.
PaRRuSS	Primary noun [giš]*ša-ku-li* (a type of wood) Billa 25:1.
PaRuSSat	Deverbal noun: *a-ḫu-ze-te* 'marriage gift' MAL A § 30:28.
PiRaSS	Primary noun: *ši-pa-si-ni* 'our sealings' MARV 1 71:14.
PiRiSS	Deverbal noun: [m]*Gi-mil-li* KAJ 1:22; *Gi-mi-li* KAJ 79:23 (all PNs). A variant of PiRS.
PuRuSS	Primary noun *ḫu-ru-up-pa-a-te* (sg. *ḫuruppu*) 'dishes' MAL A § 42:17. Deverbal nouns: *ḫu-bu-ul-li* 'debt' MARV 4 151:9; *ku-nu-ki-(...)* 'seal' KAV 99:29; *pu-ṣu-ni* 'veil' Lambert 1969:45.
PuRRiSS	A Primary noun: *ku-di-mu* 'cress' MARV 1 9:17; [ú]*ku-di-mi* MARV 2 28:7 (Stol 1983/84, 29).

5.1.3 Expanded patterns

§ 251 Various patterns occur.

a) Prefixed vowel:

iPRiS	Probably a variant of *PiRS* (GOA § 4.2.2.6): [*i*]*k-ri-be-(...)* 'blessings' Coronation Ritual i 22; *ip-ṭí-ri-(...)* 'ransom' AO 20.154:10; KAJ 167:8. Both are deverbal nouns.

b) Prefixed mV-:

maPRaS	The *maPRaS* is a non-verbal noun pattern that has various functions (see Streck 2002a). Most of the patterns using afformative *ma-* are variants of *maPRaS*. Some attestations indicate a place of verbal action: *maš-ka-an* 'place of putting' MAPD § 9:53; *ma-qe-e* (=*manquʾu*) 'place of pouring' Ištar Ritual:7; *ma-ia-*[*li*] 'bed' MAPD § 17:80; *me-re-še* 'cultivated land' MARV 2 23:7. Instrument of verbal action: *maḫ-li-še* 'chisels' KAJ 178:9; *ma-áš-ḫi-li* 'sieve' PKT 3 i 17; *ma-áš-le-ú* 'leather bucket' KAJ 303:9. See also the result of verbal action: [zì]*ma-áš-ḫe-te* '*m*.-flour' New Year Ritual:17'; *ma-al-ṭi-ri* 'prescription' A 300:8.[6]
maPRaSt	Feminine variant of *maPRaS*. Place of verbal action: *ma-áš-ka-at-ta* 'depot' MAL A § 6:70; *ma-ṣar-te* 'protection' MATSH 22:5. Instrument of verbal action: *ma-kal-ta* 'bowl' Ištar Ritual:6; *ma-na-aḫ-*⌜*ta*⌝ 'equipment' MAL B § 11:8; [dug]*mar-sa-tu* 'one soaking-vessel' KAJ 182:7. See also the result of verbal action: *ma-da-te* (=*mandantu*) KAJ 106:13; *ma-ak-na-*⌜*ak*⌝*-tu* 'envelope' MATSH 9:14; *ma-al-qe-tu* 'revenue' Coronation Ritual i 37; *ma-šar-tu* 'review' MARV 2 23:21'.
maPRāS	Rare variant of *maPRaS* with similar functions (Streck 2002, 242–43): *na-at-ba-ka-ni-ka* 'your pourings' PKT 1 I right:20.
maPRiS(t)	Rare variant of *maPRaS* with similar functions (Streck 2002, 243–44): *ma-zi-iz pa-ni*[meš] 'court attendants' MAPD § 8:50; *na-ak-ri-me* 'a leather container' KAJ 225:16. This also includes feminine III/ē-ī *mapras* nouns: *mar-ši-ti* 'property' RS 18.54a:18'; *ma-al-ti-tu* (*maltittu*) 'allowance of drink' MATC 53:6.
muPaRRiS	The patterns with affirmative *mu-* are essentially lexicalized participles of different verbal stems. In the case of *muPaRRiS(t)* this is the D-stem: *mu-be-i-še* 'instrument

6 The use of the value <ṭi> in A 300 cannot be checked on a copy or photo; it may be omitted in the transliteration. Cf. Donbaz (2010).

for stirring' PKT 4 r. left 4; [lúm]*u-ra-qi-e* 'perfume maker' MAH 16467:6; *mu-si-pi* 'scoop' (*esāpu*) PKT; 304:21; *mu-ta-e-r*[*u*] 'fire-rake' MAH 16130 i 2'.

muPaRRiSt Feminine variant of *muPaRRiS*: f*mu-um-me-er-ta* 'procuress' MAL A § 23:21; f*mu-ra-qi-te* 'perfume maker' PKT 6 ii 31.

muPaSS giš*mu-ger-re* A 1828 (NTA, 25):4; giš*mu-gi-ru-(...)* KAJ 310:4; ⌜*mu*⌝*-ger-ri-šu* MARV 10 4:2. All attestations can be translated as either 'wheel' or chariot and may derive from *qarāru* (CAD, 215a).

muPtaRiS Lexicalized participle pattern form of the Gt-stem. *mu-ut-taḫ-iṣ* 'warrior' Lambert 1969:40.

multaPRiSt Lexicalized participle pattern form of the Št-stem: *mul-te-ṣi-tu-(...)* 'expenses' KAJ 307:14; *mu-ul-te-še-er-te* 'maintenance' KAJ 130:15.

c) Prefixed nV-:

naPRaS For the change *mV- > nV-*, see § 234. These are essentially *maPRaS* forms: túg*na-ak-bu-su* 'mat' MARV 10:18; *na-ak-re-me* KAJ 225:16; *na*[*m*]*-ḫi-ri* (a vessel) MARV 10 69:4; *nap-se-me* 'nose bag' BVW Ko Vs. 17; *nap-ti-ni* 'meal' A 113 (NTA, 15):18; *nàr-ki-*[*b*]*i-(...)* 'grinding stone' KAJ 123:3; *ni-pa-ša* 'procedure' A 1724 (NTA, 17):4, cf. *ni-pi-še* A 1724 (NTA, 17):2; ⌜*ni-re*⌝*-be* 'entrance' MARV 1 27+:25.

naPRaSt Feminine variant of *naPRaS*: *na-ma-te* (*namāttu* < *maʾādu*) 'increase(?)' KAJ 146:6; *nam-šar-te* 'threshing sledge?' MATC 46.2:7'; [*na-a*]*p-pal-te-e-en* 'two shares' MAL B § 19:16; *nap-šal-ti* 'salve' (< *mapšaštum*) MARV 2 28:12; é*nap-ṭar-ta* 'guest house' MATC 12:15; *na*[*r*]*-kab-tu* 'chariot' BVW Ko:20; *nàr-ma-ak-tum* 'washing bowl' KAJ 303:1; *na-aṣ-be-te* 'a festival' KAJ 226:4; *na-aš-*la*lam-ti* 'security' KAJ 28:12; *na-áš-pér-tu* 'message' MATSH 12:42; *ni-mat-te* (*emēdu*) KTN inventory ii 9.

na/uPRā/iS(t) See above under *maPRā/iS(t)* and *muPRaS*.

naPRuSt Deverbal nouns: *na-mu-ra-a-tu* 'audience gifts' KAJ 203:7; *na-mur-tu* 'audience gift' A 1738 (NTA, 19):2.

nuPRaS Deverbal noun with *mV- > nV-*; found in one nomen temporis: *nu-bat-ti* 'evening (rest)' MATSH 12:30.

d) Prefixed šV-:

šaPRuSt This is pattern for the substantivized adjectives of the Š-stem. As expected, the suffix is *ša-* rather than Bab *šu-*: *še-bu-ul-ta* 'gift' MATC 22:11; *ša-ku-ul-te* 'feeding' MAL A § 42:16; *ša-kúl-te* LB 1848:13; *še-ru-ub-te* '(a ritual/ceremony?)' Ali 11:4.

e) Prefixed ta-:

taPRāS In the case of forms such as *tarbāṣi*, the presence of a long vowel can be deduced from the lack of VA: *ták-ba-a-ru* 'fattened sheep' A 2606 (NTA, 28):10; lú*ta-ka-ru* (< *tamkāru*) 'merchant' T 97-18:16; *tar-ba-ṣi* 'animal stall' MATC 81:5; MARV 2 23 r. 18'. This rare type of noun is semantically related to the Gt-stem (GAG, 82 § 56k). See also Kouwenberg 2010, 397ff.

taPRāSt Feminine variant of *taPRāS*: *tal-lak-tu-šu* 'its procedure' PKT 5 r. 3: *tal-la-ka-tu* 'procedures' Ištar Ritual r. 9'.

taPRiS Forms of the pattern *taPRiS* can generally be generated with substantivized forms of the verbal D-stem (cf. Kouwenberg 2010, 397–402 § 14.6): *ta-bi-li* 'powder' MATC 11:15; *tal-mi-du* 'apprentices' KAJ 180:3; *tam-li-e* 'terrace' Coronation Ritual ii 44.

taPRiSt Feminine variant of *taPRiS*: *ták-li-mu* (offering) A 602:8; *ták-pir-ti* 'purification ritual' KAJ 192:26; *ták-pír-ti* A 3188 (NTA, 36):9; *ta-li-ta* (< **tawlidtu*) 'offspring' KAJ 96:16; *ta-li-tu-(...)* 'its offspring' LVUH 42:21; *tal-mi-da-tu* 'apprentice' (pl.) MATC 70:58; *tal-pi-it-te* (passim but meaning uncertain) MARV 3 9:2 *tam-li-*[*t*]*e-(...)* 'inlay' Coronation Ritual i 35; *ta-ás-ḫi-ra-te-(...)* (meaning uncertain) KTN inventory ii 17; *ta-az-ki-te* 'clearance' KAJ 310:11; *te-lil-te* 'purification' A 295

(NTA, 16):2: *te-li-it* 'proceeds (of harvest)' KAJ 80:7; 262:3; LVUH 60:11.

taPRuS — Abstract nouns of the G-stem: *ta-lu-uk* 'coming' MARV 6 34:15; *tág-mur* 'completion(?)' T 97-10:24.

taPRuSt — Feminine variant of *taPRuS*: *ta-kúl-te* 'consumption' CTMMA 1 99:17; KAJ 92:4; *tar-ku-ub-ta* 'cargo' MARV 5 5:18; *te-ru-bat* 'entry' MATC 80:1; *ti-ru-ub-ti* (*tērubtu*) 'certification(?)' KAJ 79:16.

f) With infixed *-t-*:

PitRāS — Derived pattern of the Gt-stem (Kouwenberg 2010, 34): *mi-it-ḫa-ar* 'equal' MAL A § 43:35; *mi-it-ḫar-(...)* MAL K § 3:9; MARV 5 85:21'; *me-et-ḫar-(...)* KAJ 91:22. Primary nouns: *šil*$_4$*-ta-ḫi*^{meš} 'arrows' KAM 11 59:5'.

PitRāSat — *mi-it-ḫa-ra-tu* Giricano 12:21' feminine form of *mitḫār?* (see Giricano, 93).

PitRuS — Only one primary noun attested: *it-qu-ru* 'spoon' KAJ 310:41. Otherwise attested in Akkadian as an infinitive and adjective of the Gt-stem. Cf. GAG, 83–84 § 56n.

g) With affirmatives:

PaRāSi — Found in *ša-la-ši-a* KAJ 139:4. Limited to numerals, see § 340ff.

PuRuSSā — Discussed in more detail in UGM, 45. However, the pattern is not limited to MA.[7] All examples refer to things provided and are usually plurale tantums referring to judicial or commercial assets: *nu-du-un-na-a* 'dowry' MAL A § 27:105; *su-lum-ma-e* 'peace-making' KUB 3 73:11'; T96-1;16; *zu-bu-ul-la-a* 'marriage gift' MAL A § 30:29 cf. *zu-bu-ul-la-e* OIP 79 5:2; *ú-ku-ul-la-a* 'provisions' MAL A § 36:87; *ú-ku-la-i-ša* MAL A § 45:65. The examples are deverbal nouns.

PuRuSSāna — Nominal pattern presumably limited to MA; see also UGM, 45. Two attestations of the same substantive. Due to the accusative case they are found in, they cannot be regarded as plural forms with plural marker *-ānu/i*: *bu-qu-ra-*[*n*]*a-e* 'legal claim' VAT 9034:13; *bu-qur-ra-na-e* KAJ 10:8; *ru-gu-u*[*m-ma-n*]*a-a* 'claim' MAL A § 39:38; *ru-gu-um-ma-na-a* MAL A § 55:12.

taPRuSann — In *tar-gu-ma-nu* 'dragoman' MARV 2 17a+:45, 58. Possibly an Anatolian loan transmitted through OA (see Dercksen 2007, 37 no. 15).

h) Quadriradical roots:

PvRSvD — Primary nouns, most of them animals names often used as PNS: ^{m}*Ak-bi-ru* 'Jerboa (PN)' KAJ 214:16; *e-re-bi-ú* 'locust' MATSH 2:7; ^{anše}*ku-du-nu* (< **kawdan*) 'mules' MATC 24:9; ^{m}*še-lu-bu* (< **ṯaˤlab*) 'Fox (PN)' KAJ 55 r. 6'; ^{uzu}*šu-me-la* (√*šmʔl*) 'left side' Adad Ritual r. 10'.

i) Reduplicated two-radical roots:

PaSPaS — Primary nouns, usually with assimimlated second radical: *qa-qar* 'ground' KAJ 53:15; *qa-qa-sa* 'her head' TR 2083a+:2; *sa-ap-si-pi* 'fringe' MARV 1 24:11, cf. *la-li-ú* 'kid (of an animal)' Billa 36:9. For a brief discussion of patterns based on reduplicated two-radical roots, see GAG, 87 § 57a.

PiSPiS — Hapax: *ṭí-iš-ṭí-ša* 'residue' PKT 3 iv 6.

PuSPuS(S) — Primary nouns: *bu-bu-a-te* 'hunger' MATSH 12:33; VAT 8851:7; *šur-šur-ra-te* 'chains' KAV 96:6. All provided attestations are plurale tantums. Note that *bubu'ātu* 'hunger' appears in Babylonian and OA/NA as the singular *bubūtu* (AHw, 135b; CAD B, 301–2).

---

7 Cf. GAG. 84 § 56o; OA in GOA § 4.2.2.12; OAkk in Gelb (1961, 154–55); Hasselbach (2005, 188).

5.2 Suffixes

5.2.1 Abstract nouns with *-utt*

§ 252 The suffix *-ūt* is used for plural forms of adjectives and nouns (§ 310 and § 281), but can also indicate an abstractum (see GAG, 86 § 56s). The Assyrian variant *-utt* has already been discussed in § 113ff. It may be observed that spellings involving the gemination of /t/ in abstract nouns are slightly more preferred than they are with adjectives. The multifunctionality of *-utt* can cause nouns to have different meanings, e.g., *šēbuttu* 'testifying' (abstract) ~ 'witnesses' (plural). It seems, though, that the latter plural forms are a secondary development derived from the abstractum. The suffix can be added to a base of Semitic/Akkadian origin, but it is also found on bases of foreign origin (e.g., *ḫaziānuttu* 'governing').

In the function of the abstractum of bases designating persons and professions:

aḫuttu	ŠEŠ-*ut-te* 'brotherhood' KBo 28 61/62:14'
	aḫ-ḫu-tu T 04-3:8
aʾīluttu	*ritti a-i-lu-ut-te* 'the hand of a human' KTN inventory iv 23'
	a-i-lu-tu 'humanity' MATSH 2:21
ālāyuttu	*a-la-iu-ú-t*[*i*] 'citizenship' KAJ 7:24
bārīuttu	[*ba*]*-ri-ú-ut-ta* 'divination' MATSH 9:19
ḫaziānuttu	*ḫa-zi-a-nu-ut-te* 'governing' KAV 217:4
līmuttu	*li-mu-ut-te* 'eponymy' KAM 11 96:16
marʾuttu	*mar*$_5$*-ut-ti-šu* 'his adoption' MAL A § 28:5
	mar-ú-ut-ti 'adoption' (*marʾuttu*) KAJ 1:6
muraqqīuttu	*mu-ra-qi-ú-ti-ki-na* 'your (f.) perfume-mixing' MARV 3 64:37
mututtu	*mu-tu-ut-*<*ta*> ''(status of a) husband' TIM 4 45:4
šanguttu	*ša-an-gu-ta* 'priesthood' Coronation Ritual ii 33
šarruttu	MAN-*ut-te* 'kingship' Coronation Ritual ii 47
	šar-ru-ut-ti-⸢*ia*?⸣ 'my kingship' KUB 3 73:3'
šēbuttu	*a-na še-bu-ut-te uššabū*(sic) 'they will sit down for testifying' T 04-37:21
ṭābuttu	*ṭa-bu-t*[*u*] 'friendship' T 04-3:8

Other various types of nouns:

ayyāruttu	*ayya-a-ru-ut-te* (unclear meaning) PKT 6 ii 24
ba??eruttu	⸢*ba*⸣*-e-ru-*⸢*ta*⸣ 'extispicy' MAL A § 1:9
	ba-e-ru-te Ali 7:9
eṭuttu	*e-ṭu-tu* 'darkness' A 602:1
massuttu	[*m*]*a-ás-su-ú-tu* 'washing' PKT 2 ii 9
nērāruttu	*n*[*i-r*]*a-ru-*[*t*]*e* 'aid' T 98-119:13
rāqu	*ra-qu-te-e-ša tuṣṣa* 'she will go out empty handed' MAL A § 37:19
šalimuttu	*ša-li-mu-ut-ti* 'debt(?)' KAV 209:2
	ša-li-mu-ti-šu-nu 'their debt(?)' KAJ 47:16[8]
šamnuttu	*ša-am-nu-ti-šu* (uncertain meaning) MATSH 2:50

Nouns ending with a feminine ending have it deleted when *-utt* is added.

amuttu	*a-mu-*[*u*]*t-ti-ša* (< *amtu* 'slave girl') 'her slavery' KAJ 7:8; but OA *am-tù-tim* I 490:3 (GOA § 4.3.2)
aššuttu	*aš-šu-ut-ta* '(status of a) wife' TIM 4 45:4

8 Following Faist (2001, 160 n67). Cf. CAD Š$_1$, 246b.

aš-šu-ut-ti-šu '(status of) his wife' KAJ 7:9

In some nouns, the etymology is probably not Akkadian. In this case, the morpheme *-utt* is probably different from the abstractum suffix and probably has no function in these nouns.

rīmuttu	*ri-mu-ut-te* 'gift' MATSH 1:13
sabsuttu	ᶠ*sa-ab-su-tu* 'midwife' MAPD § 1:11

As both the infinitive and the suffix *-utt* have an abstract meaning, they are sometimes interchangeable. Consider the following standard phrase, with the infinitive: *a-na ra-a-e ta-ad-na* 'they gave if for pasturing' Ali 1:8–9. The passage uses the preposition *ana*+infinitive as the direct object of *tadānu* 'to give'. A variant with the same meaning is found in another passage, wherein the abstractum with *-utt* replaces the infinitive: *a-na re-ú-te i-di-nu-ni* Billa 6:17-18. Nonetheless, it seems that constructions with the infinitive remained more common in the MA corpus. Consider the following similar passages:

ḫaziānuttu	*a-na ḫa-zi-a-nu-ut-te il-*[...] 'for governing' KAV 217:4'
rēʾuttu	*a-na re-ú-te iddinūni* 'they gave if for pasturing' Billa 6:17–18
šatûttu	*a-na ša-tu-ti-šu* (…) *ta*??*erā* 'return if for its weaving' KAV 103:13–15
šēbuttu	*a-na še-bu-ut-te uššabū*sic. 'they will sit down for testifying' T 04-37:21
ṭēʾinuttu	*a-na ṭé-i-nu-te tadnūni* 'it is given for grinding -corvée' KAV 107:12

As the object of a clause:

muraqqīuttu	*mu-ra-qi-ú-ta lā lamdā* 'they (f.) must not learn to mix perfume' MARV 3 64:41

5.1.2 Suffix *-ān*

§ 253 The morpheme *-ān* occurs frequently in MA in a number of different functions. It is sometimes spelled plene (e.g., *be-ta-a-nu* MAPD § 8:49; *šul-ma-a-na* T 98-134:23), more often defectively (e.g., *šul-ma-nu* 'bribe' KAJ 72:10) and once with the metathesis of quantity (e.g., ˡᵘ́*ḫa-zi-an-ni* A 1736 (NTA, 18):13). It is found as a morpheme among the plurality of masculine nouns (§ 281); it is secondly found in substantivizing participles and adjectives. However, as these are essentially nominal verbal forms, they are discussed in § 324f. Not all forms with *-ānu* are participles or adjectives. A few non-verbal nominal patterns with Semitic roots use the suffix as well. In these cases *-ān* seems to build concrete substantives from existing nouns (Streck 2005, 236–70), e.g., *šulmu* 'greeting' > *šulmānu* 'greeting gift'. [9] A number of these concrete substantives refers to people and are thus semantically similar to the participles and adjectives with *-ān*.[10]

susānu	*su-sa-ni* 'horse trainer' BVW A r. 5
	[ˡᵘ́?] ⌜*su*⌝*-sa-a-n*[*u*] MARV 10 70:6
pargānīu (?)	26 UDU.NÍTAᵐᵉš *pár-ga-ni-ú-te* '26 grazing sheep' KAJ 115:2–3[11]

9 Cf. Syriac, e.g., *mawtānā* (ܡܘܬܢܐ) 'plague' of the root √*mūt* 'to die' (see Nöldeke 1904, 77f § 128).

10 It is not clear to what extent bases of non-Semitic etymology belong in this category, e.g., *ummiānu* 'creditor' (< UM.ME.A) and *um-mi-a-nu* 'creditor' MAL A § 39:29. This Sumerian loan is also notable for having a feminine plural, e.g., ⌜*um*⌝*-mi-a-na-ti* MAL C+ § 11:21. Perhaps also *ḫarrānu* 'road', which may be related to Hurrian *ḫari* with a similar meaning (CAD Ḫ, 106; Richter 2012, 133a). However, in MA, this word in only rarely attested: *ḫar-ra-a-na* 'road' MAL A § 22:107; pl. *ḫar-ra-na-te* KAJ 103:15, being replaced mostly by *ḫūlu*; also *ḫaziānu* 'mayor', e.g., *ḫa-zi-a-nu* MAL B § 6:35; *ḫa-zi-a-ni* KAJ 103:9, note ˡᵘ́*ḫa-zi-an-ni* A 1736 (NTA, 18):13.

11 This form is a nisbe of the noun *pargānu* 'meadow'. The etymology remains unclear and thus the presence of suffix *-ān* is uncertain.

We also find *-ān* suffixed to a number of inanimate words. Many of them are used adverbially with the locative *-u(m)*, resulting in the longer ending *-ānu(m)* (see § 483).

arsānu	*ar-sa-a-nu* 'barley-groats' NBC 4599:8 ; cf. NA lex. *arsu* 'a cereal'.
ēdānu	*e-da-nu* (< *wēdu* +*ān*) 'appointed time' MAL B § 6:21; C+ § 7:8; KAJ 63:15
šulmānu	*šul-ma-nu* '*šulmānu*-gift' KAJ 72:10

Plural forms:

šulmānu	*šul-ma-na-te* '*šulmānu*-gift' Coronation Ritual iii 4

5.2.3 Nisbe

§ 254 The nisbe is a special type of adjective. It can be said that the nisbe suffix is used to create a noun or proper name (mostly GNs) from an adjective. MA demonstrates two different nisbe suffixes: *-āy* and *-īy*. They are inflected in a similar manner to normal nouns, rather than adjectives (cf. below). Semantically, both nisbe endings seem identical, with only a dialectal difference (Lipiński 2001, 229f § 29.41). Given that *-āy* is also found in the Amorite-influenced Old Babylonian era texts from Mari, von Soden suggested WS influences.[12] Feminine substantives take the short feminine morpheme *-t*. Moreover, gemination is attested as an instance of the metathesis of quantity: *Aš-šu-ri-it-tu* KAJ 167:3. As we discussed above, this happened in order to compensate for the shortening of the preceding vowel (*Aššurītum* > *Aššurittu*; see § 115). As with all other forms of the metathesis of quantity, the two forms may indicate variation within the Assyrian dialect. The occurrence of nisbe *-āy* is a new feature in MA, which had mostly removed the original *-īy* by the NA period.[13] However, attestations of *-āy* are already more broadly attested in the earliest MA texts, while *-īy* seems mostly limited to a few lexicalized words. The replacement of *-īy* by *-āy* was, therefore, already largely completed before the start of the MA archives.

§ 255 Spellings of the nisbe *-āy* usually apply the sign IA when followed directly by a case ending. As IA is used for any vocalic reading, an extra vowel sign is necessary to specify the case ending. In most cases, an extra vowel sign Ú or E is added to indicate a nominative or genitive case ending.

Aššur	*šumma* ^{lú}*Aš-šu-ra-iu-ú u šumma* ^{f}*Aš-šu-ra-i-tu* 'if an Assyrian man or if an Assyrian woman' MAL A § 44:40–41
	Aš-[*šu*]*-ra-ie-e* 'Assyrian' KAJ 2:11
	ina qāt Áš-šu-ra-ie-e 'from the hand of an Assyrian' Hall 1983:19
Kargamis	*šarru* ^{uru}*Kar-ga-mis-a-iu-ú* 'the Carchemishean king' MATSH 6:2'; cf. *šarru* ^{uru}*kar-ga-mis-a-IA* l. 6'

12 GAG, 85 § 56p; cf. Finet (1956, 90–93 § 37). Of course, *-āy* is well attested as a hypocoristic suffix in the Amorite onomasticon (see Streck 2000, 352–53 § 5.80; Golinets 2010, 451–52). In light of possible West Semitic/Aramaic influence on Akkadian, it should be pointed out that the Aramaic nisbe ending is *-āy* as well. (cf. Syriac in Nöldeke 1904, 80ff § 135; Old Aramaic in Degen 1969, 50). However, any direct connection would be highly hypothetical and unlikely, given the early attestations in MA of nisbe *-āy*.

13 The nisbe *-āy* was virtually non-existent in OA, although *-y-* was attached directly to geographical designations ending in *-a*, e.g., Waḫšušanā > Waḫšušanāyum (GKT, 89 § 57b; GOA § 7.2.10). For the situation in NA, see Deller (1959, 86ff); SNAG, 84 § 3.10b.

Ninūʾa	^{m}*Ni-nu-a-ie-e* 'man from Nineveh' KAJ 129:7
Uššukani	*ṣabʾu* ^{uru}*Áš-šu-ka-na-iu-ú* 'Uššukannian troops' MATSH 2:15

There are no attestations of an accusative with an extra vowel sign A. It is doubtful whether they existed, as it can be assumed that, analogous to identical spellings for the pronominal suffix *-ya* 'mine', scribes did not consider its use obligatory. Defective spellings are also frequently found for the nominative and genitive case endings.

Aššur	1 *Áš-šu-ra-iu* 'one Assyrian' MATC 9:6
	Áš-šu-ra-a-ie^{meš} 'Assyrians' MARV 7 3:5
Ḫatti	*ubru Ḫa-ta-iu* 'the Hittite envoy' MATC 56:2
Muṣru	*ša* ^{m}*Mu-uṣ-ri-ie* 'from the Egyptian' LVUH 104:14
Ninūʾa	*ina muḫḫi* ^{m}*Ni-nu-a-ie* 'on account of Ninūʾa' Giricano 8:7

We, therefore, have to wonder whether the plene spellings are a hypercorrection on the scribe's part or whether they reflect actual pronunciation (cf. for NA LAS 2, 152 n294). In fact, when we compare the MA nisbe with NA, we find new defective spellings that have largely taken over IA. NA often applies A-A spellings, regardless of the case ending (SNAG, 84). Given these NA spellings, it is not clear if the nisbe is inflected according to case ending (SNAG, 84). This type of spelling is uncommon in MA, although one attestation for *bēlu* with a similar variant can be found in the following passages:

Aššur	13 *emmerātu* (…) *Aš-šu-ra-a-TUM* 5 *emmerātu* (…) *Ḫa-ab-ḫa-a-TUM* '13 Assyrian sheep, five Ḫabḫian sheep' Billa 36:2-3
bēlu	EN-*a-a* 'Bēlāya (a PN)' A 1476 r. 6' (cf. NA in PNAE 1.II B–G, 285)

Masculine plural *-āyū*:

Aššur	*Áš-šu-ra-iu-ú* 'Assyrians' Faist 2001, 252:18 (pl.)
	Aš-šu-ra-ie-e^{meš} KAJ 310:22
	ana $^{\text{uru.d}}$*A-šur-a-ie*^{meš} 'for Assyrians' KAV 217:16'
Qairān	*Su-ti-ú*^{meš} *Qa-i-ra-na-i*[*u*]*-ú* T 96-36:20–21 cf. *Su-ti-ú*^{meš} *Qa-i-ra-na-ia-e* l. 27–28

Below are a few examples of the masculine singular nisbe *-īy*. Note that, as for orthography, many commonly attested forms, such as *Sūtīu* and *Šubrīu*, use defective spellings. However, forms such as ^{kur}*Mu-uṣ-ri-ie*, with the sign IA, show the presence of the semivowel /y/.

ēššīu	PN *ālu* GIBIL-*iu*$^{!}$*-ú* 'PN of the new city' MATC 66:2-3
Kargamis	[^{l}]^{ú}[*K*]*ar-ga-mis-ie-e* 'man from Carchemish' T 93-6:4
Muṣrīu	26 ^{kur}*Mu-uṣ-ri-ie* '26 Muṣrean people' MARV 1 12:10
Sūtīu	*Su-ti-ú iqtibia* 'a Sutean told me' T 93-2:3
Šubrīu	ŠE-*um damqu Šu-ub-ri-ú* 'good-quality Hurrian barley' KAJ 63:2

As for the positioning of the nisbe, there are a few cases where *-āy* is added to a word construction ending with a vowel:

Elam	^{kur}*E-la-mi-a-ie-e* 'Elamite' MATC 46.2:5'
	^{kur}*E-la-mi-a-ie-e* MATC 70:59
Ninūʾa	*līme* ^{m}*Ni-nu-a-ie-e* 'the eponymy of Ninūʾa' MARV 1 17:2

In some cases, we find morphographemic spellings of *-āy*, although it is attested for nisbe constructions of the GN Carchemish:

Aššur	*a-na* $^{\text{uru.d}}$*A-šur-a-ie*^{meš} 'for Assyrians' KAV 217:16'
Kargamis	*šarra* ^{uru}*Kar-ga-mis-a-ia* 'the Carchemishean king' T 96-1:14–15

šarru ^uru^*Kar-ga-mis-ayu-ú* 'the Carchemishean king' MATSH 6:2'

It seems that MA has a preference for using *-āy* on substantives ending in a single consonant or vowel, whereas *-īy* is found most frequently with consonant clusters (e.g., Muṣrīu; Kaššīu etc.).

§ 256 The feminine inflection *-āy* of the nisbe shows an unusual development. It was naturally absent from OA and NA, but common in MA (Deller 1959, 87–88), e.g., *Aš-šur-i-tú* SAA 7 145:7. There are only few examples of the feminine singular *-āyittu*. The metathesis of quantity forces normalization with both /y/ and an extra vowel /i/, since a form such as **-āyttu* is impossible.

Aššur	^f^*Aš-šu-ra-i-tu* 'if an Assyrian woman' MAL A § 44: 41
	Áš-šu-⸢*ra-it*?⸣*-te* MARV 5 71:9
šaddû	^f^KUR-*da-it-te* (*šaddāyttu*) KAJ 201:2
	^f^KUR-*da-i-te* A 3193 (NTA, 38):4

Feminine singular *-ittu* (< *-ītu*):

Aššur	*Aš-šu-ri-it-tu* 'Assyrian' KAJ 167:3
	^d^*Iš*~8~*-t*[*ár*] *Aš-šu-ri-t*[*u*] 'Assyrian Ištar' MARV 8 56 :2'–3'
	⸢*A*!?*-šu-ri*!?*-i*?*-te*⸣ MARV 4 78:33'
	⸢*Áš-šu*⸣*-ri-*⸢*te*⸣ MARV 4 95 i' 9'
	⸢*A*?*-šu*?*-ri*?*-te*?⸣ MARV 4 116:6
Šubrīu	^f^*Šu-ub-ri-it-tum* 'Hurrian' KAV 211:3
Sūtīu	*Su-ti-tu* 'Sutean' MPR 55:34

The feminine plural is attested as *-āyātu*. It is unclear why the two examples from MARV 3 64 take the singular accusative ending *-a*. These two examples would be expected to occur in the genitive, making the case ending unsuitable for singular as well as plural morphology.

Aššur	*Aš-šu-ra-*[*ia*]-⸢*a*⸣*-ta* 'Assyrian' MARV 3 64:7
Katmuḫu	*Ku-ut-mu-ḫa-ia-a-ta* 'Katmuhean' MARV 3 64:8
Kilizu	*zamārātu Ki-li-za-i*[*a*]*-tu* '(female) Kilezean singers' T 93-54:21

Feminine plural *-īātu*:

Sūtīu	*emmerātu* (…) *Su-ti-a-te* 'Sutean sheep' MATC 1:12–13

Having established the occurrence of the feminine nisbe *-āytu* in MA, Deller explains its absence from NA as being due to the contraction of the diphthong /āy/: *Aššurāytu* > *Aššurētu*. This explanation may not apply to MA *-īytu*, since it would presume the replacement of *-īy* by *-āy*, followed by the contraction of the diphthong and ultimately the metathesis of quantity. All developments would have been completed within the period between OA and MA. As this would seem to represent too short a time period, it is likely that the *-īy* nisbe was better preserved in the feminine rather than the masculine gender.

§ 257 The basic function of the nisbe can be summarized as making adjectives from substantives, although they are inflected as normal nouns rather than adjectives. The nisbe is usually used as a gentilic ending for the geographical origin of people and other beings.

Often, nisbe endings are used to describe the origin of a product or concept, such as 'Dutch cheese' or 'Moroccan leather'.

Aššur	*lišāni Áš-šu-ra-i-*[*t*]*i* 'the Assyrian language' VAT 8722:3
	2 *niksu* 1 *lubēru Áš-šu-ra-iu-ú* 'two *n* textiles, one garment, (all) Assyrian' Faist 2001, 251:6–7
Kargamis	*ana muḫḫi šarre* ^{uru}*Kar-ga-mis-a-ia* 'to the Carchemishean king' T 96-1:14–15
	šarru ^{uru}*Kar-ga-miš-a-iu-ú* MATSH 6:2' cf. *šarru* ^{uru}*Kar-ga-miš-a-IA* l. 6'
Muḫāyu	*šuḫuppātu* ^{kur}*Mu-ḫa-ia-tu* 'Muḫean boots' Postgate 1973 1:18–19
Muṣrīu	*šarre* ^{kur}*Mu-uṣ-ri-ie-e* 'the Egyptian king' MATC 22:15
Qutīu	1 *ṣubātu Qu-ti-ú* 'one Qutean textile' Postgate 1973 1:7

In the list of examples below, it is not always clear whether the nisbe is adjectival or independent. With logograms such as ÉRIN^{meš} 'people' or LÚ^{meš} 'people', it is likely that they have to be interpreted as determinatives.

Elam	ÉRIN^{meš} *E-la-mi-a-iu-ú* 'Elamite troops' MATC 71:53
Kaššīu	ÉRIN^{meš} *Kaš-ši-ú*$^{!}$ 'Kassite troops' MATSH 2:18
Kulišḫinu	LÚ^{meš} ^{uru}*Ku-liš-ḫi-na-ie-e* 'Kulišḫinean people' MARV 1 73A:11
Šubrīu	ÉRIN^{meš} *Šu-ub-ri-ú* 'Hurrian troops' MATSH 2:19-20
Uššukannu	ÉRIN^{mes} ^{uru}*Áš-šu-ka-na-iu-ú* 'Uššukanian troops' MATSH 2:15

Some substantives derive from this function, most notably *alāyu* 'villager'. Nisbes are also used for substantive designations of professions (GAG, 85 § 56q), although this is rare in MA (cf. Jakob 2003). We have many instances of nisbe *sirašû* 'brewer', but they are always written logographically (^{lú}LUNGA).

ālāyu	[^{f}]⸢*a*⸣*-la-i-tu* 'villager (f.)' MAL A § 45:52
	al-la-iu-ú^{meš} 'villagers' AO 20.154:6 (*alāyu* is limited to Assyrian and Nuzi; see CAD A$_1$, 390f)
	a-la-iu-ú 'villagers' KAJ 7:22

Some unclear cases of a possible nisbe:

erbīu	*e-re-bi-ú* 'locust' MATSH 2:7
parrāṣu	DUMU *pár-ra-ṣa-ie-e* 'liar' MATC 2:13

§ 258 As a secondary function, the nisbe ending can also be found in a number of non-gentilic adjectives. It may be observed that the nisbe ending *-īy* is still dominant here. Although more functions occur in Akkadian, in general (cf. GAG, 56 § 56q), in MA, the nisbe seems to refer to temporal matters, such as 'earlier', 'first' and 'later'. In the Adad Ritual, *panīu* refers to something spatial: the front (of an animal). Some examples:

panīu	*ummiānu pa-ni-ú* 'an earlier creditor' MAL A § 39:29
	šulmāna pa-ni-a 'the first gift' Coronation Ritual iii 5
	kursinnāte pa-ni-a-te 'the front ankles' Adad Ritual r. 12'
	šamaššammū pa-ni-ú-te 'old sesame' MATC 29:7
	unūta pa-ni-ta 'the earlier equipment' MCS 2 1:12–14
	ina lēʾe (…) *pa-ni-e u ur-ki-e* 'on the earlier and later wooden tablets' KAJ 260:7–9
	tuppāti[*š*]*u pa-ni-a-ti* 'the earlier tablets' KAJ 26:2
šaplīu	*nakkamte šap-li-te* 'the lower storehouse' KAJ 310:65
urkīu	*mussama ur-ki-ú* 'her later husband' MAL A § 45:78
	šumma ur-ki-it-tu šīt 'if she is secondary' MAL A § 46:99

It should not come as a surprise that some of these adjectives can also function as adverbs: ⸢*i+na ur-ki*⸣*-it-te* 'afterwards' MAL A § 24:51; *i+na pa-ni-te* 'earlier' MATSH 12:27 etc. (see § 496). This type of abbreviated nisbe may not be directly related to the nisbes directly attached to substantives and GNs.

§ 259 In light of the morphologically similar hypocoristic suffix *-āy*, we may briefly discuss the profession *šellipāyu* derived from the PN Šalim-pî-Ea (cf. Jakob 2003, 461ff).[14] It is first attested in texts from the reign of Tukultī-Ninurta until the NA period. Although most of our MA attestations date from the reign of TN, we can partly follow the development of the pronunciation during this period. From the beginning, we find the shortened form *Šalimpīya*, which is quite common for PNs in Akkadian; cf. MB Enlil-kidinni > Ellīya (Hölscher 1996, 67). Yet, even here, we find alternations between *Šalimpīya* and *Šalippīya*. The assimilation of /m/ to a following consonant is otherwise rare in MA, with the exception of the reflections of dropped mimation and the Kassite PN Melissaḫ (< Melimsaḫ). That said, it could, as these two PNs demonstrate, have been more common in the vernacular language. The early occurrences of this assimilation in a TN text shows that it was present from the beginning and that other spellings likely retained it based on historical grounds. The change /a/ > /i-e/ in the two later forms is very unusual for MA. Rather, it seems that a folk etymology was created where the word was connected to *šeleppīu* 'turtle'.[15] The two cases with the sound change /a/ > /e/ allow us to date this folk etymology to the later MA period. An exceptional case of Assyrian VA seems to take place here in the two later spellings ^{lú}*še-lip-pa-iu-ú*/^{lú}*ši-lip-pa-ie*, where the sound change occurs in the initial syllable, rather than the normal penultimate or antepenultimate. Rather unexpectedly, in NA, the /i/ of the second syllable changed to /a/ in a kind of reverted VA: *še-lap-pa-a-a* SAA 7 13:7; SAA 1 95 r. 1 (*šelappāya*, for spelling A+A, see W. R. Mayer 2003; Luukko 2004, 37 § 3.9.). The PN Šalim-pî-Ea does not otherwise occur in MA; the same is true of comparable names with different DNs in common (cf. OMA 1, 429). Interestingly, we once find a stylized version of the name as a PN in a letter: ^{m}*Ša-li-pi-ii* Hall 1983:1. This PN has the nisbe ending *-īy* rather than the expected *-āy*. Therefore, a different analysis of the name exists as Ša-lipīya (OMA 1, 482; II, 134, 229). However, for difficulties cited elsewhere (Hall 1983, 78), it may be best to assume an early abbreviation of Šalim-pî-Ea. A list of attestations is presented below:

Transcription	Orthography	Text
mar Šalim-pî-Ea	DUMU *Ša-lim-pi-i-*^{d}*É-a*	MARV 1 14:34 (TN)
marʾū Šalim-pî-Ea	DUMU^{meš} *Ša-lim-pi-i-*^{d}*É-a*	MARV 2 17A+:5 (TN); 17B+:⸢4⸣
šalimpāyu	*ša-lim-pa-iu-ú*	MARV 4 1:16 (TN)
	ša-lim-pa-ie-e	MARV 1 27: ⸢21⸣, 33 (TN); MARV 2 17A+:77 (TN); MARV 4 34:13' (TN)
šalippāyu	*ša-li-pa-ie-e*	MARV 4 34:15' (TN)
šelippāyu	^{lú}*še-lip-pa-iu-ú*	KAJ 188:22 (NtA)
šilippāyu	^{lú}*ši-lip-pa-ie*	KAJ 300:6 (Tp)
Šalippīu (PN)	^{m}*Ša-li-pi-ii*	Hall 1983:1 (TN)

14 See Freydank (1985a; Jakob 2003, 461–65); in the dictionaries: AHw, 1210; CAD Š2, 270–71. Note also *šelenāyu* (see Deller 1987, 61). However, this seems to refer to people of a specific geographical origin. See Jakob (2003, 46 n324); CAD Š2, 270.

15 See AHw, 120; CAD Š2, 271–72.

All attestations, except for the PN (mŠa-li-pi-ii), include the ending *-pāyu*, which was derived from *-pî*-Ea. It is difficult to establish how the original form changed into the derived abbreviation. This supports the claim we made above (§ 153) that the MA spelling *pi-i* 'mouth' is learned, whereas the underlying form is *pāʾi*. A similar spelling is found once independently in *pa-i* KAJ 6:4.

5.3 Loans

5.3.1 West-Semitic loans

§ 260 Loans from other Semitic languages may have occurred in MA, but are difficult to identify. Kouwenberg was unable to list any examples of Amorite loans in OA with certainty (GOA § 4.4.4). For MA, the situation is not much better, despite the rise of Sutean/Aramaic tribes in the Ḫanigalbat region.[16] Some Northwest Semitic loans may be attested in the peripheral MA archives, including the Tell Aš-Šēḫ Ḥamad letters. West-Semitic loans in TŠḤ letters are rather unexpected because they are written by high officials of the Assyrian administration, meaning that it is unlikely that the proposed loans are due to local influence.[17] One suggested loan is the verb *ḫabāqu* (MATSH, 110 l. 23). As we discussed in § 179, Bloch has tried to argue that the forms from √*ḥbq* are of genuine Akkadian origin. However, due to the absence of compelling evidence for his claim, we have to maintain the likelihood of a West-Semitic loan. That said, the Northwest Semitic root √*ḥbq* is, admittedly, not very common and its meaning does not really help in explaining its presumed Akkadian cognate.[18]

Infinitive G		*ba-lu-ut ḫa-ba-a-q*[*i*] T 93-54:16
		ba-lu-ut ḫa-ba-qi T 96-36:31
Imperative D	mp	*ḫa-bi-i-qa* MATSH 3:23
Substantive		*ḫa-bi-iq-t*[*i*] MATSH 7:19''
		ḫa-bi-iq-⸢*te*⸣ MATSH 19:6'
		[*ḫa*]*-bi-iq-te* MATSH 18:12'

§ 261 The other unusual word from the TŠḤ letters is *ia-a-bi-li* MATSH 14:15, which has been suggested in the commentary to be a *PaRīS* form of √*ybl* (MATSH, 167). The root is typical Northwest-Semitic, where the initial /w/ > /y/. Thus, the root is the cognate of MA *ubālu* 'to bring'. According to Streck (1997, 275), the form from *yabālu* is the participle *yābil* of West-Semitic/Sutean origin. This interpretation is better because of the plene-written A; however, it would make the noun identical to *yābilu* 'battering ram', which is an Northwest Semitic loan, cf. BH *yōḇēl* (יוֹבֵל).[19] The metathesis of quantity (thus *yabbilu*) remains possible, as the relevant passage is not entirely clear:

16 For the West Semitic origin of the logogram lúA.BA 'scribe', see de Ridder (2017a, 300 § 1.3).

17 For instance, MATSH 3 was written by Sîn-mudammeq, who, according to Kühne, was an official located in Uššukanni, the former Ḫanigalbat capital and a Hurrian stronghold. See MATSH, 23 n79.

18 Most attestations seem to occur in Ugaritic; see Del Olmo Lete/Sanmartín (2003, 352–53): the G-stem 'to embrace, take in one's arm, cover'. In BH, see HALOT, 287a: √*ḥbq* (חבק) 'clasp, embrace'. For limited use in Syriac, see Sokoloff (2009, 409b): √*ḥbq* (ܚܒܩ) Peʿal 'to surround'.

19 See AHw, 411a; CDA I/J, 321a; CDA, 440a.

> 30 *emāra* ŠE-*am ša rāminīya ina ia-a-bi-li ša sūte attabak* '30 homers of my own barley, with the *yābilu* of the seah measure I have poured out' MATSH 14:14–16

§ 262 In Ḫana texts, we find the noun *naṣbu*. Its West-Semitic etymology has most recently been discussed and reasserted by Yamada (2011, 66); cf. from Tell Ṭābān: *na-aṣ-bu* TabT09-47:25 (MB). The noun would have derived from the root √*nṣb*. In the following passage, it is used as an adjective in a comparable function to the more common MA *tuppu dannutu* 'an incontestable tablet'.[20]

> *tuppu na-aṣ-bu ša lā baqre* '(this is) an incontestable tablet; free from claims' HSM 1036688:13–14; Kümmel 1989:22–23

5.3.2 Babylonian loans

§ 263 It is very likely that MA uses a considerable number of loans from other Akkadian dialects, most notably OB and MB. As might be expected, these loans are actually difficult to isolate because phonology and nominal construction do not differ significantly between the dialects. One may also wonder whether a word is a loan or simply shared, albeit written in Babylonian fashion. This is probably true for some nominal verbal forms found in literary texts and administrative documents. A few other examples of possible loans may be given.

§ 264 In the Assyrian laws, we once find the noun *biblu* 'dowry', which is probably Babylonian as its root appears as √*bbl* in this dialect (AHw, 94a). At the same time, we cannot exclude the possibility of the word-initial shift /w/ >/b/, as occurs in the intervocalic position. In fact, we have already discussed some possible examples (§ 178). Another clear example is *pētḫallu*, which derives from *pētû+ḫallu*, literally 'the opener of thighs' (AHw, 858a). Note the Babylonian VA in the participle of *patāʾu* 'to open'. This indicates that *pētḫallu* itself is a loan from Babylonian. Kouwenberg referred to some OA nouns with the III/weak root as being loans from Babylonian because they seem to have had an non-etymologic lengthening of the vowel between R_2 and R_3, e.g., *ṣābum* < *ṣābʾum* 'people'; *mārum* < *marʾum* 'son' (GOA § 4.4.5). Curiously, these examples appear to have retained their R_3 in MA and are thus genuine Assyrian nouns (see § 168), e.g.:

marʾuttu	*mar-ú-ut-ti* 'adoption' KAJ 1:6
ṣābʾu	*ṣab-e annūte lišši lēmur* 'he should bring and inspect these troops' MATC 11:28

5.3.3 Sumerian loans

§ 265 Sumerian loans in Akkadian are a large group. Most words are rather technical, designating pottery types, stone or other natural materials. Professions are common, as well such as *asūʾu* 'physician' or *etû* 'porter'. Places and buildings also occur, such as *altammu* 'tavern' and *kāru* 'harbour'. Other Sumerian loans, such as *tuppu* 'tablet' and *tappāʾu* 'friend', are very common in Akkadian, meaning that the loans are not restricted to technical jargon. Kouwenberg pointed out that there are no loans in OA that do not occur in

---

20 For other Semitic languages: e.g., Syrian, see Sokoloff (2009, 938–39): √*nṣb* (ܢܨܒ) 'to plant' or 'to found, establish' etc.; Arabic, see Wehr (1979, 1136): √*nṣb* (نصب) 'to raise, rear, erect' etc.

OB, concluding that Babylonian must have been the transmitter language (GOA § 4.4.1). I have not been able to test this claim for MA, but it is unlikely that it includes many loans that were unknown in OB.[21] The contraction of the aleph may or may not have taken place in the loans. It is retained in ^{lú}*a-su-e* Postgate 1973, 1:21; *tap-pa-i-šu* MAL B § 8:12 and *ki-ta-e* MATSH 3:5, 9; but notice *e-te* KAJ 102:7 (*etû*). A selection of nouns is given below:

altammu 'tavern'	< ÉŠ.DAM	*al-tam-me* MAL A § 14:31
arsānu 'barley groats'	< AR.ZA.NA	*ar-sa-nu* KAJ 226:10
asūʾu 'physician'	< ^{lú}A.ZU	^{lú}*a-su-e* Postgate 1973, 1:21
ašnugallu 'alabaster'	< $^{\text{na4}}$GIŠ.NU$_{11}$.GAL (?)	$^{\text{na4}}$*iš-nu-gal-li* KTN inventory i 23
bappiru 'beer-bread'	< BAPPIR	*pa-pi-[ri]* MARV 2 23:12'
erēnu 'cedar'	< EREN	*e-re-na* New Year Ritual:16'; *e-re-ni*^{meš} MARV 1 23:1
erretu 'weir of reeds'	< ^{giš}IR	*er-re-te* MATSH 2:9
etû 'porter'	< Ì.DU$_8$	GAL *e-te* KAJ 102:7; *e-te-e* MARV 2 17a+:7
ginā'u 'regular offerings'	< GI.NA	*gi-na-e* MARV 5 2:26; *gi-na-ú* MARV 6 13:2
gugallu 'irrigation controller'	< GÚ.GAL	^{lú}*gu-gal-li* MARV 5 20:13
isinnu 'festival'	< EZEN	*i-si-ni* MAL A § 55:19
iškāru 'corvée'	< GIŠ.GÁR	*iš-ka-ri-šu* Billa 25:7
kabšarru 'stone carver'	< KAB.SAR	^{lú}*kab-ša-ru* A 2613 (NTA, 30):2
kalgukku (red mineral paste)	< KAL.KU$_7$.KU$_7$	*kal-gu-qa* KAV 98:27
kāru 'harbour'	< KAR	*ka-a-ri* MATSH 9:44
kirru 'a big jar'	< ^{dug}KÍR	*ki-ir-ru* KAJ 303:6
kisallu 'forecourt'	< KISAL	*ki-sa-li* KAJ 178:6; *ki-⸢sa-li⸣* MARV 1 27+:25
kitāʾu 'flax'	< GADA	*ki-ta-e* MATSH 3:5, 9
kurultu 'fodder'		*ku-ru-ul-te-e* KAJ 127:11
kutallu 'back'	< GÚ.TÁL	*ku-tal-li-šu* MAL A § 40:86 *ku-tal-li-(...)* MATSH 6:23'
laḫannu (a flask)	< LA.ḪA.AN	*la-ḫa-na* New Year Ritual:17'
malāḫu 'sailor'	< ^{lú}MÁ.LAḪ$_5$	^{lú}*ma-la-ḫu* MARV 1 66:9
niggallu 'sickle'	< NÍG/NI.GÁL.LA	*ni-gál-lu* T 96-3:1
nikkassu 'account'	< NÍG.KA$_9$	*ni-ka-si* VS 1 105:6†
paššuru 'table'	< BANŠAR	$^{\text{giš!}}$*pa-šu-ru* KAJ 179:18
sabsuttu 'midwife'	< ^{f}ŠÀ.ZU	^{f}*sa-ab-su-tu* MAPD § 1:11
šamallāʾu 'merchant's assistant'	< ^{lú}ŠÁMAN.LÁ	^{lú}*[š]a-ma-la-e* MARV 5 85:18; *⸢ša⸣-ma-al-li-a* MARV 10 3:6
šuḫuppātu (SB *suḫuppatum*)	< ŠUHUB	[^{ku}]^{š}*šu-ḫu-pa-a-te*/^{kuš}SUḪUB^{meš} MAPD § 6:43; ^{kuš}*šu-ḫu-pa-tu* Postgate 1973, 1:18
tallu (a container)	< DAL	*tal-lu* KAJ 310:30
tappāʾu 'friend'	< TAB.BA	*tap-pa-i-šu* MAL B § 8:12
tappinnu 'bread'	< DABIN	^{ninda}*tap-pi-nu* MARV 6 27:20'
tuppu 'tablet'	< DUB	*tup-pi* MATC 3:14
ugāru 'meadow'	< A.GÀR	*ú-ga-ri* KAJ 121a:2
ūru 'roof'	< ÙR	*ú-ra-su* A 3061 (NTA, 33):3†
uššu 'dead reed'	< ÚŠ	^{ú}*uš-še* KAJ 133:12
utullu 'herdsman'	< UDUL	^{lú}*ú-tu-li* Billa 26:6

21 Some exceptions may occur, e.g., *tallu* (< ^{dug}DAL) 'a container', attested from MA/MB onwards. See CAD T, 101.

suluppu 'dates'	< ZÚ.LUM	*su-lu-pu* MARV 10 1:6

5.3.4 Hurrian loans

§ 266 MA contains a relatively large number of Hurrian loans due to contact with Hurrian-speaking people in the areas surrounding Assyria. Analysing non-Semitic nouns as Hurrian is not an easy task, as many nouns do not occur in our small corpus of Hurrian texts, with *alaḫḫenu* 'baker' being the prime example. Moreover, although we have Laroche 1980, we still need an updated Hurrian-Urartian dictionary with all lexica from Akkadian included. Richter (2012) is a very helpful addition, yet this work gathers together all the previous literature, rather than passing judgement on etymologies. As Richter's entries show, it is often very difficult and uncertain as to whether a noun is of Hurrian origin or from other unattested languages. We are somewhat helped by the fact that we can often recognize the Hurrian suffix chain, added to a nominal base. By these means, some otherwise incomprehensible words can still be analysed as Hurrian. The most common suffixes are -*nni* (cf. Wegner 2007, 54–56) and -*uḫli* (ibid.57–58) for professions.[22] On the other hand, it is possible for Hurrian to add suffixes to Akkadian nouns or loans from other languages (e.g., Richter 2012, 121–22). Many Hurrian loans in MA are in congruence with case, gender and number, e.g., *a-la-ḫi-na-a-tu* 'female a.' MATSH 10:12; ^túg^*iš-ḫa-na-be-a-te* '(a garment, fem. pl.)' MAH 15854 A:7'.[23] One can group the Hurrian loans according to two different conditions. This distinction is chronological; most Hurrian words came into Assyria during the crossover conquests between Aššur and Ḫanigalbat, where eventually a part of the Ḫanigalbat administrative system was introduced in Assyria, with many Hurrian names of professions in the military or administrative sphere. It is, however, not entirely clear to what extent this system was introduced before Aššur-uballiṭ, or whether it was mostly incorporated along with the conquests of Ḫanigalbat in the 13th century (Jakob 2003, 7). On the other hand, contact with Hurrian-speaking communities went back at least as far as the OA period. Admittedly, the group of Hurrian loans in OA is very small.[24] Among this small lexicon, only the nomen *alaḫḫenu* seems to have survived in MA (cf. Jakob 2003, 386–94). We find a small number of odd spellings, most noticeably two from Tell Billa. It is possible that the attestation from Aššur is a scribal mistake *a-*<*láḫ*>*-ḫi-ni* MARV 6 24:20, but the same cannot be said for the two Billa spellings, since this would require us to reconstruct an extra sign, which leads to an erroneous doubling of /l/. Note that the form changed again in NA, where the first syllable had dropped off, e.g., ^lú^*láḫ-ḫi-nu* KAV 112:1.

mas. Sg.	*alaḫḫinu*	*a-láḫ-ḫi-nu* MARV 5 8:19; *a-láḫ-ḫi-ni* MARV 9 23 r. 4'; *a-láḫ-ḫi-na* T 93-54:24 (et passim)
	alaḫnu	^lú^GAL *a-láḫ-ni* KAM 11 92:8
	alaḫḫenu	*a-láḫ-ḫe-e-nu* MARV 3 6:5
	alḫinu	^lú^*al-ḫi-nu* Billa 7:7; ^lú^*al-ḫ*[*i-n*]*u* Billa 8:5
	aḫḫinu	*a-ḫi-ni* MARV 6 24:20 (Tp)
mas. pl.	*alaḫḫinū*	^lú^*a-láḫ-ḫi-nu*^meš^ MARV 5 6:6; ^lú^*a-láḫ-ḫi-ni*^meš^ A 1750 (NTA, 24):10

22 Notice also the Hurrian genitive *-ve* > *-be*, which occurs only in GNs, e.g., Ḫarbe (modern Tell Ḫuwīra). See MATC, 4; UGM, 20; cf. Wegner (2007, 65).

23 The origin of the said word remains disputed, but is included in Richter (2012, 105b). Note that CDA (133) suggests either a Hurrian or a Hittite origin.

24 See Dercksen (2007, 37–38, 40); GOA § 4.4.3.

fem. sg.	*alaḫḫinutu*	–
fem. pl.	*alaḫḫinātu*	*a-la-ḫi-na-a-tu* MATSH 10:12

§ 267 The second group of nouns, which first occurred in Assyrian in the MA corpus comprises nouns, can also largely be found in the Nuzi texts, which fell under the same Mittani influence as Assyria. It is impossible to include all loans; therefore, we will have to satisfy ourselves with a small selection of some of the more common examples. All instances of lemna are found in Richter's dictionary and have therefore been connected with Hurrian, although this does not guarantee that all nouns have an actual Hurrian origin.

aššiannu	^{túg}*a-ši-a-nu*^{meš} 'a garment' MARV 10 69 :1 (see Richter 2012, 54a; Postgate 2014, 417)
ḫawiluḫḫu	*rēš ḫa-me-lu-ḫi* 'head of the *ḫ*.' Coronation Ritual ii 42 (*ḫawiluḫḫu* seems to refer to ground/fields; see AHw, 338; Richter 2012, 122b)
ḫurādu	*ḫu-ra-di* '*ḫ*.-soldier' MATSH 8:25' (perhaps genuine Akkadian; see Richter 2012, 169–70)
išḫanabe	^{túg}*iš-ḫa-na-be-a-te* 'a garment' MAH 15854 A:7' (see Richter 2012, 105; Postgate 2014, 418)
kakardinnu	*ka-kar-di-nu* 'victualler' MATC 4:27 (base of disputed etymology, but with Hurrian suffix *-tennu*; see Richter 2012, 180)
šiltāḫu	*šil*$_4$*-ta-ḫu* 'arrows' MARV 1 72:1 (Richter 2012, 377)
šiluḫlu	*ši-luḫ-li* (a class of persons) MARV 2 23:7' (see Freydank 1971, 536; Richter 2012, 378a etc.)
taḫapšu	*ta-ḫap-še* 'felt' MARV 3 53:2 (Richter 2012, 425–26)
tartānu	*tar-ta-a-ni* Stelen 66:3; *tar-ta-nu* GAL-*ú* MARV 1 63:11 (Richter 2012, 448)
tupninnu	*tup-ni-na* 'box' KAV 103:8; pl. ^{giš}*tup-ni-na-te* KAV 105:5. Previously read as *umninnu*. (see von Soden 1977, 237–39; Richter 2012, 474)
turēzu	⸢*tu*⸣*-ú-re-e-ze* 'harvest' MAL B § 19:11; *tu-re-zi-šu-nu* KAJ 101:4 (Richter 2012, 478a)
umzarḫu	*um-za-ar-ḫu* 'local' MATSH 12:31; Hall 1983:13 (Richter 2012, 491)[25]

§ 268 Beyond substantives, Hurrian has not left any impression on the Assyrian dialect. No verbal forms or prepositions appear to be of foreign origin, although we do find two adjectives: *talmu* 'big' and *sillunu* 'old' (see § 317). It should be noted that some Hurrian loans remain indifferent to gender or number. This is true for the two adjectives, which are always in congruence with the singular; the same applies to ^{f}PN ⸢*um*⸣*-za-ar-ḫu* '^{f}PN the homeborn slave' KAJ 100:2–3. In addition, there is the adverb *entu* of Hurrian origin (§ 494).

25 For the use of *umzarḫu* to designate (houseborn) slaves, see de Ridder (2017b, 53).

Chapter 6: Inflection of Nouns

6.1 Genus

§ 269 As with Akkadian and Semitic in general, MA differentiates between two different genders: masculine and feminine. The masculine gender has no specific markers for singular forms; however, the feminine uses the suffix *-(a)t*. The distribution between the short (*-t*) and long (*-at*) ending can usually be determined, with the short ending being preferred in most instances. The long ending is added to words ending in a consonant cluster, usually a geminated consonant: *ši-il-la-ta* MAL A § 2:16; *qi-im-ma-te* (√*qamāmu*) KTN inventory i 11. According to von Soden, it is possible for *PvRS* patterns to receive the long suffix *-at*, rather than opening the second syllable. This was more likely to happen to the second syllable in *PaRS* patterns than with *PiRS*; *PuRS* (GAG, 91 § 60b). The evidence from MA shows a preference for a short suffix for all three patterns. In fact, the *PvRSat* pattern is rarely attested in MA, occurring in *pu-uq-du-tu* 'spike' KAJ 310:61, UDU *zi-bu-tu*^{meš} (< **zinb*) 'fat-tailed sheep(?)' Ali 9:5 and perhaps *te-er-ḫe-te* 'bridal gift' MAL A § 38:23. As can be seen in the examples below, the forms with the long ending *-at* are affected by VA:

aḫuzzutu	*a-ḫu-ze-te* 'marriage gift' MAL A § 30:28
ḫūrutu	*ḫu-ru-tu* 'madder' KAJ 130:3
šapputu	⌜1 ^{dug}⌝ *šap-pu-tu* '(a vessel)' MARV 7 5:11
šillutu	*ši-il-la-ta* 'slander' MAL A § 2:16
piššutu	*piš-še-te* 'ointment' T 93-10:17

Examples of short ending *-t*:

lubultu	^{túg}*lu-bùl-ta* 'clothing' Coronation Ritual i 35
nārtu	*na-ar-te* 'canal' KAJ 13:17
nīktu	*ni-ik-tu* 'sexual victim' MAL A § 23:20
rebītu	*re-be-e-ti* 'square' MAL A § 12:14
ṣāltu	*ṣa-al-te* 'quarrel' MAL A § 8:78
šaqultu	*ša-qúl-te* 'weight' KAJ 178:18

§ 270 There is a number of primary nouns in Akkadian that are Common Semitic (although some loans occur as well), which are not marked with the ending *-at*. In some cases, the feminine gender of the noun may already be obvious in the meaning, for instance, a feminine person such as *ummu* 'mother'. In other cases, we find a substantive with the adjective or verb inflected according to the feminine gender, e.g., IGI^{meš} (sg. *ēnu*) *dāgilāte* 'the seeing eyes' KTN inventory i 27. In the plural, all feminine substantives take the feminine ending *-āt*, so that the gender becomes visible. We can arrange these unmarked feminine substantives in a number of categories following previous grammatical treatments of Akkadian/Assyrian.[1] Although it should be noted that many technical terms are loans, especially from Sumerian.

---

1 Cf. GAG, 92 § 60d; GKT, 89f § 58a; Streck (2010b, 294–97).

1) Female creatures:
ummu 'mother': ⸢*um*⸣*-mi-(...)* MAL A § 49:61; *um-me* 'trunk' KTN inventory ii 17; *um-ma-(...)* MARV 4 28:14'; pl. ⸢*um-ma-te*⸣*-šu-nu* 'their mothers' MARV 1 61:8

2) Body parts, usually dual:
ēnu 'eye': pl. IGI^{meš} *dāgilāte* KTN inventory i 27
išku 'testicle': *iš-ku šanittu iltēšama* 'with the (testicle) a second testicle' MAL A § 8:82
kursinnu 'ankle': pl. *kur-si-na-te* Adad Ritual:12
labiānu 'neck': pl. *la-ba-n[a-t]i-(...)* MARV 3 64:42
lišānu 'tongue, language': EME *Aššurāyi[tt]e* 'the Assyrian language' VAT 8722:3
purīdu 'leg': pl. *pu-ri-*⸢*da*⸣*-tu-(...)* 'legs' KTN inventory i 31
qātu 'hand': pl. *qa-ta-t[e]* KAJ 259:7
rāmunu 'self': pl. *ra-ma-na-tu-(...)* KTN inventory i 17
ṣupru 'fingernail': pl. *ṣu-up-ra-at* KTN inventory ii 8
ubānu 'fingers': pl. *ú-ba-na-te-(...)* PKT 4 obv. left 16

3) Parts of buildings:
adru 'threshing floor': pl. *ad-ra-te* Giricano 3:7
igāru 'wall': pl. *i-ga-ra-te-ma* MATSH 6:10'
kisallu 'forecourt': pl. *ki-sa-la-te* A 3187 (NTA, 36):2

4) Domestic utensils and containers:
asallu (a copper vessel): 1 *a-sa-lu šanāyittum* 'a secondary *asallu* bowl' KAJ 303:4
ḫurrupu 'dish': pl. *ḫu-ru-up-pa-a-te* MAL A § 42:17
kablu 'foot (of furniture)': *ka-ab-la-a-te*^{meš} KAJ 121a:3
kallu '*k*.-bowl': ^{dug}*kal-la-a-te* New Year Ritual:16'
kammu '*k*.-tool': pl. *kám-ma-te* KTN inventory i 24
kāsu 'cup': pl. *ka-sa-a-te* 'cups' MARV 1 7:8
laḫannu '(a flask)': pl. *la-ḫa-na-a-te* New Year Ritual:23'
šuḫuppu 'boot': pl. [^{ku}]^{š}*šu-ḫu-pa-a-te* MAPD § 6:43
tarīḫu 't. bowl': ^{dug}*ta-ri-ḫa-te*' MATC 12:13
tuppu 'tablet': pl. *tup-pa-tu* 'tablets' KAJ 110:13; *tup-pu* (...) *tattalkamma* 'the tablet came' MATSH 19:7'–8'; *tup-pí dannata* 'strong tablet' KAJ 12:18
zīqu 'torch': *zi-qu annītu* 'this torch' Ištar Ritual:12

5) Means of transport:
eleppu 'boat': [^{giš}M]Á *š[i]-*⸢*i*⸣*-it* 'that boat' MAL M § 1:3

6) Geographical terms:
ḫarrānu 'road': pl. *ḫar-ra-na-te* KAJ 103:16; [*ḫar*]*-ra-na-tu* T 93-20:18
mātu 'country': *ana ma-a-te šanittem-ma* 'to another country' MAL A § 36:4-5

7) Natural products:
ḫaṭṭu 'stick': 4 ^{giš}GIDRU (...) *šāḫuzā* 'four sticks (...) are reserved' KAJ 310:49–50
kitāʾu 'flax': *ki-ta-e* (…) *lā bašlat* 'flax (…) is not ripe' MATSH 3:5–9
miḫḫu (kind of beer): ⸢^{kaš}*miḫ*⸣*-ḫa-tu* MATC 12:29
nušḫu '*nušḫu*-nut': pl. ^{giš}*nu-uš-ḫa-te* KTN inventory ii 18
šinna 'ivory': *ši-in-na ša* (…) *šēṣuʾatanni* 'ivory that is brought out' KAV 205:6

8) Abstract:
ḫamsu 'maltreatment': *ḫa-am-sa-tu* ' T 93-2:13; *ḫa-am-sa-te*^{meš} PRU 4, 289:5

9) A small group of deverbal nouns remains:

kanīku 'sealed document': *ka-ṇi-ka-te-*(...) George 1988 1 r. 16'
niqīu 'offering': ⸢*ni*⸣*-qi-a-te* 'MARV 4 59:14
riksu 'agreement': pl. *ri-ik-sa-a-te* MAL A § 17:70 cf. *ri-ik-sa-ni* KTN inventory i 3
maškanu 'settlements': *ma-áš-ka-na-te* T 04-37:8

§ 271 The list given above is not without its problems, such as the number of noun variations or changes in gender that take place. In the case of *tuppu*, this noun used to be masculine in OA.[2] As noted by Streck (2010b) for OB, there is a number of unmarked nouns where gender may vary between singular and plural. Even variation in the singular itself is possible. Some examples given by Streck (e.g., *ḫaṭṭu*) are also found in the list above; however, variation can only rarely be proven based on the MA material. Some nouns that fit into the categories given above are congruent as a masculine noun or have a masculine plural. In the case of a noun following a number, it is also possible that a singular is meant (§ 336).

appu/uznu	*ap-pi-šu-nu uz-ni-šu-nu unakkusū* 'they will cut of their noses (pl.) and ears (pl.)' MAL A § 4:49–50
biršu	2 ^{túg}*bir-še* 'two felt textiles (pl.)' Coronation Ritual ii 17
gašūru	^{giš}*ga-šu-ri* 'beams' T 97-17:18
mašḫuru	^{túg}*maš-ḫu-ru maḫruttu* 'received *m.*-textiles (pl.)' MPR 26:19
qaqqudu	*qa-qa-sa kazir* 'her head is shaven' TR 2083+:20
qaqquru	*qa-qú-ru paṣīuttum* 'white (=empty) ground (pl.)' KAJ 174:3
rīqu	ŠIM^{meš} *ballutte* 'mixed aromatics' Ištar Ritual:7–8

There are also a few nouns that are masculine in meaning, but morphologically and syntactically feminine. These seemingly masculine nouns have a feminine plural. Note that, in the two examples of *ummiānātu* 'creditors' (OA *ummiānū*, e.g., AKT 6a 208:19), the verb agrees with as a feminine plural, while, in the other phrase, a masculine pronominal plural suffix is used to refer to them. One may guess that, in this case, the gender is analogous to the feminine noun *ummu* 'mother', with a similar base.

ḫurādu	*ḫu-ra-da-te* '*ḫurādu*-soldiers' KAV 119:13
	PN *rab ḫu-ra-da-a-te* MARV 1 5:1
ummiānu	*um-mi-a-na-tu* (...) *lā iṣabbatāšunu* 'the creditors will not seize them' KAV 211 r. 5'–7'
	$^{\text{lú.meš}}$*um-mi-a-na-a-tu* [*š*]*a* PN *ḫabbulaššununi* 'the creditors to whom PN was indebted' MARV 4 151:62–63
urû	'team of oxen' in pl. *ú-ra-te* Giricano 15:5
UDU.NÍTA	While the meaning 'ram' or 'male sheep' is expected, we may point out the feminine plural UDU.NÍTA^{meš}*-tu* A 1741 (NTA, 20):1. Yet the noun, as in other texts, agrees with verbs as a masculine plural: *pa-aq-du* l. 10. Possibly it has a masculine plural ending *-utt*.

Nouns with both genders attested in the plural are rare, although a number of examples can be found in OA (GOA § 5.2.2.4). For MA, we have attestations for *riksu* 'decree' involving the masculine plural *ri-ik-sa-ni* KTN inventory i 3 and feminine plural *ri-ik-sa-a-te* MAL A § 17:70. We also find two plural forms for *bētu* 'house' in É^{meš}*-ni* (*bētāni*) 'houses' KAJ 223:10; Faist 2001:24 ~ É^{meš}*-ti-*[*ia*] (*bētātīya*) Billa 61:5. This alternation is a feature that is

---

2 E.g., *tup-pí-im la-bi-ri-im* 'old tablet' TCL 20 184:5. Late OA shows feminine forms, e.g., *tup-pì dan-na-tí* 'strong tablet' MAH 15962:35 (Gelb/Sollberg 1957). Cf. GOA § 5.2.2.1.

described for NA (GAG, 94 § 61j). Another example is *ūmu* 'day', which can take both a masculine and a feminine plural gender.

Masculine plural and masculine verbal congruence:

ūmū	*tūr* UD^{meš} *ikaṣṣuˀū* 'again, the days will be cold' MATSH 6:11'
	ina šanīe *u*$_4$*-me* 'on the second day' MARV 1 10:11
	adi ú-mu^{meš} *iṭibbūni* 'as long as the days are good' MATC 3:7
	UD^{meš} *lā šaˀiˀū* 'days not propitious' TabT05A-134:16[3]
	UD^{meš} *šaˀiˀ⸢uttu⸣* 'days propitious' TabT05A-134:18

Feminine plural:

ūmātu	*ù*$^{!}$*-ma-te* MATSH 4:15'
	UD^{meš}*-te-šu-nu* MATC 40:13

The categories used above thus provide little more than a theoretical framework to explain the feminine inflection of forms without feminine markers.

6.2 Status rectus and it declinations

§ 272 Most substantives occur in the status rectus, which features full declination of the three Common Semitic case endings: nominative, genitive and accusative. Akkadian is unique in having an additional dative case, but restricted to verbal pronominal suffixes. The status rectus does not take pronominal suffixes, in contrast to the status constructus. It occurs without governing noun or pronominal suffixes. MA retains the triptotic declination of the case endings, possessing a nominative, a genitive and an accusative. The mimation of case endings was already in decline in the OA period and is no longer productive in MA. In some instances, the case endings are replaced with adverbial terminative or locative suffixes (see § 483 and § 489). The function of the case ending is discussed in the chapter on the syntax of nouns (Chapter 7). Nonetheless, a short summary follows:

Number	Case	Masculine	Feminine
Singular	Nominative Genitive Accusative	*šipr-u* *šipr-e* *šipr-a*	*šarr-utu* *šarr-ete* *šarr-ata*
Dual	Nominative Oblique	*šipr-ān* *šipr-ēn*	**šarr-atān* **šarr-etēn*
Plural	Nominative Oblique	*šipr-ū* *šipr-ī*	*šarr-ātu* *šarr-āte*

Figure 19: Inflection of nouns.

Note that open syllables with short /a/ preceding the case ending are susceptible to VA: *qaqqare* > *qaqqere*. In the plural, the case ending lengthens, except for the feminine. Declination is diptotic, with the genitive and accusative merged in an oblique case *-ē*.

3 This follows the etymology of these forms, according to Shibata (2015b, 148), who connected it to Babylonian equivalent *šemû*. I have assumed an adjective *ša*^{w}*iˀu*, rather than *šaˀû*, in analogy with the ordinal *šanīu* 'second'. The orthography allows for this.

§ 273 The original genitive ending *-i(m)* has changed into *-e*, possibly under the influence of the original mimation (to this end, see § 240).[4] Evidence for *-e* can be found in the instances where the case ending is written with the vocalic sign E (e.g., *gi-na-e* MARV 9 9:21') or with a sign that specifically has the syllabic value Ce (e.g., *ṭé-me*). Despite the many attestations of the said orthography, exceptions are frequent (e.g., *nu-bat-ti* MATSH 12:30). A quantitative survey of the genitive orthography in LVUH (see table below) shows that the Ci spelling usually occurs next to Ce and represents the minority. The exception *qātu* could be a historic orthography.

Word	I	E
anniʾu		20x E
asaʾittu	1x TI	3x TE
karmu	7x MI	20x ME
bēt nakkamte		1x TE
bēt pāšerte		1x TE
bēt rugbe		1x BAD
erābu	1x (BI)	6x BAD
ikkartu		2x TE
karuʾu		30x E
lubultu		2x TE
mētu		7x TE
nussuḫtu		1x TE
pāḫutu		1x TE
parrutu		8x TE
rēḫtu	⸢2x⸣ TI	1x TE
tamliʾu		2x E
umāmu	1x MI	

Figure 20: The genitive in LVUH.[5]

§ 274 Most proper names do not take case endings, such as the deities Aššur, Šamaš and Ištar. In some cases, a proper name can also end in an invariable vowel, e.g., DN. However, it should be noted that PNs are usually written logographically. Normal PNs are often compounds and, as a result, not inflected, e.g., Sîn-balassu-ēriš, Aššur-taklāk and Adad-šarra-uṣur. This is also true for compounds in which the final element ends in a vowel, e.g., Kidin-Gula; Marduk-nādin-aḫḫe; Šamaš-ālik-panē. Exceptions occur, but are rare, e.g., Naḫiš-šalmu: ᵐ*Na-ḫi-iš-šal-mu* KAJ 27:15 and ᵐ*Na-ḫiš-šal-me* KAJ 175:40. Proper nouns with nisbe endings seem to be inflected, although the extent to which this is only orthographic remains debatable (see § 255). For other proper names, it is usually possible for proper names to be inflected, such as the former Ḫanigalbat capital of Uššukannu, e.g., ⸢*Uš*⸣*-šu-ka-nu* MARV 5 2:17; ᵘʳᵘ*Áš-šu-ka-ni* MARV 5 10:16; Taʾidu: ᵘʳᵘ*Ta-i-du* MARV 9 9:7'; *iltu* ᵘʳᵘ*Ta-*⸢*i*⸣*-di* MARV 9 26:8; Katmuḫḫu: ᵏᵘʳ*Kat-mu-ḫu* MARV 6 51:7; *ša* ᵏᵘʳ*Kat-mu-ḫi* MARV 6 82:7.

4 For the OA evidence, see GKT, 94f § 60b.; GOA § 3.4.5.3. The change became standard at the end of the OA period, as some scribes started to use the phonetic complement E, instead of mimation at the end of a word, in order to emphasize the correct pronunciation, e.g., *ṣa-al-me-e* AKT 5 64:27. See Veenhof (2010, 31).

5 Broken attestations and signs with equal e/I readings are not taken into account, unless indicated.

§ 275 First millennium Akkadian is well known for its decline in terms of case endings. In NA, the accusative ending assimilated into the nominative *-u*, while losing the nominative plural case endings (see SNAG, 77 § 3.9.1). In fact, it seems that all three case endings declined in the first millennium with the genitive being retained the longest. Similar developments are known for NB.[6] The decline of the case endings is already visible in MA, where the NA/NB nominative/accusative *-u* already occurs.[7] Note that mistakes in case endings are not uncommon in Akkadian.[8] The oldest cited passage occurs in a text from the reign of Abn (KAJ 22). Other examples are numerous; a selection follows:

Nominative for genitive:

maškan it-ḫu-ru 'tent of the *itḫuru*' MAPD § 9:53

a-na e-mi-it-ta-a-na ^giš^BANŠUR (< *ana emitte ana*) 'to the right side, to the table' Ištar Ritual:2 (possibly crasis)

ana É-⸢*tu*?⸣ 'for the house' KAJ 220:2 (BAI) (possibly a modified TU > TE)

aššum a-bu šuāte 'concerning that father' KAJ 93:6† (M 8 50)

1 *sūtu burāšu kīmū* ^šim^*ka-ak-*⸢*ku*⸣ 'one seah juniper instead of chickpeas' KAJ 248:6 (Nae)

ezib tup-pu-šu 'aside from his tablet' KAJ 22:2 (Abn)

iltu ^iti^*ku-zal-lu* 'from the month of *Kuzallu*' A 300:1[9] (TN) (no copy/photo available)

Nominative for accusative:

aʾīlu a[*l-m*]*a-at-tu ētaḫaz* 'a man has seized a widow' MAL A § 34:71

ša (…) ^lú^*pa-gu-ú ina nāre taššianni* 'the *pagû* she carried from the river' Franke/Wilhelm 1985:2–3 (Tp)

pa-gu-ú lā ipuggū 'they will not take away the *pagû*' Franke/Wilhelm 1985:8-9 (Tp)

a-ba-ru-ḫu ana PN *dinā* 'give *abaruḫu* to PN' K9-T1:16–18

qaqqad AN.NA-*ku išaqqal* 'the amount of lead he will pay' KAJ 38:7 (M 9 86); also KAJ 141:6 (EAd/Aub)

Genitive for nominative:

DAM-*ti šīt lā aššat* 'that wife is not a (proper) wife' MAL A § 41:9

---

6 See GAG, 99 § 63e; Woodington (1983, 63ff § 27); Streck (2014b). Cf. Arabic, where only the masculine singular accusative is still preserved in writing, e.g., *malik-an* (ملكاً) 'king'. Even Ge'ez involves the non-nominative *ḥaqla* (ሐቅለ) 'field', as opposed to the nominative *ḥaql* (ሐቅል); cf. Lipiński 2001, 269ff. For the plural, we may draw a parallel with BH, where the oblique became standard when the nominative was lost, e.g., *mlāḵīm* (מְלָכִים) 'kings'; likewise, Syriac *dayyānin* (ܕܝܢܝܢ) (absolute). In general, it can be said that most Semitic languages started to lose case endings at the end of the second millennium BCE, much like Akkadian. The only 'classical' Semitic language, where case endings are still fully functional, is classical Arabic.

7 See Franke/Wilhelm (1985, 21); Giricano, 53.

8 Cf. UgAkk: Huehnergard (1989, 143); Emar: Seminara (1998, 287–89).

9 Similar constructions with other month names generally show the correct genitive case ending, e.g., *iltu* ^iti^*kal-mar-te* VAT 9410:20.

tup-pi iḫappi 'he will break (his!) tablet' MARV 3 55:16'–17' (i/o passim *tuppušu*) (TN–Nae)

8 *su-ḫi-ra-te ša irte* 'eight foals of the breast' (list) LVUH 8:15 (Sa)

ŠE-*um an-ni-e* (…) *sasi* 'this barley is declared' A 320:20–22 (Aub)

ikkuru de-ke 'a killed farmer' MPR 60:50 (list, no predicate)

PN *me-te* 'PN, dead' MPR 66:50 (list, no predicate)

ana ḫalzīka gabbe maš-ri 'your entire district is wealthy' A 877:4

Genitive for accusative:

adi tup-pí dannata išaṭṭurū<ni> annītuma dannat 'until he writes a (new) strong tablet this one is valid' KAJ 12:20–21; cf. *adi tup-pa* (…) KAJ 148:26 (Adn/Sa); KAJ 151:21 (Aub)

šumma ša-ni-ta tup-pí ultēb[*ilakku*] 'when I send you my second tablet' KAV 169:14–15 (TN)

ú-nu-ti ḫaliqta (…) *izzuzū* 'they have divided the lost property' KAV 168:7–10 (TN)

ikarrurū rab liqtāni ki-si-šu rab zammāre sa-am-me-šu u attamannu bēl pāḫete ša ukallūni 'the *l.*-official his bag, the chief singer his lyre and each one and every governore (whatever) he is holding they will lay down' Coronation Ritual iii 9–11

[*a*]*lpa lā še-bi* (…) *iddan* 'he will give a young bull (=not old)' Giricano 10:17–18 (Abk)

Accusative for a nominative:

ša-an-gu-ta (…) *lu ṭāba*[*t*] 'may the priesthood be good' Coronation Ritual ii 33–34

tapp[*aḫ*]*ḫu sipar<ru> u paššūru mimma an-ni-a ana nīšēšuma* 'a copper cauldron and table, all this is for his installation' KAJ 179:17–20 (M 9 100)

e-da-na ētiqma 'the term is passed' TR 3007:10 (Sa)

1 ^{túg}*maš-ḫa-ra* PN 'one *mašḫuru* textile for PN' MPR 26:1[10]

Accusative for genitive:

aššat na-i-ka-a-na 'wife of the rapist' MAL A § 55:24

mulṭu ša il-da 'the comb of the base' KAJ 310:6 (Sa)

ana e-me-ta tabik 'it is poured to the right' LVUH 93:10–11 (TN)

Oblique plural for nominative plural:

kī DINGIR^{meš}*-ni ana bēte sa-si-ú-ni* 'when the gods are called to the house' KAJ 232:3–4 (Adn)

For the following attestations from Giricano (Abk), it should be pointed out that all texts are from the hand of the same scribe. This anonymous individual is named 'Schreiber X' by Radner (Giricano, 62). The passage, Giricano 7:18–19, is therefore found in another text by another scribe with the correct case ending (Giricano 4:28).

ma[*nnu*] *ša de-nu ubta*$^{??}$*u*$^{?}$*ūni* 'whoever seeks a lawsuit' Giricano 7:18–19 cf. *ša de-na ubta*$^{??}$*ûni* Giricano 4:28

---

10 It is possible that, as a form with Assyrian VA, a pausal form is intended, in which case we have an epenthetic vowel.

[*ina adr*]*āte* [ŠE-*um*] *ù* ^{še}[À]RA^{meš}-*šu-ú* [n *e*]-*ṣi-du idd*[*a*]*n* 'on the threshing floor, he will give two reapers, the barley and its grinded barley' Giricano 2:9–12

ina adrāte 2 *e-ṣi-du ŠE-um* [*u* ^{še}]ÀRA^{meš} *idd*[*a*]*n* 'on the threshing floor, he will give two reapers, the barley and the grinded barley' Giricano 3:7–9

ina adrāte ŠE-um u ^{še}ÀRA 5 *e-ṣi-du-ú pa-ḫa-nu* PN$_2$ *iddan* 'on the threshing floor (PN$_1$) will give the barley, grinded barley and five reapers, under the p. of PN$_2$' Giricano 9:6–10

[*ina a*]*drāte* [*ŠE-um*] *u* ŠE.ÀRA-*šu*-[*ú n e-ṣi*]-*du* [*idd*]*an* 'on the threshing floor, he will give *n* reapers, the barley and its grinded barley' Giricano 13:6–9

Perhaps in PN:

[^{m}]*Pu-ú-ie-e* DUMU *Bulīe ilqe* 'Pūyû son of Bulīya took it' AO 19.228:5–6 (Arn)

A problematic form is the sign UD, which could be read *-tú* (nominative), as well as *tam* (accusative). This would be a case where the accusative is erroneously used for the nominative.

As nominative:

UDU.NÍTA-*tú* KAJ 283:6 (NtA)

riḫṣu ši-iḫ-tú Giricano 8:4 ~ cf. *ri-iḫ-ṣu ḫi-iṣ-nu* Giricano 1:3 (Abk)

3 *gurrātu an-na-*⸢*tú*$^{!}$⸣ *šulmānu* 'the three ewes are a *šulmānu*-gift' KAJ 94:6–7 (Sa)

Once, the value <tú> is used for a wrong case ending, in this case the oblique feminine plural ending *-āte*.

nap-⸢*ša*⸣*-a-tú ša šarre bēlišu izzīar* 'he has hated the life of the king his lord' A 2994:24–25 (TN)

The editors (Brinkman/Donbaz 1985, 86) of this text defended the reading <tú> (UD) over <te$^{!}$>, even though the plurale tantum *napšātu* is the object of the verb. We find *nap-*⸢*ša*⸣*-a-te* in Freydank (2009a, 69). Unfortunately, the latter author does not elaborate on his corrected reading.

§ 276 There is a number of nouns that frequently, and sometimes almost inevitably, take a wrong case ending. We will briefly discuss this matter below. The most prominent example is probably the semi-logographic spellings of ŠE 'barley'. Cancik-Kirschbaum (2012, 28 n30) suggested that this was due to Babylonian influence, where phonetic complements of logograms were common, but absent in the MA tradition. This assumption is incorrect as ŠE with a phonetic complement is attested in OA (cf. Dercksen 2011). The mistakes seem to have their origin in the discontinuation of -UM/IM/AM as markers of case endings, which in turn was due to the loss of mimation. The mistakes are so common in MA that we may suspect that the frozen case endings were added randomly following the logogram ŠE. For this reason, we provide only a very small selection of phrases:

[*k*]*ī našlamte anneke ù* ŠE-*um annie* 'as security for this lead and barley' KAJ 28:12–13

qaqqad ŠE-*um imaddudū šumma* ŠE-*um lā imaddudū* 'they will measure the capital of the barley, and if they do not measure it (…)' KAJ 85:17–18

4 *emāru* 1 *sūtu* ŠE-*im* (…) *rēḫu* 'four homers and one seah of barley is left' Maul 2004 2:10–12, cf. 3 *emāru* ŠE-*um* 'three seahs of barley' MARV 1 9:14

ŠE-*am utru ša* PN 'the extra barley of PN' LVUH 75:35

Another noun used in loans with a regular erroneous case ending is *kātu* 'pledge'. The case ending varies mostly between the correct nominative and the erroneous genitive, although an attestation of the accusative is also found. This is somewhat unexpected as it is fully syllabic and does not have special case ending signs, such as ŠE-*um*. A possible alternative explanation is to transcribe the noun as *katû*, taken from the root *katāʾu* 'to take as security'. In this case, we could take the spelling *ka-te* as representing the status constructus. This does not account for the variation between the status rectus and status constructus in similar constructions.

Nominative:

ka-tum [*ṣar*]*pe eqlu*^{meš} *u bētānūšunu* 'the pledge for the silver are the fields and his houses' KAJ 32:16–17

ka-tu libnāte eqalšu u bēssu 'pledge for the bricks are his field and his house' KAJ 87:8–9 (EAd/Aub)

Genitive:

ka-te annuku(^{sic}) *eqalšu u bēssu* 'the pledge for the lead are his field and his house' KAJ 34:13–14; KAJ 40:13–14

ka-te ṣarpe u ŠE-*im eqal*^{meš}-*šunu u bētānu-šunu* 'the pledge of the silver and barley are their fields and their houses' KAJ 47:25–26

Accusative:

ka-ta annaku$^{sic.}$ *eqalšu u bēssu* 'the pledge for the lead is his field and his house' KAJ 38:14–15

A third noun with similar behavior is the collective word *ṣēna* 'flock'. It occurs most frequently in accounts from Tell Ali and Tell Aš-Šēḫ Ḥamad, when the flock is counted. As such, it would occur in the nominative or alternatively in the status absolutus; yet, the form is almost exclusively written *ṣe-na*. We should possibly regard this form as an Akkadogram, similar to MA.NA.

Nominative:

ṣe-na sammuḫātu 'mixed flock' LVUH 29:9–10; Ali 4:9–10

ŠU.NIGÍN 5 ME 29 *ṣe-na*^{meš} 'total of 529 flocks' Ali 3:6

ŠU.NÍGIN 41 *ṣe-ni ana qaqqede umtaṭṭi* 'a total of 41 flocks, he has reduced the capital with' LVUH 56:10'–11'

ŠU.NÍGIN 5⸢8⸣ *ṣe-na* 'total of 58 flocks' MARV 2 6:7

Genitive (the case ending is grammatically correct in the following examples):

ŠU.NÍGIN 35 *maškātu ša ṣe-ni sammuḫāte* 'total of 35 hides of mixed flocks' LVUH 56:5

ša l[*ē*]*ʾāni* [*š*]*a ṣe-ni* 'from the list of the flock' MARV 1 27:24

Accusative:

ṣe-ni ina muḫḫīšu ukarruʾu 'they will deduct the flock from his (account)' LVUH 51:12

6.2.1 Dual

§ 277 While the dual case was still frequently used in the OA period (GKT, 92 § 59b; GOA § 5.4.2), only remnants are found in the NA corpus (SNAG, 77f). This latter situation is reflected in MA where the dual is only seldom found. Most cases where it is preserved concern body parts: *ēnu* 'eye'; *qarnu* 'horn'; *rēš* 'head'; *ṣupru* 'fingernail'; and *uznu* 'ear'. It is no coincidence that many body parts usually occur in pairs. In other cases, the dual ending is frozen: *battubattēn* 'both sides'; the adverb *ebertān* 'on the other side'; and *kilallān* 'both'. As for the nunation of the case endings, as far as can be seen, it is retained in MA, unlike mimation.

Nominative:

ēnu	*e-na-šu* 'both his eyes' KAJ 179:14
qarnu	*qar-na-šu-nu* 'their horns' KTN inventory iv 10'
ṣupru	*ṣu-up-ra-šu-nu* 'their hooves' KTN inventory iv 9' [11]

Oblique:

battubattēn	*bat-tu-ba-te-en* 'both sides' New Year Ritual:18'
	bat-tu-ba-te-e[n] 'both sides' A 1947+:21
naḫallu	*ša iltu na-ḫa-al-te-en* 'from the two wadis(?)' A 1947+:8
nappaltu	*[na-a]p-pal-te-e-en* 'two shares' MAL B § 19:16
rēš	*ana ša re-še-en* 'eunuch' MAL A § 20:97
ša battēn	túg⸢*ša*⸣ *bat-te-en* (type of textile, perhaps 'of two sides') KAJ 316:9 (Postgate 2014, 423–24)

When pronominal suffixes are added to the oblique case, there is no morphological difference with the oblique plural. In these cases, we have to use context, such as the basic fact that a wife could have no more than two ears in MAL A § 4:51 (sg. would have been *uznaša*).

kisitte qar-ni-šu-nu 'the stem of their horns' KTN inventory i 20

aʾīlu ša aššassu uz-ni-ša unakkaš 'the man will cut off the ears (2) of his wife' MAL A § 4:51–52

The quantifying pronoun *kilallān* 'both' (§ 397) appears to use a hybrid form of the dual case endings. In the nominative, the adjective ends in the mixture *-ūn* (*-ū* and *-ān*) and, in the oblique case, as the real dual *-ān*. Likewise, the non-congruent adverb *ebertān* 'on the other side' probably derives from the idea that a river has two riverbanks, e.g., *iš-tu e-be*!*-er-ta*!*-a-an* MAL M § 2:9 (cf. § 457). Instead of the dual, we find the number 2 usually written preceding a plural noun, a practice already known in OA (GKT, 92 § 59b), e.g.:

Arrapḫāyu	2 *Ar-rap-ḫa-iu-ú* 'two Arraphaeans' MARV 2 17a+:44
ebertu	2 *eb-ra-a-te* 'two steps' Aššur ritual ii 7'
kāsu	2 *ka-sa-a-te* 'two cups' PKT 1 I right:5

11 Even though animals usually have more than two hooves each, it seems likely that this was a dual in analogy with the preceding *qarnāšunu*. The dual can be used for substantives relating to body parts involving a stable number; see GAG, 93 § 61c.

laḫannu	2 *la-ḫa-na-a-te* 'two flasks' New Year Ritual:23'
makkusu	2 $^{d[u]g}$*ma-ku-su* 'two bowls' T 98-131:3
niggallu	2 *ni-gal-la* 'two sickles' A 845:15
talmittu	2 ^{f}*tal-mi-da-tu* 'two pupils' MATC 70:57

6.2.2 Plural

§ 278 In MA substantives have morphologically singular and plural forms. Remnants of the dual can still be found, although the material is scarce. As mentioned by Hämeen-Anttila and Luukko, there are four different plural endings for MA/NA, of which three are restricted to masculine nouns.[12] This is an increase in respect of the situation in other dialects of Akkadian, where there are only two plural endings for normal nouns. Unlike the singular, the plural has only two case endings, in which the genitive and accusative cases merged into one oblique case ending for non-subject forms. The disappearance of the nominative case ending, as it occurred in NA (Luukko 2004, 136), is not attested for MA.

	Masculine		Feminine	
	Nominative	Oblique	Nominative	Oblique
-ū	*alaḫḫinn-ū*	*alaḫḫin-ē*	–	–
-ānu	*riks-ānu*	*riks-āni*	–	–
-uttu	*šēb-uttu*	*šēb-utte*	–	–
-ātu	*(ummiān-ātu)*	*(ummiān-āte)*	*riks-ātu*	*riks-āte*

Figure 21: Plural morphemes.

§ 279 The situation for the feminine plural has not changed and is marked by the ending -*āt*, which can easily be confused with the short ending *-at*. This problem is partly solved by plene spellings of the plural morpheme:

Nominative:

mugil(l)u	2 *mu-gi-la-a-tu* (type of container) MARV 4 13:8'
nāmurtu	*na-mu-ra-a-tu* 'presents' KAJ 203:7
qumāšu	4 *qu-ma-ša-a-tu* 'four capitals (of columns)' MARV 1 14:12
tuppu	*tup-pa-a-tu* 'tablets' KAJ 115:13'
utnānu	6 ^{giš}*ut-na-na-a-tu* 'six carriages' MATSH 10:14

Oblique:

adru	*ad-ra-a-te* 'threshing floor' Giricano 9:6
pāḫutu	*pa-ḫa-a-te* 'provinces' MARV 6 70:1
qimmutu	*qi-m[a]-a-te* 'capitals of (column)' MARV 1 14:14
qiltu	*qi-ša-a-te* 'wood' MARV 1 29:17
riksu	*ri-ik-sa-a-te* 'agreements' MAL A § 17:70
siqqurrutu	4 *si-qu-ra-a-te*^{meš} (uncertain meaning) MARV 1 33:7
šēḫtu	*še-ḫa-a-te*^{meš} 'incense burners' Coronation Ritual i 39
tuppu	*tup-pa-a-te* 'tablets' MATC 25B:17

MA is rather inconsistent regarding these plene spellings. The defective spellings for the feminine plural are just as frequent. Morphologically, the only factor that visibly distinguishes these forms from the singular is the lack of VA. Although, in most cases,

12 See SNAG, 77 § 3.9.1; Luukko (2004, 136–39 § 5.3).

these nouns are either plurale tantum or do not have the long feminine ending *-at* in singular numbers.

adru	*ad-ra-tu* 'threshing floors' KAJ 66:18
abātu	*a-ba-tu-šu* 'his words' MATSH 8:41'
maʾdu	*ma-da-te* 'many' OIP 79 2:5
nupāru	*nu-pa-ra-*⸢*te*⸣ 'working houses' MARV 10 51:7
pāḫutu	*pa-ḫa-te-ia* 'my provinces' MATSH 26:12†
šuršurrātu	*šur-šur-ra-te* 'chains' KAV 96:6
talmittu	2 ^{f}*tal-mi-da-tu* 'apprentices (f.)' MATC 70:57
tuppu	*tup-pa-tu* 'tablets' KAJ 110:13

The patterns *PvRvSt* change to *PvRSāt* in the plural in order to prevent two successive unstressed open syllables.

bitiqtum	*bi-it-qa-a-te* 'compensation' MAL A § 22:6
	bit-qa-te KAJ 274:16
damiqtu	*dam-qa-te-ka* 'your good (words)' Ištar Ritual:11
esertu	*és-ra-a-te* 'concubines' MAL A § 41:12
	[*é*]*s*$^{?}$-⸢*ra-a*⸣*-te*(?) TabT05a-134:7
	cf. sg. *e-se-er-tu-šu* MAL A § 41:1
kiṣirtu	*ki-iṣ-ra-te* 'envelopes' MATC 22:23
	cf. sg. *ki-ṣir-ta* MATC 83:15
napšātu	*nap-ša-a-te* 'life' MAL B § 2:16
	cf. sg. *na-pal-tu* 'life' KAJ 316:15

The plural ending *-āt* is also found with some masculine nouns, such as *ummiānu* 'creditor' and *ḫurādu* 'soldier'. How these plural forms agree with adjectives and verbs is not entirely clear. The first example (KAV 211) contains a feminine plural verb (*iṣabbatā*), whereas the second phrase (MARV 4 151) uses the masculine pronominal suffix *-šunu*. Meanwhile, the verbal forms suggest that we have to regard the plural as feminine in terms of gender. Both examples deal with the *ummiānu*, while the plural *ḫurādu* is only attested in a context without other nouns in agreement.

um-mi-a-na-tu (...) *lā iṣabbatāšunu* 'the creditors will not seize them' KAV 211 r. 5'–7'

$^{lú.meš}$*um-mi-a-na-a-tu* [*š*]*a* PN *ḫabbulaššununi* 'the creditors to whom PN was indebted' MARV 4 151:62–63

ḫu-ra-da-tu '*ḫ*.-soldiers' YBC 12862:6

One feminine noun *rīmuttu* has the irregular plural *rimuātu*. Although it has previously been analysed as an abstractum of *riāmu* 'to grant' (AHw, 987; CAD R, 364), this etymology is not without problems (Llop 2007, 115–16).

rīmuttu	*ri-mu-ut-te* 'gift' (sg.) MATSH 1:13; MARV 4 59:20
	ri-mu-a-tu 'gifts' (pl.) KAJ 192:20; KAJ 213:14
	[*ri*]*-mu-a-te* VAT 9410:45

§ 280 The masculine plural was traditionally *-ū* (nominative) and *-ī* (oblique) in Akkadian. The latter ending is likely to have changed to *-ē*. We have already discussed the use of extra plural markers on syllabically written substantives (§ 77). The cause for these markers is not entirely clear, although it may have been caused by the shortening of final vowels, which is a feature known from NA (SNAG, 78). This would cause confusion with the masculine plural forms, thus prompting their use with logographic plural markers. Analogous to the regular masculine plurals, plural markers were capable of extending to all plural substantives, especially if the concerned nouns were little known to the scribe. On the other hand, it could just as well have been started by the lack of plene spellings involving the long vowel, regardless of whether they were short or long in spoken language. As of yet, this cannot be claimed with certainty for MA.

Examples of *-ū*:

azamru	*a-za-am-ru*^meš^ 'fruit' MARV 5 42:4
erēnu	*e-re-nu*^meš^ 'cedar' MARV 1 23:1
ēṣidu	7 ^lú^*e-ṣi-du* 'reapers' KAJ 11:3
qermu	*qé-er-mu*^meš^ (type of cloak) MARV 10 18:3
šerku	*šer-ku*^meš^ (palace functionary) MAPD § 20:97
tuttubu	^túg^*tu-ut-tu-bu*^meš^ (woollen fabric) MARV 10 14:1

Examples of *-ē*:

alaḫḫinu	*a-láḫ-ḫi-ni*^meš^ 'bakers' A 1750 (NTA, 24):10
nakrumu	*na-ak-ri-me* (leather containers) KAJ 225:16[13]
ēṣidu	*e-ṣi-di* 'reapers' KAJ 11:17

The length and difference between /i/ and /e/ are not apparent in the examples above. In some cases, an extra vowel sign E gives decisive information. When Cv signs differentiate between /i/ and /e/, a Ce sign is usually found.

abu	*a-ba-e* 'fathers' KAJ 6:13
ikribu	[*i*]*k-ri-be-šu-nu* 'blessings' Coronation Ritual ii 37
kunukku	^na4^KIŠIB^meš^-*e* 'seals' KAV 99:35
maḫlušu	*a-na maḫ-li-še* ZABAR 'for chisels of bronze' KAJ 178:9
mullāʾu	*mul-la-e* (…) *lā nimaḫḫar* 'we will not accept the compensations' MATSH 2:59
mutu	*mu-te-ši-na* 'their husbands' MAPD § 3:23
uznu	*uz-NI-e-šu* 'his ears' MAPD § 5:36

However, note that the long final /ī/, in conjunction with *kī*, is almost always written as *ki-i*. Similar in this respect is *pî: pi-i* MAL A § 40:71 passim, but only rarely *pe-e* MAL A § 2:17.

§ 281 As we mentioned above, MA and NA developed a number of new plural constructions by taking the adjectival plural *-utt* and the archaic *-ān* for normal nouns (SNAG, 78f § 3.9.2; Luukko 2004, 136–39 § 5.3.). This change is probably caused by the following changes in MA/NA: the loss of mimation (§ 236ff); the possible shortening of long final vowels (cf. § 97); and the decay of case endings (§ 275). These three changes made the singular and plural of the masculine indistinguishable, leading to the innovation of new plural morphemes. In MA, the beginning of this development can be observed, but NA plural constructions only occur in a minority of substantives. The plural marker *-utt*,

---

13 This is likely to be a plural because of the many hides that are used to make (multiple?) containers: 21 *mašku*^meš^ (…) *ana nakreme ša šizbe* '21 hides are meant for leather containers (to hold) milk' KAJ 225:14–16.

which derives from the plural marker of adjectives and the abstractum marker, is found in different nominal patterns: adjectives (*šēbu* 'old'); participles (*nāšīu* 'carrier'); and various types of deverbal nouns (*ubru* 'foreigner'). Only once does a plural appear to have been derived from an abstractum (*aʾīluttu*). All attestations are used as plurals for personal entities. They are not collectives because they are inflected as plural nouns (as in OA; see GOA § 4.3.2).

aʾīlu	*a-i-lu-tu* 'people' MATSH 2:21
	a-i-lu-ut-te 'people' T 93-2:9
ḫubšu	*ḫu-ub-šu-te* 'foot soldiers(?)' MARV 3 53:13 (Postgate 2000, 214)
lissik (-)	^{d}*li-sí-ku-ti* (uncertain meaning) VAT 8923:2, 8.
nāšīu	*na-ši-ú-[te]* 'carriers' Coronation Ritual i 26
perru	$^{\text{érin.meš}}$*per-ru-te* MARV 2 17a+:34 (*perru*, see Freydank 1976, 115ff)
qēpu	*qé-pu-ú-te* 'officials' MAL B § 6:43
	qe-pu-tu^{meš} MAPD § 8:51
sarru	*sa-ru-tu izzuzzū* 'the criminals have divided it' KAV 168:9–10
ṣabbutu	*ṣa-bu-tu-tu* 'prisoners' MATSH 2:19
šēbu	*še-bu-tu ubta*$^{??}$*erūš* 'the witnesses have proven him' MAL A § 12:22
	še-bu-te-ka 'your witnesses' KAV 168:19
	cf. OA pl. *šībū*: *ší-bi* VS 26 2:4
šipru	DUMU *ši-ip-r⸢u-ut-te⸣* 'messengers' MATSH 9:25
ubru	*ub-ru-te* 'foreigners' CTMMA 1 99:4
usbu	*us-bu-tu* 'inhabitants' Billa 49:11
zīb/pu	5 UDU *zi-pu-te* 'five of (a type of) sheep' KAJ 230:8 (possibly an adjective)

The plural marker is a common feature in Akkadian for some Semitic nouns, such as *šarrānu* 'kings' and *alānu* 'cities'. Pace von Soden: this suffix did not originally refer to specific groups, in the same way that *ilu* > *ilānu* is no more specific than *ilū* (cf. GAG, 94 § 61j). Rather, it seems that this plural was originally limited to monosyllabic stems, slowly spreading to longer substantives (Streck 2005, 240f). While the suffix was rare in OA (GOA § 5.4.3.2), it had spread to a considerably larger group of nouns in MA and NA.

Nominative:

lidu[14]	*li-da-nu-[ša]* 'her children' KAJ 7:21
ṣuḫāru	2 TUR^{meš}-*nu* (*ṣuḫārānu*) 'two servants' K9-T3:12'; cf. OA: *ṣú-ḫa-re-e* 'servants' AKT 6 329:15
šarru	LUGAL^{meš}-*nu* 'kings' T 02-32:10
urdu	ÌR^{meš}-*nu-ú-<a>* (*urdānu*) 'my slaves' KBo 28 61/2:18', cf. OA *wa-ar-dí* 'slaves' BIN 4 200:5.

Oblique:

agru	*ag-ra-ni* 'hirelings' MATC 4:10; cf. OA: *ag-ri* 'hirelings' TCL 14 14:38
ālu	URU^{meš}-*ni* 'cities' KAJ 193:5
bētu	É^{meš}-*ni* (*bētāni*) 'houses' KAJ 223:10; cf. OA *bi-ta-tù-ni* 'our houses' CCT 5 1b:9. Both plural forms occur in NA.

14 I prefer to analyse this noun as having a singular (*lidu*) with the plural form *lidānu*. This goes against the CAD, which takes *līdānu* (sic) as the singular form (CAD L, 182). There does not seem to be any compelling reason to accept this interpretation, given that all attestations are plural. I, therefore, follow von Soden who takes all attestations of the (also singularly attested) noun *līdu* (AHw, 552a; cf. CAD L, 183a). Neither am I convinced by the negative translation of the CAD as 'bastard' or 'child of slave girl'.

ebūru	*e-bu-ra-ni* ‘harvests’ KAJ 80:8
ḫalzu	*ḫal-za-a-ni* ‘districts’ MARV 1 5:12
	ḫal-za-ni MARV 4 39:8; cf. OB: *ḫa-al-ṣú-ú-a* ‘my fortresses’ YOS 2 90:4.
ḫīṭu	*ḫi-ṭa-a-ni* ‘sins’ MAL A § 58:54
karmu	^{é}*kar-ma-ni* ‘granaries’ LVUH 90:2
lēʾu	13 *le-a-ni* ‘13 wooden tablets’ KAJ 109:4, cf. sg. *le-ʾi* KAJ 245:7
līdu	*li-da-ni-ša-ma* ‘her children’ MAL A § 36:14
	li-da-ni-[*ša*] ‘her children’ KAJ 7:28
	li-da-ni-ša ‘her children’ KAV 211:4; KAM 11 2:7
liqtānu	GAL *liq-ta-ni* ‘commander of the *liqtu*-people (=type of official)’ Coronation Ritual iii 9
natbāku	*na-at-ba-ka-ni-ka* ‘your pourings’ PKT 1 I right:20
pilku	*píl-ka-ni* ‘*pilku*-duty’ MATC 3:5; MARV 4 25:6
pūru	*pu-ra-a-ni* ‘lots’ MAL B 9:21
	3 *pu-ra-ni* ‘three lots’ KAJ 139:6’
riksu	*ri-ik-sa-ni* ‘knots’ KTN inventory i 3; cf. OA: *ri-ik-sí* ‘bundles’ CCT 6 22a:8
ṣirpu	*ṣir-pa-ni* ‘coloured wool’ KTN inventory iii 31’
šaduʾu	*ša-du-a-ni* ‘mountains’ Giricano 12:17’; cf. OA SÁ.TU-*e* ‘mountains’ kt 98/k 118:7
ṭēmu	*ṭé-ma-a-ni* ‘reports’ T 93-12:10; cf. NA *ṭè-ma-te* SAA 1 77 r. 12’ (both plural forms attested in Akkadian; see CAD Ṭ, 85a)
urdu	$^{\text{érin.meš}}$ÌR^{meš}-*ni* ‘slaves’ T 97-2:11; for OA plural *urdū*, see above.

A number of bi-radical substantives in Akkadian, usually referring to male family members, demonstrate an irregular plural with gemination (GAG, 93 § 61g: Luukko/Van Buylaere 2017, 326). This is also attested in MA, albeit only rarely.

abu	*ab-ba-ú-ia* ‘my forefathers’ EA 15:9 cf. *a-ba-e* KAJ 6:13
aḫu	^{d}UTU-*aḫ-ḫe*-KAM (=*aḫḫē* ‘brothers’) TR 3019:10 (see Aynard/Durand 1980, 45)

§ 282 There is a number of collective nouns in MA, which are morphologically always singular, even when counted.[15] Semantically, the collective indicates groups of beings taken as a whole, e.g., *ṣabʾu* for a troop of people or *ṣēnu* for cattle (=flock).

erbīu	*e-re-bi-ú lā e*⸢*k*⸣*ul* ‘the locust swarm did not eat it’ MATSH 3:7
nakru	*na*!*-ak*!*-* ⸢*ru*⸣ <<*ru*>> *ilteqešunu* ‘the enemy took them’ MPR 66:50
ṣabʾu	*aššum* ÈRIN^{meš}-*ma*! (...) *ša lā unammešanni* ‘concerning the soldiers who have not set out (towards you)’ MATSH 3:33–34
	[ER]ÍN^{meš} *na-ak-ru ša ina pî* GN [*i*]*ḫbutūni* ‘the hostile troops that plundered at the entrance of GN’ MATSH 7:17’’–18’’
ṣēnu	*ṣe-na* ‘flock’ Ali 2:9

We already mentioned the noun *ḫurādu* (type of soldier) having a feminine plural. At the same time, it is attested as a collective, with the congruence of a singular noun.

ḫurādu	*ḫu-ra-du* (…) *inassaḫa* ‘the soldiers marched here’ DeZ 2521:1–2
	ḫ[*u-r*]*a-*[*d*]*u ana kāri lā ikaššad* ‘the soldiers will not reach the quay’ MATSH 9:44
	78 *ḫu-rad* PN ‘78 troops of PN’ MARV 2 17a+:4

Given that collective nouns are plural in character, they are congruent as normal plurals. This is well attested with adjectives, especially the noun *ṣabʾu* (ÉRIN) ‘troops’, which often

15 Cf. GAG, 92 § 61b; Streck (2014a, 51–52 § 148).

takes plural adjectival forms. Note the difference between gender: whereas *ṣabʾu* is in congruence with the masculine gender, *ṣēnu* takes feminine adjectives and verbs.

ṣabʾu	ÉRIN^{meš} *nasḫutte* 'deported people' KAJ 121:6
	ÉRIN^{meš} *u emārē ḫalqutte* 'lost troops and donkeys' MATSH 2:55
	ÉRIN^{meš} *ma*⸢*?du*⸣*tte* 'many people' MATSH 10:25
	ÉRIN^{meš} *balṭutte* 'living soldiers' MATSH 18:32
	ÉRIN^{meš} *šalluttu* 'deported people' KAJ 180:11
	ÉRIN^{meš} *mētuttu* 'dead people' MARV 1 6:7
riqīu	ŠIM^{meš} *ballutte* 'mixed aromatics' Ištar Ritual:7–8
ṣēnu	*ṣe-na* (…) *šāludā {BA} baqnā* 'flock is made to give birth and plucked' LVUH 28:8–12
	ṣe-na sammuḫātu 'mixed flock' LVUH 29:9–10

The singular masculine morphology seems to conform to the OA material (cf. GOA § 5.4.1), e.g., 5: *ṣa-ba-am: a-ḫi-ú-tim* 'a group of five strangers' CCT 5 3a:30. Nonetheless, there is some material that points to a plural variant of these collective nouns; one letter from Tell Ḫuwīra has *ṣabʾu* inflected on one occasion as a masculine plural with the oblique ending *-ē*, rather than as the singular accusative *-a*. In this study, we always transcribe this type of noun as morphologically singular, unless phonologically indicated otherwise.

ṣab-e annūte liššī lēmur 'he should bring in(?) these troops and inspect (them)' MATC 11:28

lū qēma lū arša lū ⸢MUNU$_5$⸣ *muḫur* ÉRIN^{meš}-*i*[*a*] *ḫu-ra-di emda* 'receive the flour, groat and malt and impose it on my soldiers' T 97-10:9–12

Note also this unusual passage where *ṣabʾu* is seemingly used for a singular noun.

PN ÉRIN^{meš} *šarre* (…) *iššiʾanni* 'PN, the man of the king, brought it here' MARV 4 31:4–5

A similar category comprises the mass nouns that are plural in character, but singular in morphology. This is because their meaning does not allow for a singular form: for instance, an individual cannot have 'one' barley, but they can have multiple goats or litres of barley. Semantically, many of these nouns deal with natural materials. As can be seen in this example, Akkadian does not essentially differ from English in this respect. Mass nouns behave in congruence usually like a plural

kitāʾu	*ki-ta-e* 'flax' MATSH 3:5
ŠE-*um*	ŠE-*um*^{meš} *anniu* 'this barley' KAJ 91:12[16]
	ṣarpu u ŠE-*um rakis* 'the silver and barley is bound (legally)' KAJ 47:23–24

The scribes were aware of the plurality of the semantic aspects of collective and mass nouns. We often find plural markers on some of the more frequent nouns, such as ŠE-*um*. For other collective nouns, such as KÙ.BABBAR 'silver', a plural marker is rarer.

ṣabʾu	ÉRIN^{meš} 'troops' passim
ṣarpu	KÙ.BABBAR^{meš} 'silver' Giricano 12:21'
ṣēnu	*ṣe-ni*^{meš} 'flock' MARV 3 73:3
	ṣe-na^{meš} 'flock' Ali 3:6
ŠE-*um*	ŠE-*um*^{meš} 'barley' passim

16 Cf. *šamaššammū* 'sesame', which is usually spelled ŠE.Ì.GIŠ, but, when in congruence, behaves as a plural: ŠE.Ì.GIŠ^{meš} *la-be-ru-tu* 'old sesame' LVUH 83:2.

Conversely, we also find plural forms that cannot have a singular for the same reason as the collectives. These plurales tantums are relatively frequent.

dumāqū	*du-ma-qi* 'jewels' Adad Ritual:6'
ḫašlātu	*ḫa-áš-la-tu* 'bruised (grain)' KAJ 226:11
ḫimsātu	*ḫi-im-sa-a-te-šu-nu* (*ḫimsātu*) 'their wrongful possessions' KAV 217:11'
	ḫi-⌜im⌝-sa-⌜te⌝-e-ni 'our wrongful possessions' KAV 217:13'
kišpū	*kiš-pi* 'witchcraft' MAL A § 47:2[17]
šiʾamātu	*ši-a-ma-at* PN *abi abīšu* 'property of PN, his father's father' KAJ 149:6
šīmātu	*ši-ma-tu-šu* 'his purchase' KAJ 179:10
tamuātu	*ta-mu-a-ti* 'oath' Giricano 14:7

Some nouns, which are otherwise singular, occur as plurales tantums in MA. Most notable is *napšātu*. In OB, this form is *napištum*, while MA usually uses the plural, e.g., *nap-ša-a-te(-ma)* MAL A § 50:69, 73, 81; MAL B § 2:16, 17, 18: *nap-šá-a-te* MAL A § 52:9; *nap-ša-te* MARV 4 119:29; *nap-ša-a-*[*te*] MARV 10 3:45'; *nap-ša-te-šu* OIP 79 1:3'. The variant *napultu* is not used in the core MA corpus, but can be found in some literary texts. On one occasion, we find the variant *na-pal-tu* (*napaltu*) KAJ 316:15. However, the orthography also allows us to read *na-pùl-tu* (CAD N_1, 300). It is possible that there was a difference in function or meaning between *napšātu* and *napaltu*, although this remains unclear. The attestation of the latter suggests some kind of abstract meaning, or fixed expression: *mūtu napaltu* '(it is a case) of life and death' KAJ 316:14–15. On the other hand, *napšātu* is found here in an identical context in T 02-3:20 and Cohen/Llop 2017:12–13. Another noun that appears as a plurale tantum in MA is *ši-a-ra-a-te* 'morning' PKT 1 I right:18, usually *šiāru* (CAD $Š_2$, 370ff). In the case of *billu*, there seems to be free variation between the singular *billu* (CAD B, 228–29) and the plural *billātu* (CAD B, 225–28).

billātu:

1 *mana eria* x 7½ *šiqla ann*[*aka*] *paṣīa bi-la-te-šu ultēbil*[*a*] 'one mina of copper x 7½ shekels of white tin, its alloy he sent (to you)' KAV 205:16–17

bi-la-te liblu[*l*] 'he must mix the alloy' KAV 205:25

billu:

[*b*]*i-i-⌜la⌝ ana šiltaḫḫē lēpuš* 'I want to make the alloy into arrows' MATSH 16:18–19

bi-il-lu lū mād liblulū 'should there be much alloy, they must mix it' OIP 79 2:8–9[18]

6.3 Status constructus

§ 283 The second frequent state of nouns and adjectives is the status constructus, which deals with the so-called bound forms of nouns. With some special exceptions (see below), the status constructus is built by omitting normal case endings and, when necessary,

17 Probably a plurale tantum (CAD K, 454b), confirmed by the fact that the noun is used as a direct object (i.e., no *kišpa).

18 The original edition and CAD B (228b) translate *billu* as beer, but I see no compelling reason for this assumption.

replaces them with a bound vowel. The status constructus is found in the (synthetic) genitive construction. The simplest variant consists of two parts: a noun in the genitive, preceded by a governing noun in the status constructus. As such, the case endings of the genitive construction are fixed, no matter which syntactical position it takes in the sentence. The noun in the genitive specifies the noun in the status constructus. However, it is the status constructus that is the actual object. We also find it used to express possession of a noun, e.g., *bēt šarre* 'the house of the king'. Constructions with multiple governing nouns and governed nouns are attested:

ṭí-ri NA₄ É *a-lim* 'the stamp? of the stone of the house of the city' KAJ 12:3[19]

tup-pí 1 *šu-ši* IKU A.ŠÀ *u du-un-ni ad-ri* ^giš^KIRI₆ *u* PÚ ⸢*ū lū*⸣ *qa-qa-ar* URU 'a tablet of 60 *iku* of the field and *dunnu*, threshing floor, orchard and well or land of the city' KAJ 160:2–4

It should be noted that the sequence of nouns are similar in English. The genitive construction and, with it, the status constructus, are in the process of disappearing in MA and are relatively rarely attested. In its place, we find the particle *ša* between the governing noun and the genitive (see below). We cannot be absolutely certain whether this new construction lies behind logographic spellings, such as KIŠIB DUB.SAR 'seal of the scribe' KAJ 14:25=*kunukku ša tupšarre*. If this is correct, the status constructus has indeed become rare in MA. However, in prepositional expressions, such as *ina libbi* and *ina pî*, it can still be found (see Chapter 13 for similar expressions).

	Normal		Cluster	
	Before noun	Before suffix	Before noun	Before suffix
Nom. sg.	*bēt*	*bēt-*	*šipar*	*šipar-*
Gen. sg.	*bēt*	*bēti-*	*šipar*	*šiprī-*
Acc. sg.	*bēt*	*bēt-*	*šipar*	*šipar-*
Nom. pl.	*bētū*	*bētū-*	*šiprū*	*šiprū-*
Obl. pl	*bētē*	*bētē-*	*šiprē*	*šiprē-*

Figure 22: Status constructus.

§ 284 The construction of the bound form mostly does not differ from the other dialects. As such, we can follow the rules, which have been most extensively laid out by von Soden (GAG, 101–7 § 64–5) and Huehnergard (2005, 57–63 § 8.3). The basic principles are summarized in the following table, although there is a number of special circumstances and changes to the base of the bound form, which we will present in more detail below.

Only masculine plural nouns generally retain their case endings (GAG, 103 § 64l).

maḫlušu *a-na maḫ-li-še* ZABAR (a bronze scraper)? KAJ 178:9
sikkātu *a-na si-ka-te* ZABAR 'for pegs (pl.) of bronze' KAJ 178:8[20]

Feminine nouns, ending with the long ending *-at* or with the plural ending *-āt*, lose their vocalic endings (GAG, 101 § 64d, 104 § 64n). To this group, we may add nouns with the short ending *-t*, which is preceded by a vowel, for instance, because the root is weak.

abātu *a-bat* LUGAL 'words of the king' MATSH 1:4

19 Passim, but on one occasion: ²/₃ MA.NA KÙ.BABBAR *ṭi-ir-ru* NA₄ É *a-lim* KAJ 32:1–2.

20 Note that the noun *sikkatu* (unclear etymology) never seems to involve Assyrian VA, cf. *si-ka-te* KAJ 310:50 and CAD S, 247–51. We should therefore read either *sikkattu* or preferably *sikkātu*. A feminine plural is not possible as case endings drop in the status constructus.

dannutu	*dan-na-at* LUGAL 'royal holdings' MAL A § 45:82
šiʾamātu	*ši-a-ma-at a-bi-šu* 'property of his father' KAJ 153:6
šūkultu	⸢*šuk*⸣*-la-at* DINGIR 'feeding of the god' MARV 3 9:30
tēlītu	*te-li-it* BUR[U$_{14}$] 'the yield of the harvest' MPR 76:94

Forms ending in a consonant cluster with the feminine suffix *-t* cannot keep their consonant cluster according to the basic rules of Akkadian. There are two solutions. In most cases, the suffix lengthens to the long version *-at* (GAG, 102 § 64g):

bēltu	GAŠAN-*at šamāʾe* 'mistress of heaven' MARV 8 56:4'
biltu	⸢*bi*⸣*-la-at* A.ŠÀ 'yield of the field' MAL B § 19:15
damiqtu	⸢f⸣*Dam-qa-at-*^{d}*Taš-me-tu* KAJ 100:22
maḫirtu	*ina ma-ḫi-ra-at* 3 MA.NA$^{\text{ta.àm}}$ 'at the value of three minas each' A 320:20–21
pūḫtu	*pu-ḫa-at* GÉME *za-ku-e* 'responsible for clearing the slave woman' KAJ 100:20–21
tērubtu	*te-ru-bat* É 'entrance of the temple' MATC 80:1

Alternatively, a bound vowel /i/ is added. This vowel is never written plene, unlike OA (GKT, 107–8 § 63k):

ebertu	*e-be-er-ti Ši-iš-ša-ar* 'across the Šiššar' KAJ 177:2
eriltu	*i+na e-ri-il-ti li-be* 'according to (my?) wish' 93-11:34–35
kišittu	*ki-ši-it-ti* ^{uru}*Na-ḫur* 'spoil of Naḫur' MARV 1 14:24
pišertu	*pi-šèr-ti ka-ru-e* 'clearance of the grain heap' MARV 3 10:20'; LVUH 63:29 (passim LVUH)
rēḫtu	[*re*]*-eḫ-ti* DINGIR^{meš}*-ni* 'the remaining gods' New Year Ritual:12'
	re-eḫ-ti ŠÁM 'the rest of the price' KAJ 159:3
ṣimittu	3 *ṣi-mi-te* ^{anše}*ku-di-ni* 'three yokes of donkeys' MATC 25A:9
šīmtu	*ši-im-ti* É*-šu* 'the testament of his house' MARV 8 47:5

§ 285 Normal multiple-syllable nouns ending in a single consonant simply lose their case ending (GAG, 101 § 64c). This also applies for nouns with a weak root, of which the base ends with a glide or stop (e.g., *nāšiʾu* 'carrier'):

edānu	*e-da-an* Ì^{meš} 'term of oil' T 93-11:10
ēpišu	*e-piš ši-ip-ri* 'doer of work' MAPD § 5:36
nāšīu	*na-ši tup-pí-šu* 'the carrier of his tablet' KAJ 19:16
qaqquru	*qa-qar* URU 'terrain of the city' KAJ 149:15
sassuʾu	*ša sa-su na-gi-ri* 'of the proclamation of the herald' KAJ 310:20
tarbāṣu	*ina tar-ba-aṣ* ^{d}NIN-É.GA⸢L-*LIM*⸣ 'in the courtyard of *Bēlet-ēkallim*' MARV 1 28:16
tēlitu	*te-l*[*i*]*-it e-bu-ri* 'harvest produce' KAJ 262:3
	te-li-it BURU$_{14}$ LVUH 60:11
unūtu	*ú-nu-ut* É*-šu* 'equipment of his house' T 97-10:21

Forms with a one-syllable base ending in a single consonant form their status constructus in a similar way to nouns with a base of more than one syllable. Those ending in a single consonant lose their case ending, as can be seen in the table for *bētu* 'house'. These are often short nouns of the type PvS or PvP. Other examples include:

ḫūlu	*ḫu-ul* MAN 'expedition of the king' A 1051:5
īlu	*ina ūm il* KASKAL*-ni* 'on the day of the travel of the god' MAPD § 8:48
mazzizu	*ma-zi-iz pa-ni*^{meš} 'courtiers' MAPD § 20:97
mutu	*mu-ut* MUNUS 'husband of the woman' MAL A § 22:111
qātu	*qa-at* DAM*-at* 'the hand of the wife' MAL A § 3:40–41
rēšu	*re-eš ḫa-me-lu-ḫi* 'head of the *ḫawalḫu*' Coronation Ritual i 42

ri-iš ur-ḫi 'beginning of the month' TabT05a-134:19
tūru — *tu-ur* UD^{meš} *ikaṣṣuʾū* 'the days become cold again' MATSH 6:11'
ṭēmu — *ṭé-em na-ak-ri* 'news (concerning) the enemy' T 93-2:3

Sometimes, a bound vowel *-i* can be added to these one-syllable bases, but this is rare and I only know of examples that tend to come as a variation in the short form. The latter form, *pani*, is likely to be a plural (cf. § 465) and thus transcribed as *panē* in this study:

aḫu — *a-ḫi* GN 'at the bank of GN' MARV 1 20:14
līmu — *ša li-me* PN_1 *u li-im* PN_2 'of the eponymate of PN_1 and the eponymate of PN_2' KAM 11 40:1–4
pan(ē) — *ana pa-an Aš-šur* Coronation Ritual i 23
šarru pa-ni DINGIR^{meš}*-ni iṣabbat* 'the king will take (his place) before the gods' New Year Ritual:10'

Perhaps we should add *lēʾu* 'wooden tablet' if we observe that spellings such as *le-ḫi* reflect the original /ḥ/ (see § 199).

lēʾu — *ša pi-i le-ḫi ša* É.GAL*-lim* 'according to the wording of the wooden tablet of the palace' MARV 3 5:36
ša ki le-ḫi ša PN 'according to the wording of the wooden tablet of PN' MAH 1608 ii 5'

Note *kalû* sometimes takes a bound vowel *-a* (see § 492):

kalû — *ka-la* u_4*-mi-šu* 'all day' PKT 1 I right:6
ina kal u_4*-me* 'during the entire day' MAPD § 6:41

In the case where a noun ends in a consonant cluster, there are three solutions to build a construct form. Similar to the one-syllable bases, it is possible to add an additional bound vowel /i/. This is true for nouns with a one-syllable base.

libbu — *ana lìb-bi* ^{giš}*tup-ni-na-te* 'inside the boxes' KAV 98:4
rittu — *ri-it-ti a-i-lu-ut-te* 'the hand of a human' KTN inventory iv 23'
šiddu — *iltu ši-id-di* ÍD 'from along the river' MATSH 2:6–7[21]

In the case of the noun *pittu* 'responsibility', forms with and without the bound vowel *-i-* are attested in a similar fashion as *pan(ē)*. One case (*PI-et ḫa-*[*š*]*i-me* KAJ 101:5) was discussed by Harrak (1989), who suggested that they be read as *bēt(i)* of the *bēt ḫašīme* structure (§ 204). Other examples of the short construct form *pit* are very limited.

pittu — *ina pi-it* ^{giš}GU.ZA Coronation Ritual ii 47†
ša pit PN 'of the responsibility of PN' KAJ 219:5
ša pi-it-ti PN 'of the responsibility of PN' KAJ 230:9-10; MARV 3 59:4–5
ša ilt[*e*] *pi-it-ti* PN 'which is within the responsibility of PN' KAJ 238:5–7; MATC 11:14–25

If a noun with more than one syllable ends in geminated consonant, it is possible for the consonant cluster to be degeminated:

isinnu — *ina i-si-ni a-li* 'during the festival of the city' MAL A § 55:19
kutallu — *ina ku-tal* É.GAL*-lim* 'at the rear of the palace' MARV 4 35:10
pirikku — *pi-ri-ik* KÁ.G[A]L New Year Ritual:25'

21 For the idiomatic expression (*ina*) *šiddi* 'alongside' in NA, see Luukko 1997, 32.

§ 286 Common noun patterns of the type *PvRS* have a base ending in a cluster consisting of two different consonants, with an extra vowel inserted in between them (GAG, 102 § 64f). This vowel generally corresponds with the preceding vowel:

ašlu	*a-šal* LUGAL 'the rope of the king' KAJ 153:17
meḫru	*me-ḫi-ir tup-pi* 'copy of the tablet' MARV 5 12:13
miqtu	*mi-qí-it pe-e* 'offensive speech' MAL A § 2:17
muḫru	*mu-ḫur ni-qi-*[*e*] 'the offering(?) of the sacrifice' MATC 17:7
qablu	*qa-bal* É 'middle of the house' VAT 8923:1
ṣalmu	*ṣa-lam* LUGAL 'statue of the king' KAJ 273:6
šaplu	[*š*]*a-pal* ÚTUL 'bottom of the cauldron' PKT 2 i 16

If the *PvRS* is an adjective, the vowel /i/ of the original *PaRiS* pattern resurfaces:

šaknu	*ša-kín* KUR 'governor of the country' MARV 3 31:7
	šá-kin É 'governor of the house' A 3196 (NTA, 39):28

A feature of Assyrian is a secondary /a/ in *PiRS* and *PuRS* constructions.[22] We could assume another instance of a *Murmelvokal* (§ 131). Already in the OA period, this construction was anything but obligatory, while, for the MA period, we usually find the preceding vowel used (see examples above). Given the scarcity of attestations, we will quote some examples with attached pronominal suffixes, which will be otherwise discussed in § 287ff. Matouš/Petráček pointed out the occurrence of *šipru* > *šipar*, which is attested in all MA subgenres and the most common form.

šipru	*ši-pár* LUGAL 'labour of the king' MAL A § 21:104; MAL B § 9:28
	ši-pár ^{giš}GIGIR 'assignment of the chariot' KAJ 223:2
	ši-pár ša-kúl-te 'assignment of a meal' LB 1848:13
	ší-pár-ka 'your task' MATC 4:17; T 02-32:35
	ši-pár pi-ir-ki MARV 8 21:16
	a-na ši-pár tal-pe-te 'for the smearing work' ADD 1 713:3'

Three further unusual attestations can be given. The case of *meḫru* is actually a status absolutus; yet, as this form is morphologically identical in the status constructus, it is also relevant here. The second form from *milku* derives from an incantation in mixed language. The form from *riksu* can only be accepted if we assume that it has an added pronominal suffix -*ša*.

meḫru	1 TUR *mi-ḫa-ar lā iddina* 'he will not give one equal boy' Giricano 4:29–30
milku	*mi-lak-šu-nu* 'their minds' Rm 376 r. 5
riksu	*ri-ka-sa lā rakis* 'her marriage contract is not bound' MAL A § 34:72

Another possibility is *mišlu* > *mišal* 'half', but this depends on how the sign of the final syllable is read, that is, either as <šal> (SAL) or as <šil> (TAR) (see MATSH, 95 n6–7). Note also OA *mì-ša-al* TCL 19 69:15.

mišlu	*mi-šal/šil-šu-nu-*(*ma*) MATSH 2:8 (2x)

For the pattern *PuRS*, a few bound forms of *PuRaS* are known:

ḫubtu	*ḫu-ba-su-nu* 'their spoils' MATSH 7:18''
	ḫu-bat ṣe-ri 'the spoils of the countryside' MATSH 8:55'
ṣupru	*ṣu-pár-šu* 'his fingernail' Giricano 2:1

22 For OA, see Matouš/Petráček (1956); GKT, 105f § 63h; GOA § 5.5.1.4.2-3; GAG, 102 § 64f; Reiner (2001, 389–90). For NA, see Luukko (2004, 140 § 5.4).

ṣu-pa-ar-šu 'his fingernail' MARV 8 70:17

Moreover, in royal inscriptions, we find *kubru*: > *kubar*:

kubru	*ku-bar-šu* 'its thickness' RIMA 1 A.0.76.10:38 (Adn)

It seems likely that the bound vowel /a/ was actually disappearing from Assyrian. Hämeen-Anttila quotes the bound form *ṣu-pur* 'fingernail' SAA 1 51:5 (SNAG, 81) contra MA *ṣu-pár-šu* 'his fingernail' (*ṣupru*) Giricano 2:1, while stating that /a/ is only regularly retained in bound forms with suffixes (see below). However, from NA administrative documents, note also *ṣu-pár-šú-nu* 'their fingernail' SAA 6 100:2. Hämeen-Anttila gives two examples of *PiRaS* in the status constructus, of which *bilat* 'talent' must be rejected because it is likely to have derived from the root *ubālu* (AHw, 126a) and thus it is not a *PiRaS* form. This leaves us with only one other available form in NA: *i-lak* 'service' SAA 1 183:12'.

6.3.1 Bound forms with pronominal suffixes

§ 287 The status constructus is used as the base when pronominal suffixes are attached, indicating possession, e.g., *bēt-ka* 'your house'. Despite the fact that the base of the status constructus, with and without suffixes, remains identical, there are some differences in the vocalic endings of the construct nouns. These vocalic endings can, in addition to indicating the unsuffixed status constructus, indicate case endings. The different rules for these vocalic endings will be discussed below.

§ 288 Masculine plural forms are normally declined in the nominative and oblique cases. This also applies to the few dual forms, which are attested. To date, no feminine plural nouns have been found whose construct certainly involves a nominative case ending. However, we may expect that the nominative ending *-u* was lengthened, e.g., *tuppātuka* 'your tablets' (GAG, 107 § 65k). The masculine plural endings *-utt* and *-ān* probably behaved similarly to the feminine plural nouns (GAG, 107 § 65k).

Examples for the dual:

ēnu	*e-na-šu* 'his two eyes' KAJ 179:14
uznu	*uz-ni-ša unakkas* 'he will cut of her ears' MAL A § 5:65
	ap-pu-šu uz-né-e-šu inakkisū 'they will cut off her nose and her ears' MAPD § 5:36

Examples for the masculine plural:

abu	*ab-ba-ú-ia* 'my fathers' EA 15:9
igru	*ig-ri-šu-⸢nu limḫu⸣ rū* 'they shall receive their loans' MATSH 3:37
qēpu	lú*qe-pu-tu-ia* 'my representatives' KAV 98:7

Feminine plural:

damiqtu	*dam-qa-te-ka* (…) *liqbi* 'may he speak your good (words)' Ištar Ritual:11
šīmātu	*ši-ma-tu-šu* 'his purchase' KAJ 179:10
tuppu	*tup-pa-te-šu-nu* 'their tablets' MAL B § 6:16
	tup-pa-te-ia 'my tablets' KAV 217:7'

§ 289 The situation is more complicated for the singular nouns, where a differentiation exists between the case endings. Nouns that function as subject or direct object (nominative and accusative in status rectus) involve the basic form and have the pronominal suffix directly attached to the base when ending with a closed syllable ending in a consonant (GAG, 104–105 § 65b). If the final consonant is a dental or sibilant and the suffix starts with /š/, both phonemes often merge into double /ss/ (see § 224). The nasal /n/ can be assimilated into the suffix, but is often retained (see § 228).

bātiqānu	*ba-ti-qa-an-šu* ‘his informer’ MAL A § 40:82
mutu	*ša mu-us-sa balṭūni* ‘whose husband is alive’ MAL A § 3:33
nāʾikānu	*na-i-ka-an-ša* ‘her fornicator’ MAL A § 55:36
	ana na-i-ka-ni-ša MAL A § 55:36
pāḫutu	[*pa-ḫ*]*a-su* ‘his office’ Coronation Ritual iii 13
pūru	*pur-šu* ‘his lot’ MAL B § 1:14
šulmānu	*šul-*[*m*]*a-šu* ‘his *šulmānu*-gift’ (*šulmān-šu*) T 97-2:16
šumu	*šúm-šu* ‘his name’ MARV 4 151:19

Note that, when a base ends in *-ī*, the final vowel is retained without regard to the case:

bāšīu	*bēssu u ba-ši-šu* ‘his house and his property’ KAM 10 18:16
panīu	*pa-ni-šu gabba inaqqurū* ‘they will scarify his entire face’ MAL A § 15:55

If a noun ends in a consonant cluster of two different phonemes, an extra vowel is inserted with the colour of the preceding vowel similar to the normal status construct. This often includes nouns with the short feminine ending *-t* directly attached to the root (GAG, 105 § 65e), e.g.:

adru	*a-da-ar-šu* ‘his threshing floor’ Jankowska 1962 r. 1
	ad-ar-šu ‘his threshing floor’ MARV 1 36:7’
arnu	*a-ra-an-ša* ‘her offense’ MAL A § 2:20
aššutu	DAM-*su* ‘his wife’ VAT 9034:14
puḫru	*pu-ḫu-ur-šu-nu* ‘their assembly’ MATSH 2:47
ṣupru	*ṣu-pár-šu* ‘his fingernail’ Giricano 2:1
šaptu	[*ša*]*-pa-as-su* ‘his lip’ MAL A § 9:94
šik/qtu	*ši-qat-ka* ‘your slag’ PKT 3 i 6

§ 290 In a few types of nouns, a bound vowel /a/ is placed between the base and suffix when the noun would otherwise occur in the nominative/accusative.[23] This bound vowel is often changed to /u/ as a result of Assyrian VA. A few exceptions without VA do occur and are mentioned in § 146. Nouns receiving the bound vowel /a/ can be divided into a few categories. The first group are nouns, which have a bound vowel /i/ in the status constructus without pronominal suffixes. Many are one-syllable nouns ending in a geminated consonant (GAG, 105 §f).

appu	*ap-pa-ša inakkis* ‘he will cut off her nose’ MAL A § 5:69
	ap-pu-šu uz-né-e-šu inakkisū ‘they will cut off her nose and her ears’ MAPD § 5:36
gabbu	*gab-bu-šu* KAV 109:16
rittu	*mamma ri-tu-šu lā umalli* ‘nobody filled his hand’ MATSH 4:17’
tuppu	*tup-pa-ša* (…) *išaṭṭurū* ‘they will write her tablet’ MAL A § 45:71
	tup-pa-ka šuṭar ‘write your tablet’ KAV 104:16
	tup-pu-šu ṣabtā ‘seize his tablet’ KAV 102:17–18
zittu	*zi-te-ki-na* (< *zittakina*) ‘your (2fp) share’ KAV 194:21

23 One may draw parallels between the /a/ and the status constructus in Ge‘ez (see Lipiński 2001, 263 § 32.5).

zi-tu-šu 'his share' KAJ 178:9

The second group of nouns ends in a consonant cluster with the feminine marker *-t*, although not all forms receive a bound vowel (GAG, 105–106 § 65f).

lubultu	*lu-bu-ul-ta-ša ṣābitāšša ilaqqe* 'her arrester will take her clothing' MAL A § 40:73–74
mazzaltu	*ma-za-al-ta-šu-nu uššurū* 'they will relinquish their post' Coronation Ritual iii 11
nubattu	*nu-bat-tu-šu-nu* 'their night' MATC 41:7'
piriltu	*pi-ri-il-ta-ša lā tattaṣarma* 'you have not guarded her secret' Ištar Ritual r. 7'
sinniltu	MUNUS-*šu* (=*sinniltušu*) (…) *tamaggar* 'his wife agrees' Giricano 8:19–21
šapārtu	*šá-pár-tu-šu i*[*šakkan*] 'he will place his pledge' T 04-37:25

There are also feminine participle patterns:

multēṣittu	*mul-te-ṣi-tu-šu-nu* 'their expenses' KAJ 307:14

There are a few attestations of nouns with bound vowels, which are not expected to have them, according to the rules laid out here.

ḫīṭu	*ḫi-ṭa-šu* 'his punishment' MAL A § 16:66 (perhaps *ḫiṭaʾšu*; see § 168)
šulmānu	*šul-ma-nu-šu-nu maḫir* (i/o *šulmānšunu*) 'he received their *šulmānu*-gift' KAJ 91:20

§ 291 All singular bound forms with pronominal suffixes receive a bound vowel /i/ when in the genitive. We already saw some plene spellings of this vowel, as it is likely that it was lengthened (GAG, 104 § 65a). It must be emphasized that MA has a slight, but clear, tendency to use <I> signs, rather than <E> signs.[24] Some spellings seem to be fixed, such as the preposition *il-te-šu*, but never **il-ti-šu*. It is not entirely clear what this tendency reflects. We have claimed that the change /i/ > /e/ was connected to mimation and the loss of it (see § 240). Assuming that it is correct, the bound vowel /i/ was not affected by mimation and can thus be expected to have retained its original value. The fixed spellings make the situation more complicated; for instance, *libbu* is usually written with BI, including in genitive constructions (e.g., MATSH 1:6). At the same time, *lìb-be* is also attested, e.g., *lìb-be-ši-na* KAJ 277:6; *lìb-be-ku-nu* MATSH 9:31. Consider the following spellings:

E signs:

maddattu	*ma-da-te-šu* 'his payments' KAJ 307:6
mazzaltu	*ina ma-za-al-te-šú* 'at his position' Coronation Ritual iii 14
mutu	*mu-te-ki* 'your husband' T 93-17:4
ṣibtu	*ṣi-*[*i*]*b-te-šu* 'its interest' MARV 1 8:2
šanûttu	*ša-nu-te-šu* 'a second time' A 1828 (NTA, 25):10
šēbu	*še-bu-te-ka* 'your witnesses' MARV 1 1:9
šillutu	*ana ši-il-li-te-š*[*a*] 'her impudence' MAPD § 18:89
tamlītu	*adi tam-li-*[*t*]*e-ša* 'her inlay' Coronation Ritual i 35
tuppu	*tup-pa-te-šu* 'his tablets' KAJ 119:1
urkittu	*ur-ki-te-*⸢*šu*⸣ 'after him' MATSH 4:7

24 In order to reinforce this tendency, here are a few statistics based on the texts in KAJ: 4x sequence *-te-šu/a* against 25+x *-ti-šu/a*; 1x *-be-ši* ~ 15x *-bi-šu/a*. Admittedly, the differences are less pronounced, while, in some texts, more E signs can be found, e.g., MAPD 6x *-te-šu/a* ~ 4x *-ti-šu/a*. Nevertheless, the tendency is clear.

I signs:

abu	*a-bi-š*[*u*] 'his father' KAV 156:1
aššutu	DAM-*ti-šu* 'his wife' MAL A § 56:44
aššuttu	*aš-šu-ut-ti-šu* 'his wife (being)' KAJ 7:9
bētu	*iltu* É-*ti-ša* 'from her house' MAL A § 13:25
	É-*ti-šu* 'his house' KAJ 145:7
dabābu	*da-ba-bi-ka* KAV 168:17
gināʾu	*gi-na-i-šu-nu* 'their regular offerings' MARV 7 86:13
libbu	*lìb-bi-šu-nu* 'their midst' A 1737 (NTA, 19):7
marʾuttu	[*m*]*a-ru-ut-ti-šu* 'his adoption' KAJ 4:7
mātu	KUR-*ti-šu* 'his land' MATC 23A:16
meḫertu	*me-ḫi-ir-ti-ša* 'her rank' MAPD § 21:104
migru	*mi-ig-ra-ti-ša* 'her own will' KAJ 3:2
qātu	*ina qa-ti-šu-nu* 'from their hands' MAL A § 47:3
	qa-ti-šu MAL A § 29:10; KAJ 179:22
ṣāltu	*ina ṣa-al-ti-ši-na* 'their (f.) quarrel' MAPD § 10:57
šēbu	*še-bu-ti-ka* 'your witnesses' KAV 202:19
ṣibtu	MÁŠ-*ti-šu* 'its interest' KAJ 25:16
tappāʾu	*ša tap-pa-i-šu* 'his comrade' MAL B § 8:12
tuppu	*tup-pa-ti-šu* 'his tablets' KAJ 26:1
zittu	ḪA.LA-*ti-šu* 'his share' KAJ 155:5

Many signs do not have a specific i/e value. A few examples should suffice:

dēnu	*de-ni-ka* 'your case' MARV 1 13:14
muḫḫu	*ana muḫ-ḫi-ša* 'to her' MAPD § 21:108

In the case of an otherwise degeminated final consonant, gemination is retained when a bound vowel is added:

kutallu	*ina* ⸢*ku-tal*⸣-*li-šu* 'on his back' MAL A § 40:103

A special group of construct forms includes a small group of primary nouns built on a monosyllabic basis, which refer to family members (e.g., father, mother, aunt). They are fully declined in all three cases when pronominal suffixes are added. Despite this group of nouns having an irregular status constructus, an archaic regular form is still attested in the month name *Ab šarrāni* (CAD A_1, 2a); otherwise:

abu	*aʾīlu lā a-bu-ša lā aḫuša* 'a man; not her father, not her brother' MAL A § 22:105-106
	a-bu-ša išaʾʾal 'he will ask her father' MAL A § 48:35
	a-bu-ša mēt 'her father died' MAL A § 48:38
	ana bēt a-bi-i-ša 'for the house of her father' MAL A § 55:13
aḫu	*aʾīlu lā abuša lā a-ḫu-ša* 'a man; not her father, not her brother' MAL A § 22:105-106
	a-ḫi-šu 'his brother' MAL D § 2:5
emu	*e-mu-ú-ša* 'her father-in-law' MAL A § 29:14
	e-mu-ša u marāša laššu 'her father-in-law and son are not available' MAL A § 45:48

§ 292 As for the orthography of the construct with pronominal suffixes, the vast majority spell the bound vowels /i/ defectively. However, in MAL A-B, plene spellings are found. A relatively large portion consists of the family members mentioned above, including an example of the nominative case. It is likely that these plene spellings refer to the lengthening of the bound vowel /i/ and all cases for family members (cf. OA in GOA § 5.5.1.8.1). Additionally, we discussed the possibility that spellings in MAL A–B indicate stress (see § 107ff). In any case, this type of spelling is also attested for NA (Deller/Parpola 1966).

abu	*a-bi-i-ša* 'her father' MAL A § 55:13
	a-bi-i-šu-ma 'his father' KAJ 6:5
emu	*e-mu-ú-ša* 'her father-in-law' MAL A § 29:14
ḫimsātu	*ḫi-*⌜*im*⌝*-sa-*⌜*te*⌝*-e-ni* 'our wrongful possessions' KAV 217:13'
ilku	*il-ki-i-šu* 'his *ilku*-service' Giricano 4:26
libbu	*li-ib-bi-i-šu* 'his desire' MAL B § 3:26
qaqquru	*qa-qí-ri-i-šu* 'his territory' MAL B § 13:19; § 14:26; 15:34
šākulu	*a-na ša-ku-li-i-ša* 'for her care' MAL A § 46:104

6.4 Status absolutus

§ 293 In a few MA instances, a number of substantives and nominal verbal forms does not take case endings. These forms are used for the few cases of the syllabically written cardinal numbers (§ 333ff). The function of the status absolutus is often not easy to define. Von Soden recognizes a category for "*bestimmte Preis- und Massangaben*" for MA/NA and lists the examples with *šim gamer* 'complete price' and *ana mitḫār* 'equal' (GAG, 97 § 62f). However, the first example is known from OB (CAD G, 37) and thus seems to be part of the OB influence on MA scribal traditions. Likewise, *mitḫār* already occurs in OB and, relatively frequently, in the status absolutus (CAD M_2, 135b). As von Soden only provides these two examples, his motivations for claiming that this category is something typical for M/NA remain puzzling. In any case, they seem to be learned Babylonian forms and have little to do with the Assyrian dialect. A list of attestations is given below:

meḫru	1 TUR *mi-ḫa-ar lā iddina* 'he will not give one equal boy' Giricano 4:29-30
muttaḫṣu	*kī* UR.SAG *mu-ut-taḫ-iṣ* 'like a fighting warrior' Lambert 1969:40
panīu	*pa-a-ni ša* 6 ITI.UD^{meš} *maḫrū* 'earlier (rations) of six months are received' MPR 66:43–44
rākibu	*ra*$^{?}$*-ki-ib šaliṭ* 'the rider is in authority' T 97-22:12–13 (uncertain)
utru[25]	4 *sūtu* ŠE *ú-tar ša* ŠU PN 'four seahs of extra barley is from the hand of PN' LVUH 68:8
	9 *sūtu* ŠE *ú-ta-ar* 'nine seahs of barley is extra' LVUH 63:14
	6 *sūtu ú-tar* PN 'six seahs extra from PN' LVUH 81:5

A significant number of attestations follows the preposition *ana*:

balluṭu/laqā'u	*a*[*na*] *ba-lu-uṭ u le-qé* 'to be provided for and to be adopted' KAJ 167:4
dēnu/dayyānu	*ana de-en da-a-an* 'for the judgement by the judge' KAV 159:7
mitḫāru	*ana mi-it-ḫa-ar uta*$^{??}$*ar* 'he will return it for an equal share' MAL A § 43:35
šīmu gamru	*ana ši-im ga-me-er* 'for the complete price' KAJ 147:10; KAJ 149:7
urḫu	<*ana*> 1 ITI-*aḫ qaqqad anneke išaqqal* 'after one month, he will pay the capital of lead' KAJ 19:6–7, cf. *ana n* ITI-*ḫi qaqqad* x *išaqqal* passim

25 Examples are not to be confused with a nominal stative. In this regard, note the attestation of the plural form *utruttu* (MPR 46:16).

I know of only one example in which the status absolutus form follows *ina*:

tuāru *ina tu-a*[*r*] *iltēn ra-di iddan* 'upon returning, he shall give one r.' TR 2021+:10–12

§ 294 The status absolutus is sometimes used for adverbial expressions of a local and temporal character (GAG, 97 § 62h). Most attestations are from *ūmu* 'day', but also derived forms, such as *ummākal*, can be found. These are discussed in § 492.

ūmu *u*4*-um* 1 *marsattu* 'daily, one soaking vessel' KAJ 182:7

Adverbial expressions remain rare in MA in the status absolutus (cf. GAG, 97 § 62i):

maʾdu *e-ṣú ù ma-du* 'as much as it is' KAJ 149:3

ana 2*-šu ma-a-ad ina ḫ̮ūle* [*tukaššad tapaṭṭar*] 'a second time more you will make a journey and release (them)' BVW F r. 1–2

Chapter 7: Syntax of Nouns

§ 295 In the chapter of the status rectus, we already mentioned the three case endings, which nouns can take. In the following chapter, we will list and discuss the function of the three cases. A noun's syntactical case is not always clear, not only when written logographically, but also when in the plural, when we can only distinguish a nominative vs. oblique case (genitive/accusative). Likewise, in bound forms with suffixes, there is only a morphological distinction between the genitive and the nominative/accusative case.

7.1 Nominative

§ 296 The nominative in MA has three basic functions. Its first and basic function is its use as the subject of a clause, when the subject occurs in the status rectus. The nominative is also used for the predicative of the nominal clause, e.g., *sinniltu annītu* *<u>šul-ma-nu</u>* 'this woman is a gift' KAJ 98:4. In many administrative documents, the object of the verb is placed in front of a long legal formula and occurs in the nominative. This feature is known as the casus pendens (§ 673f), e.g., 10 *e-ṣi-du iltu* PN_1 PN_2 *ilqe* '10 reapers PN_2 took from PN_1' KAJ 29:3–6. Unexpected cases of a nominative sometimes occur and are either explained as an archaic locative adverbial ending (§ 483) or due to the decay of case endings. In lists, where the syntactical context is absent, forms are sometimes cited in the status absolutus (e.g., *šēbat* 'old woman'), but more frequently in the nominative. Consider these designations following different PNs in a list of people: *pír-su* 'weaned (child)' 2:8 (et passim); *ta-ri-ú* 'young child' MARV 2 6 vi 8 (et passim); *ta-ri-tu* 'young child (f.)' MARV 3 80:14' (et passim); *pa-ḫa-ru* 'potter' MARV 3 80:11'. We should also mention the date formula of texts, where (in the absence of prepositions), the month names occur in the nominative as does the noun *līmu* 'eponym', with the PN following in apposition.

7.2 Genitive

§ 297 The genitive is used as the case ending for all nouns following a preposition, regardless of that noun's function as object. In this respect, the genitive is rather different from the other two case endings. With the preposition *ana*, it often becomes an indirect object, but this is due to the preposition and not because the noun takes the function of the indirect object. We already discussed how the genitive is used as a case ending for the governing noun in the synthetic genitive construction (see § 283ff). Note that the genitive does not always directly follow the status constructus, as can be observed in the following clause where the governing and governed nouns are separated by negation *lā*:

> *ina libbi* GIŠ.GÀR *la-a maḫ-ri* 'from the unreceived assignment' KAV 98:42

§ 298 The status constructus was in the process of being replaced in the Assyrian dialect. In its place, we find the multifunctional particle *ša* (here called a genitive marker) used in order to express genitive relations.[1] This construction can be referred to as an analytic genitive construction, as opposed to the synthetic genitive construction with status constructus. It is also found in the literature as the periphrastic genitive (SNAG, 80) or unbound genitive construction (Haber 2013). We already find this type of construction in the OA period (GKT, 202ff, § 121; GOA § 6.3.4) and it was prominent in the NA corpus (SNAG, 80 § 3.9.5). There is a general tendency to replace the synthetic constructions with analytic ones in Semitic languages.[2] The decay and eventual loss of case endings may have added to this development, since the status constructus is basically formed by removing the case ending, making the status constructus and status rectus indistinguishable. In any case, the MA evidence is abundant. Here is a selection:

abu	*a-bu ša* DUMU.MUNUS 'the father of the daughter' MAL A § 43:33
agāʾu	*a-ga-a ša Aš-šur* 'the crown of Aššur' Coronation Ritual ii 15
appu	*ap-pa ša* DAM-*šu* 'the nose of his wife' MAL A § 15:53
aššutu	DAM^{meš}-*te ša* É.GAL-*lim* 'women of the palace' MAPD § 2:15
azaʾīlu	34 *a-<za>-i-lu ša* IN.NU '34 bales of straw' KAJ 122:3
emu	É *e-me ša* DUMU-*šu* 'the house of the father-in-law of his son' MAL A § 30:20
gimru	*gi-im-ru ša* ^{giš}GIGIR 'the expenses of the chariot' KAJ 122:16
ḫīṭu	*ḫi-i-ṭu ša* LÚ 'sin of the man' MAL A § 16:60
lišānu	*li-ša-na* ⸢*ša*⸣ AN.BAR 'tongue of iron' MATSH 16:9
lubultu	*lu-bu-ul-te ša* PN 'the clothing of PN' KAV 98:16
malqētu	*ma-al-qe-tu ša* ^{lú}SANGA 'revenue of the priest' Coronation Ritual i 37
maṣṣartu	*a-na* ⸢*ma*⸣*-ṣar-te ša* URU 'for the guard of the city' MATSH 22:5
pāḫutu	*pa-ḫe-te ša* EN-*ni* 'the district of our lord' MARV 1 71:7
pūru	*pu-ri ša* PN 'lot of PN' AO 19.228:10
riksu	*ri-ik-si ša* MAN 'decree of the king' MAPD § 2:19
	ri-ik-si ša LUGAL 'edict of the king' TR 3004:13'–14'
ṣabʾu	ÉRIN^{meš} *ša* É.GAL-*lim* 'personnel of the palace' MAPD § 2:20
	ÉRIN^{meš} *ša ma-ṣar-te* MARV 4 60:19
šēpu	GÌR^{meš} *ša* MAN 'the feet of the king' Coronation Ritual iii 3
šīpātu	SÍG^{meš} *ša* É.GAL-*lim* 'wool of the palace' Ali 24T:10
tuppu	*tup-pa ša* ^{lú}DI.KU$_5$^{meš} 'tablet of the judges' MAL B § 17:14

As can be seen in the following examples, the governed noun in the analytic genitive construction always occurs in the genitive:

kunukku	^{na4}KIŠIB^{meš} *ša ki-iṣ-ra-te* 'the seals of the *k*.-documents' MATC 23A:20
marīnu	1 *ma-ri-nu ša ta-kil-te* 'one *m*.-cloth of blue-purple' A 305:1
muppišānu	*mu-up-pi-ša-na ša kiš-pi* 'the committer of witchcraft' MAL A § 47:6
naruqqu	1 *na-ru-qu ša sa-me-di* 'one sack with *s*.-spices/vegetables' KAJ 277:8
piqittu	*pi-qi-te ša ub-ri* 'maintenance of the foreigner' MATC 54:2
qātu	[*q*]*a-tu ša* EN-*ia* 'the hand of my lord' KAV 159:9
ṣubātu	TÚG *a-ḫa-tu ša ṣir-pi* 'a textile with sleeves of red dye' KAV 105:12

1 See GAG, 238f § 138; cf. UgAkk in Huehnergard (1989, 226ff).

2 This process is typical for Semitic languages. In Syriac, the status constructus is mostly replaced by the particle *d-*, e.g., *ruḥā d-qudšā* (ܪܘܚܐ ܕܩܘܕܫܐ) 'the spirit of holiness' (Nöldeke 1904, 161–64), and has totally replaced the status constructus in modern dialects, such as Ṭuroyo and Mlaḥsô, e.g., *barṯo d-malko* 'daughter of the king' (Jastrow 1992, 42–43 § 5.5; 1994, 60–61 § 5.1.5). Moroccan Arabic in fact has two particles, which occur side by side with the original status constructus (Arabic. إضافة), e.g., *z-znaqi d-le-mdna* 'streets of the city' and *ž-žmel dyal l-qoyyad* 'the camel of the judges' (Harrel 1962, 202–3). On the other hand, the loss of case endings did not affect the status constructus in Hebrew (e.g., Joüon/Muraoka 2006, 253–54 § 92).

Some mixed forms are found where the governing noun occurs in the status constructus:

batqu *a-na ba-ti-iq ša pu-ri ša* PN *ilteqe* 'for the disruption of the loss of PN, he has taken it' MARV 3 37:9–12

suḫīru *sú-ḫi-ir ša* ANŠE 'foal of the donkey' BM 103203:9–10 (Nuzi/Ass.)[3]

The governing noun and genitive may be separated by the particle *-ma*:

ēnu *e-na-ma ša* URU 'spring of GN' MATSH 3:30

pû *a-na* KA-*ša-ma ša* ^{f}PN 'according to PN's own declaration' KAJ 7:6

ṣabʾu ÉRIN^{meš}-*ma*$^{!}$ *ša* GN 'troops of GN' MATSH 3:33

šamaššammû ŠE.Ì.GIŠ^{me}[^{š}]-*ma ša* ⸢*li*⸣-*me* 'sesame oil (of the period) of the eponym' MARV 3 30:8

Separation with an independent personal pronoun is attested:

bēlu EN [*at*]-*ta ša ba-la-ṭí-ia* 'you are the lord of my life' VAT 8851:30

In one instance, the governing and governed noun are even separated by a dependent clause:

ruqqu *adi ru-uq-qi ša pa-ni-šu ša* ZABAR 'with a cauldron, which is in front of it, of bronze' KTN inventory iv 14'

§ 299 A construct with a pronominal suffix for the noun it modifies also occurs in Akkadian, which is sometimes described as the anticipatory genitive in the literature. This construction, consisting of a bound form+pronominal suffix+genitive marker *ša*+governed noun, can be called a double analytic genitive construction, since the relation between the governing noun and the governed noun is expressed twice: by the pronominal suffix and by *ša*. In OA, this construction is still rare (GKT, 203 § 121e; GOA § 6.3.4), but also occurs in NA (SNAG, 81). In MA, it is only rarely attested. Nonetheless, because of its early attestations, it is unlikely to have been influenced by Aramaic (cf. Kaufman 1974, 131):

aḫu PN_1 DUMU-*šu* ŠEŠ-*šu ša* PN_2 'PN_1, his son, the brother of PN_2' Snell 1983/84:21

ālu *qa-qar a-lim-šu ša* PN 'the terrain of the city of PN' KAJ 53:15–16

ipṭiru ^{f}*Šu-ub-ri-ta ip-ṭí-ri-ša ša* ^{f}PN 'a Hurrian girl, the substitute of ^{f}PN' KAJ 167:8–9

Curiously, the genitive marker *ša* can also be placed before the governing nouns (cf. OA in GOA § 6.3.5). This occurs more frequently in Mittani Akkadian and the suggestion of Hurrian influence here has been made (Adler 1976, 110 § 76).

abātu *ša* EN-*ia a-ia-a-tu a-ba-tu-šu* 'which are the words of my lord?' MATSH 8:41'

aḫu *ša* PN ŠEŠ^{meš}-*šú* UN^{meš}-*šu* EN *il-ki-i-šu* 'of PN his brothers, people and lord of his *ilku*' Giricano 4:24–26

appu *ša* ÌR *ù* GÉME *ap-pi-šu-nu uz-ni-šu-nu ú-na-ak-ku-su* 'they will cut off the nose and ear of the slave and the maid' MAL A § 4:49–50

ḫīṭu *ša* MUNUS *ḫi-i-ṭu la-áš-šu* 'there is no sin of the woman' MAL A § 12:24

rēšu *ša la a-ka-a-li* SAG.DU-*ma ilaqqe* 'what is not edible, he will take the capital' MAL A § 30:37–38

sinniltu *šumma ša-a mu-ut* MUNUS *ši-a-ti marāšu laššu* 'that wife's husband does not have a son' MAL A § 50:74–75

sisīu *iltaʾlanni* [*mā š*]*a ma-an-ni* ⸢ANŠE⸣.[KUR].RA^{meš} 'he asked me: 'from whom are the horses?' MATC 15:13–15

3 Freydank (2016b, 97) reads *su-ḫi-ir-*[*ta*].

§ 300 When it comes down to the difference between the synthetic genitive construction and the analytic genitive construction, there does not seem to be a fundamental distinction in function. On the other hand, many frequently occurring constructions seem semantically motivated. For instance, we always find *abāt šarre* 'words of the king', but never *abātu ša šarre*. When we zoom in on this semantic distribution, there are a few remarks that can be made (for OA see GOA § 6.3.8–9). We already pointed out that the genitive construction remains preserved in prepositional phrases (e.g., *ina muḫḫi*; *ana libbi*). Some archaic fossilized constructions could maintain the genitive construct out of tradition, most notably *Libbi-āle* 'the inner city (Aššur)' passim spelled uruŠÀ-*bi*-URU and variations. One cannot take the construction apart; *ālu* could still refer to Aššur, but *libbu* could not. This observation is also true for institutions, e.g., *bēt āle* 'the city hall'; *pišerti karūʾe* 'clearance of the grain heap'; *šakin māte* 'governor'; *tupšar šarre* 'royal scribe. The governing noun can be used independently (e.g., *tupšar šarre* 'royal scribe > *tupšarru* 'scribe'), but the governed noun means nothing on its own when used in the same context. Perhaps we should add some institutional instruments, such as the *ašal šarre* 'rope of the king' or *abāt šarre* 'words of the king'. These constructions cannot be taken apart; if they are, only the governing noun maintains function. This is also true for genealogies, as far as we can conclude, based on mostly exclusive logographic spellings, such as DUMU PN 'son of PN'. We always find the genitive construction in nominal verbal forms, such as the participle or the infinitive:

nāšīu	*nāši tuppe* 'carrier of the tablet' passim (cf. OA *wābil tuppim*)
ṣabātu	*i+na ṣa-bat* NÍG.KA$_9$^{meš} 'at the settling of accounts' KAJ 225:4
šēzubu	*ša še-zu-⸢ub⸣ ra-mi-šu* 'his own saving' MATSH 9:42

A problematic exception:

puāgu	*kē šumma* GÁNA.A.ŠÀ *a-na pu-a-g[i ša] ur-di* 'how can it be that a slave takes a field by force?' T 02-32:29–31

§ 301 In OA, the synthetic genitive construction is used when the governing noun represents part of the whole of the governed noun. In MA, this seems to have been changed, in some cases, to the analytic genitive construction, e.g., *mišal ša* (...) 'half of (...)' (see § 344). In related prepositional positions, such as *ina libbi*, the synthetic construction is retained. The analytic genitive construction seems to be especially preferable when the governing noun expresses a main characteristic of the governing noun, for instance, the main material or another major feature. The content of a tablet or vessel is also possible:

ellabbuḫḫu	*el-la-bu-ḫa ša* Ì 'bladder with oil' KAV 200:10
ēṣu	GIŠ *ša šu-uq-di ma-at-qi* 'wood of sweet almond' KAJ 310:51
kunukku	na4KIŠ[IB-*k*]*i-ma ša* [*l*]*a-aḫ-mi* 'the seal with the *laḫmu*-picture' KAV 98:8–9
šaḫḫu	12 giš*ša-aḫ*!*-ḫu* SIG$_5$ *ša* giš*ša-aḫ-šu-ri* '12 good bowls(?) of apple wood' KAJ 310:41–42
šinnu	*ši-in-na ša pi-ri* 'ivory of elephant' KAV 205:6

It could be suggested that the synthetic was preferred over analytic genitive constructions when expressing the physical relations between objects, such as family members, building parts or limbs. However, the analytic genitive construction is attested with body parts too, e.g., *ap-pa ša* DAM-*šu* 'the nose of his wife' MAL A § 15:53. The analytic genitive construction is also preferred in order to avoid a double synthetic genitive construction:

pāḫutu	*ina muḫḫi* EN^{meš} *pa-ḫa-te ša* ^{kur}KASKAL-*ni* 'it is (incumbent) on the lords of the province of Ḫarrān' T 98-119:9–10
quppu	1 *qu-pu ša sa-su na-gi-ri* 'one box of the proclamation of the herald' KAJ 310:19–20

When the governing noun has an adjective, the analytic genitive construction is used:

ṣabʾu	ÉRIN^{meš} *ù* ANŠE^{meš} *ḫal-qu-te ša* GN 'the lost troops and donkeys of GN' MATSH 2:55
tāḫumu	*ta-ḫu-ú-ma* GAL *ša-a tap-pa-i-šu* 'the large boundary of his comrade' MAL B § 8:11–12

This is probably also the case when there are two governing nouns used in combination with each other:

ḫaziānu	*ḫa-zi-a-nu* 3 GAL^{meš} *ša* URU 'the mayor and three noblemen of the city' MAL B § 6:35
nāgiru	^{lú}IL *ù qé-pu-tu ša* LUGAL 'the herald and representatives of the king' MAL B § 6:31–32
ṣabʾu	ÉRIN^{meš} *ù* ANŠE^{meš} *ḫal-qu-te ša* GN 'the lost troops and donkeys of GN' MATSH 2:55

The same tendency is attested for the two governed nouns used in combination with each other:

māʾu	*lu* A^{meš} *ša ḫi-ri-ṣi ù lu na-qu-ri gab-bu e-*⸢*ṣu*?⸣ 'be it the water of the canal or (the water) of the *n.*-canals, all will be little' MATSH 8:33'
quppu	*qu-up-pa ša ši-in-ni ù* ^{giš}*a-ši-e pitʾā* 'open the box of ivory and ebony' KAV 99:25–26

When the governed noun is followed by a demonstrative pronoun, the analytic genitive construction is found:

tuppu	*tup-pa ša pi-i an-ni-te-ma altaṭar* 'I have written the tablet of this wording' MATSH 22:22–23

§ 302 It should be pointed out that we cannot always trust the MA material. In the text A 3310, we find the same genitive construction twice; once as an analytic construction and once as a synthetic construction. It appears that, in the synthetic construction, the particle *ša* is forgotten or simply omitted, which is furthermore obscured by the logographic character of the governed noun: 10 ^{giš}*na-al-ba-tu*^{meš} *ša* SIG$_4$-*tu* '10 brick moulds' A 3310:1–2 ~ 12 ^{giš}*na-al-b*[*a-tu*^{meš}] <*ša*> SIG$_4^{\text{meš}}$ *ša-ḫa-*[*a-ṭí*] 12 moulds for brick making' A 3310:5–6. Variation is also found in the construction *sūtu* (*ša*) *ḫiburne* 'seah of the *ḫiburnu* house', e.g., *i+na* ^{giš}BÁN *ša* ^{é}*ḫi-bur-ni* KAJ 66:3 KAJ 219:2 et passim; but *a-na* ^{giš}BÁN *ḫi-bur-ni* MARV 1 1 i 57'; *i+na* ^{giš}BÁN *ḫi-bur-ni* MPR 44:22. Note that the analytic genitive construction is found in a few lexicalized constructions as well (cf. Luukko/Van Buylaere 2017, 325):

ša abbašše	*ša ab-ba-še* (a textile worker) MARV 3 5:40'
ša kurulte	(PN) *ša ku-ru-ul-te-e* 'PN the animal-fattener' KAJ 127:11
ša muḫḫi bēte	*ša* UGU É 'housemaster' KAV 99:19 et passim
ša muḫḫi ēkalle	*ša* UGU É.GAL 'palace administrator' MAPD § 8:49; cf. § 20:96, 99
ša rēšēn	*a-na ša re-še-en* 'eunuch' MAL A § 15:54

ša rēš šarre	*ša* SAG LUGAL 'royal eunuch' MARV 2 20:12
	šá SAG MAN^{meš} 'royal eunuchs' MAPD § 21:103
	^{lú}*ša* SAG MAN^{meš}-*nu* Coronation Ritual iii 2[4]
ša Sarrāte	^{iti}*ša sa-ra-te* (a name of the month) passim

7.3 Accusative

§ 303 The primary function of the accusative is to indicate the direct object in the status rectus. It is nonetheless found in a number of secondary functions, most importantly, as a case marker of adverbial nouns (see Chapter 14). The accusative is also used for the infinitive in the paronomastic infinitive, which, for this reason, is often referred to as a paronomastic accusative. In this construction, the verbal root of the predicate is repeated in a preceding infinitive (cf. GOA § 6.4.1.3). Although widely attested in Akkadian, examples in MA remain limited to one occurrence:

nappušu *nu-pu-ša na-pí-ša* 'air (the textiles)!' KAV 99:14

§ 304 It has been pointed out that some Akkadian verbs alternate between taking a direct object (accusative) and an indirect object.[5] As there is only a limited number of attestations of these verbs available in MA, this alternation between direct and indirect objects can only be highlighted in a few cases. Most amply attested is the verb *dagālu* 'to see'. The use of a prepositional phrase marks the shift in meaning to 'to wait for' (see CAD D, 21ff).

dagālu+direct object:

aʾīlu ša še-zu-⸢ub⸣ ra-mi-šu la-a i-da-gal 'a man who does not look at his own salvation' MATSH 9:42

dagālu+(*ana*) *panē* (indirect object):

MUNUS *ši-i-it* 5 MU^{meš} *pa-ni mu-ti-ša ta-da-gal* 'that woman will wait five years for her husband' MAL A § 36:91–92

a-na pa-ni-ka a-da-gal 'I will wait for you' MATC 1:9–10

pa-ni ṭé-mi ša EN-*ia a-da-gal* 'I await the message of my lord' MATSH 6:12'–13'

The double-weak verb *qaʾʾû* 'to wait' is also known to alternate, although its attestations in MA always seem to use a direct object. There is one possible exception:

[*a-n*]⸢*a* LUGAL EN-*i-ni*⸣ *ú-qa-a-ʾu* 'they wait for the king our lord' KAV 217:16'†

Similarly, we should also mention *kašādu* 'to reach/arrive', which usually takes a prepositional phrase and/or dative. However, there is also an alternative meaning 'to seize',

4 In this attestation, the phonetic complement *-nu* is used to indicate that *ša rēš šarrāni* is used as the subject of the clause. Similar cases are found in a Babylonian-style letter from Tukultī-Ninurta for the noun *mār šipre* 'messenger', e.g., DUMU KIN-*ra lā ašpura* 'I did not send a messenger' RS 34.165 r. 6'. Nonetheless, there is no evidence from core MA texts that compound nouns (with or without *ša*) had a governed noun with variable case ending.

5 See GAV, 97; cf. OA GOA § 6.4.1.1.

in which case the verb changes from intransitive to transitive and takes a direct object (CAD K, 276b).

ina muḫḫi aššat a'īle ik-šu-du-uš 'they have caught him on top of (another) man's wife' MAL A § 12:20

§ 305 The accusative is commonly attached to nouns functioning as adverbs, some of which are fixed, while others are found as normal nouns in MA.[6] This application of the accusative is still visible in Modern Arabic.[7] Most of the adverbial attestations of the accusative occur with a limited number of fixed forms, e.g., *ūma* 'day' (§ 492). Active application is rare, but attested in the following passages.

mussa É (=*bēta*) *ana batte ú-še-ši-ib-ši* 'her husband settles her elsewhere' MAL A § 36:83–84

7 *e-bir-ta*^{meš} *ana muḫḫīša la-a i-qar-ri-ib* 'he will not go nearer to her (than) seven paces' MAPD § 21:108

1 *mašiānu erīe ṣar-pa qa-ri-im* 'one tongue of copper is inlayed with silver' KTN inventory iv 27'

PN *abušu* A.ŠÀ (=*eqla*) *ù li-ba a-la i-pá-la-aḫ-šu* 'PN will honour his father on the field and in the city' KAJ 6:10–12

ša e-bir-ta ina GN *ana napāle im-ḫur-ú-ni* 'which he received for demolition on the other bank in GN' KAJ 129:10–13

ŠE-*um ḫi-iṣ-na ma-di-id* 'barley, measured in a dehusked manner' MARV 2 20:11 (Postgate 2006)

ŠE *ši-iḫ-ṭa ma-di-id* barley, measured in a stored manner' LVUH 98:1–3 cf. ŠE (…) *ši-iḫ-*[*t*]*a ma-di-id* MARV 2 20:25; ŠE-*u*[*m š*]*a*$^{?}$*-aḫ-ṭa ma-di-id* MARV 4 113:2 (see Postgate 2006)

ka-ra ana kāre ta-ḫu-ma ana taḫūme za-ku-e PN *na-a-ši* 'quay to quay, border to border; PN bears the responsibility for clearing' KAJ 169:17-20 cf. KAJ 171:25–29

pa-ḫa-at pu-qu-ra-[*n*]*a-e ša* PN *za-ku-e ka-ra kāre ta-ḫu-ma taḫūme* (…) PN-*ma na-ši* 'PN bears the responsibility to clear the claims, quay (to) quay, border (to) border'' VAT 8722:13–20

e-mu-qa-ma iṣ-ṣa-ba-as-si 'he seized her with force' MAL A § 12:18

šumma e-mu-qa-a-ma it-ti-ak-ši 'if he had intercourse with her, with force' MAL A § 16:63

PN (…) *qa-ta mi-it-ḫa-ar* 'PN is entitled to an equal share'KAJ 1:22–24

[^{Í}]^{d}*Pu-ra-ta ētabra* 'he crossed the Euphrates (to him)' MATSH 17:8'

§ 306 While a clause usually has only one direct object, there are a few circumstances where there is a double accusative in one clause[8]. Kouwenberg distinguishes different types of double accusatives. A first type is the transitive verb in the causative Š-stem (GOA §

6 See GAG, 246f § 146; Ungnad (1992, 104 § 90a).

7 Cf. Lipiński (2001, 462 § 47.2); Ryding (2005, 276f).

8 Cf. OA in GKT, 212 § 126; MA in UGM, 105 § 94. Many examples given by W. Mayer in UGM do not, on closer inspection, seem to be valid as double accusatives. Some objects should be read either with an extra determinative (TÚG) or as *ša*-constructions, rather than as relative clauses (*šakaršu ša eṣṣe* 'handle of wood').

6.4.1.2), which turns the would-be subject of the G-stem into a second object. In our attestations, all cases of the first direct object are expressed by a pronominal suffix. Instances of *šēbulu* 'to make someone carry' are considerably rarer in MA, as the verb seems to have a modified nuance into 'to send (something)'.

aḫāzu Š	DAM-*ta ú-ša-aḫ-ḫa-sú* 'he will make him take a wife' MARV 1 37:6
ṣabātu Š	*ḫar-ra-a-na ul-ta-aṣ-bi-si* 'he will make her travel' MAL A § 22:107–108
ṣalāʾu Š	*ša-a lìb-bi-ša ú-ša-aṣ-li-ši* 'he caused her to have a miscarriage' MAL A § 51:84

A second group has a second accusative to indicate a beneficiary or goal of the verb (GOA § 6.4.2.4). For instance, the verb *emādu* is used to indicate the imposing of a fine, in which the fine is the object and the person receiving the fine is the beneficiary. Note that the phrase from DeZ 2495 actually has three direct objects: six *manā šipāta* (etc.), *mašḫirī* and *epāša*:

emādu	*ḫi-i-ṭa* (…) *ma-ḫi-ra-a-na e-em-mi-du* 'a punishment he will impose on the receiver' MAL A § 3:43–43
	gab-bi ḫi-ṭa-a-ni[meš] GAL É.GAL-*lim e-mi-du* 'they will impose all punishments upon the palace commander' MAPD § 21:111
kallumu D	EME5 *uk-tal-li-ma-an-ni* 'he showed me the she-ass' Hall 1983:20
šakānu	*ša ṭé-ma áš-ku-nu-ka-ni* 'of which I instructed you' Billa 60:5; MATC 4:19
	pa-ni-ma ṭé-e-ma al-ta-ka-an-ka 'earlier I gave you the order' T 93-20:6–7
	šam-⸢ma⸣ li-iš-ku-nu-ú-ka 'they should prescribe herbs for you' TabT05a-134:15
šaṭāru	*lu-bu-ul-ta ammar ušēlûni ka-ni-ka-te šu-uṭ-ra* 'inscribe the seals according to the textiles, as much as they brought up' KAV 98:22–23
tadānu	6 MA.NA SÍG[meš] (…) *ina* UGU PN *maš-ḫi-ri e-pa-ša i-ta-na* 'he(?) gave six minas of wool (…) to PN in order to make *mašḫuru* textiles' DeZ 2495:1–12

A third group has a second object that seems to function as an instrumental, which is at least true for the examples provided below (cf. GOA § 6.4.2.1):

labāʾu	*mamma lā iṣbassu* DU6-*šu* BÀD *lā ilbi* 'nobody seized it and surrounded its tell with a wall' Maul 1992, 23:5
kanāku	[giš]*tup-ni-na-te* [na4]KIŠIB[meš]-*ia kunkā* 'seal the boxes with my seal' KAV 99:31
	[é]*na-kám-ta* [na4]KIŠIB *an-ni-a-ma kunkā* 'seal the treasury with the same seal' KAV 105:21–22
maḫāṣu	PN *šur-šur-ra-te* ZA[BAR] *amtaḫaṣ* 'I have put PN in copper chains' KAV 96:5–7

7.4 Apposition

§ 307 A noun can be followed by another noun, which is used to specify a characteristic of the preceding noun (cf. OA in GOA § 6.7). The use of substantives in this position is similar to that of adjectives and occurs when a characteristic cannot be expressed by an adjective, for instance, when it is a proper name. Nouns in apposition take the same case ending as the noun they stand in apposition to, making them distinct from the genitive constructions. However, they do not have to take the same number or gender, e.g., *annūte alpīšu rēḫta* 'these bulls of his, the rest'.

When the apposition is a profession (cf. Huehnergard 1989, 231):

mušaqqīu	*ina muḫḫi* PN *mu-ša-qí* 'it is (incumbent) on PN, the water carrier (for animals)' MARV 3 25:5–6

nāgiru	PN ⌜lú⌝NAGAR gišGIGIR? *imtaḫranni* 'PN the carpenter of the chariot has confronted me' Hall 1983:4–5
qēpu	PN_1 PN_2 *u* PN_3 lú*qe-pu-tu-ia kunukkī* (…) *naṣṣū illukūnekkunu* 'PN_1, PN_2 and PN_3 my representatives are coming to you to bring my seal' KAV 98:5–10
tupšarru	PN lúDUB.SAR *altaprakku* 'I sent PN the scribe to you' KAV 104:18–19

When the apposition is a proper name:

abu	*ana pā'i tuppe ša a-bi-i-šu-ma* PN 'according to the tablet of his father, PN' KAJ 6:4–6

When the apposition follows a proper name:

nupāru	*ina* GN é*nu-pa-*[*ri*] *usbū*[*ni*] '(who) dwells in GN, in the prison' MATC 79:8–10

Other nouns are used to specify the preceding noun or proper name. This is similar to the use of adjectives; yet, for some of the following examples, such as *dunnu*, no corresponding adjective exists:

dunnu	*ša Dunni-Aššur du-un-ni-a* 'from Dunni-Aššur, my *dunnu*' MATSH 2:6
ḫubtu	*ša l*[*ē*]*'āni* [*š*]*a ṣēne ḫu-ub-te ša* GN 'from the list of the flock, spoils of GN' MARV 1 27:24
rēḫtu	*annūte alpī*meš*-šu re-eḫ-ta šūt lilqe* 'may he take the remainder of his oxen' T 97-17:15–17[9]

Note also the following phrase, where the apposition indicates the material it is made from. Normally, we would expect an analytic genitive construction here:

fPN *lu* 2 *ni-gal-la* ⌜ZABAR⌝ *ù lu* URUDU fPN *lū tušēbila* 'fPN, may fPN send me two sickles of copper or bronze' A 845:14–18

The difference between an adjective and an apposition can be observed in *ḫalqu* or *ḫulqu*. The first pattern is better attested in Akkadian and behaves as a true adjective with the plural morpheme *-ūt/-utt* (CAD Ḫ, 50), whereas the second behaves as a noun with the plural morpheme *-ū/ē* (CAD Ḫ, 230–31). It should be noted that *ḫulqu* is attested with some rather dubious spellings, including epenthetic vowels. It is possible that these forms should be analysed as *ḫuluqqû* (CAD Ḫ, 233b), although we would expect to find the Assyrian variant *ḫaluqqā'u*. In any case, we find *ḫulqu* used in apposition of the noun it specifies.

ḫalqu	*ḫal-qa u mēta umalla* '(for the) lost and dead he will compensate' LVUH 22:27–8
	GU_4meš *ḫal-qu-te* 'lost oxen' AO 19.227:6
	ÉRINmeš *ù* ANŠEmeš *ḫal-qu-te* 'lost troops and donkeys' MATSH 2:55
	5 *ši-luḫ-lu mētuttu ù ḫal-qu-tu* 'five *šiluḫlu* dead or lost' MPR 66:51
ḫulqu	1 *emāru ḫu-ul-qú* 'one donkey, loss' LVUH 17:16
	1 *emā*[*ru ḫ*]*u-ul-*<*qu*> 'one donkey, loss' LVUH 2:15
	2 *emāru*(pl.) *ḫu-lu-q*[*u*!] 'two donkeys, losses' LVUH 6:14
	6 *mašku*(pl.) [*ḫu*]*-lu-qú* 'six hides, losses' LVUH 43:10

Following measurements, the noun being measured follows in apposition, always in the singular. In the case of mass nouns, a plural marker is sometimes added.

GUN	4 GUN AN.NA 'four talents of lead' KAJ 155:9
IKU	3 IKU A.ŠÀ 'three-*iku* field ' KAJ 50:11
MA.NA	5 1/3 MA.NA *ḫu-ru-tu* '5 1/3 minas of gall nuts' KAJ 130:3
	24 MA.NA *an-nu-ku* '24 minas of lead' KAJ 37:2.

9 See § 367 for a discussion on this clause.

SÌLA	2 SÌLA LÀL 2 SÌLA Ì^{meš} 'two litres of honey, two litres of oil' MARV 3 16 iii 23

Once, a logographically written cardinal number is placed in apposition, rather than preceding the counted noun.

2	*liāte* 2 *ša pitti* PN 'two cows of the responsibility of PN' T 97-17:6–7

Chapter 8: Adjectives and Participles

8.1 Adjectives

§ 308 We can divide adjectives into two main groups: verbal adjectives and primary adjectives.[1] The difference between the two groups is not always entirely clear because the distinction is one of semantics rather than morphology. It comes down to the difference between the adjectives that usually correspond to transitive verbs of action, which have a resultative meaning, e.g., *duāku* 'to kill' > *dēku* 'killed' or *muātu* 'to die' > *mētu* 'dead', cf. the participle in *aʾīluttu dāgilū* 'seeing people (=people with sight)' KAJ 180:2. This group always has the pattern *PaRiS* in the G-stem. Secondly, there is a group of primary adjectives that usually has a corresponding adjectival verb, e.g., *damqu* 'good'; *ṣeḫru* 'small' (cf. Kouwenberg 2010, 58ff § 3.3.2). This group can also take a different pattern (see below), although *PaRiS* is preferred here as well. Adjectival verbs (e.g., *damāqu* 'to be good'), which have primary adjectives other than verbal adjectives, cannot have a participle.

§ 309 Morphologically, MA adjectives are mostly identical to other Akkadian dialects, except for some phonologic and morphologic features not restricted to adjectives. The base form is most notable, which is usually *PaRiS*, but differs in the other stems: when two successive short open syllables follow, the vowel of the second syllable is omitted according to the Akkadian rules of vowel syncope: *PaRiSu* > *PaRSu*. It is, therefore, often not possible to say whether all adjectives have a *PaRiS* construction or whether the second vowel varies. We will assume that this is not the case unless there is clear evidence for it. Adjectives are generally inflected similarly to normal nouns; the only point where the inflection partly differs is the masculine plural.

Number	Case	Masculine	Feminine
Singular	Nominative	*damq-u*	*damiq-tu*
	Genitive	*damq-e*	*damiq-te*
	Accusative	*šarr-a*	*damiq-ta*
Plural	Nominative	*damq-uttu* (or *-ūtu*)	*damq-ātu*
	Oblique	*damq-utte* (or *-ūte*)	*damq-āte*

Figure 23: Inflection of adjectives.

G-stem masculine singular:

balṭu	1 SILA₄ *bal-ṭa* 'one living lamb' New Year Ritual:14'
ḫalqu	*mu-us-sa ḫal-qu* 'her lost husband' MAL A § 45:72–73
ḫarpu	*i+na tu-re-zi ḫar-pi* 'at early harvest time YBC 12860:14–15
kasmu	*e-re-na ka-ás-ma* 'chopped cedar' New Year Ritual:6'

1 Some disagreement exists among Assyriologists about what is a verbal adjective and what is not. According to von Soden, non-verbal adjectives have a pattern that is distinct from the G-stem *PaRvS* and derived stems (GAG, 66 § 52a; 125 § 77b). Adjectives with corresponding adjectival verbs are also considered to be verbal adjectives. This chapter uses the definition employed by Kouwenberg, which differs with regard to the position of the latter group (GOA Chapter 6).

maʾdu	*e-ṣú ù ma-du* 'little or much' KAJ 149:3
malʾu	1 ITI *la ma-al-ʾa* 'one month not full' MATSH 12:23
nakru	ÉRIN^{meš} *na-ak-ru* 'hostile troops' MATSH 2:10
qatnu	1 TÚG$^{ḫi.a}$ *qa-at-nu* 'one thin garment' VAT 8236:7
ṣeḫru	DUMU-*ú ṣe-eḫ-ru* 'the youngest son' MAL B § 1:10
	AN.BAR *ṣe-eḫ-⸢ra⸣* 'little (piece) of iron' MATSH 16:22
tārīu	*ta-ri-ú* 'child' KAJ 180:4
uldu	[...] *ša* GABA *ul-du* 'x of the breast, just born' LVUH 5:20†(?)

§ 310 Masculine plural adjectives in Akkadian take the endings *-ūtu* (nominative) or *-ūte* (oblique). As discussed in § 281, some of these adjectives were substantivized, causing the abstractum/plural ending *-uttu* to be used as a plural for normal nouns. Cases where nominal inflection occurs with the endings *-ū/ē* are very rare. It may be noted that no plene spellings for the gemination in *-uttu* and *-utte* can be found as they occur for the abstractum/masculine plural nouns. This led Kouwenberg to believe that gemination did not take place with plural adjectives (GOA § 7.4.1 n22). If Kouwenberg is correct, this suggests a morphological difference between the abstract *-uttu* and the plural morpheme *-ūtu*, which is absent in Babylonian. However, the endings of the plural adjectives are, in most instances, spelled defectively, providing no information about the length of the vowel or consonant in *-ūt/utt*. As there is no etymological difference with the ending *-uttu* on nominalized plural adjectives, the matter remains undecided.

G-stem, masculine plural:

ballu	ŠIM^{meš} *bal-lu-te* 'mixed aromatics' Ištar Ritual:7–8
balṭu	ÉRIN^{meš} *bal-ṭu-te* 'living soldiers' MATSH 18:32
barīu	ÉRIN^{meš} *ba-ri-ú-te* 'hungry troops' MARV 1 1 iv 33
ḫalqu	ÉRIN^{meš} u ANSE^{meš} *ḫal-qu-te* 'lost troops and donkeys' MATSH 2:55
labēru	ŠE.Ì.GIŠ^{meš} *la-be-ru-tu* 'old sesame' LVUH 83:2
kamṣu	13 SAG.DU^{meš} *bur-ḫi-iš kám-ṣu-tu* (meaning uncertain) KTN inventory ii 5
maʾdu	ÉRIN^{meš} *ma-⸢a-du⸣-te* 'many people' MATSH 10:25
mētu	ÉRIN^{meš} *me-tu-tu* 'dead people' MARV 1 6:7
paṣīu	*qa-qú-ru pa-ṣi-ú-tum* 'white (=empty) ground' KAJ 174:3
nasḫu	ÉRIN^{meš} *na-ás-ḫu-te* 'deported people' KAJ 121:6
šallu	ÉRIN^{meš} *šal-lu-tu* 'deported people' KAJ 180:11
zarīu	80 KUŠ MÁŠ^{meš} *⸢za⸣-ri-ú-tu* 'eighty goat skins, skinned(?)' MARV 3 7:1; cf. 1 2; VAT 19545.[2]

G-stem, masculine plural, nominal inflection:

ašru	*ši-luḫ-lu*^{meš} *aš-⸢ru⸣* 'reviewed *šiluḫlu*-personnel' MPR 69:28
šiāmu	*a⸢na⸣ šīme* 5 LÚ^{meš} *ši-i-me* 'for the price of five bought men' MARV 3 2:18'

§ 311 The feminine forms of the *PaRiS* construction have the second vowel maintained and become *PaRiSt*. Note that II/gem verbs always maintain their geminated R_2, e.g., *tuppu dannutu* 'strong tablet' (KAJ 35:19–20).

G-stem, feminine singular:

dannu	*tup-pa* [*da*]-*na-ta* 'the strong tablet' KAJ 35:19–20
kanku	1 ^{dug}ŠAB *ka-nik-tu* 'one sealed bowl' MARV 5 24:11

2 This is an unclear adjective, which could mean 'skinned', according to Jakob (in Faist 2001, 88 n33).

malīu	^{giš}MÁ *ma-li-ta* 'a loaded boat' MAL M § 2:10
naṭīu	[GEME] *na-ṭí-i-tu* 'the beaten maid' MAPD § 18:85
nīktu	DAM-*su ni-ik-ta* 'his fornicating wife' MAL A § 23:20
ṣabtu	*tup-pi ṣa-bi-te* 'drawn-up tablet' KAJ 122:4–5
tarīu	3 MUNUS^{meš} *ta-ri-*[*t*]*u* 'three female children' KAJ 180:8

Feminine plural:

eliʾu	*ša-pa-tu-šu-nu el-li-a-tu* (*elīʾātu*) 'their upper lips' KTN inventory i 19
maʾdu	SÍG^{meš} *ma-da-te* 'much wool' KAV 106:5
malʾu	*ma-al-ʾa-tu* MARV 7 5 r. 3'†
šaʾmu	10$^{?!}$ *li-tu* (…) [*š*]*a-a*$^{?}$*-ma-tu* '10 bought cows' AO 21.157:1–2

8.2 Adjectives: secondary stems

§ 312 As we have already mentioned, the nominal base for the D-stem *PaRRuS* (Bab. *PuRRuS*) is also found with adjectives. All attested forms seem to be verbal adjectives.

D-stem, masculine singular:

gammuru	*ga-mu-ur ta-din* 'it is completely given' LVUH 66:21 (also *ga-mur* LVUH 77:22) cf. *a-na ší-im ga-me-er* (…) *i-din* KAJ 146:7–11
pattu	SAG.DU-*sa pa-at-tu* 'her uncovered head' MAL A § 40:64
ṣaʾʾupu	1 $^{\text{túg.ḫi.a}}$*bi-ir-ša er-qa ṣa-ú-pa* 'a green decorated felt' KAV 99:18–19
	1 TÚG$^{\text{ḫi.a}}$ *qa-at-nu ṣa-ú-pu* 'one thin decorated$^{?}$ textile' VAT 8236:9
taqqunu	*ṭé-ma táq-qu-na* 'a secure order' MATSH 12:10
zakkuʾu	*mi-mu-šu za-ku-a* 'his cleared property' Billa 3:16; 4:12
	zak-ku-ú 'cleared' MARV 9 9:21'

D-stem, masculine plural:

arruku	NINDA^{meš} *ar-ru-ku-*⌜*tu*⌝ 'long breads' MARV 1 7:6
ḫammuru	4 *ar-mu*^{meš} *ḫa-am-mu-ru-tu* 'four crippled *armu*-goats' KTN inventory iv 8'
kassupu	14 *ni-gal-lu*^{meš} x$^{?}$ *ka-su-pu-tu* '14 broken sickles' MARV 10 75:1–2
labbuku	ŠIM^{meš} *la-bu-ku-ú-te* 'steeped aromatics' PKT 1 I right:10, 29
maḫḫuṣu	ÉRIN^{meš}*-šu-nu ma-ḫu-ṣu-tu* 'their wounded troops' MATSH 6:34'
sammuḫu	13 KUŠ^{meš} *sa-mu-ḫu-tu* '13 mixed hides' KAJ 225:5–6

D-stem, masculine plural, nominal inflection:

arruku	NINDA^{meš} *ar-ru-ku-tu* 'long breads' MARV 1 7:6
paṭṭuru	KUŠ^{meš}*-ša pa-ṭu-ru* 'its leather straps undone' KAJ 310:4

D-stem, feminine singular:

malluʾu	*anāku ma-lu-ta ina muḫḫīšunu ašakkanma* 'I will impose a compensation payment upon them' Ni 669:19–21
paṣṣunu	DAM-*šu pa-ṣu-un-te* 'his veiled wife' MAL A § 41:11–12
zakkuʾu	*tup-pí* 2.KÁM-*ma zak-ku-tu* 'second(?) cleared tablet' MARV 6 31:31; cf. MARV 5 12:26

D-stem, feminine plural:

ḫappuʾu	PÈŠ^{meš} *ḫap-pu-a-tu* 'broken dates' MARV 3 32:2
paʾʾugu	*tup-pa-te pa-ú-ga-te* 'p. tablets' KAJ 310:14
ṣaʾʾupu	[… *ṣ*]*a-ú-pa-tu* (broken, said of textile) MAH 16086 i 4

	TÚG$^{hi.a.meš}$ *ṣu-pa-a-t*[*u*] 'embroidered(?) textiles' KAV 108:4 (Bab.)
ta$^{??}$*uru*	*ta-ú-ra-te* (broken context) KAJ 5:7
zakkuʾu	(PNs) *za-ku-a-tu* 'cleared women' MPR 66:34

For the Š-stem we find *šaPRuS* (Bab. *šuPRuS*). Only a few forms are attested, mostly masculine plural forms of the verb *akālu*. Note that adjectives of other verbal stems, such as the N-stem are not attested in MA.

Š-stem, feminine singular:

ešāru Š	6 ANŠE 1 BÁN *še-šur-tu* 'six homer and one seah, processed(?) (barley)' T 99-21:10–11

Š-stem, masculine plural:

šākulu	2 GU$_4$^{meš} *ša-ku-lu-tu* 'two fattened oxen' MARV 4 65 iv 1, 2
	30 GUKKAL *ša-ku-lu-tu*^{meš} '30 fattened sheep' A 3186 (NTA, 35):3
	6 GUKKAL *šá-ku-lu-tu* 'six fattened sheep' A 3186 (NTA, 35):6
	2 GU$_4$ *ša-ku-lu-ú-tu* 'two fattened oxen' A 3191 (NTA, 37):1
	a-di ša-ku-lu-te 'with the fattened (sheep)' Ali 10:2

8.3 Adjectives: secondary patterns

§ 313 Adjectives with different patterns are rare, but mostly of Semitic etymology. We can divide the other patterns into different groups. The first group consists of the patterns *PaRaS* and *PaRuS*, which are found for strong roots; but these patterns are usually not attested with certainty in MA because of the aforementioned vowel syncope (cf. GOA § 7.2). We find *PaRaS* attested a number of times for the root *utāru* 'to be surplus'. All attestations are found in the agricultural texts from Dūr-Katlimmu and occur in the status absolutus, so that the vowel of the second syllable is visible.

utru	9 BÁN ŠE *ú-ta-ar* 'nine seahs of barley is extra' LVUH 63:14, cf. plural *ut-ru-te* MPR 46:16
	6 BÁN *ú-tar* PN 'six seahs extra of PN' LVUH 81:5

The other pattern *PuRuS* is attested in multiple forms in the Assyrian dialect, although it is limited in MA to *qurbu* 'nearby'. As *qurub* is a rare instance of an adjective without /a/ in the first syllable, it has been suggested that it is a secondary form where /a/ assimilated into successive /u/ (LAS 2, 220; Kouwenberg 2010, 65). If this is the case, *qurub* would be an original *PaRuS* adjective with a rare instance of VA on the first syllable. The occurrence of a *PuRuS* form has been used in the case of *qurub* for the argument that /a/ > /o/ (e.g., GAG, 14 § 9e; SNAG, 26: Luukko 2004, 85 n262). However, its occurrence in both OA and MA makes this unlikely (Kouwenberg 2005/6, 332). Edzard (1983, 135) suggested that *qurbu* is an analogue pattern to the contraction in Assyrian *raʾuqu* > *rūqu*. This is, of course, possible; however, most *PuRuS* patterns in the Assyrian dialect have strong roots (cf. OA in GOA § 7.2.3), making it unlikely that these adjectives were influenced by *rūqu*.

qurbu	*ina* URU^{didli} *qur-bu-ú-te* 'in nearby cities' MAL A § 24:44
	1 *up-ru* (…) *qur-bu* 'one head cover is available' A 893:8–10

§ 314 The second distinct group of adjectival patterns results from the irregularities of the II/weak roots. For this class, we find the nominal base *PāS* in Assyrian for a limited number of roots, rather than Babylonian *PīS*. This subject will be discussed in more detail with the stative in § 562. However, it should be pointed out that this nominal base is frequently found for adjectives. The adjective *ṭābu* 'good' is shared by both Babylonian and Assyrian (Kouwenberg 2010, 479).

rāqu	*ra-qu-te-e-ša* 'empty-handed' MAL A § 37:19
	ina u$_4$*-mi ra-a-qí* 'holiday' MAL A § 42:14
	5 ^{giš}*maḫ-ḫu-lu ra-qu-tu* 'five empty *m.*-baskets' KAJ 125:2–3
	1 *el-la-bu-ḫa ra-aq-ta-*[*m*]*a* 'one empty bladder' KAV 103:28
	ra-qu-ta liddin 'he will give *rāqūtu*'[3] A 2704:22
	GÌR^{meš}-*šu ra-qa-a-te* (meaning uncertain) KBo 28 64:9'
ṭābu	^{kaš}SA.MAR *ṭa-bu* 'good SA.MAR-beer' MATC 23:5

At the same time, the same adjectives that are attested with *PāS* pattern can also be found with *PīS* pattern in other texts.[4] We can assume an Assyrian form *PēS*, rather than *PīS*, since it is likely that these forms derive from a diphthong *rayqu* > *rēqu*. Alternatively, they may be direct loans from the Babylonian dialect, but this cannot be decided, based on the present evidence. Note that the pattern *PēS* is used for the majority of II/weak roots, e.g., *mētu* 'dead' (never **mātu*).

rēqu	⸢UD⸣^{meš} *re-qu-te* 'holidays' VS 1 103:10†
	ina UD^{meš} *re-qu-te* RE 19:21
	1 *mana*$^{a.àm}$ <AN.NA> *re-qa-a-tu* RE 19:23-24[5]
sēqu	*se-qu* 'they are narrow' VAT 8236 r. 12 (cf. stative, 3fs: *sa-qa-at* Lambert 1969:44)

Examples of other II/weak adjectives:

dēku	^{lú}ENGAR *de-ke* 'a killed farmer' MPR 60:50
	⸢DUMU⸣^{meš} SIG$_5$ *de-ku-ú-te* 'killed elite troops' MATSH 8:42' cf. ⸢*di-ku-te*⸣ l. 43'
mētu	DAM-*šu me-et-te* 'his deceased wife' MAL A § 31:44
šēb	PN *še-eb* 'PN, an old man' MPR 18:1 et passim
	^{f}PN *še-bat* 'PN, an old lady' MPR 3:14
zēzu	*ina* A.ŠÀ *la-a ze-e-zi* 'on an undivided field' MAL B § 4:27
	ŠEŠ^{meš} *la ze-zu-ú-te* 'brothers who have not divided' MAL B § 2:15

§ 315 One case of *PaRīS* can be found in *labēru* 'old', which has a long /ī/ in most dialects of Akkadian. The MA attestations point to a long /ē/ instead, presumably caused by its vicinity to /r/.[6]

labēru	ŠE.Ì.GIŠ^{meš} *la-be-ru-tu* 'old sesame' LVUH 83:2
	2 TÚG (…) 1 GIBIL 1 *la-be-ru* 'two textiles, one new, one old' KAJ 256:1–2

§ 316 There is a small group of adjectives that has an irregular plural where *PaRS* > *PaRRaS*. Note that the feminine plural marker *-āt* is added to some of the given examples.[7] The attested adjectives seem to indicate dimension: 'small' and 'low'.

---

3 For a translation and discussion of this passage, see Brinkman/Donbaz (1985, 81–82).
4 See Deller (1999, 35); cf. GAG, 180 § 104j.
5 For a translation and discussion of this passage, see Deller (1999, 32, 35).
6 See CAD L, 26–31; AHw, 525.

ṣaḫḫaru	*ana ṣa-ḫa-ra-te* 'for the small ones' VAT 9410:32
ṣeḫḫeru	*ana qāt* 10 *šanāte marʾū marʾe ṣe-eḫ-ḫe-ru* 'the sons of the son are younger than 10 years' MAL A § 43:31–32 (stative use)
šappalu	^{giš}GU.ZA^{meš} *šap-pa-la-te* 'the low stools' Ali 23:13

§ 317 Some adjectives are loans. This category consists of the Hurrian adjectives *talmu* 'big' and *sillunu* 'old'. Neither of them is inflected according to number or gender, although different case endings are attested. The first adjective, *talmu* 'big', seems to be used exclusively with the logogram ÙZ.[8]

talmu	1 ÙZ *tal-mu* 'one big goat' KAJ 120:12
	5 ÙZ^{meš} *tal-mu* 'five big goats' Billa 36:15
	23 ÙZ *tal-mu* '23 big goats' Ali 4:5
	ÙZ^{meš} *tal-mu* 'big goats' LVUH 11:4'

It is also the case that *sillunu* 'old' derives from the Hurrian base *zill-* 'to be old' (Richter 2012, 375a). It occurs in both MA/NA and Nuzi.[9] Note that, while different case endings are attested, the adjective is not in agreement with the gender and number, similar to *talmu*.

sillunu	11 GU_4.NÍTA^{meš} *si-lu-nu* '11 old oxen' KAJ 289:5
	2 *si-lu-nu* 'two old ones' LVUH 8:5
	1 GU_4 *si-lu-nu* 'one old ox' LVUH 13:5
	1 KUŠ GU_4 *si-lu-ni* 'one hide of an old ox' LVUH 40:3

Finally, there is one attestation of *šiḫlu* 'second quality', which is believed to derive from Hurrian as well.[10]

2 *šaḫḫu ša ḫašḫūre ši-iḫ-lu* 'two second-class *šaḫḫu*-containers of apple wood' KAJ 310:42–43

8.4 Syntax of the adjective

§ 318 Above, we listed a large number of attestations of the adjective in its main function: attributive to a noun. There are a few remarks to be made on their function and structure. Adjectives agree with nouns with respect to gender, number and case ending. A structural exception is the morphologically singular collectives (see § 282). When an adjective is used as an attributive with a noun, it is placed directly after it, e.g., *erīna kasma* 'chopper cedar' New Year Ritual:16'. A pronominal suffix is only added to the governing noun with the adjective following, e.g., *mussa* (< *mutu+ša*) *ḫalqu* 'her lost husband' MAL A § 45:72–73. Opposites are usually created by negating the adjective with *lā*, e.g., *urḫu lā malʾu* 'a month not passed' MATSH 12:23; *lā magrūtu* '(who) do not agree' MAL B § 18:33. Adjectives are in agreement with the nouns to which they are attributive, according to case ending, gender and number. Multiple adjectives may follow each other, e.g., *ṣubātu qatnu ṣaʾʾupu* 'a thin decorated textile' VAT 8236:9. There are a few exceptional attestations of the adjective, which are not common in Akkadian. First of all, adjectives preceding the noun are also attested (UGM, 104).

7 See Reiner (1966, 64); GAV, 52–55; cf. OA in GOA § 7.4.4.
8 See AHw, 1312; Richter (2012, 432–35).
9 See AHw, 1044a; CAD S, 265–66.
10 See CAD $Š_2$, 415–15; Richer 2012, 371a; cf. AHw. 1232a.

ešartu *ina e-šar-te* ^{giš}GIDRU-*ka* 'with your righteous sceptre' Coronation Ritual ii 34–5
šaknu *ša-kín* KUR 'governor of the country' MARV 3 31:7 (lexical, et passim.)

Regarding adjectives following a status constructus form (UGM, 104–5 § 93), in the examples given below, the adjective modifies the governing noun:
rabʾu DUMU É GAL (=*marā bēte rabʾe*) 'the oldest son of the house' KAJ 1:21
zēzu *aḫḫē mutīša la-a ze-zu-ú-tu* 'her brothers-in-law, who did not divide' MAL A § 25:88–89

An attributive adjective can be separated from the governing noun by the conjunction *u*:
aḫīu NA_4^{meš} *ša muḫḫi kalamme u a-ḫi-a-te laššu* 'stones that are on the *kalammu* and the other (stones) are absent' KAJ 310:8[11]

Notice also the following construction where the adjectives (*riḫṣu ḫiṣnu*) are separated from the noun (ŠE-*um*^{meš}):

8 *emāru* 7 *sūtu* ŠE-*um*^{meš} *ina sūte ša allāni ri-iḫ-ṣu ḫi-iṣ-nu* 'eight homers and seven seahs of barley, in the oak-seah, threshed and crushed' Giricano 1:1–3

§ 319 Adjectives can also be used independently where they function as normal nouns. Only very rarely is a substantivized adjective used for the designation of a profession or activity of individuals. This can only happen in a passive meaning, as participles are just for that function. Thus, we have *qēpu* 'representative' or from *qiāpu* 'to (en)trust'. Consider these examples:
damqu *dam-qa-te-ka* (…) *liqbi* 'may he speak favourably of you' Ištar Ritual:11
dannu *da-an-ni* 'my valid declaration' KAV 159:4
labēru 2 TÚG (…) 1 GIBIL 1 *la-be-ru* 'two textiles, (…) one new (garment), one old (garment)' KAJ 256:1–2
magru *ma-ag-ru* (…) *i-šaʾʾal* 'the one who agrees will ask' MAL B § 17:12–13
la-a ma-ag-ru-tu ibašši 'there are those who do not agree' MAL B § 18:33
marṣu *iltu mar-ṣu-te* 'with the sick men' CTMMA 1 99:2
nakru *na-ak-ru ana* GN *imtuqut* 'the enemy attacked GN' MATSH 4:7–8 vs. ÉRIN^{meš} *na-ak-ru* 'hostile troops' MATSH 2:10
qēpu *qe-pu-tu-šu*^{meš} 'his representatives' MAPD § 21:109
ṣaḫḫaru *ana ṣa-ḫa-ra-te* 'for the small ones' VAT 9410:32
ṣabbutu *lū līṭu lū ṣa-bu-tu-tu* 'be it hostages or captives' MATSH 2:19
zēzu *la-a ze-zu-ú-tu* 'who did not divide' MAL A § 25:89

§ 320 Two more rare functions of the adjective remain to be mentioned. It is possible for an adjective to be used as a predicate; but this is usual, considering that Akkadian normally uses the stative. In the case of the expression *mētu šūt* 'he is dead', it may be observed that nominal clauses with the anaphoric pronoun cannot use a stative, even though stative forms of the nominal predicate exist (see § 513).
mētu *me-e-tu šūt* 'he is dead' MATSH 8:49'

11 This translation was suggested by Postgate in UŠA (110–11 no. 50). As indicated in the commentary, the translation of the CAD A_1 (58a) is equally possible, which reads that the stones are on the *kalammu* and the borders.

8.5 Participles

§ 321 A morphologically and semantically similar group to the adjectives are the participles, which are inflected in a similar manner. The base of the G-stem is likewise similar to the adjectives, but lengthening takes place on the penultimate /ā/ > *PāRiS*, preventing /i/ from being elided. Note that the secondary D, Š and N-stems take the prefix *mu-* and the basic preterite forms are *muPaRRiS(u)*, *mušaPRiS(u)* and *munPaRS(u)*.

§ 322 Participles are used for active verbs, substantivizing the root to indicate the agent of a verb, e.g., *maḫāṣu* 'to hit' > *māḫiṣu* 'the person who hits'. Participles of adjectival verbs do not occur. We mostly find adjectives being used as normal nouns, rather than an actual verb.

zāʾiru	lú*za-i-ru* 'enemy, opponent' MATSH 2:51; lú*za-i-ri* T 98-42:18'
multapšiqu	*mu-ul-tap-ši-iq-te* 'woman having difficulty in childbirth' Lambert 1969:50

Participles can be used to introduce a kind of dependent clause. Similar to the relative clauses with *ša*, the participle is used to describe the directly preceding head of the clause. Further parallels may be drawn with the Arabic *ḥāl* clauses (جملة الحال), where a participle in the accusative is used in a singular fashion to describe the subject (or head) of a sentence.[12] This construction remains rare in MA:

> *ṣab qalte a-li-ku-t[u] ša ḫu-ra-di ša ina ḫalze* [...] 'bowmen, serving in the army, who are in the province (the remaining text is partly damaged)' MARV 4 119:6–7

> *šumma* 1 *aʾīlu a-li-ku ša ḫu-ra-di ina panē paḫitīšu lū āla iṣbat* 'if one man, coming from battle, settled on (the land of) his province or city' MARV 4 119:25–26

In MA, the use of participles is rather limited. They are naturally common in royal inscriptions as an independent function: *mu-šá-ter* RIMA 1 A.9.78.1:13; ⌜*mul-tas*⌝*-ḫir* l. 14 However, in the core corpus, the use of participles mostly remains limited to the designations of different types of professions (cf. Jakob 2003), where they are lexicalized. Consider the following examples:

G-stem, masculine singular:

āliku	lú*a-lik urke* 'retainer' KAJ 118:10 cf. MARV 1 41:12
āpīu	lú*a-pi-ú* 'bakers' MARV 9 110:12
	lú*a-pi-e* 'baker' MATSH 12:33
dāgilu	PN lú*la da-gi-lu* 'PN, the blind one' MPR 3:13
ēpišu	*e-piš* GUŠKIN 'gold smith' MCS 2 1:7
ēṣidu	lú*e-ṣi-du* 'reaper' KAJ 11:3
kāṣiru	lú*ka-ṣi-ra* 'knotter' KAV 109:8
māḫiṣu	lú*ma-ḫi-ṣu* 'weaver' Billa 61:21
mākisu	lú*ma-ki-*⌜*su*⌝ 'tax-collector' KAJ 301:6 ~ *ma-ki-sa* MCS 2 1:6
nāgiru	*na-gi-ri* 'herald' KAJ 310:20
nāšīu	*a-na-ši* (*ana nāši*) *tuppīš[u]* KAJ 52:19
	na-ši tuppīšu KAJ 67:18–9

12 For example, *ġādara l-madīna ʾamsi mutawaǧǧihan ʾila r-rīfi* (غادر المدينة أمس متوجهاً إلى الريف) 'he left the city yesterday, heading for the countryside' (e.g., Fischer 2006, 173–74 § 380; Badawi/Carter/Gully 2004, 156–59 § 2.4.6).

	^{lú}*na-ši-a-na* 'the one who carried' MAL F § 1:6
rākibu	*ra*$^{?}$*-ki-ib* 'the rider' T 97-22:12
sāpīu	^{lú}*sa-pi-ú* 'felt-worker'' MARV 3 53:11
sāḫiru	*sa-ḫi-ra* 'peddler' MCS 2 1:8
	sa-ḫi-ri 'peddler' AO 19.229:7
ṣāḫitu	^{lú}*ṣa-ḫi-tu* 'oil presser' T 93-7:5
šāqīu	^{lú}*ša-qi-e*$^{!}$ 'cup bearer' KAJ 310:33
ṭēʾinu	^{lú}*ṭé-[i]-ni* 'miller' MARV 9 23 r. 2'
	ṭé-i-nu MPR 2:44
zāʾiru	^{lú}*za-i-ru* 'enemy' MATSH 2:51
zāriqu	^{lú}*za-ri-qi* 'overseer' A 2605 (NTA, 27):9; A 2609 (NTA, 29):11

G-stem, feminine singular:

bānitu	*ba-ni-tu* 'mother' (Bab. *bāntum*) Lambert 1969:37
tārīu	*ta-ri-te* 'nurse' MARV 1 40:17

Gt-stem, masculine singular:

muttaḫṣu	*mu-ut-taḫ-iṣ* (< *maḫāṣu*) 'warrior' Lambert 1969:40

Gtn-stem, masculine singular:

mumtalliʾu	*mu-te-li-ú* 'replacement(?)' MPR 69:27

D-stem, masculine singular:

mudammiqu	^{m}*Mu-dam-me-eq* A 3196 (NTA, 39):19
murabbīu	10-*mu-ra-bi* TR 102:13
muraddīu	^{md}UTU-*mu-ra-di* KAJ 59:16
muraqqīu	*mu-ra-qi-e* 'perfume maker' KAJ 192:18
	mu-ra-qi-te MARV 2 22:24
mušallim	^{m}*A-šur-mu-šal-lim* KAJ 114:23
	^{m}EN-*mu-sal-la-e* Billa 37:3(?)
	$^{m\,d}$30-*mu*-SILIM 'Sîn-mušallim' MARV 9 96:3
mušaqqīu	*mu-ša-qí* 'giver of water (to cattle)' MARV 3 25:6
mutaʾʾeru	*mu-ta-e-r[u]* 'fire-rake' MAH 16130 i 2'

D-stem, feminine singular:

mukannišu	^{f}*Mu-ka*$^{!}$*-ni-šat-*^{d}*Taš-me-ti* MARV 1 57 iv 16'
mummertu	^{f}*mu-um-me-er-ta* 'procuress' MAL A § 23:21

Š-stem, masculine singular:

mušabšīu	^{d}*A-šur-mu-šab-ši* MARV 1 6:31
mušākilu	*mu-ša-ki-il* MUŠEN^{meš} 'feeder of birds' KAJ 218:6
	^{lú}*mu-šá-ki-lu* A 1735 (NTA, 18):16
mušakšidu	^{md}*A-šur-mu*-KUR-*id* (*Aššur-mušakšid*) KAM 10 10:5
mušarkisu	^{lú}*mu-ša-ar-k[i-su]* MARV 10 70:10
	⸢^{lú}⸣ *mu-šar-*⸢*ki*⸣*-su* MARV 10 28:21
mušašrīu	^{m}10-*mu-šá-aš-*⸢*ri*⸣ KAJ 224:8
mušēlīu	^{d}*Adad-mu-še-li* KAJ 76:6
mušēzibu	^{d}UTU-*mu-še-zi-ib* KAJ 165:29[13]
	^{d}*Iš*$_{8}$*-tá[r-m]u-še-zi-bat* TR 2069A+:14

13 Note that *mušēzib* is usually written as *mu*-KAR in PNs.

Št$_1$-stem:

multēṣittu *mul-te-ṣi-tu-šu-nu* 'their expenses' KAJ 307:14

Št$_2$-stem:

multēšertu *mul-te-šèr-tu* 'maintenance' T 98-7:13; cf. T 98-30:15

N-stem:

munnabdu *mu-nab-di* 'refugee' MARV 4 30:17'

§ 323 According to common grammar, the participle is inflected in a similar way to adjectives. This would mean that they receive the adjective masculine plural suffix *-ūt*.[14]

G-stem, masculine plural:

ētiru *e-ṭí-ru-tu* 'saviours' Rm 376 r. 21 (incantation)
nāšīu $^{\text{lú.meš}}$*na-ši-ú-*[*te*] 'carriers' Coronation Ritual i 26
ṣāpīu *ṣa-pi-ú-tu* 'dyers' Whiting 1988:2

G-stem, feminine plural:

dāgilu IGI^{meš} *da-gi-la-te* 'seeing eyes' KTN inventory i 27

D-stem, feminine plural:

muraqqīu *mu-ra-qi-a-tu* 'perfume makers' MARV 3 1 vi 13'

In most cases, the participles have become substantives and are, as such, lexicalized. For this reason, we find the masculine plural participles inflected as if they were normal nouns.[15]

dāgilu $^{\text{lú.meš}}$*da-gi-lu* 'people with sight' KAJ 180:2
munnabdu *mu-nab-du* 'refugees' KBo 1 20:17'
nāgiru *na-gi-ri* 'heralds' MARV 1 iv 32
sāmidu *sa-mi-di-šu*^{meš} 'his grinders' MARV 1 49:10
ṭāʾinu *ṭa-i-nu*^{meš} 'grinders' MARV 6 90:14
zāriqu GAL *za-ri-qi*^{meš} 'chief of the overseers' MAPD § 9:55

8.6 Participles with suffixed *-ān*

§ 324 We already discussed the use of the suffix *-ān* on a number of substantives. In the MAL and MA edicts, we find *-ān* to be frequently suffixed to participle forms. It has traditionally been assumed that, in this context, *-ān* had the function of individualizing the participles. Thus, a form such as *tādinānu* refers to a specific seller, whereas *tādinu* is indefinite, as suggested by Goetze (1946; also GAG, 85f § 56r). However, objections were raised against this opinion due to the lack of any actual foundation for these claims.[16] Streck continued to emphasize an example from the Codex Hammurapi (§ 9), where *nādinānum* and *nādin* are used in succeeding order, although both refer to an unspecified seller (Streck 2005, 235). Rather, it seems that *-ān* had no function other than to turn true

14 Cf. GAG, 138 § 85d; Ungnad (1992, 47 § 38l).
15 See GAG, 94 § 61k; Streck (2014a, 93–93 § 206); cf. GOA § 19.7.
16 See Gelb (1955, 106); Streck (2005).

participles into substantives.[17] It should be noted that *-ān* participles usually occur in the context of the verb it derives from (cf. Kouwenberg 2010, 208).

> *ma-ḫi-ra-a-nu ša ina qāt aššat aʾīle im-ḫu-ru-ú-ni* 'the receiver who has received it from the hand of (another man's) wife' MAL A § 3:40–41
>
> *nāgira* 3-*šu* (…) *ú-sa-ás-sa* (…) *ana mu-sa-as-si-a-ni ša nāgire zakku* 'he will make the herald proclaim three times (…) to the one who made the herald proclaim it is cleared' MAL B 6:5–6/46–47
>
> *šumma lā marʾassu ana mute it-ti-din* (…) *ummiānu panīu ittalka ina muḫḫi ta-di-na-a-ni ša šinnilte šīmi šinnilte išallim* 'if someone has given someone other than his daughter to a husband (…) an earlier creditor comes forward and from the one who sold the woman he will receive the value of the woman' MAL A § 39:26–41

This is not always the case in MA:

> *ba-ti-qa-an-šu lubultušu ilaqqe* 'his informer will take his clothes' MAL A § 40:82–83
>
> PN *maḫi*[*r*] PN *mu-šal-lim-a-nu* 'PN received it, PN is the one who will pay in full' KAJ 92:7–10

In other cases, the action of the participle is at least implied:

> *ana pî ēkalle ubbalašši* (…) *ṣa-bi-ta-an-ša ṣubāta*$^{\text{hi.a}}$-*ša ilaqqe* 'he will bring her to the palace entrance (…) her arrester will take her clothes' MAL A § 40:91–93
>
> ^{f}*batulta iṣbatma ú-ma-an-ze-e-eʾ-ši abu ša batulte aššat na-i-ka-a-na* (…) *ilaqqe* 'he seized a young girl with the intent to rape her, the father of the girl will take the wife of the rapist' MAL A § 55:21–25
>
> [*šum*]*ma* [*al*]*mattu ana bēt aʾīle te-ta-ra-ab* (…) *ina bēt a-ḫi-za-ni-ša irtibi* 'if a widow has entered the house of a man (…) (her son) will grow up in the house of he who married her' MAL A § 28:1–14

§ 325 It may be pointed out that actual participles are very rare in MA and mostly limited to professions. The occurrence of *-ān*-formed participles, in MA, may simply have replaced the forms that are without. Since these kinds of participles with *-ān* are only required on a regular basis in laws, it should not come as a surprise to find most MA examples confined to laws, with the exception of *mu-šal-lim-a-nu* 'escort(?)' KAJ 92:10 and *ba-ti-qa-an-šu* 'his informer' MARV 1 41:12.[18] Likewise, this kind of word formation seems to be frequent in all Mesopotamian law cases. As may be expected, the use of this morpheme is rare in OA.[19] However, in NA, its function has shifted to intensifying and, perhaps in some cases, become lexical (SNAG, 84 § 3.10a). Most participles are basic G-stem and, sometimes, D-stems; other stems are not attested. The plural is usually formed with the adjectival *-uttu*. Below is a list of MA attestations of the morpheme *-ān* (at least one per substantive); no female forms are attested:

---

17 Notice the parallel function of *-ān* in Syriac (cf. Nöldeke 1904, 79 § 130), where one finds participles such as *manhrānā* (ܡܢܗܪܢܐ) (< ptc. *aphel*) 'enlightener' or *mettsimānā* (ܡܬܬܣܝܡܢܐ) (< ptc. *ethpeel*) 'to be ordained'.

18 Cf. Huehnergard (1995, 198 § 20.2), who gives three examples, all of which are common in the Mesopotamian law codices.

19 Cf. GKT, 89 § 57c; GOA § 4.3.3; Kouwenberg (2010, 209 n44).

G-stem, masculine singular:

āḫizānu	^{lú}*a-ḫi-za-a-*[*nu*] 'bridegroom' MAL A § 39:36
ālidānu	*a-li-da-ni-šu* 'his begetter' MAL A § 28:9
āmirānu	*a-me-ra-a-ni* 'eyewitness' MAL A § 47:9
	a-me-ra-na 'eyewitness' MAPD § 19:94
bātiqānu	*ba-ti-qa-an-šu* 'his informer' MAL A § 40:82; MARV 1 41:12 (Arn)
	ba-ti-qa-šu-nu 'their informer' RE 92:12 (Sa/TN)
ērišānu	[*e-ri*]-⸢*ša*⸣-*a-nu* 'cultivator' MAL B § 19:10
lāqiāni	*la-qí-a-nu* 'buyer' MAL C+ § 1:2; § 6b:2
māḫirānu	*ma-ḫi-ra-a-nu* 'recipient' MAL A § 3:40
māḫiṣānu	*ma-ḫi-ṣa-a-na* 'the one who struck' MAL A § 50:79
nādiānu	*na-di-a-ni* 'the one who laid out' MAL B § 12:17
nāʾikānu	^{lú}*na-i-ka-a-nu* 'fornicator' MAL A § 14:38
nāšiānu	^{lú}*na-ši-a-na* 'the one who carried' MAL F § 1:6
šāmiānu	*ša-me-a-nu* 'hearsay witness' MAL A § 47:12
tādinānu	*ta-di-na-a-nu* 'the seller' MAL A § 39:41

D-stem, masculine singular:

muballiṭānu	*mu-bal-li-ṭa-ni-*⸢*ša*⸣ 'maintainer' MAL A § 39:35
muppišānu	*mu-up-pi-ša-na ša kišpe* 'the committer of witchcraft' MAL A § 47:6
murabbiānu	*mu-ra-bi-a-ni-šu* 'his foster father' MAL A § 28:6
musassiānu	*mu-sa-as-si-a-ni* 'the one who made a proclamation' MAL B § 6:46
mušallimānu	*mu-šal-lim-a-nu* 'escort(?)' KAJ 92:10

As these forms are basically participles, they are treated as adjectives and thus receive the ending *-uttu* in the masculine plural. This is somewhat unexpected, as most normal participles have switched to the paradigm of nouns and receive the *-ū/ē* plural ending (see § 323).

dāʾikānu	⸢*da*⸣-*i-ka-nu-te* 'murderers' MAL A § 10:100
māḫirānu	*ma-ḫi-ra-nu-te-ma* 'recipients' MAL A § 3:30

Instead of participle forms, adjectives can be used as well (Streck 2005, 237). So far, only one example is extant:

qayipānu	*qa-ia-pa-nu* 'creditor' MAL K § 3:7

Unlike NA (Kouwenberg 2010, 209), it should be noted that these nominalized participles and adjectives are not found in the semantic class of professions (cf. Jakob 2003). The morpheme *-ān* seems to be limited to persons with a more vague or general activity, such as 'killing' or 'buying', rather than actual professions.

Chapter 9: Numbers

§ 326 Numbers in many ancient Semitic languages remain a terra incognita. As nowadays, scribes preferred to use simple symbols, instead of writing them out. Consequently, and due to the fact that a text corpus of a dead language is limited, the material on exceptional plene-written spellings remains generally insufficient for a detailed reconstruction of the numeral systems of these languages. Akkadian and especially MA are no exceptions here, while the existence of some unknown numeral patterns only adds to the confusion.

§ 327 In this chapter, no attempt is made to extensively discuss the logographic system for indicating numbers. MA has its own ways in this respect, but it appears that they are mostly similar to the contemporary Babylonian system and add little to our knowledge of MA grammar. The exceptions here are the cases where phonetic complements are added. These are of interest because they add to the evidence of true syllabic spellings, which remains rather slim. Adverbs of number are discussed in the chapter on adverbs (§ 485ff).

9.1 Logographic numbers

§ 328 A very brief summary of the logographic numbers may be given. Signs used for logographic numbers can also be found in the sign list. Units are counted in the decimal system with every number below 10 counted with a vertical sign (DIŠ). Higher numbers with one sign are 10 (U), 100 (ME) and 1,000 (LIM). The last two are semisyllabic (see § 335 below). Tens are counted by writing an additional *Winkelhaken* (U) with regard to number 60, which is usually written GÉŠ or, semisyllabically, ŠU-ŠI. This second alternative was probably introduced to avoid confusion with the graphic number '1', as DIŠ and GÉŠ are the same sign (MZL no. 748). Thus, the number 80 would be written as GÉŠ+NEŠ (U+U), e.g., 𒁹𒌋𒌋 MARV 9 17:6. Higher numbers, such as 200 or 3,000, would be MIN (DIŠ 2x) ME (𒈫𒈨) and EŠ$_5$ (DIŠ 3x) LIM (𒐈𒇷). Below is a table with the most important logographic cardinal numbers; the MZL numbering is provided with numbers in brackets, where applicable.

1	2	3	4	5	6
DIŠ 𒁹 (748)	MIN 𒈫 (825)	EŠ$_5$ 𒐈 (834)	LIMMU[1] 𒐉 (860)	ÍA 𒐊 (861)	ÀŠ 𒐋 (862)
7	8	10	60	100	1000
IMIN 𒐌 (866)	USSU 𒐍 (864)	U 𒌋 (810)	GÉŠ/ŠU-ŠI 𒁹 (748)/𒋗𒅆	ME 𒈨 (753)	LIM 𒇷 (724)

Figure 24: Cardinal numbers.

§ 329 There are a few special types of numbering that differ from the usual type described above. Most important is the measurement seah (*sūtu*), which is counted in units of six: one *sūtu* (BÁN), two *sūtu* (BANMIN), three *sūtu* (BANEŠ), four *sūtu* (BANLIMMU), five *sūtu*

1 LIMMU is preferred over LIMMU$_5$, e.g., KAJ 37:2; LVUH 48:1.

(BANIA), six *sūtu* (NIGIDA). Graphically, each seah is indicated by a horizon line drawn upon a vertical. The fourth and fifth seahs are more redolent a *Winkelhaken* and attached on the right side of the first three. The sixth seah is simply indicated by one horizontal, with each additional seah drawn at the right side in a new seah sign. Rather than applying these complicated sign names in the transcriptions of this study, we simply count the number of seahs followed by BÁN. For a discussion and another opinion on the notation of the seah measure, see Postgate (2013, 55–56).

1	2	3	4	5	6
BÁN 𒑏 (122)	BANMIN 𒑐 (465)	BANEŠ 𒑑 (549)	BANLIMMU 𒑒 (550)	BANIA 𒑔 (551)	NIGIDA (749)

Figure 25: Seah measures.

§ 330 A talent *biltu* (GUN) (𒄘) is counted with horizontal lines, which are drawn preceding it, e.g., 3 GUN KAJ 146:8; 4 GUN KAJ 155:9; 5 GUN KAJ 145:2. Higher numbers are also possible, but fall back on the normal notation: 80 (GÉŠ+NEŠ) GUN KAJ 158:2; also in combination: 12 GUN (U+MIN$_5$) KAJ 159:2. Horizontal lines are also used to count years, where they succeed the logogram, e.g., MU.4 KAJ 313:4. For the underlying Akkadian numerals counting years, see § 347.

1	2	3	4	5	6
AŠ 𒀸 (1)	MIN$_5$[2] 𒐀 (209)	EŠ$_6$[3] 𒐁 (4)	LÍMMU[4] 𒐂 (215)	IA$_7$[5] 𒐃 (216)	AŠ$_4$[6] 𒐄 (217)
7	8	9			
ÍMIN[7] 𒐅 (218)	ÚSSU[8] 𒐆 (219)	ÍLIMMU[9] 𒐇 (220)			

Figure 26: Counting of talents.

§ 331 Fractions can also be found, e.g., ½ KAJ 66:14; ⅓ KAJ 130:3; T 98-63:3; ⅔ KAJ 16:2; KAJ 130:2; MARV 4 114:11'; ⅚ KAJ 40:9; MARV 10 81:1. I know of no attestation involving smaller fractions, such as ¼ and ⅙, but they may have been used.

½	⅓	⅔	⅚
SA$_9$ (120)	ŠUŠANA 𒑚 (826)	ŠANABI 𒑛 (832)	KINGUSILA 𒑜 (838)

Figure 27: Fractions.

§ 332 Lastly, we should make a quick reference to the different measurements used in the MA documents. As it falls outside the scope of this study to attempt to approach the exact value of the original amounts, we must refer to the entry in the RlA by Powell (1989/90).

2 MIN$_5$ is preferred over MIN$_6$, e.g., KAJ 293:17.
3 EŠ$_6$ is preferred over EŠ$_{16}$, e.g., KAJ 54:2.
4 LÍMMU is preferred over LIMMU$_4$, e.g., KAJ 155:9; KAJ 168:2; T 98-63:4.
5 IA$_7$ is preferred over IA$_9$, e.g., KAJ 144:2; KAJ 145:2; KAJ 169:10.
6 AŠ$_4$ is preferred over AŠ$_9$, e.g., T 98-63:1.
7 ÍMIN is preferred over ÌMIN, e.g., MARV 3 2:11'.
8 ÚSSU is preferred over ÙSSU, e.g., LVUH 51:4.
9 ÍLIMMU is preferred over ÌLIMMU, e.g., Ali 24T:9.

Moreover, a more extensive summary of the system is found in Postgate (2013, 53–56). The *šeqlu-manāʾu-biltu* triad indicates weight, which approaches (but is not identical to) eight grams - 500 grams - 30 kilograms. The *qāʾu-sūtu-emāru* refers to the weight, which approaches (but is not identical to) one litre - 10 litres - 100 litres. Furthermore, it has been pointed out that, while seah and homer are common transliterations for *sūtu* and *emāru* coming from Hebrew, it would be logical to transcribe *qāʾu*; the same applies to qav (Postgate 2013, 55). For area measures, we only have the *iku* (IKU no. 174)( ), which indicates around 60 x 60 m (about 3,600 m^2).

šeqlu (shekel)	*manāʾu* (mina)	*biltu* (talent)
GÍN (836)	MA.NA 60 *šeqlu*	GUN (GÚ.UN) 60 *manāʾu* (179)
qāʾu	*sūtu* (seah)	*emāru* (homer)
SÌLA (QA) (99)	BÁN 10 *qāʾu* (122)	ANŠE/I/U 10 *sūtu* (353)

Figure 28: Different measures of weight and capacity.

9.2 Cardinal numbers

§ 333 Cardinal numbers are only scarcely attested in the MA corpus. As with modern script nowadays, they are usually written with symbols, instead of being spelled out. In a few cases, a phonetic complement is added, but both syllabic and semisyllabic spellings remain uncommon in MA. Most syllabically written numbers are in the status absolutus, which is common for cardinal numerals.[10] In 1 *li-me* 5 *ME* SIG$_4$^{meš} '1,500 bricks' KAJ 161:3, we find *līmu* '1,000' written in the genitive. Common Semitic 'gender polarity' is not attested in MA, but again our evidence is very flimsy.[11] As gender polarity does not occur with the numerals 1 and 2, we do find *iltēn* MAL A § 46:101 referring to a brother and *iltēt beritte* 'one clasp' KAJ 123a:3.[12] In this light, the reading 2 *ši-na* DUMU.MUNUS ^{d}*A-nim* 'two are the daughters of An' Lambert 1969:59 (in Veldhuis 1991, 12f, 64) is preferable to Lambert's original reading 2-*ši-na* DUMU.MUNUS ^{d}*A-nim* 'two daughters of An'.

§ 334 Cardinal numbers with phonetic complements are as rare as fully syllabic numerals. Still, we have both feminine and masculine forms of the number '1'. Some distinction can be made between the adjectival use 1-*et be-ri-it-te* 'one clasp' KAJ 123a:3; 12 and the independent use *iltu il-te-en tuššab* 'she will live with one' MAL A § 46:101. The numeral precedes the noun in attributive function.

iltēn 1-*en ina aḫḫēša* 'one of her brothers' MAL A § 48:39
1-*en* *u*$_4$-⸢*me*⸣ 'one day' MARV 7 1:15

10 For example, Ungnad (1992, 57 § 47b); GAG, 96 § 139d; 241 § 139i.

11 Cf. CGSL, 116; Lipiński (2001, 293f § 35.6).

12 Gender polarity is not attested with the numerals 1 and 2 in Akkadian (see Streck 1995, 12–13 § 17; cf. the higher numbers in Streck 1995, 35 § 30). As he continues to point out, gender polarity is expected to be on the way out in later forms of Akkadian, in analogy with the other Semitic languages, where it is more or less totally lost in modern vernacular (see Streck 1995, 35–39 § 31).

ina tūa[r] 1-*en ra-di iddan* ‘upon returning he shall give one r.’ TR 2021+:10–12
ka-al-bi$_4$ 1-*en* ‘one dog’ RS 18.54a:12’ (probably not Assyrian)
iltēt 1-*et beritte* ‘one clasp’ KAJ 124a:3; 12
šitta 2-*ta qa-ta-ti i-la-aq-qé-ma* ‘he will take two shares’ KAM 10 25:15–16

Syllabic spellings are found for the number ‘1’, although they remain rare. Note the erroneous case ending in MATC 15, possibly a locative.

iltēn *iltu il-te-en tuššab* ‘she will live with one (stepson)’ MAL A § 46:101
ana il-te-⸢nu⸣$^?$*-na mamma lū lā idabbub* ‘alone(?), nobody may speak’ MATC 15:33–34

Rather than assume a new type of adverb (as in UGM, 55), we may add *il-ta-a-nu* BVW F: eight to the list of cardinal numbers. Unfortunately, the context of this form is broken. There is only one possible syllabic attestation for the number ‘2’ in a rather broken context (see Freydank 1992a). Notice the unexpected aleph sign, which does not belong there, such that the reading is therefore probably incorrect and the translation makes little sense.

šitta [*ši*]-⸢*it*⸣*-ta-*ʾ*e ḫimsātēšunu* ‘two(?) (is$^?$) their wrongful possessions’ KAV 217:11’

§ 335 Larger numbers are usually written with one sign: ŠU-ŠI ‘60’, ME ‘100’ and LIM ‘1,000’. These logograms are based on the underlying Akkadian forms: *šūši; mētu/meʾat; līmu*. The Assyrian word for *mētu/miʾat* ‘100’, despite being written with the sign ME, derives from PS *miʾ-(a)t*.[13] It is therefore not entirely clear whether ME is purely logographic or syllabic. These logograms occur frequently in lists and notes (cf. LB Streck 1995, 45–46).

meʾat 5 *me emāru* ‘500 homers’ MARV 8 19:8
šūši 1 *šu-ši* ‘sixty’ MARV 10 22:3
līmu 2 *lim emāru* ‘2,000 homers’ MARV 8 19:6

Rarely do we find syllabic spellings:

meʾat 1 *li-im* 2 *me-ti libnātu* ‘1,200 bricks’ KAJ 87:1
1 *me-*[*a*]*t emāru* ŠE ‘100 homers of barley’ T 98-105:4’
līmu 1 *tuppu ša* 1 *emāru* ŠE 1 *li-me* 5 ME *libnātu* ‘one tablet of one homer of barley and 1,500 bricks’ KAJ 161:2–3
gabbe LIM-ma ia-ú ūl ma[*ti*] ‘a total of 1,000 (troops), not one missing’ A 1947+:6 (obscure text)

In the case of KAJ 87, the counted bricks are a casus pendens and would be expected to occur in the nominative. The false genitive is probably a rare case of an anaptyctic vowel in MA (cf. NA Luukko 2004, 102 § 4.8). The example in A 1947+ is probably not a syllabic accusative, but involves the particle *-ma*. Still, we need to await a decent publication of this text to be certain.

§ 336 The logographic spellings of numerals are abundant in MA. This is mostly due to the character of our corpus, which consists of many transactions of goods and lists. The numerals always precede the nouns in these texts, as they would have in spoken language.[14]

13 See Fox (2003, 73); GOA § 8.2.5.

14 Very rarely does a cardinal numeral occur in apposition: ^{gu4}ÁB 2 *ša pi-ti* PN ‘two cows of the responsibility of PN’ T 97-17:6–7. This example is even more problematic because the numeral is

Unfortunately, the substantives themselves are usually written logographically and refer to a small number of items or variations of them, e.g., UDU ‘sheep’ with variations, such as UDU.NIM. They usually take a plural marker, although instances that are without can occasionally be found. It should be mentioned that measurements, such as IKU and MA.NA, always remain singular.

Plural numbers with a plural logographic noun:

abnu	56 NA$_{4}^{\text{meš}}$ ‘56 stones’ MATC 63:6
alpu	PAP 21 GU$_{4}^{\text{meš}}$ ‘a total of 21 oxen’ A 3194 (NTA, 38):10
	17 GU$_4$.NÍTA^{meš} KAJ 289:6
emmeru	26 UDU.NÍTA^{meš} ‘two sheep’ KAJ 115:2 idem. passim
	PAP-*ma* 1 *LIM* 7 *ME* [1]4 UDU^{meš} ‘a total of 1714 sheep’ A 113 (NTA, 15):7
emāru	3 ANŠE^{meš} ‘three donkeys’ MATC 22B:7
kakkallu	3 GUKKAL^{meš} ‘fat-tailed sheep’ KAJ 314:3
libittu	1 LIM SIG$_{4}^{\text{meš}}$ ‘1,000 bricks’ KAJ 112:8
mašku	ŠU.NIGÍN 13 KUŠ^{meš} ‘a total of 13 skins’ KAJ 225:5
sīrāšu	5 ^{lú}LUNGA^{meš} ‘five brewers’ MATC 12:4
ṣubātu	2 TÚG$^{\text{ḫi.a}}$ ‘two textiles’ KAV 99:15

Plural numbers with a singular logographic noun:

emmeru	4 UDU ‘four sheep’ KAJ 189:6
mašku	11 KUŠ MÁŠ ‘11 goat hides’ KAJ 224:12
urīṣu	ŠU.NÍGIN 11 KUŠ MÁŠ ‘a total of 11 goat skins’ KAJ 224:12

With syllabically written nouns, the situation is more varied, with singular nouns regularly following a logographic number. In some cases, these singular nouns receive a plural marker. Similar spellings are well attested in LB (Streck 1995, 48-52).

Plural numbers with a singular syllabic noun:

agannu	4 *a-ga-nu* ‘four cauldrons’ KAJ 292:4
ebertu	7 *e-bir-ta*^{meš} ‘seven steps’ MAPD § 21:108
kibsu	17 *ki-ib-su* ‘17 treads’ KAJ 128:3
lītu	10$^{?!}$ *li-tu* (…) [*š*]*a*$^{?}$*mātu* ‘10 bought cows’ AO 21.157:1–2
nalbattu	10 ^{giš}*na-al-ba-tu*^{meš} *ša* SIG$_4$-*tu* ‘10 brick moulds’ A 3310:1–2
niggallu	20 *ni-gál-lu* ZABAR T 93-3:1
ṣimittu	3 *ṣi-mi-te* ^{anše}*ku-di-ni* ‘three yokes of donkeys’ MATC 25A:9
šabārtu	8 *ša-bar-tu* ‘eight bars’ MARV 3 19:14
šaḫḫu	12 ^{giš}*ša-aḫ*$^{!}$-*ḫu*^{meš} SIG$_5$ ‘12 good bowls(?)’ KAJ 310:41
tarīu	3 MUNUS^{meš} *ta-ri-*[*t*]*u* ‘three female children’ KAJ 180:8

Plural numbers with plural syllabic nouns:

ku(k)ku(b)bu	5 *ku-ku-ba-tu* ‘five k bowls’ KAJ 292:6
gurrātu	48 U$_{8}^{\text{meš}}$-*ra-tu* ‘48 ewes’ T 98-43:2
pursītu	5 ^{dug}*pu-ur-s*[*i*]-*a*-[*t*]*u* ‘five p bowls’ T 98-131:9
qūpu	ŠU.NÍGIN 24 *qu-pa-tu* ‘a total of 24 boxes’ KAJ 310:38
umū	15 UD^{meš}-*te-šu-nu* MATC 40:13

---

written with two horizontal wedges, instead of vertical ones. This would normally suggest the counting talents (GUN). The numeral reading is therefore likely to be a mistake, which is difficult to check because of the absence of a photo. Alternatively, it may refer to an adjectival number (see § 340ff).

An overview of the (semi)syllabic attestations of cardinal numbers:

1	m	abs.	*iltēn*	*il-te-en*	MAL A § 46:101
				1-*en*	MAL A § 48:39; TR 2021+:11; RS 18.54a:12’
		nom.?	*iltēnu*	*il-te-*⸢*nu*⸣?*-na*	MATC 15:33
				il-ta-a-nu	BVW F:8
	f	abs.	*iltēt*	1-*et*	KAJ 124a:3; 12
2		?	*šitta*	[*ši*]⸢*-it*⸣*-ta-ʾe*	KAV 217:11’
60	–	–	*šūši*	*šu-ši*	passim
100	–	–	*meʾat*	*me*	passim
				me-ti	KAJ 87:1
1,000	–	–	*līmu*	*lim*	passim
				li-im	KAJ 87:1
				lim-ma	A 1947+:6
		gen.		*li-me*	KAJ 161:3

9.3 Ordinal numbers and adjectives

§ 337 The ordinal numbers are not well known in Akkadian, while the situation in MA is rather confusing. An ordinal form of the number ‘1’ is not attested and generally replaced in Akkadian with the cardinal number or a substantive, such as *panûm*, which can be translated as ‘first’ or ‘previous’. In this sense, it is the opposite of *urkīu* ‘last’, e.g.:

panīu	*pa-ni-a ša a-na šarre* [*u*]*qarribūni* ‘the first (gift), which they brought to the king’ Coronation Ritual iii 5-6
	[^{ku}]⸢*Imarāyu pa-ni-ú* ‘the first Emariote’ MATSH 13:10
	pa-a-ni ša 6 ITI.UD^{meš} *maḫrū* ‘earlier (rations) of the six months are received’ MPR 66:43–44
panittu	*marʾū pa-ni-te* ‘the sons of first (=previous wife)’ MAL A § 46:104
panīuttu	*lū pa-ni-*⸢*ú-tu ulū ur*⸣*-ki-ú-tu* ‘the first and the last’ MATSH 10:32-33
	[*n*+]14 *ṣabʾu ša lēʾāni lū* ⸢*pa*⸣*-ni-ú-te ulū ur-ki-ú-*⸢*te*⸣ *ša* (…) *itūrūnenni* ‘*n*+14 troops of the tablets, be it the first and last, who returned’ MARV 4 27:18-21
paniyātu	*tuppātēšu pa-ni-a-te* ‘his previous tablets’ KAJ 119:1-2

§ 338 From the number ‘2’ onwards, a type of numeral pattern *PaRāSi* occurs. W. Mayer claimed that it was the ordinal replacement of the Assyrian ordinal pattern *PaRiS* (OB *PaRuS*) and this has since been followed by other scholars, even though the phenomenon would be unique in Semitic languages.[15] Consider the following two examples, which both seem to indicate the ordinal number ‘2’:

(A) *marāšu ša-ni-ú* (…) *mēt* ‘his second son is dead’ MAL A § 30:23–25

(B) *ana marʾīšu ša-na-i-e* ‘to his second son’ MAL A § 30:26

It appears that both numbers are morphologically not identical (A: *šanīu*; B: *šanāyiu*). However, it is clear that *šanīu* is more closely related to the ordinal pattern of OB (*šanûm*)

15 See UGM, 53f § 55; GAG, 115 § 70c, 241 § 139l; Lipiński (2001, 302 §35.27); Streck (2011, 372 § 4.5). As pointed out by Lipiński, there is a number of Semitic languages that have an ordinal number with an added nisbe (or related) morpheme added. Most noticeable is Ge‘ez, where forms with and without a nisbe seem to be used in free variation (Tropper 2002, 83 § 43.22). In other languages, the nisbe ending is fixed (e.g., Amharic in Leslau 2000, 52 § 46.1; BH in Joüon/Muraoka 2006, 301 § 101; Syriac in Ungnad 1932, 52 § 24k). It is important to note that, in Amharic and Hebrew, the nisbe is attached directly to the cardinal construction.

and especially OA (*šanīum*) with the *PaRiS* pattern.[16] Likewise, the NA evidence points to the *PaRiS* pattern for ordinal numbers (SNAG, 85f § 3.11.2), making the occurrence of *parāsīu* rather unusual and unexpected. Other attestations of *šanīu* include:

šanīu — *šumma aššat aʾīle ina bēt aʾīle ša-ni-e-ma mimma taltiriq* 'if a wife has stolen something from another man's house' MAL A § 5:57–58

šumma aššat aʾīle lā abuša lā aḫuša lā marāša aʾīlu ša-ni-um-ma ḫarrāna ultaṣbissi 'if another man, not her father, neither her brother, not her son, nor her son, arranged to have a wife travel with him' MAL A § 22:105–107

[*aḫu ša-ni-u*]*m-ma ittalka* 'another brother came' MAL B § 4:31 (admittedly hardly legible)

ana ṣarpe ana aʾīle ša-ni-im-ma [*iddin*] 'he has sold it to another man' MAL C+ § 2:9

ana libbi ḫersi ša-ni-e tuzakka 'you will clear it into a second *ḫersu*-vessel PKT 3 i 9

ṣibta [...] *ša Sūtīe ša-ni-im-ma lā i*[*laqqe*] 'he may not take interest from another Sutean' T 04-37:26–27

šanittu — *išku ša-ni-tu iltēšama tattalpat* 'the second testicle is also infected' MAL A § 8:82–83 cf. *ša-ni-ta* l. 86

ana māte ša-ni-te-em-ma il-ta-pár-šu 'he sent him to another country' MAL A § 36:4–5 cf. l. § 47:86

ana māte ša-ni-ti ana ṣarpe iddin 'he will sell it in another country' MAL C+ § 3:15

ša-ni-tam-ma MAPD § 18:87†

tuppu ⸢*ša-ni*?⸣-[*tu*] *šēṣuata*sic. 'a second tablet has been issued' KAJ 122:10–11

šarrānu ša māte ša-ni-it-te ittalkūni ibtikiū 'kings of another country (=other countries) came and cried' T 02-32:10–13

Preceding the noun:

šanīu — *ina* 2-*e ūme* 'on the second day' MARV 1 10:11

ina ša-ni-e ū-mi 'on the second day' KUB 3 77:12'

šanittu — *ša ša-ni-te qātīšu iltu aḫḫēšu puršu iṣalli* 'for what is his second share, he will cast his lot with his brothers' MAL B § 1:13–14

šumma ša-ni-ta tuppī ultēb[*ilakku*] 'when I sent you my second tablet' KAV 169:14–15

With *mamma* 'somebody/who(so)ever', the meaning of *šanīu* changes to 'somebody else/who(so)ever else'. With negation *lā*, it becomes 'nobody else':

šanīu — *lū ana aʾīle lū ana sinnilte ana ma-am-ma ša-ni-im-ma tattidin* 'she gives it either to a man, a woman or somebody else' MAL A § 3:26–28 cf. l. 36–37

ma-am-ma ša-ni-ú-um-ma la-a išaqqi 'nobody else may irrigate' MAL B § 17:19–20

[*an*]*a* ⸢*ma*?⸣-*am-ma ša-ni-im-ma* ⸢ *la*?-*a*? ⸣ *ta-e-*⸢*ra*?⸣-*an-ni* 'it is not returned to anybody else' MARV 4 24:5'–6'[17]

On two occasions, we find the ordinal number *šanīu* inflected as a plural noun. This demonstrates that the ordinals were in full congruence with number and gender, similar to adjectives. A similar plural is attested in OA as well.[18]

16 See GKT, 115 § 69; GOA 8.4.1; cf. GAG, 115 § 70c.

17 This passage is damaged and reading remains uncertain. The verbal form, here analysed as a stative, would be ungrammatical.

18 A plural form is attested in the passage *ša-ra-né-e ša-ni-ú-tim* 'other kings' Kt g/t 35:10, 14. See GOA §

šanīuttu *ūmū ša riqie*^{me}[^{š}] *šēbulika ša-ni-ú-tu*$^{!}$ *ibašši* 'the days when you are to send aromatics are there again' T 96-1:4-7
lū Sūtīū ša-ni-ú-tu-ma 'other Suteans' T 04-37:2

In the same texts, we also find the adverbial *šanittu* (AHw, 1164) in the meaning 'something else' or 'secondly' in order to introduce a new subject:

šanittu *š*[*a*]*-ni-ta ša Aššurāyē* [...] 'secondly, concerning Assyrians' T 04-37 r. 7

§ 339 Initially, no ordinal numbers, other than *šanīu* (m.) and *šanittu* (f.), were known in MA, until the following improved reading of the palace decrees and *šalšu* > *šaššu* 'third' was claimed (CAD Š$_{1}$, 264; Roth 1997, 205 for MAPD § 19:92). The same sound change /lš/ > /šš/ was attested in *ša-áš-šu-te-šu* 'the third time' PKT 4 obv. left 5 (§ 242 and § 485).

šaššu *ša-áš-šu iltēšunu* [*l*]*aššu* 'a third (person) is not with them' MAPD § 19:92

For the number 10, we have a few attestation referring to groups of people. These are likely substantivized collective forms based on the ordinal numbers. It is possible that the underlying form is *ešertu* (see MATC, 154), or *ešartu* (cf. GOA § 8.4.4).

ešertu 10 *ka-nu ša* 10*-te ša* PN '10 k. of 10 of PN' KAJ 292:15–17
ina UD.14.KÁM 10^{meš}*-tu gab-bu* 'on the 14th day all groups of 10' MATC 80:4
ina UD.16.KÁM 10^{meš}*-tu-ma* 'on the 16th day (all) groups of 10' MATC 80:5 cf. l. 9, 12
ina UD.17.KÁM 10*-tu* 'on the 17th day (all) groups of 10' MATC 80:6
10*-tu* PN MARV 4 127:20
rab 10*-ka aʾīlutte* 'your commander-of-ten (men)' T 93-2:9
GAL 10*-te* 'your commander-of-ten men' KAM 11 49:36; T 98-6:9; T 98-7:18
[G]AL ^{lú}10*-te* T 98-28:6

8.4.1.

The occurrence of *šaššu* 'third' next to *šanīu* (m.) and *šanittu* (f.) clearly shows that the expected form *paris* was the pattern for ordinal numbers. A summary of the attestations follows:

2	ms	nom	*šanīu*	*ša-ni-ú*	MAL A § 30:24
				ša-ni-um-ma	MAL A § 22:107
				ša-ni-ú-um-ma	MAL B § 17:19
				2-*ú*	Coronation Ritual iii 8
				⸢2?-*ú*⸣	VAT 19655:21
		gen		*ša-ni-e*	PKT 3 i 9; KUB 3 77:12'
				ša-ni-e-ma	MAL A § 5:58
				ša-ni-im-ma	MAL C+ § 2:9; MARV 4 24:5'; T 04-37 r. 27
				ša-ni-ma	KBo 28 61/2:25'
				2-*e*	MARV 1 10:11
				⸢2?⸣-*e*	MARV 5 18:8
				2-⸢*e*?⸣	MARV 7 91 r. 10'
		acc		–	–
	fs	nom	*šanittu*	*ša-ni-tu*	MAL A § 8:82
				⸢*ša-ni*?⸣-[*tu*]	KAJ 122:10
		gen		*ša-ni-te*	MAL B § 1:13
				ša-ni-ti	MAL C+ § 3:15
				ša-ni-it-te	MPR 75:45b'; T 02-32:11
		acc		*ša-ni-ta*	MAL A § 8:86; KAV 169:14; T 04-37 r. 7; KBo 1 20:6
				ša-ni-tam-ma	MAL C+ § 2:9; MAPD § 18:87
	mp	nom	*šanīuttu*	*ša-ni-ú-tu-ma*	T 04-37 r. 2
3	ms	nom	*šaššu*	*ša-áš-šu*	MAPD § 19:92
4	ms	nom	*rab'u*	4-*ú*	MARV 5 13:12
10	fs	nom	*ešertu*	10-*tu*	MARV 4 127:20
				10^{meš}-*tu(-ma)*	MATC 80:4, 5, 6
		gen		10-*te*	KAJ 292:16
				^{lú}10-*te*	T 98-28:6

It should be noted that most of these examples derive from literary texts, leading to the suggestion that they are archaisms. As we have mentioned many times, the degree of the MA character of MAL A-B is disputed. However, the occurrence of one attestation in a private letter, an administrative document and a treaty (KAV 169:14, KAJ 122:10 and T 04-37 r. 2) shows that these forms occur in colloquial MA as well. Moreover, the discovery of the ordinal number 'third' a (*šalšum* > *šaššu*) and the OA and NA cognates makes the replacement of the ordinal pattern *PaRiS* unlikely. The cause of the almost equal distribution of *PaRiS* and *PaRāSī* between literary and private texts is unknown.

9.4 Adjective number *PaRāSī*

§ 340 The exact origins of the number pattern *PaRāSi* are not clear.[19] Attestations are limited to MA and do not occur in any other variant of the Akkadian language.[20] One

19 I have discussed the numbers of the pattern *PaRāSī* in de Ridder (2015a). The following discussion follows the conclusions drawn in the said study.

important feature is that *PaRāSi* is always used attributively, following a noun. This is unlike *PaRiS*, which can also be used independently.[21] In this respect, *PaRāSi* is morphologically and syntactically no different than normal adjectives. An additional problem is that most of the probable attestations are logographic with a phonetic complement. In the case of those attestations, such as 2-*i-ú*, we cannot be certain whether to read *šan/īu* or *ša/nā/yī/yu*. On high numbers, such as 3-*i-ú-tu* (KTN inventory i 14), there does not seem to be any possible reading other than *šalāšīuttu*. Moreover, attestations such as 2-*ú* in Coronation Ritual iii 8 seem to be the norm for normal ordinal numbers. However, as we will see below, this assessment does not hold. For these reasons, the assumptions made below are based on semantic considerations, which, in turn, are based on their syllabic attestations.

§ 341 In MA, the function of *PaRāSi* seems to differ slightly from *PaRiS* by having a couple of different meanings. We will start to make a comparison based on the literary genre. Unfortunately, there is only one text where *PaRāSi* occurs. On the other hand, we also find *PaRiS* in the same passage, providing us with the sole opportunity to directly compare the two. As the text only provides one example of *PaRāSī*, we cannot draw any firm conclusions on this matter and interpretation remains subjective. Still, in the very least, it does demonstrate that a difference in function is a possibility.

(A) *marāšu ša-ni-ú* (…) *mēt* 'his second son is dead' MAL A § 30:23–25

(B) *ana marʾīšu ša-na-i-e* 'to his second son' MAL A § 30:26

The first passage introduces this son in relation to his earlier-mentioned brother, which prompts the use of the ordinal number. In the second passage, *šanāyīu* has a more general adjectival meaning 'aforementioned'. In this case, the difference between the two forms is between referential and non-referential. Alternatively, *šanāyiyu* could refer to the secondary age or status of the son in question. This fits well with a number of passages where *PaRāSī* refers to secondary quality. There is some evidence that the ordinal numbers of the pattern *PaRiS* can be used to indicate secondary quality in Akkadian (CAD Š$_1$, 396-7 2), but the evidence is relatively slim, making it likely that an innovated form was used in MA. Note the following examples:

šanāyīu	2 *mana ḫurāṣu* 2-*i-ú* 'two minas of second-quality gold' KAV 164
šanāyittu	1 [túg][K]IMIN *ša argamanne* 2-*i-tu* 'one similar purple textile of secondary quality' MAH 16086 B 10'
	ša bir-me 2-*i-te* 'of secondary quality *birmu*-cloth' YBC 6956:7
šanāyīātu	1 [túg]*na-ḫa-ÁB-ta* [*š*]*a-na-i-ta* 'one secondary quality cloak' KAJ 77:9-10
	naḫlapātu ša PN$_1$ *u* PN$_3$ 2-*ia-a-tu* 'secondary quality cloaks of PN$_1$ and PN$_2$' KAJ 279:9

§ 342 In a number of texts, we find *PaRāSi* used when referring to sizes. Here, we find the number '2' used again in the same way as the higher numbers. The exact meaning often remains unclear. Clearer examples include:

---

20 However, an early root of the pattern may be found in the following passage from OA (cf. GKT, 116 § 69; GOA § 8.4.1.; GAG, 115 § 70c): 2 *me-at* 60 MA.NA *i-tup-pì-im ša-li-ší-im* 2 *me-at* URUDU *i-tup-pì-im* <u>*ša-da-ší-im*</u> É *kà-ri-im i*-GN *na-dá-ku* 'I have deposited 260 minas (of copper) on the third tablet, 200 (minas of) copper on the sixth tablet at the office of the colony at Purušḫattum' TMH 1 27b (complete translation following Dercksen 2004, 196 n529).

21 Admittedly, this usage is only attested twice in MA: MAL B § 1:13; MAPD § 19:92.

šanāyittu	1 *asallu rabīu* 1 *asallu ša-na-i-tum* 'a big asallu bowl, secondary size *asallu* bowl' KAJ 303:3–4 (list)
	ina muḫḫi larie 2-*i-ú-te* 'on the secondary (size) branches' KTN inventory i 30–31
	3 *emāru* 2 *sūtu kubarinnu ša-na-i-tu* '182 seahs (in) a *kubarinnu*-vessel of secondary size' CUSAS 34 44:2
	1 *naḫlaptu ša birme* 2-*i-tu* 'one multicoloured coat of secondary quality' MAH 16086 A ii 8
šalāšittu	3 *emāru* 2 *sūtu kubarinnu ša-la-ši-i-tu* '182 seahs (in) a *kubarinnu*-vessel of the third size' CUSAS 34 44:3
šanāyīuttu/ šalāšīuttu	16 *ayyurū rabīuttu* 9 *ayyurū* 2-*i-ú-tu* 9 *ayyurū* 3-*i-ú-tu* '16 large roses, nine secondary (size) roses, nine third (size) roses' KTN inventory i 13–14
šanāyīātu/ šalāšīātu	26 *ēnātu* 2-*i-a-tu* 3 *ēnātu* 3-*i-a-t*[*u*] '26 secondary (size?) eyes, three of third (size?) eyes' KTN inventory ii 14 cf. i 12

All these passages refer to a different size. The other attestations are used for land lots, although the exact meaning is unknown. Note the use of the sign PI to indicate either wV or yV. Both values would be unique in MA and uncommon in late second millennium Akkadian, with yV (or jV) being typical for OB Mari (cf. MZL no. 598).

šanāyīu/ šalāšīu/ rabāʾīu	[*eqla p*]*u-ra ša-na-i-PI* PN_1 KIMIN *eqla pu-ra ša-la-ši-*[*PI*] PN_2 KIMIN *eqla* 3 *pūrāni* [x] *ra-ba-i-ú*?! [PN_3?] 'a field, the second lot is of PN_1, likewise a field, the third lot is of PN_2, likewise three lots [x], fourth of PN_3' KAJ 139:2'–7' cf. 12'–16'
ḫamāšīu/ tašāʾīu	1 *pūru* 5-*ši-ú*/9-*i-ú* 'a fifth/ninth of a lot' KAV 127:2/128:2

Despite some small broken sections, it can be observed that, in KAJ 139, the scribe enumerates to four, although, in both instances, the number '1' is not preserved. On one occasion, the preceding lots are even counted: A.ŠÀ 3 *pu-ra-ni* 'field, three lots' KAJ 139:6'. If this total refers to the preceding three aforementioned lots, we can exclude the possibility that three different sizes are intentional.

§ 343 If our claim is correct, *PaRiS* is used for ordinal numbers and *PaRāSī* in an adjectival meaning for items of different size and quality. Below is the list of known attestations. Note that many forms are written logographically with a phonetic complement. The occurrence of a nisbe and/or an adjectival ending, together with the context, is convincing enough that these should be analysed as *PaRāSi* patterns.

2	ms	nom	*šanāyīu*	2-*i-ú*	KAV 164:3
				2?-*i*!-*ú*	KAJ 317:11
	ms	gen	*šanāyīe*	*ša-na-i-e*	MAL A § 30:26
				2-*i-šu*	KAJ 317:7
		acc	*šanāyīa*	*ša-na-i-PI*	KAJ 139:2
				ša-na-⌜*i*⌝-[?]	KAJ 139:12
	mp	nom	*šanāyīuttu*	2-*i-ú-tu*	KTN inventory i 13
		obl	*šanāyīutte*	2-*i-ú-te*	KTN inventory i 31
	fs	nom	*šanāyittu*	*ša-na-i-tu*	CUSAS 34 44:2
				ša-na-i-tum[22]	KAJ 303:4
				2-*i-tu*	MAH 16086 A i 3, 7, 12, 14. ii 7, 16, 23, B ii 10', 17'
		gen		*ša-na-it-*[*te*]	MARV 10 63:3'

22 The reading of CAD A_2, 327: *ša na-kám*!*-tum* cannot be excluded here.

				ša-na-ˀi-⌜*te*?⌝	MARV 10 20:10[23]
				2-i-te	YBC 6956:7
	fp	nom	*šanāyiātu*	*2-i-a-tu*	KTN inventory i 8; 12; ii 14
				2-ia-a-tu	KAJ 279:9
3	ms	nom	*šalāšīu*	–	–
		acc	*šalāšīa*	*ša-la-ši-a*	KAJ 139:4; 14
	mp	nom	*šalāšīuttu*	*3-i-ú-tu*	KTN inventory i 14
	fs	nom	*šalāšittu*	*ša-la-ši-i-tu*	CUSAS 34 44:3
	fp	nom	*šalāšīātu*	*3-i-a-t*[*u*]	KTN inventory ii 14
4	ms	nom	*rabāˀīu*	*ra-ba-i-ú*	KAJ 139:7
				4-ú	KAV 126:2
		acc	*rabāyīa*	*ra-ba-i-PI*	KAJ 139:16
5	ms	nom	*ḫamāšīu*	*5-ši-ú*	KAV 127:2
7	ms	nom	*sabāyīu*?	*7-ú*	KAV 125:2
9	ms	nom	*tašāˀīu*?	*9-i-ú*	KAV 128:2
[…]				[…]*-í-ú*	KAV 129:2

9.5 Fractions

§ 344 We already discussed the possibility for *parāsi* numbers to refer to fractions. However, it must be noted that *mišlu* is used, as well in MA, to indicate halves.[24] The plural form *mišlātu* 'halves' is attested.

mašil	*ana* GN *u₄-mu ma-ši-il ṭēma ittablūne* 'at noon, they brought the report to me to GN' MATSH 2:23–24
mišlu	*qaqqad* ŠE*-im mi*!*-iš-la ina* GN$_1$ *imaddad u mi-iš-la* [*ina*] GN$_2$ [*imadd*]*ad* 'he will measure the capital of barley, half in GN$_1$ and half in GN$_2$' KAJ 67:7–11
	karpatu mi-iš-lu ša 'one container half of […]' KAJ 277:4†
	1 *ME-iš-lu ša* (…) 'one half of (…)' KAJ 310:28
	mi-šil-šu-nu GN$_1$ *mi-šil-šu-nu-ma* GN$_2$ *ultaṣbit* 'I provisioned half of them in GN$_1$ and half of them in GN$_2$' MATSH 2:8–10[25]
mišlātu	*gi-na-ú a-na mi-iš-la-*⌜*te*⌝ 'the regular offerings at half' MARV 2 14:6'
	[*gi-na-ú a-na*] ⌜*mi*⌝*-iš-la-te (...)* [*i*]*-ša-ka-an* 'he will place the regular offerings at half (volume)' MARV 7 52:2–4 cf. 8

Cancik-Kirschbaum (MATSH, 95 n6) notes that the CvC sign in *mi-šil* MATSH 2:8 can be read as either <šil> (TAR) or <šal> (SAL). As we discussed in § 286, an infixed /a/ in a construct form is especially common in substantives of the types *PiRS* and *PuRS*. On the other hand, cases where the infixed vowel takes the colour of the preceding vowel are also known, e.g., *mi-qí-it pe-e* (*miqtu*) MAL A § 2:17. The matter remains undecided, although it may be noted that LB has *mišil* (Streck 1995, 63 § 54). The form *mašil* only occurs in the adverbial expression *ūm mašil* 'midday' and the (unattested in MA) *mūšu mašil* 'midnight' (CAD, 379f). This is actually a frozen stative contained in these adverbial expressions.
One attestation of a higher number occurs:

23 This is an uncertain attestation with unusual spelling in a broken context.

24 Note that the syllabic writing for third, found in UGM (54), is not correct (see Freydank 1975, 143).

25 Note that some doubt exists about whether to read <šil> (TAR) or <šal> (SAL). Both forms are possible in MA (see MATSH, 95 n6–7). However, the occurrence of *ma-ši-il* MATSH 2:24 in the same text favours TAR.

[*n em*]*āru* ŠE-*um*$^{[\text{me}]\text{š}}$ ⸢8⸣-[*t*]*i-šu* (…) [*idda*]*n* 'he will give n homers of barley and a one-eighth share' Giricano 5:10–12

9.5 Nouns derived from numerals

§ 345 We find *iltēnīuttu* 'set, unit' (cf. CAD I/J, 282; OA in GOA § 8.2.1) in a few MA texts written logographically with a phonetic complement.[26] As all spellings use the sign <ni>, it appears that *iltēnīuttu* has a nisbe ending. We should read 1-*ni-ú-tu* as the masculine plural *iltēnīuttu* and 1-*ni-a-tu* as the feminine plural *iltēniātu*.[27] As the feminine ending *-at* does not normally occur on a nisbe, the nisbe has to be regarded as fossilized. Moreover, it seems to be used with feminine nouns. Postgate (1988, 87–88) analysed these forms as adjectives, which confirms the adjective character of the nisbe suffix. However, adjectives normally follow the noun. They seem to be used with plurale tantum nouns, or nouns that usually do not come in singles (e.g., *šuḫupputu* 'boot'). It should be translated as 'set' or (when going in two) 'pair'. When multiple sets of a plurale tantum are counted, the quantifying adverb n-*šu* is used (see below).

mp	*iltēnīuttu*	1-*ni-ú-tu mašiānu* 2 *mana šuqultu* 'one pair of fire tongs, two minas is (its) weight' MAH 16130:3' cf. l. 7', 8', 9'
fp	*iltēniātu*	1-*ni-a-tu šuršurrātu siparre* 'one set of bronze chains' KAJ 124a:2, 11
		1-*ni-a-tu ḫurātu* GIBIL SIG$_5$ 'one set of good new steps' KAJ 128:2[28]
		1-*ni-a-tu aḫātu* 'one set of sleeves (?)' MARV 1 24:6
		⸢1⸣-*ni-a-te-ma šuḫḫupāte ša Aššurā*[*y*]*āta*$^{\text{sic.}}$ 'one set of Assyrian boots' MARV 3 64:6–7
		1-*ni-a-te-ma šuḫḫupāte ša Kutmuḫāyāta*$^{\text{sic.}}$ 'one set of boots that are Kutmuḫean' MARV 3 64:7–8
		1-*ni-a-tu ṣubātu ša-ḪAR-ra-tu ša šēpē šarre* 'one set of š. textiles for the feet of the king' MAH 16086 B ii 13'
		1-*ni-a-tu šuḫuppātu* 'one pair of boots' Postgate 1973, 1:18 cf. l. 28

In apposition, *iltēniuttu* does not seem to agree with the preceding noun (cf. de Ridder 2015b, 123–24).

mp	*iltēniuttu*	2 *ḫullānātu* 1-*ni-ú-tu* 'two wraps, one pair' MARV 10 54:1–2
		2 *šaḫarrātu*$^{?}$ 1-*ni-ú-tu* 'two š.-garments, one pair' MARV 10 64:3'

§ 346 Higher numbers are only attested logographically in MA. They are built with a grapheme of a number. So far, they are only attested for the numbers one to four, with the pronominal suffix -*īšu* attached and usually the preposition *ana*. In comparison with the multiplicative adverbs (§ 486), they were probably built on the base of the cardinal numbers.

1	mp	*iltēniuttu*	1-*ni-ú-tu*	MARV 10 54:1; MARV 10 64:3'; MAH

26 Cf. CAD I/J, 278f; GAG, 118 § 71c.

27 Given the lack of VA in spellings such as 1-*ni-a-tu*, such forms can only be morphologically plural. It is, therefore, better to take 1-*ni-ú-tu* as the corresponding masculine plural (pace AHW, 401a).

28 Not to be confused with *gišḫurru* (pace CAD G, 102a); the translation follows Postgate in UŠA, 86–88 no. 41 (cf. AHW, 358a).

			16130:3',7', 8', 9'
fp	*iltēniātu*	1-*ni-a-tu*	KAJ 124a:2, 11; KAJ 128:2; MARV 10 7:1; MARV 10 64:2'; MARV 10 71:1; MAH 16086 B ii 13'; Postgate 1973, 1:18 cf. l. 28
2	*šinīšu*?	2-*šu*	KAV 105:14; KAV 205:19; KAJ 303:8; KAJ 310:59
		2-*i-šu*	MARV 1 58:6, 8
4	*arbʾīšu*?	4-*i-šu*	MARV 1 58:11

As we discussed above, these adjectival numeral forms are used to count sets of plural substantives following *iltēnīu* 'one set', e.g., *a-na* 2-*šu šur-šu-ra-a-te* 'two chains' KAJ 310:59. Here *šuršurrātu* 'chain' is plural because it consists of multiple parts.

2-*i-šu* *ana* 2-*šu ṣubāte* (…) *šēliāne* 'take out two sets of textiles' KAV 105:14-17
ana 2-*šu na*[*gl*]*ibe* 'for two sets of razors' KAV 205:19
2-*šu urrutḫu* 'two sets of *urrutḫu*' KAJ 303:8
ana 2-*šu šuršurāte* 'two sets of chains' KAJ 310:59

Similar spellings with adverbial forms meaning 'once, twice etc.' are likely to represent quantifying adverbs with the *PaRSēšu* pattern. They are discussed in § 486.

9.6 Other numerals

§ 347 We may further note the numeral *šun(n)uʾû* 'two years old' (GAG, 118 § 71d; 313). It is attested once as the feminine *šunuʾittu* (Freydank 2003, 247):

1 udu*gurrutum*sic *šu-nu-i*!*-tum damiqtu* 'one good two-year-old ewe' KAJ 96:2

Usually, this type of numeral is written logographically as MU.2 (CAD Š3, 313–14).

1 gudÁB MU.2 SIG5 'one good two-year old cow' KAJ 115:6

2 gudÁB.MEŠ MU.2 'two good two-year old cows' LVUH 1:2

Chapter 10: Personal Pronouns

10.1 Independent personal pronouns

10.1.1 Nominative independent pronouns

§ 348 MA personal pronouns in the nominative case mainly follow the OA example, while NA is more distant from the two earlier phases of the language (SNAG, 43–44 § 3.1.1.) The 3ms and 3fs forms both have a suffixed morpheme *-t*: *šūt/šīt*. This has to be regarded as an Assyrian innovation, probably by analogy with the accusative case *šuātV/šiātV*. The plural is relatively poorly attested. Fortunately, since the publication of UGM, attestations of the plural have risen somewhat, although they remain scarce. The broken 3fp attestation ([*š*]*i-i-n*[*a*] TR 2028:10) has an unexpected plene vowel. For 2mp *attunu*, we find another broken plene spelling (*at-tu-*[*nu*]*-ú-ma*), which may have been caused by the shift of stress caused by the particle *-ma* (cf. NA *at-tu-ú-ni* SAA 5 81:13).[1] A similar case of lengthening due to a change of stress is found in *at-ta-a-ma* T 97-10:13. An attestation of 1cp has been found, i.e., *né-e-nu* T 04-37:17, but it occurs more frequently in PNs, e.g., ([m])*Ša*-[d]IŠKUR-*ni-nu* KAJ 90:19; 145:17.[2] The long vowel /ē/, instead of /ī/, in *nēnu* is confirmed by NA evidence (e.g., *né-e-nu* SAA 1 133 r. 7; *a-né-e-nu* SAA 15 98:16).

3ms	*šūt*	*šu-ú-ut*	MAPD § 21:104; § 21:106
		šu-ut	e.g., MAL A § 47:25; § 48:40; KAV 127:5; MATSH 8:48'; 24:14; KAJ 4:8; TR 2048 13'; 2903:10; T 02-32:14; KBo 28 64:5'; Franke/Wilhelm 1985:4; Giricano 4:23; T 02-32:25; etc.
		šu-ut-ma	MAL A § 38:22; MAL M § 1:5; KAJ 180:15, 29
		šu-ú	Billa 24:9; T 93-28:8
3fs	*šīt*	*ši-i-it*	MAL A § 2:19; § 33:69; § 34:74; § 36:91; § 41:4.5.10; § 45:55; 46:99; T 98-125:10
		ši-it	MAL A § 26:102; § 41:9; § 45:52; § 50:70; § 53:102; Lambert 1969:32; KAJ 142:12
		ši-it-ma	MAL A § 26:102
		ši-i	MAL A § 24:51
2ms	*atta*	*at-ta*	e.g., KAV 168:21; MCS 2 1:15; VAT 8851:19; MATSH 1:16; 26:4'; 15.8.21; T 97-17:14
		at-ta-ma	MARV 10 90:20; VAT 8851:17; MATC 10:7
		at-ta-a-ma	T 97-10:13
2fs	*atti*	–	–
1cs	*anāku*	*a-na-ku*	e.g., MAL A § 18:75; § 47:10; KAJ 316:5; AO 19.227:11; RS 06.198:24; Billa 64:23; MATSH 2:25; 3:17; 4:1'; 6:5'; 7:4''; 8:47'; 9:43; 12:18.45; 17:18'; 22:20; 26:3'; 27:5'; 28:4'; 30:11''; MATC 2:16; 4:10; 9:12.22; 15:15.23; KBo 28 61 vs. 6'; 64 vs. 13'
		a-na-ku-ma	MARV 3 63:9'†
		in a PN	[m]*A-na-ku-a-na*-[d]UTU George 1988 2:16

1 The only example of feminine 2fp (*at-te-n*[*a*] KAV 194:14) has unfortunately been corrected to another reading (see BAI, 70; cf. UGM, 28 § 24.2).

2 An additional case of *né-e-nu* is found in the predominantly Babylonian letter RS 34.164:38, 43, which was written by Tukultī-Ninurta I.

3mp	*šunu*	*šu-nu*	KAJ 7:23; 118:19; MATSH 7:8''; Faist 2001, 252:26, 32; T 97-6:11; RE 92:12
		šu-nu-ma	KAJ 307:15
3fp	*šina*	*ši-na*	MARV 1 38:8; Lambert 1966:59 (cf. Veldhuis 1991, 12)
		[*š*]*i-i-n*[*a*]	TR 2028:10
		ši-ME?(?)	KAJ 94:8
2mp	*attūnu*	*at-tu-nu*	KAV 102:9; KAV 105:8, 27; KAV 205:11
		at-tu-nu-ma	KAV 105:29
		ma-at-tu-nu	MATSH 7:12''
		at-tu-[*nu*]*-ú-*(*ma*)	MATSH 7:6''
2fp	*attīna*	–	–
1cp	*nēnu*	*né-e-nu*	T 04-37 r. 17
		in PN	e.g., (m)*Ša*-dIŠKUR-*ni-nu* KAJ 90:19; 145:17

10.1.1.1 Function of nominative independent pronouns

§ 349 As with all Akkadian dialects, the nominative and accusative independent pronouns of the third-person function as anaphoric pronouns, which refer to the antecedent (or postcedent). In practice, this means that pronouns in the third person are also used as a demonstrative.[3] They refer back to an antecedent, but do not occur on the same spatial deixis as the normal demonstrative pronouns (cf. OA in GOA § 9.3.9). Here, we find them used attributively following a noun. This function can be demonstrated by the following examples:

> *sinniltu ši-i-it* 5 *šanāte panē mutīša tadaggal* 'that woman will wait five years for her husband' MAL A § 36:91–92
>
> *šumma sinniltu ši-it mītat a'īla idukkū* 'if that woman dies, they will kill the man' MAL A § 50:70–71
>
> *eqlu šu-ut uppu l*[*aqi*] 'that field is acquired and taken' KAM 10 33:9
>
> *tuppātu ši-na naḫrā* 'those tablets are invalid' MARV 1 38:8–9
>
> *tup-pu ši-it* (…) *lā gamrat* 'this tablet is not finished' Lambert 1969:32

§ 350 Aside from the demonstrative pronoun, there is no difference in function between the anaphoric and other independent personal pronouns. It is well known that the subject of the verb is enclosed in the finite verb and, as such, does not require an independent personal pronoun, unlike many Indo-European languages, including English. Akkadian and MA are no exceptions to this rule, which can be sufficiently demonstrated with one example.

> *lubulta* (…) *ša* (…) *ana kurille ilqeūnenni ultēbilakkunu* '<u>I</u> have sent you the clothing that <u>they</u> took to the harvest-festival' KAV 99:37–40

The use of independent personal pronouns as the subject of verbs happens frequently and is often explained as an emphasis of the subject (e.g., GAG, 49 § 41a). What this emphasis means and how it was motivated are often vague, although a few remarks can be made. Sometimes, the emphasis on the pronominal element is so explicit that we find the pronoun in an unusual place in the sentence (usually upfront):

> *mā š*[*u*]*-ut ana'īne lā illika* 'but he, why did he not come?' T 02-32:14–15

3 See GAG, 49 § 41a; Reiner (1966, 101 § 5.5.3).

The emphasis of the personal element can also be negative, such as in the following statement of denial:

ina telīt ebūrišunu a-⸢na⸣-ku lā aku[*l*] 'I did not consume (any part) of the tax on their harvest' A 2994:13–14

This type of topicalization can also be found in the following similar nominal polar question, where the emphasis lies on the subject of the clause, which is therefore placed upfront:

GÁNA.A.ŠÀ *mīnu šu-ut* 'a field? Why is that?' T 02-32:25

§ 351 Frequently, the personal pronouns indicate that the subject is personally carrying out the action of the verbal predicate. This type of emphasis of the pronoun is most frequently found with the first-person *anāku*. We may translate this as 'I personally':

mā a-na-ku uba$^{??}$*ar* 'saying, 'I will personally prove it' MAL A § 18:75

a-na-ku ātamar iqbiaššunni 'I have personally seen it, he said to him' MAL A § 47:10–11

a-na-ku agrāni uggara 'I will personally hire hirelings' MATC 4:10–11

a-na-ku Šubrīe ša uddûni alt[*aʾalma*] 'I have personally questioned the Hurrians who know about it' MATSH 6:5'

a-na-ku ina GN *ātamaršunu* 'I personally saw them in GN' MATSH 7:4''

a-na-ku iššerte ammīša ana biāde allaka 'I will come there tomorrow to rest' MATC 2:16–18

né-e-nu nušallamk[*unu*] 'we will make it up to you' T 04-37:17

ana šumeka a-na-ku malluta ina muḫḫīšunu ašakkanma 'in your name, I will impose a compensation payment upon them' Ni 669:19–21

In the Tell Šayḫ Ḥamad letters, we find a personal pronoun twice for a stative describing an emotion:

a-na-ku ḫadiāku 'I am happy' MATSH 9:43

a-na-ku palḫāku 'I am afraid' MATSH 22:20 cf. *balu bēlīya palḫāku* 'I am afraid without my lord' Billa 63:21

With imperatives, a complementary pronoun is only rarely used. It is attested in two letters, where it could specify the addressed person 'you personally', rather than somebody else being allowed to carry out the command instead.

at-ta šuṭur 'you, write (it) down!'MATSH 1:16

3 *alpē* (...) *at-ta usuq* 'you, select three oxen!' T 97-17:12–14

Sometimes, the independent personal pronouns are used to introduce direct speech:

a-na-ku akkīa aqtibiaššu 'I told him thus' T 96-15:10; MATC 15:15–16

a-na-ku annāka [*a*]*-na* PN *aqtibi* 'I said to PN here' MATC 15:23–24

There remains a final group of passages where the third person is used to refer to human subjects in verbal clauses. These cases may again indicate an emphasis of the agent of the verb or be used in order to avoid one-word (dependent) clauses.

šumma mar'ū mutīša laššu ši-it-ma talaqqe 'If there are no sons of her husband, she will take it' MAL A § 26:101–102

šu-ut ana aḫḫēša iqabbi 'he will speak with her brothers' MAL A § 48:40

u šu-ú-ut izzâz iltanamme 'and he holds still, listening' MAPD § 21:103

šu-ut-ma imḫurū[ni] 'he received it' KAJ 180:29

annūte alpēšu rēḫta šu-ut lilqe 'may he take these, the remainder of his oxen' T 97-17:15–17

šu-nu ḫiṭṭa ša šarre inaššiū 'they will personally carry the penalty of the king' RE 92:14–16

The use of pronouns to indicate the change of subject is almost unattested in MA, as this type of clause is more typical for letters. One phrase from a diplomatic letter can be given.

abūya bēl nukurtika šu-ut [?] *a-na-ku bēl sulummā'e ša aḫīya* 'my father was your enemy, but I am the ally of my brother' KUB 3 73:10'–11'

§ 352 In the case of a non-verbal sentence, the personal pronoun becomes obligatory as there is no finite verb available to indicate the agent. Despite being the subject, the pronoun is in clause-final position.

mā abīya at-ta bēlīya ⸢*at-ta*⸣ 'saying, "you are my father, you are my lord"' VAT 8851:19–20

almattu ši-i-it 'she is a widow' MAL A § 33:69

ŠE-*um*^{meš} *anniu pūḫu šu-ut* 'this barley is a substitute' Giricano 1:9–10

mētu šu-ut 'is he dead?' MATSH 8:49'

When the pronoun is not the subject, it remains in the final position and functions as a kind of copula. We will discuss the subject in more detail in § 675ff. Below is a selected example:

ŠE-*um anniu šulmānu šu-ut* 'this barley is a *šulmānu*-gift' KAJ 73:9–11

10.1.2 Dative and accusative independent pronouns

§ 353 The oblique paradigms seem to be built out of the pronominal suffixes, with a suffixed morpheme *-ātV* for the accusative, e.g., *šu+ātV* > *šuātV*. The third-person forms are shared with many other Semitic languages, whereas the first- and second-person forms (e.g., *iyāti* and *kuāti*) are an archaic feature lost in other Semitic languages for unknown reasons (Huehnergard 2006, 11). It is therefore important to note that MA seems to have lost **iyāti* and **kuāti* as well, while they were still present in OA (cf. GKT, 74 § 48b; GOA § 9.2). Morphologically, the 3ms and 2fs of the accusative have not changed significantly since OA. The OA forms 3mp *šunūti* and 3fp **šināti* have changed considerably to *šunātunu* and *šinātina*. According to von Soden, this occurred through a process where the original suffix *-āt*, as found in the singular forms, became an infix: *šunu+āt* > *šunu-āt-nu* (GAG, 50 § 41d, cf. MB *šuātunu*). The extra syllable *-nu* must have been added by analogy with the nominative pronouns. It is possible that we have an attestation of the OA morphological form in *šu-nu*$^{?}$- ⸢*te*$^{?}$⸣ LVUH 36:8. As with the singular, there are no plural oblique forms attested for the first and second person.

§ 354 While OA had one oblique paradigm for the dative/accusative (GKT, 74 § 48b; GOA § 9.2), this situation had drastically changed in MA with the paradigm split into a new dative paradigm and an accusative paradigm that seems etymologically closest to the OA. The paradigm for the dative was morphologically similar to the accusative, but with the morpheme *-āšV*, rather than *-ātV* i.e., *šu+āšV* > *šu*^{w}*āV*. The second-person singular takes its base from the dative suffix *-ku(m)*: *ku+āša* > *ku*^{w}*āša* and the first person from the genitive pronominal suffix *-ya*, i.e., *yā+ašV* > *iyāšV*. Von Soden suggested that the dative and accusative paradigms already existed in complementary distribution in OA, but were represented identically in the orthography. He explained this by assuming a spirantized /ṯ/ for the dative, which was written with <Š>, albeit only in MA (von Soden 1968, 219; GAG, 50 § 41c*). There is some evidence in MA of /ṯ/ in forms where the expected /š/ is written as <T> (see § 214).

§ 355 Alternatively, the dative paradigm could have spread from the dative pronominal suffix present in MA, perhaps influenced by Babylonian. It is also possible that MA is not a direct descendant of OA. This would explain the large differences in the pronouns between the two stages of the language, which is also true for the pronominal suffixes (see also Huehnergard 2006, 12 n57). It is not unlikely that the tripartite paradigm (nominative/dative/oblique), as known from OB, was influenced by its Sumerian counterpart (cf. Pedersén 1989, 436f). In fact, Akkadian is the only Semitic language with such an extended paradigm, with only traces from an oblique case in a few languages, such ase Ugaritic and Sabaic (Lipiński 2001, 308 § 36.3). If we assume that the dative case was borrowed by Sumerian, we should be no longer surprised by its absence from OA, which had less contact with Sumerian. Furthermore, the independent accusative pronouns were gradually lost, resulting in the independent dative pronouns taking their place in NA (SNAG, 44–45 § 3.1.1) and MB (Aro 1955a, 51ff). Some Babylonian forms can be found like *ka-ša* EA 15; *ka-a-ša* BE 17 77:4. However, these texts may be regarded as non-Assyrian. The MA paradigm of the new dative pronoun is mostly inflected on a regular basis, with only an irregular 1cp *nâši(n)* (Bab. *niāšim*). The second- and third-person plural forms are constructed in a similar way to the accusative case: *šun+āš+unu* > *šunāšunu* (Bab. *šunūšim*) and 2mp *kun+āš+unu* > *kunāšunu* (Bab. *kunūšim*).[4]

§ 356 A feature of the dative pronouns is the differentiation between genders through the final vowel. This suggestion is made by Hämeen-Anttila in his treatment of NA grammar (SNAG, 44), where he included this differentiation in his paradigms for the NA third and second persons of the oblique paradigm (*šâš-; kâš-*). These forms are clearly the equivalent of MA bases *šuāš-* and *kuāš-*, where no contraction has taken place. However, Hämeen-Anttila did not discuss how he came to this conclusion; in fact, some of the attestations that he discussed oppose this assumption, e.g., masculine: [*a*]*-na ša-ši-*[*ma*] SAA 5 108:16; feminine: *a-na šá-ši* RIMA 2 A.0.101.38:24 (Grayson: *ía-ši!*). A similar differentiation of the vowel is not attested in 1cs *iyāši*, as Semitic languages do not generally distinguish

4 Many of the plural dative personal pronouns are only rarely attested. For instance, we find *šunāšunu* for the first time in MARV 10 3:8 (Zomer 2015, 178).

between gender in the first person.[5] It seems, however, that the vowels are based on the pronominal suffixes for nouns, which form the base of these independent pronouns. Thus, the vowel has moved to the end of the pronoun: *-šu* > *šuāšu*; *-ša* > *šuašā*; *-ka* > *kuāša*; *-ki* > *kuāši*.

		Masculine	Feminine
Oblique	3s	*šâšu*	*šâša*
	2s	*kâša*	*kâši*

Figure 29: NA ending vocals on the oblique pronouns according to SNAG, 44.

In MA, Hämeen-Anttila's assumption seems to work for the dative paradigm, whereas, for the accusative, any vowel can be used, which is indifferent to the case of the phonetic environment and not affected by a successive vowel, e.g., *tuppa ši-a-ti* KAJ 165:16 ~ *qaqqara šu-a-tu* KAJ 175:27. According to W. Mayer (UGM, 17 § 11.1), the final vowel had weakened to a schwa, meaning that scribes were indifferent in their use of the final vowel. If this were so, however, we should expect many sandhis where schwa had assimilated into a successive vowel. To add to the confusion, the sign TUM was sometimes used erroneously, whereas the original never had mimation, e.g., *šu-a-TUM* KAJ 175:8.

	Old Assyrian	Middle Assyrian		Neo-Assyrian
	oblique	Dative	accusative	oblique
3ms	*šuāti*	*Šuāšu*	*šuātV*	*šâšu*
3fs	*šiāti*	*šuāša*	*šiātV*	*šâša*
2ms	*kuāti*	*kuāša*	–	*kâša*
2fs	~	*kiāši*	–	**kâši*
1cs	*(i)yāti*	*iyāši*	–	*(i)yāši*
3mp	*šunūti*	*šunāšunu*	*šunātunu*	*šunāšunu*
3fp	*šināti*	**šināšina*	*šinātina*	*šunāšina*
2mp	*kunūti*	*kunāšunu*	–	*kunāšunu*
2fp	*kināti*	*kināšina*	–	**kunāšina*
1cp	*niāti*	*nâši(n)*	–	*nâši*

Figure 30: Dative/accusative pronouns in Assyrian.

3ms	*šuāšu*	Dative	*šu-a-šu*	MAL A § 22:12; Adad Ritual r. 8; KAJ 149:22; MATSH 9:45; KUB 3 77 r. 9'†
		Oblique	*šu-a-šu-ma*	MATSH 2:50
	šuātV	Genitive	*šu-a-tu*	MAL A § 18:77; § 19:89; § 40:80; § 45:64; KAJ 132:16; KAJ 175:27
			šu-a-tum	KAJ 175:8
			šu-a-te	KAJ 101:12; MARV 1 47:10, 16, 35, 40, 46
			šu-a-ti	MAL D § 1:6
		Accusative	*šu-a-tu*	MAL A § 18:77; § 19:89; § 40:89; KAJ 175:27
			šu-a-tum	KAJ 175:8
3fs	*šuāša*	Dative	*šu-a-ša*	MAL A § 36:13(?); Billa 19:6, 18
	šiātV	Genitive	*ši-a-ti*	KAJ 79:17; KAJ 165:5, 11; KAJ 172:8; MAL A § 50:74

5 This does not necessarily mean that Semitic languages cannot distinguish between the two genders; especially in innovative forms, this is more common, e.g., in Syriac, the participle in the status absolutus is used to express the present tense by adding enclitic personal pronouns, masculine: *qāṭel-nā* 'I kill' (ܩܳܛܶܠ ܐ̱ܢܳܐ > ܩܳܛܶܠܢܳܐ) feminine: *qāṭlā-na* (ܩܳܛܠܳܐ ܐ̱ܢܳܐ > ܩܳܛܠܳܢܳܐ). In modern Aramaic languages, such as Ṭūroyo, this has resulted in two fully distinguished forms: masculine *qoṭálno* ~ feminine *qəṭlóno* (cf. Jastrow 1992, 61).

			ši-a-tum	KAJ 154:6
		Accusative	*ši-a-ti*	KAJ 132:12; KAJ 160:11; KAJ 161:8; KAJ 165:15; KAJ 172:5
2ms	*kuāša*	Dative	*ku-a-ša*	VAT 8851:4; NP 46:4; T 02-32:4; RS 20-18:5; KBo 28 64:6'
			ku-a-ša-a	KBo 1 14: 27
			ka-ša	EA 15:4
			ka-a-ša	MARV 10 90:4; BE 17 77:4
2fs	*kuāši*	Dative	*ku-a-ši*	T 96-36:4
			[*k*]*u-ia-š*[*i*$^{?}$]	T 02-05:5[6]
			ku-š[*a*]	T 93-17:4
1cs	*iyāši*	Dative	*iya-a-ši*	AO 19.227:22; T 96-36:5; MATSH 26:5; KUB 3 75:6'
			A-A-ši	K9-T1:4; T 97-32:16'†
			a-ia-ši	T 93-17:3
3mp	*šunāšunu*	Dative	*šu-na-šu-nu-ma*	MARV 10 3:8
	šunātunu	Accusative	*šu-na-a-tu-nu*	MAL B § 17:16
			šu-na-tu-nu	MAL O § 5:9
			šu-nu$^{?}$- ⸢*te*$^{?}$/*tu*$^{?}$⸣	LVUH 36:8
3fp	**šināšina*	Dative	–	–
	šinātina	Accusative	*ši-na-ti-na*	KAJ 164:12
2mp	*kunāšunu*	Dative	*ku-na-šu-nu*	KBo 1 20 r.7; RS 18.54a:19'
			ku-na-[*šu-nu*]	KAV 96:16
2fp	*kunāšina*	Accusative	*ku-na-*[*š*]*i-na*	T 93-8a:5
1cp	*nāši(n)*	Dative	[*n*]*a-ši-*⸢*in*⸣	MATSH 22:17; MATSH 27:5''†
			ni-ši-in	KAM 7 150:4

Figure 31: Independent dative and oblique personal pronouns.

10.1.2.1 Function of accusative and dative independent pronouns

§ 357 We find the accusative and dative cases of the independent pronouns divided between the direct and indirect object. Again, the pronouns can be used independently or attributively. The second and first person of the accusative case are not attested at all, which may signal the decay of this paradigm. Curiously, new textual material provides us with very few new attestations of the accusative paradigm, meaning that we must rely on the material already known to W. Mayer (UGM).

§ 358 The accusative case can be used independently as an anaphoric pronoun, but this is only very rarely attested. Two passages from the same text are given below:

> ŠE-*um* (…) *ilqe* (…) *ina la šu-a-te iddini*$^{sic.}$ 'he took the barley and gave it in the absence of any of his own' MARV 1 47:9–11
>
> ŠE-*um anniu ina la-a šu-a-te bēssu uballiṭi* 'this barley will support his house in the absence of his (own barley)' KAJ 101:11–13 cf. MARV 1 47:10–11

More frequently, the accusative is used attributively with a noun. It functions as a demonstrative pronoun in the same sense that we discussed for the nominal case.

Apposition to genitive:

6 An exceptional spelling with IA in a badly damaged letter. Perhaps it is better to read the line [*a*]-⸢*na*⸣ *ku*$^{!}$*-ia-š*[*i*$^{?}$], instead of [*a-na k*]*u-ia-š*[*i*$^{?}$].

ša mut sinniltu ši-a-ti marāšu laššu 'that wife's husband does not have a son' MAL A § 50:74–75

ina qaqqere šu-a-tum 'from that terrain' KAJ 175:8

šumma ina pūre ši-a-tum lā išallim 'if he cannot take all of the lot' KAJ 154:6–7

ina pî tuppi ši-a-ti 'according to this tablet' KAJ 165:5

Apposition to accusative:

aʾīla šu-a-tu 40 *ina ḫaṭṭāte imaḫḫuṣūš* 'they will hit that man 40 times with rods' MAL A § 18:77–78 (cf. § 19:89; § 40:89)

qaqqara šu-a-tum (…) *ú-ba-ʾa-PI ù ilaqqe* ' (the buyer) may select that terrain and take it' KAJ 175:35–38

šumma tuppa ši-a-ti PN_1 *ana* PN_2 *lā inaddin* 'if PN_1 does not give that tablet to PN_2' KAJ 132:12–15

pāḫat eqle šu-a-tu zakkue PN *ittanašši* 'PN will bear the responsibility for clearing that field' KAJ 132:16–18

tuppāti ši-na-ti-na u eqle ša pîšina (…) *ana* ŠÁM *gamer iddin* 'he sold these tablets and the field recorded on them' KAJ 164:12–18

§ 359 We already stated that the dative paradigm was a new feature in the MA dialect. Interestingly, in a pure dative function, it is only rarely attested, mostly in the introduction formula of letters. We always find it preceded by the preposition *ana*.

a-na ku-a-ša bētīka pāḫitīka lū šulmu 'may it be well with you, your house and your province' T 02-32:4–5

a-na ia-a-ši [šu]lmu 'all is well with me' T 96-36:5

gabbi maršīti ša bētīya a-na ku-na-šu-nu 'all of the property of my house is for you' RS 18.54a:17'–18'

⌜*a*⌝*-na šu-na-šu-nu ana epāše iddinūni* 'that they gave to them to process' MARV 10 3:8

a-na šu-a-šu 'to him' KUB 3 77 r. 9'†

a-na ku-a-ša pa[qd]āku 'I am entrusted to you' T 97-22:10–11

It should be noted that, in verbal clauses, the dative pronoun repeats the pronominal suffix attached to the verb.

sarta (…) *a-na ia-a-ši lēmedūnni* 'may they impose the penalty on me' AO 19.227:21–23

[šu]prā a-na ia-a-ši 'send it to me' MATSH 26:5'

§ 360 In NA, the accusative had merged with the dative into one oblique paradigm (SNAG, 44f § 3.1.1). This development is visible in MA in the lack of independent accusative pronouns aside from the third-person anaphoric pronouns. The use of the dative is confusing, while some examples can be presented where it is used for the grammatical direct object. In one example (Adad Ritual), the morphologic dative is used attributively and without the preposition *ana*. Yet, the uncontracted form (*šuāšu* i/o *šâšu*) distinguishes it from later NA. Examples are given below:

ina emmere šu-a-šu (…) '(pieces of meat) from that sheep' Adad Ritual r. 8'

tuppu dannutu <*ša*> *eqle šu-a-šu* (…) *ana* PN *zakkuat* 'the valid tablet of that field is cleared for PN' KAJ 149:22–25

[*ša/i+na*] *pi*$^{?}$ DUB$^{?}$ *šu-a-ša* 'according to the wording of that tablet' Billa 19:18

Perhaps we find an intermediate stage in the following phrases, where the dative construction *ana šuāšu* is used as a direct object. Note that in all cases except MATSH 2, the direct object is repeated as a pronominal suffix attached to the verb. The use of the pronouns in this construction continues in the NA period (Vinnichenko 2016a, 64–66).

kī mut sinnilte sinnilassu eppušūni a-na šu-a-šu e-ep-pu-ú-šu-uš 'as the husband treated his wife, they will treat him' MAL A § 22:11–13

a-na šu-a-ša u lidānīšama i-laq-qé-šu-nu 'he will take her and her children' MAL A § 36:13–14

a-šam-me a-na ku-na-[*šu-nu*] *la ú-ba-la-aṭ-ku-n*[*u*] '(if) I hear it, I will not let you live' KAV 96:16–17

ma$^{!}$*-a-na šu-a-šu-ma ana šamnuttīšu utta*$^{??}$*erūni* 'they have returned him to his *šamnu*-position' MATSH 2:50

a-na šu-a-šu na-aṣ-ṣu-uš ubbulūneššu 'they carry and bring him to me ' MATSH 9:45–46

Rarely do we find the accusative *šuātu* used for a nominative subject. This has already been observed in a peripheral royal inscription of Tall Bdēri. This use also occurs in NA.[7]

abu šu-a-te 'that father' KAJ 93:6†

The accusative independent pronoun *šuātu* is used attributively in relation to the subject in the Māri royal inscriptions. This is attested in two different passages:

enūma tillu šu-a-tu šumšu ūl idē ellān GN_1 *ina aḫ* GN_2 *šaknu* 'when this hill, its name was not known, was situated in GN_2, upstream of GN_1' Maul 1992, 22:2–3

enūma ālu u ēkallum šu-a-tu a-[*na* ....] 'when the city and that palace' Maul 1992, 38:8

At the same time, one passage uses the accusative pronoun correctly as an attributive in relation to an object:

šum āle šu-a-tu (…) *lū aškunu* 'I indeed established the name of that city' Maul 1992, 24:8

Maul (1992, 18) explained this as a typical feature for NA, where *šuātu* is frequently used as an attributive for a subject. Deller (1959, 142–44 § 34d) presented a large number of attestations for *šuātu*; however, Hämeen-Anttila highlighted that all attestations occur in the administrative documents and are not representative of spoken Assyrian (SNAG, 44). Upon checking, most, if not all, of the attestations occur in a variation of the same clause regarding the sale of slaves:

LÚ *šu-a-te za-rip laq-qe* 'that man is purchased and taken' SAA 6 244:8; cf. *šu-a-tú* in SAA 14 67:7; *šú-a-tu* SAA 6 346:6'

7 See Deller (1959, 142); Maul (1992, 18).

UN[meš] *šu-a-tú zar₄-pu la-qe-u* 'these people are acquired and taken' SAA 6 110:11

We already mentioned that the accusative *šuātu* was replaced by the morphological dative *šâšu* in NA. It seems likely that the function of *šuātu* was in the process of being forgotten in the MA corpus. This would explain why *šuātu* could be erroneously used as an attributive for the subject in the later NA texts.

10.2 Pronominal suffixes

§ 361 In common with all Semitic languages, personal pronominal suffixes can be attached to verbs, nomina and some prepositions. Although the suffixes are, for the most part, similar, there still remain some significant differences in the paradigms of the nominal and verbal suffixes in the accusative and the dative case.[8] Nomina receive pronominal suffixes directly on the status constructus form or have an extra vowel inserted (see § 287ff). The suffixes on nouns are usually used to indicate possession of the object in question, e.g., *uz-ni-šu-nu* 'their ears' MAL A § 4:50; *tup-pa-te-ia* 'my tablets' KAV 217:7'. A limited number of prepositions (see Chapter 13) and infinitives can take the genitive pronominal suffixes, e.g., *qa-ra-ab-ša-ni* MAPD § 7:47. When the sibilant of a suffix comes in contact with an interdental or sibilant, assimilation takes place (see § 224ff). In cases where the pronominal suffix follows /n/, assimilation usually remains absent (see § 228), e.g., *i-din-šu* 'he gave him' TR 2082:18.

§ 362 Unlike the independent pronouns, OA already possessed two different paradigms for the dative and accusative pronominal suffixes. The accusative forms mostly follow the genitive paradigm and do not differ morphologically. The dative pronominal suffixes in the singular follow the Babylonian suffixes; thus, we find the 3ms genitive *-šu*, the oblique *-šu* and the dative *-šum*.[9] In MA, mimation has dropped off, such that the three paradigms are more or less identical, with the exception of the 2ms dative *-kum* > *-ku* vs. the accusative *-ka*. For this reason, the distinction between dative and accusative appears to be in decline because the characteristic ending *-m* was elided when mimation was dropped in Assyrian. Indeed, in NA, all differences seem to be lost according to the paradigm given by Hämeen-Anttila (SNAG, 49 § 3.1.3). At the same time, the dative case has become almost inseparable with the ventive that precedes the suffix. Still, some exceptions remain, e.g., *i-di-nu-na-ši* 'they gave to us' MARV 1 71:22. Plural forms have *-ni(m)-* prefixed to the suffix, which is etymologically a plural ventive (§ 654ff), e.g., *id-du-nu-ni-šu* T 04-37:26. Dative suffixes following a ventive on a 2fs prefix verb *-(m)* are not attested, but would be similar to the singular *-a(m)* without the vowel. It is possible that the NA dative suffix *-(an)ni* was used in this instance (SNAG, 48). The only case of such a feminine verb ending in *-ī* is unfortunately broken at the end of the line.[10] Note also that one accusative suffix with the ventive is attested where no dative is needed: *i-pa-ša-ra-ku-nu* 'he will release

8 One could also refer to these nominal suffixes as being in the genitive case. However, this definition is not entirely correct, as the suffixes can also be added on nominative/accusative forms.

9 Cf. GAG, 53–54 § 42g–h; GOA § 9.4.1.

10 *a-na-i-*[*ni*] *la ta-šap-pi-ri-*[?] 'why do you not write to me?' T 97-32:12-13'.

you' MAL A § 47:28 (see Kouwenberg 2010, 240). A dative without preceding ventive is also once attested:

> 12 ^{giš}*nalb*[*attu*] <*ša*> *libitte šaḫā*[*ṭe*] (…) *ta-ad-na-šu ana šaḫāṭe* '12 moulds for brick making are given to him for brick making' A 3310:5–11

Similar cases of the dative without a preceding ventive are found in the literary TSA text T 96-31, which was probably not written in the Assyrian dialect.

§ 363 The third-person singular renders some interesting forms with apocopation, which only appears if the preceding vowel has the same quality as the apocopate vowel. In other words, *-š(u)* follows the ending of the finite 3mp verbs *-ū*, e.g., *ik-šu-du-uš* MAL A § 12:20; *ú-tar-ru-uš* § 20:97; *ub-ta-e-ru-ú-uš* § 21:100; *i-du-nu-uš* B § 2:17. The masculine *-š* is very common in MAL A, but can also be found elsewhere: *e-tam-ru-uš* TR 2031:7; *li-di-nu-uš* KAV 107:17. The apocopate suffix is fairly optional, while we also find 3mp with long suffixes: *ú-ba-ru-šu* MAPD § 2:21; *ú-še-šu-bu-šu* Coronation Ritual iii 1. Considering that there is only one example of an apocopate 3fs (*ul-ta-aṣ-le-eš* MAL A § 21:99), it is notable that, in the same text, we find a similar form without apocopate (*ú-ša-aṣ-le-ši* MAL A § 51:84). It is not unlikely that all III/weak verbs would come with an apocopate 3fs suffix, but we simply lack the evidence for it. Apocopate suffixes are quite common in the Akkadian dialects (cf. GAG, 53–54 § 42g–h) and quite similar to the situation in vernacular Arabic (e.g., Moroccan: 2ms *-ka* > *-ek*; see Harrel 1962, 134). Apocopate pronominal suffixes are also attested in the other stages of the Assyrian dialects, although they are never common (OA in GKT, 75 § 49a; GOA § 9.4.3, e.g., *e-mu-ru-uš* TCL 21 248:16; see also 2ms in *ma-lá-ak* I 437:33 and NA SNAG, 50 § 3.1.3). Moreover, while apocopate suffixes are rarer in OA, they do occur in relation to a wider variety of forms, including dative suffixes (see GOA § 9.4.3, e.g., *i-na-pu-lu-uš* JCS 26 68:10). Contemporary Babylonian usage of the apocopate *-š(u)* is uncommon, but found a few times in literary compositions and only on nomina, instead of the accusative on verbal forms (Aro 1955a, 54). The apocopate suffixes are, therefore, best explained as an Assyrian feature, rather than Babylonian influence. As such, it is also found once in the Ḫurro-Akkadian Amarna letter EA 16: *i-is-si-pu-uš* 'they gather it' l. 15 (Artzi 1997, 328). The dative 3fs underwent the sound change /i/ > /e/ in *-šim* > *-še*, probably under the influence of mimation, which was lost in MA. This allows for the possibility of making a better distinction between the accusative and the dative, e.g., *iq-ti-bi-a-áš-še* MAL A § 12:16. Unfortunately, we also find *-ši* for the dative, e.g., *ud-du-ši-i-ni* 'which he assigned her' MAL A § 24:45 from *udāʾu* (see § 607), which must be a dative pronominal suffix by analogy with OA *ú-da-a-ku-nu-tí* 'I shall inform you' BIN 4 32:22.

§ 364 The 2ms form *-ka* differs from the dative *-ku*. The dative form clearly derives from -*kum*, but this was shortened because of the disappearance of mimation. By analogy with the dative 3fs *-še*, one could expect a similar sound change in the form of *-kim* > *-ke*. Unfortunately, only one example of 2fs is known, in the accusative: *la-ni-ik-ki-me* 'I want to lie with you' MAL A § 12:16. The first-person singular is different in all paradigms. With nomina, it is simply *-ī* in the nominative/accusative singular case and follows the stem directly. In genitive or plural nomina, the suffix is *-ya* and follows the preceding /ē/ of the genitive (*ba-la-ṭí-ia* 'my life' VAT 8851:30), /ū/ of the nominative plural (*qe-pu-tu-ia* KAV 98:7) or /ē/ of the oblique plural (*tup-pa-te-ia* KAV 217:7). The accusative is basically the ventive+the suffix *-ni*. However, up until now, only the variation of the singular ventive is known: *-anni* (< *-am+ni*), but not **-nni* (on pc 2fs) nor **-nenni* (on plural forms). The broken spellings of *-anni* could signal that it was added directly to the base of a verb, separated by a stop, e.g., *ip/rus/an/ni*. However, broken spellings with added morphemes are common in MA, meaning that this assumption is questionable.[11] While there are no attestations of the accusative *-ni* on plural nouns, we would expect to find *-nenni* by analogy with Babylonian (GAG, 53–54 § 42g–h); however, OA material suggests that this form did not exist in the Assyrian dialect.[12] However, in this stage of the language, the accusative *-ni* and *-anni* were interchangeable, whereas, in MA, *-anni* was obligatory.

§ 365 The plural paradigm of the accusative and dative pronominal suffixes represent a departure from the situation in OA. The initial stage of the Assyrian dialect built the plural suffixes by putting a *-ti* ending on the dative, while both the nominative and accusative had -Ø; e.g., genitive: *-šunu*; accusative: *-šunu*; dative: *-šunūti* (cf. Reiner 2001, 391–92). Babylonian plural suffixes have a nominal ending -Ø, an accusative ending *-ti* and dative -*šim*; e.g., genitive: *-šunu*; accusative: *šunūti*; dative *šunūšim* (GAG, 53–54 § 42g–h). On first sight, the accusative and dative in OA are reversed from Babylonian. In MA, the paradigm was simplified considerably, with some forms being identical in all three cases (e.g., *-šunu*). More curiously is the 1cp *-nâši* for the accusative/dative, which comes from the Babylonian dative paradigm (*-niāšim*), replacing the OA *-niāti*. It is possible that this suffix is a sign of Babylonian influence on the pronominal paradigm (cf. Kouwenberg 2010, 12 n22). If this is the case, we should assume that the contraction (*-niāši* > *-nâši*) must have taken place in Babylonian before it was introduced in Assyrian.[13] Alternatively, presumable Babylonian pronouns in Assyrian could just as well be the result of an otherwise unknown dialect of Akkadian, which was spoken in the vicinity of Aššur.[14] We simply lack the evidence to explain the precise origin of these developments. Another development regarding the pronominal suffixes involves the loss of variation in the genitive plural forms with the vowel syncope *-knu*, *-šnu*, *-šna*, as they occur in OA following the construct vowel *-a-* (GOA § 9.5.3). The possibility of hypercorrection by Assyrian scribes can be excluded given that the construct vowel *-a-* becomes affected by VA, which is not possible with the apocopate variants., as they close the preceding syllable. The short OA forms may be another case of allegro forms vs. lene forms of MA (cf. Sommerfeld 2006).

11 For example, *mu-šal-lim-a-nu* KAJ 92: 10; *áš-šúm-i-ka* T 02-32:7; [iti]*Ab Šar-a-nu* KAV 212:12 (Aub); cf. § 119.

12 Cf. 3mp *ú-wa-šé-ru-ni-ma* KTH 3:6, instead of **uwaššerūnenni-ma*, GKT, 75 § 49a; cf. GOA § 9.7.1.

13 Curiously, MB seems to have the dative and accusative reversed; accusative: *-nâši*; dative: *-nâti*. See Aro (1955a, 57–58).

14 The idea that MA is not a direct descendent of OA was suggested by Huehnergard (2006, 12 n57).

		Old Assyrian		Middle Assyrian		Neo-Assyrian
	Genitive	Dative	Accusative	Dative	Accusative	Dative/accusative
3ms	*-šu*	*-šum*	*-šu*	*-šu*	*-š(u)*	*-šu*
3fs	*-ša*	*-šim*	*-ši*	*-še*	*-š(i)*	*-ši*
2ms	*-ka*	*-kum*	*-ka*	*-ku*	*-ka*	*-ka*
2fs	*-ki*	*-kim*	*-ki*	*-ke?*	*-ki*	*-ki*
1cs	*-ī/ya*	*-am/m/nim*	*-(an)ni/ī*	*-a, -Ø*	*-anni*	*-(an)nī*
3mp	*-šunu*	*-šunūti*	*-šunu*	*-šunu*		*-šunu*
3fp	*-šina*	*-šināti*	*-šina*	*-šina*		*-šina*
2mp	*-kunu*	*-kunūti*	*-kunu*	*-kunu*		*-kunu*
2fp	*-kina*	*-kināti*	*-kina*	**-kina*		*-kina*
1cp	*-ni*	*-niāti*	*-niāti*	*-nâši(n?)*		*-nāši*

Figure 32: Pronominal suffixes in Assyrian.

Examples:

3ms	Genitive	*-šu*	*-šu*	*a-ra-an-šu* 'his offense' MAL A § 15:46
				il-ki-i-šu 'his service' Giricano 4:26
				il-te-šu 'with him' MATC 9:7
			-šu-ú	ŠE.ÀRA-*šu-ú* 'its grinded barley' Giricano 2:10, 13:7
			-šú	*a-bu-šú* 'his father' TR 3029:4.
				bi-ḫir-šú KAJ 306a:9
				tup-pu-šú 'his tablet' Giricano 1:15
	Accusative	*-š(u)*	*-šu*	*ú-kal-lal-šu* 'he will crown him' Coronation Ritual ii 26
				la i-ka-la-šu 'he will not stop him' T 97-17:24
				še-bi-la-šu 'send him here!' MATC 32:3
			-uš	*i-maḫ-ḫu-ṣu-uš* 'they will hit him' MAL B § 7:9
				i-ša-ku-nu-uš 'they will place him' MATSH 2:52
				li-di-nu-uš 'they must give him' KAV 107:17
	Dative	*-aššu*	*-šu*	*iq-bi-áš-šu* 'he said to him' MAL A § 19:86
				iq-bi-áš-šu-un-ni 'he said to him' MAL A § 47:11
				di-na-áš-šu 'give to him' MATC 5:22
			-šu-ú	*ta-at-ta-an-na-šu-ú* 'you have given it to him' MARV 4 8:19
3fs	Genitive	*-ša*	*-ša*	*ap-pa-ša* 'her nose' MAL A § 5:69
				lìb-bi-ša TR 3002:5
				mi-ig-ra-ti-ša 'her own will' KAJ 3:2
	Accusative	*-š(i)*	*-ši*	*ú-ša-ḫi-zu-ši-ni* 'I have instructed her' MAL A § 5:61
				e-te-zi-ib-ši 'he has left her' MAL A § 38:21
				uz-zak-ki-ši 'he will free her' KAJ 7:8
			-š	*ul-ta-aṣ-le-eš* 'he has caused her abortion' MAL A § 21:99
	Dative	*-ašše*	*-še*	*e-zi-ba-áš-še* 'he left to her' MAL A § 36:88
				iq-ti-bi-a-áš-še 'he told her' MAL A § 12:16
				iq-bi-a-še-ni 'he has said to her' MAPD § 15:75
			-ši	*lā i-ka-la-ši* 'he will not withhold from her' TR 2037:36
				id-di-na-aš-ši 'he gave to her' KAJ 9:22
2ms	Genitive	*-ka*	*-ka*	DAM-*ka* 'your wife' MAL A § 17:68
				pi-i-tu-uk-ka 'your responsibility' MATSH 1:17
				ši-pár-ka 'your message' MATC 4:17
	Accusative	*-ka*	*-ka*	*ú-ba-ar-ka* 'I will prove you' MAL A § 19:87

				ṭēma áš-ku-nu-ka-ni 'I instructed you' MATC 4:19
				la-áš-pur-ka 'I want to send you' MAPD § 21:106
	Dative	*-akku*	*-ku*	*i-lu-ku-ni-ku* 'they will come to you' MATC 18:6
				a-šap-pa-ra-ku 'I will write to you' A 877:7
				lid-da-na-ku 'may he give to you' Coronation Ritual ii 36
2fs	Genitive	*-ki*	*-ki*	*a-na a-ma-ri-ki* 'to see you' A 845:8
				ṣu-u[ḫ-r]i-ki 'your children' T 93-17:5
				ÌR-⸢*ki*⸣ 'your servant' TabT05a-134:2
	Accusative	*-ki*		*la-ni-ik-ki-me* 'I want to lie with you' MAL A § 12:16
	Dative	*-akke*		[*a-š*]*a-pa-ra-ak-ki-m*[*a*] 'I will write to you' T 97-32:10'
				ul-te-bi-la-ak-ki 'I have sent to you' A 845:13
1cs	Genitive	*-ī*	*-i*	*ú-nu-ti* 'my property' KAV 168:7
		-ya	*-ia*	*ba-la-ṭí-ia* 'my life' VAT 8851:30
				bi-it-qi-ia 'my accusation' A 748:8
				qe-pu-tu-ia 'my representatives' KAV 98:7
			-a	*du-un-ni-a* 'my fortress' MATSH 2:6[1]
	Accusative	*-anni*	*-an-ni*	*uk-tal-li-ma-an-ni* 'he showed me' Hall 1983:20
				i-it-ti-ka-an-⸢*ni*⸣ 'he lied with me' MAL A § 22:5
				i-ṣe-ḫa-an-ni '(I rejoiced)' T 93-8a:12
			-an-ni-i	*ta-an-ti-ši-an-ni-i* 'did you forget me?' T 93-12:4
			-a-ni	*lā i-la-qe-a-ni* 'he will not take me' KAV 159:7
				im-taḫ-ra-a-ni 'he has confronted me' KAV 169:5; MARV 1 13:5
				il-ta-ʾa-la-a-ni 'he has questioned me' T 02-32:8
	Dative	*-a/ne*	*-a*	*iq-ti-bi-a* 'he said to me' T 93-2:4
				i-di-na-ni (< *iddin-am-ni*) 'he gave to me' MATSH 16:6
			-ne	*it-tab-lu-ni* 'they brought to me' MATSH 2:24
3mp	Genitive	*-šunu*	*-šu-nu*	*ap-pi-šu-nu* 'their nose' MAL A § 4:49
				ki-la-al-li-šu-nu-ma 'them both' MAL A § 15:44
				tup-pa-te-šu-nu 'their tablets' MAL B § 6:16
			-šú-nu	*ina pa-ni-šú-*⸢*nu*⸣ 'in front of them' Coronation Ritual i 28
	Accusative	*-šunu*	*-šu-nu*	*i-du-uk-ku-šu-nu* 'they will kill them' MAL A § 3:31
				i-kar-ru-ru-šu-nu 'they will throw them' MAPD § 19:94
				ù-uš-šu-ru-šu-nu 'they will release them' MAL A § 23:26
	Dative	*-aššunu*		*i-qa-bi-ú-ni-šu-nu-ni* 'he said to them' MATC 83:14
				⸢*i*⸣*-di-na-šu-nu-ú-ma* 'he gave to them' MATSH 7:3''
				ta-ad-na-ta-šu-nu 'it is given to them' VAT 8236 r. 16
3fp	Genitive	*-šina*	*-ši-na*	*adi e-li-ti-ši-na u i-ga-ra-ti-ši-na* 'with their upperpart and their walls' VAT 8923:7
				bu-qu-ni-ši-na 'their wool yield' KAJ 88:13
				ina ṣa-al-ti-ši-na 'during their quarrel' MAPD § 10:57
	Accusative	*-šina*	*-ši-na*	*ú-pa-aṭ-*[*ṭa-ar-ši*]*-na* 'he will clear them' MAPD §

1 The copy of the text is unclear regarding the sign reading.

				21:112
	Dative	*-aššina*	*-ši-na*	*ta-ad-na-ši-na* 'it is given to them' MARV 4 113:20' ⸢*ta-ad-na-ši*⸣*-na* MARV 4 59:20; MARV 10 40:15
2mp	Genitive	*-kunu*	*-ku-nu*	*ḫu-ra-ad-ku-nu* 'your *ḫurādu*-troops' MATSH 7:12' *ku-nu-ki-ku-nu* 'your seals' KAV 99:29 *ina* UGU-*ku-nu* 'in your responsibility' VS 1 105:17
	Accusative	*-kunu*	*-ku-nu*	*lā ú-ba-la-aṭ-ku-n*[*u*] 'I will not let you live' KAV 96:17 *i-pa-ša-ra-ku-nu* 'he will release you' MAL A § 47:28 *ú-šal-lam-ku-nu-ma* 'I will compensate you' T 04-37:12
	Dative	*-akkunu*	*-ku-nu*	*i-lu-ku-ni-ku-nu* 'they will come to you' KAV 98:19 *i-qa-bi-a-ku-nu-ú-ni* 'he will say to you' MATSH 7:15'' *ul-te-bi-lak-ku-n*[*u*] 'I have sent to you' KAV 96:8
2fp	Genitive	*-kina*	*-ki-na*	*a-na a-ma-ri-ki-na* 'to see you' T 93-8a:11 IGI^{meš}-*ki-n*[*a*] 'your eyes' T 93-8a:13 *zi-te-ki-na* 'your share' KAV 194:21
	Accusative	*-kina*	*-ki-na*	–
	Dative	*-akkina*	*-ki-na*	–
1cp	Genitive	*-ni*	*-ni*	EN-*ni* 'our lord' MATSH 2:59 *ḫi-im-sa-te-e-ni* 'our wrongful possessions' KAV 217:13 *ši-pa-si-ni* 'our sealing' MARV 1 71:14
	Accusative	*-nâši(n)*	*-na-ši-ni*	*tu-ša-ra-na-ši-ni* 'you will release us' MATSH 22:16
			-na-ši-in	*lu ni-{ib}-il-qu-na-*[*š*]*i-*[*in*] 'we want to take it for us' MATSH 22:18 *ú-še-ra-*[*n*]*a-ši-in* 'release us' MATSH 22:17
	Dative	*-annâsi*	*-na-ši*	*e-*⸢*ep*⸣*-pa-ša-na-ši-in-ni* 'he will do to us' MATSH 11:17 *ip-táq-da-na-ši-na* 'he entrusted us' KAV 217:15 *la i-di-nu-na-ši* 'they did not give us' MARV 1 71:22

10.2.1 Function of the pronominal suffixes

§ 366 The three paradigms of pronominal suffixes come with different functions. The genitive is usually attached to nouns and some prepositions. On nouns, it indicates possession, e.g., *bēt-ka* 'your house'; *pāḫussunu* 'their province'; *lidān-ni* 'our children'. On prepositions, the meaning is usually adverbial, e.g., *iltē-ka* 'with you'; *ina libbī-šu* 'inside it'; *balukkunu* 'without you'. The dative is attached to verbs and (as its name suggests) indicates the indirect object, e.g., iddanakku 'he will give it to you'. The accusative, therefore, indicates the direct object, e.g., *iṣṣabat-anni* 'he seized me'.

§ 367 A finite verb normally does not take a pronominal suffix to refer to a direct object mentioned in the same sentence. A few exceptions have been found.

> *šumma aššat aʾīle lā abuša lā aḫuša lā marāša aʾīlu šanīumma ḫarrāna ul-ta-aṣ-bi-si* 'if another man, neither her father, nor her brother, nor her son, arranges for a wife to travel (with him)' MAL A § 22:105–108

kī kallete ša-a i-ra-ʾu-mu-ši-ni irakkusūnešše 'like a daughter-in-law that they love, they draw up (an agreement) for her' MAL A 46:97–98

½ *mana ṣarpa ana panē Adad i*⌜*q*⌝*-bi-šu* 'he promised him half a mina of silver before Adad' KAM 10 25:6–7

PN *abušu eqla u libba-āla*[sic.] *i-pá-la-aḫ-šu* 'PN will honour his father on the field and in the city' KAJ 6:10–12

When an (indirect) object is already mentioned earlier in the text, it is not obligatory to refer to the antecedent again in the finite verb by adding a pronominal suffix.

šumma iṣ-ṣa-ab-ta lū ana muḫḫi šarre lū ana muḫḫi dayānē it-tab-la 'if he seized (him) and brought (him) either before the king or before judges' MAL A § 15:47–48

ana ša ḫadiūni i-id-dan 'he will give (her) to the one he wishes' MAL A § 43:26

šumma adi 1 ITI.UD[meš] *la-a i-ti-din ina muḫḫīšu ire*[??]*a u ú-*⌜*la*[?]⌝ {x} *ibaqqan ina ūme gurrāte iddunūni tuppušu i-ḫap-pi* 'If he has not given them within one month, they will pasture on his expense and he may not pluck them. On the day he will give the ewes, he will break his tablet' KAJ 88:16–21

When the object is referred to in the subordinate clause, it does not need to be repeated in the main clause:

ina ūme erišūšuni iddan 'when he requests it from him he will give it' KAJ 97:8–9

When the object is mentioned in the main clause, the predicate does not take the pronominal suffix, although the predicate of the following clauses does:

mā ina muḫḫi GN_1 GN_2 *u* GN_3 *lā amlik la-a áš-pur-šu-nu la-a ás-si-šu-nu* 'I did not give advice to the GN_1 GN_2 and GN_3, I did not write them, I did not call upon them' A 2994:6–10

Here is an unclear use:

annūte GU_4[meš]*-šu rēḫta šūt lilqe* 'may he take these, the remainder of his oxen' T 97-17:15–17[2]

§ 368 Although pronominal suffixes are usually applied correctly, some mistakes surface. In the OA, mistakes in gender occur in texts written in Anatolia as a result of a lack of gender distinction in the Anatolian languages (cf. GOA § 9.4.1). Similar mistakes are attested in a peripheral Assyrian letter from Carchemish, written to a few women (T 93-8a). The masculine plural is applied a number of times instead of the feminine; however, note that the correct feminine suffix *-kina* is also found in the text. As highlighted by Wiggermann (private correspondence), confusion in the gender of pronominal suffixes is attested in Akkadian texts from Carchemish (Huehnergard 1979, 32).

[*ana*] [f]PNs *u* DUMU[meš]*-š*[*u*]*-nu qi*[*bima*] *umma* PN Š[E]Š*-ku-nu-ma* 'speak to [f]PNs and their children, thus (says) PN your brother' T 93-8a:1–4

[*n*]*ap-šá-*[*t*]*i-ku-nu liṣṣurū lušall*[*imū*] 'may they fully guard your lives' T 93-8a:9–10

---

2 Llop (2012, 294) takes *annūte* GU_4[meš] as the object of the preceding finite verb, which would create a rare case of the verbal predicate in the first position of the sentence: *liqe annūte* GU_4[meš] 'take these oxen'. However, it is preferable to regard the verbal form as part of a normal asyndetic construction of two succeeding imperatives: GU_4[meš] (...) *atta usuq liqe* 'you select the bulls and take them' T 97-17:12–15.

Moreover, texts concerning female persons are rare in MA, whereas females are often the object of OA Anatolian slave contracts. In texts from Aššur, we find a handful of mistakes concerning gender (regarding agreements, see also § 665ff).

⌜*iṣ*⌝*-ṣa-ba-a-sú* for *iṣṣabassi* MAL A § 12:15

ni-še-sà-ma for *nišessuma* KAM 10 25:8

Mistakes between dative and accusative pronominal suffixes are rare. This may be related to the fusion of the MA and NA dative and accusative paradigms, which included the accusative (*-an*)*ni*, which in turn replaced the dative *-a*(*m*); see SNAG, 49 § 3.1.3.

anaʾīne ṭēma la taš-pu-ra-ni 'why did you not write me a message?' K9-T1:8–10

a[*šš*]*um* ŠE *u qēme* x *ša ta-áš-pu-ra-ni-*[*n*]*i* 'concerning the barley and flour, about which you wrote to me' T 93-46:17–18

§ 369 The traditional distinction between the 1cs genitive suffix *-ī* for nominative/accusative singular nouns and *-ya* for genitive singular nouns and all plural nouns was disappearing in MA. According to Hämeen-Anttila, *-ī* was used, following a consonant, and *-ya*, following a vowel (SNAG, 49 § 3.1.3). In MA, the decay of this distinction can be observed in a number of nouns referring to family members, which take *-ya* instead of the expected *-ī*. Another explanation is the logographic spellings, where scribes may have had problems adding the pronominal suffix *-ī* by writing the sign I. Spellings with I are, as far as I know, not attested in MA and may have motivated the choice to write IA instead.

a-bi-ia atta 'you are my father' VAT 8851:19 (cf. OA *a-bi a-ta* AKT 6 53:4)

mā PN_1 DUMU-*ia rabīu u* PN_2 DUMU-*ia-ma* (….) [*z*]*itta iltu aḫāmiš*[sic.] [(…) *li-zu*]*-SU* 'PN_1 my oldest son and PN_2, my son, will together divide the inheritance' Snell 1983/84:6–12

ilānu (...) ŠEŠ-*ia liṣṣurūka* 'may the gods protect you, my brother' RS 06.198:5–6

[*mī*]*nummê* ŠEŠ-*ia* [*i*]*ṣabbutū*[*ni*] 'whatever my brother wants to take' RS 06.198:24–25

With logographic writings, the first-person pronoun *-ī/ya* is not always visible following the logogram, such as in the case of EN (*bēlu*) 'lord' and NIN (*bēltu*) (cf. SNAG, 49). This was probably because the combination 'my lord' was in the process of becoming lexicalized, as 'my lord' is addressed in the third person.[3]

abāte ša EN *idbubanni* 'the words that my lord said to me' Tsukimoto 1992 D:7

ana kaṣāre EN *lišpura* 'may my lord send it here for knitting' MATSH 6:13'

iltu EN *namāšīšu* (…) 'after my lord's departure' MATSH 8:25'

[*a*]*mma*[*r*] *ina pitti* NIN-*ia ibaššiūni* NIN *lū tušēbila* 'as much as there is in the responsibility of my lady, may my lady send me' TabT05a-134:26–29

Nonetheless, in most cases we still find the sign *-ya* attached and, when EN occurs in the nominative/accusative, even the semisyllabic spelling EN-*li* (*bēlī*) is commonly used in the

3 Cf. Aramaic *mārā* (ܡܪܐ) 'lord' to > *mār-Ø* (ܡܪܝ) 'my lord' as standard for ecclesiastical and saint titles (see Smith 1903, 298).

TŠḪ correspondence (passim). However, it remains relatively rare elsewhere, e.g., T 02-32:20.

10.3 Possessive personal pronouns

§ 370 MA independent genitive pronouns are found, however they are relatively rare, such that we only have a small part of the paradigm. Following the OA and OB dialects, it seems that MA and NA are the only dialects of Akkadian, other than the literary forms, where they were retained: in MB, they were replaced (Aro 1955a, 53–54), the grammars of WPA make no mention of them.[4] They function as an adjective to a noun, but also independently as the examples below illustrate. They are the only group of independent pronouns that are inflected according to number and gender of the nomen they are attributed to, but they retain the person of the possessor.

§ 371 The morphology of the pronouns has changed little since OA, aside from the dropped mimation. Etymologically, they are inflected according to the stem of the oblique paradigms (*šuā-*; *kuā-* etc., see GOA § 9.8.1). In the paradigm, a glide /y-w/ is reconstructed under the assumption that this helped the pronunciation. This is confirmed by some of the OA evidence that still show /w/ (e.g., *šu-wa-am* VS 26 37:25), the same can be said for the genitive/accusative and dative pronouns (e.g., *ku-wa-tí* BIN 4 79:12). No contraction took place, even in the double-weak forms (*ku*^{w}*āʾu*). An exception is perhaps the sequence of similar vowels, attested in the following feminine plural form: *niā-+ātu* > *ni-a-tu* (*niâtu*) 'our' MATSH 10:10. Another interesting feature is the metathesis of quantity found in the feminine singular form *ni-a-at-tu* (*niāttu* < *niātu*) 'our' MATC 80:7. On the basis of this form, we should also expect this metathesis to take place in the masculine plural forms ending in *-ūt*. In NA, the pronouns have developed a prefix iC-, where the C is a geminated first consonant. Perhaps we can explain the first-person singular (*yāʾû* > *iyû*) this way. The example, *i-IA-ú* MATSH 29:7' is better explained if we assume the reading <iya>, rather than <ia>, because it explains the use of the sign I in this context (cf. § 170). This conclusion is consistent with the other examples, except *iya*$^{!}$*-i*$^{!}$*-e* MATSH 17:11'.

§ 372 The possessive personal pronouns occur in a number of different functions. In some cases, they act as predicates (e.g., 'the country is yours'). In this case, the pronominal suffixes cannot be used and are thus replaced by the independent possessive pronouns:

GN *ia-a-ú* GN *ka-a-*[*ú*] '(the city) GN is mine (or) GN is yours' KBo 1 14:10

ālānu u munnabdū ku-na-ú-[*tu*] 'the cities and refugees are yours' KBo 1 20:17'

When the possessive pronoun is used to negate possession, the pronominal suffixes cannot be used and instead we find independent possessive pronouns (e.g., 'I crossed the country, that is not mine'):

4 For example, Izre'el (1991); Huehnergard (1989); Seminara (1998).

4 *sinnišātu la iya-a-tu ša kī ṣarpe tadnāni u sinniltu ku-a-tu iltu annākamma udduat* 'Four women, not mine, who are sold and your wife, who is assigned there' MATC 15:4–7

When an opposition is used in combination with the particle *lū* (e.g., be they yours or be they mine), the possessive pronouns are used attributively with the noun:

lū sinnišātu damqātu ni-a-tu KIMIN *lū kaššiātu* 'be it our good women, or be it a Kassite good woman' MATSH 10:10–11

rabuttu gabbu lū ni-a-⸢ú-tu⸣ KIMIN *lū kaššiū* 'All the elite, be they ours, or be they Kassite' MATSH 10:31

emmerāte lū ša iltu GN *naṣṣākuni lū ku-a-ú-te (…) altaḫal* 'sheep, be it those that are brought to you from GN, be it yours (…) I have selected' MATC 10:16–22

4 *sinnišātu la iya-a-tu ša kī ṣarpe tadnāni u sinniltu ku-a-tu iltu annākamma udduat* 'Four women, not mine, who are sold, and your wife, who is assigned there' MATC 15:4–7

In some cases, a special emphasis must be presumed, as the possessive pronouns could also have been expressed by pronominal suffixes.

ina qaqqere ii[!]*-i*[!]*-e ḫalaq* 'he disappeared on my territory' MATSH 17:10'–11'

ešartu ni-a-at-tu 'our group of 10' MATC 80:6–7 cf. l. 8–10, 11–12

It is possible for the pronoun to precede the noun, as is attested on one occasion. Unlike OA, we have no attestations of the noun taking an extra pronominal suffix when the possessive pronoun precedes it (GOA § 9.8.3.1).

ku-a-ú-te ṣabʾa aʾīlutta lā alqea 'I have not taken your troops and men' MATC 4:14–16

Apparently, the possessive pronouns can be used independently in the sense of 'property'. This function is better attested in OA (GOA § 9.8.3.3). The following example also seems to be a prime example of strengthening involving the suffix *-ma* (§ 411f), again as in OA (GOA § 9.8.3.1).

šu-a-am-ma ilaqqe 'he will take his possessions' MAL A § 27:106–107

3s	ms	*šu-a-am-ma*	MAL A § 27:106
	fs		
	mp		
	fp		
2s	ms	*ku-a-ú*	KBo 1 14:10, 15, 16; MATSH 29:7', 8'
		ku[!]*-a-ú-um-[ma]*	MATSH 29:8'
	fs	*ku-a-tu*	MATC 15:6
	mp	*ku-a-ú-te*	MATC 4:14; 10:19
	fp	–	
1cs	ms	*i-iya-ú*	MATSH 29:7'; Cohen/Llop 2017:4, 5
		iya-a-ú	KBo 1 14:9, 10, 16
		iya[!]*-i*[!]*-e*	MATSH 17:11'
		ia-a-ma	T 93-46:22
	fs	–	
	mp	–	
	fp	*iya-a-tu*	MATC 15:4
3p	ms	–	
	fs	–	
	mp	–	

	fp	–	
2p	ms	–	
	fs	–	
	mp	*ku-na-ú-*[*tu*]	KBo 1 20:17'
	fp	–	
1cp	ms	–	
	fs	*ni-a-at-tu*	MATC 80:7, 10, 12
	mp	*ni-a-*⌈*ú-tu*⌉	MATSH 10:30
	fp	*ni-a-tu*	MATSH 10:10

Figure 33: Independent possessive personal pronouns.

Chapter 11: Other Types of Pronouns

11.1 Demonstrative pronouns

11.1.1 *anniu* 'this'

§ 373 The most common demonstrative pronoun is *anniu* (OB *annûm*). Unlike in Babylonian, there is no vowel contraction except in the plural. In the common orthography of the genitive *an-NI-e*, contraction is not clear, but NA evidence seems to suggest the opposite, e.g., *an-ni-i-e* SAA 10 39:16; *ḫa-an-ni-i-e* SAA 56:16 (SNAG, 50 § 3.1.4.1), cf. spatial deixis *ammiu*: *am-mi-e-em-ma* MAL A § 24:43. In the feminine inflection (*annītu*), it is not clear what happens to the aleph, as the orthography shows neither a long vowel nor a geminated /t/. The pronoun is fully in congruence according to the case, gender and number of the noun it refers to. As such, it can be used either adjectivally or as a substantive. A dual form was already rare in OA (*an-né-en-ma* ATHE 48:35) and has not been found in MA. The core of *anniu* is the base *ann-*, which was originally part of a person-orientated tripartite system of *ann-* (first person), *amm-* (second person) and *all-* (third person). All three bases are part of the spatial deixis, which "refers to the spatial location of an entity relative to the deictic centre, which is canonically the speaker" (Kouwenberg 2012, 18). For the demonstrative pronouns, the system was stripped down and the basis *ann-* replaced *amm-* and *all-* for the second and third person, respectively. We still find *amm-* in some adverbs of location (see § 483).

§ 374 The demonstrative pronouns basically function as (non-verbal) adjectives in terms of inflection, as well as syntactical position. They usually follow a head noun and are inflected according to number and gender of the head.

> *ina* 2 *šanāte an-na-te šumma ša akāli la*[*š*]*šu tallakamma taqabbi* 'If there is no food in these two years, she will come forward and say so' MAL A § 45:50–51
>
> *abnū an-nu-te ana niqie iddan* 'he will give these stones as a gift' Coronation Ritual ii 13
>
> *ša riksa an-ni-a etiqūni* '(…) who has violated this decree (…)' MAPD § 21:108
>
> *ana muḫḫi mā'ē an-nu-ti* (…) *tatabbak* 'you will pour it on top of this water' PKT 3 i 5–6
>
> *iltu libbi ḫerse an-ni-e ana libbi ḫerse ša*[*n*]*īe tašaḫḫal* 'from this *ḫersu*-vessel to another *ḫersu*-vessel, you will filter it PKT 3 i 10
>
> *ṣab'ē an-nu-te lišši lēmur* 'he should bring and inspect these troops' MATC 11:28
>
> *ina mūše* ⌜*an*⌝*-ni-e* 'during this night (i.e. tonight)' T 93-2:6
>
> *annuku an-ni-ú šulmānu* 'this silver is a *šulmānu*-gift' KAJ 54:9–10

On rare occasions, the demonstrative pronoun precedes the noun it qualifies (cf. OA GOA § 10.2.2).

> *an-ni-tu tuppu dannat* 'this is a strong tablet' KAJ 148:28

According to Kouwenberg, the pronoun changes meaning with the suffix *-ma* to 'the (very) same'. This is part of the function of the suffix, which will be discussed in § 412.

> *nakkamta kunukka an-ni-a-ma kunkā* 'seal the treasury with the same seal' KAV 105:21–22

Despite the character of the adjective, we also find the demonstrative pronouns used independently, referring to an antecedent.

> *adi tuppi dannata išaṭṭuru an-ni-tu-ma dannat* 'until he writes a (new) strong tablet, this one is valid' KAJ 12:20–21; cf. KAJ 151:21–23
>
> 5 *lim ṣabʾu* (…) *an-nu-tu āla lilbiū an-nu-tu ana* GN *lušēber* '5,000 troops (…) these (people) must lay siege to the city, but these (others) I shall bring (across the river) to GN' MATSH 8:25'–27'
>
> *an-nu-ú-tu ītašerūni*[sic.] 'these (people) came straight to me' MATSH 3:35

In nominal clauses:

> *šumma aʾīlu aššat aʾīle ša murabbita imḫaṣma ša libbīša ušaṣliši ḫiṭṭu an-ni-ú* 'If a man hits a wife who raises a child and he caused her to have a miscarriage, it is a crime' MAL A § 51:82–85
>
> *mimma an-ni-ú qēlt*[*u*] 'all this is a gift' New Year Ritual:7'
>
> *šiqatka an-ni-ú* 'this is your slag' PKT 3 i 6
>
> *an-ni-a ša iltu māʾē bē*[*dūni qātika*] *tumarraṭ* 'This, from the water that stood at night, your hand will scrape off' PKT 3 iii 1–2
>
> *mīnumma an-ni-ú* 'what is this?' T 93-3:4

After prepositions:

> *urki an-ni-e* […] (context broken) MAL O § 2b:5
>
> *kī an-ni-e e-pa*[*l* …] (context broken) New Year Ritual r. 20
>
> *aššum an-n*[*i-te*] *lammuš* 'I want to depart because of this' MATSH 4:7'–8'
>
> *kīmū an-nu-te mazzalta iṣabbutū* 'instead of these, they will take position' MATSH 8:47'

Pronominal suffix+demonstrative:

> *an-nu-te* $GU_4^{meš}$*-šu* 'these oxen of him' T 97-17:15–16

ms	nom	*an-ni-ú*	PKT 3 i 6; MATC 40:17
		an-nu-ú	KAJ 83:9
	gen	*an-ni-e*	LVUH 73:14
		an-ni	MATSH 26:5'
		an-ni-ma	Adad Ritual:3
		an-ni-e-ma	KAJ 182:6; 291:3; 307:13; MARV 2 14 r. 2; MARV 5 57:4; MARV 6 14:6; MARV 10 52:9
		an-ni-im-ma	MARV 3 16 passim
	acc	*an-ni-a*	PKT 3 iii 1; MATSH 1:12
		an-ni-a-ma	KAV 105:22; KAV 200:7
fs	nom	*an-ni-tu*	KAJ 98:8
		an-ni-TUM	KAJ 89:7
		an-ni-TUM-ma	BM 108924:22
		an-ni-tu-ma	KAJ 12:21; KAJ 151:23
	gen	*an-ni-te*	
		an-ni-te-ma	MATSH 22:22

		an-ni-ti	KAJ 165:21
	acc	*an-ni-ta*	MATC 12:15
		an-ni-ta-ma	KBo 1 14 r. 10’
mp	nom	*an-nu-tu*	MATSH 6:32’
		an-nu-ú-tu	MATSH 3:35, 39
		an-ni-ú-tu	MCS 2 1:9
		an-nu-TUM	KAJ 303:12
	obl	*an-nu-te*	PKT 1 I right:21; MATC 11:27
		an-nu-te-ma	PKT 3 i 12; PKT 6 i 32
		an-nu-ú-te	MATSH 3:39
		an-nu-ti	PKT 3 i 15
fp	nom	*an-na-tu*	–
	obl	*an-na-te*	–
		an-na-a-te	MATSH 3:36; MAL B § 6:20; New Year Ritual:9’
		an-na-ti	CT 33 15b:5†; MARV 1 20:11
		an$^{!?}$*-ni*$^{?}$*-a-te*	T 93-3:23
		a-na-te-ka(?)	MATSH 29:10†

11.1.2 *ammiu* ‘that’

§ 375 In the OA period, *ammiu* lost its original association with the second person, instead it replaced *allium* in MA for the distal spatial deixis (Kouwenberg 2012, 30; cf. GKT, 81 § 54b; GOA § 10.3.2). It can roughly be distinguished from *anniu* in translation as ‘this’ (*anniu*) vs. ‘that’ (*ammiu*). Examples in MA are nonetheless scarce. However, in NA, *ammiu* can still be found and is in congruence according to number and gender (SNAG, 50 § 3.1.4.1). There are three attestations of the masculine singular in MA:

ina libbi āle am-mi-e-em-ma ‘in that city’ MAL A § 24:43

ina qaqqare$^{sic.}$ *am-mi-e-ma* ‘on that terrain’ KAJ 175:20

sarta ša am-me-a ana emādini ana iyyāši lēmedūnni ‘may they impose the penalty on me, which is there to impose’ AO 19.227:21–23

ms	nom	–	–
	gen	*am-mi-e-ma*	KAJ 175:20
		am-mi-e-em-ma	MAL A § 24:43
	acc	*am-me-a*	AO 19.227:21

11.1.3 *alliu* ‘that’

§ 376 The original third element *allium* (OB *ullûm*) seems to have been used in OA for an entity, mentioned only indirectly, but is not the one the discourse available.[1] While it is usually maintained that *allium* disappeared in MA, it is noted that it has been preserved in WPA (Kouwenberg 2012, 72), especially in Nuzi (CAD A_1, 158). Apparently, in Alalaḫ (Giacumakis 1970, 35 § 4.36) and Ḫattuša (Kouwenberg 2012, 72), Babylonian *ullû* was used, while, in Emar, both forms are found (Seminar 1998, 245–46).[2] It is therefore not impossible that these WPA dialects based themselves on an active use of these particles in contemporary Akkadian. Rather typical is the contracted Assyrian *allû* (< OA *alliu*). A case of *alliu* is attested in the Cypriote letter, which is regarded by some as MA. Although its

1 See Kouwenberg (2012, 33 § 3.5); GOA § 10.3.3.

2 A form of *allû* in the WPA dialects, influenced by Canaanite, could have involved a different etymology (Rainey 1988, 214–19; Rainey 1996c, 159–167).

usage in this instance does not conform to OA usage, we quote the passage here for the sake of completion. However, as we stated in the introduction, the letter is not MA; thus, we can maintain that *alliu* is still not attested in MA.

> *aš-šum a-ma-te*^meš^ *ša* ^lú^KÚR^meš^ *al-lu-ti* DUMU^meš^ KUR-*ti-ka₄* ^giš^MÁ^meš^*-ka₄-ma a-ba-ta an-ni-ta i-te-ep-šu-ni* 'concerning the words of those enemies, your citizens and your ships, this thing they did to me' RS 20.18:7–11

11.2 Demonstrative pronouns referring to quantity

§ 377 Amongst the MA pronouns, we find three forms that describe unknown quantities or entities. With the exception of isolate *annannia*, they also occur in other dialects of Akkadian and are therefore not Assyrian innovations. However, only *annanna* is known from the OB period, while *akukia* first occurs in Late Bronze Age Akkadian. It is notable that, among the four texts, we find the pronouns in three, which are from the BAI archive (*akukia* and *annannia*); it may therefore be argued that they were limited to the writing of this particular scribe. Moreover, in the three BAI texts, the pronouns are used in quasi-direct speech, i.e., a message, which the author of the letter instructs the recipient to answer him with, with the pronominal marking the place where the recipient should add the requested information. The three pronouns are presented in semantical comparison below:

- *akukia* 'so-and-so-much'
- *annanna* 'so-and-so (for PNs)'
- *annannia* 'so-and-so (for objects)'

11.2.1 *akukia* 'so-and-so-much'

§ 378 This rare pronoun only occurs in two letters from the BAI archive, with an unclear etymology (cf. AHw, 30). It could be argued that the pronoun belonged to the language of one anonymous scribe, who wrote KAV 98 directly for his master, Bābu-aḫa-iddina, and MCS 2 14 2 for another servant of his. *Akukia* functions as a placeholder for an exact amount and could be roughly translated as 'so-and-so-much'. As such, we find it in both letters in a quasi-direct speech, i.e., the author of the letters instructs the recipient of the message that he should reply back, with *akukia* used where new information is requested. NB and LB *akkāikī* 'how much?' (CAD A_1, 273; AHw, 29) is clearly related.

> *ṭēma šuprāne mā a-ku-ki-a iškūru mā a-ku-ki-a* gi mu^?^ me ši ⸢e⸣ [*t*]*a*^??^*uru* 'send me a message, thus: 'so much wax and so much […] is placed back'' MCS 2 2:14–17 (TN)

> *tuppukunu šuṭrā mā a-ku-ki-a lubulta ina libbi tupninnāte a-ku-ki-a ina libbi iškāre lā maḫri a-ku-ki-a ina libbi lubult*[*e*] *ša* PN *uta*^??^*eranni ittaṣṣū* 'write your tablet, thus: 'so much clothing from the chests and however much from the work assignment was not received and however much from the clothing that PN returned, they took out'' KAV 98:40–45 (Sa)

11.2.2 *annanna* 'so-and-so (for PNs)'

§ 379 Similar in meaning to *akukia* is the pronoun *annanna*. It is written in place of an undefined PN. Although there are only two attestations in the same sentence, *annanna* can be found in other Akkadian dialects (CAD A_2, 129f):

eqla u bēta ša an-na-na marā an-na-na 'the field and the house of so-and-so, the son of so-and-so' MAL B § 6:9–10

11.2.3 *annannia* 'so-and-so (for objects)'

§ 380 Morphologically and semantically similar to *annanna* is the pronoun *annannia*, which is only attested once in the entire Akkadian corpus (cf. CAD A_2, 130; AHw, 52). Although labelled by von Soden as unclear in meaning (AHw, 52), in comparison with *akukia* and *annannia*, the meaning is quite clear, as all three pronouns seem to be only used in limited contexts for undefined quantities and entities: *akukia*=amounts; *annanna*=persons; *annannia*=objects. Consider the sole example:

tuppukunu šuṭrā šēbilāni mā an-[na-n]i-a an-na-ni-a nul[tēṣi]a ni[tt]idin 'write your tablet and send it here, thus: 'so-and-so and so-and-so we have taken out and issued'' KAV 100:27–29

11.3 Reflexive and reciprocal pronouns

11.3.1 *rāmunu* 'self'

§ 381 Reflexive pronouns function as anaphoric expressions, which refer back to their antecedents, which occur in the same sentence. In Akkadian, the antecedent would usually be the finite verb and thus the reflexive pronoun would mostly precede the antecedent. In MA we find the Akkadian noun *ramānum* 'self' functioning as the reflexive pronoun.[3] The affect of VA on the long /ā/ in MA would suggest that the vowel was, in fact, short and explains the NA allophone *ramnu*. Perhaps this form is observable in *ra-mi-šu* < *ramni-šu* MATSH 9:42, although one may just as well presume a scribal mistake. In order to account for the VA of the second syllable, it has been suggested that the first syllable had a long /ā/, > *rāmunum*.[4] As for the utilization of *rāmunu* as a reflexive pronoun, in order to indicate the number and gender of the pronoun, a possessive suffix is added. In this sense, its construction is similar to English (pronoun+self >, e.g., himself). Examples are given below:

i+na ra-mi-ni-šu lā ikkalʾūni 'he was not held because of himself' MAL A § 36:104–105

šumma sinniltu i+na ra-mi-ni-ša ša libbīša taṣṣili 'if a woman herself caused her abortion' MAL A § 53:92–93

a-na ra-mi-ni-šu ilaqqe 'he will take it for himself' MAL B § 17:17

As the governing noun in the genitive construction.

ina migrāt ra-mi-ni-šu (…) *iddinšu* 'out of his own consensus (…) he gave him' KAJ 1:3–6 cf. KAJ 2:3; KAJ 4:4; KAJ 8:5; MARV 1 37:3; Snell 1983/84:4

aʾīlu ša še-zu-⸢ub⸣ ra-mi-šu 'a man of his own salvation' MATSH 9:42

Damaged:

3 Cf. GAG, 55 § 43a; NA: SNAG, 51 § 3.1.4.2; MB: Aro (1955a, 58f); NB: Woodington (1983, 52 § 22); Semitic: Lipiński (2001, 319 § 36.28).

4 See Goetze (1947, 249–50); GOA § 21.3.2.

> […] ⸢*ī*⸣+*na ra-mi-ni-š*[*u*] […] > ‘ [if a boat drifts(?)] out of his own’ MAL M § 1:1 (Roth 1997, 189)

§ 382 The reflexive pronouns represent an innovation confirming that the agent of the verb is identical to the antecedent. In the case of the first and second person, little confusion is possible; but, in the case of third-person pronouns, multiple parties can exist at the same time, e.g., he saw him ≠ he saw himself. On the other hand, one may notice an application of *rāmunu* in an adjectival function, where a possessive pronoun would be expected on the possessive noun. Here, we need to assume an emphatic function:

> *ina bēt marʾē ra-mi-ni-ša* (…) *tuššab* ‘she will live in the house of her own sons’ MAL A § 46:105–107
>
> *marʾē ra-mi-ni-ša-ma ušakkulūši* ‘her own sons will feed her’ MAL A § 46:107–108
>
> 30 *emāra* ŠE-*am ra-mi-ni-ia attabak* ‘I poured out 30 homers of barley of my own’ MATSH 14:14–17 cf. l. 9–10

Note also *n* ŠE-*um* (…) *ša* PN *ša ra-m*[*i*]-*ni-šu* ‘*n* barley of PN is at his own disposal’ MARV 3 34:1–4

11.3.2 *aḫāʾiš* ‘together’

§ 383 The adverb *aḫāʾiš* (< SB *aḫāmiš*) has a couple of functions: it can function as a pronoun as well as an adverb, although the latter is probably the original function in the majority of cases in our corpus. Etymologically, *aḫāʾiš* is built from base *aḫa(m)* (cf. *aḫu(m)* ‘side’)+adverbial ending *-iš* (see § 489). Apparently the /m/ in Babylonian became a glide [w], which is represented in MA as two uncontracted vowels (see § 233).

§ 384 As *aḫāʾiš* can sometimes be used in a reciprocal function, it has sometimes been analysed as a reciprocal pronoun.[5] Reciprocal pronouns function as both agent and patient of the finite verb to which they belong, e.g.:

> […] *a-ḫa-iš idūkāni* ‘they have fought with each other’ MAPD § 10:57
>
> [*a-ḫ*]*a-iš etarbū a-ḫa-iš ittanablakutū* ‘when (the components) go through one another and when they mingle with each other’ PKT 4 obv. left 20 cf. PKT 3 ii 15–16; iv 2’

With *ša*:

> *pāḫat buqurrānāʾe ša a-ḫa-iš lā inaššiū* ‘they do not assume the responsibility of the claims of each other’ KAJ 10:9

§ 385 When *ahāʾiš* follows a preposition, its function varies between reciprocal and adverbial. This seems to be mostly dependent on the type of preposition and can also be observed in the available MB passages (Aro 1955a, 117f). For NB, we only have examples of these prepositional expressions used reciprocally (Woodington 1983, 52 § 22). The prepositional expressions mostly have an adverbial meaning ‘together’, as opposed to the reciprocal ‘each other’. The difference becomes apparent in examples such as *iltu aḫāʾiš tattanaddanū* ‘together you keep giving’ KAV 194:15-16, as opposed to the reciprocal ‘you keep giving to each other’.

---

5 For example, Woodington (1983, 52 § 22); cf. also Aro (1955a, 117f); UGM, 34f § 30; GAG, 55 § 43b.

With *ana* (reciprocal):

a-na a-ḫa-i[*š*$^{?}$] *ittan*[*nū*] 'they gave it to each other' MATSH 13:15–16

a-na [*a*]-*ḫa-i*[*š* ....] MATSH 21:1'

a-na a-ḫa-iš [*mi*]*mma lā epāše* 'for each other nothing to do' (context broken) MATSH 26:15'–16'

With *iltu* (adverbial):

iš-tu a-ḫa-iš [*iz*]*zazzū* 'they will stand with each other' MAL B § 17:6–7 cf. § 18:25

dišpa iš-tu a-ḫa-iš tasūak 'you pound honey (…) together' PKT 6 i 28–29

ina sikkāte ša siparre iš-tu a-ḫa-iš rabqū 'they are riveted together with bronze pegs' KTN inventory iv 14'–15'

iš-tu a-ḫa-i-i[*š*] *tattanadnū*-[x]$^{sic.}$ 'together you keep giving' KAV 194:15–16

With *kī* (adverbial):

ki-i a-ḫa-iš lū epšat 'it must be done together' MATSH 10:22–23

With *urki* (reciprocal):

aḫḫūšu ur-ki a-ḫa-iš inassuqū ilaqqeū 'his brothers will choose after one another and take (a share)' MAL B § 1:6–7

11.4 Indefinite pronouns

11.4.1 *mamma* 'somebody

§ 386 The indefinite pronoun mamma is used with the meaning 'somebody' in positive clauses. It is commonly used in Akkadian (CAD M_1, 195ff), but is not declined. For the combination with the ordinal *šanīu*, see § 338. The orthography is the invariable *ma-am-ma*.

a-na ma-am-ma šanīemma tattidin 'he has given it to another person' MAL A § 3:27–28 (cf. l. 36–37)

mar$^{?}$*u ma-am-ma ša kalze ēkalle* 'somebody from the palace precinct' MAPD § 1:4

ma-am-ma mimma [*ušē*]*ṣiūni* 'somebody takes something out' MAPD § 6:41

When the verb is negated, it is better to translate 'nobody' instead of 'somebody did not'.

ma-am-ma šanīumma lā išaqqi 'nobody else may irrigate' MAL B § 17:19–20

ina āle ma-am-ma laššu 'there is nobody in the city' MATSH 2:18

ma-am-ma lū lā uṣṣa 'nobody may leave' MATSH 4:12'

ma-am-ma rittušu lā umalli 'nobody may fill his hand' MATSH 4:17'

panē ma-am-ma lā tapul 'formerly you responded to nobody' T 97-10:20

ma-am-ma ana dēn dayyān lā ilaqqeanni lā ekalla$^{?}$*anni*$^{sic.}$ 'nobody can take me to court or detain me' KAV 159:6–8

It seems that *mamma* cannot occur in a genitive construction as it is indeclinable. As such, we find it once in opposition to a noun:

> *ki-i-k*[*i*?*-m*]*a ṭēma m*[*a-a*]*m-ma t*[*a*]*l*[*q*]*e* 'how could you appropriate somebody else's report' T 93-12:6–7

11.4.2 *mimmû* 'something/property'

§ 387 The pronoun *mimmû* has lost its function in MA and can hardly be attributed to this grammatical category of pronouns. We find *mimmû* in different orthographical forms. The long /û/ is confirmed by some plene spellings, while *mi-i-mu-ú-šu* KAJ 6:9 (Aub) seems to have a plene /i/ as a replacement for gemination.

mimmû	*mi-mu-šu*	KAJ 58:21; KAJ 101:20; Billa 2:16; 3:16; 4:12; 4a:3
	mi-mu-ka	Cohen/Llop 2017:20
	mi-mu-ia	Cohen/Llop 2017:19
	mi-mu-ú-šu	KAJ 58:25
	mi-i-mu-ú-šu	KAJ 6:9
	mi-im-mu-šu	KAJ 67:15; 310:9; AO 21.380:15
	me-mu-šu	KAJ 29:17; 65:19
	mìm-mu-ú	MAL C+ § 2:12; § 3:17; § 4:25
	mìm-mu-šu	MAL C+ § 6:37, 41

§ 388 We find it in the meaning of 'property' as a substantive, often used in connection with *gabbu*.[6] Unlike the words its stands in relation to, *mimmû* is never inflected. We usually find *mimmû* with the pronominal suffix *-šu,* as *mimmûšu,* where it can be translated as 'his property' or, better still, 'all his things'. Two times in a private letter (Cohen/Llop 2017), we find other pronominal suffixes: *anāku lā mimmukka* 'I am nothing for you' (l. 20). Normal status rectus forms can be found in MAL C+ in the status constructus EN *mimmû* 'owner of the property'.

> *ana* EN *mìm-mu-ú iddan* 'he will give to the proprietor' MAL C+ § 2:12; § 3:17

> [E]N *mìm-mu-ú mìm-mu-šu* [*ilaqqe*] 'the owner of the property will take his property' MAL C+ § 6:37

> *ḫa-laq mìm-mu-šu* 'the loss of his property' MAL C+ § 6:41

> *kī šapārte ME-mu-šu zakkua ša* PN_1 PN_2 *iṣabbat uka*??*al* 'PN_2 will seize as pledged by PN_1 his cleared property and hold it' Billa 3:16–17; 4:12–15 cf. *me-mu-šu za-ku-a* KAJ 29:17

> *mi-mu-ú-šu ipaṭṭar* 'he will release his property' KAJ 58:25

> *mi-mu-šu gabba* 'all his possessions' KAJ 101:20–22; cf. *mi-i-mu-ú-šu ga-BI-e* KAJ 6:9; *mi-im-m*[*u*]*-šu* [*ga*]*bba* KAJ 67:15–16

> *ina bētīšu ina mi-mu-š*[*u*] *išallim* 'he will redeem with his house and with his property' KAJ 58:21–22

> [1 *s*]*assu ša mugerre mi-im-mu-šu laššu* 'one floorboard of a chariot with all (accessories) is not available' KAJ 310:9

6 See UGM, 42; CAD M2, 80ff; GAG, 62 § 48f.

11.4.3 *mimma* 'something'

§ 389 The pronominal *mimma* derives from *mīnu(m)+ma* in order to form an indefinite pronoun (Cohen 2000, 207). There is some variation in the orthography caused by plene/defective spellings and two different CvC signs (MUNUS and MAN).

mimma	*mi-im-ma*	MAL A § 3:25; § 26:97; MAL B § 1:8; KAV 99:20; KAV 168:15; MATSH 2:12; 8:44'; T 96-8:16
	mi-ma	KAV 107:18 (BAI); MAL M § 2:12
	mim-ma	MATSH 4:11
	mìm-ma	MAL A § 37:16; § 46:92

§ 390 As an indefinite pronoun, *mimma* is used independently with the meaning 'something' as can be observed from the following examples (GAG, 270 § 168d):

mi-im-ma taltiriq 'she stole something' MAL A § 3:25

lū mìm-ma ša akāle 'whatever there is to eat' MAL A § 31:47–48

ana mi-im-ma taˀˀerā 'return it to something (=wrapping)' KAV 99:20 (see CAD M_2, 74a)

mi-im-ma ša ana dabābika illukūni 'all that is suitable for your case' KAV 168:17–18

šumma lā tuddaˀāšu mi-ma pîšu šaˀlā 'if you do not know him, ask what is said about him' KAV 107:18–19

Alternatively, *mimma* can also be used attributively, either preceding or following a noun. According to Kouwenberg, for OA, *mimma* preceded the noun when used in the meaning 'all, every' (GOA § 12.7). If this is correct for MA, it may explain why this construction is not attested more commonly, as MA seems to prefer *gabbu* in this function (see § 395).

mi-im-ma dumāqē ša mussa ina muḫḫīša iškunūni 'all the jewels her husband placed upon her' MAL A § 25:86–87

This small group may be expanded in combination with the demonstrative pronoun *anniu*, which we can usually translate as 'all this'. Following this sequence, a specification of *mimma* is given.

mi-im-ma an-ni-ú gimru ša mugerre iddan 'he will give all this, the expenses of the chariots' KAJ 122:15–17

mi-im-ma an-ni-ú aššum lā mašāˀe šaṭir 'all this is written down in order not to be forgotten' KAJ 256:12–14

mi-im-ma an-n[i-ú] ša ana šarre qarrubūni 'all this, which was presented for the king' Postgate 1994:7'–9'

Similarly, Kouwenberg explained the cases where *mimma* follows the noun as "some, any" (GOA § 11.5). This can be illustrated by the following phrases:

šiluḫlē mi-im-ma u mānaḫāte gabbe 'any *šiluḫlu*-personnel and all equipment' MAL B § 1:8–9

[l]ū sarta mi-im-ma tētapaš 'or she has committed any crime' MAPD § 18:83

inba mi-ma šēbila 'send me some fruit' T 93-12:14–12

gabba mi-im-ma lū lā imaṭṭi 'may he not deduct all of it with anything' T 96-8:16–17

§ 391 Frequently, the indefinite pronoun *mimma* is preceded by the negation *lā mimma*. This addition changes the basic translation from 'something' to 'nothing'.

> *la-a mi-im-ma ēzibašše la-a mi-im-ma šubulta iltu eqle ušēbilašše* 'he left her nothing and sent her nothing of provisions from abroad' MAL A § 36:88–90

Usually, the negation is placed before the verb. The translation as 'nothing' remains identical.

> *mìm-ma lā eppaš* 'he will do nothing' MAL A § 23:23

> *emittu mi-im-ma laššu* 'there will not be any sanctions' MAL A § 24:81

> *libbušuma mìm-ma iddanašše la-a libbušuma mi-im-ma la-a iddanašše* '(if) he likes, he will give her something, and if he does not like, he will give her nothing' MAL A § 37:16–18

> *mìm-ma la-a ilṭurašše* 'he has not written anything to her' MAL A § 46:92

11.4.4 *mīnummê* 'everything'

§ 392 This indefinite pronoun is more typical for WPA Akkadian than for MA (cf. M_2, 97-98). As such, it occurs only twice in one letter found in Ugarit and once in Ḫattuša. Nevertheless, these specific letters show sufficient MA features (see § 23).

> *u anāku* ⸢*mi*⸣*-nu-me-e aḫūya* [*i*]*ṣabbutū*[*ni an*]*āk*[*u*] *ušēbbala* 'and I shall send to my brother whatever my brother wants to take' RS 06.198:24–27

> *mi-mu-*⸢*um-mi-e*⸣ [*ša*] *ana māte ša aḫīya aḫṭiūni* 'what sin (is it) [that] I committed against the land of my brother?' KUB 3 73:3'–4'

11.4.5 *iyāmattu* 'each, everyone'

§ 393 The pronoun *(i)yāmattu* is only attested three times in two texts. It is only found in MA and NA.[7]

iyāmattu	*iya-ma-tu*	Coronation Ritual iii 12, 14
	iya-a-ma-at-tu	KAV 205:29

The meaning of the pronoun overlaps partly with *attamannu* (see below); however, with only four attestations of both pronouns, it is hard to draw any conclusions. As we discussed in § 170, we should read the initial sign IA as either <iy> or <ay>; the occurrence of a spelling such as *IA-ma-tu* is not problematic since similar forms occur in NA as well (*i-*⸢*mu*⸣*-tú* SAA 1 223 r. 9'). For MA, the following attestations can be given:

> *iya-ma-tu* [*pāḫ*]*assu luka*$^{??}$*il* 'everyone may keep his office' Coronation Ritual iii 12–13

> *iya-ma-tu ina mazzaltēšu izzâz* 'everyone will stand in his position' Coronation Ritual iii 14

> *ina rāṭ siparre ana be-ta-te iya-a-ma-at-tu ana ṭēmīšu lišpuk* 'may he pour it into bronze tubes separately, each into its mould(?)' KAV 205:28–29

11.4.6 *attamannu* 'each one'

§ 394 This pronoun occurs in a number of Akkadian dialects from the Late Bronze Age onwards (CAD A_2, 509). In MA, there is only one example:

> *at-ta-ma-nu* [*b*]*ēl pāḫete* 'each governor' Coronation Ritual iii 10

---

7 See AHw, 411a; CAD I/J, 322; SNAG, 53–54.

11.4.7 *gabbu* 'all, everything'

§ 395 The pronoun *gabbu* broadly occurs in the Akkadian dialect from the Late Bronze Age onwards (AHw, 272; CAD G, 4–5). The pronoun *gabbu* is fully declined according to its syntactical position. The meaning 'all, everything' makes *gabbu* the equivalent of *kalu*, which was in the process of being replaced. In its place, *gabbu* is used syntactically as an adjective, or even independently, not necessarily referring to a specific antecedent. Orthographically, the spelling *gab-bv* is predominant, although we once find *ga-BI-e* KAJ 6:9 and perhaps, in a broken context, *gáb-bì* A 1020:13'. The pronoun is inflected according to its grammatical case:

> *panīšu gab-ba inaqquru* 'they will destroy his complete face' MAL A § 15:55
>
> *ša šiddi māti gab-ba* 'of the extent of the entire country' MAPD § 20:96
>
> *gišmugerrumeš-ka* ⌜*gab-bu*⌝ (…) *lū tallika* 'may all your chariots come T 93-2:7–8

With a pronominal suffix:

> *gab-be-ni šulmu* 'we all are well' KAM 7 150:5
>
> *gab-bu-šu-nu-ma* 'all of them' KBo 28 61/62:26'

While *gabbu* is declined according to the three case endings, plural forms are not attested. We have to regard *gabbu* as a collective. At the same time, when used attributively as an adjective, *gabbu* occurs in the genitive when the head noun is an oblique plural noun.

> *šiluḫlē mimma u mānaḫāte gab-be* 'whatever *šiluḫlu*-personnel and all equipment' MAL B § 1:8–9
>
> [*r*]*ēḫti ilāni gab-ba lā ušēššub*[*ū*] 'they will not seat all the remaining gods' New Year Ritual:12'
>
> *gab-bi ḫiṭṭāni rab ēkalle emmidū* 'they will impose all of the punishments upon the palace manager' MAPD § 21:111
>
> *mimma ammar naṣṣatūni gab-bu ša mutīša* 'everything she brings (with her) is of her husband' MAL A § 35:77–78
>
> *iltu nikkassūšu ṣa*[*bt*]*ūni gab-bu tušaḫaruṣūni* 'after his accounts were settled, all will be deducted' KAJ 120:5–7
>
> *iltu nikkassūšu* (…) *gab-bu ṣabtūni* 'when his accounts (from the period) are entirely settled' KAJ 40:1–5
>
> *gab-bu uppuš* 'all is done' MATC 53:12
>
> *lū māʾū ša ḫirīṣe ulū naqqure gab-bu eṣū* 'be it the water of the *ḫ*.-canal or of the *n*.-canal, all will be little' MATSH 8:33'
>
> *mimmûšu ga-BI-e* 'all his possessions' KAJ 6:9

Status constructus:

> *ina gab-bi qa-*⌜*qi*⌝*-*[*ri*] 'on the entire earth' MATC 10:8

11.4.8 *kalu* 'all'

§ 396 The original *kalu* can still be found in the construct form within the expression *kal(a) ūme* 'all day'.

ina kal u$_4$-me 'during the entire day' MAPD § 6:41; 9:52

ka-la ūmīšu 'all day' PKT 1 I right:6, 16; II right:11, 30; II left:12; 5:1, 24

bēssu šīmta ka-la-ma 'the entire price of the house(?)' MARV 4 151:56

Once *kalu* may appear as *kulu*:

ina kúl-<lat> libbīka 'with all your heart' KBo 28 61 Rd. 1'

11.4.9 *kilallān* 'both'

§ 397 This Akkadian quantifier derives Proto Semitic **kilˀ*, which is a common root **ṯin* (MA *šanīu*) that is used in Semitic for the number '2'.[8] The ending *-ān* is a leftover of the dual. It is retained in MA while, in LB, the form was shortened to > *-ē* in all cases (see Streck 1995, 75 § 72). The apparently nominative ending *-ūn* occurs rarely in Akkadian and is only found once in MA where we should expect an oblique (see GAG, 100 § 63h).

[...] *ki-la-lu-un inappulū* 'both [...] will be gouged out' MAL A § 8:87[9]

ki-la-al-li-šu-nu-ma idukkūšunuma 'they will kill them both' MAL A § 15:44–45

11.5 Determinative pronouns

11.5.1 *ša* as determinative pronoun

§ 398 Akkadian has one shared determinative pronoun *ša* (UGM, 38–39 § 37; GAG § 46). The pronoun *ša* used to be inflected, according to number and gender, in Akkadian, of which we still find remnants in OA (GOA § 12.2.1). The typical OA name construction *Šu*-DN, may only be attested in MA in ^{m}*Šu*-^{d}IM KAJ 156:5. As for its function, *ša* is used in the analytic genitive construction (§ 298ff) and marking particle of a relative clause (§ 714ff). There is one attestation that seems to be the feminine variant *šāt*, which is so unusual that it is probably a mistake. If correct, the feminine gender of the relative particle in the following clause refers to the plural of *ūmu* 'day' (pl. *ūmū/ūmātu*).

12 *umātu ša-at ina* GN *usbākūni lā aklu ū lā māˀū* 'the 12 days that I have been in GN, there has been neither bread nor water' T 93-11:16–18

11.6 Interrogative pronouns and adverbs

§ 399 The interrogative pronouns are relatively rare in the MA corpus. As their function makes them useful for direct speech, we find them almost exclusively in quotations within letters. No attestations in literary or administrative texts are known, with one important exception: the PNs. In light of the scarceness of some of the interrogative pronouns, we will

---

8 Cardinal numbers derived from **kilˀ* occur most prominently in South Semitic languages (cf. Lipiński, 292f § 35.4; Ge'ez *kəlˀe* (ክልኤ) Dillmann 1907, 364; also Amharic *hulätt* (ሁለት) Leslau 2000, 50). We find *kilallān* in OA (GKT, 117 § 71d; GOA § 8.7.2), as well as NA (SNAG, 53 § 3.1.4.6).

9 Based on the seemingly nominative ending *-ūn*, it seems preferable to interpret an N-stem here in order to make the sentence intransitive. However, sanctions in MAL A, such as the cutting of a nose, always occur as transitives. For this reason, an N-stem would be a break in style.

also briefly discuss the PNs in the following section. Interrogative pronouns can be used to turn a sentence into a question, even though not all types of question require one (see § 682). The interrogative adverbs (GAG, § 118a; 119a; 120a) belong in this section as well, but only *alē* 'where?', *ayyēša* 'whither?' and *kē maṣi* 'how much?' are attested in MA. It may also be noted that the interrogative pronoun *mīnu* 'what?' developed into an adverb of this manner, especially in combination with the preposition *ana*, merging into *anaʾīne* 'for what?' > 'why?'. When it comes to a difference, the pronouns naturally refer to the object or subject of the verb, whereas the adverbs refer to an adverbial element.

11.6.1 *alē* 'where?'

§ 400 This interrogative adverb is only attested once.

mā ṣabʾa ša iddinūni a-le-e 'where are the troops that they gave?' MARV 4 8:11–12

11.6.2 *ayyānu* 'where?'

§ 401 The existence of this interrogative pronoun was proposed by Bloch (2017, 124), on the assumption that the previous reading *yānu* 'there is not' could not be correct since this verbal expression is unknown in Assyrian (where *laššu* is used instead).[10] Moreover, *ayyānu* is attested in OA (AHw, 24b; CAD A_1, 226–27). In Bloch's translation, the subject of the question remains unexpressed and seems to be replaced by a relative clause. Nonetheless, this interpretation is preferable over the semiverb *yānu*.

ay[a-n]u ša libbe niḫr[iū]ni 'where is (the barley) from (that) which we dug out?' T 96-36:23–24

11.6.3 *ayyû* 'which?'

§ 402 The preposition is inflected according to number and gender.[11] However, only in MATSH 8 do we find traces of this.

[*šar*]*ru a-iu-ú* [...] (broken context) Ni 669:9

ša bēlīya a-ia-a-tu abātušu 'which are the words of my lord?' MATSH 8:41'

11.6.4 *ayyēša* 'whither?'

§ 403 This adverb is based on the pronoun *ayyu* 'which?' with the suffix *-ēša(m)*, which has an allative meaning (see Kouwenberg 2012, 64). A possible alternative form, *ayyišāmmê*, seems to be suggested by the CDA (33) in the lemma *ayyišamma*, which is based on an entry in AHw (25) that cites one attestation from a letter from Ugarit written in the Hittite kingdom (cf. Huehnergard 1979, 275 n421). Alternatively, the particle *-mi* (see § 418) may be attested twice on *ayyēša*.

[*a*]*-ie-e-ša tubil* 'where did you bring it?' KAV 104:11–12

ma-a-ie-e-ša-mi emaqqatūni lā udda 'where will they 'attack'? I do not know it' MATSH 3:11–12

mā ušappulūš a-ie-e-ša ušappulūš 'they will lower him; how far will they lower him?' MATSH 9:40

ana a-ie-e-ša-mi-ni iḫtaliq 'to wherever he has fled' Giricano 12:18'–19'

---

10 Earlier interpretations can be found in Minx (2005, 91 no. 78). The verbal expressions *yānu* and *laššu* are discussed in § 593ff.

11 See GAG, 60 § 47c; cf. OA in GKT, 79f § 51; GOA § 11.7.

adi ayye-e-ša!-am-ma lā nillukūni ŠE-*am laddinakku* 'before we go anywhere, I want to give you the barley' NP 46:18–20

11.6.5 *kē* 'how?'

§ 404 The interrogative adverb *kē* (spelled *ke* or *ke-e*) is attested only a few times in MA.[12]

mā ḫurādkunu ke-e nakirma 'thus, your *ḫurādu*-troops, how are they hostile?' MATSH 7:12''[13]

⌜*ke*⌝ *lā naqid* 'how is that not difficult? (=it is not difficult!)' MATC 7:20 (cf. commentary MATC, 47)

A variant *kīkī* is once attested. It occurs in MB and NB, although nowhere does it seem to be common.[14]

ki-i-k[*i*?-*m*]*a ṭēma m*[*a*]*mma t*[*a*]*l*[*q*]*e* 'how could you appropriate somebody else's report' T 93-12:6–7

The compound interrogative *kē maṣi* is built from a combination of the conjunction *kī* 'how?' and a grammaticalized stative *maṣi* 'it is sufficient'. This compound is known in OA and NA (GOA § 12.8; Parker 1997), but only attested three times in MA. One passage is broken.

šīpātu ša qātika ke-e ma-ṣi ibašši iriḫḫa 'the wool that is at your disposal, how much is available as a remainder?' KAV 106:9–11; cf. *ke ma-ṣi* [...] KAV 106:13†

šarru ke [*m*]*a-ṣi kitāʾa*[meš] *ana muḫḫi bē*[*līya*] *ušebbala* 'how much flax will the king send to my lord?' MATSH 7:19'–20'

11.6.7 *mannu* 'who?'

§ 405 This pronoun is frequently attached to PNs especially in the type Mannu-balum-DN 'Who-is-without-DN' and, less frequently, in Mannu-kī-DN' (see UGM, 38 § 36.1).[15] A number of these attestations involves PNs:

[m]*Man-nu-ki-i-*[d]*A-nim* Who-is-like-An?' KAV 26 r. 20'

Ma-nu-bal-DINGIR 'Who-is-without god?'[16] KAJ 51:15

[m]*Ma-nu-lu-iu-ú* (abbreviation? see OMA I, 308) KAJ 195:4

[[m]] ⌜*Ma*⌝-*nu-ki-a-bi* 'Who-is-like-the-father' MARV 7 72:12

M⌜*a*⌝-*nu-i-qip* 'Who-believed' YBC 12862:22+commentary

⌜*Ma-nu-šá-nin*⌝-[d]⌜IM⌝ 'Who-is-second-to-Adad?' MARV 4 103 r. 20'

Newer text publications provide a number of questions built with *mannu*. It should be noted that *mannu* is still inflected according to case ending. This is especially clear in the

12 See GAG, 217 § 120a; cf. GOA § 12.7.

13 Cancik-Kirschbaum interprets this passage as a statement rather than a question. See MATSH, 125.

14 See AHw, 474b; CAD K, 351; Aro (1957, 43).

15 See OMA 2, 135, but read *balum* i/o *gēr*. See also § 448 for this improved reading.

16 According to MZL no. 5; BAL ≠ *gēru* 'enemy', as opposed to OMA 1, 306f; cf. OA *Mannum-balum*-DN, e.g., Hirsch (1972, 27). However, how should the syllabic ([m])*Ma-nu-ge-er-*[d]*A-šur* KAJ 119:8; LVUH 92:10 be explained?

following example, which features two questions; one where *mannu* is the subject and the other where it is the object:

> *ma-an-na-ma lēriš ma-nu-ma liddina* 'who can I ask, who will give it to me?' T 93-3:20–22

Other attestations are available, including a genitive:

> *iltaʾlanni* [*mā š*]*a ma-an-ni sī*[*sā*]*ʾu*^{meš} 'he asked me: 'from who are the horses'' MATC 15:13–15

> *ma-an-nu ēnāta damqāta* [*l*]*ēm*[*ur*] *u dabābki ṭāb*[*a*] *lišme* 'who may see (your) beautiful eyes and hear your speaking sweet words?' A 845:6–8

> *ma-nu ēnātīkin*[*a damqāt*]*i* [*lēmur*] 'who may see your beautiful eyes (again)?' T 93-8a:13–14

Note that, in the following phrase, *mannu* is not used as a question word:

> *ma*[*nnu*] *ša dēnu ubtaʾʾeʾū-ni sinnilta lušērib* '(the one) who will seek legal action must make the woman enter' Giricano 7:18–20

11.6.8 *mīnu* 'what?/why?' and *anaʾīne* 'why?'

§ 406 The original interrogative pronoun of substance ('what?') was *mīnu* in Akkadian and OA. It is found twice in a fossilized accusative, despite it being inflected in OA (GOA § 11.4). In these two cases, *mīnu* has acquired a secondary meaning 'why?'

> [*m*]*ā ḫurādkunu mi-na nakirma* '(concerning) your troops, why are they hostile?' MATSH 7:5''

> *mā attu*[*n*]*ūma ana mayyirāni mi-na tattanarr*[*ad*]*āne* 'thus (I said), "why do you keep coming down to the *m.*-troops?"' MATSH 7:6''–7''

A similar accusative is found in one PN (cf. UGM, 38 § 36.2). A possible meaning ('what did I do, DN?') is discussed by von Soden (1973, 191; also CAD M_2, 93a; PNAE 2.II, 754b).

> *Mi-na-e-pu-šu* KAJ 141:1,4

On two occasions, we find *mīnu* still occurring in the nominative, both times in texts from Tell Ṣabī Abyaḍ.

> *mi-nu-*⸢*ú-ma*⸣ *anniu ša ammar aqabbiakkunni kī pî*[*y*]*a lā teppušūni* 'what is this, that whatever I say to you, you do not act according to my words?' T 93-3:4–6

> GÁNA.A.ŠÀ *mi-i-nu šūt* 'a field, why is that?' T 02-32:25

An additional attestation of *mīnu* in the genitive occurs in the rare expression ⸢*áš-šúm*⸣ *mi-ni* 'for what? > why?' T 97-32:14. This expression is more commonly found with the preposition *ana* (see below).

§ 407 A variation of *mīnu* occurs in combination with the preposition *ana*, in a construction that is very similar to the Arabic equivalent: *li-* (ل) 'to'+*mādā* (ماذا) 'what?' > *limādā* (لماذا) 'why?' According to the Assyrian sound rule where the intervocalic /*m*/ elides, both components are merged into one, resulting in *anaʾīne* (< *ana mīne*).

> *ma-a-a-na-i-ni ina bubuāte amūat* 'why should I die from hunger?' VAT 8851:7–8

> *a-na-i-ni lā illikū* 'why did they not go?' MATSH 2:16

> *ma!-a-na-i-ni mullāʾe* (…) *lā tamalli* 'why did you not compensate?' MATSH 2:54–56

a-[na-i]-ni lā ēṣid 'why is it not harvested?' MATSH 3:8

ma-a-na-i-ni ṭēm bēte lā tašappara 'thus, why do you not send me news about the house?' MATSH 12:41

a-na-i-ni tuššaršu 'why do you not release him?' MATC 2:23–24

a-na-i-ni lā tallika ina dēnika lā tadbub 'why did you not come and speak during your case?' KAV 169:10–13

a-na-i-ni PN *marā šipre ana muḫḫīya illikamma u šulmākka lā tašp[u]ra* 'why did PN, the messenger, come to me, but you did not send me your greetings (with him)?' RS 06.198:7–11

a-na-i-ni lā tamli[ka] 'why did you not take counsel' KBo 1 20:8'

⸢*a*⸣*-na-*⸢*i-ni*⸣ *ṭēma lā tašpuranni*$^{\text{sic.}}$ 'why did you not write me a message' K9-T1:8–10

However, in itself, the resulting form *anaˀīne* is unexpected, since, by analogy with crasis spellings of *ana* and *ina*, we should expect the final /*a*/ of the preposition to elide and /*n*/ to assimilate into the following consonant > *ammīne*. Alternatively, /m/ could still have been elided despite its gemination (cf. § 233) > **a*^{w}*īne*. The latter form is not attested in MA texts, yet *ammīne* is.

am-mi-ni i+na IGI^{meš}*-ka i-sa-aḫ-ḫu-ur* 'why does it linger in your sight' EA 16:15–16

a-mi-ni-i i+na ṣe-ti ⸢*i*⸣*-ma-at-*⸢*tu*⸣*-[ú-ma]* 'why should they die from a sunstroke?' EA 16:50–51

am-mi-ni a-na ia-ši UR.MAḪ (…) *ú-uz-za-nu-ni-ni* 'why are they making the lion angry with me?' KBo 1 14:18'–19'

am-mi-ni-e ta-al-li-ka 'why did you come?' RS 34-165:17–18

As the careful reader may have noticed, these phrases all derive from letters that we discussed in the introduction (§ 40), which we concluded were not written in Assyrian but rather in a Babylonian dialect. At the same time, *ammīne* is, in fact, attested in OA.[17] It seems that the occurrence of *ammīni* in OA is unrelated to the occurrences in the quoted letters, given that *ammīne* is well known from MB (Aro 1955a, 11). The form *ammīni* is also attested in NA, while *anaˀīne* is not (SNAG, 63–64 § 3.3). The only explanation for the difference between OA *ammīni* and MA *anaˀine* is variation in spoken language and the absence of the lexicalization of *ammīni* in MA. If we assume that the Assyrians remained aware of the composition of both variants by *ana* and *mīnu*, a form such as *ammīni* was actively created by the phonetic rules in OA. In pausal form, the interrogative would still have been *ana mīnim*. Upon the introduction of the sound change involving intervocalic /m/ > /ˀ/, the realization of the composite form would change accordingly.

17 See GKT, 175 § 102c; GOA § 11.8; CAD M_2, 94b.

Chapter 12: Enclitic Particles

12.1 The particle *-ma*

§ 408 The enclitic particle *-ma* can basically be attached to any word. It is the last in a chain of added morphemes and follows optional pronominal suffixes. In MA, the particle is always spelled with one single sign, i.e., *-ma*. No plene spellings are known to me, unlike those in OA (vs. GOA § 15.3). As such, the particles written this way can have different functions. The function of *-ma* as conjunction is discussed in detail in § 693f. Fossilized -*ma*, which is also omitted from the discussion, is standardly attested in a number of pronouns, such as *mimma* and *mamma*, and the conjunction *šumma*, but rarely attested *kīma*. Although all instances of *-ma* on these particles probably derive from the same suffix, its fixed use makes them unqualified for anything but an etymologic discussion. In the following section, we will follow Kouwenberg's classification of three different functions in OA (GOA § 15.3ff):

1. Marker of focus
2. Marker of identity
3. Marker of distinction

We will apply these three categories for the evidence in the MA corpus. The first category seems to be standard and can be applied to the vast majority of cases.

12.1.1 Focus marker

§ 409 Frequently, the particle *-ma* is found on nouns and adjectives in the function of bringing emphasis or focus to the object. This main point of the sentence could be labelled as a 'logical predicate' as opposed to the normal grammatical predicate.[1] Usually, the finite verb is also the logical predicate unless the emphasis lies on an element in the sentence, such that the grammatical and logical predicates become two different items. As such, the logical predicate can be the subject of a sentence. This function is already known from OA (GKT, 186 § 106e; GOA § 15.3ff) and also very common in MA. In NA, it is attested, with its function described by Hämeen-Anttila as indicating emphasis and opposition in terms of function (SNAG, 65 § 3.4.). In general, the function of a focus marker has become rather weak in MA. In contrast to some studies proposed for OB, it does not often warrant translation with cleft clauses. It is preferable to translate with an adverbial 'self' or 'only', or similar adverbs.[2] That said, it would be better to refrain from translating this particle.

§ 410 The focus marker *-ma* can be added on every word of a sentence, regardless of case ending or grammatical function.

---

1 Here is a selection of the literature: GAG, 221 § 123a; Finet (1956, 279-81 § 100); Rainey (1976, 51); Huehnergard (2005, 325 § 29.2); Cohen (2000, 214).

2 Cf. AHw, 569–70; GOA § 15.3.2; see also Faist (2001, 160 n68).

Nominative:

umma PN-*ma* 'thus PN' passim in letters

mu-us-sa-ma urkīu ilaqqe 'her later husband will take (them)' MAL A § 45:78

50 *ṣabʾu Kaššiū lū līṭu lū ṣabbututtu u* 50-*ma ṣabʾu Šuburiū li-ṭu-ma ina āle usbū ana maṣṣartema ša āle aʾīluttu laššu* '50 Kassite troops, be they hostages, be they captives, and 50 Hurrian troops, hostages dwelling in the city, but for the guarding of the city there is nobody' MATSH 2:18–21

Genitive:

sinniltu ina bēt a-bi-ša-ma usbat 'a woman dwells in the house of her father' MAL A § 17:103

tuppaša kī al-ma-te-ma išaṭṭurū 'they will write on her tablet that she is a widow' MAL A § 45:71

ana lìb-bi-ma kamer 'it has been added to it' TabT05a-151:14–15

aššum ÈRIN^{meš}-*ma*$^{!}$ (...) *ša lā unammešanni* 'concerning the soldiers who have not set out (towards you)' MATSH 3:33–34

ana UGU-*ia-ma lublūni* 'may they bring it to me' KAV 98:35

nakkamta $^{\text{na4}}$KIŠIB^{meš}-*ia-ma kunkā* 'seal the treasury with my seals' KAV 99:33–34 cf. KAV 105:5–6, 21–22

ina pitti ša muḫḫi É-*ma lu šaknat* 'may it be placed in the responsibility of the housemaster' KAV 99:41–42

qaqqad ṣarpe u ŠE-*im ši-im-*⌜*ta*$^{!}$⌝-*am-ma iddunū* 'they will pay the the capital of the silver and barley' KAJ 47:20–22 (see Faist 2001, 160 n68)

ṭēḫi eqle pūre ša PN_1-*ma u ṭēḫi* <*eqle*> *pūre ša* PN_2 *aḫīšu* 'adjacent to the field, lot of PN_1, and adjacent to the lot of PN_2, his brother' AO 19.228:10–11

50 *emāru i+na* ^{giš}5 BÁN-*te-ma madid* 'the 50 homers (barley) is measured with a five-seah measure' MARV 7 7:6

Accusative:

aššat aʾīle aššat LÚ-*ma ana bētīša talteqe* 'a wife took a(nother man's) wife to her house' MAL A § 23:14–15

šumma (…) *aššassu lā unakkis* DAM-*su-ma ilaqqe emittu mimma laššu* 'if he has not mutilated his wife and he will take his wife, there is no punishment' MAL A § 24:79–81

izzazzū ^{lú}ÍL-*ma usassû* 'they stand ready and make the herald proclaim' MAL B § 6:35–36

i-ga-ra-te-ma u tarbāṣa (…) *liqâl*$^{\text{sic.}}$ 'may he take care of the walls and the courtyard' MATSH 6:10'

When multiple nouns have the focus, the final term receives the suffix (GOA § 15.3.1):

LÚ *ù* MUNUS-*ma idukkū* 'they will kill man and woman' MAL A § 13:29

PN_1 PN_2 *ù* PN_3 ^{lú}*qe-pu-tu-ma altaprakkunu* 'I sent you the representatives PN_1 PN_2 and PN_3' KAV 100:6–8

$^{\text{na4}}$KIŠIB *ša pi-i* ^{giš}*tup-ni-na-te ù* $^{\text{na4}}$KIŠIB-*ma ša pî nakkamāte naṣṣū* 'they are bringing the seal of the opening of the boxes and the seal of the opening of the treasury' KAV 100:8–10

ŠE *ù* ^{še}ZÌ-*ma lā tumaṭṭa* 'do not reduce the barley and flour' A 877:9–10

Exceptions:

ana pā'i tuppe ša a-bi-i-šu-ma PN *ša ana mar'utti* (...) *šaṭrū*<*ni*> 'according to the wording of the tablet of his father PN, which was written for adoption' KAJ 6:4–7

50 *ṣab'u Kaššiū lū līṭu lū ṣabbututtu u* 50-*ma ṣab'u Šuburiū līṭumma ina āle usbū ana maṣṣartema ša āle a'īluttu laššu* '50 Kassite troops, be they hostages, be they captives and 50 Hurrian troops, hostages dwelling in the city, but for the guarding of the city there is nobody' MATSH 2:18–21

The particle is rarely attached to adjectives, nonetheless it is attested with the ordinal number *šanīu* 'second' (cf. GOA § 15.3.1; 15.3.2.4):

lū ana mamma ša-ni-im-ma tattidin 'or she has given it to another person' MAL A § 3:36–37

aššat a'īlē ina bēt a'īlē ša-ni-e-ma mimma taltiriq 'a wife has stolen something from another man's house' MAL A § 5:57–58

1 *ellabuḫa ra-aq-ta-*[*m*]*a ultēbilakkunu* 'I sent you one empty bladder' KAV 103:28–29

12.1.1.1 The particle -ma with pronouns

§ 411 The particle *-ma* is attached frequently to independent personal pronouns, where it brings about the focus of the aforementioned subject on the agent. These examples can usually be translated as 'himself' or 'personally' or left untranslated. It may be observed that the usage of the enclitic particle *-ma* is double; the independent pronouns themselves are already emphatic, meaning that *-ma* is not required.

šūt — *dumāqē ša šu-ut-ma iškunūšini* 'the jewels that he himself placed upon her' MAL A § 38:22

atta — *at-ta-ma tudda* 'you yourself know' VAT 8851:17
at-ta-a-ma tudda 'you yourself know' T 97-10:13–14

attūnu — *at-tu-nu-ma leqyāne* 'you yourself must take it to me' KAV 105:29–30
ma-at-tu-nu-ma ana mayyirāni tattanarradāne 'now you, you keep descending to the *m.*-troops' MATSH 7:12''–13''

A similar function can be observed when *-ma* is added to pronominal suffixes; however, relevant examples are few and largely limited to MAL A (cf. GOA § 15.3.2.2).

-šu — *ana pā'i tuppe ša a-bi-i-šu-ma* PN *ša ana mar'utti* (...) *šaṭrū-*<*ni*> 'according to the wording of the tablet of his father PN, which was written for adoption' KAJ 6:4–7
riksa a-ki-šu-ma irtaksū 'thus they have issued a decree' MATSH 17:9–10
ina šērte ana mu-ši-šu-ma litūra 'in the morning until the night, he must return' 'MATC 5:11–13
[*k*]*ī pa-ni-ti-šu-ma* PN-*ma uka''al* 'PN will hold it as before' AO 19.228:22–23

-ša — *sinniltu ina bēt a-bi-ša-ma usbat* 'a woman lives in the house of her own father' MAL A § 25:82
mar'ū ra-mi-ni-ša-ma ušakkulūši 'her own sons will feed her' MAL A § 46:107–108
ana KA-*ša-ma ša* ^{f}PN 'according to PN's own declaration' KAJ 7:6

-ī/ya — *ana* UGU-*ia-ma lublūni* 'may they bring it to me' KAV 98:35
$^{\text{na4}}$KIŠIB^{meš}-*ia-ma kunkā* 'seal with my seals' KAV 99:34

-šunu *ki-la-al-li-šu-nu-ma idukkūšunu* 'they will kill them both' MAL A § 15:44–45

The enclitic *-ma* is attested once on a possessive independent pronoun, again giving emphasis.

šuāʾu *mimma nudunnāʾa ša mussa iddinaššenni šu-a-am-ma ilaqqe* 'whatever bridal gift her husband has given her; he will take his (property)' MAL A § 27:105–107

§ 412 Kouwenberg points out that a demonstrative pronoun rarely takes *-ma* (GOA § 15.3.2.5), probably because it is already identifying by itself. Nonetheless, emphasized demonstrative pronouns are attested relatively often in MA. According to Kouwenberg, *anniu-ma* functions in these cases with the meaning 'the (very) same' (GOA § 10.2.2; 15.3.2.5).

anniu *iltu ū-me an-ni-e-ma multēṣittušunu ša mugerre kī panitti šunuma iddunū* 'From this day, they will pay their chariot expenses themselves, as before' KAJ 307:13–15

kunukka an-ni-a-ma kunkā 'seal this seal' KAV 105:22

ina libbi an-ni-ma 'among this' Adad Ritual:3

annītu *adi tuppi*[sic.] *dannata išaṭṭurū an-ni-tu-ma dannat* 'until they write a strong tablet, this one is valid' KAJ 12:20–21

tuppa ša pî ạn-ni-te-ma altaṭar 'I have written the tablet of this wording' MATSH 22:22–23

According to Hämeen-Anttila, *-ma* can be used in NA to make interrogative pronouns adverbial (SNAG, 64 § 3.3.1). He provides only one adverb (*immate*) that takes *-ma*, which is attested once in MA as well.

immate *im-ma-te-ma ṭē*[*m* PN] *ana muḫḫi bē*[*līya*] *lā ašp*[*ur*] 'I have not, at any time, sent the news of PN to my lord' MATSH 11:10–12

The focus marker is also attached behind interrogative pronouns in the letter T 93-3. This seems to be exceptional and is not attested in OA (GOA § 15.3.2.6), but is attested in NA (SNAG, 52 § 3.1.4.4). Cohen (2000, 222–23) tries to explain similar phrases as indicating a cleft clause:

mannu *ma-an-na-ma lēriš ma-nu-ma liddina* 'who can I ask, who will give it to me?' T 93-3:20–22

mīnu *mi-nu-⌜ú-ma⌝ anniu ša ammar aqabbiakkunni kī pî*[*y*]*a lā teppušūni* 'what is this, that whatever I say to you, you do not act according to my words?' T 93-3:4–6

12.1.1.2 The particle -ma with adverbs

§ 413 With adverbial expressions, a similar contrastive or emphasizing function occurs. Kouwenberg refers to a number of adverbs that frequently take *-ma* (GOA § 15.3.2.1). Most of these are only attested a few times in MA, such is the nature of our limited corpus. Some cases, such as *annāka* (and thus *amīša*) or *kīam*, are attested with *-ma*; on the other hand, *arḫiš*, *danniš* and *uma* are not. Here, it should be noted that there may be a negative relation between the terminative-adverbial and the emphatic *-ma* (cf. *ša-da-aq-de-eš* MARV 7 14:16 ~ *ša-da-aq-di-ma* MATSH 4:15'). Only one terminative-adverbial is attested with *-ma*: *il-te-níš-ma* KAV 103:24. Sometimes, the particle seems to indicate contrast, such as in MATC 9: here vs. there. In other cases, the function is more difficult (MATSH 4:15'–16'). Cohen (2000, 223) highlights the possibility that *-ma* has lost its function here, as it appears to occur in free variation with adverbs with or without the particle.

akkī	*riksa a-ki-šu-ma irtaksū* 'thus they have issued a decree' MATSH 17:9–10
ammīša	*anāku* [lú]*sīrāšê*[meš] *ša annāka am-me-e-ša-ma alaqqea* 'I will take the brewers, who are here, there' MATC 9:22–25
annāka	(...) *iltu an-na-ka-am-ma udduat* 'she is assigned from here' MATC 15:6–7
emūqu	*e-mu-qa-ma iṣṣabassi* 'he seized her with force' MAL A § 12:18
iltēniš	[*i*]*l-te-ni-iš-ma* [*u*]*ttammiš* 'together I sent (them) off' MATSH 14:17–18
kīam	*lū ša ki-am-ma šaknūni* 'or it is placed in a similar manner' MCS 2 2:11–12
panīu	*pa-ni-ma iltu aḫā'iš niddubub tattatlak* 'Previously, we talked together but you departed' NP 46:6–8
šaddaqdi	*ša-da-aq-di-ma ina ūmē annūte* 'last year on these days' MATSH 4:15'–16'

Similar to the adverbs, we find *-ma* attached to a number of nominal adverbial constructions and adverbial expressions.

ina mā'ē u riqie[meš] *an-nu-te-ma tamassi* 'you will wash it in this water and perfume' PKT 3 i 12

[*k*]*ī pa-ni-ti-šu-ma* PN-*ma uka''al* 'PN will hold it as before' AO 19.228:22–23

ina mūše ba-ra-re-ma ittaṣṣū 'at dusk, they went off' MATSH 2:22–23

ina šērte ana mu-ši-šu-ma litūra 'in the morning until the night, he must return' MATC 5:11–13

Unlike OA (GOA § 15.3.2.7), the particle *-ma* is only very rarely used on adverbial dependent clauses. The available passages occur in the literary corpus.

kī ta-ad-nu-ni-ma iddan u ilaqqe 'he will give and take as much as was given' MAL A § 45:83–84

ša ina tuppe qa-bi-ú-ni-ma ana bētāni ilāni (...) *errab* 'what is mentioned on the tablet will enter the temple' Coronation Ritual iii 39–40

12.1.2 The particle *-ma* of identity

§ 414 MA legal documents often revolve around one central person; a person who sells something or takes a loan and therefore carries responsibility for the transaction. Frequently, this central person is already identified at the head of a tablet with his seal. In any case, when the legal responsibility is described for this person, the particle *-ma* is added to indicate that this is the same person that features in the transaction. This function of *-ma* more or less conforms to what Kouwenberg called the *-ma* of identity (GOA § 15.3.3).

PN (...) *ittidin* (...) *pāḫat buqurrā*[*n*]*ā'e* (...) PN-*ma naši* 'PN sold to (...) (this) PN bears the responsibility of claims' VAT 8722:1–20

PN *ilqe* (...) *pāḫat eqle zakkue* PN-*ma ittanašši* 'PN took it (...) (this) PN will carry the responsibility' AO 19.228:5–24

PN_1 DUMU PN_2 *ù* PN_3 DUMU PN_4 DUMU PN_2-*ma* 'PN_1, the son of PN_2, and PN_3, the son of PN_4, (also) the son of PN_2' KAJ 79:5–7

[ŠE[?]] (...) *ša* PN (...) *tuppi* (...) *ša* PN-*ma* 'barley of PN (...) the tablet of (this) PN' Billa 13:1–12

1 *emāru abšu ša šibše ina sūte ša ši-ib-še-ma* 'one homer of lentils of the *šibšu* in a seah (also) of the *šibšu*' KAJ 134:2–4

> *ana* PN *iddinma ušappim[a]* (…) *ana* PN-*ma zakkuat* 'it is given to PN and caused to acquire (…) it is cleared to (the aforementioned) PN' KAJ 149:11–25

In addition, note:

> IGI PN-*ma t[up]šarru* 'witnessed by PN, the scribe (and also seller)' KAJ 168:23–24 (see commentary UŠA, 51)

Note also a preposition in combination with a pronominal suffix:

> *išku šanittu il-te-ša-ma tattalpat* 'a second testicle has become infected with it' MAL A § 8:82–83

§ 415 Demonstrative pronouns are used independently in order to indicate the date of a tablet as mentioned earlier. In this function, it seems to indicate a syllabic spelling of the logogram KIMIN-*ma*. This claim is not without its problems; a number of the few attestations that are available refers to elements of dating not previously mentioned. This will be indicated by the character †. It is quite possible that administrative notes, with a short span of relevance, did not need to mention month or year because the tablet would be thrown away before these facts changed. Alternatively, *annie-ma* could refer to the date at the bottom of the tablet.

> *iltu Allanātu* UD.19.KÁM *līme PN adi Ša Sarrāte* UD.⌜20⌝[+n.KÁ]M *līme an-ni-e-ma* 'from the month *Allanātu*, 19th day, eponym PN until the month of *Ša Sarrāte*, 20+n day, the same eponym' MARV 2 14 r. 1–2

> *ina ūme an-ni-e-ma* 'on this day' MARV 5 57:4, 8†

> *[i]ltu Ṣippe* UD.12.KÁM *līm[e a]n-ni-e-ma* 'from the month of *Ṣippu*, 12th day, the same eponym' MARV 5 57:12†

> *ina* iti KIMIN-*ma* UD.18.KÁM *līme* KIMIN-*ma* 'in the same month, 18th day, the same eponym' MARV 7 7:9–10 (referring back to an earlier passage)

> *[iltu] Ṣippe* UD.20[+n.KÁM *l*]*īme* PN *[ad]i* iti *an-ni-e-ma [l]īme* PN MARV 7 73:5'–8'

> *ina urḫe an-ni-e-ma* 'in the same month' KAJ 291:3†

We should also consider the following phrases, where the demonstrative pronoun with *-ma* is to be translated as 'the same':

> *ina kāse an-ni-te-ma* 'with the same cup' Aššur Ritual ii 15'

> *ina* UD.24.KÁM 1 *emmer* PN_1 *ina* <u>UD.24.KÁM-*ma*</u> 1 *emmer* PN_2 *ina* UD.25.KÁM 1 *emmer* PN_3 *ina* UD.25.KÁM 2 *emmer*meš PN_4 *maḫir* 'on the 24th day, one sheep of PN_1, <u>(also) on the 24th day</u> one sheep of PN_2, on the 25th day one sheep of PN_3, on the 25th day one sheep of PN_4' A 2608 (NTA, 29):1–5

12.1.3 The particle *-ma* of distinction

§ 416 The particle *-ma* is also applied in a few cases on a PN in the lists of witnesses in legal documents or date formulas, e.g., KAJ 8:32; KAJ 13:30; KAJ 168:13; KAJ 197:3; KAJ 236:3; A 297 (NTA, 16):13; MATC 67:9. The reasons for this are not exactly clear, given that, for the list of witnesses, the application of *-ma* seems to be related to the fact when the same PN is mentioned elsewhere in the text. In that case, *-ma* is probably used to indicate that the PN is a different person from the aforementioned PN. Kouwenberg calls this the '-*ma* of distinction' (GOA § 15.3.4). This -*ma* is also attested elsewhere:

RN$_1$ *uklu marā* RN$_2$ UGULA-*lim-ma* 'RN$_1$, the steward, son of RN$_2$, (also a) steward' MAPD passim

ša qāt PN$_1$ PN$_1$-*ma maḫir* 'PN1 received it from (the man with the same name) PN$_1$' AO 21.381:5–8

ša GN$_1$ *mišilšunu* GN$_2$ *mi-šil-šu-nu-ma* 'half of them from GN$_1$ and (the other) half of them from GN$_2$' MATSH 2:7–8

ina UD.14.KÁM *ešartu gabbu ina* UD.16.KÁM 10^{meš}-*tu-ma* MATC 80:4–5

12.1.4 Unclear usage of *-ma*

§ 417 A small category remains, where parts of the formula in administrative documents receive the particle -*ma*.

PAP-*ma* 1 LIM 7 ME [1]4 UDU^{meš} A 113 (NTA, 15):7

ŠU.NÌGIN-*ma* 36 MUNUS 'total of 36 women' MARV 1 57 iv 43'

ŠU.NÍGIN-*ma* 1 ME 5 ANŠE^{meš} 'total of 105 donkeys' LVUH 3:21

tup-pí 2.KÁM-*ma* 'second(?) cleared tablet' MARV 7 8:25

1 UDU *i+na* UD.14.KÁM-*ma* 'one sheep on the 14th day' KAJ 221:5

In relation to these cases, we can also point to the two instances where the negation *lā* received the emphatic particle (see commentary LVUH, 176):[3]

la-ma maḫrū 'it is not received' LVUH 97:10

la-ma zārū 'it is not sowed' LVUH 106:8

Instead of the logical predicate, we sometimes find -*ma* attached to the grammatical predicate when it is a finite verb. This function of -*ma* could have developed out of the instances where it is added to the nominal predicate (cf. Cohen 2000, 217).

šumma mut sinnilte aššassu idūak u aʾīla i-du-ak-ma 'if the husband kills his wife, then he will kill the man as well' MAL A § 15:51–52

ša 10 *šanātīšuni ibašši eḫ-ḫa-az-ma* 'if he is at least 10 years old, he will marry' MAL A § 43:29–30

[*it*]*talkū la-*⸢*a i*⸣*-di-na-šu-ú-ma* 'they came but he did not give them' MATSH 7:3''

uradka lā ušeṣṣušu la-a$^{!}$ *ul-te-ṣi-ú-šu-m*[*a*] 'I will not let your servant go as they have not let him go (earlier)' MATSH 8:35'

[*a*]*l-te-me-ma nakru ina šad*[*ue*] 'I heard that the enemy is in the mountains' MATSH 4:4'

Cases where the particle -*ma* marks the nominal predicate are rare and limited to literary texts (cf. Cohen 2000, 217).

---

3 Cf. the Alašia letter: 20 ^{giš}MÁ^{meš} (…) *l*[*a*]*-a-ma it-*⸢*tu*$^{?}$⸣*-*[*ra*$^{?}$]*-ni-*⸢*me*$^{?}$⸣ '20 ships did not return' RS 20.18:17–19.

tallaktušu išāssu kī an-ni-im-ma 'its procedure and its fire are as this' PKT 5 r. 3

DAM-*ti šīt lā aššat e-se-er-tu-ú-ma šīt* 'that wife is not a (proper) wife, she is a concubine' MAL A § 41:9–10

ḫiṭaʾšu kī ša DAM-*at* LÚ-*ma* 'his punishment will be (equal to) that of the other man's wife' MAL A § 16:66

12.2 The particle *-mi/me*

§ 418 More exceptional is the usage of *-mi* to indicate direct speech (UGM, 109 § 98c). This particle, while common in OB, is rare in OA and mostly occurs in incantations.[4] For this reason, a Babylonian loan may be expected in that genre. In MA, our stock of attestations has grown somewhat. I discussed its function in MA and its limited examples elsewhere (de Ridder 2014, 176). Spelling varies between ME (in MAL) and MI (in other texts), but this does not necessarily mean anything (cf. Huehnergard 1989, 209). The placement of *-mi* is usually on verbs and twice on the adverb *ayyēša(m)* 'where', although, in OB, its placement was free (Wasserman 2012, 199–201).

Direct speech in MAL:

la-ni-ik-ki-me iqtibiašše '"I want to fornicate", he said to her' MAL A § 12:16

ḫal-laq-me iqbi '"it is lost", he said' MAL M § 3:6

Direct speech in letters:

ma-a-ie-e-ša-mi emaqqatūni lā udda 'Where will they attack? I do not know it' MATSH 3:12–13

Direct speech in contracts:

šumma PN *la*[?!] *a-mi-gi-ir-mi iqabbi* 'if PN declares "I do not agree"' KAJ 57:16–18 cf. 19–21

la a[š-š]a-ti-mi iqabbi ''she is not my wife', he says' TIM 4 45:10

la mu-ti-mi iqabbi ''he is not my husband', she says' TIM 4 45:14

Conditional clauses in contracts:

šumma ana šaduāni ana a-ie-e-ša-mi-ni iḫtaliq[sic.] 'if he has fled to the mountains or wherever' Giricano 12:17'–19'

§ 419 The particle *-me/mi* is quite common in late second millennium Akkadian. In WPA, it is often identified with direct speech: AmurA (Izre'el 1991, 329–30 § 4.7.2.1); UgarA (Huehnergard 1989, 209–10); MittA (Adler 1976, 101–3). Meanwhile, in MB, it is used for direct speech (Aro 1955a, 120). As for the origin of the particle, we need to look at OB and OAkk. A recent study by Wasserman (2012, 184ff) systematically describes the function of this model particle as indicating the words of someone else, from which the speaker takes distance. In other words, the particle is often found in OB in bad news, of which the messengers try to stress that it is not their own words. In literary texts, the function is

4 For OA, see GOA § 15.5 (cf. GKT, 219f § 130; Veenhof 1996, 432). Incantations are discussed in Wasserman (2012, 189).

different and the public is addressed instead, a function that is far from our corpus. Thus, applying this knowledge to our examples, we only find *-mi* used once in a letter (MATSH 3), where the speaker distances himself from any knowledge about enemy attacks. We may also accept *-mi* on other occasions. In the case of MAL A § 12, the scribe of the text may have wished to distance himself from the words of the rapist. MAL M § 3, however, is rather fragmentary. In the case of the marriage contract TIM 4 45, distance is inserted from the possibility of divorce, just as in KAJ 57 and Giricano 12, in which an unwanted hypothetical situation is indicated with *-mi.* Based on the examples at hand, there seems little reason to assume the WPA nominalizing particle *-me* (cf. MATSH, 109 n44). At the same time, it is not unthinkable that *-mi/me* is related to the OA irreal particle *-men/m.*[5] The usage of *-mi* in contracts is also known from MB (Aro 1955a, 120), where it was also used to indicate unwanted hypothetical situations.

§ 420 It seems possible that, in the case of *ayyēša+mi* (MATSH 3:12; Giricano 12:18'), a nominalizing meaning is interpretable, changing the meaning of *ayyēša* 'whither' to 'wherever'. This usage of the particle is known from AmurA.[6] This particle is suggested to have a Hurrian origin, where *-me* is also present as nominalizing (cf. Wegner 2007, 59). Provided that this connection is correct, this would be one of the few direct influences of Hurrian on MA grammar. However, the two examples given are open to multiple interpretations.

5 See GKT, 186 § 106e; GOA § 23.5.1.
6 See Izre'el (1991, 333–37 § 4.7.3); MATSH, 109 n44.

Chapter 13: Prepositions

§ 421 Semitic languages make extensive use of their stock of different prepositions to make up for the lack of a complex system of case endings. For instance, *ana* is used where we would otherwise find a dative case and *ina* instead of a locative. Moreover, Akkadian is unique among the Semitic languages in its set of primary prepositions; MA is no different. These primary prepositions (*ana*, *ina*, *adi* and *iltu*) have no common pairs with other West Semitic languages, save for an attempt by von Soden (1987) to identify some prepositions with Ethiopian and Arabic counterparts. The set of prepositions in MA is a growing one. This has two reasons. New prepositions can be created by unrelated word forms, such as the imperative *ezib* 'leave it' gradually turning into 'save for/except'. There are, therefore, a few secondary prepositions found in MA from different origin, including verbs (*uššer*), adverbs (*kī-*) and negations (*balu(t)*). However, most new prepositions are in fact compounds, that is, a preposition followed by a standard noun, e.g., *ina ṣēr* or *ina muḫḫi* (Rubin 2005, 46–48 § 3.3.). When nouns or compound prepositions are used with the original meaning of the noun retained, we may speak of prepositional phrases, e.g., *šaplu* 'bottom, underside' can be used as the prepositional *šapal* 'below, under(neath)' in the status constructus, or as a compound *ina šapal* (§ 474). Other prepositional phrases, such as *ellān(u)* (§ 483), even have an adverbial ending.[1] At the same time, we can observe a tendency in Akkadian to use prepositions as conjunctions in adverbial clauses (see § 723ff). Prepositions are, without exception, always followed by a genitive or the first term of a genitive construction. Another general observation is that prepositions normally do not take pronominal suffixes, aside from *iltu*, *ellān*, *urki* and various prepositional phrases, such as *ina libbi*.

§ 422 According to Cancik-Kirschbaum, *ina/ana* is often omitted in NA following *ša*, which is already visible in MA (MATSH, 121). She presents MATSH 6 as an example, which looks similar to an analytic genitive construction ^{túg}GAD^{meš} *ša šatte annite*, were it not for the verb *eṣidūni*.

> ^{túg}*katāʾa*^{meš} *ša <i+na> šatte annīte ēṣidūni* 'the flax that they harvested this year' MATSH 6:8'
>
> *ina libbi eṣe*^{meš} *ša <i+na> āle lēpušū* 'may they make it from the wood of the city' A 1476 r. 8'–9'

Note that the preposition *ina* is also frequently omitted from the PN Ina-Aššur-šumī-aṣbat.

> ^{m}*I+na-*^{d}*A-šur-*MU*-aṣ-bat* MATSH 2:68; MATSH 3:45; MATSH 4:18'; MATSH 6:3'''; MARV 4 33:3
>
> ^{md}*A-šur-*MU*-aṣ-b*[*at*] MATSH 13:30
>
> ^{md}*A-šur-*MU*-aṣ-*[*bat*] MATSH 22:30
>
> ⸢^{md}⸣*A-šur-*MU*-aṣ-bat* MARV 4 46:8

This type of omission is more common when *ša* is followed by compound prepositions found under the prepositional phrase (see § 452).

---

1 See GAG, 207–8 § 115a–b; Streck 2014a, 115–16 § 267).

13.1 Primary prepositions

13.1.1 *ana* 'to(wards)'

§ 423 In Akkadian and MA, *ana* is one of the most common prepositions. In its basic function, it indicates motion towards location. As we have briefly mentioned (§ 125f), prepositions are often part of sandhi spellings. In the case of the prepositions, for example, this caused a successive short unstressed syllable, while the vowel was often dropped and the /n/ in the prepositions *ana* or *ina* assimilated. While not as commonly attested as in OA (cf. *a-ṣé-er* CCT 4 25b:3, see GKT, 177f § 103b; GOA § 3.2.4.1), there is still a relatively large number of attestations in MA of both *ana* and *ina* (for the latter, see below). In NA, we find this type of assimilation to be rare; Hämeen-Anttila suggested that it most often occurred with adverbs (SNAG, 68).

> *aq-qa-at* (*ana qāt*) *šina bēr eqle* 'more than two double-hours' MAPD § 2:18
>
> *a-na-ši tuppiš*[*u*] *inaddinū* 'they will give to the carrier of his tablet' KAJ 52:19–20; cf. KAJ 71:16
>
> *a-pa-ni šarre išaṭṭar* 'he writes in the presence of the king' KAJ 150:17 cf. KAJ 151:20, 22
>
> *a-pa-an šarre išaṭṭar* 'he writes in the presence of the king' BM 108924:19–20 cf. l. 21
>
> *aššum* (< *ana šum*) compound preposition (see § 442), passim
>
> *am-mal-la kāse* (< *ana mala*) 'as much as a cup' MARV 10 23:4

Logographic spellings may occur with the sign DIŠ, although only in some administrative documents:

> *ana* IGI *Aššur tabik* 'it is poured out before Aššur' MARV 6 31:3

§ 424 The main function of *ana* is to indicate motion towards location, conforming to the dative/allative case. In its function as dative, the preposition of *ana* marks the indirect object.[2] It occurs frequently with verbs that require an indirect object, such as verbs for giving and addressing someone (e.g., *qabāʾu*; *tadānu*). Note that the preposition *ana* in these cases is usually expressed by a dative pronominal suffix when the indirect object is not specified, e.g., *aq-ti-bi-áš-šu-nu* 'I said to them' MATSH 7:4'' ≠ **ana šunāšunu aqṭibi*.

> *a-na šu-a-šu eppušūš* 'they will do for him' MAL A § 22:12–13
>
> *aʾīlu a-na* LÚ *iqtibi* 'a man said to a man' MAL A § 17:67
>
> *a-na mu-ut* MUNUS *iddan* 'he will pay the husband' MAL A § 22:111
>
> *a-na* MAN *lā ibtatqūni* 'he did not denounce it to the king' MAPD § 5:37
>
> *a-na* DN *išakkan* 'he will place it (before) DN' Ištar Ritual:9
>
> *a-na a-ḫe-e lā taddan* 'she will not give it to strangers' KAJ 9:27
>
> *a-na na-ši tup-pí-šu annaka iḫīaṭ* 'he will weigh out the lead to the carrier of his tablet' KAJ 22:16–17
>
> *a-na* PN (…) *tadnā* 'it is given to PN' Ali 1:7–9

2 Cf. Kouwenberg (2002); OA in GOA § 14.4.5.

a-na LÚ (…) *din* 'give it to the man' MATC 3:14–15

[*a*]-*na* PN *aqtibi* 'I said to PN' MATC 15:24

ana PN *qibīma* 'speak to PN' passim letters

a-na ku-a-ša (…) *gabbe lū šulmu* 'may it be well with you' VAT 8851:4–6

§ 425 In its allative function, the preposition indicates a direction of an object towards location. For this purpose, we find *ana* with motion verbs, such as *erābu*, *alāku* and *šapāru* (Kouwenberg 2002, 202).

sinniltu qa-ta a-na LÚ *tattabal* 'a woman put her hand on a man' MAL A § 7:74

a-na ÌD-*i-id illukū* 'they will go to the river ordeal' MAL A § 17:71

aššat aʾīle aššat aʾīlema a-na É-*ti-ša talteqe* 'a wife took a(nother man's) wife to her house' MAL A § 23:14–15

a-na É *aš-šu-ra-ie-e tētarab* 'she entered the house of an Assyrian' MAL A § 24:46

a-na ma-a-te ša-ni-te-em-ma iltaparšu 'he sent him to another country' MAL A § 36:4–5

qīra a-na SAG.DU-*ša itabbukū* 'they will pour liquid bitumen over her head' MAL A § 40:76

šarru a-na qa-qi-ri inaqqi 'the king pours (a libation of wine) onto the ground' New Year Ritual:23'

a-na mi-im-ma taʾʾerā 'put it back in something' KAV 99:20

a-na tar-ba-ṣ[*i*] *ša kīdānu uṣṣâ*[*kkunu*] '(if) he goes out to you to the outer courtyard' KAV 96:14–15

a-na ḫu-ra-di illukū 'they will go on campaign' MATC 4:12–13

a-na KUR-*ti-šu i*[*m*]*mušūne* 'he departed to his land' MATC 23A:16–17

a-na šu-ub-te (…) *ētarbūne* 'they went into position' T 93-2:5–6

a-na ÉRIN^{meš}[^{eš} *š*]*a ḫ*[*u-r*]*a-di itbeūni* 'they stood up(?) for the *ḫurādu*-soldiers' T 04-35:13–14 (uncertain)

Sometimes, the difference between the allative and dative is not entirely clear when verbs experience a shift in meaning, e.g., *qarābu* 'to approach' > 'to claim'.

a-na mu-ti-ša (…) *lā iqarribū* 'they will not have a claim against her husband' MAL A § 2:21–22

a-na te-er-ḫe-te ša ublūni lā iqarrib 'he will have no claim of the bridal gift, which he brought' MAL A § 38:23–24

a-na id-ri ù gi-ri la iqarrib 'he may not encroach on the threshing floor and road' KAM 10 14:3

§ 426 We often find *ana* with a referential meaning, which can be translated as 'concerning', 'because of'.[3] One of the main examples of this function is the interrogative

3 See GOA § 14.4.5 (cf. Huehnergard 1989, 184).

pronoun *ana mīni* > *anaʾīni* 'because of what (=why)?' (see § 407). Other examples include:

a-na ri-ḫa-a-te 'as for the rest' MAL A § 25:90

eqla u bēta a-na ú-ku-la-i-ša ša 2 *šanāte uppušū* 'they will assign a field and house for her provisions of two years' MAL A § 45:65–66

a-na mar-ú-ut-ti iddinšu 'he gave him for adoption' KAJ 1:6

a-[*na m*]*a-ru-ut-ti-šu ērub* 'he entered adoption status' KAJ 4:7

a-na MÁŠ *annuku illak* 'the lead will go for interest' KAJ 19:9

a-na šal-lu-um ša-li-mu-ti-šu-nu 'for the payment of their debts' KAJ 47:15–16

ŠE-*um anniu a-na pu-ḫi ilqe* 'he took this barley on exchange' KAJ 91:13

a-na GIŠ.GÀR *ša* ^{lú}ZADIM *dinā* 'give it for the corvée of the bowmaker' KAV 100:21–22

a-na ḫa-mu-ṭí dinā 'give it with haste' KAV 103:30

ṣabʾa gabba a-na SIG$_4$^{me}[^{š}] *šērid* 'make all the troops go down for mudbricks' MATC 4:22–23

a-na SIG$_4$^{meš} *urrudūne* 'they will descend for mudbricks' MATC 3:8

šumma Sūtīu šikara a-na qi-ip-te išatti 'if a Sutean drinks beer on a loan' T 04-37:25

a-na di-na-an EN-*ia attalak* 'I will have gone substitute for my lord' MATSH passim

a-na pu-uḫ-ri-šu-nu ušakkulūši 'they will provide for her commonly' MAL A § 46:102

For an amount of:

a-na ŠÀM *ga-me-er laqiūni* 'he is taken for the full price' MAL A § 44:43

a-na KÙ.BABBAR [*ilaq*]*qe* 'he will take for silver' MAL B § 6:2

Only very rarely is *ana* is used temporally; this is usually the domain of *adi*:

a-na 6 ITI-*ḫi qaqqad anneke iddan* 'within a period of six months, he will pay for the capital of the lead' KAJ 11:7–8

a-na li-di-iš 'the day after tomorrow' MATC 5:18

§ 427 Rather unusual is the following passage, where *ana* occurs in a temporal meaning ('until'), which is mostly covered by *adi* (see below).

ina šērte a-na mu-ši-šu-ma litūra 'in the morning until the night, he must return' MATC 5:11–13

Negation following ana is very rare, except in the following clause that is typical of legal transactions:

a-na la ma$^{!}$*-ša-e šaṭir* 'it is written down in order not to forget' MARV 1 10:20 et passim

A final and frequent function of *ana* to be mentioned is its usage in the infinitive constructions. When a clause has an adverbial final clause, it is almost always preceded by *ana*.[4] Infinitive constructions will be discussed in more detail in § 647ff. Two examples are given here:

a-na ta-da-a-ni maḫrū 'they received it in order to give it (away)' MARV 1 1 iv 35

ammīša a-na bi-a-di allaka 'I will come to rest there' MATC 2:17–18

13.1.2 *ina* 'in'

§ 428 This Common Akkadian preposition is written with the ligature *i+na*, indicating that *ina* is learned, rather than being an actual representation of the language (cf. *iltu* below). The logographic <ina> (DIL) is common in NA, with Hämeen-Anttila claiming it has the value <in$_6$> (SNAG, 69 § 3.8.1); but such a reading is unnecessary if it is only based on the preposition. Moreover, if the reading is based on phonology, it does not account for the assimilation of /n/ into the following consonant. The preferred reading of the sign thus remains <ina>, while keeping in mind that the spelling is actually logographic.[5] This logographic spelling is attested in MA in the Coronation Ritual and some administrative documents. Some examples:

ša ina šēpē ile šaknūni 'which is placed at the feet of the god' Coronation Ritual i 37

šarru adi muḫḫi ina kussīe ina labāni naṣṣū 'they carry the king up until this point on a throne on (their) neck' Coronation Ritual ii 48–49

ina ^{iti}KIMIN-*m*[*a*] UD.25.KÁM 'in the same month, 25th day' MARV 5 25:8

n emāru ina qāt PN 'n homers in the responsibility of PN' MARV 6 34 passim

11 *emāru* 5 *sūtu ina sūte* 6 *sūte* '11 homers, five seahs (measured) by the six-seah (measure)' MARV 7 7:24

It is clear that the ligature *i+na* and the semi-logographic sign <ina> do not represent the spoken language. This is confirmed by spellings where the /a/ of the preposition elides and the /n/ assimilates into the following consonant, similar to the preposition *ana*. This phenomenon can also be found in OA (GKT, 178f § 103c; GOA § 3.2.4.1) and NA (SNAG, 69), but is also attested in other forms of Akkadian (GAG, 204 § 114c). Note also that MA consistently spells the OA conjunction *inūmi* as *i+na u*$_4$*-mi*, which is no doubt an institutionalized hypercorrection of Assyrian scribes.

i-qí-bi ilāni 'at the command of the gods' Franke/Wilhelm 1985:8

im-ma-te-ma (*ina+mati+ma*) 'when?' MATSH 11:10

i-⸢*tup*⸣*-pi* 'from the tablet' TR 2015:10 (Sa)

§ 429 In the following categories of the function of *ina*, we follow Kouwenberg on OA (GOA § 14.4.8). Slightly different categories are found in GKT (178–79 § 103c). The main

4 See Aro (1961, 119); Ungnad (1992, 118–19 § 109h).

5 Luukko (2004, 45) finds in$_6$ in only one attestation where it is not a preposition. According to Borger, the value *ina* is also used for the present of I/n verbs (MZL, 145 no. 1). However, this use is acceptable since it applied the 'correct' value *ina* in another context, according to the rebus principle, which is frequently applied in cuneiform. The value *in*$_6$ does not occur in MA outside its use in relation to the preposition.

function of *ina* is locative. Other functions seem to be secondary and are derived from it (cf. GAG, 204 § 114c). Consider the following locative attestations:

i+na É-*šu usbutūni* 'she dwelled in his house' MAL A § 24:69

i+na ki-i-di mēt 'he dies outside' MAPD § 2:14

ina UGU [giš]GÚ.ZA *ušeššab* 'he will make sit on the throne' Coronation Ritual ii 16

tuppāte (…) *ša i+na* É *ma-ia-li-ia šaknāni* 'tablets that are placed in the sleeping room' KAV 102:11–15

i+na ad-ra-ti uta??ar 'he will return it at the threshing floors' KAJ 74:7–8

i+na qa-qí-ri paṣīutti 'on cleared ground' KAJ 175:2

ANŠE.KUR.RA[meš] (…) *i+na* GN *lu us-bu* 'the horses dwell in GN' MATC 4:3–5

i+na pi-i-tu-uk-ka šukun 'place it in your responsibility' MATSH 1:17–18

i+na URU *mamma laššu* 'there is nobody in the city' MATSH 2:18

kī alpe mēte ša i+na GN *mītūni* 'instead of a dead ox that died in GN' DeZ 3389:10–12

§ 430 A secondary function is ablative '(away) from', e.g., *i+na* É-*šu mi-im-ma tal-ti-ri-iq* 'she stole something from his house' MAL A § 3:24–25. In this passage, the action took place in the house, which is locative. However, at the same time, the verbal predicate describes how the object was removed from location, which favours a secondary ablative interpretation. It should be pointed out that this function of *ina* conflicts with *iltu*, which is also ablative in its basic function. Some attestations are given below:

15 *emmeru*[meš] (…) *i+na qa-at* PN_1 PN_2 *maḫi[r]* 'PN_2 received 15 sheep from the charge of PN_1' KAJ 92:1–8

i+na ḪA.LA-*šu* (…) *damqa išallim* 'he will obtain compensation from his share' KAJ 148:30–31

⌜*i*⌝*+na qa-at ṭé-em* PN (…) *lā nilammudūni* '(since) we are not finding out the news of PN' MATSH 11:6–8

ša (…) *pagû*[sic.] *i+na* ÍD *taššianni* 'she carried the *pagû*-man away from the river' Franke/Wilhelm 1985:2–3

Among the uses of the ablative, there is a group that can be regarded as separative, in the meaning 'one from' (cf. GKT, 178 § 103c.3):

šumma i+na DUMU[meš] *mu-ti-sa-a-ma ša-a ēḫuzūšini i[baš]ši* 'if amongst the sons of her husband there is one who married her' MAL A § 46:109

iltēn i+na ŠEŠ[meš]*-ša iša??al* 'he will ask one of her brothers' MAL A § 48:39

i+na DUMU[meš]*-šu ri-ḫa-a-te* (…) *ana ša ḫadiūni iddan* '(one) from his remaining sons he will marry to whom he pleases' MAL A § 43:23–26

§ 431 The preposition is also used temporally, with a present aspect (cf. OA GOA § 14.4.8.1) As such, we often find it with adverbial expressions of time, such as *i+na na-ma-ri* 'at dawn' BVW A:8.

i+na ṣa-al-te 'during a fight' MAL A § 8:78

⌜*i+na ur-ki*⌝*-it-te* 'afterwards' MAL A § 24:51

i+na mu-še lu-ú i+na kal u₄-me 'during the night or day' MAPD § 6:41

[*i*]*kribēšunu ina ga-am-mu-ri* 'as their blessings ended' Coronation Ritual ii 37

i+na tu-re-zi ēṣidē iddan 'he will give the reapers at the harvest time' KAJ 11:11–12

i+na u₄-me annaka iḫīṭūni 'on the day that they weigh out the lead' KAJ 17:13–14

i+na e-ri-ib KASKAL*-ni-šu-nu* 'at the arrival of their caravan' KAJ 32:7–8

i+na li-me PN 'during the eponymate of PN' KAJ 113:13–14 (with variation passim)

PN *i+na tu-a-ri-šu šēbila* 'send me PN when he returns' MATC 4:32–33

i+na ^{iti}*Ḫi-bur* ^{iti}NE UD.20.KÁM (…) *maḫir* 'it is received on the 20th day of the month of *Ḫibur/Abu*' MARV 1 73a:5–13

In combination with *ana*:

i+na še-er-te a-na mu-ši-šu-ma 'from morning to the night' MATC 5:11–12

§ 432 Instrumental usage is attested relatively frequently (cf. OA in GOA § 14.4.8.3):

20 *i+na* ^{giš}GIDRU^{meš} *imaḫḫuṣūši* 'they shall hit 20 twenty times with rods' MAL A § 7:77

i+na GIŠ^{meš} *izaqqupūši* 'they will impale her with stakes' MAL A § 53:96

30 *i+na* ^{giš}GIDRU^{meš} *tamaḫḫassi* 'she will hit her 30 times with rods' MAPD § 18:85

2$^{ta.àm}$ *i+na up-ni* ŠE*-am tašappakaššunu* 'you will pour out barley for them two times with the palm (of your hand)' BVW A:6

i+na kám-ma-te ša ḫurāṣe rapqā 'they are fastened with plaques of gold' KTN inventory i 25

i+na a-šal LUGAL *imaddudū* 'they will measure with the royal measuring line' KAJ 12:17–18

i+na KIN *me-il-te mētā* 'they died because of the flood' LVUH 48:23

With measurements (cf. OA GOA § 14.4.8.4):

3 *emāru* ŠE *i+na* ^{giš}BÁN SUMUN 'three homers of barley in an old seah measure' KAJ 59:1 (passim with small variation)

ŠE*-um annie i+na ma-ḫi-ra-at* 3 MA.NA$^{ta.àm}$ 'this barley at a rate of three minas (of lead) each' A 320:20–21

2 *mana* 5 *šiqlu ṣarpu i+na* NA₄^{meš} *ša* GN '125 shekels of silver by the weight stones of GN' Faist 2001, 251:5

1 KIMIN 10 *i+na am-mi-te arik* 'likewise one (column) 10 cubits long' MARV 1 14:7 and passim in this text

§ 433 There are various adverbial expressions in which *ina* is attested, but they do not belong to the previous categories (cf. OA in GOA § 14.4.8.4).

i+na pu-uz-ri 'secretly' MAL A § 18:73

i+na de-ni-ka dubbu 'speak at your case' KAV 201:23–24

i+na mi-ig-ra-at ra-mi-ni-šu 'at his own free will' KAJ 1:3

i+na muḫ-ḫi šal-mi-šu ù ke-ni-šu annuku rakis 'on his credibility and legal position the lead is bound' KAJ 43:10–11

i+na a-bat LUGAL 'according to the word of the king' KAJ 121:5

The preposition *ina* can be succeeded by a negation. It seems to occur often in a locative meaning as illustrated by the following examples. When *ina* indicates the adverb of manner (instrumental), in combination with negation, it has the same meaning as *balu* 'without' (cf. OA in GOA § 14.4.8.4). For this reason, it is probably attested on only rare occasions:

šumma aʾīlu i+na la-a A.ŠÀ-*šu būrta iḫri* 'if a man dug a well in a land, not his' MAL B § 10:29

i+na la-a qa-qí-ri-i-šu 'in a plot of ground (that is) not his' MAL B § 13:19

i+na la-a šu-a-te 'in the absence of his own' KAJ 101:12; MARV 1 47:10

i+na la-a ú-ša-a!-bi 'in his absence' MARV 10 81:7

i+na la-a ÉRIN^meš^ *lā ašḫul* 'I could not filter without people (personnel)' MATSH 3:32

13.1.3 Confusion between *ana* and *ina*

§ 434 It has been stated that *ina* is sometimes used instead of *ana* (cf. UgAkk in Huehnergard 1989, 184 n335). As this confusion between the prepositions is also found in NA, it is unlikely that these are accidents.[6] While W. Mayer attributed the confusion to phonetic grounds (UGM, 14), this attribution was criticized in two other studies.[7] Once, we find this preposition used erroneously with an indirect object in a text from the M 6 archive.

ša i+na É ^lú^LUNGA *ù* ^lú^*a-láḫ-ḫi-ni paqqudūni* 'which were entrusted to the house of the brewer and baker' KAJ 185:13–15

That *ina* is erroneous, but is not used in a locative function can be seen in similar phrases from the same archive, where ana is always used. Below are two examples:

ša a-na É ^lú^*a-láḫ-ḫi-ni ù* É ^lú^LUNGA *paqqudūni* 'which were entrusted to the house of the brewer and baker' KAJ 214:22–23

a-na É ^lú^*a-láḫ-ḫi-ni*^meš^ *ša* É DINGIR *paqqudū* 'which were entrusted to the house of the bakers of the temple' A 1750 (NTA, 24):10–12

The confusion is especially frequent with the D-stem stative *ta??ur* in the expression *ana sūtu x ta??ur* 'it goes back to the x seah measure'.

ŠU.NÍGIN 1 *me* 23 *emāru* 5 *sūtu* ŠE *ina sūte ṣeḫre ana* 99 *emāre* ŠE <u>*a-na ḫi-bur-ni ta-ur*</u> 'a total of 123 homers and five seahs of barley, in a small seah goes back to 99 homers of barley in the (seah) of the *ḫiburnu*' MPR 49:42–44

(…) *a-na* ^giš^BÁN *ḫi-bur-ni ta-ur* MARV 1 1 i 57'; MARV 4 31:2; LVUH 75:20

---

6 Cf. NA LAS 2 47–48; SNAG 69–70. The sole example, which is given in UGM is KAJ 214:22–23, does not correspond with the copy or its edition in MAOG 7 1/2, 35f.

7 See Freydank (1975, 143); Postgate (1974, 143).

In the Tell Aš-Šēḫ Ḥamad texts, we often find the preposition *ina* instead of *ana*:

(…) *i+na* ^{giš}BÁN *ḫi-bur-<ni> ta*$^{??}$*ur* MPR 18:60

(…) *i+na* ^{giš}BÁN *ša ḫi-bur-n[i ta*$^{??}$*ur*] MPR 19:15

(…) ŠE *i+na* ⌜^{giš}BÁN⌝ [*ḫi-bur-ni*] *ta*$^{??}$*ur* MPR 71 r. 6’–7’

Without a preposition:

<a-na> ḫi-bur-ni ta$^{??}$*ur* MPR 42:56

In barley loans, we find the location *ana adrāti* ‘on the threshing floor’ as an adverbial clause for the verb *madādu* ‘to measure’. For instance:

a-na ad-ra-ti qaqqad ŠE *imaddad* ‘on the threshing floor, he will measure out the capital of the barley’ KAJ 77:6–7 cf. KAJ 71:7–8; KAJ 78:8–9

§ 435 In the expression *ana/ina muḫḫe dabābu* ‘to lodge a complaint against someone’, both prepositions are attested. Following the CAD D (9ff), both expressions are attested in Akkadian. The difference may occur in the context of complaining. The expression *ina muḫḫe* occurs in the court, where a complaint is lodged against someone (locative), whereas *ana muḫḫe* occurs outside a court where people are complaining to someone (directive).

i+na UGU-*šu* [*i*]*dabbubū* “they will lodge a complaint against him” MARV 5 71:13–14; cf. KAJ 102:12–13

a-na UGU-*k*[*a*] *idabbubū* “they will lodge a complaint against you” T 97-1:10–11

It seems unlikely that a mistake is meant here, as the phrase is attested in three different texts by different scribes. At the same time, the expected preposition *ina* is attested more frequently in this type of phrase. One example:

i+na ad-ra-te qaqqad ŠE *imaddad* ‘on the threshing floor, he will measure out the capital of the barley’ KAJ 81:9–10

Similar phrases occur in NA, although apparently with the verb *tadānu* instead of *madādu.*

ŠE.PAD^{meš} *ina ad-ri a-na* DN *id-dan* ‘he will give the barley on the threshing floor to DN’ SAA 14 205:9’–10’

Note also that the name of the eponym Ana-pî-Aššur-lišlim is written in various ways:

^{m}*I+na*-KA-^{d}[*A-šur-liš-lim*] TR 3006:15

^{m}*Ina-pi-*^{d}*A-šur-liš-l*[*im*] OIP 79 7 r. 3’

^{m}*A-na*-KA-^{d}*A-šur-liš-lim* KAJ 190:25

^{m}*I+na*-KA-^{d}*A-šur-liš-lim* LVUH 71:22

13.1.4 *adi* ‘until, up to, together with’

§ 436 The preposition *adi* is common in MA and always written as *a-di*. It is morphologically identical to the conjunction ‘while’ (see § 724ff), but remains easily distinguishable because the conjunction takes a subjunctive on the verbal predicate. Within the meaning of the preposition, we can roughly divide between spatial and temporal.

Temporal:

aḫātī a-di 1 ITI UD^{meš} *apaṭṭar* ‘I will redeem my sister before a month (has passed) MAL A § 48:42

a-di 1 ITI.UD^{meš} *itūar* ‘he will return it within one month’ TR 2028:18

a-di 1 ITI UD^{meš} *gurrāte* (…) *iddin* ‘within one month, he will have given the ewes’ KAJ 88:10–14

Once, this typical construction is replaced with a kind of relative clause:

ša 6 ITI UD^{meš} *tadnaššu* ‘it was given to him for six months’ KAJ 106:16–17

The second function of *adi* is spatial, which can be translated as ‘up until’.

qabal bēte iltu igāre ša DN *a-di i-ga-ra-ti-šu* ‘the midst of the house from the wall of DN up until its walls’ VAT 8923:1–2

a-di A.ŠÀ-*šu ù* É-*šu u mimmûšu gabbe* ‘up until his field and his house and everything else’ KAJ 6:8–9

We also find *adi* with the meaning ‘concerning’ instead of *aššum* (cf. OA GKT, 259 § 156c). Note also that an accusative is used instead of a genitive. This is probably caused by the verbal form of *šakānu*, which takes *za*$^{??}$*eru* as the direct object (cf. MATSH, 128).

a-di za-i-ra-ma ša bēlī išpurūni ṭēma išakkunūni ‘concerning the enemy, about whom my lord wrote (*to me*), they will instruct me’ MATSH 7:15’’–16’’

Often *adi* is used in combination with *iltu*, thereby creating a sequence *iltu* (…) *adi* (…) ‘from (…) up until (…)’. This construction is most frequently found in date formulas to indicate a temporal meaning, yet spatial usage is also observable.

iltu <date$_1$> *a-di* <date$_2$> ‘from <date$_1$> up until <date$_2$> ‘KAJ 20:2–4 et passim; cf. MARV 4 57:13–14

ilte GN$_1$ *a-di* GN$_2$ *ultaṣbit* ‘from GN$_1$ up to GN$_2$, I have settled them’ MATSH 2:9–10

§ 437 It appears that *adi* also takes the position of the Common Akkadian preposition *qadu* ‘with’. This is surprising as *qadu* is attested frequently in OA (GOA § 14.4.16). Only once do we find the morphologic form *qadu* used as a conjunction in KAJ 9:23 (see § 725). In its place, *adi* is used in MA to specify a previous noun (cf. Edzard 1978):

kirā^{ʾ}*a a-di ma-ni-ḫa-te-šu ilaqqe* ‘he will take the orchard with its installations’ MAL B § 13:25

1 *lubulta a-di tam-*[*l*]*i-te-ša* ‘one textile with decoration’ Coronation Ritual i 35

2 *ṣubātu*$^{hi.a}$ *ša šipāte ša ṣēre a-di ma-ak-li-l*[*i*]*-šu-nu* ‘two woollen textiles of the steppe with their accessories’ KAV 99:15–16

gurrātu a-di SILA$_4$^{meš}*-ši-na* ‘the ewes with their lambs’ KAJ 88:11–12

1 *gurrutu a-di pa-ri-ti-ša* ‘one ewe with her young’ KAJ 97:1

This is followed by a relative clause instead of a noun:

[*a*]*-di ša* PN ⸢*il-ti*⸣*-ú-ni gab-bu uppuš* ‘everything is recorded together with what PN drunk’ MATC 53:10–12

13.1.5 *iltu* 'with'

§ 438 The Common Akkadian prepositions *ištu* ('from') and *itti* ('with') are indistinguishable from each other in Assyrian and are both represented in *iltu* (cf. GKT, 180 § 103d–e; Vinnichenko 2016b). In MA, the orthography is predominantly *iš-tu* in independent usage, while we only find *ilte* (*il-te* T 04-3:13) and *ultu* (*ul-tu* KÁ *ú-*⸢*ṣi*⸣ KAJ 209:13 Ad), both on a single occasion.[8] This is probably a direct Babylonian loan as *ultu* is the form that became common in MB (Aro 1955a, 98f; GAG, 206 § 114k). Its orthography *iš-tu* conflicts with the MA/MB sound change /št/ > /lt/ [lt]. That the spelling is not representative of the realization is also confirmed by its NA equivalent *issu* (SNAG, 69), which shows the NA sound change /lt/ > /ss/. This is one of the two simple prepositions that takes pronominal suffixes. Moreover, as the bound form of *iltu* is inflected, the phonetic reality is represented, as expected, with the spelling *il-te-(e)-*, e.g.:

- 3ms: *il-te-šu* MARV 1 34:9; KI-*šu* George 1988 1 r. 4'
- 3fs: *il-te-ša-ma* MAL A § 8:82; § 24:56 ~ *il-te-e-ša* MAPD § 21:106
- 2ms: *il-te-ka* MATC 5:23
- 1cs: *il-te-ia* MATC 4:11
- 3mp: *il-te-šu-nu* MAPD § 19:92; KAV 99:8
- 2mp *il-te-ku-nu* KBo 1 20 r. 4'†

§ 439 As for its function, *iltu* usually has an ablative meaning '(away) from', which is similar to the ablative usage of *ina* (see above).

> *aššat aʾīle iš-tu* É-*ti-ša tattiṣiʾma* 'a wife has gone out of her house' MAL A § 13:25–26
>
> *iš-tu* A.ŠÀ *ušēbilašše* 'he sends to her from abroad' MAL A § 36:90
>
> *iš-tu* É.GAL-*lim lā ušeṣṣuʾū* 'they will remove nothing from the palace' MAPD § 6:44
>
> *iš-tu* ŠÀ *ḫi-ir-si an-ni-e ana libbi ḫersi ša*[*n*]*īe* 'from this *ḫersu*-vessel to another *ḫersu*-vessel' PKT 4 r. left 10
>
> *ša iš-tu* ᵉ*na-kám-te šēṣuʾatanni* 'which is brought out from the storehouse' KAV 205:6
>
> *ḫu-ra-du iš-tu* GN *inassaḫa* 'the *ḫurādu* will depart from GN' DeZ 2521:1–2
>
> *ša iš-tu Su-ti-e* (…) *ilqeūni* 'which he took from the Sutean' AO 21.382:3–5
>
> *erēne*ᵐᵉˢ *ša tamkārē iš-tu* GN *ušēṣiūnenni* 'cedar which the merchants brought out from GN' MARV 1 23:1–3
>
> ŠE-*um anniu š*[*a*] *i+na* GN *iššiūni* 'this barley that they will have brought from GN' T 97-7:14–16

With pronominal suffixes:

> 3 *emāra*ᵐᵉˢ (…) *uṣṣabit il-te-šu* 'I seized three donkeys from him' Hall 1983:7–8

§ 440 We have already mentioned that *iltu* replaced *itti* 'with' in MA. This can be observed in the following examples. Notice also the expression *iltu aḫāʾeš* 'with each other' (attestations § 385):

---

8 In OA, we once find *uš-tù* OIP 27 15:20; see GKT, 181 § 103e. Note that the editors of the CAD insist on reading *ul-tu* in KAJ 179:21; see CAD K, 377b; CAD Q, 197a. It is probably better to read *kim-tu* 'family'; see Schwemer (2001, 579).

aʾīla iš-tu DAM-*ti-šu aʾīlu iṣṣabat* 'If a man has seized "another" man with his wife' MAL A § 15:41

iš-tu il-te-en tuššab 'she will live with one (son)' MAL A § 46:101

iš-tu ŠEŠ^{meš}-*šu pūršu iṣalli* 'he will cast his lot with his brothers' MAL B § 1:14

iš-tu a-ḫa-iš izzazzū 'with each other, they stand ready' MAL B § 18:25

ša iš-tu MAN *illakūni*$^{sic.}$ 'who go (on campaign) with the king' MAPD § 6:40

ṣalta [i]š-tu me-ḫe-er-ti-ša garʾat 'she quarrels with her equal' MAPD § 21:103–104

ana qēputte ša iš-tu mar-ṣu-te 'for the representatives who are with the sick men' CTMMA 1 99:2

PN_1 *i[š-t]u* PN_2 *ētamar* 'PN_1 met PN_2' TabT05a-134:9–10

With pronominal suffixes:

šūt iltuḫur il-te-e-ša idabbub 'he tarries to speak with her' MAPD § 21:106

attunu il-te-šu-nu izizzā 'you, stand ready with them' KAV 102:9–10

il-te-šu (…) *alik* 'go with him' Billa 66:7–9

il-te-ia ana ḫurāde illukū 'they will go with me on campaign' MATC 4:11–13

il-te-šu izuzzūni 'they divided with him' MARV 1 6:5

EN-*li* (…) *il-te-šu lā ṭāb* 'my lord is not on good terms with him' T 02-32:20–22

In Röllig's publication on the administrative documents from Dūr-Katlimmu, an attestation of *itti* is listed. The reading of *itti* is damaged and cannot be confirmed.

⌜*it*!-*ti*!⌝ *aḫāʾiš izzūzū* 'together they have divided it' LVUH 22:35

§ 441 In temporal functions, *iltu* indicates a departure point. We can translate the preposition with 'after/(onward) from'. We have already looked at some examples in combination with the preposition *adi* 'until'. This also led to the usage of conjunctions for temporal adverbial clauses.

iš-tu ^{iti}*ša-sa-ra-a-te* UD.11.KÁM *li-me* PN 'from the 11th day of the month of *Ša sarrāte*, eponymy of PN' MARV 1 17:1–2 cf, MARV 1 56:41

13.2 Secondary prepositions

13.2.1 *aššum* 'concerning, because of'

§ 442 While *aššum* is seemingly one word, it is derived from the prepositional compound *ana šum* (AHw, 84). However, as the form is fossilized, it has become a secondary preposition. It may also occur in adverbial clauses (§ 728). We find *aššum* used with the meaning 'concerning, because of' (GAG, 207 § 114s; GOA § 14.5.19). Spellings vary between *aš-šum* (KAJ 8:12, Aub), *aš-šúm* (VAT 8851:24) and *áš-šúm* (MARV 1 71:25). The spelling **áš-šum* is not attested. Only once is the original long form written, albeit in a letter from Nippur of questionable Assyrian character:

a-na šu-me-ka anāku mallūta ina muḫḫīšunu ašakkanma 'in your name, I will impose a compensation payment upon them' Ni 669:19–21

Other attestations:

áš-šúm GU_4^{meš} *ḫalqutte* (...) *ša bēlī išpuranni* (...) *anāku uṣabbit* 'concerning the lost oxen of which my lord wrote me (...) I have seized (them)' AO 19.227:6–11

áš-šúm KUŠ *mar-še ù* KUŠ *ap-pa-te*^{meš} *ša bēltī tašpuranni* (...) *attidin* 'concerning the leather straps and reins about which my lady wrote me (...) I have given (them)' A 2704:6–11

áš-šúm ŠUK-*at* ÉRIN^{meš} (...) *ša maḫrūni* 'concerning the rations of the troops (...) that they received' MARV 1 71:25–27

[áš]-šúm tup-pi ša ul[tēb]ilakkunni 'concerning the tablet that I sent to you' MATC 7:4

áš-šúm ki-ta-e (...) *altapar* 'concerning the flax I wrote' MATSH 3:5–6

áš-šúm UDU^{meš} *ša ṭēma aškunūkani* 'concerning the sheep about which I instructed you' Billa 60:4–5

ša dēna u dab[ā]ba aš-šum si-ki-il-ti-šu iltēšu u<ba>⸢ʾʾû⸣-ni whoever seeks a lawsuit or complaint against him because of his acquisition' KAJ 8:11–13

Uncertain:

áš-šúm a-bu šu-a-te 'concerning that father' KAJ 93:6†

With an infinitive:

áš-šum la ma-ša-e šaṭir 'in order not to forget it is written down' KAJ 256:13–14, usually written *ana la mašāʾe* (e.g., KAJ 268:14)

With a pronominal suffix (also Ni 669 above):

áš-šúm-i-ka PN *iltaʾlanni* 'PN questioned me concerning you' T 02-32:7–8

13.2.2 Preposition *kīma* and related *kī*, *akī*, *kīmū* and *kumu*

§ 443 The preposition *kīma* 'like, instead of' occurs very rarely in MA (perhaps once as *ki-i-ma* in MATC 20:6, but the context is broken). A few attestations are found in the same position in the Giricano archive (see below). Instead of *kīma*, we usually find *kī*, which is in contrast to most Akkadian instances where *kī*, in its function as a preposition, is mostly limited to literary texts, while *kīma* is used in private archives (GAG, 205 § 114f–g). In OA, *kīma* still occurs, yet *kī* already appears, although mostly in PNs.[9] In NA, *kī* had all but replaced *kīma* (SNAG, 68). As for orthography, we mostly find spelling *ki-i*, but the defective *ki* is common as well. We may wonder what caused the reappearance of *kī* in MA, since it is likely that *kīma* is a secondary development with a fossilized enclitic *-ma* (cf. GOA 14.29). It seems most likely that both prepositions had existed next to each other in the spoken language during the OA period, whereas *kīma* was ultimately reduced in popularity, which led to the reappearance of *kī* in MA. The spelling *ke-e* could denote a semantically (and perhaps morphologically) different particle, as it exclusively occurs as a question word (see § 403f).

9 See GAG, 205 § 114f; GKT, 190f § 103f; GOA § 14.4.11.

§ 444 As for its function, *kī* is rather uniform and used to indicate a kind of comparison identical to *kīma*, which can be translated as 'like' (GAG, 205 § 114a). For the meaning of 'instead of', a different preposition is used (see below).

ki-i bu-ri ēpussi 'like a bull he has done (to) her' MAL A § 9:89

zitta ki-i qa-ti-šu ilaqqe 'he will take a part according to his share' MAL A § 28:10

ki-i sa-ar-[*ri*] *ṣabitma* 'he was arrested like a criminal' MAL A § 36:107–108

ki-i ša-pár-te šēšubat 'she has been made to sit as a pledge' MAL A § 39:28–29

eqlu u bētu ša ki-i ú-kúl-la-i-ša 'a field and house as her provisions' MAL A § 45:79

ki-i pi-i ri-ik-si ša LUGAL *i-ba-ki-a* 'in accordance with the decree of the king, (the women) will cry' MAPD § 2:19

ina abat šarre ki-i ri-mu-ut-te tadin 'it is given as gift according to the king's word' MARV 1 40:18–19

1 *pasru* ⸢*ki-i*⸣ *an-ni-im-ma* 'one tray like this' MARV 3 16 passim

šarru ⸢*ki-i*⸣ *ri-mu-ut-te ana t*[*ad*]*āne iq-t*[*i*]⸢*bi*⸣ 'the king commanded it to be given as a gift' MATSH 1:13–15

ki-i ut-ru-te (…) *tadin* 'it was given as overflow' MPR 46:16–17

mīnumma anniu ša ammar aqabbiakkunni ki-i pi-[*i*]*a lā teppušūni* 'what is this, that whatever I say to you, you do not act according to my words?' T 93-3:4–6

ki-i pi-i ri-ik-si ša šarre nāgiru usassa 'the herald will proclaim according to the wording of the decree of the king' TR 3004:13'–14'

Note also the following possible case of an adverbial expression *kī maḫar* 'as before' (see Bloch 2012, 221–22 n73):

ki IGI *ana mu*[*ḫḫīya*] *urrudūni* 'they will come down to me as before' MATSH 11:14–15

Very rarely is *kī* affected with spoken speech:

ša ki-i a-na-ku akkīa 'that I said like this' T 02-32:19–20 cf. *ša ki-i* PN l. 22

In one case, *kī* seems to occur instead of the prepositional *pû* (§ 470); consider the following two phrases:

ša pi-i le-ḫi ša É.GAL-*lim* 'according to the wooden tablet (*lēʾu*) of the palace' MARV 3 5:36

ša ki le-ḫi ša PN 'according to the wooden tablet (*lēʾu*) of PN' MAH 1608 ii 5'

§ 445 From OB onwards, Akkadian features the preposition *kīmū*, which seems to replace *kīma* in the meaning 'instead of' or 'as a substitute of'.[10] The preposition *kīmū* appears to have two long vowels based on spellings such as *ki-i-mu-ú* KAJ 100:7. Its meaning 'instead of' developed in a rare spatial form, i.e., 'at the place of': *ki-mu pi-ri-ik* KÁ.G[A]L 'at the place of shrine of the gate' New Year Ritual:25'. We also find the preposition used to refer to a substitute for a crime, i.e., *ki-i-mu-ú sa-ar-te* KAJ 100:7–8, where a person has taken a

10 See AHw, 479; CAD K, 37.

slave as substitute for the committer. The replacement of *kīma* by *kīmū* is clearly shown in the Giricano corpus, where we find *kīma* twice and, on one occasion, a damaged *kīmū*, both of which were extraordinary for MA. Rather than an archaism, the usage of *kīma* seems to be a sign for the younger stage of the dialect, as NA disposes of both *kīma* and *kīmū* and uses a new form, i.e., *kūm*, instead (SNAG, 72).

> *ki-ma* ^{na4}KIŠIB-*šu ṣu-pár-šu* 'instead of his seal, his fingernail' Giricano 8:1; 14:1
>
> [*ki-m*]*u* ^{na4}KIŠIB-*šu* UM[BIN]-*šu* 'instead of his seal, his fingernail' Giricano 7:1[11]

Cf. NA:

> *ku-um* ^{na4}KIŠIB^{meš}-*šú-nu ṣu-pur-šú-nu iš-ku-nu* 'instead of their seals, they placed their fingernail s' SAA 6 19:1

According to Güterbock in his text edition (OIP 79, 89), we once find *kūmu* instead of *kīmū* in one of the Tell Faḫariyya texts (also in CAD K, 531). This would conform to NA (SNAG, 72) and NB (Woodington 1983, 175). However, the copy itself seems to suggest KI, rather than KU, even though the necessary wedge at the beginning of KI is hardly visible. Its existence in MA therefore remains tentative.

> *ku*$^{?}$*-mu zu-bu-ul-la-e ša ana bēt emēšunu izbilūni* 'instead of the marriage that he brought to the house of their father-in-law' OIP 79 5:7–9

§ 446 Note that normal *kī* can also be used where usually *kīmū* is found, with the meaning 'instead of':

> *ki-i* DAM-*šu me-et-te* 'instead of his deceased wife' MAL A § 31:44
>
> *rab ikkarē ki-i* GU_4 *me-te* (…) *tadin* 'the head ploughman is given instead of the dead ox' DeZ 3389:9–13

Other examples of *kīmū* include:

> *ki-mu-ú ša lìb-bi-ša* 'in place of her foetus' MAL A § 50:78
>
> *šarru ki-mu* ^{lú}SANGA *isarraq* 'the king sprinkles instead of the priest' New Year Ritual:17'
>
> *ki-i-mu-ú sa-ar-te* 'as substitute of the crime' KAJ 100:7–8
>
> *qaqqara šuātu ki-i-mu-ú* PN *ú-ba-*$^{?}$*a-PI* 'instead of PN, they may select this terrain' KAJ 175:35–38
>
> *ki-i-mu an-nu-te mazzalta iṣabbutū* 'they will take position instead of these' MATSH 8:47'
>
> PN_1 *ki-i-mu* PN_2 *maḫir* 'PN_1 received (it) as a substitute of PN_2' LB 2532:5–7
>
> *ki-i-mu-ú* [^{giš}]BAN^{meš} *an-na-ti* [*n*] *iku eqlīšu uka*$^{??}$*al* 'he holds *n iku* of his field instead of these bows' MARV 1 20:10–16
>
> *ki-mu* MÁŠ AN.NA *an-ni-e* 'instead of the interest of this lead' AO 19.228:7
>
> 1 *sūtu burāšu ki-mu ṣum-la-le-*⸢*e*⸣ 'one seah of junipers instead of spices' KAJ 248:7

With a prepositional suffix:

> [*ki*]-*mu-šu-nu* 'instead of them' MARV 6 40:16†

11 The reading of *kīmū* in the Giricano is in all reconstructed texts; even in this passage, the copy shows hardly any remnants of MU, so even here it can be contested.

[k]i-i-mu-ka lu-ša-k[íl] 'instead of you, I must feed' T 98-129:9'

Note the following case where no genitive follows the preposition:

1 *sūtu burāšu ki-mu* [šim]*ka-ak-⸢ku⸣* 'one seah of junipers instead of chickpeas' KAJ 248:6

13.2.3 *balu(t)* 'without'

§ 447 The preposition *balu(t)* occurs in two different forms. We find *balut* limited to MAPD (see CAD B, 76), where it is found multiple times. It seems to derive from *balātum* (CAD B, 45), which appears to have had a locative ending *-um*.[12] For this reason, we find OA forms, such as *ba-lá-tù-ká* 'without you' CCT 3 34a:11. Moreover, the locative ending is also found in the short form, e.g., *ba-lu-um* BIN 4 64:19 (GKT, 175 § 102d). Concerning the long and short forms in MA, we may assume that *balut* derives from *balātum* when affected by VA > *balutu(m)* > *balut*. This also implies that the long /ā/ in *balātu* was actually short or, more likely, shortened. The short form *balu* is identical to OA, but with mimation dropped. We usually find the preposition in combination with an infinitive, but sometimes the preposition and the infinitive are separated by a noun, so that we have a three-part construction.[13]

ba-lu EN-*šu ša-a-li* 'without asking his lord' MAL F § 2:10

ba-lu-ut MAN *ša-ʾa-[li]* 'without asking the king' MAPD § 3:24

ša ba-lu-ut GAL É.[GAL-*lim*] 'without the palace overseer' MAPD § 6:41

ba-lu-ut ḫi-a-ri [an]a ēkalle lā errab 'he will not enter the palace without inspection' MAPD § 20:97–98

ba-a-lu de₄-e-ni ù da-ba-bi (…) *iddinšu* 'he will sell him off without (any) a case and complaint' KAJ 6:20–23

mullāʾā ša ṣabʾe ba-lu EN-*ni la mimaḫḫar* 'we will not accept compensation for the soldiers without (asking) our lord' MATSH 2:59

ba-lu EN-*ia palḫāku* 'without my lord, I am afraid' MATSH 16:19–20 cf. Billa 63:21

šumma ba-lu [lú]*ma-zi-i-zu immaggar* 'if it be agreed upon without witness(?)' MARV 1 41:8–9

ba-lu-ut ḫa-⸢ba-a⸣-q[i] aššatu[sic.] *lū lā tu[dda]* 'the woman may not know it without inspecting' T 93-54:16–17

ba-lu-ut ḫa-ba-qi lū lā uddiū 'without an inspection(?), they should not make it known' T 96-36:31–32

With a pronominal suffix:

ba-la-tu-k[a] lū lā ettiqāne 'without your (consent), they may not cross' T 93-20:11–12

Its occurrence in PNs is more problematic; consider the following examples from OA (see Hirsch 1972, 9):

Ma-nu-ba-al-ma-Aš-šur 'Who-is-without-Aššur?' AKT 2 8:2

12 See GAG, 108 § 66c; Kouwenberg (2012a, 325).

13 See Aro (1961, 293); cf. Izre'el (1991a, 290–91 § 4.2.4).

Ma-num-ba-lúm-A-šùr 'Who-is-without-Aššur?' TCL 19 67:2

§ 448 The onomastic evidence shows that Mannum-balum-Aššur was a popular name in OA with many different patronymics. In MA, we have the same type of name, but with the sign BAL following *mannu(m)*. Saporetti makes a claim for the reading *gēru* 'equal, adversary', seemingly basing this conclusion, in part, on the syllabically written name (^{m})*Ma-nu-ge-er-*^{d}*A-šur*, which is attested two or three times in KAJ 119:8; KAJ 310:30(?); Billa 57:15 (see OMA 1, 306–7; OMA 2, 121-2; cf. value <gér> in AHw, 287a). This reading is not accepted by others, while Saporetti distanced himself from it in later instances.[14] It is furthermore rejected in this study by analogy with the OA material and the lack of attestations of the logographic *gēru* in other dialects. There is nothing to prevent us from accepting the existence of two similar PNs. As a result, we may assume that the logographic ending *-um* had totally dropped off in these MA PNs, thus creating an extra short form of the original *balūtum*.

Ma-nu-bal-DINGIR KAJ 51:15

Ma-nu-bal-⌜^{d}*A*$^{!}$⌝*-šur* KAJ 79:9

13.2.4 *ezib* 'apart from'

§ 449 This preposition derives from the root *ezābu*, the grammaticalized imperative 'leave it', gradually developing into 'aside from/safe from' (cf. CAD E, 430a) or 'excluding' (UŠA, 56). Its prepositional usage is not unique to MA and also occurs in other Assyrian and Babylonian dialects (sometimes as *ezub*). The morphologically identical conjunction and interjection *ezib* is not attested in MA, but can be found in OA.[15]

⌜*e*⌝*-zi-ib tup-pu-šu* 'apart from from his tablet' KAJ 22:2

e-zi-ib KA-*i tup-pí-šu pa-*⌜*ni*⌝*-ti* 'apart from the wording of his previous tablet' KAJ 31:1

e-zi-ib KA-*i tup-pa-te-šu pa-ni-a-te* 'apart from the wording of his previous tablets' KAJ 119:1–2

e-zí-ib pí-i t[*up-pí-šu pa-ni-t*]*i* 'apart from the wording of his previous tablet' KAM 10 2:2

e-zi-ib 35 ANŠE ŠE-*i*[*m*] 'apart from the 35 homers of barley' MARV 6 40 r. 11

e-zi-ib [^{gi}]^{š}PAN^{meš} *šil*$_{4}$*-ta-ḫu*^{meš} *ša* LUGAL 'apart from the bows and arrows of the king' MARV 10 3:10

Once with *ša*, without a clear differentiation in function:

⌜*e*⌝-[*z*]*i-ib ša* KA-*i tup-pa-ti-*⌜*šu*⌝ *pa-ni-a-ti* 'apart from the content of his previous tablets' KAJ 26:2

⌜*e*⌝*-zi-ib ša* (…)⌜*ša*⌝ (…) *a-na e-pa-še id-di*$^{!}$*-nu-*⌜*ni*⌝ 'apart from what they gave for processing' MARV 10 3:7–8

---

14 For example, Weidner (1973, 141); Freydank/Saporetti (1979, 160); MZL no. 5.

15 See CAD E, 429ff; cf. UGM, 100.

13.2.5 *uššer* 'excluding that'

§ 450 We find this preposition limited to Nuzi and MA (CAD U/W, 304). It obviously derives from an imperative of the verb *uššuru* in its meaning 'to let go of'. This is similar to the preposition *ezib*, which has a similar origin in an imperative. Examples in MA are rare.

> *uš-šìr ḫi-ṭa-a-ni ša* [DAM-*at* LÚ] *ša i+na tup-pi* [*šaṭ-ru-ú-ni*] 'excluding the sins of the wife, which are written on the tablet' MAL A § 59:58–59
>
> *uš-še-er* UDU^{meš} *ša re-ša a-na qa-ú-e ta-ad-nu-*[*š*]*u-ni* 'excluding the sheep that were given to him to be held in readiness' KAJ 120:1–4

13.3 Prepositional phrases

§ 451 We already mentioned how prepositional phrases consist of nouns, which are used prepositionally to maintain their original meaning. As such, these nouns could also be used independently in the contemporary language, even though this is not attested in many cases. While some adverbs are used as prepositional phrases, most instances consist of compounds, e.g., *ina muḫḫi*. The noun succeeds the preposition and always occurs in the status constructus following another noun. Alternatively, it can take a pronominal suffix, which simple prepositions cannot normally take, except for the few that are mentioned above. This is part of a process of the grammaticalization of substantives into prepositions. Sometimes, the original prepositions are not even used anymore with the grammaticalized counterparts (cf. Rubin 2005, 46–47 § 3.3.1–2). The distinction between prepositional phrases and secondary prepositions is not always unambiguous and depends on how far a prepositional phrase is lexicalized. A case such as *uššer* has lost its function as an original imperative and is fossilized in terms of prepositional meaning; it can therefore be regarded as a lexicalized secondary preposition. In the case of *šaplu*, its original adjectival meaning 'below' is not only retained, but it is also used freely as a status constructus or as a compound. In a case such as *urku* (Bab. *warkum*), one could argue it is secondary (Streck 2014a, 114) or a prepositional phrase (GAG, 209 § 115n).

§ 452 According to Kouwenberg, for OA, in a compound preposition, the first element following the genitive marker *ša* is omitted (GOA § 14.3.1). This does not seem different in MA, e.g., the following phrases of *ša (ina) libbi*.

> *ša lìb-bi* G[I]G^{meš} 'from the arrows' MARV 1 26:5
>
> 2 UDU^{meš} (…) *ša lìb-bi* UDU^{meš} *ša* PN 'two sheep from among the sheep of PN' A 3199 (NTA, 41):1–6
>
> *ay*[*a-n*]*u ša* ŠÀ *ni-iḫ-r*[*i-ú*]*-ni* 'where is (the barley) from (that) which we dug out?' T 96-36:23–24
>
> *ša* ŠÀ ŠE-*im*^{meš} 'from among the barley' A 981:6'
>
> *ša* ŠÀ 10 MA.NA DU$_{8}$.LÀL 'which is from the 10 minas of wax' A 1065:3
>
> ⸢*ša*⸣ ŠÀ *gi-na-*[*e*] 'which is from the *ginā*ʾ*u*-offering' MARV 7 87:6
>
> ½ MA.NA *ṣip-pu-tu*^{meš} *ša* ŠÀ GUN *ṣip-pe-*⸢*te*⸣ 'half a mina of *ṣipputu*, which is from one talent of *ṣipputu*' MARV 10 49:1–2

However, *ina* is preserved in the compound preposition *ša ina pî*:

> [*ṣab*]*ʾu nakru ša i+na pi-i* GN [*i*]*ḫbutūni* 'the hostile troops that plundered at the entrance of GN' MATSH 7:17''–18''

Other cases where the prepositions are omitted are discussed in the individual sections. The situation is more complicated for the compound preposition *ina muḫḫi*. A distinction is made between the genitive marker *ša* (omission > *ša muḫḫi*) and the relative pronoun *ša* (preservation = *ša ina muḫḫi*). See the discussion and examples in § 463.

13.3.1 *bēt*

§ 453 According to Streck (1997, 273) we find the compound preposition *ana bēt* in MATSH 2, which is otherwise limited to NA. Freydank (2016b, 106) reads Ú instead of É.

> *ina panīya panē a-na* É *qa-qe-re tariṣ* 'before me with face it was placed on the ground' MATSH 2:13–14

13.3.2 *battubattēn* 'both sides'

§ 454 This word is only once attested in MA (cf. GAG § 115r) and derives from a reduplicated *battu* 'side' (AHw, 115b).

> *i+na bat-tu-ba-te-en ša ka-nu-ni* 'on both sides of the brazier' New Year Ritual:18'

That its etymology is a reduplicated *battu* 'side' becomes clear from some semi-attestations (cf. CAD B, 169):

> *mussa bēta a-na ba-at-te ušēšibši* 'her husband settles her elsewhere' MAL A § 36:83–84

> 2 $^{\text{na4}}$*uḫinnu ša pappardalīe bat-ta ù bat-ta šaknū* 'two date stones of agate placed on both sides' BE 17 91:5

> *ina rāṭ siparre a-na be-ta-te iyāmattu ana ṭēmīšu lišpuk* 'may he pour it into a bronze tub separately, each into its mould(?)' KAV 205:28–29

13.3.3 *bere* 'among, between'

§ 455 While OA is the only Akkadian dialect that uses *bari* (CAD B, 246), in MA, the Common Akkadian variant *beri* is found as the value <be> (BAD) is preferred over <bi> (KAŠ). This is probably a case in which /r/ colours the preceding /a/ > /e/. Babylonian uses *biri* (GAG, 210 § 115q). It should be noted that *beri* always takes a pronominal suffix. It is attested a number of times following *ša*, where the preposition is, in some cases, omitted.

ana beri:

> *a-na be-*⌜*ri*?⌝*-šu-nu* 'among themselves' (full clause) MARV 4 114:4'

ina beri:

> *ša i+na be-ri-šu-nu i-pa-si-lu-ni* 'whoever among them that distorts' KAJ 1:25

> *i+na bi-ri-šu-nu tar-ṣú-ma* 'among each other they are *t.*' KAJ 39:15

The preposition *beri* occurs three times with a locative. It is also attested in OA (GOA § 14.5.3). The locative version is probably preceded by *ina*, but this preposition is omitted twice following *ša*.

> 21 *mašku*^{meš} *ša be-ru-šu-nu* '21 hides are (owned by) them jointly' KAJ 225:14

i+na be-ru-un-ni 'among us' MARV 2 5:12, 13

ša be-ru-šu-nu šalim 'which is paid in full(?) among them' MARV 2 12:9

Without pronominal suffixes, the longer form *berti* is used. Attestations remain very limited.

ina berti:

i+na ber-ti KUR^{meš}*-ni usbāku* 'I dwell between the mountains' MATSH 12:29

On one occasion, the preposition *ina* is omitted, as it follows *ša*; thus we find *ša berte:*

šigare$^{\text{sic.}}$ *ša be-er-ti* ⌜KÁ⌝ 'the lock that is between the gate' Aššur Ritual ii 4'

ša be-er-te i-ga-ra-te 'which is between the walls' KAJ 119:4–5

13.3.4 *eberti* 'the other side'

§ 456 This preposition is derived from the substantive *ebertu* 'the other side'. It is found in MA in prepositional usage, as well as in adverbial usage (see Chapter 14). According to the CAD (E, 9f; cf. AHw, 182a; UGM, 100), it can also be used as a preposition; in MA, we find the following examples:

20 *iku eqalšu damqu e-be-er-ti Ši-iš-ša-ar* '20 *iku* of his good fields across the Šiššar' KAJ 14:9–10 (Adn/Sa)

3 *iku* (…) *e-bir*$_5$*-ti Ši-šar* 'three *iku* (…) across the Šiššar' KAJ 149:2–4 (Aub); cf. KAJ 20:11 (EAd); KAJ 135:6 (M 9); KAJ 151:2–3 (Aub)

1 *me iku eqlu dunnu u adru e-be-er-ti Ši-iš-ša-ar* '100 *iku* field, a *dunnu* and threshing floor across the Šiššar' KAJ 177:2 (Aššnīr II)

e-be-er-ti Ši-šar$^!$ 'across the Šiššar' KAJ 146:2 (Aub)

[*n*] *iku eqlu* [*e*]-⌜*be-er*⌝*-ti Ši-iš-šar* '*n iku* field across the Šiššar' KAM 10 4:2 (Aub)

§ 457 There is a considerable number of passages where *ebertu* is followed by the ending -*ān*, written as *-A-AN*. This resembles the nominative dual ending *-ān*. However, this interpretation is problematic as, in the first examples, it follows the preposition *iltu*, such that we should expect the oblique ending *-īn*. Saporetti seems to prefer to read the composite sign <àm> (e.g., on MAL M in DSC 2, 179). It is difficult to decide which reading is favourable, as *ebert-A-AN* occurs roughly in the same context as *eberti*.

lu iš-tu e-be$^!$*-er-ta*$^!$*-a-an e-be-ra* 'or crossed from the other side' MAL M § 2:9

ina qaqqere paṣīutti e-be-er-ta-a-an A.GÀR URU 'on cleared terrain from across the meadow of the city' KAJ 175:2–3 (EAd/Aub)

20 *iku eqlu e-be-er-ta-a-*[*an* …] '20 *iku* field across (…)' KAJ 9:5 (M 9)

1 *iku eqalšu e-bir*$_5$*-ta*$^!$*-a-an* A.GÀR 'one *iku* of his field, across the meadow' KAJ 19:11–13 (Aub)

nāru e-bir$_5$*-ta-a-an* A.GÀR 'river across the meadow' KAJ 142:10–11 (Aub); KAJ 27:13–14 (EAd).

[*n*] *iku eqalšu e-be-er-ta-a-an a-ḫi* GN '*n iku*, his field, on the other side of the bank of GN' MARV 1 20:12–13 (EAd)

One may argue that a simple reading *a-an* is preferred over <*àm*>, which would be a case of unexpected mimation in MA. A form of *ebirta* without mimation or nunation, is attested in a text, which is considerably later than other non-literary texts: *e-bir-ta ina* GN 'on the other side, in GN' KAJ 129:10–11 (Ad). It seems that, in this phrase, *ebirta* is used as an adverb rather than a preposition. Moreover, while *ebirta(m)* would not be limited to MA, spellings with A-AN would be (CAD E, 8b), but defective spellings of *ebirtān* are also known outside MA (CAD E, 8–9).

13.3.5 *ellān(u)* 'above, over'

§ 458 Prepositions derived from the root *elāʾu* are rare in MA, for example, the preposition *eli*, '(up)on, over', common in Babylonian, is not found in MA. Similarly, *ellān* is only attested in a handful of texts. The preposition appears to be built out of the base *elli+ān(um)*. It is included in the dictionaries under the lemma *elēnu* (AHw, 198; CAD E, 83), which shows that *ellānu* may be the Assyrian variant. Nonetheless, *ellānu* ended up in some late Babylonian texts and NA royal inscriptions. NB letters seems to have *elēnu* (Woodington 1983, 174).

el-la-an a-li ina muḫḫi larīe 'above the a., on the branches' KTN inventory i 30

il-la-nu-ka naplis 'look after yourself' MARV 1 22:6–7

Furthermore, note its occurrence in Māri MA royal inscriptions:

i+na el-la-an GN 'upwards from GN' Maul 1992, 22:2

13.3.6 *libbu* 'heart'

§ 459 The noun *libbu* (ŠÀ) 'heart' can be combined with *ana/ina* in MA, where it is used to indicate a centre.[16] In combination with *ana*, it has an allative meaning and indicates the direction of the verb. Usually, it is used to refer to where something is stored or placed (cf. OA in GOA § 14.5.5).

a-na Š[À U]DUN *ikarrurūšunu* 'they will throw them into the oven' MAPD § 19:94

a-na lìb-bi takarrar 'you will pour it into (the bowl)' PKT 1 I right:6

a-na lìb-bi ^{giš}*tup-ni-na-te ṣilʾā* 'lay it down inside the boxes' KAV 98:24–25

a-na lìb-be ŠE-*im maḫ-ri lā kamir* 'it is not stored among the received barley' MARV 2 20:28

a-na lìb-be-ši-na [...] 'on them(?)' KAJ 277:6

a-na ŠÀ KASKAL-*ni* (...) *karru* 'they (arrows) are deducted (from stock) on the road' MARV 1 10:13–14

a-na lìb-bi lā kamir 'it is not added to it' MARV 9 112:22

16 Cf. GAG, 208 § 115d; MB: Aro (1955a, 103–104); NA: SNAG, 72 § 3.8.2. The noun *libbu* can also be found in the literal meaning 'heart' e.g., *a-na a-ma-ri-ki-na l*[*ìb-bi*] *i-ṣe-ḫa-an-ni* 'my heart was happy to see you' T 93-8a:11–12; cf. A 845:9–10 (see CAD Ṣ, 65a).

With *ina*, the prepositional phrase can have different meanings. The phrase can have a locative meaning 'at, in its midst'. In combination with plural pronominal suffixes the meaning changes to 'among them'.

Locative:

[*iltēn aḫu*] *i+na lìb-bi-šu-nu* 'one brother among them' MAL B § 4:28

šumma i+na lìb-bi-šu-nu lā magruttu ibašši 'if there are unwilling people among them' MAL B § 17:10–11

šamnu^{meš} *i+na lìb-b*[*i-š*]*u tabek* 'oil is poured in it' Coronation Ritual i 33

*ṣab*ʾ*u annūtu marṣuttu ša* ŠÀ ^{giš}MÁ *lā iddinū* 'these men sick inside the boat (…) did not give' MARV 1 71:38–40

More commonly, the prepositional phrase *ina libbi* has an ablative meaning:

i+na ŠÀ *an-ni-ma* 'from this: (list follows)' Adad Ritual:3

i+na lìb-bi (…) *maḫir* 'it was received from (PN$^{?}$)' A 1051:6-8

40 *em*[*āru*] ŠE-*um* (...) *i+na lìb-bi* ŠE *ša* É.GAL-*lim* '40 homers of barley (…) from the barley of the palace' MATSH 1:5–6

ša pî tuppi (...) *ša i+na lìb-bi-ša akkīa šaṭrūni* 'in accordance with the tablet on which is written thus' KAJ 159:4–5

i+na lìb-bi-šu-nu 1 *emeru* (…) *paqdū* 'from among them, one sheep was entrusted' A 1737 (NTA, 19):7–12

*ṣab*ʾ*u Šelenāyū u piqd*[*ū*] *ša i+na* ŠÀ [*ši*]-*luḫ-li* (…) *eliūni* 'the Šelenean-people and entrusted representatives who went up from among the *siluḫlu*-people' MARV 1 28:13–17

i+na lìb-bi ŠE É.GAL-*lim* from the barley of the palace' MATSH 1:6

20 *šiltāḫē i+na lìb-bi-šu ētapaš* 'I made 20 arrows from it' MATSH 16:7–8

i+na ŠÀ GIŠ^{meš} *ša āle lēpušū* 'May they make it from the wood of the city' A 1476 r. 5'–7'

13.3.7 IGI = *maḫar*$^{?}$

§ 460 On a list of witnesses of legal documents, the reading of this logogram is not entirely clear, since it could refer to both the prepositional *panu* and *maḫru*. The latter is more common in the context of witness lists in Mesopotamian scribal culture.[17] It appears not to be an actual preposition, since inflected PNs that follow it occur in the nominative.

IGI *Bu-ḫu-nu* KAJ 25:19; KAM 10 26:26 (cf. OMA 1, 183)

IGI ^{d}UTU-*ki-di-nu* KAJ 8:25 (cf. OMA 1, 441)

One TSA text has the phonetic complement *-bu* on the witness lists, which strongly suggests a reading of *šēbu* 'witness', with the PN following in apposition, e.g., IGI-*bu* in T 97-37:18, 19, 21, 23. If this is the case, MA legal documents follow NA practice where the

17 See MZL, 407 no. 725; cf. OA in GOA § 14.5.6.

transcription of *šēbu* for the logogram IGI has been known for some time.[18] Otherwise, our attestations of the prepositional *maḫru* are very limited. We only once find the prepositional phrase *ina maḫar* written syllabically in a literary text:

> *i+na ma-ḫar Aš-šur* DINGIR-*ka* 'before Aššur, your god' Coronation Ritual ii 33

13.3.8 *muḫḫu* 'top'

§ 461 While *muḫḫu* does not occur in OA (GAG, 208 § 115h), it is frequently found in MA in a number of prepositional expressions. Spellings are logographic, with or without a phonetic complement (UGU ~ UGU-*ḫi* to be read *muḫ-ḫi*). Alternatively, we find *mu-ḫi* on a number of occasions in early texts (KAJ 23:5; KAJ 66:4 etc.; see also TSA *mu-ḫi-ia* T 93-11:21). Interestingly, phonetic complements are not used in combination with the preposition *ana*, albeit with a limited number of exceptions in the peripheral letters (e.g., *a-na muḫ-ḫi-ia* KBo 28 82:10; RS 06.198:8; RS 85.54:10). In the absence of a better explanation, we must regard this uneven distribution as being due to chance.

§ 462 The phrase *ana muḫḫi* indicates the direction 'towards', which seems to have mostly replaced *ana panē* in this function (see below), as such a prepositional phrase is not found in OA.

> *a-na* UGU LÚ (…) *ta-ta-lak* 'she has gone to a man' MAL A § 13:26–27
>
> *lū a-na* UGU LUGAL *lū ana muḫḫi dayyānē ittabla* 'he has brought (them) either before the king or before judges' MAL A § 15:47–48
>
> *aʾīla a-na* UGU-*ša tultērib* 'she has brought the man upon her' MAL A § 23:30–31
>
> *tuppa* (…) *a-na* UGU *lā magrutte ilaqqe* 'he will take the tablet to those who do not agree' MAL B § 18:32–34
>
> *tuppaka a-na* UGU PN *šuṭar*^sic.^ 'write your tablet to PN' KAV 104:21–22
>
> *a-na* UGU ⌜LUGAL⌝ *ana tarāṣe tadnaš*[*šu*] 'it is given to the king in order to expand(?)' MARV 10 45:19–21
>
> *a-na* UGU LÚ *ittablašu* 'he has brought it to the man' MARV 10 59:9

Note also the following expression:

> *a-na* UGU *du-a-ki telli* 'you are approaching death' OIP 79 3:19–20

It is also attested in a slightly different form without *muḫḫu*:

> *adi rēssu lā inaššiūne*[*nni*] *a-na du-a-ki la še-li-na-ni-ni* 'as long as they do not bring his head here, do not put me to death' T 02-3:22–25

With pronominal suffixes:

> *a-na* UGU-*ia-ma lublūni* 'may they bring (it) to me' KAV 98:35
>
> *a-na* UGU-*ia šēbilāne* 'send it to me' KAV 100:26
>
> *a-na* UGU-*ia illukūne* 'they will come to me' OIP 79 2:7

18 See Postgate (1973, 46); also, MZL, 407 no. 724.

a-na [U]GU-*šu tabik* 'it is poured out upon it' MARV 2 22:5

a-na UGU-*k*[*a*] *ultēbilašš*[*i*] 'I will have sent her to you' VAT 8851:13–14

§ 463 The expression *ina muḫḫi* 'on top of' is spatial, as it refers specifically to something that is on top of the object.

i+na UGU DAM LÚ *ikšudūš* 'they have caught him on top of (another man's) wife' MAL A § 12:20

i-na UGU ^{túg}*bir-še* 'on top of the felt' Coronation Ritual ii 25

peʾetta i+na muḫ-ḫi itabbak 'he will lay down charcoal on top of it' New Year Ritual:13'–14'

ṣubāta$^{\text{ḫi.a}}$ *i+na* UGU ^{giš}GU.ZA *liškun* 'may he place the textiles upon the throne' Snell 1983/84:16–17

Alternatively, *ina muḫḫi* means 'concerning'. Von Soden rightfully translates 'zu Lasten von'.

i+na UGU *tap-pa-i-šu abāta iškun* 'he started rumours about his friend' MAL A § 19:83

12 *mana annuku* (…) *i+na muḫ-ḫi* PN *ilqe* '12 minas of lead, it is (incumbent) on PN, he took it' KAJ 11:2–7 passim in KAJ

i+na UGU-*šu lā idabbub* 'he will not complain against him' KAJ 102:12–13

i+na UGU *šal-mi-šu-nu ù ke-ni-šu-nu ṣarpu rakis* 'the silver is bound on their credibility and legal position' VAT 8873:9–12

ša dēna dabāba i+na UGU-*šu ubtaʾʾuʾūni* 'whoever seeks a case and complaints against him' Franke/Wilhelm 1985:5–6

i+na UGU *Šu-ub-ri-e* (…) *lā amlik lā ašpuršunu* 'concerning the Hurrians, I did not counsel nor write them' A 2994:6–9

Following *ša*, the prepositional phrase *ina muḫḫi* is used to indicate someone's responsibility over something. This stands in relation to the phrase *ina pitte* (see below), to indicate that something is in someone's responsibility. The preposition *ina* is omitted following the genitive marker *ša*, not including clauses where the latter functions as a relative pronoun (see below).[19] This is frequently attested in the administrative documents and some lexicalized constructions, e.g.,

10 ANŠE ŠE *ša* UGU PN '10 homers of barley of the responsibility of PN' KAJ 110:7–8

PN *ša* UGU É 'PN the housemaster' KAJ 123:6–7

ša UGU É '(the official) responsible for the house' KAV 99:19

ŠE-*im* LAL.ME *ša* UGU ^{lú}MÁ.LAḪ$_5$ *lā šēlu* 'the deducted barley was not added to the responsibility of the shipper' MARV 2 20:28–29

PN *ša* UGU A.ŠÀ 'PN who is responsible for the field' MARV 4 106:9–10

19 See GAG, 208 § 115h; GOA § 14.3.1.

ana PN *ša* UGU ANŠE.KUR.RA^{meš} 'for PN, (the official) in charge of the donkeys' MARV 8 51:19–21

PN *ša* ⌜UGU ANŠE.KUR.RA^{meš}⌝ 'PN, responsible for the horses' T 93-2:9–19

In its function as a relative pronoun, *ina* is retained. The difference between the two types is further strengthened by the presence of a subjunctive.

ša i+na UGU LUGAL [*an*]*a ḫurāde* (…) *illikūni* 'who went with the king on campaign' MARV 4 27:21–22

ša i+na UGU PN *šaknūni* 'which are added to the debt of PN' MARV 1 30:18–19

ša i+na UGU PN (…) *šaṭrutūni* 'which was recorded in the debt of PN' KAJ 114:6; cf. KAJ 115:4

2 *emmeru*$^{pl.}$ *ša i+na* UGU PN 'two sheep, which (are incumbent) on PN' KAJ 120:13–14

ša i+na UGU-*šu iššaknūni* 'that is placed upon him (as debt)' MARV 3 55:14'–15'

§ 464 Combinations with *adi* are rare; a handful of passages can be given with two different meanings:

adi muḫḫi 'until; up to':

iltu muḫḫi marʾe rabīe a-di UGU DUMU *ṣe-eḫ-ri* 'from the oldest son up to the youngest son' MAL A § 43:24–25

šarra a-di UGU *ina* ^{giš}GU.ZA *ina la-ba-ni naṣṣū* 'they carry the king up until this point on a throne on (their) neck' Coronation Ritual ii 48–49

adi muḫḫi 'while':

a-di UGU *ša ḫarr*[*āni*] 'while on journey' MAL M § 3:4

13.3.9 *panū* 'front, face'

§ 465 Both *ana* and *ina* occur in combination with *panu* 'front, face', involving various meanings to indicate the direction of movement, location and tempora. For adverbial usage, see § 496. Morphologically, *pan(i)* is difficult, as there are two frequent variations. One of them has a vowel /i/ attached to the base, including the preceding pronominal suffixes. This form is common in OA, where plene spellings led Kouwenberg to the assumption about a plural form *panē* (GOA § 14.5.8). A plural form *panū* may be attested: *pa-ni-šu ana panē ili bēte iša*[*kkan*] 'he will set his attention to the temple' Aššur Ritual ii 6'. In this phrase, the vowel /i/ can only present the oblique of the dual/plural, or be part of the stem of the noun. Another case is the logographic IGI^{meš}-*ki-n*[*a*] T 93-8a:13, although one may argue that this refers to multiple faces of multiple people. In MA, no plene spellings of *panu* are known to me (only *pa-a-ni* MPR 66:43) and thus a short vowel must be assumed. There is no obvious difference in meaning, nor is there a different distribution over the corpora, although it should be noted that, in the M 6 archive (NtA), *ana pan* is preferred, while, in the MATSH correspondence, we always find *ana pani*. This points to a personal preference of scribes to favour one variant over another (cf. MB Aro 1955a, 107). NA seems to favour *pan*, judging by the examples gathered by Hämeen-Anttila. Both combinations with *ana* and *ina* occur, while forms without both are also frequent (SNAG, 73–74 § 3.8.2). It seems possible that the short form *pan* is influenced by Babylonian, where the short form seems to have become common (cf. GAG, 209 § 115l). Spellings with the logographic IGI can be found in combination with the preposition *ana*. In the case of the logographic spelling IGI, it is not entirely certain whether to read *pan(ē)* or *maḫar*. The latter is attested syllabically in the Coronation Ritual, but its absence in other texts suggests that the reading *pan(ē)* is preferable.

§ 466 As for its function, we have already stated that *ana pan(ē)* indicates a motion of direction, usually towards a location (allative), i.e., 'to'.[20] This is sometimes indeed the case, but, in many examples, the said meaning is lacking. An actual direction, similar to the (also present) ventive, can best be observed in the examples below:

a-na pa-ni LUGAL [*u*]*qarrabanni* 'he will bring it before the king' MATSH 12:24–25

iltu ammāka ṭēma a-na pa-ni-ia lilqeūni 'from there, they must bring news to me here' MATC 9:9–11

However, *ana pan(ē)* usually seems to have an allative function, indicating the goal of motion, which is characteristic of late second millennium Akkadian.[21] In this case, it is not an object of the predicate, but indicates an adverbial element. It should be noted that *ana pan(ē)* is often used before DNs, especially in administrative documents. In this context, *ana pan(ē)* is used to indicate being in front of the object or opposite to where it is placed (Aro 1955a, 107). At the same time, *ina pan(ē)* seems to be used in similar contexts (see below), where no real difference is distinguishable.

ša a-na pa-ni ÉRIN^{meš} *lā paṣṣunutūni* 'who is not veiled in public' MAL A § 41:5–6

a-na pa-an MAN *ikarrurū* 'they will lay (it) down before the king' Coronation Ritual iii 9

a-na pa-ni qé-pu-⸢ú-te⸣ liškunū 'may they place (it) before the officials' MAL B § 6:17

a-na pa-ni ^{d}AMAR.UTU *eppaš* 'he will do before Marduk' New Year Ritual:22'

[1] *emmeru* (…) *a-na pa-an* DN (…) *epiš* 'one sheep was sacrificed before DN' A 1765 (NTA, 25):1–6 cf. A 2609 (NTA, 29):13–15 cf. Ali 7:7

tuppa dannata a-na pa-ni LUGAL *išaṭṭar* 'he will write a strong tablet in the presence of the king' KAJ 153:18–19

1 *emmeru a-na* IGI DN 'one sheep (is sacrificed) in the presence of DN' MARV 3 75 passim; cf. MARV 2 29; MARV 6 76 passim

a-na pa-ni-ka adaggal 'I will wait for you' (lit. 'I will look at your face') MATC 1:9–10

marāšu a-na pa-ni ^{d}IM *iššiššu* 'he dedicated his son before Adad' KAJ 179:3–4

a-na pa-ni-šu-nu šuknā 'place it before them' KAV 98:13

ṣabʾu anniu šēbuttu ša a-na pa-ni-ka ubaʾʾerūni 'these people are the witnesses whom I established in your presence' MCS 2 1:9–11

ṭēma a-na pa-ni-ia lilqeūni 'they must bring the message to me' MATC 9:10–11

20 Cf. OA in GOA § 14.5.8.1; MB in Aro (1955a, 107).
21 See GAG, 209 § 115l; MB in Aro (1955a, 107).

a-na pa-an [*ša*]*r-ri lā terra*[*b*] 'she shall not enter before the king' MAPD § 7:47

Often, *ana panē* stands in the context of a verbal predicate of speech (e.g., *qabāʾu* 'to say'), but it is not part of direct speech. One would expect that *ana pan(ē)* is used as an indirect object to whom the speech is addressed, but again it seems to involve location, e.g., speaking before a statue of a god.

a-na IGI ÉRIN^meš^ *iqbiaššu* 'he said to him in public' MAL A § 19:85–86

a-na pa-ni DN *iqabbi* 'he shall declare before the god' MAL A § 47:16

a-na pa-ni ^d^IM *inaddiā* 'they will recite before Adad' Adad Ritual:4

a-na pa-ni-ia taddubub 'you spoke in my presence' KAV 201:10–11

a-na pa-an LUGAL E[N-*š*]*u* [*akk*]*īa iqṭibi* 'he spoke thus before the king, his lord' KAV 217:9'–10'

a-na pa-ni MUNUS.LUGAL-*ti sisima* 'read it before the queen' RS 06.198:15–16

ana pan 'upon' instead of expected *ina muḫḫi*:

1 *emmera* (…) *a-na pa-an pe-ʾe-te uštabšilū*^sic.^ 'they roasted one sheep upon charcoal' A 1748 (NTA, 8):9–11

ana panē 'in accordance with'; it is unclear, as it could be similar to the unattested *kī panē* 'at will' in MA (MATC, 57; cf. AHw, 819b):

alākta a-na pa-ni-šu-nu utarrūni 'they will continue the journey at (their) will' MATC 18:8–9

§ 467 The prepositional phrase *ina pan(ē)* is only attested a few times and with various different meanings (cf. GOA § 14.5.8.2).

Locative *ina pan(ē)* 'on':

šumma 1 *aʾīlu* (…) *i+na pa-ni pa-ḫi-ti-šu lu*^!^ URU *iṣbat* 'if one man settled on (the land of) his province or city' MARV 4 119:25–26

In a semi-locative function, *ina pan(ē)* is used in a more literary sense 'before the face of' or 'in the presence of':

i+na pa-ni-šu ana bēte erāba lâlaʾʾe 'I am not able to enter the house in his presence' MATSH 12:27–28

akla^meš^ *i+na pa-ni-ia ekkulūni* 'they eat bread in my presence' T 93-3:18–19

ubruttu i+na p[*a-n*]*i* PN *akla*^meš^ *ētanakkulū* 'the delegates eat bread in the presence of PN' T 97-10:15–17

alpēšu gabba lupaḫḫira i+na pa-ni-ka lu[*š*]*azziz* 'may he gather all his oxen and station (them) to your presence' T 97-17:8–11

ša i+na pa-ni na-ak-ri lā inniṣidūni 'which could not be harvested in the presence of the enemy' LVUH 79:11–12

ina ḫūle i+na pa-ni-ia iltaʾlanni 'on the road, in my presence, he asked me' MATC 15:11–12

Temporal *ina panē* 'at the beginning of':

2 ITI 12 UD^{meš}*-ti i+na pa-ni* MU *eppaš* ''he will do work for two months, 12 days at the beginning of the year (=spring)' KAJ 99:7–8

ina panē 'within':

i+na pa-ni 5 MU^{meš} *ana mute tattašab* 'within five years, she has lived with (another) husband' MAL A § 36:8–9

ina panē 'before (temporal)':

i+na pa-ni-šu ma-am-ma lā ēriš 'nobody requested it before him' KAJ 177:13–14

i+na pa-ni na-áš-pér-te ša bēlīya ana Libbi-āle ēt[*abra*] 'he entered the Inner City (Aššur) before the writing of my lord' MATSH 13:11–12

ina panē in its ablative function 'from' is attested a few times, mostly in similar clauses in MAL A:

i+na pa-ni mu-ti-ša ramanša taltadad 'she has withdrawn herself from the presence of her husband' MAL A § 24:41–42 cf. MAL A § 24:72–73, 77–78

šumma i+na pa-ni mu-ra-ri-[*t*]*i lā išallim* 'If he does not obtain compensation from the *m*-field' KAJ 148:29–30

§ 468 We have already discussed how, following *ša*, the prepositions *ana* and *ina* are frequently omitted. This is attested a number of times with the prepositional phrases *ina/ana pan(ē)*. A few examples, with various functions, such as those given above, follow:

a[*būsā*]*tu ša <i+na> pa-ni-š*[*u*] 'the stall, which is in front of it' VAT 8923:13–14

adi ruqqe ša <i+na> pa-ni-šu ša siparre 'with a cauldron, which is in front of it, of bronze' KTN inventory iv 14'

ina pūre ša <i+na> pa-ni ḫa-ri-be-ti 'on the lot that is situated (facing) the wasteland' KAJ 164:3

áššum piqitte ša <a+na> pa-ni ÉRIN^{meš} 'concerning the rations, which are for the troops' MATSH 10:16-17

[*mimma a*]*nniu išḫu ša <i+na> pa-ni Aš-šur* 'all this *assignment*, which is before Aššur' MARV 3 16 i 8'

ša bēt asaʾīti ša <a+na> pa-ni KÁ *tabik* 'which is poured at the tower house, which is opposite the gate' LVUH 86:12

Once, *panē* is used without the preposition *ana/ina* preceding an infinitive:

1 *šappu* (…) *pa-ni ta-ú-ri* 'one vessel set for returning' KAV 98:30

13.3.10 *pû* 'mouth'

§ 469 It has previously been suggested that *ina/ana pî* could be regarded as a prepositional expression.[22] This more or less seems to be a misnomer, as the combination is not used prepositionally and *pû* is often used in a literary sense. Postgate (1986, 29) notes that *pû*, within administrative documents, refers to the wording of a tablet, rather than an actual mouth. Possibly for this reason, it is not mentioned in the NA (SNAG, 70ff § 3.8.2.) or NB

22 See Aro (1955a, 110); UGM, 100; GAG, 210 § 115t.

(Woodington 1983, 176ff § 76) grammars. Spellings have already been discussed on multiple occasions; see § 153 and § 259.

§ 470 In MA, we find *ana pî* used once with a motion verb to indicate the movement of direction. In this case, we would usually expect *ana pani*. The exception seems to be caused by the understanding of buildings or other inanimate objects, which have a *pû* rather than a *pan(ē)* (CAD P, 469b). As attestations without prepositions show, these are not real prepositional phrases; rather, *pû* is meant as an actual element of an inanimate object.

a-na pi-i É.GAL*-lim ubbalašši* 'he will bring her to the palace entrance' MAL A § 40:71

i+na pi-i ḫu-li-šu-nu 'at the entrance of their processional residence' MAPD § 21:112

IŠ-TU pi-i ḫu-ú-[*li*] *upaṭ*[*ṭarši*]*na* 'he will clear them from the entrance of the processional residence' MAPD § 21:112

i-na pi-i ^na4^KIŠIB*-ia kunukkēkunu kunkā* 'seal my seal with your seals' KAV 105:23–24

ša i+na pi-i GN [*i*]*ḫbutūni* 'who plundered at the entrance of GN' MATSH 7:17''–18''

More common is the meaning 'in accordance with'. This is usually related to the wording of a tablet or any type of (spoken) message:

a-na pa-i tup-pé-e 'according to the wording of the tablet' KAJ 6:4

a-na pi-i PN (…) *ša*[*ṭ*]*ir* 'it is written in accordance with the wording of PN' KAV 156:3

[*a+n*]*a pi-i tup-pi ša ma-mi-te ša nitmuʾūni* 'in accordance with the wording of the tablet of the oath which we swore' KAV 217:14'

[*šumma mam*]*ma a-na pi-i* PN (…) *lā imtagrūni* 'if somebody does not agree with PN' Snell 1983/84:13–15

i+na KA*-i tup-pi akkīa išakkan* 'in the wording of the tablet, he will put as follows' KAJ 83:17–18 (cf. CAD A_1, 266)

[*a-n*]*a pi-šu šukuššu* 'instruct him according to his word' MATC 11:31

We have already mentioned how, following *ša*, prepositional phrases omit the first term *ana/ina*. As can be seen in the following examples, this is also attested with *pû*:

ša KA*-i tup-pi* (...) *ša ina libbiša akkīa šaṭrūni* 'in accordance with the tablet on which is written thus' KAJ 159:4–5

tuppa ša pi-i an-ni-te-ma altaṭar 'I have written the tablet of this wording' MATSH 22:22–23

kunukkī (…) *ša pi-i* ^giš^*tup-ni-na-te naṣṣū* 'they bring my seal for the opening of the boxes' KAV 98:7–10

13.3.11 *ina pitte* 'in the responsibility of'

§ 471 Another common, albeit limited, prepositional phrase is *ina pitti* 'in the responsibility of' (GAG, 210 § 115s; cf. SNAG, 75). It is usually found in administrative documents, as well as a few letters (CAD P, 443–44):

i+na pi-ti PN 'in the responsibility of PN' KAJ 261:3–4

ša iš-t[u] PN *pi-it-ti* 'from the responsibility of PN' KAJ 238:5–6

i+na pi-ti ša UGU É-*ma lū šaknat* 'may it be placed in the responsibility of the housemaster' KAV 99:41–42

suḫīrta le'atta ša i+na pi-ti PN *ēzibanni* 'the usable foal, which I left in the responsibility of PN' MATC 3:9–13

1 *alpu šēbu ša i+na pi-ti* PN 'one old ox in the responsibility of PN' LVUH 41:16–17

Literary:

i+na pi-it ^{giš}GU.ZA <broken context> Coronation Ritual ii 47†

It seems that, when pronominal suffixes are added, an archaic form with locative ending is applied, i.e., *ina pittu(m)*-. These forms are discussed in § 487.

13.3.12 *qablum* 'middle'

§ 472 This is very rarely used in compound prepositions (but GAG, 208 § 115f; cf. GOA § 14.5.12):

i+na qa-bal É.GAL-*lim* 'in the centre of the palace' MAPD § 21:111

ša rēš qa-bal É-*te šaknū<ni>* 'which are placed on top, inside of the house' KAJ 240:16–17

With the omitted *ana/ina* following *ša*:

ša qa-bal tar-ba-ṣi 'in the middle of the animal stall' MATC 81:15

13.3.13 *qātu* 'hand'

§ 473 The noun *qātu* 'hand' occurs in combination with *ana* and *ina*, largely confined to stock phrases from legal documents. It is, in most cases, written logographically as ŠU.

ana qāt 'to the extent of':

a-na qa-at 5 MA.NA AN.NA *tuttattir* 'it exceeded five minas of lead' MAL A § 5:59–60

a-na qa-at 6 MU^{meš} *uḫḫiranni* 'if he is delayed beyond six years' MAL A § 36:103–104 cf. § 36:6

ana qāt 'to the hand of':

mā'ē a-na [Š]U DN *sangû inašši* 'the priest will bring the water to DN' New Year Ritual:19'

Ablative *ina qāt* 'from the possession of':

ša i+na qa-at DAM-*at* LÚ *imḫurūni* 'who received (something) from (another man's) wife' MAL A § 3:40–41

i+na qa-ti-šu-nu iṣṣabtū 'they caught them in the act' MAL A § 47:3

⸢*i*⸣*+na qa-at ṭé-em* PN (…) *lā nilammudūni* '(since) we are not finding out the news of PN' MATSH 11:6–8

i+na qa-at PN_1 PN_2 *maḫi[r]* 'from PN_1, PN_2 received it' KAJ 92:6–8

i+na ŠU PN_1 PN_2 *maḫir* 'from PN_1, PN_2 received it' MARV 7 12:11–14

i+na ŠU PN_1 PN_2 (…) *imtaḫar* 'from PN_1, PN_2 received it' KAJ 109:15–17

ŠE-*um*^{meš} *i+na qa-at* PN *ittakal* 'barley from the possession of PN was consumed' MARV 1 49:17–18

13.3.14 *šaplu* 'bottom'

§ 474 The noun *šaplu* 'bottom' is used in a number of different prepositional expressions (GAG, 208 § 115g). None of them is frequently attested.

ina šapal 'below':

i+na ša-pal ÚTU 'underneath the bowl' PKT 5:29

i+na šap-la-an GN *ētabrūni* 'they crossed over (the river) below GN' MATSH 6:18'

ša-pal sa-x[…] 'lower part of […]' KAJ 310:3

Once we find a variation with a locative case in *ana šaplušššu*:

a-na ⸢*šap*$^{?}$⸣*-lu-šu turad*[*di*] 'you will add to its bottom' PKT 4 r. left 9

It seems that *šaplu* could also be used independently in the genitive construction *(ša) šapal*:

išāta ša ša-pal ÚTUL 'fire that is below the bowl' PKT 3 iii 14 cf. *ša-pal* ÚTUL PKT 4 obv. left 14

ḫurše ša ša-pal$^{!}$ *si-mil-ti* 'the storage beneath the stairs' VAT 8921:3

^{giš}NÁ ⸢^{meš}⸣*-te ša ša-*⸢*pal* LUGAL⸣ 'the beds below (=used by) the king' MARV 10 14:7'–8'[23]

13.3.15 *tarṣu* 'extent/duration'

§ 475 The noun *tarṣu* 'extent/duration' is used in a number of compound prepositions (GAG, 210 § 115p; cf. SNAG, 76).

ana tarṣe 'towards' or 'opposite':

a-na tar-ṣi DN *ana 2-šu ibattuqū* 'opposite DN, they cut it in two' New Year Ritual:14'–15'

a-na ṭar-ṣi ^{uru}[*... att*]*alak* 'I went towards the city […]' MATSH 7:22''–23''

a-na tar-ṣi PN$_1$ *ù* PN$_2$ *billāte liblu*[*l*] 'may he mix the alloy in the presence of PN$_1$ and PN$_2$' KAV 205:23–25

a-na tar-ṣi-šu ana suqinni uṣṣa 'it goes out opposite of it to the alley' VAT 8923:4

Following *ša*, the preposition *ana* is omitted in this prepositional phrase. This is attested a number of times in the agriculture texts from Tell Aš-Šēḫ Ḥamad (LVUH), on each occasion in an identical context:

ša tar-ṣi KÁ *tabik* 'it is poured out opposite the gate' LVUH 84:3–4 cf. LVUH 82:26

13.3.16 *ṭiḫi* 'adjacent to'

§ 476 The preposition *ṭiḫi* is an original construct from *ṭiḫ*^{ʾ}*um* 'proximity', now used in the prepositional meaning 'adjacent to' (GOA § 14.5.20). Saporetti (1966, 276–77) discussed *tiḫi*, as expressed with the Sumerogram SUḪUR, highlighting the relation to syllabic writings (cf. AHw, 1383; MZL, 173 no. 646). Summarizing the discussion, the logographic

23 For the meaning of the logogram NÁ and the phrase in general, see the commentary in Prechel/Freydank (2014, 33).

reading seems to refer back to the palaeographic difference between <*ṭí*> (TÍ) and <*ḫi*> (ḪI) in OA. In MA, the two signs had merged into one sign, which resulted in a spelling of two identical signs following each other, e.g., *ṭé-ḫi* KAV 127:3. Apparently, some scribes had difficulties with this sequence, which perhaps resulted in spellings such as *TI-ḫi* Jankowska 1962:9. Another possible graphic solution was the insertion of a remnant of the old OA palaeographic form ḪI: (from TC 2, 5 no. 201). This form is visible, for instance, in the copy of KAJ 154:5. Accordingly, it is perhaps more correct to transcribe *ṭé-*^{ḫi}*ḫi* and abandon SUḪUR. The spelling is furthermore notable as a rare remnant of OA scribal traditions; cf. OA *ṭé-ḫi-i* KTK 103:17.

> *TI-ḫi ad-ri*$^{!}$ *š*[*a*] É PN 'adjacent to the threshing floor of the house of PN' Jankowska 1962:9
>
> *ṭí-ḫi* KASKAL *Lìb-bi*-URU 'adjacent to the road of Aššur' KAV 127:3
>
> SUḪUR A.ŠÀ 'adjacent to the earth' KAJ 13 passim
>
> SUḪUR *qa-qí-ri* 'adjacent to the ground' TR 2037:17
>
> *ša* SUḪUR É 'which is adjacent to the house' LVUH 76:21

13.3.17 *urki* 'after, behind'

§ 477 The preposition *urki* derives from *warki* according to the MA sound changes. It can be roughly translated with 'after' indicating something that follows either in place or time. Typically, its spelling is simply *ur-ki*; however, the logographic EGIR is also attested.

Place:

> *ur-ki a-ḫa-iš* 'after each other' MAL B § 1:7
>
> 1 *pitnu ša* EGIR$^{?}$ ^{giš}GU.ZA *izzazzū*<*ni*> 'one chest that stands behind the throne' KTN inventory iii 11'

Temporal:

> *ur-ki* ÉRIN^{meš} *ša* (...) *innabidūni* (…) *attalak* 'I went after the people who fled' MATSH 2:4
>
> *ṣabʾu gabbu ur-ki ba-la-a-ṭé ittaparku* 'all the soldiers disappeared after the provisions' MATSH 3:27–28
>
> *ša ur-ki* ⸢*an*⸣*-ni-e* MARV 4 151:42
>
> *ša ur-ki* ^{iti}[K]IMIN MARV 4 151:8
>
> *li-me* 2-⸢*e*$^{!?}$ *šá*⸣ EGIR PN 'the second eponym who (comes) after PN' MARV 7 91 r. 10'–11'
>
> *li-me ša* EGIR PN 'eponym who (comes) after PN' MARV 10 4:20'

Uncertain:

> *ur-ki an-ni-e* <broken context> MAL O § 2b:5; KBo 28 61 rd. 3'
>
> *ur-ki* A.ŠÀ-*šu* SIG_5 KAM 10 15:6

Once, we find *urkittu* used as a preposition. It seems that *urkittu* can be used as a bound form of *urki* in order to take a pronominal suffix. Note that *urkittu* is otherwise used adverbially (§ 495).

ur-ki-te-⸢*šu*⸣ *na-ak-ru ana* GN *imtuqut* 'after his (departure), the enemy attacked GN' MATSH 4:7–8

Chapter 14: Adverbs

§ 478 The category of adverbs is somewhat similar to adjectives, irrespective of whether they modify any word or part of a sentence, except for nouns (Valin 2001, 7). They are related to adverbial phrases and adverbial dependent clauses. Adverbial dependent clauses will be discussed in Chapter 21.2, whereas we will list here the most important stock adverbial phrases, together with the adverbs. Adverbs are one of the more neglected parts of Akkadian grammar. In this section, some short adverbial phrases are included, as they are expected to have been used frequently in the language. Some of these adverbial phrases were grammaticalized by the language itself and turned into compound time adverbials (cf. Ryding 2005, 293ff), e.g., *ūmakkal* (< *ūma(m)+kal*) 'every day=daily'. Alongside the adverbial accusative is a number of suffixes found on different adverbs. The most important ones are the terminative-adverbial *-iš* and the locative *-u(m)*. The terminative-adverbial denotes direction and can be compared to the preposition *ana*+genitive (GAG, 109 § 67a). However, the occurrence of preceding prepositions, which became common in MA when used as directives, takes away any function of the terminative (cf. GAG, 110 § 66b). Examples involving the terminative in a directive function are nonetheless rare and only occur with *eliš*:

> [*šumm*]*a eleppu lū iš-tu e-li-iš iqqalpua* 'if a boat drifts down' MAL M § 2:8
>
> *išātu a-na e-liš* [*tellia*] 'the fire goes up' PKT 1 II right 26
>
> *a-na e-li-iš it-ta-al-ka*! 'it went upwards' LVUH 87:13–14

Other forms of the terminative-adverbial are usually used for adverbs of manner, e.g., *arḫiš* 'quickly', *danniš* 'severely, very', *lemniš* 'badly' and *mādiš* 'greatly, very', all of which are discussed in § 489. The form *aḫāʾiš* 'together' occurs as the reciprocal pronoun 'each other', which is reviewed in § 383ff. Adverbs of number are found in § 488: *iltēniš* 'together'; *šanîš* 'secondly'. Adverbs of time are also found: perhaps *līdiš* 'day after tomorrow'; *šaddaqdiš* 'last year' (§ 493); *urkiš* 'afterwards' (see § 495).

14.1 Adverbs of location

14.1.1 Spatial deixis

§ 479 Akkadian uses a number of adverbs of location. These consist of two opposing pairs, the first being *anna-*, the proximal deixis, or whatever is close to the speaker. The opposite is *amma-*, the distal deixis, which refers to what is distant from the speaker (Kouwenberg 2012, 18). This system derived from a three-term system, which also included a medial term, distinguishing between the first, second and third person (Kouwenberg 2012, 51ff). While this system was still active in OB and OA, from MA, there is only evidence or the third person. At the end of the OA period, the morphological third person (*ull-*) was abandoned and replaced by the morphological second-person *amma-* (Kouwenberg 2012, 30). Evidence is not abundant, with some forms missing. Some of them reappear in NA, suggesting that the system was retained in MA/NA. The lack of attestations is probably best explained by the nature of our text corpus. For OA traders who communicated over large distances, an extended terminology for 'here' and 'there' was a necessity. Therefore, it comes as no surprise that most of our MA examples are from letters from the colonies. Given the scarceness of the sources, all known examples are quoted.

14.1.1.1 Suffix -ānu

§ 480 It has been demonstrated previously that the meaning of the suffix is 'from here/there'.[1] This is more or less confirmed by our sole example of the proximal deixis, *annānu(m)*. *⸢a⸣-na-nu unakkusū* 'from here they will cut off' A 877:7–8. Unfortunately, there are no attestations of the distal *ammānu* to date; however, this adverb was already rare in OA.

14.1.1.2 Suffix -āka

§ 481 The suffix *-āka* has a locative meaning (Kouwenberg 2012, 64ff). It is attested for both *ann-* and *amm-* in MA. The list of attestations for *annāka* 'here' is relatively abundant. As for the context where these adverbs occur, it may be noted that there are a few passages from letter introductions. These describe the situation for the author 'it is well here' or express desire for the recipient 'may it be well there' (e.g., Wilhelm 1997; A 845; KAM 7 150).

The proximal deixis *annāka* 'here':

an-na-ka a-na iyāši [šul]mu 'here everything is well with me' A 845:5

a-na-kám šaqqul 'it is weighed here' KAV 106:6

an-na-ka ana ṣabʾe Kaššīē ša ina GN *usbūni šulmu* 'here it is well with the Kassite troops who dwell in GN' MARV 1 71:8–9

an-na-ka ana É *gab<be> šulmu* 'everything in all of the house is well' Wilhelm 1997:9–10

iš-tu an-na-ka-am-ma udduat 'she is assigned from here' MATC 15:6–7

anāku an-na-ka ana PN *aqtibi* 'I said to PN here' MATC 15:23–24

⸢a-na-ka$^{?!}$ lā⸣ ipallahši 'he will not serve her here' Tsukimoto 1992 D r. 5'

The distal deixis *ammāka* 'there' has more attestations. Usually, this adverb is written with gemination (*am-ma-ka*), although it is exceptionally found with the defective writing, *a-ma-ka* T 96-14:17.

am-ma-ka ana kuāša lū šulmu 'may it be well there with you' KAM 7 150:5–6

iš-tu am-ma-ka itūranni '(when) he returned from there' LVUH 92:19–20

iš-tu am-ma-ka ina tuāre 'as soon as he returns from there' MATC 6:8–9

iš-tu am-ma-ka ṭēma ana panīya lilqeūne 'they must take a message from there for me' MATC 9:9–11

1 See Lewy (1938); Kouwenberg (2012, 59).

anāku ^lú^*sirašê*^meš^ *ša an-na-ka am-me-e-ša-ma alaqqea* 'I will take the brewers, who are here, there' MATC 9:22–25

am-ma-ka [*l*]*idbub* 'he should speak there' MATC 11:31–32

at-ta am-ma-ka kī ḫadiātane epuš 'you there, do as you please!' MATC 15:8–9

atta am-ma-ka marʾē āle ṭēma šukun 'you, instruct the citizens there!' MATC 15:21–23

PN *am-ma-ka-ma* É 'PN (has?) a house there' MATSH 22:27–28

ammar am-ma-ka laššūni anāku upaḫḫar 'I will gather (here) whatever is not there' TabT05a-134:28–30

šarru naptanšu am-ma-ka-ma ekkal 'the king will eat his meal there' T 04-2:28–29

14.1.1.3 Suffix -ēša

§ 482 The suffix *-ēša* has an ablative function, meaning 'to this place' (*annēša*) vs. 'to that place' (*ammēša*) (Kouwenberg 2012, 64). The proximal deixis *annēša* is not attested in MA, but does occur in OA and NA. On the other hand, we find the distal deixis on three occasions:

anāku iššērte am-mi-ša ana biāde allaka 'I will come tomorrow to spend the night there' MATC 2:16–18

anāku ^lú^*sirašê*^meš^ *ša an-na-ka am-me-e-ša-ma alaqqea* 'I will take the brewers, who are here, there' MATC 9:22–25

PN *am-mi-ša illaka* 'PN will come there' MATC 12:3–4

14.1.2 Locative *-um* and *-ānum*

§ 483 The so-called locative ending *-um* has sometimes been called a case ending (Streck 2014a, 52, 53 § 149, 151). However, as it is invariable, even when a preposition precedes it or when occurring in the status constructus, it could be better labelled as an adverbial ending. Furthermore, the assumed locative meaning is anything but absent in a number of important forms, e.g., *balu(t)* 'without' (preposition) and *apputum* 'please' (interjection). In MA, its usage is very limited and only occurs in a few fixed expressions, in addition to the aforementioned two. In any case, one could argue that, especially with a locative function, -*um* functions as an adverb. Yet, as it could be argued that most of the examples presented here are locative, we may categorize most locatives as belonging to the adverbs of location. The most important fixed expression with a locative is the prepositional *i+na pittu(m)* 'in the responsibility of'. Although the attestations are frequent, those without a locative occur as well, e.g., *i+na pi-te-*[*ka*] MATSH 16:28. The locative always appears before a pronominal suffix; however, the occurrence of /u/, followed by a geminated consonant of the assimilated suffix, betrays its presence; e.g.:

i+na pi-tu-uk-ka šukun 'place it in your responsibility' MATSH 1:17–18

i+na pi-tu-ia usbū 'they live under my responsibility' MATSH 8:34'

emmera^meš^ (...) *ša pi-tu-ka* 'sheep of your responsibility' MATC 1:12–13

ANŠE.KUR.RA EME₅^meš *ša pi-tu-ka lirkusū* 'may they tie the horses (and) she-asses of your responsibility' MATC 4:6–7

ina nupāre i+na pi-tu-ka usbūni 'he stays under your responsibility in the prison' T 98-3:7–9

As indicated elsewhere (GAG, 107f § 66b; MATSH, 146), the occurrence of the preposition *ina* makes the usage of the locative unnecessary and demonstrates that it was no longer functional in MA and limited to fixed expressions. On the other hand, Streck (2011, 36 § 79; for OA, see GKT, 112 § 66) noted that the combination of prepositions with the locative was already common in OB. Other cases of *-um* with a locative meaning can be found in the opposition *šaplu(m)/šaplānu(m)* 'below' and *ellān(um)* 'above'.

[*lū sinnilta*] *ša šap-la-nu-ša tātarar lemniš* 'or she spitefully curses a woman who is below her in rank' MAPD § 17:80–81

i+na šap-la-an GN *ētabrūni* 'they crossed over (the river) below GN' MATSH 6:18'

IL-la-nu-ka naplis 'look after yourself' KAJ 316:6–7

el-la-nu-šu-nu ipallisū 'they look after them' MATSH 8:30'–31'

We find the locative attested a few times with the preposition *beri* 'among, between' (cf. MARV 2, 9 no. 5). This is attested in Akkadian in general (AHw, 128a; CAD B, 247a), but the attestations in MA are often in damaged or unclear context.

21 *mašku*^meš *ša be-ru-šu-nu* '21 hides are (owned by) them jointly' KAJ 225:14

ša be-ru-šu-nu šalim 'between them it is well(?)' MARV 2 12:9

The opposition between *bētānu* 'inside' and *kīdānu* 'outside' is attested in a few passages. These forms take the adverbial ending *-ānu*.

ana tarbāṣ[*e*] *ša ki-da-nu uṣṣâ*[*kkunu*] '(if) he goes out to you to the outer courtyard' KAV 96:14–15

i+na ki-⌜*da*⌝*-a-nu i+na be-*[*ta*]*-a-nu* 'in the exterior, in the interior' MARV 1 17:8–9

*ēpiš šipre ša ki-da-a-nu/*É*-ta-a-nu* 'the worker of the exterior/interior' MARV 3 43:1–2/5–6

naggāru be-ta-⌜*nu*⌝ 'carpenter of the inner parts' MARV 10 56:15''

14.1.3 Other adverbs of location

§ 484 Two adverbs of direction are found in the Tell Aš-Šēḫ Ḥamad corpus, which are opposite to each other: *šumēla* 'on the left' and *emitta* (Bab. *imitta*) 'on the right'. They are notable because the adverbial accusative is not subjected to inflection of the genitive case ending when a preposition precedes them. Note the variation of *šumēla* in *šu-ma-la* LVUH 69. Moreover, on some forms, a subjunctive *-ni* is added, which indicates that they have to be analysed as the predicate of a dependent adverbial clause.

emitta 'on the right':

a-na e-mi-ta tabkū '(the barley) is poured out to the right side'LVUH 83:4–5

ina karmi ša ⌜*e*⌝*-mi-ta*? 'on the granary of the right side' LVUH 84:6

a-na e-me-ta tabik 'it is poured out to the right side' LVUH 93:10–11

1 *me* 20 *emāru* ŠE (…) *ana šumēlāni* 80 *emāru* ŠE (…) *a-na e-mi-ta-ni* ŠU.NÍGIN 4 *me* 1 *šūši tabkū* '120 homers of barley to the left side, 80 homers of barley to the right side, a total of 460 homers of barley is poured out' LVUH 91:4–13

šumēla 'on the left':

⌜*ša*⌝ *šu-me-la išaqqi* 'it goes up to what is of the left side' Aššur Ritual ii 5'; cf. ii 8'

ina karme a-na šu-mi-la t[*abik*] 'it is poured out on the granary to the left side' LVUH 69:21

a-na šu-ma-la tabik 'it is poured out to the left side' LVUH 69:30–31

a-na šu-mé-la tabik 'it is poured out to the left side' LVUH 86:4

ša ana erābe a-na šu-mi-la-a-ni (…) *tabik* … 'which is at the entrance, to the left side (…) it is poured out' LVUH 89:15–17

14.2 Adverbs of number

14.2.1 Quantifying adverbs of the type n-*ātu*

§ 485 A few attestations for multiplying adverbs are known, all of which are logographic with phonetic complements. A form similar to Babylonian has been suggested to have been hiding beneath these logograms.[2] However, until a more extensive spelling surfaces, the actual underlying form remains uncertain.

3-*a-te iddan* 'he will pay three times' MAL A § 24:64, 71

3-*a-te ṣarpa šīm batulte* (…) *iddan* 'he will give (…) three times the silver the price of the girl' MAL A § 55:34 cf. l. 39–40; § 56:46–47

eqla ammar usammeḫūni 3$^{\text{ta.àm}}$-*a-te iddan* 'as much field as he incorporated he will pay back three times' MAL B § 8:16

eqla ammar usammeḫūni 3-*ti iddan* 'as much field as he incorporated he will pay back three times' MAL B § 9:25–26

14.2.2 Quantifying adverbs of the type *PaRSišu*

§ 486 There is a number of attestations where quantifying adverbs are spelled logographically with a phonetic complement -*ēšu* added to them. It is likely that the underlying forms may have been built on the base of the cardinal numbers of the type *šinēšu*, *šalāšēšu* etc., as found in OA and NA.[3] The adverbs are used in multiplicatives meaning 'once, twice etc.', 'one time, two times etc.' or distributive with the preposition *ana* 'into one, two, etc..

a-na 2-*šu ma-a-ad ina ḫūle* [*tukaššad tapaṭṭar*] 'a second time more you will make a journey and release (them)' BVW F r. 1–2

2 One suggestion is to read *šal(a)šiātu* (see GAG, 118 § 71c; UGM, 56 § 59.4). Alternatively, *šalultu* (Ass. *šaliltu*?, cf. OA in GOA § 8.4.2) 'a third' > 'tripe' may be a possibility (see CAD Š$_1$, 288a).

3 For OA, see GKT, 116–17 § 71a; GOA § 8.5.1; for NA, see Postgate (1976, 63 § 6.1.3); SNAG, 86–87 § 3.11.3. For LB, see Streck (1995, 73 § 70). For Akkadian, in general, see GAG, 117 § 71a. For alternative explanations of the suffix -*īšu*, see GAG, 117 § 71a and Lipiński (2001, 303–4 § 35.31).

šīra 2-*šu* (…) *ittablūne lā iddinūnâši* 'they brought meat twice but gave us nothing' MARV 1 71:21–22

usbuttu ša 2-*šu* (…) [Š]E[?] *ušēliūni* 'the inhabitants who brought barley twice' Billa 49:11–13

a-na 3-*e-šu piqitta ana panē ṣabʾe* [*ša*] *ēkalle litruṣū* 'into three (groups) let them distribute the rations for the personnel of the palace' MATSH 10:19–21

As in OA (GKT, 117; GOA § 8.5.1), MA uses the adjective *mala* (better *malla*: *ma-al-la* MARV 1 14:4) as an adverb of time in the meaning 'once, one time' (MAL M_1, 146f). We always find *malla* in the status absolutus.

ma-la ḫūla (…) [… *illukū*] 'one time they will go on the road' BVW B:4–10

šamnu[meš] *ma-l*[*a*] *ri-te* 'a handful of hay' BVW F:5

ma-la tunassa[*ḫ*] 'you will extract once' PKT 6 i 4

ma-la ina bēt gināʾe imaddad u tuppušu iḫappi 'he measures it once in the *gināʾu* house and he will break his tablet' MARV 7 71:8–10

The adverb probably derives from the conjunction *mala* 'as much as'. In some passages, we can translate it as 'as much as', e.g., *malla ritte* 'as much as one hand' BVW F:5. However the difference with the original conjunction can be seen in the absence of a subjunctive on verbs:

ma-la sipsāte talabbi 'you will make one round …' BVW B:11; F r. 13

[*šamm*]*ē ma-la ṣibte turaddaʾaššunu* 'you will add for them one portion of fodder' BVW F r. 11; cf. D:4

An overview of the attestations:

1	*mala*	*ma-la*	BVW B:4; BVW F:5; PKT 6 i 4; MARV 7 71:8
		ma-al-la	MARV 1 14:4, 6
2	*šanīšu*	⌜*ša*⌝-*ni-šu*	MAL O § 2a:4†[4]
	šinēšu[?]	2-*šu*	BVW F r. 1; MARV 1 71:21; MARV 4 146;18'; Billa 49:11
3	*šalāšēšu*	3-*e-šu*	MATSH 10:19
		3-*šu*	T 04-2:26

14.2.3 Quantifying adverbs of the type *PaRSutte-*

§ 487 In MA, we find a number of quantifying adverbs of the meaning 'second, third etc. time'.[5] They are built by using the base of the ordinal numbers *paris* and thus not *parāsī*. These adverbs are inflected as masculine plural adjectives, with the ending *-utt* and usually an additional suffix *-īšu*. Consider the following list of attestations:

2	*šanûttēšu-*	*ša-nu-te-šu*	MAL B § 4:33; Aššur Ritual ii 12'; A 1828 (NTA, 25):10; MATSH 4:11[!]†
		ša-nu-ut-te-šu	MAPD § 8:50; § 20:98
	šanûttēka	*ša-nu-ut-te-ka*	PKT 5 r. 9
	šanûttēya	*ša-nu-te-ia*	MATSH 8:53†

4 This broken attestation may refer to incompetence (*ṭēmšu šanīšu*) (see also DSC 2, 180; Roth 1997, 191; CADT Ṭ, 95b).

5 See GAG, 118 § 71b; cf. for MB, see Aro (1955a, 71); NA SNAG, 87 § 3.11.3.

	šanīuttu	*ša-ni-ú-tu*!	T 96-1:6
3	*šaššuttēšu*	*ša-áš-šu-te-šu*	PKT 4 obv. left 5
		ša-šu-te-šu	Aššur Ritual ii 14'
4	*rabuttēšu*	*ra-bu-te-šu*	PKT 3 ii 3
		4-*šu*	PKT 5:20
19	–	19-*šu*	PKT 5 r. 1
20	–	20-*šu*	PKT 5 r. 1

The adverbs are used to indicate how many times an action is performed. It has been suggested before that a pronominal suffix is attached to the adverb, which refers to the subject of the sentence (UGM, 55; GAG, 118 § 71b). However, the only well-preserved case with a pronoun, other than -*šu*, is found in PKT 5 r. 9.[6]

[ŠE.NUMUN *mēr*]*eše ša aḫīšu* [*i+na*] *ša-nu-te-šu* [*ilqe*] 'for a second time, he took his brother's seeds of cultivation' MAL B § 4:32–34

i+na ra-bu-te-šu ta-[*ba-ki*] 'at the fourth time of pouring (of the perfume)' PKT 3 ii 3

[*massuttu*] *annītu ša ša-áš-šu-te-šu* 'this cleaning is of the third time' PKT 4 obv. left 5[7]

ša-nu-ut-te-ka (...) *tak*[*appar*] 'you will wipe (clean for) a second time' PKT 5 r. 9–10

ša-šu-te-šu i-ḫa-bu 'a third time he will draw (beer)' Aššur Ritual ii 14'

As the predicate of a sentence shows, regarding the grammatical number and person of the subject, the function of these pronominal suffixes is unnecessary in this position. In later Akkadian dialects, we only find the suffixes -*šu* (GAG, 118 § 71b; SNAG, 87). Already in MAPD, we find two passages where two plural verbs take the singular suffix -*šu*:

ša-nu-ut-[*te-š*]*u* (…) *iddunūš* 'they will give him a second time' MAPD § 8:50–51

ša-nu-ut-te-šu (…) *panutte uta*[*rr*]*ūšu* 'a second time (…) they will return him' MAPD § 20:98

Sometimes, forms without pronominal suffixes occur as well. Given that, in the following passage, the verbal predicate *ibašši* is impersonal, the adverb takes the place of the subject and does not take a pronominal suffix:

ūmū ša riqqe^{me}[^{š}] *šēbulika ša-ni-ú-tu*! *ibašši* 'it is time again for you to send the perfume' T 96-1:4–7

14.2.4 Other adverbs of number

§ 488 Below is a list of the main attested adverbs of number, with selected passages:

***iltēniš* 'together, jointly':** In all instances, it is placed directly in front of the verbal predicate. In addition to the terminative-adverbial, the adverb takes the particle -*ma* for further emphasis.

quppa ša šinne ašie (…) *il-te-ni-iš-ma šēbilāne* 'send me the box with ivory (and) ebony together' KAV 109:25–29

---

6 While similar, it appears that there is no relation with the adverb of number of the type *šanīšu* (§ 486). A connection with the adverbial locative has also been suggested (see MATSH, 138; GAG, 109 § 66e).

7 In contrast to claims made by some authors (PKT, 405; UGM, 55; CAD Š2, 177), the base *šaššu* cannot be derived from 'six', as this number usually has /e/ in the base (e.g., GAG, 115 § 70b); cf. *ša-áš-šu* MAPD § 19:92 (see § 242 for the assimilation of /l/).

34[+1 *em*]*āra* Š[E] (…) [*at*]*tabak* (…) 30 *emāra* ŠE-*am* (…) *attabak* [*i*]*l-te-ni-iš-ma* [*u*]*ttammiš* '35 homers of barley I poured out, 30 homers of barley I poured out; together I sent it off' MATSH 14:8–19

šanîš **'secondly':** The adverb *šanîš* 'secondly' with a terminative-adverbial is only attested once:

⌜*ša*⌝-*ni-iš adi balṭūni* 'secondly, as long as he is alive' KBo 1 20 r. 11'

udē **'alone':** The adverb 'alone' derives from the Proto Semitic root **waḥd*, which is one of the Semitic roots for the number 'one', similar to **ˁišt*, which we find, for instance, in the Akkadian cardinal numbers (cf. Lipiński 2001, 289 § 35.3). It is followed by pronominal suffixes (also NA, see SNAG, 57 § 3.2.1:

ú-di-šu-nu izzazzū 'they stand by themselves' MAPD § 19:92

1 *Sūtīu* (...) [...] *ina* GN *ú-di-šu šakin* 'one Sutean is placed alone in GN' MATSH 2:42–43

ēdēnu **'alone':** This adverb, also from Proto Semitic root **waḥd*, may occur in the following text (cf. Freydank 2010c, 668–69):

ana atān[*āte*] *annā*[*te*] *uššer*[*šu*] *e-de*!?-*nu*-[*šu*] ŠE-*am lēku*[*l*] 'leave him (the horse) to these she-asses, he alone may eat the barley' MATC 17:11–15

14.3 Adverbs of manner

14.3.1 Terminative-adverbial -*iš*

§ 489 Most adverbs of manner are marked by the terminative-adverbial ending -*iš*. Other adverbs or adverbial expressions in this category are relatively rare. Here we will list their attestations briefly.

arḫiš 'quickly':

ar-ḫiš ana GN *šēbilāneššu* 'send it quickly to GN' KAV 107:14–15

ar-ḫiš muḫuršu 'receive it quickly' MARV 7 14:22; T 97-2:12–13

kannamāre ar-ḫiš lublūni 'they must quickly bring (them) in the early morning' MATC 1:5–6

ar-ḫiš nammiš 'make (them) depart quickly' MATC 1:15

ar-ḫi-iš EN (...) *lišpura* 'may my lord quickly write to me' MATSH 12:38–39

ar-ḫiš alka 'come quickly' T 93-2:13–14

ar-ḫiš šēbila 'send it quickly to me' T 93-3:24

ar-ḫi-[*iš*] *li-ḪI-*[*lu-ṣu*] 'they must filter quickly' T 93-7:22–23

The position of *arḫiš* is not always at the beginning of a clause (Llop/Luukko 2014, 214–15):

bēlī [*šu*]*lmānaka ar-ḫiš liqīš lušēbila* 'may my lord quickly present your[sic.] gift and send it to me' A 1947+:25–26 (obscure text) *ša pî tuppi annīte ar-ḫi-iš leqyā alkā* 'according to the wording of this tablet, take it quickly and come here' MCS 2 1:18–19

leqya ar-ḫi-iš 'quickly take it here' NP 46:12–13[8]

ūšēbbala [ar-ḫi]š 'I will send to my brother quickly' RS 06.198:27

danniš 'severely, very':

dan-iš! lā [t]aṣ[arr]aḫ 'you will not heat it severely' PKT 1 I right:3

dan-niš lā tutaḫḫaḫ 'you will not vigorously moisten(?)' PKT 4 obv. left 23

lemniš 'badly':

tātarar lem-niš 'she spitefully cursed' MAPD § 17:81

mādiš 'greatly, very':

ana amārīki [libb]ī ma-di-iš [i-ṣa]-⸢ḫa⸣-an-ni 'my heart very much longs to see you' A 845:8–10 (reading of the verb as suggested by M. Luukko)

14.3.2 Other adverbs of manner

§ 490 Below is a list of the main attested adverbs of manner, with selected passages:

***akkīa/kīam* 'thus':** This adverb is attested only a few times.[9] Following the spelling *ki-a* (KAV 105:29), *kīam* usually loses its mimation, although this is nullified by the addition of the particle *-ma* in other examples: *ki-a[m-m]a* MARV 3 64:30†. We may also note the etymologically related *akkīa* (< *ana kīam-ma*), introducing direct speech (see § 739).

ū la ki-a attunuma leqyāne 'and if it is not so, you take it to me' KAV 105:29–30

lū ša ki-am-ma šaknūni 'or it is placed in a similar manner' MCS 2 2:11–12

la ki-am-ma iššaprūne '(if) it is not that they were sent here' T 99-10:16 (interpretation uncertain)

The short form *kī* (cf. prepositions in § 443ff) is also attested with the preposition *ana* assimilated, resulting in *akkī*:

riksa a-ki-šu-ma irtaksū 'thus they have issued a decree' MATSH 17:9–10

[t]ēma a-ki-šu-ma anaʾīne tēp[uš] 'why did you prepare (*your*) report like this?' KUB 3 73:13'

qibyā mā ṣālāte a-ki-šu-ma lā tuga[mmirā] 'speak, thus you have not ended (your) quarrels' MARV 3 64:36–37

***assurrē* 'hopefully':** The adverb *assurrē* is frequently attested in Akkadian, including both OA and NA.[10] In MA, it is only attested in unpublished TSA material. As for a study of its function (in OB) and presumed etymology (*ana/adi+surru*), it is sufficient to refer to Wasserman's recent study (2012, 154–78). However, it should be pointed out that the writer and recipient of the following letter are in conflict, confirming the negative context

8 I am reluctant to take *arḫiš* as the beginning of a new clause, as it would be followed directly by a dependent clause. Admittedly, the preceding lines become difficult.

9 Cf. GAG, 217 § 120a; UGM, 98 § 85.

10 For OA, see GKT, 185 § 106b; GOA § 13.5.6; NA: CAD S, 411–12.

in which *assurrē* usually occurs in OB letters (Wasserman 2012, 156).A threat may even be suspected:

> *a-su-ri atta tanammuš* 'presumably you will depart' T 93-11:11–12

***emūqa(mma)* 'by force':** This adverb occurs twice in MAL A in connection with rape. MA shares the adverb *emūqa(mma)* with Nuzi (CAD E, 156b), whereas OA uses *emūqattam*.[11] Nuzi texts show the attestation of *emūqa(mma)*, with and without *-ma*. It is therefore unclear whether this particle is part of the adverb or not, but the particle *-ma* is attested on a few adverbs (§ 413).

> *e-mu-qa-ma iṣṣabassi* 'he seized her with force' MAL A § 12:18; cf. MAL A § 16:63

***ana kallīe* 'promptly, posthaste':** This adverb is attested on a few occasions in MA (cf. AHw, 426; CAD K, 84):

> *⸢a⸣-na kal-li-e [a/i+na líb(?)-b]i tettiqa* 'you will *get there posthaste*' MATSH 5:10'–11' (a tentative reconstruction follows a suggestion by M. Luukko).

> *a-na kal-li-e [ana ...] attalak attūra* 'I went and returned posthaste to [...]' MATSH 9:34–35

The adverb is probably etymologically related to *kallīu* '(post) station' as found in MARV 2 17a+ (cf. Deller 1984, 59–60; Freydank 2014, 71–72; 2015, 86–87, 111). Cf. *kallīu* 'messenger' (§ 250c).

> *ša ištu* GN$_1$ *adi* GN$_2$ *a-na kal-li-e sadrūni* 'they are placed in order of stations from GN$_1$ to GN$_2$' MARV 2 17a+:16–17

> *š[a n]ašperāte a-na kal-li-e (...) ana muḫḫi šarre ⸢a⸣na tušēbule usbūni* '(the horses) *are ready* for continues letting bring messages to the king in stages' MARV 2 17a+:98–99

***malama* 'once again':** Only one attestation is known to me:

> *ma-la-ma tušāḫaz* 'you ignite (it) once again' PKT 1 I right:18

14.4 Adverbs of time I: specific

14.4.1 *kannamāre* 'in the early morning' and *namāru* 'at dawn'

§ 491 This adverb is the equivalent of the NA *kallamāre*.[12] It can be found in a number of identical passages in BVW, which Ebeling partly reads logographically as KA *na-ma-ri*. Due to new attestations from Tell Ḫuwīra, we can be certain that the spelling in BVW is fully syllabic, as one attestation shows the gemination of /n/ (*ka-an-na-ma-ri* MATC 5:9). Unlike the etymology given by the AHw (*kallû* 'haste?'+*amāru* 'to see'), the occurrence of *kannamāri* shows that the second component was *namāru* 'to shine'. Freydank (2010c, 665) suggests an etymology *kī ana namāre* 'when it becomes light'. A sandhi spelling of the preposition *ana*, where /n/ assimilates into the first consonant of the succeeding noun, is common in MA and especially in OA. Streck (2017, 598–99) lists some objections. The contraction of /ī/+/a/ > /ā/ is unexpected.[13] Moreover, the usage of the conjunction *kī* and

11 See GOA § 13.5.4; AHw, 215; CAD E, 157a; cf. the OA expression *emūqīn atawwum* 'to speak harshly' (see de Ridder 2012, 557).

12 See CAD K, 78; AHw, 425; MATC, 41.

13 Contraction to > /ē/ is known, which is in the present of II/ī verbs, e.g., *iḫīaṭū* > *iḫēṭu* 'they will weigh'.

the preposition *ina* to express the temporal aspect is unnecessary, as we would expect either *kī namāre* or *ina namāre*. Streck suggests an etymology with an initial element, i.e., *kal* 'all', and draws parallels with similar Akkadian adverbial expressions, such as *kal ūmim* 'all day' and *kal mūšim* 'all night'. In this case, the regressive assimilation /l/+/n/ > /nn/ occurs and, in the case of our adverb, *kal+namāre* > *kannamāre*.

ka-na-ma-ri šamma^{meš} [*ekkulū*] 'they will eat grass at dawn' BVW Ab:7 cf. D:5; M+N r. 5 cf. H:2

ka-na-ma-ri arḫiš lublūne 'they must quickly bring (them) in the early morning' MATC 1:5–6

ūma ka-an-na-ma-ri lillik 'may he go the same day, in the early morning' MATC 5:9–10

An alternative form, i.e., *ina namāre* 'at dawn', seems to occur in roughly the same context. The following passage from BVW suggests that *ina namāre* may be slightly later in the day than *kannamāri* or is contemporaneous, as it directly follows the latter adverbial expression:

[*ka-n*]*a-ma-ri šamma*^{meš} *ekkulū ina namāre tara*[*kkas*] 'in the early morning they will eat plants, (then) you will bind them at dawn' BVW A:8

Another passage from PKT further describes the period, such as when the sun rises:

i+na na-ma-re ^{d}*šamšu ina napāḫe* (...) *tašaḫḫal* 'at dawn, when the sun rises, you will sieve it' PKT 3 i 8–9

Note also the following passage:

ittaṣṣū i+na na-ma-re 'at dawn, they (=the pursuers) went off' MATSH 2:22–23

14.4.2 *ūma* 'today' and variations

§ 492 We find *ūmu* used as an adverb in a reasonable number of texts, most frequently in the Tell Aš-Šēḫ Ḥamad letter correspondence. It is related to the conjunction *ina ūme* 'when', which introduces a dependent clause. As an adverb, *ūmu* is one of the cases where the adverbial accusative is attested frequently. A selection of attestations follows:

u$_4$*-ma* 1 EME$_5$ *ātamar* 'today I saw a she-ass' Hall 1983:18

kurummutu (…) *ša* 1 *u*$_4$*-ma* (…) <*ēkul*>*ūni*(?) 'rations that they ate in one day' MATC 43:19–21

u$_4$*-ma uttammešamma* 'today (the troops$^?$) departed' MATSH 3:39

u$_4$*-ma mā*$^?$*ē*^{š} *abattaq* 'today I will cut off the water' MATSH 8:30'

u$_4$*-ma alteme* 'today I heard' MATSH 12:11

u$_4$*-ma anāku altaprakku* 'today I write you' EA 15:11

ūma ^{kur}*Ḫa-ni-gal-bat ki-i iggam*[*erūni*] 'the day that Hanigalbat was annihilated' KBo 1 20 r. 6'

We also find *ūmu* in the status absolutus used as an expression for 'for a day'. (MATSH, 161 and CAD U/W, 143). This goes against CAD (U, 143a), which suggests 'daily' as a translation of KAJ 182. However, in the same text, there is a note suggesting a one-time transaction, rather than an iterative delivery.

i+na u$_4$*-um il ḫarrāne kī ana ēkalle errabūni*$^{sic.}$ (…) *iqabbiū* 'on the day of the road deity, when (the statue) enters the palace (…) they shall report' MAPD § 8:48–50

u$_4$*-um* 1 *tarīḫa*$^{sic.}$ (…) *tadin* 'one vessel is given for a day' A 300:5–10 *u$_4$-um* 1 *marsattu* (…) *ana ēkalle rakis* 'one soaking vessel for a day established as dues for the palace' KAJ 182:7–12

u$_4$-um 1 BÁN GA 'daily, one seah of milk' KAJ 184:5

u$_4$-um 5 *sūtu miṭru tadnū* 'five seahs of *miṭru*-bread is given for a day' MARV 2 14:8'

u$_4$-um 2 *sūtu* 6 *qa aklu* 'two seahs, six litres of bread for a day' MARV 9 19:38

u$_4$-um 2½ *azaʾillu ša tibne* '2½ sacks of straw for a day' Billa 23:3

i+na u$_4$-um šarru ana GN *illikūni* '(unpublished section), on the day the king went to GN' DeZ 4022:9–11

u$_4$-um (…) *kurummata bila* 'bring me rations for a day' MATSH 12:26

***kal(a) ūme* 'all day':** This adverb is rather similar to *ūmakkal* 'for one day', as both refer to the period of one day (cf. CAD K, 89; AHw 427b). The usage of *kalāʾu* 'all' in this adverb is archaic, since we already saw it replaced by *gabbu* in MA (§ 395).

ša […] *lu-ú i+na mu-še lu-ú i+na kal u$_4$-me* (…) *mamma mimma* [*ušē*]*ṣiūni* 'whoever, either at night or during the day, took something away' MAPD § 6:41

i+na kal u$_4$-me (…) *išappar* 'during the day he sends (someone)' MAPD § 9:52

ṣabʾu ana maṣṣarte ša āle [*la-a*] *ša mu-še ù la-a ša ka$^!$-⸢lu⸣-mi* […]*-ti-ú-ni* 'troops for the protection of the city […] not during the night or day' MATSH 22:5–7

***ūmakkal* 'for one day':** This adverb is a compound of *ūmu* 'day' and *kalu* 'all', of which the latter occurs in the status absolutus. So far, only two attestations in MA are known. In both cases, *ūmakkal* is written with <ú>, rather than <u$_4$>, unlike OA (GOA § 13.5.2).

ana ṣēne^{meš} *⸢ú⸣-[ma]-ka-al iqtual* 'he looked after the cattle for one day' MATC 15:28–29

ú-ma-kal ina panīya panē ana bēt qaqqere tariṣ 'for the length of one day before me, it stretched (its) face to the ground' MATSH 2:13–14

***ūmu mašil* 'noon':** This adverbial construction consists of the compound *ūmu* in the status rectus with *mašil* 'half', which is used attributively. Unexpectedly, *ūmu* is not used in the accusative case. The variant *mūšu mašil* 'midnight' is attested a number of times in Akkadian (AHw, 628; CAD M$_1$, 379–80).

a-na GN *u$_4$-mu ma-ši-il ṭēma ittablūne* at noon, they brought the report to me to GN' MATSH 2:23–24

14.4.3 Other specific adverbs of time

§ 493 Below is a list of the main attested specific adverbs of time, with selected passages:

***līdiš* 'day after tomorrow':** This is actually a short form of *allītiš* (Bab. *ullītiš*; see AHw, 1409f; CAD U/W, 81). It is only once attested in MA. The exact etymology is not clear, but it has a terminative-adverbial ending.[14]

a-na li-di-iš (...) *litūra* 'the day after tomorrow, he must return' MATC 5:18–20

14 Von Soden (AHw, 1409b) makes no remarks on etymology. Could it be derived from the root √*wld*, with the feminine marker *-t*?

***mūšu* 'night':** We find the noun *mūšu* 'night' used for adverbial phrases. It usually follows prepositions and appears in combination with another temporal designation.

> *lū i+na mu-še* (...) *aʾīlu kī daʾāne batulta iṣbatma* 'or at night (...) a man seized the girl with force' MAL A § 55:17–21
>
> *ki-i mu-ši-šu liškunū* 'may they place (them) like its night' MATC 15:14
>
> *lā ša mu-še ū lā ša ka!-⸢lu⸣-mi* 'not during night or day' MATSH 22:6

We may also note the expression *ina mūše barāre* 'at dusk':

> *ṣabʾu kī innābidūni i+na mu-še barārema* 'the troops that fled at dusk' MATSH 2:22–23

***nubattu* 'evening':** This adverb from the root *biādu* show the sound change /n/ > /m/, which is caused by the labial /b/ (§ 234). The ending *-u* in KAJ 192 has to be regarded as a nominal relative clause with conjunction *kī* (§ 732).

> 3 UDU (…) *ana takpirti* (...) *ki-i nu-bat-tu ina* <UD>.15.KÁM *epšū* 'three sheep are prepared for the *t.*-ritual at night on the 15th day' KAJ 192:26–28
>
> 1 *emmeru ana naptini nu-bat-tu-šu epiš* 'one sheep was prepared for a meal in that evening' KAJ 207:1–3 cf. KAJ 200:1–5; A 1746 (NTA, 22):1–4

***simānu* 'time':** While *simānu* is not really used in a pure adverbial sense, it is fitting to include it here with other designations of time. It is perhaps better to assume an (Assyrian) variant *simunu* in order to understand the occurrence of VA and the lack of elision regarding the vowel in the second short syllable.

> *tallakātu ša si-mi-ni ša bēt ēqe rabīe* 'procedures of the (right) time of the great *bēt-ēqe*' Ištar Ritual r. 9'–10', cf. Ištar Ritual:1

***šaddaqda* 'last year':** This adverb broadly occurs in Akkadian (cf. CAD Š$_1$, 38–40), but is only attested once in MA. A variation with the terminative-adverbial ending *-iš* is found in a broken context. The change from *šaddaqda* to *šaddaqdiš* is a diachronic development, in which the latter form replaced the form without a terminative in NA (cf. CAD Š$_1$, 40). Note the usage of the genitive case instead of the accusative in the phrases without a terminative-adverbial, which perhaps harks back to the root if we accept von Soden's etymology of a composite noun of *šattu* and a form of √*qdm* (AHw, 1123). However, there are also reasons to assume that /q/ was instead realized as /g/ in this adverb, going against the etymology of von Soden (CAD Š$_1$, 40b).

> ^{lú}(…) *ša* PN (…) *ša-da-aq-di ina ša nāre ušēribanni* 'the ^{lú}(…), whom PN brought over the river last year' KAV 107:5–11
>
> *ša-da-aq-di-ma ina ūmē annūte* 'last year on these days' MATSH 4:15'–16'
>
> *ša-da-aq-de-eš* MARV 7 14:16†

***šattu* 'year':** The noun *šattu* (pl. *šanātu*), usually written logographically as MU, is attested in the adverbial expression *šattu lā šattu*, the meaning of which, as used in a loan text, was suggested by Donbaz (2009, 359) to be either 'year by year' or 'within a year', depending on whether the loan was long or short term.

> *ana adrāti ina libbi* GN ⸢*ša*⸣*-at-tum la ša-tum qaqqad* ŠE *imaddad* 'he will measure out the capital of the barley on the threshing floor of GN, year by year' A 333:7–8

Otherwise, attestations of syllabic *šattu* are:

ša 7 pa-ni ša-na-te 'of seven springs(?)' MARV 2 9:6'†

^{túg}*katāʾa*^{meš} *ša ša-at-te an-ni-te ēṣidūni* 'the flax that they harvested this year' MATSH 6:8'

***šērtu* 'morning':** This adverb can also be used in the sense of the next morning, as in the first example, thus creating a secondary meaning of tomorrow (cf. CAD Š$_2$, 321f). Often, the preposition *ina* is used, once the preposition is assimilated into the adverb, creating the compound adverb *iššērte*.

šumma sisīu^{meš} *ana ḫarrāne še-er-te* 'if the horses are for the road in the morning' BVW A:10

anāku iš-še-er-te ammīša ana biāde allaka 'I will come in the (next) morning to spend the night there' MATC 2:16–18

i+na še-er-te a-na mu-ši-šu-ma litūra 'in the morning until the night, he must return' MATC 5:11–13

The variant *šiārātu* is attested twice (cf. CAD Š$_2$, 341a; AHw, 1226):

e-mi-šu i+na ši-a-ra-a-te malama tušāḫaz '(to keep$^{?}$) it hot, you ignite (it) once again in the morning' PKT 1 I right:18

ŠE-*um*^{meš} *i+na še-a-ra-te maḫrū* 'they received the barley in the morning' MARV 1 11:9–10

14.5 Adverbs of time II: unspecific

14.5.1 *entu* 'at that time; when'

§ 494 The adverb/conjunction *entu* derives from Hurrian *undo*.[15] The conjunction is common in the other WPA Akkadian dialects (CAD U/W, 157f). We also find the original Hurrian form on one occasion as *un-du* in the Amarna letter EA 16:19. It was already noted that these letters were in the Nuzi-Akkadian dialect, *undu*, representing one of the arguments favouring this view (Artzi 1997, 329). The Assyrian for *entu* remains restricted to a few examples in the Tell Billa texts, one of the few hints of regional differences in MA. Unfortunately, both letters where *entu* occurs are from different authors. However, Arigi, the name of the author of Billa 64, could be Hurrian.[16] In the two examples of EA 16, *undu* is a conjunction and comes with a subjunctive (here Bab. -*u*), but this does not follow from the Tell Billa letters. Nonetheless, in Billa 67, *entu* functions as a conjunction, which introduces a nominal adverbial clause. The attestation of Billa 67 is different from the other in that it forms a conditional sentence, referring to future events.

en-tu iqtibia 'at the time he said to me' Billa 63:18

en-tu ina muḫḫīya anāku lalli[*k*] 'when (she is) before me, I will go' Billa 67:9–10

Amarna:

un-du PN *abī ana Miṣri išpuru* 'when PN, my father, wrote to Egypt' EA 16:19–20

---

15 See CAD U/W, 157; Wegner (2007, 290); Richter (2012, 492); cf. MA: de Ridder (2017a, 302 § 3.1).

16 Cf. the PN Arikke in the Nuzi onomasticon (Gelb/Purves/MacRae 1943, 26b; Cassin/Glassner 1977, 27). The name is explained as Hurrian in Richter (2016, 588).

[un]-du šarru Ḫanigalbatû [a]na muḫḫi abika ana Miṣri [iš]puru when the king of Ḫanigalbat wrote to your father in Egypt' EA 16:22–24

14.5.2 *urkīu, urkittu* and *urkiš* 'afterwards'

§ 495 The base of *urku* (< *warkum*) forms various adverbs referring to what happens in the future. The simple form is *urkīu*, which carries a nisbe and, from this sole example, cannot be distinguished from the frequent *urkittu*:

enūšu ur-ki-ù mamma rittušu lā umalli 'then (and) later nobody filled his hand' MATSH 4:16'–17'

The feminine *urkittu* is found more often adverbially used, mostly in combination with the preposition *ina*, e.g.:

⌜*i+na ur-ki*⌝*-it-te sinniltu šī*[sic.] *tattaṣbat* 'later, that woman is seized' MAL A § 24:51–52

i+na ur-ki-ti ina ālim 'afterwards, in the city …' KAJ 1:12

i+na ur-ki-it-ti š[a P]N *marāša* 'in the future, it is of PN, her son' KAJ 9:25

i-na ur-ki-ti kimtu āḫḫūšu kī qātīšu 'in the future, the family, his brothers are equal his share' KAJ 179:21–22

ur-[k]i-ta a-na-k[u] x [(x x)] T 99-10:19

Once we find an adverbial phrase with Babylonian *(w)arkatum*:

i+na ar-kat UD^{meš} *mussa ḫalqu ana māte ittūra* 'in later days, her lost husband has returned to the country' MAL A § 45:72–73

Note that the base *urku* is not always used adverbially; in the following phrase, it is used adjectivally:

šumma ur-ki-it-tu šīt 'if she is secondary' MAL A § 46:99.

Adverbs of the base *urku* can also be found involving adjectival use:

ana marʾē ša ana mu-ti-ša ur-ke-e uldutūni 'to the sons whom she bore to the later husband'.MAL A § 45:76–77

mu-us-sa-ma ur-ki-ú ilaqqe 'her later husband shall take (them)' MAL A § 45:78

ina le-e ša ŠE *maḫ-ri* ⌜*pa-ni*⌝*-e* ⌜*ù*⌝ *ur-ki-e [lā] ēmurū* 'they did not find it on earlier or later wooden tablets of grain deliveries' KAJ 260:7–10

ina 5 UDU (….) *ša pi-it-te* PN *ur-ki-ú-te* 'from the later (delivery of) five sheep in the responsibility of PN' KAJ 230:8–11

Even as a preposition:

ur-ki-te-⌜*šu*⌝ *na-ak-ru ana* GN *imtuqut* 'after his (departure), the enemy attacked GN' MATSH 4:7–8

urkiš 'afterwards' occurs multiple times:

ur-k[i]-iš ētamrū 'afterwards, they notice' MAPD § 20:100

ur-ki-iš MAN *[ḫi]ṭṭa ilteme* 'afterwards, the king hears of the sin' MAPD § 21:110

14.5.3 Other unspecific adverbs of time

§ 496 Below is a list of the main attested unspecific adverbs of time, with selected passages:

***annîša* 'hither':** Only attested in the Amarna letter EA 15 (see Moran 1984, 297–98).

> *a-di an-ni-ša abbāʾūya lā išpurū ūma anāku altaprakku* 'up until now, my forefathers did not write, but today I have written to you' EA 15:9–11 (Aub)

***ḫaramma* 'afterwards':** This NA adverb is attested a few times in MA. According to the CAD Ḫ (89a), it derives from *uḫḫuru*, although the AHw (323a) gives a rather different etymology, taking it as a compound from *aḫar+amma*.

> *billāte liblu[l] u ḫa-ra-ma nagle[b]e* (…) *lišpuk u ḫa-ra-ma a[na] epāše liṣbat* 'may he mix an alloy and afterwards may he cast a nail clipper and afterwards may he take it to finish it' KAV 205:25–29

> *riqīa*^meš^ *ina libbīšunu* [*bē*]*dūni ḫa-ra-ma-ma* (…) [*tatabbak*] 'the perfume in which it was soaked overnight, you will afterwards pour' PKT 6 i 24–25; cf. PKT 6 ii 22–23

***dāria* 'forever':** This adverb is only once attested, but the interpretation of the phrase is not entirely certain:

> *an-ni-a da-ri-a šarru naptanšu ammākama ekkal* 'this constantly (?), the king will eat his meal there' T 04-2:27–29

***enūšu* 'then':** This adverb is attested a number of times in Akkadian (AHw, 384; CAD I/J, 162f). Only one attestation so far has been found in MA:

> *e-nu-šu urkīu mamma rittušu lā umalli* 'then (and) later nobody filled his hand' MATSH 4:16'–17'

***inanna* 'now':** While common in Akkadian, there is only one attestation in MA, which appears on two occasions. The adverb is followed in RS 06.198 by *anumma*, with a presumed identical meaning, which is a construction found more often in Ugaritic letters (Huehnergard 1989, 197). The double adverbial expression has been suggested to indicate emphasis (CAD I,/J, 144).

> *i-na-an-na a-nu-um-ma tuppātēya* (…) *sisima* 'now hereby read (…) my tablets' RS 06.198:12–16

> *i-na-na a-za-ni-a-ku* 'now, I am angry with you' T 93-11:23

***immatēma* 'at any time, ever':** This adverb is attested only once or twice with the assimilated preposition *ina*. Note that *immatēma* is also found as a conjunction to introduce a temporal adverbial clause (§ 731).

> *im-ma-te-ma ṭē*[*m* PN] *ana muḫḫi bē*[*līya*] *lā ašp*[*ur*] 'I have not, at any time, sent the news of PN to my lord' MATSH 11:10–12

***panēma* 'previously':** This adverb with the enclitic particle *-ma* is only attested a few times.[17]

> *šumma pa-ni-ma abuša ḫabbul* 'if, in the past, her father was indebted' MAL A § 39:27–28

> *pa-ni-ma iltu aḫāʾiš niddubub* 'Previously, we talked together' NP 46:6

---

17 See UGM, 99 § 85/7; GAG, 216 § 119h; Llop/Luukko (2014, 212–13).

pa-ni-ma bēlī i[špura] 'previously, my lord wrote me' MATSH 4:9'

Despite the fact that this adverb refers to past events, in the following phrase it is accompanied by a present:

pa-ni-ma ina muḫḫīya tuttazzam 'previously, you raise(d) a complaint against me' T 93-11:20–21

***tūr* 'again':** This adverb may be a grammaticalized imperative of the verb *tuāru* 'to return, do again'. It is otherwise only attested in NA and possibly SB (AHw, 1372; CAD T, 483), but can be found on three occasions in the Tell Aš-Šēḫ Ḥamad correspondence (MATSH, 146 l. 32). The adverbial ending *-a*, which is only standard in the first millennium attestations, occurs in one of three attestations, in a broken context.

tu-ur ūmū ikaṣṣuʾū 'again, the days will be cold' MATSH 6:11'

tu-ú-ur (...) *šupur* 'send again' MATSH 9:32–33

tu-ra x x-⌜*šu*⌝ *attūra* 'again, I returned' MATSH 15:17

***udīni* '(not) yet':** So far, there are only two attestations of this adverb in the same paragraph of MAL B. The CAD (U/W, 21) points out that this adverb must be followed by a negation, as indicated by the more abundant NA material. While it is related to the Babylonian *adīna*, the change /a /> /u/ cannot be explained as of yet (GAG, 215 § 119d).

ú-di-ni eqla u bēta ana ṣarpe lā [ilaq]qeūni 'he has not yet bought the field and house' MAL B § 6:3–4

ú-di-i-ni edānu lā mašāʾe 'the term is not yet forgotten' MAL B § 6:21–22

14.6 Interjections

§ 497 Interjections form a class of words that express a certain remark, which is syntactically independent from any clause that follows or precedes it, e.g., 'fire!', 'please!' 'sorry'. In MA, interjections are only expected in letters and texts that quote direct speech, since interjections generally express a certain emotion that does not fit into administrative formula. MA attestations remain rare, due to the limited character of the Assyrian letters corpus to which they belong.

***appūtu* 'please' or 'it is urgent':** This interjection, while frequent in OA (see CAD A_2, 191), is only attested once in MA:

arḫiš leqya alka a-pu-tu 'quickly take (it) and come, it is urgent!' MCS 2 1:19

Chapter 15: The Verb: Regular Inflection

15.1 General remarks

§ 498 As with all classical Semitic languages, Akkadian uses three main types of finite verbal forms: prefix conjugation, suffix conjugation and the imperative next to the normal infinitive. Similar to some South Semitic languages, such as Geʿez, the prefix conjugation is divided into different temporal categories for different past and present tenses. This is unlike other Northwest and Central Semitic languages, where past and present tenses were divided between prefix- and suffix-conjugations. In Akkadian, we have the preterite (*PvRS* base), perfect (*PtvRvS* base) and present (*PaRRvS* base). The name prefix conjugation can be somewhat misleading, since it also takes suffixes. Verbs are conjugated after the gender and number of the agent, tempus and mood. A direct or indirect object can be added by means of optional pronominal suffixes. The dialectal differences inside Akkadian are not significant, while the verbal system remained mostly intact during the known history of the language, although it simplified somewhat during the later period, for example, the loss of the infixed T-stems and the decay of the preterite tense.

§ 499 Verbs are built out of three- or, very rarely, four-radical roots (§ 547f). We usually indicate the radicals as R_1, R_2 and R_3. Weak and some irregular verbs have one or more radicals omitted or replaced by a weak reflex, e.g., II/ū stative *māt* 'he is dead' or the imperative *din* 'give' from *tadānu*. We may argue that II/weak verbs often have R_2 as a vowel, e.g., *muātu* with R_2/ū. However, the verbal paradigm generally conjugated all different roots according to a three-radical system, such that this was mostly invisible. The verbal roots are put in different bases or patterns for each different mood or tempora, which can be conjugated in the case of finite verbal forms. The consonants, which can be used for roots, are bound to different laws, also known as 'incompatibility rules' (Kouwenberg 2010, 43). For instance, R_2 and R_3 are never two homorganic consonants, but they can be identical, e.g., *dabābu*, *karāru*, *madādu* and *marruru* (see § 567). Similarly, R_1 and R_3 can be identical: *izuzzu*; *kanāku; ziāzu*. While R_1 and R_2, ideally, are never identical, this has changed in MA with the root *sasāʾu* 'to call', which derives from earlier *šasāʾu* (cf. Kouwenberg 2010, 43–44).

§ 500 Usually, verbal bases/patterns have alternative forms with different functions, which modify the basic function. The normal base/pattern is called the G-stem, after the German *Grundstamm*. We have a secondary base, where R_2 is geminated, which is called the D-stem from 'double', along with the *ša-* prefix, which is called the Š-stem and finally a *na-* prefix, which is called N-stem. Moreover, these four stems have an alternative form with the *-ta-* suffix and the Gt, Dt, Št and Nt-stems, but also a *-tan-* infix called Gtn, Dtn, Štn and Ntn. This system of alternative verbal stems is typical for Semitic languages, which, with the exception of the *tan*-stems, can be found in most classical languages in different forms. In the prefix conjugations, the different types of the D and Š-stems alter the vowel of the prefixes /i-a / > /u/.

§ 501 The conjugated verb is subjected to a number of secondary suffixes, which are added according to a strict pattern (they are numbered I–V in the table below). Their function and morphologic form are discussed in further detail in their respective paragraphs. The first and second suffixes (I–II) are the subjunctive or ventive. Both suffixes are strictly connected to the verb and not (or rarely) attested on non-verbal forms. In the first category (I), the subjunctive cannot be attached to a verb ending in a vowel, while the dative in that case changes to an alternative form *-ne*. It is possible for the dative to follow the subjunctive */ū/* with the suffix *-ne*. The third category (III) is filled by the different pronominal suffixes, of which the dative usually takes a preceding ventive, e.g., *-a(m)* + *šu(m)* > *-aššu(m)*. Pronominal suffixes are followed by the second part of the subjunctive (IV), which must follow the initial subjunctive marker, but is sometimes separated by the ventive or pronominal suffixes. Finally, the chain of suffixes is ended by the different particles (V). The suffixes can build long verbal forms: *iprusūneššunnima*, which derives from *iprus+ū+ne(m)+šu(m)+ni+ma*. Admittedly, forms with all V particles are rare.

I *-ū* subjunctive I	II Ventive	III Pronominal suffix	IV Subjunctive II	V Particle
-ū	*-a/ne/*	*-šu*, *-ka*, *-ku*, etc.	*-ni*	*-ma/mi* etc.

Figure 34: Particle chain for verbs.

The verb itself does not change when a suffix is added, except for the penultimate vowel, which may elide when it becomes part of the second unstressed open syllable in a row:

balāṭu *ib-ta-al-ṭa* (< *ibtalaṭa*) 'he lived' MATSH 8:50'
batāqu *ib-ta-*⌜*aq*⌝*-qu-ni* (< *ibtataq-ūni*) 'he has denounced' MAPD § 5:37
rakāsu *ra-ak-su-ú-ni* (< *rakis-ūni*) 'it is committed' KAJ 225:18
ṣabātu *ṣa-ab-ta-ni-šu* (< *ṣabitā-neššu*) 'seize him!' TR 2031:13

15.2 The prefix conjugation

§ 502 In MA, the three Akkadian types of the prefix conjugation are present: the preterite and perfect for the past tense and the present for the present/future tense. As we will see, the function of the preterite for past tenses was becoming more limited, as it was being slowly replaced with the perfect. The present was used for the present and future tenses; for a more extensive discussion of the usage and function of the tenses, see Chapter 17. All three conjugations use a different base, but are otherwise identically conjugated by a set of prefixes and suffixes to indicate person, number and gender. These are also used for the imperative, which is basically the preterite without prefixes. As the imperative is, by definition, in the second person, it does not need a prefix to indicate this, but does use the suffixes *-ī/ā* to indicate gender and number. As can be seen in the table below, the vowel of the prefixes differs in some cases: in the regular G-stem there is a morphologic difference with /i/ only occurring in the short prefix and *ni-*. In the I/voc weak verbs, there is some alternation due to original gutturals, while the vowel is /u/ in the D/Š-stem.

		Prefix conjugation				Imperative
		G/N-stem			D/Š-stem	
		Regular	I/ā	I/ē	Regular	
Singular	3m	*i --- Ø*	*e --- Ø*	*e --- Ø*	*u --- Ø*	
	3f	*ta --- Ø*	*ta --- Ø*	*te --- Ø*	*tu --- Ø*	
	2m	*ta --- Ø*	*ta --- Ø*	*te --- Ø*	*tu --- Ø*	*--- Ø*
	2f	*ta --- ī*	*ta --- ī*	*te --- ī*	*tu --- ī*	*--- ī*
	1c	*a --- Ø*	*a --- Ø*	*e --- Ø*	*u ---- Ø*	
Plural	3m	*i --- ū*	*e --- ū*	*e --- ū*	*u ---- ū*	
	3f	*i --- ā*	*e --- ā*	*e --- ā*	*u --- ā*	
	2m	*ta --- ā*	*ta --- ā*	*te --- ā*	*tu --- ā*	*--- ā*
	1c	*ni --- Ø*	*ni --- Ø*	*ne --- Ø*	*nu --- Ø*	

Figure 35: Prefix conjugation.

§ 503 Archaic Akkadian recognized two conjugated persons, a recognition that disappeared in later stages of the language: the third-person dual *-ā* and the third-person feminine singular *ta-*. Of these two forms, the dual is still attested in OA, but has become rare in MA.[1] So far, we only have one exception in a peripheral MA text from Tell Barri (see Salvini 1998, 192):

izuzzu 2 TUR^{meš}*-nu ša* AGRIG GAL PN$_1$ PN$_2$ *liz-zi-za-a-niš-šu* 'two servants of the steward, PN$_1$ and PN$_2$, must stand ready for him' K9-T3:12'–15'

Note that the noun *ṣuḫārānu* 'servants' occurs in the plural, rather than dual *ṣuḫārān*.

§ 504 We find the feminine personal ending *ta-* has become a characteristic of the Assyrian dialect as opposed to the Southern Babylonian language, where it does not occur in the vernacular language (cf. OA, see GKT, 121 § 73a). The vowel of the prefix differs between the G-stem (*ta-*) and D/Š-stem (*tu-*).

dagālu *ta-da-gal* 'she shall look' MAL A § 45:49
ḫapāʾu *ta-ḫap-pi* 'she will break' TabT05-11:10
kaʾʾulu D *tu-ka*$^{!}$*-al* 'she will hold' KAJ 9:24
magāru *ta-ma-ga-ar* 'she agrees' Giricano 8:21
malāʾu D *tu-ma-al-la* 'she fills' MAL A § 45:69
maṭāʾu *ta-am-ti-ṭí* 'it is lacking' MARV 3 38:10
ragāmu *tar-tu-gu-um* 'she shall summons' MAPD § 21:105
šapāru *ta-šap-pa-ra-am-ma* 'she shall send' MAPD § 6:43

See also PNs:

balāṭu ^{md}*Iš*$_8$*-tár-tu-bal-li-s*[*u*] (Ištar-tuballissu) MARV 7 28:4'
⌜^{d}*Iš*$_8$*-tár*⌝*-tu-*TI*-su* MARV 9 95:21

For irregularities in the agreement of the gender of verb and subject, see § 665ff.

§ 505 It should be expected that the feminine marker *-ī* in the second-person singular becomes *-ē* in MA. While no attestations are available for the 2fs form *taprusī*, we should compare the imperative feminine singular form *PaRSī* with *laqāʾu*. Contraction cannot be excluded in this example (*leqê*):

laqāʾu *l*[*e-q*]*e-e* (< *leqy-ī*) 'take!' T 96-36:25

1 Cf. OA in GKT, 121 § 73a; GOA § 22.1.6.

§ 506 Unlike OA (cf. GOA § 16.6.2), the final morpheme *-ī/ū/ā* indicating gender or number is only rarely written plene (cf. § 96). Verbs in questions are an exception (§ 682). This could be due to the shortening of this final vowel, as is believed to have been the case in NA (SNAG, 29 § 2.4.3). Two out of three attestations occur with the verb *tadānu*:

tadānu	*i-ta-nu-ú* 'they have given' AO 20.154:13
ubālu	*it-ta-ab-lu-ú* 'they have brought' KAJ 212:9

As we will see below, the infixed *-ū-* of the subjunctive *-ūni* is usually written plene. This strengthens the idea that, in this position, /ū/ was stressed and remained long (see also § 106).

§ 507 The vowel of the 3ms prefix is /i/ in the G-stem, while we find /e/ in I/weak verbs. Sometimes, we find exceptions of /i/ > /e/ (for the exceptions of I/weak verbs, see § 555):

ḫiāṭu	*e-ḫi-aṭ* 'he will pay' KAJ 57:19 vs. *i-ḫi-at* KAJ 57:22
kaʾʾulu D	*la e-ka-la-an-ni* 'he does not detain me' KAV 159:8
našāʾu	*e-ta-na-ši* 'he will continue to carry' KAJ 57:24
sasāʾu	*li-is₅-si-ú* 'they must read' MATSH 9:11'
tadānu	*e-dan* 'he will give' RE 19:15
uṣābu	*e-ta-aṣ-bu-ú-ni* (*ittaṣbūni*) 'they have added' MKA 95:22
zamāru	⸢*e-za-mu-ra-ni*⸣ 'they will sing' MARV 4 59:18
zarāʾu	*e-za-ru-ú* 'they will sow' LVUH 103:16

Cf. a literary text:

zaqāpu	*e-za-qa-ap* ''he planted' BWL, 162:12

Exceptions remain rare, but are nonetheless noteworthy, as they seem relatively more frequent than in the other Assyrian dialects.[2] As it has been suggested that these alternations are a reflection of actual pronunciation, it is not unthinkable that the prefix *i-* became *e-*, but with the old spelling retained on historical grounds.[3] However, it is just as likely that the variation is the result of the confusion between the two vowels, as we discussed in § 133. In any case, unlike Parpola's suggestion in LAS 2, it seems unlikely that /e/ > /i/ in I/weak verbs, since the e-prefixes in I/weak verbs are actually an Assyrian realization.

15.2.1 The theme vowel

§ 508 We have already discussed how the vowel of the prefixes was determined. As such, there is no trace of the Barth-Ginsberg law in MA, which dictates that the vowel of the prefixes stands in relation to the theme vowel of the base.[4] The base of the verb in the G, Gt and N-stems use different theme vowels, which are unpredictable and do not seem to have any special semantic function. There is often a difference in the theme vowel between the present/perfect on one side and the preterite/imperative on the other. Similar to some dictionaries (AHw; CDA), we indicate the vowel pattern $V_1 \sim V_2$ or V_1/V_2, where V_1 stands for the present/perfect and V_2 for the preterite/imperative. The situation of the N-stem will be discussed in § 532; however, there are not enough attestations for the Gt-stem to draw

2 Cf. OA: in GOA §16.6.4; NA: in Luukko (2004, 86–87 § 4.3.4).
3 See Luukko (2004, 87 § 4.3.3); LAS 2, 48 r. 5.
4 This phonetic rule is usually applied on a number of Northwest Semitic languages; cf. Lipiński (2001, 376 § 40.16); Joüon/Muraoka (2006, 118 n1).

any conclusions about their theme vowel in MA. Weak radicals of the II/weak and III/weak verbs determine the theme vowels; otherwise, there are four different patterns attested in MA.

(a/u) class
kanāku; maḫāru; šakānu; šapāru; tabāku; rakāsu; šaṭāru

(a/a) class
maḫāṣu; ṣabātu

(i/i) class
kašāru; labānu; raṣāpu; šarāqu; zabālu

(u/u) class
magāru

§ 509 The theme vowel patterns themselves are no different from the other dialects. As such, an (i/u) or (a/i) pattern does not exist. The vowel /e/ is used in verbs, but only as an allophone of /i/ and is not part of any pattern. Changes in vowel patterns are attested. Note the verb *magāru*: *la-a ta-ma-gu-ur* MAL A § 12:17; *ta-ma-ga-ar* Giricano 8:21. According to von Soden (AHw, 575a), the vowel pattern changed from (a/u) to (u/u), meaning that the attestation in MAL A reflected a younger stage of the language, despite being written before the text from Giricano. As cases of (a/u) are attested in MB (CAD M_1, 37a), it is perhaps likely that the form was influenced by Babylonian. Moreover, not all vowel patterns are shared among the different Akkadian dialects. For instance, the verb *erābu* has an (a/u) pattern in Assyrian, but is (u/u) in Babylonian (AHw, 234a). Differences in the vowel patterns between Babylonian and Assyrian are listed in Kouwenberg (2010, 75-81 § 3.5.3). In addition, there is the deviating *PiRaS* imperative vocalic pattern, which is usually confined to III/weak verbs (§ 574); also note, in relation to PNs, the verb *palāḫu* 'to fear': ^{md}*A-šur-pí-láḫ* KAJ 19:1 (cf. Kouwenberg 2010, 134).

15.2.2 The *i-modus*

§ 510 The occurrence of an added *-i* vowel to a finite verb (cf. UGM, 67 n4, GAG, 134 § 82e) has been called a typical NA characteristic (UŠA, 38; Streck 2001, 517). However, NA with a changed final vowel has been referred to as being a coloured ventive (GAG, 134 § 82e) or having the final syllable opened due to a change of stress (Luukko 2004, 128ff § 4.15). Both causes are not expected in the so-called *i-modus* of MA, given that a ventive does not belong in the attestations and the preceding syllable has been maintained. We can, therefore, draw closer parallels with the features described by Kraus (1973b) for OB. For MA, consider the following attestations:

arāšu	*la-a i-na-re-še* 'it is not grown' LVUH 79:14 (TN)
balāṭu D	ŠE-*um anniu* (...) *bēssu ú-ba-li-ṭí* 'this barley (…) will support his household' KAJ 101:11–13 (Adn$^?$)
eṣādu	*eqla e-ṣi-*⸢*di*⸣ *u tuppuš*[*u*] *iḫappi* 'he shall reap the field and break his tablet' KAJ 81:12–14 (Sa)
	šumma (...) *eqla la e-te-ṣi-di* [*b*]*ilat eqle inašši* 'if (…) he did not reap the field he

	shall be liable for the yield of the field' KAJ 81:19–21 (Sa)
kamāṣu	*ik-ta-mi-ṣi i-ḫa-al* 'she crouched down, went into labour' Rm 376:26 (probably sandhi; see Röllig 1985, 266)
makāsu	*ina* GN *ētamar im-ti-ki-si* 'he saw it in GN and levied dues' AO 21.382:10 (Sa) [*eta*]*mar* [*im-ti*]*-ki-si* TR 3027 r. 4'–5' (Sa)
saḫāru	*lā ta-sa-ḫu-ri* 'do not delay' Cohen/Llop 2017:16
tadānu	*i-di-ni* 'he will give' MARV 1 47:5, 11, 17, 36, 41, 47 (TN)

§ 511 Not all attestations can be accepted without doubt. It is likely that Rm 376:26 is sandhi (Röllig 1985, 266), while *imtikisi* KAJ 81:21 may be defective writing for *imtikis+ši* (Farber 1990, 93), although this interpretation would represent an additional problem in itself. Postgate also proposed a new modus, since the preterite *uballiṭi* and *iddini* could hardly refer to past events (UŠA, 134f l. 13). On the other hand, both *uballiṭi* and *iddini* can be analysed as present, if we explain the theme vowel /i/ as being caused by VA through the *i-modus* (Aynard/Durand 1980, 42 n52). Yet, this conflicts with the OB *i-modus*, which seems to follow a geminated third radical (see Kraus 1973b, 257). Still, southern influences cannot be excluded as the *i-modus* occurs in MB as well.[5] Oelsner (1975, 291) believed these forms to be scribal mistakes. Considering Oelsner's opinion (for MA, see also Farber 1990, 93), three texts with an attested *i-modus* derive with certainty from the UŠA archive (KAJ 81; 101; MARV 1 47) and possibly the same scribe. We may assume a reoccurring mistake from a scribe having difficulties using his vC and CvC signs; additionally, *eṣṣidi* may very well be caused by the occurrence of *ēṣidī* 'reapers' in the same text.[6] Luukko (2004, 108f § 4.8.3) suggested an epenthetic vowel added to verbal forms, replacing *-ma* in NA. However, *-ma* still occurs in MA, while some attestations (MARV 1 56; KAJ 101; AO 21.382) have the verb in the final position. Summarizing, we cannot be sure of the cause and meaning of the *i-modus* in MA due to the limited evidence available (cf. Kouwenberg 2010, 211 n3).

15.2.3 Examples

§ 512 Below is a selected list of attestations for strong roots in the G-stem:

G	3ms	*i-ba-qa-an* KAJ 88:18
		i-ba-táq-šu George 1988 2 r. 9'
		i-da-gal MATSH 9:42
		i-ḫa-ṣi-in MARV 2 8:10
		i-kar-rab Ištar Ritual:10
		i-ka-sa-ap Ištar Ritual:6
		i-la-bi-in[!] KAJ 111:12
		i-la-pat Coronation Ritual i 25
		i-ma-ag-gu-ur MAL A § 30:31
		i-maḫ-ḫa-ar MAL A § 31:49; *i-ma-ḫar* T 97-2:16
		i-maḫ-aṣ Coronation Ritual i 28
		i-pa-láḫ-šu Giricano 4:23; *i-pa-*⌜*al-làḫ-ši*[?]⌝ Tsukimoto 1992 D r. 5'
		i-pa-si-lu-ni KAJ 1:25
		i-pa-ša-ḫu-ni PKT 5 r. 9'

5 Cf. Aro (1955a, 74f); Petschow (1974, 30); Gurney (1983, 109); Stein (2000, 43).

6 Although this assumption is, admittedly, not without its problems, e.g., *ú-ba-li-ṭí* KAJ 101:13 is followed by *me-ID-ḫa-ar-šu* l. 13, while, in MARV 1 47, we find *i-di-ni* passim, as well as [d]UTU-*di-in-de-ni* l. 32.

i-pa-aṭ-ṭar-ši MAL A § 5:64
i-qar-rib MAL A § 37:24; Ištar Ritual:3; Coronation Ritual i 39
i-qar-ri-ib Aššur Ritual ii 9’
i-ra-gu-um KAJ 10:7
i-ra-ḫi-iṣ MARV 8 2:9
i-ra-kas Coronation Ritual iv 17; *i-ra-ka-su-ni* i 40
i-sa-ma-ak-ši MAL A § 55:37
i-sa-ra-aq New Year Ritual:17’
i-sa-ḫa-ra-áš!-[...] MATSH 27:7’
i-ṣa-bat MAL B § 17:14
i-ša-ka-an MARV 6 37:19
i-ša-lim KAJ 61:20
i-šap-pak Ištar Ritual:5; KAV 205:31
i-šap-pa-ar MAPD § 9:53
i-ša-rap MARV 1 23:10; ⸢*i*⸣*-ša-ra-ap* MATSH 4:7’
i-ša-aṭ-ṭa-ar KAJ 153:19
i-tab-ba-ak MAL B § 19:12
i-za-bi-lu-ni KAJ 267:19†
i-za-kar MAPD § 11:61

3fs *ta-da-gal* MAL A § 45:49
ta-ma-gu-ur MAL A § 12:17; cf. *ta-ma-ga-ar* Giricano 8:21
ta-ma-ḫa-si MAPD § 18:85
ta-šap-pa-ra-am-ma MAPD § 6:43
ta-ša-qa-al TIM 4 45:16
ta-z[*a-m*]*u-ur* MAPD § 21:103

2ms *ta-bal-laṭ* Ištar Ritual:6’
ta-ka-pár PKT 1 I right:9; *ta-kap-pár* PKT 2 i 5
ta-ka-ša-ad MCS 2 1:20
ta-kám-mar MARV 3 9:22
[*ta*]*-ma-ri-iṭ* PKT 1 II right:23
ta-par-ri-ik PKT 3 iv 5
ta-pa-ṭar BVW A:9
ta-qar-ra-ab MATSH 1:19
ta-ra-kas BVW A:15
ta-ṣa-ra-aḫ PKT 1 II right:27
ta-ša-ḫal PKT 3 i 10
ta-ša-ka-an MARV 6 37:4
ta-šal-lim Ištar Ritual:7’
ta-šap-pa-ka-šu-nu BVW F r. 10
ta-šap-pa-ra T 98-134:24
ta-tab-ba-ak PKT 1 I right:5

2fs *ta-šap-pi-ri-*[?] T 97-32:13’

1cs *a-ba-ta-aq* MATSH 8:30’
a-da-gal MATSH 6:13’; MATC 1:10
a-pa-láḫ KAV 159:5
a-pa-ṭar MAL A § 48:42
a-ṣa-bat MATSH 8:36’; MARV 2 25:17
a-šap-pa-ra-ku MATC 12:32

3mp *i-bat-tu-qu* New Year Ritual:15’
i-ga-ad-di-mu-uš MAL A § 18:80
i-ka-ṣu-ru-ni-ku MATC 22:27
i-ka-šu-du MATSH 3:43
i-⸢*ka*⸣*-šu-du-ni-ni* TabT05a-134:19
i-la-bi-nu KAM 10 9:9
i-ma-gu-ru MATSH 7:12’; T 93-11:17

		i-maḫ-ḫu-ṣu-uš MAL A § 40:83
		i-pal-lu-šu MAPD § 17:81
		i-pa-ṭu-ru Adad Ritual r. 7'; KAJ 21:25
		i-qa-ab-bi-ru-ši MAL A § 53:97
		i-qar-ri-bu MAL A § 29:17
		i-ra-gu-mu KAJ 167:13
		i-ra-ak-ku-su MAL A § 40:86
		i-ša-ak-ku-nu MARV 4 151:57
		i-šaṭ-ṭu-ru MAL A § 45:68
		i-tab-bu-ku MAL A § 40:76
		i-za-am-mu-ru Coronation Ritual iii 2
		i-za-qu-pu-ú-ši MAL A § 53:96
	3fp	*i-la-be-ra-*[*ni*$^?$] MATC 12:11†
		i-la-ma-da-ni MARV 3 64:35
		i-pa-ša-ra Adad Ritual:4
		i-ṣa-ba-ta-šu-nu KAV 211 r. 9'
		⸢*e-za-mu-ra-ni*⸣ MARV 4 59:18
	2cp	*ta-ma-gu-ra* KAV 194:18
		ta-sa-da-ar-a$^?$ MARV 3 64:39[7]
	1cp	*ni-ma-ḫar* MATSH 2:59

Perfect:

G	3ms	*ib-ta-*⸢*at*⸣*-qu-ni* MAPD § 5:37
		ib-ta-al-ṭa MATSH 8:50'
		iḫ-ta-li-iq Giricano 12:19'; T 98-94:18
		ik-tal-da$^!$ MATSH 14:5
		im-ti-ki-is$_5$ TR 2059:11
		im-ta-ḫar KAJ 109:17
		im-tu-qu-ut MATSH 4:7
		ip-tu-ḫu-u[*r*] MATSH 2:47
		ip-ta-ṭa-ar T 98-94:14
		il-tu-ḫu-ur MAPD § 21:106
		iṣ-ṣa-ba-as-si MAL A § 12:18
		iṣ-ṣa-bat MAL A § 15:41
		il-ta-par-šu MAL A § 36:5
		il-ta-ṭar MAL C+ § 11:20
		iz-zi-bi-il$_5$ MAL A § 30:21
	3fs	*tar-tu-gu-um* MAPD § 21:105
		tal-ta-ka-an MAL A § 6:71
		tal-ti-ri-iq MAL A § 3:25
	2ms	*ta-am-ta-ḫar* KAV 104:10; Faist 2001, 252:21
	1cs	⸢*ak-ta*⸣*-na-ak* MATSH 9:6
		am-ta-ḫa-aṣ KAV 96:7
		[*a*]*m-ta-šar* MATSH 2:11
		aq-ti-ri-ib MATSH 2:29
		aṣ-ṣa-bat Hall 1983:19
		al-ta-ka-an-ka T 93-20:7
		al-tap-ra-ku T 96-7:4
		al-ta-ṭar MATSH 22:23; VAT 8851:9
		[*a*]*t-ta-ba-ak* MATSH 14:11
	3mp	*iḫ-ta-al-qu* RS 18.54a:2'
		im-ta-aḫ-ru MAL A § 4:48; MATC 40:15

7 I cannot explain the presence of the sign A$^?$ for the *-ā* morpheme of the second-person plural.

		im-taḫ-ru MARV 1 48A r. 5'; MPR 31:16
		ip-ta-áš-[*r*]*u* LVUH 66:24
		iq-tar-bu KAV 159:4
		ir$^{!}$*-ták-su* MATSH 17:10
		ir-ta-ap-su Billa 63:17
		il-ta-ak-nu-ú-ni MAL B § 6:25
	2cp	*ta-ṣa-ba-ta-ni* KAV 102:19
	1cp	*ni-*<*il*>*-ta-ka-an* T 96-9:14
		ni-ta-ba-ak MARV 1 71:14

Preterite:

G	3ms	*ig-mu-ur* MAL B § 2:16
		iḫ-l[*u*$^{!}$*-ṣ*]*u-ni* T 98-1:2
		ik-šu-da-ku-<*ni*> T 93-11:7
		ik-šìr MARV 1 10:19
		il-bi-in MAL B § 13:27
		im-⸢*gur*⸣ MATSH 2:65
		im-ḫur KAJ 234:11
		im-ḫa-aṣ-ma MAL A § 51:83; *im-ḫa-aṣ* MAL E § 2:11'
		im-li-ku-ú-[*ni*$^{?}$] KBo 28 61/2 r. 12'
		ip-šu-ru-ú-ni KAJ 113:9
		ir-ku-ús MAPD § 7:46; MARV 1 17:6
		iṣ-bu-tu-ni KAJ 311:13
		iš-kun MAL A § 18:83
		iš-pu-ra-an-ni AO 19.227:8
		[*i*]*š-ri-qu-ni* T 98-42:3'†
		il-ṭu-ru-ni KAV 119:15;
		it-bu-uk MAL A § 42:15
		it-ru-uḫ MAL B § 20:19
		iz-bil MAL A § 31:41
	2ms	*ta-ak-nu-ku-ni* MCS 2 1:15
		tam-ḫur Faist 2001, 252:23
		ta-aṣ-bu-tu-ni T 98-3:6
		la-a ta-áš-p[*u*]*-ra* RS 06.198:11
		ta-at-bu-ku-ni PKT 5 r. 1
	1cs	*la-a am-li-ik* A 2994:9
		ap-ṭu-ra-ni MAL C+ § 1:3
		áš-ḫu-ul MASH 3:32
		áš-ku-nu-ka-ni MATC 4:19; Billa 60:5
		áš-pu-ra MATSH 26:3'
	3mp	*ib-tu-qu-ni* MATSH 2:49
		[*i*]*ḫ-bu-tu-ni* MATSH 7:18''
		ik-šu-du-uš MAL A § 12:20
		im-ḫu-ru-ni KAJ 109:11; KAJ 252:9
		il-ṭu-ru RE 92:11
		ip-šu-ru-ú-ni MARV 3 4 r. 9'
		ir-ṣi-pu-ú-ni MARV 1 1 iv 56'
		iṣ-bu-tu MARV 4 151:65
		iz-ku-ru-ni-šu-ni MAL M § 1:7
	1cp	*ni-*[*ip*]*-qi-id* Billa 66:18

Precative:

G	3ms	*lim-ḫur* MAL E § 3:5'
		[*l*]*i-iṣ-bat* Ištar Ritual:12

		le-eš-ḫu-ut MAL K § 3:8
		li-iš-pu-ra MATSH 6:13'; 12:21
	3fs	*lu taš-pu-ra* A 845:22
	1cs	*la-áš-pur* MATSH 7:19'
	3mp	*li-ik-ṣu-ru* MATSH 6:14'
		⌜*lim-ḫu*⌝*-ru* MATSH 3:37
		li-im-ḫi-ṣu MATSH 6:14'
		li-iš-ku-nu MATC 12:14
		li-it-ru-ṣu MATSH 10:21
		li-iz-bu-lu-ú-ni MATSH 4:3'
		li-iz-qu-pu T 97-34:22
	1cp	*lu ni-ib-la-aṭ* MATSH 22:19
		lu ni-iš-⌜*pur*⌝ MATSH 17:23'

Imperative:

G	2ms	*mu-ḫu-ur-šu* MARV 7 14:22
		pu-uš-ra-n[*i*] MAL M § 1:2
		[*r*]*u-ku-ús* T 93-4:13
		ṣa-bat T 96-7:5
		šu-ku-un MATSH 1:18
		šu-pu-ur MATSH 9:33; MATC 5:5
		šu-ṭu-ur MATSH 1:16
		tu-bu-[*uk*] MATC 17:10
		ṭu-ru-ud MATSH 21:4'
		zu-kur Billa 66:18
	2fp	*ši-ir-qí* MAL A § 5:62
	2cp	*ku-un-ka* KAV 98:21
		mu-uḫ-ra KAV 99:40
		šu-up$^{!}$*-ra-ni* MCS 2 2:14
		šu-uṭ-ra KAV 98:22

15.3 The suffix conjugation: the stative

§ 513 The Akkadian stative is formed by conjugating a nominal base with its specific paradigm pronominal suffixes. This nominal base mostly consists of the adjectival patterns. The stative itself is the equivalent of the West Semitic perfect paradigm; however, unlike West Semitic, the Akkadian stative does not simply designate the past tense, but has a number of different functions. Basically, every substantive or adjective can be turned into a stative and conjugated as such (GAG, 124f § 77a). Morphologically, the nominal stative of masculine/feminine third-person singular is identical to the status absolutus.

aššutu	*aššiti*$^{\text{sic.}}$ *šīt lā áš-ša-at* 'that wife is not a (proper) wife' MAL A § 41:9
iššakku	*lā u-bar u iš-šak* 'he is not a stranger but an *iššakku*-farmer' RE 19:15 (peripheral)
mitḫāru	PN (…) *qāta mi-it-ḫa-ar* 'PN is entitled to an equal share'KAJ 1:22–24
Sūtīu	*atānu lā su-ti-a-at* 'the she-ass is not Sutean' Hall 1983:12
šēbu	PN *šé-eb iškāra lā eppaš* 'PN, old man, does not do the work assignment' MPR 18:1
šēbtu	PN *emāssina še-bat* 'PN, their mother-in-law, old woman' MARV 4 89 v 45'
	PN *še-bat iškāra lā teppaš* 'PN, their mother-in-law, is an old woman' MPR 3:14–15

There may be some instances involving PNs for the third-person feminine singular, but these could also be instances of the status absolutus:[8]

dayyānu	^{d}*Iš$_8$-tár-* DI.KU$_5$-*at* (*Ištar-dayyānat*) 'Ištar-is-judge' MARV 2 27 v 24
iltu	^{fd}NIN.LÍL-DINGIR-*at* (*Mulliltu-ilat*) 'Mullissu-is-goddess' MARV 2 6 ii 69
mušēzibtu	^{d}*Iš$_8$-tá*[*r-m*]*u-še-zi-bat* TR 2069A+:14

Attestations of the nominal stative in the first-/second-person singular and plural forms are considerably rarer in MA:

sarru	*lā sa-ra-a-ku* 'I am not a criminal' KAV 201:7
	lā sa-ra-ku A 133:7
	lā sa-ar-ra-ku A 748:7[9]
ṣeḫḫeru	*ṣe-eḫ-ḫe-ru* 'they are (very) young' MAL A § 43:32

The last form is distinguishable from an adjective by the lack of the plural suffix *-utt*. Other examples are uncertain.[10]

§ 514 As these nominal statives are equally rare in NA (SNAG, 90 § 3.1.2.3), it may be assumed that they were gradually lost over time. The main form of the stative is thus the adjective construction *PaRiS*, which we find in the form 3ms with a zero ending. With other suffixes attached, the second short vowel disappears according to the rules of vowel syncope. As such, it has led many grammarians to conclude that the stative derived from nominal sentences, with a nominal base and an additional pronominal element. However, some disagreement exists as to whether the stative is still nominal in Akkadian or whether it has developed into a verbal form; most recent studies suggest the latter.[11] For the sake of our research into MA, this question appears to be of little relevance, although we do conclude, to a certain extent, that we are talking about a nominal verbal form with the infinitive and participle, in light of the related base of all three forms. One distinction between nominal forms and a stative can be found in the following phrase of MAL A:

(A) *aḫḫū mutīša la-a ze-e-zu* 'her brothers-in-laws did not divide' MAL A § 25:84

(B) *aḫḫū mutīša la-a ze-zu-ú-tu ilaqqeū* 'her brothers-in-law, who did not divide, will take it'MAL A § 25:88–89

The difference between the two quotes relates, of course, to the fact that (A) involves an independent clause and *zēzū* as the predicate, whereas, in (B), *zēzuttu* is merely an adjective and *ilaqqeū* is the predicate.

§ 515 In previous research into MA, the paradigm for statives was not well attested among the different persons (UGM, 57). Unfortunately, the situation nowadays is not much better,

8 The occurrence of a similar PN for the stative verb *laʾû* 'to be able' suggests that a status absolutus is the correct analysis: ^{fd}*Iš$_8$-tár-le-at* YBC 12862:3.

9 It is possible to take these statives from the verb *sarāru* 'to be a cheat, criminal' (CAD S, 174–75). In general, this verb seems to occur in the prefix conjugation; thus, we agree with CAD that takes this stative from the noun *sarru* 'criminal' (CAD S, 183a).

10 The occurrence of *pa-ni-a-ku* MATSH 2:25 does not make sense. For this reason, we will have to go with the solution presented in MATSH (102-103), which reads: *pa-ni-<i> a-<na>-ku*. Although not entirely satisfying, it could say something about the pronunciation of the language, where some syllables and word borders were elided.

11 Cf. Kouwenberg (2000); Streck (2007, 51f § 2.2.5); Kouwenberg (2010, 161ff).

with a number of gaps in the paradigm as can be seen below. A normal stative is built on the adjectival pattern *PaRiS* and likewise on the patterns of the derived stems (e.g., D-stem *PaRRuS*). According to Kouwenberg, the Assyrian dialect, in general, involves more variation in patterns than Babylonian, including *PaRaS* and *PuRuS*. He pointed out that, aside from the normal pattern *PaRiS*, we also find *PaRaS* for *balāṭu*, *ušābu* and *ḫalāqu*. Statives derived from adjectives, such as *marāṣu*, have the pattern *PaRuS*, whereas the vowel /u/ is directly copied from the adjectival pattern (Kouwenberg 2010, 162). These variations are only rarely attested in MA, but we do find the *PaRaS* pattern of the verb *ḫalāqu* on a few occasions:

balāṭu ŠEŠ-*ka ba-la-aṭ* 'your brother is alive' KBo 28 61/62:17'
ḫalāqu *ḫa-laq* 'it is lost' MAL C+ § 6:41; MATSH 17:9', 11', 20'
ḫa-la-qa RE 19:16

Note, however, *ḫa-li*[*q*] in T 98-132:18. We probably find some instances of the stative *ušab*. In the first example, from the Adad Ritual, the orthography does not allow for a distinction. The second example, from a letter, only allows for a precative as an alternative interpretation. However, the fact that the precative would have been *lūšib* makes this unlikely.

ušābu *šangû ú-šab* 'the priest sits' Adad Ritual:13
lū ú-šab 'he must settle down' KAV 194:5

The pattern *PuRuS* is extremely rare in MA regarding statives, with only one of the verbs given by Kouwenberg (2010, 162) attested in a PN. Moreover, the evidence from other Assyrian dialects remains flimsy.

ruāqu ^{f}*Ṣi-iḫ-ti-*⸢*ru*⸣*-qa*!*-a*[*t*]! (Ṣīḫtī-rūqat) KAJ 16:14 (Kouwenberg 2010, 64–65 n88).

The pattern *PaRuS* is also very rare, but could be common with III/ū verbs (see § 572). For strong roots, it may be noted that the Babylonian stative *maruṣ* is attested in MA as *PaRiS*, e.g., *ma-ri-iṣ* MAL A § 3:23; MAL D § 1:4 (cf. Kouwenberg 2010, 64 § 3.3.4).

	OA	MA	NA	OB
3ms	*paris*	*paris*	*paris*	*paris*
3fs	*pars-at*	*pars-at*	*pars-at*	*pars-at*
2ms	*pars-āti* *pars-āt*	*pars-āta*	*pars-āka*	*pars-āta*
2fs	*pars-āti*	–	*pars-āki*	*pars-āti*
1cs	*pars-āku* *pars-āk*	*pars-āku* (*pars-āk*)	*pars-āku* *pars-āk*	*pars-āku*
3mp	*pars-ū*	*pars-ū*	*pars-ū*	*pars-ū*
3fp	*pars-ā*	*pars-ā*	*pars-ā*	*pars-ā*
2mp	*pars-ātunu*	*pars-ātunu*	*pars-ākunu*	*pars-ātunu*
2fp	*pars-ātini*	–	–	*pars-ātina*
1cp	*pars-āni*	*pars-āni* *pars-ānu*	*pars-āni*	*pars-ānu*

Figure 36: Stative paradigms of Assyrian and Old Babylonian.

§ 516 The above figure presents an overview of the conjugation of the stative in Assyrian. Note that, in some attestations, the syllabic signs point to *PaReS*, rather than *PaRiS*, e.g., *ka-me-er* TabT105A-151:15 (perhaps caused by /r/; see § 135). Other forms, such as *ba-ti-iq* MARV 6 65:24, have a true <I> sign to indicate *PaRiS*, while, in *ra-ki-i-EŠ* MAL A §

34:72, we find both. In the irregular verb *našāʾu* (etymologic III/ʔ), both variations are attested: *na-a-ši* KAJ 169:20 ~ *na-še* MARV 1 47:56. It can be observed that, especially in the second-person singular, some diversity exists. In OA, the main form 2ms is *parsāti*, which is identical to the feminine form.[12] In MA, we only find the Babylonian variant: *tamʾāta* MAL A § 47:31; *šaknāta* MATSH 9:39. In NA, the situation is again different, with the singular and plural forms having changed from /t/ > /k/, probably by analogy with the 1cs suffix *-āku*.[13] Moreover, apocopate forms, such as *parsāt(i)* and *parsāk(u)*, which occur in both OA and NA, are not found in MA, except in some forms with crasis in the onomasticon, e.g., ᵐ*Ták-lak-ana-*ᵈ*Aššur* (< *Taklāku-ana-Aššur*) KAV 217:21'; ᵐᵈ*Aššur-ták-lak* KAJ 252:7. The OA stative 1cp *parsāni* does occur in other WPA dialects and is found in Amurru (Izre'el 1991, 128), while in the MA corpus we find once Assyrian *PaRSāni* in *us-ba-ni* T 96-36:12, 25 and once Babylonian *PaRSānu* in *naḫsānu* MATSH 2:45. This is remarkable: in NA, we find the OA *PaRSāni*, while the ending with /i/ seems to be Common Semitic (cf. Lipiński 2001, 374 § 40.12). It seems that Babylonian had a large influence on the paradigm of the Assyrian stative, similar to the pronominal paradigm. It led to the reintroduction of a distinction between masculine and feminine in the second-person singular. This distinction remained in Assyrian as indicated by the NA endings with /k/, which are dialectal forms that retain the distinction between the two genders. The apocopate forms, which are attested in both OA and NA, are not found in MA, except for the PNs. Here, it seems that these forms were regarded as incorrect and therefore not written in their natural form. The introduction of the Babylonian 1cp *PaRSānu* in MA seems to have only been scriba convention, as it disappeared in NA.

§ 517 Statives can take all the five suffixes discussed above in Figure 34. This includes the pronominal suffixes, although they are not frequently attested in Akkadian (Kouwenberg 2010, 162–63). While stative forms with pronominal suffixes are frequently found in OA (GOA § 16.7.2; cf. GKT, 118–19 § 72a), similar forms in MA are rare.[14] In the few attestations available to us, both accusative (*naṣṣū-š* MATSH 9:45) and dative (*naṣṣ-akku-ni* MATC 10:18) pronominal suffixes are attested. Most attestations come with the irregular verbs *našāʾu* 'to bring' and *tadānu* 'to give':

našāʾu	3ms	*+akku(m) (+ni)*	*na-ṣa-ku-ú-ni* MATC 10:18
	3fs	*+akku(m) (+ni)*	*na-ṣa-ta-ku-ni* MATC 5:16
	3mp	*+šu*	*na-aṣ-ṣu-uš* MATSH 9:45
naṭāʾu	3ms	*+aššu(m)*	*na-ṭu-a-šu-ni* MATSH 10:27
tadānu	3ms	*+aššu(m) (+ni)*	*ta-ad-na-áš-šu* KAJ 83:13
	3fs	*+aššunu*	*ta-ad-na-ta-šu-nu* VAT 8236 r. 16
	3mp	*+neššu(m) (+ni)*	*ta-ad-nu-ni-[š]u-ni* KAJ 120:4

12 This is probably a merging of the masculine and the feminine form, and therefore an OA simplification, rather than an archaism. A similar merging of the two genders is attested in Moroccan Arabic (Harell 1962, 41), e.g., *mšiti* 'you (m/f) went'; *neqqiti* 'you cleaned'.

13 It seems that these forms developed following a tendency to make the personal morphemes more regular, in analogy with the 1cs morpheme *-āku*. We may draw parallels with the South Semitic languages, for instance, the Ge'ez paradigm, where all forms (except 1cp) start with /k/, e.g., 1cs *naṣṣar-ku* (**ነጸርኩ**); 2ms *warad-ka* (**ወረድከ**); 2mp *śarab-kəmu* (**ሠረብክሙ**); cf. Tropper (2002, 88 § 44.122). It also occurs in South Modern Arabic, e.g., *matk* 'you died' with *-(ə)k* in Mehri (see Rubin 2010, 121).

14 Unfortunately, as Hämeen-Anttila (SNAG) makes no reference to the situation in NA, we are left in the dark regarding the situation at this stage of Assyrian.

šakānu	3ms	+*aššunu*	*ša-⸢ak⸣-na-áš-šu-nu* MARV 7 2:8

§ 518 Below is a selected list of attestations for strong roots in the G-stem:

G	3ms	*ba-la-aṭ* KBo 28 61/62:17'
		ba-ti-iq MARV 6 65:24
		ḫa-laq MAL C+ § 6:41; MATSH 17:9', 11', 20'
		ka-me-er TabT105A-151:15; MARV 5 2:29
		ka-ṣi-ir T 98-41:8'
		ka-zi-ir TR 2083a+:18
		la-at-ku-ú-<*ni*> MARV 3 38:7
		ma-gi-ir MAL A § 5:63
		ma-ḫi-ir KAJ 233:6; *ma-ḫír* MARV 8 88:16
		ma-ri-iṣ MAL A § 3:23
		pa-qi-id KAJ 210:10
		ra-ki-i-és MAL A § 34:72; *ra-ki-is* KAJ 39:12; *ra-ke-és* KAJ 182:12
		ša-kín PKT 1 I right:1; LB 1848:10;
		ša-ak-nu-ú-ni MATC 22:19
		ša-li-iṭ T 97-22:13
		ša-ṭí-ir KAV 156:5
		ta-bi-ik MATC 80:3; MARV 2 22:11; *ta-be-ek* Coronation Ritual i 33
	3fs	*⸢bal⸣-ṭa-at* MAL A § 39:34
		ba-áš-la-at MATSH 3:9
		ḫal-qa-at KAM 10 31:8
		kat-ma-at MAPD § 19:94
		ma-ḫa-rat LVUH 105:8
		mar-ṣu-tu-ú-ni A 1765 (NTA, 25):5
		nam-ra-tu-ni Ištar Ritual:12
		pár-ka-at KAV 159:10
		ra-ap-ša-a[*t*] Billa 22:5
		ṣa-ar-ḫa-at PKT 4 obv. left 17
		ša-ak-na-at KAV 99:42
		šaṭ-rat MAL A § 28:5; *šaṭ-ra-at* KAJ 122:14
		táq-na-at MATSH 2:66
	2ms	*ša-ak-na-ta* MATSH 9:39
	1cs	*pa-al-ḫa-a-ku* Billa 63:21; *pal-ḫa-ku* MATSH 16:20
		bal-ṭa-ku-ma KBo 28 64:10'
	3mp	*bal-ṭu-ni* KAJ 7:12
		bat-qu-ú-ni MPR 23:22
		ḫal-qu-ú-ni MAL A § 25:88
		la-ap-tu KAJ 230:12
		maḫ-ru KAJ 66:29
		pa-aq-du A 297 (NTA, 16):7 passim; *pa-qi-du* A 3196 (NTA, 39):4
		ra-ak-su KAM 10 9:16
		sa-ad-ru-ni MARV 2 17a+:17
		ša-ak-nu MATSH 15:22
		ra-ap-qu KTN inventory iv 15'
		ṣab-tu MARV 6 22:13'
		tab-ku-ni MARV 1 119:14
	3fp	*ba!-aq-na* LVUH 21:19
		la-am-da MARV 3 64:41
		ra-ap-qa KTN inventory i 25
		ra-ak-sa Wilhelm 1997:18
		ša-aṭ-ra-ni MARV 1 38:7
		šap-ka KAJ 249:13

1cp	(*na-aḫ-sa-nu* MATSH 2:45)

15.4 The Infinitive

§ 519 The group of infinitives is another group of verbal nouns, as the name already suggests. They morphologically take the same base as the adjective/stative, but with normal case endings. The only exception is the G-stem, which involves *PaRāS* vs. the stative *PaRiS*. The difference is especially visible in the II/weak verbs where, due to the long vowel, no contraction takes place (e.g., *muāt*) as it does in the stative (*mēt*). Unlike normal nouns, the infinitive in MA is never conjugated according to number or gender, but only after case. A number of attestations of the infinitive in the status absolutus and constructus is also known. It is essentially an action noun, expressing a verbal action, although, in some instances, the infinitive was lexicalized. We find a relatively large number of Babylonian-shaped infinitives in MA, which could be partly explained by the lexicalized character of some infinitives.

G-stem:

erēbu	*i+na* <u>*e-re-eb*</u> KASKAL-*ni*(-*š*[*u-nu*]) 'at the return of their caravan' KAJ 32:7-8; 39:8
ḫapā'u	*a-na* <u>*he-pí*</u> 'for breaking' KAJ 142:15 (etc. see § 570)
laqā'u	*a-na* (…) *le-qé* 'for taking' KAJ 167:4
šamā'u	*še-ma-a* 'hearing' Coronation Ritual ii 35

D-stem:

kallulu	*ku-lu-li* (Ass. *kallulu*) 'crowning' Coronation Ritual ii 30
mallu'u	*i+na mu-le-e* 'at the filling(?)' MATSH 7:22''
nappušu	*nu-pu-ša* 'airing' KAV 99:14; KAV 109:12

The infinitive may be negated in similar way to adjectives and finite verbs (§ 688). Genitive pronominal suffixes are added as if they were nouns, e.g.:

alāku	*i+na a-la-ki-ia* 'at my arrival' MATC 11:12

The infinitive can be used in the status constructus as observed in the following passage:

ṣabātu	*i+na ṣa-bat* NÍG.KA$_9$^{meš} 'at the settling of accounts' KAJ 255:4

Sometimes, the infinitive occurs in the status absolutus. This is also attested for OA (GOA § 16.9.6), but the function is not clear.

balāṭu D	^{f}PN *ša a-na* <u>*ba-lu-uṭ*</u> *ù* <u>*le-qé*</u> (…) *laqiutūni* 'PN who is taken to be provided for and adopted' KAJ 167:3–6
palāḫu	*a-di bal-ṭu-ni* A.ŠÀ *ù* ŠÀ-URU <u>*pa-la-aḫ*</u> *a-ḫa-iš e-pu-šu* 'they will do for each other (their) obligation in field and city as long as they live' KAJ 7:12–13

Infinitives have often become substantivized, e.g., *alāku* 'to come' > 'arrival'; *eṣādu* 'to harvest'. There is no clear distinction between the 'nominal' infinitives and the verbal infinitives Some differences can be observed in the infinitive constructions, which are all verbal with *ana*, whereas nominal infinitives are more frequent (but not exclusive) with the preposition *ina* and in the status constructus.

alāku	*i+na* <u>*a-lak*</u> LUGAL 'at the proceedings of the king' Ali 7:14
arāšu	A.ŠÀ <u>*a-ra-*⌜*še*⌝</u> 'land of cultivation' MARV 3 10:7'
danānu	*aʾīlu ki-i* <u>*da-ʾa-ni*</u> *ᶠbatulta iṣbatma* 'the man seized the girl with force' MAL A § 55:20–21
eṣādu	<u>*e-ṣa-da*</u> *ana šaṣbute atta*[*lak*] 'I went to organize the harvest' MATSH 2:26
šalāmu D	*pa-ḫa-at* <u>*šal-lu-me*</u> 'the responsibility of paying in full' Billa 20:18–19

§ 520 Below is a selected list of attestations for strong roots in the G-stem:

urki ba-la-a-ṭé MATSH 3:27
ina ka-ba-a-si MAL A § 36:99
ana ka-ṣa-ri MATSH 6:13'
ka-ša-a-di MAPD § 7:46
*ana la-ba-n*i KAJ 111:10
ma-ga-ra Coronation Ritual ii 35
ana ma-ḫa-re MATSH 2:57
ana ma-qa-te MASTH 3:15
ša ma-ta-ḫi KAJ 310:58
ana pa-ša-ri KAJ 316:6
ana pa-ṭa-ri-ša MAL A § 5:66
ša lā qa-ra-ab-ša-ni MAPD § 7:47
ša ra-ma-ki PKT 4 obv. left 17
ra-ma-ki KAJ 205:9
ina ṣa-bat KAJ 255:4
ana ša-ḫa-a-li MATSH 3:31
ana ša-ḫa-a-ṭí MARV 1 67:13
ša-ka-a-ni MAL B § 18:23
ana ṣa-ra-pí A 305:14
ana ša-pa-⌜*ri*⌝ MATSH 9:9
ana ša-ra-pi MARV 1 23:8
ina 10-*šu ta-ba-ki* PKT 1 I right:3

15.5 The derived stems

15.5.1 The D-stem

§ 521 The D-stem occurs frequently in MA. Its main morphological feature is the gemination of R_2, hence its name deriving from (D)ouble. The pattern of the D-stem is similar to OA and NA, which are, to a certain extent, different from MB. Consider the following table, which is slightly edited from Kouwenberg (2010, 269) for a comparison with OB and contemporary MB. As can be observed, in forms without a prefix, Babylonian placed /u/ between the first and second radical. This is certainly secondary (as in the case of the imperative), as the same base as the preterite would be expected. Moreover, Babylonian recognizes a number of 'Assyrian forms' (Kouwenberg 2010, 269f). The MB form *uperris* is likewise not found in Assyrian. The nominal base, as used for the stative, adjective and infinitive, is different from its Babylonian counterpart: *PaRRuS* vs. the Babylonian *PuRRuS*. Likewise, the imperative involves the infinitive *PaRRiS* vs. Babylonian *PuRRiS*. The slightly different pattern with the vowel /a/ instead of /u/ can also be observed in the Š-nominal base: *šaPRuS* vs. *šuPRuS*. Reiner (2001, 390) assumes that this vowel in the first syllable is a *Murmelvokal*, as she describes it as being inverted in order to prevent a three-consonant cluster. Kouwenberg argues that *PaRRuS* is the original form by analogy with the *šaPRuS* pattern, which is also attested in Babylonian, with /a/ being the basis vowel in verbal forms to separate R_1 and R_2. In any case, we do find Babylonian infinitives in MA, e.g., *ku-lu-li* 'crowning' Coronation Ritual ii 30; *nu-pu-ša* KAV 99:14; KAV 109:12 (cf. GAG, 143 § 88b) and the substantive *bu-qu-ni-ša* 'her sheep ready for plucking' (< D *baqāmu*) KAJ 97:2; *bu-qu-ni-ši-na* KAJ 88:13. As Kouwenberg (2010, 271) argued for the gradual spread of *PuRRuS* northwards, these forms may actually be a reflection of that development.

	MA	OB	MB
Present		*u-parras*	
Perfect		*u-ptarris*	
Preterite		*u-parris*	*u-perris*
Imperative	*parris*		*purris*
Stative/adjective	*parrus*		*purrus*
Infinitive/past participle	*parrusu*		*purrusu*
Present participle		*muparrisu*	

Figure 37: Overview of the D-stem.

§ 522 A small number of D-tantum verbs can be found in MA; these are: *ba*$^{??}$*û* 'to search'; *ka*$^{??}$*ulu* 'to hold'; *kallulu* 'to crown'; and *qa*$^{??}$*û* 'to wait'. The D-stem occurs in a number of different functions. Its meaning is most clear in the case of intransitive G-stems, which become transitive in the D-stem. This function of the D-stem is usually called "factitive", e.g., G *balāṭu* 'to live' > *balluṭu* 'to let live'.[15] Some intransitive action verbs retain their intransitivity in the D-stem, but these are rare; indeed, I found no examples in MA.[16] A number of examples of factitive D-stems follows:

balāṭu (G) 'to live' > *balluṭu* (D) 'to let (someone) live:

> *la-a ú-bal-lu-ṭu-ši* 'they will not allow her to live' MAPD § 11:63

kuāšu (G) 'to linger' > *ka*$^{??}$*ušu* (D) 'to make linger=to delay':

> [*mar š*]*ipre* (…) [*l*]*a tu*$_4$*-ka-*⌜*as*⌝*-sú* 'do not delay the messenger (sg.)' EA 15:16–18

paḫāru (G) 'to gather' > *paḫḫuru* (D) 'to gather (something)':

> *alpēšu gabba lu-pa-ḫi-ra* 'may he gather all his oxen' T 97-17:8–9

pašāḫu (G) 'to rest' > *paššuḫu* (D) 'to make something rest':

> *tu-pa-ša-aḫ-šu* 'you will let it rest' PKT 5 r. 6

qarābu (G) 'to be near' > *qarrubu* (D) 'to make something near=present something':

> *nāmurāte ana šarre ú-qar-ri-bu-ni* 'they presented the audience gifts to the king' Coronation Ritual iii 7–8
>
> *kī nāmurte ú-qar-ri-bu-ni* he brought it as a present'KAJ 274:13–14

rapāšu (G) 'to be broad' > *rappušu* (D) 'to make something broad=expand':

> *mātka ra-pi*[*š*] 'expand your country!' Coronation Ritual ii 35

raṭābu (G) 'to be damp' > *raṭṭubu* (D) 'to moisten':

15 See GAG, 143 § 88c; GAV, 237–80; Kouwenberg (2010, 272–74 § 11.3.1).
16 See GAV, 281–86; Kouwenberg (2010, 274 § 11.3.2).

buqla (…) *ú-ra-ṭu-bu* 'they will make the barley humid' MATC 12:32–33

samāḫu (G) 'to mix' > *sammuḫu* (D) 'to mix (something):

eqla ammar ú-sa-me-ḫu-ú-ni 'as much field as he confused (< to mix)' MAL B § 9:20

tuāru (G) 'to go back, return' > *ta*[??]*uru* (D) 'to return (something)':

[*e*]*rīu an-nu-tum* (...) *ú-ta-e-ru-ni-ni* 'they returned this copper' KAJ 303:12–14

ušāru (G) 'to hang down' > *uššuru* (D) 'to release':

bitqīšu la-a tu-še-er '(if) you do not let go of (your) claim against him' KAV 201:17–18

Sometimes, the factitive D-stem can be used without an object (GAV, 261–65 § 7.4.2–3). This is attested for the verb *šalāmu* (G) 'to be whole' > *šallumu* 'to make complete':

[8] *šanātu ú-šal-la-ma* 'the eight years will complete' AO 19.228:15

niqīa[meš] (…) *ana šal-lu-mi illikanni* 'he has come to complete the offerings' MARV 1 10:5

In the stative, an agent is not expressed; however, the context implies the factitive meaning. For instance, a motion such as *tuāru* 'to turn back' has a different meaning in the D-stem 'to return (something)', which results in a clear difference in the stative G: 'to have returned' vs. D: 'to have been returned'.

šumma la-a ma-ru-ur 'if he is not made bitter (=castrated)' MAPD § 20:98

3 *mana gabīu* (…) *ana šarre qar-ru-bat-ni* 'three minas of alum are presented to the king' KAJ 223:1–4

ša ana šarre qar-ru-bu-ú-ni '(textiles) that are presented to the king' KAV 108:12–13

rēḫtu ana kunuk šarre ta-ur 'the rest was returned to the seal of the king' LVUH 71:18–19

§ 523 The D and Š-stem share the function of making intransitives transitive by providing an agent to them. The differences between them are sometimes difficult to observe on individual bases (e.g., see Kouwenberg 2010, 328–29). A general rule of thumb should be sufficient for this study: the D-stem is mostly used for adjectival verbs, whereas the Š-stem is found mostly with motion verbs. Some verbs can be used adjectivally and also as motion verbs (e.g., *elāʾu* 'to go up/be high'); thus, there is an overlap with verbs having both stems, sometimes with almost identical meanings. A similar, but smaller, group comprises the transitive process verbs in the D-stem. As with the intransitive process verbs, their D-stem is factitive, with the difference being that they already took an object in the G-stem: *labāšu* 'to wear' > *labbušu* 'to make someone wear'. Note that, in the following examples, the verbs occur in the stative, meaning that there is no agent:

šumma panima abuša ḫab-bu-ul 'if previously her father was indebted' MAL A § 39:27–29

[*amtu a*]*nnītu* x x *sa la-bu-ša-*[*a*]*t*[?] 'this slave girl is clothed' TR 2083+:17–18 (see Postgate 1979b, 92)

mā la ha-bu-la-ku 'saying, "I am not indebted"' MARV 1 13:6

§ 524 For transitive action verbs, the D-stem is used to indicate the plurality of the participants, most frequently, the direct object. However, the plurality of the participants is not always clear and may also refer to the event itself or the intensity of the action itself.

Some verbs feature a more lexicalized meaning, such as *rakāsu* 'to bind' > *rakkusu* 'to bind (with bandages)' (GAV, 119–46; Kouwenberg 2010, 274ff), e.g.:

asû ur-ták-ki-is-ma 'a physician bound it (with bandages)' MAL A § 8:81

uznēšu ú-pal-lu-ú-šu 'they will pierce his ears' MAL A § 40:84

1$^{\text{ta.àm}}$ *šepēšunu ú-ba-at-tu-qu* 'they will cut one foot each of them' MAPD § 20:101

[ÉRIN^{meš}] *bal-ṭu-te ša* <*la-a*> *nu-ṣa-bi-ta-ni* 'the living troops, which we did not seize' MATSH 18:33

emmera^{meš} (…) *nam-mi-iš* 'make the sheep depart' MATC 1:12–15

4 *alpē* (...) *ú-ṣa-bi-it* 'I seized the four oxen' AO 19.227:9–11

The plurality of the object is well attested for *nakāsu* 'to cut off' (see GAV, 123–24). In the following phrases, we find the G-stem with a singular object:

appaša i-na-ak-ki-is 'he will cut off her nose' MAL A § 5:69

1 *uzanšu i-na-ki-su* 'they will cut off one of his ears' MAPD § 21:104

1 *ubanša i-na-ki-su* 'they will cut off her finger' MAL A § 8:80

appa ša aššitīšu i-na-ke-és 'he will cut off the nose of his wife' MAL A § 15:53

In the following passage, it seems that the primary object of the verb is *appušu* 'her nose'. Thus, the G-stem is used:

appušu uznēšu i-na-ki-su 'they will cut off her nose and her ears' MAPD § 5:36

Thus, with a plural object, the D-stem is used:

ša urde u amte appēšunu uznēšunu ú-na-ak-ku-su 'they will cut off of the slave and maid their noses and their ears' MAL A § 4:49–50

uznēša ú-na-ak-ka-ás 'he will cut off her ears' MAL A § 5:65

The plurality is found in the character of the verb to cut off (G) > to mutilate (D):

aššassu la-a ú-na-ak-ke-és 'he will not mutilate his wife' MAL A § 24:79

It is also possible that the plurality of the subject causes the verb to occur in the D-stem. This is exclusive to the verb *našāqu*, but other examples may be given as well (GAV, 148–49 § 6.5.1):

šēpē ša šarre ú-na-šu-qu 'they will kiss the feet of the king' Coronation Ritual ii 38 (see GAV, 149)

emārašu$^{\text{sic.}}$ *lu-ḫa-ti-pu* 'may they slaughter his donkey' VAT 8851:26

kunuk PN *ka-nu-ku* 'the (textiles) are sealed with the seal of PN' VAT 8236 r. 13'–14'; yet, more often, the G-stem: *ku-nu-*[*ki*]*-ku-nu ku-un-ka* 'seal with your seals' KAV 99:21

unūta panitta ša PN *ú-ṣa-bi-tu-ni* 'the earlier equipment that PN seized' MCS 2 1:12–14

Examples are found in the stative, without an object:[17]

---

17 An alternative suggestion from Kouwenberg for the following two passages would be to analyse the verbal forms as nominal statives, whereas *arrukū* would derive from the adjectival pattern *PaRRaS*. As

4 KIMIN 10$^{\text{ta.àm}}$ *ina ammete* KIMIN *malla eṣemte ar-ru-ku* 'likewise four (columns), which are 10 each in cubits, one *eṣemtu* long' MARV 1 14:5–6

1 KIMIN 10 *ina ammete a-ri-ik* 'likewise one (column), is 10 cubits long' MARV 1 14:7 and passim in this text

Plurality of the indirect object is rare, but Kouwenberg (GAV, 149–50; cf. 2010, 275) argued for it in a few cases of the M 6 archive, where sometimes the D-stem is used in the case of a plural indirect object, e.g.:

5 *emmeru*^{meš} (…) *ana bēt alaḫḫinē ša bēt ile pa-qu-du* 'five sheep are entrusted to the house of the bakers of the temple' A 1750 (NTA, 24):9–12

2 *emmeru*$^{\text{pl.}}$ (…) *ša abullāte pa-qu-du-ni* 'two sheep, which are entrusted to gate-keepers' A 2611 (NTA, 30):7–9

As a result, one may note that, when the indirect object is singular, *paqādu* occurs in the G-stem, e.g.:

10 *ḫurāpu*^{meš} (…) *ana* PN *pa-aq-du* '10 sheep are entrusted to PN' A 1741 (NTA, 20):1–10 cf. A 1749 (NTA, 23):1–9

A similar distinction can be noted for the verb *tabāku*:

3 *sūtu šamnu* (…) *ina šēpē ilāni ta-bu-uk* 'three seahs of oil are poured out onto the feet of the gods' MARV 2 22:1–3

Vs.:

3 *qa šamnu* (…) *ana* PN *ta-bi-ik* 'three litres of oil are poured out before PN' MARV 2 22:10–11

§ 525 There seems to have been a difference between Babylonian and Assyrian in the use of different D-stems. Kouwenberg suggested that this difference could have been caused, in part, by the one-sided character of the OA corpus. In cases where OA uses an otherwise rare or unattested D-stem, this may be due to their relation to mass nouns, such as metals, textiles and other merchandise (GAV, 184–85 § 6.9.1.2). However, some of the verbs listed for OA can also be found in MA. In addition to the clauses given below, we should briefly mention *talpittu* 'booked out' from *lapātu* 'to touch', which, as a *taPRiSt* noun, is connected with the D-stem. The exact meaning of this noun remains disputed, but seems to be related to the D-stem with the meaning 'to write'. [18]

šarru (…) *lā* ^{túg}*kitāʾa*^{meš} *la-a ú-ša-la lā erraš* 'the king does not ask around for flax, nor does he (himself) plant for it' MATSH 6:7'[19]

---

nominal statives are very rare in MA, I prefer to read a D-stem.

18 E.g., *tal-pi-tu* KAJ 281:6; *ta-al-pi-tum* A 776 (NTA, 17):6. See Postgate (2013, 143 n147); Johnson (2016, 443–44). Alternatively read *ripītu*, see Freydank (2016b, 101–6); especially *ri-pi-*⸢*a*?⸣*-te* MARV 2 22:24 (p. 103).

19 Note that the D-stem of *šaʾālu* is uncertain in both MATSH examples and extensively discussed in MATSH, 120-21. However, Cancik-Kirschbaum thinks its meaning would not fit into the context, since we expect the king to sell, not buy, linen (flax). Unless an otherwise unknown double-weak verb in the Š-stem is to be considered here, there is no option other than *šaʾālu*. Perhaps we should consider the factitive meaning for *šaʾālu* as a transitive process verb, in the case, 'to make (someone) ask for it', i.e., 'to try to sell it'. This meaning is otherwise unknown, but does fit well into the function of the D-stem. Alternatively, the verbal expression *lā ušaʾʾala lā erraš* could be interpreted as 'neither does he ask for

[^{túg}*kitāʾa*]^{meš} *lā ú-ša-ʾa-al lā erraš* 'he does not ask around here for flax, nor does he (himself) plant for it' MATSH 7:21'–22'

anāku agrāni ú-ug-ga-ra 'I will hire hirelings' MATC 4:10–11

Kouwenberg suggested, based on the technical character of some of the verbs, that the usage of the D-stem was more semantically defined in Assyrian than in Babylonian, where plurality remained important (GAV, 184–85 § 6.9.1.2). If this is correct, we may explain some of the transitive verbs in the D-stem which lack any sign of plurality in their specific context.

kamāsu 'to kneel':

ina muḫḫi kussie ka-mu-ús '(the king) is seated on the throne' Coronation Ritual iii 4

nasāqu 'to select' (cf. GAV 140):

20 *iku eqlīšu* (…) *i-na-ás-sa-aq* 'he will select 20 *iku* of his field' KAJ 14:9–11

PN *ú-ta-si-iq* 'PN selected' VAT 8923:20

ṣabātu 'to seize':

kī nēšu ú-ṣa-bi-tu-šu-ni 'after the lion seized him' A 3196 (NTA, 39):11

§ 526 Below is a list of attestations of strong roots in the D-stem:

Present:

D	3ms	*ú-ga-mar* New Year Ritual:19; MARV 1 23:10; MARV 5 82:9'
		ú-⸢pa⸣-ṣa-an MAL A § 41:1
		ú-pa-aṭ-ṭa[*r*] MAPD § 22:120
		ú-qar-ra[*b*] MARV 5 82:8'
		ú-ša-lam KAM 10 12:8
	2ms	*tu-kal-lam* BVW B:7
		tu-ka-šad BVW B:5
		tu-ka-tam PKT 1 I right:17
		tu-mar-ra-aṭ PKT 3 iii 2
		tu-pa-ša-aḫ-šu PKT 5 r. 6
		tu-sa-ḫar Billa 60:9
		tu-š[*á*]*-ra-aḫ* BVW Ab:6
	1cs	*ú-ba-la-aṭ-ku-n*[*u*] KAV 96:17
		ú-pa-ḫar TabT05a-134:30
		ú-tab-ba-ak T 97-34:16
	3mp	*ú-ba-la-ṭu* KAJ 168:13
		ú-ba-at-tu-qu MAPD § 20:101
		ú-pal-lu-ú-šu MAL A § 40:84
		ú-ra-ṭu-bu MATC 12:33
		ú-ṣa-bu-tu George 1988 2 r. 15'
	3fp	*ú-la*[!]*-ba-ša-*[*ni*] MARV 2 27 iv 5'
		ú-šal-la-ma AO 19.228:15

Perfect:

D	3ms	*uk-tal-li-ma-an-ni* Hall 1983:20

---

it (= buy it), nor does he produce it himself', i.e., the king is not interested in trading in linen to any extent. This fits better with the OA evidence, where no factitive meaning for *šaʾālu* is known.

		⸢up⸣-ta-ṭir MARV 5 12:24
		ur-ták-ki-is-s[*u*?] MARV 1 119:5
		ús-sa-am-me-eḫ MAL B § 8:12
		uṣ-ṣa-bi-it KAV 217:6
	2ms	*tu-ḫu-ta-li-qa* T 93-11:28†
		tu-uḫ-tam-mi-iṣ MAL N § 1:3
	1cs	*uṣ-ṣa-bi-it* Halle 1983:8
	3mp	*up-ta-zi-r*[*u*] RE 92:10
		uq-ṭa-ri-bu-ni-šu KAJ 205:11
Preterite:		
D	3ms	*ú-ba-li-ṭí* KAJ 101:13
		ú-ḫal-li-pu-ú-⸢ni⸣ A 842:23
		ú-ḫal-li-qu-ú-ni KAJ 128:13
		ú-ka-⸢ad⸣-di-ir MAL B § 20:20
		ú-⸢pa-[*qi*]*-du*?⸣*-ú-ni* KAJ 254:19
		ú-qar-ri-bu-ni KAJ 274:14 (Sa/TN)
		ú-sa-aḫ-ḫi-ru-ni KAJ 177:9
		ú-sa-am-me-ḫu-ni MAL B § 8:15
		ú-ṣa-bi-tu-ni MCS 2 1:14
	2ms	*tu-qa*[*r*]*-ri-ba-ni* MATSH 5:13'
	3mp	*ú-pa-ḫi-r*[*u-ni*] T 04-14:3''†
		ú-qar-ri-bu-ni A 1812 (NTA, 25):15
		ú-⸢rak⸣-ki-su MARV 10 4:31'
		ú-ra-ṭí-bu-ú-ni MARV 3 27:14
		ú-sa-ḫi-ru KBo 1 20:19'
Precative:		
D	3ms	*lu-pa-ḫi-ra* T 97-17:9
	3mp	*lu-ḫa-mi-ṭu* KAV 103:30
		lu-ḫa-ri-ṣu T 93-54:20
		lu-ḫa-ti-pu VAT 8851:26
		lu-šal-lim-mu MARV 7 14:10
		lu-šal-li-qu T 97-34:21
	1cp	*lu nu-ḫal-li-iq* KBo 28 82:6
Imperative:		
D	2ms	*dal-li-iḫ* T 99-10:14
		[*ḫa*]*r-ri-⸢im⸣* MATSH 9:14
		ka-ni-ik T 93-20:23
		lab-bir Rm 376:9
		[*q*]*ar-ri-ib-šu* Billa 66:9
		ra-pi[*š*] Coronation Ritual ii 35
		táq-[*q*]*i-in* T 93-6:7
	2cp	*ḫa-bi-i-qa* MATSH 3:23
Stative:		
D	3ms	*ḫab-bu-ul* MAL A § 39:28
		ka-mu-ús Coronation Ritual iii 4
		kat-tu-um MARV 3 4:10
		la-pu-ut MATC 54:23
		pa-at-tu MAL A § 40:64
		ša-lu-um MARV 5 66:14

ta-bu-uk MARV 2 22:3
3fs *ga-mu-rat* MPR 76:100;
ḫab-bu-da-at MPR 3:4 MPR 6:4[20]
la-bu-ša-[*a*]*t*? TR 2083a+:18
qa-bu-da-at MPR 12:56[21]
qa-bu-[*d*]*a*!*-at*! MPR 42:27[22]
ka-at-tu-ma-at MAPD § 21:105
pa-aṣ-ṣu-ú-na-at MAL A § 40:60
qar-ru-bat-ni KAJ 223:4
1cs *ḫa-bu-la-ku* MARV 1 13:6
3mp *ḫa-mu-ṣu*! T 96-15:11
[*ká*]*m*?*-mu*?*-su-ú* T 96-1:19
ka-nu-ku VAT 8236 r. 14
ma-ḫu-ṣu MATSH 6:32'
pa-qu-du A 1747 (NTA, 23):14
qar-ru-bu-ú-ni KAV 108:13
ṣa-ab-bu-tu-⌈*ni*⌉ MATSH 8:39'

Infinitive:
D *ana bal-lu-ṭí* MARV 4 5:18'
ina ga-am-mu-ri Coronation Ritual ii 37
ana ḫa-mu-ṭí KAV 103:30
šal-lu-me KAJ 224:13
ana šal-lu-mu MARV 1 10:5

15.5.2 The Š-stem

§ 527 The Akkadian Š-stem is used to make a verb causative. The Assyrian form is built by adding the prefix *ša-* to the base *PRvS*, making the base of the prefix and suffix conjugations mostly identical: stative *šaPRuS-* ~ prefixed *-šaPRVS*. Babylonian uses *šu-* for the stative and other nominal forms, which appears to be a secondary development (Kouwenberg 2010, 324f), similar to the difference we observed in the D-stem: Babylonian *PuRRuS* ~ Assyrian *PaRRuS*. The more archaic *šaPRvS* pattern continued to be used in the Assyrian dialect and is thus also found in MA. Babylonian forms are rare; indeed, there is only: ⌈*šuk*⌉*-la-at* DINGIR 'feeding of the god' MARV 3 9:30. The following table presents a comparison between the two dialects following Kouwenberg 2010, 324:

<table>
<tr><th></th><th>Assyrian</th><th>Babylonian</th></tr>
<tr><td>Present</td><td colspan="2">u-šapras</td></tr>
<tr><td>Perfect</td><td colspan="2">u-štapris</td></tr>
<tr><td>Preterite</td><td colspan="2">u-šapris</td></tr>
<tr><td>Imperative</td><td>šapris</td><td>supris</td></tr>
<tr><td>Stative</td><td>šaprus</td><td>šuprus</td></tr>
<tr><td>Infinitive</td><td>šaprusu</td><td>šuprusu</td></tr>
<tr><td>Participle</td><td colspan="2">mušaprisu</td></tr>
</table>

Figure 38: Overview of the Š-stem.

§ 528 The main function of the Š-stem as a marker of causativity is amply attested in MA. According to Kouwenberg (2010, 327), this function was fully productive in Akkadian,

20 For the discussion as to whether this verb is *ḫappudu* or a by-form of *kabādu*, see § 208.

21 See the note above on the verb *ḫappudu*.

22 See the note above.

although it may be noted that the Š-stem in general, is seldom attested in MA in a relative sense. Nonetheless, there are still plenty of examples:

libbīša ú-ša-aṣ-li-ši 'he caused her to have a miscarriage' MAL A § 51:84

4 *ḫaṭṭātu* (…) *ana sikkātē ša-ḫu-za* 'four sticks (…) reserved for pegs' KAJ 310:49–50

ŠE *annia ú-šá-dan* 'he shall cause to give (=distribute) this barley' KAJ 119:10–11

21 *emmeru*^{meš} *ša* RN *alaḫḫinū*$^{\text{sic.}}$ *u sirāšê ú-šá-ku-lu* '11 sheep, which RN will give the bakers and brewers to eat' A 1735 (NTA, 18):19–21

aššata ú-ša-aḫ-ḫa-sú 'he will make him take a wife' MARV 1 37:6

Some transitive verbs do not receive a causative meaning in the Š-stem; rather, their meaning could be semantically influenced. For instance, the verb *ubālu* 'to bring' would change into 'to make one bring', effectively creating a double object (§ 306): the object that is to be carried and the person who would carry the object. This is amply attested in OA (cf. GOA § 6.4.1.2), while, in MA, the verb had developed into 'to send', making it rarely attested with a double accusative.

1 *ellabbuḫḫa rāqta*[*m*]*a ul-te-bi-lak-ku-nu* 'I sent you one empty bladder' KAV 103:28–29

§ 529 Additionally, there is a number of attestations of intransitive verbs. We already discussed the difference between the D-stem of intransitive verbs above. The basic meaning is the causative:

a'īlu ana muḫḫīša tu-ul-te-ri-ib 'she brings a man upon her' MAL A § 23:30–31

kī šapārte še-šu-bat 'she has been made to sit as a pledge' MAL A § 39:28–29

ú-ša-aq-ba 'he will make him say' MAL A § 47:24

lā marrura ana ēkalle ul-te-ri-bu 'they allowed an uncastrated man to enter the palace' MAPD § 20:100

(...) *a-na še-šu-ru* [...] *maḫir* 'he received it for processing (the goods)' Billa 29:9–10

ŠU.NÍGIN 20+n *lubultu* (...) *iltu tupninnāte* (...) [*u*]*l-te-li-ú-ni* 'a total of 20+n textiles they took out of the boxes' VAT 8236 r. 3'–12'

A few adjectival verbs receive a Š-stem rather than the expected D-stem to indicate change of state (Kouwenberg 2010, 328). This is attested in a damaged passage with the verb *muātu* 'to die':

⌜*lu uš*⌝-*ma-at* 'I will put (you) to death' KAV 194:14†

§ 530 Below is a list of attestations of strong roots in the Š-stem:

Present:

Š	3mp	*ú-šal-pu-tu* Adad Ritual:5'†

Perfect:

Š	3ms	*ul-ta-aṣ-bi-si* MAL A § 22:108
	3mp	*uš-ta-ab-ši-lu* A 1748 (NTA, 23):10

Preterite:
Š 3ms *ú-ša-aṣ-bi-⌜tu⌝-ni* MARV 3 8:36'†

Imperative:
Š 2ms *šal-bir* Rm 376:9

Stative:
Š 3fs *šap-šu-qa-at* Lambert 1969:33

Infinitive:
Š *a-na ša-aṣ-bu-te* MATSH 2:26

15.5.3 The N-stem and passive voice

§ 531 In Akkadian, we find verbs conjugated as an N-stem in order to make an active verb passive. Morphologically, the N-stem attaches an *n*-morpheme before the first radical of a root. This usually leads to the assimilation of /n/ into the following consonant; however, we find double /nn/ when the first radical is weak. In nominal forms, /n/ is word-initial; thus, an extra vowel /a/ is inserted by analogy with the Š-stem. Statives in the N-stem are only once attested (*naškun* stative 3ms).

	(a/i) class		(i/i) class	
	No ending	Vowel ending	No ending	Vowel ending
Present	*i-mmaggar*		*i-ppaqqid*	
Perfect	*i-ttamgar*		*i-ttapqid*	
Preterite	*i-mmigir*	*i-mmagr(ū)*	*i-ppiqid*	*i-ppaqd(ū)*
Imperative	*namgir*		*napqid*	
Stative	*namgur*		*napqud*	
Infinitive	*namgur*		*napqudu*	
Participle	*mummagru*		*muqqapdu*	

Figure 39: Overview of the N-stem.

§ 532 The theme vowel patterns, as discussed for the G-stem, are not valid for the N-stem. The preterite/imperative always seems to have an /i/ theme vowel, while the perfect and present can have either an /i/ or an /a/. I have found no attestations of a /u/ theme vowel in MA, except for the possibility of *la-sa-ḫur* KAJ 316:15 see § 157, although this is more likely to have been an epenthetic vowel. This leaves us with two different classes: an a-class (a/i) < (a/u)/(a/a) and an i-class (< i/i) (cf. Kouwenberg 2010, 288–90). The vast majority involve (a/a) class verbs.

(a/i) class:
lapātu; magāru; maḫāṣu; ṣabātu; šahāru; šakānu; tabāku

(i/i) class:
palāsu

§ 533 Morphologically, the construction of the N-stem in Assyrian was extensively discussed by Hecker (GKT, 143) and Kouwenberg on two occasions (2004; 2010, 288ff). The situation in OA shows VA penetrating /a/ between the first and second radical in the preterite and becoming a permanent part of the structure of the conjugation. Thus, we find the 3ms *ippiris* instead of the Babylonian *ipparis*. This change took place irrespective of whether new morphemes were added to the base of the verb; thus, also note *i-ší-ik-nu-ma* BIN 4 10:19. This forms an interesting contradiction with the lack of VA in OA before the construct vowel /a/ preceding a bisyllabic pronominal suffix (§ 146). In MA, the situation is reversed and we do not find the VA in most N-stem preterites, e.g., *iš-ša-ak-nu-ni* KAJ 107=117:12 UŠ; *iṣ-ṣa-ab-tu* MAL A § 47:3. However, in the cases without a vocalic ending attached to it, we still find the OA version: *im-me-gi-ir-ma* KAJ 3:2; *la-pi-ṭí-ir* Faist 2001, 252:22; *it-ti-bi-ik* KAJ 306a:4. These forms continued to be used up to the NA period (Kouwenberg 2010, 289). This accords well with the rules of VA, which stipulate that VA is penultimate; however, it remains unexplained as to how this change did not apply in OA (Kouwenberg 2010, 18 n44). Again, change of stress would be the most probable conclusion. The preterite *it-ti-ba-ak* Maul 2004 1:14 cannot be explained according to either OA or MA vowel patterns (cf. Maul 2004, 132). I/ā verbs, such as *innāmmer*, can be reconstructed with a long vowel because of the lack of VA (Kouwenberg 2004, 336), e.g., *in-na-bi-id* MAL A § 36:106; 43:22; MAL B § 3:24; *In-na-me-er* (PN) KAJ 146:19 (however, I/ē: *ta-an-ni-di-ip* KAV 168:22). The paucity of gemination in MA orthography is reflected in some N-stems, e.g., *a-na* UGU *šarre ta-ka-ša-ad ta-ka-la* 'upon your reaching the king, you will be detained' MCS 2,16:21.

§ 534 As already stated, the main function of the N-stem was to make an active verb passive. Although the N-stem certainly has more functions in Akkadian, the vast majority of attestations in MA show it as a marker of ditransivity.

išku (...) *ta-at-ta-al-pa-at* 'the testicle is affected' MAL A § 8:82–83

marʾūša (...) *in-na-gu-ú-ru* 'her sons will be hired' MAL A § 36:93–94

1 *me im-maḫ-ḫ*[*a-a*]*ṣ* 'he will be beaten 100 (times)' MAPD § 21:104

sinniltu šī^sic.^ ⌜*ta-at*⌝*-ta-aṣ-bat* 'that woman is seized' MAL A § 24:52

^giš^*riqīū*^meš^ *iṣ-ṣa-ru-ḫu* 'the aromatics will become hot' PKT 1 I right:12

The N-stem is also found on one occasion for *magāru* 'to agree', which has been claimed to have had a reciprocal function.[23] All attestations occur in the singular, without any second agent expressed or referred to; thus, *magāru* cannot be regarded as being reciprocal here (cf. Streck 2003a, 83). It seems that the verb has obtained a lexicalized meaning 'to agree with each other' > 'to agree'. In the case of the MA *magāru*, then, there is no difference in meaning between the G and N-stem. A similar lexicalization is also attested for reciprocal Gt-stems (Streck 2003a, 84–86 § 6.3).

panūšuma im-ma-an-ga-ar [*u*] *zittušu ilaqqe* 'should he chose to come to an agreement, he will take his share' MAL B § 2:20

PN *im-me-gi-ir-ma* 'PN agreed' KAJ 3:2

šumma PN *la*^!^ *a-mi-gi-ir-mi iqabbi* 'if PN says: 'I did not agree'' KAJ 57:19–21

šumma (…) *im-ma-ag-ga-ar ilaqqe* 'if he agrees, he will take it' MARV 1 41:8–10

23 See Kouwenberg (2010, 294–95); cf. OA in GKT, 140; GOA § 17.5.2.

We find one verb as an N-tantum: *nābudu* (Bab. *nābutu*, see § 213), which occurs quite frequently in our corpus, e.g., *in-na-bi-id* MAL A § 36:106; 43:22; MAL B § 3:24. According to Kouwenberg (2010, 299), the intransitive character of the verb links it to the ingressive N-stems.

§ 535 The passive function of the N-stem was apparently in decline, as we are informed that it is only rarely used in NA, which involves a 3mp in this function (SNAG, 88). Due to the sketchy character of the grammar, it is hard to see how Hämeen-Anttila came to this conclusion. While attestations of the N-stem are still common in MA, it should be noted that the third-person plural form of the verb may be used for an unnamed generic subject, which could also be expressed by an N-stem.

> *ina muḫḫi aššat aʾīle ik-šu-du-uš* 'they have caught him on top of (another) man's wife' MAL A § 12:20
>
> *ana lib[be ut]ūne i-kar-ru-ru-šu-nu* 'they will throw them in the oven' MAPD § 19:93
>
> 1 *kalūma balṭa* (...) *ana 2-šu i-bat-tu-qu* 'they will cut one living lamb in two' New Year Ritual:14'–15'
>
> *n rēḫtu ša* (…) *i-ba-tu-qu-ú-ni* '*n* is the remainder, which will be selected' MARV 1 18:4–6

Arguably, these forms are not uncommon in Akkadian and could just as well be found in OA, e.g., *la i-ṣu-bu-tù-kà-ni* 'they may not seize you' OAA 1 11:25.

§ 536 Below is a list of attestations of strong roots in the N-stem:

Present:

N	3ms	*im-ma-an-ga-ar* MAL B § 2:20; *im-ma-ag-ga-ar* MARV 1 41:9
		im-maḫ-ḫ[a-a]ṣ MAPD § 21:104
		iš-ša-ka-an MARV 8 35:20''
		it-ta-ba-ak KAJ 306a:11
	3mp	*i-pal-li-su* MATSH 8:30'
		iṣ-ṣa-ab-bu-ú-tu MAL A § 25:94
		iṣ-ṣa-ru-ḫu PKT 1 I right:12
	3fp	*i-ba-qa-an-na* LVUH 48:26
		i-ša!*-ka-na*!*-n[i]* KAJ 179:15

Perfect:

N	3ms	*it-ta-aṣ-bat* MAL C+ § 9:14
		i-ta-áš-ḫ[a-ar-...] MATSH 27:8'
		it-ta-ás-ḫa-x-x-[*ni*] MARV 8 76 r. 8'†
		it-ta-áš-ka-an MARV 6 22:11
	3fs	*ta-at-ta-al-pa-at* MAL A § 8:83
		⌜*ta-at*⌝*-ta-aṣ-bat* MAL A § 24:52
	3mp	*i-ta-pàr-ku* MATSH 3:28

Preterite:

N	3ms	*ig-ga-m[e*?!*-ru-ni]* KBo 1 20 r. 6'
		iš-ša-ak-nu-ú-ni MARV 7 3:7; *i-ša-ak-nu-ni* VS 1 105:9
		it-ti-bi-ik KAJ 306a:4; *it-ti-ba-ak* Maul 2004 1:14
	3fs	*im-me-gi-ir-ma* KAJ 3:2

	1cs	*a-mi-gi-ir-mi* KAJ 57:17, 20
	3mp	*iṣ-ṣa-ab-tu* MAL A § 47:3; MARV 6 86 env. 8'
		iš-ša-ak-nu-ú-ni KAJ 255:7
		i-šap-ru-ni T 99-10:16

Precative:

N	3ms	*la-pi-ṭí-ir* Faist 2001, 252:22

Imperative:

N	ms	*nap-le-és* KAJ 316:8

Infinitive:

N		*ša nap-lu-si* KAJ 303:10
		na-áš-ku-ša-ni KAV 99:38

15.5.4 The *tan*-stems

§ 537 One of the features unique to Akkadian involves the *-tan-* stems, which occur as a variation of all main stems (G-, D-, Š-, N-), giving them an iterative or frequentative meaning (GAG, 147–49 § 91). As the difference between the different *-tan-* stems is not indicated by the *-tan-* infix, but by the main stems, we will discuss them here together. According to W. Mayer, the *-tan-* stems have become relatively rare in MA (UGM, 64 § 71). However, this does not seem to agree with the evidence where the Gtn occurs frequently (Kouwenberg 2010, 421 n213). On the other hand, only one quadradical verb is attested in the Ntn-stem so far. Still, the situation for OA is not much better for the Štn and Ntn-stems (cf. GOA § 17.4.5; 17.5.3). Theme vowels of the Gtn-stem seem to correspond with the G-stem, but there are too few attestations to demonstrate this.

	Gtn	Dtn	Štn	Ntn
Present	*i-ptanarras*	*u-ptanarras*	*u-štanapras*	*i-ttanapras*
Perfect	*i-ptatarras*			
Preterite	*i-ptarras*			
Imperative	*tiparras*			
Stative/adjective				
Infinitive	*tiparrusum*	*putarrusu*	*tušaprusu*	
Present participle	*muptarris*			

Figure 40: Overview of the *tan*-stems.

§ 538 Morphologically, the *-tan-* stems are characterized by the *-tan-* infix between the first and second radical. The /n/ is usually assimilated into the second radical, with the exception of the present, where the second radical is already geminated and a vowel is inserted between it and the *-tan-* infix. In the infinitive, the /n/ seems to be absent all together, making the *-tan-* infinitive morphologically indistinguishable from the Gt infinitive. At the same time, it must be noted that an infinitive metathesis can take place when a /t/ (infix) follows /š/ (Š-stem or radical) (see § 226; cf. Gt-stems below). Additionally, the *tan*-stems are rare in the perfect; indeed, there is only *al-ta-ta-pa-ra-šu-nu* MATSH 8:40' (for MA/NA, see Kouwenberg 2010, 419 n207). They are not attested in OA (GKT, 125 § 76b; 145 § 86e; GOA § 17).

§ 539 For the function of the *-tan-* stems, we follow its description in GAV (also Kouwenberg 2010, 416–17). The most common function of the *-tan-* stems is to express frequency. This is the continued carrying out of the action of the verb on multiple occasions, which can be referred to as habitual if the verb has an animate agent (GAV, 80–81 § 4.2.2).

šumma sinniltu ina bēt abīšama usbat mussa e-ta-na-ra-ab 'if a woman dwells in the house of her father but her husband continually comes in' MAL A § 27:103–104

šumma bēl mārte ša zubullāʾa im-ta-aḫ-ḫu-ru-ú-ni (…) *lā imaggur* 'if the master of the girl, who will receive the marriage gift on various occasions, does not agree' MAL A § 30:29–32

ú-ia pîša ik-ta-na-at-tam 'the woe of her mouth keeps covering her' Lambert 1969:43 (incantation)

adi balṭūšunu it-ta-na-bal-šu-nu 'he will continue to take care of them as long as they live' KAJ 1:8–9

ŠU.NÍGIN 9 [*iku eqla*] (…) *ukaʾʾal e-ta-na-ra-aš* 'he will hold and continually cultivate a field with a total of nine *iku*' KAJ 13:22–25

al-ta-ta-pa-ra-šu-nu 'I have kept writing them' MATSH 8:40'

ul-te-n[*i-ba-la*] *lū* 2 *bilta lū* 3 *biltamma lū* 10 *b*[*ilta* túg*kitāʾa*meš] 'he will successively send two, three or 10 talents of flax' MATSH 6:3'–4' (cf. Streck 1997, 274)

kī RN *ana muḫḫi kisallāte mê ramāke it-ta-na-ra-du-ú-ni epšū* 'when the king goes repeatedly down with water to wash the forecourts, they are sacrificed' KAJ 204:8–12

PN *Imarāy*[*ū*] *ana muḫḫi šarre* (…) *ša sulummāe il-ta-nap-pu-ru* 'PN (and) the Emariotes keep sending peace proposals to the king' T 96-1:12–17

Sometimes, it seems that the *-tan-* stem is used to indicate the plurality of the subject. This is somewhat similar to the D-stem, but, unlike the latter, it indicates that an action is carried out multiple times as the result of the plurality of the subject.[24]

iqtibi mā aššatka it-ti-ni-ik-ku 'he said, thus 'everybody has slept with your wife' MAL A § 17:67–68

ina muḫḫi tappāʾīšu abāta iškun mā it-ti-ni-ku-ú-uš 'he has started a rumour about his comrade, saying: "everybody fornicates with him"' MAL A § 19:83–84

šulmānāte [*ana*] *šarre uq-ṭa-na-ra-bu* '(the palace officials) will present *šulmānu*-gifts to the king (each after another)' Coronation Ritual iii 4–5

ubruttu (…) *akla*meš *e-ta-na-ku-lu qaqquru bari ša nillukūni* 'the delegates eat, but the territory that we travel through is starving' T 97-10:15–19

Rarely, the *tan*-stems have an iterative function, where the action indicated by the verb could be plural, but can be summarized as occurring on one occasion, e.g., *alāku* 'to go' > Gtn 'to go around' (GAV, 80 § 4.2.1). There are a few examples of this in MA:

24 See GKT, 144 § 86b; GAV, 81–84 § 4.2.3.

a'īlu iṣṣabassu[sic.] *lānīkkime iqtibiašše lā tamaggur ta-ta-na-ṣa-ar* 'a man has seized her(!) and says to her that he wants to lie with her, she should not agree but must protect herself' MAL A § 12:15–16

šumma tuppa šiāti PN_1 *ana* PN_2 *lā inaddin pāḫat eqle šuātu zakkue* PN *it-ta-na-aš-ši* 'if PN_1 does not give that tablet to PN_2, PN1shall bear the responsibility for clearing that field' KAJ 132:12–18

§ 540 Below is a list of attestations, including the weak and irregular verbs for the Dtn/Štn/Ntn-stems, due to their rarity:

Gtn-stem:

Present	3ms	*ik-ta-na-at-tam* Lambert 1969:43
	3mp	*il-ta-nap-pu-ru* T 96-1:17
Perfect	3ms	*iḫ-ta-tab-bi-lu-ni* MARV 4 151:60
	1cs	*al-ta-ta-pa-ra-šu-nu* MATSH 8:40'
	3mp	*iḫ-ta-tab-bu-tu* KUB 3 73:6', 7
Preterite	3ms	*im-ta-aḫ-ḫu-ru-ú-ni* MAL A § 30:30
	1cs	*la al-ta-ap-pa-a*[*r*] MATSH 27:4'†
	3mp	*i-ta-ḫa-ṣu-ni* T 96-15:12
		il-ta-ka-nu-ni T 96-15:13
Imperative	ms	^{d}*Aššur-ti-šam-me* MARV 4 151:59
Infinitive		*ana ti-šap-pu-r*[*e*] MARV 2 17b+:97

Dtn-stem:

Present	3mp	⌜*uk-ta*⌝*-na-*⌜*lu-ú*⌝ KAM 10 13:16
		uq-ṭa-na-ru-bu Coronation Ritual iii 5
Infinitive		^{túg}*ša tu-sa-ḫu-ri* MAH 16086 A ii 10; B ii 11'

Štn-stem:

Present	3ms	*ul-te-n*[*i-ba-la*] MATSH 6:3'
	2ms	*tul-ta-na-kal* (< *akālu*) PKT 1 I right:16
		[*tu*]*-ul-*[*t*]*a-na-aḫ-ra-ar* MATSH 9:36
	3mp	*ul-ta-na-ak-na-nu* Coronation Ritual iii 3; cf ii 38
Infinitive		*ina tu-ša-aḫ-ru-ri-ma* MATSH 9:37
		⌜*a*⌝ *na tu-še-bu-le* MARV 2 17a+:99

Ntn-stem::

Present	3mp	*it-ta-nab-la-ku-tu* PKT 2 i 16

15.5.5 The *ta*-stems

§ 541 The ta-infix stems have become rare in MA and the statistics clearly show a stark decline in attestations from OA to NA.[25] This was no doubt caused by the MA/MB development of the perfect to cover the past tense and the decline of the preterite. This made the infix -t- increasingly difficult to use for anything but the past tense (Kouwenberg 2005, 96). It has been suggested that another contributing factor to the decay of the G-stem was the replacement of the reciprocal function of the Gt-stems by the pronouns *aḫā'iš* and the reflexive *rāmunu* (e.g., Kouwenberg 2010, 365 § 14.3.2; cf. SNAG, 88 § 3.12.1). It

25 See Streck (2003a, 89ff). Note that the table does not account for the difference in sizes in the multiple corpus, meaning that there would not have been a light revival in the NA period and first millennium Babylonian.

appears that *ramumu* was already used in OA for this function (Streck 2003a, 97–98 § 10.2), whereas *aḫāʾiš* was not yet attested in this period. As a result, we may conclude that the Gt-stem in general, was more limited in the Assyrian dialect (Kouwenberg 2010, 363). In this respect, there does not seem to be a significant development from OA to MA, as the lack of attestations for the *ta*-stems can, to a large extent, be explained by the more limited character of the corpus. While the reciprocal and reflexive pronouns may have replaced the Gt-stem, this is visible only in a few attestations, e.g.:

> [...] *a-ḫa-iš i-du-ka-a-ni* 'they have fought with each other' MAPD § 10:57 (cf. Streck 2003a, 23 no.12)

However, none of these forms appears to occur with verbs that would otherwise be expected to occur in the G-stem.[26] In most cases, they do not refer to the verb; instead, they occur in apposition or in the genitive construction of a noun (e.g., *ina migrāt rāminīšu* 'out of his own consensus'). In other cases, a ta-stem is not attested or occurs with other meanings.

> *a-na ra-mi-ni-šu i-laq-qé* 'he will take it for himself' MAL B § 17:17 (no Gt-stem)

> *kī a-ḫa-iš lu ep-ša-at* 'it must be done together' MATSH 10:22–23 (cf. *itpušu* 'to do thoroughly', Streck 2003a, 61 no. 142)

> *aʾīlu ša še-zu-⌜ub⌝ ra-mi-šu* 'a man of his own salvation' MATSH 9:42 (only Št *šutēzubu* 'to be saved', Streck 2003a, 116 no. 332)

The claim that *aḫāʾiš* and *rāmunu* replaced the Gt-stem could be true for the other phases of the Akkadian dialect; however, a visible decay and the replacement of the Gt-stem cannot be demonstrated with regard to the rather limited MA corpus.

	Gt	Dt	Št2
Present	*i-ptarrus*	*u-ptarras*	
Perfect	*i-ptatrus*		
Preterite	*i-ptaras*	*u-ptattir*	
Imperative	*pitras*		
Stative	*pitrus*		*tušaprus*
Infinitive			*tušaprusu*
Present participle	*muptarsu*		

Figure 41: Overview of the ta-stems.

§ 542 In MA, the only verb with a productive Gt-stem is *alāku*, or *atluku*, with the meaning 'to leave' (already UGM, 92). This Gt-verb has an ingressive meaning, which is a lexicalized root, whereas the Gt-stem usually has a ditransivation or reciprocal value (Kouwenberg 2005, 80–86; 2010, 360–61). Although *atluku* is often morphologically identical to a normal perfect, its occurrence can definitively be proven with the precative 1cs *la-tal-ka* Faist 2001, 252:32. Nonetheless, it often remains difficult to distinguish between the perfect and the Gt-stem. W. Mayer referred to three instances involving the verb *alāku* (UGM, 92). His first example concerned the present *i-it-ta-lak* MAL A § 36:85, which was unlikely as the verb occurs in the protasis of law paragraph, which was always written in the past tense. However, a preterite Gt cannot be completely ruled out here. His

26 Cf. the list of Gt-verbs in OA in Kouwenberg (2010, 362f § 14.3.1.2); in SB, see Kouwenberg (2010 § 14.3.3, 367ff).

second example, *i-it-tal-ka-an-ni* MAL B § 19:9, uses a ventive, which points to *alāku* with the meaning of 'leaving towards' (cf. Streck 2003a, 48f); although it should be noted that the passage is damaged. Meanwhile, Roth (1997) translated it as a perfect, but both examples were rejected by Kouwenberg (2010, 365 n40). Additionally, *tu-na-kar ta-at-ta-lak* 'you will remove and you will take it away' PKT 3 iv 7 appears plausible; however, the function of *alāku* as a transitive verb, taking an object, remains problematic here. This could be solved if we were to take *ṭí-iš-ṭí-ša ù mi-du-uḫ-ra* l. 6' as the subject; however, these two obscure words are in the accusative and take, in the following relative clause, the expected masculine plural verb *i-ri-ḫu-ni* l. 7'. The occurrence of *ta-at-ta-lak* as a transitive verb could actually be an indication of an almost complete decay of the Gt-stem. Scribes may have learned some Gt-verb verbs during their education, which would have been influenced by an OB tradition; however, they seldom applied them. In this case, where we do find a Gt form, it is used erroneously. Indeed, it is unlikely that the Gt of *alāku* was actually used as a transitive verb in the spoken language. Nonetheless, the Gt of *alāku* survived into NA, albeit in a somewhat different form. Already in the MA/MB, the perfect had become so dominant that a normal Gt-stem could not be recognized. As a result, several derived stems were created with the double *-ta-* infix to distinguish them from the perfect: the Gtt, Dtt and Štt-stems. One of the verbs that underwent this transition is *alāku*, which has a double *-ta-* infix attested in the precative and perfect (Kouwenberg 2005, 97; 2010, 357 n10, 388–91 § 14.5.3; cf. Parpola 1984: SNAG, 96 § 3.13.1).[27] An early attestation is found in MA in a Tell Ḫuwīra letter *[it]-ta-at-la-ak* MATC 15:30 and also *ta-at-ta-at-la-ak* NP 46:8.

§ 543 Beyond *alāku*, we find the Gt in a number of PNs, e.g., *apālu*: ^{d}*A-šur-mu-tap-li* KAJ 165:14; *šamāru*: ^{d}IŠKUR-*tíš-mar* KAJ 75:17. Additionally, we find lexicalized Gt-stem nominal constructions, e.g., *mi-it-ḫa-ra-tu* Giricano 12:21' and the participle *mu-ut-taḫ-iṣ* 'warrior' Lambert 1969:40 (Kouwenberg 2010, 365f). Another Gt-preterite, *im-tág-ru-ú-ni* Snell 1983/84:15, occurs in a text of a rare 'peripheral Assyrian' dialect, which deserves to be mentioned here (cf. Kouwenberg 2010, 365). In the same text, we find another Gt-precative of *alāku*: *li-it-ta-a-lak* Snell 1983/84:18. A true Gt-present is also found in *e-te-li* CTMMA 100:9, while a Gt-stative is found in *mi-ta-aḫ-ru* 'they are equal' KAM 10 25:18. This form is typical of the Assyrian dialect; when a vocalic ending is added to the base form, *PitRuS* becomes *PitaRS-* (GAG, 149 § 92a; GOA § § 17.2.1). On the other hand, we once find *mi-it-ḫu-ru* MARV 8 7 47:37†.

§ 544 For the Dt, we have a couple of attestations for the verb *paṣānu* 'to cover', all clustered in MAL A § 40, which deals with the head covering of women. All three examples involve the present in the third-person feminine (singular: *tu-up-ta-aṣ-ṣa-an* MAL A § 40:65, 66; plural: *up-ta-ṣa-na-ma* MAL A § 40:88). The meaning is clearly

---

27 Note that, because of the absence of attested Gtt-forms in the present, Kouwenberg (2010, 390) rejected the term Gtt-stem since the forms for the precative and perfect are occasional analogical formations. Other than the Dtt and Štt-stems, there are probably no more than two 'Gtt-stems', of which *alāku* is the most important root.

reflexive, as the woman is the object of her own action ('to veil herself') (GAV, 324–25 § 9.1.2).

ḫarimtu la-a tu-up-ta-aṣ-ṣa-an 'a prostitute will not veil herself' MAL A § 40:66

amātu la-a up-ta-ṣa-na-ma 'slave girls will not veil themselves' MAL A § 40:88

There is a clear Dt-stem attested for the verb *nazāmu* 'to complain'. How it compares to the D-stem is not entirely clear. It is possible that the verb is used as an intransitive version of a transitive D-stem, which is the most basic function of the Dt-stem (GAV, 318). However, forms of *nazāmu* are not well attested, resulting in some confusion. We should probably translate the D-stem *nazzumu* as 'to cause to complain', compared with the Dt-stem 'to raise a complaint' (AHw, 772a; CDA, 248):

panēma ina muḫḫīya tu-ta-za-am 'previously, you raised a complaint against me' T 93-11:20–21

Another example given by W. Mayer is *ú-tar-ri-šu-nu* MAL A § 55:9 from an I/w root, which comes in a broken context (UGM, 76). Von Soden takes the verb as a Dt from *ešāru* 'to wish'.[28] However, as this is the only Dt example provided, with no normal D-stem forms of this root otherwise known, the claims from both Mayer and von Soden are not very strong. A clearer example from *labāšu* occurs in a MARV text, while *uššuru* occurs in a text from Tell Ḫuwīra:

ina bēt PN *ekkal ul-ta-ba-aš* 'he will eat and be clothed in the house of PN' MARV 1 37:8

1 *biltu* ^{na4}Ú^{meš} *ina pitti* PN *lu-ta-áš-ši-⸢ir⸣* One talent of moonstone must be removed from the responsibility of PN' MATC 5:6–8

Here, the meaning of the Dt-stem appears to be the passive/intransitive of the D-stem, which is again the most common meaning of the Dt-stem (GAV, 318). Röllig proposed the occurrence of a Dt-stem of *maṭāʾu* (LVUH, 16), which was attested passim in TŠḪ agriculture texts, e.g., *um-ta-ṭí* LVUH 48:22. This has been rejected by others on the basis that the finite verb and its alleged subject *ṣēnu* 'flock' (fp) are in incongruence (e.g., Llop 2010, 129).

§ 545 We find one Št_2 verb in MA, occurring as a stative from *ḫarāṣu*: *tu-ša-ḫa-ru-ṣu-ni* KAJ 120:7. According to the discussion of the verb by Streck (1994, 179; 2003a, 122 no. 377), we should analyse the *ḫarāṣu* form as a Št_2 in its function to make the G-stem reciprocal. Morphologically, both forms of Št_1 and Št_2 feature two rare cases of metathesis in MA (see § 226). Kouwenberg's suggestion (2010, 404 n166), that *tušaḫaruṣūni* (KAJ 120) was borrowed from Babylonian technical jargon, is probably not correct because metathesis of this kind is typical for MA. Some cases of lexicalized participles are found, e.g., *multēšertu* 'maintenance'. Additionally, the Št participle *multēpiš/muštēpiš* in the PNs, ^{d}*A-šur-mul-te-piš* KAJ 54:20 and ^{m}*Muš-te-piš*-DINGIR KAJ 173:3, is presumably a Št_2 (Kouwenberg 2010, 404 n166). This name construction was possibly borrowed from the Babylonian onomasticon (Kouwenberg 2010, 404 n166).

§ 546 Below is a list of attestations of strong roots:

28 See AHw, 1433 (cf. Roth 1997, 193 n31).

Gt-stem:

Present	3ms	*e-te-li* CTMMA 1 100:9
	2ms	*ta-at-ta-lak* PKT 3 iv 7
Perfect	3ms	[*it*]*-ta-at-la-ak* MATC 15:30
Preterite	3ms	*im-tág-ru-ú-ni* Snell 1983/84:15
Precative	3ms	*li-it-ta-a-lak* Snell 1983/84:18; *li-it-ta-al-ka* EA 15:22
	1cs	*la-tal-ka* Faist 2001, 252:32
Imperative	ms	^d^*Adad-tíš-mar* KAJ 75:17
Stative	3mp	*mi-ta-aḫ-ru* KAM 10 25:18
		mi-it-ḫu-ru MARV 8 7 47:37†

Dt-stem:

Present	3ms	*ul-ta-ba-aš* MARV 1 37:8
	2ms	*tu-ta-za-am* T 93-11:21
	3fs	*tu-up-ta-aṣ-ṣa-an* MAL A § 40:65, 66
	3fp	*up-ta-ṣa-na-ma* MAL A § 40:88
Preterite	3ms	*ú-tar-ri-šu-nu* MAL A § 55:9
Precative	3ms	*lu-ta-áš-ši-*⸢*ir*⸣ MATC 5:8

$Št_1$-stem:

Participle	fs	*mul-te-ṣi-tu-šu-nu* 'their expenses' KAJ 307:14

$Št_2$-stem:

Stative	3ms	*tu-ša-ḫa-ru-ṣu-ni* KAJ 120:7
Participle	ms	*mul-te-šèr-tu* 'maintenance' T 98-7:13

15.6 The quadradical verbs

§ 547 Quadradical verbs are relatively rare in Akkadian as opposed to some Semitic languages, such as Arabic. The term is often a misnomer, since verbs such as *šugarrur* have only two radicals: R_1=g ~ R_{2-3}=r. The quadradical verbs always occur in a type of Š or N-stem, never in the G or D-stem. The small group occurring in MA can be divided into two groups: the roots with four different radicals (e.g., *šabalkutu*; see Kouwenberg 2010, 307ff) and the roots where r_2 and r_3 are identical and liquid, e.g., *šagarruru*. They always have R_2 geminated, which sets them apart from II/gem verbs, even though the forms with this unexpected gemination are not attested in MA (cf. Kouwenberg 2010, 301ff § 12.3). The latter group of verbs differs from a normal Š or N-stem in the gemination of r_2 and/or possibly r_3 (in *ig-ga-ra-ru* 'they grovel' Coronation Ritual iii 13) (Kouwenberg 2010, 303). For the peculiarities of *šukayyunu* and *šapayyulu*, see Kouwenberg (2010, 346ff). Its MA attestations only differ from Babylonian due to the lack of e-colouring. While R_2 is maintained in the perfect (*ul-ta-ka-in* passim), in the present, it contracts (e.g., *uš-ka-an* Coronation Ritual i 31).[29] The verbal form *ul-tum-ḫe-ḫi-in* (*ultuḵe*ˀˀ*in*) KBo 28 82:3 derives from *šakayyunu* in a letter of questionable Assyrian character (§ 40). It features the spirantization of /k/ > <Ḫ>, while R_2/ˀ is represented here as <Ḫ> (see Tropper 1999). Given its frequency in letters from Hurrian-speaking areas, it cannot be regarded as a genuine feature of MA.[30]

---

29 For OA, see GKT, 174f § 101; GOA § 17.6.2; for NA, see SNAG, 101 § 3.14.6.
30 Cf. CAD $Š_3$, 218a; GAG, 198 § 109m.

§ 548 Below is a list of attestations of strong roots of the quadradical verbs:

Quadradical		Geminate		$R_{2\text{-}3}$=y	
nabalkutu	'to cross over'	*nagarruru*	'to grovel'	*šakayyunu*	'to prostrate'
naparkāʾu	'to cease'	*šaqallulu*	'to hang (down)'	*šapayyulu*	'to exchange'
naparšudu	'to flee'	*šaḫarrruru*	'to be silent'		
naqalpāʾu	'to float'				

Š-stem:

Present	3ms	*uš-ka-an* Coronation Ritual i 31; Ištar Ritual:9
	2ms	*tu-uš-ba-la-kat* PKT 3 i 16
		tu-uš-ga-ra-a-ar BVW F:4; *tu-UZ-ga-[ra-a]r*[31] BVW A:12
		ip!-par-rak-ku IM 60240 r. 4'
	3mp	*uš-ka-nu* Coronation Ritual iii 13
Perfect	1cs	*ul-ta-ka-in* passim in letters, e.g., KAJ 302:4; MATSH 10:3
		ul-tum-ḫe-ḫi-in (*ultuk̲e??in*) KBo 28 82:3 (peripheral)
	1cp	*nu-ul-ta-ka-in* MARV 1 71:4
Preterite	3ms	*us-bal-ki-it* MAL B § 9:21
		us-qa-al-pí-ú-⸢ni⸣ MARV 4 35:7
Imperative	ms	*⸢šu⸣-ga-ar-ri-ir* MATSH 9:15
Stative	3ms	*šu-bal-ku-ut* MATC 67:32

Štn-stem:

infinitive		*ina tu-ša-aḫ-ru-ri-ma* MATSH 9:37

N-stem:

Present	3ms	*i-ba-la-ku-tu-ni* VAT 8722:19
		ig-ga-ra-ar Coronation Ritual i 32; cf. l. 31
	3mp	*ig-ga-ra-ru* Coronation Ritual iii 13
Perfect	3mp	*it-ta-pàr-ku* MATSH 3:28; 12:35
Preterite	3ms	*ib-bal-ki-tu-ni* Ali 19:13
		⸢ip⸣-pár-ši-du-ni MARV 10 6:35'
		iq-qa-al-pu-a MAL M § 2:8

Ntn-stem:

Present	3mp	*it-ta-nab-la-ku-tu* PKT 2 i 16

Substantives:

šupêlu	*šupa??ultu*	*ana šu-pa-ul-ti* KAJ 175:6
		šu-pél-te T 04-2:8 (Bab.)

31 See Girbal (1997, 174).

Chapter 16: Weak Verbs

16.1 R_1/weak

16.1.1 I/u and I/i

§ 549 In MA, the first radical /w/ has fully developed into a vowel. As such, /w/ is never written as a consonant, except in some uncertain spellings. We will mention the main characteristics shortly and compare them with other Assyrian dialects. The class of I/i verbs was still a distinct group in OA (see Kouwenberg 2010, 464f); but, in MA, they have become rare and are mostly limited to the irregular *idāʾu* (§ 607). Among the secondary stems, the Š-stem *šēšuru* occurs; however, no differences with the normal I/u class are expected here (cf. UGM, 67 n2). There is also the possibility of the D-stem *ussuku*, although, in this study, the verb is categorized as the I/e root *ussuqu*.[1] Akkadian includes two types of I/w verb: fientive and stative. The difference is not only semantic, but also morphologic. The stative-type verbs are conjugated according to the I/i verb pattern in the prefix conjugations of the G-stem, e.g., the preterite *ubil* vs. *ītir*. The stative verbs are rare in MA, with *utturu* and possibly *uppāʾu* as the only examples, of which *utturu* occurs only in the D and Š-stems.

I/u				I/i	
Fientive		Stative/adjectival (I/a)		I	
ubālu (a/i) *ulādu* *urādu (a/i)* *uššuru*	'to bring' 'to give birth' 'to go down' 'to release'	*utturu*	'to be excessive'	*šēšuru*	'to direct'

§ 550 The fientive I/u verbs are conjugated with u- replacing i- as the prefix vowel, thus *tubil* vs. *tiprus* etc. This phenomenon also penetrated the stative and infinitive; however, the imperative is conjugated as a two-radical verb, e.g., *bil*.[2] In the perfect and Gtn-stem, the original /w/ assimilated into the infixed /t/, which resulted in gemination. This was probably also true for the Dt-forms. In OB, plene spelling of the present prefix u- occurs, just as it does with the I/voc verbs. Kouwenberg (2003/4, 451) argued that these cases were analogue spellings of the latter group, which can be confirmed by the relative scarceness of these plene forms. This is also true for MA, with only a handful of examples for the second person (e.g., *tu-ú-uš-šab* MAL A § 46:101), while two D-forms of *uššuru* (e.g., *ú-uš-šu-ru* MAL A § 23:34) can be found in MAL A. Unlike the I/voc verbs, forms with a vocalic ending are affected by vowel syncope. This is easily explained by the conclusion that prefixed *u-* is short, thereby resulting in two successive open syllables, *u/bi/lū* > *ub/lū*. As a

1 The etymology of *ussuku* is not entirely clear since there are two verbs, *esēku* (< √*ysk*) and *esēqu* (< √*ʿzq*), with similar meanings found in AHw (248-249), which are gathered under one root, *esēqu*, in CAD E (331–32). Modern studies seem to prefer *esēqu* (DSC 2, 10; Roth 1997, 176); this is the reading used here as well.

2 Cf. the Arabic imperative of I/w verbs *ḍaʿ* (ضع) 'place!' or *ṣil* (صل) 'arrive!'.

result, geminated forms in the present and D-stem are not affected. For the unexpected geminated /t/ of the perfect, see Kouwenberg (2010, 452f). All verbs have a theme vowel pattern (a/i).

§ 551 In OA, we still find strong conjugated verbal forms, where R_1 was represented as /w/ in the D preterite *ú-wa-šé-er* TCL 4 37:22 and the G infinitive *wa-ra-dí-ni* CCT 5 10b:2 (GKT, 156f § 93). These reflections of /w/ have disappeared in favour of a short word-initial *u*-. Some exceptions may be found in a peripheral letter (*ú-ma-ša-ar-šu-n*[*u*] RS 18.54a:6') and once for the irregular *ušābu* (*muš-ba-a-ku* TR 2083a+:9). Babylonian influence is likely here, since I/w verbs are conjugated as I/m in the prefix conjugation (Aro 1955a, 32–33). As a result, a G present has become inseparable from a D present, e.g., *ur-ra-da* Coronation Ritual i 38 (G) vs. *ú-uš-šu-ru* MAL A § 23:34 (D). The NA perfect **ittubil* is not found in MA (cf. SNAG, 96 § 3.13.2).[3] In the D-stem, the typical Assyrian pattern *PaRRuS* is not retained, due to the loss of the initial *w*-, which changed it into *uBBuL*: *uš-šur* KAJ 102:1.

§ 552 In the Š-stem, the prefix conjugation of Akkadian can have either /ū/, /ā/ or /ē/ following /š/, while /ū/ seems to be original (ū < ūw). In MA, we exclusively find /ē/, which seems to be caused by the change of /w/ > /y/ in this position, which in turn is triggered by the expected diphthong sound change /ay/ > /ē/.[4] We still find -*šā*- variants in the two other stages of the Assyrian dialect (NA: SNAG, 151). In OA, there are two variations for *wašābum*: *nu-ša-bi-lam* TTC 6:11 ~ *tù-šé-bi-lam* BIN 4 222:10, although the latter is significantly more common. In MA, no attestations for the *šū*- prefix are known, while -*šā*- is found in *ušappi* passim (§ 585). Kouwenberg (2010, 456; cf. GAG, 178 §103v) pointed out that the -*šā*- morpheme was especially frequent in adjectival verbs occurring in non-literary Babylonian. There are also two exceptional attestations of the stative *šāludā* 'they are caused to give birth'. This could be a Babylonian influence (cf. GAG, 178 § 103v). Based on their preference of the morpheme -*šā*- (Kouwenberg 2010, 456), we indicate I/u adjectival verbs as I/a verbs. In the case of the present, the second radical of the I/u verb geminates as if it were a strong verb (cf. § 557 for I/voc). However, this is only visible in two attestations of two special verbs: *ú-še-eṣ-ṣa-*⸢*a*⸣ KAV 217:8 (*uṣāʾu* § 608) and *ú-še-iš-šu-b*[*u*] New Year Ritual:11, 12 (*ušābu*, § 609) (Kouwenberg 2010, 456 n34). We have one case of a reconstructed Štn in *ul-te-n*[*i-ba-la*] MATSH 6:3'. Streck (1997, 274) suggested that this form should be read as *ultēnebela*. This pattern is attested in OA; however, it suggests Babylonian VA, such that *ultēnebala* is the more likely candidate.[5]

G-stem:

Present	*u*	3ms	⸢*ub*⸣*-ba-la* MATSH 12:11; *ub-ba-la-a-ši* MAL A § 40:71
			ur-ra-da Coronation Ritual i 38
		2ms	*tu-ba-la* MATC 22:22

3 Hämeen-Anttila suggests another difference for NA: "The short unstressed i after the second radical does not normally disappear (**ušbu* < *ūšibu*), but this sometimes happens in the perfect" (SNAG, 96 § 3.13.2), e.g., *i-tu-bu-lu* SAA 15 59 r. 13'. There are no attestations for MA, but similar forms without syncope can also be found in OA, e.g., *lu-bu-lu-nim* TCL 21 25:21 (GKT, 51).

4 See GAG, 177 § 103s; Kouwenberg (2010, 455ff).

5 Cf. GKT, 158 § 93g; GOA § 18.2.3.4.; GAG, paradigm 30*.

		1cs	*ú-bal* AO 19.227:24, 25
			ú-ma-ša-ar-šu-n[u] RS 18.54a:6'† (peripheral)
		3mp	*ub-bu-lu* Coronation Ritual iii 6; *ú-bu-lu-ni* KAJ 121:16
			ú-ub-bu-lu-né-eš-šu MATSH 9:46
			ul-lu-du LVUH 48:25
			ur-ru-du BVW O:9; *ur-ru-du-ú-n[i]* MATSH 11:15†
			uš-šu-ru MARV 4 119:32
		3fp	*ul-la-da* LVUH 48:25
Perfect	*u*	3ms	*it-ta-bal* MAL A § 30:21; *it-tab-la* LVUH 4:12
		3fs	*ta-ta-bal* MAL A § 6:74
			ta-at-ta-la-ad MAL A § 36:10
			ta-ta-rad A 3184 (NTA, 34):2
		2ms	⸢*ta-ta*⸣*-bal* MATC 22:25; *ta-tab-la* KAV 168:21
		1cs	*[u]l-te-bi-lak-ku* MARV 7 14:21
			ul-te-bi-lak-ku-n[u] KAV 96:8
		3mp	*it-ta-ab-lu-ú* KAJ 212:9; *it-tab-lu-ni* MARV 1 71:22
			e-ta-aṣ-bu-ú-ni MKA 95:22
Preterite	*u*	3ms	*ú-bi-il* MAL A § 42:17; *ú-bíl* MAL A § 43:20
			ur-da T 04-13:15
		3mp	*ub-lu-ni-šu-ni* MATC 38:7
			ur-du-ú-ni-ni T 04-13:10
		2ms	*[t]u-bi-il* KAV 104:12
			tu-r[i$^{?}$*-d]u*$^{?}$*-ni* BM 103203:17 (Nuzi/Ass.)
		3mp	*ub-lu-ni* KAV 119:7
Precative	*u*	3ms	*lu-ub-l[a]* KAV 102:20
		3mp	*lu-ub-lu* MATC 9:9; *lu-ub-lu-ni* KAV 98:35
Imperative	*u*	ms	*bi-il* MATC 11:20
		cp	*bi-la* VS 1 105:12, 20, 27; *bi-la-*⸢*an*⸣*-ni* MATSH 3:23
Stative	*u*	3fs	*ul-du-tu-ú-ni* MAL A § 45:77
Infinitive	*u*		*ana ú-ba-l[i]* MATC 79:16

Gtn-stem:

Present	*u*	3ms	*it-ta-na-bal-šu-nu* KAJ 1:9
			it-ta-na-ra-du-ni A 1748 (NTA, 23):12
			it-ta-na-ra-du-ú-ni KAJ 204:11
		2ms	*ta-ta-na-ra-da*$^{!}$*-ni*$^{!}$ MATSH 7:13''
		3fs	*ta-ta-na-bal* KAJ 9:24

D-stem:

Present	*u*	3ms	*ú-ba-la* MARV 4 5:20'
			uš-šar Coronation Ritual ii 14†
		2ms	*tu-uš-šar-šu* MATC 2:24; *tu-šar-šu* MATC 2:23
		3mp	*ú-uš-šu-ru* MAL A § 23:34; *uš-šu-ru-ú-ni* T 97-22:6
Perfect	*u*	3ms	*u-ta-áš-šir* MAL A § 40:78
		3mp	*ú-ta-še-ru* MATSH 12:35
	a	3ms	*ú-ta-tir* MAL C+ § 11:20
		3fs	*tu-ta-at-ti-ir* MAL A § 5:60
Preterite	*u*	3ms	*ú-uš-šìr* MAL A § 4:53
		3ms	*tu-še-er* KAV 201:18
Imperative	*u*	ms	*uš-še-er* MATC 4:22; *ú-še-er* KAV 201:16
	a	ms	*ut-te-er* T 97-34:9
Stative	*u*	3ms	*uš-šur* KAJ 102:15
	a	3fs	*mu-tu-rat* Rm 376:20

Dt-stem:

Preterite	*u*	3ms	*ú-tar-ri-šu-nu* MAL A § 55:9
Precative	*u*	3ms	*lu-ta-áš-ši-*⸢*ir*⸣ MATC 5:8

Š-stem:

Present	*u*	3ms	*ú-še-ba-la* MATSH 6:3'; 12:43
		2ms	*tu-še-rad* BVW B:6
		1cs	*ú-še-ba-al* T 96-15:8
Perfect	*u*	1cs	*ul-te-bi-il* MATC 11:21 *ul-te-bi-la* TabT05a-134:25
Preterite	*u*	3ms	*ú-še*[!]*-ri-du*[!]*-ni* LVUH 92:18
		2fs	[*tu-š*]*e-bi-li* T 02-05:10
		1cs	*ú-še-bi-la-ku-ni* RS 06.198:14
	e	2ms	*tu-še-še-*⸢*ir*[!?]⸣*-šu*[?] BM 103203:16 (Nuzi/Ass.)
Precative	*u*	3ms	*lu*[?]*-še-bi-la* MKA 95:26
		3fs	*lu tu-še-bi-la* A 845:18; TabT05a-134:27-28
Imperative	*u*	ms	*še-bi-il* MATSH 9:16; *še-bi-la* T 93-3:24
			še-ri-id MATSH 9:13; MATC 4:23
		fs	*še-bi-li* T 93-46:27
		mp	*še-bi-la-ni* KAV 98:21
Stative	*u*	3ms	*še-bu-ul* KAJ 178:13; KAJ 298:14
		3mp	*še-ru-du-ni* T 93-1:5
		3fp	*še-ru-da-ni* KAJ 178:6
			ša-lu-da LVUH 21:18; LVUH 28:12
Infinitive	*u*		*ana* ⸢*še*⸣*-bu-li* MARV 8 88:19
			še-ru-di BVW B:7; [*š*]*a še-ru-di-ka* MATSH 9:13
	i		*ana še-šu-re* Billa 29:9

Štn-stem:

Present	*i*	3ms	*ul-te-n*[*i-ba-la*] MATSH 6:3'
Infinitive	*i*		⸢*a*⸣*-na tu-še-bu-le* MARV 2 17a+:99

16.1.2 I/voc

§ 553 The so-called I/voc verbs are of two different types: those with and those without e-colouring, which is caused by the gutturals /ˁ-ḥ/ as opposed to /ˀ- h/. When looking at the list of attested I/voc verbs in MA, the picture can be simplified, as the vast majority of the roots are divided between etymologic I/ˀ and I/ˁ verbs. Roots with other gutturals are considerably rarer. I/h is attested only in double-weak *arāˀu* 'to be pregnant' (§ 588) and irregular *alāku* 'to go' (§ 598f). Another possibility is the verb *edāpu* (see below). The class of I/ḥ is relatively common in Akkadian (Kouwenberg 2010, 538), but is nonetheless only found in MA in the frequently used *eṣādu* 'to harvest'. In the infinitive of I/e verbs, e-colouring affects the /a/ following R_1 (e.g., *e-ṣa-du* Billa 1:9). Through Babylonian VA, I/e verbs have /e/ carried over to a following /a/ in the forms *ezābum* > *ezēbum*. We do find some of this Babylonian infinitive attested in *i+na e-re-eb* KASKAL-*ni*(-*š*[*u-nu*]) KAJ 32:7-8; 39:8. The NA development to conjugate I/voc verbs similar to I/w verbs (SNAG, 95–96 § 5.13.1) is not attested in MA. It should be noted that VA affects the infix *-ta-* of the perfect, cf. *e-te-zi-ib-ši* MAL A § 37:21 ~ *e-ta-az-ba* MATC 4:30. Thus, the change *-ta-* > *-te-* in I/e verbs is not caused by e-colouring.

§ 554 There are a few cases where the analogy between e-colouring and etymology does not hold. The root *erāšu* 'to request' has cognates in Northwest Semitic in √*ˀrš* (AHw, 239), but has e-colouring. On the other hand, *arāšu* 'to cultivate', which despite having a second radical /r/ and an original guttural (< *ḥrṯ*), has become an I/a verb in Assyrian, as opposed to the expected I/e, which is found in Babylonian (Kouwenberg 2010, 538). Moreover, the vowel patterns of *ašāru* (a/u) seem to follow OAkk, whereas, in Babylonian, it is an (i/i) verb (CAD E, 285). The theme vowels of the two verbs can be derived from the following attestations: *a-ra-áš* Wilhelm 1997:19 (present) ~ *e-ru-uš* MAL B § 4:30 (preterite). We can add to these two verbs *nēdupu* 'to be blown away', which is attested once in an obscure context (*ta-an-ni-di-ip* KAV 168:22) and shows e-colouring, even though von Soden gives the root √*hdp* in his entry for *edēpu* (AHw, 186). We also find e-colouring in *te-és-si-ip* PKT 4 obv. left 3, which has an etymologic root √*ʾsp* (AHw, 248). A new I/e verb is *egāru* 'to write down', which is found in the phrase *ana lā mašāʾe egir* 'in order not to forget, it is written down'. In this position, it replaces the commonly attested stative *šaṭir*. Note also the nominal *ú-gu-ra-t*[*e*] 'documents' KAJ 310:37.[6] Attestation of this verb in MA is significant as the nominal form was originally thought to be a loan from Aramaic (see Postgate 1980, 68a).

§ 555 The difference between I/a and I/e verbs is stronger in Babylonian than Assyrian, not only because of the lack of Babylonian VA, but also because of the vowel of the prefix conjugation in the G-stem, which Babylonian clearly divided between /i/ for I/a verbs (e.g., 3cs *i-mur*) and /e/ for I/e verbs (e.g., 3cs *e-puš*). Assyrian uses the /e/ for both classes when no consonant is prefixed to it; in the case of one, however, the Babylonian model is retained (*tāmur* 'you saw' ~ *tēpuš* 'you did'). This feature, which should be regarded as secondary, could be an analogous development with the I/e class (cf. Kouwenberg 2010, 543), or have been due to the sound /ia/ > /ē/, as we find in OB Mari (cf. Finet 1956, 8f § 6), which would have led to the development of *yiʾamur* > *ēmur* 'he saw'. We have already seen cases of strong verbs, where the prefix vowel /i/ is written <E>, while the opposite is also attested fairly frequently for I/voc verbs (cf. UGM,15 § 9):

akālu	*i-ta-kal* Aynard/Durand 1980 12:10 (Sa)
amāru	*la i-ta-mar* KAJ 89:15'
ašāru	*i-ta-*⌜*še*⌝*-ru-ni* MATSH 3:35 (TN)
elāʾu	*ti-li-ni* KAJ 143:23 (Ead/Aub)
	I-lu-ú-ni MARV 8 7:11 (TN)
epāšu	*i-pu-šu* TIM 4 45:9 (pre-MA)
erābu	^{d}*Šamaš-i-ri-ba* 'Šamaš, enter!' (PN) KAV 119:8 (Sa)
	^{m}*I-ri-ib-*^{d}*Adad* KAM 10 25:2 (Aub)
erāšu	*i-ri-šu-šu-ni* KAJ 48:11 (Sa)
eṣādu	*i-ṣi-id* T 96-3:7 (TN)
etāqu	*i-te*$^{!}$*-te-eq-šu-ma* KAJ 101:19 (Adn$^{?}$)
	i-ti$_{4}$*-iq-ma* KAM 10 20:8 (pre-Aub)

Related is the spelling *e-tam-ra* 'I have seen' MATC 10:16, where we would otherwise expect a 1cs prefix *ā-* in a form such as *ātamar* (MAL A § 47:10). We may also note an attestation of *alāku* 'to go', where an <E> is written for the prefix rather than an <I>.

alāku	*ni-EL-lu*$^{!}$*-ku-ú-ni* T 97-10:1 (Aššnīr III)

6 See UŠA, 113; Postgate (2013, 242); cf. CAD U/W, 40.

§ 556 This brings us to the plene spelling for the first radical, which can be found in the present of the G-stem and the present/preterite of the D-stem. These are used to indicate a long vowel of I/voc verbs (Kouwenberg 2003/4). As discussed in § 101ff, this type of 'initial plene spelling' still occurs in MA (mostly in MAL A–B) for forms of the present tense, but their relative scarceness suggests that they are a leftover of an OB scribal tradition (Kouwenberg 2003/4, 98ff). The most common spelling is the defective spelling (e.g., *e-pa-áš* KAJ 108:7), whereas 'normal spellings' (e.g., *er-rab* MAPD § 9:55) are mostly limited to MAPD, with only a few attestations found elsewhere (e.g., *er-ra-áš* MATSH 6:7').[7] According to Kouwenberg (2003/4, 84; 2010, 543), this type of spelling was already unusual in OB. The defective spellings and VA may cause some confusion about how to analyse a verbal form. In the case of the VA of I/voc verbs with a vowel pattern (a/u), it is often impossible to morphologically distinguish between present and preterite, e.g., *e-pu-šu-ú-ni* (< *eppašūni* or *ēpušūni*) A 1724 (NTA, 17):5. More confusing are the (i/i) forms, of which some attestations (e.g., *e-ti-qu-ni* MATC 43:15) can indicate present, preterite or stative. The tempora of this type of verb can often only be decided on the basis of context.

§ 557 In the Š-present, the second radical geminates, although this doubled consonant is rarely indicated in the orthography, e.g., *ú-še-el-la* Coronation Ritual iv 21; *ú-še-et-tu-qu* MAL A § 25:91; *ú-ša-aḫ-ḫa-sú* MARV 1 37:6. It must be noted that the same sound change took place in the I/w verbs as well, resulting in all three types of I/weak verbs (I/voc; I/n; I/w) having a geminated second radical in the Š-present.

§ 558 The lengthening of the first radical is still preserved in the N-stem stem of I/a, although the VA present is not present in other N-stems (e.g., *in-na-bi-id* MAL A § 36:106=*innābid* i/o *innibid*). The occurrence of this long vowel, in addition to a double /n/, is unexpected as a strong /ʾ/, while /n/ would give a geminated aleph. This long vowel is confirmed by the lack of vowel syncope of the theme vowel in the preterite when vocalic suffixes are attached (*in-na-bi-du-ni* MATSH 2:4=*in/nā/bi/dū/ni* ≠ *in/nab/dū/ni*). According to Kouwenberg, the N-stem of I/a verbs is derived from the base of the stative. This would be *naʾMvR*, to which the /n/ of the N-stem was again attached *i+n+naʾmur* > *innāmur* (Kouwenberg 2004, 340; 2010, 550ff). A similar change took place in the I/e verbs, where a double /n/ also occurs; however the following /ē/ is expected, according to the rule of e-colouring (*in-ni-pa-áš* MATSH 8:44'=*innēpaš*).

7 The terminology for initial plene spelling, normal spelling and defective spelling corresponds to definitions used by Kouwenberg (2003/4).

I/a		I/e	
agāru	‘to hire’	*ebāru* (?/i)	‘to cross’
aḫḫuru D	‘to delay’	*egāru*	‘to write’
aḫāzu (a/?)	‘to take’	*emādu* (i/i)	‘to impose’
akālu (a/u)	‘to eat’	*epāšu* (a/u)	‘to do’
amāru (a/u)	‘to see’	*erābu* (a/u)	‘to enter’
apālu (a/u)	‘to answer’	*erāšu* (i/i)	‘to request’
apāru	‘to cover’	*esāpu* (i/i)	‘to gather’
arāku	‘to be long’	*eṣādu*	‘to harvest’
arāšu (a/u)	‘to cultivate’	*etāqu* (i/i)	‘to pass’
ašāru	‘to review’	*ezābu* (i/i)	‘to leave’
nābudu N	‘to flee’	*ussuqu* D	‘to select’
		nēdupu	‘to be blown away’

G-stem:

Present	*a*	3ms	*e-gu-ru-ni* KAJ 50:16
			eḫ-ḫa-az-ma MAL A § 43:30
			e-kal T 04-2:29
			e-em-mar MAL A § 47:22; *e-mar* Coronation Ritual iv 20
			e-pal New Year Ritual r. 24
			er-ra-áš MATSH 6:7’
		3fs	*ta-kal* MPR 3:16
			ta-mar T 97-5:11
			ta-ap-pa-al MAPD § 10:59
		2ms	*ta-pa-la-ni* OIP 79 2:12
		1cs	*a-ra-áš* MATSH 25:11’; Wilhelm 1997:19
		3mp	*e-ek-ku-lu* MAL A § 36:94
			e-ku-lu BVW A:4
			e-em-mu-ru MARV 2 20:20
			e-er-ru-⸢*šu*⸣ KAJ 52:18
			e-šu-⸢*ru*⸣-x VAT 8236 r. 19
	e	3ms	*e-em-mi-id* MAL A § 16:62; *e-em-me-ed* MAL A § 3:39
			e-ep-⸢*pal*⸣ MARV 4 151:61
			e-ep-pa-áš MAL B § 17:8; *e-pa-aš* KAJ 99:13
			er-rab MAPD § 9:55; *e-rab* Coronation Ritual iii 40
			e-ri-šu-šu-ni KAJ 17:8; *i-ri-šu-šu-ni* KAJ 48:11
			e-ṣi-⸢*di*⸣ KAJ 81:12
			e-ez-zi-ib MAL A § 37:15
		3fs	*te-ep-pa-áš* MAL A § 45:53; *te-pa-áš* MPR 3:15
			te-er-ra-[*ab*] MAPD § 7:47
			e-ri-šu-n[*i*] KAJ 90:9
		2ms	*te-ep-pa-áš* MATSH 9:40; *te-pa-áš* BVW E r. 2
			te-és-si-ip PKT 4 obv. left 3
			te-zi-ba T 93-2:11
		3mp	*e-em-mi-du* MAL A § 3:45
			e-pu-lu-ma KAJ 32:10; KAJ 47:19
			e-ep-pu-šu-ni MARV 4 34:20’; *e-pu-šu* MAL A § 14:35
			er-ru-bu T 04-35:5
		3fp	*er-ra-ba* MAPD § 1:12
		1cp	*ni-pa-áš* MATSH 19:9’
Perfect	*a*	3ms	*e-ta-ḫa-az* MAL A § 34:71
			e-ta-kal MATSH 2:17; *i-ta-kal* Aynard/Durand 1980 12:10
			e-ta-mar AO 21.38:9; *et-ta-mar* TabT05a-134:10

		2ms	*ta-ta-pa-al-šu* OIP 79 3:16
		1cs	*a-ta-ḫa-az* MARV 2 8:8
			a-ta-mar MAL A § 47:10; *e-tam-ra* MATC 10:16
			a-ta-ra-áš-š[*u*] MARV 7 14:19†
		3mp	*e-ták-lu* BVW A:2; *e-ta-ak-lu* MATSH 2:17
			e-ta-am-ru MAPD § 20:100; *e-tam-ru* MARV 7 4:32'
	e	3ms	*e-tab-ra* MATSH 17:8'
			e-ta-pa-áš Ali 8:4
			e-ta-rab MAPD § 9:55
			i-te!*-te-eq-šu-ma* KAJ 101:19
			e-te-ri-iš KAV 106:6
			e-ti-ṣi-di KAJ 81:19
			e-ta-šar A 3204:18
			e-te-ze-eb-ši MAL A § 37:21; *e-ta-az-ba* MATC 4:30
		3fs	*te-ta-pa-áš* MAPD § 18:83
			te-ta-rab MAL A § 24:46; *te-ta-ra-ab* MAL A § 28:2
			te-te-te-eq MAL A § 12:15
		1cs	*e-tab-ra* MATSH 2:14
			e-ta-pa-aš MATSH 16:8
		3mp	*e-tab-ru* MATSH 6:24'
			e-tar-bu Ali 11:5
			i-ta-⸢*še*⸣*-ru-ni* MATSH 3:35
			e-ta-az-bu-ú-ni MATSH 7:19''
Preterite	*a*	3ms	*e-mur* T 02-32:18; *e-mu-ru-ú-ni* MAL A § 47:8
			e-ru-uš MAL B § 4:30
			e-šu-ru-ni KAJ 311:11; Ali 3:13
		3fs	*ta-mu-ru-ši-ni* MAPD § 19:93
		2ms	*ta-pùl* T 97-10:20
		1cs	*a-mur* MATSH 3:30
			a-ku-[*u*]*l* A 2994:14
		3mp	*e-ku-lu* MATSH 23:5'
			e-mu-⸢*ru*⸣ KAJ 260:10
			e-ru-šu A 2994:12
			e-šu-ru-ú-ni MARV 1 6:30
	e	3ms	*e-mi-du-šu-ni* MAPD § 21:109
			e-pu-⸢*uš*⸣ MAL B § 10:30
			e-ru-ub MAL A § 45:82
			e-ti-iq KAJ 66:23; *e-te-qa-an-ni* MATSH 4:6
			e-zi-ba-áš-še MAL A § 36:88
		3fs	*e-be-ra* MAL M § 2:9
		2ms	*te-ti-qa* MATSH 5:11'†
			te-p[*u-uš*] KUB 3 73:13'
		1cs	*e-zi-ba-ni* MATC 3:13
		3mp	*e-pu-šu* Billa 62:7
			e-ṣi-du-ni MATSH 7:16'
			e-ti-qu-ú-ni MARV 1 6:3
			e-zi-bu-ú-ni T 97-22:8
Precative	*a*	3ms	*le-e-kúl* MATC 5:24
			le-⸢*mur*?⸣ MATC 11:28
			le-šur KAV 195+:22
		3fs	*le-ku-u*[*l*] MATC 17:15
		3mp	*le-ku-lu* MATC 4:5; 18:11
	e	3ms	*le-pu-uš* MATSH 10:28
			le-r[*i*]*-iš* T 93-3:21
			le-ri-su K9-T1:14

		1cs	⸢*le*⸣*-pu-uš* MATSH 16:19
		3mp	*le-me-du-un-ni* AO 19.227:23
			le-ru-bu KAV 102:9
			le-ru-šu MATSH 4:15’
			le-pu-šu MATSH 8:24’; 13:9
		3fp	*lu la e-ti-qa-ni* T 93-20:12
		1cp	*lu ni-pu-uš* MATSH 6:11’
Imperative	*a*	mp	*áš-ra* KAV 99:41
	e	ms	*e-mi-i-id* T 97-10:25; *em-da* T 97-10:12
			e-pu-uš MATC 4:17
			e-ri-iš MATC 9:6
Stative	*a*	3ms	*aḫ-zu-ši-ni* MAL A § 40:61
			a-píl passim, e.g., KAJ 12:16
			a-ri-ik MARV 1 14:3
			a-ri-ši LVUH 80:17
		3fs	*aḫ-zu-tu-ú-ni* MAL A § 45:75; ⸢*aḫ*⸣*-za-tu-ú-ni* MAL A § 55:11
			am-rat KAJ 48:9; KAJ 90:8; KAJ 73:13
		3mp	⸢*ak-lu*⸣ TabT105A-182:7
			ap-lu KAJ 66:29; KAJ 170:17
			ar-ku MARV 1 10:2
		3fp	*ar-ka* KAJ 128:4
			áš-ra-a-ni LVUH 51:19
	e	3ms	*e-gi-ir* MARV 1 4:10;
			e-piš A 1742 (NTA, 21):4
			e-ti-qu-ni MATC 43:15
			e-ṣi-id MATSH 3:8
		3fs	*ep-ša-at* MATSH 9:22
		3mp	*em*$^{?}$*-du-ni* Billa 30:5
			ep-šu KAJ 192:28
			e-ri-šu MARV 1 71:24
		3fp	*ep-ša* KAJ 247:7; *e-pa-ša-ni* Tsukimoto 1992 B:10, r. 9’
Infinitive	*a*		*ša lā a-ka-a-li* MAL A § 30:37
			iltu tuppi a-ma-ri-ka MATC 5:3; *ana a-ma-ri-ki-na* T 93-8a:11
			ana a-ra-še LVUH 39:2; *ša* IKU *a-ra-še* LVUH 60:18
			ana a-ša-ri VAT 8236 r. 16
	e		*ana e-ma-di-ni* AO 19.227:22
			e-pa-a-ša MAL A § 47:7; *ana e-pa-še* MATSH 16:6
			e-ra-bi-ša MAL A § 29:15
			ana bēte e-ra-a-ba MATSH 12:27
			ina e-re-eb ḫarrāni(*-š*[*u-nu*]) KAJ 32:7-8; 39:8 (Bab.)
			e-ṣa-du Billa 1:9

Gtn-stem:

Present	*a*	3ms	*e-ta-na-ra-aš* AO 19.228:12
		3mp	*e-ta-na-ku-lu* T 97-10:17
	e	3ms	*e-ta-na-ra-ab* MAL A § 27:104
Precative	*a*	3mp	*li-t*[*ep-p*]*u-ru-ka* Coronation Ritual ii 31

D-stem:

Present	*a*	1cs	*ú-ug-ga-ra* MATC 4:11
	e	3ms	*ú-pa-aš-ma* MAL C+ § 7:11; *ù-pa-us-sí* KAJ 2:12(!)
			ús-sa-aq MAL B § 1:10
		3mp	*ú-up-pu-šu* MAL A § 45:66; *ú-pu-šu* TabT05a-134:22
Perfect	*a*	3ms	*ú-taḫ-ḫi-ra* MAL A § 36:6

		3mp	*ú-ta-ḫi-ru-*<*ni*> MKA 95:14
	e	1cs	*ú-ta-mi-id* Billa 62:6
			ú-ta-gi-⸢*ir*⸣ TabT05a-134:24
Preterite	*a*	3ms	*ú-ḫi-ra-an-ni* MAL A § 36:104
	e	3ms	*ú-up-pi-šu-ú-ni* DeZ 2521:19
		2ms	*tu-mi-da-an-*[*ni*] MARV 7 17:7’
		3mp	*ú-up-pi-šu-ma* MAL A § 47:2
Precative	*e*	3ms	*lu-up-pi-iš* MATSH 9:18
Stative	*a*	3mp	*aḫ-ḫu-zu* MARV 1 53:3
			ar-ru-ku MARV 1 14:6
		3fp	*aḫ-ḫu-za-a-ni* MAPD § 3:22
			ap-pa-⸢*ra*⸣ MARV 4 34:17’
	e	3ms	*up-pu-uš* MATC 53:12; MARV 3 10:17’
		3mp	*up-pu-*⸢*šu*⸣ TabT105a-085:12
		3fp	*up-pu-ša* MAH 15854 A:3’
Infinitive	*e*		*ša ú-up-pu-še* KAM 11 82:16

Š-stem:

Present	*a*	3ms	*ú-ša-ḫa-az* Ištar Ritual:4
			ú-ša-kal A 113 (NTA, 15):29; *ú-šá-ka*[*l*] T 98-17:15
		2ms	*tu-ša-ḫa-az* PKT 1 I right:2
		3mp	*ú-šá-ku-lu* A 1735 (NTA, 18):21; *ú-ša-ku-lu-ú-ši* MAL A § 46:95
	e	2ms	*tu-še-ra-ab* BVW Ko:8
		3mp	*ú-še-pu-šu-šu-nu* MAL J § 5:4†
			ú-še-et-tu-qu MAL A § 25:91; *ú-še-tu-qu* MARV 5 85:25’
Perfect	*a*	3ms	*ul-ta-ki-il* MARV 4 40:13; *ul-ta-kil* CTMMA 1 101:8
		3mp	*ul-t*[*a*]*-ki-lu* T 98-119:18
	e	3fs	*tu-ul-te-ri-ib* MAL A § 23:31
		3mp	*ul-te-be-ru* MARV 1 14:36
			ul-te-ri-bu MAPD § 20:100
Preterite	*a*	1cs	*ú-ša-ḫi-zu-ši-ni* MAL A § 5:61
	e	3ms	*ú-še-ri-ba-ni* KAV 107:11
			ú-še-ti-qu-[*šu*] MATC 55:9
Precative	*a*	3ms	*lu-ša-k*[*íl*] T 98-129:9’
	e	3ms	*lu-še-ri-ib* Giricano 7:20
		1cs	*lu-ú-še-be-er* MATSH 8:27’
		3mp	*lu-še-še-ru* MATC 12:16
Imperative	*e*	ms	*lu* ḪU *še-mi-da-ni-šu-*[*nu*] T 02-3:21 (obscure)
			še-ti-iq MATSH 12:38
			dŠ*erūa-še-zi-ba-a-n*[*i*] TR 3022:14 (PN)
Stative	*a*	3fp	*ša-ḫu-za* KAJ 310:50
			še-ru-ba-a-ni AO 19.227:10
	e	3mp	*še-ru-bu-ni* LVUH 51:1
Infinitive	*a*		*ana ša-ku-li* KAJ 213:13; *ana šá-ku-li* A 2606 (NTA, 28):12
	e		*ana še-tu-qe* KAJ 248:15
			ša še-zu-⸢*ub*⸣ MATSH 9:42

N-stem:

Present	*a*	3mp	*in-na-gu-ú-ru* MAL A § 36:94
			in-na-ka-al MARV 7 4:30’; *in-na-kal* MARV 6 35+:48
			in-na-mu-ru MAPD § 23:127
	e	3ms	*in-ni-pa-áš* MATSH 8:44’
		2ms	*ta-an-ni-di-ip* KAV 168:22
		3mp	*in-ni-p*[*u-šu*] Adad Ritual r. 7’

Perfect	*a*	3ms	*it-ta-kal* MARV 1 48:18; *i-ta-kal* CTMMA 1 101:5
		3mp	*it-ta-ku-lu* VAT 9410:39; *i-ta-ku-lu* Ali 9:5
Preterite	*a*	3ms	*in-na-bi-id* MAL A § 36:106; *i-na-bi-da-an-ni* MATSH 12:8
			In-na-me-er KAJ 146:19 (PN)
			la-a i-na-re-še LVUH 79:14
		3fs	*ta-na-ḫi-zu!*(SU)-*ú-ni* MAL A § 36:13
		3mp	*in-na-bi-du-ni* MATSH 2:4, 22
			in-na-ki-lu-ni MARV 3 34:8; *i-na-ki-lu-ni* Ali 11:21
			⌈*i*⌉-*na*-⌈*kil*⌉-*ú-ni* MARV 5 70:18
	e	3ms	*in-ni-ṣi-id* LVUH 70:16; *i-ni-ṣi-id* LVUH 74:22
Precative	*a*	3ms	*li-na-me-ru*! MATC 11:29
Imperative	*a*	ms	*na-me-er* T 97-1:15

16.1.3 I/n verbs

§ 559 The I/n verbs have /n/ as their first radical, which is susceptible to assimilation when in direct contact with a preceding or successive consonant. As for R_2, no such (regressive) assimilation is attested (e.g., *li-ib-ni-*[*ú*] MATSH 8:23'). In III/n verbs, regressive assimilation is attested in the perfect (e.g., *i-ta-nu* MATSH 6:21'), but not in the stative of *tadānu* (e.g., *ta-ad-nu* KAV 119:17); otherwise, assimilation is usually omitted for a following morpheme (e.g., *ú-pa-ṣa-an-ši* 'he will veil her' MAL A § 41:3). Assimilation of /n/ in I/n is therefore exceptional rather than representative of MA phonology. In the paradigm of this group of verbs, R_1/n behaves regularly and according to the conventions of the Akkadian language, making the paradigm almost identical to the strong verbs. For instance, there is no difference in either the present of the G or the present and preterite of the D-stem as no assimilation takes place. The absence of assimilation is attested in OA (GKT, 154 § 92a; GOA § 18.4.1), but not in the younger dialects. We can be certain of the verbs attested with theme vowels:

I/n		
G	*naḫāru*	'to be invalid'
	naḫāsu	'to withdraw'
	nakāru (i/i)	'to become hostile'
	nakāsu (i/i)	'to cut'
	napālu	'to gouge out'
	naqādu	'to be in danger'
	naqāru	'to demolish'
	nasāḫu	'to tear out'
	nasāqu (a/u)	'to select'
	naṣāru (a/u)	'to protect'
	našāqu (i/i)	'to kiss'
	našāru	'to deduct'
	naṭālu	'to look'
D	*nazzumu*	'to raise a complaint'
N	*naḫḫutu*	'to diminish'
	nappušu	'to air'

The double-weak verbs are presented in Chapter 16.4. Notice also that Common Akkadian *nadānu* 'to give' is realized as *tadānu* in Assyrian (§ 604ff).

§ 560 As the imperative derives from the base of the preterite, we find /n/ omitted from the imperative: *iṣṣur* > *uṣur*. It has been suggested that the primary vowel is representative of the sonar /*ṇ*/; thus *uṣur*=*ṇṣur* (Tropper 1998, 13). There seems to be no convincing argument for this claim, while the suggestion that such a phoneme is unnecessary as the imperative of I/n is not problematic. Rather, *uṣur* seems to be based on two principles: it is bisyllabic in the same shape as *purus* (Cv/CvC), while the first radical /n/ is not visible in the base of the preterite from which the imperative derives (also Kouwenberg 2010, 471). The two-consonantal origin of the I/n verbs is still visible in the irregular verb *tadānu* (OB *nadānum* 'to give'), where the imperative is *din* (e.g., *di-in* MATSH 1:11, see § 604ff). This is similar to the imperative of the I/w verbs, which also go back to a two-consonant root (e.g., *bi-la-⌜an⌝-ni* MATSH 3:23). The first radical /n/ also disappears in the non-prefixed forms of the Gt and Gtn- stems.[1] However, these forms are not attested in MA.

G-stem:

Present	3ms	*i-na-ke-és* MAL A § 15:53
		i-na-sa-aq KAJ 155:21; *i-na-ás-sa-aq* KAJ 14:11
		i-na-ás-sa-ḫa DeZ 2521:2
		i-na-su-qú-ni BM 108924:7
	2ms	*ta-na-mu-uš* T 93-11:12
	3mp	*i-na-ki-su* MAL A § 9:92
		i-na-pu-lu MAL A § 8:87
		i-na-pu-šu BVW C:5
		i-na-qu-ru MAL A § 15:55
		i-na-su-qu MAL B § 1:7
Perfect	3ms	*it-ta-as-ḫu-ú-ni* MARV 4 151:60
		it-ti-ši-iq-ši MAL A § 9:93
		it-ta-áš-ra KAJ 220:4
	3fs	*ta-tu-mu-uš* Maul 2004 1:9
	2ms	*la ta-ta-ṣar-ma* Ištar Ritual:7'
	1cs	*at-ta-ṣa-ar* MATSH 2:11
	3mp	*it-tu-um-šu-ni* MATSH 6:25'
Preterite	3ms	*ik-ki-ru-ú-ni* MAL A § 47
		im-mu-šu-ú-ni MATC 22:20
		iq-qu-ru-⌜ú-ni⌝ MAL B § 7:5
		is-su-uḫ MARV 3 24:10
	3mp	*iq-qu-ru-⌜ú-ni⌝* MAL B § 7:5†
		iṭ-ṭu-lu MAPD § 21:110
	1cs	*ni-ki-s[u!]-ni* T 96-9:7
Precative	3fs	*lu ta-ṣur!* Ištar Ritual:8'
	1cs	*la-am-mu-uš* MATSH 4:8'
	3mp	*li-su-ḫu* T 97-10:19
		li-iṣ-ṣu-ru MARV 7 14:9; *li-ṣu-ru* T 93-8a:10
Imperative	ms	*ú-ṣur* MARV 8 41:11
		ú-su-uq T 97-17:14
	fs	[fd]*Tašmētu-šarra-uṣ-ri* MARV 1 57 iv 11'
	mp	*ik-sa* KAV 100:25
Stative	3ms	*na-qi-id* MATC 7:20
		na-še-er KAJ 219:9; MARV 8 51:12
		na-áš-ra T 97-26:15†
	3fs	*na-aḫ-ra-at* KAM 10 31:10; *na-ḫa-rat* TR 2061:11
	1cp	*na-aḫ-sa-nu* MATSH 2:45
	3fp	*na-áš-ra-ni* KAJ 119:5
		na-aḫ-ra MARV 1 38:9

1 Cf. OA in GKT, 154§ 92b; Kouwenberg (2010, 470f).

Infinitive		*na-ma-ši-šu* MATSH 8:25'; *ana na-ma-še* Billa 63:20
		ana na-pa-li KAJ 129:12
		ana GN *l*[*ā*] *na-sa-ḫi-šu* T 98-125:12–13
		na-ša-a-ri-i-ka MATC 4:20

Gtn-stem:

Present	3fs	*ta-ta-na-ṣa-ar* MAL A § 12:17

D-stem:

Present	3ms	*ú-na-ma-áš* New Year Ritual:28'
	2ms	*tu-na-kar* PKT 1 I right:14
		tu-na-sa-aḫ PKT 7:7
	1cs	*ú-na-ka-*[*a*]*s* MARV 3 64:43
	3mp	*ú-na-ku-ú-su* MAL A § 40:92
		ú-na-šú-qu Coronation Ritual ii 38
Perfect	3ms	*ú-ta-me*[!]*-ša-ma* MATSH 3:39
		ú-ta-si-iq VAT 8923:20
	1cs	[*u*]*t-ta-mi-iš* MATSH 14:18
Preterite	3ms	*ú-na-ak-ki-is* MAL A § 4:54
		ú-na-me-ša-ni MATSH 3:34
Precative	3mp	*lu-na-ḫi-tu* MATC 29:6
Imperative	ms	*na-aḫ-ḫi-it* MATC 29:8
		nam-mi-iš MATC 1:15;*na*[*m*]*-meš* T 93-6:12
	mp	*na-pí-ša* KAV 99:14; KAV 109:12
Stative		*na-as-su-ḫa-an-ni* MARV 6 40 r. 12; *na-su-ḫa-an-ni* MARV 6 40:10
Infinitive		*nu-pu-ša* KAV 99:14; KAV 109:12 (Bab.)
		*ana nu-su-uḫ te-*x[…] LVUH 78:29 (Bab.)

Dt-stem:

Present	2ms	*tu-ta-za-am* T 93-11:21

16.2 R$_2$/weak

16.2.1 II/voc

§ 561 The core group of this verb type comprises verbs with a vowel as a second radical consonant, that is, II/ī and II/ū. The development of this verb type can be explained by a base form in the preterite, e.g., *imūt* 'he died'. This form would be expanded when a vowel was added by gemination in the present: *imūt* > *imuttū*. When this was not possible, an extra /a/ was added, which is not a theme vowel, as it is invariable: *imūt* > *imūat* (cf. Reiner 2001, 393). No doubt, the original vowel /ū/ or /ī/ was followed by a glide, which is sometimes visible in OA orthography for II/ū verbs, e.g., *i-tù-wa-ri-šu* (< *ina tu*^{w}*ārīšu*) TCL 4 24:8 (see Kouwenberg 2010, 476f). To the normal II/voc roots, we may add a class of verbs with /ḫ/ as an etymologic second radical. These verbs do not behave any differently from the normal II/ī class.[2] We should expect e-colouring of the preceding /a/ in these

2 The situation is represented in a somewhat overcomplicated manner by Kouwenberg (2010), who discusses the II/ḫ and II/y separately with two different paradigms. However, no difference can be indicated other than a cautious assumption that /a/ > /e/ ≠ /i/ in II/ḫ verbs. As can be seen below, this assumption is not supported by orthographic evidence.

etymologic /ḫ/ verbs as opposed to their II/ī counterparts. However, the few known examples are conflicting, so that even here no difference can be seen. A difference between the /i/ and /e/ distribution is not visible in the available evidence. According to e-colouring, /a/+/ḫ/ > /e/ in II/ḫ verbs, just like /a/+/y/ > /e/. While either vowel typically remains open to interpretation (e.g., *i-ḫi-ṭu-ni* KAJ 17:14), we also find the unexpected i-forms: *i-ši-im* MAL O § 1:1; *ta-bi-ar* PKT 2 ii 17 etc. Some roots, such as *raʾābu* 'to shake', are etymologically II/ḫ, yet behave as a II/ū verb (AHw, 932a).

§ 562 The orthographic evidence for the stative shows the theme vowel /ē/ for all three categories of II/ī, II/ḫ and II/ū. This is likely to be caused by the original stative pattern *PaRiS* to which the sound change of diphthongs applies: **mayit* > *mēt* (cf. Kouwenberg 2010, 478–79). There are a few forms that suggest a vowel /i/ (e.g., *mi-tu-ni* DeZ 3389:12), but these are exceptional and not limited to the II/ī category. Sometimes, II/ī verbs take an /ā/ instead of /ē/ in the stative, e.g., *ṭa-bu-ni* KAJ 209:7; *sa-qa-at* Lambert 1969:44. Similar constructions also occur in OA (GKT, 159 § 94b; GOA § 18.5.2) and NA (SNAG, 154). The /ā/ theme vowel seems to be restricted to a small number of verbs: *riāqu*; *siāqu* and *ṭiābu* are so far attested in MA. The construction *ṭāb* also occurs in Babylonian, but otherwise the *PāS* pattern is limited to Assyrian as opposed to Babylonian *PīS*. According to Kouwenberg (2010, 65–66, 479), these forms derive from the *PaRaS* adjectival pattern and are more original than the Babylonian *PīS* since *ṭayabum* > *ṭābu* ~ *ṭaybum* > *ṭēbu*.[3] On the other hand, the attestations outside *ṭiābu* are limited at best. Note that the infinitive (e.g., *mūātu* sic. 'to die') has a similar base to the present, but with the long vowel /ā/. The first long vowel /ū/ is caused by a contraction of the diphthong. As there are, however, no plene spellings for this long vowel available, it is considered a short vowel in most grammars.[4] While shortening of this long vowel cannot be excluded, there is no additional evidence to support this possibility.

§ 563 In the D-stem Assyrian differs from Babylonian in the absence of vowel contraction in the perfect/preterite: Babylonian *ukîl* Babylonian ~ Assyrian *ukaʾʾil*, e.g., *ú-ba-e-er* MAL A § 18:89. The only II/ḫ verb shows e-colouring: *tu-bi-áš* PKT 1 II right:4; *tu-be-áš* PKT 1 II right:17; *tu-be-šú-ni-ma* +subjunctive PKT 4 r. left 5. This feature of original II/ḫ verbs is also attested in OA (GOA § 18.8). There is some evidence of vowel contraction in the unsuffixed D-stem present: *ú-tar* MAL A § 15:54; *ú-kal* Billa 61:15 (this can also be found in OA and NA, which could in part be the result of Babylonian influences; see Kouwenberg 2010, 484). On the other hand, it is possible that these are simply short forms for the scribe's convenience, as undisputed preterite forms with contraction (like **ú-ki-il*) do not occur. Akkadian, in general, is reluctant in spelling intervocalic glides, especially between two identical vowels; as such, these short forms should come as no surprise. The character of the glide is therefore not certain as no aleph sign is used and a /y/ cannot be indicated in this position. The occurrence of the present *tu-be-áš* (*tubeʸʸaš* < *tubaḫḫaš*) PKT 1 II right:17 suggests a /y/ in this II/ḫ verb, making it likely that, in other verbs, it was an aleph.

3 Note also a possible instance of *PūS* for *ruāqu* 'to be far' in ᶠ*Ṣīḫtī-*⸢*ru*⸣*-qa*ʾ*-a*[*t*]ʾ KAJ 16:14 (OMA 1, 413; Kouwenberg 2010, 64f n88). This verb is not to be confused with *riāqu* 'to be empty', which has a *PāS* and a *Pē/īS* adjective in MA (see § 314).

4 Cf. UGM, 77 § 79.1; GOA § 18.5.2.

As no Assyrian VA took place in the D-stem preterite and perfect, it is likely that R_2 was geminated. However, in the G present the second radical assimilates into the third in forms with the vocalic suffix **uka*ˀˀ*alū* > *ukallū*, e.g., *ú-kal-lu-ni* MARV 1 12:13; *ú-tar-ra* MATSH 25:10'; *ú-ba-ar-ru* MAL A § 25:91. This assimilation does not take place in the preterite, e.g., *ú-ba-e-ru-ni* MCS 2 1:11; *ú-ta-e-ru-ni-ni* KAJ 303:14, as it does in the perfect, e.g., *uk-ta-i-lu-ni* MATSH 6:20'.

§ 564 The construction of the Š-stem in the II/voc verbs in Akkadian resembles the literary ŠD-stem *ušparris* (cf. GAG, 153 § 95a). They show the /a/ elided in the prefix *ša*-, resulting in a form, e.g., *ušpās*. Moreover, the paradigm of these verbs differed again between the Babylonian and OA, even though information is scarce.[5] NA shows a tendency to replace these irregular forms with a regular one and restore the /a/ between *š*- and the first radial (SNAG, 97): *ušPāS* > *ušaPāS*. Our information on MA, then, is based on only one attestation, which is a present of the Babylonian construction, that is, *ut-ra-a-aq*[sic.] (< *ušrāq*) MAL B § 19:12 (cf. § 214) and perhaps ⌜*lu uš*!⌝*-ma-at* KAV 194:14†. We should also point out that the Š-stem of the irregular verb *izuzzu* is *ušazzaz* in all Assyrian dialects, rather than the OB *ušzāz* (see § 601). Regarding the developments in NA, we can expect similar forms to eventually turn up in the MA corpus.

ē				ū	
II/ī		II/ē		II/ū	
daˀˀumu D	'to make dark'	*beˀāru*	'to check'	*baˀˀuru* D	'to convict'
biādu	'spend the night'	*beˀāšu*	'to stir'	*duāku*	'to kill'
diānu	'to judge'	*reˀāmu*	'to be merciful'	*kaˀˀulu* D	'to hold'
ḫiāru	'to check'	*seˀaru*	'to smear'	*kuānu*	'to be firm'
ḫiāṭu	'to weigh'	*ṣeāḫu*	'to laugh'	*kuāṣu*	'to skin'
qiāpu	'to (en)trust'	*ṭeˀānu*	'to grind'	*kuāšu*	'to delay'
qiāšu	'to present'			*muātu*	'to die'
riābu[6]	'to replace'			*puāgu*	'to take away'
riāḫu	'to remain'			*quālu*[7]	'to be silent'
riāqu	'to be far'			*raˀābu*	'to shake'
šiābu	'to be old'			*suāku*	'to pound'
šiāmu	'to decree'			*ṣaˀˀupu* D	'to rub'
ṭiābu	'to be good'			*tuāru*	'to return'
ziāru	'to hate'			*zuāzu*	'to divide'

G-stem:

Present	*ī*	3ms	*i-bi-ad* DeZ 2521:8
			i-ḫi-a-aṭ MARV 8 47:31; *i-ḫi-aṭ* KAJ 1:26;
			i-ṭí-bu-ni MATC 3:6
		3mp	*i-bi-id-du* PKT 1 I right:28; *i-bi-du* PKT 1 I right:9
			i-ḫi-ru-ú-ni MAPD § 8:50

5 See GKT, 160f § 94e; GOA § 18.5.6; Kouwenberg (2010, 485ff).

6 See Kouwenberg (2010, 475).

7 A verb with uncertain etymology, cf. similar II/weak verbs *qâlu* (AHw, 895) and *qiālu* (AHw, 918). Of these, *qâlu* is attested as a II/ū verb (*taqūal*). The two attested precative attestations appear to behave as a II/ˀ or II/ā weak verb, which suggests a different etymology than the two aforementioned verbs. However, the place of R_2 in these two precatives is not entirely certain. Moreover, as both II/ū and II/ā forms of (seemingly) the same verb are attested in KBo 28 61/2, all forms are taken as being derived from *qâlu* (*quālu*). It is also possible that this is in fact a II/h verb (see Kouwenberg 2010, 564 n182).

			i-ḫi-ṭu RE 19:26; *i-ḫi-ṭù* KAJ 85:21
			i-ri-ab-bu T 97-7:20[8]
			i-ri-qu MATC 3:4
		3fp	*i-ri-ḫa* KAV 106:11
	ē	3ms	*i-ṭé-an* KAJ 318:9; CTMMA 1 100:6; ⸢*i*⸣-*ṭé-a-an* CUSAS 34 40:10
		2ms	*ta-bi-ar* PKT 2 ii 17
			ta-be-šú-ni PKT 4 r. left 3
			ta-se-a-a[*r*] BVW O r. 2; *ta-se-ar* BVW B:8
		3mp	*i-se-er-ru* MAPD § 1:8
			i-ṭé-nu George 1988 1:10
	ū	3ms	*i-du-ak* MAL A § 15:51
			⸢*i-mu-ut*⸣-*tu-ni* MATSH 12:32
			i-pu-ag-ši MAL A § 29:18
			i-tu-ur-ra MAL M § 1:7
		2ms	*ta-ku-un-na* MATC 11:24[9]
			ta-qu-al KBo 61/62:23’
			ta-su-ak PKT 6 i 29
		1cs	*a-mu-at* VAT 8851:8
		3mp	*i-duk-ku* MAL A § 13:29; *i-du-uk-ku-uš* MAPD § 6:41
			i-mu-ut-tu T 93-11:35
			i-pu-gu Franke/Wilhelm 1985:9
			i-tu-ru-ni Adad Ritual r. 6’
		2cp	*ta-ku-ša* KAV 105:27
			⸢*ta*⸣-*tu-ra* MARV 3 64:38
Perfect	*ī*	3ms	*ir-ti-aḫ* MARV 6 86 env. 5’; KAJ 257:13
			i-ṣe-ḫa-an-ni T 93-8a:12
			iz-zi-ar A 2994:25
		3fs	*tar-ti-aḫ-ma* MATSH 12:10
		3fp	*ir-ti-ḫa* KAV 106:15
		3mp	[*i*]*ḫ-ti-ṭu* KAJ 124a:7
			ir-te-ḫu A 113 (NTA, 15):28; KAJ 190:23
	ū	3ms	*ip-tu-ag-šu-nu* MATSH 6:31’; *ip-tu-ga-ni* T 96-3:7
			ir-⸢*tu-ba*⸣-*áš-šu* T 96-14:7
			it-tu-ar MARV 9 112:6; *it-tu-ra* MAL A § 22:10
		1cs	*at-tu-ra* MATSH 9:35
		3mp	*id-du-ku* MATSH 2:49
			ip-tu-gu-šu-nu Kbo 28 59 r. 5’†
			iz-zu-ú-zu LVUH 22:36; *iz-zu-zu* KAV 168:10
Preterite	*ī*	3ms	*i-ḫi-ṭu-ni* KAM 10 13:17
			i-ši-im MAL O § 1:1; *i-ši-*[*im*] TR 105:5
		3mp	*i-ri-ḫu-ni* PKT 3 iv 7
	ē	2ms	*ta-ṭé-en* Billa 62:9
	ū	3ms	*i*!*-ku-su* (*ikūṣ+šu*) LVUH 43:4’
			i-tu-ra-ni Ali 8:7; T 99-12:13’
			i-zu-zu-ú-ni MARV 1 6:5
		3fs	*ta-du-ku-ú-ni* MAPD § 18:89
		2ms	*ta-tu-ra* NP 46:9
		1cs	*a-ku-s*[*ú*] (*akūṣ+šu*) LVUG 37:20
			a-ke-e-sú LVUH 48:11(?)

8 While the transliteration follows Wiggermann’s notes, it is not supported by the copy, which indicates heavy damage with illegible signs. In any case, the spelling is a mixed form (it should either be 3ms *irīab* or 3mp *iribbū*).

9 Very uncertain. Alternatively, this may be a Hurrian substantive, see Postgate 2013, 68 n87.

		3mp	*i-zu-zu-ú-ni* OIP 79 6:12; *i-zu-zu-ni* KAV 168:13
		3fp	*i-du-ka-a-ni* MAPD § 10:57
Precative	*ī*	3ms	*li-qiš* MKA 95:26
		2cp	[*lu-ú*] *ta-ṭí-i-ba* MATC 15:32
	ē	3mp	*li-se-e-*[*er*]*-ru* MATC 12:18
	ū	3ms	*li-tu-ra* MATC 4:13
	ā	3ms	*li-qa-a-al* MATSH 12:3; *li-qa-al* MATSH 6:10'
Imperative	*ī*	mp	*ḫi-ṭa* KAV 99:28
	ē	ms	^{d}*Aššur-re-ma-ni* Billa 1:20
			ṭé-en MARV 5 89:12
		fs	^{fd}ḪU.TI-*re-mi-ni* Franke/Wilhelm 1985:1
	ū	ms	[*p*]*u-ug*$^{?}$ T 96-8:12
			zu-ú-uz PKT 3 i 6
Stative	*voc*	3ms	*be-du-ni* MATC 50:9; *bi-du-ni* MATC 43:13
			me-e-et MAL A § 25:25; *me-et* MAL A § 3:24
			qé-ep MAL E § 4:10'
		3fs	*be-da-at* MAL A § 24:48
			me-ta-at MAL A § 31:42; *mi-ta-at* MAL A § 49:57
			pe-gu-tu-ú-ni MARV 3 19:16
		1cs	*be-da-ku* TR 2083a+:9
			me-ta-ku-ma KBo 28 64:10'
		3mp	*be-du-ni* PKT 2 i 10
			de-ku-ú-ni MATSH 8:39'
			me-tu-ni MARV 1 71:38
			re-e-ḫu MARV 1 49:21
			ze-e-zu MAL A § 25:26; *ze-zu* KAJ 10:6
		3fp	*me-e-ta* LVUH 48:23
	ā	3ms	*ṭa-a-ab* T 97-34:13; *ṭa-ab* T 02-32:22
			ṭa-bu-ni KAJ 209:7
		3fs	*sa-qa-at* Lambert 1969:44
			ṭa-ba-a[*t*] Coronation Ritual ii 34
		2ms	*qa-la-ta* KBo 61/2:16'
		2mp	*qa-la-tu-nu* KBo 61/2:13'
Infinitive	*ī*		*a-na bi-a-di* MATSH 10:38; MATC 2:17
			ša ḫi-a-qi PKT 3 iii 8
			balūt ḫi-a-ri MAPD § 20:97
			ana hi-a-ṭí MARV 5 45:6
	ē		*ana ṭé-a-ni* MATC 44:6
	ū		*ina tu-a-ri* KAV 194:20; *tu-a-ru* KAM 10 15:17
			ina tu-a[*r*] TR 2021+:10
			ina tu-a-ri MATC 6:9
			⸢*ša* (...) *tu*⸣*-a-ri* MATC 22:20

D-stem:

Present	3ms	*ú-ba-ar* MAL A § 3:38; *ú-ba-a-*⸢*ar*⸣ MAL A § 36:1
		ú-kal Billa 61:15; *ú-ka-al* MARV 1 20:16
		ú-tar MAL A § 15:54; *ú-ta-a-ar* MARV 9 33:16
	3fs	*tu-ka*$^{!}$*-al* KAJ 9:24
	2ms	*TUM-ka-*⸢*as*⸣*-sú* (+*šu*) EA 15:18
		tu-ṣa-ap BVW A:5; *tu-ṣa-a-ap* BVW G:12
		tu-ta-ar MATC 22:24; *tu-tar-šu* PKT 5 r. 7
		tu-ṭa-ab PKT 3 iv 4
	1cs	*ú-ba-ar-ka* MAL A § 19:47
	3mp	*ú-ba-ar-ru* MAL A § 25:91; *ú-ba-ru-šu* MAPD § 2:21

			ú-ka-lu MKA 95:20; *ú-kal-lu-ni* MARV 2 20:27
			ú-ta-ar-ru MAL A § 42:18
	(ḫ)	2ms	*tu-be-áš* PKT 1 II right:17; *tu-bi-áš* PKT 1 II right:4
Perfect		3ms	*ut-ta-er* Postgate 1973 1:17
		3mp	*ub-ta-e-ru-ú-uš* MAL A § 21:100
			uk-ta-i-lu-ni MATSH 6:20'
			ut-ta-e-ru-ni-šu MAPD § 21:110
Preterite		3ms	*ú-ba-e-er* MAL A § 18:89
			ú-ka-i-lu-ni LVUH 21:18; *ú-ka-i-la-ni* MATC 48:3'
			ú-ta-e-ra-ni KAV 98:17; *ú-t*[*i*]*-ra* TR 2910:15
		2ms	*tu-ta-er* MATC 22:26
		1cs	*ú-ba-e-ru-ni* MCS 2 1:11
		3mp	*ú-ta-e-ru-ni-ni* KAJ 303:14
Precative		3ms	*lu-ka-il* Coronation Ritual iii 13
		3fs	*lu ta-ši-ma-ku* Ištar Ritual:13
		3mp	*lu-ka-i-*[*lu*] MATC 7:15
Imperative		mp	*ta-e-ra* KAV 98:20; 99:20; 103:15
Stative		3ms	*ta-ur* MPR 49:44; *ta-ú-ru-ni* MATSH 25:9''
		3mp	*ta-ú-ru* KAJ 245:18
		3fp	*ta-ú-ra* KTN inventory iv 18'
Infinitive			*ba-ú-ra* MAL A § 18:76; MAL N § 2:8
			ana da-ú-[*me*] MARV 3 77:4
			ana ṭa-ú-be MARV 10 29:13
			ta-ú-re KAV 98:44

Š-stem:

Present	3ms	*ut-ra-a-aq* MAL B § 19:12
	1cs	⌜*lu uš*!⌝*-ma-at* KAV 194:14†[10]
Perfect	3ms	*ul-ti-mi-it* MARV 3 18:6

16.2.2 II/aleph verbs

§ 565 The II/ˀ aleph verbs all have $ˀ_1$ as a second-root consonant.[11] This group of verbs is relatively small in MA, consisting of only four or five roots. No II/ˀ verbs of the type $ˀ_2$ (ayin) have been found to date, while their change to the II/y paradigm in NA suggests that they died out as a distinct group after OA (see Kouwenberg 2010, 562). As an exception, the verb *ṣaˀālu* 'to quarrel' is attested with e-colouring (*i-ṣe-ˀa-la* MARV 8 62:6'†), which may point to an original ayin. However, the etymologic root of this verb is uncertain (cf. AHw, 1079b). The verb *raˀāmu* is known from Arabic with the root √*rym* (رئم). Akkadian evidence is conflicting, showing either /ˀ/ as a second radical or a geminated /m/, as if it were a II/ā verb (CAD R, 137ff). The verb *danānu* has become II/ˀ in MA. However, as forms with the original root occur as well, this verb is regarded as being irregular (discussed in § 600). In general, it can be said that our evidence for II/ˀ verbs in MA is

10 This form cannot be a precative, as that would be *lūšmēt*.

11 According to W. Mayer, there was also an e-group of II/ˀ verbs (see UGM, 69–71 § 74). However, one of the verbs (*beāšu*) is etymologically II/ḫ, which more or less behaves like II/ī verbs (see § 563). The etymology of *beāru* remains uncertain, while the other verb *seāru* shows gemination of the third radical with a suffixed vowel (*i-se-er-ru* MAPD § 1:8). This would be unexpected if a strong aleph was present in the verb, as can be seen in other examples, such as *il-ta-aˀ-la-a-ni* T 02-32:8.

limited, especially for the preterite and the perfect. The sign ˀA is usually used, but not in all instances. As it can be seen in the preterite *la-a iš-ˀu-lu-n*[*i*] (*lā išˀulūni*) MAPD § 3:25, the sign ˀA can also be used if in contact with a consonant, which argues against assimilation. Only three examples show a vowel sign, instead of ˀA: *ša-a-le* MAL F § 2:10; *ma-a-ad* BVW F r. 1; *ni-ša-a-al* MATSH 2:60.

§ 566 A curious phenomenon in MA is the occurrence of ˀA in positions where it is believed to have been lost in OA: in a syllable-final position followed by a consonant, e.g., perfect ⌜*il-ta*⌝*-a*ˀ*-la-ni* MATC 15:12 (OA *ištāl-*); and in the imperative mp *ša-a*ˀ*-la* KAV 107:99 (OA *šālā*). However, other forms show no trace of an aleph where it is expected, which would be incorrect in any case, according to syllabic rules: *i-ša-mu-ú-ni* KAJ 175:25 (expected *iš/*ˀ*a/mū/ni*); *i-ša-mu-ši* KAV 195+:18 (see Kouwenberg 2010, 562). For this reason, the forms that carry an unexpected aleph are likely to have been formed by analogy with the forms that still contain it.[12]

G	*maˀādu*	'to be many'
	raˀāmu (a/a)	'to love'
	ṣaˀālu	'to quarrel'
	šaˀālu (a/a)	'to ask'
	šaˀāmu (a/a)	'to buy'
D	*šaˀˀulu*	D-stem of *šaˀālu*? 'to ask'

G-stem:

Present	*a*	3ms	*i-ša-ˀa-al* MAL A § 48:35; MAL O § 5:8
			i-ša-ˀa-la-ni KAV 106:8
		3mp	*i-ra-ˀu-mu-ši-ni* MAL A § 46:97
			i-ša-ˀu-ú-lu MAL A § 45:63
			⌜*i*⌝-[*š*]*a-ˀu-*[*ú-lu*] MAL A § 1:10
		2mp	*ta-*⌜*ra*⌝*-a-ma-ni-ni* KBo 28 61 Rd. 1'
		1cp	*ni-ša-a-al* MATSH 2:60
	e	3ms	*i-ṣe-ˀa-la* MARV 8 62:6'†
Perfect	*a*	3ms	*il-ta*ˀ*-ˀa-a*[*l*] T 96-15:9
			il-ta-ˀa-la-a-ni T 02-32:8; ⌜*il-ta*⌝*-a*ˀ*-la-ni* MATC 15:12
		1cs	*al-ta-ˀa-al* Billa 62:8; MATSH 7:21'; T 04-13:11
			al-ta-a-a[*l*] MARV 4 8:10; *al-ta-al-šu* MATSH 6:37'
Preterite	*a*	3ms	*i-ra-a*ˀ*-ši* Lambert 1969:54
			i-ša-mu-ú-ni KAJ 175:25
		1cs	*áš-ˀa-al* T 04-13:16
		3mp	*iš-ˀu-lu-n*[*i*] (*išˀulūni*) MAPD § 3:25
			i-ša-mu-ši KAV 195+:18†[13]
Imperative		ms	*ša-ˀa-al* AO 19.227:18
		mp	*ša-a*ˀ*-la* KAV 107:99
Stative	*a*	3ms	*lu ma-ad* OIP 79 2:8
			ša-im LVUH 74:24
		3mp	*lu ma-du* MATC 10:23

12 Kouwenberg suggested that, on the basis of the paradigm of the strong verbs II/ˀ, one can restore the aleph to the paradigm, as long as it is still retained in some forms. However, he could not explain the spellings without an aleph (see Kouwenberg 2010, 562). In NA, aleph is known to have assimilated into preceding consonants in a number of instances, suggesting a gradual loss over the course of Assyrian history (see SNAG, 13 § 2.1.4).

13 Broken context (see UGM, 70). In BAI, we read *ki-i ša-mu-šu*; no translation is given.

			ša-mu KAV 103:12
Infinitive	*a*		*ša-a-le* MAL F § 2:10; *ša-ʾa-le* MAPD A § 3:24; 6:44

Gtn-stem:

Present	*a*	3ms	*il-ta-na-ʾa-al-šu* MAL A § 47:21

D-stem:

Present	*a*	3ms	*ú-ša-ʾa-al* MATSH 7:22'; *ú-ša-la* MATSH 6:7'

N-stem:

Preterite	*a*	3ms	*i-ši-ma* KAJ 150:8

16.2.3 II/gem verbs

§ 567 The verbs *mediae geminatae* are mostly conjugated as strong verbs in Akkadian and MA. For this reason, they do not need to be extensively discussed (for a more detailed discussion, see Kouwenberg 2010, 491ff § 16.6). A monosyllabic stative is attested for the irregular *danānu* 'to be strong' (see § 600). Two other characteristics should be briefly mentioned:

1) The imperative is an irregular construct, with the theme vowel attached after the base: *DuBBu*. This construction spread in NA to strong verbs as well (Kouwenberg 2010, 136).

2) Unlike the four radical verbs of the type *šagarruru*, the final radical does not geminate with vocalic endings. There is usually no gemination in the G-stem, e.g., *i-ša-ak-ku-ku* MAL A § 40:85; *ú-ta-ḫu-ḫu-šu* MAPD § 5:37; *i-ba-lu-lu* MATC 12:34. At the same time, the perfect *im-ta-du-du* MARV 7 7:8 appears to have R_3 geminated because it is retained. However, as *madādu* is an (a/u) verb, we need to construct *imtadudū*, rather than *imtaduddū* (sic). In this case, we have an epenthetic vowel between R_2 and R_3, which is affected by VA. Another possible example is the Štn-stem *ul-ta-na-ak-na-nu* (*ultanaknannū*) Coronation Ritual iii 3, given the lack of VA (Kouwenberg 2010, 425).

G	*balālu*	'to mix'
	dabābu (u/u)	'to speak'
	dalālu	'to praise'
	ḫaṭāṭu	'to dig out'
	karāru (a/u)	'to discard'
	lapāpu	'to wrap around'
	kašāšu (i/i)	'to acquire'
	madādu (a/u)	'to measure'
	maḫāḫu (a/?)	'to soak'
	šadādu	'to pull'
	šakāku	'to harrow'
	šalālu	'to plunder'
D	*kallulu*	'to crown'
	marruru	'to make bitter'
	taḫḫuḫu	'to drench'
Š	*šaknunu*	'to bend down completely'
	šarbubu	'to tire'
N	*nagruru*	'to roll'
	napšušu	'to be anointed'

G-stem:

Present	3ms	*i-da-bu-ub* KAJ 102:13
		i-ma-ad-da-ad Jankowska 1962:17; *i-ma-da-ad* KAJ 81:10
	2ms	*ta-kar-ra-ar* PKT 1 I right:28
		ta-ma-da-ad PKT 2 i 13; *ta-ma-da-da* T 93-6:20
		ta-ma-ḫa-aḫ PKT 6 i 29
	1cs	*a-da-bu-ub* Faist 2001, 252:28; MATSH 28:4'
	3mp	*i-ba-lu-lu* MATC 12:34
		i-da-bu-bu T 97-1:11
		[*i-dal*]-*lu-lu-ni-ma* Coronation Ritual iii 4
		i-kar-ru-ru Coronation Ritual iii 9
		i-ma-du-du KAJ 134:16
		i-ša-ak-ku-ku MAL A § 40:85
Perfect	3ms	*im-ta-da-ad* KAJ 81:16
	3fs	*tal-ta-da-ad* MAL A § 24:42
	1cs	*ad-du-bu-ub* Tsukimoto 1992 D:8
	3mp	⌜*i*⌝-*du-bu-bu* T 96-14:9
		im-ta-du-du MARV 7 7:8
	1cp	*ni-id-du-bu-ub* NP 46:7
Preterite	3ms	*id-bu-ba-ni* Tsukimoto 1992 D:7
		ik-ru-ru-ni Coronation Ritual ii 27
	2ms	*ta-ad-bu-ub* KAV 169:13
	1cs	*ad-bu-b*[*u-šu*] MATSH 17:17'
		ak-ru-ra-ni KAJ 302:11
		ak-ši-šu-ni MATC 9:16
	3mp	*id-bu-bu* TIM 4 45:5
		iḫ-ṭu-ṭu MATC 3:6[1]
Precative	3ms	*li-ib-lu-u*[*l*] KAV 205:25
		[*l*]*i-id-bu-ub* MATC 11:32; [*li*]-*id-bu-ba-ak-ku* MATSH 9:21
	3mp	*li-id-bu-bu* MAL B § 6:18
Imperative	ms	*du-ub-bu* MARV 1 13:15

1 I see no reason to interpret this form as a perfect (see MATC, 43 Com. 6), since the grammatical form *iḫtuṭū* (or *iḫtuṭṭū*) would not explain the change *-ta-* > *-ṭa-*.

		mu-ud-du MARV 1 15:7
Stative	3ms	*ma-di-id* MARV 2 23:6
	3mp	*ša-ak-ku* KTN inventory i 29
Infinitive		*da-ba-bu* Jankowska 1962 r. 3
		da-ba-ba Franke/Wilhelm 1985:5
		⸢*da-ba*⸣*-a-ab-šu-nu* MAL B § 6:14
		ana ma-da-di KAJ 83:20
		ina mu-še ba-ra-re-ma MATSH 2:22

Gtn-stem:

Present	2ms	[*ta-ad*]*-da-na-*⸢*ab*⸣*-bu-ub* MATSH 9:37

D-stem:

Present	3ms	*ú-kal-lal-šu* Coronation Ritual ii 26
	2ms	[*la*]*-a tu-ta-ḫa-aḫ* PKT 4 obv. left 3
	3mp	*ú-ta-ḫu-ḫu-šu* MAPD § 5:37
Preterite	2ms	*tu-ma-ri-ra-ni* MATC 2:18
Precative	3mp	*lu-pa-ši-i-šu* MATSH 3:37
Stative	3ms	*ma-ru-ur* MAPD § 20:98
Infinitive		*ku-lu-li* Coronation Ritual ii 30; cf. ii 31 (Bab.)
		ša lā mar-ru-ru-ni MAPD § 8:50
		ana ⸢*pa-šu-še*⸣ MATSH 3:40

Š-stem:

Perfect	3mp	⸢*ul*⸣*-ta-ar-bi-bu* MATSH 6:27’

Štn-stem:

Present	2ms	[*tu*]*-ul-*[*t*]*a-na-aḫ-ra-ar* MATSH 9:36
	3mp	*ul-ta-na-ak-na-nu* Coronation Ritual iii 3; ii 38

N-stem:

Infinitive		*ša na-ap-šu-ši* KBo 1 14 r. 9’
		ana nap-šu-u[*š-ši*] MARV 4 146:5’[2]

16.3 R_3/weak verbs

§ 568 The III/weak verbs can essentially be divided into two groups. The first group consists of verbs with a guttural as R_3: /h/; /ḥ/; /ˁ/; /ˀ/. The second group has a vowel as R_3: /ū/ or /ī/. We will not touch upon the subject of whether some of the verbs in this group originally had a semivowel /w/ or /y/ as R_3, as it is not relevant to MA. On the other hand, the original III/h and III/ḥ have lost their original R_3 as an actual consonant and merged with the III/ū and III/ī verbs as III/voc verbs against the III/ˀ, which derive from /ˁ/ and /ˀ/. It is generally assumed that the weak R_3 caused the preceding vowel to lengthen, while it shortened in later Akkadian (GAG, 184 § 105d; Kouwenberg 2010, 499).

2 The reading follows Llop (2015a, 253). However, this leaves the gemination of /š/ unexplained. Perhaps it is necessary to assume a status constructus with the governed noun written in the damaged part.

§ 569 The various etymologic origins of R_3 are the same in the D and Š-stems. As such, e-colouring never takes place, as it would make the present and preterite tenses morphologically identical. Neither is there VA with suffixes in the present of the D and Š-stems (e.g., *ú-zak-ka-a-ši* MAL A § 48:44; *tu-ma-sa-šu* PKT 3 i 2; *ú-ma-al-la-ku-nu* T 04-37:13). It is possible that the vowel retained length, or was either lengthened before suffixes (GOA § 18.10.1) or at least replaced by anceps (cf. Edzard 2001, 134 n7). Before the plurality morpheme *-ū*, VA does take place, e.g., *ú-kar-ru-ú* KAJ 159 r. 13; *ú-za-ku-ú* KAJ 66:30. Vowel contraction is attested in this position: *ú-zak-ku* KAJ 12:17. Once, we find a Babylonian D-stem pattern in the stative *mu-ṭu*$^!$*-ú-ni* (Ass. *maṭṭuˀūni*) LVUH 37:10. As the copy shows the sign LU rather than <*ṭu*> GÍN, Röllig's reading in his edition must be doubted.

§ 570 In the infinitive, we find no indication of the character of the third radical, e.g., *a-na la ma-ša-e* KAJ 268:14; *a-na la-qa-e* Faist 2001, 252:25. Kouwenberg argued that, in the case of a glide, we should expect spellings such as **la-qa-i-ú* (Kouwenberg 2010, 579), but I am not convinced that a glide would be indicated at all in orthography. For OAkk, there is one attestation available with an aleph spelling in *ra-da-ì* (=*radāˀi*) Gir 33:12 (Hasselbach 2006, 210; for *ì* see p. 76). In any case, a non-etymologic aleph does occur in Semitic languages, e.g., participle forms of II/voc verbs in Arabic: *qāˀilan* (قائلا) 'saying' √*qūl*. Moreover, MA recognizes a number of problematic infinitives: *ṣa-le-e* √*ṣlˀ* MAL A § 53:99. This form can be analysed in one of three ways: either it has vowel contraction (*ṣalāˀe* > *ṣalê*) or unexpected VA (*ṣalāˀe* > *ṣalēˀe*), or perhaps a combination of both (*ṣalāˀe* > *ṣalēˀe* > *ṣalê*). Another common MA verb, *ḫapāˀu*, allows us to study this process in more detail. Below is a brief overview of the attestations that occur in the expression *tuppu ana ḫapāˀu nadˀat* 'the tablet is liable for destruction':

ana ḫapāˀe	Not applicable	Not applicable
ana ḫapê	*a-na ḫa-pí*	MARV 1 38:10 (Ead/Aub); KAM 10 31:11 (Aub–Adn)
ana ḫepê	*a-na ḫe-pi*	MARV 3 11:22 (UŠA); MARV 4 151:41; TR 115:20; CUSAS 34 41:14 (TN$^?$)
ana heBê	*a-na ḫe-pí*	KAJ 142:15 (Aub)

Unfortunately, not all variations are attested, while the attested forms do not allow for an estimated dating of the sound change. Still, these attestations show that VA remained an active sound change, which gradually affected the first syllable of the III/weak infinitives after the third radical of this verb disappeared and vowel contraction took place. It is also not unlikely that the expression where this infinitive is used is actually taken from Babylonian legal formulae. It should be noted that the Babylonian infinitive is *ḫepû*, which is similar to what is attested here. If this is correct, a spelling such as *ḫa-pí* is actually a mixed form with Babylonian and Assyrian characteristics.[3] Mixed forms are found in MA and not unexpected, e.g., *ú-ter-šu-nu* for Babylonian *utēršunūti* and Assyrian *utaˀˀeršunu* Rm 376 r. 17, 18. Moreover, the usage of <pí> (BI) can be explained as a remnant of

3 Another mixed form can be found in *še-ma-a* (*šemāˀa*) 'hearing' Coronation Ritual ii 35. The Babylonian infinitive would be *šemē-*, in which contraction would have taken place when an accusative ending was added (> *šemê*).

OA/OB orthography, where PI was often limited to wa/i/e/u. Note the following attestation of the expression in OB Susa:[4]

[*tup*]-*pu* (…) [*a-na*] *ḫe-pé-e ta-da-a-at* 'this tablet is liable to break' MDP 22 160:38–40

iš-tu tup-pa-šu (...) *a-na ḫe-pi na-du-ma* MDP 23 275:11–12

tup-pu (…) *a-na ḫe-pi na-di* MDP 24 387:14–15

16.3.1 III/ū verbs

§ 571 The first group of verbs to be discussed comprises III/ū verbs. Orthographic evidence for the glide /w/ following ū is found in OA, e.g., *la i-za-ku-wa* 'they (3fp) will not become available' BIN 6 59:29; *za-ku-wa-ku* 'I am free' ICK 1 183:5 (see GOA § 18.10.3). Most of the verbs go back to etymologic R_3/w verbs, with a few exceptions, such as *ṭabāʾu* 'to sink' < √*ṭbʿ* (AHw, 138). The verb *ḫadāʾu* 'to rejoice' was still a III/ū verb in OA (GKT, 161 § 95c; 18.10.3), but is only attested in MA as a III/ī stative and is discussed as a III/voc verb (already a III/voc stative in OA), e.g., *ḫa-di-a-ku* 'I rejoice' MATSH 9:43. Another possible case is the verb *šaqāʾu* 'to be high', which used to have an (u/u) pattern (AHw, 1180a), but is attested as *i-šá-qi* Aššur Ritual ii 4'. Vowel contraction with the intervocalic R_3 is frequent, e.g., *i-za-ar-ru* (< *izarru*^{w}*ū*) MARV 3 10:18'. This is also attested in the 3mp forms *ú-zak-ku* KAJ 12:17; *i-na-aṭ-ṭu* MAL A § 44:44. Progressive assimilation of the glide is attested: *i-zu-ku* (*izzuk*^{w}*ū* < *iztuku*^{w}*ū*) KAJ 162:19.

§ 572 At least originally, the stative of III/ū verbs had a *PaRuS* pattern. As /u/ is a root radical and not a theme vowel, it is not elided in stative forms with added morphemes, e.g., *naṭu*(*^{w}*)*aššunni* 'it was suitable to him' MATSH 10:27.[5] It is therefore difficult to distinguish between the G and D-stems (*PaRRuS*), which mostly affect the verb *zakāʾu* 'to clear'. The stative is attested in a number of purchases and similar texts, which refer to the clearance of claims, e.g., *a-píl za-ku* 'he is paid and cleared (of claims)' KAJ 165:22. The G-stem has an intransitive meaning 'to be clear' against the factitive meaning of the D-stem 'to clear (something)'. However, as is natural for stative verbs, its function is intransitive as the verb does not take an object. For this reason, the difference between the two stems remains vague. On the other hand, the presence of D-stem statives in MA is proven by forms with gemination: *maḫ-*⸢*ru*⸣ *ap-lu zak-ku-ú* 'they are paid and cleared (of claims)' KAJ 175:34; *zak-ku-ú* 'cleared' MARV 9 9:21' and also *a-píl za-ak-ku* BM 108924:17. In its entry of the verb, CAD Z (27) ignores KAJ 175 and analyses all attestations of the stative as the G-stem. Von Soden analyses the spelling as a mistake and agrees with CAD (AHw, 1506), while W. Mayer analyses all stative forms, except for KAJ 175, as a G-stem and does not explain the form *zakku* as a D-stem (UGM, 82–84). Moreover, other verbal forms of the root in similar texts do not give decisive answers. The difference is that both of the similar passages can only be explained by the plurality of the subject in the D-stem (cf. GAV, 148–49, 264). For the adjective, probably both the G-stem (*zakuʾu*) and D-stem (*zakkuʾu*) are attested, again with the same problem of differentiation between the two.

4 See CAD Ḫ, 172; CAD N_1, 88; Deller/Saporetti (1970a, 44).

5 We may also note the noun *maḫḫû* 'ecstatic' from the original III/ū root *mahāʾu* 'to rave' (AHw, 586b). The noun is attested in MA, as a masculine and feminine plural, without contraction as a *PaRRuS* pattern, in *maḫ-ḫu-e maḫ-ḫu-a-te* MARV 1 1 i 38'.

Postgate (UŠA, 111) believes that all instances are D-stems based on the occurrence of the noun *tazkītu*, which is an example of a D-stem nominal form of the *taPRīSt* pattern: 1 *qu-pu ta-az-ki-te* 'one box of obligations' KAJ 310:11. We may furthermore note the occurrence of a *PaRiS* adjective (TÚG[ḫi.a] *za-ki-a* Coronation Ritual iii 35) and a *PaRRuS* adjective (*tup-pí* 2.KÁM-*ma zak-ku-tu* MARV 6 31:31). This makes it likely that the discussed stative forms in the expression from loan contracts (*apil zakku* 'it is paid and cleared (of claims)') are all D-stems.

G	*ḫabāʾu*	'to draw water'
	maḫāʾu	'to rave'
	naṭāʾu I	'to be suitable'
	naṭāʾu II	'to hit'
	panāʾu	'to face'
	ṣapāʾu	'to soak'
	ṭabāʾu	'to sink'
	zakāʾu	'to clear'
	zarāʾu	'to sow'

G-stem:

Present	*u*	3ms	*i-ḫa-bu* Aššur Ritual ii 12'; 14'
			i-na-aṭ-ṭu MAL A § 44:44
			i-za-ru-a LVUH 96:16'
		1cs	*a-za-ru-ka* Cohen/Llop 2017:22
		3mp	*i-za-ar-ru* MARV 3 10:18'; *i-za-ru* LVUH 73:26
	i		*i-pa-an-ni-*[…] MAL E § 3:7'†
Perfect	*u*	3mp	*i-zu-ku* KAJ 162:19
		3fp	*ta-tu-ṭu* MAPD § 18:88
Preterite	*u*	3ms	*iz-ru* MAL B § 4:29
		3fs	*iṭ-bu* MAL M § 1:3 (possibly 3ms)
Precative	*u*	3mp	*li-iṣ-pu-ú* MATSH 8:29'
Imperative	*u*	ms	*zu-ú-ru* MCS 2 2:17
Stative	*u*	3ms	*na-ṭu-a-šu-ni* MATSH 10:27
Infinitive			*ša za-ka-i-ša* KAJ 7:32

D-stem:

Present	3ms	*ú-zak-ka* KAJ 149:19; *ú-za-ak-ka-ma* KAV 212:10
	2ms	*tu-zak-ka* PKT 2 i 11
	3mp	*ú-za-ku-ú* KAJ 66:30; *ú-zak-ku* KAJ 12:17
Perfect	3ms	*uz-zak-ki-ši* KAJ 7:8; *ú-za-ki* Billa 66:11
Precative	3mp	*lu-*⸢*zak-ki*⸣*-ú-ma* MAL B § 6:18
Stative	3ms	*za-ak-ku* BM 108924:17; *za-ku-ú* KAJ 12:16
		za-ku KAM 10 14:16; *za-a-ku* MAL A § 14:38;
	3fs	*za-ku-at* KAJ 149:25; *za-ku-a-at* MAL A § 23:34
	3mp	*zak-ku-ú* KAJ 175:34; *za-ku-ú* KAJ 170:18
Infinitive		*za-ak-ku-e* KAJ 139:18'; 167:16
		za-ku-e KAJ 100:21; 132:17; 165:23; VAT 8722:15

16.3.2 III/ī and III/ē verbs

§ 573 The second group of verbs to be discussed comprises III/ī and III/ē verbs. Morphologically, they only differ in their final vowel, which is caused by a weak R_3. Similar to the II/ī and II/ē verbs, the difference is caused by the etymology of R_3. We can divide the verbs into three groups. The first group is of the type R_3=ī. The second group of the type R_3=ḫ features Assyrian VA, which was caused by the weakening of /ḫ/ to a glide, e.g., *iptaḫ* > *iptaʸ* > *iptē* > *ipte* 'he opened'.[6] The third group consists of some III/h verbs (e.g., *karruʾu*), that is, verbs with an unclear etymologic root, of which *qabāʾu* 'to speak' is one example, strictly speaking.[7] Other verbs are rare and therefore have an unclear meaning, such as *kaṣṣuʾu* (most recently: Meinhold 2009, 352). Given that it is often not clear from orthography whether a verb is III/ī or III/ē, I have been strict in ordering several verbs in relation to this particular category, even though, to be precise, all verbs in this category seem to be conjugated as true III/ī verbs. The category also includes some verbs, which originally belonged to a different class. We have already mentioned how *ḫadāʾu* 'to rejoice' was in OA as a III/ū verb, while, in MA, it is found as a III/ī verb, e.g., *ḫa-di-a-ku* 'I am happy' MATSH 9:43.

§ 574 Unlike the II/ḫ and II/ī verbs, evidence from the orthography is fairly consistent and abundant. Consider the following examples for III/ī: *la-a ib-ki* T 02-32:16; *aq-ti-bi* MATC 15:16. Contrast these examples with III/ḫ: *i-laq-qé-e-ši* MAL A § 5:68; *i-pa-at-te* MAPD § 6:40; *al-te-qe-ma* KAV 217:7; *i-la-qé-e* AO 19.228:20; *pe-te* MATSH 9:23. Evidence mostly remains limited to roots with clear vocalic patterns, that is, *qabāʾu*; *patāʾu* and *laqāʾu*, but that evidence is, so far, mostly uniform. A few exceptions can be found, e.g., *ip-ti-ú-ni* MARV 3 23 r. 7 (for an explanation of *pe-ti-a* KAV 98:12, see § 187). In the imperative, the theme vowel carries over to the first syllable, as well as in the case of e-colouring: *pe-ti-a* KAV 98:12. As the verbs of the type III/ḫ have replaced their guttural with the glide /y/, no aleph spelling can be found in their paradigm. With a suffixed vowel, the glide does not contract, e.g., *i-laq-qé-ú* MAL A § 41:13. This is also true for instances involving the second- and third-root consonant cluster, e.g., *il-te-qi-ú-ni* 'they took' KAJ 132:6 (*iPtaRSūni*); *pi-ti-a* 'open' KAV 98:12 (*PuRSā*). A similar solution is found for III/ī verbs, e.g., *iq-ṭí-b*[*i*]*-ú* MAPD § 8:51. As we discussed in § 173, it is likely that R_3 is realized as the semivowel /y/, rather than having an epenthetic vowel: *il/teq/yū/ni*; *pit/yā*. The glide spellings of these III/voc verbs thus contrast with the broken spellings of the III/ʾ verbs, e.g., *ṣi-il-a* (*sel/ʾā*) 'lay down' KAV 98:25. Unlike III/ū verbs, vowel contraction of the intervocalic glide does not occur, with only one exception: *i-la-qu-ú!-ni* MARV 1 71:19. Note that some III/ē verbs, which originally had an (a/a) theme vowel, have an /i/ in the first syllable of the imperative. These verbs belong to the group of verbs that has a *PiRaS* imperative pattern, e.g., *li-qe* T 97-17:15; *pi-te* MATSH 9:23.

6 For the etymology of *mesāʾu* 'to wash', see Kouwenberg (219, 473 n206). Von Soden provides no Semitic root (AHw, 647).

7 In OAkk, *qabāʾu* had /y/ as a strong consonant, which should have led to /ē/ in Assyrian: *iqabbay* > *iqabbē* (Kouwenberg 2010, 110–11).

III/ī		III/ḫ		Other/unknown (III/ī)	
bakāʾu	'to cry'	*barāʾu*	'to be hungry'	*ḫapāʾu*	'to break'
labāʾu	'to surround'	*laqāʾu*	'to take'	*ḫaṭāʾu*	'to sin'
mašāʾu	'to forget'	*masāʾu*	'to wash'	*ḫadāʾu*	'to rejoice'
rabāʾu	'to grow'	*patāʾu*	'to open'	*ḫarāʾu*	'to dig'
rašāʾu	'to acquire'	*raqquʾu* D	'to process oil'	*karruʾu* D	'to deduct'
salāʾu	'to slander'			*kaṣṣuʾu* D	'to cool'
šaqāʾu	'to give to drink'			*maṭāʾu*	'to be little'
šarruʾu D	'to make rich'			*qabāʾu*	'to speak'
šašnuʾu Š	'to alter'			*raqquʾu* D	'to hide'
šašluʾu Š	'to neglect'			*ṣabbuʾu* D	'to inspect'[8]
				šaqāʾu	'to be high'
				šatāʾu	'to drink'
				zanāʾu	'to be angry'

G-stem:

Present	ī	3ms	*i-ḫap-pi* KAJ 73:16; [*i*]-*ḫe-pi* TR 3022:10 (Bab.)
			⌜*i-ma-aṭ*⌝*-ṭé* T 93-20:26
			i-qa-ab-bi MAL A § 24:66; *i-qa-bi* KAJ 57:21
			i-šá-aq-qi MARV 6 40 r. 19; *i-ša-qí* KAJ 147:4
		3fs	*ta-ḫap-pi* TabT05-11:10
			ta-qa-bi MAL A § 45:51
		2ms	*ta-la-bi* BVW F:7
			t[*a*]-*qa-bi* T 93-2:12
			ta-ša-aq-qi BVW A:9; *ta-šá-qi* BVW Ac:5
		1cs	*a-qa-bi-ú-ni* Billa 19:7; *a-qa-bi-a-ku-ni* T 93-3:5
		3mp	*i-ḫap-pi-ú* MATC 83:18; *i-ḫa-pí-ú* KAJ 134:17
			i-qa-bi-ú MAPD § 8:50; *i-qa-bi-ú-ni-šu-nu-ni* MATC 83:14
		3fp	*i-ba-ki-a* MAPD § 2:19
			i-ra-bi-a LVUH 48:26
	ē	3ms	*i-la-aq-qe* MARV 6 37:20; *i-la-aq-qé* KAV 212:11
			i-laq-qé-e-ši MAL A § 5:68
			i-la-qe KAJ 98:10; *i-la-qé* KAJ 146:4; *i-la-qé-e* AO 19.228:20
			i-pa-at-te MAPD § 6:40
		3fs	*ta-la-qe* T 97-5:12; *ta-la-qé* MAL A § 26:102
			ul ta-pa-te Lambert 1969:42
		2ms	*ta-ma-as-si* PKT 1 I right:4; *ta-ma-si* PKT 1 II right:8
		1cs	*a-la-aq-qe* MARV 5 89:13; *a-laq-qe-a* MATC 9:25
			a-za-ni-a-ku T 93-11:23[9]
		3mp	*i-la-aq-qé-ú* MARV 1 41:7; *i-laq-qé-ú* MAL A § 41:13
			i-la-qu-ú!*-ni* MARV 1 71:19
			[*i*]-*pa-te-ú* Coronation Ritual iii 12
Perfect	ī	3ms	*iq-ti-bi* A 2994:5; *iq-ṭí-bi* MAPD § 2:20
			ir-ti-bi MAL A § 28:3
			il-ti-ti T 04-2:26
		3fs	*ta-am-ti-ṭí* MARV 3 38:10
			táq-ti-bi MAL A § 2:16; *táq-ṭí-bi* MAPD § 14:71
			tar-ti-i-ši MAL A § 8:84(?)

8 Note that the few attestations of this D-tantum verb vary between /b/ and /p/, visible in T 04-37:20 (with PI). The analysis of the verb in T 04-35:16 follows a suggestion by Wiggermann.

9 The verb *zanāʾu* 'to be angry' (Bab. *zenû*) usually takes its object with the preposition *itti* (or MA *iltu*); see CAD Z, 85ff. This is, in fact, attested in the preceding clause (l. 22), making this attestation of the verb rather unusual.

		2ms	*ta-an-ti-ši-an-ni-i* T 93-12:4
		1cs	*aq-ti-bi* MARV 3 63:11'; *aq-ti-ba-a-áš-šu* MATC 15:16
		3mp	*ib-ti-ki-i-ú* T 02-32:13
			iq-ti-bi-ú MATSH 2:58; *iq-ṭí-b*[*i*]*-ú* MAPD § 8:51
			i-ti-bi-ú MKA 95:10
	ē	3ms	*il-te-qe* A 1765 (NTA, 25):15; *il-te-qé* MAL A § 45:47
			ip-te-te MAPD § 22:118; KAM 10 43:7
		3fs	*taḫ-te-pe* MAL A § 8:86; *ta-aḫ-te-e-pe* MAL A § 8:79
			ta-al-ti-qe-ú-ši-ni MAL A § 23:29
		1cs	*al-te-qe-ma* KAV 217:7
		3mp	*il-te-qi-ú* KAV 217:12; *il-te-qi-ú-ni* KAJ 132:6
		2cp	*tal-ti-qi-*[*a*] KAV 217:17'
Preterite	*ī*	3ms	*ib-ki* T 02-32:16
			il-be-ú-ni KAV 119:11; *il-bi* MAL B § 20:20
			⸢*iq*⸣*-bi-a* KAJ 121a:4; *iq-bi-a-ni* MATSH 3:31
			il-ti-ú-ni KAJ 221:4; ⸢*il-ti*⸣*-ú-ni* MATC 53:11
		2ms	*táq-bi-an-ni* Billa 67:5
		1cs	*aḫ-ṭí-ú-ni* RS 18.54a:13'; KUB 3 73:4'
			aq-bi-a-ku-ú MATC 2:22
		3mp	*iḫ-pi-ú-ni* T 93-44:17
			⸢*iq*⸣*-bi-ú* MAL A § 53:105
			ir-di-ú-ni Billa 63:16
		1cp	*ni-iḫ-r*[*i-ú*]*-ni*(?) T 96-36:24
	ē	3ms	*iḫ-ri* MAL B § 10:29
			il-qe KAJ 3:4; *il-qé-ú-ni* KAJ 8:22
		3fs	*ta-al-qe-ú-ni* TR 2059:6
		1cs	*al-qe-a* MATC 4:16
		3mp	*il-qe-ú* Billa 1:12; *il-qe-ú* MATC 9:19
			ip-ti-ú-ni MARV 3 23 r. 7
Precative	*ī*	3ms	*li-iq-bi* KAJ 316:18; *liq-bi* Ištar Ritual:11
		3fs	*lu tàq-bi* Ištar Ritual:3'
		1cs	[*l*]*a*$^{?}$- ⸢*aq*⸣*-bi-a-ku-nu* KBo 1 20:67'
		3mp	*li-ib-ni-*[*ú*] MATSH 8:23'
			li-il-bi-ú MATSH 8:26'
			li-iq-bi-ú MATSH 7:11''
			liš-qi K9-T1:15
			li-il-ti-ú MATC 18:13
	ē	3ms	*li-il-qe* T 96-7:7; *li-il-qe-a* KAV 105:25
		3mp	*li-il-*⸢*qé*⸣*-ú* MAL B § 6:19; *li-il-qe-ú-ni* MATC 9:11
			li-im-si-ú MATSH 6:15'
		1cp	*lu ni-{ib}-il-qu-na-*[*š*]*i-*[*in*] MATSH 22:18
Imperative	*ī*	ms	*qí-bi-ma* passim letters; [*q*]*í-bi-a* OIP 79 3:24
		mp	*qí-bi-a* MARV 3 64:6
	ē	ms	*li-qe* T 97-17:15; *li-qí-a* MCS 2 1:18
			pi-te MATSH 9:23
		fp	*l*[*e-q*]*e-e* (< *leqy-ī*) T 96-36:25
		mp	*pi-ti-a* KAV 98:12
			li-qi-a MARV 3 64:17
Stative	*ī*	3ms	*ḫa-di-ma* MAL A § 24:58; *ḫa-a-di* MAL A § 55:38
			ma-ši TabT05a-134:23
			ma-ṭí LVUH 42:10
			qa-bi KAJ 132:11
		3fs	*ḫa-di-ú-tu-ú-ni* MARV 8 47:35
		2ms	*ḫa-di-a-ta-a-ni* MATC 12:9
		1cs	*ḫa-di-a-ku* MATSH 9:43

			la-a-ma-ku-ma (*labāʾu*) Lambert 1969:47
			sa-la-ku KAV 169:7
		3mp	*ma-si-ú-ni* KAV 108:6
			ṭa-bu-ni MATSH 6:15'
	ē	3ms	*ba-a-ri* T 97-10:18
			la-qi Postgate 1973, 1:3; *la-qí* KAJ 12:14
			la-qú-ú-ni MAL C+ § 3:21
		3fs	*la-qí-a-at* MAL A § 32:52; *la-qí-ú-tu-ni* KAJ 167:6
			pa-te-at MARV 8 33 r. 4'; *pa-te-a-tu-ú-ni* MAL A § 55:10
		3mp	*ba-ri-ú* MARV 1 71:20
		3fp	*la-qí-a* KAJ 170:13
Infinitive	ī		*ana ḫa-pí* MARV 1 38:10; *ana ḫe-pé* KAJ 142:15
			ma-⸢ša⸣-e MAL B § 6:22[10]
			ana lā ma-ša-e KAJ 268:14; *ana lā ma-šá-e* MARV 5 65:12
			aššum lā ma-ša-e KAJ 256:13
			[*q*]*a-ba-a* Coronation Ritual ii 35
			kī ra-qa-e MARV 4 119:27
	ē		*ša ⸢la⸣-qa-šu-nu* MAL B § 6:13
			ana la-qa-e Faist 2001, 252:25; MARV 10 8:10
			a[*na*] *balluṭ u le-qé* KAJ 167:4
			ana ma-sa-e MAL M § 3:5; MATSH 6:12'

Gtn-stem:

Present	ē	2ms	*tal-ta-na-qe* PKT 3 iv 5

D-stem:

Present		3ms	*ú-ḫap-pa* MAL A § 44:45
			ú-ka-ṣa Ištar Ritual:6
			ú-ra-qa MAH 16467:10'†
			ú-š[*ar-r*]*a* Coronation Ritual i 31
		2ms	*tu-kàṣ-ṣa* PKT 3 iv 3; *tu-ka-ṣa* PKT 4 obv. right:22
			tu-ma-sa-šu KAR 220 i 2
			tu-ma-ṭa-a A 877:10
			tu-ra-aq-qa PKT 3 i 1
			tu-šar-ra BVW Ab:3
		3mp	*ú-kar-ru-ú* KAJ 159 r. 13; *ú-kar-ú* TR 102:11
Perfect		3ms	*um-ta-ṭí* LVUH 48:22; *um-ta-aṭ-⸢ṭí⸣-ú-ni* MARV 4 24:12'†
			ú-ṣ[*a-b*]*i-šu-n*[*u*] T 04-35:16
		3fs	*tu-ur-tab-bi-šu* Franke/Wilhelm 1985:4
		3mp	[*ú*]*-ṣa-pi-ú* T 04-37:20
Preterite		3ms	*ú-la-qi-šu* MATSH 19:2'†
			ú-ma-ṭí-ú-ni KAJ 129:14
			ú-rab-bi MAL B § 13:21
Imperative		ms	*za-ni-i-ni* T 93-11:22†[11]

10 CAD A₁, 99; CAD U/W, 21a reads *ma-la-e*. The reading *ma-la-e* does not follow from the copy, which shows ⸢*ša*⸣ (a reading that is also found in Driver/Miles 1935, 169; AHw, 184; CAD M₁, 400; DSC 2, 160; Roth 1997, 177). The infinitive is found with a legal term (*edānu*). The verb *malāʾu* 'to fill (the term)' is uncommon; instead, *etāqu* 'to pass the term' is used. No other attestations of *malāʾu* or *mašāʾu* occur with *edānu*, making *mašāʾu* the preferable reading.

11 Morphologically, this verb can only be an imperative of *zanāʾu* (Bab. *zenû*) 'to be angry'. This fits well into the context of conflict in the letter that these attestations derive from. However, the exact translation is unclear; presumably, *-ni* is the accusative pronominal suffix (< *-anni*), although, in this case, it repeats the object of the verb, as can be seen in the full phrase (which in itself makes little

Precative		3ms	*lu-ra-qi* KAV 194:6
		3mp	*lu-ra-qi-ú* KAV 194:24; T 97-34:11
Stative		3ms	*pa-at-tu* MAL A § 40:67
			ra-qu?*-ni* MARV 4 146:19'
		3mp	*ka-ar-ru* MARV 1 10:14; *kar-ru-ú* LVUH 34:3'
			mu-ṭu!*-ú-ni* LVUH 37:10
			lu-ú pa-tu MATSH 12:38
		3fp	*ḫap-pu-a-ni* MARV 7 33:20'†
			pa-at-tu-a MAPD § 21:105
Infinitive			*ana ra-bu-e* MATC 44:3
			[*a*]*na ra-qu-e* MAH 16467:9'

Š-stem:

Present		3ms	*ú-šal-ba* TR 3004:12'
			ú-ša-aq-ba MAL A § 47:24
			ú-ša-šá-qa T 98-17:16
Preterite		3ms	*ú-ša-áš-ni-ma* MAL F § 1:5
		2ms	*tu-ša-áš-ni* KUB 3 73:12'
		3mp	*ú-ša-as-le-ú-n*[*i-ni*] MPR 58:59

Št$_2$-stem:

Participle		ms	*mul-te-šèr-tu* 'maintenance' T 98-7:13; T 98-56:11

N-stem:

Present	*ē*	3ms	*i-la-aq-qe* KAJ 306a:9

16.3.3 III/aleph verb

§ 575 The group of III/aleph verbs consists of verbs with an etymologic aleph or ayin as R_3. As we discussed in § 182, both consonants merged into an aleph in Assyrian, the only difference being the VA that comes with etymologic ayin verbs. A distinction must be made between the two vowel classes (*a/a*) and (*i/i*) for the III/ˀ verbs. The latter group consists only of two verbs, *ḫaṭāʾu* and *ṣalāʾu*. The latter group sometimes resembles the III/ī verbs, despite having R_3/ˀ as an etymologic radical (cf. Kouwenberg 2010, 577 n220), e.g., *taḫ-ṭí-a-ši-ni* MAPD § 18:84. However, some attestations of these verbs with broken spellings show the presence of an aleph, e.g., *ṣi-il-a-šu-nu* MATC 3:5; *ṣa-al-ʾa-at* Coronation Ritual ii 46. The etymologic root of *ṣalāʾu* remains unclear (cf. AHw, 1076) and, although orthography does not directly support e-colouring (e.g., *ṣi-IL-a* KAV 98:25), it is possible that the verb ultimately belongs in the III/ˁ class of verbs. The occurrence of *kaṣāʾu* 'to become cold' is unexpected in *i-ka-ṣu-ú* MATSH 6:11'. Von Soden qualifies it as an (i/i) verb, which would put it with the III/ī verbs, but does not give an etymology (AHw, 477). Kouwenberg (2010, 573) analyses the verb as III/ā, which would explain the VA. There is one case of a III/ˀ verb with clear aleph spellings (*ga-ar-ʾa-at* MAPD § 21:104), although this is given the etymologic root √*grī* by von Soden (*gerû* in AHw, 286). Another unclear root is *mazzuʾu* 'to rape', linked by von Soden to the Arabic √*mzz* (مزز) (AHw, 637). A stop is indicated with Aˀ in the attestation *ú-ma-an-ze-e-ʾe-ši* MAL A § 55:22. Note that the usage of the sign E is not a sign of e-colouring, since this sound change does not take place in the D and Š-stems of III/weak verbs.

---

sense): *il-te-ia za-ni-i-ni* N[I] 'make me angry (with me?)' T 93-11:22. See also the discussion above on *a-za-ni-a-ku* T 93-11:23.

§ 576 The III/ˁ verbs are relatively rare, but we can add the irregular verb *idāˀu* 'to know' (see § 607). Most attestations consist of *šamāˀu*, which usually show e-colouring: *iš-me-ú-ni-ma* MAL A § 47:10. We could add *radāˀu* 'to lead' and *tabāˀu* 'to get up' (Kouwenberg 2010, 573-4 n207), although von Soden gave the Semitic root √*rdī*, while refraining from giving an etymology (AHw, 965, 1375). The III/ˁ verbs generally use E signs to indicate e-colouring, e.g., *iš-me-ú-ni-ma* MAL A § 47:10; *a-šam-me* KAV 96:16 (there are a few exceptions: *iš-mi-ú-ni* MAPD § 21:109). Note that, similar to the III/ē verbs, a *PiRaS* imperative is attested in *ši-me* A 850:18.

III/ˀ (a/a) class		II/ˀ (i/i) class		III/ˁ	
garāˀu	'to attack'	*ḫaṭāˀu*	'to sin'	*idāˀu*	'to know'
kalāˀu	'to hold'	*ṣalāˀu*	'to throw'	*radāˀu*	'to lead'
kaṣāˀu	'to become cold'			*šabāˀu*	'to satisfy'
malāˀu	'to become full'			*šamāˀu*	'to hear'
maṣāˀu	'to be able'			*tabāˀu*	'to get up'
mazāˀu	'to squeeze'				
tamāˀu	'to swear'				

§ 577 There are a few instances where Aˀ is used for R_3, although this is rare in MA, e.g., *ta-am-ˀa-a-ta* MAL A § 47:31; *ú-ma-an-ze-e-ˀe-ši* MAL A § 55:22; *ga-ar-ˀa-at* MAPD § 21:104; [*u*]⸢*m*⸣*-ta-zi-iˀ-ù* KAV 217:12. Except for the final example, all attestations of Aˀ occur in literary texts. These examples also show that the post-consonantal aleph is usually retained, as can be observed in broken spellings, e.g., *ṣi-il-a* KAV 98:25; *ṣi-il-a-šu-nu* MATC 3:5. There are some cases with progressive assimilation, e.g., *ma-ṣa-ta* (*maṣṣāta* < *maṣˀāta*) MARV 1 15:13. This is discussed in more detail in § 162. There are few orthographic indications for the realization of the syllable-final aleph, although the following Š-stem with the apocopate dative suggests that it was lost: *ul-ta-aṣ-le-eš* (*ultāṣlēš* < *ultāṣliˀ-šim*) MAL A § 21:99. In the G-stem, the loss of the syllable-final aleph causes VA. Thus, we find forms with the aleph retained: *ik-la-šu* MAL B § 19:6; ⸢*ak*⸣*-ta-la-*⸢*šu*⸣*-ni* MATSH 7:13. The intervocalic aleph is usually retained, e.g., *i-ṣa-li-ú-ni* Coronation Ritual ii 28; *ir-de-ú-ni* KAJ 134:15; *it-be-ú-ni* T 04-35:14. In the case of VA, orthography allows for both options. For instance, *ú-ma-lu-ú* (MAL A § 4:56) can be read as *umalluˀu* or *umallû*. The latter form with vowel contraction is indeed attested in defective spellings, *li-ik-lu-šu-nu* (*liklû-šunu*) MATSH 7:11".

G-stem:

Present	ˀ	3ms	*i-ka-la-šu* T 97-10:24
			e-ka-la-an-ni KAV 159:8
			i-ṣa-al-li MAL B § 1:14
			i-tam-ma MAL A § 5:60; *i-ta-ma* LVUH 48:24
		2ms	*ta-kal-la* T 96-11:14
			ta-ṣa-al-li MATSH 9:39
		3mp	*i-kal-lu-ú* MPR 59:15; *i-ka-lu-ú* MPR 56:12
			i-ka-ṣu-ú MATSH 6:11'
		1cp	*ni-tam-ma* T 04-37:18
	ˁ	3ms	*i-rad-de* George 1988 1 r. 6'
		2ms	*ta-ra-ad-de-šu* PKT 6 i 33
			ta-šam-m[*e*] KBo 28 64:12'

		1cs	*a-šam-me* KAV 96:16
Perfect	ʾ	3ms	*it-ta-ma* LVUH 48:12, 24; MARV 4 119:30
		3fs	*ta-aṣ-ṣi-li* MAL A § 53:93
		1cs	⸢*ak*⸣*-ta-la-*⸢*šu*⸣*-ni* MATSH 7:13'
			a-ṣi-li AO 19.227:13
	ʿ	3ms	*il-te-me* MAPD § 21:110; MATSH 17:9'
			it-te-be MATSH 8:50'
		3fs	*ta-te-be* T 04-2:17
		1cs	*al-te-me* MATSH 12:11
Preterite	ʾ	3ms	*ik-la-šu* MAL B § 19:6†
			it-ma LVUH 43:5'
		3fs	*taḫ-ṭí-a-ši-ni* MAPD § 18:84
			ta-aṣ-li MAL A § 50:77
		3mp	[*i*]*t-*⸢*mu*⸣*-ú* T 04-34:5†
		2cp	*ta-at-ma-a-ni* KAV 217:17'
		1cp	*ni-it-mu-ú-ni* KAV 217:17'
	ʿ	3ms	*iš-me-ú-ni-ma* MAL A § 47:10
			iš-mi-ú-ni MAPD § 21:109
			ir-de-a-ni Ali 11:11
		3fs	*ta-áš-me-ú-ni* MAPD § 14:72†
		2ms	*ta-áš-me-ú-ni* T 93-12:12
		3mp	*ir-de-ú-ni* KAJ 134:15
			it-be-ú-ni T 04-35:14
Precative	ʾ	3mp	*li-ik-lu-šu-nu* MATSH 7:11''
	ʿ	3ms	⸢*liš-me*⸣ A 845:8
Imperative	ʾ	ms	*ṣi-il-a-šu-nu* MATC 3:5
		mp	*ṣi-il-a* KAV 98:25
	ʿ	ms	*ši-me* A 850:18
Stative	ʾ	3fs	*ga-ar-ʾa-at* MAPD § 21:104
			ṣa-al-ʾa-at Coronation Ritual ii 46
			ṣa-la-at Lambert 1969:40
		2ms	*ma-ṣa-ta* MARV 1 15:13
			ta-am-ʾa-a-ta MAL A § 47:31
Infinitive	ʾ		*ina ka-ṣa-e* MARV 3 64:32†
			ana ṣa-la-e MARV 7 45:9'; *ina ṣa-le-e* MAL A § 53:99
	ʿ		*a-na* ⸢*ša*⸣*-ba-e* KAJ 217:4, 9
			ša šá-ba-e NBC 4599:26
			še-ma-a Coronation Ritual ii 35

Gtn-stem:

Present	ʿ	3ms	*il-ta-nam-me* MAPD § 21:104
Imperative	ʿ	ms	^{d}*Aššur-ti-šam-me* MARV 4 151:59 passim MARV 4

D-stem:

Present		3ms	*ú-ka-ṣa* Ištar Ritual:6
			ú-ma-al-la LVUH 22:28
		3fs	*tu-ma-al-la* MAL A § 45:69
		2ms	*tu-kàṣ-ṣa* PKT 3 iv 3
			tu-ma-al-la$^{!}$ MATSH 12:23
			tu-[*r*]*a-da-a-šu-nu* BVW F r. 11
			tu-ša-ba-šu-nu BVW Ac:10
		1cs	*ú-ma-al-la-ku-nu* T 04-37:13
		3mp	*ú-ma-lu-ú* MAL A § 4:56
Perfect		3ms	*ú-ṣ*[*a-b*]*i-šu-n*[*u*] T 04-35:16

	1cs	*um-ta-al-li* MATSH 2:56
	3mp	[*u*]⌜*m*⌝*-ta-zi-i*$^{?}$*-ù* KAV 217:12’
Preterite	3ms	*ú-ma-li* MATSH 4:17’
		ú-ma-an-ze-e-ˀe-ši MAL A § 55:22
	3mp	*ú-tam-mi-ú-šu-nu-n*[*i*] T 04-5a r. 7’
Imperative	ms	*ma-a-al-li* MATC 11:19(?)
Stative	3ms	*ra-*⌜*ad*⌝*-du* KAV 209:7
Infinitive		*mu-le-e* MATSH 7:22’’ (Bab.)

Dtn-stem:

Present	3mp	⌜*uk-ta*⌝*-na-*⌜*lu-ú*⌝ KAM 10 13:16

Š-stem:

Present	2ms	*tu-ša-aḫ-*[*ṭa*] KAJ 291:9
Perfect	3ms	*ul-ta-aṣ-le-eš* MAL A § 21:99
Preterite	3ms	*ú-ša-aṣ-li-ši* MAL A § 52:88

N-stem:

Present	2ms	*ta-ka-la* MCS 2 1:21
Perfect	3ms	*it-ta-áš-me* MAL M § 3:9
Preterite	3ms	*ik-kal-ú-ni* MAL A § 36:105

16.4 Double-weak verbs

§ 578 In Akkadian, there is a large number of double-weak verbs, which are difficult to arrange according to previous categories with one weak radical. Sometimes, due to MA sound changes, some verbs appear to be irregular. As such, it will be helpful to present the attestations below. We have arranged the verbs following the first irregular radical.

16.4.1 *baˀˀû* ‘to seek for’

§ 579 The etymologic root of this verb has been suggested as √*bġī* (cf. AHw, 145). As we have already discussed, none of the attestations features e-colouring (cf. Kogan 2001, 275). The verb *baˀˀû* ‘to seek for’ occurs a number of times in the D-stem. According to Radner, the earliest attestations occur in the Giricano archive before becoming a common verb in NA (Giricano, 53). However, there is a number of attestations outside this small archive (UGM, 91). There is a semantic difference between the MA and NA variants of the verb, as MA also applies the D-stem in the meaning ‘to select (a piece of land)’.[12] Similar to *uṣāˀu*, the third weakness sometimes seems to elide in the Giricano examples, e.g., *ub-ta-ˀu-ni* Giricano 4:27 (< *ubtaˀˀe*^{y}*ūni*), which can still be observed in the older texts, as in the case of *ub-ta-ˀe-ú-ni* Franke/Wilhelm 1985:6. Notice also the rare occurrence of <*ja*> (PI) in *ú-ba-ˀa-PI* KAJ 175:38. It has been suggested for NA that the perfect forms could be Dt-stems.[13]

D-stem:

Present	3ms	*ú-ba-ˀa-a* KAJ 161:14

12 See Deller (1961, 33); CAD P, 362b.

13 See Deller (1961, 31 n6; Postgate 1976, 189; however cf. Kouwenberg (2010, 155 n52). I thank M. Luukko for pointing this out to me.

		ú-ba-ˀa-PI KAJ 175:38
		ú-ba-a KAJ 163:29; 172:14
Perfect	3ms	*ub-ta-e-ú-ni* VAT 8722:22
		ub-ta-ˀe-ú-ni MARV 5 71:16; OIP 79 6:18; Giricano 7:19; Franke/Wilhelm 1985:6
		ub-[*ta-ˀ*]*e-ú-ni* Giricano 14 r. 4
		ub-ta-ˀu-ni Giricano 4:27
		⸢*ub*!*-ta*⸣*-ˀe-e-ni* MARV 8 47:30
	3mp	*ub-ta-ˀe-e-ú* KBo 28 59 r. 4'†

16.4.2 *elāˀu* 'to go up'

§ 580 This well-attested Semitic verb has the etymologic root √*ˁlī* (cf. AHw, 206). For this reason, it is surprising that we often find instances with /i/ in the prefix, e.g., *I-lu-ú-ni* MARV 8 7:11. This is an orthographic irregularity as e-colouring did take place in these prefixes. This can be observed in 3fs conjugated forms of the present (e.g., *TI-li-ni* KAJ 149:23), in the same way that, in I/a verbs, we would find /a/ in the prefix (e.g., *ta-mar* T 97-5:11). Therefore, the orthographic <I> can only represent /e/. Vowel contraction in relation to R_3 is attested (e.g., *I-lu-ú-ni* MARV 8 7:11; *ú-<še>-e-lu-ni* KAJ 104:4), and perhaps also in *TI-li-ni* (=*tellêni* < *telianni*) KAJ 149:23 cf. *te-li-a-ni* TR 3001:8.

G-stem:		
Present	3ms	*e-el-li* KAM 11 2:5'; *el-li* Coronation Ritual i 32; *e-li* KAJ 8:15
	3fs	*te-el-li* OIP 79 6:20; *TI-li-ni* KAJ 149:23
		te-li-a-ni TR 102:10; *TI-li-a-ni* KAJ 142:13
Perfect	3ms	⸢*e-te*⸣*-li* MATSH 14:20; *e-te-li-ú-ni* MAPD § 1:9
	3mp	*e-te-li-ú* MATSH 14:13
	3fp	*e-te-li-a-ni* T 93-54:9
Preterite	3ms	*I-lu-ú-ni* MARV 8 7:11
	3mp	*e-li-ú-ni* MARV 2 5:8†; [*e*]*-li-ú-ni* MARV 4 146:14'†
Gt-stem:		
Gt	3ms	*e-te-li* CTMMA 1 100:9
D-stem:		
Present	3fp	*ú-la-a* Adad Ritual:5, 9, 10
Imperative	ms	*ul-li* MATC 4:21
Š-stem:		
Present	3ms	*ú-še-el-la* Coronation Ritual iv 21; *ú-še-la* iv 22
	2ms	*tu-še-la-a* BVW F r. 4
Perfect	3ms	*ul-te-li-šu* T 98-94:16
	3mp	[*u*]*l-te-li-ú-ni* VAT 8236 r. 12
	1cp	*nu-ul-te-li-a* T 06-9:9
Preterite	3mp	*ú-še-li-ú-ni* MATSH 21:2'†; *ú-še-*⸢*li*⸣*-ú-ni* Billa 49:13
		⸢*ú*⸣*-še-*⸢*lu*⸣*-ú* MARV 10 76:15; *ú-še-lu-ni* KAV 98:22
		ú-<še>-e-lu-ni KAJ 104:4[14]
Precative	3mp	*lu-še-*⸢*li-a*⸣*-nim-ma* MAL B § 6:16[15]

---

14 Pace Deller/Saporetti (1970b, 308f); see CAD B, 20: GAV, 205.

Imperative	ms	*še-li* MATSH 9:12; Lambert 1969:48
	mp	*še-li-na-ni-ni* T 02-3:25(!)
Stative	3fs	*še-⌜lu⌝-a-ta-an-ni* A 1722:10
	3mp	*še-lu-ú* MARV 3 9:2; MARV 10 75:5
Infinitive		*še-lu-e* MAL C+ § 11:20
		ša še-lu-i-ka MATSH 9:12

16.4.3 *nadāˀu* 'to lay down'

§ 581 The verb *nadāˀu* is mostly found in loans with variations of the expression *tuppušu ana ḫepê naṭṭat* 'his tablet is liable to break'. Other attestations are limited to literary texts, where we may furthermore point to a case of nasalization with /m/ (see § 231). The verb should not be confused with III/ū *naṭāˀu* 'to be suitable', as *nadāˀu* is a III/ˀ verb. Once, the theme vowel /i/ merges with the ventive in *la-a ta-na-da-šu-nu* 'you will not put down for them' (< *lā tanaddi-aššunu*) BVW G r. 5. Vowel contraction is to be expected for this verb, since, with the stative, the third radical assimilates regressively in most instances, e.g., *na-da-at* Billa 18:11, while it is retained only once in *na-ad-at* KAM 10 31:11. As for the third radical, from an etymological point of view, it is most likely to have been/y/, since von Soden connects the root to the Hebrew √*ydī* and the Geʿez √*wdy* (AHw, 705). As for the orthographic evidence, it seems that the third radical was reflected by a stop, which caused /d/ to be post-glottalized. For this reason, both R_2 and R_3 were represented by one geminated double consonant: *nadyat=nadˀat* > *naṭṭat* (see Kouwenberg 2010, 577-8). We will see the same sound change with *našāˀu,* for which we find the stative base *naṣṣ-* (see § 602).

§ 582 In addition to the post-glottalization of III/ˀ verbs, Kouwenberg (2003, 85) made some additional notes on the verb *nadāˀu* in MA. He claimed that *nadāˀu* has disappeared from daily speech in MA, basing this on the absence of the verb outside of the formulaic expressions of the stative in the loans. He furthermore added that the spelling *na-TA-at* TR 3012:12 is a remnant from OA, due to the absence of the value <ṭá> (TA) in MA. Kouwenberg's conclusions seem to be overly hasty. First of all, we already noted that the verb does in fact occur in literary compositions. Moreover, the verb is conjugated in the contracts as we find an instance of the feminine plural form when the subject is *tuppātu* 'tablets'. The evidence therefore does not support a disappearance of the verb in MA, the more so because our evidence for MA is limited, compared to OA and NA. Therefore, the absence of attestations in letters and administrative documents in other contexts could be a matter of chance. As for the OA spelling with the value <*ṭá*> (TA), this cannot be retained. Archaic orthographic spellings occur in the early MA period (up until EAd/Aub), but mostly disappear afterwards. This text dates from the period of Shalmaneser I. Additionally, the text originates from Tell Ar-Rimāḥ, which makes local influence possible. As a matter of fact, Syllab, no. 102 notes that the value <*ṭá*> can be found in peripheral Akkadian, meaning there is therefore no reason to assume an archaic OA spelling. On the other hand, it is correct to assume that the formula, *tuppušu ana ḫepe naṭṭat* 'his tablet is liable to break', was not a local invention, but borrowed from OB. We already discussed

15 The occurrence of A instead of Ú in this 3mp form is problematic and made extra difficult by the damaged signs. W. Mayer restores Ú instead (UGM, 87), while Saporetti (DSC 2, 169) and Roth (1997, 177) maintain the reading A.

how the variations of the infinitive *ḫepê* seem to represent a Babylonian rather than an Assyrian form (see § 570).

G-stem:

Present	3ms	*i-nam-di* PKT 1 I right:15
	2ms	*ta-na-da-šu-nu* BVW G r. 5
	3fp	*i-na-di-a* Adad Ritual:4
Perfect	3ms	*it-ti-di* PKT 1 II left:25
Preterite	3ms	*id-di* MAL B § 13:20
Stative	3fs	*na-ad-at* KAM 10 31:11 (Aub/En)
		na-ṭa-at Billa 18:11 (Adn); KAJ 142:15 (Aub); TR 3001:10
		na-ṭa-TA CUSAS 34 41:14 (TN$^{?}$)
		na-TA-at TR 3012:12 (Sa)
	3fp	[*n*]*a-aṭ-ṭa* MARV 4 151:41 (TN)
		na-⌜*ṭa*⌝*-a* MARV 1 38:11 (EAd/Aub)
Infinitive		*ana na-da-a-e* A 1828 (NTA, 25):11

Gtn- stem:

Present	2ms	*ta-ta-na-di* BVW F r. 15

Š- stem:

Preterite	3ms	*ú-ša-ad-di* MAL C+ § 7:12

16.4.4 *niāku* 'to have intercourse'

§ 583 This verb is exclusively attested in MAL A for the MA corpus. Note the VA in the *tan-* infix of the Gtn-stem present *ittinīk* < *ittanīk*, e.g., *it-ti-ni-ik-ku* MAL A § 17:68 (Kouwenberg 2010, 481).

G-stem:

Perfect	3ms	*i-it-ti-a-ak-ši* MAL A § 14:37; *it-ti-ak-ši* MAL A § 12:19
		i-it-ti-ka-an-⌜*ni*⌝ MAL A § 22:5
Preterite	3ms	*i-ni-ik* MAL A § 20:93; *i-ni-ku-ú-ni* MAL A § 12:21
Precative	1cs	*la-ni-ik-ki-me* MAL A § 12:16
Stative	3fs	*ni-ku-tu-ú-ni* MAL A § 23:33
Infinitive		*ana ni-a-ki* MAL A § 23:16

Gtn-stem:

Present	3mp	*it-ti-ni-ik-ku* MAL A § 17:68
		it-ti-ni-ku MAL A § 18:74
		it-ti-ni-ku-ú-uš MAL A § 19:84

16.4.5 *qa*ʾʾ*û* 'to wait'

§ 584 Although the etymologic second radical points to ū/w, we instead find it represented with /y/ in *qa-iyi-ni* Billa 63:20.[16] This appears to be a reflection of the glide, which occurs in the D-stem. No attestations of the G-stem are known from MA.

D- stem:

Present	3fs	*tu-qa-*ʾ*a-a* MAL A § 36:98; *tu-ú-qa-a* MAL A § 36:95

16 Cf. Syriac √*qwy* (ܩܘܝ); see Sokoloff (2012, 1327f).

	3mp	*ú-qa-a-ʾu* KAV 217:16’
Preterite	3fs	*tu-qa-i-ú-ni* MAL A § 36:12
	1cs	^{d}*Adad-ú-qa-i*
Precative	3ms	*lu-qa-i-a* MATC 12:6
	1cs	*l*[*u*]*-ú-qa-i* T 98-134:21†
Imperative	ms	*qa-iyi-ni* (*qa*^{yy}*ī-ni*) Billa 63:20
Infinitive		*re-ša* <*a-na*> *qa-ú-e* A 297 (NTA, 16):9; *re-ša a-na qa-ú-e* KAJ 120:3; KAJ 223:11; A 3185 (NTA, 35):6–7 ‘in order to mature’ see CAD Q, 331 3a)

16.4.6 *uppuʾu* ‘to obtain’

§ 585 The verb *uppuʾu* only occurs in the D and Š-stem; however, it can be reconstructed as belonging to the I/u verbs, based on the root √*wfy* in Ge‘ez/Arabic (AHw, 1459). If this is correct, we cannot explain the Š-stem preterite *ušāppi*, which should be **ušēpi* (according to other I/w verbs). In fact, the vowel /ā/ suggest that this form belongs to the small group of I/w adjectival verbs, which is otherwise not attested in MA administrative documents (cf. Kouwenberg 2010, 449 n12). On the other hand, gemination of R_2 in the Š-stem preterite suggests assimilation of R_1. Therefore we should read *ušappi* instead. The D-stem is limited to the stative with the meaning ‘to cause to acquire’, whereas the Š-stem occurs in the preterite in the meaning ‘to make acquire’. Attestations are limited to the jargon in transaction contracts, it first appears in this context in the MA texts (cf. UGM, 89). It may be attested in the post-OA document MAH 15962: *i-dí-nu-ma ú-ša-pì-ú* ‘he gave it and made it acquired’ l. 23–24, although this verb was understood by the original editors as a D-stem form of *šabāʾu* ‘to satisfy’. The sequence of *iddinma ušappi* ‘he has given it and made it acquired’ is the common expression found in MA, e.g., *i-di-ma ú-ša-pi* KAJ 169:12. Notice, also, the geminated *ù-ša-áp-pè-ú-*[*šu*] on the envelope of said post-OA text MAH 16123:24, which also has a parallel in MA *ú-šap-BI* KAJ 154:12.

§ 586 An additional problem is the character of R_2. In the stative *uppu,* both the sign UB and BU can represent either /b/ or /p/. Moreover, in the preterite, attestations with <pí> (BI) are more frequent than the expected PI. If we are dealing with an archaic spelling, it is not clear where it comes from, since it does not seem to have been a regular verb in OA or WPA dialects.

D-stem:

Stative	3ms	*up-pu* KAJ 12:14; *ú-pu* KAJ 169:13
	3fs	*up-pu-at* KAJ 160:17; *up-pu-a-*[*a*]*t* Jankowska 1962 r. 2
	3fp	*up-pu-a* KAJ 170:13

Š-stem:

Preterite	3ms	*ú-šap-BI* KAJ 154:12; *ú-šap-BI-m*[*a*] KAJ 149:12
		ú-ša-ap-BI KAJ 79:13; ⸢*ú*⸣-[*š*]*ap-pi* KAJ 147:12
		ú-ša-BI KAM 10 15:16; *ú*$^{?!}$*-ša*$^{?!}$*-pi* KAJ 169:12
	3mp	*ú-šap-BI-ú* KAJ 170:12; *ú-šap-pi-*⸢*ú*⸣ KAJ 175:31

16.4.7 *raʾāʾu* ‘to pasture’

§ 587 The root derives from √*rʿī* (AHw, 976–77), where ayin would inflect the e-colouring of the preceding /a/; however, this is absent from both attestations of the infinitive. On the other hand, the expected present *ireˀˀa* is found in KAJ 88:17 (ARu 68). An explanation of the difference cannot be given on the basis of only three examples, although the literary *i-ra-ˀu-ši* 'he pastures her' Rm 376:23 and *ir-ta-na-ˀi* Lambert 1969:54 may be considered. Comparing OA and NA shows that e-colouring originally took place in OA, but had disappeared from NA verbal forms.[17] The substantivized participle *rēˀû* (*PāRiS*) is amply attested, but exclusively logographic (Jakob 2003, 357ff; cf. OA *re-i-um* ICK 1 13:16 in Kouwenberg 2010, 503 and NA *re-ˀi-šu-nu-u* SAA 5 256:8).

G-stem:

Present	3ms	*i-ra-ˀu-ši* Rm 376:23[18]
	3fp	*i-re-a* KAJ 88:17
Infinitive		*ra-ˀa-e* KAJ 127:13
		a-na ra-ˀa-e LVUH 22:26; *a-na ra-a-e* Ali 1:8

Gtn-stem:

Present	3ms	*ir-ta-na-ˀi* Lambert 1969:54

16.4.8 Less commonly attested double-weak verbs

§ 588 There is a number of verbs with a guttural as the first radical and a weak third radical: *arāˀu* 'to be pregnant'; *ebāˀu* 'to be thick'; *epāˀu* 'to bake'; *urāˀu* 'to lead'. The etymology proposed by von Soden for *arāˀu* (√*hrī* AHw, 72b) does not support e-colouring following R_1 in the G-stem stative. We also present two adjectival forms of the root; once seemingly with a nisbe ending (*arāˀittu*) and once with the normal PaRiS pattern (*arīˀātu*). The verb *epāˀu* is only attested as a G-stem infinitive in the harvest texts from Tell Aš-Šēḫ Ḥamad; however, note the substantive 'baker' from the same archive and Aššur: ^{lú}*a-pi-ú* MARV 9 110:12; ^{lú}*a-pi-e* MATSH 12:32. The etymology seems to derive from Common Semitic √*ˀpī* (AHw, 231a). This is actually unexpected, as R_1/aleph usually does not cause e-colouring, as found in the infinitive (e.g., Syriac *ēfā* ܐܦܐ Smith 1903, 26a).

G-stem:

Present	3ms	*ur-ra-šu-ni* (*urrâššuni* < *urraˀaššuni*) Giricano 10:13
		ú-ra-šu KAJ 89:16'
Stative	3fs	*e-bi-at* PKT 4 obv. left 15
	3mp	[*e*]-*ri-ú* LVUH 48:13
	3fp	*e-ri-a* LVUH 48:25
Infinitive		*ana e-pa-e* LVUH 80:30; cf. LVUH 63:27; 67:32; 69:37
Adjective	fs	42 *atānu a'-ra-it-tu* LVUH 43:6'–7'
	fp	[…] *a'-ri-a-tu* LVUH 5:21†

§ 589 Two II/gem verbal roots are attested, which have a weak first radical: *allulu* (Bab. *elēlum*) 'to purify'; *arāru* 'to insult' The latter verb is only attested in MAPD. Note that, in one copy of the texts, we find a perfect *tātarur*, rather than the expected *tātarar*.

G-stem:

Perfect	3fs	*ta-ta-ru-ur*/*ra-ar* MAPD § 17:79; *ta-ta-ra-ar* MAPD § 17:81

17 OA, e.g., *i-re-e-ú* CCT 6 28c:18 ~; NA, e.g., *i-ra-ˀu-u-ni* Iraq 28, 182 no. 87: 10; see also SNAG, 158.

18 The orthographically identical form in Lambert 1969:54 derives from *raˀāmu* 'to love' (see Röllig 1985, 261).

D-stem:

Present	3ms	*ú-lal* Adad Ritual:5, 8, 10 14
		ul-lu-lu-ú-ni MAL A § 47:23

§ 590 There is a number of double-weak verbs with /n/ as the first radical: *naʾʾuḫu* 'to rest'; *naqāʾu* 'to pour'; *nêʾu* 'to overturn'. Note that attestations for *naṭāʾu* 'to beat/to be suitable' are discussed with the III/ū verbs. The verb *naʾʾuḫu*, of the Semitic root √*nūḫ* (AHw, 716, Bab. *nâḫum*), is attested only once in MA in the D-stem, with the meaning 'to appease'. According to Saporetti, an imperative of the D-stem with a Babylonian pattern is attested in the PN *Nūḫi-mātum*.[19]

G-stem:

Present	3ms	*i-na-aq-qi* New Year Ritual:23'; *i-na-qi* Adad Ritual:12
	2ms	*ta-na-qi* BVW L: 6
Preterite	3fs	*in-né-e* MAL M § 1:3

D-stem:

Present	3mp	*ú-na-aḫ-ḫu* New Year Ritual:26'
Imperative	fs	^{f}*Nu-ḫi-mātum* KAJ 2:17
		Nu-ḫi-mātum KAJ 2:16

§ 591 Of II/III-weak verbs, we should mention common *laʾû* 'to be able' and *šaʾû* 'to seek'. The presence of the Common Akkadian verb *laʾû* 'to be able' in the MA corpus remains uncertain; see also the footnote of the following attestation. The root of *laʾû* appears to be the etymologic √*lʾī*, based on the Ugaritic cognate (cf. AHw, 547). The MA present is thus in line with this assumption, *ilaʾʾe*. However, in OA, we find the VA of /a/ between the first and second radical (GKT, 170 § 98; GOA § 18.10.7). Moreover, in an attested adjective, we find this OA form attested as *le-a-at-ta* (*leʾâttu*) MATC 3:10. Note that *laʾû* is a stative verb, which is neutral in terms of tense (cf. GOA § 16.5), e.g.:

> *baʾʾura la-a i-la-ʾe-e lā ubaʾʾer* 'he was not able to prove it and did not prove it' MAL A § 18:16–76

G-stem:

Present	3ms	*i-la-a-ʾe-e* MAL A § 19:88; *i-la-ʾe-e* MAL A § 18:76
	1cs	*la-la-ʾe* MATSH 12:28
Perfect	1cp	[*ni*]-*il-ta-ʾe-e-ma* MATSH 18:34[20]

PNs:

littu	^{md}*Bēr-bēl-li-it-te* KAJ 217:12
	^{fd}*Ištar-le-at* YBC 12862:3

19 See OMA 1, 358; 2, 145; cf. CAD N_1, 146.

20 Streck's (1997, 275) suggestion to analyse this form as a perfect from *labāʾu*, cannot be accepted for two reasons. Firstly, the etymologic /w/ is always written <B> for this root. Secondly, the etymologic /w/ is never written with the sign ʾA in MA (cf. § 175).

16.5 Irregular verbs

§ 592 MA recognizes one basic type of irregular verb, where unexpected differences occur between the various verbal forms. Verbs in this group are *tadānu* (present *iddan*), *udāʾu* (pret. *ide*) and *alāku* (pret. *illik*). Most other so-called irregular verbs behave differently because of a sound change; on closer examination, however, they are regularly conjugated. One example is the verb *qabāʾu*, which, under the influence of the emphatic /q/, has an infixed /ṭ/ instead of /t/ in the perfect. In the case of changes so minor, such verbs are discussed in the section on phonology. What is distinct here is the verb *našāʾu*, which rather unpredictably changes two root radicals and shows unexpected gemination in the orthography. Verbs altered by typical Assyrian sound changes are listed here, except for *qabāʾu* and *qarābu* (/q+t/ > /qṭ/, see § 211), as their peculiar sound change is only found in some perfect forms. Some of these verbs are built analogously to each other. This is particularly clear in the cases of *izuzzu* and *tadānu* in relation to *alāku*; however, *našāʾu/naṣṣ-* and *uṣāʾu* behave rather similarly. These, among some other verbs, are also found in the paradigms.

16.5.1 The existential verbs *ibašši* and *laššu*

§ 593 There are two main existential verbs in MA, which stand in direct opposition to each other, namely, the two semantically related verbs *ibašši* (< **bašāʾu*) 'to be available' and *laššu* 'to not be available'.[21] Neither of the verbs is inflected according to gender or tense, aside from some archaic exceptions in PNs. The verb *laššu* is typical of the MA dialect, whereas the Babylonian counterpart *yānu* does not occur (see below).

> *i-ba-ši ù la-šu ana* PN_1 *u* PN_2 '(what) there is and (what) there is not (belong) to PN_1 and PN_2' KAJ 79:19–21

§ 594 Of the two verbs, *laššu* is typical of the Assyrian dialect (GAG, 201 § 111a). Alternatively, Babylonian *yānu* 'there is not' is attested once, although it does not seem to belong to the Assyrian dialect, as it mostly has the same function as *laššu*.[22] In fact, these existential verbs may not be verbs in the true sense of the word, as they are not conjugated according to tense, gender or number. Von Soden called both *laššu* and *yānu* 'Verbale Ausdrücke' (GAG, 201 § 111). Kouwenberg referred to *laššu* as an existential adjective (Kouwenberg 2010, 467 n76). However, *laššu* was originally conjugated as a substantive stative, while some remnants may be found in OA, e.g., *lá-šu-a-tí-ni* 'you were absent' I 610:7 (GKT, 168 n1). This resembles the Arabic perfect-only verb *laysa* (ليس) 'not to be', even though a direct etymologic relation remains disputed (Rubin 2005, 46; Kouwenberg 2010, 467 n76). However, no such examples exist in MA, which means that *laššu* is better labelled, in a more general sense, as a copula than as an actual verb.

§ 595 Below is a list of spellings of *ibašši* (G) and *bašāʾu* forms in the Š and N-stem:

---

21 Although a proposed etymologic relation is not unproblematic, see Kouwenberg 2010, 467 n76; also note Al-Fatlawee (2005, 217–18).

22 It is only found in an Assyrian letter from Nippur: ⸢DIRIG⸣ [*i*]*a-a-nu* 'there is no surplus' Ni. 669:17-18. The attestation alone is reason to exclude this letter from the MA corpus. Akkadian has developed the negative existential verb *yānu* 'there is not' out of *ayyānum* 'who'. The verbal expression seems more closely connected to Babylonian (GAG, 201 § 11a), especially to MB where laššu is not attested in the letter corpus (Aro 1957, 42).

Present	3cs/p	*i-ba-aš-ši* MAL A § 26:100; *i-ba-áš-ši* KAV 103:24
		i-ba-ši-i K9-T1:6
		i-ba-ši-ú-ni MARV 1 13:12; *i-ba-aš-*⸢*ši-ú*⸣-[*ni*] IM 61027:8†
	3mp$^{?}$	*i-ba-áš-ši-ú* MATC 11:10†
Š present	3ms	*ú-ša-ab-šu-ú-*<*ni*> KAM 10 25:14
Š participle		^{d}*Adad-mu-šab-ši* KAJ 73:22; [^{m}*M*]*u-ši-ib-ši-Sibitta* Billa 3:27 (Bab.)
N present	3ms	[*i*]*b-ba-šu-ni* MAPD § 2:16†
N perfect	3ms	^{m}*It-tab-ši-dēn-Aššur* KAV 99:47; *It-tab-ši* MARV 1 14:34 (PN)
	3mp	*it-tab-ši*$^{!}$*-i-ú* MARV 8 47:34 (TN)

As can be seen, the spellings with <aš> DIL are uncommon and occur in literary texts or peripheral letters, which were not written in the Assyrian dialect. The existence of the 3mp plural form is possible, but it is often clouded by the addition of the subjunctive *-(ū)ni*. Its existence is unlikely but cannot be excluded. Moreover, one N-stem may be suspected ([*i*]*b-ba-šu-ni* MAPD § 2:16), while more remnants of an N-stem perfect are found in PNs, e.g., ^{m}*It-tab-ši*-DI-^{d}*A-šur* KAV 99:47 (UGM, 5 n1). Likewise, a Š-stem participle is attested in PNs, e.g., ^{d}IŠKUR-*mu-šab-ši* KAJ 73:22. Semiverbs are not to be regarded as copula verbs, as there are no such verbs in Akkadian (the former tend to have an existential meaning).[23] For NA, see SNAG, 103 § 3.16.

ḫaʾu lā masīuttu i-ba-áš-ši 'if there are uncleaned *ḫaʾu* textiles (pl.)' KAV 103:23–24

šīpātu ša qātika kē maṣi i-ba-áš-ši iriḫḫa 'the wool that is at your disposal, how much is available as a remainder?' KAV 106:9–11

šēbutteka u mimma ša ana dabābika i-ba-ši-ú-ni 'your witnesses and what there is, is for your speaking' MARV 1 13:10–12

Substantives *bāšīu* and *bušīu* derive of *ibašši* (**bašāʾu*):

bu-ši-ú ù ba-ši-ù ina GN 'whatever possessions and holdings in GN' KAJ 174:5

kāte anneke eqalšu bēssu u ba-ši-šu 'the guarantee of the lead is his field, his house and his possessions' KAM 10 18:15–16

ina bu$^{!}$*-ši ù ba-ši-e* 'possessions and holdings' KAM 10 25:11

kāte ŠE *ba-ši-šu bu-ši-šu* 'the guarantee of the barley is his possessions and holdings' Jankowska 1962 r. 4

§ 596 The negated counterpart of *ibašši* is *laššu*. There are considerably fewer derived forms, while remnants of secondary stems are absent.

laššu	*la-áš-šu* MATSH 2:18; *la-aš-šu* T 05-1:6; *la-a-áš-šu* T 93-6:18
	la$^{!}$*-šu* KAJ 153:20; *la-šu-ú* K9-T1:7
laššūni	*la-áš-šu-ni* MATSH 6:9'

Plene spellings are more common than defective spellings. Note that <aš> and <áš> are in free variation.

23 Pace SNAG, 103 § 3.16; in response, see Streck (2003b, 128). One cannot use these verbs as true copulas, as in *awīlum ibašši šarrum* 'the man is a king', for instance; instead, a nominal sentence would be required here.

ana maṣṣartema ša āle aʾīluttu la-áš-šu 'there are no men (pl.) for the protection of the city' MATSH 2:21

šumma eqlu ina ugāre PN *la!-šu* 'if there is no field in the meadow of PN' KAJ 153:20

iltu túg*kitāʾu*meš *la-áš-šu-ni* 'since there is no flax' MATSH 6:9'

Attestations with a subjunctive are rare. Note that, in some cases, the expected subjunctive is not written:

ša sinnilte ḫiṭṭu la-áš-šu 'there is no crime of the woman' MAL A § 12:24

One curiosity of MA is a substantivized form of *laššu*, which is attested twice as the plural *laššuttu* in the letter correspondence of Tell Faḫariyya and once in a fragment (of a letter?) from KTN. All three passages occur in combination with the verb *apālu* 'to answer'. Presumably, *laššuttu* refers to the content of the answer. The dictionary translates it as follows: 'Neinwort, Ablehnung' (AHw, 540a); 'empty(?) answers' in the context of the passage (CAD L, 110); 'lack of things' (Parpola 2007, 54). According to Freydank (MARV 9, 4-5 Commentary no. 20), *laššuttu* indicates a status, rather than the answer itself (pace CAD L); cf. also Freydank (2009a, 61 n105).

mimma la-áš-šu-ta lā tappalanni 'do not answer me that there is nothing whatsoever' OIP 79 2:10–12

šumma mimma la-áš-šu-ta tātapalšu if you answer him that there is nothing whatsoever' OIP 79 3:14–16

ša la-áš-šu-ta ēpulūne 'they answered me that nothing is available' MARV 9 20:8'–9'

Cf. the literary corpus:

la-áš-šu-tu mut-tag-gi-[…] 'they do not exist, those who wander about' KAR 24+ i 6

§ 597 The verb *išû* 'to have' is frequently attested in OA (GKT, 16 § 97d; GOA § 18.11.1). It was conjugated according to number and gender and is therefore different from the existential verbs. That said, as it could be etymologically related to *ibašši* and *laššu,* here, we present the few examples in MA. The rarity of the verb suggests that it was on its way out. It was replaced in MA with constructions involving the verb *ibašši.*

būlta ūl ti-šu 'she has no shame' Lambert 1969:45 (incantation)

annak ṣibte la i-šu [*eq*]*līšu* <*ša*> *igre la i-šu* 'he does not have lead for the interest, he does not have a field for hire' AO 19.228:13–14

[*eqla igra*] *la? i?- šu* 'he has no hired field (?)' Billa 5:21 (cf. Saporetti 1981, 12)

16.5.2 *alāku* 'to go'

§ 598 The verb *alāku* is, aside from its morphological character, interesting in two respects: its translation in English is directly altered by a ventive (going ~ coming) and, secondly, it is the only verb in MA with a regular Gt-stem. The verb differs from the other I/ā-ē verbs by the regular gemination in the preterite. This gemination is absent in the perfect, where we find double *-tt-* instead. Unlike the I/ā-ē verbs, the vowel of the third person in the prefix conjugations is always /i/, never /e/ (Kouwenberg 2010, 546). Note the lack of plene spellings of the prefixes, unlike other I/weak verbs (cf. § 101ff). Otherwise, *alāku* is not different from its occurrence in the other Akkadian vernaculars. For OA, see GKT, 172f § 100a; GOA § 18.11.2; for NA, see SNAG, 148. Note the double *-ta-* infix in the Gt-perfect [*it*]*-ta-at-la-ak* MATC 15:30 (Kouwenberg 2010, 357 n10) and *ta-at-ta-at-la-ak* NP 46:8. Statives of *alāku* do not occur in MA, yet they are theoretically possible (GAG, 126 § 77g). Originally, *alāku* was a dynamic verb; however, over time, it developed a stative meaning 'to be liable for/worth'. Similar to *ibašši,* it continued to be used in the prefix conjugation, despite its stative character. However, unlike *ibašši*, we find *alāku* conjugated in all tempora:

> [*š*]*umma eqla ana ṣarpe iddan kī eqlu i-lu-ku-ni* PN *ilaqqe* 'if he sells the field for silver, PN shall take it according (to the price) the field goes for' AO 19.228:18–20
>
> *lišāna ša parzille ša bēlī ḫaṭṭa* [*an*]*a e-pa-še* [*idd*]*inanni* [*an*]*a ḫaṭṭe* [*an*]*a epāše la i-lak* 'The tongue of iron that my lord gave me to make a stick is not suitable to make a stick' MATSH 16:9–15
>
> ŠE-*um ana ṣibtīšu i-lak* 'the barley will go for interest' Giricano 1:19–20
>
> *mimma* [*ša*] *ana dabābika* [*i*]*-lu-ku-ú-ni* 'everything that is suitable for your case' KAV 201:19–21
>
> *ana* 6 *ēṣidē it-ta-lak* 'he will be liable for six reapers' Giricano 1:12–13

§ 599 The verb *alāku* is also unique due to its relatively frequent Gt-stem. Even though some examples previously given by W. Mayer prove to be incorrect (§ 542), new texts have since made up for this with some new attestations. The Gt meaning of this verb is irregular and has a separative meaning, rather than the reciprocal or reflexive meaning, which is standard for this stem (Streck 2003a, 48-49 no. 93). The attestations may be translated as 'to go away', instead of the more basic 'to go' of the G-stem. A different opinion was voiced by Kouwenberg (2005, 80ff), who suggested an ingressive meaning of 'to start to go'. This interpretation has two advantages. First of all, it accounts for the frequent occurrence of *atluku* with a ventive, which conflicts with an otherwise proposed separative meaning, since one would otherwise have to translate with an undesirable double meaning 'to go away from there, coming here'. Secondly, it accounts for its alternation with the G-stem, since both meanings are similar, although *atluku* is merely more precise when describing the action (Kouwenberg 2005, 80ff), e.g., *a-na-ku a-na* GN (…) *la-li-ik* 'I want to go to GN' MATSH 4:1'-2', cf. Billa 67:10. This irregular ingressive meaning of the Gt-stem has, therefore, been analysed as a lexical form (Kouwenberg 2010, 361), which also explains that it was still maintained in the MA period, as opposed to the functional Gt-stem. On the other hand, many of the MA examples do not fit the ingressive meaning of 'to start to go'. In fact, the separative meaning 'to go away' is preferable. This is perhaps most visible in the following phrase:

> 1 *me* 44 *talpittu ša it-ta-lu-ku-ni* '144 (people) written off, who will be going away' MARV 1 18:1–3

Other examples include (note that a considerable number occur in the precative):

> *anāku la-tal-ka* 'I want to depart (to you)' Faist 2001, 252:32
>
> *ṭēm mātika lēmur u li-it-tal-ka* 'may he hear (lit. see) the news of your country and then depart to me' EA 15:20–22

iltu bēte (…) *li-it-ta-a-lak* 'may he go away from the house' Snell 1983/84:18 (peripheral)

ana ṣēne ū[*ma*]*kkal iqtual* [*it*]-*ta-at-la-ak* 'a full day he attended to the flocks and departed' MATC 15:28–30

In a different meaning, we find *atluku* in the PKT texts:

[*ša i*]*na ilde diqāre irīḫūni tunakkar ta-at-ta-lak* 'you will remove and *take away* what remains at the base of the vessel' PKT 3 iv 7

Here, *alāku* appears to have become a transitive verb by having an object. This is unprecedented in Akkadian and may point to a faulty reading by Ebeling.

G-stem:

Present	3ms	*i-il-la-ak* T 97-15:15; *i-la-a-ka* MATC 12:4
		il-la-ak MARV 3 14:15; *il-lak* MAL A § 22:8;
		i-lak MATSH 16:15; *i-lak* Giricano 1:20[24]
	3fs	*ta-al-lak* MAL A § 33:70; *tal-la-ka-ma* MAL A § 45:51
	1cs	*al-la-ka* KAJ 316:6; *a-la-a-ka* MATC 2:18
	3mp	*il-lu-ku* MATC 4:13: *i-lu-ku-ni-n*[*i*] T 93-3:18
		il-lu-ú-ku MAL A § 17:71; *i-lu-ku* BVW Ab:5
	3fp	*il-la-ka* Adad Ritual:13; *il-la-ka-ni* T 93-54:22
	1cp	*ni-la-ka-ni* KAJ 316:17
		ni-il$_5$-lu$^{!}$-ku-ú-ni T 97-10:1; *ni-lu-ku-ni* NP 46:19
Perfect	3ms	*i-it-ta-lak* MAL A § 36:85; *it-ta-lak* Giricano 1:13
		it-tal-ka MARV 3 4:6; *it-tal-ka-an-ni* MAL B § 19:9
	3fs	*ta-ta-lak* MAL A § 13:27; *ta-at-ta-al-ka* T 04-2:20
	1cs	*at-ta-lak* MATSH 2:5; *at-ta-al-ka-áš-šu* Hall 1983:15
	3mp	*it-tal-ku-ú-ni* T 02-32:12; *i-tal-ku-ú-ni* A 1947+:12
	3fp	*ta-tal-ka-ma* MATSH 19:8'
Preterite	3ms	*il-li-ka-ni* MATC 43:13; *i-lik-a-ni* CTMMA 1 101:4
	3fs	*tal-li-ik* T 04-2:16
	2ms	*ta-li-ka* KAV 169:11
	3mp	*il-li-ku* MATSH 2:16
Precative	3ms	*li-il-li-ik* MATC 5:10; *li-il-li-ka* KAV 103:22
	3fs	*lu tal-li-ka* T 93-3:14
	1cs	*la-li-ik* MATSH 4:2'; *la-al-li-*[*ik*] Billa 67:10
	3mp	*li-il-li-ku-ú-ni* MATSH 8:24'; *li-li-ku* MATSH 7:14''
	3fp	*lu tal-li-ka* T 93-2:8 (pl$^{!}$)
Imperative	ms	*a-lik* Billa 66:9; T 02-3:16
		al-ka Halle 1983:24; *a-al-ka* T 93-7:13
Infinitive		*ina a-la-a-ki* MAL A § 36:11; *ina a-la-ki-ia* MATC 11:12
		⸢*ša a-la-ki*⸣ MATC 22:21

Gt-stem:

Present	3ms	*it-tal-la-ka* DeZ 2521:15
	2ms	*ta-at-ta-lak* PKT 3 iv 7
	3mp	*ša it-ta-lu-ku-ni* MARV 1 18:3
Perfect	3ms	*it-ta-at-lak* KAM 11 21:5; [*it*]-*ta-at-la-ak* MATC 15:30

24 The spelling of *i-lak* in KAJ (KAJ 11:12, 13, KAJ 29:11, 13, 14; KAJ 99:16, 17) is probably erroneous for *i-dan*$^{!}$, given that, in all cases, the subject would be given in the accusative (see CAD T, 486a). However, note the comparable, albeit intransitive, passage *šumma eqlu ina turēze ḫarpe lā i-ta-lak* 'if at early harvest time the field does not return' YBC 12860:14–15.

	2ms	*ta-at-ta-at-la-ak* NP 46:8; *ta-at-ta-at-lak* T 93-12:5
Precative	3ms	*li-it-ta-a-lak* Snell 1983/84:18
		li-tal-ka MARV 7 14:24; *li-it-ta-al-ka* EA 15:22
	1cs	*la-tal-ka* Faist 2001, 252:32

16.5.3 *danānu* 'to be strong'

§ 600 Although originally a normal II=III verb, *danānu* is susceptible to II/n in terms of being elided when intervocalic. Its occurrence in the D-stem as *uda*^{ʔʔ}*in* shows that the change II/n > II/^{ʔ} had become part of the root and is conjugated as such. For the sound change n > ^{ʔ},see § 233; for its usage in NA, see SNAG, 100 § 3.14.3. As *danānu* is an adjectival II/gem verb, it has a monosyllabic 3ms stative attested: *dan* or *dān*, e.g., *da-an* PKT 1 I right:18. In other persons, the stative becomes regular and geminates R_2/R_3 as expected: *dan-na-at* KAJ 12:21 (see Kouwenberg 2010, 492).

G-stem:

Stative	3ms	*da-an* PKT 1 I right:18
		^{m}*Da-an-*^{d}*Aššur* KAJ 142:17; ^{m}*Dan-*^{d}*Aššur* KAJ 96:23
	3fs	*dan-na-at* T 96:36:30; KALAG-*at* BM 108924:22
Infinitive		*kī da-*^{ʔ}*a-ni* MAL A § 55:20
		da-a-an KAV 159:7

D-stem:

Present	2ms	*tu-da-*^{ʔ}*a-an* PKT 1 II left:29; *tu-da-an* PKT 1 II right:6
	3mp	*ú-*⸢*dan-nu*⸣ Billa15:16'
Imperative	ms	^{md}*Aššur-da-i-su-nu* 'Aššur-make-them-strong!' VAT 8009:8

16.5.4 *izuzzu* 'to stand'

§ 601 The etymologic origin of *izuzzu* is not entirely clear, although it has been suggested that it is essentially an N-stem from the root *ZvZ* (cf. Huehnergard 2002, 175; Streck 2014a, 112 § 256 with literature). In general, many of the patterns of the conjugation of *izuzzu* are analogous to *alāku* (Huehnergard 2002), which is in itself not unusual, as the same can be said for the verb *tadānu* (§ 604ff).[25] Attestations for MA are, as of yet, relatively few and limited (cf UGM, 95). For instance, all attestations of the imperative occur in letters from Bābu-aḫa-iddina to his representatives, usually in the expression *iltu aḫā*^{ʔ}*iš izizzā* 'stand ready together'. Gemination of the first /z/ in the imperative has been claimed (Abusch 2016, 69 n43), however there are not attestations to support this (Schwemer 2017, 77 n169). The Š-stem of *izuzzu* is *ušazzaz* (or *ušazāz*) in all Assyrian. This is significantly different from OB *ušzāz*. Apparently, this construction was made by analogy with the Š-stem of *alāku* (*ušallak*) (see Huehnergard 2002, 170–71).

G-stem:

Present	3ms	*iz-za-az* MAPD § 9:54
		iz-za-zu-ni KUB 3 77 r. 11'†; *i-za-za-a-ni* MARV 3 1 vi 12'
	1cs	*la-za-az* MCS 2 1:23[26]

25 For OA see GKT, 173f § 100c; GOA § 18.11.4; for NA see SNAG, 99 § 3.14.2.

26 This is probably crasis instead of precative, as the theme vowel should have been /i/ in that case (see Kouwenberg 2010, 489 n143).

	3mp	*iz-za-zu* MAL B § 6:32
Preterite	3ms	*iz-zi-zi* New Year Ritual:25
Precative	3dual	*liz-zi-za-a-niš-šu* K9-T3:15’
Imperative	mp	*i-zi-za* KAV 98:11; KAV 100:13; KAV 109:10; ⸢*i*⸣*-zi-za* KAV 99:12

Š-stem:

Present	3ms	*ú-[ša$^{?}$]-za-az* MARV 4 5:21’
	2ms	*[t]u-ša-za-[su]* T 97-22:15
Perfect	3ms	*ul-ta-zi-za-an-ni* MARV 3 63:8’
Precative	3ms	*lu-ú-[š]a-zi-iz* T 97-17:11
Stative	3mp	*ša-zu-zu* Ali 11:8

Note also the substantive forms of this irregular verbal root:

mazzaltu	*ma-za-al-ta-šú-nu* ‘their post’ Coronation Ritual iii 11; *ma-za-al-te-šú* iii 14
mazziz panē	*ma-zi-iz panē*^{meš} ‘courtiers’ MAPD § 8:50
mazzizzu	^{lú}*ma-zi-i-zu* ‘witnesses(?)’ MARV 1 41:8

16.5.5 *našāʾu/naṣṣ-* ‘to carry’

§ 602 This verb mostly behaves as a normal double-weak verb. The irregularities come in the forms where the second and third radicals are in direct contact and create double *-ṣṣ-* in MA and NA. This has led some earlier studies to assume two different verbs, instead of one.[27] Parpola (1974; see also SNAG, 100 § 3.14.4) pointed out that *naṣṣ-* forms belonged to *našāʾu* as well, only occurring in forms where second third radicals are directly in contact.[28] Exceptions are uncommon, save for a stative 3fs from an MA incantation, where the aleph is not present: *na-ša-at* (*našat* < *našʾat*) Lambert 1969:59 (cf. Parpola 1974, 7). Thus, we find a stative *na-aṣ-ṣu-ú-ni* MAL A § 35:80, but *na-ši* KAJ 5:4. Despite *-ṣṣ-* never occurring before the vowel /i/, we find *-šš-* once, possibly by analogy with *-ṣṣ-* in *na-aš-ši* KAJ 165:23.[29] The sound change underlying this change in spelling is discussed in § 162. Because of this sound change, there is no morphologic difference between *našāʾu* and *uṣāʾu* in verbal forms such as the perfect 3mp *ittaṣṣū*, which can derive from either verb. Note also the nominal forms of *našāʾu*: *ni-še-ti-šu* ‘his installation’ KAM 10 25:5; *ni-še-šu-ma* KAJ 179:20.

G-stem:

Present	3ms	*i-na-áš-ši* KAJ 81:21
		i-na-ši-a Coronation Ritual ii 15; *i-na-ši-ú-ni* ii 17
	3fs	*ta-na-áš-ši* MAL A § 2:20
	2ms	*ta-na-ši-a* PKT 5 r. 7; *ta-na-áš-[ši]* PKT 6 i 13
	1cs	*a-na-*⸢*ši*⸣*-a* MARV 2 25:16
	3mp	*i-na-áš-ši-ú* MARV 4 140:20; *i-na-ši-ú* KAJ 10:9
		i-na-ši-ú-ni-ni KAV 98:18
Perfect	3ms	*i-ti-ši* KAJ 293a; *it$^{?}$-te-ši* KAJ 293a:8; *it-ti-ši* T 04-37:23
	3mp	*it-ta-aṣ-ṣu* MARV 7 48:13; *it-ta-ṣu* KAV 98:45

27 See von Soden (1952b, 178f); AHw, 757; UGM, 87f (*našāʾu*) ~ 95 (*naṣṣ-*).

28 Pace Parpola, the quality of the vowel is not important here, as forms with /i/ directly following a consonant cluster of /š/+/ʾ/ are not attested (see Voigt 1986, 57 n28).

29 Parpola (1974, 10 n12) assumes that gemination is here caused by stress, but only refers to supporting evidence from NA.

		i-ta-aṣ-ṣu MARV 7 7:13; *i-ta-ṣu* MARV 7 7:3[30]
Preterite	3ms	*iš-ši* KUB 3 73:9'
		i-ši-iš-šu KAJ 179:4; *iš-ši-šu-ma* KAM 10 25:4
		⸢*iš*⸣*-ši-a-ni* MARV 9 88:9; *iš-ši-an-ni* MARV 9 58:8
	3fs	*ta-ši-a-ni* Franke/Wilhelm 1985:3
	3mp	*iš-ši-ú-ni* MARV 1 1 iv 43; *i-ši-ú-ni* T 97-7:16
		iš-ši-ú-ni-ni MARV 8 4:6'
Precative	3ms	*liš-ši* MATC 11:28; *liš-ši-a* MATC 5:17
	3mp	*liš-ši-ú* MATC 9:8; *li-ši-ú-ni* KAV 98:19
Imperative	mp	*iṣ-ṣa* VS 1 105:9
Stative	3ms	*na-ši* MATSH 2:54; *na-še* MARV 1 47:56
		na-aš-ši KAJ 165:23; *na-a-ši* KAJ 169:20
		na-aṣ-ṣa Billa 64:25†; *na-ṣa* MARV 7 5:8
		na-ṣa-an-ni MARV 1 40:14; *na-ṣa-a-ni* MATC 3:14
		na-aṣ-ṣu-ú-ni A 1746 (NTA, 22):6; *na-ṣu-ú-ni* MATC 22:16
		na-aṣ-ṣú-ni TabT105A-151:12; *na-ṣu-ni* MATC 23:11
	3fs	*na-ṣa-at* KAJ 178:16; *na-ša-at* Lambert 1969:59
		na-ṣu-tu-ú-ni MAL A § 29:13; *na-ṣa-tu-ú-ni* MAL A § 35:77
	3mp	*na-aṣ-ṣu* Coronation Ritual ii 49; *na-ṣu* T 93-20:24
		na-aṣ-ṣu-uš MATSH 9:45; *na-aṣ-ṣú-ni* TabT05a-151:12
		na-ṣu-ú-ni KAJ 131:8;
Infinitive		*ana na-ša-en-ni* MAPD § 17:81
		ana na-ša-e-ni MARV 8 51:18
		ana ⸢*na*⸣*-ša-e* MARV 4 34:19'; cf. MARV 2 17b+:20

Gtn-stem:

Present	3ms	*it-ta-na-aš-ši* KAJ 132:18; *i-ta-na-ši* AO 19.228:24'
		e-ta-na-ši KAJ 57:24
	3mp	*it-*⸢*ta-na*⸣*-aš-ši-*[*ú*] KAJ 20:18

16.5.6 *sasāʾu* 'to call'

§ 603 Perhaps this is not an irregular verb in the traditional sense, since it behaves as a normal III/weak verb. However, the contrast with the normal Babylonian variant *šasûm* makes it necessary to consider the few attestations here. Note also that only one consonant is visible in the precative (*li-is₅-si-ú* MATSH 9:11'), making it a double-weak verb. The Assyrian change in verbal root is also visible in the participle *mu-sa-as-si-a-ni* 'announcer' MAL B § 6:46.

G-stem:

Present	3ms	*i-*⸢*sa*⸣*-si-ú-ni* MAL B § 6:29
	1cs	*a-sa-si* Cohen/Llop 2017:7
	3mp	*i-sa-si-ú* MAPD coll. 3; KAJ 168:14
Perfect	3ms	*is-si-si* MAL B § 6:40
Preterite	3ms	*i-si-ma* KAJ 150:8
	1cs	*ás-si-šu-nu* A 2994:10
Precative	3ms	*li-is₅-si-ú* MATSH 9:11'
Imperative	ms	*si-si* MATSH 9:23; *si-i-si* RS 06.198:16
		⸢*si-si*⸣*-a* MARV 3 64:10
Stative	3ms	*sa-si* A 320:22
	3mp	*sa-si-ú-ni* KAJ 232:4

30 Both are attested as a perfect of *našāʾu*, rather than *uṣāʾu* by analogy with KAJ 293a:5.

D-stem:

Present	3ms	*ú-sa-ás-sa* MAL B § 6:6, 8; *ú-sa-sa* TR 3004:14'[31]
	3mp	*ú-sa-su-ú* MAL B § 6:36
Preterite	3ms	*ú-sa-si* MARV 4 151:6
Infinitive		*ša sa-su* KAJ 310:20

16.5.7 *t/nadānu* 'to give'

§ 604 One of the main features of the Assyrian dialect is the irregular verb *tadānu* 'to give', where Babylonian uses *nadānu*.[32] We find *tadānu* as a standard verb in OA (GKT, 173 § 100b; GOA § 18.11.3; Veenhof 1972, 441) and NA (SNAG, 98f § 3.1.14.1). The differences between the Babylonian and Assyrian paradigms prompts the question as to which is the original root. The evidence carefully points to the Babylonian form (see Kouwenberg 2010, 473). However, if we assume that both forms derive from a bi-consonantal root, which is supported by the Assyrian imperative *din*, then we may just as well assume both forms to be secondary. However, as the PS root may have been √*ntn*, the imperative would have been secondary (Kouwenberg 2010, 474).

§ 605 The verb *tadānu* only occurs in the nominal verbal forms of the G-stem, with all three radicals visible. In the prefix conjugations, it behaves as a true irregular verb with the first radical being absent in the present *iddan*. This makes it only marginally different from the preterite *iddin*, where presumably *t-* (or *n-*) has assimilated into the second radical. The formation of *iddan* ~ *iddin* was probably formed by analogy with *illak* ~ *illik* from *alāku* (Huehnergard 2002, 163 n8). In the case of the perfect, the first radical occurs in the regular position by being assimilated into the infix *-ta-*, e.g., *it-ti-din* KAV 212:9. Some plural forms appear odd at first sight, e.g., *i-ta-nu* MATSH 6:21', instead of **itadnū*. In these forms, /d/ has assimilated into /n/ (cf. OA *i-ta-ad-nu* TCL 14 51:24), which again becomes apparent if we compare the orthography of perfect 1cs with and without suffixes: *at-⌈ti⌉-din* Faist 2001, 252:17 ~ *at-ta-na-šu-nu* Faist 2001, 252:16. In the stative, no assimilation of /d/ takes place and thus we find *ta-ad-nu* KAV 119:17, rather than **tannū*. Another difference with Babylonian is the theme vowel, as in the Assyrian *tadānu,* which is a (*a/i*) verb, while in Babylonian it is *nadānu (i/i/)*. From the derived stems, the Gtn is only found in some examples from the BAI archive, where the /a/ between second and third radicals is suddenly elided (see § 122).

§ 606 Despite *tadānu* being commonly used in Assyrian texts, we do find instances of *nadānu* in MA, e.g., *i-na-din* KAJ 87:6. Instances of *nadānu* in OA are disputed.[33] They also occur in MAL A-B texts known for their archaic character and Babylonian influences. Otherwise, the Babylonian forms occur in administrative texts mostly from the early M 9 archive (mainly EAd-Aub), although this is not the case for all attestations: KAJ 77:15-16 (UŠA). In the case of KAJ 87, the text is short and there are too many Sumerograms to be positive as to whether this text was actually written in the Assyrian dialect, but the text is

31 According to the collations of Postgate (1982, 309 n11). Only the sign Ú is visible on the original copy.

32 Attestations of the verb were collated in Saporetti (1967); cf. UGM, 93–94 § 82.3.

33 See Kouwenberg (2010, 472); cf. GKT, 173 § 100b; GOA § 18.11.3.

peculiar for twice using *inaddin* in the present (l. 5, 6) and being from the hand of a scribe with an Assyrian name (Aššur-mudammeq). KAJ 132, which is slightly longer with Babylonian forms, does in fact use the Assyrian infinitive *tadānu* (l. 11). As noted by Kouwenberg (2010, 473; GOA § 18.11.3), *nadānu* is the base of the derived stems. This is visible in MA in the N-stem: *in-na-di-in* MARV 2 14 r. 4. This shows that *tadānu* is a secondary Assyrian development. Presumably, we should find that substantives of the verb show both *tadānu* and *nadānu* in the two known lexica *nu-du-un-na-a* 'dowry' MAL A § 27:105 and *ta-di-na-a-nu* 'the seller' MAL A § 39:41. That said, it should be admitted that the latter is little more than the participle of *tadānu*+suffix *-ān* (§ 324f). However, in PNs, we find the Babylonian participle *nādin* instead of *tādin*, which is usually written logographically (SUM passim), but also syllabically, e.g., ^{md}*Aššur-na-din-aḫḫē* KAJ 161:5. This would suggest a Babylonian influence as there seems to be no OA name with the participle *nādin*.

G-stem:

Present	3ms	*i-id-da-an* MAL A § 3:42; *id-da-a-an* MARV 3 52:10
		id-dan MAL A § 5:64; *id-da-an* MAPD § 18:87
		i-dan KAJ 110:20; *i-da-an* KAJ 120:25; *e-dan* RE 19:15
		i-na-dan^{an}/ *i-na-⸢da!⸣-a-an* KAJ 146:6[34]
		i-na-da-an KAJ 124a:7'
		i-na-ad-di-in MAL B § 19:16; *i-na-din* KAJ 77:15
	3fs	*ta-ad-dan* MAL A § 7:76; *ta-da-an* KAJ 9:8
	2ms	*ta-dan* MATC 2:9
		ta-ad-da-na MATC 4:27; *ta-da-na* MARV 5 89:15
	1cs	*ad-da-na-a[k-kum]* KAJ 121a:6
	3mp	*i-id-du-nu* MAL B § 6:38; *id-du-nu-ú* MATSH 12:44
		id-du-nu MATC 20:7; *id-du-ú-nu* KAM 11 79:29
		id-du-nu-uš MAPD § 8:51; *i-du-nu-uš* MAL B § 2:17
		i-na-di-nu KAM 10 9:13
	2cp	*ta-da-na-ni* KAV 99:23
		ta$^{?}$*-na-di-na-ni* KAV 194:22
	1cp	*[n]i-id-dan* T 04-37:18; *ni-da-na-šu-nu-ú* MARV 1 71:28
Perfect	3ms	*it-ti-din* MARV 1 71:11; *i-ti-din* KAJ 172:12
		i-ti-di-in KAJ 172:11; *i-te-⸢din⸣* YBC 12860:12
		it-ti-di-ši TR 2083+:16
		it-ta-din Giricano 12:9', 11';*i-[t]a-din* TR 2015:10
	3fs	*ta-ti-din* KAJ 100:19; *ta-ti-di-in* TabT05A-43:10
	2ms	*ta-at-ti-din* MAL A § 3:37
		ta-at-ta-an-na-šu-ú MARV 4 8:19
	1cs	*at-ti-din* A 2704:11; *a-ti-di-in-[š]i* VAT 8851:12
		at-ta-na-šu-nu Faist 2001, 252:16
	3mp	*it-ta-nu* MARV 10 3:3; *i-ta-nu* MATSH 6:21'
		i-ta-nu-ú AO 20.154:13
		it-ta-an-nu-ni MARV 4 8:15
	3fp	*i-ta-na* DeZ 2495:12

34 An unclear spelling. CAD (N_1, 223) reads *i-ša*$^{?}$*-ka*$^{?}$*-an*, but this does not fit into the context. In DSC 1 (124), we find *i-na-da*$^{!}$*-a-an*. Weeden (2012, 306) suggested *i-na-⸢dá⸣-a-an*. Judging by the copy, it seems to be similar to the section *da-a* = *dan* with the extra phonetic complement *-an* added. The scribe seems to have made a mess out of this line by all accounts, as *inaddan* should be a mixed form of the Assyrian present *iddan* and Babylonian *inaddin*.

Preterite	3ms	*id-din* MAL C+ § 3:15
		i-din-ma KAJ 149:12; *i-di!-im-ma* KAM 10 7:11'
		id-di-nu-ú-ni KAJ 242:3; *i-di-nu-ni* KAJ 113:27
		i-di-ni MARV 1 47:5
	2ms	*ta-di-nu-ni* KAV 104:17
	3mp	*id-di-nu* MARV 10 3:17
		id-di-nu-ni Giricano 14:15; *i-di-nu-ni* MARV 3 23 r. 8
		i-din-nu KAJ 163:25; *id-din-nu-ni* KAJ 157:6
	1cp	*ni-di-na-šu-nu* MARV 1 71:15
Precative	3ms	*li-din* Giricano 4:31; *li-di-in* T 93-3:20
		li-di-na T 93-3:22; *lid-di-na-ku* Coronation Ritual ii 36
	1cs	*la-a-din* Faist 2001, 252:22; *la-a-d[i-i]n* T 96-15:13
		la-a-ad-di-na-ak-ku NP 46:17; *la-a-ad-di-na-ku* NP 46:20
	3mp	*li-di-nu* T 93-11:15
		li-di-nu-uš KAV 107:17
Imperative	ms	*di-in* MATSH 1:11; MATC 2:7; 3:15; Faist 2001, 252:30
		di-na-áš-šu MATC 5:22
	fs	*di-ni* T 96-36:16
	mp	*di-na* KAV 99:23; *di-i-⸢na⸣* KAV 217:19'
		di-na-ni-šu TR 2031:14
Stative	3ms	*ta-din* MARV 1 12:14; *ta-a-din* A 842:3
		ta-ad-na-áš-šu KAJ 83:13; KAJ 106:17; MARV 1 23:9
	3fs	*ta-ad-na-at* Billa 9:12; *ta-ad-na-TA* KAJ 114:14
		ta-<ad>-na-at MARV 10 73:7
		ta-ad-na-ta-šu-nu VAT 8236 r. 16
		ta-ad-nu-tu-ni MARV 4 25:7;
	3mp	*ta-ad-nu* KAV 119:17; KAJ 225:19; MARV 1 72:6; VAT 9363:8
		ta-ad-nu-ni-[š]u-ni KAJ 120:4
		ta-ad-nu-ni KAJ 120:20; KAJ 245:15; KAV 107:13
	3fp	*ta-ad-na* KAJ 249:19
		ta-ad-na-ni MATC 15:5; *ta-ad-na-ni-šu* KAJ 111:11
Participle	ms	*ta-di-na-a-nu* 'the seller' MAL A § 39:41
Bab. Part.	ms	^{md}*Aššur-na-din-aḫḫē* KAM 10 9:4 (et passim PNs)
Infinitive		*ana ta-da-ni* MATSH 16:20; *ana ta-da-a-ni* MAL A § 30:31
		lā ta-da-a-ni T 97-2:14
		ta-da-šu-nu-ni MARV 3 35:6[35]
		ta-⸢da⸣-šu-ni MARV 3 40:6[36]

Gtn-stem:

Present	1cs	*a-ta-na-ad-nu-[ni]* KAV 96:12
	2cp	*ta-ta-na-ad-nu-⸢ni?⸣* KAV 194:16

35 This verbal form is problematic. Freydank (1992, 289) analysed the form as the present 3fs *taddanšununi* and seems to have taken *paḫutu* (l. 4) as the subject of the verb and *azamru* (l. 4) as the object. It seems rather unlikely that an inanimate noun is used as the agent of *tadānu*. Postgate (2013, 116 n94) suggests an infinitive. The occurrence of a subjunctive in this position would be possible, but very rare (cf. § 664). A similar form is found in an N-stem infinitive: *na-áš-ku-ša-ni* KAV 99:38. Alternatively, it may be possible to assume a stative 3ms, with the barley/flour in l. 1–2 figuring as a subject and the *gina'ū/bēt Aššur* as an indirect object (*taddaššununi* < *tadn-aššunu-ni*). The direct object is repeated in the dative pronoun *-aššunu*. For MARV 3 35, this leads to the following text interpretation: (1) 2 ANŠE 8 BÁN ŠE-*um* (…) (3) *ša ki-mu a-za-am-ri* (4) *ša pa-ḫe-te ša* PN (5) *ša a-na gi-na-e* (6) *a-na* É ^{d}*A-šur ta-da-šu-nu-ni* 'two homers and eight seahs of barley, which instead of the fruit, from the responsibility of PN, which is given for the *ginā'u* of the temple of Aššur'.

36 As above.

		ta$^{?}$*-na-di-na-ni* KAV 194:22
Š-stem:		
Present	3ms	*ú-ša-da-an* KAJ 115:19
		ú-ša-dan T 98-33:10; *ú-šá-dan* KAJ 119:11
		ù-ša-dá-na KAJ 114:15
Perfect	3ms	*ul-ta-di-in* TR 3003:4
Preterite	3ms	*ú-ša-di-nu-ni* KAJ 274:9
Infinitive		*ana ša-ad-du-ni* KAJ 109:20; *ana ša-du-ni* AO 19.229:22
		[*ana š*]*a-du-ú-ni* KAJ 113:31
N-stem:		
Preterite	3ms	*in-na-di-in* MARV 2 14 r. 4; *in-na-din* MARV 6 37:17
Substantives:		
maddattu		*ma-da-te-šu* 'his payments' KAJ 307:6
		ma-da-te 'tribute' KAJ 106:13
nudunnāʾu		*nu-du-un-na-a* 'dowry' MAL A § 27:105

16.5.8 *udāʾu* 'to know'

§ 607 The verb *udāʾu* 'to know' derives from the OA *idāʾum* or *idû* in SB. In Common Semitic, the root of the verb is √*ydˁ*, whose effects of III/ˁ can still be seen in the e-colouring of theme vowel /a/ in the form *idē*. As is common in Akkadian, OA used the conjugated G form *idē* as an unaltered base for all tenses (see GKT,168 § 97d; GOA § 18.11.1). Moreover, 3ms and 1cs are morphologically identical due to the first radical R_1/y; even the 2ms prefix is exceptionally *ti-*. Probably for these reasons, the geminated D-basis, which was sometimes already built to a weak extent, was carried over to the G-stem. That this was the D-form can be confirmed by the lack of e-colouring through /ˁ/, as this does not take place in the D present.[37] Eventually, *udda* removed the original preterite *idē* in NA as well (SNAG, 102 § 3.14.7). However, in MA, we still find both *idē* in the MAL texts and *udda* in the rest of the corpus. According to W. Mayer, these forms were used to distinguish between the preterite and present (UGM, 90). Kouwenberg (2010, 466) objected, pointing out the difference in the distribution of the two forms over the corpus and suggesting that *idē* was either archaic or Babylonian. The latter option is not unthinkable as the fragments of MAL also feature Babylonian forms of the verb *tadānu*. However, despite clear Babylonian influences, these texts are also archaic. On the other hand, there seems to be good reason to support the claim for *idē*, as it was seemingly still a known form. Moreover, the forms *idē* and *udda* are indeed used separately for preterite and present as far as can be discerned from the presently known texts. Therefore, Mayer may very well have been correct in his assumption. Furthermore, the Assyrian change *idē* > *udda* can best be explained by assuming that the introduction of *udda* in the G-stem differentiated from *idē*.[38] A transition period with both forms should also be expected. The present *udda* seems to

---

37 Kouwenberg (2010, 466) takes *udda* as deriving from the alternate root √*wdˁ*. He believes this form to be used for all tenses, but does not explain the apparent replacement of the morphologic preterite form with a present involving a geminated second radical. In combination with the lack of e-colouring, a form such **udē* would be expected instead.

38 Alternatively, it is also possible that the preterite was, in fact, a stative (cf. Streck 1995, 144 § 28b).

have derived from I/w, in the same way as the other verbs in this group.[39] No perfect is attested and the lack of evidence from NA, as well as the scarcity in OA, makes it likely that it was not used for this verb. The D-stem in the present would be undistinguishable from the present in the G-stem; however, the D present is not attested so far (as opposed to UGM, 90). Note that the third radical can disappear, e.g., D-stem *ud-du-ši-i-ni* (< *uddiˀū-*) MAL A § 24:45 (cf. § 194). Twice, the peripheral Alašia letter RS 20.18 (see discussion § 40) wrongfully uses the preterite form for the present tense: *la ni-i-de*$_4$*-me* RS 20.18:24; [*l*]*u-ú ti-i-de*$_4$*-me* RS 20.18:28. An adjectival form is attested in *bēlšu la ú-du* 'its owner is not known' MARV 1 56:69. Note also a substantive of the verbal root: *mu-du* (< *mudiˀu*) 'experience' Giricano 10:2.

G-stem:

Present(?)	2ms	*tu-ud-da* MARV 10 90:21; *tu-da* VAT 8851:17
	1cs	*ud-da* KAV 156:2; MATSH 3:13, 16
	3mp	*ú-ud-du-ni* MATSH 6:5'
	2cp	*tu-da-a-šu* KAV 107:18
Preterite(?)	3ms	*i-de* MAL A § 13:29
	3fs	*ti-i-di* MAL A § 23:27
	1cs	*i-de* MAL A § 22:109; *i-de-e-ma* MAL A § 24:66
Precative	3ms	*li-de-e-*[*ma*] MAL A § 58:56†

D-stem:

Preterite	3ms	*ú-ud-di-ú-ni-šu-ni* MAL A § 43:28
		ú-di-ú-ni-šu-ni MAL A § 43:21
		ud-du-ši-i-ni MAL A § 24:45
		u-d[*u*]*-ú-ni* MATSH 18:29
	3mp	*ú-di-ú* T 96-36:32
Imperative	ms	*ud-di-a-*⸢*ni*⸣ MARV 7 14:18†
Stative	3fs	*ud-du-a-at* MATC 15:7

16.5.9 *uṣāˀu* 'to go out'

§ 608 This verb is a cognate of the Babylonian *waṣûm*. Notice the third radical, which derives from aleph (cf. Leslau 1987, 605f). While this verb may be regarded as mostly regular, its similarities with *našāˀu/naṣṣ-* makes it more suitable to be discussed in connection with the irregular verbs. Sometimes, vowel contraction takes place with this verb: *ú-še-ṣi-ú-ni-ni* (*ušēṣiˀūnenni*) MATC 42:10 > *ú-še-ṣu-ni* (*ušēṣûni*) Adad Ritual:1. One case of a substantivized Babylonian form of the infinitive is attested: *a-ṣi-e* 'departure' Billa 62:5. However, we normally find the Assyrian *uṣāˀu*. The verb is one of the cases where the process of the post-glottalized realization of R_2, when followed directly by R_3, can be observed; we discussed this process from a more general perspective in § 162. For *uṣāˀu*, this meant a seemingly progressive assimilation of R_3 when directly following R_2, e.g., *uṣ-ṣa-ni* (< *uṣˀanni*) Giricano 4:21. This orthographic gemination is not a case of vowel contraction or the weakening of the aleph, but rather a symptom of the realization of emphatic consonants in MA, often with this orthographic doubling omitted, e.g., *ú-ṣa-an-ni* A 3196 (NTA, 39):22. The situation becomes more problematic in perfect forms where a vowel is attached to the base, e.g., 3mp *ittaṣˀū* > *ittaṣṣū* (*it-ta-ṣu* MATSH 2:23). The third

39 Note that little outside of the Akkadian evidence points to an etymologic I/w verb, as opposed to I/y (cf. the collections of roots in Leslau 1987, 626a).

radical disappeared as it does in some other attestations, but this also resulted in the absence of VA because the second syllable became closed, e.g., 3mp *it/taṣ/ṣū*, cf. 3fs *ta-at-ti-ṣi-ma* (*tat/ti/ṣiʾ/ma)* MAL A § 13:26. This shows that VA is still an active phenomenon, as it had not become a fixed part of the base; otherwise, we would have found *ittiṣū*. The assimilation of aleph is also attested for the same verb in OA (Kouwenberg 2003, 77f) and similarly for *našāʾu*. Regarding *našāʾu*, it is to be expected in an orthographical sense between *našāʾu* and *uṣāʾu* in verbal forms such as *ittaṣṣū*. Caution should be taken when analysing such forms for either verb. Note also the nominal forms of this verbal root: *mu-ṣa-i-ša* 'right-of-way' KAJ 20:9; *mu-*⸢*ṣa*⸣*-e* 'exit' KAM 10 26:5.

G-stem:

Present	3ms	*uṣ-ṣa-a* Coronation Ritual ii 39; *ú-ṣa* MATSH 4:12'
		ú-ṣa-k[*u-nu*] KAV 96:13
	3fs	*tu-ú-uṣ-ṣa* MAL A § 37:19; *tu-uṣ-ṣa* MAL A § 34:74
		tu-uṣ-ṣa-a-an-ni MATC 32:2; *tu-ṣu-ú-ni* MAPD § 6:45
	1cs	*ú-*⸢*uṣ*⸣*-ṣa* MATSH 12:28
	3mp	*ú-ṣu-ni* Adad Ritual:6
	3fp	*uṣ-ṣa-a* MAPD § 1:12
		uṣ-ṣa-a-ni MAPD § 9:54; *uṣ-ṣa-ni-en-ni* T 93-20:10
Prefect	3fs	*ta-at-ti-ṣi-ma* MAL A § 13:26
	3mp	*it-ta-ṣu* MATSH 2:23, 31; *i-ta-aṣ-ṣu* MARV 7 7:13
		it-ta-ṣu-ú-ni MATC 15:27
Preterite	3ms	*ú-*⸢*ṣi*⸣ KAJ 209:13
		ú-ṣa-an-ni A 3196 (NTA, 39):22; *uṣ-ṣa-ni* Giricano 4:21
Precative	3cs	[*lu*$^{?}$]*-ṣi-i* Giricano 14 r. 7
	1cs	^{m}*Ana-nūr-Sîn-lu-ṣi* KAJ 27:29
Imperative	mp	*ṣi-a* KAV 105:16; A 877:6
Stative	3mp	*ṣe-e-ú-ni* KAV 108:8(?)[40]
Infinitive		*ina ú-ṣa-i-ša* MAL A § 23:32
		ina ú-ṣa-e New Year Ritual 52:24'
		[*ú*]*-ṣa-e* MATSH 22:8†
Bab. infinitive		*a-ṣi-e* 'departure' Billa 62:5

D-stem:

Precative	3ms	*lu-ú-ṣa-ma* Lambert 1969:49

Š-stem:

Present	3ms	*ú-še-ṣa-šu* Franke/Wilhelm 1985:7
	2ms	*tu-še-ṣa-šu* PKT 5 r. 8; *tu-še-ṣa-šu-nu* BVW M+ r. 6
		tu-še-ṣu-ni PKT 5 r. 10
	1cs	*ú-še-ṣu-*⸢*šu*⸣ MATSH 8:35'
	3mp	*ú-še-ṣu-ú* MAPD § 6:44; VAT 8236 r. 18
		ú-še-ṣu-ni Adad Ritual:1
	3fp	*ú-še-eṣ-ṣa-*⸢*a*⸣ KAV 217:8'†[41]

40 Opinions on the root of this stative are divided: *ṣi-rip*$^{!}$*-ú-ni* from *ṣarāpu* (CAD Ṣ, 105a) can be excluded because of the abnormal syllabification and the simple fact that the vocalic pattern is unexpected. A more acceptable possibility is the verb *ṣuāʾu* 'to dry' (AHw, 1107a; CAD P, 444a), if only for the fact that it remains limited to this passage. For this reason, the verb *uṣāʾu* (BAI, 28) is preferable, even though the apparent loss of word-initial /u/ remains unexplained and the G-stem stative of *uṣāʾu* is not common in the Assyrian dialect.

Perfect	3ms	*ul-te-ṣi* MAPD § 5:34
	2ms	*tul-te-ṣi-ma* Ištar Ritual:6'
	3mp	*ul-te-ṣi-ú-šu-m[a]* MATSH 8:35'
Preterite	3ms	*ú-še-ṣi-an-ni* KAJ 249:10; [*ú-š*]*e-ṣi-a-ni* KAJ 171:13
		[*ú-še*]*-ṣi-ú-ni* MAPD § 6:41; [*ú*]*-še-ṣi-ú-ni* MARV 10 3:46'†
	3mp	*ú-še-ṣi-ú-ni-ni* MARV 1 23:3
		ú-še-ṣu-ú-ni MAL J § 5:1†; *ú-še-ṣu-ni* Adad Ritual:1
Precative	3ms	*lu-še-ṣi* Giricano 4:32
Stative	3ms	*še-ṣu-ni* PKT 5 r. 5; MARV 4 146:18'
	3fs	*še-ṣu-a-at* LVUH 101:12
		še-ṣu-a-ta KAJ 122:11; *še-ṣu-a-ta-ni* KAV 205:6
	3mp	[*še*]*-ṣu-ú-ni* MARV 8 7:13
	3fp	*še-ṣi-a-ni-ma* AO 21.157:7
Imperative	ms	^{md}*Nabû-ketti-še-ṣi* MARV 6 27:23'
	mp	*še-ṣi-a-ni* KAV 98:12
Infinitive		*še-ṣu-e* MATSH 8:27'

Št_1-stem:[42]

Participle	fs	*mul-te-ṣi-tu-šu-nu* 'their expenses' KAJ 307:14

16.5.10 *ušābu* 'to sit'

§ 609 The verb *ušābu* 'to sit' is an I/ū found as *wašābum* in OB and OA. It is different from the other I/ū in the sound change /š/ > /s/ when in direct contact with radical /b/. This phenomenon is extensively discussed in § 222. It should be enough to simply state the paradigm of the attested forms here. The change in root is also found in the adjectival form *us-bu-tu* Billa 49:11. It is furthermore often difficult to distinguish between the preterite and stative as the third-person masculine is identical in both cases. The attestation of a number of statives with attached suffixes suggest that most cases of the unambiguous forms should be interpreted as statives as well.

G-stem:

Present	3ms	*ú-uš-šab* MATSH 2:64[43]
		ú-šab Adad Ritual:13; TabT05a-134:11
	3fs	*tu-ú-uš-šab* MAL A § 46:101; *tu-ú-uš-ša-ab* MAL A § 45:70
		tu-uš-šab MAL A § 36:92; *tu-ša-ab* KAJ 9:29, 30
	3mp	*uš-šu-bu* MATC 18:7; ⸢*uš-šá-bu*⸣ T 04-37:21
Perfect	3fs	*ta-*⸢*ta*⸣*-ša-ab* MAL A § 36:9
Preterite	3ms	*us-bu-ni* T 98-94:10; T 98-132:7
Precative	3mp	*lu-us-bu* MATC 4:5; MATSH 4:2'
Stative	3ms	*lu ú-šab* KAV 194:5
		us-bu-ú-ni MAL A § 13:27; *us-bu-ni* MARV 9 73:4
	3fs	*ú-us-bat* MAL A § 24:47; *us-bat* T 04-2:24
		us-bu-tu-ú-ni MAL A § 30:24; *us-bu-tu-ni* MAL A § 24:57

41 Kouwenberg (2010, 456 n34) analyses this form as 3fp, but gives no reason why. As can be seen in Freydank (1992, 225), there seems to be no contextual certainty for the exact analysis.

42 Probably a Št_1 participle (cf. Postgate 1982, 306; 2013, 23; Streck 2003a, 118 no. 358). Note that a Št_2-stem of *uṣā'u* is also attested (see Streck 2003a, 128 no. 410). Pace Postgate, I would not totally exclude the reading *mul-te-šèr-tu-šu-nu*.

43 The correct reading is not entirely clear. According to the copy, it is *ú-uš-*<*šab*>, while the transliteration gives us *ú-šab*. I could not find ŠAB in the photo, but admittedly the quality of the print may be the cause here (cf. Streck 2007, 273).

	2ms	*lu us-ba-ta-ma* TabT05a-134:21
	1cs	⸢*us*⸣*-ba-a-ku* MATSH 12:29; *us-ba-ak-*[*k*]*u* T 96-6:10
		muš-ba-a-ku TR 2083a+:9
		us-ba-ku-ni NP 46:14
	3mp	*us-bu* Coronation Ritual iii 41
		us-bu-ni MARV 1 71:9
	3fp	*us-bu-ú-*⸢*ni*⸣ KAV 217:18’ (sic)
	1cp	*us-ba-ni* T 96-36:12, 25
Infinitive		*ina lā ú-ša-a!-bi* MARV 10 81:7

Š-stem:

Present	3ms	*ú-še-šab* MAL A § 41:2; Coronation Ritual ii 16
	3mp	*ú-še-iš-šu-b*[*u*] New Year Ritual:11, 12
		ú-še-šu-bu-šu Coronation Ritual iii 1
Preterite	3ms	*ú-še-ši-ib-ši* MAL A § 36:84
	3mp	*ú-še-ši-bu-ú-ni* RE 19:11
Stative	3ms	*še-šu-ub* KAJ 16:15
	3fs	*še-šu-bat* MAL A § 39:29
	3mp	*še-šu!-bu-ni* KAJ 150:5; *še-šu-b*[*u-ú-ni*] KAV 211 r. 2’

Chapter 17: Function of Verbal Categories

17.1 Tenses and mood in Middle Assyrian

§ 610 MA has three morphologically distinguishable tenses: the present, the perfect for past tense and the preterite for past tense in relative clauses. The situation of future events is more complicated and can be expressed by both the perfect and the present, depending on the sequence of the events. There are three types of modal verbs: imperative, precative and prohibitive. The stative and infinitive fall into none of these categories. The function of verbal tenses differs significantly between the main categories of literary texts, letters and administrative texts. There are two main reasons for this. The varying function of the different texts is the first cause. When a ritual is consequently described in the present, we cannot derive much information on how tenses compare to each other. The second reason is that the literary and administrative texts are sometimes archaic in their usage of the verbal system. In the case of some texts, such as MAL, this could have been due to an earlier composition, while, in administrative texts, the legal formulae are archaic. We can link this usage in the latter corpus directly to the OB texts from Tell Muḫammad. We have already seen similarities in the usage of the Sumerian verbs, and the same can be said for syllabic attestations.

Example 1:

a-na ^{iti}DU$_6$.KÙ KÙ.BABBAR (…) *i-na-ad-di-in-ma ka-ni-ik-šu i-ḫe-ep-pí* 'he will pay the silver and break his seal in the month of DU$_6$.KÙ' IM 90602:6–9

ŠE-*um*^{meš} (…) *i-da-an tup-pu-šu i-ḫap-pi* 'he will pay the barley and break his tablet' KAJ 101:15–17

Example 2:

a-da-an-šu i-ti-iq-ma KÙ.BABBAR *a-na* MÁŠ *i-ir-ru-ub* '(when) his term passes, the silver will go for interest' IM 90602:10–11

e-da-nu e-ti-iq-ma SIG$_4$ *a-na* MÁŠ DU-*ak* '(when) the term passes, the bricks will go for interest' KAJ 86:8–9

While the differences between OB and MA are especially notable in the relation with the perfect/preterite, these examples clearly show how MA administrative documents were influenced by earlier examples. As such, we may venture to suggest that verbal tense and syntax, generally in relation to literary and administrative texts, actually tell us little about the Assyrian dialect.

17.2 The present: general remarks

§ 611 The present is usually used for the present habitual tense or for the future. Sometimes, its usage is more specific and does not fit in this category. For the usage of the present in the prohibitive, see § 641. Some irregular verbs, such as *ibašši*, are always used in the present (see § 593ff). We may also add these verbs the stative verb *laʾû* 'to be able' (see § 591).

17.2.1 The present in the literary corpus

§ 612 The corpus of literary texts in MA covers three basic types: (1) descriptions of an event, occurring in rituals: Adad Ritual, Coronation Ritual, Ištar Ritual, New Year Ritual; (2) the apodosis of conditional clauses used in law texts to describe the consequence of a hypothetical situation of the protasis: MAL and MAPD; (3) instructions to an unspecified second person, occurring in PKT and BVW. In all three categories, the present is the predominant tense. Only in the law texts (2), in the protasis, which describes a hypothetical situation in the past tense, does MA make use of the preterite and perfect, while, in the apodosis, the present is used. Even in (3), the present is preferred above a possible imperative or precative, although alternation with an imperative is attested: *zu-ú-uz* 'divide!' PKT 3 i 6. The usage of the present tense in these categories has been described by von Soden as 'zeitlose Tatsachenfeststellung' (GAG, 127 § 78d). This designation is perhaps less fortunate as all three categories feature cases of the preterite/perfect, which suggests a sequence of events. The first category of various rituals (1) consists of texts that are almost exclusively written in the present tense. It seems therefore that the present is used descriptively for hypothetical future events:

> *simunu ina kašāde bēl niqie ana bēt ēqe er-rab* 'when the time arrives, the sacrificer will enter the *bēt-ēqe*' Ištar Ritual:1
>
> *qaldātu ana ḫamre il-la-ka šangû ú-šab* 'the *qadiltu*-priestesses go to the *chapel* and the priest sits down' Adad Ritual:13
>
> *šarru panē ilāni i-ṣa-bat [šarru u šan]gi Marduk ina parakki šī[m]āte ú-še-iš-š[u-bu rē]ḫ-te ilāni gabba la-a ú-še-IŠ-šu-b[u]* 'the king marches before the (statues of) the gods, the king and the priest seat Marduk in the Dais of Destinies, the rest of the gods they do not seat' New Year Ritual:10'–12'
>
> *šarru paššūra ana panē Aššur i-ra-[kas] ur-ra-da ana muḫḫi šēḫāte i-qar-rib* 'the king sets up a table before Aššur and steps down, (and then) he approaches the incense burners' Coronation Ritual i 37–39
>
> *rabīuttu ša-rēš-šarrāne [ul-ta]-na-ak-na-nu šēpē ša šarre ú-na-šu-qu* 'the elite and royal eunuchs prostrate themselves and kiss the feet of the king' Coronation Ritual ii 37–38

§ 613 In law texts (2), we find the present in the apodosis of a conditional clause. A law paragraph generally starts with the description of an event in the protasis involving the preterite/perfect. The judicial consequences in the apodosis are then described in the present, which is here used as a future tense. When the present is used in the protasis, it indicates intention (see § 632):

> *appēšunu uznēšunu ú-na-ak-ku-su* 'they will cut off their noses and ears' MAL A § 4:49–50
>
> *batulta iṣbatma ú-ma-an-ze-e-eʾ-ši abu ša batulte aššat nāikāna (…) ilaqqe* 'he seized a young girl with the intent to rape her, the father of the girl will take the wife of the rapist' MAL A § 55:21–25

i-du-ak-šu u panūšuma im-ma-an-ga-ar [*u*] *zittušu i-laq-qé* 'he will kill him, or should he agree to it, he will take his share' MAL B § 2:19–21

ina ūme bēl eqle illakanni kiria adi mānehātešu i-laq-qé 'on the day the owner of the field comes, he shall take the orchard with its installations' MAL B § 13:24–25

lū sinnilta lū a'īla āmerāna ana lib[*bi a*]*tūne i-kar-ru-ru-šu-nu* 'they shall throw the witness, be he woman or man, in the oven' MAPD § 19:94

ša qēputte annūte $1^{\text{ta.àm}}$ *šēpēšunu ú-ba-at-tu-qu* 'they will cut off one foot each of these representatives' MAPD § 20:101

§ 614 In prescriptive texts (3), the present is always used for the future tense, rather than an imperative or precative. This is because precatives in the second person usually do not occur and are not attested in MA. The imperative is not used because the situation is theoretical, as there is nobody dictating the actions, which is different from letters where the imperative is used for direct orders.

ina namāre ta-ra-[*kas* ...] *ta-pa-ṭar mā'ē ta-ša-aq-qi* 'at dawn you will harness (the horses) [...] (then?) you will loosen (them) and give (them) water to drink' BVW A:8–9

[ŠE-*am*] *ta-ša-pa-ka-šu-nu e-ku-lu* 'you will pour barley for them and they will eat' BVW A:13

ina 12-šu tabāke šamna te-si-ip utūna ta-ka-pár mā'ē ta-ṣa-ra-ah ana harīe ta-tab-ba-ak 'at the 12th pouring, you will gather the oil, wipe the vessel, heat the water (and then) pour it into a vat' PKT 1 I right:23–24

šumma tu-ma-sa-šu ÚTUL *ša ah-ti-ṣi ta-ša-kan* 'when you are to wash it, you will place a bowl of ...' PKT 3 i 2

ina namāre šamšu ina napāhe mā'ē u riqīa^{meš} *annūte ina sūne ana libbi herse ta-ša-hal* 'at dawn, when the sun rises, you will filter this water and perfume through a cloth into the *hersu*-vessel' PKT 3 i 8–9

§ 615 The present is also used in dependent clauses. Its position in adverbial clauses, in order to indicate a simultaneous action, is well described for NB.[1] Of course, the present is also found in the corresponding main clause. Adverbial clauses of all types are more extensively discussed in Chapter 21.2. The most common type of adverbial clause involving time constructions, with *inā ūme* and *adi*, is attested in the literary corpus:

ina ūmi ina rebēte e[*diš*] *il-la-ka-a-ni uptaṣṣa*[*nāma*] 'when they go out alone, they will be covered' MAL A § 40:56–57

ina ūmi bēl eqle il-la-ka-an-ni kirīa adi mānehātešu ilaqqe 'on the day the owner of the field comes, he shall take the orchard with its installations' MAL B § 13:24–25

a[*di*] *šarru paššūra ša mahar Aššur i-ra-ka-su-ni šangû paššūrē ša ilāni* (...) *ira*[*kkas*] 'while the king will set up the table before Aššur, the priest will set up the tables of the gods' Coronation Ritual i 39–41

Adverbial clauses of comparison start with *kī*:

1 See Streck (1995, 99–102).

kī ša mut sinnilte aššassu nēkta ep-pu-šu-ú-ni mummerta eppušū 'as the husband will treat his fornicating wife, they will treat the procuress' MAL A § 23:19–21

kī kallete ša i-ra-ʾu-mu-ši-ni irakkusūnešše 'like a daughter-in-law whom they love, they draw up (an agreement) for her' MAL A 46:97–98

The present is also attested as a predicate of normal relative clauses. In some cases, it seems to indicate intention.

Following the particle *ša*:

3-*šu-ma ina libbi-āle eqla u beta ša i-laq-qe-ú-ni usassa* 'three times (the herald) will proclaim in the Inner City (Aššur) the field and house that he wants to take,' MAL B § 6:7–8

(…) *u attamannu [bē]l pāḫete ša u-kal-lu-ni* '(…) and each governor, whatever he is holding' Coronation Ritual iii 10–11

ṣabʾu ša ēkalle ša iltu šarre ana ḫarrāne il-la-ku-ú-ni 'personnel of the palace who go with the king on a campaign' MAPD § 6:39

Following *ašar*:

eqalšu u bēssu ašar šarru id-du-nu-ú-ni iddan 'his house and field, wherever the king (wants) to give it, he will give it' MAL A § 45:87–88

17.2.2 The present in contracts and other administrative documents

§ 616 In administrative documents, the present is used in a similar way to the apodosis in the conditional clauses of laws. It describes the consequences of a loan or other contractual obligations, which is usually a payback and/or interest. Administrative documents can only describe events in the past and conditional future, since they record either completed events or future events that are conditional, while matters that are still valid in the present use the stative, e.g., *ana lā mašāʾe šaṭir* 'in order not to forget it is written down' or *maḫir* 'it is received'. The usage of the present is thus called 'heischendes Präsens' by von Soden (GAG, 127 § 78d). Most of the attestations are slight variations of each other due the formulaic character of most documents. A list of the usage of the present as future tense in these clauses is given below:

[b]ilat eqle i-na-áš-ši 'he shall be liable for the yield of the field' KAJ 81:20–21

abāssu e-MUR (=emmar) šulmāššu i-la-qe 'he will investigate his case and take his *šulmānu*-gift' KAJ 98:9–10

ŠE (…) *ana ḫašīme i-ta-ba-ak* 'he will store the barley in the granary' KAJ 119:12–16

ŠE-*um*^{meš} *ana ṣibte i-lak* 'the barley will go for interest' Giricano 1:19–20

ŠE *ana* PN *i-dan u tuppa ša* PN *i-ṣa-ba-ta ina pî tuppi akkīa i-ša-ka-an* 'he will give the barley to PN and he will draw up a tablet of PN and, in the wording of the tablet, he shall put as follows' (direct quotation) … KAJ 83:14–18

sinnilta ú-ba-la-ṭu šīm sinnilte i-sa-si-ú 'they will maintain the woman and declare the price of the woman' KAJ 168:13–14

§ 617 Similar to the literary corpus, the present can be found in adverbial and relative clauses.

Adverbial:

ina ūme (…) *i-du-nu-ni*[!] *eqalšu ipaṭṭar* 'on the day that he pays, he shall redeem his field' KAJ 11:17–18; cf. KAM 10 10:14–16

ina [*ūme*] ŠE-*im u ṣibātēšu i-ma-du-du-ni mimmûšu ipaṭṭar* 'on the day that he measures out the barley and its interest, he shall redeem his property' KAJ 58:22–23

ina ūmi er-ri-šu-⸢šu⸣-ni iddan 'when he requests it from, he will give it' MARV 3 44:14–16

Relative:

ša ina bērīšunu i-pa-si-lu-ni 5 *mana iḫīaṭ* 'whoever among them distorts will weigh out five minas' KAJ 1:25–26

3 *iku eqla ina āle ša i-qa-bi-ú-ni-šu-ni eṣṣid* 'he will reap a 3 *iku* field in the city that they will tell him' KAJ 50:11–13

šumma ŠE-*am lā imaddad maḫīrat* ŠE-*um i-lu-ku-ni* [*a*]*nnaka iḫīaṭ* 'if he does not measure out the barley, he will weigh out lead at the going rate of barley' KAJ 53:9–11

ašar i-qa-bi-ú-ni-šu-nu-ni iddunū 'wherever they will say to them, they will give (the barley)' MATC 83:14–15

sinniltušu [*ša*] *ina* É [*ša*] PN *i-ba-laṭ-ṭú-ni* [*amutt*]*īša ta-ma-ga-ar* 'his wife, who lives in the house of PN, agrees on her status of maid' Giricano 8:19–21

17.2.3 The present in letters

§ 618 When we consider the letter corpus, we find a considerable number of atelic verbs, which are expressed in the present with a habitual function. It is seldom totally clear if a clause refers to the present tense or future, as this remains partly open to interpretation. However, in the following cases, it may be reasonably assumed that the verbs refer to events, which coincide with the moment when the letter was written.

qēputtūya kunukkī (…) *naṣṣū i-lu-ku-ni-ku-nu* 'my representatives come to bring you my seal' KAV 98:7–10

aššum šīpāte mimma i-ša-ʾa-la-ni šīpātu ša qātika kē maṣi ibašši iriḫḫa 'concerning the wool, he asks me something: "the wool that is at your disposal, how much is available as a remainder?"' KAV 106:7–11

ubruttu (…) *akla*[meš] *e-ta-na-ku-lu qaqquru bari ša ni-il₅-lu-ku-ú-ni* 'the delegates eat, but the territory that we travel through is starving' T 97-10:15–19

ammar i-na-ši-ú-ni-ni liššiūni 'may they bring here as much as they can carry' KAV 98:18–19

lišāna ša parzille ša bēlī ḫaṭṭa [*an*]*a epāše* [*idd*]*inanni* [*an*]*a ḫaṭṭe* [*an*]*a epāše la i-lak* 'The tongue of iron that my lord gave me to make a stick is not suitable to make a stick' MATSH 16:9–15

mimma [*ša*] *ana dabābika* [*i*]-*lu-ku-ú-ni* 'everything that is suitable for your case' KAV 201:19–21 *mīnumma anniu ša ammar a-qa-bi-a-ku-ni kī pī*[*y*]*a la te-pu-šu-ni* 'what is this, that whatever I say to you, you do not act according to my words?' T 93-3:4–6

ana panika a-da-gal 'I will wait for you' MATC 1:9–10

Frequently, the present has a nuance of willingness/intention. In this case, it is used to refer to events that are intended to be carried out in the future, thus enabling the present to express the future tense.

ammîša ana biāde a-la-a-ka 'I will come there to spend the night' MATC 2:17–18

šumma attunu ta-ku-ša PN *lilqea* 'if you are delayed, PN must take it here' KAV 105:27–28

panē ṭēmīšunu i-da-gal ṭēma i-ša-ku-nu-uš i-na-am-mu-ša 'he awaits their instructions, (and once) he is given orders, he shall depart' MATSH 2:52–53

anaʾīne ina bubuāte a-mu-at 'why should I die from hunger?' VAT 8851:7–8

marʾū damquttu [...] *ina erilti libbe i-mu-ut-tu* 'the good people would die according to (my?) wish' T 93-11:33–35

In Akkadian, it is possible for the present to refer to the past tense when an action is incomplete. As such, we find it a few times with the verbs *šapāru* and *šamāʾu* when something is perceived, such as a rumour or a message that is written by a party different from the author of the letter. Apparently, the perceiving of such as message was regarded as incomplete (cf. GOA § 19.1.3).

ašamme u la ú-bal 'I hear that he does not bring [...]' KAV 194:8

§ 619 As we have already seen in the literary corpus and the administrative documents, the present can also be used in dependent clauses. Both adverbial and relative constructions are attested.

Adverbial:

iltu ūme ša ú-ru-du-ni 'on the day that they come down' MATC 4:24

kī ša bēlni i-ša-pa-ra-ni šunu 1 *qa*$^{\text{ta.àm}}$ 2 *qa*$^{\text{ta.àm}}$ *i-la-qu-ú*$^{!}$*-ni* 'as our lord writes me, they will take one or two litres' MARV 1 71:16–19

ūmti S[*ū*]*tīu i-lu-ku-ni-n*[*i*] *akla*^{meš} *ina panīya e-ku-lu-ni liddin* 'may he give it the day the Suteans come to eat bread in my presence'T 93-3:17–20

[*b*]*aʾerutta lā eppušū* [*m*]*ādi ūmū šaʾuttu ša rēš urḫe i-*⸢*ka*⸣*-šu-du-ni-ni* 'they will not perform extispicy until the propitious days of the beginning of the month arrive' TabT05a-134:17–19

In a relative clause:

tuppušu ṣabta tuppa ša ta-ṣa-ba-ta-ni PN *li*[*lqe*]*a* 'seize his tablet, the tablet that you will have seized, PN must take' KAV 102:17–19

mimma ša ana dabābika i-lu-ku-ú-ni leqya alka 'take everything that is suitable for your case and come here' A 133:12–15

qul[*lula*] *ša ana atānāte* x x *uš-šu-ru-ú-ni ša ina du*[*nn*]*e ēzibūni* 'the q. that they will release to the she-asses, which they left in the *dunnu*' T 97-22:4–8 *mīnumma anniu ša ammar a-qa-bi-a-ku-ni kī pi[y]a lā teppušūni* 'what is this, that whatever I say to you, you do not act according to my words?' T 93-3:4–6

ŠE-*am ša Ḫurrīu la i-la-qe-ú-*[*ni*?] *laqya* 'the barley that the Hurrians will not take is taken here' T 93-46:19–21

qaqquru bari ša ni-il₅-lu-ku-ú-ni 'the territory, which we travel through, is starving' T 97-10:18–19

ana sinnišāte ša ina pitti PN *i-la-ma-da-ni qibyā* 'speak to the women who learn of the responsibility of PN' MARV 3 64:35

17.3 Past tense: the perfect and preterite - general remarks

§ 620 The traditional conjugation for the past tense, i.e., the preterite, was in the process of being replaced by the perfect as the main indicator of the past tense. This was already observed by Hirsch (1969, 130–31) for the law texts, but is just as well true for the letters (MATSH, 62–65). This is a development that MA shares with MB, although, as we will see, the preterite was still common in a number of texts, such as MAL A–B. It appears that these texts are rather more archaic in character than those texts where the perfect is dominant. For LB, Streck pointed out that, especially in the letter corpus, the preterite was replaced by the perfect; the letter corpus is closer to the spoken language than the more archaic corpus of administrative documents (Streck 1995, 153–54; Kouwenberg 2010, 154).[2] It is probably better to study this development according to genre and chronology. However, in general, we may state the following: the perfect is used in main clauses for the past tense. The preterite is still dominant in the relative clauses, following the negation *lā* and in questions (*Wortfragen*). Its position in the precative has also not changed with the increasing usage of the perfect. This general differentiation between the two tenses is especially valid for the letter corpus, although, as we will see, there are exceptions everywhere. The perfect and preterite are used for future events as well; these will be discussed below in § 628ff.

17.3.1 The perfect and preterite in letters

§ 621 The small letter corpus is probably the closest representative of the contemporary vernacular language as it features direct quotations. This is especially apparent in the expression of the past tense, as it is most regular in its expression of the past tense and almost free of archaic formulaic expressions. For normal events in the past tense, the perfect has fully replaced the preterite. The preterite itself remains limited to three specific environments: dependent clauses, negated past tense and the precative. When the perfect is used in this domain, it has a different function, as we will argue below. Exceptions where the preterite is used in main clauses will be referred to as the *zero preterite* from now on. As stated above, the perfect completely replaces the zero preterite for past action in the MA epistolary corpus. It is probably sufficient to provide some basic passages, as this change is relatively unproblematic:

bitqīya ib-ta-{*ta*}*-táq* 'he has accused me' MARV 1 13:7–8

2 This explanation seems more tenable than Aro's claim (1955, 81) that the difference between genres is due to the meaning of the preterite for *Feststellung* and the perfect as *Behauptungsform* (see also GAG, 131 § 80f, cf. Kouwenberg 2010, 154). For MA, this becomes especially clear from the common use in MAL A–B, which are known for their archaic character.

ina našpertika ta-al-⸢ta?⸣-ṭar tu-ul-te-bi-la 'you wrote and sent me in your message, (thus ...)' MARV 4 8:4–5

PN *raqi ina* GN *e-tam-ru-uš* 'PN was hiding, but they saw him in GN' TR 2031:6–7

3 *ḫarrānātu ša Sūḫāyē e-te-li-a-ni* 'three Suḫean caravans have come here' T 93-54:7–9

§ 622 The preterite is still found as referring to the past tense in specific environments. It can mainly be found in dependent clauses with the subjunctive. In this case, it usually refers to past events, unlike the perfect in dependent clauses, which seems to have a slightly different function (see below).

ḫiṭṭa ša šarru iš-pu-⸢ra-an-ni⸣ 'the penalty of which the king wrote me' MARV 4 153:9–10

aššum alpē ḫalqutte (…) *ša bēlī iš-pu-ra-an-ni* 'concerning the lost oxen of which my lord wrote me' AO 19.227:6–8

ina lubulte ša (…) *tamkāru ú-ta-e-ra-ni* 'from the clothing, which the merchant returned' KAV 98:16–17

ašar ta-di-nu-ni tuppaka ana muḫḫi PN *šuṭar*[sic.] 'write (on) your tablet to PN where you sold it' KAV 104:20–22

urki ṣabʾu ša GN_1 *ša in-na-bi-du-ni ana* GN_2 *attalak* 'after the troops fled from GN_1, I went to GN_2' MATSH 2:4–5

This is basically true for the negated past tense as well, where the preterite is used rather than the perfect:

anaʾīne paḫāra (…) *la t[a-á]š-pu-ur* Why did you not send a potter?' T 93-3:7–10

Aššurāyu mamma la-a ur-da ṭēma la áš-ʾa-al 'no Assyrian came down, so I did not ask for a report' T 04-13:14–16

sirāšû[meš] *emmera*[meš] *la il-qe-ú* 'the brewers did not take the sheep' MATC 9:18–19

šumma ṣarpa la-a tam-ḫur 'if you did not receive the silver' Faist 2001, 252:23

ana maḫārīya la-a im-gúr 'he did not agree to receive for me' MATSH 2:65

eribīu la-a e-⸢ku⸣-ul a[naʾī]ne la-a ēṣid 'locusts did not eat (the crops), why is there no harvest?' MATSH 3:7–8

The zero preterite also occurs in questions or *Wortfragen*, which are questions with question pronouns or adverbs.[3]

anaʾīne (…) *marā šipre ana muḫḫīya il-li-ka-ma* 'why did the messenger come to me?' RS 06.198:7–9

tamtaḫar [a]yyēša [t]u-bi-il 'you did receive it, but where did you take it?' KAV 104:10–12

mānaʾīne la-a il-li-ka 'why did he not come?' T 02-32:9

In other epistolary texts I know of only a few examples of a zero preterite, which are not

3 See Kouwenberg (2010, 128); cf., for NB, Streck (1995, 21 § 19). The term "*Wortfrage*" follows GAG, 254 § 153b.

unambiguous because of the absence of (preserved) question words:

ḫirīṣaḫe iḫ-ṭu-ṭu '(have) they (already started) digging the ditches?' MATC 3:6[4]

[... *kus*]*sîya iṣ-bat* '[why(?)] did he seize my throne?' KBo 28 61/62:15'

Rarely, the perfect occurs in dependent clauses when referring to past events. Note also the phrases of the badly published A 1947+.

iqtibia mā 30 *ṣabʾu Suḫāyū ana šubte ina mūše* [*an*]*nie e-tar-bu-ú-ni* 'he told me, thus: '30 Suḫean men took positions this night' T 93-2:4–6

[*š*]*a al-ta-ap-ru-ni* 'what I wrote' A 1947+:17†

pil-ka-a-na ša bat-tu-bat-te-e[*n*] *e-ta-aṣ-bu-ú-ni* (...) 'the districts that they added of both riverbanks (...)' A 1947+:21–22

§ 623 Cancik-Kirschbaum argued for the occurrence of a pluperfect expressed in MA (MATSH, 63). According to her, the preterites of the verb *šapāru* referred to an action in the past, which chronologically preceded what followed. This claim was criticized by Streck (1997, 272), who doubted all provided instances in the corpus. Indeed, as most attestations of *šapāru* occur in relative sentences or in negation, very few attestations remain. One instance (*i*[*š-pu-ra*] MATSH 4:9') is too damaged to be sure that the reading of the only sign IŠ is correct. This leaves us with two more passages, but here the broken context does not allow us to draw any meaningful conclusion about their syntactic constructions.

[*an*]*āku áš-pu-ra* 'I myself wrote' MATSH 26:3'

5-*ma kitāʾa*^{meš} *bēlī iš-p*[*u*]-⸢*ra*⸣ 'five times my lord wrote to me about linen' MATSH 7:27'

Otherwise, it should be noted that MA does not always bother to distinguish between sequences of the past tense. This can be demonstrated easily by the following passage from another letter in the Tell Aš-Šēḫ Ḥamad corpus:

aššum kitāʾe ša GN *al-ta-pár ṭēma il-te-qe-ú-ni eribīu lā ēkul a*[*naʾī*]*ni lā ēṣid mā lā bašlat il-tap-ra* 'I wrote (them) concerning the flax of GN, and they brought me the news (that) the locust did not eat it. Why is it not harvested? 'It is not ripe', he wrote to me' MATSH 3:5–9

As can be seen, the first perfect *altapar* 'I wrote' precedes the two perfects dealing with the reply that was brought: *ilteqeūni* 'they brought me' and *iltapra* 'he wrote me'. If Cancik-Kirschbaum's claim is correct, we certainly would have had *altapar* occurring in the preterite. On the other hand, it may be noted that the preterite in relative clauses is already a kind of past perfect tense, as, by definition, it denotes a completed action (Kouwenberg 2010, 128). Other examples of the pluperfect, when expressed with the perfect, were provided by Streck (1997, 272).

4 Jakob's suggestion about reading this form as perfect from *ḫaṭātu* (*iḫṭuṭṭu*) is not without problems (MATC, 43). The change of the perfect infix /t/ > /ṭ/ is difficult to explain. As for the change a > u, which Jakob attributes to the emphatic consonant, there is very little evidence to support this claim in MA. Alternatively, it is possible to interpret this passage as a rhetorical question, which could explain the use of a preterite (§ 680). Admittedly, the use of preterite is only clear for *Wortfragen*, which requires a question word.

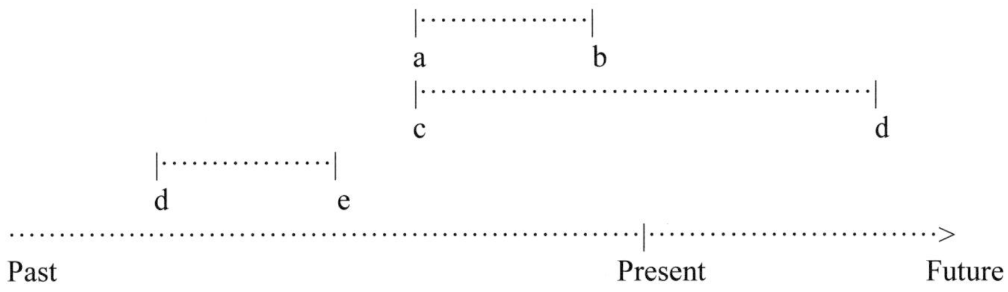

a–b=preterite as in the dependent clause; c–d=perfect in the main clause; d–e=present
Figure 42: Tenses found in letters.

17.3.2 The perfect and preterite in administrative documents

§ 624 Despite being largely replaced in the letter corpus, the zero preterite can still be found in administrative documents. We already mentioned the formulaic character of many administrative documents; especially when it comes to legal formulae, there was little room for innovation, other than the occasional variation in syllabic spelling and the possibility to use a logogram. It may therefore not surprise us that some verbs always occur in the preterite, such as *rakāsu* (including MAPD). Others have a tendency to involve the zero preterite, such as *laqāʾu* and *tadānu*.[5] An additional number of miscellaneous attestations of the preterite may be given.

The preterite in adoption and marriage contracts:

ina migrātīšunu (…) *id-bu-bu* 'they voluntary declared' TIM 4 45:3–5

PN_1 *im-me-gi-ir-ma* (…) PN_2 *ana maruttīša*$^{\text{sic.}}$ *il-qé* 'PN agreed and PN_2 adopted her' KAJ 3:1–4 (Ead/Aub)

PN_1 PN_2 (…) *ip-ṭu-ra-ši-*⸢*ma*$^{!}$⸣ PN_2 released PN_1' KAJ 7:2–5 (Ead/Aub)

ana aš[*šuttīšu*] *iš-ku-nu-ši* ''they made her his wife' KAJ 7:18–19 (Ead/Aub)

The preterite in loans and purchases:

36 *mana annuku iltu* PN_1 (…) PN_2 *il-qé* 'PN_2 has taken as a loan 36 minas of lead from PN_1' KAJ 18:2–7 (Ead/Aub) cf. KAJ 18:2–7 (EAd/Aub); KAJ 19:2–6 (Aub); KAJ 28:2–7 (Aššrnīr II) KAJ 62:2–10 (Sa) etc.

PN_1 *ana* PN_2 *i-din* 'PN_1 gave (it) to PN_2' KAJ 79:9–13 (Aub)

ŠE-*um*^{meš} *anniu il-qe* 'he took this barley' KAJ 91:12–13 (Sa$^{?}$)

ana 30 *mana anneke i-din-ma ú-*[*š*]*ap-pi* 'he sold it for 30 minas of lead and made it acquired' KAJ 147:11–12 cf. KAJ 148:18; KAJ 149:12; KAM 10 14:11

5 This situation regarding the formulaic choice of tenses is not unique for MA (cf. UgAkk in Huehnergard 1989, 249–51).

12 *emāru* ŠE (…) *i+na* UGU PN (…) *il-qé* '12 barley homers he loaned to' Billa 3:2–9 (Sa); cf. *il-qé-ú* Billa 1:12 (Sa)

6 *mana annaka* (…) PN *il-qé* 'PN took (as a loan) six minas of lead' MARV 1 19:2–8 (Aub)

ŠE-*um*^{meš} *anniu ana pūḫe il-qe* 'he took this barley as exchange' MARV 1 47:9 (TN)

The preterite in testaments and decrees:

PN *tupšarru* [*i*]*na migrāt ramānīšu* [*š*]*īmti š*[*a bētī*]*šu i-ši-im-*<*ma*> 'PN the scribe decreed the testament of his house in full agreement' MARV 5 71:2–6 (Sa)

PN *ina migrāt rāminīšu šīmti bētīšu i-ši-im-ma* 'PN decreed the testament of his house in full agreement' MARV 8 47:2–5 (TN) cf. TR 105:3–5; TR 2037:1–4

The preterite in treaties/edicts:

PN *r*[*ik*]*sa ir-ku-ús* 'PN issued a decree' MARV 1 17:3–6 (TN; edict); MARV 4 116:1–3

ana GN *lū lā er*[*rab*] *šum-ma* 1 *aʔīlu āliku ša ḫurāde ina panē paḫitīšu lū āle iṣ*$^{!}$*-bat ū lū kī raqāʔe ana* GN *e-ru-ub* 'he should not enter GN, even if one man coming from battle settled on (the land of) his province or city, or secretly entered GN' MARV 4 119:24–28 (TN; treaty)

mimma lū kī bitqi ib-[*tu*]*-qu ū lū kī šapa*[*rti*] *iṣ-bu-tu* '(if) they made any kind of accusation or seized (something) as a pledge' MARV 4 151:63–65 (TN)

lū kī bitqi ib-[*tu*]*-qu ū lū kī šapa*[*rti*] *iṣ-bu-tu ana* PN *zakk*[*u*] 'be it that what they accused as an accusation or seized as a pledge, it is cleared to PN' MARV 4 151:64–65 (TN)

Miscellaneous:

ina migrāt rāminīšu riksa ir$^{!}$*-ku-ús* 'he issued a decree out of his free will' Snell 198/84:4–5 (testament)

ana panē Adad i-ši-iš-šu 'he dedicated him to Adad' KAJ 179:4

kī Aššurāyu anāku (…) *aq-ti-bi* 'that I am Assyrian, I said' MARV 3 63:10'–11'

§ 625 At the same time, MA also uses the perfect in administrative documents in its normal function of indicating past tense:

ana muḫḫi PN *marā šarre iq-tar-bu* 'they approached PN, the son of the king' KAV 159:3–4

1 *sūtu* ŠE (…) *ana susīe*^{meš} (…) *it-ti-din* 'he has given one seah of barley to the horses' MATC 38:1–8

ina migrāt <*rāminīšunu*$^{?}$> *ipṭirēšunu ana* PN *bēlīšunu i-ta-nu-ú* 'they gave their ransom to PN their lord at their own free will' AO 20.154:9–13

mākisu (...) *e-ta-mar im-ti-ki-si* 'the tax collector has inspected it and levied tax' AO 21.382:7–10

ina muḫḫi PN *ir-te-ḫu* 'they were left (incumbent) on PN' A 113 (NTA, 15):27–28

PN_1 *iq-ṭí-bi mā* PN_2 *il-te-qe* 'PN_1 said thus: PN_2 took it' A 1765 (NTA, 25):11–15

ŠE-*um*^{meš} *anniu pūḫu šūt* (…) *ana* 6 *ēṣidē it-ta-lak* 'this barley is a substitute, it went for six reapers' Giricano 1:9–13 *ṣarpa an[nia] ana [p]ū[ḫe] it-ta-din* 'he gave this silver as a substitute' Giricano 12:7'–9'

The perfect is attested in dependent clauses, where it indicates the past tense:

2 *emmera*^meš PN *ša nāmurta ana muḫḫi* RN *naṣṣūni piqitta it-ta-nu-ni-šu-ú-ni* 'two sheep (for) PN, who has brought a present to RN (and) to whom (RN) gave provisions' A 1746 (NTA, 22):1–8

17.3.3 Historical development of the past tense in late Middle Assyrian

§ 626 According to W. Mayer, the preterite disappeared from main clauses by the reign of Aššur-dān I (1178/1168–1133), as can be observed in the M 6 archive.[6] The problem with this claim lies in the fact that Mayer did not possess a significant number of post-TN texts, other than the M 6 archive (NTA). The variety of verbal forms in this archive is low and mostly limited to statives for the main verbal predicate and preterites for the predicate in subordinate clauses. Furthermore, this does not account for the fact that the literary texts still possess a zero preterite and all date from the post-TN period (cf. Weeden 2012, 236). Arguably, their composition is earlier, but the same can be said for the standard formulae of the texts in the M 6 archive.[7] It is therefore difficult, if not impossible, to distinguish between standard formulae and improvisation on the scribe's part. Upon checking Mayer's claim with the MARV publications, the former does not hold up to scrutiny and we find the preterite in the main clause in other archives prior to the reign of Tp (MARV 1 10). Examples of a normal preterite after TN include:

(…) PN_1 *ana* PN_2 *id-din* 'PN_1 gave (…) to PN_2' MARV 1 53:2–10 (Nae)

ina muḫḫi PN *il-qe* 'it is (incumbent) on PN, he has taken it' MARV 3 22:4–7: MARV 3 50:8–11 (both Nae)

ana UD.5.KÁM *il-qe* 'he has taken it for five days' MARV 3 32:13–14 (Nae)

ana paddugāni is-su-uḫ 'he has taken it away for the *paddugānu*' MARV 3 24:9–10 (Nae)

PN *mugerra ik-šìr* 'PN repaired the chariot' MARV 1 10:19 (Tp)

ina nikkassī[šu]nu iš⌉-ku-nu 'they placed it on their account' MARV 5 6:12 (Tp)

iš-ku-un MARV 5 80:4† (Tp)

Comparing this usage with the situation in NA, Mayer's claim is further invalidated, since the preterite occurs frequently in the main clauses of NA in all types of administrative documents. A small selection now follows:

É (…) *ina* 1 MA.NA (…) *il-qe* 'he took the house for one mina' SAA 6 17:7–14

zi-kir ^d*A-šur be-lí-ia* (…) *ma-a*^?*-d*[*i*]*-iš ap-*⌜*làḫ*⌝*-ma* 'I greatly respected the command of Aššur, my lord' SAA 12 19:28–29

tu-piš-ma PN *i+na* ŠÀ 9 GÍN^meš (…) *tal-qe* 'she has contracted and bought (her) for nine shekels (of silver)' SAA 14 10:2'–5'

6 See UGM, 58; cf. Kouwenberg (2010, 155).

7 For example, the clause, *ana la mašā*^ʾ*e šaṭir* 'it is written down in order not to forget' M 6 (NTA) passim, is already found in texts such as KAJ 255:8–9 (TN).

We can also offer a few attestations of OA contracts, where the preterite seems to have been standard:

PN *am-tám* (...) *a-ší-mì-im i-dí-in-ma* 'PN sold a maid' KUG 3:1–3

$^1/_3$ MA.NA 2½ GÍN KÙ.BABBAR *ší-im* PN$_1$ PN$_2$ *a-na* PN$_3$ *ta-áš-qú-ul* 'PN$_2$ paid 22½ shekels of silver to PN$_3$, the price of PN$_1$' BIN 4 183:1–7

ší-im ṣú-ḫa-ri-im (...) PN *il$_5$-qé* 'PN took the price of a boy' ICK 2 160:1–6

Clearly, MB deals with the same problem involving the preterite that is still found in administrative texts (Aro 1955a, 81), while some WPA dialects lack a clear set of rules for the past tense as a result of it (cf. Huehnergard 1989, 249–57).

§ 627 In order to deal more definitively with Mayer's claim, one needs to look at the actual types of texts and their formulae, rather than restricting oneself to mere statistics. We can safely state that the preterite was in the process of being replaced by the perfect in most functions under the circumstances stated above. The usage of a zero preterite in administrative documents can thus be regarded as formulaic; however, this did not prevent them from being used. In order to prove that these forms disappeared from younger texts, we need to compare identical formulae from the earlier and later periods. When looking at verbs in the corpus of administrative texts, one may note that the present and stative make up the majority of finite verbs, followed by preterites with negation or with the subjunctive. Finally, we have a relatively small group of perfect and zero preterites. Of these attestations, there is a number of instances of the futurum exactum (see below), which is usually not expressed with the preterite; as such, these instances are out of this discussion. The actual group of attestations is thus considerably smaller than one might expect. Analysing the attestations of the zero preterite, we find miscellaneous verbs in adoption and marriage texts (which all date from the Ead/Aub period) without later parallels. This is also true for treaties/edicts from the period of TN, which have closest parallels with the law texts and NA edicts (cf. SAA 12), both of which also show usage of the preterite. The final significant group comprises loans and purchases. The following formulae with preterites can be found, which occur frequently:

n X iltu PN$_1$ *ina muḫḫi* PN$_2$ *ilqe* '*n* amount of X from PN$_1$ (incumbent) on PN$_2$; he has taken it' (common in loans, small variations exist)

iddin ušappi uppu laqe 'he has paid it and made it acquired and taken' (with an additional preterite ušappi in some purchases)

The zero preterite of *laqāʾu* is common; however, it is usually replaced with the Sumerian verb Ì.LÁ.E and variations. When the Assyrian verbal form is written, we always find the preterite, not the perfect. In the later MA corpora, not many loans and purchases are found and, as a result, we cannot compare the two groups, although the perfect *ilteqe* is not frequent in these later texts. The loans in the Giricano texts (Abk) avoid the usage of *laqāʾu* altogether. The other common verb is *tadānu*, which is used passim in the preterite in loans, purchases and similar texts.[8] However, some cases of the perfect occur, most notably in

8 See the following texts: KAJ 1:6; KAJ 6:23; KAJ 114:17; KAJ 146:11; KAJ 147:12; KAJ 148:18; KAJ 149:12; KAJ 151:12: KAJ 153:11; KAJ 154:12; KAJ 155:12; KAJ 164:18; KAJ 165:19; KAJ 174:12;

Abk texts from Giricano, the youngest group in the corpus, but also in older texts from Aššur.[9] Admittedly, the amount of perfects is considerably smaller and, with the exception of Giricano, none of the texts date from the 11th century. A select group, which only uses the perfect are the royal documents (or royal land grants), is notable as these documents belong to the earliest MA texts:

it-ti-din (broken context) KAJ 177:12 (Aššrnīr II)

PN1 *ana* PN2 *it-ti-[din]* 'PN1 gave it to PN2' KAJ 183:4–7 (EAd/Aub); cf KAV 212:9 (Aub) (probably also KAJ 173:8 Aub); MARV 1 41:5 (Arn)

ukl[um] *[an]a PN* *[i]t-ti-din* 'the steward has given it to PN' KAM 10 8:4–7 (EAd/Aub)

KAJ 172:11, which is comparable, is, strictly speaking, a purchase, but also features the same formula as a royal grant. While we cannot be certain about the reasons why the perfect is used here, this shows that we can usually explain the difference between preterite and perfect on the bases of formulaic grounds.

17.4 The perfect and preterite for the future tense

§ 628 Akkadian uses the preterite and perfect to indicate special cases of the future tense, which we will refer to as the futurum exactum. This function of the perfect is often found in the literature with the German term "*Vorzeitigkeit in der Zukunft*" (e.g., GAG, 274 § 171h). It has also been compared with the German tense "*Futur II*" (Streck 1995, 160–65 § 36). The futurum exactum is attested in all three main categories of MA texts: literary, epistolary and administrative. As in other main clauses, the perfect is chosen in MA over the preterite to indicate these future tenses. In general, in Akkadian, the futurum exactum is expressed by the perfect, rather than the preterite (Streck 1998b, 305–6; 1999, 103–8). The fact that the perfect has also replaced the preterite in main clauses for the past tense does not change this. Moreover, it may be expected that the perfect, when indicating future events, penetrates the environments that are otherwise restricted to the preterite, which comprises negation and dependent clauses. Thus, although we may argue that the difference between the preterite and perfect in MA is mostly not related to tense, this seems only partly true for instances when used for the future tense. If we were to represent this futurum exactum in a graph, we would place it on the right side of the present as in the graph below:

KAM 10 5:8; KAM 10 14:11; Billa 12:20.

9 See the following texts: KAV 212:9; KAJ 88:16; KAJ 109:21; KAJ 167:14; KAJ 172:11; KAJ 173:8; KAJ 177:12; KAJ 183:7; KAM 10 8:7; Billa 2:14; Giricano 1:18; Giricano 12:9', 11'; TR 2083+:16.

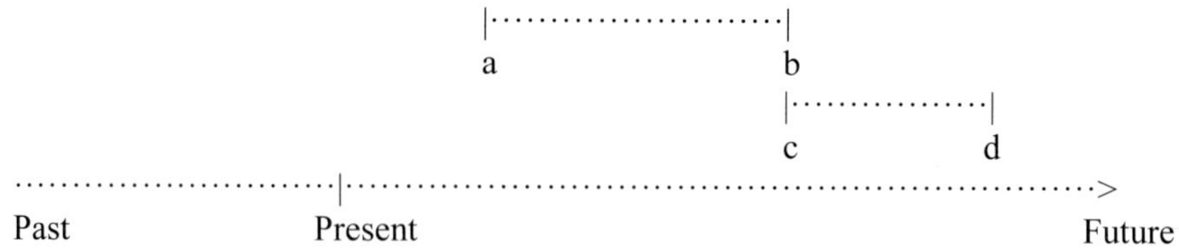

a–b=perfect in the dependent clause, c–d=present in the main clause
Figure 43: Future tenses.[10]

The present on the right side of the figure can be used to indicate the present tense itself until the indefinite future is in play. Somewhere in the middle, the perfect (exactum) is placed, which can be used for the future, but always precedes another further act. The existence of a futurum exactum has earlier been suggested for MA by a number of different scholars, including von Soden.[11] The futurum exactum often occurs in the protasis of conditional clauses. However, as this futurum exactum precedes other future events, it generally occurs in dependent clauses penetrating the domain of the preterite, which is usually used in this situation.[12]

17.4.1 The perfect and preterite in MAL A–B

§ 629 The commonly used tense of the protasis of the law texts is either the perfect or preterite. The protasis expresses action that precedes the apodosis, which has been argued to be the reference time of laws.[13] In the law text MAL A, the perfect is already the common verbal form to express the past tense, although, as Kouwenberg pointed out, these texts are expected to go back to a phase of the language that is older than contemporary private archives (Kouwenberg 2010, 155).[14] As we will see, the situation in MAL B is different, where the preterite is more or less prevalent in the protasis. In MAL A, for the most part, we usually find *šumma*+ perfect, e.g.:

> *šumma* (…) *šillata táq-ti-bi* 'if she has spoken slander' MAL A § 2:14–16
>
> *šumma* (…) *aššassu ina bētīšu mimma tal-ti-ri-iq* 'if his wife has stolen something from his house' MAL A § 3:24–25
>
> *šumma sinniltu qāta ana aʾīle ta-ta-bal* 'if a woman has put (her) hand on a man' MAL A § 7:74
>
> *šumma aʾīlu iltu aššatīšu aʾīla iṣ-ṣa-bat* 'if a man has seized a man with his wife' MAL A § 15:41

---

10 Note, in the table, the following: the stative has been omitted because it is independent of tense. The present is used for the present and future, whereas the perfect and preterite are used for the past tense. Given that the preterite usually occurs in dependent clauses, which chronologically precede the main clause, it is placed further back in the past tense than the perfect.

11 See GAG, 267 § 165h; cf. UGM, 112 § 102.1.

12 See GAG, 131 § 80e; 267 § 165h; UGM, 112 § 102.1a.

13 Cf. OB Metzler (2002, 64–65); Loesov (2005, 713).

14 The other law fragments and MAPD are unfortunately too damaged to give a general statement about their temporal system, although the perfect seems to be dominant in MAPD (Hirsch 1969, 131). Note that other literary prescriptive texts, such as the Coronation Ritual and the Ištar Ritual, for the most part, use the present tense and thus provide few attestations of the preterite and perfect.

šumma aššat aʾīle ina panē mutīša ramanša tal-ta-da-ad 'if a wife has withdrawn herself from her husband' MAL A § 24:41–42

However, in a significant minority of cases, we find the preterite in MAL A. Selected examples include:

[*šum*]*ma aʾīlu qāta ana aššat aʾīle* [*ú*]-⌜*bíl*⌝ *kī būre e-pu-us-si* [*ub*]*ta*??*erūš ukta*??*inūš* 'if a man has put (his) hand on a man's wife *and attacked her like a bull*, they will have him charged and convicted' MAL A § 9:88–89

[*šumma*] (…) *e-ru-bu-ma* (…) *i-du-ku* 'if (…) (they) entered and (…) (they) killed' MAL A § 10:97–100

šumma aʾīlu ana tappāʾīšu (…) *iq-bi* (…) *la-a ú-ba-e-er* 'if a man has said (something) to his friend, but he did not prove it' MAL A § 18:72–77

šumma aʾīlu ina puzre ina muḫḫi tappāʾīšu abāta iš-kun (…) *lu-ú ina ṣālte* (…) *iq-bi-áš-šu* 'if a man in secret has put out a rumour about his comrade (…) or said to him during a fight (so-and-so)' MAL A § 19:82–86

šumma aʾīlu tappāʾšu i-ni-ik 'if a man has sodomized his comrade' MAL A § 20:93

Similarly, many attestations are available for a preterite in MAL B, although, here, they are more frequent than in MAL A.

šumma aʾīlu (…) *napšāte ig-mu-ur* 'if a man (…) has ended a life' MAL B § 2:15–16

[*šum*]*ma aʾīlu* (…) *lū šillata* [*iq*]*-bi ū lū in-na-bi-it* 'if a man (…) spoke treason or fled' MAL B § 3:23–24

šumma aʾīlu taḫūma ṣeḫra ša pūrāni us-bal-ki-it 'if a man has transferred a small border of lots' MAL B § 9:20–21

šumma aʾīlu ina lā qaqqirīšu [*i*]*g-lu-šu-ma libnāte il-bi-in* 'if a man in a plot not his, *dug a pit* and made bricks' MAL B § 14:26–27 (see Roth 1997, 180)

[*šumma*] (…) *id-din* 'if (…) he gave' MAL C+ § 3:14–15

The combination *šumma*+perfect is restricted to one passage:

šumma aʾīlu taḫūma rabīa ša tappāʾīšu ussammeḫ 'if a man has incorporated a larger border of his comrade' MAL B § 8:11–12

§ 630 If we compare MAL A and MAL B with each other, it becomes obvious that, in the latter, *šumma*+preterite is the dominant construction. We are able to provide some statistics based on the first *šumma* main clause in a law paragraph. Especially in MAL A, multiple conditional clauses in one law edict are attested; however, these are omitted in order to retain a better overview of the statistics. This provides us with the following numbers:

	MAL A §			MAL B §		
Preterite	9–10, 18–21, 31, 42–43, 47, 50–52, 55	14	24%	2–4, 9–10, 12–15, 20	10	50%
Perfect	1–8 12–15, 17, 22–24, 28–30, 34-35, 39, 53, 56	24	41%	8	1	5%
Present	37, 41, 46, 48	4	6%	19	1	5%
Stative	25–27, 32–33, 36, 38, 45	8	14%	–	–	–
Semiverb	–	–	–	17–18	2	10%
Unknown	11, 16, 49, 54	4	6%	1, 5–7, 11, 16	6	30%
Other	40, 44, 57–59	5	9%	–	–	–
		59	100%		20	100 %

Figure 44: Tenses in the protasis of MAL A-B.

As can be observed, MAL B uses the preterite in the main clause in 10 out of 20 conditional clauses, against one out of 20 for the perfect. In MAL A, the distribution of the past tense is mostly equally divided. The reason for the difference is not clear, but MAL B contains fewer than half of the paragraphs of MAL A, with six out of 20 damaged paragraphs. Chance therefore cannot be excluded. The usage of the preterite as the common tense in the protasis is not standard in earlier law codices. The statistics presented by Hirsch (1969, 126) show that, the perfect was already preferred in the Ḫammurapi. Nonetheless, the preterite for the futurum exactum can still be found in main clauses (Streck 2014a, 76 § 178l). In a few passages of MAL A, the preterite is actually followed by a perfect in the protasis. This is a common sequence in the Codex Ḫammurapi (Hirsch 1969, 126). In MAL, it can be observed with the commonly used clause *ubtaʾʾerūš uktaʾʾinūš* 'they will have him charged and convicted'.

> *šumma aʾīlu tappāʾšu i-ni-ik ub-ta-e-ru-ú-uš uk-ta-i-nu-ú-uš i-ni-ik-ku-ú-uš ana ša rēšēn ú-tar-ru-uš* 'if a man has sodomized his comrade, they will have him charged and convicted, sodomize him and turn him into a eunuch' MAL A § 20:93–97

In this passage, we have the temporal progress of three tenses; in the protasis, the events of the preterite are followed by the perfect, which is again followed in the apodosis with the present tense. This construction with a phrase other than *ubtaʾʾerūš uktaʾʾinūš* remains rare in the law texts. A few exceptions are:

> *šumma aʾīlu mārat aʾīle im-ḫa-aṣ-ma ša libbīšu ul-ta-aṣ-le-eš* 'if a man has hit a woman of the *awīlu*-class and caused her to have a miscarriage' MAL A § 21:98

> [*šumma*] *aḫḫū ina eqle lā zēze* [*iltēn aḫu*] *ina libbīšunu* [...] *zerʾa iz-ru* [...] *e*⌉*qla e-ru-uš* [*aḫu šanīu*]*mma ittalka* [ŠE *mēr*]*eše ša aḫīšu* [*ina*] *šanuttēšu* [*il(te)qe*] 'if brothers, on an undivided field, one brother from them (...) has sown and tilled the field (and) another brother has come and has taken the seed of cultivation of his brother for a second time' MAL B § 4:27–34

It is clear that this difference between preterite and perfect has more or less lost it function, as indicated by other passages in which the same phrase follows a perfect, rather than a preterite:

> *šumma aʾīla iltu aššatīšu aʾīlu iṣ-ṣa-bat ubtaʾʾerūš uktaʾʾinūš* 'if a man has seized a man with his wife, they will have him charged and convicted' MAL A § 15:41–43

In a few clauses in the protasis, a perfect is followed by a present tense: thus (*šumma*) perfect+present:

šumma bēl mārte ša zubullāʾa im-ta-aḫ-ḫu-ru-ú-ni (…) *la-a i-ma-ag-gu-ur* 'the master of the girl, who will receive the marriage gift on various occasions, does not agree' MAL A § 30:29–32

ša ḫarimta paṣṣunta e-tam-ru-ú-ni i-<ṣa>-ba-as-si 'whoever sees a veiled prostitute will seize her' MAL A § 40:68–69

§ 631 We have already mentioned that, in general, the preterite in MA has become limited to dependent clauses when preceded by negation. This is partly confirmed in the law texts where the preterite mostly occurs in relative clauses referring to events that precede the main clause. Following Streck (2014a, 76 § 178k), the preterite was already being used in the OB period in dependent clauses for the futurum exactum, e.g., CḪ § 179.

mimma dumāqē ša mussa ina muḫḫīša iš-ku-nu-ú-ni lā ḫalqūni 'whatever jewels, which her husband placed upon her, are not lost' MAL A § 25:86–88

mimma nudunna ša mussa id-di-na-aš-še-ni šu-a-am-ma ilaqqe 'whatever marriage gift that her husband gave her, he will take his (due)' MAL A § 27:105–107

abu ša zubullāʾa iz-bi-lu-ú-ni kallassu ilaqqea 'the father, who brought the bridal gift, shall take his daughter-in-law' MAL A § 30:33–35

Nonetheless, there is a significant number of cases where the perfect is used:

sinniltu ša ana bētīša ta-al-ti-qe-ú-ši-ni 'the woman, who has taken her to her house' MAL A § 23:28–29

bēl mārte ša zubullāʾa im-ta-aḫ-ḫu-ru-ú-ni 'the master of the girl, who has received the bridal gift on various occasions' MAL A § 30:29–30

ša ḫarimta pa-aṣ-ṣu-un-⌜ta⌝ e-tam-ru-ú-ni 'whoever has seen a veiled prostitute' MAL A § 40:68–69

ša ina 1 ITI.UD^{meš}*-te annāte tuppušu la-a it-tab-la-an-ni ana panē qēputte la-a il-ták-nu-ú-ni* 'whoever that, within this one month, has not brought his tablet (and) placed it before the representatives' MAL B § 6:41–44

Again, in the negated past tense, the distribution between the two tenses seems to be more or less equal, as demonstrated by a few selected examples.

Preterite:

uznīša la-a ú-na-ak-ki-is 'he did not cut off her ears' MAL A § 4:53–54

la-a ú-ba-e-er 'he did not prove it' MAL A § 18:77

šumma ana dannat šarre la-a e-ru-ub 'if it (a field) does not enter the royal holdings' MAL A § 45:82

šumma mussa mimma la-a il-ṭu-ra-áš-še 'if her husband did not bequeath anything for her' MAL A § 46:92

Perfect:

šumma sinniltu la-a táq-ti-bi 'if the woman has not declared it' MAL A § 23:37

šumma la-a it-tu-ú-ra 'if he has not returned' MAL A § 45:85

šumma adi 1 ITI.UD^{meš} *la-a ip-ta-ṭar* 'if he has not redeemed (her) within one month' MAL A § 48:3

§ 632 The protasis of conditional clauses from law texts is not limited to the perfect and preterite. In a number of cases, the present is found instead. By definition, the apodosis takes place later than the protasis, meaning that we should expect a perfect/preterite or stative in the protasis. However, as already indicated by Hecker for OA, in the case of expressing an intention or ability, the present is used instead.[15] This indicates to the reader that the action is not completed (Kouwenberg 2010, 95):

šumma aʾīlu aššassu e-ez-zi-ib 'if a man wants to leave his wife' MAL A § 37:15

šumma aʾīlu esertušu ú-⸢pa⸣-ṣa-an 'if a man intends to veil his concubine' MAL A § 41:1

šumma sinniltu ša mussa mētūni mussa ina mūate iltu bētīša la-a tu-ú-uṣ-ṣa 'if a wife whose husband is dead and, upon her husband's death, she does not intend to go out' MAL A § 46:89–91

This present of the futurum exactum is also found on a few occasions in the protasis of conditional clauses in loans:

šumma ēṣidē la i-dan! ēṣidu ½ mana annaka iḫīaṭ 'if he does not give the reapers, the reaper will weigh out half a mina of lead' KAJ 11:13–15

šumma ana 6 *urḫe annaka la i-ḫi-aṭ eqalšu uppu laqi* 'if he does not weigh the lead out within six months, his field will be acquired and taken' KAJ 14:12–14

17.4.2 The perfect and preterite in MAPD and rituals

§ 633 The language of MAPD is closer to letters than to MAL A–B with respect to its tense system, in the sense that the zero preterite is almost totally replaced by the perfect. This is actually a strong argument for it being a contemporary MA composition, whereas MAL A–B follows an older tradition. As such, we will start with an overview of past tense in MAPD, which will nevertheless be limited due to its damaged character. First of all, there are no instances of a zero preterite. As expected, this is rare as the perfect replaced the zero preterite in MA. There is one common passage introducing each edict, which is a genuine case of the past tense:

RN (…) *riksa* (…) <u>*ir-ku-ús*</u> 'RN issued a decree' MAPD § 7:46 (passim MAPD)

This is a formulaic example. In other documents, we find *irkus* instead of perfect *irtakas* (§ 624); the latter form would be expected in the letter corpus where it is not attested. In another passage from MAPD, a negated preterite (*lā iṭṭulū*) occurs with two perfects (*ilteme* and *uttaʾʾerūneššu*) used as the futurum exactum.

šumma (…) *qēputtušu ana šidde ēkalle la-a iṭ-ṭu-lu ḫiṭṭāni la-a ut-ta-e-ru-ni-šu urkiš šarru* [*ḫi*]*ṭṭa il-te-me gabbī ḫiṭṭāni rab ēkalle emmidū*[*šu*] 'if his representatives have not checked the environment of the palace and have not reported on (their) crime to him, but afterwards the king has heard of the crime, they will impose the entire punishment on the palace manager' MAPD § 21:109–111

In other instances, MAPD resorts to the perfect for the futurum exactum. Most instances occur in the protasis of a conditional clause, which is part of a larger edict:

15 See GKT, 235 § 137; cf. GAG, 262 § 161i; for NB, see Streck (1995, 99–106).

šumma (...) [*an*]*a ṣabʾe ša ēkalle iq-ṭí-bi ubarrūšu* 'if he has spoken to the people of the palace, they will charge him' MAPD § 2:20–21

[*šumma* (...) ...] *rab ēkalle ul-te-ṣi sinnilta ša ēkalle la-a uš-šu-ru* 'if the palace manager has let (him/her) go, they will not release the woman of the palace' MAPD § 5:34–35

šumma qēputtu annūtu la-a iq-ṭí-b[*i*]*-ú ḫiṭṭa inaššiū* 'if these representatives have not reported it, they will carry the penalty' MAPD § 8:51

šumma ša rēš šarre balut qēp[*utte*] *annūte e-ta-rab ḫiṭṭa inašši* 'if the royal eunuch has entered without these representatives, he will carry the penalty' MAPD § 9:55

(...) *aššat šarre* [...*šumma amassa* ... *l*]*ū sarta mimma te-ta-pa-áš* [*aššat šarre* (...)] (...) [*ša am*]*assa ḫiṭṭa taḫ-ṭí-a-ši-ni* 30 *ina ḫaṭṭāte tamaḫḫassi* 'the queen (...) if her slave [...] or has committed whatever crime, the queen (...) whose slave girl committed a crime, she will hit her 30 times with a stick' MAPD § 18:82–85

It is furthermore noteworthy that MAPD applies the perfect in dependent clauses, which is otherwise the domain of the preterite when referring to past events. Despite the damaged character of both passages, we can safely regard the perfect of the following phrases as a futurum exactum in the apodosis of a conditional clause:

[*ša ... ana ūr ēkal*]*le e-te-li-ú-ni ḫiṭṭa inašši* 'who(ever) went up to the roof of the palace will carry the penalty' MAPD § 1:9

ēpiš šipre [*ša* (...)] *im-taḫ-ru-ni* (...) [... *aʾīlu ša*] *ana šarre la-a ib-ta-⸢at⸣-qu-ni utaḫḫuḫūšu* 'a craftsman, who will have received things [...], the man who will not have denounced (the craftsman) to the king, they will drench him (in oil)' MAPD § 5:36–37

In addition, note a broken negated perfect in a broken context:

la-a ip-te-te 'he has not opened' MAPD § 22:118†

Normal relative clauses with a preterite can also be found:

šumma lū mazziz panē lū sinniltu kēnatt[*eš*]*a ša ta-mu-ru-ši-ni* [...] 'if a court attendant or a woman of her status who has seen her (or...)' MAPD § 19:93

ša riksa annia e-ti-qu-ni [*rab ē*]*kalle iš-mi-ú-ni ḫiṭṭa lā ēmidūšuni rab ēkalle ḫiṭṭa inašši* 'whoever violated this decree (and) the palace manager heard (about it but) did not impose a punishment, (then) the palace manager will carry the penalty' MAPD § 21:108–109

§ 634 Outside the law texts, this futurum exactum is rare, save for the following passage from the Ištar Ritual:

abāta ša Ištar tul-te-ṣi-ma lā taballaṭ u piriltaša lā tattaṣarma lā tašallim 'should you divulge the word of Ištar, you shall not live, and should you not protect her secret, you shall not prosper' Ištar Ritual r. 6'–7'

Only rarely do we find a preterite in the rituals, which is used as a futurum exactum to describe events preceding the present. The usage of the preterite over the perfect in both clauses has to be explained by its position in dependent clauses.

1 *mana*$^{\text{ta.àm}}$ *ṣarpa aʾīluttu ša šarre iš-ši-ú-ni i*[*laqq*]*eū* 'the men who carried the king, take one mina of silver each' Coronation Ritual ii 40–41

šulmānāte [*ana*] *šarre uqṭanarrubū šulmāna panīya ša ana šarre* [*ú*]*-qar-ri-bu-ni ana bēt Aššur ubbulū* 'they present *šulmānu*-gifts for the king, the first gift they present they bring to the temple of Aššur' Coronation Ritual iii 4–6

17.4.3 The perfect and preterite in letters and administrative documents

§ 635 When it comes to the letter corpus, the attestations of the futurum exactum is limited to the protasis of conditional clauses. Attestations derive from letter orders where orders to subordinates are sometimes accompanied by threats in the case of negligence:

šumma ṣabʾa u unūta gabba ⸢*la*⸣*-a ta-tab-la* 'if you have not brought the people and all property' KAV 168:19–21

ana muḫḫi PN *našperta ultēbil šumma susīa*^{meš} *u* ^{giš}*mugerra*^{meš} *la-a it-ta-na-ku suḫīrē ta-ku-un-na* 'I have sent a message to PN, if he has not given you horses and chariots, *assign* foals' MATC 11:20–24

šumma dēnīšu ú-za-ki liqešu 'if he cleared his case, take him' Billa 66:11–12

šumma mimma laššutta ta-ta-pa-al-šu u arḫiš la-a ta-ta-na-áš-šu ana muḫḫi duāke telli 'if you answer him that there is nothing whatsoever and you do not give him quickly, then you will meet death' OIP 79 3:14–20

šumma aʾīlu iḫ-ta-li-iq aʾīla uma[*lla*] 'if the man will be lost, PN will replace (him with another) man' T 98-94:17–19

We also find the perfect negated in this position, whereas a negated perfect in subordinate and conditional clauses was still rare, including in the case of the futurum exactum (GKT, 127 § 76f; GOA § 19.3.4):

šumma adi 1 ITI.UD^{meš} *la ta-ta-bal la tu-ta-ir lā ikaṣṣurūnekku* 'if you do not bring and return (the tablet) within a month, the (costs) will not be deducted (from your account)' MATC 23A:21–24

§ 636 For administrative documents the perfect exactum is again frequent in conditional clauses, involving a usage that is very similar to the aforementioned law texts (§ 629ff). Most attestations derive from loans and *šulmānu* contracts, where the conditional clauses discuss the proceedings. Examples of the negated perfect exactum are found in the protasis:

šumma ina adre qaqqad ŠE *la im-ta-da-ad* ŠE *ana* <*ṣibte*> *illak* 'if does not measure out the capital of the barley at the threshing-floor, the barley shall bear <interest>' KAJ 81:15–17

šumma adi 1 ITI.UD^{meš} *la-a i-ti-din* 'if he will not have given (them) within a month (then…)' KAJ 88:15–16 (TN)

[*šum*]*ma abāssu la i-ta-mar tuppušu urrâššu* 'if he does not examine his case, he shall deliver his tablet to him' KAJ 89:14'–16'

[*šu*]*mma ad*[*i* 1 *urḫe*] *annaka* ⸢*la*⸣ *i-t*[*i-din*] AN.NA *a-na* MÁŠ 'if he does not give the lead within a month, the lead will go for interest' Billa 2:13–15

šumma ina adre la it-ti-din ŠE*-um*^{meš} *ana ṣibtīšu illak* 'if he does not give it on the threshing floor, the barley will go for interest' Giricano 1:17–20 *šumma ina adrāte la i-ta-nu* ŠE-*um ana ṣibte illak* 'if they do not give it at the threshing floors, the barley shall go for interest' OIP 79 5:17–19

A preterite used for futurum exactum is attested in a few relative clauses, where it precedes the actions of the main clause:

mardiātu ša ḫurāde ša PN (…) *ú-up-pi-šu-ú-ni* 'the travel stations of the *ḫurādu*, which PN will have prepared' DeZ 2521:16–19

iltu GN *i-tu-ra-ni ina māte usbāni* 'after he has returned from GN, we will dwell in the country' T 96-36:11–12

Relative clauses are especially frequent for the verb *baʾāʾu* 'to seek' (cf. § 579), which describes the consequences of violating a contract.

[*š*]*a dēna u da*[*bāb*]*a* [*ina*] *bēruššunu ub-ta-ʾe-ú-ni* (…) *qāssu* 'whoever among them will seek a case and complaint shall forfeit his share' OIP 79 6:16–20

ša dēna u dabāba ub-ta-e-ú-ni 10 *bilta annaka* (…) *iḫīaṭ* 'whoever seeks a case and complaint will weigh out 10 talents of lead' VAT 8722:21–24

ša dēnu ub-ta-ʾu-ú-ni sinnilta lūšērib 'whoever seeks legal action must make the woman enter' Giricano 7:19–20

A case of the futurum exactum outside a conditional or relative clause is found in the following passage. Note that, as the clause is not followed by a present, the futurum exactum precedes any other action in the future, as is the case in normal conditional and relative clauses. Perhaps this phrase is comparable to the epistolary perfect of letters (see below).

5 *emmeru*$^{pl.}$ (…) *ina ālik šarre i-ta-ku-lu* 'five sheep will be eaten at the procession of the king' Ali 9:1–5

17.4.4 The epistolary perfect

§ 637 An additional kind of perfect for the future tense is found in MA letters, where the author writes according to the perspective of the recipient. As explained by Cancik-Kirschbaum, this refers to events that are ongoing or take place in the near future at the moment of writing, but are in the past at the moment that the recipient reads the letter. For this reason, we find the perfect in such instances. We may call this tense, according to Pardee/Whiting's (1987) definition of 'epistolary perfect', similar to the futurum exactum found in MA administrative documents (§ 635f), which is common in OB (cf. Kouwenberg 2010, 147) and later LB (Streck 1995, 155–59 § 35). The main examples, according to Cancik-Kirschbaum (MATSH, 62), are as follows:

ana dinān bēlīya attalak 'I will have gone as a substitute for my lord' MATSH et passim

ina abāt šarre al-tap-[*ra-ku*] 'I will have written to you at the command of the king' MATSH 21:4

Otherwise, examples are not unambiguous and mostly revolve around the sending verbs, such as *ubālu*:

PN *šuršurrāte sipa*[*rre*$^{pl.}$] *amtaḫaṣ ul-te-bi-lak-ku-n*[*u*] 'I will have put PN in fetters and sent (him) to you' KAV 96:5–8 *ina pî kunukkīya* ^{na4}*kunukku*^{meš}*-ia kankū al-tap-ra-ku-nu* 'my seals are sealed with my seal, I will have sent it to you' KAV 99:10–11

PN *al-tap-ra-ku* 'I will have sent you PN' Billa 67:4

iš-tu ta-at-ta-na-šu-ni x x *ana muḫḫīya* [*a*]*lka* 'come to me as soon as you have given it to him' OIP 79 3:21–23

mā ina 2 ITI.UD^{meš} *kurummassunu tar-ti-aḫ* 'thus, for two months, their rations remained' MATSH 12:9–10

In some texts, we find an unexpected perfect, which is used in instances that have not yet taken place at the moment of writing. They may be explained as other instances of the past tense in the perception of the recipient.

qāssunu la ú-ṣa-li-ú (*uṣṣaliū*) 'they may not have been idle' T 93-7:6

A preterite for the future exactum can be used in the specific case where it is not replaced by the perfect. This is only rarely attested; however, note a passage with a negated preterite:

bitqēšu la-a tu-še-er šēbuttika (…) *leqya alka* '(if) you do not drop his accusation, take your witnesses and come here' KAV 201:17–22

17.5 The imperative, precative and prohibitive

§ 638 Aside from the indicative, we find a number of other modi in Akkadian. The most morphologically basic form is the imperative, which derives from the base of the preterite *PRvS*. As Akkadian knows no consonant cluster at the start of a word, in the G-stem an additional vowel is inserted between the first and second radicals. Gender and plural markers are added, namely, *-ī* (fs) and *-ā* (mp). According to the rules of vowel elision, in forms where a vocalic morpheme is added, the second vowel is deleted in the G-stem *áš-ra* (< **ašarā*) 'check it!' KAV 99:40–41. With III/voc verbs, the R_3 is a (semi)vowel and thus not elided: *qí-bi-a* 'speak!' MARV 3 64:5–6. The imperative is restricted to the second person and used to express commands, wishes and desires. It remains optional in instructional texts, such as perfume recipes (PKT), where we find the present instead: [IZI] *tu-ša-ḫa-az* 'you will ignite the fire' PKT 1 I right:2; *a-na lìb-be ta-tab-ba-ak* 'you will pour it into it' PKT 1 I right:8. An imperative with an additional personal pronoun is not common, but can be found:

ū lā kīa at-tu-nu-ma le-qe-a-ni 'and if it is not so, you take it to me' KAV 105:29–30

at-ta ú-su-uq 'as for you, select' T 97-10:14

Imperatives in administrative documents are rare, as they do not belong in contracts. An exception is found in a note:

[*i*]*na nikkasse ana panīya* (...) *a-na* PN *di-in* 'at the accounting before me, give it to PN' KAJ 308:5–9[16]

16 Previously considered to be a letter (Saporetti 1970, 147 no. 38); however, this claim is now rejected (MATSH, 236).

§ 639 As the imperative can only be used for the second person, the volitive mood of the other persons is expressed in Akkadian. Morphologically, the precative is built with *lū*+preterite conjugation. Assyrian differs slightly from Babylonian in 1cs *laprus*, as opposed to *luprus* (Reiner 2001, 390-91). Moreover, in the D and Š and their secondary stems, the vowel of the prefix colours /u/ in a similar way to the normal prefix conjugation. Thus, we find *luparris* in MA, rather than Babylonian *liparris*. There is little reason to assume that *lū* was long in the precative, although there are a few cases of weak roots where it is written plene (e.g., *lu-ú-še-be-er* MATSH 8:27'). This feature is probably related to the purely orthographic spelling of some I/weak roots (see § 101ff).

> *tuppātēšunu lu-še-⸢li-a⸣-nim-ma ana panē qēputte liš-ku-nu li-id-bu-bu lu-zak-k*[*i*]*-ú-ma li-il-⸢qé⸣-ú* (in case there are written opposing claims) '(in case there are opposing claims written) 'they should bring up their tablets and place them before the officials, contest, clear (the field of claims) and take it ' MAL B § 6:16–19

> *la-áš-pur-ka* 'I wish to send you' MAPD § 21:106

> *iyāmattu* [*pāḫ*]*assu lu-ka-il* 'everyone may keep his office' Coronation Ritual iii 12–13

> *anāku la-tal-ka* 'I want to leave (to you)' Faist 2001, 252:32

> [*a*]*mma*[*r*] (…) *ibaššiūni bēltu ⸢lu tu⸣-še-bi-la* 'may my lady send to me as much as there is' TabT05a-134:26–28

> *šalāma Ištar lu ta-ši-ma-ku* 'may Ištar decree your well-being' Ištar Ritual:13

Fincke (2014, 25) translates the following phrase as an apparent form of the second person, but with *lū* omitted. As this letter was written by a scribe from a Hurrian (Arrapḫa) background, it is questionable to what extent this is representative of the MA system of tenses.

> *tu-še-še-⸢ir*$^{!?}$⸣*-šu*$^{?}$ *arḫiš tu-r*[*i*$^{?}$*-d*]*u*$^{?}$*-ni* 'you must prepare it and quickly come down here' BM 103203:16–17 (Nuzi/Ass.)

An Assyrian 1cp precative (or cohortative) appears as *lū niprus*, rather than expected Babylonian *i niprus* (cf. GOA § 19.8.1.1). We may also consider the following possibility (Billa 66), with a normal preterite used in this function, although the passage is damaged. Likewise, in NA the cohortative occurs without *lū* (SNAG, 93 § 3.12.7).

> *zukur mā ni-*[*ip*]*-qi-id* [x x] *a'īla išarriqū*<*ni*> 'let us *hand over* […] the man who steals'' Billa 66:18–19 (see commentary on p. 136; also notice the seemingly Babylonian subjunctive)

> *lu ni-iš-⸢pur⸣* '[…] we want to send' MATSH 17:23'†

> *lu ni-{ib}-il-qu-na-*[*š*]*i-*[*in*] *lu ni-ib-la-aṭ* 'we want to take it for us (so that) we may live' MATSH 22:18–19

§ 640 The prefixed *l-* in the precative is probably directly related to the particle *lū* (cf. Bab 1cs *luprus*). As such, we find *lū* also used with statives in order to express the wish for a status.[17]

17 See GAG, 131 § 81b; UGM, 60; Freydank (1975, 143); cf. GKT, 128 § 77a; GOA § 19.8.1.3.

ina pitti ša muḫḫi bētema lu ša-ak-na-at 'may it be placed in the responsibility of the housemaster' KAV 99:41–42

PN *lu ú-šab* 'may (PN) sit down' KAV 194:4–5

billu lu ma-ad 'may the mixed beer be much' OIP 79 2:8

kī aḫāʾiš lu ep-ša-at 'it must be done together' MATSH 10:22–23

luḫammiṭū lu ša-ak-n[*u*] 'they must hurry and place it' KAV 205:15

lu us-bu lēkulū 'they must sit and eat' MATC 4:5

emeru^{meš} *lu ma-du* 'the sheep should be numerous' MATC 10:23

For 1cs, we can give *lu* ⸢*šal-ma-a-ku*⸣ 'I want to be well' KAV 194:19.[18] However, this reading is contestable.[19] Similar to the stative, non-verbal forms can also receive *lū* (cf. SNAG, 94 § 3.12.7):

ana kuāši lu-ú šul-mu 'may it be well with you' A 845:5

§ 641 For a negated version of the precative, early Akkadian uses the vetitive, which is still attested in OA (GKT, 129f § 77d; GOA § 19.8.3), but does not occur in MA. Instead, a finite verb can be negated by inserting the particle *lā* between *lū* and the verbal base. In combination with a present, this becomes a kind of prohibitive in Akkadian (GAG, 133 § 81h). Apparently, this form was used to replace the vetitive, which is built in closer analogy to its positive counterpart, the precative.

ilu lu-ú la-a i-qa-bi 'may the god not say (i.e. forbid)' MAPD § 2:13[20]

[*šu*]*m ile lu-ú la-a i-za-kar* 'he may not invoke the name of god' MAPD § 11:61

lu la ú-ṣa-k[*u-nu*] 'may he not go out to you' KAV 96:13

lu la i-ma-[*ṭí*] 'nothing may be missing' KAV 168:15

iltu a[*ḫā*^{w}*i*]*š* [*l*]*u la-a i-šap-*⸢*pa-ak*⸣ 'together they must not cast' KAV 205:31

lu la-a i-ṣa-ab-bat 'he must not seize' MARV 4 119:22

⸢*a-na*⸣ *il-te-*⸢*nu*$^{?}$⸣*-na ma-am-ma lu-ú la i-da-bu-ub* 'alone(?), nobody may speak' MATC 15:33

mamma lu la ú-ṣa 'nobody may leave' MATSH 4:12'

balātukk[*a*] *lu la e-ti-qa-ni* 'without you(r consent), may they not cross' T 93-20:11–12

gabba mimma lu la-a i-ma-a-ṭí 'may he not deduct all of it with anything' T 96-8:16–17

ana PN (…) *din* (…) [*l*]*u la ta-kal-l*[*a*(*-šu*)] 'give (him) to PN, you should not detain him' T 98-3:10–14

Sometimes a stative can be used to indicate a status:

18 See Freydank (1975, 143); BAI, 30, 70.

19 See CAD S, 288; MAOG 7/1–2, 5–6; Jakob (2003, 484–89).

20 Cf. the OA expression *lā libbi ilim*, introducing the death of someone, e.g., CCT 6 15a+I 633, 763:4; TCL 4 30:3–4.

lu la ba-re-ú 'they may not be hungry' MARV 1 71:20

lu-ú la-a ra-qu 'they may not be idle' T 96-1:10

§ 642 As is well known from Akkadian (and Common Semitic), a negated imperative is ungrammatical. Therefore, either a negated precative or present is used in MA. Nonetheless, we may point to the following unusual phrase from a TSA letter:

adi rēssu lā inaššiūne[nni] ana duāke la še-li-na-ni-ni 'as long as they do not bring his head here, do no put me to death' T 02-3:22–25

Of course, we can easily reconstruct an omitted <tu> or <ú> before the verbal form in both cases, reducing these phrases to simple scribal mistakes. That said, in general, the phrases remain difficult, as the imperative seems to have a plural agent, followed by a ventive, and then one or two times by the suffix *-ni*, possibly part of the accusative *-(a)nni* 'me'. However, the plural agent does not follow from the context of T 02-3. Alternatively, we may not totally exclude some kind of 'modus attraction' where the subjunctive of the adverbial clause spreads to the imperative of the main clause. In this case, the suffix chain would be reduced to a pronominal suffix with the subjunctive. The interpretation remains open until the respective text is edited and context is provided. I still have no idea what the *-na-* particle in T 02-3 should represent; perhaps it is nasalization (see § 231). We should also note the following passage, again from T 02-3, which features what seems to be an imperative following the particle *lū* with the unexplained sign ḪU:

qāta[k]a lu ḪU *še-mi-da-ni-šu-[nu]* 'you must impose your hand on them' T 02-3:20–21

17.6 The stative

§ 643 The Akkadian stative is tense neutral. However, it is most frequently used for past and present tense events, while its use for the future tense is uncommon. According to Cancik-Kirschbaum, the stative is replaced by the present for the future tense (cf. MATSH, 65). She gives the following two examples where the future or the present occurs in contrast to the continuous character of the stative.

tūr ūmū i-ka-ṣu-ú 'the weather will be cold again' MATSH 6:11'

adi ūmū ṭa-bu-ni 'as long as the weather is (still) good' MATSH 6:15'

However, a similar instance of case is found in the Tell Ḫuwīra corpus, where the same verb *ṭiābu* 'to be good' is used in the present to specify the continuous character of the weather.

adi ūmū i-ṭí-bu-ni ana libnāte urrudūne 'as long as the weather is good, they will come down for bricks' MATC 3:7–8

There is a number of other instances where the stative is found to refer to a future event, disproving Cancik-Kirschbaum's claim.

šumma ina adrāti ŠE *lā imaddad kī panittīšuma ina muḫḫi šalmīšu u kēnīšu* ŠE *ra-ki-is* 'if he does not measure out the barley on the threshing floor, according to earlier agreements, the barley will be bound on his credibility and legal status' KAJ 69:7–12 *iltu* GN *ittūranni ina māte us-ba-ni* 'after he has returned from GN, we will dwell in the country' T 96-36:11–12

šumma ḫa-li[*q*] PN [L]Ú *uma*[*ll*]*a* 'if he is lost, PN will replace (him with another) man' T 98-132:18–20

In theory, any verb can take a stative in MA, with the possible exception of some irregular roots.[21] Still, there are a few cases where a stative is absent, even though we would nonetheless expect it. The distinction between stative and fientive verbs in Akkadian, in general, is not always clear (cf. Kouwenberg 2010, 54–55):

šīpātu ša qātika kē maṣi ibašši i-ri-ḫa 'the wool that is at your disposal, how much is available as a remainder?' KAV 106:9–11

ša i-la-be-ra [x x x] 'who are old' MATC 12:11†

§ 644 In Akkadian, when a noun is used as a predicate, it may be conjugated as a stative. In MA, this type of nominal clause is rare. Most instances can alternatively be explained as a status absolutus, although the actual difference between a third-person singular stative and a status absolutus could be superficial. Otherwise, we have a 1cs *pa-ni-a-ku* MATSH 2:25, but see the commentary MATSH (102) for difficulties.[22] Statives of primary adjectives are more frequent in MA, e.g., *ṭāb-* 'to be good', which derives from the adjective *ṭābu* rather than verbal *ṭiābu*.[23] Other examples include:

šumma aʾīlu lu-ú ma-ri-iṣ lu-ú me-et 'if a man is either sick or dead' MAL A § 3:23–24

šang[*utta*]*ka* (…) *lu ṭa-ba-a*[*t*] 'may your priesthood be good' Coronation Ritual ii 33–34

išātu la da-an 'the fire is not strong' PKT 1 I right:18

aḫuka ba-la-aṭ 'your brother is alive' KBo 28 61/62:17'

annītu tuppu dan-na-at 'this is a strong tablet' KAJ 148:28

kī TI-ru (…) *la-a ṭa-bu-ni* 'because the flesh (of sheep) was not good' KAJ 209:5–7

---

21 Cancik-Kirschbaum lists a few verbs, which she believes could only occur in the present and never as a stative: *alāku*, *dagālu*, *magāru* and *udāʾu* (MATSH, 64). It is undoubtedly correct that there is no stative of *idāʾu* 'to know', as it is irregular and weak. A stative of *alāku* is possible, but not common due to it being a verb of movement without a resultative meaning (GAG, 126 § 77g). However, Cancik-Kirschbaum refers more specifically to *alāku* in the meaning 'to be suitable', e.g., *a-na ma-sa-e la-a i-lak* 'it is not suitable for washing' MATSH 6:12'. Indeed, in this context, *alāku* never occurs in the stative, although this stative derivative meaning of the fientive *alāku* 'to go' is unexpected. On the other hand, statives of *magāru* are, in fact, attested in MA: *ma-gi-ir* MAL A § 5:63; see also the preterite *ana maḫārīya la-a im-gúr* 'he did not agree to receive me' MATSH 2:65. The verb *dagālu* 'to wait upon' can certainly occur in the stative, but not in the active meaning (cf. CAD D, 23b). There does not seem to be a reason why these verbs could not be used in the stative.

22 Cancik-Kirschbaum points out that *panāʾu*, as an original III/ū, would have a /u/ vowel. We already noted how *ḫadāʾu* (§ 573) changed to the III/ī class.

23 See GAG, 125 § 77b; Kouwenberg (2010, 166f). The difference between statives derived from primary adjectives and verbs goes back to the difference between adjectival and fientive verbs. For a discussion, see Kouwenberg (2010, 58–60 § 3.3.2, 166). In MA, this group is largely limited to *danānu* 'to be strong' and *ṭiābu* 'to be good'. Morphologically, verbs with a different nominal construction to that of the common *PaRiS* seem to belong to this category (see also Kouwenberg 2010, 162)

makuttu ša āl[āni] lu dan-na-at 'the destitution of the settlements should be severe' T 96-36:29–30

māna'īne la-a ṭa-ab 'why is it not good?' T 02-32:23

Probably:

12 *ina ammete ar-ka* '12 cubits long' KAJ 128:4

2 *ammutu ra-ap-ša-a[t]* 'two cubits wide' Billa 22:5

§ 645 Most statives derive from (fientive) verbs in different stems. They have a resultative meaning, describing the result of the action of the verb as occurring in the prefix conjugation. Here, we can distinguish between transitive and intransitive verbs. The group of intransitive verbs, which cannot take an object, only concerns verbs in the G-stem.

mussa ma-gi-ir 'her husband agrees' MAL A § 5:63

ša libbīša (…) *mi-ta-a-at* 'her foetus dies' MAL A § 53:99

ina eqle u bēte qāssu e-li '(his claim) on the field and house forfeits' MAL B § 6:45

kī zīqu annītu nam-ra-tu-ni 'as this torch is bright' Ištar Ritual:12

ammar zabāle ma-ṣa-ta 'as much as you are able to carry' MARV 1 15:12–13

19 *ṣab'u ša Kalmarte me-tu-ni* '19 men died in the month of *Kalmartu*' MARV 1 71:37–38

5 *sūtu* ŠE *ma-ṭí* 'five seahs of barley are missing' LVUH 70:20

kī ḫa-di-a-ta-a-ni epuš 'do as you please' MATC 15:8–9

be-da-ku 'I spent the night' TR 2083a+:9

qaqquru ba-a-ri 'the territory is starving' T 97-10:18

If a stative derives from a transitive verb, it usually does not take an object. As such, we usually translate it as a passive.

tuppu ša mar'uttīšu la-a šaṭ-rat 'a tablet of his adoption was not written' MAL A § 28:5

lū a[na] bēt emīša la-qé-a-at lū la-a la-qé-a-at 'she is either taken or not taken to the house of her father-in-law' MAL A § 32:52–53

abuša ḫab-bu-ul 'her father was indebted' MAL A § 39:28

esertu (...) *pa-aṣ-ṣu-ú-na-at* 'a concubine (…) will be veiled' MAL A § 40:58–60

ša bēssu qé-pu-ni lā iq[bi] 'he did not say that it was entrusted (to) his house' MAL C+ § 9:13

šumma la-a ma-ru-ur 'if he is not turned into a eunuch' MAPD § 20:98

šamnu^{meš} *i+na lìb-b[i-š]u tabek* 'oil is poured in it' Coronation Ritual i 33

eqalšu up-pu la-qé 'his field is acquired and taken' KAJ 14:14

abāssu am-rat 'his case is examined' KAJ 48:8–9

ana lā mašā'e ša-ṭí-ir 'it is written down in order not to forget' MARV 5 32:8–9

balu bēlīya pa-al-ḫa-a-ku 'I am afraid without my lord' Billa 62:21

iltu nakkamte še-ṣu-a-at 'it was brought out from the storehouse' LVUH 101:11–12

qaqqassa ka-zi-ir 'her head is shaven(?)' TR 2083a+:20

§ 646 Some transitive verbs remain active in the stative and retain their objects. The examples are nonetheless limited. Kouwenberg noted that the resultative character of the stative verbs makes them fit for the protasis of law paragraphs, whereas other more frequently used active statives have developed a lexicalized meaning, e.g., *maḫāru* 'to receive' or *našāʾu* 'to carry'.[24]

[*šum*]*ma* [*al*]*mattu ana bēt aʾīle tētarab u marāša ḫurda iltēša na-ṣa-a-at* 'if a widow has entered the house of a man and she took her posthumous son with her' MAL A § 28:1–3

māmīta ša (…) *ta-am-ʾa-a-ta-ni* 'the oath that you swore' MAL A § 47:26–27

PN *u aḫḫūšu* (…) *eqla u Libbi-āle ze-zu* 'PN and his brothers divided (the land) of the countryside and the inner city (Aššur)' KAJ 10:3–6

pāḫat šallume PN *na-ši* 'PN bears the responsibility for the payment (of the debt)' KAJ 224:13–17

luḫammiṭū lu ša-ak-n[*u*] 'they must hurry and place (it)' KAV 205:15

[*r*]*abê ṣabʾē ša simta la ša-ak-nu-ú-n*[*i*] 'the commandants of troops who were not regarded as appropriate' MARV 1 5:29

emmera^{meš} *lū ša iltu* GN *na-ṣa-ku-ú-ni* 'sheep, be it those that are brought to you from GN' MATC 10:16–18

1 *sūtu* ŠE (…) PN *ma-ḫi-ir* 'PN received one seah of barley' MATC 38:1–4 (variant passim)

ana šuāšu na-aṣ-ṣu-uš 'they carry him' MATSH 9:45

Note that the active usage of these verbs is not obligatory as can be observed on the base of the following two examples of *aḫāzu* 'to seize', with and without direct object:

qadiltu ša mutu aḫ-zu-ši-ni 'a *qadiltu*-priestess, whom a husband married' MAL A § 40:61

aššassu ša a-na kīdi aḫ-zu-tu-ú-ni ilaqqeašši 'he will take his wife who married outside (the family)' MAL A § 45:74–75

17.7 The infinitive

§ 647 Similar to the stative, the infinitive is not used as a tense; instead, it mostly complements the finite verbs. Considering the usage of infinitives, the study by Aro (1961) is still valid today. Since he made extensive usage of the MA evidence, the following section can do little more than repeat and summarize his study to a certain extent, while adding attestations from new texts. The infinitive is generally used in a fairly frequent and wide-ranging way, compared to some other Semitic languages, for instance, the resultative construction with the following preposition *ana*, e.g., *mullāʾē ša ṣabʾe lā imaggurū a-na ma-ḫa-ri* 'they did not want to receive compensation for the troops' MATSH 2:57.

24 See Kouwenberg (2010, 172–73); cf. OA GOA § 19.4.3.

§ 648 Attestations of the infinitive in the nominative are very rare in MA. So far, they only occur in similar constructions as the subject of existential verbs. Both attestations are also found in Aro 1961, 21:[25]

tu-a-ru ù da-ba-bu laššu ‘there will be no coming back or complaining’ KAJ 27:18; KAJ 149:13 et passim

ša [l]a-qa-šu-nu ù d⸢a-ba⸣-a-ab-šu-nu ibaššiūni ‘those who are there to claim or complain’ MAL B § 6:13–15

It is possible for the infinitive to occur as the object of a verb, which is attested for the verbs *amāru*, *laʾāʾu* and *tadānu*:[26]

ba-ú-ra lā ilaʾʾe ‘he will not be able to prove it’ MAL A § 18:76

aʾīlu ša kišpe e-pa-a-ša ēmurūni ‘a man who saw witchcraft performed’ MAL A § 47:7–8

[q]a-ba-a še-ma-a ma-ga-ra ketta u sa[lī]ma Aššur liddinakku ‘may Aššur give you command, obeying, agreement, justice and reconciliation’ Coronation Ritual ii 35–36

pāḫat šal-lu-me PN *[n]aši* ‘PN bears the responsibility for the payment (of the debt)’ KAJ 224:13–17 (Aro 1961, 38)

(…) *mašḫerē e-pa-ša ittannā* ‘they gave (raw material) to make *mašḫuru* textiles’ DeZ 2495:10–12

ana bēte e-ra-a-ba lālaʾʾe ‘I will not be able to enter into the house’ MATSH 12:27–28

ša dēna da-ba-ba ina muḫḫīšu ubtaʾʾuʾūni ‘whoever seeks a case and complaints against him’ Franke/Wilhelm 1985:5–6

Otherwise, examples are rare:

ša-la-ma Ištar lū tašīmakku ‘may Ištar decree your well-being’ Ištar Ritual:13

Note also the following passage with a pronominal suffix. The passage is notable for the adjective that stands attributively in relation to the infinitive.

mannu (…) *da-ba-ab-ki* DÙG.G[A] *lišme* ‘who (…) may hear your speaking sweet words?’ A 845:7–8

§ 649 In paronomastic constructions, where the finite verb is repeated in an infinitive, the locative is usually used in Akkadian (Aro 1961, 111–15). For MA, we have very few examples, which have the infinitive in the accusative. According to Aro (1961, 114), this became the replacement in MA, while von Soden argued that the accusative only replaced the locative in Assyrian with singular transitive verbs (GAG, 250 § 150a).

nu-pu-ša nappišā ‘air it’ KAV 99:14 cf. KAV 109:12

Semi-paronomastic infinitives are more frequent, where the root of the finite verb is repeated in the infinitive, usually following a preposition.

a-n[a t]a-da-ni tadnaššu ‘it is given to him in order to give (again)’ KAJ 83:12–13

ša la-a ba-ta-qa tabtuqūni ‘that what is not to accuse, you accused’ KAV 201:12–13[27]

---

25 Cf. OA in GKT, 213 § 127a; GOA § 20.3.1.1.

26 See Aro (1961, 74–110); GOA § 20.3.3.

ša libbika ša še-lu-i-ka šēli [u š]a še-ru-di-ka šērid 'remove, what you want to remove, and add, what you to add' MATSH 9:12–13

§ 650 The infinitive can also be found as the governed noun of a synthetic genitive construction (Aro 1961, 31–32). Most attestations given below stem from different variants of the *pāḫat* x *zakkue* 'the responsibility to clear (something)':

ina šurrât še-ru-di-ka 'when you begin to bring down (the horses)' BVW F r. 3

SIG$_4$^{meš} *ša-ḫa-[a-ṭí]* 'bricks making' A 3310:6

puḫat$^{\text{sic.}}$ GÉME *za-ku-e* PN *[n]aṣṣat* 'PN bears the responsibility for clearing the slave girl' KAJ 100:20–23

kī RN *ana muḫḫi kisallāte* A^{meš} *ra-ma-ki ittanaradūni epšū* 'when the king goes repeatedly down with water to wash the forecourts, they are sacrificed' KAJ 204:8–12

pāḫat puqurrā[n]āʾe ša PN *za-ku-e kāra kāre taḫūma taḫūme* (…) PN-*ma na-ši* 'PN bears the responsibility to clear the claims, quay (to) quay, border (to) border' VAT 8722:13–20

Once, the construction is reversed and the infinitive is the governed noun:

ḫa-laq mìm-mu-šu 'the loss of his property' MAL C+ § 6:41

Separated by a pronoun:

pāḫat A.ŠÀ *šu-a-tu za-ku-e* PN *ittanašši* 'PN will bear the responsibility for clearing that field' KAJ 132:16–18

Note also the following construction where the infinitive is separated from the governing noun by an adverbial construction:

pāḫat pu<qu>rrānāʾe ša sinniltīšu kāra ana kāre taḫūma ana taḫūme za-ku-e PN *naši* 'PN bears the responsibility for clearing the claims of his woman, quay to quay, border to border' KAJ 169:16–20

§ 651 The infinitive can follow the particle *ša*. As explained by Kouwenberg, the meaning of the infinitive here roughly corresponds to its English counterpart in sentences, such as 'a lesson to be learned', when indicating something that is to be done.[28]

lū mimma ša a-ka-li 'or whatever there is to eat' MAL A § 31:47–48

mimma ša la a-ka-li qaqqadamma uta$^{??}$*ar* 'he will return the capital of anything not edible' MAL A § 43:37–38

māʾū kī ša ḫi-a-qi iṣ[ṣarruḫū] 'the water that is for mixing will be heated' PKT 3 iii 8

kī māʾē ša ra-ma-ki ṣarḫat 'when it is hot as water for bathing' PKT 4 obv. left 17

eqla u Libbi-āle ša pa-la-ḫi-šu-nu e-pa-aš 'he will serve them outside and in the inner city (Aššur)' KAJ 1:10–11

ša ipṭiri ša PN *ša za-ka-i-ša ina bēte* (...) *šaknat* 'concerning the ransom (money) of ^{f}PN, for her clearance, it is placed in the house' KAJ 7:31–33

27 The original copy of KAV 201 is erroneous; for an improved version, see Freydank (1997b).
28 See GOA § 20.3.2.2; cf. GAG, 250 § 150b.

1 *quppu ša sa-su nāgire* 'one chest with proclamations of the herald' KAJ 310:20

ša a-la-ki ù tu-a-ri din 'give it for going and returning' MATC 24A:19

ša libbika ša še-lu-i-ka šēli [u š]a še-ru-di-ka šērid 'what you want to remove, remove it! And what you want to add, add it!' MATSH 9:12–13

Rarely do we find the infinitive as the verbal predicate of a main clause. This only occurs in administrative documents, such as notes:

qaqqad ŠE *i+na ad-ra-te a-na ma-da-di* 'for measuring out the capital of barley at the threshing floors' KAJ 83:19–20

5 *emāru* ŠE PN *zarʾu a-na ra-bu-e* 'five homers of barley (for) PN to increase the seed (for agriculture)' MATC 44:1–3

2 *emāru* ŠE PN *a-na ṭé-a-ni* 'two homers of barley (for) PN are for grinding' MATC 44:4–6

§ 652 Infinitives are most frequently used following a preposition. With the preposition *ana*, the infinitive occurs in its most basic function, i.e., to specify the resultative action of the finite verb. In this respect, *ana* functions in a similar way to the English 'to' before infinitives in constructions, such as 'he went home to sleep'. This construction is partly replaced in MA with the abstractum (see § 252).

šumma mussa a-na pa-ṭa-ri-ša lā imaggur 'if her husband does not agree to release her' MAL A § 5:66–67

ana aʾīle a-na ni-a-ki tattidinši ''she gave her to the man for fornicating' MAL A § 23:16

1? *marīnē* (…) *a-na ṣa-ra-pí tadnaššu* 'one(?) *m.*-textile is given to him for tanning' A 305:12–15

a-na ša-ad-du-ni ittidin 'he has given it for distribution' KAJ 109:20–21

a-na ḫa-mu-ṭí dinā luḫammiṭū 'give it with haste, they must make haste' KAV 103:30

a-na la ma-ša-e šaṭir 'it is given in order not to forget' A 1724 (NTA, 17):11–12

ammīša a-na bi-a-di allaka 'I will go there to spend the night' MATC 2:17–18

20 *niggallu* (…) PN *a-na e-ṣa-di maḫir* 'PN received 20 sickles for harvesting' T 96-3:1–6

With the preposition *ina*, the infinitive is usually used in an adverbial manner. As such, the preposition occurs in its temporal function. As von Soden states, this construction often replaces dependent clauses (GAG 251 § 150g).

i+na a-la-ki la-a iqarribašše 'upon returning he will not approach her' MAL A § 36:101

i-na 19-*šu ù* 20-*šu ta-ba-ki* 'at the 19th and 20th time of pouring' PKT 5 r. 1

i+na na-ma-re 'at dawn' MATSH 2:23

iltu libbīka [tad]danabbub i+na tu-ša-aḫ-ru-ri-ma a-di […] *taṣalli* 'you keep *poundering* while you keep silent' MATSH 9:36–37

Sometimes, this infinitive construction is used as an attributive to another noun:

mussa i+na mu-a-te iltu bētīša lā tuṣṣa 'when her husband died, she does not leave the house' MAL A § 46:90–91

ana bāb DN *i+na ka-ša-di šarru ana bēt ile [er]rab* 'when arriving at the gate of DN, the king will enter the temple' Coronation Ritual i 30

[i]kribēšunu ina ga-am-mu-ri (…) *[ulta]naknannū* 'when they finish their blessings, they prostrate themselves' Coronation Ritual ii 37–38

simunu i+na ka-ša-di bēlu (…) *errab* 'when the time arrives, the lord will enter' Ištar Ritual:1

3 *me* 95 *emāru* ŠE *a[n]a tarbā[ṣe an]a karme i+na e-ra-be ana e[m]i[tte š]a karmi ša qanni ša a[tū]n pappi[re]* '395 homers of barley in the courtyard of the granary, at the entrance to the right side, which is at the granary, which is at the fringe of the beer-bread oven' MARV 2 23 r. 10'–12'

This temporal adverbial construction is also attested in the status construct:

i+na e-ri-ib ḫarrānīšunu 'upon the return of their caravan' KAJ 32:7–8

i+na ṣa-bat nikkasse^{meš} 'at the settling of accounts' KAJ 255:4

Another temporal adverbial construction is found with the preposition *iltu* (Aro 1961, 258–59). The nuance is slightly different from *ina* as the *iltu* construction indicates duration, similar to the present perfect. It could be argued that *iltu* is used in this infinitive construction as a conjunction, as it is attested with a number of finite verbs (§ 729). Under this assumption, the examples below can be regarded as temporal dependent clauses with an infinitive as verbal predicate.

iltu niqiāte ka-ša-a-di sinniltu (…) *ana pan [ša]rre lā terra[b]* 'when the time for making sacrifices draws near, a woman shall not approach the king' MAPD § 7:46–47

iltu asāyāte (…) *na-ša-a-ri-i-ka ammar qable ulli* 'as soon as you have deduced the towers, raise it as much as the middle' MATC 4:18–21

iltu ammāka i+na tu-a-ri (…) *din* 'when he returns from there, give!' MATC 6:8–12

iltu EN *na-ma-ši-šu* (…) […] 'after my lord's departure' MATSH 8:25'

The preposition *kī* is rarely attested, but it can express a comparison in the sense of 'like' or even a complement clause. In this sense, the following two passages are similar to infinitive constructions with *ana*:

šumma 1 *a'īlu āliku ša ḫurāde ina panī paḫitīšu lū āla iṣbat ū lū ki-i ra-qa-e ana* GN *ērub* 'if one man coming from battle settled on (the land of) his province or city, or *like secretly* entered GN' MARV 4 119:25–28

annūte ana bīr[āte] lušēber kī ina āle la-a še-ṣu-e u āle la-a š[e-l]u-⸢e⸣ 'I shall bring those (troops) across to the fortifications, so that there is no exit or entry in the city' MATSH 8:26'–27'

Following the preposition *aššum*, the infinitive is only rarely attested. It is used in the sense of 'in order to' (Aro 1961, 266–67).

mimma anniu aššum la ma-ša-e šaṭir 'all this is written down in order not to be forgotten' KAJ 256:12–14

According to Aro (1961, 277), *ana muḫḫi* replaces *aššum* in this construction in NA. However, it is also attested in one passage from MA.

ana muḫḫi du-a-ki telli 'you are approaching (your) death' OIP 79 3:19–20

§ 653 Note that the infinitive can take some syntactical features, which are typical of a finite verb, where the infinitive takes a subject and a direct object (cf. Kouwenberg 2010, 197). It is especially common to find the subject expressed as a pronominal suffix (Aro 1961, 200ff).

ša emuša i+na e-ra-bi-ša iddinaššenni 'what her father-in-law gave her upon her entering' MAL A § 29:14–15

iltu asāyāte (..) *na-ša-a-ri-i-ka ammar qabli ulli* 'as soon as you have deduced the towers, raise it as much as the middle' MATC 4:18–21

i+na tu-a-ri-šu šēbila 'send him here when he returns' MATC 4:32–33

iltu EN *na-ma-ši-šu* 'after my lord's departure' MATSH 8:25'

ša libbika ša še-lu-i-ka še-li [*u š*]*a še-ru-di-ka šērid* 'what you want to remove, remove it and what you want to add, add it!' MATSH 9:13

In the case of the third-person singular, a pronominal suffix is not obligatory, similar to the stative.

mussa i+na mu-a-te iltu bētīša lā tuṣṣa 'since her husband's death, she does not leave her house' MAL A § 46:90–91

iltu niqiāte ka-ša-a-di 'when the time for making sacrifices draws near' MAPD § 7:46

i+na tu-a-ri ŠE-*am u tibna ana sisīe*^{meš}-*šu din* 'give barley and straw to his horses on his return' MATC 6:9–12

Note that, in many cases, this 'finite' construction of the infinitive forms the predicate of an adverbial clause, although none of these cases takes a subjunctive.

iltu tuppī a-ma-ri-ka (…) *šupur* 'when you see my tablet (…) send' MATC 5:3–5

17.8 The ventive

§ 654 The MA ventive is represented by two different morphemes: *-a* (< *-am*) and *-ne* (< *-nim*). The first morpheme is attached to a verbal stem ending in a consonant (*iprus+a*), while the second morpheme is attached to a stem ending in a vowel: (*iprusū+ne*). This effectively divides the two between verbs in the singular (*-a*) and verbs in the plural (*-ne*). For the sound change *-im* > *-em*, see § 240. The ending for the prefix conjugation 2fs (*taprusī*) was *-m* in older Akkadian. Verbs of the 2fs type are almost non-existent in the MA corpus, but it is likely that this type of verb simply lost the possibility of a ventive. Alternatively, it is possible that *-ī* > *-ē*, under the influence of the dropped mimation, although there is no material to back this up. In the chain of morphemes added to the finite verb, the ventive follows directly before the subjunctive or pronominal suffixes. Ventives can be attached to statives, although available examples continue to be rare. Attestations remain limited to 3ms and 3fp, which were probably not common, as they are not attested in OA either (GKT, 130f § 67b). In MA, the ventive is also attested on the 3fs stative (*šēṣuatanni* KAV 205:6), which is a feature that it has in common with MB.[29]

elāʾu Š — *še-⸢lu⸣-a-ta-an-ni* A 1722:10
uṣāʾu Š — *še-ṣu-a-ta-ni* KAV 205:6; MATC 64:30
še-ṣu-a-ta KAJ 122:11

§ 655 The functions of the ventive, as first described by Landsberger (1923) and more recently by Kouwenberg, are also valid for MA.[30] We can divide the ventive into three different groups: the ventive used as an allative, as a dative and as a linking morpheme between the accusative/dative pronominal suffixes (Kouwenberg 2010, 233–34). The allative is a directional element, indicating motion towards the speech event. This feature can drastically change the meaning of a verb, at least in our perception. The verb *alāku* 'to go (away from the speech event)' becomes, with the ventive, 'to come (towards a speech event)'. Thus, we find *al-la-ka* 'I will come' Faist 2001, 252:27 (with the ventive) vs. *a-na* ÌD-*i-id il-lu-ú-ku* 'they will go to the river' MAL A § 17:71 (without the ventive). As an allative, the ventive is mostly used on motion verbs, such as *alāku* 'to go'; *ubālu* 'to bring'; *šapāru* 'to send'. W. Mayer offered a list of such verbs often carrying a ventive in MA (UGM, 71), while Hecker did the same for OA (GKT, 131–32 § 78d). There does not seem to be a verb that cannot take a ventive when used as an allative, while any verb that can take an indirect object will have a ventive preceding the dative pronominal suffix. Only very rarely can a ventive remain unexplained:

agāru D — *anāku agrāni ú-ug-ga-ra* 'I will hire hirelings' MATC 4:10–11
amāru — *ēnē n[āqidē] e-ta-am-ra* 'I met the herds' MATC 10:15–16
balāṭu — *ù*$^{!}$ *ib-ta-al-ṭa ittebe* 'and he became healthy (and) stood up' MATSH 8:50'
kaʾʾulu D — *ša* PN (...) *panēšunu ú-ka-i-la-ni* 'of whom PN was in charge' CTMMA 1 99:5–6
qaʾʾû D — 5 ^{lú}*sirašû*^{meš} (…) *a[mmāk]a* (?) *lu-qa-i-a* 'he should wait for five brewers there' MATC 12:6
zarāʾu — 2 *sūta*$^{\text{ta.àm}}$ *i-za-ru-a* 'they will sow two seahs each' LVUH 96:16

§ 656 Kouwenberg (2002) distinguished three main functions of the allative: referring to an unspecific goal, a specific locational goal and a specific personal goal. All three are attested in MA. The unspecified goal is not mentioned in the context and does not refer directly to the location of the speaker him/herself or the recipient.

išātu ana eliš te-el-li-a 'the fire rises upwards' PKT 1 II right 19

ša iltu GN *<ú>-še-ṣi-a-ni-ma* 'who brought out (a cow) (towards this direction) from GN' AO 20.157:6–7

ša ḫarrāni (…) *ub-la-an-ni* 'as for the caravan (…) he brought here' KAJ 274:3–5

siparru$^{\text{pl.}}$ *annūtu* [*ša*] *ēkalle ú-ta-e-ru-ni-ni* 'these bronzes, which they returned the palace' KAJ 303:12–14

ša PN *tamkāru ú-ta-e-ra-ni* 'what PN the merchant put back' KAV 98:16–17

29 See GAG, 134 § 82d; cf. Kouwenberg (2010, 223 n76).

30 Kouwenberg (2010, 235 n85) complained about the lack of studies on the Assyrian ventive, but noted that there did not seem to be much difference between Assyrian and Babylonian dialect. Upon inspection, this indeed seems to be the case for MA; in any event, we seem to be able to distinguish the main functions of the ventive, according to Kouwenberg (2002), with only ventive anticipation missing.

ša rēš šarre ina ^{giš}*eleppe*$^{\text{<meš>}}$ *iltu* GN *iš-ši-an-ni* 'which the eunuch of the king brought here in ships from GN' MARV 9 58:6–8

kī marʾu ana bētīšu ú-ṣa-an-ni 'when the son goes out to his house' A 3196 (NTA, 39):21–22

adi ūmū iṭibbūni ana libnāte ú-ru-du-ni 'as long as the weather is good, they will come down for bricks' MATC 3:7–8

aššum ṣabʾemma (…) *ša la-a ú-na-me-ša-ni* 'concerning the troops (…) who have not set out (towards you)' MATSH 3:33–34

ana bābe la-a ⌜*uṣ*⌝*-ṣa-a* 'he does not go out to the gate' MATSH 8:51'

m[*unna*]*bdu ša i-na-bi-da-an-ni* 'the refugee, who fled to this place/me' MATSH 12:8

Sūtīū iltu GN *e-te-li-ú-ni iqtibiūne* 'Suteans from GN came up and said to me' T 93-54:4–6

As an unspecified goal can be rather subjective, we may also add to this category some cases where we cannot directly pinpoint a general direction:

ana qāt 5 *šanāte ú-taḫ-ḫi-ra* 'he was delayed beyond five years' MAL A § 36:6

šumma ana qāt 6 *šanāte ú-ḫi-ra-an-ni* 'if he was delayed beyond six years' MAL A § 36:103–104

ša amta paṣṣunta ētamrūni i-ṣa-ba-ta-aš-ši 'whoever will have seen a covered maid will seize her' MAL A § 40:89-90 ~ *i-<ṣa>-ba-as-si* MAL A § 40:69

sinniltu ša ēkal[*le*] *la-a ta-šap-pa-ra-am-ma* 'a woman of the palace shall not send (for anything)' MAPD § 6:42–43

[*i*]*ltu bēt Adad ú-ṣu-ni* 'they go out from the Temple of Adad' Adad Ritual:6

rēḫti ḫarrānātīšunu [*i*]*l-te-qe-ú-ni it-tu-um-šu-ni* 'they continued the rest of their journey and set out towards (the speaker/recipient)' MATSH 6:24'–25'

alpēšu gabba lu-pa-ḫi-ra 'may he gather all his oxen' T 97-17:8–9

With a specified goal, the location of the directed motion is mentioned, which is usually a GN. It is necessary that the speaker identifies this location as his general direction or the direction of the recipient (Kouwenberg 2002, 206–7):

PN *ammīša i-la-a-ka* 'PN will come there' MATC 12:3–4

ana panē māte e-tab-ra 'I crossed over (the river) to the entrance of the land' MATSH 2:14

tamkārū (…) *ina šaplān* GN *e-tab-ru-ni* 'the merchants (...) crossed over here below the land of GN' MATSH 6:16'–18'

PN [*ša ana muḫ*]*ḫi šarre i-li-ka-ni Puratta e-tab-ra* 'PN, who came to the king, crossed the Euphrates (to him)' MATSH 17:7'–8'

30 *ṣabʾu* (…) *ana šubte ina mūše annie e-tar-bu-ú-ni* '30 troops took position this night' T 93-2:4–6

§ 657 The allative can also have a personal goal. In this case, the allative is rather similar to the dative in usage and function. However, for an allative direction/dative to the first person, there is no morphological difference, although, in many cases, we find the personal goal expressed with additional prepositional phrases, such as *ana muḫḫīya*, to indicate the goal specifically (Kouwenberg 2002, 208):

ana muḫḫīyama lu-ub-lu-ni 'may they bring it to me' KAV 98:35

anaʾīne PN *marā šipre ana muḫḫīya il-li-ka-ma* 'why did PN the messenger come to me?' RS 06.198:7–9

Such an extra marker is not obligatory when the goal is clear from the context:

mānaʾīne ṭēm bēte la ta-šap-pa-ra 'thus, why do you not send me news about the house?' MATSH 12:41

ṭēmu iktalda 'a report has arrived here (with me)' MATSH 14:5

An allative ventive referring to direction in the second person only requires a ventive, rather than a ventive and a dative pronominal suffix: short *altapra* 'I sent (towards you)' instead of longer *altaprakku* 'I sent to you'/'I wrote to you'. Similar to the first person, a pronominal suffix is instead found on a prepositional phrase, such as *ana muḫḫīka* (see Kouwenberg 2002, 210–13 § 3.3.2; cf. 2010, 234–35; GOA § 19.10.2):

adi 5 umē ana muḫḫika anāku (…) *al-la-ka* 'within five days I will come (to you)' KAJ 316:4–6

1 *mana erīu* x 7½ *šiqlu ann*[*uku*] *paṣīu billātēšu ul-te-bi-l*[*a*] 'one mina of copper x 7½ shekels of white tin, its alloy he sent (to you)' KAV 205:16–17

panēma iltu aḫāʾiš niddubub tattatlak ⸢*la-a*⸣ *ta-tu-ra* 'previously, we talked together, but you left and did not return (to me/here)' NP 46:6–9

[*an*]*āku áš-pu-ra* 'I wrote (to you)' MATSH 26:3'

ana muḫḫīk[*a*] *ul-te-bi-la-š*[*i*] 'I will have sent her (to you)' VAT 8851:13–14

anāku la-tal-ka 'I want to leave (for you)' Faist 2001, 252:32

The same phenomenon is likewise attested for the third person (cf. Kouwenberg 2002, 214–15):

ša ana eleppe ša PN *ak-ru-ra-ni* 'that I loaded on the boat of PN' KAJ 302:11

suḫīrta [...] *ša ina pitti* PN *e-zi-ba-ni* 'a foal that I left in the responsibility of PN' MATC 3:9–13

ana muḫḫi PN *ul-te-bi-la* 'I sent it to PN' MATSH 22:23–25

While not obligatory, a pronominal suffix is added to a number of phrases (cf. Kouwenberg 2002, 211). In this case, only a dative pronominal suffix can be used, since it is used as an indirect object, rather than a direct object of the verb.

PN *šuršurrāte sipa*[*rre*$^{\text{pl.}}$] *amtaḫaṣ ul-te-bi-lak-ku-n*[*u*] 'I will have put PN in fetters and sent (him) to you' KAV 96:5–8

MUNU$_4$? *ma-a-ki*? *a-šap-pa-ra-ku* 'I will send you …' MATC 12:32

PN$_1$ *u* PN$_2$ *i-lu-ku-ni-ku* 'PN$_1$ and PN$_2$ will come to you' MATC 18:4–6

PN *ul-te-bi-*⸢*lak*⸣*-ku* 'I have made PN bring them to you' MATSH 9:6

§ 658 Very rarely, a ventive occurs in combination with an accusative pronominal suffix. This seems to be (at least in MA) limited to the cases where the ventive and accusative are not complementary to each other (cf. Kouwenberg 2002, 222):

$^{f}PN_1$ PN_2 iltu *bēte* PN_3 *ip-ṭu-ra-ši-⌜ma⌝* ‘PN_2 has released $^{f}PN_1$ from the house of PN_3’ KAJ 7:2–5

ūma iltu mugerre ša tuṣṣaʾanni še-bi-la-šu ‘send him to me today with the chariot that goes out to me’ MATC 32 (full)

This ventive is not uncommon for the *paṭāru*, but it usually appears to take an accusative, rather than a dative (CAD P, 292–95). The action seems to consist of releasing the female pledge (*-ši* i/o dative *-še*) and taking her away from the house (ventive *-a*) where she was detained.

17.9 The subjunctive

§ 659 The subjunctive in Akkadian is used to mark a verb in a relative clause. Morphologically, the Assyrian version *-ūni* is more complicated than the Babylonian *-u*. Unlike the situation in the OA corpus (GKT, 133f § 79; GOA § 16.9.10), the short and long forms do not occur next to each other; in the few cases where short forms do occur, they have to be regarded as Babylonianisms. The Assyrian subjunctive *-(ū)ni* is already found in OAkk, although the Babylonian *-u* is clearly favoured (Hasselbach 2005, 207). An explanation for its appearance in Akkadian has still to be found (cf. Streck 1998a, 527), although Hecker (GKT, 133f § 79) assumed that the co-existence of the short and long form in OA was due to an initial differentiation in function. It was suggested by Kouwenberg (2010, 228) that the subjunctive *-ūni* derived from a longer Proto-Akkadian plural form *yiprusūni*, which is similar to the Arabic *yafʿalūna* (يفعلون). This long form would later remain limited to subordinate clauses in the Assyrian dialect. In OA, *-u* is mostly used for forms ending in a radical, while *-ni* follows a vowel. The occurrence of the combination form *-ūni* is likely to have been a later development (Bar-am 1938, 27). This longer form became standard in MA, although we also find attestations in OA, where it was already optional (GKT, 134 § 79d).

§ 660 The /u/ of the subjunctive is added directly to the root of the verb, even if the final radical is a vowel: *iqbiūni*. In the cases of a plural marker, the /u/ elides: 3fp *išpurā+ūni* > *išpurāni*.

aḫāzu D	*aḫ-ḫu-za-a-ni* MAPD § 3:22
duāku	*i-du-ka-a-ni* MAPD § 10:57
laqāʾu	*il-qé-ú-ni* KAJ 8:22
našāru	*na-áš-ra-ni* KAJ 119:5
qabāʾu	*iq-bi-ú-ni* MAL A § 41:8
ṣalāʾu	*i-ṣa-li-ú-ni* Coronation Ritual ii 28

The /ū/ also elides on plural verbs ending in a vowel. The 3mp of the finite verb has become indistinguishable from the 3ms:

ḫapāʾu	*iḫ-pi-ú-ni* T 93-44:17 (3mp)
laqāʾu	*il-qe-ú-ni* T 96-8:15 (3ms)
maḫāru	*im-ḫu-ru-ú-ni* MAL A § 3:41 (3ms)

	im-ḫu-ru-ni KAJ 109:11 (3mp)
rakāsu	*i-ra-ka-su-ni* Coronation Ritual i 40 (3ms)
šaṭāru	*il-ṭu-ru-ni* KAV 119:15 (3ms)

The subjunctive comes after the ventive in the chain of added suffixes to the verb. As the ventive ends in a vowel, the vowel /u/ of the subjunctive elides; however, the final *-m* of the ventive assimilates into /n/ of the subjunctive: 3ms *išpuranni*; 3mp *išpurūnenni*.

alāku	*il-li-ku-ni-ni* MARV 1 1 iv 34
etāqu	*e-te-qa-an-ni* MATSH 4:6
laqāʾu	*il-qe-ú-ni-ni* KAV 99:39
qabāʾu	*táq-bi-an-ni* Billa 67:5
ṣalāʾu	[*i-ṣ*]*a-li-ú-ni-ni* Coronation Ritual iv 23†
šapāru	*iš-pu-ra-ni* MATSH 2:15
tuāru D	*ú-ta-e-ru-ni-ni* KAJ 303:14
ubālu	*it-ta-ab-lu-né-en-ni* MAL B § 6:23
uṣāʾu Š	*ú-še-ṣi-ú-ni-ni* MARV 1 23:3

In MA, the subjunctive *-ūni* is taken apart when a pronominal suffix is added: *išpur* +*ūni* +*šu* > *išpurū-šu-ni*. This distinguishes it from the ventive on plural verbs, which should come before the pronominal suffix: *išpurūneššu*.

aḫāzu	*aḫ-zu-ši-ni* MAL A § 40:61
amāru	*ta-mu-ru-ši-ni* MAPD § 19:93
emādu	*e-mi-du-šu-ni* MAPD § 21:109
epāšu	*e-*⸢*ep*⸣*-pa-ša-a-ši-in-n*[*i*] MATSH 11:17
ḫapāʾu	*taḫ-ṭí-a-ši-ni* MAPD § 18:84
laqāʾu	*ta-al-ti-qi-ú-ši-ni* MAL A § 23:29
qabāʾu	*iq-bi-áš-šu-un-ni* MAL A § 47:11
ṣabātu D	*ki-i* PN *ú-ṣa-bi-tu-šu-ni* A 3196 (NTA, 39):11

It is also possible for the *-ni* of the subjunctive to follow the plural ventive *-ni(m)*:

alāku	*il-lu-ku-ú-ni-ni* T 97-10:23
laqāʾu	*il-qe-ú-ni-ni* KAV 99:39
qabāʾu	*i-qa-bi-ú-ni-šu-nu-ni* MATC 83:14
uṣāʾu Š	*ú-še-ṣi-ú-ni-ni* MARV 1 23:3; MATC 42:10

§ 661 Although arguably not a verbal form, Assyrian has no problem adding the subjunctive to the stative. While, in Babylonian, the subjunctive was limited to the third person (Kouwenberg 2010, 221), the subjunctive is more widespread in the MA paradigm. Examples are abundant in MA; however, as with the prefix conjugation, masculine plural forms with the plural marker *-ū* remain morphologically identical to the singular. In OA, the situation was different, as3ms *PaRiS* received *-u*, while all other forms received *-ni* (GOA § 16.9.10.3). As such, the 3fs stative *qar-ru-bat-ni* KAJ 223:4 may be an exceptional archaic form in MA (Kouwenberg 2010, 223), such that we cannot assume a missing sign due to syllabic borders (*qar/ru/bat/ni* ~ **qar/ru/ba/tū/ni*). At the same time, /ū/ of *-ūni* is frequently omitted in NA (Luukko 2004, 36 § 3.8). Unfortunately, there are no attestations of a subjunctive on statives of the first- and second-person plural forms. From OA, we know that *-ūni* could also be used for first- and second-person forms, e.g., *na-áš-a-ku-ni* BIN 4 7:21; *wa-áš-ba-tù-nu-/ni* CCT 5 80:6 (cf. Bar-am 1938, 19). In OA, the stative 3fs was built by adding only *-ni*, e.g., *da-am-qá-at-ni* CCT 4 24b:19; however, in MA, the normal *-ūni* is found (GAG, 135 § 83b). We have a few examples of a stative in combination with the singular ventive and subjunctive, but no plural forms. We thus find *-a(m)+ni*, but never *-ne+ni*.

3ms:

balātu	*bal-ṭu-ú-ni* MAL A § 3:33
muātu	*me-tu-ú-ni* A 3197 (NTA, 40):11
rakāsu	*ra-ak-su-ú-ni* KAJ 225:18
šakānu	*ša-ak-nu-ú-ni* MATC 22:19

3ms with ventive *-a(m)*:

erābu Š	*še-ru-ba-a-ni* AO 19.227:10
našā'u	*na-ṣa-a-ni* MATC 3:14

3fs *-ni*:

qarābu D	*qar-ru-bat-ni* KAJ 223:4
šaṭāru D	*šaṭ-ru-ut-ni* TR 2018:4; TR 3012:7

3fs *-ūni*:

marāṣu	*mar-ṣu-tu-ú-ni* A 1765 (NTA, 25):5
našā'u	*na-ṣa-tu-ú-ni* MAL A § 35:77
šakānu	*ša-ak-nu-tu-ni* KAV 205:7

3fs with ventive *-a(m)*:

uṣā'u Š	*še-ṣu-a-ta-ni* KAV 205:6

2ms:

ḫadā'u	*ḫa-di-a-ta-a-ni* MATC 15:9

1cs:

ušābu	*us-ba-ku-ni* T 93-11:17

3mp:

maḫāru	*maḫ-ru-ni* MARV 1 34:6
šakānu	*ša-ak-nu-ni* Coronation Ritual i 37; KAJ 120:9; KAV 103:12

3fp:

aḫāzu D	*aḫ-ḫu-za-a-ni* MAPD § 3:22
šaṭāru	*ša-aṭ-ra-ni* MARV 1 38:7
tadānu	*ta-ad-na-ni* MATC 15:5

Moreover, the 3fs stative is also notable for its alternation between VA and the absence of VA. We have already discussed the development of the secondary /a/ [ə] before a subjunctive, instead of the expected VA (see § 151). This seems to be the case with these stative forms, where the sound change that resulted in [ə] had not fully spread throughout the paradigm, such that we still find alternations.

With VA:

aḫāzu	*aḫ-zu-tu-ú-ni* MAL A § 45:75

ḫadāʾu	*ḫa-di-<ú>-⌜tu⌝-ú-ni* MAL A § 33:70
laqāʾu	*la-qé-ú-tu-ni* KAJ 167:6
marāṣu	*ki-i* PN *mar-ṣu-tu-ú-ni* 'when PN (f.) was sick' A 1765 (NTA, 25):4–5
qarābu D	*a-na* LUGAL *qar-ru-bat-ni* 'which was offered to the king' KAJ 223:4
ulādu	*ul-du-tu-ú-ni* MAL A § 45:77
ušābu	*us-bu-tu-ni* MAL A § 24:57

Without VA:

aḫāzu	⌜*la-a aḫ*⌝*-za-tu-ú-ni* MAL A § 55:11
namāru	*nam-ra-tu-ni* Ištar Ritual:12
našāʾu	*na-ṣa-tu-ú-ni* MAL A § 35:77
patāʾu	*pa-te-a-tu-ú-ni* MAL A § 55:10

§ 662 Frequently, we find a short subjunctive *-u* on the prefix conjugation. We have to regard these forms as due to Babylonian influence, although an OA archaism cannot be totally excluded:

aššassu <*ša*> *im-ḫu-ṣu-ú-ma* 'his wife whom he hit' MAL A § 50:75–76

1 *pitnu ša urki kussīe iz-za-zu* 'one chest that stands behind the throne' KTN inventory iii 11'

ina libbi GIŠ^{meš} *ša* PN *li-pu-šu dinā ina libbi* GIŠ^{meš} *ša āle li-pu-šu* EN *ṭēma lišpura* 'may they make it from the wood of PN, give (them). May they make it from the wood of the city, may my lord send me instructions' A 1476 r. 5'–10'

annuku anniu ša (…) *ša*$^{!}$*-aṭ-ru* 'this lead, which is recorded' AO 19.229:19–20 (EAd/Aub)

adi tuppi dannata i-ša-ṭu-ru annītuma dannat 'until they will write a valid tablet, this one is valid' KAJ 12:20–21 (Aub) cf. KAJ 152:18–20 (Aub)

ammar i-ba$^{!}$*ši-ú* 'as much as there is' KAJ 67:16 (Aub)

ša PN (…) *id-di-nu* 'which PN has given' KAJ 175:4–7 (EAd/Aub)

ina mimma mānaḫāti ša PN *abušu ú-ša-du-šu* 'from whatever equipment that PN, his father, had gathered for him' KAM 10 25:12–14 (Aub)

zukur mā ni[*ip*]*qid* [x x] *aʾīla i-šar-ri-qu* 'let us *hand over* […] the man who steals'' Billa 66:18–19

ina ūme annaka u ṣibtušu i-ḫi-ṭu šaprātema ipaṭṭar 'he will release the pledges on the day that he will weigh out the lead and its interest' TR 3021:15–17

Similar to the prefix conjugation, sometimes the Babylonian subjunctive *-u* is attached to the third-person masculine singular stative, instead of the longer form *-ūni*:

ana pāʾi tuppe ša abīšuma PN *ša ana marʾutti* (…) *ša-aṭ-ru* 'according to the wording of the tablet of his father PN, which was written for adoption' KAJ 6:4–7

ša šume PN *ina pî tuppi šiāti ša-ak-nu* 'that the name of PN is put on this tablet' KAJ 165:4–6

kī šapārti ša-ak-nu 'it is placed as a pledge' KAJ 165:12

In some cases, the subjunctive is absent from the prefix conjugation and stative:

ša iltu šarre ana ḫurāde (…) *it-ti-ši*<*-ú-ni*> 'who set out with the king on campaign' MARV 1 1 iv 40–41 (TN) *ammar zabāle ma-ṣa-ta-*<*ni*> 'as much as you are able to carry' MARV 1 15:12–13 (TN)

ša la-at-ku-ú-<*ni*> 'which are tested' MARV 3 38:7 (Nae)

^{giš}*eleppa*^{meš} *ša ḫurdāte ša ap-pa-*⸢*ra*⸣ (≠ *appurā-ni*) 'ships of beams, which are covering (the boats)' MARV 4 34:16'–17' (TN)

LÚ *ša šēzub rammīšu la-a i-da-gal* 'a man who does not look at his own salvation' MATSH 9:42 (TN)

The omission of /ū/ in *-ūni* is regarded as a scribal convention, rather than representing a phonologic change.[31] Attestations are found more frequently in NA, although there are one or two possible cases in MA:

laqā'u	*il-qe-ni* TR 121:7'†
šaṭāru	*il-ṭu-ur-ni* MAL C+ § 11:23[32]

§ 663 The verbal predicate of the dependent clause always takes the subjunctive *-ūni*, which is an important marker of the end of the relative clause, as it is often directly followed by the verbal predicate of the main clause. In the case of the lack of a verbal predicate in the relative sentence, a substantive or pronoun carries a subjunctive similar to the one attested in OA.[33]

šumma kī DAM-*at* LÚ-*ni lā ide* 'if he did not know that she is a wife' MAL A § 14:36 cf. MAL A § 13:28–29; MAL A § 14:32

iltu muḫḫi mar'e rabīe adi muḫḫi mar'e ṣeḫre ša 10 MU^{meš}-*šu-ni ana ša ḫadiūni iddan* 'from the oldest to the youngest son, who is at least 10 years old, he will give (her) to whomever he wishes' MAL A § 43:24–26

ina bēt mar'ēša ašar pa-nu-ša-a-ni tuššab 'she shall reside in the house of (one of) her own sons, wherever she chooses' MAL A § 46:93–94

1 *iku eqlu kirīu ša būrtu ina lib-bi-šu-n*[*i*] '1 *iku* field (and) orchard, in which there is a well' KAJ 13:13–14

ina zittīšu ašar A.ŠÀ-*šu-ni damqu išallim* 'he will obtain compensation from his share, wherever his field is' KAJ 148:30–31

tupni[*nna*] *ša ṣubāte* (…) *i+na lìb-bi-ni šēṣiāne* 'take out the box with textile in it' KAV 105:11–13

kī ša ṭé-mu-ni bēlī lišpura 'may my lord write me what (his) orders are' MARV 1 71:29–30

EN *kī ša ṭé-mu-un-ni lišpura* 'may my lord write me what (his) orders are' MATSH 12:39

ammar šu-ut-ni ṭēma šuṭrāne 'as much as it is, write me a message' MCS 2 2:13–14

iltu ṭé-mu-k[*a*] *ana* PN *qibya* 'say to PN according to your report' MATC 7:8–9

31 See Parpola (1972, 24); Postgate (1974, 274); Luukko (2004, 36 § 3.8).

32 According to Freydank (1994, 207), Schroeder erroneously copied UR, instead of RU in KAV 6, as is visible on the tablet.The available photos of the tablet (VAT 10093) are not convincing in my opinion.

33 Cf. GKT, 134 § 79c; GOA § 16.9.10.5; MA UGM, 112 § 102.3.

kanīka ša ŠIM^{meš}*-ni ūtaggir* 'I have written a sealed document that is about aromatic plants' TabT05a-134:23–24

The subjunctive is not always marked:

anāku ^{lú}*sirašê*^{meš} *ša an-na-ka ammēšama alaqqea* 'I will take the brewers, who are here, there' MATC 9:22–25

ki-ma PN *marā šipre* [*an*]*a muḫḫīya il-la-*⸢*ka*⸣ *u anāku mīnummê aḫūya* [*i*]*ṣabbutū*[*ni an*]*āk*[*u a*]*na muḫḫi* [*aḫ*]*īya ušebbala* [*arḫi*]*š* 'when PN, the messenger, will come to me then I shall send to my brother quickly whatever my brother wants to take' RS 06.198:21–27

§ 664 Very rarely do we find a subjunctive added to an infinitive (see UGM, 107 § 96.2). The case ending is retained in these attestations. With the subjunctive attached directly to the base, the status rectus is used; however, when the subjunctive is preceded with a pronominal suffix, we find the status constructus.

sinniltu ša ēkalle ša lā qa-ra-ab-ša-ni 'a palace woman who is not to be approached' MAPD § 7:47 (cf. Aro 1961, 297–98)

ša la-a mar-ru-ru-ni iqabbiū 'they will report, who is not turned into a eunuch' MAPD § 8:50[34]

sarta ša ammea a-na e-ma-di-ni ana iyāši lēmedūnni 'may they impose the penalty on me, which is there to impose' AO 19.227:21–23

lubulta (…) *ša ina pitti ša muḫḫi bēte na-áš-ku-ša-ni* 'clothing that is to be placed in the responsibility of the housemaster' KAV 99:37–38 (Sa)

2 *emāru* 8 *sūtu* ŠE-*um* (...) *ša ana ginā*ʾ*e* (….) *ta-da-šu-nu-ni ša qāt* PN$_1$ (…) [*in*]*a muḫḫi* PN$_2$ (…) *iddan* 'two homers and eight seahs of flour that are given for the *ginā*ʾ*u*, (and) which are in the charge of PN$_1$, (incumbent) on PN$_2$, he will give it' MARV 3 35:1–13 (Aššnīr III/Eku)

5 *emāru* 2 *qa qēmu* (…) *ša ana ginā*ʾ*e* (…) *ta-*⸢*da*⸣*-šu-ni ša qāt* PN$_1$ (…) *ina muḫḫi* PN$_2$ (…) *iddan* 'five homers and two litres of flour, which is given to him for the *ginā*ʾ*u* (and) which are in the charge of PN$_1$, (incumbent) on PN$_2$, he will give it' MARV 3 40:1–12 (Aššnīr III/Eku)

⸢*ša*⸣*-ma-al-li-a a-na* ⸢*e*!⸣*-pa-še-ni* 'which the apprentice will execute (?)' MARV 10 3:6 (see de Ridder 2015b, 121)

ša ana tamlê rabīe a-na e-ra-bi-ni […] 'which is at the entrance to the large terrace' LVUH 87:9–11

In a broken context, we find two passages with the irregular verb *našā*ʾ*u*:

a-na na-ša-en-ni 'for carrying' MAPD § 17:81†

ša sariyāne ⸢x x x x x⸣ LUGAL *a-na na-ša-e-ni* 'which the armour x x x x the king is to bring' MARV 8 51:16–18

On the other hand, most infinitives that are constructed with *ša* do not take a subjunctive. This is also true for other types of dependent clauses, which take the infinitive as the verbal predicate:

---

34 I prefer to analyse this form as an infinitive by analogy with the *ša lā* construction in *ša lā qarābšani*.

tuppu (…) *ša za-ka-i-ša ina bēt* PN *šaknat* 'the tablet (…) was placed in the house of PN for her clearance' KAJ 7:30–33

1 *kappu ša nap-lu-si* (…) *šaknū* 'one *kappu* for display (and other commodities) are placed' KAJ 303:10

iltu ammāka i+na tu-a-ri (…) *din* 'when he returns from there, give!' MATC 6:8–12

[*š*]*a še-ru-di-ka šērid* 'add, what you want to add!' MATSH 9:13

Chapter 18: Syntax: Simple Clause

18.1 Congruence of subject and predicate

§ 665 The verbal predicate is usually in agreement with the gender and number of the subject. There are some exceptions to this rule, which have sometimes become regular in their own way. We have already discussed how the two existential verbs *ibašši* and *laššu* are quasi-finite and do not agree in terms of gender and number with their subject. Another group concerns a number of instances, which could be regarded as mistakes, since they cannot be explained grammatically. Relatively often, a verb is not inflected as per its feminine subject:

[*ele*]*ppu šīt* (…) *lū iṭ-bu lū in-né-e* 'that boat (…) whether it sinks or capsizes' MAL M § 1:3

ina ūme e-ri-šu-n[*i*] *iddan* 'on the day she requires it, he shall pay it' KAJ 90:9

ᶠPN (…) *ša kīmū sarte* (…) *ṣa-ab-tu-ni* 'ᶠPN was seized as a substitute for a crime' KAJ 100:1–14

[*aššāt*]*u mārātu ša us-bu-ú-*⌜*ni*⌝ 'women and daughters who are present' KAV 217:19'

1 *maššartu* (…) *pa-*⌜*qi-id*⌝ 'one *maššartu*-container is entrusted' MARV 4 146:5'–6'

20+*n lubultu* (…) [*u*]*ltēliūni si-qu kunuk* PN *ka-nu-ku* 'n-textiles^(feminine sg.) 'they took out n-textiles^(feminine sg.), they are narrow^((mp)) (and) sealed^((mp)) with the seal of PN' VAT 8236 r. 3'–14'

sinniltušu [*ša*] *ina bēte* (…) *i-bal-laṭ-ṭú-ni* 'his wife who lives (m.) in the house' Giricano 8:19–20 (however, the following line is: [*amti*]*īša ta-ma-ga-ar* 'she acknowledges her (status of being a) slave girl' Giricano 8:21)

ana atān[*āte*] *annā*[*te*] *uššer*[*šu*] *ēdēnu*[*ššu*] ŠE-*am le-ku-u*[*l*] 'leave him (the horse) to these she-asses, he alone may eat the barley' MATC 17:11–15

3 *ṣimitte kūdenē* (…) *e-ku-*[*lu-ni*] 'three donkey teams which (…) eat' MATC 25A:9–10 passim with *ṣimittu* in MATC

[*š*]*a maltītu ana muḫḫi* PN *na-ṣu-ni* 'what was brought to PN as the shipment of consumption' MATC 53:6–9

Kouwenberg argued that, in OA administrative documents, they may have been simple scribal mistakes due to stereotyped phraseology (GOA § 22.1.2). In support of this claim, the text KAJ 3 consistently applies the masculine verbal form for a feminine subject. On the other hand, this text led Lambert (1973, 126) to believe that this particular text betrayed the Babylonian linguistic background of the scribe, where there is no differentiation between the masculine and feminine in the third-person verbal forms of the prefix conjugation.

ᵐ.ᶠ*Am-mi-ni-ši-na mārat* PN *im-me-ge-er-ma* 'Amminišina, daughter of PN, agreed' KAJ 3:2

ana māruttīša il-qé 'she took her in adoption' KAJ 3:4

ana PN *i-qa-bi* 'she will say to PN' KAJ 3:13

Recently, another text was published in MARV 10; the text is so confusing in terms of gender, that I remain uncertain about the gender of the subject of the text:

> *ina muḫḫi* ^{f}⌜*Ḫa*⌝*-ta-a-ie*$^{\text{(hybrid f. and m.)}}$^{lú}*mu-raq-qi-*⌜*e*⌝$^{\text{(m.)}}$*šamna*^{meš} (…) *ana raqqu*[*e*] *ta-ad-na-á*[*š*$^{?}$*-ši*$^{?}$]$^{\text{(gender uncertain)}}$ *ú-ra-qa*$^{\text{(m.)}}$*i-dan* ⌜*ù*⌝ *tup-*⌜*pu-ša*⌝$^{\text{(f.)}}$*i-ḫap-*[*pi*]$^{\text{(m.)}}$ '(these commodities) (are incumbent) on the Hittite perfume maker, the oil is given to him/her for aromatic mixing. S/he will mix it, give it and break his/her tablet' MARV 10 30:9–16

Mixed gender agreement is also found in KAV 108. The plural logogram TÚG (Akk. *ṣubātu*) takes one feminine plural adjective, despite being masculine according to the CAD Ṣ (p. 221), but the following adjectives and statives are masculine:

> *ṣubātu*$^{\text{ḫi.a.meš}}$ *ṣu-pa-a-t*[*u*]$^{\text{(fp)}}$ SIG$_5$^{meš} *ša*$^{!}$*-ḫu-tu*$^{\text{(mp)}}$ *ša ma-si-ú-ni*$^{\text{(mp)}}$ *ina pittukka ṣe-e-ú-ni*$^{\text{(mp)}}$ *ša-ak-nu-ú-ni*$^{\text{(mp)}}$ 'the embroidered(?), good (but) dirty textiles, which were washed, are dried out and placed in your responsibility' KAV 108:4–9

Lack of agreement is also attested in pure orthographic inconsistency. In the following phrase, the PN is indicated as masculine, but this 'he' is specified as being a daughter (DUMU.MUNUS):

> ^{md}30*-še-zib-a-ni* DUMU.MUNUS *lu-i-ṣi* MARV 2 27 v$^{?}$ 13

Masculine+feminine subject=masculine plural inflection (common Semitic):

> *lū aʾīlu lū sinniltu kišpē ú-up-pi-šu-ma* 'whether a man or woman performed witchcraft' MAL A § 47:1–2

> *alpu u atānu annītu šulm*[*ā*]*nu šu-nu* 'the ox and this she-ass are a *šulmānu*-gift' T 97-6:8–11

But exceptionally a masculine+feminine subject=feminine verb:

> 1 *me* 1 *šūši* 2 UDU.U$_8$^{meš} 35 UDU *pa-ra-tu*^{meš} 1 *šūši* 3 UDU.NÍTA^{meš} 26 UDU.NIM^{meš} 15 UDU.MÁŠ^{meš} (…) *ana raʾāʾe ta-ad-na* '162 ewes, 35 female lambs, 63 sheep, 26 male spring lambs, 15 male goats are given for pasturing' Ali 1:1–9

Masculine subject(s) with a feminine verb in singular:

> *šang*[*utta*]*ka u šangutta ša marʾēka* (…) *lu ṭa-ba-a*[*t*] 'may your priesthood and the priesthood of your sons be well' Coronation Ritual ii 33–34

Masculine plural subject with a feminine plural verb:

> *ša* [*l*]*aqāšunu u dabābšunu ibaššiūni tuppātēšunu lu-še-*⌜*li-a*⌝*-nim-ma* 'may those bring forth their tablets who are there to take and complain' MAL B § 6:13–16

Masculine adjective for a feminine noun:

> *kī martušuma Aš-*[*šu*]*-ra-ie-e uppaussi*$^{\text{sic.}}$ 'he will treat her as his Assyrian daughter' KAJ 2:10–12

As has been observed for OA, the usage of the feminine prefix *tV-* in the prefix conjugation is uncommon for inanimate words, although it is still attested in a few cases.[1] Apart from the phrases in MAL M and MATC 53 above, the situation is different in MA. The opposite is attested, as can be seen in the phrases below where *tV-* is found for inanimate words. We may therefore wonder whether its usage increased during the MA period.

> *išātu ana eliš te-el-li-a* 'the fire will go up' PKT 1 II right 9

1 See Veenhof (1972, 115–16 n185); GOA § 22.1.2.

ēm našpertu [*ša*] *šarre tal-la-ka-ni* 'when the message of the king comes' MATSH 12:42

qāssu te-el-li 'his hand will go up (=forfeit his claims)' OIP 79 6:20

našpe[*rt*]*aka ana muḫḫi sirašê* (…) *lu tal-li-ka* 'your message must go to the brewer' T 93-3:11–14

§ 666 A second group, where the verb is not in agreement with its subjects, revolves around numbers rather than gender.

Singular for plural:

tuppātu šina naḫrā za-ku 'these tablets are cancelled (fp) and cleared (ms$^{?}$)' MARV 1 38:8–9

kīmū 1 *ikkuru damqu* PN (…) *e-dan* 'instead of PN, they (sg$^{!}$) will give one good farmer' RE 19:12–15[2]

mugerra^{meš}*-ka gabbu* (…) *lu tal-li-ka* 'may all your chariots come' T 93-2:7–8

Plural for singular:

PN$_1$ (…) *ana pî* PN$_2$ *šaṭ-ru* 'PN$_1$ written down at the word of PN$_2$' KAV 156:6–8

According to W. Mayer (UGM, 104 § 92.4), for some cases where the gender and number of the finite verb do not agree with the subject, there may instead be a logical predicate to which the verb refers:

qaqqad ṣarpe u ŠE-*im* (…) *iddunū* (…) *ṣarpu* ŠE-*um ra-ki-*[*i*]*s* 'they will pay the capital of the silver and barley (…) the silver and barley is$^{\text{sic.}}$ bound'KAJ 47:20–24 (stative refers to *qaqqudu*)

1 *marsattu ša šizbe* (…) *ana ēkalle ra-ke-és* 'one *marsattu*-vessel of milk (…) for the palace is bound' KAJ 182:7–12 (stative refers to *šizbu*)

7 *kukkalla*[^{m}]^{eš} *nāmurtu ša* PN$_1$ *a-na* PN$_2$ *uqarribūni* (…) *rēḫtušunu ana bēt alaḫḫinnē pa-qu-du* 'seven fat-tailed sheep, (they are) the gift, which PN$_1$ presented to PN$_2$. The rest of them are entrusted to the house of the bakers'A 1747 (NTA, 23):1–14 (stative refers to *kukkallu*)

§ 667 Regarding the subject, we may note that, in some letters, the subject is repeated within the same clause. This is probably caused by a scribe working on citation; thus, when the message was dictated to him, the scribe erroneously repeated the subject within his train of thought, such as happens frequently in daily speech.

^{f}PN *lū* 2 *niggalla siparra ū lū eria* ^{f}PN *lū tušēbila* '^{f}PN, may ^{f}PN send me two sickles of copper or bronze'A 845:14–18

kīma PN *marā šipre* [*an*]*a muḫḫīya illaka u anāku mīnummê aḫūya* [*i*]*ṣabbutū*[*ni an*]*āk*[*u a*]*na muḫḫi* [*aḫ*]*īya ušebbala* [*arḫi*]*š* 'when PN, the messenger, will come to me then I shall send to my brother quickly whatever my brother wants to take' RS 06.198:21–27

2 Note that, in addition to the singular morphology of the plural verb, we find *kīmū* and 1 ENGAR reversed (see Deller 1999, 33–34).

18.2 Hendiadys

§ 668 Hendiadys, which is a term derived from the Greek *hen dia duoin* (ἓν διὰ δυοῖν) 'one through two', connects substantives or verbs.[3] In Akkadian, it is usually applied to a sequence of two verbs, of which "the first qualifies or restricts the meaning of the second".[4] Nominal hendiadys are present in Akkadian (cf. Wasserman 2003, 5–19), but, in general, studies tend to concentrate on the verbal version. The main study on hendiadys is Kraus (1987), who introduced the term 'Koppelungen'. Rather than nouns (as in Greek), it connects two finite verbs of one main clause, where one of the verbs receives an adverbial translation in English. A classic example of a hendiadys in OB would be the *tasaḫḫurma tamarraq* 'you will rub it again' (Kraus 1987, 13). As can be seen, the two finite verbs are connected with *-ma*, even though they do not necessarily have to follow each other. Two observations on the constructions that are not valid for MA must be made. First of all, the sentence connector *-ma* is not used structurally anymore in MA, removing an important characteristic of the construction. On the other hand, hendiadyses are still found in NA (SNAG, 114 § 4.2.2.2.4). Additionally, it may be noted that the first verb in our example is translated adverbially as 'to do again.' There is a number of verbs in Akkadian that are found frequently in this function, e.g., *ḫarāpu* 'to do early' *saḫāru* 'to do again', *šanāʾu* 'to do a second time', *tuāru* 'to do again' (cf. Wasserman 2003, 19–22). Many of these verbs do not occur in MA, or only rarely. As a result, hendiadys in MA are difficult to recognize and W. Mayer (UGM) did not mention them. Only one case is available:

> *šumma* ⌜*ta*⌝*-tu-ra ṣalta ta-sa-da-ar-a*ˀ (…) *mā labān*[*āt*]*īkina unakkas* 'if you keep quarrelling, I will cut off your necks' MARV 3 64:38–43

On the other hand, Shibata (2007, 71 n51) analysed the following passage as a hendiadys:

> *ṣubāta*$^{\text{ḫi.a.meš}}$ (…) *ana* GN [*i*]*-ta-ṣu it-*⌜*tu*⌝*-um-šu* 'they have brought the textiles to GN and departed' TabT05a-623:610

This is no real hendiadys, but a sequence of two separate actions since the perfect of *našāʾu* does not support *namāšu*.[5] Although the distinction between hendiadys and two different sequences is often a matter of the interpretation of the Assyriologist involved (cf. Wasserman 2003, 22–23), we may note that Kraus (1987) did not include a category with either *našāʾu* or *namāšu* as a hendiadys. That said, he did include a category for this type of action in two different sequences (3. Teil). Although we cannot provide examples of a true hendiadys in MA, we may offer some passages where a close connection of succeeding verbs can be found:

> *bibla it-ta-bal iz-zi-bi-il*$_5$ 'he has brought and delivered a marriage gift' MAL A § 30:21

> *qēputtūya kunukkī* (…) *na-aṣ-ṣu i-lu-ku-ni-ku-nu* 'my representatives carry and bring my seal' KAV 98:7–10

> *kunukkātēkunu ku-un-ka še-bi-la-ni* 'seal your seals and send (them) to me' KAV 98:20–21

---

3 Despite being derived from it, Greek uses hendiadys in a slightly different function to express a single idea through two nouns or verbs, e.g., 'in the sea and the waves' or 'he prayed and asked' (cf. Morwood 2001, 237).

4 See Huehnergard (2005, 125–26 § 14.5).

5 Cf. the similar construction *na-aṣ-ṣu i-lu-ku-ni-ku-nu* 'they are coming to you to bring' KAV 98:10.

aššum šīpāte mimma išaʾʾalanni šīpāte ša qātīka kē maṣi i-ba-áš-ši i-ri-ḫa 'concerning the wool, he asks me something: "the wool that is at your disposal, how much is available as a remainder?"' KAV 106:7–11

anaʾīne la ta-li-ka *ina dēnīka* la ta-ad-bu-ub 'why did you not come to speak during your case?' KAV 169:10–13

anāku al-la-ka *ina dēne* a-da-bu-ub 'I will come to speak in trial' Faist 2001, 252:26–28

A hendiadys generally demonstrates the irreversible order of the two succeeding verbal forms, although not always (cf. Wasserman 2003, 17–18). Although not a true hendiadys, we may note the following passage where the order of succeeding verbs is confused and not chronological:

1 *qalta šēṣi[āne]* še-bi-la-ni ⌜ku⌝-[un-ka] 'take one bow out, send and seal it (=seal and send it)' KAV 98:47–48

18.3 Word order and topicalization

§ 669 The main feature of MA (and Akkadian grammar, in general) is the clause-final position of the finite verb. The main sequence of word order is subject - object - verb (SOV). The verbal predicate stands in the final position of tge clause, while the subject, following by the object, comes at the beginning. The subject is often not expressed explicitly as it is frequently mentioned earlier or is enclosed in the verb.

sinniltu šīt aranša tanašši 'that woman carries (the punishment for) her sin' MAL A § 2:19–20

aššat aʾīle ina rebēti tētitiq 'a wife crossed the street' MAL A § 12:14–15

lū aʾīlu lū sinniltu kišpi uppišūma 'whether a man or woman performed witchcraft' MAL A § 47:1–2

nagāra u pirʾa kannamāri arḫiš lublūni 'may they quickly bring a carpenter and student tomorrow morning' MATC 1:4–6

anāku iššērte ammīša ana biāde allaka 'I will come there tomorrow to spend the night' MATC 2:16-18

anāku agrāni uggara 'I will hire hirelings' MATC 4:10–11

kakardinnu elammaṣa ētazba 'the victualler left me *e.*' MATC 4:28–30

The sequence direct ~ indirect object seems to be more or less free and dependent on topicalization. For instance, in the following clauses, the sequence is direct ~ indirect object:

šumma sinniltu qāta ana aʾīle tattabal 'if a woman placed the hand on a man' MAL A § 7:74

anaʾīne paḫāre ana GN *la t[a]špur* 'why did you not send the potter to GN?' T 93-3:7–9

našpe[rt]aka ana muḫḫi sirašê (…) *lū tallika* 'your message must go the brewer' T 93-3:11–14

šamaššammē ana ṣā[ḫ]ite dina 'give sesame to the oil presser' T 93-7:14–15

The other way around (indirect ~ direct object):

ana muḫḫi PN *našperta ultēbil* 'I have sent a message to PN' MATC 11:20–21

The position of adverbs and adverbial phrases are more or less free, but they occur most frequently at the beginning of a clause, e.g.:

an-na-ka ana iyāši [*šul*]*mu* 'here everything is well with me' A 845:5

i+na pa-ni-šu ana bēte erāba lâla??*e* 'I am not able to enter the house in his presence' MATSH 12:27–28

*u*4*-ma* 1 *atāna ātamar* 'today I saw a she-ass' Hall 1983:18

An adverb is also often found before the finite verb:

ana ṣēni ⌜*ú*⌝*-*[*ma*]*-ka-al iqtual* 'he looked after the cattle for one day' MATC 15:28–29

*mā*ʾ*ē u*4*-ma lā abattaq* 'today I will not block the water' MATSH 8:28'

Note also $_{\text{indirect}}$O-A-$_{\text{direct}}$O-V:

ana GN *ūmu mašil ṭēma ittablūne* at noon, they brought the report to me to GN' MATSH 2:23–24

§ 670 While, in OA, the OSV word order was still common (GOA § 22.4.3), it was not noted by Hämeen-Anttila for NA (SNAG, 116ff § 4.3). It is, of course, possible that, while word order was relatively free in OA, the decay of case endings in MA/NA made it increasingly necessary to follow the SO(V) order more strictly in order to avoid confusion. As such, it seems that the OSV order in MA is more or less limited to the casus pendens (see § 673f below). Only a few other examples can be given:

mussa nakru ilteqe 'the enemy took her husband' MAL A § 45:47

šumma tuppa šiāti PN$_1$ *ana* PN$_2$ *lā inaddin* 'if PN$_1$ does not give that tablet to PN$_2$' KAJ 132:12–15

ŠE *annia šarru kī rīmutte ana t*[*ad*]*āni iqt*[*i*]*bi* 'the king commanded this barley to be given as a gift' MATSH 1:12–15

§ 671 It can be stated though, that as far as MA can deviate from the SOV order, we sometimes find that the clause continues after the verb. It is possible that parts were added to a complete clause as an afterthought.[6] Usually this concerns adverbial constructions and specifications of the verbal action. For instance, there are the following cases of an adverb following the verb in letters:

[*lū sinnilta*] *ša šap-la-nu-ša tātarar lem-niš* 'or she spitefully curses a woman who is below her in rank' MAPD § 17:80–81

[*a*]*na muḫḫi* [*aḫ*]*īya ušebbala* [*ar-ḫi*]*š* 'I shall send to my brother quickly' RS 06.198:26–27

alik ar-ḫi-iš leqyaššu 'go quickly, take him there' T 02-3:16–17

As an infinitive construction in letters:

ina GN *qayyini ana na-ma-še* 'wait for me for departure in GN' Billa 63:20[7]

6 Cf. OA GKT, 189 § 190c; GOA § 22.4.1.

7 According to the Finkelstein edition. However, we may also translate l. 18-21 as follows: *'when he said to me: 'wait for me in GN!' I am afraid to move without my lord'*. In this case, the infinitive precedes the finite verb *palḫāku* 'I am afraid' (l. 21); I leave this possibility open due to the lack of a clear

ana panīka adaggal a-na nam-ma-⸢še⸣ 'I wait for you to depart' MATC 1:10–11

annūtu āla lilbiū u annūte ana bir[*āte*] *lušēber ki-i i+na* URU *la-a še-ṣu-e ù* URU *la-a* [*še-l*]*u-⸢e⸣* 'these (troops) must lay siege to the city and I shall bring those (troops) across to the fortifications, so that there is no exit or entry in the city' MATSH 8:26'–27'

Miscellaneous constructions in letters:

ana iltēnunna mamma lū lā idabbub lu-ú Áš-šu-ra-iu-ú lu-ú Kaš-[*ši-ú*] 'alone(?), nobody may speak, be he Assyrian or Kassite' MATC 15:33–35

lu ni-{*ib*}*-il-qu-na-*[*š*]*i-*[*i*]*n* 'we want to take for us' MATSH 22:18

3 *emāra*^{meš} (…) *uṣṣabit il-te-šu* 'I seized three donkeys from him' Hall 1983:7–8

These types of clauses with non-final verbs are also attested in the administrative documents, albeit on a smaller scale (UGM, 103 § 91). Again, the sections following the verbs are probably added as an afterthought; this is most likely the case in such a formulaic loan as KAJ 46, which forms an exception to the standard formulae.

12 *nalb*[*attu*] <*ša*> *libnāte šaḫā*[*ṭe*] (…) *tadnāšu ⸢a-na ša-ḫa-a-ṭí⸣* '12 moulds for brick making are given to him for brick making' A 3310:5–11

$3^{2}/_{3}$ *mana ṣarpu* (…) *ilqe a-na* KASKAL É ^{lú}*Su-ti-e* 'he took 3 2/3 minas of silver for the caravan (or caravanserai?) of the Suteans' KAJ 39:2–7

[n+]7 *mana annuku* (…) *ilqe a-na ú-si-ti-šu* 'he took *n* minas of lead for his assistance' KAJ 46:1–5

ana ēkalle ilaqqe bi-ḫir-šú 'to the palace he will take his *b.*' KAJ 306a:9

§ 672 Cases of clause-initial finite verbs are very rare in MA. Of course, direct speech can be introduced by a verb, e.g., *alteme mā* 'I heard (that)'; *iqṭibi mā* 'he said (that)'. Although, in this case, it is better to regard the direct speech as a separate clause. Similar to OA, the verb is sometimes initial in PNs (cf. GKT, 188 § 109a):

^{m}*Ṭà-ab-*^{d}*A-šur* KAJ 37:23

Šal-lim-pi-i-^{d}*É-a* MARV 1 14:32

Clauses with verbs at the beginning of a clause are otherwise very rare (cf. OA GKT, 188 § 109b):

la-a tu-ma-ri-ra-ni ina ṣabʾe Imarāye 'you did not frustrate me, concerning the Emariote troops' MATC 2:18–19

ul-te-n[*i-ba-la*] *lū* 2 *bilta lū* 3 *biltamma lū* 10 *b*[*ilta kitāʾa*] 'he will successively send two, three or 10 talents of flax' MATSH 6:3'–4'

An infinitive is also attested at the beginning of a sentence:

a-na ṭa-ú-be ^{kuš}*dušû* (…) [*t*]*adnaššu* 'untanned leather was given to him for improving' MARV 10 29:13–16

---

context.

18.4 Casus pendens

§ 673 As explained clearly by Huehnergard, in language, one can place a special focus or emphasis on a part of a sentence, often expressed by the stress put on it by the speaker; this is called topicalization.[8] In MA texts, this is in fact marked by the emphatic particle *-ma* (§ 409ff) or by the occurrence of the casus pendens. This feature, also visible in other forms of Akkadian, such as OB and UgAkk, has the object of the predicate at the beginning of the sentence, thus creating an OSV sentence, rather than the usual SOV.[9] Moreover, the object occurs in the nominative case, e.g.:

> ⅔ MA.NA KÙ.BABBAR *ṭi-ir-ru* NA$_4$ É *a-lim iltu* PN$_1$ PN$_2$ *u tappāʾūšu* (…) *ilqeū* '⅔ mina of silver of the weight of the city, PN$_2$ and his colleagues took it from PN$_1$ KAJ 32:1–7

§ 674 As for the translation of these examples, it is probably best to put the object at the beginning of the sentence, as in the original text, in order to preserve its emphasis. MA attests many examples of the casus pendens, which will not all be given here. As the verbal predicate takes this first sentence as object, it could be argued that both parts are two separate sentences, with the object not repeated in the second. In any case, this MA feature seems to be formulaic, rather than grammatically motivated. Still, it is sometimes difficult to distinguish between the casus pendens and the decline of case endings (§ 275): there are no examples of the casus pendens in the literary corpus.[10]

Administrative texts:

> 10 *e-ṣi-du iltu* PN$_1$ PN$_2$ *ilqe* '10 reapers PN$_2$ took from PN$_1$' KAJ 29:3–6
>
> ŠE-*um an-ni-ú ana pūḫe ilqe* 'this barley he took in exchange' KAJ 91:13 (cf. UŠA, 130 also MARV 1 47 passim).
>
> *ad-ru qa-qar* URU *e-ṣú ma-du* (…) *ana šīmi ana šīm g[a]mer* PN$_1$ *ana* PN$_2$ *iddinma* 'threshing floor, territory of the city, little and much, PN$_1$ sold it for the complete price to PN$_2$' KAJ 149:3–12
>
> 1 ^{kuš}*ḫi-im-t[u]* PN (…) *maḫir* 'one leather skin PN received' KAJ 250:1–5
>
> 1 GÍN ⸢KÙ⸣.GI *sa-ag-ru ša* PN$_1$ PN$_2$ *kīmū* PN$_3$ *maḫir* 'one shekel of *sagru*-gold of PN$_1$, PN$_2$ received instead of PN$_3$' LB 2532:1–7 cf. LB 1848:1–6; envelope 1–5

With two predicates, taking the entire previous sentence as the object:

> NINDA *an-ni-ú ša* (…) *ina muḫḫīšu iššaknūni ušaddan* 'this bread, which has been put to his debit, he shall collect' KAJ 107:7–12

This also takes place in short sentences (O-V), where the agent of the verb is unnamed:

> ^{gud}ÁB *an-ni-tu iddan* 'this cow; he will give (it)' KAJ 95:9–10

---

8 See Huehnergard (2005, 211–12 § 21.5); Streck (2014a, 144 § 343); cf. GAG, 22 § 128.

9 See Huehnergard (1989, 369); but not in OA, cf. GKT, 190 § 11a.

10 W. Mayer (UGM, 106-7 § 95) presented one example from the Coronation Ritual. However, I feel that it is better to divide his example into two sentences, since there are two verbal predicates (*tabik* ~ *naṣṣū*): 1 *kapp[u] ša ḫurāṣe šamnu ina libb[īš]u tabek iltu [ēkal]le iltu šarre naṣṣū* 'one golden bowl with oil is poured out in its midst. They brought it from the palace with the king' Coronation Ritual i 32–34.

mi-im-ma an-ni-ú gi-im-ru ša ^{giš}GIGIR *iddan* 'all these are the expenses of the chariot; he will give it' KAJ 122:15–17

20 ^{giš}BAN^{meš} *la sa-aḫ-pa-tum* (…) *maḫir* 'he received 20 unwrapped bows' MARV 1 20:2–5

But very rarely in letters:

2 MA.NA 5 GÍN *ṣar-pu* (…) 2 ^{túg}*ni-ik-su* 1 *lu-be-ru ana* (…) *attannaššunu* '125 shekels of silver, two *n.*, one *l.* I gave to them (…)' Faist 2001, 251:5–16

18.5 Nominal clauses

§ 675 As a result of a (partial) absence of copula verbs in Semitic languages in general, nominal clauses are a common feature. This is also true for MA, where no verbal copula exists and thus nominal clauses occur regardless of the temporal context. Among the many administrative documents, groups of one or two words are frequently listed out of syntactical context. This is most noticeable in the *ginā'u* tables (e.g., MARV 9 12), but we may also regard the casus pendens (§ 673f) as a kind of nominal clause. Such examples are excluded from the passages quoted here.

§ 676 As for word order, it should be pointed out that the predicate is still final in most cases. The situation reverses when an independent personal pronoun is used; in this case, the predicate precedes the pronoun, which is final. This can be explained by analogy with the usage of the nominal personal pronouns as a copula, where the pronoun takes the place of the verbal predicate and is thus placed in the clause-final position. This can be illustrated by the following theoretical examples: MA can express the clause 'Aššur-uballiṭ is king' in two ways: *Aššur-uballiṭ šar(ru)* or *Aššur-uballiṭ šarru šūt* (Huehnergard 1986, 235–41). In general, the latter three-part construction, where subject, predicate and pronoun are explicitly expressed, is thought to be typical for NA and influenced by Aramaic.[11] Huehnergard (1986, 235) pointed out that the earliest examples are OB, but we may conclude that they were also common in MA.

PN_1 *u lidānu*[*ša*] *a-la-iu-ú ša* PN_2 *ù* DUMU^{meš}-*šú šu-nu* 'PN_1 and her children, they are villagers of PN_2 and his sons' KAJ 7:20–23 (EAd/Aub)

6 *iku* 1 KU 6½ GÌR *eqlu* 1 *pu-ru* 5-*ši-ú ša ṭé-ḫi* KASKAL *Lìb-bi*-URU *ša* PN *šu-ut* '6 *iku* field (…), is a one fifth lot, which is adjacent to the road of inner city (Aššur) and which is (owned) by PN' KAV 127

ŠE-*um*^{meš} *anniu pu-ḫu šu-ut* 'this barley is a substitute' Giricano 1:9–10; Giricano 6:6–7

PN_1 ÌR *ša* PN_2 *šu-ut* 'PN_1 is the slave of PN_2' Giricano 4:22–23

[…] *ša* ŠEŠ-*ia* EN *ṭa-ab-ti-ka šu-ut* '[…] of my brother, he *was* your friend (lit. 'lord of your favour')' KUB 3 73:5'

11 See GAG, 302 § 196c, cf. 224 § 126f; SNAG, 45–48 § 3.1.1.

In one instance, the pronoun stands at the beginning of a clause, instead of in final position. This was caused by the subject change of two succeeding nominal clauses, which stand in contrast to each other.

abūya bēl nakrika šūt [?] *a-na-ku bēl sulummāʾe ša aḫīya* 'my father was your enemy, but I am the ally of my brother' KUB 3 73:10'–11'

As the pronoun functions as copula and thus takes the position of the verb, it can carry a subjunctive in this position:

ammar šu-ut-ni ṭēma šuprāne 'as much as it is, write me a message' MCS 2 2:13–14

§ 677 As MA is unlikely to have been in intensive contact with Aramaic, influence from this Northwest Semitic language is unlikely. In fact, we may consider Hurrian as a more likely source, where the verb *mān(n)=* 'to be' is often used as a copula in the clause-final position (Dietrich/W. Mayer 2010, 221–22 § 2.5.8.2), e.g.:

PN_1 *at-*[*ta*]*-*⌜*íw-wu*⌝*-ú-e* PN_2 *ša-a-la* ⌜*ma-a-an-né*⌝ 'PN_1 is the daughter of my father PN_2' EA 24 i 47–48

ta-a-an-ki-ma-a-an an-ti ma-a-an-né 'this one is beautiful' EA 24 iv 60

If this is correct, the construction must have been introduced between the OA and MA periods, as it was not present in OA texts, where the nominal clause was similarly constructed, but without the pronoun (GOA § 22.4.6 n39). In this light, we may point to the clause *anniu šulmānu šūt* 'this is a *šulmānu*', which is common in the eponymous *šulmānu* texts. It uses an independent pronoun as a copula.

ḫurāṣu anniu šul-ma-nu šu-ut 'this gold is a *šulmānu*-gift' KAJ 49:8'–10' (Sa)

annuku anniu šul-ma-nu šu-ut 'this lead is a *šulmānu*-gift' KAJ 56:10–12 (Sa)

ŠE *anniu šul-ma-nu šu-ut* 'this barley is a *šulmānu*-gift' KAJ 72:9–10 (Adn)

aʾīlu anniu šul-ma-nu šu-ut 'this man is a *šulmānu*-gift' T 97-2:8–10 (TN)

emāru anniu šul-ma-nu šu-ut 'this donkey is a *šulmānu*-gift' T 97-5:7–9 (TN)

ṣeḫru anniu šul-ma-nu šu-ut 'this child is a *šulmānu-gift*' T 98-85:7–10 (TN–Eku)

gurrātu annāt[*u*] *šul-ma-nu* [*š*]*i-i-n*[*a*] 'these ewes are a *šulmānu*-gift' TR 2028:8–10 (TN)

The exception here is formed by the Urad-Šerūa archive (M 10), where about four of the *šulmānu* texts can be demonstrated to have the copula omitted. This is certainly not the majority (although some texts have this passage damaged), but it is nonetheless a significant number.

annuku šul-ma-nu 'the lead is a *šulmānu*-gift' KAJ 51:8

annuku anniu šul-ma-nu 'this lead is a *šulmānu*-gift' KAJ 54:9–10

atānu annītu šul-ma-nu 'this she-ass is a *šulmānu*-gift' KAJ 90:8

sinniltu annītu šul-ma-nu 'this woman is a *šulmānu*-gift' KAJ 98:4

§ 678 These examples clearly show that the pronouns were not obligatory in the way they would be in the NA texts. There are a few more exceptions involving various word classes and constructions.[12] The first to be mentioned are the normal nouns.

kātu libnāte A.ŠÀ[!]-*šu u* É-*sú* 'the pledge for the bricks are his field and his house' KAJ 87:8–9 (EAd/Aub)

PN *qe-pu* 'PN was representative' MARV 1 12:15–16

PN *marā šarre qe-pu* 'PN, the son of the king, was representative' A 1746 (NTA, 22):9–10

[f]PN GÉM[E]-*su* '[f]PN is his slave girl' Giricano 7:21

With adjectives:

ana ḫalzīka gabbe maš-ri 'your entire district is wealthy' A 877:4

ṣarpu ša PN *mi-it-ḫa-ra-tu* 'the silver of PN is in accordance' Giricano 12:20'–22'

lū māʾū ša ḫiriṣe ū lū naqqure gabbu e-ṣ[*u*] 'be it the water of the *ḫ*.-canal or be it the *n*.-canal, all will be little' MATSH 8:33'

Noun phrases:

tallaktušu iššāssu ki-i an-ni-im-ma 'its procedure and its fire are as like this' PKT 5 r. 3

ana šarre ēkalle mārʾē šul-mu 'the king, the palace and the sons are well' MATSH 10:5

aḫḫēšu ki qa-ti-šu 'his brothers (are entitled to) a share equal to his' KAJ 179:22

PN_1 *i*[*lt*]*u* PN_2 *ettamar šul-mu* 'PN_1 met PN_2: he is in good health' TabT05A-134:9–10

ki-ma [na4]KIŠIB-*šu ṣuparšu* 'his fingernail is instead of his seal' Giricano 8:1

mēt ḫalaqa i+na muḫ-ḫi-šu-nu '(if) he dies or flees, the responsibility is theirs' RE 19:16–17

With a possessive personal pronoun:

4 *sinnišātu la iya-a-tu* (…) *u sinniltu ku-a-tu* 'four women, not mine (…) and your wife' MATC 15:4–6

[[uru]]*Tūrira ia-a-ú* [uru]*Tūrira ka-a-*[*ú*] 'the city *Tūrira* is mine (or) *Tūrira* is yours' KBo 1 14:10

ālānu u munnabdu ku-na-ú-[*tu*] 'the cities and refugees are yours' KBo 1 20:17'

Infinitive:

iltu ammāka i+na tu-a-ri 'as soon as he returns from there' MATC 6:8–9 (subordinate clause)

5 *emāru* ŠE PN *zarʾu a-na ra-bu-e* 'five homers of barley (for) PN to increase the seed (for agriculture)' MATC 44:1–3

2 *emāru* ŠE PN *a-na ṭé-a-ni* 'two homers of barley (for) PN are for grinding' MATC 44:4–6

---

12 Huehnergard (1986, 222 n16) adds KAV 98:1–7 and takes *qēputtūya* 'they are my representatives' as the nominal predicate. It seems more likely that this noun stands in opposition to the aforementioned PNs, whereas we find the verbal predicate later in the text, i.e., *naṣṣū illukūnekkunu* 'they come to you to bring' l. 10.

iltu [*t*]*uppī a-m*[*a-r*]*i-ka* 'when you see my tablet' T 93-20:4–5 (no main clause)

Genitive marker (cf. Vinnichenko 2016a, 143–44):

mimma ammar naṣṣūni gabbu ša-a MUNUS 'everything, as much as he brought in, is of the woman' MAL A § 35:80–81; cf. MAL A § 35:77–78

[*massuttu*] *annītu ša-áš-šu-te-šu* 'this cleaning is of the third time' PKT 4 obv. left 5

[ŠE *an*]*niu ša pi-i* 5 *le-a-ni* 'this barley is in accordance with the five wooden tablets' KAJ 113:32

mā sisīu^{meš} *ša Šu-ti-e u kūdunū ša Šu-ub-ri-e* 'the horses are from the Suteans and the mules of the Hurrians' MATC 15:17–19

Adverbial:

[…] *ša a-ḫa-iš šunu* 'they are held in common(?)' KAJ 118:19 (Huehnergard 1986, 224)

Aššurāyu il-te-šu 'an Assyrian is with him' MATC 9:6–7; cf. KAV 200:7–8

In some cases, a nominal stative is used. In the example of MAL A § 41, this is caused by the usage of the *šīt* attributive with the preceding noun, making it impossible to repeat it again as a copula. It is also possible to regard these examples as indeterminate rather than determinate examples with a pronoun as a copula (Buccellati 1988, 174). Buccellati's claim has been criticized and elaborated on by Kouwenberg (2000, 51–52), who stated that the stative of nouns is rather adscript and adjectival in nature.

aššiti$^{sic.}$ *šīt la-a áš-ša-at* 'that wife is not a (proper) wife' MAL A § 41:9

šumma ana qāt 10 *šanāti marʾū marʾe ṣe-eḫ-ḫe-ru* 'if the sons of the son are younger than 10 years' MAL A § 43:31–32

PN (…) *qāta mi-it-ḫa-ar* 'PN is entitled to an equal share' KAJ 1:22–24

atānu la su-ti-a-at 'the she-ass is not Sutean' Hall 1983:12

§ 679 It should be pointed out that the pronouns can also function as the subject, in which case they are still clause-final. This construction is already well known from OA, although normal Subject-Predicate occurs in this period as well (GOA § 23.1.1.2). Nonetheless, the frequency of this construction may have caused the increase in pronouns as copulas. This explanation is not favourable to the Aramaic and the even more probable Hurrian influence. Although it cannot be excluded that Hurrian contributed to the change.

al-ma-at-⸢tu⸣ šīt 'she is a widow' MAL A § 33:69

DAM-*ti šīt iqabbi* ''she is my wife', he will say' MAL A § 41:4

aššiti$^{sic.}$ *šīt lā aššat e-se-er-tu-ú-ma šīt* 'that wife is not a (proper) wife, she is a concubine' MAL A § 41:9–10

šumma ur-ki-it-tu šīt 'If she is a second (wife)' MAL A § 46:99

6 IKU (…) A.ŠÀ (…) *ša* PN *šūt* '6 *iku* field is of PN' KAV 127

mā da-an-ni šūt 'this is my valid declaration' KAV 159:4

ÌR *ša* EN-*ia anāku* 'I am the servant of my lord' KAV 159:6

mā Áš-šu-ra-iu-ú anākuma '(saying,) I am Assyrian' MARV 3 63:9'

mā a-bi-ia atta EN-⸢*ia*⸣ *atta* 'saying, "you are my father, you are my lord"' VAT 8851:19–20

me-e-tu šūt 'is he dead?' MATSH 8:49'

táq-qu-nu-ú šūt 'is it confirmed?' T 93-6:6

GÁNA.A.ŠÀ *mīnu šūt* 'a field? Why is that?' T 02-32:25

DUMU-*ša šu-ut* 'he is her son' Franke/Wilhelm 1985:4

There are a few cases where the pronouns are omitted:

mu-tu na-pal-tu '(give it, it is a question of) death or life' KAJ 316:14–15

mu-tu nap-ša-tu '(it is a question of) death or life' T 02-3:20

12 *umātu* (…) *lā aklu ū lā māʾū* '(for) 12 days there has been neither bread nor water' T 93-11:16–18

Instead of pronouns, the particle *-ma* can be added to the predicate of nominal clauses (GAG, 224 § 126c). This is not attested in OA.[13]

ḫiṭaʾšu kī ša DAM-*at* LÚ-*ma* 'his punishment will be (equal to) that of the other man's wife' MAL A § 16:66

lìb-bu-šu-ma mimma iddanašše '(if) it is his will, he will give her something' MAL A § 37:16

pa-nu-šu-ma bēl napšāte idūakšu '(if) it is his will, the *next-of-kin* will kill him' MAL B § 2:18–19 (see Roth 1997, 176)

mimma anniu a-na ni-še-šu-ma 'all this is for his installation' KAJ 179:19–20

[*m*]*ā ḫurādkunu mīna na-ki-ir-ma* '(concerning) your troops, why are they hostile?' MATSH 7:5"

As for animate nouns, in some cases, the stative of a noun is used (cf. Kouwenberg 2000, 43):

la-a ḫa-bu-la-ku ù la-a sa-ra-a-ku 'I am not indebted and not a criminal' KAV 201:6–7; (*sarru*) *la sa-ra-ku* A 133:7; *la sa-ar-ra-ku* A 748:7[14]

la u-bar u iš-šak 'he is not a stranger but an *iššakku*-farmer' RE 19:15

The following clause likely features a stative noun, but the translation is difficult to perform:

PN *ammākamma* É 'PN (has?) a house there' MATSH 22:27–28

13 See GKT, 186 § 107b, cf. GOA § 23.1.

14 It is possible to take these statives from the verb *sarāru* 'to be a cheat, criminal' (CAD S, 174–75). In general, this verb seems to occur in the prefix conjugation; thus we agree with CAD to take this stative from the noun *sarru* 'criminal' (CAD S, 183a).

18.6 Questions

§ 680 There are two main types of questions in MA: content questions (also called pronominal questions), which contain a question word, and polar questions (also called nexus questions).[15] We already discussed the first category of content questions with attestations (Chapter 11.7), so we will limit ourselves here to some irregularities of word order. Content questions are special sentences (together with dependent clauses) where the preterite is still applied for the past tense rather than the perfect. The situation regarding the past tense in polar questions is not unambiguous; possibly, the preterite was used here as well (see § 622).

§ 681 It can easily be observed that a question word is placed at the beginning of the sentence; however, there are also many exceptions to this. For extra emphasis, the subject may be placed before the question word:

> *šīpātu ša qātika ke-e ma-ṣi ibašši iriḫḫa* 'the wool that is at your disposal, how much is available as a remainder?' KAV 106:9–11
>
> [*ṭ*]*ēma akkīšuma a-na-i-ni tēp*[*uš*] 'why did you change the message this way?' KUB 3 73:13'
>
> [*m*]*ā ḫurādkunu mi-na nakirma* '(concerning) your troops, why are they hostile?' MATSH 7:5''
>
> *mā attu*[*n*]*ū ana mayyirāni mi-na tattanarr*[*ad*]*āne* 'thus (I said), "why do you keep coming down to the *m*.-troops?"' MATSH 7:6''–7''
>
> *šūt a-na-i-ni lā illika mēta lā ibki u balṭa lā ēmur* '(but) he, why did he not come to mourn the dead one and see the living one?' T 02-32:14–18
>
> *eqlu mi-i-nu šūt* 'a field? Why is that?' T 02-32:25

Once, when asked about the identity of the owner of horses, an analytic genitive construction is used. The question pronoun *mannu*, which is used as a governing noun, is thus placed at the start of the question, preceded only by *ša*:

> *ilta'lanni* [*mā š*]*a ma-an-ni si*[*sī*]*su*^{meš} 'he asked me: 'from whom are the horses?'' MATC 15:13–15

Similarly:

> *ša bēlīya a-ia-a-tu abātušu* 'which are the words of my lord?' MATSH 8:41'

Only once do we have a question word at the end of the question. Kouwenberg argued that, for OA, similar question clauses were formed because of the topicalization of the object at the beginning of the sentence (GOA § 23.2.1).

> *mā ṣab'a ša iddinūni a-le-e* 'where are the troops that they gave?' MARV 4 8:11–12

Some questions are likely to have been rhetorical, but can only be established by textual interpretation. Jakob (MATC, 47) pointed out that the interrogative adverb *kī* (or *kē*) could particularly be used with rhetorical questions (cf. AHw, 467b):

15 This division into two groups is found in GAG, 254–55 § 153; however, for different English terminology, see GOA § 23.2 and Izre'el/Cohen (2004, 110–1 § 4.5.2.3).

⌜*ke*⌝ *lā naqid* 'how is that not difficult? (i.e., it is not difficult)' MATC 7:20 (cf. commentary MATC, 47)

iltu kitāʾu laššūni igārātema u tarbāṣa ša ṣubāte liqâl[sic.] *lu ni-pu-uš* 'since there is no flax, he should look after the walls and the courtyard of the textile(?), or should we do it?' MATSH 6:9'–10'

mā ḫurādkunu ke-e nakirma 'thus, 'your *ḫurādu*-troops, how are they hostile?' MATSH 7:12''

§ 682 The section category of polar questions can only receive a yes/no answer; they do not have a question word and are therefore only recognized by context.

mīmummê [*ša*] *ana māte ša aḫīya aḫṭiūni* 'what sin (is it) [that] I committed against the land of my brother?' KUB 3 73:3'–4'

ša bēlī išpura[*n*]*ni* [*mā*] *me-e-tu šu-ut* '(concerning) whom my lord wrote to me, 'is he dead?'' MATSH 8:48'–49'

Sometimes scribes write a final open syllable plene. Perhaps this is done because of the change in intonation or simply to indicate a question by the absence of formal question words. The problem with the first solution is the lack of similar plene spellings in content questions. This is a common feature of Akkadian, which is also attested in OA and MA.[16] This study indicates such plene spellings in transcription with a circumflex on the vowel (^).

aššum kurummat ṣabʾe ša urḫe annie ša maḫrūni ni-da-na-šu-nu-ú kī ša ṭēmunni bēlī lišpura 'concerning the rations of the troops for this month, which they received, shall we give (them) to them? May my lord write me what (his) orders are' MARV 1 71:25–30

kuriangu i-ba-ši-i la-šu-ú 'is there *k.*-barley or not?' K9-T1:5–7

kī ina ⌜[lú]GIGIR⌝ (…) *tumarrirannini la aq-bi-a-ku-ú* 'that you annoyed me concerning the charioteer, did I not say to you (the following…)?' MATC 2:20–22

id-du-nu-ú la id-du-nu-ú bēlī lišpura 'will they give or not give? May my lord write it to me' MATSH 12:44–45

ta-an-ti-ši-an-ni-i 'did you forget me?' T 93-12:4

In the following passage, the lengthening falls on the nominative case of an adjective, rather than a finite verb:

ṭēm [*K*]*argamisīe ša taš*[*p*]*uranni táq-qu-nu-ú šūt* '(concerning) the news of the man of Carchemish about whom you wrote me, is it confirmed?' T 93-6:4–6

mā at-tu-[*nu*]*-ú-ma ana mayyirāni mi-na tattanarr*[*ad*]*āne* 'thus (I said), "why do you keep coming down to the *m.*-troops?"' MATSH 7:6'''–7''

We should also note the following damaged phrase with plene spelling, from a letter of questionable Assyrian character:

la-[*a*? *a*]*q*?*-ta-ba-ku-ú anāku* [lú][…]*-za*?*-a arḫiš lu nuḫalliq* 'did I not say to you: "we should quickly get rid of the […]-man"' KBo 28 82:5–6

16 Cf. GAG, 255 § 153d; GOA § 23 .2.2; SNAG, 35 § 2.4.10.

18.7 Negation

§ 683 Negation of verbs in MA is expressed by the usage of the particle *lā*. The Babylonian *ul* (GAG, 220f § 122b) and the OA *ūla* (GKT, 183f § 105; GOA § 23.3.1) are basically absent; thus, the distribution of *ul* and *lā* over different types of sentences is not found here.[17] Likewise, the vetitive (*ē*), which was still known in OA (GKT, 129f § 77d; GOA § 19.8.3), is not attested in MA, with *lā* used here for negative wishes and commands.[18] The OA negation *ūla* is still attested in PNs, but only rarely:

^{md}UTU-*ú-la-am-ši* (< *Šamaš-ūla-amši*) 'I-did-not-forget-Šamaš' KAJ 234:4

The Babylonian negation *ul* is also found in PNs:

^{m}*A-ba-ul-i-de* 'He-does-not-know-(his)-father' T 98-112:11

Only once do we possibly find it as a negation of the verbal predicate. It occurs in a main clause, describing something that may not be done, similar to OA. On the other hand, it is unfortunate that the signs of the passage are somewhat damaged, with an additional *ša* visible on the copy, which does not belong here.

ina muḫḫišu ire$^{??}$*â u ú-*⌜*la*$^{?}$ {*ša*$^{?}$}⌝ *i-ba-qa-an* '(the sheep) will pasture at his expense, but he shall not pluck (them)' KAJ 88:17–18

Alternatively, Saporetti (1981, 20) reads *ú-*⌜*la*$^{!}$⌝*-da*$^{!}$ *i-ba-qa-an*, which should be translated 'he (may) pluck the offspring.' The noun *ulādu* used for offspring is unexpected and would appear to be an infinitive. Therefore, this reading remains tentative.

§ 684 Mostly, we find *lā* used on verbal forms. The function of negated verbs differs slightly across the tenses. We already discussed the negated counterparts of the precative and imperative, which seems to come down to a combination of *lū lā* and a present form, e.g., *lū lā takkal* 'do not eat!' (see § 641). However, the negated second-person present is, in most cases, to a certain degree, a negative command or instruction. Note, in particular, the PKT clauses in which non-negated verbs occur in the present rather than the imperative.

la tu-na-kar 'you must not remove it' PKT 1 I right:14

[*išāta*] *la-a tu-da-*ˀ*a-an* 'you will not make the fire too strong' PKT 1 II left 29

[*la*]*-a tu-ta-ḫa-aḫ* 'you will not drench it' PKT 4 obv. left 3 cf. obv. right 21

ŠE *u qēmamma la-a tu-ma-ṭa-a* 'do not reduce barley and flour' A 877:9–10

[*mar š*]*ipre* (…) [*l*]*a tu*$_4$*-ka-*⌜*as*⌝*-sú* 'do not delay the messenger' EA 15:16–18

la-a tu-šar-šu 'do not let him go' MATC 2:23

mimma laššutta la ta-pa-la-ni 'do not answer me that there is nothing whatsoever' OIP 79 2:10–12

PN (…) *la-a te-zi-ba* 'do not leave PN behind' T 93-2:9–11

la-a t[*a*]*-qa-bi* 'do not say' T 93-2:12

---

17 Note that *ul* occurs passim in two incantation tablets (Lambert 1965, 1969).

18 Cf. GAG, 133 § 81i and, in response, Kouwenberg (2010, 219 n35).

The difference is clearest in the following example: *la ta-bal-laṭ* 'you will not live' Ištar Ritual r. 6'. Naturally, this is no negated command, i.e., 'do not live' (sic). Rather, it is expressed as undesirable that the addressed person will live. However, the difference is superficial as it is limited to the perspective from an English language point of view. In MA, there was no difference, so the problem is semantic with there being no negative imperative for *balāṭu*.

§ 685 Similar to the second-person cases, the third person frequently occurs in descriptions of future events, which are therefore often close to the negated counterparts of the precative.

> *šumma* (…) [*uz*]*nēša la-a ú-na-ak-ki-is ša urde u amte la-a ú-na-ku-su-ma* 'if he did not cut off her ears (i.e., of the wife), they should not cut (the ears) of the slave and maid' MAL A § 4:53–55
>
> *la-a ta-šap-pa-ra-am-ma* 'she shall not send' MAPD § 6:43
>
> *šumma* PN_1 PN_2 *la i-pá-la-aḫ* 'if PN_1 will not serve PN_2' KAJ 6:17–19
>
> *ana aḫê la ta-da-an* 'she will not give it to strangers' KAJ 9:27
>
> *mamma ana dēn dayyān la i-la-qe-a-ni la e-ka-la-an-ni* 'nobody may take me to court or detain me' KAV 159:6–8
>
> *šamna la i-ṣa-ḫu-tu* 'they will not press the oil' T 93-7:18
>
> *zammārātu Kilizāy*[*ā*]*tu la-a il-la-ka-ni* 'the Kilizean singers may not come' T 93-54:21–22
>
> *la-a er-ru-bu akla la-a ú-šá-ku-lu-šu-nu* 'they will not enter and they will (also) not provide them with bread' T 04-37:5

The first person:

> *la ú-ba-la-aṭ-ku-n*[*u*] 'I will not keep you alive' KAV 96:17

The preterite maintains its past meaning (for exceptions, see § 631).

> *la-a ub-la-áš-ši* 'he did not bring her' MAL A § 40:79
>
> *panē mamma la ta-pùl* 'formerly, you responded to no one' T 97-10:20
>
> *mēta la-a ib-ki u balṭa la-⸢a⸣ e-mu-ur* '(he did not come) to mourn the dead one and see the living one?' T 02-32:16–18
>
> *Aššurāyu m*[*a*]*mma la-a ur-da ṭēma la áš-ʾa-al* 'no Assyrian came down, so I did not request a report' T 04-13:14–16
>
> *šumma ṣarpa la-a tam-ḫur* 'if you did not receive the silver' Faist 2001, 252:23

§ 686 As we have discussed elsewhere (§ 631), the cases of a negated perfect should be regarded as a future tense of the futurum exactum type.

> *šumma sinniltu la-a taq-ti-bi* 'if the woman has not declared it' MAL A § 23:37
>
> *piriltaša la ta-ta-ṣar-ma la ta-šal-lim* '(if) you did not guard her secret, you will not prosper' Adad Ritual r. 7'

šumma ina adre qaqqad ŠE *la im-ta-da-ad* ŠE *ana* <*ṣibte*> *illak* 'if he has not measured out the capital of the barley at the threshing-floor, the barley shall bear <interest>' KAJ 81:15–17

šumma adi 1 ITI.UD[meš] *la-a i-ti-din* 'if he has not given (them) within a month (then…)' KAJ 88:15–16 (TN); et passim

[*šum*]*ma abāssu la i-ta-mar tuppušu urrâššu* 'if he has not examined his case, he shall deliver his tablet to him' KAJ 89:14'–16'

šumma ina ad-ri la it-ti-din ŠE-*um*[meš] *a-na* MÁŠ-*šu i-lak* 'if he will not have given it on the threshing floor, the barley will go for interest' Giricano 1:17–20

šúm-ma i+na ad-ra-te la i-ta-nu ŠE-*um a-na* MÁŠ *i-lak* 'if they do not give it at the threshing floors, the barley shall go for interest' OIP 79 5:17–19

qāssunu la ú-ṣa-li-ú (*uṣṣalliʾū* < *uṣtalliʾū*) 'they should not put down their work' T 93-7:16

Negation *lā* with a stative:

aḫḫū mutiša la-a ze-e-zu 'her brothers-in-law did not divide (the inheritance)' MAL A § 25:84

abu la-a ḫa-a-di 'the father is not happy' MAL A § 55:38

ša la-a mar-ru-ru-ni 'who is not castrated' MAPD § 8:50

Sūtīu ina māt x[...] *la-a ša-ak-nu* 'Suteans are not stationed in the country […]' MATSH 2:41–42

la ḫa-bu-la-ku ù la sa-ra-ku 'I am not indebted and not a criminal' A 133:6–7

šamaššammū ša PN *la maḫ-ru* 'sesame of PN is not received' LVUH 104:12–14

PN *iltēšu la-a ṭa-ab* 'PN is not on good terms with him' T 02-32:21–22

§ 687 While *lā* is mostly used to negate verbs, it is also required to negate nouns and other substantives. Unlike, for instance, the Arabic *ġayra* (غير), MA has no special negator for substantives. In general, the dialect is noticeable for its simplicity in indicating negation, where one form fits all and difference in meaning only follows out of context. In the category of substantives, a defective spelling for the negation is preferred over plene *la-a*. Often, the negated substantive is also the nominal predicate or possibly a nominal stative:

šumma aššat aʾīle la-a a-bu-ša la-a a-ḫu-ša la-a DUMU-*ša aʾīlu šanīumma ḫarrāna ultaṣbissi* 'if another man, neither her father, nor her brother, nor her son, arranges for a wife to travel (with him)' MAL A § 22:105–108

la-a mi-gi-ir-mi iqabbi 'he declares it to be not free will' KAJ 57:20–21

la mu-ti-mi taqabbi '(he) is not my husband', she says' TIM 4 45:14

Negation *lā* with participles and adjectives:

aḫḫū mutiša la-a ze-zu-ú-tu 'her brothers-in-law, who did not divide' MAL A § 25:88–89

la-a ma-ag-ru-tu ibašši 'there are people not willing' MAL B § 17:11

ina la ze-zi-[*šu-nu*] 'from their undivided (property)' KAJ 8:19

Adjectives in negation:

[G]UD *la še-bi*$^{\text{sic.}}$ (…) *iddan* 'he will give a young ox' (lit. 'not old') Giricano 10:17–18

i+na ŠÀ GIŠ.GÀR *la-a maḫ-ri* 'from the non-received assignment' KAV 98:42

šúm-ma TÚG$^{\text{ḫi.a.meš}}$ *ḫa-ˀu la-a ma-si-ú-tu i-ba-áš-ši* 'if there are unwashed *ḫ*.-textiles' KAV 105:22–24

20 ^{giš}BAN^{meš} *la sa-aḫ-pa-tum* (…) *ma-ḫi-ir* 'he received 20 unwrapped bows' MARV 1 20:2–5

Negation *lā* with an adverbial:

šattum la ša-tum 'year by year' A 333:7[19]

§ 688 The negation *lā* is often preceded by a preposition, sometimes altering the meaning slightly. In combination with *ina*, the negation sometimes (but not always) receives a meaning 'without' (cf. GOA § 23.3.1); cf. the more common preposition *balu* 'without' (§ 447).

ŠE-*um anniu i+na la-a šu-a-te bēssu uballiṭi*$^{\text{sic.}}$ 'this barley will support his house in the absence of his (own barley)' KAJ 101:11–13

i+na la šu-a-te iddini$^{\text{sic.}}$ 'he will give in his absence' MARV 1 47:10–11

i+na la ÉRIN^{meš} *lā ašḫul* 'I could not filter without people (personnel)' MATSH 3:32

The combination can also be used as a locative:

šumma aʾīlu i+na la-a qa-qí-ri-i-šu lū kirāʾa iddi 'if a man either planted an orchard in a plot of ground (that is) not his' MAL B § 13:19–20

In this locative construction, the negation usually precedes the preposition:

la-a ina GN_1 *u la-a ina* GN_2 *aʾīlutta a-mur* 'I saw troops neither in GN_1 nor in GN_2' MATSH 3:28–30

la-a ina bēt āpiē u la ina bēt sīrāšê^{meš} *i-ba-áš-ši* 'there are no bakers in the house and no brewers in the house' MATSH 12:33–34

la-a ina qaqqere iyê ḫa-laq 'he did not disappear in my territory' MATSH 17:10'–11'

Combinations with *kī* are rare. The attestation given below seems to be a mimationless *kīam*, rather than *kī*, which otherwise rarely occurs in MA (see § 732f; cf. CAD K, 327).

ù la ki-a attunuma leqyāne 'and if it is not so, you take it to me' KAV 105:29–30

With the preposition *ana*:

šum ile a-na la-a ki-it-te [...] 'the name of god for improper [...]' MAPD § 11:62

Infinitives, with and without prepositions, also occur:

udīni edānu la-a ma-⸢*ša*⸣*-e* 'the term not yet forgotten' MAL B § 6:21–22

a-na la ma-ša-e šaṭir 'it is written down in order not to be forgotten' KAJ 197:8–9

ša a-na la a-la-ki 'whom for not going' MARV 4 5:4

[*mi*]*mma* ⸢*la*⸣*-a e-pa-še* 'nothing to do' MATSH 26:16'

19 The interpretation of this difficult phrase follows Donbaz. Similar 'Noun *lā* Noun' expressions are discussed by W. R. Mayer (1989).

Chapter 19: Syntax: Coordination

19.1 The conjunction *u*

§ 689 The most common MA conjunction, *u,* is found in most Semitic languages as *w(a)-* and is used to connect sentences in the most basic meaning 'and.' Unlike suffixed *-ma*, there does not need to be a direct relationship between the two sentences.[1] Huehnergard (2005, 49f § 7.4) added that the connected sentences are interchangeable, unlike *-ma.* Orthographically, the sign Ù is almost exclusively used for the conjunction. Plene spellings are unknown. In a few cases, we find the other common values for *u*; however, in percentage terms, the share of Ù is much higher than the 85% suggested for NA (SNAG, 66). Spellings with <ú> are extremely rare, as the sign is used for syllabic spellings. Nonetheless, two uncontested attestations are found in the M 9 archive:

tuppi 1 *šūši iku* A.ŠÀ *ú du-un-ni* (…) 'a tablet of a 60 *iku* field and *dunnu* (…)' KAJ 160:2 (Ead)

tu-a-ru ú da-ba-b[*u*] *laššu* 'there is no renewal of litigation' KAM 10 15:17–18 (Aub)

Spellings with <u$_1$> are more common. Attestations are found in various documents from the capital up until the reign of TN. Additionally, passages with <u$_1$> are found in the Coronation Ritual:

^{d}BAD *u* ^{d}*Da-gan* 'Ellil and Dagan' Coronation Ritual i 44

aga'a ša Aš-šur u ^{giš}TUKUL^{meš} *ša Mulliltu inaššia* 'he will carry the crown of Aššur and the weapons of Mullissu' Coronation Ritual ii 15

A.ŠÀ^{meš} u É ⸢^{meš}⸣-*šú-nu* 'fields and their houses' KAJ 32:17

A.ŠÀ-*šu u* É-*sú* 'his field and his house' KAJ 44:14; cf. KAJ 69:13

ŠE-*um u* SIG$_4$ *raksū* 'the barley and bricks are bound' KAM 10 9:16

É-*sú u ba-ši-šu* 'his house and his property' KAM 10 18:16

1 *emāru* ŠE *u* ^{lú}⸢*e*⸣-[*ṣi-di*] 'one homer of barley and a reaper' KAM 10 32:3'

§ 690 In terms of its funcion, we can divide the usage of *u* into two categories. As we have already described, the first connects the interchangeable clauses. Nonetheless, the two parts stand in relation to each other in the context of the text (cf. GAG, 257 § 156b–c). One would expect that *u* expanded to cover the function of the nearly obsolete conjunction *-ma*, whose possibilities we will discuss below (§ 693f). The tempus of the two connected main clauses needs to be identical (GKT, 225 § 134a; GOA § 24.4.2):

šumma sinniltu ina bēt abīšama us-bat ù mussa me-e-et 'if a woman dwells in the house of her father and her husband is dead' MAL A § 26:95–96

mā lā ḫa-bu-la-ku ù lā sa-ra-ku 'I am not indebted and not a criminal' A 133:6–7

---

1 See GAG, 212 § 117a; also, SNAG, 124f § 4.4.1.2.

šumma lā tudda'āšu mimma pîšu ša-a'-la ù šumma mēt tuppukunu šu-uṭ-ra 'if you do not know him, ask what is said about him and, if he is dead, write your tablet' KAV 107:18–20

nikkassa[meš] *i-ṣa-bat ù tuppušu i-ḫap-pi* 'he will settle accounts and break his tablet' Billa 7:11–13

annūtu āla li-il-bi-ú ù annūte ana bir[āte] lu-ú-še-be-er 'these (troops) must lay siege to the city and I shall bring those (troops) across to the fortifications' MATSH 8:26'–27'

šumma mimma laššutta ta-ta-pa-al-šu ù arḫiš la-a ta-ta-na-áš-šu 'if you answer him that there is nothing whatsoever and you do not give him quickly' OIP 79 3:14–18

mēta la-a ib-ki ù balṭa la-⌜a⌝ e-mu-ur '(he did not come) to mourn the dead one and see the living one?' T 02-32:16–18

This is not the case when both sentences are nominal, a stative verbal predicate or an imperative:

ina bēt āḫizānīša ir-ti-bi ù tuppu ša mar'uttīšu la-a šaṭ-rat 'he grows up in the house of the one who married her, but the tablet of his adoption is not written' MAL A § 28:4–5

PN_1 *ša* PN_2 (…) *ú-še-ri-ba-ni ù ana ṭē'inutte ta-ad-nu-ni* 'PN_1, whom PN_2 brought and gave for grinding' KAV 107:5–13

Another type of connection is an opposition, which we can translate as 'but' or 'however':

la-a ḫa-bu-la-ku u la-a sa-ra-a-ku ⌜ù⌝ {ù} bitqīya ib-ta-ta-aq 'I am not indebted and not a criminal, but he made accusations against me' KAV 201:6–9

la u-bar u iš-šak 'he is not a stranger but an *iššakku*-farmer' RE 19:15

Connecting direct speech:

mā 2 sisīu[meš] *ša Sūtīē iltēya it-ta-ṣu-ú-ni ù ma-a ana ṣēne ū[ma]kkal iq-tu-a-al* 'thus, two Sutean horses went out with me', and 'thus, he took care of the cattle for a day' MATC 15:25–29

§ 691 Given the loss of *-ma* (see below), we may expect *u* to partly replace it. However, there are in fact a few cases where *u* covers the syntactic function of *-ma*. Instead, as we will see below, instances with *-ma* are usually replaced with an asyndetic construction.

u connects two verbs:

šumma mussa magir šurqa id-dan ù i-pa-aṭ-ṭar-ši 'if her husband agrees, he will give the stolen goods and ransom her' MAL A § 5:63–64

ša-lu-da ù ba-aq-na 'they are caused to give birth and be plucked' LVUH 28:23

§ 692 The second function of *u* is enumerating objects. In MA, these are usually two objects. For instance:

LÚ *ù* MUNUS-*ma idukkū* 'they will kill the man and woman' MAL A § 13:29

ana [d]ÍD-*i-id ù ma-mi-te lā iṣṣabbutū* 'they will not be taken for the river ordeal and oath' MAL A § 25:93–94

[lú]NAGAR *ù pír-'a* 'the carpenter and apprentice' MATC 1:4

ŠE-*am ù* IN.NU 'barley and straw' MATC 6:10

la-a i+na GN_1 *ù la-a i+na*! GN_2 *aʾīlutta āmur* 'neither in GN_1 nor in GN_2 did I see the people' MATSH 3:28–30

KAŠ^{meš} *ù* ^{dug}*ta-ri-ḫa-te* 'beer and vessels' T 93-3:15–16

Often, the two enumerated objects are expanded into a relative clause:

4 MUNUS^{meš} *la ia-a-tu ša kī ṣarpe tadnāni ù* MUNUS *ku-a-tu iltu annākamma* 'four women, not mine, that are sold and your woman from there' MATC 15:4–7

3 *ṣi-mi-[te* ^{anše}*]ku-di-ni ša* 3 *qa*$^{ta.àm}$ ŠE-*am ekkulūni ù* 6 ANŠE^{meš} *ša* 2 *qa*$^{ta.àm}$ *ekkulūni* 'three spans of donkeys that will each eat three litres of barley and six donkeys that will each eat two litres' MATC 24A:9–12

Multiple objects:

ana PN_1 PN_2 *ù* PN_3 *qibīma* 'speak to PN_1, PN_2 and PN_3' KAV 99:1–3

In multiple genitive constructions, governed nouns may be coordinated with the conjunction *u*:

šurista$^{sic.}$ *ša ši-in-ni ù* ^{giš}*a-ši-e* 'the *š*. of ivory and ebony wood' KAV 99:26–27

Enumerations of objects without *u* or any other conjunction occur:

5 6 *tap-pa-e-šu ušeššab* 'he will seat five or six comrades' MAL A § 41:2

2 BÁN ŠE-*am* 1 *a-za-i-la ša tibne* (…) *din* 'give two seahs of barley (and) one sack with straw' MATC 6:4–7

19.2 The sentence connector *-ma*

§ 693 We already discussed *-ma* as a marker of focus (see Chapter 12.1); however, *-ma* is also common in Akkadian as a conjunction and a sentence connector. As such, we find it used in OA (GKT, 225ff § 135; GOA § 24.4.3), but, over time, this function fell into decay, while, in NA, it is not used anymore (SNAG, 66). In MA, the sentence connector function can still be observed (cf. UGM, 101 § 87), although von Soden labelled its frequency as '*selten*' (GAG, 221 § 123a). It may be observed that it has indeed become rare in some texts, as it only occurs twice in the Coronation Ritual and is absent in the New years ritual. Similarly, the function of conjunction is rare in WPA in contrast to its usage in the core Akkadian dialects.[2] Unlike the conjunction *u*, enclitic *-ma* connects sentences, which are related to each other, following in a chronological sequence that cannot be reversed. It may be noted that *-ma* is especially frequent in MAL A, more so than in the other literary texts. Again, this is a reflection of the more archaic syntax of the text. Some attestations from MAL A are given below:

šumma asû ur-ták-ki-is-ma išku šanittu iltēšama tattalpat 'if a physician bandages it, but then the second testicle becomes infected with it' MAL A § 8:81–83

kišpē ú-up-pi-šu-ma ina qātīšunu iṣṣabtu 'they performed witchcraft and were caught in the act' MAL A § 47:2–3

2 See WPA in Huehnergard (1989, 203ff); Izre'el (1991, 323ff); cf. MB in Aro (1955a, 136ff) and NB in Woodington (1983, 307ff § 117).

ša kišpē iš-me-ú-ni-ma anāku ātamar iqbiaššunni 'who heard of the witchcraft and who said to him 'I saw it'' MAL A § 47:10–11

When combining a sequence of two verbs:

iṣ-ba-at-sú-ma innābit 'he seized him and he fled' MAL A § 36:106

e-ta-mar-ma ūtaššir 'he saw (her) and let (her) go' MAL A § 40:78

In some cases, the sequence of connected clauses may not be chronological (cf., for OB, Cohen 2000, 209ff):

ša urde u amte la-a ú-na-ku-su-ma šurqa lā umalluʾū 'they will not cut off (the ears) of the slave and maid and they will not compensate the stolen goods' MAL A § 4:55–56

When *-ma* connects a sequence of verbs, it is added to the penultimate verb (Streck 2014a, 135–36 § 318):

tuppātēšunu lušēliānimma ana panē qēputte liš-ku-nu li-id-bu-bu lu-zak-k[*i*]*-ú-ma li-il-*⸢*qé*⸣*-ú* 'they should bring up their tablets and place them before the officials, speak, clear (the field from claims) and take it' MAL B § 6:16–17

§ 694 Attestations of *-ma* in letters are very rare and most instances should be regarded as markers of the logical predicate (Chapter 12.1), rather than as sentence connectors. In letters *-ma* is thus rather exceptional, but always attested in the formulaic standard introduction (see the first example).

ana PN$_1$ *qí-bi-ma umma* PN$_2$*-ma* 'speak to PN$_1$, so (says) PN$_2$' passim in letters

i-[*l*]*u-k*[*u*]*-ni-ma ikaššudū* 'they will come and arrive' MATSH 3:42–43

In contracts, *-ma* is especially frequent. In addition to the examples presented below, we may also note that *-ma* links the protasis and the apodosis in some cases of conditional clauses without *šumma* (for a discussion on this matter, see § 709f).

pāḫassunu e-pu-lu-ma (…) *ṣarpa u* ŠE*-im* (…) *iddunū* 'they will answer to their responsibilities and pay for the silver and barley' KAJ 57:18–22

i-din-ma ušapp[*i*] 'he will give it and make it acquired' KAJ 148:18

ú-za-ak-ka-ma ilaqqe 'he will clear it and take it' KAV 212:10–11

Pleonastic sequences of *-ma+u* are rare (cf. HurAkk Adler 1976, 73 § 52a). Moreover, it is questionable how far *-ma* is used as a sentence connector or logical predicate (see Chapter 12.1).

ṭiḫi eqle pūre ša PN$_1$*-ma ù ṭiḫi* <*eqle*> *pūre ša* PN$_2$ *aḫīšu* 'adjacent to the field lot of PN$_1$ and adjacent to the lot of PN$_2$, his brother' AO 19.228:10–11

iltu ^{túg}*katāʾu*^{meš} *laššūni i-ga-ra-te-ma ù tarbāṣa ša* TÚG *liqâl*$^{\text{sic.}}$ *lū nēpuš* 'since there is no flax, he should look after the walls and the courtyard of the textiles(?), or should we do it?' MATSH 6:9'–10'

anaʾīne PN *marā šipre ana muḫḫīya il-li-ka-ma ù šulmaka lā tašp*[*u*]*ra* 'why did PN, the messenger, come to me, but you did not send me your greetings (with him)?' RS 06.198:7–11

19.3 Asyndetic constructions

§ 695 As the particle *-ma* has mostly lost its function as a conjunction, the number of asyndetic clauses has increased in MA. This not only covers clauses where we would expect *-ma*, but also *u*, which remains absent from a number of cases. This does not mean that asyndetically connected clauses are a new feature in MA; they are well attested in OA and OB. Moreover, it often remains difficult to establish whether clauses are semantically connected. When two verbs are directly connected, they indicate (an often chronological) sequence of actions. In MA, this construction is usually indicated as asyndetic:

> PN *šuršurrāte sipa*[*rre*$^{\text{pl.}}$] *amtaḫaṣ ul-te-bi-lak-ku-n*[*u*] 'I will have put PN in fetters and sent (him) to you' KAV 96:5–8
>
> *tuppukunu šu-uṭ-ra še-bi-la-ni* 'write your tablet and send it here' KAV 100:27
>
> *ga-mu-ur ta-din* 'it is completely given' LVUH 66:21
>
> *sisīū*^{meš} (…) *lu-us-bu le-ku-lu* 'may the horses stay and eat' MATC 4:3–5
>
> *al-ta-ḫa-al ut-ta-mi-i*[*š*] 'I selected and made depart' MATC 10:22
>
> *ṣab'ē*$^{\text{sic.}}$ *annūte liš-ši li-*⌜*mur*⌝$^{?}$ 'he should bring in(?) these troops and inspect (them)' MATC 11:28
>
> *Sūtīū* (…) *e-te-li-ú-ni iq-ti-bi-ú-ni* 'the Suteans came up and said to me' T 93-54:4–6
>
> *mu-ḫur di-na-áš-šu* 'receive it and give it to him' T 97-17:7–8
>
> *it-tal-ku-ú-ni ib-ti-ki-i-ú* 'they came and wept' T 02-32:12–13

The same is true for clauses where the verbs do not follow each other directly, but still indicate a chronological sequence.

> *mimma la-a id-da-na-áš-še rāquttēša tu-ú-uṣ-ṣa* 'he will give her nothing and she will leave empty-handed' MAL A § 37:17–19
>
> *šumma a'īlu esertušu upaṣṣan* 5 6 *tappā'ēšu ú-še-šab ana panēšunu ú-pa-ṣa-an-ši* 'if a man intends to veil his concubine, he will seat five or six witnesses and veil her in their presence' MAL A § 41:1–3
>
> *šūt il-tu-ḫu-ur iltēša i-da-bu-ub* 'he tarries to speak with her' MAPD § 21:106
>
> *kanīkāte šu-uṭ-ra ana libbi tupninnāte ṣe-el-a* 'inscribe your sealed documents and deposit them in the boxes' KAV 98:23–25
>
> *nakkamta pi-ti-a iškāra* (…) *še-ṣi-a-ni di-na* 'open the storage, take out the assignment and give it' KAV 100:16–18
>
> *ana muḫḫi šarre ta-ka-ša-ad ta-ka-la ana pāḫitīka la-za-az* 'should you be detained upon reaching the king, I shall not stand for you' MCS 2 1:20–23
>
> *šumma ana muḫḫi annie i-ba-áš-ši up-ta-zi-r*[*u*] *la-a il-ṭu-ru* 'if there is (something more) in addition to this (inventory) they have concealed and did not register' RE 92:7–11
>
> *alpēšu gabba lu-pa-ḫi-ra ina panēka lu-ú-*[*š*]*a-zi-iz* 'may he gather all his oxen and transfer (them) to your presence' T 97-17:8–11

A number of enumerations is also asyndetic, whereas, in normal circumstances, we would expect the conjunction *u* to be used (cf. OA in GOA § 24.2.1).

ana ub-ru-te EN^{meš} URU^{didli} 'for the foreign envoys and the lords of the cities' CTMMA 1 99:4

PN ^{kur}*I-ma-ra-a-i[u] ana muḫḫi šarre* (…) *ša sulummāʾe iltanappurū* 'PN (and) the Emariote are sending peace proposals to the king' T 96-1:12–17

e-ṣu-tu ma-du-tù 'little and much' TR 3025:16

Compare the following two similar clauses, with and without the conjunction *u*:

kāte annuku eq[al]šu bēssu marʾūšu mārāt[šu] 'the pledge for the lead are his field, his house, sons and daughters' KAJ 16:15–16; cf. KAJ 37:13–14; KAJ 40:13–14

kāte annuku eqalšu ù̲ bēssu 'the pledge for the lead are his field and his house' KAJ 34:13–14; cf. KAJ 47:25–26; KAM 10 29:12–15

19.4 *ū* 'or'

§ 696 This conjunction is always written with <Ù>, making it orthographically identical to the other conjunction *u* 'and', despite having a different etymological background: *ū* (< *aw*).[3] It is therefore often unclear whether *ū* or *u* is intended. Despite the confusion, some likely attestations may be given:

šumma attunu takuššā PN *lilqea ù lā kīa attunuma leqyāne* 'if you are delayed, PN must take it and, if it is not so, you must take it' KAV 105:27–30

5 *šiluḫlū mētuttu ù ḫalquttu* 'five *šiluḫlu*-personnel dead or lost' MPR 66:51

12 *umātu* (…) *lā aklu ū lā māʾū* '(for) 12 days there has been neither bread nor water' T 93-11:16–18

We find *ū* probably in combination with the particle *lū*, when indicating alternatives in the construction *lū* (…) *ū lū* (…) 'be it (…) or be it (…)' (see also below):

lu-ú ana aʾīle lu-ú ana sinnilte ù̲ l̲ú̲ ana mamma šanīemma tattidin 'she gives it either to a man, a woman or somebody else' MAL A § 3:26–28

There is a number of asyndetic constructions where *ū* should have been used, yet it is not found. It should be pointed out that most of the examples concern question clauses.

māna GN_1 *māna* GN_2 *māna* GN_3 *ana maqāte mā lā [u]dda* 'whether they are to attack GN_1, GN_2 or GN_3, I do not know' MATSH 3:13–16

kuriangu ibaššî laššû 'is there *k.*-barley or not?' K9-T1:5–7

iltu ^{túg}*kitāʾu*^{meš} *laššūni igarātemma u tarbāṣa ša ṣubāte liqâl*$^{sic.}$ *lū nēpuš* 'since there is no flax, he should look after the walls and the courtyard of the textile(?), or should we do it?' MATSH 6:9'–10'

iddunû lā iddunû bēlī lišpura 'will they give or not give? May my lord write it to me' MATSH 12:44–45

3 See GAG, 212 § 117b; cf. the Arabic *ʾāw* (أو) (Fischer 2006, 156 § 331).

mēt ḫalaqa ina muḫḫīšunu '(if) he dies or flees, the responsibility is theirs' RE 19:16–17

19.5 *lū* 'be it, or'

§ 697 The conjunction *lū* should not be confused by the identical particle used for verbs and attached directly to precative basis. We find it in the construction *lū* (…) *lū* (…), where it arranges different objects in a clause, which, together, form one grammatical element (cf. GAG, 212 § 117d). In OA, this conjunction is usually spelled defectively as *lu* (GOA § 24.3.4). For NA, Hämeen-Anttila claimed a differentiation between the spelling *lu-ú* for precatives and *lu-u*$_1$ for the conjunction (SNAG, 66 § 3.5). MA does not have this innovation; the spelling remains almost exclusively *lu-ú*. Nonetheless, defective *lu* is still found in all kinds of texts. It is unlikely that this is a reflection of OA; most likely, it is applied because it is shorter and thus easier to use. Here are a few examples:

šumma aʾīlu ana tappāʾīšu lu-ú ina puzre lu ina ṣālte iqbi 'if a man said (so-and-so) to his comrade in private or in a quarrel' MAL A § 18:72–74

ugār GN_1 *lu* GN_2 'the meadow of GN_1 or GN_2' KAM 10 7:6'–7'

lu ina eqle lu ša ina Libbi-āle 'either in the countryside or in the inner city (Aššur)' KAM 10 31:8

lu Kaššīū lu Sūḫāyū 'be it Kassites or Suḫeans' T 04-37:1

§ 698 We have already mentioned that the sequence *lū* (…) *lū* (…) is used to enumerate items, indicating different alternatives. We can usually translate 'either (…) or (…)':

šumma sinniltu lu-ú aššat aʾīle lu-ú mārat aʾīle šillata taqtibi 'If a woman, be she a wife or of the *awīlu*-class, spoke slander' MAL A § 2:14–16

šumma aʾīlu lu-ú mariṣ lu-ú mēt 'if a man is sick or dead' MAL A § 3:23–24

ugāru (…) *lu-ú ina zittīšu lu-ú šiāmātī*[*š*]*u* [*lu*]*-ú šiāmāt abīšu* 'the meadow, be it his share or his purchase or the purchase of his father' KAJ 153:4–6

lu-ú ugār ḫarībete lu-ú ugār GN_1 *lu-ù ugār* GN_2 *lu-ú zittušu ù-lu-ú šīmātušu lu-*⌜*ú*⌝ *ḫarībete* ⌜*lu*⌝*-*[*ú*] GN_1 *ù-*[*lu*]*-ú* GN_2 *maškan ēnāšu iššakkanān*[*i*] 10 *iku eqla inass*[*a*]*q* '10 *iku* field – be it the meadow of the steppe or the meadow of GN_1 or the meadow of GN_2 or his share or be it his purchase or of the steppe or of GN_1 or be it of GN_2 – he will select the place of his choosing (lit. the place his eyes are put on)' KAJ 179:6–16

In the following phrase, *lū* is omitted before the last term of the enumeration and replaced by *u*:

emmera^{meš} *lu-ú ša iltu* GN *naṣṣakkūni lu-ú kuāʾuttu ù emmera*^{meš} *umzarḫē ša libbi ṣēnīya altaḫal* 'sheep, be it those that are brought to you from GN, be it yours or *umzarḫu*-sheep, I have selected from my livestock' MATC 10:16–22

Sometimes, *lū* directly follows the conjunction <Ù>. In this case, we should probably analyse it as *ū* 'or', as, in these constructions, it indicates an alternative. Some studies prefer to read the compound *ūlu* (e.g., GAG, 212 § 117c–d). In OA, this construction is still rare (GOA § 24.3.6).

^{f}PN *lu 2 niggalla siparra ù lu eria* ^{f}PN *lū tušēbila* '^{f}PN, may ^{f}PN send me two sickles of copper or bronze' A 845:14–18

tuppi 1 *šūši iku eqle u dunne adre kirīe u būrte* ⸢*ù lu-ú*⸣ *qaqqar āle* 'a tablet of 60 *iku* of the countryside and *dunnu*, a threshing floor, an orchard, terrain or a well of the city' KAJ 160:2–4

lu-ú zittušu ù lu-ú ši-ma-tu-šu lu-⸢*ú*⸣ *ḫarībete* ⸢*lu*⸣-[*ú*] GN$_1$ *ù* [*lu*]-*ú* GN$_2$ or be it his purchase or of the steppe or of GN$_1$ or be it of GN$_2$ KAJ 179:9–13

ina panē pāḫitīšu lu$^{!}$ *āla iṣbat ù lu-ú kī raqāʾe ana GN ērub* 'he settled on (the land of) his province or city, or secretly entered GN' MARV 4 119:26–28

§ 699 Veenhof (1972, 18 n35) pointed out that, for OA, while the previously offered translation suggests that *lū* is used to enumerate alternatives, this is certainly not always the case. More often than not, all elements are used to enumerate elements that are available, as is suggested by constructions, such as *lū* (…) *lū* (…) *u*. He therefore suggested the translation 'whether (…) or (…)'. We can also apply this claim at least to some MA phrases, as can be observed in the following example:

šumma aʾīlu ina lā qaqqirīšu lu kirīa iddi lu-ú būrta iḫri lu-ú urqē lu GIŠ^{meš} *urabbi* 'if a man in a plot not his own, either established an orchard, or dug a well, or grows vegetables or trees' MAL B § 13:19–22

It is unlikely that the man is expected to have dug a well, established an orchard or cultivated the ground. The opposite may be true: he probably dug a well to provide water for the orchard that he had established on the land.The only possible case of an alternative in this passage is whether he planted vegetables or trees. However, there is no reason to assume that he could not have done both. Other examples are plentiful:

lubulta lu ša libbi tupninnāte ša kunukkēya ù lu i-na lubulte ša PN *tamkāre utaʾʾeranni* 'clothing either from the chests with my seals, or from the clothing which PN, the merchant, returned' KAV 98:14–17

50 *ṣabʾu Kaššīū lu-ú līṭū lu-ú sabbututtu ù* 50-*ma ṣabʾu Šubrīū līṭūma ina āle usbū* '50 Kassite troops, be they hostages, be they captives and 50 Hurrian troops, hostages dwell in the city' MATSH 2:18–20

ēkallu rabiʾtu ^{f}PN *u* 2 *aḫātīša* 13 *sinnišātu lu-ú mārātu damqātu niātu* KIMIN *lu-ú Kaššīātu* '(it will be) a great court (with) ^{f}PN and her two sisters (or colleagues); (a total of?) 13 women, both our fine (Assyrian) ladies (lit. daughters/girls) and the fine$^{?}$ Kassite ladies' MATSH 10:8–11

lu-ú iškāre lu-ú lubulte ša PN 'be it the corvée or clothing of PN' MPR 47:25–26

lu-ú qēma lu ar-ša lu-ú [MUNU$_5$] *muḫur ṣabʾēya ḫurādē emda* 'receive the flour, groats and malt and impose it on my soldiers' T 97-10:9–12

Note that, when *lū* is used for multiple subjects, the verb likewise occurs in the plural (see UGM, 103–4 § 94):

šumma lu-ú urdu lu-ú amtu ina qāt aššat aʾīle mimma im-ta-aḫ-ru 'if either a slave or a slave girl, received something from the hand of a wife' MAL A § 4:46–48

> *šumma lu-ú aʾīlu lu-ú sinniltu kišpē uppišūma* 'if either a man or a woman performed witchcraft' MAL A § 47:1–2

In most cases, *lū* is used to specify a subject. In this case, the verb occurs in the singular, unless the specified subject itself is plural.

> *šumma sinniltu lu-ú aššat aʾīle lu-ú mārat aʾīle šillata tàq-ti-bi* 'if a woman, whether a wife or a woman of the *awīlu*-class, spoke slander' MAL A § 2:14–16

> *tuppu lu-ú ša* x *lu-ú* U_8.UDU$^{\text{hi.a}}[^{\text{-me}}]^{\text{š!}}$ *lu-ú ša* ŠE-*im* (…) *ša ina muḫḫi* PN *ša-aṭ-ra-ni* 'a tablet, be it of … or of ewes or of barley, which is written as the responsibility of PN' MARV 1 38:1–7

19.6 *ula*

§ 700 This is only attested once in Giricano. Radner regarded *ula* as an NA conjunction.[4] It is, however, well known in OA.[5] Regarding the distribution across OA and NA, we must view the almost total absence of *ula* in MA as a matter of chance, rather than as a characteristic of the dialect.

> PN_1 *urad* PN_2 *šūt ú-la ipallaḫšu* 'PN_1 is the slave of PN_2, or he will serve him' Giricano 4:22–23

19.7 *šumma/entu* 'when'

§ 701 The particle *šumma*, which is used as a conjunction to introduce a conditional sentence, and will be discussed in detail in Chapter 20, can also be used as a conjunction with the meaning 'when':

> *šum-ma šanitta tuppī ultēb*[*ilakku*] 'when I sent you my second tablet' KAV 169:14–15

In addition, *entu* is found once with this function:

> *en-tu ina muḫḫīya anāku lalli*[*k*] 'when (she is) before me, I will go' Billa 67:9–10

4 See Giricano, 53; cf. SNAG, 66 § 3.5, 122 § 4.4.
5 See GKT, 183 § 104df; GOA § 24.3.5.

Chapter 20: Syntax: Conditional clauses

20.1 Conditional sentence with *šumma* in law texts

§ 702 Conditional sentences introduced with the particle *šumma* 'if' or 'when' are constructions that are typical of the MA law texts (cf. UGM, 110–11 § 101). They generally start with the *šumma* clause (protasis), followed by consequences (the apodosis), although some exceptions are found. In the protasis, all four verbal categories are attested: the preterite, perfect, present and stative. Usually, the construction is followed by the apodosis, which presents the verbal predicate in the function of a futurum to indicate the consequences. Conditional clauses can also be built from nominal parts. It should be noted that conditional clauses are dependent clauses in function, but not in form, as they, by default, do not take relative pronouns or subjunctives, which are the formal markers in Akkadian for a relative clause (GOA § 26.1). There is some evidence from Giricano that local scribes had started to regard the protasis as a dependent clause and started marking it with a subjunctive ending (see § 713).

§ 703 Most of the conditional clauses in MAL start with a protasis involving a perfect or preterite. We discussed this aspect in § 629ff. It is likely that the perfect and preterite are used in the function of the futurum exactum, indicating that events of the protasis precede the apodosis. However, we have seen that cases with the stative and present are also present.

> *šum-ma aššat aʾīle maškatta ina kīde tal-ta-ka-an māḫirānu šurqa inašši* 'if a wife has placed deposits outside (the family), the receiver will carry (liability for) stolen property' MAL A § 6:70–73
>
> *šum-ma aʾīla iltu aššitīšu aʾīlu iṣ-ṣa-bat ubtaʾʾerūš uktaʾʾinūš kilallēšunuma idukkūšunu* 'if a man has seized (another) man with his wife, they will have him tried and convicted (and then) they will kill them both' MAL A § 15:41–45
>
> *šum-ma aʾīlu ana tappāʾīšu* (…) *iq-bi* (…) *aʾīla šuātu* 40 *ina ḫaṭṭāte imaḫḫuṣūš* 'if a man has said (so and so) to his comrade, they will hit that man 40 times with sticks' MAL A 18 § 72–78
>
> *šumma aʾīlu* (…) *napšāte ig-mu-ur ana bēl napšāte iddunūš* 'if a man ended a life, they will give him to the *next-of-kin*' MAL B § 2:15–17

In the case of a protasis with a stative, a continuous state is expressed. This is especially visible in the following passage:

> [*šum*]*ma sinniltu ta-ad-na-at u mussa nakru ilteqe* (…) 2 *šanāte panē mutīša tadaggal* 'if a woman is given (for marriage) and the enemy has taken her husband (…), she will wait two years for her husband' MAL A § 45:46–49

As can be seen in this example, the phrase differentiates the stative verb indicating marriage of the woman, which is still valid, from the telic event of the taking of the husband, as indicated with a perfect (cf. GKT, 234 § 137e). Other examples include:

šum-ma sinniltu ina bēt abīšama us-bat mussa ētanarrab (…) *šuā'amma ilaqqe ana ša bēt abīša lā iqarrib* 'if a woman dwells in the house of her father and her husband keeps visiting her, he will take his (property), but will not have a claim against the house of her father' MAL A § 27:103–108

šum-ma sinniltu ina bēt abīšama us-bat u mussa me-e-et 'if a woman dwells in the house of her father and her husband is dead' MAL A § 26:95–96

Conditional sentences with a present in the protasis seem to have an intentional meaning. These passages express something that has not yet happened, but require a further action expressed in the apodosis:

šum-ma a'īlu aššassu e-ez-zi-ib 'if a man wants to leave his woman' MAL A § 37:15

šum-ma a'īlu esertušu ú-⌜pa⌝-ṣa-an 5 6 tappā'ēšu ušeššab ana panēšunu upaṣṣanši 'if a man intends to veil his concubine, he will seat five or six witnesses and veil her in their presence' MAL A § 41:1–3

šum-ma sinniltu (…) *iltu bētīša la-a tu-ú-uṣ-ṣa* 'if a woman does not want to go out of her house' MAL A § 46:89–91

§ 704 If *šumma* is preceded by the conjunction *u*, an alternate protasis is introduced. These clauses are used to specify the consequences in the apodosis of the preceding conditional clause they follow. While the construction frequently occurs in the longer and more complicated law paragraphs, a few examples suffice:

a'īlu ša aššassu uznēša unakkas ù šum-ma aššassu ú-uš-šìr [uz]nēša la-a ú-na-ak-ki-is ša urde u amte lā unakkusūma 'the man, who intends to cut off the ears of his wife, but if he lets his wife go (with impunity) and does not cut off her ears, they will (likewise) not cut off (the ears) of the slave and maid' MAL A § 4:51–55

nāikāna u mummerta i-du-uk-ku ù šum-ma sinniltu lā taqtibi a'īlu aššassu ḫiṭṭa kī libbīšu emmid 'they will kill the fornicator and the procuress, but if the woman does not declare it, the husband will punish his wife as he desires' MAL A § 23:35–39

ù šum-ma a'īlu (…) *aššassu lā unakkis* 'and if a man has not mutilated his wife' MAL A § 24:79

šum-ma Aššurāyu ù šum-ma Aššurāyittu ša kī šapārte (…) *ina bēt a'īle usbūni* 'if (it) is an Assyrian man or if (it) is an Assyrian woman who dwells as a pledge in the house of a man' MAL A § 40:40–43

However, in this light, we should also point to the following passage from MAL A. It contains two conditional clauses, which together form the apodosis of the law paragraph. In this somewhat complicated construction, both conditional clauses form equal alternatives to each other and are thus not introduced with *u šumma*:

šum-ma mut sinnilte aššassu idūak u a'īla idūakma šum-ma appa ša aššitīšu i-na-ki-eš a'īla ana ša rēšēn utâr 'if the husband kills his wife, then he will kill the man (as well), but if he cuts off the nose of his wife, he will turn the man into a eunuch' MAL A § 15:51–54

20.2 Conditional clauses outside law texts

§ 705 Outside MAL and MAPD, conditional clauses are frequently found, especially in loans and treaties where they stipulate legal obligations. Most of the attestations are therefore rather formulaic, although there is still a number of attestations in the letter corpus. A significant proportion of this type of formulaic clause is found in loans. They have a present in the protasis in order to stipulate a possible future scenario. We have already discussed their character as the future (exactum) indicating an (un)ability or intention (see § 628).

> *šum-ma ēṣidē la i-dan*[!] *ēṣidu ½ mana annaka i-ḫi-aṭ* 'if he does not give the reapers, the reaper will weigh out half a mina of lead' KAJ 11:13–15
>
> *šum-ma ana* 6 *urḫe annaka la i-ḫi-aṭ eqalšu uppu laqi* 'if he does not weigh out the lead within six months, his field is acquired and taken' KAJ 14:12–14
>
> *šum-ma eqla la e-ṣi-id kī* PN_1 *ēṣidē ēgurūni* PN_2 *annaka iḫīaṭ* 'if he does not harvest the field, PN_2 will weigh out as much lead as PN_1's hired reapers' KAJ 50:13–17
>
> *šum-ma* PN *lā ammigirmi i-qa-bi* 1 *bilta ḫurāṣa eḫīaṭ*[sic.] 'if PN declares 'I do not agree' he will weigh out one talent of gold' KAJ 57:16–19
>
> *šum-ma ina eqlātīšu bētānīšu la i-ša-lim ina marʾēšu mārātī*[*šu*] *išallim* 'if he (cannot) obtain satisfaction from his fields or houses, he will obtain it from his sons and daughters' KAJ 61:19–21
>
> *šum-ma ina adrāti* ŠE *la i-ma-da-ad kī panittīšuma ina muḫḫi šalmīšu u kēnīšu* ŠE *rakis* 'if he does not measure out the barley on the threshing floor, according to earlier agreements, the barley will be bound on their credibility and legal status' KAJ 69:7–12
>
> [*šum*]*-ma abāssu la i-ta-mar tuppušu urrâššu* 'if he has not examined his case, he shall deliver his tablet to him' KAJ 89:14'–16'
>
> *šum-ma ina panēšu mamma la e-ri-iš u ta-ad-na-aš-šu uzakkama tuppa dannata išaṭṭurūneššu* 'if nobody has requested it before him and it was given to him, he will clear it and they will write a strong tablet for him' KAJ 177:13–17

Treaties:

> [*šúm-m*]*a dēnāni ša ḫimsāte ana šallume* [*ú*]*-ṣa-pi-ú* [GAL^{meš}]*-nu* (…) *a*⌉*na šēbutte uššabū*[sic.] 'if they observe to compensate with substitutes for the stolen goods, the elders will sit as witnesses' T 04-37:19–21
>
> *šúm-ma Sūtīu ana āle it-ta-lak panē sirāšê ši*[*karšu lā išatti*] 'if a Sutean has gone to the city, he will not drink his beer before the brewer' T 04-37:22
>
> *šúm-ma Sūtīu sikara ana qīpte i-šat-ti šapārtušu i*[*šakkan*] 'if a Sutean intends to drink on a loan, he will place a security' T 04-37:25

Rather unique is the following attestation where the apodosis precedes the protasis:

> *a-na* GN *lu*[!] *la-a er-*[*rab*] *šúm-ma* 1 *aʾīlu āliku ša ḫurāde ina panē pāḫitīšu lū āla iṣbat ū lū kī raqāʾe ana* GN *ērub* 'he will not enter GN, even if one man coming from battle settled in a city, or secretly entered GN' MARV 4 119:24–28

Testimony with a perfect for the futurum exactum:

šumma PN GNs ⸢*il*⸣*-ta-pa-ar* x*-si-šu* ^giš^*epinni*^meš^*-šu* ⸢*uk-ta*⸣*-i-lu telīt ebūrišunu e-ta-kal* PN *napšātu ša šarre bēlīšu iz-zi-ar* 'if PN has written to the GNs, (and) … they have used his ploughs, (but) he has consumed the tax on their harvest, PN is guilty of treason' A 2994:15–25

A conditional clause with a precative in the apodosis:

šúm-ma ša PN *aḫḫūšu nišūšu bēl ilkīšu dēna ana muḫḫi* PN *ub-ta-ʾu-ni ša dēna ub-ta-ʾu-ú-ni šúm-ma* 1 *ṣeḫra mi-ḫa-ar la* SUM*-na* 6 *naḫlapātu* 4 ^túg^*ni-ik-si li-din* PN *lu-še-ṣi* 'if because of PN, his brothers, his people or the lord of his work task began a procedure concerning PN, the one who started the procedure, if he did not give an equal boy, he shall give six cloaks, four cut textiles and release PN' Giricano 4:24–32

§ 706 While not very common, there is also a number of conditional clauses found in letters. Most of them involve no further difficulties:

šúm-ma ṣubātu^ḫi.a.meš^ *ḫa-ʾu lā masīuttu i-ba-áš-ši iltēnišma šēbilāne* 'if unwashed *ḫ*-textiles are available, send them to me together' KAV 103:22–24

šum-ma attunu ta-ku-ša PN *lilqea* 'if you will be delayed, PN must take it here' KAV 105:27–28

šum-ma la tu-da-a-šu mimma pîšu šaʾlā ù šum-ma me-et tuppukunu šuṭrā ana muḫḫi PN *šēbilāne* 'if you do not know him, ask what is said about him and, if he is dead, write your tablet and send it to PN' KAV 107:18–23

šúm-ma sisia^meš^ *u mugerra*^meš^ *la-a it-ta-na-ku suḫīrē tak-ku-un-na ša ina pit*[*ti*] PN *ekulūni* 'if he did not give you the horses and chariots, you will select foals that eat in the responsibility of PN' MATC 11:22–25

šúm-ma adi 1 ITU UD⸢^meš^⸣ *la ta-ta-bal la tu-ta-ir lā ikaṣṣurūnekku* 'if you do will not have brought and returned it within a month, it will not be deducted from your (account)!'MATC 22A:24–27

šúm-ma mimma laššutta ta-ta-pa-al-šu u arḫiš la-a ta-ta-na-áš-šu ana muḫḫi duāke telli 'if you answer him that there is nothing whatsoever and you do not give him quickly, then you will meet death' OIP 79 3:14–20

šúm-ma ṣarpa la-a tam-ḫur šubta erṣāte bētātini ana laqāʾe šukun 'if you have not received the silver, then put up the dwelling, lands and our houses for sale!' Faist 2001, 252:23–25

Note the following phrase, with a question as the apodosis:

šúm-ma (…) *ibašši ay*[*a-n*]*u ša* ŠÀ *ni-iḫ-r*[*i-ú*]*-ni*(?) 'if they are available, where is (the barley), from (that) we dug out?' T 96-36:20–24

20.3 Oaths and irrealis

§ 707 A special '*šumma*' sentence is used for oaths. In MA, this construction is attested three times in MAL A, albeit once in a very broken context. In all examples, the oath represents spoken speech, thus it is introduced with a finite form of either *qabāʾu* 'to say' or *tamāʾu* 'to swear' and the particle *mā*. The negation or lack of it represents the opposite situation, as intended, thereby creating a kind of irrealis: 'if so-and-so was the case, (then I am cursed)', whereas the last part is never written. This type of oath also occurs in other Akkadian dialects (see GAG, 293 § 185h–j; cf. UGM, 109 § 99). The usage of a subjunctive on this type of clause indicates that they are regarded as dependent clauses. While this type of clause does not occur in OA (GKT, 221 § 131b n1), the clauses form a kind of irrealis, which resembles the OA counterparts in as far as they are introduced by the particle *šumma* (cf. GOA § 23.5):

> *i-tam-ma ma-a šum-ma ú-ša-ḫi-zu-ši-ni ma-a i+na* É-*ia ši-ir-qí* 'he will swear, saying: "I did not instigate her", saying: "steal from my house"' MAL A § 5:60–62
>
> [*i-tam-ma ma*]-⌜*a*⌝ *šum-ma a-ni-*[*ik-ku-ši-ni*] 'he will swear, saying: "I did not fornicate with her"' MAL A § 22:2–3
>
> *i-qa-bi ma-a šum-ma la-a iq-bi-an-ni* 'he shall say (before DN), thus: "he told me (so)"' MAL A § 47:16–17

§ 708 Related, but different in function, is the use of *šumma* to express a kind of irrealis in letters.[1] According to W. Mayer, the passage in KAV 194 is an oath (UGM, 109); however, this is unusual in the middle of a letter in MA. [2] Moreover, an oath taken by someone for somebody else in the second person is not an oath but a command. This has only been attested twice so far, both times with a subjunctive on the predicate, similar to the oaths:

> *ma-a šum-ma ina tuārīš*[*u*] *zittekina la ta*ˀ*-na-di-na-ni* 'thus, "you shall give your share at his return"' KAV 194:20–22
>
> *šúm-ma umzarḫu ina bubuāte* ⌜*la-a i-mu-ut*⌝*-tu-ni* 'if a houseborn slave will die from the hunger (then…)' MATSH 12:31–32

The following clause from a letter (T 02-32), which is introduced by *šumma*, is probably related. The use of *šumma* intensifies the question:

> *ma-a ke-e šúm-ma eqlu ana puāg*[*e ša*] *urde* 'thus (he said): "how can it be that a slave takes a field by force?"' T 02-32:29–31

In the question of T 02-32, the particle *kē* is used as a question adverb of manner, i.e., 'how?'. The sentence expresses an unwanted situation, 'how could it be that something like that happened?'. Another possible case of an irrealis can be found in the following clause:

> *ana tarbāṣ*[*e*] *ša kīdānu uṣṣâ*[*kkunu*] *a-šam-me a-na ku-na-*[*šu-nu*] *la ú-ba-la-aṭ-ku-n*[*u*] 'should he go out to you in the courtyard that is outside and I hear it, I will not keep you alive!' KAV 96:14–17

20.4 Conditional sentence without *šumma*

§ 709 This type of conditional sentence is formed by two main clauses (GAG, 260–61 § 160). MA uses two types of constructions of the conditional clause without *šumma*. The first uses the particle *-ma* on the predicate of the protasis. This construction is also known

1 Cf. NA in GAG, 288 § 180b; SNAG, 134 § 4.5.10.

2 Oaths are more common in NA letters, e.g., SAA 1 179 r. 3–4; SAA 5 117:15–19; SAA 10 285 r. 4'–8'; SAA 15 108:9'–11' (M. Luukko, private communication).

in OA and OB. Nonetheless, the construction is not specifically conditional and clauses can often be translated as temporal (GOA § 25.5; Streck 2014a, 135 § 317 on OB). Regarding the usage of *-ma*, we have already discussed many of the examples in § 693f. Von Soden claims that this type of conditional clause with a stative in the protasis of a conditional clause without *šumma* is a feature that is unique to MA (GAG, 260 § 160d). This has only been attested with the stative *ḫadi* in MAL A. Note, however, that Cohen presented claims for similar construction in OB (Cohen 2005, 174–75).

ḫa-di-ma mussa (…) *šīmša iddan* 'if it pleases him, then her husband will pay her price' MAL A § 24:58–59

ù ḫa-di-ma aššassu ilaqqēu 'and, if it pleases him, they will take his wife' MAL A § 24:60

ḫa-di-ma mārassu iddan ú ḫa-di-i-ma tūrta ana mitḫār uta??ar 'if he wishes, he will give his daughter and, if he wishes, he will make an equal return' MAL A § 43:33–35

billu lu ma-ad liblulū 'should there be much alloy, they must mix it' OIP 79 2:8–9

The expression *libbu-šu-ma* 'if he likes', which is attested in MAL A (GAG, 261 § 160e), is similar. This expression is actually a shortened form from the OA prepositional expression *šumma libbīšu*, where similar expressions, such as *ašar libbīšu* 'wherever he likes', occurred as well.[3]

šumma aʾīlu aššassu ezzib lìb-bu-šu-ma mimma iddanašše la-a lìb-bu-⸢šu⸣-ma mimma lā iddanašše rāquttēša tuṣṣa 'if a man wants to leave his wife, he can give her something if he wants to, but if he does not want to, he will give her nothing and she will leave empty-handed' MAL A § 37:15–19

The second construction of the conditional clause without *šumma* is asyndetic. Since, in MA, *-ma* had become disused as a sentence connector, its loss resulted in the creation of this construction.

idūakšu u panūšuma im-ma-an-ga-ar [*ù*] *zittušu ilaqqe* 'he will kill him, or should he agree to it, (then) he will take his (inheritance) share' MAL B § 2:19–21

abāta ša Ištar tul-te-ṣi-ma la taballaṭ ù piriltaša la ta-ta-ṣar-ma lā tašallim 'should you divulge the word of Ištar, you shall not live, and should you not protect her secret, you shall not prosper' Ištar Ritual r. 6'–7'

a-šam-me a-na ku-na-[*šu-nu*] *lā uballaṭkun*[*u*] '(if) I hear it, I will not let you live' KAV 96:16–17

panē ṭēmīšunu idaggal ṭēma i-ša-ku-nu-uš inammuša 'he awaits their instructions, (and once) he is given orders, he shall depart' MATSH 2:52–53

ana muḫḫi šarre ta-ka-ša-ad ta-ka-la ana pāḫitīka lâzzâz 'should you be detained upon reaching the king, I shall not stand for you' MCS 2 1:20–23

§ 710 In the administrative documents most cases are variations of each other, belonging to the standard formulae of administrative documents concerning loans. The protasis of these clauses presumably contains a preterite (*ētiq-ma*) followed by an apodosis with present or stative. The limited context of this type of conditional clause can be explained by the

3 See GKT, 181 § 103j; GOA § 14.4.18.

decline of sentence connector *-ma* in contemporary spoken Assyrian, which is better reflected in the letter corpus.

Preterite (protasis)+present (apodosis):

> *ēdānu e-ti-iq-ma kī panitti illak* '(if) the term has passed; it will go (for interest) according to earlier (agreements)' KAJ 38:8–10
>
> *ēdānu e-ti-iq-ma* ŠE *ana ṣibte illak* '(if) the term has passed; the barley will go for interest' KAJ 65:8–10
>
> *ēdānu e-ti-*[*i*]*q-*[*ma*] *buqūna u tāli*[*tt*]*a iddan* '(if) the term has passed; he will give the yield and the offspring' KAJ 96:7–10

Preterite (protasis)+stative (apodosis):

> *ēdānu e-ti-iq-ma eqalšu up-pu la-qé* '(if) the term has passed; his field is acquired and taken' KAJ 27:16–17

A variant form with perfect reflects the actual temporal system, with the verb *etāqu* occurring in the perfect rather than the preterite:

> *īdānu*[sic.] *i-te*[!]*-te-eq-šu-ma* (…) *mimmûšu gabba za-ku-a iṣabbat* '(if) his term has passed he will seize all his cleared property' KAJ 101:19–21

This type of clause is also attested without the particle *-ma*:

> *ēdānu e-ti-iq šaprāt*[*ēšunu*] *la*[*q*] '(if) the term has passed, their pledges will be taken' KAJ 66:23–25
>
> *ēdānu e-ti-iq* ŠE *annuku ana ṣibte illak* '(if) the term passes, the barley and lead will go for interest' KAJ 70:9–10
>
> *ēdānu e-ti-qú-ni uppu laqi qabiūni* '(that the tablet) says, (if) the term has passed, it will be acquired and taken' KAJ 142:7–8

Chapter 21: Syntax: Dependent Clauses

§ 711 Dependent clauses are an important and complex aspect of Akkadian grammar. They are clauses that do not stand on their own, but are dependent on the main clause, which either precedes or succeeds them, or is even built around the dependent clause. Most of them are syndetic, using one sort of relative pronoun or conjunction to introduce the start of the dependent clause. A large number of conjunctive constructions are summarized by Dietrich (1969) for NB, which is also relevant for MA, although MA conjunctions do not display the same number of constructions. The verbal predicate of the relative clause always takes a subjunctive *-ūni*, this is an important marker of the end of the relative clause as it is often directly followed by the verbal predicate of the main clause. In case of the lack of a verbal predicate in the relative sentence a substantive or pronoun carries a subjunctive similar to OA.[1]

> *ki-i aššat* LÚ*-ni idē* 'he knew that she was a wife' MAL A § 13:28–29; cf. MAL A § 14:32, 36
>
> *iltu muḫḫi marʾe rabīe adi muḫḫi marʾe ṣeḫre ša-a* 10 MU^{meš}*-šu-ni ana ša ḫadiūni iddan* 'from the oldest to the youngest son, who is at least 10 years old, he will give (her) to whomever he wishes' MAL A § 43:24–26
>
> *ina bēt marʾēša a-šar pa-nu-ša-a-ni tuššab* 'she shall reside in the house of (one of) her own sons, wherever she chooses' MAL A § 46:93–94
>
> 1 *iku eqlu kirīu ša būrtu ina lib-bi-šu-n*[*i*] '1 *iku* field (and) orchard, in which there is a well' KAJ 13:13–14
>
> *ina zittīšu a-šar* A.ŠÀ*-šu-ni damqa išallim* 'he will obtain compensation from his share, wherever his field is' KAJ 148:30–31
>
> *tupni*[*nna*] *ša ṣubātu* (…) *i+na lìb-bi-ni šēṣiāne* 'take out the box with textile in it' KAV 105:11–13
>
> *kī ša ṭé-mu-ni bēlī lišpura* 'may my lord write me what (his) orders are' MARV 1 71:29–30
>
> *am-mar šu-ut-ni ṭēma šuṭrāne* 'as much as it is, write me a message' MCS 2 2:13–14
>
> 6 *emāru* 6 *sūtu zaruʾšunu ša* 22 *iku* A.ŠÀ*-ni*? '6 homer, 6 seah their seed, which is for(?) 22 *iku* field ' MATC 69 r. 11''–12'' (uncertain translation, perhaps a mistake)
>
> *bēlī kī ša ṭé-mu-un-ni lišpura* 'may my lord write me what (his) orders are' MATSH 12:39

Infinitive in the relative clause:

> *lubulta ša muḫḫi šarre ša ina pitti ša muḫḫe bēte na-áš-ku-ša-ni ana kurille ilqeūnenni ultēbilakkunu* 'the clothing for the king that is placed in the responsibility of the housemaster and which they took for the harvest-festival, I have sent to you' KAV 99:37–40

---

1 Cf. GKT, 134 § 79c; GOA § 16.9.10.5; MA in UGM, 112 § 102.3.

2 *emāru* 8 *sūtu* ŠE-*um* (...) *ša ana ginā'e* (....) *ta-da-šu-nu-ni ša qāt* PN$_1$ (...) [*in*]*a muḫḫi* PN$_2$ (...) *iddan* 'two homers and eight seahs of barley that are given for the *ginā'u*, (and) which are in the charge of PN$_1$, incumbent on PN$_2$, he will give it' MARV 3 35:1–13

5 *emāru* 2 *qa qēmu* (...) *ša ana ginā'e* (...) *ta-*⸢*da*⸣*-šu-ni ša qāt* PN$_1$ (...) *ina muḫḫi* PN$_2$ (...) *iddan* 'five homers and two litres of flour, which is given to him for the *ginā'u* (and) which are in the charge of PN$_1$, incumbent on PN$_2$, he will give it' MARV 3 40:1–12

The nominal predicate of a dependent clause does not always take a subjunctive:

a-na ša a-ka-⸢*li*⸣ *lā iqarrib* 'he shall not have a claim to anything edible' MAL A § 30:39

anāku sīrāšê^{meš} *ša annāka am-me-e-ša-ma alaqqea* 'I will take the brewers, who are here, there' MATC 9:22–25

ša dannutte ša lìb-bi-šu-nu PN *lir*[*kus*] 'may PN hitch (them) regarding the strength among them' MATC 11:26–27

§ 712 As can be expected, no wish forms, such as the precative or imperative, can be used in the relative sentence (GKT, 240 § 141a), although they can be found in the main clauses. It was noticed by W. Mayer that the tempus of the dependent clause is in agreement with the main clause (UGM, 112 § 102.2). However, this claim does not take into account the usage of the imperative, stative and nominal clauses. Mayer explains some relative clauses with the perfect, as opposed to the present, in the main clauses as instances of the 'futurum exactum'. This is a circular argumentation, since it requires verbal forms to be translated in specific ways to support this claim. However, as we discussed elsewhere, these cases of a perfect refer to future events preceding the action of the present, which makes them two different tempora in form and function (§ 628). However, even when we accept this part, Mayer's claim is, by definition, incorrect and even illogical, since the main clause could refer to items in the present/future in relation to events of the past in the relative clause, or vice versa (GAG, 264 § 163b).

1 *mana*$^{\text{ta.àm}}$ *ṣarpa a'īluttu ša šarra iš-ši-ú-ni i-*[*la-q*]*e-ú* 'the men who carried the king, take one mina of silver each' Coronation Ritual ii 40–41

Additionally, the perfect in the following two clauses is used for the futurum exactum:

ša ḫarimta paṣṣunta e-tam-ru-ú-ni i<*ṣa*>*bbassi* 'whoever sees a veiled prostitute shall seize her' MAL A § 40:68–69

ša (...) *tuppātēšunu it-ta-ab-lu-né-en-ni ana panē qēputte il-ta-ak-nu-ú-ni a'īlu* (...) *eqalšu išallim ilaqqe* '(of those) who will bring their tablets and place them before the representatives, the man (the righful owner) shall redeem and take his field' MAL B § 6:20–27

§ 713 There are three types of dependent clause: relative, adverbial and complement. They will be discussed individually in different categories. The Giricano archive added a new type of dependent clause, namely, the protasis of the conditional clause. Unfortunately, the attestations are mostly limited to text no. 4, whereas the particle *šumma* in Giricano 10 is restored, meaning that we cannot be entirely certain that the passage is valid. Unfortunately, as the relevant texts Giricano 4, 10 and 12 were written by three different scribes (see Giricano, 62), we cannot ascribe this characteristic as a particularity of one individual scribe, unlike some other features of the Giricano archive.

šú[*m-ma* PN_1 *ana urduttīšu l*]*a im-*⌜*ma*⌝*-gur-ú-ni ana* PN_2 *id-di-nu-ú-ni ša nupāre uṣṣanni* PN_1 *urdu ša* PN_3 *šūt ūla ipallaḫšu* 'If PN_1 does not agree to become a slave and they gave (him) to PN_2, but he left the prison; PN_1 is the slave of PN_3 or he will serve him' Giricano 4:15–23

[*šúm-ma l*]*a ur-ra-šu-ni* PN *u*[*k*]*aššadsu*^sic.^ 'if he does not fetch it (i.e., the ox), PN will prosecute him' Giricano 10:13–15

In the following passage from Giricano 4, the subjunctive may be applied erroneously as the scribe was influenced by the common phrase *šā dēnu dabābu iltu* PN *ubta*$^{??}$*ūni* 'whoever seeks a lawsuit with PN'. This phrase was common in NA, but is already found in MA (cf. Deller 1961, 31).

šumma ša PN *aḫḫūšu nišūšu bēl ilkīšu dēna ana muḫḫi* PN *ub-ta-ʾu-ni* 'If, because of PN, his brothers, his people or the lord of his work task began a procedure concerning PN' Giricano 4:24–27

Already at the start of Giricano 4, the main clause receives a subjunctive. It is not unthinkable that the erroneous usage of the subjunctive is caused by the clumsy wording of the scribe, rather than a new type of dependent clause. It is possible that the subjunctive was carried over from this asyndetic dependent clause as a kind of modus attraction.

PN (...) *sārta e-p*[*u-š*]*u-ni* PN *aḫu*[*šu*] (...) [*an*]*a u*[*rdutt*]*i* [*iltaka*]*n* 'PN_1 (...) who (...) has committed a crime, he put PN_2, his brother (...) into slavery' Giricano 4:2–14

Not all scribes in Giricano use the subjunctive for the protasis. This is noticeable, since the passage of Giricano 1 is from the same scribe as Giricano 4 (see Giricano, 62). On the other hand, this may be explained from the formulaic character of the protasis in Giricano 1.

šúm-ma ina adre la it-ti-din 'if he will not have given it on the threshing floor' Giricano 1:17–18

šúm-ma PN *ana niggalle la it-tal-ka* 'if PN does not go for the harvest time (lit. to the sickle)' Giricano 12:12'–14'

Additionally, I am uncertain about the following passage that originates from the hand of the scribe of Giricano 4 (Aḫu-teribīya, according to Giricano, 62). We may conditionally accept that the first verb in the following broken passage occurs in a dependent clause; but, if this were so, the following asyndetical dependant clause would be unusual. Note also a similar problematic passage in Giricano 12:

(...) [*id*]*-di-nu-ú-ši-ni* [*ṣarpa*]^meš^*-ša il-qe-ú-ni* '(that$^?$) he gave her, that he took her silver' Giricano 14:11–12

šumma ana šaduāni ana a-ie-e-ša-mi-ni iḫtaliq^sic.^ 'if he has fled to the mountains or wherever' Giricano 12:17'–19'

Outside Giricano, this type of dependent clause is rarely attested. Perhaps this is an example:

šum-ma ana qāt 6 *šanāti ú-ḫi-ra-an-ni ina rāminīšu la-a ik-kal-ú-ni* 'if he has been delayed beyond six years (but) was not detained of his own will' MAL A § 36:103–105

21.1 Relative clause and the particle *ša*

§ 714 Relative clauses are usually constructed with the particle *ša*.[2] As a conjunction, *ša* is neutral and has no other semantic function other than to indicate the start of a relative clause. For these reasons, we will discuss the construction of relative clauses that use this relative pronoun. Relative clauses generally modify a noun phrase, which we will call the "head" from now on, following Kouwenberg.[3] There are two main groups of relative clauses, those with a head and those without an external head. The first and main groups have the relative clause following the apposition of an antecedent noun, together with optional adjectives. The following relative clause, standing in relation to the head, also gave rise to the *ša*-type analytic genitive construction, which was in the process of replacing the status constructus (see § 298ff). One theoretical example is:

> *šarrāqa lemna*$^{\text{(head/noun phrase)}}$ *ša*$^{\text{(particle)}}$ *ina bēte iṣbutūni*$^{\text{(relative clause+subjunctive)}}$ *idukkū*$^{\text{(verbal predicate)}}$ 'the evil thief$^{\text{(head)}}$ who$^{\text{(particle)}}$ was caught in the house$^{\text{(relative pronoun)}}$ they will kill$^{\text{(verbal predicate)}}$

It should be noted that relative sentences of all sizes occur. A relative clause can be a short nominal clause or one finite verb. One may argue that some cases of the unbound genitive construction form perhaps involve the shortest form of the relative clause in Akkadian. Some examples are:

> *ša la a-ka-a-li qaqqadma ilaqqe* 'what is not edible, he will take the capital' MAL A § 30:37–38

> *a*[*di*] *šarru paššūra ša* IGI *Aš-šur irakkasūni* (...) 'when the king sets up a table that will be before Aššur' Coronation Ritual i 39–40

> *ḫimsātēšunu ša ta-at-ma-a-ni talteqe*[*a*] 'their stolen goods, of which you swore, you have taken' KAV 217:17' (uncertain translation)

> UDU^{meš} (...) *ša pi-tu-ka arḫiš nammiš* 'the sheep, which are in your responsibility, make (them) depart quickly' MATC 1:13–15

> 1 *sūtu* ŠE *ša* ŠU PN$_1$ PN$_2$ *maḫir* 'one seah of barley, from the hand of PN$_1$, PN$_2$ has received' MATC 38:1–4

Multiple relative clauses may follow each other. In this case, each individual relative clause is introduced with a new particle.

> [...] *ša erēne ša ina qumāšātēšunu ēkallu* (...) *kišitti* GN$_1$ *ša-aṭ-ru-ú-ni ša ina ēkalle* (...) *ša-ak-nu-ú-ni ša ina ūme šarru* (...) *niqia*^{meš} (...) *ana šallum*[*e*] *ana* GN$_2$ *e-be-ra-an-ni ina abāt šarre* PN$_1$ *ú-ma-di-*[*du*]*-ni* PN$_2$ *u* PN$_3$ *ana* GN$_3$ *ultēberū* '[In total, n columns] of cedar, which with their capitals (belonging to) the palace, were recorded as the spoils of GN$_1$ (first), that was placed in the palace (second), on the day that the king crossed over to GN$_2$ to complete the offerings (third), according to the word of the king (whom) PN$_1$ has given orders(?) (fourth), PN$_2$ and PN$_3$ have brought it across (the river to) GN$_3$' MARV 1 14:19–36

---

2 The common nomer "relative pronoun" is incorrect for *ša*, since it is invariable, unlike different kinds of relative pronouns in European languages, which represent the duplicate noun in the relative sentence. Instead, it has no other function than marking the start of a relative clause. See Deutscher (2002, 89–92).

3 See GOA § 26.2.1 (cf. Huehnergard 2005, 185).

10 *emāru* ŠE (…) *ša ina ūmi* PN ŠE-*am ana* GN *ú-še!-ri-du!-ni ki-i iltu ammāka i-tu-ra-ni ana kurummat sisīe*meš (…) *tadin* ‘10 homers of barley, on the day which PN brought it down to GN (first), when he returned from there (second), it was given as rations for the horses’ LVUH 92:13–21

Not always is *ša* repeated:

2 *sūta akla* (...) *kurummat* 1 *ṣimitte sisīe*meš *u* 3 *emāre*meš *ša* 2 *qa*ta.àm ŠE-*am e-ku-lu-ú-ni ša* (…) *ubre* (…) *ša tuppāte* (...) *na-ṣu-ú-ni ana muḫḫi šarre ana Libbi-āle il-li-ka-an-ni ṭē*[*ma*] *ša-ak-nu-ú-ni ana mātīšu im-mu-šu-ú-ni* [*ša alāke u tu*]*āre din* ‘two seahs of bread (…) is the ration for one span of horses and three donkeys that each eat two litres of barley (first), for the foreigner, who has brought the tablets (second) (and) come to the king to the Inner City (Aššur) (third), (and once) the order was given (fourth), he had departed to his land (fifth), give it for (his) going and returning’ MATC 22A:5–22

ša riksa annia e-ti-qu-ni [*rab ē*]*kalle iš-mi-ú-ni ḫiṭṭa la-a e-mi-du-šu-ni rab ēkalle ḫiṭṭa inašši* ‘whoever violated this decree (first), (of which/whom) the palace manager heard (second), (but of which) he did not impose a punishment on him (third), the palace manager will carry the penalty’ MAPD § 21:108–109

Note also the following text, where the head is a nominal clause (*mīnumma anniu*), followed by two dependent clauses, both following the same *ša*:

mīnumma anniu ša am-mar a-qa-bi-a-ku-ni ki-i pi-[*i*]*a la te-pu-šu-ni* ‘what is this, that whatever I say to you, you do not act according to my words?’ T 93-3:4–6

No subjunctive:

PN_1 *ša* PN_2 (…) *it-ti-din* ‘PN_1 who sold PN_2’ VAT 8722:2–11

No main clause:

mardiātu ša! ḫurāde ša PN (…) *ú-up-pi-šu-ú-ni* ‘the travel stations of the *ḫurādu*, which PN will have had prepared’ DeZ 2521:16–19

21.1.1 Head of the relative clause

§ 715 We already discussed the head of a relative clause. However, there are many ways in which the relative clause with a head can be built (this will be discussed below). First of all, the head can have any syntactical function in the main clause, as can be seen in the following examples.

Subject:

šumma a-me-ra-a-nu ša ana šarre iqbiūni itteker ‘if the witness, who reported to the king, denies it’ MAL A § 47:14–15

ēm na-áš-pér-tu ša LUGAL *tallakanni našperta ana* [UG]U-*ia ušebbala* ‘when the message of the king comes, he will send the message to me’ MATSH 12:42–43

Direct object:

túg*lu-*[*bal*]*-ta* (...) *ša ina šēp ile ša-ak-nu-ni malqittu* ‘a textile (…), which is placed before the feet of the god, is revenue’ Coronation Ritual i 36–37

2 *urḫē· urki adrāti ši-ip-ra ša iqabbiūneššunni eppaš* 'for two months after threshing time, he will do the work that they assigned to him' KAJ 99:11–13

4 ÉRIN^meš (…) *ša ina ēkalle* PN (...) *ilṭurūni* (...) *tadnū* 'four people, whom PN recorded in the palace, are given' KAV 119:12–17

ÉRIN^meš *ša unūta ina bētīka izūzūni* (...) *leqya alka* 'take the troops, who divided the property in your house, and come' KAV 168:10–19

ši-in-na (...) *ša iltu nakkamte šēṣuatanni* (...) *ta*^??*erā* 'return the ivory, which is brought out from the storehouse' KAV 205:6–8

MUNUS *ša taqbianni ana* PN *din* 'sell the woman, about whom I spoke to you, to PN' Billa 67:5–6

su-ḫi-ir-ta le-a-at-ta ša ina pitti PN *ēzibanni ana aʾīle ša tuppi naṣṣanni din* 'give the usable foal, which I left in the responsibility of PN, to the man, who brought the tablet' MATC 3:9–15

adi za-i-ra-ma ša bēlī išpurūni ṭēma išakkunūni 'concerning the enemy, about whom my lord wrote (*to me*), they will instruct me' MATSH 7:15''–16''

Indirect object:

a-na ^giš^GIGIR *ša tuppī naṣṣatakkuni din* 'to the chariot that brings you my tablet, give it' MATC 5:14–17

a-na ⌜ŠÀM UDU⌝^meš *ša* PN_1 *ù* PN_2 *ublūnenni uppušū* 'as for the payment of the sheep that PN_1 and PN_2 brought in, they are acquired' TabT05-85:6–12

Adverbial:

šalāšēšuma i+na ŠÀ URU A.ŠÀ *ù* É *ša ilaqqeūni usassa* 'he shall proclaim three times in the city of the field or house that he wants to take' MAL B § 6:6–8

3 *iku eqla i+na* URU *ša iqabbiūneššunni eṣṣid* 'he will reap a 3 *iku* field in the city that they will tell him' KAJ 50:11–13

ūma iš-tu ^giš^GIGIR *ša tuṣṣaʾanni šēbilaššu* 'send him to me today with the chariot that goes out to me' MATC 32 (Complete)

When the head of the relative clause is the object, it can be preceded by the subject:

anāku Šu-ub-ri-e ša uddûni alt[*aʾalma*] 'I have personally questioned the Hurrians who know about it' MATSH 6:5'

anāku ^lú^LUNGA^meš *ša annāka ammēšamma alaqqea* 'I will take the brewers, who are here, there' MATC 9:22–25

With negation:

sinniltu ša ēkalle ša la-a qa-ra-ab-ša-ni 'a palace woman who is not to be approached' MAPD § 7:47

ša la-a ba-ta-qa ta-ab-tu-qu-ú-ni lā i-mi-id-ka 'that what is not to accuse, you accused; it is not your assignment' KAV 201:12–14

1 *me* 10 *ṣabʾu muṭāʾu ša la-a ub-la-an-ni* '110 men deducted, whom he did not bring' MARV 1 6:6

ṣab'umma (…) *ša la-a ú-na-me-ša-ni ilmil*[*ta*] *errišū* 'the troops, who did not depart, request chickpeas' MATSH 3:34–35

zar'a (…) *ša la-a im-ḫu-ru-ni dinī* 'give the seed that they did not receive' T 96-36:13–16

Negation preceding the particle *ša*:

ṣab'u ana maṣṣarte ša āle ⌜*la-a*⌝ *ša mu-še* ⌜*ù*⌝ *la-a ša ka*!-⌜*lu*⌝-*mi* x x x [x x x]-*ti*-⌜*ú*⌝-*ni* […] 'troops for the protection of the city, not during the night and not during the day […]' MATSH 22:5–7

§ 716 As can be seen in the examples above, the relative clause is usually placed after the head. This is not always the case, as sometimes the relative clause is placed after the main clause (GOA § 26.2.2):

panē mamma lā tāpul (…) *ša il-te-ka il-lu-ku-ú-ni-ni* 'formerly, you responded to nobody, (including) those who come with you' T 97-10:20–23

This is similar to the cases in which the head is the nominal main clause, with the relative clause standing in opposition to it, but without being followed by the predicate. This construction is found in lists:

5 *sūtu* (…) *ana qēputte ša iš-tu mar-ṣu-te* 'five seahs for the representatives who are with the sick men' CTMMA 1 99:1–2

5 *mana lulīu* (…) *ša* PN *ki-i na-mur-te ú-qar-ri-bu-ni* 'five minas of antimony that PN presented as a gift' KAJ 274:10–14

ḫurādu ša $SIG_4^{meš}$ (…) *il-be-ú-ni* 'the contingent, which laid out bricks' KAV 119:10–11

(…) *ana kurummat sisīe*^{meš} (...) *ša a-na ḫu-ra-di* (…) *il-li-ku-ni* '(n barley) is for the ration of the horses that went on campaign' MARV 1 1 iv 36–38

1 *me* 30 *ṣab'u* (…) *ša i+na* GÌR^{meš}-*šu-nu e-ti-qu-ú-ni* '130 troops who passed through on their feet' MARV 1 6:13–14

3 *emāru* 1 *sūtu šamaššammū* (…) *ša* PN *ub-la-an-ni* 'three homers and one seah of sesame, which PN brought' MARV 1 56:50

Sometimes, a main clause is not written as it assumed to be obvious. This is also attested in the adverbial clauses with *kī* (§ 732).

m[*unna*]*bdu ša i-na-bi-da-an-ni ma-a* 'the refugee, who fled to me, (said)' MATSH 12:8–9

The head of the relative clause can also be a pronoun (cf. OA in GOA § 26.2.1.1). Note that the examples of MAL have the head of the relative clause specified and repeated in the main clause.

mi-im-ma ša la a-ka-li SAG.DU-*ma ú-ta-*⌜*ar*⌝ 'he will return the capital of anything not edible' MAL A § 43:37–38

mi-im-m[*a ša … ḫal-q*]*u-ni* SAG.DU-*ma ana x* [*umalla*] '[he will restore] that what is lost to …' MAL M § 3:6–7

mi-nu-⌜*ú-ma*⌝ *an-ni-ú ša am-mar a-qa-bi-a-ku-ni ki-i pi-*[*i*]*a la te-pu-šu-ni* 'what is this, that whatever I say to you, you do not act according to my words?' T 93-3:4–6

§ 717 Usually, the head in the case corresponds to its relation with the predicate; however, it sometimes adopts the case ending in accordance with its position of the relative clause. This phenomenon is called case attraction (GOA § 26.2.5) and is attested a few times in MA:

Su-ti-ú^{meš} *ša iltu* GN *urdūnenni altaʾal* 'I questioned the Suteans, who came down from GN' T 04-13:8–11

Cf.

anāku Šu-ub-ri-e ša uddûni alt[*aʾalma*] 'I have personally questioned the Hurrians who know about it' MATSH 6:5'

When separating the head and relative clause (GOA § 26.2.2.):

pa-ni ma-am-ma la ta-pùl lu-ú ša LUGAL^{meš}-[*n*]*i ù lu-ú ša il-te-ka il-lu-ku-ú-ni-ni* 'formerly, you answered no one, be it the king, or those who go with you' T 97-10:20–23

21.1.2 Relative clause without a head

§ 718 The particle *ša* can also function as a subject or direct object on its own, without taking a head.[4] In this case, the subject/object specified by the relative clause is sometimes undetermined. In this respect, the following clauses are similar to those with an indefinite pronoun, such as *mimma* 'something' as the head (see above).

ša ḫarimta paṣṣunta ētamrūni i<*ṣa*>*bbassi* 'whoever sees a veiled prostitute shall seize her' MAL A § 40:68–69

ša-a [*l*]*aqāšunu u dabābšunu i-ba-áš-ši-ú-ni tuppātēšunu lušēliānemma* 'those who are there to take and complain will bring forth their tablets' MAL B § 6:13–16

ša (...) *tuppātēšunu ittablūnenni ana panē qēputte iltaknūni aʾīlu* (…) *eqalšu išallim ilaqqe* '(of those) who will bring their tablets and place them before the representatives, the man (the righful owner) shall redeem and take his field' MAL B § 6:20–27

ša ina bērīšunu i-pa-si-lu-ni 5 *mana iḫīaṭ* 'whoever amongst them distorts will weigh out five minas' KAJ 1:25–26

ša dēna u dab[*ā*]*ba aššum sikiltīšu iltēšu ú-*<*ba*>*-*⸢*ú*⸣*-ni ina zittīšu* [*qāta*] *elli* 'whoever seeks a lawsuit or complaint against him because of his acquisition, he shall forfeit his share' KAJ 8:11–15

ša dēna u dabāba ⸢*il*!*-ta*⸣*-ʾe-e-ni* 6? *mana ḫurāṣa ana* DN *iḫīaṭ* MARV 8 47:29–31

ša dannutte ša lìb-bi-šu-nu PN *lir*[*kus*] 'may PN hitch (them) regarding the strength among them' MATC 11:26–27

ša teppušūni libbi bēlīka 'what you do is of the satisfaction of your lord' T 02-32:36–37

In this independent usage, *ša* can also be preceded by the preposition *ana* to make it an indirect object:

a-na ša É *a-bi-ša lā iqarrib* 'he shall not have claim to anything belonging to the house of her father' MAL A § 27:107–108

4 See GAG, 267 § 165g; cf. OA in GKT, 241 § 142b; GOA § 26.2.6.

mārassu a-na ša ḫa-di-ú-ni iddan 'he will give his daughter to who he wants' MAL A § 55:40–41

A similar prepositional construction is created with *adi*:

šikur[u] (…) *[a]-di ša* PN *⸢il-ti⸣-ú-ni gabbu uppuš* 'all beer (…) is recorded together with what PN drunk' MATC 53:1–12

21.1.3 Asyndetic relative clauses

§ 719 There is a number of cases where the particle *ša* is omitted. The presence of an actual relative clause can still be observed with the help of the subjunctive marking the predicate.

šumma sinniltu ša mussa mētūni mu-us-sa i+na mu-a-te iltu bētīša lā tuṣṣa 'if a woman, whose husband is dead, upon the death of her husband, does not leave her house' MAL A § 46:89–91

riqqia^{meš} *i+na lìb-bi-šu-nu [be]-du-ú-ni ḫarammama* (…) *[tatabbak]* 'the perfume, in which it was soaked overnight, you will afterwards pour' PKT 6 i 24–25; cf. ii 22–23

12 *emāru* ŠE-*um i+na* ^{giš}BÁN *il-qé-ú-ni ša* PN (…) *ilqeūni ana* 5 *urḫē qaqqad* ŠE-*um imaddudū* '12 homers of barley, (which) were taken by the seah measure, which PN took, they will measure out the capital of barley within five months' KAJ 85:14–17

lū ugār ḫarībete lū ugār PN (…) *ma-áš-ka-an e-na-šu i-ša-ka-na-n[i]* 10 *iku eqla inass[a]q* '10 *iku* field – be it the meadow of the steppe or the meadow of PN (…), – he will select the place of his choosing (lit. the place his eyes are put on)' KAJ 179:6–16

§ 720 We may expect that letters were written by scribes upon the citation of the 'author.' As a result, it is expected that a scribe or author could have lost themselves in the main sentence, resulting in incorrect grammatical constructions. This is rarely attested in MA, but the following text, possibly sent from the household of Bābu-aḫa-iddina (Jakob 2003, 301), is a rare exception:

kīma PN *marā šipre [an]a muḫḫīya illaka u anāku ⸢mi⸣-nu-me-e* ŠEŠ-*ia [i]-ṣa-bu-tu-[ni an]āk[u a]na muḫḫi [aḫ]īya ušebbala [arḫi]š* 'when PN, the messenger, will come to me then I shall send to my brother quickly whatever my brother wants to take' RS 06.198:21–27

As can be seen in this example, the usage of *kīma* instead of *kī* is already obscure. The scribe then changes the temporal adverbial clause in a main clause by forgetting or losing the subjunctive on *illaka*, as he follows the finite verb with the conjunction *u*, rather than a governing main clause. The scribe follows with the subject *anāku* and continues with an asyndetic relative clause without *ša*, before continuing with the main clause by repeating the subject *anāku* and ending by putting an adverbial component behind the verbal predicate. Perhaps something similar is at play in the following unclear passage from a TSA letter:

ḫammuṣū 1 *me* 1 *šu-ši* ^{giš}GIDRU^{meš} *i-ta-ḫa-ṣu-ni* ZABAR^{meš} *il-ta-ka-nu-ni* 'they (=the oxen) are stolen; they hit (the thieves) 160 (times with) sticks (and) put them in fetters' T 96-15:11–13

§ 721 In some texts, there are also multiple relatives, with the first in sequence introduced with the particle *ša* or an alternative adverbial clause, while succeeding relative clauses are asyndetic.

ṣubātu$^{\text{ḫi.a.meš}}$ (…) *ša masiūni i-na pi-it-tu-ka ṣe-e-ú-ni ša-ak-nu-ú-ni iškā*[*ru*] 'the textiles (…) which were washed (and) dried out, are placed in your responsibility, (this is) a work assignment' KAV 108:4–10

[...] *ša erēne ša ina qumāšātēšunu ēkallu* (…) *kišitti* GN$_1$ *ša-aṭ-ru-ú-ni ša ina ēkalle* (…) *šaknūni ša ina ūme šarru* (…) *niqia*^{meš} (…) *ana šallum*[*e*] *ana* GN$_2$ *ēberanni i+na a-bat* LUGAL PN$_1$ *ú-ma-di-*[*du*]*-ni* PN$_2$ *u* PN$_3$ *ana* GN$_3$ *ultēberū* '[In total, n columns] of cedar, which with their capitals (belonging to) the palace, were recorded as spoils of GN$_1$ (first), which were placed in the palace (second), on the day that the king crossed over to GN$_2$ to complete the offerings (third), according to the word of the king (whom) PN$_1$ has given orders(?) (fourth), PN$_2$ and PN$_3$ have brought it across (the river to) GN$_3$' MARV 1 14:19–36

2 *emmera*^{meš} (…) PN *ša nāmurta ana muḫḫi RN naṣṣūni pi-qi-it-ta it-ta-nu-ni-šu-ú-ni* 'two sheep (for) PN, who has brought a present to RN (and) to whom (RN) gave provisions' A 1746 (NTA, 22):1–8

Adverbial:

ina ūmi ṭēma šaknūni a-na KUR*-ti-šu im-mu-šu-ni* (…) *din* 'on the day the order was given, he departed to his land (…) give it' MATC 24A:16–18

3 *emāru aklu* 6 *emmeru*^{meš} (…) *kī* [P]N (…) *illikanni i+na* GN$_1$ *be-du-ni a-na* GN$_2$ *e-ti-qu-ni* 'three homers of bread and six sheep (…) when PN came, he stayed in GN$_1$ and continued to GN$_2$' MATC 43:6–15

21.1.4 Relative clauses with *ammar* and other constructions

§ 722 MA only recognizes one other particle for use in normal relative sentences: *ammar* 'as much as' replaces the earlier *mala*, which is also absent from NA (CAD M$_1$, 148, one broken attestation). We may find the sound change /l/ > /r/ in *ammar*, if we assume it derives from *ana mala* (AHw, 43b). As with *mala* (see below), the usage of *ammar* for a relative clause initiates the usage of a subjunctive. No instances of *ammar*+infinitive have been attested so far, as they occur in other dialects with *mala* or in NA with *ammar* (Aro 1961, 69). Once, it is written as *a-mar* KAJ 135:3.

mimma am-mar na-ṣa-tu-ú-ni gabbu ša mutīša 'everything she brings (with her) is of her husband' MAL A § 35:77–78

am-mar im-ḫu-ru-ú-ni 'as much as they received' MAL A § 43:36

eqla am-mar ú-sa-am-me-ḫu-ni 3$^{\text{ta.àm}}$*-āte iddan* 'field, as much as he incorporated, he will give threefold' MAL B § 8:15–16

ina lubulte (...) *am-mar i-na-ši-ú-ni-ni liššiūni* 'may they bring from the clothing, as much as they will bring' KAV 98:16–19

lubulta am-mar ú-še-lu-ni (…) *ana libbi tupninnāte ṣelʔā* 'clothing, as much as they bring up, put it down in the boxes' KAV 98:22–25

altapra am-mar e-ṣi-du-ni 'I wrote how much they harvested' MATSH 7:16'

A combination *ša adi ammar* is attested:

ša a-di am-mar ṣe!-ni ú-ka-i-lu-nu šāludā baqnā 'as long as he kept the livestock, they gave birth and they were plucked' LVUH 21:17–19

Once ammar may appear with pronominal suffixes:

[…] *am-mar-ku-nu* […] (broken context) KUB 3 77:5'†

Nominal clauses following *ammar* are attested, where the nominal predicate in one case (MCS 2 2:13) has a subjunctive. These relative clauses can be as short as one word.

am-mar ŠÀM-*šu* 'as much as is his value' MAL A § 44:42

am-mar šu-ut-ni 'as much as it is' MCS 2 2:13

kakka am-mar i-ba-ši-ú-ni 'tools, as many as are available' MATC 1:7

am-mar qa-ab-li ulli uššer 'as much as its middle raise and release it' MATC 4:21–22

The original particle *mala* is attested in a limited number of cases. Once, according to Prechel/Freydank (2014, 40), we find *mala* with the assimilated *ana*, realized as *ammalla*:

ma-la 7 IKU A.ŠÀ 'as much as a 7 *iku* field ' BVW O r. 4

⸢*ma-la*⸣ dugBUR.ZI 'as much as (there is in) the *pursītu*-vessel' MARV 5 46:8

am-mal-la dugGÚ.ZI 'as much as a cup' MARV 10 23:4 (< *ana mala*)

A construction without any introducing particle:

šum-ma ŠE-*am la i-ma-da-ad ma-ḫi-ra-at* ŠE-*um i-lu-ku-ni* [A]N.NA *i-ḫi-aṭ* 'if he does not measure out the barley, he will weigh out lead at the going rate of barley' KAJ 53:9–11

21.2 Adverbial and complement clauses

§ 723 The second type of dependent clause is formed by the so-called adverbial clauses. These are usually placed before the actual main clause, which is introduced by a conjunction. As their name suggests, they introduce an adverbial element into the clause, be it temporal, local or causative. Given that the conjunction *kī* is multifunctional and also developed a function to introduce a complement clause (or object clause), the limited examples are discussed here as well.

21.2.1 *adi*: different functions

§ 724 The preposition *adi* (§ 436f), in relation to its temporal function, can also be frequently found as a conjunction in adverbial clauses (GAG, 277–79 § 173). Here, its meaning is again temporal. In combination with the present, the action of the relative clause is usually contemporaneous with the main clause. The common translation would be 'as soon as' or 'while' (cf. NA SNAG, 128 § 4.5.3.1). This is different from OA, where it precedes the action of the main clause and is often best translated as 'until' (an event occurs).[5]

a-di er-ra-bu-ni uṣṣaʾāne 'as soon as he enters, they go out' MAPD § 9:54

5 Cf. GOA § 26.3.1; pace GAG, 278 § 173f.

[*šumma ša*]*rra lā ikallušu a-di iltu* GN *i-tu-ra-ni ina māte usbāni* 'if they do not hold the king, as soon as he returns from GN we stay in the country' T 96-36:9–12

Sometimes, it is best translated as 'when':

a-[*di*] *šarru paššūra* (...) *i-ra-ka-su-ni šangû paššūrē* (...) *ira*[*kkas*] 'when the king sets up the table, the priest sets up tables' Coronation Ritual i 39–41

Its original meaning 'until' is still attested in some administrative documents:

a-di i-ša-li-mu-ni ilaq<*qe*> 'until he is paid off, he may take (the field)' KAJ 148:12

a-di tuppī^sic.^ *dannata i-ša-ṭu-ru-*<*ni*> *annītumma dannat* 'until they will write a valid tablet, this one is valid' KAJ 12:20–21 cf. KAJ 152:18–20

§ 725 With a stative, the function of *adi* is no different. The stative expresses a state rather than an action, similar to its usual function. However, the relative clause is still contemporaneous with the main clause; thus, we can translate it as 'as long as'. Notice the occurrence of the Babylonian *qadu* instead of *adi* in one attestation. This could be an archaism or a Babylonianism, although note that *qadu* is not attested in MB, according to Aro's (1957) glossary. In a rather different function, we find the conjunction *qadu* in OA (GOA § 26.3.22); otherwise, *qadi/u* in OA is restricted as a preposition. In general, *qadu* as a conjunction is exceptional in Akkadian (GAG, 277 § 173c).

qa-du bal-ṭú-tu-ni tuka??al tattanabbal 'as long as she is alive, she will hold (it) and provide (for herself)' KAJ 9:23–24

a-di EN *bal-ṭu-ú-ni bēlī apallaḫ* 'as long as my lord is alive, I will serve my lord' KAV 159:5

a-di us-ba-ku-ni ana GN *alka* 'as long as I stay here, come to GN' NP 46:14–16

a-di UD^meš^ *ṭa-bu-ni limsiū* 'as long as the days are good, they must wash' MATSH 6:15'

a-di re-es-su la i-na-ši-ú-ni-[*ni*] *ana duāke lā šēlinannini*^sic.^ 'as long as they do not bring his head here, do no put me to death' T 02-3:22–25 (see § 642)

It is not entirely clear whether we should translate the following passage with 'as long as' in line with Jakob's original translation. Corresponding with the above, the adverbial clause should have a stative. Alternatively, we can translate it as 'as soon as'

a-di ūmū i-ṭí-bu-ni ana libnāte urrudūne 'as long as the days are good, they must go down for bricks' MATC 3:7–8

In combination with the negation *lā*, we should translate it as 'before' (see Llop/Luukko 2014, 218):

a-di ayyēšamma la-a ni-lu-ku-ni ŠE *lāddinakku* 'before we go anywhere, I want to give you the barley' NP 46:18–20

a-di PN *la e-be-*⌜*ra*⌝*-a-ni bilā* 'bring it here, before PN crosses over' VS 1 105:10–12

§ 726 Combinations of *adi* with a preterite are not common in MA. However, the following passage has a negated preterite following the adverbial expression *adi annîša* 'up until now':

a-di annîša abbāʾūya la iš-pu-ru ūma anāku altaprakku 'up until now, my forefathers did not write, but today I have written to you' EA 15:9–11

Instead of *adi*, we sometimes find *ēm*. In the case of MATSH 11, an additional pronominal suffix, i.e., *-šu*, is attached. One broken example is also found (*e-em* George 1988 1 r. 15'†):

> *ina qāt ṭēm* PN *u ṣabā* GN *lā nilammudūni e-mi-šu ur-ru-du-ni-ni immātema ṭē*[*m* PN] *ana muḫḫi bē*[*līya*] *lā ašp*[*ur*] '(since) we are not finding out the news of PN and the troops of GN, (concerning) when they will come down, I have not ever sent a report of PN to my lord' MATSH 11:6–12

> ⸢*e*⸣*-em našperte ša šarre tal-la-ka-ni našperta ana* [*muḫ*]*ḫīya ušebbala* 'when the message of the king comes, he will send the message to me' MATSH 12:42–43

21.2.2 *ašar*: local clause

§ 727 The noun *ašru* 'place' is found frequently in MA as a conjunction.[6] It always seems to introduce a relative locative sentence, unlike OA, where it also had functions other than as a conjunction.[7] As such, it can occur with any tempora. Usually, the *ašar* relative clause is found at the beginning of a sentence:

> *a-šar bēta ud-du-ši-i-ni* (…) *tētarab* 'where he assigned a house to her (…) she entered' MAL A § 24:45–46

> *a-šar ḫa-di-*<*a*>*-*⸢*tu*⸣*-ú-ni tallak* 'she will go where she wants' MAL A § 33:70

> *a-šar* PN 'where PN (lives?)' KAJ 93:7

> *a-šar ta-di-nu-ni tuppaka* (…) *šuṭar*[sic.] *šēbila* 'where you gave it, write and send your tablet' KAV 104:20–22

> *a-šar mugerru ša š*[*arre*] *i-ba-la-ku-tu-ni* PN-*ma naši* 'where the chariot of the king passes, PN carries (it)' VAT 8722:18–20

> *a-šar i-qa-bi-ú-ni-šu-nu-ni iddunū* 'they shall give (it) wherever they order them' MATC 83:14–15

Often, *ašar* is preceded by a head. In such a case, it is more correct to speak of relative clauses, since the dependent clauses expand on the head rather than the verb.

> *ana muḫḫi aʾīle a-šar us-bu-ú-ni tattalak* 'she has gone to a man, the place where he lives' MAL A § 13:26–27

> *eqalšu u bessu a-šar šarru id-du-nu-ú-ni iddan* 'the king shall give his field and house wherever he (wants) to give it' MAL A § 45:87–88

> *ina bēt marʾēša a-šar pa-nu-ša-a-ni tuššab* 'she shall reside in the house of (one of) her own sons, wherever she chooses' MAL A § 46:93–94; cf. MAL A § 46:106

> *a-šar maškan itḫuru*[sic.] *ša-ak-nu-ú-ni* [*lā errab*] 'he will not enter the place where the *itḫuru*-tent is erected' MAPD § 9:53–54

6 See UGM, 113–14 § 104; cf. GAG, 282 § 175a. Streck (2014a, 144 § 342b) regards this type of clause as asyndetic and relative to *ašar* in the status constructus. Given the frequency of *ašar* clauses, I regard *ašar* as grammaticalized.

7 Cf. GKT, 249–50 § 150; GOA § 12.4.2.2.

12 IKU *eqla* (…) *a-šar* PN *i-na-su-qú-ni ilaqqe* 'a 12-acre field, where PN will select it, he will take it' BM 108924:1–7

ina zittīšu a-šar A.ŠÀ-*šu-ni damqa išallim* 'he will obtain compensation from his share, wherever his field is' KAJ 148:30–31[8]

tuppu dannutu <*ša*> *eqle šuāšu a-šar ti-li-ni ana* PN *zakkuat* 'the strong tablet of that field, where it comes up, will be cleared to PN' KAJ 149:22–25

In the following case, the relative clause comes behind the main clause:

tuppaka šuṭar$^{sic.}$ [*a*]-*šar ta-di-nu-ni* 'write your tablet, where you gave it' KAV 104:16–17

Some variation in these constructions is found. In the following three cases, we find multiple variants of the common clause *tuppu šīt ašar tellīanni naḫrat* 'this tablet, where it may appear, is invalid'.

[*tu*]*ppu šīt a-šar ti-li-a-ni naḫrat* 'this tablet, wherever it may appear, is invalid' KAJ 142:12–13

a-šar te-li-a-ni naḫrat '(this tablet), wherever it may appear, is invalid' TR 3002:6–7

tuppu ša a-šar te-li-a-ni naḫrat 'the tablet, wherever it may appear, is invalid' TR 3012:9–10

21.2.3 *aššum*: causal clauses

§ 728 The preposition *aššum* can be used as a conjunction with the subjunctive.[9] Examples are unfortunately very rare and I could find no more than those presented by W. Mayer (UGM, 114 § 105). Still, the conjunction is not uncommon in the Assyrian dialect, while it is also known from OA as *aššumi*.[10]

mussa ina alāke aš-šum riksa la-a tu-qa-i-ú-ni ù ta-na-ḫi-zu$^{!}$*-ú-ni ana šuāša u lidānīšama ilaqqešunu* 'upon the return of her husband, because she did not wait according to the decree but got married, he shall take her and her children' MAL A § 36:11–14

šumma ḫarimtu mītat [*aš*]-*šum aḫḫūša i-qa-ab-bi-ú-ni* (…) [*iz*]⌜*uz*⌝*zū* 'if the prostitute is dead, (and) because of that her brothers declare, they shall divide (…)' MAL A § 49:57–61

Freydank (1975, 144) pointed out that a subjunctive does not always follow *aššum*, offering the following example from VAT 8851. In addition, there are two phrases in two *šulmānu* texts where the predicate is an infinitive without a subjunctive:

(…) *iddinū* [*áš*$^{?}$]-*šúm ana lēʾe* (…) *ta-ba-ku-šu-nu* 'they gave (it) to assign them on the writing board' KAJ 91:15–18

aš-šúm PN *emāra la i-ma-gu-ur emārušu luḫattipū* 'because PN will not agree on the donkey, may they butcher his donkey' VAT 8851:24–26

áš-šúm an-n[*i-te*] *lammuš* 'I want to depart because of this' MATSH 4:7'–8'

8 Contra the CAD (M2, 218a), SIG5.GA (*damqa*) is not an adjective to A.ŠÀ-*šu-ni* because this form has a subjunctive, marking the end of the dependent clause.

9 See GAG, 211 § 116g; 283–84 § 176a.

10 See GKT, 250–51 § 151; GOA § 26.3.7.

aʾīlu anniu šulmānu šūt aš-šúm urdāni (…) *ana marʾē* ᶠPN *la-a ta-da-a-ni abā[ss]a emmar šul[m]āššu immaḫar* 'this man is a *šulmānu*-gift. (When) he examines her case concerning the servants given of to the son of ᶠPN he will receive his! *šulmānu*-gift' T 97-2:8–16

21.2.4 *iltu*: temporal clauses

§ 729 The preposition *iltu* (§ 438ff) can also be used as a conjunction in the adverbial clause.[11] Similar to *adi*, it has a temporal function, with a basic translation of 'after, from, since'. The adverbial clause functions as the starting point for the action of the main clause. In the case of the present, the action of the main clause has thus not finished if it has an adverbial clause with *iltu*.

iš-tu i-pa-ša-ḫu-ni (…) *diqāra tak[appar]* 'after it cools down, you will clean out the vessel' PKT 5 r. 9–10

iš-tu u₄-me ša ú-ru-du-ni (…) *taddana* 'from the day that they will go down (…) you will give' MATC 4:24–27

With a stative in the adverbial clause, the action of the verb continues until the moment of speech, although, as shown in these examples, the action of the main clause lies in the past:

*iš-tu nikkassušu*ᵐᵉš *ša iš-tu lime* PN_1 *a-di* (...) *lime* PN_2 *gabbu ṣa-ab-tu-ni* 'after all his accounts from eponym PN_1 until eponym PN_2 are audited' KAJ 80:1–5

iš-tu muṭṭāʾē ša karrē ša patrē ub!-lu-ú-ni 'after they brought the defects of the dagger pommels' KAJ 112:1–4 (see UŠA, 165)

iš-tu PN *me-tu-ú-ni ittablū* 'they brought it after PN died' KAJ 212:7–9

Preterite:

iš-tu nāmurāte ana šarre ú-qar-ri-bu-ni sukkallu rabīu sukkallu šanīu ḫaṭṭāte ana pan šarre ikarrurū 'after they presented the audience gifts to the king, the grand minister and second minister lay down the sceptres before the king' Coronation Ritual iii 7–9

When followed by a perfect, instead of preterite:

iš-tu ta-at-ta-na-šu-ni x x *ana muḫḫīya [a]lka* 'come to me as soon as you have given it to him' OIP 79 3:21–23

When followed by an infinitive:

iš-tu niqiāte ka-ša-a-di 'when the time for making sacrifices draws near' MAPD § 7:46

iš-tu tuppi a-ma-ri-ka (…) *šupur* 'when you see my tablet (…) send' MATC 5:3–5

Once, *panē* occurs instead of *iltu*:

pa-ni PN (…) *e-te-qa-an-ni urkittēšu nakru ana* GN *imtuqut* 'after PN moved on, the enemy attacked GN' MATSH 4:5–8

11 See GAG, 273–75 § 171; cf. OA GKT § 153; GOA § 26.3.14.

21.2.5 *ina ūme/mate*: temporal clauses

§ 730 The OA conjunction *inūmi* 'when', or literally 'on the day', is written in MA as *ina ūmi*, which identifies both elements of the conjunction.[12] This indicates that the vowel /a/ is unlikely to have been pronounced. Usually, the verbal predicate of the relative clause occurs in the present when referring to the present tense as future. A few attestations of a preterite referring to the past for time and the stative for status are known (cf. UGM, 114 § 106). Note that the subordinate clause does not necessarily stand at the beginning of a clause. There are attestations of it standing at the end or in the middle, while being preceded by the subject of the main clause.

Present in the dependent clause:

i+na u$_4$*-mi ina rēbete ē[diš] il-la-ka-a-ni uptaṣṣa[nāma]* 'on the day that they go alone in the street, they shall be veiled' MAL A § 40:56–57

i+na u$_4$*-mi nāgiru* (...) *i-⸢sa⸣-si-ú-ni* (…) *izzazzū* 'on the day that the herald proclaims, they shall stand ready' MAL B § 6:28–32

i+na u$_4$*-mi* EN A.ŠÀ *il-la-ka-an-ni* ^{giš}KIRI$_6$ *a-di ma-ni-ḫa-te-šu i-laq-qé* 'on the day the owner of the field comes, he shall take the orchard with its installations' MAL B § 13:24–25

i+na u$_4$*-me annaka ṣibātīšu ēṣidē i-du-nu-ni*$^!$ *eqalšu ipaṭṭar* 'on the day that he gives the lead, its interest and the reapers, he shall redeem his field' KAJ 11:17–18

i+na u$_4$*-me annaka i-ḫi-ṭu-ni marāšu [i]paṭṭar* 'on the day that he weighs out the lead, he shall redeem his son' KAJ 17:13–15

i+na u$_4$*-me i-ri-šu-šu-ni iddan* 'on the day that he requests it, he shall give it' KAJ 48:10–12

i+na u$_4$*-mi i-pa-ṭu-⸢ru⸣-⸢ni⸣ iddan* 'on the day he releases it, he shall give it' MARV 10 53:17–19

Preterite in the dependent clause:

i+na u$_4$*-me šarru* MAN (…) *a-na šaṣbute ana* GN$_2$ *il-li-ku-ni ana* GN$_1$ *tadna* 'when the king went to conquer GN$_2$, it was given to GN$_1$.' KAJ 249:13–19

3 *qa dišpa* (…) PN$_1$ *maḫir i+na u*$_4$*-me* PN$_2$ *ana ēkalle e-ru-bu-ni* 'PN$_1$ has received three litres of syrup on the day that PN$_2$ entered the palace' MARV 2 7:1–5

3 *qa šaman ase i+na u*$_4$*-mi šarru ṣabʾa* (…) *i-du-ku-ni* (…) *ina šēpē ilāni tabuk* 'three litres of myrtle oil, on the day that the king killed troops. It was poured before the feet of the gods' MARV 2 22:1–3

i+na u$_4$*-um šarru ana* GN *i-li-ku-ú-ni* '(unpublished section), on the day the king went to GN' DeZ 4022:9–11

ina u$_4$*-me annaka u ṣibtušu i-ḫi-ṭu-<ni> šaprātemma ipaṭṭar* 'he will release the pledges on the day that he will weigh out the lead and its interest' TR 3021:15–17

Stative in the dependent clause:

12 Cf. GKT, 251 § 152; GOA § 26.13. Notice also the NA construction *ūmu ša*; see SNAG, 128 § 4.5.3.1. We also find *ina ūme* in UgAkk (Huehnergard 1989, 245).

1 *sūtu šamnu* (…) *i+na u4-mi* PN *me-tu-ú-*⸢*ni*⸣ [x] *ana* [*mu*]*ḫḫīšu tabik* 'one seah of oil, on the day that PN died, was poured on him' MARV 2 22:4–5

i+na u4-mi ṭēma ša-ak-nu-ni ana mātīšu im-mu-šu-ni (…) *din* 'on the day that a message is placed, he departed to his land (…) give it' MATC 24A:16–19

Without a verbal predicate in the dependent clause:

šumma aʾīlu i+na u4-mi ra-a-qí šamna ana qaqqad mārat aʾīle itbuk 'if a man, on a public holiday, poured oil over the head of a woman of the *awīlu*-class' MAL A § 42:14–15

i+na u4-um il KASKAL-*ni ki-*[*i*] *a-na* É.GAL-*lim ir-ra-bu-ú-ni* (…) *i-qa-bi-ú* 'on the day of the road deity, when (the statue) enters the palace (…) they will report' MAPD § 8:48–50

A rare variant with *ūmtu* is also attested as a conjunction in a Tell Ṣabī Abyaḍ text:

šikara^meš^ *u tarīḫāte um-ti S*[*ū*]*tīu i-lu-ku-ni-n*[*i*] *akla*^meš^ *ina panīya e-ku-lu-ni liddin* 'may he give beer and *t.*-vessels on the day that the Suteans come to eat bread in my presence' T 93-3:17–20

§ 731 MA recognizes some variation with this adverbial construction. Once, we find the adverbial *ūma* in a TŠḪ letter. This is curious, as the syntax resembles the common clause from loans, i.e., *ina ūme errišūšuni* 'on the day that he requests it from him' (cf. above):

⸢*u4*⸣*-ma* PN ⸢*e*⸣*-ri-ša-a-ni* 'the day that PN requests it from me' MATSH 16:16–17

In the same type of clause, we also find the related expression *ina mate* 'whenever' (cf. GAG, 281 § 174e). Note that *mate* is also attested in OA with an apocopate vowel (GOA § 12.6.2). The two available passages derive from two loans:

i+na ma-te e-ri-šu-šu-ni 'when he requests it from him' MARV 3 49:10

i+na ma^!^*-ti e-ri-šu-*[*k*]*a-ni taddana* 'when he requests it from you, you will give it' MARV 5 89:14–15

i-ma-at e-ri-šu-šu-ni ṣabʾa iddan 'whenever he requires it from him, he will give the troops' T 98-110:9–11

Once, in a letter, *ina mate* seems to be used as the adverbial 'ever'. There is one other broken and unclear attestation, which is not further specified here ([*m*]*a*^?^*-ti-ma* T 97-32:11):

ina qāt ṭēm PN *u ṣabā* GN *lā nilammudūni ēmīšu urrudūnenni im-ma-te-ma ṭē*[*m* PN] *ana muḫḫi bē*[*līya*] *la-a áš-p*[*u-ur/ru-ni* '(since) we are not finding out the news of PN and the troops of GN, (concerning) when they will come down, I have not ever sent a report of PN to my lord' MATSH 11:6–12

21.2.6 *kī*: various adverbial and complement clauses

§ 732 As we already saw, OA usually does not use *kīma*; instead, we find *kī* used as a preposition and a conjunction.[13] Unlike other conjunctions, it has a wide array of different meanings, albeit related to each other. Originally, *kī* was used in comparative clauses, which is still its main function in MA.[14]

13 Cf. OA in GKT, 254–57 § 154; GOA § 26.3.16.

14 The development of the different syntactic function of *kī(ma)* in Babylonian is described in Deutscher (2000, Chapter 4).

'(just) as/in the same way':

šarru ki-i i-la-ʾu-ú-ni iltana$^{??}$*alšu* 'the king, as he is able, will question him' MAL A § 47:20–21

ki-i zīqu annītu nam-ra-tu-ni namāra u šalāma DN lū tašīmakku 'just as this torch is bright, may DN grant you light and well-being' Ištar Ritual:12–1; r. 3'–4'

šumma eqla ana ṣarpe iddan ki-i eqlu i-lu-ku-ni PN *ilaqqe* 'if he sells the field for silver, PN shall take it according (to the price) the field goes for' AO 19.228:18–20

šumma eqla lā eṣṣid ki-i PN_1 *ēṣidē e-gu-ru-ni* PN_2 *annaka iḫīaṭ* 'if he does not reap the field, PN_2 will weigh out (as much) lead as PN_1 hired reapers' KAJ 50:13–17

iltu asāyāte ki-i ša ṭēma áš-ku-nu-ka-ni našārīka ammar qable ulli 'as soon as you have deduced the towers as I have instructed you, raise it at much as the middle' MATC 4:18–21

ki-i ḫa-di-a-ta-a-ni epuš 'do as you please' MATC 15:8–9

rē[ḫt]a ki-i ša bē[lī] e-⌜ep⌝-pa-ša-na-ši-in-ni 'the rest, (may be) as my lord will do to us' MATSH 11:16–17

With the variant *akkī*:

a-ki-i tu-be-šú-ni-ma 'the way you stirred it' PKT 4 r. left 5

Often the construction is strengthened by an additional *ša* (UGM, 116):[15]

ki-i kallete ša i-ra-ʾu-mu-ši-ni irakkusūnešše 'like a daughter-in-law whom they love, they draw up (an agreement) for her' MAL A § 46:97–98

bēlī ki-i ša na-ṭu-a-šu-ni lēpuš 'may my lord do, as it is suitable for him' MATSH 10:27

bēlī ki-i ša ṭé-mu-un-ni lišpura 'may my lord write me what (his) orders are' MATSH 12:39

ki-i ša bēlī i-ša-pa-r[a-ni] '(it will be) according to what my lord writes to me' MATSH 16:21

'Because, as':

ki-i tīru$^{\text{sic.}}$ (…) *la-a ṭa-bu-ni* 3 *emmeru*$^{\text{pl.}}$ (…) *lā maḫrū* 'because the flesh$^{?}$ was not good, three sheep were not received' KAJ 209:5–10

lā tumarriranni ina ṣabʾe Imarāyē ki-i ina ^{lú}⌜GIGIR⌝ *ša* PN *tu-ma-ri-ra-ni-ni* 'you did not frustrate me concerning the Emariote troops, as you frustrated me about the chariot of PN' MATC 2:18–21

'When/as soon as':

i+na u$_4$*-um il ḫarrāni ki-[i] ana ēkalle ir-ra-bu-ú-ni* (…) *iqabbiū* 'on the day of the road deity, when (the statue) enters the palace (…) they shall report' MAPD § 8:48–50

ki-i PN *i-lik-a-ni ītakal* 'when PN came, it was consumed' CTMMA 1 104:2–5

1 *emāru* ŠE-*um ki-i* ŠE-*um*^{eš} *ina ugāre e-ṣi-du-ni* 'one homer of barley, when they harvested the barley in the meadow' KAJ 121a:1–2

15 Note that the use of *kī ša* is different from its temporal use as 'when' in NB. This is derived from the Aramaic (< *k dy*) (Kaufman 1974, 135), which is an Aramaism in that particular dialect of Akkadian (Woodington 1983, 275–76 § 103).

7 emmeru^{meš} *ana naptene ki-i* RN *ana muḫḫi kisallāte māʾē ramāke it-ta-na-ra-du-ú-ni epšū* 'seven sheep for a meal, when the king goes repeatedly down with water to wash the forecourts, they are sacrificed' KAJ 204:7–12 cf. KAJ 205:6–15

[1] *emmera*[sic.] (…) PN *maḫir ki-i šamma il-ti-ú-ni* 'PN received one sheep when he drank medicine' KAJ 221:1–4

ki-i ilāni[sic.] *ana bēte sa-si-ú-ni* 1 *sūtu karānu ana qilte* 'when the gods are called to the house, one seah of wine is for the forest' KAJ 232:3–6

[1] *emmeru* (…) *ki-i* [f]PN *mar-ṣu-tu-ú-ni epiš* 'one sheep, when PN is sick, will be prepared' A 1765 (NTA, 25):1–6

1 PN (…) *ki-i nēšu ú-ṣa-bi-tu-šu-ni* (…) *tadin* 'when the lion has seized them, one (ox) is given to PN' A 3196 (NTA, 39):10–12

ki-i zarʾa (…) *ú-še-ṣi-ú-ni-ni* (…) *maḫrū* 'when they brought out the seed, they received (barley)' MATC 42:8–13

ṣabʾu ki-i in-na-bi-du[!]*-ni ina mu-še barāremma ittaṣṣū* 'when the troops fled at dusk, they (the pursuers) went after (them)' MATSH 2:22–23

emmeru[meš] *annūtu ki-i* PN *a-na n[eʾr]āru[tt]e ša šarre* (...) *i-[l]i-ka-ni ina muḫḫ[i]* GN (...) *[ult]ākilu* 'these sheep, when PN went to the aid of the king, fed GN' T 98-119:11–18

With the variant *kīma*:

ki-ma PN *marā šipre [an]a muḫḫīya il-la-⌜ka⌝ u anāku mīnummê aḫuya [i]ṣabbutū[ni an]āk[u a]na muḫḫi [aḫ]īya ušebbala [arḫi]š* 'when PN, the messenger, will come to me then I shall send to my brother quickly whatever my brother wants to take' RS 06.198:21–27

Notice also that *kī* can occur without a main clause, similarly to *ša*:

ki-i ša i-qa-bi-a-na-ši[!]*-[ni]* '(we will do) that, what he will say to us' MATSH 2:60

ki-i ša i-qa-bi-a-ku-nu-ú-ni '(you will do) according to what he will command you' MATSH 7:15''

⌜*ki*⌝*-i ša bēlīma us-bu-ni* '(it was) as if my lord were here' MATSH 12:7

§ 733 We also find *kī* used to introduce a complement clause (object clause), which can also be described as a 'that clause'.[16] This may be described as the direct object of the predicate in the main clause. This is different to a normal relative clause, where the head can be a direct object, but the relative clause only functions to specify the head. In a complement clause, there is no head, while the dependent clause as a whole can be regarded as an object. This type of construction is found with verbs of notifications, such as 'to say' (e.g., 'he said that …') and 'to know' (e.g., 'he knows that …'). A complete study of complement clauses in Babylonian can be found in Deutscher (2000), although, for MA, the number of attested complement clauses is too small to allow for an extensive discussion.[17]

16 See GAG, 285 § 177; cf. OA in GKT, 256 § 154e; GOA § 27; NA in SNAG, 131–32 § 4.5.6.
17 Cf. for MB: Aro (1955a, 154); for NB: Woodington (1983, 289–90 § 110).

lū ina muḫḫi aššat aʾīle ikšudūš u lū ki-i sinnilta i-ni-ku-ú-ni šēbuttu ubtaʾʾerūš aʾīla idukkū 'be it that they have caught him on top of (another man's) wife, or be it that witnesses have proven that he raped the woman, they will kill (that) man' MAL A § 12:20–23

ki-i aššat LÚ-*ni idē* 'he knew that she was a wife' MAL A § 13:28–29; cf. MAL A § 14:32, 36

ki-i ni-la-ka-ni liqbi 'may he say that we will come' KAJ 316:17–18

attama tudda ki-i la-šu-ú-ni 'you know that there is nothing' VAT 8851:17–18

annūtu āla lilbiū u annūte ana bir[*āte*] *lušēber ki-i i+na* URU *la-a še-ṣu-e ù* URU *la-a* [*še-l*]*u-*⌜*e*⌝ 'these (troops) must lay siege to the city and I shall bring those (troops) across to the fortifications, so that there is no exit or entry in the city' MATSH 8:26'–27'

Chapter 22: Syntax: Direct Speech

22.1 Verbs introducing direct speech

§ 734 Direct speech in MA is, in most cases, indicated with the interjection *mā*. It follows a verbal form of speech. Most commonly attested is *qabāʾu* 'to say', but in the context of oaths and testimonies, we also find *tamāʾu* 'to swear':

> *i-tam-ma ma-a šumma ušāḫizūšini ma-a ina bētīya širqī* 'he will swear, thus: 'if I did instruct her', thus: "steal from my house, (*I would be damned*)"' MAL A § 5:60–62

In a legal context, we sometimes find direct speech following verbs such as *maḫāru* 'to receive' and *qarābu* 'to approach'. This is not unexpected as, already in OA, we find similar verbs, not directly related to direct speech, introducing a quote, e.g., the common phrase in testimonies: PN_1 *iṣbat-niāti-ma umma* PN_1*-ma ana* PN_2*-ma* 'PN_1 seized us (as witnesses), thus (said) PN_1 to PN_2' (BIN 4 107). The following MA examples are similar in this respect, introducing a situation in which a statement is expected:

> *ana muḫḫi* PN *marā šarre iq-tar-bu ma-a* 'they approached PN, the son of the king, saying (…)' KAV 159:3–4

> *im-taḫ-ra-an-ni ma-a* (…) *bētu ḫammuṣ* 'he has confronted me, saying: "the house was plundered"' KAV 168:5–7

> PN *im-taḫ-*⌈*ra*⌉*-an-ni ma-a* (…) 'PN has confronted me, saying: (…)' Hall 1983:4–5

With *rakkusu* 'to oblige someone (by contract)':

> *šarru ur-ták-ki-is-s*[*u*?] *ma-a* 'the king has obliged him (by contract), thus:' MARV 4 119:5–6

Direct speech can also follow a reference to a written message. This can sometimes be introduced by the verb *šapāru* (e.g., 'you wrote me that …'), but the text may also directly refer to the tablet.

> [*aš*]*šum tuppe ša ul*[*tēb*]*ilakkunni m*[*a-a*] (…) 'concerning the tablet that I sent to you, saying: (…)' MATC 7:4–5

> *ša bēlī iš-pu-ra-ni* [*m*]*a-a ṣab* GN *urkīšunu anaʾīne lā illikū* 'as to what my lord wrote me, saying: "why did the troops of GN not go after them"' MATSH 2:15–16

> *il-tap-ra ma-a ēteber ḫal*[*aq*] 'he wrote me, saying: 'he crossed and disappeared'' MATSH 17:13'

Following *šamāʾu* 'to hear':

> *al-te-me ma-a ḫarrānātu* [*i*]*ttaṣṣāne* 'I heard thus: "the caravans have gone out"' T 93-20:16–17

> *al-te-me ma-a* PN *Imarāyū ša sulummāʾe iltanappurū* 'I heard thus: "PN (and) the Emariotes keep sending peace proposals to the king"' T 96-1:11–17

Usually, the verb introducing direct speech precedes a direct quotation; however, there are a few cases where it actually follows it.

> *lā ide i-tam-ma-ma* '"I did not know", he will swear' MAL A § 22:109

lā idēma i-qa-ab-bi '"I did not know", he will declare' MAL A § 24:66

ma-a aššitī šīt i-qa-ab-bi 'thus, "she is my wife", he will declare' MAL A § 41:4

ina pî āmerāni (…) *anāku ātamar iq-bi-áš-šu-un-ni* 'from the mouth of the witness (…), who said to him, "I have seen it"' MAL A § 47:8–11

mimma laššutta la ta-pa-la-ni 'do not answer me that there is nothing whatsoever' OIP 79 2:10–12

22.2 The particle *mā*

§ 735 A particle closely connected with direct speech in MA is *mā*, spelled either defectively or plene as *ma-a*. According to the current consensus, the particle replaces *umma*, but note also *akkīa* (below).[1] Nonetheless, *umma* is still found in the letter introduction, *ana* PN_1 *qibi-ma umma* PN_2*-ma* 'speak PN_1, thus (says) PN_2'. This is clearly a fossilized construction, introducing the actual message of the letter. However, we still find a similar construction in the middle of OA letters and other texts, such as testimonies, introducing direct speech and other statements (see GOA § 27.4.2–27.4.3). The MA particle may be a weakened form of the expression of disbelief, as we find it in OA (cf. CAD M_1, 1), but it has lost its meaning in MA and been reduced to a marker of direct speech. Outside the context of direct speech, we only find *mā* on rare occasions: *lū šerku lū nāru ma-a ṣābē ēkal*[*le*] 'either a servant or a singer, indeed any official of the palace' MAPD § 22:114. Note the following phrases from literary texts:

iq-bi ma-a aššatka ittinīkū ma-a anāku uba??ar 'he said, thus: "they always fornicate with your wife (and) I shall prove it"' MAL A § 18:74–75

iq-bi-áš-šu ma-a ittinīkūkama ma-a uba??arka 'he said to him: "they always fornicate with you and I shall prove this to you"' MAL A § 19:86–87

i-qa-bi ma-a šumma lā iqbianni 'he will say, thus: "if he did not tell me, (*I would be damned*)"' MAL A § 47:16–17

i-qa-ab-bi ma-a aḫātī adi 1 ITI.UD^{meš} *apaṭṭar* 'he will say, thus: "I will redeem my sister within a month"' MAL A § 48:1–2

(…) *ma-a pu-uš-ra-n*[*i*] 'thus: "clear me (a passage)"' MAL M § 1:2

There are a few direct quotations attested where *mā* is omitted. Note that, in the two quoted phrases, the verb of speech actually follows the quote:

lā ide itammama '"I did not know", he will swear' MAL A § 22:109

lā idēma iqabbi '"I did not know", he will declare' MAL A § 24:66

ina pî āmerāni (…) *anāku ātamar iqbiaššunni* 'from the mouth of the witness (…), who said to him, "I have seen it"' MAL A § 47:8–11

---

1 See UGM, 102 § 89.2, 108–9 § 98; GAG, 219 § 121b, 256 § 155a; Streck (2011, 373); cf. also NA in SNAG, 133–34 § 4.5.10.

mimma laššutta lā tappalanni 'do not answer me that there is nothing whatsoever' OIP 79 2:10–12

§ 736 The use of the particle *mā* in letters is somewhat complicated. It usually indicates a quote inside the core of a letter, introduced by a verb introducing direct speech.

la aq-bi-a-ku-ú ma-a lā tuššaršu 'did I not say to you, thus: "do not release him (from service)?"' MATC 2:22–24

bēlī iš-pu-ra-an-ni ma-a altatapparaššunu 'my lord wrote to me, thus: "I have written them repeatedly"' MATSH 8:39'–40'

ma-a ina 2 ITI.UD^{meš} *kurummassunu tartiaḫ* 'thus:"their rations remained for two months"' MATSH 12:9–10

iq-ti-bi-a ma-a 30 *ṣabʾu Suḫāyū ana šubte ina mūše* [*an*]*nie ētarbūne* 'he told me thus: "30 Suḫean men took positions this night"' T 93-2:4–6

Frequently, but not always, each full sentence of the quote is introduced by the particle *mā*. This can be seen in the following examples:

ma-a attalkaššu ma-a emāra^{meš}*-ia bila ma-a ḫalqū ma-a laššu* 'I have gone to him, (saying:) "bring the donkeys", (but he said:) "they are lost, there are none"' Hall 1983:15–17 (section of a long quote)

anāku akkīa aq-ti-bi-a-áš-šu ma-a susīu^{meš} *ša Sūtīē u kūdunū ša Šubrīē ma ana muḫḫe* PN *naṣṣū* 'I said thus to him, thus: "the horses are from the Suteans and the mules from the Hurrians, they are brought to PN"' MATC 15:15–18

iq-ti-bi-ú-ni ma-a 3 *ḫarrānātu ša Suḫāyē ētiliāne ma-a ana Ḫarrāne tarṣū* 'they told me, thus: "three Suḫean caravans came up here, they are heading to Harran"' T 93-54:6–11

§ 737 Below, we present a number of passages where only the first clause has the particle *mā*. It should be pointed out that, statistically, these are in the absolute minority. In some cases, it may not be entirely clear where a quote ends because we do not have the necessary context. Note also the tendency to use the particle *mā* only once in summon letters, such as KAV 168 and KAV 169 (cf. Llop 2012a, 296).

ana panē šarre a-ki-a iq-ti-bi ma-a ina muḫḫi GNs *lā amlik lā ašpuršunu* 'in the presence of the king he spoke, thus: "concerning the people of GNs, I did not council nor write them (...)"' A 2994:4–9 (testimony, selected passage)

ma-a dannī šūt adi bēlī balṭūni bēli apallaḫ 'this is my valid declaration: "I will serve my lord as long as my lord is alive"' KAV 159:4–5

PN_1 *im-taḫ-ra-an-ni ma-a ina Libbi-āle bētu ḫammuṣ unūti ḫaliqta ina bēt* PN_2 *sarrutu izzūzu* 'PN_1 has confronted me, saying: "the house in the inner city (Aššur) was plundered and the thieves divided my lost property in the house of PN_2"' KAV 168:5–10

PN *im-taḫ-ra-an-ni ma-a lā ḫabbulāku u lā sallāku bit*[*qīy*]*a ibtataq* 'PN has confronted me, saying: "I am not indebted and not a fraud, yet he has accused me"' KAV 169:4–7; cf. KAV 201:4–9; A 748:4–9

§ 738 The particle *mā* does not introduce direct speech in all instances, but it may refer to the general content of a message. This can be observed in the following passage, where *mā* refers to a message that is yet to be written:

> *tuppukunu šu-uṭ-ra ma-a akukia lubulta ina libbi tupninnāte akukia ina libbi iškāre lā maḫre akukia ina libbi lubult[e] ša* PN *uta*ʾʾ*eranni ittaṣṣū* 'write your tablet, thus: "how much clothing from the chests, how much of the work assignment was not received, how much of the clothing that PN returned did they take out?"' KAV 98:40–45

In some passages, the particle *mā* is not introduced by a verb of speech, which may indicate that no quote is being indicated. In such a case, *mā* could be identical to the corresponding OA interjection, with various possible functions, such as expressing doubt or disbelief (CAD M_1, 1).[2]

> *ma-a lū sinniltu ma-a lu [a*ʾ*īlu] ma-a šumma ina tuārīš[u] zittēkina lā tanaddināne* 'be it a woman or a man, thus: "you shall give your share at his return"' KAV 194:19–22 (see oaths in § 708)

> *ma-a ana*ʾ*īne ina bubuāte amūat* 'why should I die from hunger?' VAT 8851:7–8 (*mā* continues to be used at the start of all following clauses)

22.3 The particle *akkīa*

§ 739 The particle *umma* only occurs in the introduction to letters, while, in OA, it could still be used freely (e.g., *um-ma a-na-ku-ma* 'thus I said' BIN 4 6:18) as it was in MB (*um-ma-a a-na* PN 'thus to PN' BE 92:29) (see GAG, 219 § 121b). A semantic replacement has seemingly been found in *akkīa* (< *ana+kīam*), which is placed before a finite form of *qabā*ʾ*u*. Once we find *kīam* without preposition ana (T 93-32). The particle does not replace *mā* as it is still used. Consider the following examples:

> *a-ki-a i[q]abbi* 'thus he speaks' Coronation Ritual i 28

> *šangû a-ki-a iqabb[i]* 'thus the priest speaks' Coronation Ritual ii 28–29

> *ana panē šarre a-ki-a iqtibi mā* 'in the presence of the king, he spoke thus' A 2994:4–6

> *a-ki-a iqṭibi mā* 'thus he said' KAV 217:13'

> *anāku a-ki-a aqtibiaššu mā sisīu*^{meš} *ša Sūtīe* 'I said to him, thus: "the horses are from the Suteans"' MATC 15:15–18

> *a-ki-a liqbiū mā ḫurādkunu kē nakirma* 'may they thus say: "your *ḫurādu*-troops, how are they hostile?"' MATSH 7:11''–12''

> *ētamaršu a-ki-a iqṭibiaššu [m]ā* 'he saw him and spoke to him, thus:' TabT05A-134:13–15

> *ki-am-[ma] šul-ma-an-ki a-na-i-[ni] la ta-šap-pi-ri-[ni]* 'thus, "why do you not sent me your *šulmānu*-gift?"' T 97-32:11'–13'

Besides direct speech, *akkīa* is used to indicate the written content of a tablet, rather than spoken speech:

2 See also GKT, 186 § 106d; GOA § 5.13.

ina pî tuppe a-ki[!]*-a išakkan* 'in the wording of the tablet, he will put as follows' KAJ 83:17–18

ša pî tuppi (…) *ša ina libbīša a-ki-a šaṭrūni* 'in accordance with the tablet on which is written thus' KAJ 159:4–5

Chapter 23: Paradigms

Paradigms

number	case	masculine	feminine
singular	nominative	*šarr-u*	*šarr-utu*
	genitive	*šarr-e*	*šarr-ete*
	accusative	*šarr-a*	*šarr-ata*
dual	nominative	*šarr-ān*	**šarr-atān*
	oblique	*šarr-ēn*	**šarr-etēn*
plural	nominative	*šarr-ū*	*šarr-ātu*
	oblique	*šarr-ī*	*šarr-āte*

Paradigm 1: Declination of nouns

number	case	masculine	feminine
singular	nominative	*damq-u*	*damiq-tu*
	genitive	*damq-e*	*damiq-te*
	accusative	*damq-a*	*damiq-ta*
plural	nominative	*damq-uttu*	*damq-ātu*
	oblique	*damq-utte*	*damq-āte*

Paradigm 2: Declination of adjectives

number	case	masculine		feminine	
		-āy	*-ī*	*-āy*	*-ī*
singular	nominative	*Aššur-āy-u*	*Aššur-ī-u*	*Aššur-āy-tu*	*Aššur-it-tu*
	genitive	*Assur-āy-e*	*Aššur-ī-e*	*Aššur-āy-te*	*Aššur-it-te*
	accusative	*Aššur-āy-a*	*Aššur-ī-a*	*Aššur-āy-ta*	*Aššur-it-ta*
plural	nominative	*Aššur-āy-ū*	*Aššur-ī-ū*	*Aššur-āy-ātu*	*Aššur-īy-ātu*
	oblique	*Aššur-āy-ē*	*Aššur-ī-ē*	*Aššur-āy-āte*	*Aššur-īy-āte*

Paradigm 3: Declination of the nisbe

	nom.	genitive				oblique	dative
		gen. ms	gen fs.	gen. mp	gen. fp		
3ms	*šūt*	*šuʾāʾu*	–	–	–	*šuātV*	*šuāšu*
3fs	*šīt*	–	–	–	–	*šiātV*	*šuāša*
2ms	*atta*	*kuāʾu*	*kuātu*	*kuāʾuttu*	–	–	*kuāša*
2fs	*atti*	–	–	–	–	–	*kuāši*
1cs	*anāku*	*iyû*	–	–	*iyātu*	–	*iyâši*
3mp	*šunu*	–	–	–	–	*šunātunu*	*šunāšunu*
3fp	*šina*	–	–	–	–	*šinātena*	–
2mp	*attunu*	–	–	*kunaʾuttu*	–	–	*kunāšunu*
2fp	*attina**	–	–	–	–	–	*kunāšina*
1cp	*nēnu*	–	*niātu*	*niāʾūtu*	*niâtu*	–	*nâšin*

Paradigm 4: Independent personal pronouns

	genitive	dative	accusative
3ms	*-šu*	*-šu*	*-š(u)*
3fs	*-ša*	*-še*	*-š(i)*
2ms	*-ka*	*-ku*	*-ka*
2fs	*-ki*	*-ke*	*-ki*
1cs	*-ī, -ya*	*-a, -Ø*	*-anni*
3mp	*-šunu*	*-šunu*	
3fp	*-šina*	*-šina*	
2mp	*-kunu*	*-kunu*	
2fp	*-kina*	*-kina**	
1cp	*-ni*	*-nâši(n)*	

Paradigm 5: Suffixed pronouns

	masculine[1]				feminine with -*(a)t* morpheme			
	bēlu, nom/acc	*šipru*, nom/acc	*tuppu*, nom/acc	*tuppu*, gen	-*at*, nom/acc	-*at*, gen	-*t*, nom/acc	-*t*, gen
3ms	*bēl-šu*	*šipar-šu*	*tuppu-šu*	*tuppī-šu*	*pāḫas-su*	*pāḫitī-šu*	*lubultu-šu*	*lubultī-šu*
3fs	*bēl-ša*	*šipar-ša*	*tuppa-ša*	*tuppī-ša*	*pāḫas-sa*	*pāḫitī-ša*	*lubulta-ša*	*lubultī-ša*
2ms	*bēl-ka*	*šipar-ka*	*tuppa-ka*	*tuppī-ka*	*pāḫat-ka*	*pāḫitī-ka*	*lubulta-ka*	*lubultī-ka*
2fs	*bēl-ki*	*šipar-ki*	*tuppi-ki*	*tuppī-ki*	*pāḫat-ki*	*pāḫitī-ki*	*lubulti-ki*	*lubultī-ki*
1cs	*bēl-ī*	*šipar-ī*	*tupp-ī*	*tuppī-ya*	*pāḫit-ī*	*pāḫitī-ya*	*lubult-ī*	*lubultī-ya*
3mp	*bēl-šunu*	*šipar-šunu*	*tuppu-šunu*	*tuppī-šunu*	*pāḫas-sunu*	*pāḫitī-šunu*	*lubultu-šunu*	*lubultī-šunu*
3fp	*bēl-šina*	*šipar-šina*	*tuppi-šina*	*tuppī-šina*	*pāḫas-sina*	*pāḫitī-šina*	*lubulti-šina*	*lubultī-šina*
2mp	*bēl-kunu*	*šipar-kunu*	*tuppu-kunu*	*tuppī-kunu*	*pāḫat-kunu*	*pāḫitī-kunu*	*lubultu-kunu*	*lubultī-kunu*
2fp	*bēl-kina*	*šipar-kina*	*tuppi-kina*	*tuppī-kina*	*pāḫat-kina*	*pāḫitī-kina*	*lubulti-kina*	*lubultī-kina*
1cp	*bēl-ni*	*šipar-ni*	*tuppi-ni*	*tuppī-ni*	*pāḫat-ni*	*pāḫitī-ni*	*lubulti-ni*	*lubultī-ni*

Paradigm 6: Pronominal suffixes on nouns

number	case	masculine	masculine	feminine
singular	nominative	*anniu*	*ammiu*	*annītu*
	genitive	*annie*	*ammie*	*annīte*
	accusative	*annia*	*ammia*	*annīta*
plural	nominative	*annūtu*	–	*annātu*
	oblique	*annūte*	–	*annāte*

Paradigm 7: Demonstrative pronouns

1 The noun, *tuppu* ‘tablet’, is feminine in gender but without -*(a)t* morpheme.

		present	perfect	preterite	imperative	infinitive	stative	participle
G	a-u	*iparras*	*iptaras*	*iprus*	*purus*	*parāsu*	*paris*	*pārisu*
	a-a	*imaḫḫaṣ*	*imtaḫaṣ*	*imḫaṣ*	*maḫaṣ*	*maḫāṣu*	*maḫiṣ*	*māḫiṣu*
	i-i	*ipaqqid*	*iptiqid*	*ipqid*	*piqid*	*paqādu*	*paqid*	*pāqidu*
	u-u	*irappud*	*irtupud*	*irpud*	*rupud*	*rapādu*	*rapid*	*rāpidu*
Gt		*iptarrus*	*iptatrus*	*iptaras*	*pitras*	–	*pitrus*	*muptarsu*
Gtn		*iptanarras*	*iptatarras*	*iptarras*	*tiparras*	*tiparrusu*	–	*muptarrisu*
D		*uparras*	*uptarris*	*uparris*	*parris*	*parrusu*	*parrus*	*muparrisu*
Dt		*uptarras*	–	*uptarris*	–	–	–	–
Dtn		*uptanarras*	–	–	–	–	–	–
Š		*ušapris*	*ultapris*	*ušapris*	*šapris*	*šaprusu*	*šaprus*	*mušaprisu*
Št		–	–	–	–	*tušaprusu*	*tušapərus*	–
Štn		*ultaparras*	*ultatapris*	*ultapris*	*šutapris*	*šutaprusu*	–	*multaprisu*
N	a-i	*ipparras*	*ittapras*	*ippiris*	*napris*	*naprusu*	*naprus*	*mupparsu*
	i-i	*ippaqqid*	*ittapqid*	*ippiqid*	*napqid*	*napqudu*	*napqud*	*muppaqdu*
Ntn		–	–	–	–	–	–	–

Paradigm 8: Verbal stems

	present	perfect	preterite	pret+subj	pret+ventive	prec./imper.	stative
3ms	*i-parrVs*	*i-ptarVs*	*i-prVs*	*i-prVs-ūni*	*i-prVs-a*	*li-prVs*	*paris*
3fs	*ta-parrVs*	*ta-ptarVs*	*ta-prVs*	*ta-prVs-ūni*	*ta-prVs-a*	*lū ta-prVs*	*pars-at*
2ms	*ta-parrVs*	*ta-ptarVs*	*ta-prVs*	*ta-prVs-ūni*	*ta-prVs-a*	*pVrVs*	*pars-āta*
2fs	*ta-parrVs-ī*	*ta-ptars-ī*	*ta-prVs-ī*	*ta-prVs-ī-ni*	*ta-prVs-ī-Ø*	*pVrsī*	*pars-āti*
1cs	*a-parrVs*	*a-ptarVs*	*a-prVs*	*a-prVs-ūni*	*a-prVs-a*	*lā-prVs*	*pars-āku*
3mp	*i-parrVs-ū*	*i-ptars-ū*	*i-prVs-ū*	*i-prVs-ū-ni*	*i-prVs-ū-ne*	*li-prVs-ū*	*pars-ū*
3fp	*i-parrVs-ā*	*i-ptars-ā*	*i-prVs-ā*	*i-prVs-ā-ni*	*i-prVs-ā-ne*	*li-prVs-ā*	*pars-ā*
2cp/mp	*ta-parrVs-ā*	*ta-ptars-ā*	*ta-prVs-ā*	*ta-prVs-ā-ni*	*ta-prVs-ā-ne*	*pVrsā*	*pars-ātunu*
fp							*par-ātina**
1cp	*a-parrVs*	*a-ptarVs*	*a-prVs*	*a-prVs-ni*	*a-prVs-ne*	*lū ni-prVs*	*pars-ānu*

Paradigm 9: Conjugation of regular G-stem

	present	perfect	preterite	stative
	I/*e*	I/*e*	I/*e*	I/*e*
3ms	*eppaš*	*ētapaš*	*ēpuš*	*epiš*
3fs	*teppaš*	*tētapaš*	*tēpuš*	*epšat*
2ms	*teppaš*	*tētapaš*	*tēpuš*	*epšāta*
2fs	*teppašī*	*tētapšī*	*tēpušī*	*epšāti*
1cs	*eppaš*	*ētapaš*	*ēpuš*	*epšāku*
3mp	*eppašū*	*ētapšū*	*ēpušū*	*epšū*
3fp	*eppašā*	*tētapšā*	*ēpušā*	*epšā*
2mp/2cp	*teppašā*	*tētapšā*	*tēpušā*	*epšātunu*
1cp	*neppaš*	*nētapaš*	*nēpuš*	*epšāni/u*

Paradigm 10: Conjugation of I/e verbs

	present	perfect	preterite	stative
	I/*a*	I/*a*	I/*a*	I/*e*
3ms	*emmar*	*ētamar*	*ēmur*	*amir*
3fs	*tammar*	*tātamar*	*tāmur*	*amrat*
2ms	*tammar*	*tātamar*	*tāmur*	*amrāta*
2fs	*tammarī*	*tātamrī*	*tāmurī*	*amrāti*
1cs	*ammar*	*ātamar*	*āmur*	*amrāku*
3mp	*emmurū*	*ētamrū*	*ēmurū*	*amrū*
3fp	*emmarā*	*ētamrā*	*ēmurā*	*amrā*
2mp/2cp	*tammarā*	*tātamrā*	*tāmurā*	*amrātunu*
1cp	*nemmar*	*nētamar*	*nēmur*	*amrāni/u*

Paradigm 11: Conjugation of I/a verbs

	present	perfect	preterite	imperative	stative
3ms	*ubbal*	*ittabal*	*ubil*		*ubil*
3fs	*tubbal*	*tattabal*	*tubil*		*ublat*
2ms	*tubbal*	*tattabal*	*tubil*	*bil*	*ublāta*
2fs	*tubbalī*	*tattablī*	*tublī*	*bilī*	*ublāti*
1cs	*ubbal*	*attabal*	*ubil*		*ublāku*
3mp	*ubbulū*	*ittablū*	*ublū*		*ublū*
3fp	*ubbalā*	*ittablā*	*ublā*		*ublā*
2cp/2mp	*tubbalā*	*tattablā*	*tublā*	*bilā*	*ublātunu*
1cp	*nubbal*	*nittabal*	*nubil*		*ublāni/u*

Paradigm 12: Conjugation of the I/u verbs

		present	perfect	preterite	imperative	infinitive	stative
G	I/u	*ubbal*	*uttabal*	*ubil*	*bil*	*ubālu*	*ubil*
	I/a	*emmar*	*ētamar*	*ēmur*	*emur*	*amāru*	*amir*
	I/e	*errab*	*ētarab*	*ērub*	*erub*	*erābu*	*erib*
	I/n	*inaṣṣar*	*ittaṣar*	*iṣṣur*	*uṣur*	*naṣāru*	*naṣir*
Gt		–	–	–	–	–	–
Gtn	I/u	*ittanabal*	*ittanabil*	–	–	–	–
	I/voc	*ētanammar*	–				
	I/n	*ittanaṣṣar*	–				
D	I/u	*ubbal*	*ūtabbil*	*ubbil*	*ubbil*	*ubbulu*	*ubbul*
	I/a	*ummar*	*ūtammir*	*ummir*	*ummir*	–	*ammir*
	I/e	*urrab*	*ūtarrib*	*urrib*	*urrib*	–	*urrib*
	I/n	*unaṣṣar*	*unaṣṣir*	*uttaṣṣir*	*naṣṣir*	*naṣṣuru*	*naṣṣur*
Dt		–	–	*uttabbil*	–	–	–
Dtn		–	–	–	–	–	–
Š	I/u	*ušebbal*	*ultēbil*	*ušēbil*	*šēbil*	*šēbulu*	*šēbul*
	I/a	*ušammar*	*ultāmir*	*ušāmir*	*šāmir*	*šāmuru*	*šāmur*
	I/e	*ušerrab*	*ultērib*	*ušērib*	*šērib*	*šērubu*	*šērub*
Št		–	–	–	–	–	–
Štn		–	–	–	–	*tušēbulu*	–
N	I/a	*innammar*	*ittāmar*	*innāmir*	*nāmir*	–	–
	I/e	*innerrab*	*ittērab*	*innērib*	*nērib*		
Ntn		–	–	–	–	–	–

Paradigm 13: I/weak stem overview

	present		perfect		preterite		imperative		stative
	II/*ū*	II/*ī*	II/*ū*	II/*ī*	II/*ū*	II/*ī*	II/*ū*	II/*ī*	
3ms	*imūat*	*ibīad*	*imtuat*	*ibtiad*	*imūt*	*ibīd*			*bēd*
3fs	*tamūat*	*tabīad*	*tamtuat*	*tabtiad*	*tamūt*	*tabīd*			*bēdat*
2ms	*tamūat*	*tabīad*	*tamtuat*	*tabtiad*	*tamūt*	*tabīd*	*mūt*	*bēd*	*bēdāta*
2fs	*tamuttī*	*tabiddī*	*tamtūtī*	*tabtīdi*	*tamūtī*	*tabīdī*	*mūtī*	*bēdī*	*bēdāti*
1cs	*amūat*	*abīad*	*amtuat*	*abtiad*	*amūt*	*abīd*			*bēdāku*
3mp	*imuttū*	*ibiddū*	*imtūtū*	*ibtīdū*	*imūtū*	*ibīdū*			*bēdū*
3fp	*imuttā*	*ibiddā*	*imtūtā*	*ibtīdā*	*imūtā*	*ibīdā*			*bēdā*
2cp/mp	*tamuttā*	*tabiddā*	*tamtūtā*	*tabtīdā*	*tamūtā*	*tabīdā*	*mūtā*	*bēdā*	*bēdātunu*
1cp	*nimūat*	*nibīad*	*nimtuat*	*nibtiad*	*nimūt*	*nibīd*			*bēdāni/u*

Paradigm 14: Conjugation of the II/voc verbs

	present			perfect	preterite	imperative	stative
	II/voc		II/*ē* (< II/*ḫ*)				
3ms	*ubaˀˀar* (*ubâr*)	*ubarr-ūni*	*ubēaš*	*ubtaˀˀir*	*ubaˀˀir*	*baˀˀir*	*baˀˀur*
3fs	*tubaˀˀar* (*tubâr*)	*ubarr-ūni*	*tubēaš*	*tubtaˀˀir*	*tubaˀˀir*		*baˀˀurat*
2ms	*tubaˀˀar* (*tubâr*)	*ubarr-ūni*	*tubēaš*	*tubtaˀˀir*	*tubaˀˀir*		*baˀˀurāta*
2fs	*tubarrī*	*ubarrī-ni*	*tubeššī*	*tubtaˀˀirī*	*tubaˀˀirī*	*baˀˀirī*	*baˀˀurāti*
1cs	*ubaˀˀar* (*ubâr*)	*ubarr-ūni*	*ubēaš*	*ubtaˀˀir*	*ubaˀˀir*		*baˀˀurāku*
3mp	*ubarrū*	*ubarrū-ni*	*ubeššū*	*ubtaˀˀirū*	*ubaˀˀirū*		*baˀˀurū*
3fp	*ubarrā*	*ubarrā-ni*	*ubeššā*	*ubtaˀˀirā*	*ubaˀˀirā*		*baˀˀurā*
2cp/mp	*tubarrā*	*ubarrā-ni*	*tubeššā*	*tubtaˀˀīrā*	*tubaˀˀīrā*	*baˀˀirā*	*baˀˀurātunu*
1cp	*nubaˀˀar* (*nubâr*)	*nubarr-ūni*	*nubēaš*	*nubtaˀˀir*	*nubaˀˀir*		*baˀˀurāni/u*

Paradigm 15: Conjugation of the II/voc verbs D-stem

		present	perfect	preterite	imperative	infinitive	stative
G	II/ū	*umūat*	*umtuat*	*umūt*	*mūt*	*muātu*	*mēt*
	II/ī	*ibīad*	*ibtiad*	*ibīd*	*bīd*	*biādu*	*bēd*
	II/ˀ	*išaˀˀal*	*iltaˀal*	*išˀal*	*šaˀal*	*šaˀālu*	*šaˀal*
	II/gem	*imaddad*	*imtadad*	*imdud*	*muddu*	*madādu*	*madid*
Gt		–	–	–	–	–	–
Gtn	II/ˀ	*iltanaˀˀal*	–	–	–	–	–
	II/gem	*imtanaddad*					
D	II/voc	*umaˀˀat*	*umtaˀˀit*	*umaˀˀit*	*maˀˀit*	*maˀˀutu*	*maˀˀut*
	II/ˀ	*ušaˀˀal*					
	II/gem	*umaddad*		*umaddid*		*maddudu*	*maddud*
Dt		–	–	–	–	–	–
Dtn		–	–	–	–	–	–
Š	II/voc	*ušmāt*	*ultīmīt*	–	–	–	–
	II/gem		*ultamdid*				
Št		–	–	–	–	–	–
Štn	II/gem	*ultanamdad*	–	–	–	–	–
N	II/ˀ	–	–	*iššaˀal*	–	–	–
Ntn	II/gem	–	–	–	–	*namdudu*	–

Paradigm 16: II/weak stem overview

		present	perfect	preterite	imperative	infinitive	stative
G	III/ū	*izarru*	*izzuru*	*izru*	*zuru*	*zarāʾu*	*zaru*
	III/ī	*ibanni*	*ibtini*	*ibni*	*bini*	*banāʾu*	*bani*
	III/ē	*ilaqqe*	*ilteqe*	*ilqe*	*liqe*	*laqāʾu*	*laqi*
	III/ʾ$_{1,4}$	*išamme*	*ilteme*	*išme*	*šime*	*šamāʾu*	*šami*
Gt		–	–	–	–	–	–
Gtn		*iltanaqqe*	–	–	*tilaqqe*	–	–
D		*ulaqqa*	*ultaqqi*	*ulaqqi*	*laqqi*	*laqquʾu*	*laqqu*
Dt		–	–	–	–	–	–
Dtn		*ultanaqqa*	–	–	–	–	–
Š		*ušalqa*	*ultalqi*	*ušalqi*	–	–	–
Št		–	–	–	–	–	–
Štn		–	–	–	–	–	–
N		*illaqqe*	*ittalqe*	*illeqe*	–	–	–
Ntn		–	–	–	–	–	–

Paradigm 17: III/weak stem overview

	present		perfect		preterite		imperative		stative
	našāˀu	*uṣāˀu*	*našāˀu*	*uṣāˀu*	*našāˀu*	*uṣāˀu*	*našāˀu*	*uṣāˀu*	*našāˀu*
3ms	*inašši*	*uṣṣa*	*ittiši*	*ittiṣi*	*išši*	*uṣi*			*naši*
3fs	*tanašši*	*tuṣṣa*	*tattiši*	*tattiṣi*	*tašši*	*tuṣi*			*naṣṣat*
2ms	*tanašši*	*tuṣṣa*	*tattiši*	*tattiṣi*	*tašši*	*tuṣṣi*	*iši*	*ṣi*	*naṣṣāta*
2fs	*tanaššī*	*tuṣṣaˀi*	*tattaṣṣī*	*tattaṣṣī*	*taššiˀī*	*tuṣṣī*	*iṣṣī*	*ṣiˀī*	*naṣṣāti*
1cs	*anašši*	*uṣṣa*	*attiši*	*attiṣi*	*ašši*	*uṣi*			*naṣṣāku*
3mp	*inaššiˀū*	*uṣṣuˀū*	*ittaṣṣū*	*ittaṣṣū*	*iššiˀū*	*uṣṣū*			*naṣṣū*
3fp	*inaššiˀā*	*uṣṣaˀā*	*ittaṣṣā*	*ittaṣṣā*	*iššiˀā*	*uṣṣā*			*naṣṣā*
2cp/mp	*tanaššiˀā*	*tuṣṣaˀā*	*tattaṣṣā*	*tattaṣṣā*	*taššiˀā*	*tuṣṣā*	*iṣṣā*	*ṣiˀā*	*naṣṣākunu*
2fp									*naṣṣakina*
1cp	*ninašši*	*nuṣṣa*	*nittiši*	*nittiṣi*	*nišši*	*nuṣṣi*			*naṣṣāni/u*

Paradigm 18: Conjugation of the irregular verbs *našāˀu/naṣṣu* and *uṣāˀu*

	present		perfect		preterite		imperative		stative
	alāku	*tadānu*	*alāku*	*tadānu*	*alāku*	*tadānu*	*alāku*	*tadānu*	*alāku*
3ms	*illak*	*iddan*	*ittalak*	*ittidin*	*illik*	*iddin*			*tadin*
3fs	*tallak*	*taddan*	*tattalak*	*tattidin*	*tallik*	*taddin*			*tadnat*
2ms	*tallak*	*taddan*	*tattalak*	*tattidin*	*tallik*	*taddin*	*alik*	*din*	*tadnāta*
2fs	*tallikī*	*taddinī*	*tattalkī*	*tattidinī*	*tallikī*	*taddinī*	*alkī*	*dinī*	*tadnāti*
1cs	*allak*	*addan*	*attalak*	*attidin*	*allik*	*addin*			*tadnāku*
3mp	*illākū*	*iddunū*	*ittalkū*	*ittannū*	*illikū*	*iddinū*			*tadnū*
3fp	*illakā*	*idannā*	*ittalkā*	*ittannā*	*illikā*	*iddinā*			*tadnā*
2cp/mp	*tallakā*	*taddinā*	*tattalkā*	*tattannā*	*tallikā*	*taddinā*	*alkā*	*dinā*	*tadnātunu*
1cp	*nillak*	*niddan*	*attalak*	*nittidin*	*allak*	*niddan*			*tadnāni/u*

Paradigm 19: Conjugation of the irregular verbs *alāku* and *tadānu*

	G-stem *izuzzu*			Š-stem *šazzuzu*			
	present	preterite	imper.	present	perfect	preterite	stative
3ms	*izzâz*	*izzīz*		*ušazzaz*	*ultazziz*	*ušazziz*	*šazzuz*
3fs	*tazzâz*	*tazzīz*		*tušazzaz*	*tultazziz*	*tušazziz*	*šazzuzat*
2ms	*tazzâz*	*tazzīz*	*izīz*	*tušazzaz*	*tultazziz*	*tušazziz*	*šazzuzāta*
2fs	*tazzazzī*	*tazzizzī*	*izizzī*	*tušazzazī*	*tultazzizī*	*tušazzizī*	*šazzuzāti*
1cs	*azzâz*	*azzīz*		*ušazzaz*	*ultazziz*	*ušazziz*	*šazzuzāku*
3mp	*izzazzū*	*izzizzū*		*ušazzazū*	*ultazzizzū*	*ušazzizū*	*šazzuzū*
3fp	*izzazzā*	*izzizzā*		*ušazzazā*	*ultazzizā*	*ušazzizā*	*šazzuzā*
2cp/mp	*tazzazzā*	*tazzizzā*	*izizzā*	*tušazzazā*	*tultazzizā*	*tušazzizā*	*šazzuzātunu*
1cp	*nizzâz*	*nizzīz*		*nušazzazz*	*nultazziz*	*nušazziz*	*šazzuzāni/u*

Paradigm 20: Conjugation of the irregular verb *izuzzu*

Chapter 24: Sign list

The following list represents the different uses of MA signs. It focuses on CvC-signs, logograms and determinatives. Normal Cv/vC-signs are listed as well, but their usage and distribution is discussed in more detail in the chapter of phonology with examples. All signs are ordered according to Borger's MZL.

Many texts are not included here, most notably lexical lists, incantations and other literary texts (except for the prescriptive ones such as MAL and MAPD).

It needs to be stressed that due to the large size of the corpus it is likely that a number of sign uses escaped our attention as some of them are rare, misunderstood and/or only occur in one proper name. This list should therefore merely be regarded as a representation of the MA sign uses. It also functions as a register to some sign readings that were discussed elsewhere in this study.

1	DIL	syl.:	*aš*	passim. Alternates with ÁŠ, see § 218.
			rum (*rù*)	word final, see § 241 for a discussion.
		log.:	AŠ	= preposition *ina*; Coronation Ritual passim; Billa 10:11; MARV 5 25:8; MARV 6 34 passim.
				numeral used with GUN (see § 330).
2	AŠ-AŠ	log.	DIDLI	plural marker, used almost exclusively on URU. See § 79.
			MIN$_5$	numeral used with GUN (see § 330).
3	ḪAL	syl.:	*ḫal*	e.g., *ḫal-qu-ú-ni* MAL A § 25:88; *ta-ša-ḫal* PKT 3 i 10; *ḫal-zi* MATC 79:4; *ḫal-qa-at* Giricano 8:22.
			ḪAL	in (^{lú})ḪAL = *barû*, e.g., MARV 5 8:55; MATSH 9:17.
			BULUḪ	in ^{šim}BALUḪ= *baluḫḫu*, MARV 2 28:4.
4	EŠ$_6$	log.:	EŠ$_6$	numeral used with GUN (see § 330).
5	BAL	syl.:	*b/pal*	e.g., *bal-ṭu-ú-ni* MAL A § 3:33; *ú-pal-lu-šu* § 40:101; *ša-pal* PKT 2 i 18; *i-pal-li-su* MATSH 8:31'. The signs BAL and palaeographic similar BÚR (no. 8) are used in free variation.
			b/pùl	e.g., ^{túg}*lu-bùl-ta* Coronation Ritual i 35; *la ta-pùl* T 97-10:20. Cf. no. 8.
6	GÍR	log.:	GÍR	= *patru*, e.g., Postgate 1973, 1:10; MARV 10 3:12.
8	BÚR	syl:	*búl*	in *lu-búl-ta-ša* MAPD § 6:45.
			bál	in ^{m}*Ma-nu-bál-*^{d}UTU MPR 49:18.
9	TAR	syl.:	*t/ṭar*	e.g., *ú-tar* MAL A § 15:54; *ú-tar-ru-uš* § 20:97; *ip-ta-ṭar* § 48:43; ^{lú}*tar-te-ni-šu-nu* KAJ 245:17; É *nap-tar-te* MATC 12:15; *ú-tar-ra* MATSH 25:10'.
			ḫaš	e.g., *ḫaš-la-a-te*^{meš} MARV 5 11:4.
			šil	e.g., *mi-šil-šu-nu* MATSH 2:8.
		log.:	TAR	in ^{ú}TAR.MUŠEN MARV 1 42:1, a mistake or variant of ^{ú}TAR.MUŠ 'a plant'.
10	AN	syl.	*an*	passim.
		log.	AN	= *šamaʾu,* e.g., Coronation Ritual iii 32; AN-*e* A 3196 (NTA, 39):8; MARV 3 75:2; cf. *ša-ma-e* MARV 1 2:6.
				in AN.BAR = *parzillu*, MARV 1 68:16; MATSH 16:5.
				in AN.NA = *annuku*, e.g., MAL A § 5:59. Syllabic *an-nu-ku* KAJ 37:2.
				in AN.TA = *eliʾu*, e.g., Coronation Ritual iii 32; LVUH

				22:31.
			DINGIR	= *ilu*, e.g., Coronation Ritual i 37, passim in PNs.
		det.:	d	Used before divine names, passim in theophoric elements of PNs.
11	AŠ+ŠUR	syl.	*Aš-šur*	Ligature of DIL + ŠUR. Only in DN Aššur, passim.
13	ZADIM	log.	ZADIM	in ^{lú}ZADIM = *sasinnu*, e.g., KAV 100:22; ZADIM.GI^{meš} MPR 2:43.
14	BA	syl.:	*ba*	Passim.
			(*pá*)	Scribal mistake. See § 203. For discussion and examples.
15	ZU	syl.	*zu*	Passim.
			sú	Occurs sometimes in assimilated pronominal suffix *-šu*. For examples see § 225.
			ṣú	In early texts, e.g., ^{m}*Tar-ṣú-ša-lim* KAJ 160:9; *e-ṣú* KAJ 174:7; *iḫ-mi-ZU-ku-nu-ú-ni* T 04-37:12.
16	SU	syl.:	*su*	passim.
			(*zu*$_{\text{x}}$)	Mostly limited to PNs. See § 215 for discussion.
		log.:	SU	= *riābu*, in PNs, e.g., ^{m}SU-^{d}30 KAJ 107:2.
			KUŠ	= *mašku*, e.g., A 3315:4; LVUH 21:9.
		det.:	kuš	used for hides of animals, passim.
17	ŠEN	syl.:	rug	possibly in uncertain *rug-bì* LVUH 89:15.
18	ARAD	log.	ÌR, ARAD	= *urdu*, e.g., MAL A § 4:55; ÌR-⌜*ta*⌝ Faist 2001, 252:19.
			NÍTA	= *zikaru*, e.g., KAJ 411:8.
				in UDU.NÍTA, e.g., A 3190 (NTA, 37):2 et passim.
20	ITI	log.:	ITI, ITU	= *urḫu*, e.g., MAL A § 19:91, cf. *ur-ḫi* TabT05A-134:19.
				= Sîn, in PN ^{m}ITI-*na-me-er* MARV 7 19:14.
		det.:	iti	for month names.
23	ŠAḪ	syl.:	*siḫ*	e.g., ^{lú}*ḫa-siḫ-lu* KAJ 224:13.
		log.:	ŠAḪ	= *šaḫāʾu*, e.g., MARV 3 33:2?.
				in ŠAḪ.GIŠ.GI, A 2704:15.
24	KA	syl.:	*ka*	passim.
			qà	Only in PNs, see § 206
			pi$_4$	Logographic reading for *pû* is to be preferred.
		log.:	KA	= *pû*, passim, e.g., KAM 10 15:2.
				in ^{d}KA-KA = *Pi*$^{?}$*-lišāni*, Coronation Ritual ii 10.
				in ^{lú}KA.KEŠDA = *kāṣiru,* e.g., KAV 195+:21.
			ZÚ	in $^{\text{na4}}$ZÚ = *ṣurru,* e.g., KTN inventory i 22; MARV 10 24:11.
				in ZÚ.LUM.(MA) = *suluppu* in ZÚ.LUM.MA^{meš} MARV 4 13:9'.
64	EME	log.:	EME	= *lišānu*, e.g., VAT 8722:3.
71	URU	log.:	URU	= *ālu,* e.g., MAL J § 3:5, cf. *a-lim* KAJ 63:8.
		det.	uru	For names of settlements.
73	UKKIN	log.:	UKKIN	= *puḫru*, only in ^{m}UKKIN-DINGIR^{meš}*-ni* MARV 1 59:4.
75	BANŠUR	log.	BANŠUR	= *paššūru*, Coronation Ritual i 38; Ali 11:7.
85	LI	syl.:	*li, le*	passim.
		log:	LI	in ^{šim}LI = *burāšu*, e.g., KAJ 248:8; MARV 2 28:1, cf. *bu-ra-še* 'juniper' New Year Ritual:16'.
86	TU	syl.:	*tu*	passim.
			ṭú	In private archives during the entire MA period, see § 210.
89	LA	syl.:	*la*	passim.
90	APIN	log.:	APIN	= *epinnu*, passim, e.g., ^{giš}APIN LVUH 74:18.
				= *araḫšamna*, in ^{iti}APIN Tsukimoto 2011:26.
			ENGAR	in ^{lú}ENGAR = *ikkaru* Billa 27:1; MPR 24:16; also $^{\text{lú.giš}}$ENGAR$^{!}$ MARV 8 47:10, cf. ^{lú}*i-ka-ru* T 98-58:7; *ik-kar-te* LVUH 48:2. Sometimes $^{\text{lú.giš}}$ENGAR in confusion

				with ^{giš}APIN.
91	MAH	syl.:	*maḫ*	e.g., *i-maḫ-ḫu-ṣu-ši* MAL A § 40:100; *maḫ-ru* MATC 42:13; ⸢^{kaš}*miḫ*⸣*-ḫa-tu* MATC 12:29. This sign is preferred in the 3mp stative of *maḫāru: maḫrū.*
			miḫ	Perhaps *miḫ*$^{!}$*-ḫe-te* Maul 2004 2:4, see Freydank 2012b, 111–12.
92	PAB	log.:	PAP	= *naṣāru*, PNs passim, e.g., ^{md}UTU-PAP KAJ 252:5. = *tadānu*, only in *Bābu-aḫa-iddina*, e.g., ⸢^{m}⸣KÁ-A-PAP = MARV 8 58:7. in ^{d}PAP.SUKKAL, in PNs, e.g., ^{d}PAP.SUKKAL-*na-din*-ŠEŠ^{meš} KAJ 65:24. PAP.NÍGIN = variant of ŠU.NÍGIN, e.g., MARV 5 60:30; MARV 9 14:54'.
			KÚR	in É.KÚR in PNs, e.g., ^{m}DI.KU$_5$-EN-É.KÚR MARV 1 1 iv 44.
94	BÙLUG	log.:	MUNU$_4$	= *buqlu*, e.g., MATC 82:7; T 98-31:5.
98	MU	syl.:	*mu*	passim.
		log.	MU	= *šattu,* e.g., MAL A § 36:91; KAJ 171:5. = *šumu*, passim in PNs, e.g., ^{m}*Aš-šur*-MU-SUM-*na* MARV 3 29:1. Cf. *šúm-šu* 'his name' MARV 4 151:19.
			MUḪALDIM	in ^{lú}MUḪALDIM = *nuḫatimmu*, e.g., MARV 9 83:11; A 3196 (NTA, 39):17.
99	QA	syl.:	*qa*	passim
		log.:	SÌLA	= *qaʾu*. Perhaps to be read as Akkadogram QA, see § 69,
105	GIL	syl.:	*gel*	in PN ^{m}*Gel-*⸢*zu*⸣ TR 3025:27 cf. ^{m}*Ge-el-zu* Billa 2:3.
			kíl	e.g., *ul-ta-kíl* CTMMA 1 101:8; *si-kíl-te* MARV 4 40:4; ^{lú}⸢*mu-šá*⸣*-kíl* MARV 3 3:17.
110	NA	syl.:	*na*	passim.
		log.:	NA	in ^{lú}NA.GADA = *nāqidu*, e.g., KAJ 97:4; Ali 4:12; MPR 48:22.
111	ŠUB	syl.:	*ru*	passim.
			šub/p	e.g., *šub-ta* Faist 2001, 252:24; ^{f}*Te-šub-e-li* MARV 1 iv 13'; *šub-re-*[*e*] YBC 12863:3.
112	NU	syl:	*nu*	passim.
		log.:	NU	in ^{f}NU.GIG = *qadiltu*, e.g., Adad ritual:9. in ^{giš}NU.ÚR.MA = *nurmû*, KTN inventory I 28; MARV 4 13:8'. in ^{lú}NU.^{giš}KIRI$_6$ = *nukarribu*, e.g., A 1740 (NTA, 20):13; George 1988 2:12.
113	BAD	syl.:	*be*	passim.
			bat	e.g., *iṣ-ṣa-bat* MAL A § 15:41; *us-bat* § 26:95; *i-bat-tu-qu* New Year Ritual:15'; *a-bat* KAV 104:4.
			bít	e.g., ^{m}*Ú-ṣa-bít*-DINGIR MPR 29:12; also MARV 4 59:21.
			ti/el	e.g., *til-li-ša* Coronation Ritual ii 41; *E-tel-pi-*^{d}*Taš-me-te* KAJ 113:23.
		log.:	BAD	= ^{d}BAD = *Ellil*, Coronation Ritual i 44, usually spelled with EN.LÍL.
			SUMUN	= *labāru*, e.g., KAJ 101:2; MATC 24:6; syllabic *la-be-er-*[*ti*] Billa 35:7.
			TIL	= *gamru*, e.g., MPR 66:20.
			ÚŠ	= *damu*, in MARV 2 28:10; MARV 10 1:2. = *mētu*, e.g., MPR 60:51a; MPR 61:39.
117	NUMUN	syl.:	*kul*	in ⸢^{f}⸣*Pa-iš-i-kul-*⸢*li*⸣ MPR 40:50.
		log.:	NUMUN	= *zarʾu*, e.g., ^{še}NUMUN MAL B § 4:29; KAJ 80:6, in PNs, e.g., ^{d}IŠKUR-NUMUN-NÍG.BA KAJ 224:3.

118	TI	syl.:	*ti*	passim.
			ṭì/ṭe$_6$	Rare, see § 210.
		log.:	TI	= *balluṭu*, e.g., ^{m}30-TI KAJ 280:6. Mostly written TI.LA, e.g., ^{md}30-*ú*-TI.LA KAJ 144:6.
119	DIN	syl.:	*din*	Usually used in the verb *tadānu*, e.g., *ta-ti-din* MAL A § 3:28; *id-din-šu* TR 2028:18.
120	MAŠ	syl.:	*maš*	e.g., *maš-ka-an* MAPD § 9:53; *maš-ki-ni* T 04-37 r. 23.
		log.:	MAŠ	= ^{d}MAŠ = *Ninurta*, e.g., KAR 159:7.
				in ^{lú}MAŠ.MAŠ = *āšipu/mašmašu*, MARV 1 51 r. 4'; KAJ 235:6.
				in ^{d}MAŠ.TAB.BA = *māšu*, e.g., Coronation Ritual iii 38.
			SA$_9$	= *mišlu* = ½, see § 331.
121	BAR	syl.:	*bar*	e.g., *ša-bar-tu* KAJ 178:1; *ta-bar-ri* MARV 1 24:9.
			pár	e.g., *ši-pár* MAL A § 18:79; *il-ta-pár-šu* § 36:5; *ši-pár-ka* 'your labour' MATC 4:17; *ṣu-pár-šu* Giricano 2:1; *pár-ka-at* KAV 159:10.
		log.:	BAR	= *kidinnu*, in some PNs, but usually syllabic, e.g., BAR-^{d}30 Billa 55:7.
				in ^{túg}BAR.DUL = *kusītu*, e.g., BM 108965:1; MARV 10 3:14.
122	BÁN	log.:	BÁN	= 1 *sūtu*, passim, cf. *su-ti-*⸢*e*⸣ MATSH 14:11.
124	IDIGNA	log.:	IDIGNA	in ^{íd}IDIGNA = Idiqlat, e.g., DUMU-^{d}IDIGNA-*lá* KAJ 22:21; ^{md}IDIGNA-KAM KAJ 316:1.
127	AG	syl.:	*ag/k/q*	passim.
			AG	in ^{d}AG = *Nabīu*, in PNs, e.g., ^{md}AG-KAR-ni OIP 79 4:3. Cf. ^{md}*Na-bi-um*-EN-PAP KAJ 97:12.
130	MÁŠ	log.:	MÁŠ	in MÁŠ = *ṣibtu*, KAJ 83:22, cf. *ṣi-ib-ta* T 04-37:26.
				in MÁŠ = *urīṣu*, e.g., A 295 (NTA, 16):1; KAJ 190:22, ^{udu}MÁŠ MARV 3 26:6.
131	KUN	syl.:	*kun*	e.g., *iš-kun* MAL A § 19:83.
132	ḪU	syl.:	*ḫu*	passim.
		log.:	MUŠEN	= *iṣṣūru*, e.g., KAJ 218:6; MARV 3 3:17.
				in MUŠEN.DÙ = *ušandû* e.g., MARV 4 16:2; MPR 28:27.
134	NAM	syl.:	*nam*	e.g., *il-ta-nam-me* MAPD § 21:104; *nam-mi-iš* MATC 1:15. Once in final position: ^{ú}*kur-ka-num* MARV 1 42:2.
			bir$_5$	in *e-bir*$_5$*-ta-a-an* KAJ 27:13; *e-bir*$_5$*-ti* KAJ 303:17. Following Syllab. no. 54; Luukko 2004 (50), this is an archaic value not used anymore in NA. Attestations are most frequent in the form *eberti* in the period until Aub. Replaced by <bir> no. 643. Cf. *e-bir-ta* KAJ 129:10 (Ad).
		log.:	NAM	in LÚ ^{giš}NAM.KIRI$_6$ LVUH 103:14, rare alternative for ^{lú}NU.^{giš}KIRI$_6$.
				in [^{ú}]NAM.LÚ.U$_{19}$.[LU] = *amīlānu*, in MARV 1 42:7.
135	BURU$_5$	log.	BURU$_5$	= *erbu*, e.g., MATSH 2:16; syllabic: *e-re-bi-ú* MATSH 3:7.
136	IG	syl.:	*i/eg/k/q*	Passim.
			gál	e.g., *ni-gál-lu* T 96-3:1.
		log.:	IG	in ^{giš}IG = *daltu*, e.g., KAJ 174:2; Billa 22:2.
139	ŠÌTA	syl.:	*rad/t/ṭ*	e.g., *šaṭ-rat* MAL A § 28:5; *tu-še-rad* BVW B:6; *ta-ra-rad* A 3184 (NTA, 34):2.
140	ZI	syl.:	*zi/e*	Passim.
			ṣi/e	Early texts, e.g., *e-ṣi-de* KAJ 50:6. See § 215.
			sì/è	Very rare, see § 215.
		log.:	ZI	= *napšātu*(?), MAPD § 1:4.
141	GI	syl.:	*gi/e*	passim.
			qì/è	Uncertain, see § 206.

			GI	in ^{giš}GI = *qanû*, e.g., MARV 10 41:2.
142	RI	syl.:	*ri/e*	passim.
			d/tal	e.g., *tal-ti-ri-iq* MAL A § 3:25; *tal-du-du-ú-ni* MAL A § 24:73; *ku-tal* Coronation Ritual ii 12; *tal-lak-ta-ka* PKT 1 I right:20; *it-tal-ka* Giricano 12:14'; ^{m}*Dal-lu-qi* KAJ 310:30 (cf. ^{m}*Da-lu-qu* CTMMA 1 99:5).
148	KAB	syl.:	*kap*	e.g., *kap-pi* Coronation Ritual i 35; *ta-kap-pár* PKT 2 i 5; *Kap-pu-te* (PN) MARV 3 58:20'.
			gáb	*gáb-bì* A 1020:13'.
		log.:	GÙB	= *šumēlu,* e.g., Ištar ritual:4.
149	ḪÚB	syl.:	*ḫúb*	in ^{m}*Ḫúb-bu-te* MARV 1 21:12
151	SUR	syl.:	*šur*	Usually in the (ligature) *A(š)-šur*, see no. 11. The value <šùr> (ŠIR) is more frequent in OA but does not occur in MA and NA. The value <šur> can be found a few times in other context, e.g., *šur-qa* MAL A § 3:42; *šur-rat* BVW F r. 3; *šur-šu-ra-tu* 'chain' MARV 1 4:2.
152	MÚŠ	log.:	TIŠPAK	^{md}TIŠPAK-*ia* MARV 6 19:6.
153	MÙŠ	log.:	INNIN	= ^{d}INNINA = Ištar, rarely used in true MA: [^{d}IN]NINA Coronation Ritual i 46; ^{Id}INANNA-MU-SUM-*na* Billa 52:1. For a more common spelling of Ištar see U-DAR no. 670.
157	GAD	syl.:	*kat*	e.g., *kat-ma-at* MAPD § 19:94; *kat-tu-um* MARV 3 4:10.
		log.:	GADA	^{túg}GADA = *kitāʾu*, e.g., KAJ 136:9'; MATSH 6:9'; cf. *ki-ta-e* 'flax' MATSH 3:5.
160	UMBIN	log.	UMBIN	= *ṣupru*, in Giricano 7:1$^{?}$; $^{giš?}$ ⌜UMBIN$^{?!}$⌝ $^{meš?!}$ MARV 10 56:13'', cf. *ṣu-pár-šu* Giricano 8:1.
164	EN	syl.:	*en*	Passim.
		log.:	EN	= *bēlu,* e.g., MAL A § 5:60, passim in PNs. in ^{d}EN.PI, e.g., Coronation Ritual ii 8. in ^{d}EN.ZU = *Sîn*, only in *U-tul*-^{d}EN.ZU KAM 10 30:5, 12. Once as mistake(?) for LUGAL in ^{fd}*Iš$_{8}$-tár*-EN-PAP (*Ištar-šarra-uṣrī*) MPR 53:6.
165	BURU$_{14}$	log.	BURU$_{14}$	= *ebūru*, MARV 3 4:5; MATSH 2:16 cf. *e-bu-ri* MARV 3 4 r. 6'.
166	DÀR	log.:	DÀR	in DÀRA.BAR = *ayyālu*, in MARV 2 28:9.
168	MUN	log.:	MUN	= *ṭābtu*, MATSH 15:14; MARV 1 71:25. in MUN.KUR(.RA) = *ṭabāt šadê*, in MARV 2 28:10; MARV 5 46:1.
170	LÀL	log.:	LÀL	= *dišpu*, passim, e.g., MARV 6 87:5; MARV 7 66:2.
172	SA	syl.:	*sa*	Passim.
		log.:	SA	^{lú}SA = read ZADIM, e.g., MARV 4 9:17'; MARV 7 72:12. in ^{kaš}SA.MAR, with unknown reading, e.g., MARV 6 70:15; MATC 22:6. in (^{uzu})SA.SAL = *šašallu*, e.g., KAJ 310:39; MARV 2 15:3'.
		det.	SA	Determinative used for braided materials, e.g., ^{sa}*pa-gu-me/um* (uncertain example) BVW A: 10, 11.
173	AŠGAB	log.:	AŠGAB	in ^{lú}AŠGAB = *aškāpu*, e.g., KAJ 5:3; KAJ 130:14; cf. ^{lú}AŠGAB-*pè-te* KAM 11 129:111.
174	GÁN	log.	GÁNA	= *eqlu*, in GÁNA.A.ŠÀ YBC 12860:2; T 02-32:25. Uncommon.
			ḪÉ	in ^{síg}ḪÉ.ME.DA = *tabarru, tabarriba*, e.g., KAM 11 58:7'. Cf. *ta-bar-*[*r*]*i-ba* KAV 99:43.
			IKU	= *ikû*, passim, e.g., BVW Ab:8; KAJ 11:15.
176	GÚ	log.	GÚ	= *kišādu*, e.g., KTN inventory i 30

				in ^{túg}GÚ.È (GÚ.UD.DU) = *naḫlaptu*, e.g., KAJ 256:7; Giricano 4:30.
				in GU.GAL = *gugallu*, only in ^{d}IŠKUR-⸢GÚ⸣.GAL KAJ 100:26.
				in GÚ.ZI = *kāsu*, in MARV 7 1:14, 15. Cf. *ka-si* PKT 3 I 16.
178	DUR	syl:	*túr*	in ^{md}UTU-*túr-le-šìr* MARV 2 1 vii 23; ^{md}AG-*túr*-PAP MARV 5 71:10.
179	GÚ.UN	log.	GUN	= *biltu*, passim, e.g., MAL A § 19:92.
180	GUR	syl.:	*g/qur*	e.g., *qur-bu-ú-te* MAL A § 24:44; *bu-qur-ra-na-e* KAJ 10:8; *im-*⸢*ma*⸣*-gur-ú-ni* Giricano 4:17.
181	SI	syl.:	*si/e*	passim.
			ší/é	rare, see § 218.
		log.:	SI	= *qarnu*, e.g., MARV 1 42:6, MARV 2 28:9.
				in SI.SÁ = *ešāru*, e.g., ^{m}*Ez-bu*-SI.SÁ MARV 8 22:6'.
183	DAR	syl.:	*tár*	in theophoric element of PNs *Iš*$_{8}$*-tár* passim.
184	SAG	syl.:	*šak*	in *i-šak-kan* Ištar ritual:9; *iš-šak* RE 19:15.
			riš	in ^{m}DINGIR-*i-ga-riš* KAJ 256:4; ^{f}*E-riš*$^{?}$*-te-e* Billa 59:1.
		log.:	SAG	= *rēšu*, MAPD § 9:52; T 93-18:15, cf. *ri-še-en* MAL A § 15:54.
				= *ašarēdu*, in PNs, e.g., ^{md}*Sál-ma-nu*-SAG MAPD § 5:33; ^{md}*Sa-am-nu-ḫa*-SAG MARV 5 41:3.
				in SAG.DU = *qaqqudu,* e.g., MAL A § 40:64; KAJ 83:21; also SAG.DI in LVUH 53:29; LVUH 56 r. 11'.
201	MÁ	log.:	MÁ	in ^{giš}MÁ = *eleppu*, MAL M § 2:8; MATSH 8:24'.
				in (^{lú})MÁ.LAḪ$_{5}$ = *malaḫḫu*, e.g., MAL M § 1:6; KAJ 106:13. cf. ^{lú}*ma-la-ḫu* MARV 1 66:9.
203	ÙZ	log.:	ÙZ or U(D)$_{5}$	in ÙZ = *enzu*, e.g., KAJ 120:12; KAJ 190:22; Ali 6:21.
207	DIR	log.:	SA$_{5}$	= *sâmu*, e.g., MARV 10 28:3.
209	TAB	syl.:	*tab/p*	e.g., *tap-pa-a-šu* MAL A § 20:93; *i-tab-ba-ak* New Year Ritual:14'; *al-tap-ra-a-ku* MATSH 1:4; *e-tab-ra* MATSH 2:14; ^{m}*Aš-šur-ṭab-ni-šuk-lil* A 3186 (NTA, 35):16.
		log:	TAB	in TAB.BA = *tappā'u*, e.g., KAJ 32:6 cf. *tap-pa-ú-šu* KAJ 32:5.
212	GEŠTIN	log.:	GEŠTIN	^{giš}GEŠTIN = *karānu*, e.g., KAJ 302:12.
215	LÍMMU	log.:	LÍMMU	numeral used with GUN (see § 330).
216	IA$_{7}$	log.:	IA$_{7}$	numeral used with GUN (see § 330).
217	AŠ$_{4}$	log.:	AŠ$_{4}$	numeral used with GUN (see § 330).
218	ÍMMIN	log.:	ÍMMIN	numeral used with GUN (see § 330).
219	ÚSSU	log.:	ÚSSU	numeral used with GUN (see § 330).
220	ÍLIMMU	log.:	ÍLIMMU	numeral used with GUN (see § 330).
221	TAG	syl.:	*šum*	The value *šum* is usually used in the adverb *šumma*. It seems that *šum* is more commonly used in the archaic law texts (e.g., MAL A–O; BVW), but also KAJ 11:13 (EA/AUb); KAJ 50:13 (ABN). See also *šúm* (SUM) no. 292.
			tag/k/q	Instead no. 438 is used.
222	KÁ	log.:	KÁ	in ^{d}KÁ = Bābu, e.g., ⸢^{m}⸣KÁ-A-PAP = *Bābu-aḫa-iddina* MARV 8 58:7.
				in KÁ+GAL = ABUL = *abullu*, Coronation Ritual ii 43; KAJ 254:5.
223	AB	syl.:	*ab/p*	passim.
		log.:	AB	in ^{iti}AB = *ṭebētu, kinūnu*, e.g., MARV 6 86 env. 6'; Giricano 8:37.

230	URUDU	log.:	URUDU	*erīu*, e.g., KAJ 124:1.
		det.:	urudu	e.g., ^{urudu}*ša-bar-tu* KAJ 178:1.
242	DUB	syl.:	*tup*	e.g., *tup-ni-ni* KAV 103:14; ^{giš}*tup-ni-na-te* KAV 98:14; *tup-pu* passim with variations.
		log.:	DUB	= *tuppu*, passim see § 68.
				in ^{lú}DUB.SAR = *tupšarru*, passim, e.g., MARV 5 71:2.
246	NAB	syl.:	*nab/p*	e.g., *nap-ša-a-te* MAL A § 50:73; É *nap-tar-te* MATC 12:15; *mu-nab-du* KBo 1 20:17'.
247	MUL	syl.:	*mul*	e.g., *mul-la-e* MATSH 2:57; *mul-te-ṣi-tu-šu-nu* KAJ 307:14.
248	TA	syl.:	*ta*	passim.
		log.:	TA +A+AN	= TA.ÀM, e.g., 1-TA.ÀM BVW A:16.
252	I	syl.:	*i*	passim.
253	GAN	syl.:	*ḫi/é*	rare, see § 198.
			g/kan	*i-ša-kan* Coronation Ritual i 36; ^{d}*Da-gan* Coronation Ritual i 44 and PNs; *ta-ša-kan* PKT 3 i 2.
254	KÁM	log.:	KÁM	passim.
255	TUR	syl.:	*mar*$_5$	in *mar*$_5$*-e* MAL A § 43:32; *mar*$_5$*-ut-ti-šu* MAL A § 28:5.
		log.:	DUMU	= *marā'u*(?), e.g., MAL A § 29:16.
			DUMU	in DUMU.MUNUS = *martu*, e.g., MAL A § 31:42.
				in DUMU.UŠ > IBILA = *aplu*, only in PNs, e.g., ^{md}EN.LÍL-SUM-IBILA KAJ 133:17.
			TUR	= *ṣeḫru*, e.g., MAL B § 9:20; KAJ 107:1.
258	AD	syl.:	*ad/t/ṭ*	passim.
			àb	only in ^{na4}*àb-na ga-bi-a* KAV 109:20; *àb-na ga-bi-ú* T 93-28:2.
		log.:	AD	= *abu*, in AD-KAM (PN) TR 3030:3. Rare logogram, usually written syllabically.
				in AD.KIB = *atkuppu*, e.g., ^{lú}AD.KIB MARV 4 1:3.
259	ZÍ	syl.:	*ṣi/e*	passim.
260	IA	syl.:	*ia/i/e/u*	passim, see § 170.
			a/i/e/ui	See § 170.
261	IN	syl.:	*in*	passim.
		log.:	IN	in IN.NU = *tibnu*, e.g., KAJ 118:1; Billa 23:4. Cf. *ti-ib-na* KAJ 52:14.
262	RAB	syl.:	*rab/p*	Mostly literary, e.g., *te-ta-rab* MAL A § 24:46; *er-rab* MAPD § 9:55; *i-kar-rab-šu* Ištar ritual:2'; *Ar-rap-ḫa-ie-e* MARV 1 5:27; *ú-qar-rab* MARV 5 82:8'.
266	LUGAL	log.:	LUGAL	= *šarru*, e.g., MAL A § 18:79; KAM 10 14:18. From Aššur-dān onwards, this sign occurs in alternation with MAN, but does not disappear, e.g., A 1736 (NTA, 18):2 (Ad); Giricano 8:29 (Abk).
270	ḪAŠḪUR	log.:	ḪAŠHUR	= *ḫašḫūru*, e.g., ^{giš}ḪAŠHUR KAJ 310:42.
271	EZEN	syl.:	*šì/èr*	*šèr-ki*^{meš} MAPD § 22:116; *pi-šèr-ti* MARV 3 4:7; ^{Id}30-MU-*le-šìr* MARV 4 107:2.
		log.:	EZEN	= *isinnu,* e.g., EZEN-*ni* KAJ 227:3 cf. *i-si-ni* MAL A § 55:19.
275	BÀD	log.:	BÀD	= *dūru*, in GN Dūt-Katlimmu, e.g., ^{uru}BÀD-*kat-li-mu* MATSH 8:32'.
292	SUM	syl.:	*šúm*	As opposed to *šum* (TAG) no 221, the value *šúm* is more common in somewhat later texts, in *áš-šum/šúm-ma*, e.g., MAPD passim.; Tell Ḫuēra (TN): e.g., MATC 11:20; TŠḤ: e.g., MATSH 10:6.
		log.:	SUM	= *n/tadānu*, in PNs, e.g., ^{m}DINGIR-*i*-SUM-*na* Giricano

				5:18.
293	NAGA	log.:	NAGA	^{d}NAGA = nísaba, theophoric element in PNs, e.g., [^{f}*R*]*a-ba-*⌜*at*⌝*-*^{d}*Nisaba*. Cf. ŠE.NAGA (no. 579).
				in ^{ú}NAGA.SI = *ūḫulu qarnānu*, in MARV 2 28:9.
296	UG	syl.:	*ug/k/q*	Passim.
297	AZ	syl.:	*as/ṣ/z*	Passim.
298	GAB	syl.:	*gab*	e.g., *gab-ba* MATC 4:22; *gab-bi* 10:8. This value is used in the typical Assyrian noun *gabbu*. See also § 395.
		log.:	GABA	= *irtu*, e.g., Coronation Ritual ii 32; ^{uzu}GABA TabT 07-2:1; KAJ 180:10
			DU_8	= *paṭāru* in PN ^{md}UTU-DU_8-*ir* KAJ 149:27; ^{md}UTU-*ar-ni*-DU_8 MARV 7 7:22
				in DU_8/GAB.LÀL = *iškūru*, MCS 2 2:7; A 1065:2.
300	EDIN			in ^{kuš}DU_8.ŠI.A = *du(ḫ)šû*, MARV 10 29:15.
301	TAḪ	syl.:	*d/taḫ*	e.g., *taḫ-te-pi* MAL A § 8:86; *taḫ-ṭí-a-ši-ni* MAPD § 18:84; ^{m}*Ku-taḫ-ḫ*[*u*] MARV 6 19:8.
302	KASKAL	syl.:	*kas*	e.g., *ta-ra-kas* BVW Passim (e.g., A:15).
		log.:	KASKAL	= *ḫarrānu/ḫūlu*, e.g., BVW A:10; KASKAL-*ni* KAJ 274:3.
309	AM	syl.:	*am*	passim.
		log.:	AM	in AM.SI = *pīru*, e.g., KAM 11 115:2
311	UZU	log.:	UZU	= *šīru*, e.g., MARV 1 71:21.
		det.	uzu	e.g., TabT 07-2 passim; ^{uzu}*ša-ša-lu* KAJ 130:7.
312	BÌL	syl.:	*p/bíl*	e.g., *iz-bíl* MAL A § 31:41; *ú-bíl* MAL A § 43:20; *píl-ka-ni* MATC 3:5; *ša-píl-šu-nu* 71:52; *a-píl* MARV 3, 11:16; *šu-pél-tu* T 04-2:23.
		log.:	GIBIL	= *edēšu*, e.g., KAJ 119:12; KAJ 256:2; MATC 12:17; GIBIL-*te* A 3061 (NTA, 33):3. Similar $GIBIL_4$ does not occur.
313	NE	syl.:	*pil*	Only in a few PNs: *A-pil-Ku-be* TIM 4 45:19; Billa 51:6; *Pil-ḫa-a* KAJ 47:4. Perhaps misread for graphical similar <píl> (no. 312).
		log.:	NE	= *nūru*, in PNs, e.g., ^{m}NE-^{d}IDIGNA-*lá* MPR 28:21; ^{m}NE-DINGIR MPR 29.9.
				in ^{iti}NE = *abu*, e.g., MARV 7 50:4'.
			IZI	= *išātu*, e.g., PKT 1 I right:14; ^{I}IZI-^{d}*Iš*$_8$-*tár* MATC 64:3.
320	ŠÀM	syl.:	*šàm*	⌜^{m}⌝*Iš-tu-Aš-šur-a-šàm-*⌜*šu*⌝ MARV 7 67:2.
		log.:	ŠÀM	= *šīmu*, e.g., MAL A § 24:59; KAJ 168:14.
326	ÁG	log.	ÁG	= *ra*ˁ*āmu*, only in [^{m}]^{d}*A-šur*-ÁG-UN.⌜^{meš}⌝-*šu* MARV 10 4:33'.
			Ì.ÁG.E	= *imaddad*, e.g., KAJ 67:9.
336	ZIG	syl.:	*ḫíš*	e.g., ^{uru}*Ḫíš-šu-tu* MARV 9 6:24. This value is most frequently used in *arḫiš* e.g., *ar-ḫíš* MATC 1:5; MARV 7 14:21.
			zíb	^{md}30-*še-zíb-a-ni* MARV 2 27 v$^{?}$ 13'.
339	KUM	syl.:	*kum*	rare, see § 206.
			qu	passim.
340	GAZ	syl.:	*kàṣ*	in *tu-kàṣ-ṣa* PKT 3 iv 3.
		log.:	GAZ	= *dīktu*, e.g., MAH 16086 B ii 9'.
341	ÚR	syl.:	*úr*	exceptionally in ^{m}*Úr-ḫi*-^{d}IŠ[KUR] KBo 1 14 r. 15'.
		log.:	ÚR	= *sūnu*, e.g., ÚR-*šu* MAH 16086 A i 9.
350	DU	syl.:	*du*	passim.
			ṭù	very rare, see § 210.
			qup	e.g., ^{md}*A-šur-su-qup-pa-ni* KAV 99:2; KAJ 178:20.
		log.:	DU	in DU = *alāku*, KAJ 83:22.
353	ANŠE	log.	ANŠE	= *emāru*, passim.

				in ANŠE.KUR.RA = *sisū*(?), BVW H:6; KAJ 171:5; Billa 31:5.
				in ANŠE.NÍTA = *emāru*, e.g., KAJ 311:5.
		det.:	anše	with equids, e.g., ^{anše}*ku-di-ni* 'mules' MATC 25:9; ^{anše}EME$_{5}$ = *atānu*, e.g., LVUH 10:1.
354	TUM	syl.:	*tum* (*tu*$_{4}$)	e.g., *maš-ka-tum* MAL C+ § 9:12; *nàr-ma-ak-tum* KAJ 303:10. See § 87.
		log.:	ÍB	in ^{túg}ÍB.LÁ = *nēbeḫu*, e.g., MARV 10 69:5; A 1587:5'.
356	EGIR	log.:	EGIR	= *urki*, e.g., MARV 5 18:8; MARV 10 4:20'.
357	IŠ	syl.:	*iš*	passim.
			mil	in *si-mil-ti* VAT 8923:3, mostly in PN, e.g., ^{m}*gi-mil-la* KAJ 1:4; *mil-ki-ia* KAV 119:5.
358	BI	syl.:	*bi*	passim.
			bé	Incorrect usage of the sign, see § 203.
			pí/é	Incorrect usage of the sign, unless when used as phonetic complement of DUB, which is traditional. See § 203.
			kaš	e.g., *kaš-ši-ú* MATSH 10:31; ^{m}*Kaš-til-a-šu* T 96-11:20.
		log.:	KAŠ	= *šikaru*, e.g., Adad ritual r. 7', MATSH 12:26; T 04-37:25.
		det.:	KAŠ	e.g., ⌜^{kaš}*miḫ*⌝*-ḫa-tu* MATC 12:29.
362	ŠIM	det.:	šim	for perfume(plants), e.g., ^{šim}*em-du* KAJ 248:5.
		log.:	ŠIM	^{giš}ŠIM = *riqīu*, e.g., Ištar ritual:4; PKT 1 I right:12; MARV 9 37:1'; MARV 10 1:3. cf. ^{giš}*ri-qi-ú* T 98-63:5.
				in ŠIM.LI = *burāšu*, e.g., KAJ 248:8; MARV 2 28:1.
				in ^{lú}LUNGA = *sirāšû*, e.g., MARV 5 49:5; MARV 9 14:14.
378	KIB	syl.:	*k/qib/p*	in PNs, e.g., ^{m}*Sà-kip-šu-nu* MARV 8 46:30; *M*⌜*a*⌝*-nu-i-qip* YBC 12862:22.
379	GAG	log.	GAG	in ^{giš}GAG = *sikkātu*, MAPD § 1:2; MARV 10 37:4.
				in KAK.Ú.TAG.GA = *šiltāḫu*, e.g., KAV 195+:31; MATSH 16:5.
			DÙ	= *epāšu*, e.g., Coronation Ritual ii 16.
380	NI	syl.:	*ni/é*	Passim.
			lí	limited to PNs, see § 241.
			ì	very rare only in the element *ilu* 'god' in PNs, e.g., DUMU.MUNUS-*ì-lí* A 2704:1.
			ṣal	in ^{d}*Ṣal-mu* Coronation Ritual iii 37.
			zal	^{iti}*ku-zal-lu*. Passim.
		log.:	Ì	= *šamnu,* e.g., BVW A:1; KAV 194:5.
				in Ì.GIŠ = *šamnu,* e.g., MAL A § 36:86.
				in ^{lú}Ì.DU$_{8}$ = *atā'u* MAPD § 3:26; MARV 2 17a+:57.
				in Ì.NUN(.NA) = *ḫimētu*, e.g., MARV 5 45:2; LVUH 51:6.
				in ^{lú}Ì.SUR = *ṣāḫitu*, e.g., KAJ 189:12; MARV 6 42:14; MARV 8 60:8.
				in GAG.Ú.TAG.GA = *šiltāhu*, e.g., KAJ 310:52. Syllabic *šil*$_{4}$*-ta-ḫu*^{meš} MARV 10 3:11.
				in Sumerian verbs, e.g., Ì.LÁ.E KAJ 11:8; Ì.ÁG.E (Akk. *immadad*) KAJ 67:9 (see § 70); also in PNs Ì.GÁL-DINGIR '*Ibašši-ilī*' KAJ 158:9.
381	UŠ	syl.:	*uš*	passim.
			ús	for examples and syllables, see § 221.
		log.:	UŠ	in ^{f}UŠ.BAR = *ušpartu*, e.g., KAJ 98:2; MARV 3 3:59; A 582:50.
			NITA	in ^{lú}NITA = *zikaru*, e g.MARV 7 1:13
382	AMA	log.:	AMA	= *ummu*, e.g., MARV 1 60:11; MARV 2 6 i 72''.
385	NA$_{4}$	log.:	NA$_{4}$	= *abnu*, e.g., MAPD § 5:34; NA$_{4}$^{meš} KAJ 310:8

		det.:	na$_4$	Used before types of stones and minerals, e.g., ^{na4}Ú^{meš} KAJ 178:3; ^{na4}*ga-bi-ú* KAJ 223:1
386	DÀG	syl.:	*tàk/q*	e.g., *tàq-bi* Ištar ritual:3'; *tàq-bi-an-ni* Billa 67:5; cf. no. 438. Palaeographic difference between the two signs is not always clear.
387	GÁ	syl.:	*mal*	e.g., *ú-mal-lu-ú* MAL A § 4:51; *am-mal-la* MARV 10 23:4.
408	SILA$_4$	log.:	SILA$_4$	in ^{udu}SILA$_4$ = *puḫādu*, e.g., A 1812 (NTA, 25):12; KAJ 208:1.
435	KISAL	log.:	KISAL	= *kisallu*, e.g., MARV 5 47:2.
438	DAG	syl.:	*tág/k/q*	e.g., *táq-ti-bi* MAL A § 2:16; *ur-ták-ki-is-ma* § 8:81; *ták-pír-ti* A 3188 (NTA, 36):7; *i-ba-táq-šu* George 1988 r. 9'; cf. no. 368.
			pàr	e.g., [*al*]*-ta-pàr* Wilhelm 1997:15; *it-ta-pàr-ku* MATSH 3:28. Rare, the usage of <pár> (BAR) is preferred.
464	PA	syl.:	*pa*	passim.
			ḫad/t	e.g., ^{m}*Bal-ti-ḫad-da* MARV 1 72:7; *pa-ḫat* KAJ 167:15.
		log.:	UGULA	passim in MAPD.
			GIDRU	^{giš}GIDRU = *ḫaṭṭu*, see MAL A § 18:78; MARV 4 102 iii 8'.
465	BANMIN	log.	BANMIN	= 2 *sūtu*, passim.
466	ŠAB	syl.:	*šab/p*	e.g., *šap-li-ta* MAL A § 9:94; *tu-uš-šab* § 36:92; *ta-šap-pa-ka-šu-nu* BVW F r. 10; *ú-šab* MATSH 2:64; *ú-šap-pu-lu-uš* MATSH 9:40; *ta-šap-pa-ra* MATSH 12:41; *šap-ka* KAJ 249:13.
		log.:	ŠAB	in ^{dug}ŠAB = *šappu*, e.g., MARV 10 68:3.
467	NUSKA	log.:	NUSKA	= ^{d}NUSKA = *Nusku*, e.g., Coronation Ritual i 43; ^{m}*Mu*-SIG$_5$-NUSKA OIP 79 5:27.
468	SIPA	log.:		*raʾāʾu*, e.g., ^{lú}SIPA MAL F § 2:8, KAJ 120:1; KAJ 289:15; in PNs, e.g., ^{d}UTU-SIPA KAJ 25:18.
469	GIŠ	syl.:	*i/es/ṣ/z*	Passim.
			giš	in *giš-ḫu-ra-a-te* MAPD § 1:10.
			niš	only in *il-te-niš-ma* KAV 103:24.
		log.:	GIŠ	= *iṣu*, e.g., MAL B § 12:15.
				= *ešāru*, in PN ^{m}*Ez-bu*-GIŠ*-ma* (*Ezbu-lēšir*) MARV 5 68 r. 4'.
				in GIŠ.GÀR = *iškāru*, e.g., KAV 100:21; MARV 2 15:5'. Syllabic *iš-ka-ri-šu* Billa 25:7; *iš-kàr* LVUH 39:10.
				in GIŠ.NÁ = see no. 689.
				in GIŠ.TIN = *karānu*, e.g., KAJ 252:1; MARV 3 23 r. 5.
			GIŠ.MI	read as <ṣil$_4$>, in ^{f}*I+na-ṣil$_4$-lí-ša* MPR 46:2.
472	GU$_4$	log.:	GU$_4$	= *alpu*, passim.
				in GU$_4$.NÍTA =*alpu*, e.g., KAJ 289:5; LVUH 1:5.
				in ^{iti}GU$_4$ = *ayyuru*, e.g., Giricano 14 r. 20.
		det.	gu$_4$	For bovidae, e.g., ^{gu4}ÁB = *littu*, e.g., KAJ 92:2.
474	AL	syl.:	*al*	Passim.
483	MAR	syl.:	*mar*	e.g., *e-ta-mar-ma* MAL A § 40:78; *ú-ga-mar* Aššur ritual ii 3'; *mar-ru-ru-ni* MAPD § 8:50 *am-mar*; ^{iti}*kal-mar-tv* passim.
		log	MAR	in ^{d}MAR.TU = *Amurru*, e.g., George 1988 2:1.
				in ^{giš}MAR.GÍD.DA = *eriqqu*, in KAJ 9:4; MATSH 4:8.
484	KID	syl.	*líl*	in ^{d}*En-líl* passim in PNs.
			saḫ	e.g., *Me-lim-saḫ* KAJ 48:3; ^{uru}*Saḫ-la-li* MATC 2:3: ^{uru}*Šu-ḫi-saḫ* Ali 8:12.
			síḫ	e.g., ^{lú}*ḫa-síḫ-li* Billa 6:7.

			suḫ$_4$	e.g., [^{m}]*Ú-suḫ*$_4$*-bíl-tu* MARV 2 30:24'; ^{m}*A-ri-ku-suḫ*$_4$ T 98-3:4.
485	ŠID	syl.:	*lag/k/q*	e.g., *i-laq-qé* MAL A § 10:104; *ta-ta-lak* § 13:27; *i-laq-qe-a* MATC 9:25; *ul-te-bi-lak-ku* MATC 11:15; *a-lak-ta* MATC 18:8; [*u*]*l-te-bi-lak-ku* MARV 7 14:21.
			šid	e.g., *šid-di* MAPD § 20:96.
		log.:	SANGA	^{lú}SANGA = *šangû*, Coronation Ritual i 40; MARV 3 8:23; KAV 26 obv. Passim.
486	MES	syl.:	mis/š, mèš	e.g., ^{uru}*Kar-ga-mis* MATSH 2:4
		log.:	KIŠIB	= *kunukku*, e.g., KAV 98:15; MARV 1 19:1, cf. *ku-ni-ku-*(…) KAV 99:35; ^{na4}KIŠIB in MATSH 9:5.
489	ÚMBISAG	log.:	ÚMBISAG	= *tupšarru*, Jakob (2003, 237) lists two attestations, which cannot be confirmed with the information at our disposal.
490	Ú	syl.:	*ú*	passim.
			šam	e.g., *šam-šu* BVW M:7; *šam-ma* KAJ 221:4; ^{I}10*-mu-šam-me-eḫ* MATC 78:7'.
		det.:	ú	with plants, e.g., ^{ú}*uš-še* KAJ 133:12; ^{ú}*ku-di-mi* MARV 2 28:7.
		log.:	Ú	= *šamma*, e.g., TabT05A-134:23, cf. *šam-*⌜*ma*⌝ TabT05A-134:15.
				^{na4}Ú, e.g., MATC 5:6.
			KÙŠ	= *ammutu*, e.g., MARV 10 27:2.
491	GA	syl.:	*ga*	passim.
		log.:	GA	= *šizbu*, KAJ 184:5; KAJ 225:17
				in GA.RÍG = *mulṭu*, in MARV 10 6:9, cf. *mul-ṭu* KAJ 310:6.
493	ÍL	log.:	ÍL	^{lú}ÍL = *nagīru*, MAL B § 6:28; MARV 4 151:6.
494	LUḪ	syl.:	*luḫ*	e.g., *ši-luḫ-li* MAL B § 1:8; MPR 3:17.
			làḫ	Occurs only in BVW in one verbal form, perhaps therefore erroneous: *tu-ZA-làḫ* BVW A:5. Note also the value <laḫ> (UD) and <láḫ> (ERIM) no. 612. Also in PN ^{md}⌜*É*⌝*-a-pí-là*[*ḫ*$^{?}$] KAJ 38:5. Otherwise *láḫ* (PÍR) is mostly used.
		log.:	SUKKAL	in (^{lú})SUKKAL = *sukkallu*, e.g., Coronation Ritual iii 8; MARV 4 74:25; MARV 7 22:5. cf. *su-kal*$^{!}$*-li* MPR 66:26.
495	É	syl.:	*b/pit*	e.g., *pit-te* Coronation Ritual i 41; *bit-qa-te* KAJ 274:16; *pit* KAJ 219:5.
		log.:	É	= *bētu,* passim, e.g., MAL A § 5:57.
				in É.GAL-(*lim*) passim. Cf. ^{uru}*Gu-ub-bi-e-kal-li* KAJ 157:2; *e-kal-li* MARV 3 9:27.
		det.:	é	É is also used as determinative for different types of houses and buildings (Faist/Llop 2012, 24), e.g., ^{é}*al-tam-me* MAL A § 14:31; ^{é}*kar-me* LVUH 90:8. This become clear in spellings such as accusative ^{e}*na-kám-ta* KAV 100:16, where we would otherwise expect a genitive construction.
496	KAL	syl.:	*kal*	*kal-la-a-su* MAL A § 30:34; *ú-ša-kal-ši* § 45:53; ^{dug}*kal-la-a-te* New Year Ritual:16'; ^{iti}*kal-mar-tv* passim.
			dan	Usually used in the verb *tadānu*, e.g., *ta-ad-dan* MAL A § 7:76; *ta-dan* MATC 2:9; *dan-nu-te* MATC 11:26.
			rib	e.g., *i-qar-rib* MAL A § 38:24; *ḫu-rib-te* MATSH 13:21; *ú-še-rib* Giricano 15:11
		log.:	KALAG	= *danānu*, e.g., KALAG.GA KAJ 149:22; ^{f}KALAG.GA KAJ 14:17; KALAG*-at* BM 108924:22.
			LAMMA	in ^{d}LAMMA = *Lamassu*, e.g., Coronation Ritual iii 32; ^{fd}UTU-^{d}LAMMA MARV 3 3:20.

			ESI	in ^{giš}ESI = *ušû*, e.g., KTN inventory i 26; MARV 10 4:10.
498	E	syl.:	*e*	passim.
		log.:	E	in ^{kuš}E.SIR = *šēnu*, in MARV 10 7:1.
499	DUG	syl.:	*dug/k/q*	e.g., *i-duk-ku* MAL A § 13:29.
		log.:	DUG	= *karputu*, e.g., KAJ 277:2. in ^{lú}BÁḪAR (DUG.SÌLA.BUR) = *paḫḫāru*, in T 93-3:7.
		det.	dug	For vessels, e.g., ^{dug}*šap-pat-tu* KAJ 277:1
501	UN	syl.:	*un*	passim.
		log.:	UN	= *nišū*, in [^{m}]^{d}*A-šur*-ÁG-UN⌜^{meš}⌝-*šu* MARV 10 4:33'.
502	NIR	syl.:	*nir*	in PN *Nir-bi-a* KAJ 75:18.
			nàr	e.g., *nàr-ku-m*[*u*] Köcher 1057-8 ii 21; *nàr-ki-*[*b*]*i-ši-na* KAJ 123:3; ^{na4}*nàr-ke-be-šu-nu* MARV 3 69 passim.
504	UB	syl.:	*ub/p*	passim.
			ár	Rare, § 241.
511	RA	syl.:	*ra*	passim.
514	LÚ	log.:	LÚ	= *aʔīlu*, e.g., MAL A § 3:35; Billa 62:20, cf. *a-i-la* MAL A § 15:52.
		det.	LÚ	For different types of professions or social status.
535	ŠEŠ	log.:	ŠES	= *aḫu*, e.g., MAL A § 25:84; ŠEŠ-*ša*, A 3197 (NTA, 40):10. ^{šim}ŠEŠ = *murru*, MARV 2 28:3, cf. *mur-ru* 'myrrh' PKT 6 ii 29.
540	ZAG	syl.:	*zak*	e.g., *ú-zak-ka-a-ši* MAL A § 48:44; *ta-zak-ru-ú-ni* MAPD § 10:57; *tu-zak-ka* PKT 2 i 11; *uz-zak-ki-ši* KAJ 7:8; *zak-ku-ú* 'cleared' MARV 9 9:21'.
		log.:	ZAG	=*pāṭu*, Giricano 1:11. =*imittu*, e.g., [^{d}DIN]GIR-ZAG-*ti* KAM 10 19:9.
541	SAR	syl.:	*sar*	in PN *Sar-re-ni* KAJ 158:6.
			šar	e.g., *a-šar* MAL A § 13:27; *tu-šar-ra* BVW B:9; *e-šar-te* Coronation Ritual ii 34; *tu-šar-šu* MATC 2:23.
			KIRI$_6$	in (^{giš})KIRI$_6$= *kirû* e.g., MAL B § 12:14; A 3185 (NTA, 35):6.
543	GÀR	syl.:	*k/qar*	e.g., *i-qar-ri-bu* MAL A § 29:17; *i-kar-rab* Ištar ritual:10; *ú-qar-ri-*⌜*bu*⌝*-ni* MARV 8 38:14; ^{iti}*qar-ra-tv* passim.
544	LIL	syl.:	*lil*	e.g., *te-lil-te* Adad ritual:8; A 295 (NTA, 16):2; *lil-qe-a-šu* T 98-3:13.
545	MÚRU	log.:	MÚRU	= *qablu*, e.g., MAPD § 6:43.
547	DÉ	log.:	SIMUG	in ^{lú}SIMUG = *nappāḫu*, e.g., ^{lú}SIMUG GUŠKIN A 2604 (NTA, 27):9.
548	ÁŠ	syl.:	*áš*	passim.
			ás	passim.
		log.:	ÁŠ	^{f}ÁŠ.GÀR = *unīqu*, e.g., LVUH 7:27
			ZÍZ	in ^{iti}ZÍZ = *šabātu*, Franke/Wilhelm 1985:10; Giricano 9:12.
549	BANEŠ	log.:		= 3 *sūtu*, passim, see § 329.
550	BANLIMMU			= 4 *sūtu*, passim, see § 329.
551	BANIA			= 5 *sūtu*, passim, see § 329.
552	MA	syl.:	*ma*	passim.
		log.	MA	in MA.NA = *manû*, passim in private, also in literary, e.g., MAL A § 5 59. in MA.NU = *ēru*, e.g., KAJ 310:49. in ^{giš}PÈŠ = *tittu*, e.g., MARV 3 32:2.
553	GAL	syl.	*gal*	e.g., *ta-da-gal* MAL A § 36:92; ^{d}*Ma-nu-gal* Coronation Ritual iii 22; *a-da-gal* MATC 1:10; *ni-gal-li* Giricano 12:13'.

		log.	GAL	= *rabīu*, e.g., KAJ 107:2.
				in ^{zi}GAL.GAL.LA, e.g., TabT105A-151:6.
554	BÁRA	log.:	BARAG	= *parakku*, e.g., Coronation Ritual i 44.
				in ^{iti}BÁRA = *nisannu*, in Giricano 15:7; MARV 1 25B:6'.
556	NIMGIR	syl.:	*mir*	e.g., ^{d}*Nun-nam-mir* Coronation Ritual ii 39.
		log.	NIMGIR	in (^{lú})NIMGIR = *nagīru*, MAPD § 20:95, TR 3004:14' cf. commentary on CTMMA 1 99:16.
558	GIR	syl.:	*gir*	e.g., ^{md}UTU-*ma-gir* KAJ 162:9; ⸢*mu*⸣-*ger-ri-šu* MARV 10 4:2.
			piš	e.g., *e-piš* MAPD § 5:36; ⸢*e*⸣-*piš* MATSH 19:5; ^{m}*Piš-qi-*[*ia*] T 88-1:6.
			pùs	in ^{m}*I+na-pùš-qi-lu-*⸢*ṣi*$^{!}$⸣ KAV 156:1.
		log.:	GIR	in GIR.KAL = *aplu*, in PN ^{m}GIR.KAL-*lu-ṣi* MPR 28:17. See commentary MPR, 140.
559	BUR	syl.:	*b/pur*	e.g., *pur-šu* MAL B § 1:14; *bur*$^{?}$*-ki-šu-*[*nu*] BVW A:11; *la-áš-pur-ka* MAPD § 21:106; *šu-pur* MATC 5:5; ^{iti}*ḫi-bur* passim.
		log.:	BUR	in BUR.GUL =*pa/urkullu*, e.g., KAV 100:17; MARV 4 1:10.
				in ^{dug}BUR.ZI = *pursītu*, MARV 5 46:8.
560	Á	syl.:	*i/ed/t/ṭ*	passim.
		log.:	Á	in Á = *emūqu*, in ^{d}NIN.URTA-Á-*ia* KAJ 227:7; ^{m}Á-10 MARV 2 ii 2.
				= *idu*, e.g., MARV 3 7:15.
561	DA	syl.:	*d/ṭa*	passim.
			tá	Unusual, see § 210.
562	GAŠAN	log.:	GAŠAN	= *bēltu*, e.g., GAŠAN-*at* MARV 8 56:4'.
566	ŠA	syl.:	*ša*	passim.
567	ŠU	syl.:	*šu*	passim.
		log.:	ŠU	= *qātu,* passim, e.g., BVW Ab r. 5; KAJ 252:4.
				in ^{lú}ŠU.I = *gallābu*, e.g., Ali 8:19; MATC 60:9.
				in ŠU.NIGIN = *napḫāru*, rarely used instead of ŠU.NÍGIN, e.g., MARV 3 65 iv 7'.
				in ŠU.NÍGIN = *napḫāru*, passim.
				in ^{iti}ŠU = *du*^{ʾ}*ūzu*, in ^{iti}ŠU MARV 2 2:1'.
570	LUL	syl.:	*lul*	in ^{m}*Lul-la-iu-ú* TR 3019:9.
			lib/p	e.g., ^{lú}*še-lip-pa-iu-ú* KAJ 188:22; ^{m}MU-*lib-ši* TIM 4 45:1; KAJ 132:25. Usually ŠÀ is used in *libbum* 'heart' cf. *lìb-bi* TIM 4 45:7.
		log.:	NAR	in ^{lú}NAR = *nāru*, MAPR § 22:114; MARV 10 51:4.
573	ALAM	log.:	ALAM	= *ṣalmu*, e.g., Coronation Ritual ii 7; TR 3017:14.
574	URI	log.:	URI	in URI^{ki} = *māt Akkadīe*, e.g., Coronation Ritual iv 5; MARV 6 35:18.
576	GAM	log.:	*gúr*	in *im-gúr* MATSH 2:65. Doubtfull, reading is not supported by the copy.
			GÚR	in ^{šim}GÚR.GÚR = *kukru*, MARV 1 42:4; MARV 2 28:1.
578	KUR	syl.:	*kur*	e.g., *kur-di-iš-še* MAL B § 19:14.
			kìn	(*šá-kìn* Stelen passim.[1]), cf. <kín> no. 644.
			laṭ	in *i-ba-laṭ-ṭú-ni* Giricano 8:20.
			šad/t/ṭ	e.g., *i-šaṭ-ṭu-ru* MAL A § 45:68; *tu-ka-šad* BVW B:5; ^{f}*Mu-ka*$^{!}$*-ni-šat-*^{d}*Taš-me-ti* MARV 1 57 iv 16'.
		log.:	KUR	= *mātu*, e.g., MAPD § 20:96; KAJ 100:10.

1 Generally, the combination NÍG + KUR is read as logographic GAR instead of *šá-kìn*, see MZL, 445; cf. Jakob 2003, 132.

				= *šaduʾu*, e.g., MATSH 2:47.
				= *kašādu*, in PNs, e.g., ^{m}*Bal-ṭu*-KUR-*id* KAJ 223:5.
				in ^{ú}KUR.KUR = *atāʾišu*, in MARV 1 42:3; MARV 2 28:2.
		det.:	kur	Used before countries and mountains, a few times also before cities.
579	ŠE	syl.:	*še*	passim.
		det.:	še	determinative for different types of cereals.
		log.:	ŠE	= *eyyû*, passim, see § 69.
				in ŠE.BAR = *uṭṭutu*, perhaps in MARV 4 77:2'.
				in ^{giš}ŠE.ḪAR, e.g., KAJ 275:1; KAJ 300:1. Reading unknown, see MZL, 375 no. 579.
				in ŠE.Ì.GIŠ = *šamaššammū*, e.g., T 93-7:6; MARV 3 38:6 et passim. Also variant ŠE.GIŠ.Ì in MARV 3 60:1.
				in ŠE.KIN.GU$_5$ = *eṣādu,* e.g., ^{lú}ŠE.KIN.GU$_5$^{meš} KAJ 163:9
				in ^{d}ŠE.NAGA = *nisaba*, theophoric element in PNs, e.g., $^{f!}$*Ra-ba-at-*^{d}*Nisaba*.
				in ŠE.ŠEN = *šimtu, šimdu*, e.g., A 1828 (NTA, 25):1; MARV 10 5:20; see CAD Š3, 9ff. Usually ŠE.GÍN/GIN$_7$ in Akkadian, see MZL no. 579.
				in ŠE.SA.A = *labtu*, in NBC 4599:12.
580	BU	syl.:	*bu*	passim.
			qíd/t	e.g., *pa-qíd* KAJ 178:21; *pi-qít-tu* MATC 24:13.
		log.:	GÍD	= *arāku*, e.g., GÍD-*de-en*-DINGIR MARV 1 14:22.
				also GÍD.DA = *šadādu/arāku*, e.g., TR 3017:11; TR 3020:4; Giricano 10:3.
583	UZ	syl.:	*us/ṣ/z*	passim.
584	SUD	syl.:	*sar*$_4$	e.g., ^{m}*Sar*$_4$*-ni-qu* KAJ 255:14; ^{iti}*ša sar*$_4$*-ra-te* A 2686:1'.
585	MUŠ	syl.:	*muš*	e.g., *i-ga-di-muš* MAL A § 19:92; ^{uru}*Tal-mu-šu* MARV 1 56:52.
			ṣir	e.g., DINGIR-*šu-na-ṣir* TIM 4 45:1; *ki-ṣir-ti* MARV 6 15 envl. 1.
		log.:	MUŠ	in ^{na4}MUŠ.GÍR = *muššaru*, KTN inventory i 28; MARV 4 126:12'.
587	TIR	syl.:	*ṭi/er*$_5$	^{I}EN-*le-ṭer*$_5$ VAT 8009:12.
		log.:	TIR	in (^{giš})TIR = *qiltu*, e.g., KAJ 190:20; Billa 62:5.
589	TE	syl.:	*te*	passim.
			de$_4$	Highly unusual see § 210.
			ṭe/i$_4$	In PN ^{I}EN-[*l*]*e-ṭe*$_4$*-e*[*r*] KAV 98:5; ^{I}EN-*le-ṭe*$_4$*-er* MATC 67:26.
590	KAR	syl.:	*kar*	e.g., *i-za-kar* MAPD § 11:61; *i-kar-ru-ru-šu-nu* MAPD § 19:94; *ta-kar-ra-ar* PKT 1 I right:6; *ka-kar-di-nu* MARV 10 59:13.
		log.:	KAR	in KAR.KID = *ḫarimtu*, e.g., MAL A § 40:66; ^{f}KAR.KID KAJ 309:2.
				= *ezābu*, in: ^{d}IŠKUR-*mu*-KAR KAJ 54:21; ^{m}KAR-^{d}30 MARV 6 15:2 et passim. cf. ^{d}*Še-ru-a-še-zi-ba-a-n*[*i*] TR 3022:14.
591	LIŠ	syl.:	*liš*	e.g., *liš-ku-nu* MAL B § 6:17; *e-liš* PKT 1 I right:14; *liš-ši-a* MATC 5:17.
			šil$_4$	Mostly limited to *šil*$_4$*-ta-ḫV*, see § 117.
596	UD	syl.:	*ud/t/ṭ*	passim.
			tú	See § 210.
			u$_4$	in *u*$_4$*-mv* passim.
			laḫ	e.g., ^{d}*A-šur*$^{!}$*-pí-laḫ* KAJ 57:25 cf. <láḫ> (ÉRIN) and <làḫ> (LUḪ).

			liḫ	Very rare, perhaps only in ^{uru}*Ku-liḫ-ḫi-na-áš* MARV 5 64:5. Cf. <líḫ> (no. 613).
			par	unusual, <pár> (BAR) is preferred. *ip*$^{!}$*-par-rak-ku* IM 60240 1 r. 4'.
			pi/er	in *Pir-ḫi-ta-din*$^{!}$ TR 3013:2; *na-áš-pir-te* MARV 7 3:8; *pir-su* MARV 5 53:27. Usually the similar <pír> (no. 613) is used.
			tam	e.g., *i-tam-ma* MAL A § 5:60; ^{é}*al-tam-me* MAL A § 14:31; *tu-ka-tam* PKT 1 I right:17; *e-tam-ra* MATC 10:16.
		log.:	UD	= *ūmu*, e.g., UD^{meš}*-te* MAL A § 19:91. in ZABAR(UD.KA.BAR) = *siparru*, e.g., KAJ 178:7.
			BABBAR	= *paṣīu*, MAPD § 6:43; KAV 104:7; BABBAR-*ú* KAJ 273:4. See *pa-ṣi-ú-tum* KAJ 174:3. in ^{na4}BABBAR.DILI = *pappardilû*, e.g., KTN inventory i 7.
			UTU	in ^{d}UTU = *Šamaš*, passim. especially in PNs. cf. ^{d}*Šá-maš* KAV 26 r. 16.
598	PI	syl.:	*pi/e*	passim.
			bì	very rare, see § 203.
		log.:	GEŠTU	= *uznu*, MAPD § 21:104; cf. *uz-ni-ša* MAL A § 5:65.
599	ŠÀ	syl.:	*lìb*	in *lìb-bi*, can also be read logographic (see below).
		log.:	ŠÀ	ŠÀ-(*bv*) = *libbu,* passim. See § 68.
612	ERIM	syl.:	*ṣab*	e.g., *i-ṣab-bat* Ištar ritual:4; *ṣab-tu* MARV 6 22:13'; *ṣab-e* MATC 11:28.
		log.:	ZÁLAG	= *namāru,* e.g., EN-ZÁLAG-*a-ni* KAJ 81:23.
			ÉRIN	= *ṣābu*, e.g., MAL A § 19:85, MARV 10 35:5; MPR 2:55. cf. possible *ṣab-ʾa* MATC 1:4. in ÉRIN.TÁḪ = *nērāru*, e.g., ^{md}EN.LÍL-ÉRIN.TÁḪ MARV 9 83 r. 7'; cf. ^{d}IŠKUR-*ni-ra-ri* A 3281:6'.
613	PÍR	syl.:	*pí/ér*	e.g., *pír-e* KTN inventory i 3; *pír-ṣa-du-ḫa* PKT 1 I right:7; *pír-su* MATC 64:26; *na-áš-pér-te* MATSH 12:40; ^{d}*A-šur-e-pír* KAJ 77:18; *pér-ṣa-du-ḫi* MARV 3 58:2'.
			láḫ	e.g.^{d}*Láḫ-mu* Coronation Ritual ii 10; ^{lú}*a-láḫ-ḫi-nu*^{m}[^{eš}] MARV 9 14:26; *a-pa-láḫ* KAV 159:5. Note the value <làḫ> no. 494. Cf. <laḫ> (no. 596).
			líḫ	in PNs in the element *pāliḫu*, e.g., ^{m}*Pa-líḫ-Ku-bi* KAJ 22:18. Cf. <liḫ> (no. 596).
			par₅	in *pa-par₅-da-lé-e* BE 17 91:5.
628	ZIB	syl.:	*ṣip*	e.g., ^{iti}*ṣip-pu* MARV 1 63:10; ^{iti}*ṣip-pi* MARV 8 12:1.
631	ḪI	syl.:	*ḫi/e*	passim.
			i₁₁	Rare, but best read as <ḫi/e>, see § 199.
		log.:	ḪI	in ḪI.A, plural marker, e.g., A.ŠÀ.ḪI.A MAL B § 17:6.
			DÙG	in DÙG.GA = *ṭâbu*, e.g., Coronation Ritual ii 32; in PNs, e.g., ^{m}*A-bu*-DÙG.GA KAJ 132:4.
632	ŠÀR	syl.:	*šár*	e.g., *ma-šár-te* BVW I:10; ^{m}*Tukul-ti*-A-*é-šár-ra* MAPD § 20:95; ^{uru}*ḫu-šàr-še* Billa 55:7.
633	TÍ	syl.:	*ṭí/é*	passim.
635	Aʾ	syl:	*a/i/e/uʾ*	passim.
636	AḪ	syl.:	*a/i/e/uḫ*	passim.
640	KAM	log.:	KAM	in dates. Rarely used intead of KÁM, e.g., UD.29.KAM MARV 2 32:20.
			ÚTUL	in ^{dug}ÚTUL = *diqāru*, e.g., PKT passim; MARV 1 47:6.
641	IM	syl.:	*i/em*	passim.
		log.:	IM	in ^{d}IM (^{d}IŠKUR) = Adad, passim. = *šāru*, in PNs, e.g., ^{f}IM-^{d}*Iš₈-tár*-⸢*a-al-lak*⸣ A 582:19;

				^{m}DÙG.GA-IM-^{d}*A-šur* MAH 16086 A ii 7. in IM.SAḪAR.BA[BBAR.KUR.RA] MARV 10 40:8 = *alluḫaru*.
643	BIR	syl.:	*bi/er*	^{túg}*bir-še* Coronation Ritual ii 17; *ber-ti* 'between' MATSH 12:29; *e-bir-ta* KAJ 129:10 (Ad). Replaces more archaic value <bir$_5$> no. 134.
644	ḪAR	syl.:	*ḫa/ur*	e.g., *ḫar-ra-a-na* MAL A § 22:107; *ma-ḫar* Coronation Ritual ii 33; ^{iti}*mu-ḫur*-DINGIR^{meš} passim; *ḫar-pi* YBC 12860:15.
			ḫír	e.g., *ma-ḫír* MARV 10 91:5; Giricano 15:4.
			mur	e.g., *na-mur-tu* MARV 1 68:1; ^{m}ŠEŠ-*la-mur* MARV 10 89:4.
			kín	e.g., ^{túg}*kín-da-ba-áš-še* MAPD § 21:105; *ša-kín* MARV 7 3:14. cf. <kin> no. 815; <kìn> no. 578.
		log.:	ḪAR	= *šabiru*, e.g., Coronation Ritual ii 26; MARV 10 3:13, cf. *ša-be-ru* MATC 63:5.
			ḪUR	in ^{u}ḪUR.SAG in *azupīru*, e.g., MARV 1 42:4; MARV 10 11:4.
			ÀRA	in ^{še}ÀRA = *ṭēnu*, Giricano 9:7. Spellings like ŠE.ÀRA-*šu-ú* Giricano 2:10 may be reinterpreted as ^{še}*ḫar-šu-ú* '(crumbled$^{?}$) bread'.
			UR$_5$	in ^{na4}UR$_5$ = *erāʾu*, e.g., KAJ 123:2; MARV 10 19:1.
646	SUḪUR	log.:	SUḪUR	= *ṭēḫi*, e.g., KAJ 154:5; TR 2037:16. Disputed sign, see § 476.
661	U	syl.:	*u*	as conjunction passim in Coronation Ritual also KAM 10; KAJ 69; syllabic: *i-di-nu-u-ni* TR 3025:8; *U-túl*-^{d}EN.ZU KAM 10 30:5.
			iš$_8$/eš$_{18}$	See no. 670.
		log.:	U	^{d}U = Adad, in PN, e.g., ^{d}*U-bi-ir-ti* KAJ 57:5.
			10	Numeral.
663	UGU	syl.:	*muḫ*	In *muḫ-ḫi* (passim), e.g., KAJ 11:5.
		log.:	UGU	= *muḫḫu*, e.g., *i+na* UGU MAL A § 12:20.
665	UDUN	log.:	UDUN	= *a/ūtunu*, e.g., MAPD § 19:94; U[DU]N MARV 2 23:12'.
669	U-GUR	log.:	U-GUR	= Nergal, in PNs, e.g., ^{m}*I-din*-^{d}U.GUR KAJ 110:8; ^{m}*Mu*-KAR-^{d}U.GUR MARV 1 27+:29.
670	U-DAR	syl.:	*Iš$_8$-tár*	passim for the deity Ištar. Rarely INNIN (MÚŠ) is used, see no. 153.
671	ŠAGŠU	log.:	SAGŠU	in ^{túg}SAGŠU = *kubšu*, MARV 3 53:1.
672	ÁB	syl.:	*áb*	rare, see § 201.
			lid/t/ṭ	e.g., *lid-di-na-ku* MVAeG 41:3 ii 36; *lid-din* MARV 10 70:8.
		log.:	ÁB	in ^{gu4}ÀB = *littu*, e.g., KAJ 92:2; LVUH 8:2; T 97-6:8. Also ÁB.GUD AO 21.380:1.
678	KIŠ	syl.:	*k/qiš*	e.g., *kiš-pi* MAL A § 47:6; ^{m}*I-qiš*-^{d}IM KAJ 62:21.
681	MI	syl.:	*mi*	passim.
			mé	erroneous spelling, see § 227.
			ṣíl	passim in *ṣíl-lí-* in PNs.
		log.:	GE$_6$	= *ṣalmu*, e.g., KTN inventory i 22; VAT 8236:8.
682	GUL	syl.:	*gul*	e.g., *su-gul-li* MAL F § 2:9; ^{m}*Du-gul*-DINGIR KAJ 139:3'.
			kúl	*ú-kúl-la-a-ša* MAL A § 96; *le-e-kúl* MATC 5:24; *ta-kúl-tum* TabT105A-151:13; in PN ^{md}*Nin-urta-tu-kúl-Aš-šur* KAJ 187:7, which is usually spelled with ^{giš}TUKUL.
685	ŠAGAN	log.:	ŠÁMAN	in ^{lú}ŠÁMAN.LÁ = *šamallāʾu*, in KAJ 249:4, cf. ^{lú}[*š*]*a-ma-la-e* MARV 5 85:18.

685	PAN	syl.:	pan	e.g., *pan-gu* 'a type of bread' MARV 1 7:18.
		log.:	PAN	in ^{giš}PAN = *qaltu*, e.g., KAV 98:47; ERIN PAN MARV 4 119:6.
686	GIM	log.:	ŠITIM	= *itinnu*, e.g., MARV 1 27:16; MARV 4 28 r. 21'.
689	NÁ	log.:	NÁ	in ^{giš}NÁ = *mayyālu*, e.g., KAJ 310:45. Unlike Borger (MZL, 336 no. 469), the sign GIŠ is not part of the logogram, but an optional determinative: MARV 10 3:19'. cf. *ma-ia-*[*li*] MAPD § 17:80.
690	NIM	syl.:	*nim*	e.g., *lu-še-*⌜*li-a*⌝*-nim-ma* MAL B § 6:16.
			num	e.g., ^{ú}*kur-ka-num* MARV 1 42:2.
			tum$_4$	rare: KÁ *šu-tum*$_4$*-me* George 1988 2:10.
693	LAM	syl.:	*lam*	e.g., *tu-ka-lam* BVW B:7; *ú-šal-lam-ku-nu-ma* T 04-37:12; *ṣa-lam* Stelen passim.
695	AMAR	syl.:	*ṣur*	e.g., *lu ta-ṣur*$^{!}$ Ištar ritual:8'; ^{md}IŠKUR-MU-*ú-ṣur* KAJ 181:8.
696	SISKUR	log.:	SISKUR	in ^{udu}SISKUR, e.g., Coronation Ritual ii 16; VAT 9410:26.
698	UL	syl.:	*ul*	passim.
701	GÌR	log.:	GÌR	= *šēpu*, e.g., Coronation Ritual ii 16; GÌR.2 MARV 9 63:2. = *purīdu* 'a measure of area', e.g., KAJ 147:4; KAV 127:1.
704	DUGUD	log.:	DUGUD	= *kabtu*, e.g., ^{md}IŠKUR-DUGUD KAJ 12:25.
705	GIG	log.:	GIG	in ^{še}GIG = *kibtu*, e.g., LVUH 69:3; KAM 10, 47:5; Aynard/Durand 1980 12:1.
708	MAN	syl.:	*man*	e.g., ^{m}*Man-nu-ki-i-*^{d}*A-nim* KAV 26 r. 20'.
			mìm	e.g., *mìm-ma* MAL A § 46:92; *mìm-mu-ú* MAL C+ § 2:12. cf. rare <mim> in no. 883.
			niš	e.g., *lem-niš* MAPD § 17:81; *dan-niš* PKT 2 i 16.
		log.:	MAN	= *šarru*, literary texts, e.g., MAPD; Coronation Ritual passim. Occurs regularly in alternation with LUGAL from the reign of Aššur-dān onwards in private texts, e.g., MARV 1 49:23 (Tp); MARV 1 42:10 (Abk); A 1751 (NTA, 24):4 (Ad). An odd earlier examp1e is possible, perhaps MARV 1 47:21 (broken; TN$^{?}$); VAT 9968 r. 12' (Adn$^{?}$, see Bloch 2013, 47). MAN remains the less frequently used logogram, up until NA (LAS 2, 445).
			20	Numeral.
711	EŠ	syl.:	*eš*	Rare, see § 221.
			is$_5$	passim.
		log.:	ÙŠU	Numeral. in ^{d}30 in Coronation Ritual i 45 and passim in PNs and month ^{iti}(^{d})30.
712	NIMIN	log.:	40	numeral, cf. § 328.
714	NINNU	log.:	50	numeral, cf. § 328.
715	LX	log.:	60	numeral, cf. § 328.
720	DUL	syl.:	*tul*	^{f}*ba-tul-te* MAL A § 55:39; *tul-ta-na-kal* PKT 1 I right:16.
721	DU$_6$		*tul*$_6$	As mentioned in MZL (no. 720), the sign DU$_6$ is frequently confused with DUL. This is at least attested in *tul-te-ṣi-ma* Ištar ritual r. 6 (Meinhold 2009, 350). Following MZL, the reading <tul> is maintained in this study.
		log.:	DU$_6$	= *tašrītu*, in ⌜^{iti}⌝DU$_6$ KAV 155:7.
724	IGI	syl.:	*ši*	passim.
			lim/lem	e.g., *i-šal-lim* MAL A § 39:31; ; *lim-ḫur* MAL E § 3:5'; *lem-niš* MAPD § 17:81; ⌜*lim-ḫu*⌝*-ru* MATSH 3:37
			lì/è	Reading LIM is to be preferred, see § 87.
		log.:	IGI	= *pan(ē)*, MATSH 11:14. Cf. *pa-ni* MARV 1 2:5. = *šēbu*, passim in witness lists following IGI-*bu* in T 97-

				37:18, 19, 21, 23. = *ēnu*, e.g., in ^{na4}IGI in KAJ 274 rd. 1'. in ^{ú}IGI.LIM = *imḫur-līm*, in MARV 1 42:1. in ^{ú}IGI.NIŠ = *imḫur-ešrā*, in MARV 1 42:2. in IGI.NU.DUḪ= *lā dāgilu* KAJ 180:2. ^{lú}IGI.NU.TUKU = *lā dāgilu* in LVUH 90:11, see Röllig commentary.
726	AR	syl.:	*ar*	passim.
727	AGRIG	log.:	AGRIG	in (^{lú})AGRIG = *mašennu*,[2] e.g., MARV 5 47:14.
			GIŠKIM	= *tukultu*, e.g., ^{m}MÁŠ-GISKIM-*Aš-šur* VAT 9410:4; ^{uru}Kar-^{I}GIŠKIM-⸢MAŠ⸣ MARV 4 81:3.
729	SIG$_5$	log.:	SIG$_5$	= *damqu*, e.g., KAJ 11:15; in PNs: ^{md}IŠKUR-SIG$_5$ KAM 10 3:15.
731	Ù	syl.:	*ù*	passim as conjunction, rare otherwise, e.g., *ù-ša-dá-na* KAJ 114:15.
736	DI	syl.:	*di/e*	passim.
			ti$_4$	Rare, see § 210.
			sál	e.g., ^{d}*Sál-ma-nu* Coronation Ritual iii 36; ^{md}*Sál-ma-*⸢*nu*⸣-MU-PAP MPR 69:40.
			šùl	This value should be replace by <sál>. See Radner 1998 and MZL no. 736. Perhaps *šùl-mu* in Billa 65:5 (and Nuzi TR 124:3).
		log.:	DI	= *dēnu*, MARV 4 119:32, aslo in in PNs. in ^{lú}DI.KU$_5$ = *dayyānu*, e.g., MAL B § 6:49. cf. PN ^{m}10-*da-a-an* MAR 1 73:10. in DI.KU$_5$/KUD = *dēnu*, e.g., DI.KU$_5$-*na* VAT 8722:21.
			SILIM	= *šalāmu*, in ^{m}*Mu*-SILIM-[…] Billa 35:8; $^{m\,d}$30-*mu*-SILIM MARV 9 96:3.
737	KI	syl.:	*ki/e*	passim.
			qí/é	passim. Alternates with *qi/e* (KIN), see § 206.
		det.:	ki	Does not occur.
		log.:	KI	= *iltu*, e.g., KAJ 25:4. in KI.LAL = *šuqultu*, KAJ 130:8; MARV 3 57:2. in KI.LAM = *maḫīru*, e.g., KAJ 61:10. in KI.TA = *šaplu*, e.g., MARV 9 1:15. in KI.UŠ = *kibsu*, in MATSH 2:31.
			KI+A	= PIŠ$_{10}$, in PIŠ$_{10}$.^{d}ÍD = *kibrītu*, e.g., MARV 10 11:5, cf. *kib-ri-tu*^{me}[^{š}] MARV 10 1:5.
741	KI-MIN	log.:	KIMIN	= e.g., BVW Ac:3; KTN inventory i 14; KAJ 277:2. May be read *annie-ma* according to MARV 5 57:12, see § 415.
744	ŠUL	syl.:	ŠUL	e.g., *šul-ma-nu* Coronation Ritual iii 5; EA 15:14; *šul-mu* MARV 7 14:6; MATSH 11:5 see also <šùl> (DI) no. 736.
745	KUG	log.:	KÙ	in KÙ.BABBAR = *ṣarpu*, e.g., MAL A § 31:46. Cf. *ṣar-pa* KAJ 7:15. in KÙ.GI (GUŠKIN) = *ḫurāṣu*, e.g., Coronation Ritual i 33, MATC 63:2.
746	PAD	syl.:	*pad/t/ṭ*	e.g., *i-la-pat* Coronation Ritual i 25.
			šuk	^{m}*Aš-šur-ṭab-ni-šuk-lil* A 3186 (NTA, 35):16.
		log.:	ŠUK	= *kurummutu*, passim, e.g., KAJ 218:7; ŠUK-*at* MARV 2 17a+:2.
747	XV	log.:	15	numeral, cf. § 328.
748	DIŠ	syl.:	*ana*	Perhaps in some administrative documents, e.g., MARV 6 31:3.

2 The reading *mašennu* is preferable over *abarakku*, see Jakob 2003, 94 n175.

		det.:	‘m’ or ‘I’	passim in PN, not used after the first terms in genealogies and after IGI. Exceptions, see § 73.
		log.:	DIŠ	numeral, see § 328.
			GÉŠ	numeral, see § 328.
750	LAL	syl.:	*lá*	as phonetic complement on the logogram IDIGNA in PNs, e.g., ÌR-^{d}IDIGNA-*lá* KAJ 69:3. Otherwise rare, see § 241.
			lal	e.g., *ú-kal-lal-šu* Coronation Ritual ii 26; *ú-lal* Adad ritual:8.
		log.:	LAL	= *muṭṭāʾu*, e.g., KAV 119:12; LAL^{meš} KAJ 305:4; cf. *mu-uṭ-ṭa-ú* T 98-118:7. See Postgate 1986a, 38. in NÍG.LAL = *ṣimittu*, e.g., A 1828 (NTA, 25):4; MARV 10 3:21, syllabic *ṣi-mi-tu* Billa 25:1.
753	ME	syl.:	*me*	passim.
			mì	Erroneous spellings, see § 227.
		log.:	ME	= *meʾatu*, numeral passim.
754	MEŠ	det.:	meš	Plural marker, see § 74ff.
755	LAGAB	syl.:	*ḫab/p*	^{lú}*ḫab-bu-li-ši* MAL A § 48:32; ^{kur}*Ḫab-ri-ú-*⸢*ri*⸣ MARV 6 78:5; *ta-ḫap-še* MARV 10 17:4; *i-ḫap-pi* Giricano 10:19.
			kil	Rare value, <kíl> (GIL) is preferred over this sign. Exceptions: ^{m}*Mu-*⸢*ták-kil-A*$^{?}$*-šur*⸣ MARV 6 68:6’.
			gíl	in ^{m}*Sag-gíl*-KAM KAJ 281:13.
		log.:	KUR$_4$	= *baʾālu*, in KUR$_4$.RA A 3211:5.
			ḪAB	in ^{giš}ḪAB = *ḫūratu*, e.g., KAM 11 48:19, cf. *ḫu-ru-tu* A 305:4
760	GIGIR	log.	GIGIR	in ^{giš}GIGIR = *narkabtu*/*mugerru*, e.g., KAJ 130:16; KAJ 310:1 cf. *na*[*r*]*-kab-tu* ‘chariot’ BVW Ko:20/⸢*mu*⸣*-ger-ri-šu* MARV 10 4:2.
766	U$_8$	log.:	U$_8$	in U$_8$ = *gurrutu* ‘ewe’ (Ismail/Postgate 2008, 151), e.g., KAJ 97:1; ^{udu}U$_8$ KAJ 190:6. Cf. ^{udu}*gu-ru-tum* KAJ 96:1.
767	ZAR	syl.:	*ṣar*	e.g., *ṣar-pa* MAPD § 5:34; ^{d}*Ṣar-pa-ni-ta* New Year Ritual:31’; *ik-ta-ṣar* MARV 10 70:11.
786	PÚ	log.:	PÚ	= *būrtu*, e.g., KAJ 13:14.
804	NIGIN	log.:		see no. 567.
807	IB	syl.:	*i/eb/p*	passim.
808	KU	syl.:	*ku*	passim.
		log.:	KU	‘a measurement of size’, e.g., KAV 127:1. in KU.KU ‘a plant’, e.g., MARV 2 28:9, cf. MZL, 428. in (^{d})KU(.A) = *Marduk*, very rare. Attested in MARV 3 8 e.g., ^{md}KU.A-ŠEŠ-KAM l. 52.
			TUKUL	= *kakku*, e.g., Coronation Ritual ii 15; MATSH 8:38’.
809	TÚG	log.:	TÚG	= *ṣubātu*, e.g., MAL A § 40:105; KAJ 301:1, cf. *ṣu-ba-a-ta* T 97-34:19.
810	ŠÈ	log.:	ZÌ; ZÍD	= *qēmu*, MATC 24a:4; in ZÌ(.DA= KAJ 180:31; KAJ 277:12; TabT105A-151:1. in ZÌD.KASKAL = *ṣidītu*, e.g., KAV 119:6.
		det.	zì	e.g., ^{zì}*si-im-du* TabT105A-151:2.
812	LU	syl.:	*lu*	passim.
		log.:	UDU	in UDU = *immeru*, e.g., MAL F § 1:2. in GUKKAL (LU/UDU+ḪÚL) = *g/kukkallu*, e.g., MARV 1 47:13; AO 21.382:1; A 3186 (NTA, 35):3. in UDU.NIM = *ḫurāpu*, e.g., A 3190 (NTA, 41):5; Ali 1:4. UDU.NÍTA = *immeru*, e.g., Ali 4:3.
813	DIB	log.:	DIB	= *ṣabātu*, in PNs, e.g., [^{m}]*Si-qi-Aš-šur*-DIB-*bat* MARV 7 56:23.
815	KIN	syl.:	*qi/e*	passim. Alternates with <ki/e> (KI) see § 206.

			kin	rare, in *šá-kin* A 3196 (NTA, 39):28. Usually no. 644 is used.
		log.:	KIN	= *šipru*, e.g., DUMU KIN RS 06.198:8; KIN-*šu-nu* Billa 62:23; LVUH 48:23; cf. *ši-ip-ri-ia* T 05-1:8.
				= *ulūlu*, in ^{iti}K[I]N MARV 7 46:6.
816	SÍG	log.:	SÍG	= *šīpātu*, e.g., MAL A § 36:86; VAT 8236:7
825	MIN	log.:	2	numeral, see § 328.
827	ŠUŠANA	log.:	$^1/_3$	numeral, see § 331.
828	UR	syl.:	*ur*	passim
			lig/k/q	e.g., *liq-ta-a-ni* Coronation Ritual iii 9; *liq-bi* Ištar ritual:11; ^{lú}*a-lik* KAJ 118:10; DINGIR-*ma-lik* KAM 11 2:11.
			taš	e.g., *taš-pu-ra* A 845:22; ^{f}SIG$_5$-*Taš-me-tu* MPR 12:56.
			tíš	e.g., ^{d}IŠKUR-*tíš-mar* KAJ 75:17.
		log.:	UR	in UR.MAḪ = *nēšu*, e.g., Coronation Ritual ii 9; VAT 9375:2; cf. *ni-še* KAJ 221:8.
832	ŠANABI	log.:	$^2/_3$	numeral, see § 331.
834	EŠ$_5$	log.:	3	numeral, see § 328.
836	GÍN	syl.:	*ṭu*	passim.
		log.:	GÍN	= *šiqlu*, KAJ 48:1.
838	KINGUSILA	log.:	$^5/_6$	numeral, see § 331.
839	A	syl.:	*a*	passim.
		log.:	A	= *mā*ʾ*ū*, e.g., A^{meš} BVW I:3.
				= *aḫu*, only in PN *Bābu-aḫa-iddin*, e.g., ^{I}KÁ-A-PAP KAJ 256:3
				= *aplu*, in PNs, e.g., ^{m}*Aš-šur*-A-PAP KAJ 101:1.
				= *mar*ʾ*u,* not in texts written in MA dialect, but found in other places such as seals and royal inscriptions.
				in ^{lú}A.BAL = *dalû*, MARV 3 3:54.
				in A.GÀR = *ugāru*, e.g., MAL B § 6:11; syl. *ú-ga-ri* KAJ 121a:2.
				in A.KAL = *ḫīlu*, MARV 2 28:4.
				in A.ŠÀ = *eqlu*, e.g., MAL A § 36:85; LVUH 63:13; T 96-3:7.
				in ^{lú}A.ZU = *asū*ʾ*u*, e.g., MAL A § 8:81.
				in A.ZU = *asu*, in MARV 7 10:5'.
			A+ ENGUR	= ÍD = *nāru*, e.g., KAV 107:10; ÍD-i-id MAL A § 22:10; ÍD-*te* KAJ 178:10.
				in ^{lu}A.BA = *tupšarru*, e.g., Giricano 8:36; TabT05A-43:28. Already attested in 13th century texts, e.g., KAJ 101:25 (Adn); MARV 1 47:32 (TN).
				in A.AB.BA = *tâmtu*, e.g., KAJ 106:14.
				in ÍLDAG (A.AM) = *adāru*, e.g., *Síl-lí*-ÍLDAG KAM 10 16 r. 3'.
				The sequence -A-PAP might have been used for different PNs when there was no room for the actual signs (see Freydank 2010b, 255 n9; MPR, 65 n547).
851	ZA	syl.:	*ṣ/za*	passim.
			sà	Only rarely in assimilated pronominal suffix -*ša*. See § 225.
		log.:	ZA	in $^{\text{na4}}$ZA.GÌN = *uqnû*, e.g., VAT 8236:8; New Year Ritual:6'.
				in ^{síg}ZA.GÌN.DURU$_5$ = *zagindurû*, e.g., YBC 6956:2.
				in ^{síg}ZA.GÌN.SA$_5$ = *argamannu*, e.g., MAH 15854 B:3'.

				in ^{síg}ZA.GÌN.GI$_6$ = *takiltu*$^?$, MARV 1 24:10.
				in ^{ú}ZA.ḪI.LI = *saḫliu*, in MARV 5 46:6.
852	LIMMU$_5$	log:	4	numeral, see § 328.
856	ḪA	syl.:	*ḫa*	Passim.
		log.	ḪA	in ḪA.LA = *zittu*, e.g., MAL A § 28:10; MARV 8 47:36.
858	GUG	log.	^{na4}GUG	= *sāmtu,* e.g., KTN inventory i 5; MARV 4 126:2'.
859	NÍG	syl.:	*šá*	Passim but restricted, see § 218.
			gar	in ^{m}*I-gar-še-mi-id* MARV 1 41:4.
			kar$_5$	Only in *ú-kar*$_5$*-ru-ú* in Tell Ar-Rimāh: TR 2015:11; TR 2057B:4'. See de Ridder 2017a, 299 § 1.1.
		log.:	NÍG	in NÍG.BA = *qiltu*, e.g., Coronation Ritual ii 13; in PNs, e.g., ^{d}IŠKUR-NUMUN-NÍG.BA KAJ 224:3.
				in NÍG.KA$_9$ = *nikkassu*, e.g., LB 1848:9; KAJ 255:4.
				in GAR (NÍG+KAR) = *šaknu*, e.g., MARV 1 49:6.
			NINDA	= *aklu*, e.g., Aynard/Durand 1980 12:1.
860	LIMMU	log.:	4	numeral used with GUN (see § 330).
861	IÁ	log.:	5	numeral used with GUN (see § 330).
862	ÀŠ	log.:	6	numeral used with GUN (see § 330).
863	IMIN	log.:	IMIN	In ^{d}IMIN.BI = *Sebettu* in PNs, e.g., ^{m}GAL-*ú*-^{d}IMIN.BI Billa 62:2.
			7	numeral used with GUN (see § 330).
864	USSU	log.:	8	numeral used with GUN (see § 330).
868	ILIMMU	log.:	9	numeral used with GUN (see § 330). Also in Arbail: ^{uru}4-*il* MARV 9 12:3 et passim.
869	ŠÚ	syl.:	*šú*	in late texts, see § 218.
		log.:	ŠÚ	= *kidennu*, in PN, e.g., ŠÚ-DUMU.MUNUS-*A-nim* KAV 119 3; ^{m}ŠÚ-^{d}30 Billa 1:26.
872	ŠUḪUB	log.:	ŠUḪUB	in ^{kuš}ŠUḪUB = *šuḫuppātu*, e.g., MAPD § 6:43 (var.).
881	SIG	syl.:	*sig/k*	e.g., *ma-sik-te* MAPD § 10:57; ^{m}*Siq-qi*-^{d}*A-šur*-DIB-*bat* MARV 6 24:13.
		log.:	SIG	= *qatnu*, e.g., MAH 16086 A ii 9.
883	MUNUS	syl.:	*rak/q*	e.g., ^{f}*mu-raq-qi-te* 'the perfume makster' PKT 3 iv 9; *ip*$^{!}$-*pár-rak-ku* IM 60240 r. 4'.
			šal	e.g., *i-šal-lim* MAL A § 39:31; *a-šal* KAJ 153:17; *ú-šal-ba* TR 3004:12'.
			mim	e.g., *mim-ma* MATSH 4:11 cf. more common <*mìm*> in no. 708.
		log.:	MUMUS, MÍ	= *šinniltu*, e.g., KAJ 190:10, in MUNUS-É.GAL = *iltu ēkalle*(?), in Franke/Wilhelm 1985:2; see n19. Also in ^{anše}EME$_5$ (MUNUS+ḪÚB) = *atānu*, e.g., KAJ 311:1; Hall 1983:6; EME$_5$-*nu* LVUH 43:6'. cf. *a-ta-nu* KAJ 90:8.
		det.:	'f'	Used before female personal names. passim. However it is also used for female professions and social status, much like a equivalent of the male LÚ, e.g., ^{f}*al-ma-at-tu* MAL A § 35:75; ^{f}*ba-tul-tu* § 56:42. but KAR.KID § 40:68.
884	ZUM	syl.:	*ṣu*	passim.
			rík	e.g., *pi-rík* MARV 9 14:24; [^{uru}*A*]*d-da-rík* MARV 5 53:93''.
886	NIN$_9$	log.:	NIN$_9$	= *aḫātu*, e.g., NIN$_9$-*su* MPR 20:6'; ^{f}NIN$_9$-*at*-^{d}[*Ku-be*] Giricano 14 r. 3.
887	NIN	syl.:	*nin*	e.g., ^{m}*Li-bur-za-nin*-^{d}*A-šur* KAJ 168:26.
		log.:	NIN	= *bēltu*, MATSH 10:9; TabT05A-134:4.
				in NIN.DINGIR.RA = *entu*, e.g., MARV 1 53:9.
889	DAM	syl.:	*dam*	e.g., ^{d}*Dam-ki-na* Coronation Ritual ii 11; ^{f}*Šá*-^{d}*Iš*$_8$*-tár-dam-qa* MPR 2:23.

		log.:	DAM	= *aššutu*, e.g., MAL A § 16:66; DAM-*at* Snell 1983/84:9. in ^{lú}DAM.GÀR = *tamkāru*, e.g., MATSH 6:16'; MARV 8 57:12. Cf. ^{lú}*ta-ka-ru* (< *tamkāru*) T 97-18:16
890	GÉME	log.:	GÉME	= *amtu*, e.g., MAL A § 4:49; Giricano 7:4.
891	GU	syl.:	*gu*	passim.
		log.:	GU	in ^{giš}GU.ZA = *kussiʾu,* e.g., Coronation Ritual ii 16; KAJ 108:1; Ali 23:13.
893	NAGAL	log.:	NAGAR	in ^{lú}NAGAR = *naggāru*, e.g., MARV 3 80:16'; MARV 8 10:5'.
898	NIG	syl.:	*nik*	in ^{túg}*nik-su* MARV 1 24:3; *ka-nik-tu* MARV 5 24:11.
899	EL	syl.:	*el*	passim.
			il$_5$	see § 241.
900	LUM	syl.:	*lum*	e.g., *su-lum-ma-e* 'peace-making' KUB 3 73:11'; *lum-ni* MAL A § 39:34.
905	SIG$_4$	log.:	SIG$_4$	= *libittu*, e.g., MAL B § 14:31; KAJ 87:7. = *simānu*, e.g., ^{iti}⸢SIG$_4$⸣ MARV 3 84 r. 7'.

Chapter 25: Concordances

25.1 Berlin (VAT siglum)

Number	Literature	Genre	Origin	Eponym
VAT 8009	Weidner 1959/60, AfO 19, T 7 1 BAI, 11, 53 Faist 2001, AOAT 265, 1034 Jakob 2003, CM 29, 285 Postgate 2013, Bronze age bureaucracy, 219	note	M 11 13	Usāt-Marduk (Sa)
VAT 8236	Weidner 1959/60, AfO 19, T 6 BAI, 10–11, 52 Jakob 2003, CM 29, 283–84 5–12: Postgate 2014, AT 17, 420	note	M 11 19	Ittabšī-dēn-Aššur (Sa)
VAT 8722	Weidner 1939/41, AfO 13, 122–23, 315 (studies), T 7	purchase	M 12 12	Kaštiliašu (TN)
VAT 8851	Weidner 1959/60, AfO 19 T 5 BAI, 9, 51	letter order	M 11 14	Bēr-šuma-lēšir (Sa)
VAT 8873	ARu, 14–15 no. 16 Weidner 1973, AfO 24, 141 Saporetti 1981, Mesopotamia 16, 25 DSC 3, 86, 156–57	loan	M 9 78	EN.TI-naṣir (EAd/Aub)
VAT 8923	Weidner 1963b, AfO 20, 121–122 DSC 1, 104–5, 136–37 3: Freydank 1971, OLZ 66, 533	division of inheritance	M 9 44	Tūr-kēnu (Ead–1150)
VAT 9034	Weidner 1963b, AfO 20, 123 DSC 1, 79–80, 130–31	purchase	M 9 104	
VAT 9363	Weidner 1935/36, AfO 10, 31 MAOG 7/1–2, 37	note	M 6 48	Sîn-šeya
VAT 9375	Weidner 1935/36, AfO 10, 31	note	M 6 44	Sîn-šeya
VAT 9410	Weidner 1935/36, AfO 10, 33 no. 50 39–44: Bloch 2012, Studies in MA chronology, 382	note	M 6 2	Sîn-šeya
VAT 9968	Weidner 1966, AfO 21, 44-45 Deller/Postgate 1985, AfO 32, 68 Bloch 2013, N.A.B.U. no. 28, 46–50 7', 15': Llop/Shibata 2016,	itinerary		

Number	Literature	Genre	Origin	Eponym
	JCS 68, 71			
VAT 19545	1–9: Cancik-Kirschbaum 1999, AOAT 267, 92 16–18: BMCG, 153–154		M 7	Mušallim-Aššur (Sa)
VAT 19549	1-16: Cancik-Kirschbaum 1999, AOAT 267, 92–93 17–19: BMCG, 107		M 7	Adad-bēl-gabbe (TN)
VAT 19554	1–15: Cancik-Kirschbaum 1999, AOAT 267, 93 2–6: Postgate 2014, AT 17, 405 n16 26–27: BMCG, 163		M 7	Qibbi-Aššur (TN)

25.2 Istanbul (A siglum)

Number	Literature	Genre	Origin	Eponym
A 70	Donbaz 1991, FS Garelli, 77 Faist 2001, AOAT 265, 95–96	note	M 8	Usāt-Marduk (Sa)
A 74	Donbaz 1988a, JCS 40, 71 no. 4	document	M 7 144	Ibri-šarri (Tp)
A 133	Donbaz 2004, FS Grayson, 68 no. 1 Cancik-Kirschbaum 2013, LDAS 1, 67, 79, no. 6	summon letter	M 8 23	Abattu (TN)
A 294	8–9: Donbaz 1998, Congress of Hittitology 3, 187			Sîn-apla-iddina (Tp)
A 300	Donbaz 2010, N.A.B.U. no. 68, 78	note		Abattu (TN)
A 305	Donbaz 1988a, JCS 40, 72 no. 5	note		Mušallim-Adad s. Salmānu-qarrād (TN)
A 320	Donbaz 2009, FS Parpola, 353–54 no. 1	barley loan	M 9 1	Aššur-šuma-uṣur s. o. Adad-mušēzib (Aub)
A 333	Donbaz 2009, FS Parpola, 357–60 no. 2	contract		
A 582	Weidner 1935/36, AfO 10, 42–43 no. 100 Donbaz 1969, IAMY 15/16	list	M 6 68	
A 602	Köcher 1954/56, AfO 17, 121	school text	M 3 2	
A 743	see A 1947			
A 748	Donbaz 2004, FS Grayson, 70 no. 2 Cancik-Kirschbaum 2013, LDAS 1, 66, 77–78 no. 3	summon letter	M 8 13	

Number	Literature	Genre	Origin	Eponym
A 845	Donbaz 2000, GS Cagni Llop 2012a, AuOr 30, 292	private letter		
A 850	Donbaz 2004, FS Grayson, 73–74 no. 6	letter order		
A 877	Donbaz 2004, FS Grayson, 73 no. 5	letter order		
A 981	Donbaz 1992, FS Alp, 121 no. 2 7', Donbaz 1998, Congress of Hittitology 3, 186	table		Aššur-rēša-iši (Ari)
A 983	Donbaz 1988a, JCS 40, 70 no. 3	note		Ištar-tuballissu (TN–Eku)
A 991	Donbaz 1998, Congress of Hittitology 3, 186			
A 1051	Donbaz/Harrak 1989, JCS 41, 217–18 no. 1	receipt		Kidin-Aššur (Tp)
A 1065	Donbaz 1998, Congress of Hittitology 3, 182 n13	note	M 4	Aššur-ba[?]issunu (Ad–Tp)
A 1100	Donbaz 2004, FS Grayson, 75 no. 8	letter order	M 8 25	
A 1123	Donbaz 1998, Congress of Hittitology 3, 183 n15 Llop 2003, Or 72, 208	note		Aššur-šuma-ēriš (Tp)
A 1177	10–11, Donbaz 1998, Congress of Hittitology 3, 187			Sîn-apla-iddina (Tp)
A 1476	Donbaz 2004, FS Grayson, 74–75 no. 7	letter order		
A 1587	Donbaz 1997, ArAn 3, 105 Donbaz 1998, Hittitology 3, 181 Llop 2015a, FS Wiggermann, 249			
A 1799	26–29: Donbaz 1998, Congress of Hittitology 3, 186	document	N 4 226	Enlil-nērārī s. o. Aššur-uballiṭ (En)
A 1947+743	MKA, 194 no. 95 8: Donbaz Fs Grayson, 72	letter report	M 8 15	
A 2031	Donbaz 1998, Congress of Hittitology 3, 186 (no lines)		N 4	
A 2429	Donbaz 2004, FS Grayson, 71 no. 3	letter order	M 8 27	Abattu (TN)
A 2686	1'–3', Donbaz 1998,			Bēlu-libur (Tp)

Number	Literature	Genre	Origin	Eponym
	Congress of Hittitology 3, 186			
A 2704	Brinkman/Donbaz 1985, ZA 75, 78–83 no. 1	letter order	M 11	Ubru (Sa)
A 2705	Donbaz 1991, FS Garelli, 78	letter order	M 11	
A 2824	Donbaz 1998, Congress of Hittitology 3, 185 Llop 2002, N.A.B.U. no. 35, 37			
A 2994	Brinkman/Donbaz 1985, ZA 75, 83–86 no. 2 Freydank 2009a, AoF 36, 68–69 Johnson 2013, RAI 56, 540–41 no. 14	testimony		Etel-pî-Aššur (TN)
A 3121	Donbaz 1988a, JCS 40, 69–70 no. 1	list	M 13	Enlil-nādin-apli (TN)
A 3211	Donbaz 1988b, SAAB 2/1, 5 n11 1–5: Donbaz 1988a, JCS 40, 70 no. 2	document	M 13 19	
A 3218	1'–8': Donbaz 1998, Congress of Hittitology 3, 186			Uṣur-namkūr-šarri (TN)
A 3310	Donbaz/Harrak 1989, JCS 41, 218 no. 2	contract		Kidin-Aššur (Tp)
A 3315	Donbaz/Harrak 1989, JCS 41, 224 no. 3			Aššur-nāṣir (Ead/Aub)
A 3316	Donbaz/Harrak 1989, JCS 41, 224 no. 4			

25.3 Tell Ar-Rimāḥ (TR siglum)[1]

Number	Literature	Genre	Eponym
TR 100	Deller/Saporetti 1970b, OrAnt 9, 287 2–3: Deller/Saporetti 1970a, OrAnt 9, 58	barley loan	[Abī-ilī] (Sa)
TR 101	Deller/Saporetti 1970b, OrAnt 9, 300 2: Deller/Saporetti 1970a, OrAnt 9, 58 4–5: Deller/Saporetti 1970a, OrAnt 9, 57	lead loan	Abī-ilī (Sa/TN)
TR 102	Deller/Saporetti 1970b, OrAnt 9, 289 4: Deller/Saporetti 1970a, OrAnt 9, 57	lead loan	Abī-ilī (Sa/TN)
TR 103			

[1] Copies and partial edition of tablets is found in Saggs 1968 and Wiseman 1968.

Number	Literature	Genre	Eponym
TR 104	Saporetti 1981, Mesopotamia 16, 18 4–7: Deller/Saporetti 1970a, OrAnt 9, 58	barley loan	
TR 105	Wilcke 1976, ZA 66, 208f	testament	
TR 106	25: Wilcke 1976, 210	barley debt	Bēr-šumu-lēšir (Sa)
TR 107		lead loan?	
TR 108	11–13: EMA, 78	onion loan	
TR 109	26–27: EMA, 77	lead loan	Aššur-mušēzib (TN)
TR 110	Saporetti 1981, Mesopotamia 16, 13 2–3: Deller/Saporetti 1970a, OrAnt 9, 58 20–21: EMA, 87	lead loan	Abī-ilī (Sa/TN)
TR 111	31–32: EMA, 93	mixed loan	Bēr-bēl-līte (Sa)
TR 112	29–31: EMA, 111	mixed loan	
TR 113		lead loan	
TR 114	15–18: Deller/Saporetti 1970a, OrAnt 9, 57	barley loan	
TR 115	Deller/Saporetti 1970a, OrAnt 9, 35 29–31: EMA, 108	barley loan	[…] s.o. Šamaš-tukultī
TR 116	unpublished	legal?	
TR 117	1'–7': Deller/Saporetti 1970a, OrAnt 9, 57 13' –14', 18':, Wiseman 1968, Iraq 30, 186 13'–14': Wilcke 1976, ZA 66, 222	division of inheritance	
TR 118		barley loan	
TR 119	1, 3–6: Faist 2001, AOAT 265, 126 n98 13–14: EMA, 103	barley loan	Ištu-ili-ašamšu (Adn?)
TR 120	unpublished		
TR 121			
TR 122	unpublished		
TR 123	- does not exist -		
TR 124	3: MATSH, 59	letter order	Nuzi period
TR 125		list of PNs	Nuzi period
TR 126a/b	unpublished		
TR 127	unpublished		
TR 128	unpublished		
TR 129	2'–3': Deller/Saporetti 1970a, OrAnt 9, 57	legal?	
TR 130	unpublished		
TR 131	unpublished		
TR 132			
TR 133	unpublished	witnesses/seals	
TR 134a		legal?	
TR 134b	unpublished		
TR 134c	unpublished	barley…	
TR 134d	unpublished		
TR 135a			
TR 135b	unpublished		
TR 135c			
TR 136	unpublished	letter	
TR 137		lead loan?	
TR 2000	unpublished		
TR 2001	21–22: EMA, 102	sale	Bēr-[…]
TR 2002	unpublished		
TR 2003	unpublished		

Number	Literature	Genre	Eponym
TR 2004	unpublished		
TR 2005	unpublished		
TR 2006			
TR 2007	unpublished		
TR 2008		sale of land?	
TR 2009	unpublished		
TR 2010	unpublished		
TR 2011	unpublished		
TR 2012	unpublished		
TR 2013	unpublished		
TR 2014	16–17: EMA, 124	receipt for barley	Qibi-Aššur (Sa/TN)
TR 2015	Deller/Saporetti 1970a, OrAnt 9, 290 12–13: EMA, 94	receipt for lead	Lullāyu (Sa)
TR 2016			
TR 2017		contract for lead	
TR 2018		contract for barley	
TR 2019	unpublished	letter	
TR 2020			
TR 2021+2051	21–22: EMA, 129	loan	Salmānu-šuma-uṣur (TN)
TR 2022	r. 1'–3': EMA, 91	sale? of house	Enlil-qarrād (Ead?)
TR 2023	unpublished		
TR 2024	21–22: EMA, 102		
TR 2025	14–15: EMA, 84	receipt for barley	Šamaš-tukultī (Adn?)
TR 2026	1–3: EMA, 107		Šunu-qardu (TN)
TR 2027	unpublished		
TR 2028	24–25: EMA, 115	šulmānu	Aššur-bēl-ilāni (TN)
TR 2029		letter	
TR 2030	11–12: EMA, 102	receipt	Bēr-šumu-lēšir (Sa)
TR 2031	18–19: EMA, 122	letter order	Uṣur-namkūr-šarri (TN)
TR 2032+2054		sale of property	
TR 2033	9–11: EMA, 90-91		Usāt-Marduk (Sa)
TR 2034	6–7: EMA,106	receipt for barley	Šamaš-mušēzib (Sa/TN)
TR 2035	unpublished		
TR 2036+2040		receipt	
TR 2037	Wilcke 1976, ZA 66, 225 Postgate 1979b, Iraq 41, 90 47–48: EMA, 109	testament	[...]-uṣur
TR 2038		letter order?	
TR 2039		receipt	
TR 2040	joined with TR 2036		
TR 2041	unpublished		
TR 2042	unpublished		
TR 2043	unpublished		

Number	Literature	Genre	Eponym
TR 2044	r. 1'–2': EMA, 112		
TR 2045		loan?	
TR 2046	unpublished		
TR 2047	unpublished		
TR 2048			
TR 2049		receipt for šarbu	
TR 2050	unpublished	lease of field	
TR 2051	joined with TR 2021		
TR 2052	Saporetti 1981, Mesopotamia 16, 10	loan	
TR 2053		receipt for šarbu	
TR 2054	joined with TR 2032		
TR 2055		loan	
TR 2056	EMA, 105		Libūr-zānin-Aššur (TN)
TR 2057a	Deller/Saporetti 1970a, OrAnt 9, 29 Postgate 2013, Bronze age bureaucracy, 263	loan of lead	Mušallim-Adad (TN)
TR 2057b	5'–6': EMA, 126 Deller/Saporetti 1970b, OrAnt 9, 292	contract	Mušallim-Adad (TN)
TR 2058	Deller/Saporetti 1970b, OrAnt 9, 293 15–17: EMA, 100	receipt of lead	Adad-šamšī (Sa)
TR 2059	Postgate 2013, Bronze age bureaucracy, 267 Postage 1983/84b, Mesopotamia 18/19, 233 Faist 2001, AOAT 265, 187 n184	tax payment	Adad-bēl-gabbe (TN)
TR 2060		receipt of onions	
TR 2061	Deller/Saporetti 1970a, OrAnt 9, 36 17–18: EMA, 112	loan	
TR 2062a	Deller/Saporetti 1970b, OrAnt 9, 294 4'–6': EMA, 83	contract	Mušabšiʾū-Sibitta (Sa)
TR 2062b	Deller/Saporetti 1970b, OrAnt 9, 294–95		
TR 2063a			
TR 2063b	unpublished		
TR 2063c	unpublished		
TR 2063d	unpublished		
TR 2063e	unpublished		
TR 2064			
TR 2065		receipt	
TR 2066	27–28: EMA, 99		Adad-bēl-gabbe (TN)
TR 2067	unpublished		
TR 2068	unpublished		
TR 2069a+2908	Deller/Saporetti 1970b, OrAnt 9, 295 18–20: EMA, 117	receipt for lead	
TR 2069b	unpublished		
TR 2069c	unpublished		
TR 2069d	unpublished		
TR 2069e	unpublished		
TR 2069f	unpublished		
TR 2070	unpublished		
TR 2071a	unpublished		
TR 2071b	unpublished		

Number	Literature	Genre	Eponym
TR 2071c	unpublished		
TR 2072	unpublished		
TR 2073	unpublished		
TR 2074	unpublished		
TR 2075	unpublished		
TR 2076	unpublished		
TR 2077	unpublished		
TR 2078			
TR 2079	unpublished		
TR 2080a	unpublished		
TR 2080b+2085	rd. 1’–2’: EMA, 73		Abattu (TN)
TR 2081		contract for lead	
TR 2082	unpublished		
TR 2083a-b-c+2084a+d	Postgate 1979b, Iraq 41, 92		Ilī-mu[…]
TR 2083d	unpublished		
TR 2083e	unpublished		
TR 2083f	unpublished		
TR 2084e	unpublished		
TR 2084f			
TR 2085	unpublished		
TR 2086		receipt	
TR 2087	10-16: Postgate 1982, Fs Diakonoff, 304 rd. 1’–2’: EMA, 119	contract	Nabû-bēla-uṣur (Sa)
TR 2088	unpublished		
TR 2089	unpublished		
TR 2090	r. 4’–5’: EMA, 87		Abī-ilī (Sa/TN)
TR 2091	unpublished		
TR 2092	unpublished		
TR 2093	unpublished		
TR 2094	unpublished		
TR 2095a			
TR 2095b			
TR 2096			
TR 2097	unpublished		
TR 2098	unpublished		
TR 2099	unpublished		
TR 2900	unpublished		
TR 2901	unpublished		
TR 2902	unpublished		
TR 2903	22–24: EMA,107	barley loan?	Šunu-qardū (TN)
TR 2904	17–18: EMA, 91	receipt for lead	Usāt-Marduk (Sa)
TR 2905	Deller/Saporetti 1970b, OrAnt 9, 296 13–15: EMA, 115		Aššur-bēl-ilāni (TN)
TR 2906	1–7: Jakob 2003, CM 29, 447 14’–15’: EMA, 122		Aššur-bēl-ilāni (TN)
TR 2907		loan of *šarbu*	
TR 2908	joined with TR 2069a		
TR 2909	r. 3’–5’: EMA, 105		Libūr-zānin-Aššur

Number	Literature	Genre	Eponym
			(TN)
TR 2910	21–22: EMA, 116	receipt of barley?	Aššur-dayyān (TN)
TR 2911	unpublished		
TR 2912	unpublished		
TR 2913	Saporetti 1981, Mesopotamia 16, 14 18-21, EMA, 81	loan of lead	Ištar-ēriš s.o. Salmānu-qarrād –Sa
TR 2914			
TR 2915a	unpublished		
TR 2915b	unpublished		
TR 3001	Deller/Saporetti 1970a, OrAnt 9, 37 20–21: EMA, 103	loan of barley	Ištu-ilī-ašamšu (Adn?)
TR 3002	Deller/Saporetti 1970a, OrAnt 9, 39 19–20: EMA, 103	loan of lead	Ištu-ilī-ašamšu - (Adn?)
TR 3003	1–8: Deller/Tsukimoto 1985, BaM 16, 325 12–14: EMA, 112	receipt for silver	
TR 3004	12'–14': Postgate 1982, FS Diakonoff, 309 n11 13'–14': Jakob 2003, CM 29, 72 n79	loan of lead	
TR 3005	1–8: Deller/Mayer/Sommerfeld 1987, Or 56, 180 9–11: EMA, 124–25	memo of grain	Qibi-Aššur (Sa/TN)
TR 3006	10, Postgate 1982, FS Diakonoff, 306 14–16: EMA,101	loan	Ina-pî-Aššur-lišlim (Sa)
TR 3007	Saporetti 1981, Mesopotamia 16, 10 25–27: EMA, 84	loan of barley	Ṣillī-Adad (Adn?)
TR 3008	5–7: EMA, 118	receipt for *šarbu*	Enlil-nādin-apli (TN)
TR 3009	1–3: EMA, 78	memo	Aššur-nādin-šume (Sa)
TR 3010	1-2, EMA, 100	memo of account	Adad-bēl-gabbe (TN)
TR 3011	Deller/Saporetti 1970b, OrAnt 9, 297 14–15: EMA, 94	loan of lead	Lullāyu (Sa)
TR 3012	Deller/Saporetti 1970a, OrAnt 9, 40 22–23: EMA, 79	loan of lead	Ilī-qarrād (Sa)
TR 3013	Saporetti 1981, Mesopotamia 16, 14 20–21: EMA, 117	loan of barley	Aššur-zēra-iddina (TN)
TR 3014	Saporetti 1981, Mesopotamia 16, 21 10–20: Aynard/Durand 1980, 31 l. 15–16: Postgate 1983/84, Mesopotamia 18/19, 233 27–28: EMA, 126	loan of barley	Mušallim-Adad (TN)
TR 3015	Saporetti 1981, Mesopotamia 16, 22 24–26: EMA, 125	loan of barley	Qibi-Aššur (Sa)
TR 3016	Deller/Saporetti 1970b, OrAnt 9, 298 13–15: EMA, 100	loan of lead	Adad-šumu-lēšir (Adn?)
TR 3017		census list?	Neo-Assyrian?
TR 3018		loan of lead	
TR 3019	Aynard/Durand 1980, Assur 3, 45 Postgate 1983/84, Mesopotamia 18/19, 233 Faist 2001, AOAT 265, 185-186 Jakob 2003, CM 29, 171-172	loan of lead	Nabû-bēla-uṣur (Sa)

Number	Literature	Genre	Eponym
	15-16: EMA, 120		
TR 3020		census of fields?	Neo-Assyrian?
TR 3021	Saporetti 1981, Mesopotamia 16, 9-10	loan of lead	
TR 3022	Saporetti 1981, Mesopotamia 16, 22 29–30: EMA, 125	loan of lead	Qibi-Aššur (Sa/TN)
TR 3023	5, 7: Postgate 1983/84, Mesopotamia 18/19, 233 9–11: EMA, 101	receipt of barley	Aššur-pirḫi-ēriš (Adn?)
TR 3024	4–10: Aynard/Durand 1980, Assur 3, 4 n1	census of males?	Neo-Assyrian?
TR 3025	5–8: Postgate 1983/84, Mesopotamia 18/19, 233 5–8: Faist 2001, AOAT 265, 190 n199 5–8: Jakob 2003, CM 29, 499 24–26: EMA, 106	security for loan	Mār-siki (= Masuku) (Adn?)
TR 3026	r. 1': EMA, 113	letter	
TR 3027	1–3: Faist 2001, AOAT 265, 187 n184 r. 2'–3': addional readings Postgate 1983/84, Mesopotamia 18/19, 233 r. 4'–5': EMA, 94	receipt?	Lullāyu (Sa)
TR 3028		loan	
TR 3029	11–13: EMA, 95	memo	Aššur-šad-nišēšu (Adn)
TR 3030	21–23: EMA, 79	loan of lead	Ibašši-ilī (Aub?/Adn?)
TR 3031	26-27, EMA, 108	loan? of lead	
TR 3032	unpublished		
TR 3033	unpublished		
TR 3034	unpublished		
TR 3035	unpublished		
TR 3036	Saporetti 1981, Mesopotamia 16, 22	contract re. land	
TR 3037	10'–12': EMA, 44	loan of barley	Abu-ṭāb (Aub)
TR 3038		loan	
TR 3039a			
TR 3039b		contract	Adad-bēl-gabbu? (TN)
TR 3039c			
TR 3040	unpublished		

25.4 Tell Ṣabī Abyaḍ (T siglum)

Number	Literature	Genre	Eponym
TabT03S-2	Maul 2005, ASJS 2, 18-19, 112 no. 1	fragment	
TabT05-11		disposition	Saggi'u (Nae)
TabT05A-43	Shibata forthcoming, FS Freydank 22–26: Shibata 2015, FS Wiggermann, 236	purchase	Bēr-kēna-šallim (A.n.apli–Eku)
Tab T05A-44+	Shibata forthcoming, FS Freydank	envelope	
TabT05-85	Shibata 2007, Al-Rāfidān 28, 70	receipt	Ašš[ur-…]
T 88-1	Jas 1990, Akkadica 67, 33–34	list	
T 88-3	Jas 1990, Akkadica 67, 34–35	list	

Number	Literature	Genre	Eponym
T 93-2	Minx, Die Sutäer, 85 no. 61	letter order	
T 93-3	Minx 2005, Die Sutäer, 85 no. 62 Wiggermann 2008, in Duistermaat, Pots and Potters, 561	letter order	
T 93-7	Wiggermann 2000, MOS 3, 209–10 no. 12 Jakob 2003, CM 29, 410–11	letter order	
T 93-20	18–23: Shibata 2015, FS Wiggermann, 239 23–27: CAD P, 413a		
T 93-54	Minx 2005, Die Sutäer, 97 no. 88	letter order	
T 96-3	Wiggermann 2000, MOS 3, 207 no. 8 Postgate 2013, Bronze age bureaucracy, 44-45	loan	Abattu (TN)
T 96-15	Minx 2005, Die Sutäer, 84 no. 60	letter report	
T 96-16/17	Wiggermann 2000, MOS 3, 207 nos. 6–7	list	Ninuʾāyu (TN)
T 96-23	Wiggermann 2000, MOS 3, 207 no. 9	note	
T 96-34	Minx 2005, Die Sutäer, 97 no. 87	note	
T 96-36	Wiggermann 2000, MOS 3, 208 no. 19 Bloch 2017, RAI 58, 123–26. 6–12: Llop/Shibata 2016, JCS 68, 71 13–30: Wiggermann 2000, MOS 3, 190 20–32: Minx 2005, Die Sutäer, 91 no. 78	letter order	
T 97-17	Wiggermann 2000, MOS 3, 209 no. 11 Llop 2012a, AuOr 30, 294	letter order	
T 97-26	8, 14–15: Faist/Llop 2012, AOAT 394, 24		
T 98-19	Minx 2005, Die Sutäer, 96 no. 85		
T 98-33	Wiggermann 2000, MOS 3, 205 no. 1		Salmānu-aḫa-iddina (TN– Eku)
T 98-38	Wiggermann 2000, MOS 3, 206 no. 3		
T 98-44	Wiggermann 2000, MOS 3, 206 no. 4		
T 98-58	Minx 2005, Die Sutäer, 96 no. 86		
T 98-105	Wiggermann 2000, MOS 3, 206 no. 5		
T 98-110	Minx 2005, Die Sutäer, 98 no. 89	loan	Adad-nādin-šumē (TN–Eku)
T 98-115	Wiggermann 2000, MOS 3, 205 no. 2	list	
T 98-131	Wiggermann 2008, in Duistermaat, Pots and Potters, 559		
T 02-32	Wiggermann 2006, Iconography, 94, 212 Freydank 2009b, FS Saporetti 19–37: Bloch 2012, Studies in MA chronology, 162-163	letter report	
T 04-7	Minx 2005, Die Sutäer, 95 no. 83		
T 04-13	Minx, Die Sutäer, 94 no. 82 Wiggermann 2010 Phoenix 56/1–2, 38	letter report	Adad-bān-kala (TN–Eku)
T 04-35	Minx 2005, Die Sutäer, 95 no. 84		
T 04-37	Minx 2005, Die Sutäer, 91–92 no. 79 Wiggermann 2010 Phoenix 56/1–2, 29, 55–56	treaty	

25.5 Tell Ṭābān

Number	Literature	Genre	Eponym
TabT03S-2	Maul 2005, ASJS 2, 18-19, 112 no. 1	fragment	
TabT05-11		disposition	Saggiʾu (Nae)
TabT05A-43	22–26: Shibata 2015, FS Wiggermann, 236		
TabT05-69	Shibata 2017, FS Postgate		
TabT05-85	Shibata 2007, Al-Rāfidān 28, 70	receipt	Ašš[ur-…]
TabT05a-134	Shibata 2015, ZA 105	letter order	Ellil-ašarēd (Sa)
TabT05a-151	Shibata 2012, RAI 54, 494–495 Bloch 2012, Studies in MA chronology, 103 Llop/Shibata 2016, JCS 68, 87–88	document	Aššur-nādin-šumē (Sa)
TabT05-152+	Llop/Shibata 2016, JCS 68, 88	envelope	
TabT05-182	Shibata 2007, Al-Rāfidān 28, 70	receipt	Ištar-ēriš (Sa)
TabT05-191	Shibata forthcoming, Feschrift Freydank	purchase	Adad-bān-kali (Aššnīr III/Eku)
TabT05A-192+	Shibata forthcoming, Feschrift Freydank	envelope	
TabT05A-609	16–18: Llop/Shibata 2016, JCS 68, 70		
TabT05A-623	Shibata 2007, Al-Rāfidān 28, 71		
TabT07A-2	Shibata/Yamada 2009, Excavations at Tell Taban, 88–89	fragment	Mudammeq-Bēl (Tp)
TabT09-47	Yamada 2011, RA 105, 61–84	adoption	(Ḫana)

25.6 Deir Ez-Zawr (DeZ siglum): texts from Tell Aš-Šēḫ Ḥamad

Number	Literature	Genre	Eponym
DeZ 2211	1–4: Jakob 2003, CM 29, 370 7–10: Jakob 2003, CM 29, 370 n63		
DeZ 2218	1–4: Jakob 2003, CM 29, 339 n132		
DeZ 2220	Röllig 2002, AOAT 281, 582 no. 4	note	Nabû-bēla-uṣur (Sa)
DeZ 2495	Röllig 2002, AOAT 281, 584 no. 5	note	Usāt-Marduk (Sa)
DeZ 2499	Röllig 2002, AOAT 281, 582 no. 2	note	Aššur-da'issunu (Sa)
DeZ 2503	Röllig 2002, AOAT 281, 581 no. 3	note	Lullāyu (Sa)
DeZ 2517	Röllig 2002, AOAT 281, 581 no. 1	note	Ina-pî-Aššur-lišlim (Sa)
DeZ 2521	Röllig 1983, Damaszener Mitteilungen 1 Jakob 2003, CM 29, 205	itinerary	Ina-Aššur-šumī-aṣbat (TN)
DeZ 2523	10–12: Jakob 2003, CM 29, 60 n24		
DeZ 3281	Röllig 1997, Assyria 1995		Enlil-nādin-apli (TN)
DeZ 3309+	5: MATSH, 184 12–14, 20–23: Jakob 2003, 270 n61–62		
DeZ 3358	9–11: Faist 2001, AOAT 265, 193 n210		
DeZ 3389	1–13: Jakob 2003, CM 29, 363		
DeZ 3391	9–10: Jakob 2003, CM 29, 199 n31		
DeZ 3400	1–2, 4–6: Jakob 2003, CM 29, 425 n25		
DeZ 3407	1, 4–9: Jakob 2003, CM 29, 425 n26		
DeZ 3441	Röllig 2002, AOAT 281, 587–88 no. 10		Urad-ilāni (TN)
DeZ 3810	Röllig 2002, AOAT 281, 587 no. 9		Aššur-nādin-šumē (Sa)
DeZ 3847/2	3–4: Jakob 2003, CM 29, 14 n121		

Number	Literature	Genre	Eponym
DeZ 4022	1–4: Jakob 2003, CM 29, 328 n120 9–11: MATSH, 16 9–11: Llop/Shibata 2016, JCS 68, 68		
DeZ 4029	Röllig 2002, AOAT 281, 585 no. 6		Adad-bēl-gabbe (TN)

25.7 Minor Publications

Number	Literature	Genre	Origin	Eponym
ADD 713	Postgate 1993, SAAB 7		Aššur	
AO 19.227	Aynard/Durand 1980, Assur 3/1, 29–30 no. 6 Saporetti 1981, Mesopotamia 16, 22	letter report	M 8 14	Aššur-nādin-apli (TN)
AO 19.228	Aynard/Durand 1980, Assur 3/1, 5 no. 2 Saporetti 1981, Mesopotamia 16, 11	lead loan	Aššur	Bēr-nādin-aḫḫe (Arn)
AO 19.229	Aynard/Durand 1980, Assur 3/1, 14 no. 3 1–16: Jakob 2003, CM 29, 231–32	lead loan	Aššur	Aššur-qarrād (EAd/Aub)
AO 20.153	Aynard/Durand 1980, Assur 3/1, 18 no. 4 13–14: Minx 2005, Die Sutäer, 88 no. 69	barley loan	Aššur	Aššur-dayyān (TN)
AO 20.154	Aynard/Durand 1980, Assur 3/1, 19 no. 5	exchange	Aššur	Aššur-ēriš (Aub)
AO 20.155	Aynard/Durand 1980, Assur 3/1, 29–30 no. 6 Saporetti 1981, Mesopotamia 16, 22		Kulišḫinaš	Nabû-bēla-uṣur (Sa)
AO 20.156	Aynard/Durand 1980, Assur 3/1, 35 no. 7 Saporetti 1981, Mesopotamia 16, 14	wheat loan	Kulišḫinaš	Libur-zānin-Aššur (TN)
AO 20.157	Aynard/Durand 1980, Assur 3/1, 36 no. 8 Faist 2001, AOAT 265, 186 Minx 2005, Sutäer, 72 no. 33 1–8: Jakob 2003, CM 29, 171 n10	document	Kulišḫinaš	Ittabši-dēn-Aššur? (Sa)
AO 21.380	Aynard/Durand 1980, Assur 3/1, 37-8 no. 9 Saporetti 1981, Mesopotamia 16, 17	cow loan	Kulišḫinaš	Aššur-kettī-ide (Sa)
AO 21.381	Aynard/Durand 1980, Assur 3/1, 43 no. 10	receipt	Kulišḫinaš	Aššur-kettī-ide (Sa)
AO 21.382	Aynard/Durand 1980, Assur 3/1, 44 no. 11 Faist 2001, AOAT 265, 187 Minx 2005, Die Sutäer, 71		Kulišḫinaš	Usāt-Marduk (Sa)

Number	Literature	Genre	Origin	Eponym
	no. 32:1-13 1–5: Jakob 2003, CM 29, 171 n10			
AO 28.365	LVUH, 2		TŠḪ	
BE 17 77	Von Soden 1957/58b, AfO 18, 369	letter fragment	Nippur	En
BE 17 91	Von Soden 1957/58b, AfO 18, 368 Faist 2001, AOAT 265, 19–22	Letter fragment	Nippur	En
AuOrS 1 104			TŠḪ	Qibi-Aššur (Sa/TN)
AuOrS 1 105	1–10: Minx 2005, Die Sutäer, 89 no. 74		TŠḪ	Salmānu-šuma-uṣur (TN)
AuOrS 1 106	= LVUH 83		TŠḪ	
	Aynard/Durand 1980, Assur 3/1, 46–48 no. 12		Šuri	Ištar-ēriš (Sa)
BM 103200	Fincke/Llop 2017, FS Postgate, 314–16 no. 1	Delivery note	M 7?	Ibrī-šarri (Tp)
BM 103203	Fincke 2014, AoF 41, 23–28 no. 4 Freydank 2016b, StMes 3, 96–97 no. 3	letter order	(Nuzi-style)	Kidin-Kube (Aub)
BM 103207	Fincke/Llop 2017, FS Postgate, 316–18 no. 2	Delivery note	M 7?	
BM 103395	King 1912, CT 33 pl. 15b Panayotov/Llop 2013, ArOr 81		Aššur?	Amurru-ma-ilī (Aub)
BM 108924	Postgate/Collon 1999/2001, SAAB 13, 2–4 no. 2	purchase	M 9	Enlil-taklāk (Adn?)
BM 108943	Postgate/Collon 1999/2001, SAAB 13, 7 no. 3			
BM 108960	Postgate/Collon 1999/2001, SAAB 13, 8 no. 4	delivery		Sarniqu (TN)
BM 108965	Postgate/Collon 1999/2001, SAAB 13, 1–2 no. 1	delivery		Usāt-Marduk (Sa)
BM 123367	Millard 1970, Iraq 32, 173 Postgate 1973, Iraq 35, 16–18 no. 3		Nineveh	BU.UT-nu
C 146 TF 3168	Chambon 1998, MDOG 140, 130-131	letter fragment	Tell Faḫariyya	Eru-apla-iddina (TN–Eku)
Cohen/Llop 2017	Cohen/Llop 2017, ZA 107	private letter		
CTMMA 1 99	Postgate 1988, CTMMA 1, 144–46 no. 99	allocation		Aššur-nādin-apli (TN)
CTMMA 1 100	Postgate 1988, CTMMA 1, 146–47 no. 100	memorandum		Aššur-dā'issunu (Sa)
CTMMA 1 101	Postgate 1988, CTMMA 1, 147–48 no. 101			Aššur-dā'issunu (Sa)
HSM 1036688	Tsukimoto 2011, RA 105	purchase	(Ḫana)	Aššur-kēna-šallim (Ari)
IM 60240	Laessøe 1959, Summer 15 Pl. 1	letter order	Tell Bazmusian	

Number	Literature	Genre	Origin	Eponym
	1–2: Laessøe 1959, Sumer 15, 16 n1 1–3: MATSH, 54 n26 r. 2': MATSH, 67 bottom r. 4': Kouwenberg 2010, 310			
IM 60241A	Laessøe 1959, Summer 15 Pl. 2.1	letter	Tell Bazmusian	
IM 60241B	Laessøe 1959, Summer 15 Pl. 2.2	letter	Tell Bazmusian	
IM 61025	Laessøe 1959, Summer 15 Pl. 3	letter	Tell Bazmusian	
IM 61026	Laessøe 1959, Summer 15 Pl. 4	letter	Tell Bazmusian	
IM 61027	Laessøe 1959, Summer 15 Pl. 5.1 7: Laessøe 1959, Sumer 15, 16 n6 8: Laessøe 1959, Sumer 15, 16	letter	Tell Bazmusian	
IM 61028	Laessøe 1959, Summer 15 Pl. 5.2	letter	Tell Bazmusian	
K 10135	Postgate 1973, Iraq 35, 19–20 no. 4	laws	Nineveh	
K9-T1	Salvini 1998, Tell Barri/Kaḫat 2, 187–88 no. 1	letter order	Tell Barri	
K9-T2	Salvini 1998, Tell Barri/Kaḫat 2, 189–90 no. 2	lexical list	Tell Barri	
K9-T3	Salvini 1998, Tell Barri/Kaḫat 2, 190–92 no. 3	lists of PNs	Tell Barri	
K21-E33886	Salvini 2004, Tell Barri/Kaḫat 2001, 147–49	receipt	Tell Barri	Emide (?)
LB 1848	Driel/Jas 1989/90, JEOL 31		Aššur?	Adad-šamšī (Sa)
LB 253	Hallo 1973, FS Böhl Jakob 2003, CM 29, 193 Cancik-Kirschbaum 2013, LDAS 1, 68, 79–80 no. 7	receipt	Aššur?	Ištar-ēriš (Sa)
MAH 15854	Postgate 1979a, Assur 2/4, 2		Aššur?	
MAH 16086	Postgate 1979a, Assur 2/4, 3–7 MARV 3, 9 no. 5		Aššur?	
MAH 16467	Postgate 1979a, Assur 2/4, 7 Jakob 2003, CM 29, 479	collection?	Aššur?	Aššur-da'issunu (Sa)
MAH 16130	Postgate 1979a, Assur 2/4, 8		Aššur?	
MCS 2 1	6: Faist 2001, 193 n210	letter order		Tūr-kēnu (?)
MCS 2 2	BAI, 34, 74 Postgate 2013, Bronze age bureaucracy, 226	letter order	M 11 62	Tukultī-Ninurta (TN)
Ni. 669	Von Soden 1957/58b, AfO 18, 370	royal letter	Nippur	En
NP 46	Hameeuw 2012, OLA 220, 273–75 Llop/Luukko 2014, JNES 73	letter order		

Number	Literature	Genre	Origin	Eponym
OIP 79 1	Güterbock 1958, OIP 79 (plate 81)	letter$^?$ fragment	Tell Faḫariyya	
OIP 79 2	Güterbock 1958, OIP 79, 88 no. 2 10–12: MARV 9, 5 no. 20	letter order	Tell Faḫariyya	
OIP 79 3	Güterbock 1958, OIP 79, 88 no. 3 14–20, MARV 9, 5 no. 20	letter order	Tell Faḫariyya	
OIP 79 4	Güterbock 1958, OIP 79, 88–89 no. 4	letter order	Tell Faḫariyya	
OIP 79 5	Güterbock 1958, OIP 79, 89 no. 5	disposition	Tell Faḫariyya	Mudammeq-Nusku (Adn$^?$)
OIP 79 6	Güterbock 1958, OIP 79, 89 no. 5	division of inheritence	Tell Faḫariyya	Mudammeq-Nusku (Adn$^?$)
OIP 79 7	Güterbock 1958, OIP 79 (plate 84) no. 7 r. 2'–3': EMA, 101	fragment	Tell Faḫariyya	Ina-pî-Aššur-lišlim (Sa)
OIP 79 8	Güterbock 1958, OIP 79 (plate 84) no. 8 r. 1'–2': EMA, 101	fragment	Tell Faḫariyya	Ina-pî-Aššur-lišlim (Sa)
OIP 79 9	9–11: EMA, 101	note	Tell Faḫariyya	Ina-pî-Aššur-lišlim (Sa)
OIP 79 10	Güterbock 1958, OIP 79, 90 no. 10		Tell Faḫariyya	Mušabšiʾū-Sibitta (Sa)
OIP 79 11	Güterbock 1958, OIP 79, 90 no. 11 Llop 2004, N.A.B.U. no. 65, 66 6–8: Faist/Llop 2012, AOAT 394, 24	note	Tell Faḫariyya	[...]
OIP 79 12	Güterbock 1958, OIP 79 (plate 85) no. 12	fragment	Tell Faḫariyya	
RA 19	Beckman 1996, HANE M 2, 32-34 Deller 1999, BKA 104 6, H. 1-2, Tsukimoto 1998, WO 29, 186 11, H. 1-2, Faist 2001, AOAT 265, 171 n24		Emar$^?$	Bēr-nāṣir - Nae
RA 92	Beckman 1996, HANE M 2, 116-117 2, Faist 2001, AOAT 265, 145 n3 4, Faist 2001, AOAT 265, 146 n4 LVUH, 2		TŠḪ$^?$	Šerrīya – Sa/TN
RIAA 311	BAI, 47, 85	disposition	M 11	Mušallim-Aššur – Sa/TN
RIAA 314	BAI, 35, 74	note	M 11	Bēr-šumu-lēšir (Sa)
Rm 376	Lambert 1965, AS 16	incantation	Nimrud	
RS 06.198	AO 18.889 Thureau-Dangin 1935, Syria 16	diplomatic letter	Ugarit	

Number	Literature	Genre	Origin	Eponym
	Jakob 2003, CM 29, 301–3			
RS 18.54a	Nougayrol 1956, PRU 4, 228 8', 13', 15'–16': Aro 1957/58, AfO 18, 423	diplomatic letter	Ugarit	
RS 18.268	Nougayrol 1956, PRU 4, 229	diplomatic letter	Ugarit	
RS 19.122	Nougayrol 1956, PRU 4, 289	diplomatic letter	Ugarit	
RS 20.18	Nougayrol 1968, Ugaritica 5, 83–85, 382 no. 22 Cochavi-Rainey 2003, AOAT 289, 43–46	diplomatic letter	Ugarit	
RS 34.165	Lackenbacher, 1982, RA 76 Huehnergard 1997b, Syria 74, 220 Schwemer 2006, TUAT NF 3, 254–56	diplomatic letter	Ugarit	TN
TIM 4 45	Saporetti 1968, OrAnt 7 Veenhof 1982, FS Kraus, 362 n4	marriage contract		Urad-Šerūa
VS 1 102	MKA, 119 no. 53		Aššur	
VS 1 103	MKA, 169 no. 81		Aššur	Abi-ilī (Sa/TN)
VS 1 104	MKA, 70 no. 24	disposition	Aššur	Ninuʾāyu (TN/Tp)
VS 1 105	MKA, 192 no. 192 de Ridder/Zomer 2016	letter order	Aššur	
YBC 12860	Machinist 1982, Assur 3/2, 3–5 no. 1	loan	Kulišḫinaš	Nabû-bēla-uṣur (Sa)
YBC 12861	Machinist 1982, Assur 3/2, 6–8 no. 2		Kulišḫinaš	Qibi-Aššur (Sa/TN)
YBC 12862	Machinist 1982, Assur 3/2, 8-10 no. 3		Kulišḫinaš	
YBC 12863	Machinist 1982, Assur 3/2, 10 no. 4		Kulišḫinaš	Ištar-ēriš (Sa)
YBC 12864	Machinist 1982, Assur 3/2, 11–12 no. 5		Kulišḫinaš	

25.8 Texts referred to after author

Number	Literature	Genre	Origin	Eponym
Kümmel 1989	Kümmel 1989, ZA 79 Podany 2002, The Land of Ḫana, 151–53 no. 17	purchase	(Ḫana)	Libūr-zānin-Aššur (TN)
Lambert 1969	Lambert 1969, Iraq 31	incantation	Aššur?	
Faist 2001, 251f	Faist 2001, AOAT 265, 251–52	letter report	Emar?	
Fales 1989 59	Fales 1989, Prima dell'Alfabeto, 191–92 no. 59 Fales 1989, SAAB 3 LVUH, 2		TŠḪ	Qibi-Aššur (Sa/TN)

Number	Literature	Genre	Origin	Eponym
Fales 1989 69	Fales 1989, Prima dell'Alfabeto, 193–94 no. 60	list	Aššur?	
Franke/Wilhelm 1985	Franke/Wilhelm 1985	adoption		Adad-rēša-iši (Tp)
George 1988 1	George 1988, Iraq 50, 25–30 no. 1. Freydank 1991, AoF 18, 223 no. 5	edict	Aššur?	Sa
George 1988 2	George 1988, Iraq 50, 30–32 no. 2		Aššur?	Mušallim-Adad (TN)
Hall 1983	Hall 1983, ZA 73 1–14: Faist 2001, AOAT 265, 191 9–14: Deller 1984, ZA 74, 235	letter order	M 8 28	Abattu (TN)
Jankowaska 1962	Jankowska 1962, VDI 80 Saporetti 1966, Or 35 Jankowska 1967, Or 36 Saporetti 1981, Mesopotamia 16, 16–17 11–12: Saporetti 1967, Or 36	loan of barley	Aššur	Bēr-nādin-aḫḫē (Arn)
Maul 2004 1	Maul 2004, HSAO 9, 2–5 no. 1	note	Kulišḫinaš	Mušēzib-Aššur (Ari)
Maul 2004 2	Maul 2004, HSAO 9, 5–6 no. 2 4, 7: Freydank 2012b, OLZ 107, 111–12	note	Kulišḫinaš	
Maul 2004 2	Maul 2004, HSAO 9, 6–9 no. 3	list of PNs	Kulišḫinaš	
Postgate 1973 1	Postgate 1973, Iraq 35, 14–15 no. 1 BAI, 46, 84 Postgate 2013, Bronze age bureaucracy, 225–26	note	M 11 63	Usāt-Marduk (Sa)
Postgate 1973 2	Postgate 1973, Iraq 35, 15–16 no. 2	loan?	Aššur	Adab-bān-kala (EAd/Aub)
Postgate 1994	Postgate 1994, SAAB 8 6–r. 2': Pedersén 1997, MDOG 129	memorandum	Aššur	Bēr-išmanni (TN)
Snell 1983/84	Snell 1983/84, Abr-Nahrain 22	testament	El-Qiṭār	
Tsukimoto 1992 A	Tsukimoto 1992, WO 23, 22–25 no. A		TŠḤ	Enlil-ašarēd (Sa)
Tsukimoto 1992 B	Tsukimoto 1992, WO 23, 26–31 no. B		TŠḤ	Šerrīya (Sa)
Tsukimoto 1992 C	Tsukimoto 1992, WO 23, 31–34 no. C		TŠḤ	Qibi-Aššur (Sa)
Tsukimoto 1992 D	Tsukimoto 1992, WO 23, 33–38 no. D	letter report	TŠḤ	Ina-aššur-suma-aṣbat (TN)
Wilhelm 1997	Wilhelm 1997, AOAT 247	letter order		Ištar-ēriš (Sa)
Whiting 1988	Whiting 1988, SAAB 2 Jakob 2003, CM 29, 430	note	Emar?	

Chapter 26: Bibliography

Abusch, T.: *The Magical Ceremony Maqlû: A Critical Edition*. Leiden/Boston: Brill, 2016.

Adler, H-P.: *Das Akkadische des Königs Tušratta von Mitanni*. AOAT 201. Neukirchen-Vluyn: Neukirchener Verlag, 1976.

Aitchison, J.: *Language Change, Progress or Decay?*, 3rd edition. Cambridge: Cambridge University Press, 2001.

Al-Fatlawee, S. A. E. J.: (*Laysa*) in the Semitic Language. A linguistic originating Study, *Sumer* 53 (2005/6) 207–32.

Al-Ubaid, I. J.: *Unpublished Cuneiform Texts from Old Babylonia Period Diyala Region, Tell Muhammed*. MA thesis Baghdad 1983.

Aro, J.: Abnormal Plene Writings in Akkadian Texts, *StOr* 19:11 (1953) 1–19.

—: *Studien zur Mittelbabylonischen Grammatik*. StOr 20. Helsinki: Societas Orientalis Fennica, 1955a.

—: Review of BVW, BiOr 12/3–4 (1955b) 132.

—: *Glossar zu den Mittelbabylonischen Briefen*. StOr 22. Helsinki: Societas Orientalis Fennica, 1957.

—: Review of PRU 4, *AfO* 18 (1957/58) 421–23.

—: *Die Akkadischen Infinitivkonstruktionen*. StOr 26 Helsinki: Societas Orientalis Fennica, 1961.

—: Review of AbB 3 & 4, *OLZ* 66/5–6 (1971) 245–52.

—: Review of UGM, *ZA* 62/2 (1972) 274–76.

—: Pronunciation of the "Emphatic" Consonants in Semitic Languages, *StOr* 47 (1977) 5–18.

Artzi, P.: EA 16, *AoF* 24/2 (1997) 320–36.

Aynard, M. J./Durand, J. M.: Documents d`Epoque Medio-Assyrienne, *Assur* 3/1 (1980) 1–63.

Badawi, E./Carter, M.G./Gully, A.: *Modern Written Arabic, a Comprehensive Grammar*. Abingdon: Routledge Taylor & Francis Group, 2004.

Balkan, K.: Kassiten Studien 1: *Die Sprache der Kassiten*. AOS 37. New Haven: American Oriental Society, 1954.

Bar-Am, M.: *Studies of Business Letters from Cappadocian Cuneiform Texts*. Diss. Yale, 1935.

—: The Subjunctive in Cappadocian Texts, *Or* 7 (1938) 12–31.

Barjamovic, G./Hertel, T./Larsen, M. T.: *Ups and Downs at Kanesh - Chronology, History and Society in the Old Assyrian Period*. OAAS 5. PIHANS 120. Leiden: Nederlands Instituut voor het Nabije Oosten, 2012.

Beckman, G.: *Texts from the Vicinity of Emar in the Collection of Jonathan Rosen*. HANE M 2. Padova: Sargon, 1996.

—: *Hittite Diplomatic Texts*, 2nd edition. WAW 7. Atlanta: Scholars press, 1999.

Beckman, G./Foster, B. J.: Assyrian Scholarly Texts in the Yale Babylonian Collection, in: *A Scientific Humanist: Studies in Memory of Abraham Sachs*, Occasional Publications of the Samuel Noah Kramer Fund 9, eds. E. Leichty/M. d. Ellis/P. Gerardi, 1–26. Philadelphia: University Museum, 1988.

Blasberg, M.: *Keilschrift in Aramäischer Umwelt: Untersuchungen zur Spätbabylonischen Orthographie*. Diss. Köln, 1997.

Blau, J.: *A Grammar of Biblical Hebrew*. Porta NS 12. Wiesbaden: Harrassowitz Verlag, 1993.

—: *Phonology and Morphology of Biblical Hebrew, an Introduction*. Linguistic studies in Ancient West Semitic 2. Winona Lake: Eisenbrauns, 2012

Bloch, Y.: *Studies in Middle Assyrian Chronology and its Implications for the History of the Ancient Near East in the 13th Century B.C.E.* Diss. Jerusalem, 2012.
—: *qubbatu, qubbutu* "mourning, wailing", *N.A.B.U.*/28 (2013) 46–50.
—: Nomads and the Middle Assyrian State Administration: A New Interpretation of a Letter from Tell Sheikh Hamad, in: *Private and State in the Ancient Near East Proceedings of the 58th Rencontre Assyriologique Internationale at Leiden, 16-20 July 2012*, eds. R. de Boer/J. G. Dercksen, 109–31. Winona Lake: Eisenbrauns, 2017.
Brinkman, J. A.: Foreign Relations of Babylonia from 1600 to 625 B. C.: The Documentary Evidence, AJA 72 (1972) 271–81.
Brinkman, J. A./Donbaz, V.: Two Middle Assyrian Texts from Assur, *ZA* 75/1 (1985) 78–86.
Brockelmann, C.: *Arabische Grammatik*. 14. Auflage. Porta AS 4. Wiesbaden: Harrassowitz Verlag, 1960a.
—: *Syrische Grammatik*. 8. Auflage. Porta AS 5. Wiesbaden: Harrassowitz Verlag, 1960b.
Bryce, T. R.: *The Kingdom of the Hittites*, new edition. Oxford: University Press, 2005.
Buccellati, G.: The State of the Stative, in: *Fucus: a semitic/afrasian Gathering in Remberence of Albert Ehrman*. Amsterdam Studies in the Theory and History of linguistic Science 58, ed. Y. L. Arbeitman, 153-189. John Benjamins Publishing Company: Amsterdam/Philadelphia, 1988.
—: Akkadian and Amorite Phonology, in: *Phonology of Asia and Africa,* Volume 1, ed. A. S. Kaye, 3–38. Winona Lake: Eisenbrauns, 1997.
Cancik-Kirschbaum, E.: lú*sāpi'u/sēpû*: eine akkadische Berufsbezeichnung aus dem Bereich der Textilherstellung, in: *Munuscula Mesopotamica: Festschrift für Johannes Rechner*, AOAT 267, eds. B. Böck/E. Cancik-Kirschbaum/T. Richter, 81–93. Münster: Ugarit, 1999.
—: Middle Assyrian Administrative Documents and Diplomatics: Preliminary Remarks towards an Analysis of Scribal Norms and Habits, in: *Palaeography and Scribal Practices in Syro-Palestine and Anatolia in the Late Bronze Age,* PIHANS 119, ed. E. Devecchi, 19–32. Leiden: Nederlands Instituut voor het Nabije Oosten, 2012.
—: Middle Assyrian Summonses: The Epistolary Format in Judicial Procedures, in: *The Letter. Law, State, Society and the Epistolary Format in the Ancient World Proceedings of a Colloquium held at the American Academy in Rome 28–30.9.2008*, ed. U. Yiftach-Firanko, 61–81. Wiesbaden: Harrassowitz Verlag, 2013.
Catagnoti, A.: *La Grammatica della Lingua di Ebla.* Quaderni di Semitistica 29. Florence: Dipartimento di Scienze dell'Antichità, 2012.
Chamber, J. K./Trudgill, P.: *Dialectology*, 2nd edition. Cambridge: Cambridge University Press, 2004.
Chambon, G.: Appendix I in D. Bonatz/B. Peter/A. Gilibert/C. Jauss., Bericht über die erste und zweite Grabungskampagne in Tell Fekheriye 2006 und 2007, *MDOG* 140 (2008) 130–31.
Chang, K. W.: *Dichtungen der Zeit Tukulti-Ninurta I von Assyrien*. Seoul: Sung Kwang, 1981.
Chiera, E./Speiser, E. A.: A New Factor in the History of the Ancient East, *The Annual of the American Schools of Oriental Research* 6 (1924/25) 75–92.
Cifola, B.: *Analysis of Variants in the Assyrian Royal Titulary from the Origins to Tiglathpilesar III.* Instituto Universitario Orientalie. Dipartimento di Studi Asiatici 4. Napoli: Istituto Universitario Orientale, 1995.
Cochavi-Rainey, Z.: *The Alashia Texts from the 14th and 13th Centuries BCE.* AOAT 289. Münster: Ugarit-Verlag, 2003.
—: *The Akkadian Dialect of Egyptian Scribes in the 14th and 13th Centuries BCE*. AOAT 374. Münster: Ugarit-Verlag, 2011.
Cohen, E.: Focus Marking in Old Babylonian, *WZKM* 91 (2001) 85–104.
—: *The Modal System of Old Babylonian*. HSS 56. Winona Lake: Eisenbrauns, 2005.
Cohen, Y./Llop, J.: A Private Middle Assyrian Letter Sent by Pilta-ādur to Nabbānu (with an Aphorism drawn from the World of Medicine), *ZA* 107/1 (2017) 105–110.

Cooper, J./Schwartz, G./Westbrook, R.: A Mittani-Era Tablet from Umm el-Marra, *SCCNH* 15 (2005) 41–56.
Dahood, M./Deller, K./Köbert, R.: Comparative Semitics, Some Remarks on a Recent Publication, *Or* 34/4 (1965) 35–44.
Dalley, S./Walker, C. B. F./Hawkins, J. D.: *The Old Babylonian Tablets from Tell al Rimah*. London: British School of Archaeology in Iraq, 1976.
Degen, R.: *Altaramäische Grammatik der Inschriften des 10.–8. Jh. v. Chr.* Wiesbaden: Steiner Verlag, 1969.
Deller, K.: *Lautlehre des Neuassyrischen*. Diss. Vienna, 1959.
—: Zur Terminologie neuassyrischer Urkunden, *WZKM* 57 (1961) 29–42.
—: Studien zur neuassyrischen Orthographie, *Or* 31/2 (1962) 186–96.
—: Neuassyrisches aus Sultantepe, *Or* 34/4 (1965) 457–77.
—: Notes Brèves no. 5, *RA* 61 (1967) 189.
—: Assyrisch *um/nzarḫu* und Hebräisch *ʾäzraḥ*, *ZA* 74/2 (1984) 235–39.
—: Review of MARV 2, *AfO* 34 (1987) 58–66.
—: Keilschrifttexte (ḤT 1 - ḤT 11), in: *Tall Al-Ḥamīdīya 2*, OBO Series Archaeologica 6, eds. S. Eichler/M. Wäfler/D. Warburton, 325–35. Freiburg/Schweiz: Universitätsverl, 1990.
—: Aus dem mittelassyrischen Pfandrecht: Ersatz eines Pfändlings durch eine andere, bessere qualifizierte Person, in: *Urkunden und Urkundenformulare im Klassischen Altertum und in den orientalistischen Kulturen*, ed. R. G: Khoury, 29-36. Heidelberg: Universitätsverlag Winter, 1999.
Deller, K./Finkel, I. L.: A Neo-Assyrian Inventory Tablet of Unknown Provenance, *ZA* 74/1 (1984) 76–91
Deller, K./Mayer, W. R./Sommerfeld, W., Akkadische Lexikographie: CAD N_1, *Or* 56/2 (1987) 176–218.
Deller, K./Parpola, S.: Neuassyrisch "unser Herr" = *bēlīni*, nich **bēlni*, *Or* 66/2 (1966) 121–22.
Deller, K./Postgate, J. N.: Nachträge und Verbesserungen zu RGTC 5, *AfO* 32 (1985) 68–76.
Deller, K./Saporetti, C.: Documenti Medio-Assiri Redatti per Annullare un Precente Contratto, *OrAnt* 9 (1970a) 29–59
—: Documenti Medio-Assiri Redatti a Titolo di Ricevuta Dietro Parziale Adempimento di un Debito, *OrAnt* 9 (1970b) 285–314
Deller, K./Tsukimoto, A.: Ein mittelassyrischer Protokoll über eine Rinder- und Eselmusterung, *Baghdader Mitteilungen* 16 (1985) 317–326.
Del Olmo Lete, G./Sanmartín, J.: *A Dictionary of the Ugaritic Language in the Alphabetic Tradition*. HdO 67. Leiden/Boston: Brill, 2003.
Dercksen, J. G.: *Old Assyrian Institutions*. MOS Studies 4. PIHANS 98. Leiden: Nederlands Instituut voor het Nabije Oosten, 2004.
—: Adad is King! The Sargon Text from Kültepe, *JEOL* 39 (2005) 107–29.
—: On Anatolian Loanwords in Akkadian Texts from Kültepe, *ZA* 97/1 (2007) 26–46.
—: The Barley of Life, *N.A.B.U.*/14 (2011) 17.
—: The Archive of Ali-aḫum (I): the Documents excavated in N-O-P/20 in 1950, in: *Proceedings of the 1st Kültepe International Meeting. Kültepe, September 19-23, 2013. Studies Dedicated to Kutlu Emre (Kültepe International Meetings 1)*, Subartu 35, eds. F. Kulakoğlu/C. Michel, 47–58. Turnhout: Brepols, 2015.
Deutscher G.: *Syntactic Change in Akkadian, the Evolution of Sentential Complementation*. Oxford: University Press, 2000.
Diakonoff, I. M.: Proto-Afrasian and Old Akkadian: a Study in historical Phonetics, *Journal of Afroasiatic Languages* 4 (1991/92), 1–133.
Dietrich, M.: Untersuchungen zur Grammatik des Neubabylonischen, in: *Lišān mitḫurti: Festschrift Wolfram Freiherr von Soden zum 19. VI. 1968 gewidmet von Schülern und Mitarbeitern*, ed. W. Röllig, 65–99. Kevelaer: Verlag Butzon & Bercker, 1969.

Dietrich, M./Mayer, W.: *Der Hurritische Brief des Dušratta von Mīttānni an Amenḫotep III*. AOAT 382. Münster: Ugarit-Verlag, 2010.

Dillmann, A.: *Ethiopic Grammar*, 2nd edition by C. Bezold, translated by J. A. Crichton. London: Williams & Norgate, 1907.

Dolgopolsky, A: Two Problems of Historical Linguistics, in: *Semitic Studies in Honor of Wolf Leslau*, ed. A. S. Kaye, 328–39. Wiesbaden: Harrassowitz Verlag, 1991.

Donbaz, V.: List of Female Weavers Written in the Middle Assyrian Period, *IAMY* 15/16 (1969) 221–29.

—: Complimentary Data on some Assyrian Terms (*ḫuruḫurātu*, *ḫuruḫuru*, *ḫurūtu*, *ḫuḫuru*), *JCS* 40/1 (1988a) 69–80.

—: Some Neo-Assyrian Contracts from Girnavaz and Vicinity, *SAAB* 2/1 (1988) 3–30.

—: The date of the eponym Nabû-bēla-uṣur, in: *Marchands, Diplomates et Empereurs : Études sur la Civilisation Mésopotamienne offertes à Paul Garelli*, eds. D. Charpin/F. Joannès, 73–80. Paris: Éditions Recherche sur les Civilisations, 1991.

—: The "House of Kings" in the City of Aššur, in: *Hittite and other Anatolian and Near Eastern Studies in Honour of Sedat Alp*, eds. H. Otten/E. Akurgal/H. Ertem/A. Süel, 119–25. Ankara: Türk Tarih Kurumu, 1992.

—: Bābu-aḫa-iddina's Archive in Istanbul, *Archivum Anatolicum* 3 (1997) 101–9.

—: Assur Collecton housed in Istanbul: General Outline, in: *III. Uluslararası Hititoloji Kongresi Bildirileri. Corum 16–22 Eylül 1996 / Acts of the IIIrd International Congress of Hittitology. Corum, September 16–22*, 1996, eds. S. Alp/A. Süel, 177–78. Ankara, 1998.

—: A Middle Assyrian Private Letter, in: *Studi sul vicino oriente antico dedicati alla memoria di Luigi Cagni*, ed. S. Graziani, 237–41. Napoli: Istituto universitario orientale, 2000.

—: The Eponymy of Urad-Šerua son of Aššur-bani/Inventory no. 1439, *N.A.B.U.*/55–56 (2001) 54–56.

—: Selected Middle Assyrian Private Letters housed in Istanbul, in: *From the Upper Sea to the Lower Sea: Studies on the History of Assyria and Babylonia in Honour of A.K. Grayson*, PIHANS 101, eds. G. Frame/L. Wilding, 67–80. Leiden: Nederlands Instituut voor het Nabije Oosten, 2004.

—: Two Middle Assyrian Contracts housed in Istanbul, in: *Of God(s), Trees, Kings and Scholars: Neo-Assyrian and related Studies in Honour of Simo Parpola*. StOr 106. eds. M. Luukko/S. Svärd/R. Mattila, 353–60. Helsinki: Finn ish Oriental Society, 2009.

—: A brief Note about the Name Abattu as Eponym, *N.A.B.U.*/68 (2010) 78–79.

Donbaz, V./Harrak, A.: The Middle Assyrian Eponymy of Kidin-Aššur, *JCS* 41/2 (1989) 217–25.

Driel, G. van/Jas, R.: A Second Middle Assyrian LB Text on Gold, *JEOL* 31 (1989-90) 63–65.

Driver, G. R./Miles, J. C.: *The Assyrian Laws*. Oxford: The Clarendon press, 1935.

Durham, J. W.: *Studies in Boğazköy Akkadian*. Diss. Harvard, 1976.

Edzard, D. O.: Review of Finet 1956, *ZA* 53 (1959) 304–8.

—: Zu den altbabylonischen Präpositionen *itti* und *qadum*, in: *Festschrift Lubor Matouš*, eds. B. Hruška/G. Komoróczy, 69–89. Budapest: Eötvös Loránd tudományegyetem, Ókori történeti tanszék, 1978.

—: Zu den Akkadischen Nominalformen *parsat*, *pirsat*, und *pursat*, *ZA* 72/2 (1982) 68–88.

—: Review CAD Q, *ZA* 73/2 (1983) 132–136.

—: Die 3. Person M. Pl. tiprusū im Altakkadischen von Mari, in: *Miscellanea Babylonica: Mélanges offerts à Maurice Birot*, eds. J. M. Durand/J. R. Kupper, 85–86. Paris: Éditions Recherche sur les Civilisations, 1985.

—: Review of Greenstein 1984, *JAOS* 106/2 (1986) 359–362.

—: *namir* "er ist glänzend", *Acta Sumerologica* 16 (1994) 1–14.

—: Silbenschliessendes [ʾ] im Altassyrischen, in: *Veenhof Anniversary Volume: Studies Presented to Klaas R. Veenhof on the Occasion of his Sixty-Fifth Birthday*, PIHANS 89, eds. W. H. van

Soldt/J. G. Dercksen/N. J. C. Kouwenberg/Th. J. H. Krispijn, 133–35. Leiden: Nederlands Instituut voor het Nabije Oosten, 2001.
—: LKA 62: Parodie eines Assyrischen Feldzugberichts, in: *From the Upper Sea to the Lower Sea: Studies on the History of Assyria and Babylonia in Honour of A.K. Grayson,* PIHANS 101, eds. G. Frame/L. Wilding, 81–87. Leiden: Nederlands Instituut voor het Nabije Oosten, 2004.
Fabritius, K.: Vowel Dissimilation as a Marker of Plurality in Neo-Assyrian, *JCS* 47 (1995) 51–55
Faist, B.: *Der Fernhandel des assyrischen Reiches zwischen dem 14. und 11. Jh. v. Chr.*. AOAT 265. Münster: Ugarit-Verlag, 2001.
Faist, B./Llop, J.: The Assyrian Royal Granary (*karmu*), in: *The Perfumes of Seven Tamarisks, Studies in Honour of Wilfred G. E. Watson*, AOAT 394, eds. G. del Olmo Lete/J. Vidal/N. Wyatt, 19–35. Münster: Ugarit-Verlag, 2012.
Fales, F. M.: *Prima dell'alfabeto: La Storia della Scrittura attraverso Testi cuneiformi inediti.* Venezia: Erizzo Editrice, 1989a.
—: A Middle Assyrian Text concerning Vineyards and Fruit Groves, *SAAB* 13 (1989b) 53–59.
Farber, A.: Akkadian Evidence for Proto-Semitic Affricates, *JCS* 37/1 (1985) 101–7.
Farber, W.: *Beschwörungsrituale an Ištar und Dumuzi : Atti Ištar ša ḫarmaša dumuzi.* Akademie der Wissenschaften und der Literatur, Veröffentlichungen der Orientalischen Kommission 30. Wiesbaden: Frans Stein Verlag, 1977.
—: VS 19, 47 **bīt ḫašīmi*, und ein «i-Modus» im Mittelassyrischen?, *N.A.B.U.*/117 (1990) 92–94.
—: "… But she Refuses to Take the Silver," in: *Veenhof Anniversary Volume: Studies Presented to Klaas R. Veenhof on the Occasion of his Sixty-Fifth Birthday,* PIHANS 89, eds. W. H. van Soldt/J. G. Dercksen/N. J. C. Kouwenberg/Th. J. H. Krispijn, 137–43. Leiden: Nederlands Instituut voor het Nabije Oosten, 2001.
Fincke, J. C.: Three Nuzi Texts from the British Museum and a Middle Assyrian Letter from the Aftermath of the Conquest of the Kingdom of Arrapḫe, *AoF* 41/1 (2014) 15–29.
Fincke, J. C./Llop-Raduà, J.: Two Middle Assyrian Delivery Notes from the British Museum's Tablet Collection, in: *At the Dawn of History Ancient Near Eastern Studies in Honour of J. N. Postgate*, eds. Y. Heffron/A. Stone/M. Worthington, 313–19. Winona Lake: Eisenbrauns, 2017.
Finegan, E.: *Language, its Structure and Use*, 5th edition. Sea Harbor Drive: Thomson Wadsworth, 2008.
Finet, A.: *L'Accadien des lettres de Mari*. Brussels: Duculo, 1956.
Fischer, W.: *Grammatik des Klassischen Arabisch.* Porta NS 11. Wiesbaden: Harrassowitz Verlag, 2006.
Fleming, D.: Review of Seminara 1998, *JAOS* 119/4 (1999) 701–2.
Fohrer, G.: Review of UGM, *Zeitschrift fur die alttestamentliche Wissenschaft* 84 (1972) 280–81.
Fox, J.: *Semitic Noun Patterns*. HSS 52. Winona Lake: Eisenbrauns, 2003.
Franke, S./Wilhelm, G.: Eine Mittelassyrische Fiktive Urkunde zur Wahrung des Anspruchs auf ein Findelkind, in: *Jahrbuch für Kunst und Gewerbe Hamburg 4*, ed. W. Hornbostel, 19–26. Hamburg: Paul Hartung Verlag, 1985.
Freydank, H.: Anmerkungen zu mittelassyrischen Texten, *OLZ* 66/11–12 (1971) 533–35.
—: Review of UGM, *OLZ* 70/2 (1975) 142–44.
—: Untersuchungen zur sozialen Struktur in mittelassyrischer Zeit, *AoF* 4 (1976) 111–30.
—: Zur Lage der deportierten Hurriter in Assyrien, *AoF* 7 (1980) 89–117.
—: Einige historische Nachrichten in mittelassyrischen Rechts- und Verwaltungsurkunden, in: *Gesellschaft und Kultur im alten Vorderasien*, Gesellschaft und Kultur des Alten Orients 15, ed. H. Klengel, 41–46. Berlin: Akademie-Verlag, 1982c.
—: Die „Söhne" des Šalim-pî-Ea, *AoF* 12/2 (1985a) 362–64.
—: Anmerkungen zu mittelassyrischen Texten. 2., *OLZ* 66/3 (1985b) 229–34.

—: Zur Paläographie der Mittelassyrischen Urkunden, in: *Šulmu, Papers on the Ancient Near East Presented at International Conference of Socialist Countries*, eds. P. Vavroušek/V. Souček, 73–84. Prague: Univerzita Karlova, 1988.
—: Anmerkungen zu mittelassyrischen Texten, *AoF* 18/2 (1991) 219–223.
—: KAV 217, Protokoll über eine Staatsaktion?, *ZA* 82/2 (1992) 221–32.
—: Nachlese zu den mittelassyrischen Gesetzen, *AfO* 21 (1994) 203–11.
—: Mittelassyrische Opferlisten aus Assur, in: *Assyrien im Wandel der Zeiten*, HSAO 6, eds. H. Waetzoldt/H. Hauptmann, 47–52. Heidelberg: Heidelberger Orientverlag, 1997a.
—: *bitqī batāqu* „Abschneidungen abschneiden“?, *AoF* 24/1 (1997b) 105–14.
—: Anmerkungen zu mittelassyrischen Texte. 4, *AoF* 30/2 (2003) 244–55.
—: Kār-Tukultī-Ninurta als Agrarprovinz, *AoF* 36/1 (2009a) 16–84.
—: Bemerkungen zu dem Brief T 02-32 aus Tell Sabi Abyad, in: *Dallo Stirone al Tigri, dal Tevere all'Eufrate: Studi in onore di Claudio Saporetti*, ed. P. N. Scafa/S. Viaggion, 149–55. Roma: Aracne editrice, 2009b.
—: Betrachtungen zur Weidewirtschaft in Dūr-Katlimmu, in: *Dūr-Katlimmu and Beyond*, StCh 1, ed. H. Kühne, 87–100. Wiesbaden: Harrassowitz Verlag, 2010a.
—: Perspektiven einer mittelassyrischen paläografischen Liste, *AoF* 37/2 (2010b) 252–59.
—: Anmerkungen zu mittelassyrischen Texten. 6, *OLZ* 105/6 (2010c) 663–70.
—: Anmerkungen zu mittelassyrischen Texten. 7, *AoF* 38 (2011) 348–66.
—: MARV IV 119 - ein Vertrag?, *AoF* 39/2 (2012a) 226–34.
—: Anmerkungen zu mittelassyrischen Texten. 8, *OLZ* 107/4–5 (2012b) 209–14.
—: Texte aus Kār-Tukultī-Ninurta, *StMes* 1 (2014) 43–84.
—: Texte aus Kār-Tukultī-Ninurta 2, *StMes* 2 (2015) 75–130.
—: *Assyrische Jahresbeamte des 12. Jh. v. Chr.: Eponymen von Tukulti-Ninurta I. bis Tukulti-apil-esarra I.* AOAT 429. Münster: Ugarit Verlag, 2016a.
—: Anmerkungen zu mittelassyrischen Texten. 10, *StMes* 3 (2016b) 95−108.
—: Instruktionen Tukultī-Ninurtas I, in: *At the Dawn of History Ancient Near Eastern Studies in Honour of J. N. Postgate*, eds. Y. Heffron/A. Stone/M. Worthington, 179–87. Winona Lake: Eisenbrauns, 2017.
Freydank, H./Salvini, M.: Zu den Hurritischen Personennenamen aus Kār-Tukultī-Ninurta, *Studi Micenei ed Egeo-Anatolici* 24 (1984) 33–56.
Freydank, H./Saporetti, C.: *Nuove Attestazione Dell`Onomastica Medio-Assira*. Incunabula Graeca 74. Roma: Edizioni dell` Ateneo & Bizzarri, 1979.
Friedrich, J.: *Hettitsches Elementarbuch, Teil 1: Kurzgefaßte Grammatik*, 2. Auflage. Indogermanische Bibliothek, 1. Reihe: Lehr- und Handbucher. Heidelberg: Winter, 1960.
Geers, F. W.: The Treatment of Emphatics in Akkadian, *JNES* 4/2 (1945) 65–67.
Gelb, I. J.: Notes on von Soden's grammar of Akkadian, *BiOr* 12/3–4 (1955) 93–111.
—: *Old Akkadian Writing and Grammar*, 2nd edition. Materials for the Assyrian Dictionary 2. Chicago: the university of Chicago press, 1961.
—: Comments on the Akkadian Syllabary, *Or* 39/4 (1970) 516–46.
Gelb, I. J./Purves, P. M./MacRae, A. A.: *Nuzi Personal Names*. OIP 57. Chicago: University of Chicago Press, 1943.
Gelb, I. J./Sollberger, E.: The First Legal Document from the Later Old Assyrian Period, *JNES* 16/3 (1957) 163–75.
Geller, M.: Review of SNAG, *BSOAS* 65 (2002) 562–64.
George, A. R.: Three Middle Assyrian Tablets in the British Museum, *Iraq* 50 (1988) 25–37.
Giacumakis, G.: *The Akkadian of Alalaḫ*. The Hague: Mouton, 1970.
Girbal, C.: Zur Phonologie des Akkadischen, *AoF* 24/1 (1997) 172–81.

Goetze, A.: The Akkadian Dialects of the Old-Babylonian Mathematical Texts. in: *Mathematical Cuneiform Texts*, O. Neugebauer/A. Sachs, AOS 29, 146–51. New Haven: American Oriental Society, 1945.

—: The Akkadian Masculine Plural in *-ānu/i* and its Semitic Background, *Language* 22 (1946) 121–30.

—: Short or Long a, *Or* 16/2 (1947) 239–250.

Golinets, V.: *Das Verb im amurritischen Onomastikon der altbabylonischen Zeit*. Diss. Leipzig, 2010.

Grayson, A. K.: Rivalry over Rulership at Aššur: the Puzur-Sîn Inscription, *Annual Review of the Royal Inscriptions of Mesopotamia Project* 3 (1985) 9–14.

Greenstein, E. L.: *The Phonology of Akkadian Syllable Structure*. AAL 9/1. Malibu: Undena Publications, 1984.

Greenstein, E. L./Marcus, D.: The Akkadian Inscription of Idrimi, *Journal of the Ancient Near Eastern Society* 8 (1976) 59–96.

Günbattı, C.: Kültepe'den Akadlı Sargon'a âit bir Tablet, *Archivum Anatolicum* 3 (1997) 131–51.

Gurney, O. R.: *The Middle Babylonian Legal and Economic Texts from Ur*. London: British School of Archaeology in Iraq, 1983.

Güterbock, H, G.: The Cuneiform Tablets, in: *Soudings at Tell Fakhariyah*, OIP 79, eds. C. W. McEwan/L. S. Braidwood/H. Frankfort/H. G. Güterbock/R. C. Haines/H. J. Kantor/C. H. Kraeling, 86–90. Chicago: University of Chicago Press, 1958.

Haber, E.: The Double Genitive Construction in Akkadian Literature, *N.A.B.U.*/42 (2013) 73–74.

Hall, M.: A Middle Assyrian Legal Summons, *ZA* 73/1 (1983) 75–81.

Hallo, W. W.: The Seals of Aššur-remanni, in: *Symbolae Biblicae et Mesopotamicae Francisco Mario Theodoro de Liagre Böhl dedicatae*, Studia Francisci Scholten memoriae dicata 4, ed. M. A. Beek, 180-184. Leiden: Brill, 1973.

Hameeuw, H.: 1947: Two Tablets as a Christmas Gift to a Leuven Assyriologist, in: *The Ancient Near East, a Life!: Festschrift Karel van Lerberghe*, OLA 220, eds. T. Boiy/J. Bretschneider/A. Goddeeris/H. Hammeeuw/G. Jans/J. Tavernier, 269–79. Leuven/Paris/Walpole: Peeters, 2012.

Harrak, A.: *Assyria and Hanigalbat*. Texte und Studien zur Orientalistik 4. Hildesheim: Olms Verlag, 1987.

—: Middle Assyrian *bīt ḫašīme*, *ZA* 79/1 (1989) 61–72.

Harrel, R. S.: *A Short Reference Grammar of Moroccan Arabic*, Washington: Georgetown University Press, 1962.

Hasselbach, R.: *Sargonic Akkadian*. Wiesbaden: Harrassowitz Verlag, 2005.

—: The Affiliation of Sargonic Akkadian with Babylonian and Assyrian: New Insights concerning the Internal Subgrouping of Akkadian, *Journal of the Semitic Studies* 52/1 (2007) 21–43,

Hazenbos, J.: Hurritisch und Urartäisch, in: *Sprachen des Alten Orients*, 3. Auflage, ed. M. P. Streck, 135-158. Darmstadt: Wissenschaftliche Buchgesellschaft, 2007.

Hecker, K.: Review of UGM, *WO* 7 (1973/74) 166–69.

—: Review of MARV 1, *ZA* 70/2 (1980) 275–78.

—: Zur Herkunft der hethitischen Schrift, *SCCNH* 8 (1996) 291–303.

—: Die Krönung des Königs, in: *Omina, Orakel, Rituale und Beschwörungen*, TUAT NF 4, ed. N. B. Jankowska/G. Wilhelm, 96–98. Gütersloh: Gütersloher Verlagshaus, 2008.

Hirsch, H.: Zur Fragen der t-Formen in den Keilschriftlichen Gesetztexten, in: *Lišān mitḫurti: Festschrift Wolfram Freiherr von Soden zum 19. VI. 1968 gewidmet von Schülern und Mitarbeitern*, ed. W. Röllig, 119–31. Kevelaer: Verlag Butzon & Bercker, 1969.

—: *Untersuchungen zur altassyrischen Religion*. 2nd edition. AfO Beih. 13/14. Osnabrück: Biblio Verlag, 1972.

Hoffner, H. A../Melchert, H. C.: *A Grammar of the Hittite Language, Part 1: Reference Grammar*. LANE 1, Winona Lake: Eisenbrauns, 2008.

Hout, T. van den: The Ductus of the Alalaḫ VII Texts and the Origin of Hittite Cuneiform, in: *Palaeography and Scribal Practices in Syro-Palestine and Anatolia in the Late Bronze Age,* PIHANS 119, ed. E. Devecchi, 147–70. Leiden: Nederlands Instituut voor het Nabije Oosten, 2012.

Huehnergard, J.: *The Akkadian Dialects of Carchemish and Ugarit.* Diss. Harvard, 1979.

—: On Verbless Clauses in Akkadian, *ZA* 76/2 (1986) 218–49.

—: *The Akkadian of Ugarit.* HSS 34. Atlanta: Scholars Press, 1989.

—: Akkadian Grammar (= Review of GAG), *Or* 66/4 (1997a) 434–44.

—: Notes on Ras Shamra-Ougarit VII, *Syria* 74 (1997b) 213–20.

—: *Izuzzu* and *itūlum*, in: *Riches hidden in secret places: Ancient Near Eastern Studies in memory of Thorkild Jacobsen*, ed.T. Abusch, 161–85. Winona Lake: Eisenbrauns, 2002.

—: Akkadian ḫ and West Semitic *ḥ[1], *Studia Semitica, Orientalia, Papers of the Oriental Institute, Issue III (Festschrift A. Militarev)*, ed. L. Kogan, 102–19. Moskau: Russian State University for the Humanities, 2003.

—: *A Grammar of Akkadian*, 2nd Edition. HSS 45. Winona Lake: Eisenbrauns, 2005.

—: Proto-Semitic and Proto-Akkadian, in: *The Akkadian Language in its Semitic Context: Studies in the Akkadian of the Third and Second Millennium BC,* PIHANS 106, eds. G. Deutscher/N. J. C. Kouwenberg, 1–18. Leiden: Nederlands Instituut voor het Nabije Oosten, 2006.

Ichisar, M.: *Les Archives Cappadociennes du Marchand Imdilum.* Recherches sur les grandes civilisations, cahier 3. Paris: A.D.P.F., 1981,

Ismail, B. K./Postgate, J. N.: A Middle Assyrian Flock-Master's Archive from Tell Ali, *Iraq* 70 (2008) 147–78.

Izre'el, S.: *Amurru Akkadian: a Linguistic Study, Volume I.* HSS 40. Atlanta: Scholars Press, 1991a.

—: *Amurru Akkadian: a Linguistic Study, Volume II*, HSS 41. Atlanta: Scholars Press, 1991b.

—: Review of Huehnergard 1989, *BiOr* 49/1–2 (1992) 168–78

Izre'el, S./Cohen, E.: *Literary Old Babylonian*, Languages of the World/ Materials 81. München: Lincom, 2004.

Jakob, S.: *Mittelassyrische Verwaltung und Sozialstruktur Untersuchungen*, CM 29. Leiden: Brill, 2003.

—: Zwischen Integration und Ausgrenzung Nichtassyrer im mittelassyrischen "Westreich" in: *Ethnicity in Ancient Mesopotamia: Papers Read at the 48th Rencontre Assyriologique Internationale Leiden*, 1–4 July 2002, PIHANS 102, 180–88. Leiden: Nederlands Instituut voor het Nabije Oosten, 2005.

—: The Middle Assyrian Period (14th to 11th Century BCE), in: *A Companion to Assyria*, ed. E. Frahm, 117–42. Hoboken, Wiley-Blackwell 2017.

Jankowska, N. B.: (in Russian), *VDI* 80 (1962) 69–74.

—: The Middle Assyrian Legal Document VDI 80, 71 again, *Or* 36/3 (1967) 334–35.

Jas, R.: Two Middle-Assyrian Lists of Personal Names from Sabi Abyad, *Akkadica* 67 (1990) 33–39.

Jastrow, O.: *Lehrbuch der Ṭuroyo-Sprache.* Semitica Viva, Series Didactica, 2. Wiesbaden: Harrassowitz Verlag, 1992.

—: *Laut- und Formenlehre des neuaramäischen Dialekts on Mīdin im Ṭūr ˁÂbdīn*; 4-, unveränderte Auflage. Semitica Viva 9. Harrassowitz Verlag, 1993.

—: *Der neuaramäische Dialekt von Mlaḥsô.* Semitica Viva 14. Wiesbaden: Harrassowitz Verlag, 1994.

Johnson, J. C.: Contractual Formalism and Zukunftsbewältigung in Middle Assyrian Agricultural Accounting, in: *Time and History in the Ancient Near East: Proceedings of the 56th Rencontre Assyriologique Internationale at Barcelona 26–30 July 2010*, eds. L. Feliu/J. Llop/A. Millet Albà/J. Sanmartín, 525–48. Winona Lake: Eisenbrauns, 2013.

—: Review of Postgate 2013, *BiOr* 78/3–4 (2016) 441–46.

Joüon, P./Muraoka, T.: *A Grammar of Biblical Hebrew*. Subsidia Biblica 27. Roma: Pontificio Istituto Biblico, 2006.
Jucquois, G.: *Phonétique Comparée des Dialectes Moyen-Babyloniens du Nord et de l'Ouest*. Bibliothèque du Musèon 53. Leuven: Institut Orientaliste, 1966.
Kärger, B./Minx, S.: Sutäer, *RlA* 13 (2012) 365–69.
Kaufman, S. A.: *The Akkadian Influences on Aramaic*. AS 19, Chicago: University of Chicago Press, 1974.
Keetman, J.: Wann und warum sprach man im Akkadischen einen Lateralfrikativ?, *UF* 38 (2006) 363–78.
Khan, J.: North Eastern Neo-Aramaic, in: *The Semitic Languages: An International Handbook,* HSK 36, ed. S. Weninger, 708–24. Berlin: De Gruyter Mouton, 2011.
King, L. W.: *Cuneiform Texts from Babylonian Tablets from the British Museum Part 33*, London: Harrison and Sons, 1912.
Kloekhorst, A.: The Phonological Interpretation of Plene and Non-Plene Spelled e in Hittite, in: *The Sound of Indo-European: Phonetics, Phonemics, and Morphophonemics*, eds. B. N. Whitehead/T. Olander/B. A. Olsen/J. E. Rasmussen, 243–61. Copenhagen : Museum Tusculanum Press, 2012.
Knudsen, E. E.: Cases of Free Variants in the Akkadian q Phoneme, *JCS* 15/3 (1961) 84–90
—: Spirantization of Velars in Akkadian, in: *Lišān mitḫurti: Festschrift Wolfram Freiherr von Soden zum 19. VI. 1968 gewidmet von Schülern und Mitarbeitern*, ed. W. Röllig, 147–55. Kevelaer: Verlag Butzon & Bercker, 1969.
—: Stress in Akkadian, *JCS* 32/1 (1980) 316.
Köcher, F.: Ein Mittelassyrisches Ritualfragment zum Neujahrsfest, *ZA* 50 (1952) 192-202.
—: Eine Mittelassyrischer Schülertafel mit Vokabularauszügen, *AfO* 17 (1954/56) 120.
—: Ein Inventartext aus Kār-Tukulti-Ninurta, *AfO* 18 (1957/58) 300–13.
Kogan, L.: *ġ in Akkadian, *UF* 33 (2001) 263–98.
—: Review of Buccellati 1996, *Babel und Bibel* 1 (2004) 379–89.
—: Old Assyrian vs. Old Babylonian: the Lexical Dimension, in: *The Akkadian Language in its Semitic Context: Studies in the Akkadian of the Third and Second Millennium BC,* PIHANS 106, eds. G. Deutscher/N. J. C. Kouwenberg, 177–214. Leiden: Nederlands Instituut voor het Nabije Oosten, 2006.
—: Proto-Semitic Phonetics and Phonology, in: *The Semitic Languages: An International Handbook,* HSK 36, ed. S. Weninger, 54–151. Berlin: De Gruyter Mouton, 2011.
Kouwenberg, N. J. C.: Nouns as Verbs: the Verbal Nature of the Akkadian Stative, *Or* 69/1 (2000) 21–71.
—: Ventive, Dative and Allative in Old Babylonian, *ZA* 92/2 (2002) 200–40.
—: Evidence for Post-Glottalized Consonants in Assyrian, *JCS* 55 (2003) 75–88.
—: Initial Plene Writing and the Conjugation of the First Weak Verbs in Akkadian, *JEOL* 38 (2003/4) 83–103.
—: Assyrian Light on the History of the N-stem, in: *Assyria and Beyond, Studies Presented to Mogens Trolle Larsen*, PIHANS 100, ed. J. G. Dercksen (ed.), 333–52. Leiden: Nederlands Instituut voor het Nabije Oosten 2004.
—: Reflection of the Gt-Stem in Akkadian, *ZA* 95/1 (2005) 77–103.
—: Review of Luukko 2004, *AfO* 51 (2005/6) 331–34.
—: The Reflexes of the Proto-Semitic Gutturals in Assyrian, in: *The Akkadian Language in its Semitic Context: Studies in the Akkadian of the Third and Second Millennium BC,* PIHANS 106, eds. G. Deutscher/N. J. C. Kouwenberg, 150–76. Leiden: Nederlands Instituut voor het Nabije Oosten, 2006.
—: On the Old Assyrian verb *atawwum* "to speak" and Related Issues, in: *Old Assyrian Studies in Memory of Paul Garelli*, OAAS 4, PIHANS 112, ed. C. Michel, 159–73. Leiden: Nederlands Instituut voor het Nabije Oosten, 2008.

—: *The Akkadian Verb and its Semitic Background.* LANE 2. Winona Lake: Eisenbrauns, 2010.

—: Spatial Deixis in Akkadian: Demonstrative Pronouns, Preventive Particles and Locative Adverbs, *ZA* 102/1 (2012a) 17–75.

—: Review of Streck 2011, *ZA* 102/2 (2012b) 323–32.

Kraus, F. R.: *Vom Mesopotamischen Menschen der Altbabylonischen Zeit und Seiner Welt.* Mededelingen der Koninklijke Nederlandse Akademie van Wetenschappen, Afd. Letterkunde Nieuwe reeks 36/6. Amsterdam: North-Holland Publishing Company, 1973a.

—: Ein Altbabylonischer „i-Modus"?,in *Symbolae Biblicae et Mesopotamicae Francisco Mario Theodoro de Liagre Böhl dedicatae.* Studia Francisci Scholten memoriae dicata 4, ed. M. A. Beek, 253–65. Leiden: Brill, 1973b.

—: *Sonderformen Akkadische Parataxe: die Koppelungen.* Mededelingen der Koninklijke Nederlandse Akademie van Wetenschappen, Afd. Letterkunde Nieuwe reeks 50/1. Amsterdam 1987.

Krebernik, M.: Some Questions concerning Word Formation in Akkadian, in: *The Akkadian Language in its Semitic Context: Studies in the Akkadian of the Third and Second Millennium BC,* PIHANS 106, eds. G. Deutscher/N. J. C. Kouwenberg, 84–95. Leiden: Nederlands Instituut voor het Nabije Oosten, 2006.

Kryszat, G.: The Use of Writing Among the Anatolians, in: *Anatolia and the Jazira during the Old Assyrian Period,* OAAS 3, PIHANS 111, ed. J. G. Dercksen, 231–38. Leiden: Nederlands Instituut voor het Nabije Oosten, 2008a.

Kümmel, H. M.: Ein Kaufvertrag aus Ḫana mit mittelassyrischer *līmu*-Datierung, *ZA* 79/2 (1989) 191–200.

Labat, R.: *Manuel d'Épigraphie Akkadienne*, Paris: Imprimerie Nationale, 1948.

Lackenbacher, S.: Nouveaux Documents d'Ugarit: I.- Une Lettre Royale, *RA* 76 (1982) 141–56.

Laessøe, J.: The Bazmusian Tablets, *Sumer* 15 (1959) 15–18.

Lambert, W. G.: A Middle Assyrian Tablet of Incantations, in: *Studies in Honor of Benno Landsberger in Honor of his Seventy-fifth Birthday*, AS 16, eds. H. G. Güterbock/T. Jacobsen, 283–88. Chicago: University of Chicago Press, 1965.

—: A Middle Assyrian Medical Text, *Iraq* 31 (1969) 28–39.

—: Review of UGM, *BSOAS* 36 (1973) 126–27.

Landsberger, B.: Der Ventiv des Akkadischen, *ZA* 35/2 (1923) 113–23.

—: Review of J. Lewy 1921, *OLZ* 27/12 (1924) 719–25.

Leslau, W.: *Comparative Dictionary of Geʿêz (Classical Ethiopic).* Wiesbaden: Harrassowitz Verlag, 1987.

—: *Gurage Studies; Collected articles*, Wiesbaden: Harrassowitz Verlag, 1992.

—: *Ethiopic Documents: Argobba; Grammar and Dictionary.* Aethiopische Forschungen 47. Wiesbaden: Harrassowitz Verlag, 1997.

—: *Zway Ethiopic Documents; Grammar and Dictionary.* Aethiopistische Forschungen 51. Wiesbaden: Harrassowitz Verlag, 1999.

—: Introductory Grammar of Amharic. Porta NS 21. Wiesbaden: Harrassowitz Verlag, 2000.

Lewy, J.: *Das Verbum in den »altassyrischen Gesetzen«,* Untersuchungen zur Akkadischen Grammatik I. Berlin: Selbstverlag des Herausgebers, 1921.

—: A propos des adverbs *annānum* et *ullānum*, *RA* 35 (1938) 81–91.

Lewy, J./Lewy, H.: Old Assyrian Subrum, *Hebrew Union College Annual* 38 (1967) 1–15.

Lion, B.: Assur unter Mittaniherrschaft, in: *Assur - Gott, Stadt und Land*, Colloquien der Deutschen Orient-Gesellschaft 5, ed. J. Renger, 149–67. Wiesbaden: Harrassowitz Verlag, 2011.

Lipiński, E.: Semitic Languages, Outline of a Comparative Grammar, 2nd Edition. OLA 80, Leuven: Peeters Publishers, 2001.

Llop, J.: Ein weiterer Beleg für den mA Ortsnamen Ša-Sîn-rabi, *N.A.B.U.*/35 (2002) 37.

—: Die persönlichen Gründe Tiglat-Pilesers I., Babylonien anzugreifen, *Or* 72/2 (2003) 204–9.

—: Karmu-ša-Ištar oder Speicher in Tall Faḫarīya, *N.A.B.U.*/65 (2004) 66.
—: Das Wort *rīmuttu* „Geschenk“ in der Mittelassyrischen Dokumentation, *Isimu* 6 (2007) 115–27.
—: The Food for the Gods, MARV 3, 16, A Middle Assyrian Offering List to the Great Gods of the City Aššur, *SAAB* 18 (2009/10) 1–46.
—: Review of LVUH, *BiOr* 67/1–2 (2010) 124–32.
—: The Creation of the Middle Assyrian Provinces, *JAOS* 131/4 (2011a) 591–603.
—: The Boundaries between Assyria and Babylonia in the East Tigris Region during the Reign of Tukultī-Ninurta I (1233-1197 BC), in: *Between the Cultures; The Central Euphrates Region from the 3rd to the 1st Millennium BC.*, HSAO 14, eds. P. A. Miglus/S. Mühls, 209–15. Heidelberg: Heidelberger Orientverlag, 2011b.
—: Middle Assyrian Letters: A new Survey, *AuOr* 30 (2012a) 289-306.
—: Did the Assyrians Occupy the Euphrates-Elbow in the Middle Assyrian Period (Late Bronze Age), in: *Broadening Horizons 3: Conference of Young Researchers working in the Ancient Near East*, eds. F. B. Tona/M. B. García/A. G. Bach/C. T. Dacasa/O. V. Campos., 243–73. Barcelona: Servicio De Publicaciones, 2012b.
—: Foreign Kings in the Middle Assyrian Archival Documentation, in: *Understanding hegemonic Practices of the Early Assyrian Empire: Essays dedicated to Frans Wiggermann,* Consolidatin Empires Project 1, PIHANS 125, ed. B. S. Düring, 243–73. Leiden: Nederlands Instituut voor het Nabije Oosten, 2015a.
—: Review of MATC, *AfO* 53 (2015b) 215–220.
Llop, J./Luukko, M.: NP 46: A new Middle Assyrian Letter, *JNES* 73/2 (2014) 211–18.
Llop, J./Shibata, D.: The Royal Journey in the Middle Assyrian Period, *JCS* 68 (2016) 67–98.
Loesov, S.: Akkadian Sentences about the Present Tense Part One, *Babel und Bibel* 2 (2005) 101–47.
Luukko, M.: Idiomatic Meanings of šiddu in Neo-Assyrian, *SAAB* 11 (1997) 31–35.
—: *Grammatical Variation in Neo-Assyrian*. SAAS 16. Helsinki: The Neo-Assyrian Text Project Corps, 2004.
Luukko, M./Van Buylaere, G.: Languages and Writing Systems in Assyria, in: *A Companion to Assyria*, ed. E. Frahm, 313–35. Hoboken, Wiley-Blackwell 2017.
Machinist, P. B.: *The Epic of Tukulti-Ninurta I: A Study in Middle Assyrian Literature*. Diss. Yale, 1978.
—: Provincial Governance in Middle Assyrian and some new Texts from Yale, *Assur* 3/2 (1982) 1–39.
Matouš, L./Petráček, K.: Beiträge zur Akkadischen Grammatik I, *ArOr* 24 (1956) 1–14.
Maul, S. M.: *Die Inschriften von Tall Bderi*. Berliner Beiträge zum Vorderer Orient Texte 2. Berlin: Dietrich Reimer Verlag, 1992.
—: Drei Mittelassyrische Urkunden aus Kulišḫinaš, in: *Von Sumer nach Ebla und zurück: Festschrift Pettinato*, HSAO 9, ed. H. Waetzoldt, 129–40. Heidelberg: Heidelberger Orientverlag, 2004.
—: *Die Inschriften von Tall Ṭābān (Grabungskampagnen 1997–1999), Die Könige von Ṭābētu und das Land Māri in mittelassyrischer Zeit*. ASJS 2. Tokyo: The Insititute for Cultural Studies of Ancient Iraq, 2005.
—: Ein Assyrer rezitiert ein Sumerischer Preislied auf die Schreibkunst, oder: von der unerwarteten Aussprache des Sumerischen, in: *DUB.SAR É.DUB.BA.A, Studies Presented in Honour of Veysel Donbaz*, ed. Ş. Dönmez, 205-209. Istanbul: Ege Publications, 2010.
Mayer, W.: Kultische Aspekte des Archivs Assur 6096 und zwei mittelassyrische Phantomwörter, *StMes* 3 (2016) 109–24.
Mayer, W. R.: Die Verwendung der Negation im Akkadischen zur Bildung von Indefinit- bzw. Totalitätsausdrücken, *Or* 58/2 (1989) 145–70.
—: Ein Hymnus auf Ninurta als Helfer in der Not, *Or* 61/2 (1992) 17–57.
—: Besonderheiten in der Verwendung des Graphems A.A im Akkadischen, *Or* 72/3 (2003) 293–306.

Meinhold, W.: *Ištar in Aššur, Untersuchungen eines Lokalkultus von ca. 2500 bis 614 v. Chr.* AOAT 367. Münster: Ugarit-Verlag, 2009.

Meissner, B.: *Kurzgefasste Assyrische Grammatik.* Hilfsbücher zur Kunde des Alten Orients 3. Leipzig : Hinrichs, 1907.

Menzel, B.: *Assyrische Tempel, Band 1–2.* StP s.m. 10/I–II. Roma: Pontificio Istituto Biblico, 1981.

Metzler, K. A.: *Tempora in altbabylonischen literarischen Texten.* AOAT 279. Münster: Ugarit-Verlag, 2002.

Michel, C.: *Old Assyrian Bibliography of Cuneiform Texts, Bullae, Seals and the Results of the Excavations at Aššur, Kültepe/Kaniš, Acemhöyük, Alişar and Boğazköy.* OAAS 1. PIHANS 97. Leiden: Nederlands Instituut voor het Nabije Oosten, 2003.

—: Deux Textes Atypiques Découverts à Kültepe, *JCS* 62 (2010) 71–80.

Miglus, P. A.: Middle Assyrian Settlement in the South, in: *Between the Cultures; The Central Euphrates Region from the 3rd to the 1st Millennium BC.*, HSAO 14, eds. P. A. Miglus/S. Mühls, 221–29. Heidelberg: Heidelberger Orientverlag, 2011.

Millard, A. R.: Fragments of historical Texts from Nineveh: Middle Assyrian and later Kings, *Iraq* 32 (1970) 167–76.

Minx, S.: *Die Sutäer in der Späten Bronzezeit*, Leipzig: MA thesis, 2005.

Mora, C./Giorgieri, M.: *Le lettere tra i re ittiti e i re assiri ritrovate a Hattusa.* HANE M 7. Padova: Sargon, 2004.

Moran, W. L.: Additions to the Amarna Lexicon, *Or* 53/2 (1984) 297–302.

—: *The Amarna letters*, Baltimore/London: John Hopkins University Press, 1992.

Morwood, J.: *Oxford Grammar of Classical Greek.* Oxford: University Press, 2001.

Müller, K. Fr.: *Das Assyrische Ritual Teil 1: Texte zum assyrischen Königsritual.* MVAeG 41/3. Leipzig: J. C. Hinrichs Verlag, 1937.

Müller, M.: *Akkadisch in Keilschrifttexten aus Ägypten. Deskriptive Grammatik einer Interlanguage des späten zweiten vorchristlichen Jahrtausends anhand der Ramses-Briefe.* AOAT 373. Münster: Ugarit-Verlag, 2010.

Muraoka, T.: *Classical Syriac, A Basic Grammar with a Chrestomathy*, 2nd edition. Porta NS 19. Wiesbaden: Harrassowitz Verlag, 2005.

Muraoka, T./Porten, B.: *A Grammar of Egyptian Aramaic*, 2nd edition. HdO 32. Leiden: Brill, 2003.

Nöldeke, T.: *Mandäische Grammatik.* Halle: Verlag der Buchhandlung des Waisenhauses, 1875.

—: Review of F. Schulthess, Homonyme Wurzeln im Syrischen. Ein Beitrag zur Semitischen Lexicographie, *ZDGM* 54 (1900) 152–64.

—: *Compendious Syriac Grammar*, London: Williams & Norgate, 1904.

Oelsner, J.: Review of Gurney 1974, *ZA* 75/2 (1965) 285–93.

Oppenheim, A. L.: *Ancient Mesopotamia, Portrait of Dead Civilization.* Chicago: University of Chicago Press, 1964.

Panayotov, S. V.: The tablet of the Middle Assyrian 'coronation' Ritual: the Placement of VAT 10113 and the Displacement of VAT 9978, *CDLN* 2015:7.

Panayotov, S. V./Llop, J.: A Middle Assyrian juridical Text on a Tablet with Handle, *ArOr* 81 (2013) 223–33.

Pardee, D./Whiting, R. M.: Aspects of Epistolary Usage in Ugaritic and Akkadian, *BSOAS* 50/1 (1987) 1–31.

Parker, B. J.: The Real and the Irreal: the Multiple Meanings of maṣi in Neo-Assyrian, *SAAB* 11 (1997) 37–54.

Parpola, S.: A Letter from Šamaš-šumu-ukīn to Esarhaddon, *Iraq* 34 (1972) 21–34.

—: The Alleged Middle/Neo-Assyrian Irregular Verb **naṣṣ* and the Assyrian Sound Change š > s, *Aššur* 1/1 (1974) 1–10.

—: Review of AHW Lieferung 7–12, *OLZ* 74/1 (1979) 23–35.

—: Likalka *ittatakku*: Two Notes on the Morphology of the Verb *alāku* in Neo-Assyrian, *StOr* 55 (1984), 185–209.
—: The Neo-Assyrian word for "Queen", *SAAB* 2 (1988a) 73–76.
—: The Reading of the Neo-Assyrian Logogram ^{lú}SIMUG.KUG.GI, *SAAB* 2, (1988b) 78-80.
—: Proto-Assyrian, in: *Wirtschaft und Gesellschaft von Ebla, Akten der International Tagung Heidelberg 4.–7. November 1986*, HSAO 2, eds. H. Waetzoldt/H. Hauptmann, 293–98. Heidelberg: Heidelberger Orientverlag, 1988c.
—: *Assyrian-English-Assyrian Dictionary*. Helsinki: The Neo-Assyrian Text Project Corpus, 2007.
—: Cuneiform Texts from Ziyaret Tepe (Tušḫan), 2002–2003, *SAAB* 17 (2008) 1–115.
—: *Assyrian Royal Rituals and Cultic Texts*. SAA 20. Helsinki: The Neo-Assyrian Text Project Corpus, 2017.
Pedersén, O.: Some Morphological Aspects of Sumerian and Akkadian Linguistic Areas, in: *DUMU-E$_2$-DUB-BA-BA: studies in Honor of Åke W. Sjöberg*, Occasional Publications of the Samuel Noah Kramer Fund 11, eds. H. Behrens/D. Loding/M. T. Roth, 429–438. Philedelphia: University Museum, 1989.
—: *Archives and Libraries in the Ancient Near East, 1500–300 B.C.* Bethesda: CDL Press, 1998.
Petschow, H. P.: *Mittelbabylonische Rechts- und Wirtschaftsurkunden der Hilprecht-Sammlung Jena: Mit Beiträgen zum mittelbabylonischen Recht*. Berlin: Akademie-Verlag, 1974.
Peust, C.: Zur assyrischen Vokalharmonie und zum Wortakzent des Akkadischen, *WO* 39 (2009) 223–33.
Podany, A. H.: Some Shared Traditions between Ḫana and the Kassites, in: *Crossing Boundaries and Linking Horizons: studies in honor of Michael C. Astour on his 80th birthday*, eds. G. D. Young/M. W. Chavalas/R. E. Averbeck, 417–32. Bethesda CDL Press, 1997.
—: *The Land of Hana, Kings Chronology, and Scribal Tradition*. Bethesda: CDL Press, 2002.
Pongratz-Leisten, B.: *Religion and Ideology in Assyria*. SANER 6. Boston: De Gruyter, 2015.
Postgate, J. N.: *The Governor's Palace Archive*. CTN 2. London: British School of Archaeology in Iraq, 1973.
—: Review of UGM, *BiOr* 31/3–6 (1974) 273–74.
—: *Fifty Neo-Assyrian Legal Document*. Warminster: Aris & Phillips, 1976.
—: Assyrian Documents in the Musée d'Art et d'Histoire, Geneva, *Assur* 2/4 (1979a) 93–107.
—: On Some Assyrian Ladies, *Iraq* 41 (1979b) 89–103.
—: Review of MARV 1, *BiOr* 37/1–2 (1980) 67–70.
—: Ilku and Land Tenure in the Middle Assyrian Kingdom – A second attempt, in: *Societies and Languages of the Ancient Near East: Studies in Honour of I.M. Diakonoff*, 304–13. Warminster: Aris & Phillips, 1982.
—: Review of Aynard/Durand 1980, *Mesopotamia* 18/19 (1983/84) 233–234.
—: Middle Assyrian Tablets: the Instruments of Bureaucracy, *AoF* 13/1 (1986) 10–39.
—: Administrative Archives from the City of Assur in the Middle Assyrian Period, in: *Cuneiform Archives and Libraries: Papers read at the 30e Rencontre Assyriologique Internationale Leiden 4–8 July 1983*, PIHANS 57, ed. K. R. Veenhof, 168–83. Istanbul: Nederlands Instituut voor het Nabije Oosten, 1986b.
—: Middle Assyrian Texts (Nos. 99–101), in: *Tablets, cones and bricks of the third and second millennia B.C.*, CTMMA 1, ed. I. Spar, 144–48, New York: Metropolitan Museum of Art, 1988.
—: Gleanings from ADD, *SAAB* 7 (1993) 5–7.
—: Assyria: the Home Provinces, in: *Neo-Assyrian Geography*, Quaderni di geografica storica 5, ed. M. Liverani, 1–17. Roma; Università di Roma "La Sapienza", 1995.
—: Middle Assyrian to Neo-Assyrian: the Nature of the Shift, in: *Assyrien im Wandel der Zeiten*, HSAO 6, eds. H. Waetzoldt/H. Hauptmann, 159–68. Heidelberg: Heidelberger Orientverlag, 1997.

—: Assyrian Felt, in: *Donum Natalicium: Studi in onore di Claudio Saporetti in occasione del suo 60° compleanno*, eds. P. NegriScafa/P. Gentili, 213–17. Roma: Borgia Editore, 2000.
—: "Queen" in Middle Assyrian, *N.A.B.U.*/43 (2001) 45–46.
—: *riḫṣu, ḫiṣnu* and *šiḫṭu*, but not bulgur, *N.A.B.U.*/12 (2006) 10–11.
—: The Organization of the Middle Assyrian Army: some fresh Evidence, in: *Les armées du Proche-Orient ancien (IIIe-Ier mill. av. J.C.). Actes du colloque international organisé à Lyon les 1er et 2 décembre 2006, Maison de l'Orient et de la Mediterranée*, BAR International Series 1855, eds. P. Abrahimi/L. Battini, 83–92. Oxford: Hadrian Books, 2008.
—: *Bronze Age Bureaucracy*. Cambridge: Cambridge University Press, 2013.
—: Wool, Hair and Textiles in Assyria, in: *Wool Economy in the Ancient Near East and the Agean*, AT 17, eds. C. Breniquet/C. Michel, 401–27. Oxford: Oxbow books, 2014.
Postgate, J. N./Collon, D.: More Stray Assur Tablets, *SAAB* 13 (1999-2001) 1–16.
Powell, M. A.: Maße und Gewichte, *RlA* 7 (1989–1990) 457–517.
Prechel, D./Freydank, H.: *Urkunden der königlichen Palastverwalter vom Ende des 2. Jt. v. Chr.: Das „Archiv" Assur 21101 (M7 F).* StAT 5. Wiesbaden: Harrassowitz Verlag, 2014.
Radner, K.: Der Gott Salmānu („Šulmānu") und seine Beziehung zur Stadt Dūr-Katlimmu, *WO* 29 (1998) 33–51.
Rainey, A. F.: Enclitic *-ma* and the Logical Predicate in Old Babylonian, *Israel oriental studies* 6 (1976) 51–58.
—: Some Presentation Particles in the Amarna Letters from Canaan, *UF* 20 (1988) 209–20.
—: *Canaanite in the Amarna Tablets*. HdO 1, Leiden, Brill 1996 (Volume I = 1996a, II = 1996b, III = 1996c, IV = 1996d).
Reade, J.: Assyrian King-Lists, the Royal Tombs of Ur, and Indus Origins, *JNES* 60/1 (2001) 1–29.
Reculeau, H.: *Climate, Environment and Agriculture in Assyria*. StCh 2. Wiesbaden: Harrassowitz Verlag, 2011.
Reiner, E.: Review of AfO Beih. 12, *BiOr* 19/3–4 (1962) 158–59.
—: The Phonological Interpretation of a Subsystem in the Akkadian Syllabary, in: *Studies Presented to A. Leo Oppenheim,* eds. R. D. Biggs/J. A. Brinkman, 166–180. Chicago: University of Chicago Press, 1964.
—: *A Linguistic Analysis of Akkadian.* Janua Linguarum, Series Practica 21. London: Mouton & Co., 1966.
—: How we Read Cuneiform Texts, *JCS* 25/1 (1973) 3–58.
—: The Reading of the Sign LIŠ, *RA* 76 (1982) 93.
—: Who is Afraid of Old Assyrian?, in: *Veenhof Anniversary Volume: Studies Presented to Klaas R. Veenhof on the Occasion of his Sixty-Fifth Birthday*, PIHANS 89, eds. W. H. van Soldt/J. G. Dercksen/N. J. C. Kouwenberg/Th. J. H. Krispijn, 389–94. Leiden: Nederlands Instituut voor het Nabije Oosten, 2001.
Reschid, F.: *Archiv des Nūršamaš und andere Darlehensurkunden aus der Altbabylonischen Zeit*, Diss. Heidelberg, 1965.
Richter, T.: *Bibliographisches Glossar des Hurritischen*. Wiesbaden: Harrassowitz Verlag, 2012.
—: *Vorarbeiten zu einem hurritischen Namenbuch. Erster Teil: Personennamen altbabylonischer Überliefereung vom Mittleren Euphrat und aus dem nördlichen Mesopotamien*. Wiesbaden: Harrassowitz Verlag, 2016.
Richter, T./Lange, S.: *Das Archiv des Idadda: Die Keilschrifttexte aus den deutsch-syrischen Ausgrabungen 2001–2003 im Königspalast von Qatna*. Qatna Studien 3. Wiesbaden: Harrassowitz, 2012.
Ridder, J.J. de: Review AKT 5/6a *BiOr* 69/5–6 (2012) 553–58.
—: A Late Old Assyrian Sale of a House Plot, KAM 10 1, *N.A.B.U.*/32 (2013a) 55–57.
—: Review of MARV 10, *BiOr* 70/1–2 (2013b) 139–44.
—: Review of Wasserman 2012, *BiOr* 71/1–2 (2014) 173–76.

—: Ordinal Numbers in Middle Assyrian, *ZDMG* 165/1 (2015a) 5–26.
—: Review of Prechel/Freydank 2014, *BiOr* 72/1–2 (2015b) 120–24.
—: Die b/m-Wechsel in mittelassyrischen Belegen: der Kasus Šibanibe, *N.A.B.U.*/39 (2015c) 59.
—: On the etymology of the Old and Middle Assyrian *nasbītu*-festival (< *naṣbutu*), *N.A.B.U.*/72 (2015d) 120–21.
—: Review of MPR, BiOr 73/1–2 (2016a) 122–25.
—: Review of KAM 10, *ZDMG* 166/1 (2016b) 229–32.
—: Regional Differences in Middle Assyrian, in: *Fortune and Misfortune in the Ancient Near East Proceedings of the 60th Rencontre Assyriologique Internationale Warsaw, 21–25 July 2014*, eds. O. Drewnowska/M. Sandowicz, 297–306. Winona Lake: Eisenbrauns, 2017a.
—: Slavery in Old Assyrian Documents, in: *KIM 2: Proceedings of the 2nd Kültepe International Meeting Kültepe, 26–30 July 2015*, Subartu 39, eds. F. Kulakoğlu/G. Barjamovic, 49–61. Turnhout: Brepols 2017b.
Ridder, J. J. de/Zomer, E.: The Middle Assyrian Letter Order VS 1, 105 (VAT 5385), *AoF* 43/1–2 (2016) 38–44.
Roberts, J. J. M.: Review of UGM, *Bulletin of the American Schools of Oriental Research* 20 (1972) 57.
Röllig, W.: Ein Itinerar aus Dūr-Katlimmu, *Damaszener Mitteilungen* 1 (1983) 279–84.
—: Der Mondgott und die Kuh, ein Lehrstuck zur Problematik der Textüberlieferung im Alten Orient, *Or* 54/1–2 (1985) 260–73.
—: Aspects of the Historical Geography of Northeastern Syria from Middle Assyrian to Neo-Assyrian Times, in: *Proceedings of the 10th Anniversary Symposium of the Neo-Assyrian Text Corpus Project Helsinki, September 7–11, 1995*, eds. S. Parpola/R. M. Whiting, 281–294. Helsinki: The Neo-Assyrian Text Corpus Project, 1997.
—: Aus der Kleiderkammer einer mittelassyrischen Palastverwaltung *mašḫuru*-Kleider, in: *Ex Mesopotamia et Syria Lux: Festschrift für Manfried Dietrich zu seimen 65. Geburtstag*, AOAT 281, eds. O. Loretz/K. A. Metzler/H. Schaudig, 581–95. Münster: Ugarit-Verlag, 2002.
Roth, M. T.: *Law Collections from Mesopotamia and Asia Minor*, 2nd Edition. WAW 6. Atlanta: Society of Biblical Literature, 1997.
Rubin, A. D.: *Studies in Semitic Grammaticalization*. HSS 57. Winona Lake: Eisenbrauns, 2005.
—: *The Mehri Language of Oman*, Studies in Semitic Languages and Linguistics 58. Leiden/Boston: Brill, 2010.
Rüster, C./Neu, E.: *Hethitisches Zeichenlexikon, Inventar und Interpretation der Keilschriftzeichen aus den Boğazköy Texten*. Studien zu den Boğazköy Beihefte 2. Wiesbaden: Harrassowitz Verlag, 1989.
Ryding, K. C.: *A Reference Grammar of Modern Standard Arabic*. Cambridge: Cambridge University Press, 2005.
Saggs, H. W. F.: The Tell al Rimah Tablets, 1965, *Iraq* 30 (1968) 154–74.
Salvini, M.: I Testi Cuneiformi delle Campagne 1989 e 1993 a Tell Barri/Kaḫat, in: *Tell Barri/Kaḫat 2: Relazione sulle campagne 1980–1993 a Tell Barri/Kaḫat, nel bacino del Ḫabur (Siria)*, Documenta Asiana 5, ed. P. E. Pecorella, 187–98. Roma: CNR, 1998.
—: I Documenti cuneiformi della Campagna del 2001, in: *Tell Barri/Kaḫat: la Campagna del 2001, Relazione Preliminare*, eds. P. E. Pecorella/R. P. Benoit, 147–51. Florence: Firenze University Press, 2004.
Saporetti, C.: Intorno a VDI 80 (2/1962) 71, *Or* 35/3 (1966) 275–78.
—: La Morfologia del Verbo *ndn/*tdn del Medio-Assiro, in: *Studi sull'Oriente e la Bibbia Offerti al P. Giovanni Rinaldi*, 35–48. Genova: Studio e Vita, 1967.
—: Note su TIM IV 45, *OrAnt* 7 (1968) 181–84.
—: Bibliografia delle Lettere Privata Medio-Assire, *A.I.U.O.N* 30 (*N.S.* 20) (1970) 141–52.

—: Il Prestito nei Documenti Privati dell'Assiria del XIV e XIII Secolo, *Mesopotamia* 16 (1981) 5–41.

Sassmannshausen, L.: Babylonian Chronology of the 2nd Half of the 2nd Millennium, in: *Mesopotamian Dark Age Revisited: Proceedings of an International Conference of SCIEM 2000, Wien, 8.–9. November 2002*, eds. H. Hunger/R. Pruzsinszky, 61–70. Wien: Verlag der Österreichischen Akademie der Wissenschaften, 2004.

Sasson, J.: Hurrian Personal Names in the Rimah Archives, *Assur* 2/2 (1979) 1–32.

Schrader, E.: *Die Keilinschriften am Eingange der Quellgrotte des Sebeneh-Su*. Berlin: Verlag der Königlichen Akademie der Wissenschaften, 1885.

Schwemer, D.: *Akkadische Rituale aus Ḫattuša*. THet 23. Heidelberg: Universitätsverlag C. Winter: 1998.

—: *Die Wettergottgestalten Mesopotamiens und Nordsyriens im Zeitalter der Keilschriftkulturen: Materialien und Studien nach den schriftlichen Quellen*. Wiesbaden: Harrassowitz, 2001.

—: Tukultī-Ninurta I. von Assur (?) an Ibiranu von Ugarit (?), *TUAT NF* 3 (2006) 254–56.

—: *The Anti-Witchcraft Ritual Maqlû. The Cuneiform Sources of a Magic Ceremony from Ancient Mesopotamia*. Wiesbaden: Harrassowitz, 2017.

Seminara, S.: *L'Accadico di Emar*. Münchener Vorderasiatische Studien 8. Roma: Università degli Studi di Roma "La Sapienza", 2001.

Shibata, D.: Middle Assyrian Legal and Administrative Texts from the 2005 Excavation at Tell Taban: A Preliminary Report, *Al-Rāfidān* 28 (2007) 63–74.

—: Local Power in the Middle Assyrian Period, the "Kings of the land of Māri" in the Middle Habur Region, in: *Organization, Representation and Symbols of Power in the Ancient Near East*, ed. G. Wilhelm, 489–505. Winona Lake: Eisenbrauns, 2012.

—: Dynastic Marriages in Assyria during the Late Second Millennium BC, in: *Understanding hegemonic Practices of the Early Assyrian Empire: Essays dedicated to Frans Wiggermann*, Consolidatin Empires Project 1, PIHANS 125, ed. B. S. Düring, 235–42. Leiden: Nederlands Instituut voor het Nabije Oosten, 2015a.

—: Hemerology, Extispicy and Ilī-pada's Illness, *ZA* 105/2 (2015b) 139–53.

—: The Local Scribal Tradition in the Land of Māri and Assyrian State Scribal Practice, in: *Cultures and Societies in the Middle Euphrates and Habur Areas in the Second Millennium BC I: Scribal Education and Scribal Traditions*, StCh5, eds. S. Yamada/D. Shibata, 99–118. Wiesbaden: Harrassowitz, 2016.

—: An Expedition of King Shalmaneser I and Prince Tukultī-Ninurta to Carchemish, in: *At the Dawn of History Ancient Near Eastern Studies in Honour of J. N. Postgate*, eds. Y. Heffron/A. Stone/M. Worthington, 491–506. Winona Lake: Eisenbrauns, 2017.

Shibata, D./Yamada, S.: The Cuneiform Texts from the 2007 Excavation at Tell Taban: a Preliminary Report, in: *Excavations at Tell Taban, Hassake, Syria: Preliminary Report on the 2007 Season of Excavations, and the Study of Cuneiform Text*, ed. H. Numoto, 87–109. Hiroshima: Letterpress, 2009.

Snell, D. C.: The Cuneiform Tablet from El-Qiṭār, *Abr-Nahrain* 22 (1983/84) 159–70.

Soden, W. von: Vokalfärbungen im Akkadischen, *JCS* 2/4 (1948) 291–303.

—: Zu den Amarnabriefen aus Babylon und Assur, *Or* 21 (1952a) 416–34.

—: Unregelmäßige Verben im Akkadischen, *ZA* 50 (1952b) 163–81.

—: Zur Laut- und Formenlehre des Neuassyrischen, *AfO* 18 (1957/58a) 121–22.

—: Drei mittelassyrische Briefe aus Nippur, *AfO* 18 (1957/58b) 368–71.

—: Die Spirantieserung von Verschlusslauten im Akkadischen: ein Vorbericht, *JNES* 27/3 (1968) 214–20.

—: Notes Brèves (no. 7), *RA* 67 (1973) 191.

—: Zu einigen akkadischen Wörtern, *ZA* 67/2 (1977) 235–41.

—: Review of MARV 2, *ZA* 73/2 (1983) 289–90.

—: Äthiopische-Akkadische Isoglossen, in: *Proceedings of the Fourth International Hamito-Semitic Congress, Marburg, 20–22 September, 1983*, Amsterdam studies in the theory and history of linguistic science: 4. Current Issues in Linguistic Theory 44, eds. H. Jungraithmayr/W. W. Müller, 559–67. Amsterdam/Philadelphia: John Benjamins Publishing Company, 1987.
—: Hurritisch *Uatnannu* > Mittelassyrisch *Utnannu* und > Ugaritisch ITNN > Hebräisch *ˀÄtnan* "Ein Geschenk, Dirnenlohn", *UF* 20 (1988) 309–11.
—: Deminutiva nach der Form *qutail* > *qutīl* und vergleichbare Vierkonsonantige Bildungen im Akkadischen, in: *Semitic Studies in Honor of Wolf Leslau*, ed. A. S. Kaye, 1488–92. Wiesbaden: Harrassowitz Verlag, 1991.
Sokoloff, M.: *A Syriac lexicon: A Translation from the Latin, Correction, Expansion and Update of C. Brockelmann's Lexicon Syriacum*, 2nd Edition. Winona Lake/Piscataway: Eisenbrauns/Gorgias Press, 2012.
Sommerfeld, W.: Varianten in der Keilschrift-Orthografie und die Historische Phonologie des Akkadischen, in: *Šapal tibnim mû illakū, Studies Presented to Joaquín Sanmartín on the Occasion of his 65th Birthday,* AuOrS 22, eds. G. del Olmo Lete/L. Feliu/A. M. Albà, 359–76. Barcelona: Editorial Ausa, 2006.
Stein, P.: *Die Mittel- und Neubabylonischen Königinschriften bis zum Ende der Assyrerherrschaft.* JBVO 3. Wiesbaden: Harrassowitz Verlag, 2000.
Steiner, R. C.: *The Case for Fricative-Laterals in Proto-Semitic.* AOS 59. New Haven: American Oriental Society, 1977.
Stol, M.: Cress and its Mustard, *JEOL* 28 (1983/84) 24–32.
Streck, M. P.: Funktionsanalyse des Akkadischen Št_2-Stamms, *ZA* 84/2 (1994) 161–97.
—: *Zahl und Zeit. Grammatik der Numeralia und des Verbalsystems im Spätbabylonischen.*. CM 5. Groningen: Styx, 1995.
—: Review of MATSH, *ZA* 87/2 (1997) 271–276.
—: Zur Gemination beim Akkadischen Verbum, *Or* 67/4 (1998a) 523–31.
—: Review of Roth 1995 (see Roth 1997), *Zeitschrift für Altorientalische und Biblische Rechtsgeschichte* 4 (1998b) 303–9.
—: Das „Perfekt" *iptaras* im Altbabylonischen der Hammurapi-Briefe, in: *Tempus und Aspekt in den semitischen Sprachem.* JBVO 1, ed. N. Nebes, 101–26. Wiesbaden: Harrassowitz Verlag, 1999.
—: *Das amurritische Onomastikon der altbabylonischen Zeit, Band 1: Die Amurriter , die onomastische Forschung, Orthographie und Phonologie, Nominalmorphologie.* AOAT 271/1. Münster: Ugarit-Verlag, 2000.
—: Review of Stein 2000, *OLZ* 96/4–5 (2001) 515–18.
—: Die Nominalformen maPRaS(t), maPRāS und maPRiS(t) im Akkadischen, in: *Neue Beiträge zur Semitistik.* JBVO 5, ed. N. Nebes, 223–57. Wiesbaden: Harrassowitz Verlag, 2002a.
—: Sprachliche Innovationen und Archaismen in den akkadischen Personennamen, in: *Orientalische und semitische Onomastik*, AOAT 296, eds. M. P. Streck/S. Weninger, 109–22. Münster: Ugarit-Verlag, 2002b.
—: *Die Akkadischen Verbalstämme mit ta-Infix.* AOAT 303. Münster: Ugarit-Verlag, 2003a.
—: Review of SNAG, *ZA* 93/1 (2003b) 126–28.
—: Simply a Seller, Nothing but Gods: the Nominal Suffix *-ān* in Old Babylonian, *Babel und Bibel* 2 (2005) 233–43.
—: Sibilants in the Old Babylonian Texts of Hammurapi and of the Governors in Qaṭṭunān, in: *The Akkadian Language in its Semitic Context: Studies in the Akkadian of the Third and Second Millennium BC,* PIHANS 106, eds. G. Deutscher/N. J. C. Kouwenberg, 215–51. Leiden: Nederlands Instituut voor het Nabije Oosten, 2006.
—: Akkadisch, in: *Sprachen des Alten Orients*, 3. Auflage, ed. M. P. Streck, 44–79. Darmstadt: Wissenschaftliche Buchgesellschaft, 2007.

—: Die Kardinalzahl „sechs“ im Altbabylonischen und der analogische Ausgleich der Kardinahlzahlen „sech“-„acht“, *AoF* 35/2 (2008) 246–53.
—: Review of CAD T and Ṭ, *ZA* 99/1 (2009) 135–40.
—: Großes Fach Altorientalistik: der Umfang des Keilschriftlichen Textkorpus, *MDOG* 142 (2010a) 35–58.
—: Feminine Gender of Old Babylonian Nouns, in: *Von Göttern und Menschen: Beiträge zu Literatur und Geschichte des Alten Orients. Festschrift für Brigitte Groneberg*. CM 41. eds. D. Shehata/F. Weiershäuser/K. V. Zand, 287-305. Leiden/Boston: Brill, 2010b.
—: Babylonian and Assyrian, in: *The Semitic Languages: An International Handbook,* HSK 36, ed. S. Weninger, 359–96. Berlin: De Gruyter Mouton, 2011.
—: *Altbabylonisches Lehrbuch*, 2. überarbeite Auflage. Porta NS 23. Wiesbaden: Harrassowitz Verlag, 2014a.
—: Die Kasusflexion im Status Rectus des Neu- und Spätbabylonischen, in: *Babylonien und seine Nachbarn in neu- und spätbabylonischer Zeit.* AOAT 369. ed. M. Krebernik/H. Neumann, 247–88. Münster: Ugarit-Verlag, 2014b.
—: The Terminology for Times of the Day in Akkadian, in: *At the Dawn of History Ancient Near Eastern Studies in Honour of J. N. Postgate*, eds. Y. Heffron/A. Stone/M. Worthington, 583–609. Winona Lake: Eisenbrauns, 2017.
Szuchman, J.: *Prelude to Empire: Middle Assyrian Hanigalbat and the Rise of the Aramaeans*. Diss. Los Angeles, 2007.
Tal, A.: *Samaritan Aramaic*. Lehrbücher orientalischer Sprachen III/2. Münster: Ugarit-Verlag, 2013.
Testen, D.: An Akkadian-Arabic Cognate-Pair and the Formation of stem-based Diminutives in Early Semitic, in: *The Akkadian Language in its Semitic Context: Studies in the Akkadian of the Third and Second Millennium BC,* PIHANS 106, eds. G. Deutscher/N. J. C. Kouwenberg, 140–49. Leiden: Nederlands Instituut voor het Nabije Oosten, 2006.
Thureau-Dangin, F.: Une Lettre assyrienne à Ras Shamra, *Syria* 16 (1935) 188–93.
Tropper, J.: Akkadischen */nuḫḫutu/* und die Repräsentation des Phonems /ḫ/ im Akkadischen, *ZA* 85 (1995) 58–66.
—: Zain als Affrikate im älteren Akkadischen, *UF* 28 (1996) 647–49.
—: Die Infirmen Verben des Akkadischen, *ZDMG* 148/1 (1998) 7–34.
—: Zur Etymologie von akkadischen *šukênu/šuḫeḫḫunu*, *WO* 30 (1999) 91–94.
—: *Altäthiopisch: Grammatik des Ge'ez mit Übungstexten und Glossar*. Elementa Linguarum Orientis 2. Münster: Ugarit-Verlag, 2002.
Tsukimoto, A.: Aus einer Japanischen Privatsammlung: Drei Verwaltungstexten und ein Brief aus Mittelassyrischer Zeit, *WO* 23 (1992) 21–38.
—: Review Beckman 1996, *WO* 29 (1998) 184–90.
—: Ein Neuer Text im Ḫana-Stil in Mittelassyrischer Schrift, *RA* 105 (2011) 85–94.
Ullendorff, E.: *The Semitic Languages of Ethiopia, a Comparative Phonology*. London: Taylor, 1955.
Ungnad, A.: *Syrische Grammatik mit Übungsbuch*, 2. verbesserte Auflage. Clavis linguarum semiticarum abbreviation 7. München: Beck, 1932.
—: *Akkadian Grammmar* (translation by H. A. Hoffner, Jr. from Grammatik des Akkadischen). SBL Resources for Biblical Study 30. Atlanta: Scholars press, 1992.
Valin Jr., R. D. van: *An Introduction to Syntax*. Cambridge: Cambridge University Press, 2001.
Veenhof, K. R.: *Aspects of the Old Assyrian Trade and its Terminology*. Leiden: Brill, 1972.
—: A Deed of Manumission and Adoption from the Later Old Assyrian Period, in: *Zikir Šumim: Assyriological Studies Presented to F.R. Kraus on the Occasion of his Seventieth Birthday*, ed. G. van Driel, 359–85. Leiden: Brill, 1982.
—: An Old Assyrian Incantation Against a Black Dog (kt a/k 611), *WZKM* 86 (1996) 425–33.
—: Ninive 5. Akkadische und altassyrische Periode, *RlA* 9 (2000) 433–44.

—: *The Archive of Kuliya, son of Ali-abum (Kt. 92/k 188–263)*. AKT 5. Ankara: Türk Tarih Kurumu Basimevi, 2010.

Veenhof, K. R./Eidem, J.: *Mesopotamia, the Old Assyrian Period*. Annäherungen 5. OBO 160/5. Fribourg/Göttingen: Vandenhoeck & Ruprecht, 2008.

Veldhuis, N.: *A Cow of Sîn*. Library of Oriental Texts 2. Groningen: Styx, 1991.

Vinnichenko, O.: *The Reassesment of the Influence of Aramaic on Assyrian Syntax*. Diss. Cambridge, 2016a.

—: On the prepositions issu and isse in Neo-Assyrian, *Or* 85/2 (2016b) 149–75.

Voigt, R. M.: A Note on the Alleged Middle/Neo-Assyrian Sound Change s?(*š?) → ss<ṣ>, *JNES* 45/1 (1986) 53–57.

Wasserman, N.: *Style and Form in Old-Babylonian Literary Texts*. CM 27. Leiden: Brill, 2003.

—: *Most Probably, Epistemic Modality in Old Babylonian*. LANE 3. Winona Lake: Eisenbrauns, 2012.

Weeden, M.: Assyro-Mittanian or Middle Assyrian, in: *Palaeography and Scribal Practices in Syro-Palestine and Anatolia in the Late Bronze Age,* PIHANS 119, ed. E. Devecchi, 229–52. Leiden: Nederlands Instituut voor het Nabije Oosten, 2012.

—: Hittite Scribal Culture and Syria: Palaeography and Cuneiform Traditions, in: *Cultures and Societies in the Middle Euphrates and Habur Areas in the Second Millennium BC I: Scribal Education and Scribal Traditions*, StCh5, eds. S. Yamada/D. Shibata, 157–91. Wiesbaden: Harrassowitz, 2016.

Wegner, I.: *Hurritisch eine Einführung*, 2. Veränderte Auflage, Wiesbaden: Harrassowitz Verlag, 2007.

Weidner, E.: *Politische Dokumente aus Kleinasien: Die Staatsverträge in akkadischer Sprache aus dem Archiv von Boghazköi*, Boghazköi-Studien 8, Leipzig: Hinrichs, 1923.

—: Aus den Tagen eines assyrischen Schattenkönigs, *AfO* 10 (1935/36) 1–52.

—: Das Alter der mittelassyrischen Gesetzetexte, *AfO* 12 (1937/39) 46–54.

—: Studien zur Zeitgeschichte Tukulti-Ninurtas I, *AfO* 13 (1939/41) 109–22.

—: Die Bibliothek Tiglatpilesers I, *AfO* 16 (1952/53) 197–215.

—: Säulen aus Naḫur, *AfO* 17 (1954/56a) 145–46.

—: Hof- und Harems-Erlasse assyrischer Könige aus dem 2. Jahrtausend v. Chr., *AfO* 17 (1954/56b) 257–93.

—: Der Kanzler Salmanassars I, *AfO* 19 (1959/60) 33–39.

—: Assyrische Epen über die Kassiten-Kämpfe, *AfO* 20 (1963a) 113–16.

—: Eine Erbteilung in mittelassyrischen Zeit, *AfO* 20 (1963b) 121–24

—: Assyrische Itineraire, *AfO* 21 (1966) 42–46.

—: Review OMA, *AfO* 24 (1973) 141–42.

Westenholz, A.: The Phoneme /o/ in Akkadian, *ZA* 81 (1991) 10–19.

—: Do not trust the Assyriologists, in: *The Akkadian Language in its Semitic Context: Studies in the Akkadian of the Third and Second Millennium BC,* PIHANS 106, eds. G. Deutscher/N. J. C. Kouwenberg, 252–60. Leiden: Nederlands Instituut voor het Nabije Oosten, 2006.

Whiting, R. M.: A Late Middle Assyrian Tablet from North Syria, *SAAB* 2 (1988) 99–101.

Wiggermann, F. A. M.: Agriculture in the Norhern Baliḫ Valley, the Case of Middle Assyrian Tell Sabi Abyad, in: *Rainfall and Agriculture in Northern Mesopotamia (MOS Studies 3) : Proceedings of the third MOS Symposium (Leiden 1999)*, PIHANS 88, ed. R. Jas, 171–231. Leiden: Nederlands Instituut voor het Nabije Oosten, 2000.

—: The Seal of Ilī-Padâ, Grand Vizier of the Middle Assyrian Empire, in: *The Iconography of Cylinder Seals*, ed. P. Taylor, 92-99, 212–17. Turin: Nino Aragno Editore, 2006.

—: Appendix E: Cuneiform Texts from Tell Sabi Abyad related to Pottery, in: *The Pots and Potters of Assyria:Technology and Organisation of Production, Ceramic Sequence and Vessel Function at Late Bronze Age Tell Sabi Abyad, Syria*, K. Duistermaat, 558–64. Leiden: Brepols, 2008a.

—: A Babylonian Scholar in Assur, in: *Studies in Ancient Near Eastern World View and Society: Presented to Marten Stol on the Occasion of his 65th Birthday*, ed. R. J. van der Spek, 203–34. Bethesda: CDLI press, 2008b.

—: Wein, Weiß und Gesang in een midden-assyrische Nederzetting aan de Balikh, *Phoenix* 56/1-2 (2010) 17–60.

Wilcke, C.: Assyrische Testament, *ZA* 66/2 (1976) 196–233.

—: Die Anfänge der Akkadischen Epen, *ZA* 67/2 (1977) 153–216.

Wilhelm, G.: *Untersuchungen zum Ḫurro-Akkadischen von Nuzi*. AOAT 9. Neukirchen-Vluyn: Neukirchener Verlag, 1970.

—: *The Hurrians*. Warminster: Aris & Phillips, 1989.

—: Der mittelassyrische Brief eines Verwalters an seinen Herr, in: M. Dietrich/O. Loretz, *Ana šadî labnāni lū allik: Beiträge zu altorientalischen und mittelmeerischen Kulturen. Festschrift für Wolfgang Röllig,* AOAT 247, eds. B. Pongratz-Leisten/H. Kühne/P. Xella., 431–33: Neukirchen-Vluyn: Neukirchener Verlag, 1997.

—: Hurrian, in: *The Ancient Languages of Asia Minor*, ed. R. D. Woodard, 81–104. Cambridge: Cambridge University Press, 2008. [Previously published in: R. D. Woodard (ed.), *The Cambridge Encyclopedia of the World's Ancient Languages*, Cambridge: Cambridge University Press, 2004]

—: Ein König von Ḫatti an einen König von Assyrien, *TUAT NF* 3 (2006) 238–40.

Wiseman, D. J.: The Tell al Rimah Tablets, 1966, *Iraq* 30 (1968) 175–205.

Woidich, M.: *Das Kairenisch-Arabische, eine Grammatik*, Porta NS 22. Wiesbaden: Harrassowitz Verlag, 2006.

Woodington, N. R.: *A Grammar of the Neo-Babylonian Letters of the Kuyunjik Collection*. Diss. Yale, 1983.

Worthington, M.: Some New Patterns in Neo-Assyrian Orthography and Phonology Discernible in Nouns with Monosyllabic Stems, *JNES* 69/2 (2010) 179–94.

—: *Principles of Akkadian Textual Criticism*. SANER 1. Boston: De Gruyter, 2012.

Yakubovich, I.: Review of The Akkadian Language in its Semitic Context: Studies in the Akkadian of the Third and Second Millennium BC, PIHANS 106, eds. G. Deutscher/N. J. C. Kouwenberg, *BiOr* 65/1–2 (2007) 149–54.

Yamada, S.: The Editorial History of the Assyrian King List, *ZA* 84/1 (1994) 11–37.

—: The Assyrian King List and the Murderer of Tukulti-Ninurta, *N.A.B.U.*/23 (1998) 26–27.

—: An Adoption Contract from Tell Taban, the Kings of the Land of Hana, and the Hana-Style scribal Tradition, *RA* 105 (2011) 61–84.

—: The Transition Period (17th to 15th Century BCE), in: *A Companion to Assyria*, ed. E. Frahm, 108–16. Hoboken, Wiley-Blackwell 2017.

Ylvisaker, S. C.: *Zur Babylonischen und Assyrischen Grammatik*, Leipzig: August Pries, 1911.

Zomer, E.: Review of Prechel/Freydank 2014, *Rosetta* 17 (2015) 176–178.

—: *Corpus of Middle Babylonian and Middle Assyrian Incantations*. Leipziger Altorientalistische Studien 9. Leipzig 2018.

Chapter 27: Indices

27.1 Index of selected Assyrian words

abātu (verb) § 208, 211
abātu § 158
(*ša*) *abbašše* § 250d
adi § 436f, 724ff
a/idru § 154
aḫāʾiš § 383ff, 541
aʾīlu § 180, 233
akkī § 732
akkīa § 490, 739
akukia § 378
alaḫḫinu § 266
alāku § 542, 598f
alē § 400
allulu § 589
alliu § 376
ammar § 243, 722
ammēka § 481
ammēša § 482
ammiu § 375
annāka § 481
annanna § 379
annannia § 380
annānu § 480
annîša § 496
anniu § 373f
anumma § 496
ana § 423ff, 434f
appūtu § 497
arāru § 589
arāšu § 554
arāʾu § 588
arḫiš § 489
assurrē § 490
ašar § 727
aššum § 442, 728
-āt § 98
attamannu § 394
ayyānu § 401
ayyēša § 403
ayyû § 402
baʾʾeruttu § 116
balāṭu § 515
balu(t) § 447f, 688
baqām/nu § 234
bārīuttu § 116
battubattēn § 454
baʾʾû § 522, 579
beri § 445
berti § 445
beru(m) § 483
bēt § 453
bētānu(m) § 483
bēt ḫašime § 204
biblu § 178, 264
būšu § 168
dagālu § 304
danānu § 233, 600
danniš § 489
dāria § 496
ebāʾu § 588
ebertān § 457
eberti § 456
edānu § 574
ēdēnu(m) § 488
elāʾu § 580
ellān(u) § 483
emitta § 484
emūqa(mma) § 490
entu § 268, 494, 701
enūšu § 496
epāʾu § 588
erāšu § 554
ešertu § 339
ezib § 449
gabbu § 388, 394
ḫabāqu § 179, 260
ḫ/qabbudu § 208
ḫalāqu § 515
ḫalzuḫlu § 242
ḫapāʾu § 570
ḫaramma § 496
ḫarāṣu § 545
ḫīṭu § 168
ibašši § 593ff
iltēn/t § 334
iltēniš § 488
iltēnīuttu § 345
iltu § 729
immatēma § 496
ina § 428ff, 688
inanna § 496
ištu § 438ff
-ī/ēšu § 346, 486
išû § 597
-īt/itt § 115
iyāmattu § 393
izuzzu § 601
kabādu § 213
kal(a) ūme § 492
kallamāri § 491
kallātu § 158
ana kallīe § 490
kallīu § 490
kallulu § 522
kamās/šu § 207
kannamāre § 491
kalu § 396
kaʾʾulu § 522
kē § 404, 681
kē maṣi § 404
kīkī § 404
kī § 443ff, 732ff
kīam § 490, 739
kīdānu(m) § 483

usātu § 158
uṣāʾu § 608
ušābu § 222, 515, 609
uššer § 450
-ūt/utt § 113f
yābilu § 261
zak(k)u § 572

27.2 Index of selected logograms

Ì.ÁG.E § 70
Ì.LÁ.E § 70
didili § 77
DU § 70
ḫi.a § 76
IN.NA.AN.SUM § 70
MA.NA § 69
meš § 75
NU § 70
Personenkeil § 73
QA § 69
SUḪUR § 476
ŠE-*um* § 69
ŠU.BA.AN.TI § 70

27.3 Index of quoted passages and discussed texts

A
A 133:6–7 § 686, 690
A 133:12–15 § 619
A 300:1 § 275
A 300:5–10 § 492
A 305:12–15 § 652
A 320:20–22 § 275, 432
A 333:7 § 687
A 333:7–8 § 493
A 845:5 § 481, 640, 669
A 845:6–8 § 405
A 845:7–8 § 648
A 845:8–10 § 489
A 845:14–18 § 307, 667, 698
A 877:4 § 275, 678
A 877:9–10 § 684
A 981:6’ § 452
A 1051:6-8 § 459
A 1065:3 § 452
A 1476 § 459
A 1476 r. 5’–10’ § 662
A 1476 r. 8’–9’ § 422
A 1947+:6 § 335
A 1947+:17 § 622
A 1947+:21–22 § 622
A 1947+:25–26 § 489
A 2608:1–5 § 415
A 2704:6–11 § 442
A 2994:4–6 § 739
A 2994:4–9 § 737
A 2994:6–9 § 463
A 2994:6–10 § 367
A 2994:13–14 § 350
A 2994:15–25 § 705
A 2994:24–25 § 275
A 3310:5–11 § 362, 671
A 3310:6 § 650

Adad ritual
Adad ritual:3 § 412, 459
Adad ritual:4 § 466
Adad ritual:6 § 656
Adad ritual:13 § 612
Adad ritual r. 7’ § 686
Adad ritual r. 8’ § 360

Ali
Ali 1:1–9 § 665
Ali 1:7–9 § 424
Ali 3:6 § 276
Ali 4:9–10 § 276
Ali 9:1–5 § 636
Ali 23:9–11 § 79

AO
AO 19.227:6–8 § 622
AO 19.227:6–11 § 442
AO 19.227:9–11 § 524
AO 19.227:21–23 § 359, 375, 664
AO 19.228:5–6 § 275
AO 19.228:5–24 § 414
AO 19.228:7 § 446
AO 19.228:10–11 § 410, 694
AO 19.228:13–14 § 597
AO 19.228:15 § 522
AO 19.228:18–20 § 598, 732
AO 19.228:22–23 § 411, 413
AO 19.229:19–20 § 662
AO 20.154:9–13 § 625
AO 20.157:6–7 § 656
AO 21.381:5–8 § 416
AO 21.382:3–5 § 439
AO 21.382:7–10 § 625
AO 21.382:10 § 510

APM
APM 9220: § 59

Aššur ritual
Aššur ritual ii 4’ § 455
Aššur ritual ii 5’ § 484
Aššur ritual ii 14’ § 487

Tab